D0609151

CHRISTIAN HERITAGE COLLEGE
BY HIM ALL THINGS CONSIST
SAN DIEGO, CALIFORNIA 1970

HALLAM'S WORKS.

VOLUME V.

INTRODUCTION

TO THE

LITERATURE OF EUROPE.

VOLUMES I., II.

INTRODUCTION

TO THE

LITERATURE OF EUROPE

IN THE

FIFTEENTH, SIXTEENTH, AND SEVENTEENTH CENTURIES.

By HENRY HALLAM, LL.D., F.R.A.S.,

FOREIGN ASSOCIATE OF THE INSTITUTE OF FRANCE.

De modo autem hujusmodi historiæ conscribendæ, illud imprimis monemus, ut materia et copia ejus, non tantum ab historiis et criticis petatur, verum etiam per singulas annorum centurias, aut etiam minora intervalla, seriatim libri præcipui, qui eo temporis spatio conscripti sunt, in consilium adhibeantur; ut ex eorum non perlectione (id enim infinitum quiddam esset), sed degustatione. et observatione argumenti, styli, methodi, genius illius temporis literarius, veluti incantatione quadam, a mortuis evocetur.—BACON, *de Augm. Scient.*

FOUR VOLUMES IN TWO.

VOLUMES I., II.

NEW YORK:

THOMAS Y. CROWELL,

744 BROADWAY.

1880.

University Press: John Wilson & Son,
Cambridge.

PREFACE

TO

THE FIRST EDITION.

The advantages of such a synoptical view of literature as displays its various departments in their simultaneous condition through an extensive period, and in their mutual dependency, seem too manifest to be disputed. And, as we possess little of this kind in our own language, I have been induced to undertake that to which I am, in some respects at least, very unequal, but which no more capable person, as far as I could judge, was likely to perform. In offering to the public this introduction to the literary history of three centuries, — for I cannot venture to give it a title of more pretension, — it is convenient to state my general secondary sources of information, exclusive of the acquaintance I possess with original writers; and, at the same time, by showing what has already been done, and what is left undone, to furnish a justification of my own undertaking.

The history of literature belongs to modern, and chiefly to almost recent times. The nearest approach to it that the ancients have left us is contained in a single chapter of Quintilian, the first of the tenth book, wherein he passes rapidly over the names and characters of the poets, orators, and historians of Greece and Rome. This, however, is but a sketch; and the valuable work of Diogenes Laertius preserves too little of chronological order to pass for a history of ancient philosophy, though it has supplied much of the materials for all that has been written on that subject.

In the sixteenth century, the great increase of publications, and the devotion to learning which distinguished that period, might suggest the scheme of a universal literary history. Conrad Gesner, than whom no one, by extent and variety of erudition, was more fitted for the labor, appears to have framed a plan of this kind. What he has published, the Bibliotheca Universalis and the Pandectæ Universales, are, taken together, the materials that might have been thrown into an historical form: the one being an alphabetical catalogue of authors and their writings; the other, a digested and minute index to all departments of knowledge, in twenty-one books, each divided into titles, with short references to the texts of works on every head in his comprehensive classification. The order of time is therefore altogether disregarded. Possevin, an Italian Jesuit, made somewhat a nearer approach to this in his Bibliotheca Selecta, published at Rome in 1593. Though his partitions are rather encyclopedic than historical, and his method, especially in the first volume, is chiefly argumentative, he gives under each chapter a nearly chronological catalogue of authors, and sometimes a short account of their works.

Lord Bacon, in the second book De Augmentis Scientiarum, might justly deny, notwithstanding these defective works of the preceding century, that any real history of letters had been written; and he compares that of the world, wanting this, to a statue of Polypheme deprived of his single eye. He traces the method of supplying this deficiency in one of those luminous and comprehensive passages which bear the stamp of his vast mind: the origin and antiquities of every science; the methods by which it has been taught; the sects and controversies it has occasioned; the colleges and academies in which it has been cultivated; its relation to civil government and common society; the physical or temporary causes which have influenced its condition, — form, in his plan, as essential a part of such a history, as the lives of famous authors, and the books they have produced.

No one has presumed to fill up the outline which Bacon himself could but sketch; and most part of the seventeenth century passed away with few efforts, on the part of the learned, to do justice to their own occupation: for we can hardly make an exception for the Prodromus Historiæ Literariæ (Hamburg, 1659) of Lambecius, a very learned German, who, having framed a magnificent scheme of a universal history of letters, was able to carry it no farther than the times of Moses and Cadmus. But, in 1688, Daniel Morhof, professor at Kiel in Holstein, published his well-known Polyhistor, which received considerable additions in the next age at the hands of Fabricius, and is still found in every considerable library.

Morhof appears to have had the method of Possevin in some measure before his eyes; but the lapse of a century, so rich in erudition as the seventeenth, had prodigiously enlarged the sphere of literary history. The precise object, however, of the Polyhistor, as the word imports, is to direct, on the most ample plan, the studies of a single scholar. Several chapters, that seem digressive in an historical light, are to be defended by this consideration. In his review of books in every province of literature, Morhof adopts a sufficiently chronological order; his judgments are short, but usually judicious; his erudition so copious, that later writers have freely borrowed from the Polyhistor, and, in many parts, added little to its enumeration. But he is far more conversant with writers in Latin than the modern languages; and, in particular, shows a scanty acquaintance with English literature.

Another century had elapsed, when the honor of first accomplishing a comprehensive synopsis of literary history in a more regular form than Morhof, was the reward of Andrès, a Spanish Jesuit, who, after the dissolution of his order, passed the remainder of his life in Italy. He published at Parma, in different years, from 1782 to 1799, his Origine, Progresso, e Stato attuale d'ogni Litteratura. The first edition is in five volumes quarto; but I have made use of that printed at Prato, 1806, in twenty octavo volumes. Andrès, though a Jesuit, or perhaps because a Jesuit, accommodated himself in some measure to the tone of the age wherein his book appeared, and is always temperate, and often candid. His learning is very extensive in surface, and sometimes minute and curious, but not, generally speaking, profound; his style is flowing, but diffuse and indefinite; his characters of books have a vagueness unpleasant to those who seek for precise notions; his taste is correct, but frigid; his general views are not injudicious, but display a moderate degree of luminousness or philosophy. This work is, however, an extraordinary performance, embracing both ancient and modern literature in its full extent, and, in many parts, with little assistance from any former publication of the kind. It is far better known on the Continent than in England, where I have not frequently seen it quoted; nor do I believe it is common in our private libraries.

A few years after the appearance of the first volumes of Andrès, some of the most eminent among the learned of Germany projected a universal history of modern arts and sciences on a much larger scale. Each single province, out of eleven, was deemed sufficient for the labors of one man, if they were to be minute, and exhaustive of the subject: among others, Bouterwek undertook poetry and polite letters; Buhle, speculative philosophy; Kästner, the mathematical sciences; Sprengel, anatomy and medicine; Heeren, classical philology. The general survey of the whole seems to have been assigned to Eichhorn. So vast a scheme was not fully executed; but we owe to it some standard works to which I have been considerably indebted. Eichhorn published, in 1796 and 1799, two volumes, intended as the beginning of a General History of the Cultivation and Literature of Modern Europe, from the twelfth to the eighteenth century. But he did not confine himself within the remoter limit; and his second volume, especially, expatiates on the dark ages that succeeded the fall of the Roman Empire. In consequence, perhaps, of this diffuseness, and also of the abandonment, for some reason with which I am unacquainted, of a large portion of the original undertaking, Eichhorn prosecuted this work no farther in its original form. But, altering slightly its title, he published, some years afterwards, an independent universal "History of Literature" from the earliest ages to his own. This is comprised in six volumes; the first having appeared in 1805, the last in 1811.

The execution of these volumes is very unequal. Eichhorn was conversant with oriental, with theological literature, especially of his own country, and in general with that contained in the Latin language. But he seems to have been slightly acquainted with that of the modern languages, and with most branches of science. He is more specific, more chronological, more methodical, in his distribution, than Andrès. His reach of knowledge, on the other hand, is less comprehensive; and, though I could praise neither highly for eloquence, for taste, or for philosophy, I should incline to give the preference in all these to the Spanish Jesuit. But the qualities above mentioned render Eichhorn, on the whole, more satisfactory to the student.

These are the only works, as far as I know, which deserve the name of general histories of literature, embracing all subjects, all ages, and all nations. If there are others, they must, I conceive, be too superficial to demand attention. But in one country of Europe, and only in one, we find a national history so comprehensive as to leave uncommemorated no part of its literary labor. This was first executed by Tiraboschi, a Jesuit born at Bergamo, and in his later years librarian of the Duke of Modena, in twelve volumes quarto: I have used the edition published at Rome in 1785. It descends to the close of the seventeenth century. In full and clear exposition, in minute and exact investigation of facts, Tiraboschi has few superiors; and such is his good sense in criticism, that we must regret the sparing use he has made of it. But the principal object of Tiraboschi was biography. A writer of inferior reputation, Corniani, in his Secoli della litteratura Italiana dopo il suo risorgimento (Brescia, 9 vols., 1804–1813), has gone more closely to an appreciation of the numerous writers whom he passes in review before our eyes. Though his method is biographical, he pursues sufficiently the order of chronology to come into the class of literary historians. Corniani is not much esteemed by his countrymen, and does not rise to a very elevated point of philosophy: but his erudition appears to me considerable, his judgments generally reasonable; and his frequent analyses of books give him one superiority over Tiraboschi.

The Histoire Littéraire de l'Italie, by Ginguéné, is well known: he had the advantage of following Tiraboschi; and could not so well, without his aid, have gone over a portion of the ground, including in his scheme, as he did, the Latin learning of Italy; but he was very conversant with the native literature of the language, and has, not a little prolixly, doubtless, but very usefully, rendered much of easy access to Europe, which must have been sought in scarce volumes, and was in fact known by name to a small part of the world. The Italians are ungrateful, if they deny their obligations to Ginguéné.

France has, I believe, no work of any sort, even an indifferent one, on the universal history of her own literature; nor can we claim for ourselves a single attempt of the most superficial kind. Warton's History of Poetry contains much that bears on our general learning; but it leaves us about the accession of Elizabeth.

Far more has been accomplished in the history of particular

departments of literature. In the general history of philosophy, omitting a few older writers, Brucker deserves to lead the way. There has been of late years some disposition to depreciate his laborious performance, as not sufficiently imbued with a metaphysical spirit, and as not rendering with clearness and truth the tenets of the philosophers whom he exhibits. But the Germany of 1744 was not the Germany of Kant and Fichte; and possibly Brucker may not have proved the worse historian for having known little of recent theories. The latter objection is more material: in some instances, he seems to me not quite equal to his subject. But, upon the whole, he is of eminent usefulness; copious in his extracts, impartial and candid in his judgments.

In the next age after Brucker, the great fondness of the German learned both for historical and philosophical investigation produced more works of this class than I know by name, and many more than I have read. The most celebrated, perhaps, is that of Tennemann; but of which I only know the abridgment, translated into French by M. Victor Cousin, with the title Manuel de l'Histoire de Philosophie. Buhle, one of the society above mentioned, whose focus was at Göttingen, contributed his share to their scheme in a History of Philosophy from the revival of letters. This I have employed through the French translation in six volumes. Buhle, like Tennemann, has very evident obligations to Brucker; but his own erudition was extensive, and his philosophical acuteness not inconsiderable.

The history of poetry and eloquence, or fine writing, was published by Bouterwek, in twelve volumes octavo. Those parts which relate to his own country, and to Spain and Portugal, have been of more use to me than the rest. Many of my readers must be acquainted with the Littérature du Midi, by M. Sismondi; a work written in that flowing and graceful style which distinguishes the author, and succeeding in all that it seeks to give, — a pleasing and popular, yet not superficial or unsatisfactory, account of the best authors in the southern languages. We have nothing historical as to our own poetry but the prolix volumes of Warton. They have obtained, in my opinion, full as much credit as they deserve: without depreciating a book in which so much may be found, and which has been so great a favorite with the literary part of the public, it may be observed that its errors as to fact, especially in names and dates, are extraordinarily frequent, and that the criticism, in points of taste, is not of a very superior kind.

Heeren undertook the history of classical literature, — a great desideratum, which no one had attempted to supply. But unfortunately he has only given an introduction, carrying us down to the close of the fourteenth century, and a history of the fifteenth. These are so good, that we must much lament the want of the rest; especially as I am aware of nothing to fill up the vacuity. Eichhorn, however, is here of considerable use.

In the history of mathematical science, I have had recourse chiefly to Montucla, and, as far as he conducts us, to Kästner, whose catalogue and analysis of mathematical works is far more complete, but his own observations less perspicuous and philosophical. Portal's History of Anatomy, and some other books, to which I have always referred, and which it might be tedious to enumerate, have enabled me to fill a few pages with what I could not be expected to give from any original research. But several branches of literature, using the word as I generally do, in the most general sense for the knowledge imparted through books, are as yet deficient in any thing that approaches to a real history of their progress.

The materials of literary history must always be derived in great measure from biographical collections, those especially which intermix a certain portion of criticism with mere facts. There are some, indeed, which are almost entirely of this description. Adrian Baillet, in his Jugemens des Sçavans, published in 1685, endeavored to collect the suffrages of former critics on the merits of all past authors. His design was only executed in a small part, and hardly extends beyond grammarians, translators, and poets; the latter but imperfectly. Baillet gives his quotations in French, and sometimes mingles enough of his own to raise him above a mere compiler, and to have drawn down the animosity of some contemporaries. Sir Thomas Pope Blount is a perfectly unambitious writer of the same class. His Censurá celebriorum Autorum, published in 1690, contains nothing of his own except a few short dates of each author's life, but diligently brings together the testimonies of preceding critics. Blount omits no class nor any age; his arrangement is nearly chronological, and leads the reader from the earliest records of literature to his own time. The polite writers of modern Europe, and the men of science, do not receive their full share of attention; but this volume, though not, I think, much in request at present, is a very convenient accession to any scholar's library.

Bayle's Dictionary, published in 1697, seems at first sight an inexhaustible magazine of literary history. Those who are conversant with it know that it frequently disappoints their curiosity; names of great eminence are sought in vain, or are very slightly treated; the reader is lost in episodical notes perpetually frivolous, and disgusted with an author who turns away at every moment from what is truly interesting to some idle dispute of his own time, or some contemptible indecency. Yet the numerous quotations contained in Bayle, the miscellaneous copiousness of his erudition, as well as the good sense and acuteness he can always display when it is his inclination to do so, render his dictionary of great value, though I think chiefly to those who have made a tolerable progress in general literature.

The title of a later work by Père Niceron, Mémoires pour servir à l'histoire des hommes illustres de la république des lettres, avec un catalogue raisonné de leurs ouvrages, in forty-three volumes 12mo, published at Paris from 1727 to 1745, announces something rather different from what it contains. The number of "illustrious men" recorded by Niceron is about 1600, chiefly of the sixteenth and seventeeth centuries. The names, as may be anticipated, are frequently very insignificant; and, in return, not a few of real eminence, especially when Protestant, and above all English, are overlooked, or erroneously mentioned. No kind of arrangement is observed: it is utterly impossible to conjecture in what volume of Niceron any article will be discovered. A succinct biography, though fuller than the mere dates of Blount, is followed by short judgments on the author's works, and by a catalogue of them, far more copious, at least, than had been given by any preceding bibliographer. It is a work of much utility; but the more valuable parts have been transfused into later publications.

The English Biographical Dictionary was first published in 1761. I speak of this edition with some regard, from its having been the companion of many youthful hours; but it is rather careless in its general execution. It is sometimes ascribed to Birch; but I suspect that Heathcote had more to do with it. After several successive enlargements, an edition of this dictionary was published in thirty-two volumes, from 1812 to 1817, by Alexander Chalmers, whose name it now commonly bears. Chalmers was a man of very slender powers, relatively to the magnitude of such a work; but his life had been passed in collecting small matters of fact, and he has added much of this kind to British biography. He inserts, beyond any one else, the most insignificant names, and quotes the most wretched authorities. But as the faults of excess, in such collections, are more pardonable than those of omission, we cannot deny the value of his Biographical Dictionary, especially as to our own country, which has not fared well at the hands of foreigners.

Coincident nearly in order of time with Chalmers, but more distinguished in merit, is the Biographie Universelle. The eminent names appended to a large proportion of the articles contained in its fifty-two volumes are vouchers for the ability and erudition it displays. There is doubtless much inequality in the performance; and we are sometimes disappointed by a superficial notice where we had a right to expect most. English literature, though more amply treated than had been usual on the Continent, and with the benefit of Chalmers's contemporaneous volumes, is still not fully appreciated: our chief theological writers, especially, are passed over almost in silence. There seems, on the other hand, a redundancy of modern French names; those, above all, who have, even obscurely and insignificantly, been connected with the history of the Revolution; a fault, if it be one, which is evidently gaining ground in the supplementary volumes. But I must speak respectfully of a work to which I owe so much, and without which, probably, I should never have undertaken the present.

I will not here characterize several works of more limited biography; among which are the Bibliotheca Hispana Nova of Antonio, the Biographia Britannica, the Bibliothèque Française of Goujet: still less is there time to enumerate particular lives, or those histories which relate to short periods, among the sources of literary knowledge. It will be presumed, and will appear by my references, that I have employed such of them as came within my reach. But I am sensible, that, in the great multiplicity of books of this kind, and especially in their prodigious increase on the Continent of late years, many have been overlooked from which I might have improved these volumes. The press is indeed so active that no year passes without accessions to our knowledge, even historically considered, upon some of the multifarious subjects which the present volumes embrace. An author who waits till all requisite materials are accumulated to his hands, is but watching the stream that will run on for ever; and, though I am fully sensible that I could have much improved what is now offered to the public by keeping it back for a longer time, I should but then have had to lament the impossibility of exhausting my subject. ΕΠΟΙΕΙ, the modest phrase of the Grecian sculptors, well expresses the imperfection that attaches to every work of literary industry or of philosophical investigation. But I have other warnings to bind up my sheaves while I may, — my own advancing years, and the gathering in the heavens.

I have quoted, to my recollection, no passage which I have not seen in its own place; though I may possibly have transcribed in some instances, for the sake of convenience, from a secondary authority. Without censuring those who suppress the immediate source of their quotations, I may justly say that in nothing I have given to the public has it been practised by myself. But I have now and then inserted in the text characters of books that I have not read on the faith of my guides; and it may be the case that intimation of this has not been always given to the reader.

It is very likely that omissions, not, I trust, of great consequence, will be detected; I might in fact say that I am already aware of them; but perhaps these will be candidly ascribed to the numerous ramifications of the subject, and the necessity of writing in a different order from that in which the pages are printed. And I must add that some omissions have been intentional: an accumulation of petty facts, and especially of names to which little is attached, fatigues unprofitably the attention; and as this is very frequent in works that necessarily demand condensation, and cannot altogether be avoided, it was desirable to make some sacrifice in order to palliate the inconvenience. This will be found, among many other instances, in the account of the Italian learned of the fifteenth century, where I might easily have doubled the enumeration, but with little satisfaction to the reader.

But, independently of such slighter omissions, it will appear that a good deal is wanting in these volumes which some might expect in a history of literature. Such a history has often contained so large a proportion of biography, that a work in which it appears very scantily, or hardly at all, may seem deficient in necessary information. It might be replied, that the limits to which I have confined myself, and beyond which it is not easy perhaps, in the present age, to obtain readers, would not admit of this extension: but I may add that any biography of the authors of these centuries, which is not servilely compiled from a few known books of that class, must be far too immense an undertaking for one man; and, besides its extent and difficulty, would have been particularly irksome to myself, from the waste of time, as I deem it, which an inquiry into trifling facts entails. I have more scruple about the omission of extracts from some of the poets and best writers in prose, without which they can be judged very unsatisfactorily; but in this also I have been influenced by an unwillingness to multiply my pages beyond a reasonable limit. But I have, in some instances, gone more largely into analyses of considerable works than has hitherto been usual. These are not designed to serve as complete abstracts, or to supersede instead of exciting the reader's industry; but I have felt that some books of traditional reputation are less fully known than they deserve.

Some departments of literature are passed over or partially touched. Among the former are books relating to particular arts, as agriculture or painting; or to subjects of merely local interest, as those of English law. Among the latter is the great and extensive portion of every library, — the historical. Unless where history has been written with peculiar beauty of language, or philosophical spirit, I have generally omitted all mention of it. In our researches after truth of fact, the number of books that possess some value is exceedingly great, and would occupy a disproportionate space in such a general view of literature as the present. For a similar reason, I have not given its numerical share to theology.

It were an impertinence to anticipate, for the sake of obviating, the possible criticism of a public which has a right to judge, and for whose judgments I have had so much cause to be grateful, nor less so to dictate how it should read what it is not bound to read at all: but perhaps I may be allowed to say that I do not wish this to be considered as a book of reference on particular topics, in which point of view it must often appear to disadvantage; and that, if it proves of any value, it will be as an entire and synoptical work.

ADVERTISEMENT TO THE FOURTH EDITION.

THE text of this work has been revised, and such errors as the Author detected have been removed. The few additional notes are distinguished by the dates of the publication of the different editions in the years 1842, 1847, and 1853.

CONTENTS

OF

THE FIRST VOLUME.

PART I.

ON THE LITERATURE OF THE FIFTEENTH AND FIRST HALF OF THE SIXTEENTH CENTURY.

CHAPTER I.

ON THE GENERAL STATE OF LITERATURE IN THE MIDDLE AGES TO THE END OF THE FOURTEENTH CENTURY.

CHAPTER II.

ON THE LITERATURE OF EUROPE FROM 1400 TO 1440.

CHAPTER III.

ON THE LITERATURE OF EUROPE FROM 1440 TO THE CLOSE OF THE FIFTEENTH CENTURY.

CHAPTER IV.

ON THE LITERATURE OF EUROPE FROM 1500 TO 1520.

CHAPTER V.

HISTORY OF ANCIENT LITERATURE IN EUROPE FROM 1520 TO 1550.

CHAPTER VI.

HISTORY OF THEOLOGICAL LITERATURE IN EUROPE FROM 1520 TO 1550.

CHAPTER VII.

HISTORY OF SPECULATIVE, MORAL, AND POLITICAL PHILOSOPHY, AND OF JURISPRUDENCE, IN EUROPE, FROM 1520 TO 1550.

CHAPTER VIII.

HISTORY OF THE LITERATURE OF TASTE IN EUROPE FROM 1520 TO 1550.

CHAPTER IX.

ON THE SCIENTIFIC AND MISCELLANEOUS LITERATURE OF EUROPE FROM 1520 TO 1550.

INTRODUCTION

TO THE

LITERATURE OF EUROPE

IN THE FIFTEENTH, SIXTEENTH, AND SEVENTEENTH CENTURIES.

PART I.

ON THE LITERATURE OF THE FIFTEENTH AND FIRST HALF OF THE SIXTEENTH CENTURY.

CHAPTER I.

ON THE GENERAL STATE OF LITERATURE IN THE MIDDLE AGES TO THE END OF THE FOURTEENTH CENTURY.

Loss of ancient Learning in the Fall of the Roman Empire — First Symptoms of its Revival — Improvement in the Twelfth Century — Universities and Scholastic Philosophy — Origin of Modern Languages — Early Poetry — Provençal, French, German, and Spanish — English Language and Literature — Increase of Elementary Knowledge — Invention of Paper — Roman Jurisprudence — Cultivation of Classical Literature — Its Decline after the Twelfth Century — Less visible in Italy — Petrarch.

Retrospect of learning in middle ages necessary.

1. ALTHOUGH the subject of these volumes does not comprehend the literary history of Europe anterior to the commencement of the fifteenth century, a period as nearly coinciding as can be expected in any arbitrary division of time with what is usually denominated the revival of letters, it appears necessary to prefix such a general retrospect of the state of knowledge for some preceding ages as will illustrate its subsequent progress. In this, however, the reader is not to expect a regular history of mediæval literature, which would be nothing less than the extension

of a scheme already, perhaps, too much beyond my powers of execution.[1]

Loss of learning in fall of Roman Empire.

2. Every one is well aware that the establishment of the barbarian nations on the ruins of the Roman Empire in the West was accompanied or followed by an almost universal loss of that learning which had been accumulated in the Latin and Greek languages, and which we call ancient or classical; a revolution long prepared by the decline of taste and knowledge for several preceding ages, but accelerated by public calamities in the fifth century with overwhelming rapidity. The last of the ancients, and one who forms a link between the classical period of literature and that of the middle ages, in which he was a favorite author, is Boethius, a man of fine genius, and interesting both from his character and his death. It is well known, that, after filling the dignities of consul and senator in the court of Theodoric, he fell a victim to the jealousy of a sovereign, from whose memory, in many respects glorious, the stain of that blood has never been effaced. The Consolation of Philosophy, the chief work of Boethius, was written in his prison. Few books are more striking from the circumstances of their production. Last of the classic writers, in style not impure, though displaying too lavishly that poetic exuberance which had distinguished the two or three preceding centuries, in elevation of sentiment equal to any of the philosophers, and mingling a Christian sanctity with their lessons, he speaks from his prison in the swan-like tones of dying eloquence. The philosophy that consoled him in bonds was soon required in the sufferings of a cruel death. Quenched in his blood, the lamp he had trimmed with a skilful hand gave no more light. The language of Tully and Virgil soon ceased to be spoken; and many ages were to pass away before learned diligence restored its purity, and the union of genius with imitation taught a few modern writers to surpass in eloquence the Latinity of Boethius.

Boethius: his Consolation of Philosophy.

3. The downfall of learning and eloquence after the death of Boethius, in 524, was inconceivably rapid. His contemporary Cassiodorus, Isidore of Seville, and Martianus Ca-

[1] The subject of the following chapter has been already treated by me in another work, — the History of Europe during the Middle Ages. I have not thought it necessary to repeat all that is there said. The reader, if he is acquainted with those volumes, may consider the ensuing pages partly as supplemental, and partly as correcting the former where they contain any thing inconsistent.

pella, the earliest but worst of the three, by very indifferent compilations, and that encyclopedic method which Heeren observes to be an usual concomitant of declining literature, superseded the use of the great ancient writers, with whom, indeed, in the opinion of Meiners, they were themselves acquainted only through similar productions of the fourth and fifth centuries. Isidore speaks of the rhetorical works of Cicero and Quintilian as too diffuse to be read.[1] The authorities upon which they founded their scanty course of grammar, logic, and rhetoric, were chiefly obscure writers, no longer extant; but themselves became the oracles of the succeeding period, wherein the trivium and quadrivium, a course of seven sciences, introduced in the sixth century, were taught from their jejune treatises.[2]

Rapid decline of learning in sixth century.

4. This state of general ignorance lasted, with no very sensible difference, on a superficial view, for about five centuries, during which every sort of knowledge was almost wholly confined to the ecclesiastical order; but among them, though instances of gross ignorance were exceedingly frequent, the necessity of preserving the Latin language, in which the Scriptures, the canons, and other authorities of the church, and the regular liturgies, were written, and in which alone the correspondence of their well-organized hierarchy could be conducted, kept flowing, in the worst seasons, a slender but living stream; and though, as has been observed, no great difference may appear, on a superficial view, between the seventh and eleventh centuries, it would

A portion remains in the church

[1] Meiners, Vergleichung der Sitten, &c., des Mittelalters mit denen unsers Jahrhunderts, 3 vols., Hanover, 1793, vol. ii. p. 333. Eichhorn, Allgemeine Geschichte der Cultur und Litteratur, vol. ii. p. 29. Heeren, Geschichte des Studium der classischen Litteratur, Göttingen, 1797. These three books, with the Histoire Littéraire de la France, Brucker's History of Philosophy, Turner's and Henry's Histories of England, Muratori's 43d Dissertation, Tiraboschi, and some few others, who will appear in the notes, are my chief authorities for the dark ages. But none, in a very short compass, is equal to the third discourse of Fleury, in the 13th volume of the 12mo edition of his Ecclesiastical History.

[2] The trivium contained grammar, logic, and rhetoric; the quadrivium, arithmetic, geometry, music, and astronomy, as in these two lines, framed to assist the memory: —

"GRAMM. loquitur; DIA. vera docet, RHET. verba colorat; MUS. canit; AR. numerat; GEO. ponderat; AST. colit astra."

But most of these sciences, as such, were hardly taught at all. The arithmetic, for instance, of Cassiodorus or Capella, is nothing but a few definitions mingled with superstitious absurdities about the virtues of certain numbers and figures. Meiners, ii. 339; Kästner, Geschichte der Mathematik, p. 8.

The arithmetic of Cassiodorus occupies little more than two folio pages, and does not contain one word of the common rules. The geometry is much the same: in two pages we have some definitions and axioms, but nothing farther. His logic is longer and better, extending to sixteen folio pages. The grammar is very short and trifling; the rhetoric, the same.

easily be shown, that, after the first prostration of learning, it was not long in giving signs of germinating afresh, and that a very slow and gradual improvement might be dated farther back than is generally believed.[1]

Prejudices of the clergy against profane learning.

5. Literature was assailed in its downfall by enemies from within as well as from without. A prepossession against secular learning had taken hold of those ecclesiastics who gave the tone to the rest. It was inculcated in the most extravagant degree by Gregory I., the founder, in a great measure, of the papal supremacy, and the chief authority in the dark ages.[2] It is even found in Alcuin, to whom so much is due; and it gave way very gradually in the revival of literature. In some of the monastic foundations, especially in that of Isidore, though himself a man of considerable learning, the perusal of heathen authors was prohibited. Fortunately, Benedict, whose order became the most widely diffused, while he enjoined his brethren to read, copy, and collect books, was silent as to their nature; concluding, probably, that they would be wholly religious. This, in course of time, became the means of preserving and multiplying classical manuscripts.[3]

Their usefulness in preserving it.

6. If, however, the prejudices of the clergy stood in the way of what we more esteem than they did, the study of philological literature, it is never to be forgotten, that, but for them, the records of that very literature would have perished. If they had been less tenacious of their Latin liturgy, of the vulgate translation of Scripture, and of the authority of the fathers, it is very doubtful whether less superstition would have grown up; but we cannot hesitate to pronounce, that all grammatical learning would have been laid aside. The influence of the church upon learning, partly

[1] M. Guizot confirms me in a conclusion to which I had previously come, that the seventh century is the *nadir* of the human mind in Europe, and that its movement in advance began before the end of the next, or, in other words, with Charlemagne. Hist. de la Civilisation en France, ii. 345. A notion probably is current in England, on the authority of the older writers, such as Cave or Robertson, that the greatest darkness was later; which is true as to England itself. It was in the seventh century that the barbarians were first tempted to enter the church and obtain bishoprics, which had, in the first age after their invasion, been reserved to Romans. — Fleury, p. 18.

[2] Gregory has been often charged, on the authority of a passage in John of Salisbury, with having burned a library of heathen authors. He has been warmly defended by Tiraboschi, iii. 102. Even if the assertion of our countryman were more positive, he is of too late an age to demand much credit. Eichhorn, however, produces vehement expressions of Gregory's disregard for learning, and even for the observance of grammatical rules ii. 443.

[3] Heeren, p. 59; Eichhorn, ii. 11, 12. 40, 49, 50.

favorable, partly the reverse, forms the subject of Eichhorn's second volume, whose comprehensive views and well-directed erudition, as well as his position in a great Protestant university, give much weight to his testimony: but we should remember, also, that it is, as it were, by striking a balance that we come to this result; and that, in many respects, the clergy counteracted that progress of improvement, which, in others, may be ascribed to their exertions.

First appearances of reviving learning in Ireland and England.

7. It is not unjust to claim for these islands the honor of having first withstood the dominant ignorance, and even led the way in the restoration of knowledge. As early as the sixth century, a little glimmer of light was perceptible in the Irish monasteries; and in the next, when France and Italy had sunk in deeper ignorance, they stood, not quite where national prejudice has sometimes placed them, but certainly in a very respectable position.[1] That island both drew students from the continent, and sent forth men of comparative eminence into its schools and churches. I do not find, however, that they contributed much to the advance of secular, and especially of grammatical, learning. This is rather due to England, and to the happy influence of Theodore, Archbishop of Canterbury, an Asiatic Greek by birth, sent hither by the pope in 668; through whom, and his companion Adrian, some knowledge of the Latin and even Greek languages was propagated in the Anglo-Saxon church. The Venerable Bede, as he was afterwards styled, early in the eighth century, surpasses every other name of our ancient literary annals; and, though little more than a diligent compiler from older writers, may perhaps be reckoned superior to any man whom the world (so low had the East sunk like the West) then possessed. A desire of knowledge grew up. The school of York, somewhat later, became respectable, before any liberal education had been established in France; and from this came Alcuin, a man fully equal to Bede in ability, though not in erudition.[2] By his assistance, and that

[1] Eichhorn, ii. 176, 188. See also the first volume of Moore's History of Ireland, where the claims of his country are stated favorably, and with much learning and industry, but not with extravagant partiality.

[2] Eichhorn, ii. 188, 207, 263; Hist. Litt. de la France, vols. iii. and iv.; Henry's History of England, vol. iv.; Turner's History of Anglo-Saxons. No one, however, has spoken so highly or so fully of Alcuin's merits as M. Guizot, in his Histoire de la Civilisation en France, vol. ii. pp. 344-385.

[The writings of Alcuin are not highly appreciated by the learned and judicious author of Biographia Britannica Literaria, especially in relation to their influence upon English literature. The truth is that Alcuin was a polite scholar for the age in

of one or two Italians, Charlemagne laid in his vast dominions the foundations of learning, according to the standard of that age, which dispelled, at least for a time, some part of the gross ignorance wherein his empire had been enveloped.[1]

Few schools before the age of Charlemagne.

8. The praise of having originally established schools belongs to some bishops and abbots of the sixth century. They came in place of the imperial schools overthrown by the barbarians.[2] In the downfall of that temporal dominion, a spiritual aristocracy was providentially raised up to save from extinction the remains of learning, and religion itself. Some of those schools seem to have been preserved in the south of Italy, though merely, perhaps, for elementary instruction; but in France the barbarism of the latter Merovingian period was so complete, that before the reign of Charlemagne, all liberal studies had come to an end.[3] Nor was Italy in a much better state at his accession, though he called two or three scholars from thence to his literary councils. The libraries were destroyed, the schools chiefly closed. Wherever the Lombard dominion extended, illiteracy was its companion.[4]

Beneficial effects of those established by him

9. The cathedral and conventual schools, created or restored by Charlemagne, became the means of preserving that small portion of learning which continued to exist. They flourished most, having had time to produce their fruits, under his successors, Louis the Debonair, Lothaire, and Charles the Bald.[5] It was doubtless a fortunate circumstance, that the revolution of language had now gone far enough to render Latin unintelligible without grammatical instruction. Alcuin, and others who, like him, endeavored to keep ignorance out of the church, were anxious,

which he lived, but no real poet. "He has, on the whole," says Mr. Wright, "more simplicity and less pretension in his poetry than his predecessor Aldhelm; and, so far, he is more pleasing: but unfortunately, when the latter was turgid and bombastic, the former too often went into the opposite extreme of being flat and spiritless;" p. 46. This criticism seems not unjust. Alcuin, however, is an easy versifier, and has caught the tone of Ovid, sometimes of Virgil, with some success. — 1847.]

[1] Besides the above authors, see, for the merits of Charlemagne as a restorer of letters, his Life by Gaillard and Andrès, Origine, &c., della Litteratura, i. 165.

[2] Eichhorn, ii. 5, 45. Guizot (vol. ii. p. 116) gives a list of the episcopal schools in France before Charlemagne.

[3] Ante ipsum Carolum regem in Gallia nullum fuerat studium liberalium artium. Monachus Engolimensis, apud Launoy de Scholis celebrioribus.

[4] Tiraboschi; Eichhorn; Heeren.

[5] The reader may find more of the history of these schools in a little treatise by Launoy, De Scholis celebrioribus a Car. Mag. et post Car. Mag. instauratis; also in Hist. Litt. de la France, vols. iii. and iv.; Crevier, Hist. de l'Université de Paris, vol. i.; Brucker's Hist. Phil. iii.; Muratori, Dissert. xliii.; Tiraboschi, iii. 158; Eichhorn, 261, 295; Heeren; and Fleury.

we are told, to restore orthography; or, in other words, to prevent the written Latin from following the corruptions of speech. They brought back also some knowledge of better classical authors than had been in use. Alcuin's own poems could, at least, not have been written by one unacquainted with Virgil.[1] The faults are numerous; but the style is not always inelegant: and from this time, though quotations from the Latin poets, especially Ovid and Virgil, and sometimes from Cicero, are not very frequent, they occur sufficiently to show that manuscripts had been brought to this side of the Alps. They were, however, very rare. Italy was still, as might be expected, the chief depository of ancient writings; and Gerbert speaks of the facility of obtaining them in that country.[2]

The tenth century more progressive than usually supposed.

10. The tenth century used to be reckoned by mediæval historians the darkest part of this intellectual night. It was the iron age which they vie with one another in describing as lost in the most consummate ignorance. This, however, is much rather applicable to Italy and England than to France and Germany. The former were both in a deplorable state of barbarism;[3] and there are doubtless abundant proofs of ignorance in every part of Europe. But, compared with the seventh and eighth centuries, the tenth was an age of illumination in France; and Meiners, who judged the middle ages somewhat, perhaps, too severely, but with a penetrating and comprehensive observation, of which there had been few instances, has gone so far as to say, that "in no age, perhaps, did Germany possess more learned and virtuous churchmen of the episcopal order than in the latter half of the tenth and beginning of the eleventh century."[4] Eichhorn points out indications of a more extensive acquaintance with ancient writers in several French and German ecclesiastics of this period.[5] In the eleventh century, this continued to increase; and, towards its close, we find more vigorous and extensive attempts at throwing off the yoke of barbarous ignorance, and either retrieving what had

1 A poem by Alcuin, De Pontificibus Ecclesiæ Eboracensis, is published in Gale's XV. Scriptores, vol. iii.

2 Nosti quot scriptores in urbibus aut in agris Italiæ passim habeantur. Gerbert. Epist. 130, apud Heeren, p. 166.

3 [See Tiraboschi for the one, and Turner's History of Anglo-Saxons for the other. But I do not know that England was *more* dark in the tenth century than in the ninth. —1842.]

4 Vergleichung der Sitten, ii. 384. The eleventh century he holds far more advanced in learning than the sixth. Books were read in the latter which no one looked at in the earlier; p. 399.

5 Allg. Gesch. ii. 335, 398.

been lost of ancient learning, or supplying its place by the original powers of the mind.

Want of genius in the dark ages.

11. It is the most striking circumstance in the literary annals of the dark ages, that they seem to us still more deficient in native than in acquired ability. The mere ignorance of letters has sometimes been a little exaggerated, and admits of certain qualifications; but a tameness and mediocrity, a servile habit of merely compiling from others, runs through the writers of these centuries. It is not only that much was lost, but that there was nothing to compensate for it, — nothing of original genius in the province of imagination; and but two extraordinary men, Scotus Erigena and Gerbert, may be said to stand out from the crowd, in literature and philosophy. It must be added as to the former, that his writings contain, at least in such extracts as I have seen, unintelligible rhapsodies of mysticism, in which, perhaps, he should not even have the credit of originality. Eichhorn, however, bestows great praise on Scotus; and the modern historians of philosophy treat him with respect.[1]

Prevalence of bad taste.

12. It would be a strange hypothesis, that no man endowed with superior gifts of Nature lived in so many ages. Though the pauses of her fertility in these high endowments are more considerable, I am disposed to think, than any previous calculation of probabilities would lead us to anticipate, we could not embrace so extreme a paradox. Of military skill, indeed, and civil prudence, we are not now speaking. But, though no man appeared of genius sufficient to burst the fetters imposed by ignorance and bad taste, some there must have been, who, in a happier condition of literature, would have been its legitimate pride. We perceive, therefore, in the deficiencies of these writers, the effect which an oblivion of good models and the prevalence of a false standard of merit may produce in repressing the natural vigor of the mind. Their style, where they aim at eloquence, is inflated and redundant, formed upon the model of the later fathers, whom they chiefly read, — a feeble imitation of that

[1] Extracts from John Scotus Erigena will be found in Brucker, Hist. Philosophiæ, vol. iii. p. 619; in Meiners, ii. 373; or more fully in Turner's History of England, vol. i 447; and Guizot, Hist. de la Civilisation en France, iii. 137, 178. The reader may consult also Buhle, Tennemann, and the article on Thomas Aquinas in the Encyclopædia Metropolitana, ascribed to Dr. Hampden. But perhaps Mr. Turner is the only one of them who has seen, or at least read, the metaphysical treatise of John Scotus, entitled De Divisione Naturæ, in which alone we find his Philosophy. It is very rare out of England. nor common in it.

vicious rhetoric which had long overspread the Latinity of the empire.[1]

13. It might naturally be asked, whether fancy and feeling were extinct among the people, though a false taste might reign in the cloister. Yet it is here that we find the most remarkable deficiency, and could appeal scarce to the vaguest tradition or the most doubtful fragment in witness of any poetical talent worthy of notice, except a little in the Teutonic languages. The Anglo-Saxon poetry has occasionally a wild spirit, rather impressive; though it is often turgid, and always rude. The Scandinavian, such as the well-known song of Regner Lodbrog, if that be as old as the period before us, which is now denied, displays a still more poetical character. Some of the earliest German poetry, the song on the victory of Louis III. over the Normans in 883, and, still more, the poem in praise of Hanno, Archbishop of Cologne, who died in 1075, are warmly extolled by Herder and Bouterwek.[2] In the Latin verse of these centuries, we

Deficiency of poetical talent.

[1] Fleury, l. xlv. § 19; and Troisième Discours (in vol. xiii.), p. 6. Turner's History of England, iv. 137; and History of Anglo-Saxons, iii. 403. It is sufficient to look at any extracts from these writers of the dark ages to see the justice of this censure. Fleury, at the conclusion of his excellent third discourse, justly and candidly apologizes for these five ages as not wholly destitute of learning, and far less of virtue. They have been, he says, outrageously depreciated by the humanists of the sixteenth century, who thought good Latin superior to every thing else; and by Protestant writers, who laid the corruptions of the church on its ignorance. Yet there is an opposite extreme, into which those who are disgusted with the commonplaces of superficial writers sometimes run; an estimation of men by their relative superiority above their own times, so as to forget their position in comparison with a fixed standard.

An eminent living writer, who has carried the philosophy of history, perhaps, as far as any other, has lately endeavored, at considerable length, to vindicate in some measure the intellectual character of this period (Guizot, vol. ii. p. 123-224). It is with reluctance that I ever differ from M. Guizot; but the passages adduced by him (especially if we exclude those of the fifth century, the poems of Avitus, and the homilies of Cæsarius) do not appear adequate to redeem the age by any signs of genius they display. It must always be a question of degree; for no one is absurd enough to deny the existence of a relative superiority of talent, or the power of expressing moral emotions, as well as relating facts, with some warmth and energy. The legends of saints, an extensive though quite neglected portion of the literature of the dark ages, to which M. Guizot has had the merit of directing our attention, may probably contain many passages, like those he had quoted, which will be read with interest; and it is no more than justice that he has given them in French, rather than in that half-barbarous Latin, which, though not essential to the author's mind, never fails, like an unbecoming dress, to show the gifts of nature at a disadvantage. But the questions still recur: Is this, in itself, excellent? Would it indicate, wherever we should meet with it, powers of a high order? Do we not make a tacit allowance in reading it, and that very largely, for the mean condition in which we know the human mind to have been placed at the period? Does it instruct us, or give us pleasure?

In what M. Guizot has said of the moral influence of these legends, in humanizing a lawless barbarian race (p. 157), I should be sorry not to concur: it is a striking instance of that candid and catholic spirit with which he has always treated the mediæval church.

[2] Herder, Zerstreute Blatter, vol. v. p. 169, 184; Heinsius, Lehrbuch der Deutschen

find, at best, a few lines among many which show the author to have caught something of a classical style: the far greater portion is very bad.[1]

14. The very imperfect state of language, as an instrument of refined thought in the transition of Latin to the French, Castilian, and Italian tongues, seems the best means of accounting in any satisfactory manner for this stagnation of the poetical faculties. The delicacy that distinguishes in words the shades of sentiment, the grace that brings them to the soul of the reader with the charm of novelty united to clearness, could not be attainable in a colloquial jargon, the offspring of ignorance, and indeterminate possibly in its forms, which those who possessed any superiority of education would endeavor to avoid. We shall soon have occasion to advert again to this subject.

Imperfect state of language may account for this.

15. At the beginning of the twelfth century, we enter upon a new division in the literary history of Europe. From this time we may deduce a line of men, conspicuous, according to the standard of their times, in different walks of intellectual pursuit; and the commencement of an interesting period, the later middle ages, in which, though ignorance was very far from being cleared away, the natural powers of the mind were developed in considerable activity. We shall point out separately the most important circumstances of this progress, not all of them concurrent in efficacy with each other, for they were sometimes opposed, but all tending to arouse Europe from indolence, and to fix its attention on literature. These are, 1st, The institution of universities, and the methods pursued in them; 2d, The cultivation of the modern languages, followed by the multiplication of books and the extension of

Improvement at beginning of twelfth century.

Leading circumstances in progress of learning.

Sprachwissenschaft, iv. 29; Bouterwek, Geschichte der Poesie und Beredsamkeit, vol ix. p. 78, 82. The author is unknown: "aber dem unbekannten sichert sein Werk die Unsterblichkeit," says the latter critic. One might raise a question as to the capacity of an anonymous author to possess immortal fame. Nothing equal to this poem, he says, occurs in the earlier German poetry: it is an outpouring of genius, not without faults, but full of power and feeling. The dialect is still Frankish, but approaches to Swabian. Herder calls it "a truly Pindaric song." He has given large extracts from it in the volume above quoted, which glows with his own fine sense of beauty.

[1] Tiraboschi supposes Latin versifiers to have been common in Italy. Le Città al pari che le campagne risuonavan di versi; iii. 207.

The specimens he afterwards produces, p. 219, are miserable. Hroswitha, Abbess of Gandersheim, has, perhaps, the greatest reputation among these Latin poets. She wrote, in the tenth century, sacred comedies in imitation of Terence, which I have not seen, and other poetry which I saw many years since, and thought very indifferent.

the art of writing; 3d, The investigation of the Roman law: and, lastly, The return to the study of the Latin language in its ancient models of purity. We shall thus come down to the fifteenth century, and judge better of what is meant by the revival of letters when we apprehend with more exactness their previous condition.

Origin of the University of Paris.

16. Among the Carlovingian schools, it is doubtful whether we can reckon one at Paris; and, though there are some traces of public instruction in that city about the end of the ninth century, it is not certain that we can assume it to be more ancient. For two hundred years more, indeed, it can only be said that some persons appear to have come to Paris for the purposes of study.[1] The commencement of this famous university, like that of Oxford, has no record; but it owes its first reputation to the sudden spread of what is usually called the scholastic philosophy.

Modes of treating the science of theology.

17. There had been hitherto two methods of treating theological doctrines: one, that of the fathers, who built them on Scripture, illustrated and interpreted by their own ingenuity, and in some measure also on the traditions and decisions of the church; the other, which is said by the Benedictines of St. Maur to have grown up about the eighth century (though Mosheim seems to refer it to the sixth), using the fathers themselves; that is, the chief writers of the first six hundred years, who appear now to have acquired that distinctive title of honor as authority, conjointly with Scripture and ecclesiastical determinations, by means of extracts or compends of their writings. Hence, about this time, we find more frequent instances of a practice which had begun before, — that of publishing *Loci communes* or *Catenæ patrum*, being only digested extracts from the authorities under systematic heads.[2] Both these methods were usually called positive theology.

[1] Crevier, i. 13-75.

[2] Fleury, 3me Discours, p. 48 (Hist. Ecclés. vol. xiii. 12mo ed.); Hist. Litt. de la France, vii. 147; Mosheim, in Cent. vi. et post; Muratori, Antichità Italiane, dissert. xliii. p. 610. In this dissertation, it may be observed by the way, Muratori gives the important fragment of Caius, a Roman presbyter before the end of the second century (as some place him), on the canon of the New Testament, which has not been quoted, as far as I know, by any English writer; nor, which is more remarkable, by Michaelis. It will be found in Eichhorn, Einleitung in das Neue Testament, iv. 35 [and I have learned, since the publication of my first edition, that is printed in Routh's Reliquiæ Sacræ. — 1842].

Upon this great change in the theology of the church, which consisted principally in establishing the authority of the fathers, the reader may see M. Guizot, Hist. de la Civilisation, iii. 121. There seem to be but two causes for this: the one, a consciousness of ignorance and inferiority to

Scholastic philosophy: its origin.

18. The scholastic theology was a third method: it was, in its general principle, an alliance between faith and reason, — an endeavor to arrange the orthodox system of the church, such as authority had made it, according to the rules and methods of the Aristotelian dialectics, and sometimes upon premises supplied by metaphysical reasoning. Lanfranc and Anselm made much use of this method in the controversy with Berenger as to transubstantiation, though they did not carry it so far as their successors in the next century.[1] The scholastic philosophy seems chiefly to be distinguished from this theology by a larger infusion of metaphysical reasoning, or by its occasional inquiries into subjects not immediately related to revealed articles of faith.[2] The origin of this philosophy, fixed by Buhle and Tennemann in the ninth century, or the age of Scotus Erigena, has been brought down by Tiedemann, Meiners, and Hampden[3] so low as the thirteenth. But Roscelin of Compiègne, a little before 1100, may be accounted so far the founder of the schoolmen, that the great celebrity of their dispu-

Roscelin.

men of so much talent as Augustin and a few others; the other, a constantly growing jealousy of the free exercise of reason, and a determination to keep up unity of doctrine.

[1] Hist. Litt. de la France, ubi suprà; Tennemann, Manuel de l'Hist. de la Philosophie, i. 332; Crevier, i. 100; Andrès, ii. 15.

[2] A Jesuit of the sixteenth century thus shortly and clearly distinguishes the positive from the scholastic, and both from natural or metaphysical theology: "At nos theologiam scholasticam dicimus, quæ certiori methodo et rationibus imprimis ex divina Scriptura, ac traditionibus seu decretis patrum in conciliis definitis veritatem eruit, ac discutiendo comprobat. Quod cum in scholis præcipue argumentando comparetur, id nomen sortita est. Quamobrem differt a positiva theologia, non re sed modo, quemadmodum item alia ratione non est eadem cum naturali theologia, quo nomine philosophi metaphysicen nominarunt. Positiva igitur non ita res disputandas proponit, sed pœne sententiam ratam et firmam ponit, præcipue in pietatem incumbens. Versatur autem et ipsa in explicatione Scripturæ sacræ, traditionum, conciliorum et sanctorum patrum. Naturalis porro theologia Dei naturam per naturæ argumenta et rationes inquirit, cum supernaturalis, quam scholasticam dicimus, Dei ejusdem naturam, vim, proprietates, cæterasque res divinas per ea principia vestigat, quæ sunt hominibus revelata divinitus."—Possevin, Bibliotheca Selecta, l. 3, c. i.

Both positive and scholastic theology were much indebted to Peter Lombard, whose Liber Sententiarum is a digest of propositions extracted from the fathers, with no attempt to reconcile them. It was, therefore, a prodigious magazine of arms for disputation.

[3] The first of these, according to Tennemann, begins the list of schoolmen with Hales: the two latter agree in conferring that honor on Albertus Magnus. Brucker inclines to Roscelin, and has been followed by others. It may be added, that Tennemann divides the scholastic philosophy into four periods, which Roscelin, Hales, Ockham, and the sixteenth century, terminate; and Buhle into three, ending with Roscelin, Albertus Magnus, and the sixteenth century. It is evident, that, by beginning the scholastic series with Roscelin, we exclude Lanfranc, and even Anselm, the latter of whom was certainly a deep metaphysician; since to him we owe the subtle argument for the existence of a Deity, which Des Cartes afterwards revived. Buhle, 679. This argument was answered at the time by one Gaunelo; so that metaphysical reasonings were not unknown in the eleventh century. Tennemann, 344.

tations and the rapid increase of students are to be traced to the influence of his theories, though we have no proof that he ever taught at Paris. Roscelin also, having been the first to revive the famous question as to the reality of universal ideas, marks, on every hypothesis, a new era in the history of philosophy. The principle of the schoolmen in their investigations was the expanding, developing, and, if possible, illustrating, and clearing from objection, the doctrines of natural and revealed religion, in a dialectical method, and by dint of the subtlest reason. The questions which we deem altogether metaphysical, such as that concerning universal ideas, became theological in their hands.[1]

Progress of scholasticism; increase of University of Paris

19. Next in order of time to Roscelin came William of Champeaux, who opened a school of logic at Paris in 1109; and the university can only deduce the regular succession of its teachers from that time.[2] But his reputation was soon eclipsed and his hearers drawn away by a more potent magician, Peter Abelard, who taught in the schools of Paris in the second decade of the twelfth century. Wherever Abelard retired, his fame and his disciples followed him, — in the solitary walls of the Paraclete as in the thronged streets of the capital;[3] and the impulse given was so powerful, the fascination of a science which now appears arid and unproductive was so intense, that from this time, for many generations, it continued to engage the most intelligent and active minds. Paris, about the middle of the twelfth century, in the words of the Benedictines of St. Maur, to whom we owe the "Histoire Littéraire de la France," was another Athens; the number of students

1 Brucker, though he contains some useful extracts and tolerable general views, was not well versed in the scholastic writers. Meiners (in his Comparison of the Middle Ages) is rather superficial as to their philosophy, but presents a lively picture of the schoolmen in relation to literature and manners. He has also, in the Transactions of the Göttingen Academy, vol. xii. pp. 26–47, given a succinct but valuable sketch of the Nominalist and Realist Controversy. Tennemann, with whose Manuel de la Philosophie alone I am conversant, is said to have gone very deeply into the subject in his larger history of Philosophy. Buhle appears superficial. Dr. Hampden, in his Life of Thomas Aquinas, and view of the scholastic philosophy, published in the Encyclopædia Metropolitana, has the merit of having been the only Englishman, past or present, so far as I know, since the revival of letters, who has penetrated far into the wilderness of scholasticism. Mr. Sharon Turner has given some extracts in the fourth volume of his History of England.

[M. Cousin, in the fourth volume of his Fragmens Philosophiques, has gone more fully than any one into the philosophy of Roscelin, and especially of Abelard. This is reprinted from the Introduction to the unpublished works of Abelard, edited by M. Cousin in the great series of Documens Inédits. — 1847.]

2 Crevier, i. 3.

3 Hist. Litt. de la France, vol. xii.; Brucker, iii. 750.

(hyperbolically speaking, as we must presume) exceeding that of the citizens. This influx of scholars induced Philip Augustus some time afterwards to enlarge the boundaries of the city; and this again brought a fresh harvest of students, for whom, in the former limits, it had been difficult to find lodgings. Paris was called, as Rome had been, the country of all the inhabitants of the world; and we may add, as, for very different reasons, it still claims to be.[1]

Universities founded.

Oxford.

20. Colleges, with endowments for poor scholars, were founded in the beginning of the thirteenth century, or even before, at Paris and Bologna, as they were afterwards at Oxford and Cambridge, by munificent patrons of letters. Charters incorporating the graduates and students collectively, under the name of universities, were granted by sovereigns, with privileges perhaps too extensive, but such as indicated the dignity of learning and the countenance it received.[2] It ought, however, to be remembered, that these foundations were not the cause, but the effect, of that increasing thirst for knowledge, or the semblance of knowledge, which had anticipated the encouragement of the great. The schools of Charlemagne were designed to lay the basis of a learned education, for which there was at that time no sufficient desire.[3] But, in the twelfth century, the impetu-

[1] Hist. Litt. de la France, ix. 78; Crevier, i. 274.

[2] Fleury, xvii. 13, 17; Crevier; Tiraboschi, &c. A university, "universitas doctorum et scholarium," was so called either from its incorporation, or from its professing to teach all subjects, as some have thought. Meiners, ii. 405; Fleury, xvii. 15. This excellent discourse of Fleury, the fifth, relates to the ecclesiastical literature of the later middle ages.

[The first privilege granted to Bologna was by Frederic Barbarossa in 1158. But it gives an appeal to the bishops, not to the rector of the university, in case any scholar had cause of complaint against his teacher. In fact, there was no rector, nor, properly speaking, any university, till near the end of the twelfth century. Savigny, Gesch. des Römischen Rechts, 111, 152. And as at Bologna nothing was taught but jurisprudence for some time afterwards, it is doubted by some, whether that school could be called a university, which ought to be a place of general instruction. Tiraboschi, v. 253. Upon the whole, the precedence must be allowed, I think, to Paris; but even there we cannot trace the university, as strictly such, so high as 1200. "En ces temps là, l'ensemble des écoles Parisiennes était appelé *studium generale* bien plûtot qu'*universitas;* ce dernier nom leur fut appliqué, peut-être pour la première fois, dans l'affaire d'Amaury de Chartres et de ses disciples en 1209. Il n'est point employé dans le diplome de Philippe Auguste, donné en 1201, à l'occasion d'une rixe violente entre les écoliers et les bourgeois de Paris." Discours sur l'état de lettres au treizième siècle, in Hist. Litt. de la France, vol. xvi. p. 46, par Daunou.

The University of Toulouse was incorporated with the same privileges as that of Paris by a bull of Gregory IX. in 1233; which seems to have been acknowledged as sufficient in France on several other occasions. Montpellier, which had for some time been a flourishing school of medicine, acquired the rights of an university before the end of the thirteenth century; but no other is of equal antiquity. Id. pp. 57, 59. 1842.]

[3] These schools, established by the Carlovingian princes in convents and cathedrals, declined, as it was natural to expect, with the rise of the universities. Meiners, ii. 406. Those of Paris, Oxford, and Bologna contained many thousand students.

osity with which men rushed to that source of what they deemed wisdom, the great University of Paris, did not depend upon academical privileges or eleemosynary stipends, which came afterwards; though these were undoubtedly very effectual in keeping it up. The university created patrons, and was not created by them. And this may be said also of Oxford and Cambridge, in their incorporate character, whatever the former may have owed, if in fact it owed any thing, to the prophetic munificence of Alfred. Oxford was a school of great resort in the reign of Henry II., though its first charter was only granted by Henry III. Its earlier history is but obscure, and depends chiefly on a suspicious passage in Ingulphus, against which we must set the absolute silence of other writers.[1] It became, in the thirteenth century, second only to Paris in the multitude of its students and the celebrity of its scholastic disputations. England, indeed, and especially through Oxford, could show more names of the first class in this line than any other country.[2]

Collegiate foundations not derived from the Saracens.

21. Andrès is inclined to derive the institution of collegiate foundations in universities from the Saracens. He finds no trace of these among the ancients; while in several cities of Spain, as Cordova, Granada, Malaga, colleges for learned education both existed, and obtained great renown. These were sometimes unconnected

[1] Giraldus Cambrensis, about 1180, seems the first unequivocal witness to the resort of students to Oxford as an established seat of instruction. But it is certain that Vacarius read there on the civil law in 1149; which affords a presumption that it was already assuming the character of a university. John of Salisbury, I think, does not mention it. In a former work, I gave more credence to its foundation by Alfred than I am now inclined to do. Bologna, as well as Paris, was full of English students about 1200. Meiners, ii. 428.

[2] Wood expatiates on what he thought the glorious age of the university. "What university, I pray, can produce an invincible Hales, an admirable Bacon, an excellent, well-grounded Middleton, a subtle Scotus, an approved Burley, a resolute Baconthorpe, a singular Ockham, a solid and industrious Holcot, and a profound Bradwardin? all which persons flourished within the compass of one century. I doubt that neither Paris, Bologna, or Rome, that grand mistress of the Christian world, or any place else, can do what the renowned Bellosite (Oxford) hath done. And, without doubt, all impartial men may receive it for an undeniable truth, that the most subtle arguing in school divinity did take its beginning in England and from Englishmen; and that also from thence it went to Paris and other parts of France, and at length into Italy, Spain, and other nations, as is by one observed. So that, though Italy boasted that Britain takes her Christianity first from Rome, England may truly maintain, that, from her (immediately by France), Italy first received her school divinity." Vol. i. p. 159, A.D. 1168.

[If the authenticity of the History of Croyland Abbey, under the name of Ingulphus, cannot be maintained, as both Sir Francis Palgrave and Mr. Wright contend, the antiquity of the University of Oxford must, I fear, fall to the ground. See Biographia Britannica Litteraria, vol. ii. p. 28. Whether Vacarius were the first lecturer, or chose that town because a school had already been established therein, seems not determinable, though the latter is more likely. — 1847.]

with each other, though in the same city; nor had they, of course, those privileges which were conferred in Christendom. They were, therefore, more like ordinary schools or gymnasia than universities; and it is difficult to perceive that they suggested any thing peculiarly characteristic of the latter institutions, which are much more reasonably considered as the development of a native germ, planted by a few generous men, above all by Charlemagne, in that inclement season which was passing away.[1]

Scholastic philosophy promoted by Mendicant friars.

22. The institution of the Mendicant orders of friars, soon after the beginning of the thirteenth century, caused a fresh accession, in enormous numbers, to the ecclesiastical state, and gave encouragement to the scholastic philosophy. Less acquainted, generally, with grammatical literature than the Benedictine monks, less accustomed to collect and transcribe books, the disciples of Francis and Dominic betook themselves to disputation, and found a substitute for learning in their own ingenuity and expertness.[2] The greatest of the schoolmen were the Dominican Thomas Aquinas and the Franciscan Duns Scotus. They were founders of rival sects, which wrangled with each other for two or three centuries. But the authority of their writings, which were incredibly voluminous, especially those of the former,[3] impeded, in some measure, the growth of new men; and we find, after the middle of the fourteenth century, a diminution of eminent names in the series of the schoolmen, the last of whom that is much remembered in modern times was William Ockham.[4] He revived the sect of the Nominalists, formerly

[1] Andrès, ii. 129.

[2] Meiners, ii. 615, 629.

[3] The works of Thomas Aquinas are published in seventeen volumes folio; Rome, 1570: those of Duns Scotus in twelve; Lyons, 1639. It is presumed that much was taken down from their oral lectures. Some part of these volumes is of doubtful authenticity. Meiners, ii. 718; Biogr. Univ.

[4] "In them (Scotus and Ockham), and in the later schoolmen generally, down to the period of the Reformation, there is more of the parade of logic, a more formal examination of arguments, a more burthensome importunity of syllogizing, with less of the philosophical power of arrangement and distribution of the subject discussed. The dryness again inseparable from the scholastic method is carried to excess in the later writers, and perspicuity of style is altogether neglected." Encyclopædia Metropol., part xxxvii. p. 805.

The introduction of this excess of logical subtlety, carried to the most trifling sophistry, is ascribed by Meiners to Petrus Hispanus, afterwards Pope John XXI., who died in 1271; ii. 705. Several curious specimens of scholastic folly are given by him in this place. They brought a discredit upon the name, which has adhered to it, and involved men of fine genius, such as Aquinas himself, in the common reproach.

The barbarism of style, which amounted almost to a new language, became more intolerable in Scotus and his followers than it had been in the older schoolmen. — Meiners, 722. It may be alleged, in excuse of this, that words are meant to express precise ideas; and that it was as impos-

instituted by Roscelin, and, with some important variations of opinion, brought into credit by Abelard, but afterwards overpowered by the great weight of leading schoolmen on the opposite side,—that of the Realists. The disciples of Ockham, as well as himself, being politically connected with the party in Germany unfavorable to the high pretensions of the court of Rome, though they became very numerous in the universities, passed for innovators in ecclesiastical as well as philosophical principles. Nominalism itself, indeed, was reckoned by the adverse sect cognate to heresy. No decline, however, seems to have been as yet perceptible in the spirit of disputation, which probably, at the end of the fourteenth century, went on as eagerly at Paris, Oxford, and Salamanca, the great scenes of that warfare, as before, and which, in that age, gained much ground in Germany through the establishment of several universities.

Character of this philosophy.

23. Tennemann has fairly stated the good and bad of the scholastic philosophy. It gave rise to a great display of address, subtlety, and sagacity, in the explanation and distinction of abstract ideas, but at the same time to many trifling and minute speculations, to a contempt of positive and particular knowledge, and to much unnecessary refinement.[1] Fleury well observes, that the dry technical style of the schoolmen, affecting a geometrical method and closeness, is in fact more prolix and tedious than one more natural, from its formality in multiplying objections and answers.[2] And, as their reasonings commonly rest on disputable postulates, the accuracy they affect is of no sort of value. But their chief offences were the interposing obstacles to the revival of polite literature, and to the free expansion of the mind. Italy was the land where the schoolmen had least influence; though many of the Italians, who had a turn for those discussions, repaired to Paris.[3] Public schools of theology were not opened in Italy till after 1360;[4] yet we find the disciples of Averroes numerous in the University of Padua about that time.

It prevails least in Italy.

24. II. The universities were chiefly employed upon this scholastic theology and metaphysics, with the exception of

sible to write metaphysics in good Latin as the modern naturalists have found it to describe plants and animals.

[1] Manuel de la Philosophie, i. 337; Eichhorn, ii. 396

[2] See 5me Discours, xvii. 30-50.

[3] Tiraboschi, v. 115.

[4] Id. 137, 160; De Sade, Vie de Petrarque, iii. 757.

Bologna, which dedicated its attention to the civil law; and of Montpellier, already famous as a school of medicine. The laity in general might have remained in as gross barbarity as before, while topics so removed from common utility were treated in an unknown tongue. We must therefore look to the rise of a truly native literature in the several languages of Western Europe, as a more essential cause of its intellectual improvement; and this will render it necessary to give a sketch of the origin and early progress of those languages and that new literature.

Literature in modern languages.

25. No one can require to be informed, that the Italian, Spanish, and French languages are the principal of many dialects deviating from each other in the gradual corruption of the Latin, once universally spoken by the subjects of Rome in her western provinces. They have undergone this process of change in various degrees, but always from similar causes: partly from the retention of barbarous words belonging to their original languages, or the introduction of others through the settlement of the Northern nations in the empire; but in a far greater proportion from ignorance of grammatical rules, or from vicious pronunciation and orthography. It has been the labor of many distinguished writers to trace the source and channels of these streams, which have supplied both the literature and the common speech of the south of Europe; and perhaps not much will be hereafter added to researches, which, in the scarcity of extant documents, can never be minutely successful. Du Cange, who led the way in the admirable preface to his Glossary; Le Bœuf and Bonamy, in several memoirs among the transactions of the Academy of Inscriptions, about the middle of the last century; Muratori, in his 32d, 33d, and 40th dissertations on Italian antiquities; and, with more copious evidence and successful industry than any other, M. Raynouard, in the first and sixth volumes of his Choix des Poésies des Troubadours, — have collected as full a history of the formation of these languages as we could justly require.

Origin of the French, Spanish, and Italian languages.

26. The pure Latin language, as we read it in the best ancient authors, possesses a complicated syntax and many elliptical modes of expression, which give vigor and elegance to style, but are not likely to be readily caught by the people. If, however, the citizens of Rome had spoken it with entire purity, it is to be remem-

Corruption of colloquial Latin in the Lower Empire.

bered that Latin, in the later times of the republic or under the empire, was not, like the Greek of Athens or the Tuscan of Florence, the idiom of a single city, but a language spread over countries in which it was not originally vernacular, and imposed by conquest upon many parts of Italy, as it was afterwards upon Spain and Gaul. Thus we find even early proofs that solecisms of grammar, as well as barbarous phrases and words unauthorized by use of polite writers, were very common in Rome itself; and in every succeeding generation, for the first centuries after the Christian era, these became more frequent and inevitable.[1] A vulgar Roman dialect, called *quotidianus* by Quintilian, *pedestris* by Vegetius, *usualis* by Sidonius, is recognized as distinguishable from the pure Latinity to which we give the name of classical. But the more ordinary appellation of this inferior Latin was *rusticus*: it was the country language, or *patois*, corrupted in every manner, and, from the popular want of education, incapable of being restored, because it was not perceived to be erroneous.[2] Whatever may have been the case before the fall of the Western Empire, we have reason to believe, that, in the sixth century, the colloquial Latin had undergone, at least in France, a considerable change, even with the superior class of ecclesiastics. Gregory of Tours confesses that he was habitually falling into that sort of error, the misplacing inflections and

[1] [As the word "barbarous" is applied at present with less strictness, it may be worth while to mention, that, in Latin, it meant only words borrowed from the languages of barbarians. This, of course, did not include Greek; for, though the adoption of Greek words in Latin writers was sometimes reckoned an affectation, it could not pass for a barbarism. But perhaps the provincial dialects of Italy were included; for it is said by Quintilian, that sometimes barbarous phrases had been uttered by the audience in the theatres; theatra exclamâsse barbarè. — 1847.]

[2] Du Cange, preface, pp. 13, 29. "Rusticum igitur sermonem non humiliorem paulo duntaxat, et qui sublimi opponitur, appellabant; sed eum etiam, qui magis reperet, barbarismis solœcismisque scaterat, quam apposite Sidonius squamam sermonis Celtici, &c., vocat. — Rusticum, qui nullis vel grammaticæ vel orthographiæ legibus astringitur." This is nearly a definition of the early Romance language: it was Latin without grammar or orthography.

The squama sermonis Celtici, mentioned by Sidonius, has led Gray, in his valuable remarks on rhyme, vol. ii. p. 53, as it has some others, into the erroneous notion that a real Celtic dialect, such as Cæsar found in Gaul, was still spoken. But this is incompatible with the known history of the French language; and Sidonius is one of those loose declamatory writers whose words are never to be construed in their proper meaning; the common fault of Latin authors from the third century Celticus sermo was the patois of Gaul, which, having once been Gallia Celtica, he still called such. That a few proper names, or similar words, and probably some others, in French, are Celtic, is well known.

Quintilian has said that a vicious orthography must bring on a vicious pronunciation. "Quod male scribitur, male etiam dici necesse est." But the converse of this is still more true; and was, in fact, the great cause of giving the new Romance language its *visible* form.

prepositions, which constituted the chief original difference of the rustic tongue from pure Latinity. In the opinion, indeed, of Raynouard, if we take his expressions in their natural meaning, the Romance language, or that which afterwards was generally called Provençal, is as old as the establishment of the Franks in Gaul. But this is, perhaps, not reconcilable with the proofs we have of a longer continuance of Latin. In Italy, it seems probable that the change advanced more slowly. Gregory the Great, however, who has been reckoned as inveterate an enemy of learning as ever lived, speaks with superlative contempt of a regard to grammatical purity in writing. It was a crime, in his eyes, for a clergyman to teach grammar; yet the number of laymen who were competent or willing to do so had become very small.

27. It may render this more clear if we mention a few of the growing corruptions which have in fact transformed the Latin into French and the sister tongues. The prepositions were used with no regard to the proper inflections of nouns and verbs. These were known so inaccurately, and so constantly put one for another, that it was necessary to have recourse to prepositions instead of them. Thus *de* and *ad* were made to express the genitive and dative cases, which is common in charters from the sixth to the tenth century. Again: it is a real fault in the Latin language, that it wants both the definite and indefinite article: *ille* and *unus*, especially the former, were called in to help this deficiency. In the forms of Marculfus, published towards the end of the seventh century, *ille* continually occurs as an article; and it appears to have been sometimes used in the sixth. This, of course, by an easy abbreviation, furnished the articles in French and Italian. The people came soon to establish more uniformity of case in the noun, either by rejecting inflections or by diminishing their number. Raynouard gives a long list of old French nouns formed from the Latin accusative by suppressing *em* or *am*.[1] The active auxiliary verb, than

[1] See a passage of Quintilian, l. 9, c. 4; quoted in Hallam's Middle Ages, chap. ix. In the grammar of Cassiodorus, a mere compilation from old writers, and in this instance from one Cornutus, we find another remarkable passage, which I do not remember to have seen quoted, though doubtless it has been so, on the pronunciation of the letter *M*. To utter this final consonant, he says, before a word beginning with a vowel, is wrong, "durum ac barbarum sonat:" but it is an equal fault to omit it before one beginning with a consonant; "par enim atque idem est vitium, ita cum vocali sicut cum consonante *M* literam, exprimere." Cassiodorus, De Orthographia, cap. 1. Thus we perceive that there was a nicety as to the pronunciation of this letter, which uneducated persons would naturally not regard. Hence, in

which nothing is more distinctive of the modern languages from the Latin, came in from the same cause, — the disuse, through ignorance, of several inflections of the tenses; to which we must add, that here also the Latin language is singularly deficient, possessing no means of distinguishing the second perfect from the first, or "I have seen" from "I saw." The auxiliary verb was early applied in France and Italy to supply this defect; and some have produced what they think occasional instances of its employment even in the best classical authors.

Continuance of Latin in seventh century.

28. It seems impossible to determine the progress of these changes, the degrees of variation between the polite and popular, the written and spoken Latin, in the best ages of Rome, in the decline of the empire, and in the kingdoms founded upon its ruins; or, finally, the exact epoch when the grammatical language ceased to be generally intelligible. There remains, therefore, some room still for hypothesis, and difference of opinion. The clergy preached in Latin early in the seventh century; and we have a popular song of the same age on the victory obtained by Clotaire II., in 622, over the Saxons.[1] This has been surmised by some to be a translation, merely because the Latin is better than they suppose to have been spoken. But, though the words are probably not given quite correctly, they seem reducible with a little emendation to short verses of an usual rhythmical cadence.[2]

the inscriptions of a low age, we frequently find this letter omitted; as in one quoted by Muratori, "Ego L. Contius me bibo [vivo] archa [archam] feci:" and it is very easy to multiply instances. Thus the neuter and the accusative terminations were lost.

[1] Le Bœuf, in Mém. de l'Acad. des Inscript. vol. xvii. [Liron, in a dissertation on the origin of the French language, published in his Singularités Historiques, i. 103, contends, from a passage in the Life of St. Eligius, that Latin was the vulgar tongue as late as 670. But the passage quoted is, perhaps, not conclusive. He supposes that Latin became unintelligible in the reign of Pepin, or the first years of Charlemagne; p. 116. But this is running too close; and, even if he could be so exact as to any one part of France, we have no reason whatever to suppose that the corruptions of language went on with equal steps in every province. — 1842.]

[2] Turner, in Archæologia, vol. xiv. 173; Hallam's Middle Ages, chap. ix.; Bouterwek, Gesch. der Französischen Poesie, p. 18, observes that there are many fragments of popular Latin songs preserved. I have not found any quoted, except one, which he gives from La Ravaillère, which is simple, and rather pretty; but I know not whence it is taken. It seems the song of a female slave, and is perhaps nearly as old as the destruction of the empire: —

"At quid jubes, pusiole,
Quare mandas, filiole,
Carmen dulce me cantare
Cum sim longe exul valde
Intra mare,
O cur jubes canere?"

Intra seems put for *trans*. The metre is rhymed trochaic; but that is consistent with antiquity. It is, however, more pleasing than most of the Latin verse of this period, and is more in the tone of the modern languages. As it is not at all a hackneyed passage, I have thought it worthy of quotation.

29. But, in the middle of the eighth century, we find the rustic language mentioned as distinct from Latin;[1] and in the Council of Tours, held in 813, it is ordered that homilies shall be explained to the people in their own tongue, whether rustic Roman or Frankish. In 842, we find the earliest written evidence of its existence, in the celebrated oaths taken by Louis of Germany and his brother Charles the Bald, as well as by their vassals; the former in Frankish or early German, the latter in their own current dialect. This, though with somewhat of a closer resemblance to Latin, is accounted by the best judges a specimen of the language spoken south of the Loire, afterwards variously called the Langue d'Oc, Provençal, or Limousin, and essentially the same with the dialects of Catalonia and Valencia.[2] It is decidedly the opinion of M. Raynouard, as it was of earlier inquirers, that the general language of France in the ninth century was the Southern dialect, rather than that of the North, to which we now give the exclusive name of French, and which they conceive to have deviated from it afterwards.[3] And he has employed great labor to prove, that, both in Spain and Italy, this language was generally spoken, with hardly so much difference from that of France as constitutes even a variation of dialect, — the articles, pronouns, and auxiliaries being nearly identical; most probably not with so much difference as would render the native of one country by any means unintelligible in another.[4]

It is changed to a new language in eighth and ninth.

[1] Acad. des Inscript., xvii. 713.

[2] Du Cange, p. 35; Raynouard, passim. M. de la Rue has called it "un Latin expirant." Recherches sur les Bardes d'Armorique. Between this and "un Français naissant" there may be only a verbal distinction; but, in accuracy of definition, I should think M. Raynouard much more correct. The language of this oath cannot be called Latin, without a violent stretch of words: no Latin scholar, as such, would understand it, except by conjecture. On the other hand, most of the words, as we learn from M. R., are Provençal of the twelfth century. The passage has been often printed, and sometimes incorrectly. M. Roquefort, in the preface to his Glossaire de la Langue Romane, has given a tracing from an ancient manuscript of Nitard, the historian of the ninth century, to whom we owe this important record of language.

[3] The chief difference was in orthography. The Northerns wrote Latin words with an *e* where the South retained *a*; as, "charitet, caritat; veritet, veritat; appelet, apelat. Si l'on rétablissait dans les plus anciens textes Français les *a* primitifs en place des *e*, on aurait identiquement la langue des Troubadours." Raynouard, Observations sur le Roman du Rou, 1829, p. 5.

[4] The proofs of this similarity occupy most part of the first and sixth volumes in M. Raynouard's excellent work.

[The theory of M. Raynouard, especially so far as it involves the existence of a primitive Romance tongue, akin to the Provençal, itself derived from Latin, but spoken simultaneously, or nearly so, in Spain and Italy as well as France, and the mother of the Neo-Latin languages, has been opposed in the very learned Histoire de la Formation de la Langue Française, by M. Ampère. — 1847.]

It is a common error to suppose that French and Italian had a double source, barbaric as well as Latin; and that the

30. Thus in the eighth and ninth centuries, if not before, France had acquired a language, unquestionably nothing else than a corruption of Latin (for the Celtic or Teutonic words that entered into it were by no means numerous, and did not influence its structure), but become so distinct from its parent, through modes of pronunciation as well as grammatical changes, that it requires some degree of practice to trace the derivation of words in many instances. It might be expected that we should be able to adduce, or at least prove to have existed, a series of monuments in this new form of speech. It might naturally appear that poetry, the voice of the heart, would have been heard wherever the joys and sufferings, the hopes and cares, of humanity, wherever the countenance of nature or the manners of social life, supplied their boundless treasures to its choice; and among untutored nations it has been rarely silent. Of the existence of verse, however, in this early period of the new languages, we find scarce any testimony, a doubtful passage in a Latin poem of the ninth century excepted,[1] till we come to a production on the captivity of Boethius, versified chiefly from passages in his Consolation, which M. Raynouard, though somewhat wishing to assign a higher date, places about the year 1000. This is printed by him from a manuscript formerly in the famous Abbey of Fleury, or St. Benoît-sur-Loire, and now in the Public Library of Orleans.

Early specimens of French.

Poem on Boethius.

Northern nations, in conquering those regions, brought in a large share of their own language. This is like the old erroneous opinion, that the Norman Conquest infused the French which we now find in our own tongue. There are certainly Teutonic words both in French and Italian, but not sufficient to affect the proposition that these languages are merely Latin in their origin. These words, in many instances, express what Latin could not: thus *guerra* was by no means synonymous with *bellum*. Yet even Roquefort talks of "un jargon composé de mots Tudesques et Romains," Discours Préliminaire, p. 19; forgetting which, he more justly remarks afterwards on the oath of Charles the Bald, that it shows "la langue Romane est entièrement composée de Latin." A long list could no doubt be made of French and Italian words that cannot easily be traced to any Latin with which we are acquainted; but we may be surprised that it is not still longer.

[1] In a Latin eclogue quoted by Paschasius Radbert (ob. 865), in the Life of St. Adalhard, Abbot of Corbie (ob. 826), the Romance poets are called upon to join the Latins in the following lines:—

"Rustica concelebret Romana Latinaque lingua,
Saxo, qui, pariter plangens, pro carmine dicat;
Vertite huc cuncti, cecinit quam maximus ille,
Et tumulum facite, et tumulo superaddite carmen."

Raynouard, Choix des Poésies, vol. ii. p. cxxxv. These lines are scarcely intelligible; but the quotation from Virgil, in the ninth century, perhaps deserves remark, though in one of Charlemagne's monasteries it is not by any means astonishing. Nennius, a Welsh monk, as some think, of the same age, who can hardly write Latin at all, has quoted another line:—

"Purpurea intexti tollant aulæa Britanni."

Gale, XV. Scriptores. iii. 102.

It is a fragment of 250 lines, written in stanzas of six, seven, or a greater number of verses of ten syllables, sometimes deviating to eleven or twelve; and all the lines in each stanza rhyming masculinely with each other. It is certainly by much the earliest specimen of French verse;[1] even if it should only belong, as Le Bœuf thought, to the eleventh century.

Provençal grammar.

31. M. Raynouard has asserted, what will hardly bear dispute, that "there has never been composed any considerable work in any language till it has acquired determinate forms of expressing the modifications of ideas according to time, number, and person," or, in other words, the elements of grammar.[2] But whether the Provençal or Romance language were in its infancy so defective, he does not say; nor does the grammar he has given lead us to that inference. This grammar, indeed, is necessarily framed in great measure out of more recent materials. It may be suspected, perhaps, that a language formed by mutilating the words of another could not for many ages be rich or flexible enough for the variety of poetic expression. And the more ancient forms would long retain their prerogative in writing: or, perhaps, we can only say, that the absence of poetry was the effect as well as the evidence of that intellectual barrenness, more characteristic of the dark ages than their ignorance.

Latin retained in use longer in Italy.

32. In Italy, where we may conceive the corruption of language to have been less extensive, and where the spoken patois had never acquired a distinctive name like *lingua Romana* in France, we find two remarkable proofs, as they seem, that Latin was not wholly unintel

[1] Raynouard, vol. ii. pp. 5, 6; and preface, p. cxxvii.

[2] Observations philologiques et grammaticales sur le Roman du Rou (1829), p. 26. Two ancient Provençal grammars, one by Raymond Vidal in the twelfth century, are in existence. The language, therefore, must have had its determinate rules before that time.

M. Raynouard has shown with a prodigality of evidence the regularity of the French or Romance language in the twelfth century, and its retention of Latin forms in cases where it had not been suspected. Thus it is a fundamental rule, that, in nouns masculine, the nominative ends in *s* in the singular, but wants it in the plural; while the oblique cases lose it in the singular, but retain it in the plural. This is evidently derived from the second declension in Latin. As for example:—

Sing. Li princes est venus, et a este sacrez rois.

Plu. Li evesque et li plus noble baron se sont assemble.

Thus, also, the possessive pronoun is always *mes*, *tes*, *ses* (*meus*, *tuus*, *suus*), in the nominative singular; *mon*, *ton*, *son* (*meum*, &c.), in the oblique regimen. It has been through ignorance of such rules that the old French poetry has seemed capricious, and destitute of strict grammar; and, in a philosophical sense, the simplicity and extensiveness of M. Raynouard's discovery entitle it to the appellation of beautiful. [It has, however, been since shown to require some limitation.]

ligible in the ninth and tenth centuries, and which, therefore, modify M. Raynouard's hypothesis as to the simultaneous origin of the Romance tongue. The one is a popular song of the soldiers, on their march to rescue the emperor Louis II., in 881, from the violent detention in which he had been placed by the Duke of Benevento; the other, a similar exhortation to the defenders of Modena in 924, when that city was in danger of siege from the Hungarians. Both of these were published by Muratori in his fortieth dissertation on Italian Antiquities; and both have been borrowed from him by M. Sismondi, in his Littérature du Midi.[1] The former of these poems is in a loose trochaic measure, totally destitute of regard to grammatical inflections. Yet some of the leading peculiarities of Italian, the article and the auxiliary verb, do not appear. The latter is in accentual iambics, with a sort of monotonous termination in the nature of rhyme; and in very much superior Latinity, probably the work of an ecclesiastic.[2] It is difficult to account for either of these, especially the former, which is merely a military song, except on the supposition that the Latin language was not grown wholly out of popular use.

French of eleventh century.

33. In the eleventh century, France still affords us but few extant writings. Several, indeed, can be shown to have once existed. The Romance language, comprehending the two divisions of Provençal and Northern French, by this time distinctly separate from each other, was now, say the authors of the Histoire Littéraire de la France, employed in poetry, romances, translations, and original works, in different kinds of literature; sermons were preached in it; and the code, called the Assises de Jérusalem, was drawn up under Godfrey of Bouillon in 1100.[3] Some part of this is doubtful, and especially the age of these laws They do not mention those of William the Conqueror, recorded in French by Ingulfus. Doubts have been cast by a

[1] Vol. i. pp. 23, 27.

[2] I am at a loss to know what Muratori means by saying, "Son versi di dodici sillabe, ma computata la ragione de' tempi, vengono ad essere uguali a gli endecasillabi;" p. 551. He could not have understood the metre, which is perfectly regular, and even harmonious, on the condition only that no "ragione de' tempi," except such as accentual pronunciation observes, shall be demanded. The first two lines will serve as a specimen:—

"O tu, qui servas armis ista mænia,
Noli dormire, moneo, sed vigila."

This is like another strange observation of Muratori in the same dissertation, that in the well-known lines of the Emperor Adrian to his soul, "Animula vagula, blandula," which could perplex no schoolboy, he cannot discover "un' esatta norma di metro;" and therefore takes them to be merely rhythmical.

[3] Vol. vii. p. 107.

distinguished living critic on the age of this French code, and upon the authenticity of the History of Ingulfus itself; which he conceives, upon very plausible grounds, to be a forgery of Richard II.'s time. The language of the laws, indeed, appears to be very ancient, but not probably distinguishable at this day from the French of the twelfth century.[1] It may be said in general, that, except one or two translations from books of Scripture, very little now extant has been clearly referred to an earlier period.[2] Yet we may suspect that the language

[1] [The French laws in Ingulfus are ascertained to be a translation from the Latin, made in the thirteenth century.]

[2] Roquefort, Glossaire de la Langue Romane, p. 25, and Etat de la Poésie Française, pp. 42 and 206, mentions several religious works in the Royal Library, and also a metrical romance in the British Museum, lately published in Paris, on the fabulous voyage of Charlemagne to Constantinople. [But this romance is now referred by its editor, M. Michel, to the beginning of the twelfth century; and the translations of the Books of Kings, mentioned in the text, are so far from being clearly referable to an earlier period, that their editor, M. le Roux de Lincy, in Documens Inédits, 1841, though wavering a little, evidently inclines to place them about the same time. In fact, we are not able to prove satisfactorily that any Norman French, except the version of Boethius above mentioned, belongs to the eleventh century. Roquefort and De la Rue assumed too much as to this. It may be mentioned here, that M. Michel distinguishes six dialects of Northern French in use during the twelfth century, spoken and written in Picardy, in Normandy, in the Isle of France, in Burgundy and some central provinces, in Lorraine, and, finally, in Poitou and Anjou; the last of which had a tinge of the Langue d'Oc. Id. Introduction, p. 59. — 1847.] Raynouard has collected a few fragments in Provençal. But I must dissent from this excellent writer in referring the famous poem of the Vaudois, La Nobla Leyczon, to the year 1100. Choix des Poésies des Troubadours, vol. ii. p. cxxxvii. I have already observed, that the two lines which contain what he calls "la date de l'an 1100" are so loosely expressed as to include the whole ensuing century (Hallam's Middle Ages, chap. ix.); and I am now convinced that the poem is not much older than 1200. It seems probable that they reckoned 1100 years on a loose computation, not from the Christian era, but from the time when the passage of Scripture to which these lines allude was written. The allusion may be to 1 Pet. i. 20. But it is clear, that, at the time of the composition of this poem, not only the name of *Vaudois* had been imposed on those sectaries, but they had become subject to persecution. We know nothing of this till near the end of the century. This poem was probably written in the south of France, and carried afterwards to the Alpine valleys of Piedmont, from which it was brought to Geneva and England in the seventeenth century. La Nobla Leyczon is published at length by Raynouard. It consists of 479 lines, which seem to be rhythmical or aberrant Alexandrines; the rhymes uncertain in number, chiefly masculine. The poem censures the corruptions of the church, but contains little that would be considered heretical; which agrees with what contemporary historians relate of the original Waldenses. Any doubts as to the authenticity of this poem are totally unreasonable. M. Raynouard, an indisputably competent judge, observes, "Les personnes qui l'examineront avec attention jugeront que le manuscrit n'a pas été interpolé." P. cxliii.

I will here reprint, more accurately than before, the two lines supposed to give the poem the date of 1100: —

"Ben ha mil et cent ancz compli entièrement,
Que fo scripta l'ora car sen al derier temps."

Can M. Raynouard, or any one else, be warranted by this in saying, "*La date de l'an* 1100, qu'on lit dans ce poème, mérite toute confiance"?

[The writings ascribed to the ancient Waldenses have lately been investigated with considerable acuteness and erudition in the British Magazine, and the spuriousness of the greater part seems demonstrated. But those who consider Leger as a forger do not appear to doubt the authenticity of this poem, La Nobla Leyczon, though they entirely agree with me as to its probable date near the end of the twelfth century. — 1842.]

was already employed in poetry, and had been gradually ramifying itself by the shoots of invention and sentiment; since, at the close of this age, and in the next, we find a constellation of gay and brilliant versifiers, the Troubadours of Southern France, and a corresponding class to the north of the Loire.

34. These early poets in the modern languages chiefly borrowed their forms of versification from the Latin. It is unnecessary to say, that metrical composition in that language, as in Greek, was an arrangement of verses corresponding by equal or equivalent feet; all syllables being presumed to fall under a known division of long and short, the former passing for strictly the double of the latter in quantity of time. By this law of pronunciation, all verse was measured; and to this not only actors, who were assisted by an accompaniment, but the orators also, endeavored to conform. But the accented, or, if we choose rather to call them so, emphatic syllables, being regulated by a very different though uniform law, the uninstructed people, especially in the decline of Latinity, pronounced, as we now do, with little or no regard to the metrical quantity of syllables, but according to their accentual differences. And this gave rise to the popular or rhythmical poetry of the Lower Empire; traces of which may be found in the second century, and even much earlier, but of which we have abundant proofs after the age of Constantine.[1] All metre, as Augustin says, was rhythm, but all rhythm was not metre. In rhythmical verse, neither the quantity of syllables (that is, the time allotted to each by metrical rule), nor even in some degree their number, was regarded, so long as a cadence was retained in which the ear could recognize a certain approach to uniformity. Much popular poetry, both religious and profane, and the public hymns of the church, were written in this manner. The distinction of long and short syllables, even while Latin remained a living tongue, was lost in speech, and required study to attain it. The accent or emphasis, both of which are probably, to a certain extent, connected with quantity and with each other, supplied its place; the accented syllable being, perhaps, generally

Metres of modern languages.

1 The well-known lines of Adrian to Florus, and his reply, "Ego nolo Florus esse," &c., are accentual trochaics, but not wholly so; for the last line, "Scythicas pati pruinas," requires the word *pati* to be sounded as an iambic. They are not the earliest instance extant of disregard to quantity; for Suetonius quotes some satirical lines on Julius Cæsar.

lengthened in ordinary speech: though this is not the sole cause of length; for no want of emphasis, or lowness of tone, can render a syllable of many letters short. Thus we find two species of Latin verse: one metrical, which Prudentius, Fortunatus, and others aspired to write; the other rhythmical, somewhat licentious in number of syllables, and wholly accentual in its pronunciation. But this kind was founded on the former, and imitated the ancient syllabic arrangements. Thus the trochaic, or line in which the stress falls on the uneven syllables, commonly alternating by eight and seven, a very popular metre from its spirited flow, was adopted in military songs, such as that already mentioned of the Italian soldiers in the ninth century. It was also common in religious chants. The line of eight syllables, or dimeter iambic, in which the cadence falls on the even places, was still more frequent in ecclesiastical verse. But these are the most ordinary forms of versification in the early French or Provençal, Spanish, and Italian languages. The line of eleven syllables, which became in time still more usual than the former, is nothing else than the ancient hendecasyllable, from which the French, in what they call masculine rhymes, and ourselves more generally, from a still greater deficiency of final vowels, have been forced to retrench the last syllable. The Alexandrine, of twelve syllables, might seem to be the trimeter iambic of the ancients. But Sanchez has very plausibly referred its origin to a form more usual in the dark ages, the pentameter; and shown it in some early Spanish poetry.[1] The Alexandrine, in the Southern languages, had generally a feminine termination; that is, in a short vowel: thus becoming of thirteen syllables, the stress falling on the penultimate, as is the usual case in a Latin pentameter verse, accentually read in our present mode. The variation of syllables in these Alexandrines, which run from twelve to fourteen, is accounted for by the similar numerical variety in the pentameter.[2]

[1] The break in the middle of the Alexandrine, it will occur to every competent judge, has nothing analogous to it in the trimeter iambic, but exactly corresponds to the invariable law of the pentameter.

[2] Roquefort, Essai sur la Poésie Française dans le 12me et 13me Siècles, p. 66; Galvani, Osservazioni sulla Poesia de' Trovatori (Modena, 1829); Sanchez, Poesias Castellanas anteriores al 15mo Siglo, vol. i. p. 122.

Tyrwhitt had already observed, "The metres which the Normans used, and which we seem to have borrowed from them, were plainly copied from the Latin rhythmical verses, which, in the declension of that language, were current in various forms among those who either did not understand, or did not regard, the true quantity of syllables; and the practice of rhyming is probably to be deduced from the same original." Essay on the Language and Versification of Chaucer, p 51.

35. I have dwelt, perhaps tediously, on this subject, because vague notions of a derivation of modern metrical arrangements, even in the languages of Latin origin, from the Arabs or Scandinavians, have sometimes gained credit. It has been imagined, also, that the peculiar characteristic of the new poetry, rhyme, was borrowed from the Saracens of Spain.[1] But the Latin language abounds so much in consonances, that those who have been accustomed to write verses in it well know the difficulty of avoiding them, as much as an ear formed on classical models demands; and, as this jingle is certainly pleasing in itself, it is not wonderful that the less fastidious vulgar should adopt it in their rhythmical songs. It has been proved by Muratori, Gray, and Turner, beyond the possibility of doubt, that rhymed Latin verse was in use from the end of the fourth century.[2]

Origin of rhyme in Latin.

36. Thus, about the time of the first crusade, we find two dialects of the same language, differing by that time not inconsiderably from each other,—the Provençal and French; possessing a regular grammar, established forms of versification (and the early Troubadours added several to those borrowed from the Latin[3]), and a flexibility which gave free scope to the graceful turns of poetry. William, Duke of Guienne, has the glory of leading the van of surviving Provençal songsters. He was born in 1070, and may probably have composed some of his little poems before he joined the crusaders in 1096. If these are genuine, and no doubt of them seems to be entertained, they denote a considerable degree of previous refinement in the language.[4] We do not, I believe, meet with any other Troubadour till after the middle of the twelfth century. From that time till about the close of the thirteenth, and especially before the fall of the house of Toulouse in 1228, they were numerous almost as the gay insects of spring. Names of illustrious birth are mingled

Provençal and French poetry.

[1] Andrès, with a partiality to the Saracens of Spain, whom, by a singular assumption, he takes for his countrymen, manifested in almost every page, does not fail to urge this. It had been said long before by Huet, and others who lived before these subjects had been thoroughly investigated. Origine e Progresso, &c., ii. 194. He has been copied by Ginguéné and Sismondi.

[2] Muratori, Antichità Italiane, Dissert. 40; Turner, in Archæologia, vol. xiv., and Hist of England, vol. iv. pp. 328, 653. Gray has gone as deeply as any one into this subject; and though, writing at what may be called an early period of metrical criticism, he has fallen into a few errors, and been too easy of credence, unanswerably proves the Latin origin of rhyme. Gray's Works by Mathias, vol. ii. pp. 30-54.

[3] See Raynouard, Roquefort, and Galvani for the Provençal and French metres, which are very complicated.

[4] Raynouard, Choix des Poésies des Troubadours, vol. ii.; Auguis, Recueil des Anciens Poètes Français, vol. i.

in the list with those whom genius has saved from obscurity. They were the delight of a luxurious nobility, the pride of Southern France, while the great fiefs of Toulouse and Guienne were in their splendor. Their style soon extended itself to the Northern dialect. Abelard was the first of recorded name who taught the banks of the Seine to resound a tale of love; and it was of Eloise that he sung.[1] "You composed," says that gifted and noble-spirited woman in one of her letters to him, "many verses in amorous measure, so sweet both in their language and their melody, that your name was incessantly in the mouths of all; and even the most illiterate could not be forgetful of you. This it was chiefly that made women admire you; and, as most of these songs were on me and my love, they made me known in many countries, and caused many women to envy me. Every tongue spoke of your Eloise; every street, every house, resounded with my name."[2] These poems of Abelard are lost; but, in the Norman or Northern French language, we have an immense number of poets belonging to the twelfth and the two following centuries. One hundred and twenty-seven are known by name in the twelfth alone, and above two hundred in the thirteenth.[3] Thibault,

[1] Bouterwek, on the authority of La Ravaillère, seems to doubt whether these poems of Abelard were in French or Latin. Gesch. der Französischen Poesie, p. 18. I believe this would be thought quite paradoxical by any critic at present.

[2] "Duo autem, fateor, tibi specialiter inerant, quibus feminarum quarumlibet animos statim allicere poteras, dictandi videlicet et cantandi gratia; quæ cæteros minimè philosophos assecutos esse novimus. Quibus quidem quasi ludo quodam laborem exercitii recreans philosophici pleraque amatorio metro vel rithmo composita reliquisti carmina, quæ præ nimiâ suavitate tam dictaminis quam cantûs sæpius frequentata tuum in ore omnium nomen incessanter tenebant, ut etiam illiteratos melodiæ dulcedo tui non sineret immemores esse. Atque hinc maxime in amorem tui feminæ suspirabant. Et cum horum pars maxima carminum nostros decantaret amores, multis me regionibus brevi tempore nunciavit, et multarum in me feminarum accendit invidiam." And in another place: "Frequenti carmine tuam in ore omnium Heloissam ponebas: me platæ omnes, me domus singulæ resonabant." Epist. Abælardi et Heloissæ. These epistles of Abelard and Eloisa, especially those of the latter, are, as far as I know, the first book that gives any pleasure in reading, which had been produced in Europe for 600 years, since the Consolation of Boethius. But I do not press my negative judgment. We may at least say, that the writers of the dark ages, if they have left any thing intrinsically very good, have been ill treated by the learned, who have failed to extract it. Pope, it may be here observed, has done great injustice to Eloisa in his unrivalled Epistle, by putting the sentiments of a coarse and abandoned woman into her mouth. Her refusal to marry Abelard arose, not from an abstract predilection for the name of mistress above that of wife, but from her disinterested affection, which would not deprive him of the prospect of ecclesiastical dignities to which his genius and renown might lead him. She judged very unwisely, as it turned out, but from an unbounded generosity of character. He was, in fact, unworthy of her affection, which she expresses in the tenderest language. "Deum testem invoco, si me Augustus universo præsidens mundo matrimonii honore dignaretur, totumque mihi orbem confirmaret in perpetuum præsidendum, charius mihi et dignius videretur tua dici meretrix quam illius imperatrix."

[3] Auguis, Discours Préliminaire, p. 2; Roquefort, Etat de la Poésie Française aux

King of Navarre and Count of Champagne, about the middle of the next, is accounted by some the best, as well as noblest, of French poets; but the spirited and satirical Rutebouf might contest the preference.

37. In this French and Provençal poetry, if we come to the consideration of it historically, descending from an earlier period, we are at once struck by the vast preponderance of amorous ditties. The Greek and Roman Muses, especially the latter, seem frigid as their own fountain in comparison. Satires on the great, and especially on the clergy, exhortations to the crusade, and religious odes, are intermingled in the productions of the Troubadours; but love is the prevailing theme. This tone they could hardly have borrowed from the rhythmical Latin verses, of which all that remain are without passion or energy. They could as little have been indebted to their predecessors for a peculiar gracefulness, an indescribable charm of gayety and ease, which many of their lighter poems display. This can only be ascribed to the polish of chivalrous manners, and to the influence of feminine delicacy on public taste. The well-known dialogue, for example, of Horace and Lydia, is justly praised: nothing extant of this amœbean character, from Greece or Rome, is nearly so good. But such alternate stanzas, between speakers of different sexes, are very common in the early French poets; and it would be easy to find some quite equal to Horace in grace and spirit. They had even a generic name, *tensons*, "contentions;" that is, dialogues of lively repartee, such as we are surprised to find in the twelfth century, — an age accounted by many almost barbarous. None of these are prettier than what are called *pastourelles*, in which the poet is feigned to meet a shepherdess, whose love he solicits, and by whom he is repelled (not always finally) in alternate stanzas.[1] Some of these

12me et 13me Siècles; Hist. Litt. de la France, xvi. 239.

[It ought to have been observed, that comparatively few of the poets of the twelfth century are extant: most of them are Anglo-Norman. At least ten times as much French verse of the thirteenth has been preserved. Hist. Litt. de la France, p. 239. "Notre prose et notre poésie Française existaient avant 1200, mais c'est au treizième siècle qu'elles commencèrent à prendre un caractère national." Id. p. 254 — 1847.]

[1] These have, as Galvani has observed, an ancient prototype in the twenty-seventh pastoral of Theocritus, which Dryden has translated with no diminution of its freedom. Some of the Pastourelles are also rather licentious; but that is not the case with the greater part. M. Raynouard, in an article of the Journal des Savans for 1824, p. 613, remarks the superior decency of the Southern poets, scarcely four or five transgressing in that respect; while many of the fabliaux in the collections of Barbazan and Méon are of the most coarse and stupid ribaldry, and such that even the object of exhibiting ancient manners

may be read in Roquefort, Etat de la Poésie Française dans le 12me et 13me Siècles; others in Raynouard, Choix des Poésies des Troubadours; in Auguis, Recueil des Anciens Poètes Français; or in Galvani, Osservazioni sulla Poesia de' Trovatori.

38. In all these light compositions which gallantry or gayety inspired, we perceive the characteristic excellences of French poetry, as distinctly as in the best vaudeville of the age of Louis XV. We can really sometimes find little difference, except an obsoleteness of language, which gives them a kind of poignancy; and this style, as I have observed, seems to have been quite original in France, though it was imitated by other nations.[1] The French poetry, on the other hand, was deficient in strength and ardor. It was also too much filled with monotonous commonplaces; among which the tedious descriptions of spring, and the everlasting nightingale, are eminently to be reckoned. These, perhaps, are less frequent in the early poems, most of which are short, than they became in the prolix expansion adopted by the allegorical school in the fourteenth century. They prevail, as is well known, in Chaucer, Dunbar, and several other of our own poets.

Metrical romances. Havelok the Dane.

39. The metrical romances, far from common in Provençal,[2] but forming a large portion of what was written in the Northern dialect, though occasionally picturesque, graceful, or animated, are seldom free from tedious or prosaic details. The earliest of these extant seems to be that of Havelok the Dane, of which an abridgment was made

and language scarcely warranted their publication in so large a number.

[A good many Pastourelles, but all variations of the same subject, are published by M. Michel, in his Théâtre Français au Moyen Age, p. 31. These are in Northern dialects, and may be referred to the twelfth and thirteenth centuries. Robin and Marion are always the shepherd or peasant and his rustic love; and a knight always interferes, with or without success, to seduce or outrage Marion. We have nothing corresponding to these in England. — 1847.]

[1] Andrès, as usual with him, whose prejudices are all that way, derives the Provençal style of poetry from the Arabians; and this has been countenanced, in some measure, by Ginguéné and Sismondi. Some of the peculiarities of the Troubadours, their *tensons*, or contentions, and the *envoi*, or termination of a poem, by an address to the poem itself or the reader, are said to be of Arabian origin. In assuming that rhyme was introduced by the same channel, these writers are probably mistaken. But I have seen too little of Oriental, and especially of Hispano-Saracenic poetry, to form any opinion how far the more essential characteristics of Provençal verse may have been derived from it. One seems to find more of Oriental hyperbole in the Castilian poetry.

[2] It has been denied that there are any metrical romances in Provençal; but one called the Philomena, on the fabulous history of Charlemagne, is written after 1173, though not much later than 1200. Journal des Savans, 1824. [The Philomena is in prose; but it has been pointed out to me, that four metrical romances in Provençal have been brought to light by Raynouard and others. — 1842.]

by Geoffrey Gaimar, before the middle of the twelfth century. The story is certainly a popular legend from the Danish part of England, which the French versifier has called, according to the fashion of romances, "a Breton lay." If this word meant any thing more than relating to Britain, it is a plain falsehood; and, upon either hypothesis, it may lead us to doubt, as many other reasons may also, what has been so much asserted of late years, as to the Armorican origin of romantic fictions; since the word "Breton," which some critics refer to Armorica, is here applied to a story of mere English birth.[1] It cannot, however, be doubted, from the absurd introduction of Arthur's name in this romance of Havelok, that it was written after the publication of the splendid fables of Geoffrey.[2]

1 The Recherches sur les Bardes d'Armorique, by that respectable veteran M. de la Rue, are very unsatisfactory. It does not appear that the Bretons have so much as a national tradition of any romantic poetry, nor any writings in their language older than 1450. The authority of Warton, Leyden, Ellis, Turner, and Price, has rendered this hypothesis of early Armorican romance popular; but I cannot believe that so baseless a fabric will endure much longer. Is it credible that tales of aristocratic splendor and courtesy sprung up in so poor and uncivilized a country as Bretagne? Traditional stories they might, no doubt, possess, and some of these may be found in the Lais de Marie and other early poems; but not romances of chivalry. I do not recollect, though speaking without confidence, that any proof has been given of Armorican traditions about Arthur earlier than the history of Geoffrey; for it seems too much to interpret the word *Britones* of them rather than of the Welsh. Mr. Turner, I observe, without absolutely recanting, has much receded from his opinion of an Armorican original for Geoffrey of Monmouth.

[It is not easy to perceive how the story of Arthur, as a Welsh prince and conqueror, should have originated in Brittany, which may have preserved some connection with Cornwall, but none, as far as we know, with Wales. The Armoricans, at least, had no motive for inventing magnificent fables in order to swell the glory of a different though cognate people. Mr. Wright conceives that Arthur was a mythic personage in Brittany, whose legend was confounded by Geoffrey with real history. But this wholly annihilates the historical basis, and requires us not only to reject Nennius as a spurious or interpolated writer, which is Mr. Wright's hypothesis, but to consider all the Welsh poems which contain allusions to Arthur as posterior to the time of Geoffrey. "The legends of the British kings," he says, "appear to have been brought over from Bretagne, and not to have had their origin among the Welsh. Although we begin to observe traces of the legends relating to Arthur and Merlin before Geoffrey of Monmouth wrote, yet even the Welsh of that time appear to have rejected his narrative as fabulous." Biogr. Britann. Littéraire, vol. ii. p. 145. If we can depend at all on the stories of the Mabinogion, which a lady has so honorably brought before the English public, the traditional legends concerning Arthur prevailed in Wales in an earlier age than that of Geoffrey; and perhaps William of Malmesbury alluded to them rather than to the recent forgery, in the words, "Hic est Arthurus de quo Britonum nugæ hodieque delirant; dignus plane, quem non fallaces somniarent fabulæ, sed veraces prædicarent historiæ, quippe qui labantem patriam diu sustinuerit, infractosque civium mentes ad bellum acuerit." De Gestis Reg. Angl., l. 1 Arthur's victory at Mount Badon in 516, and his death in 537, are mentioned in the Annales Cambriæ, prepared by the late Mr. Petrie for publication; a brief chronicle, which seems, in part at least, considerably older than the twelfth century, if not almost contemporary. — 1847.]

2 The romance of Havelok was printed by Sir Frederick Madden in 1829, but not for sale. His Introduction is of considerable value. The story of Havelok is that of Curan and Argentile, in Warner's Albion's England, upon which Mason founded a drama. Sir F. Madden refers the English translation to some time between 1270 and 1290. The manuscript is in the Bodleian Library. The French ori-

Diffusion of French language.

40. Two more celebrated poems are by Wace, a native of Jersey: one, a free version of the history lately published by Geoffrey of Monmouth; the other, a narrative of the Battle of Hastings, and Conquest of England. Many other romances followed. Much has been disputed for some years concerning these, as well as the lays and fabliaux of the Northern trouveurs. It is sufficient here to observe, that they afforded a copious source of amusement and interest to those who read or listened as far as the French language was diffused; and this was far beyond the boundaries of France. Not only was it the common spoken tongue of what is called the court, or generally of the superior ranks, in England, but in Italy and in Germany, at least throughout the thirteenth century. Brunetto Latini wrote his philosophical compilation, called Le Trésor, in French, "because," as he says, "the language was more agreeable and usual than any other." Italian, in fact, was hardly employed in prose at that time. But, for those whose education had not gone so far, the romances and tales of France began to be rendered into German as early as the latter part of the twelfth century, as they were long afterwards into English; becoming the basis of those popular songs which illustrate the period of the Swabian emperors, the great house of Hohenstauffen, Frederic Barbarossa, Henry VI., and Frederic II.

German poetry of Swabian period.

41. The poets of Germany, during this period of extraordinary fertility in versification, were not less numerous than those of France and Provence.[1] From Henry of Veldek to the last of the lyric poets, soon after the beginning of the fourteenth century, not less than two hundred are known by name. A collection made in that age by Rudiger von Manasse of Zurich contains the productions of one

ginal has since been reprinted in France, as I learn from Brunet's Supplément au Manuel du Libraire. Both this and its abridgment, by Geoffrey Gaimar, are in the British Museum.

[1] Bouterwek, p. 95. [Gervinus, in his Poetische Litteratur der Deutschen, has gone more fully than his predecessor Bouterwek into the history of German mediæval poetry, which was more abundant, perhaps, than in any other country. Ottfried, about 883, turned the Gospels into German verse: we here find rhyme instead of the ancient alliteration. But in the next two centuries we have chiefly Latin poetry, though some of it apparently derived from old lays of the Hunnish or Burgundian age. In the beginning of the twelfth century, the vernacular poetry revived in a number of chivalric stories, of which Alexander and Charlemagne were generally the heroes. The Franconian emperors did not encourage letters; but, under the Swabian line, poetry eminently flourished. Several epics besides the Nibelungen Lied belong to the latter part of the twelfth century or beginning of the next, and are much superior in spirit and character to any thing that followed. — 1853.]

hundred and forty; and modern editors have much enlarged the list.[1] Henry of Veldek is placed by Eichhorn about 1170, and by Bouterwek twenty years later: so that, at the utmost, we cannot reckon the period of their duration more than a century and a half. But the great difference perceptible between the poetry of Henry and that of the old German songs proves him not to have been the earliest of the Swabian school: he is as polished in language and versification as any of his successors; and, though a Northern, he wrote in the dialect of the house of Hohenstauffen. Wolfram von Eschenbach, in the first years of the next century, is perhaps the most eminent name of the Minnesingers, as the lyric poets were denominated; and is also the translator of several romances. The golden age of German poetry was before the fall of the Swabian dynasty, at the death of Conrad IV. in 1254. Love, as the word denotes, was the peculiar theme of the Minnesingers; but it was chiefly from the northern or southern dialects of France, especially the latter, that they borrowed their amorous strains.[2] In the latter part of the thirteenth century, we find less of feeling and invention, but a more didactic and moral tone, sometimes veiled in Æsopic fables, sometimes openly satirical. Conrad of Würtzburg is the chief of the later school; but he had to lament the decline of taste and manners in his own age.

42. No poetry, however, of the Swabian period, is so national as the epic romances, which drew their subjects from

[1] Bouterwek, p. 98. This collection was published in 1758 by Bodmer.

[2] Herder, Zerstreute Blatter, vol. v. p. 206; Eichhorn, Allg. Geschichte der Cultur, vol. i. p. 226; Heinsius, Teut, oder Lehrbuch der Deutschen Sprachwissenschaft, vol. iv. pp. 32–80; Weber's Illustrations of Northern Antiquities, 1814. This work contains the earliest analysis, I believe, of the Nibelungen Lied. But, above all, I have been indebted to the excellent account of German poetry by Bouterwek, in the ninth volume of his great work, the History of Poetry and Eloquence since the Thirteenth Century. In this volume, the mediæval poetry of Germany occupies nearly four hundred closely printed pages. I have since met with a pleasing little volume on the Lays of the Minnesingers, by Mr. Edgar Taylor. It contains an account of the chief of those poets, with translations, perhaps in too modern a style; though it may be true that no other would suit our modern taste.

A species of love-song, peculiar, according to Weber (p. 9), to the Minnesingers, are called Watchmen's Songs. These consist in a dialogue between a lover and the sentinel who guards his mistress. The latter is persuaded to imitate "Sir Pandarus of Troy;" but, when morning breaks, summons the lover to quit his lady, who, in her turn, maintains that "it is the nightingale, and not the lark," with almost the pertinacity of Juliet.

Mr. Taylor remarks that the German poets do not go so far in their idolatry of the fair as the Provençals, p. 127. I do not concur altogether in his reasons; but, as the Minnesingers imitated the Provençals, this deviation is remarkable. I should rather ascribe it to the hyperbolical tone which the Troubadours had borrowed from the Arabians, or to the susceptibility of their temperament.

the highest antiquity, if they did not even adopt the language of primeval bards, which perhaps, though it has been surmised, is not compatible with their style. In the two most celebrated productions of this kind, the Helden Buch, or Book of Heroes, and the Nibelungen Lied, the Lay of the Nibelungen, a fabulous people, we find the recollections of an heroic age, wherein the names of Attila and Theodoric stand out as witnesses of traditional history, clouded by error and colored by fancy. The Nibelungen Lied, in its present form, is by an uncertain author, perhaps about the year 1200;[1] but it comes,

[1] Weber says, "I have no doubt whatever that the romance itself is of very high antiquity, — at least of the eleventh century; though certainly the present copy has been considerably modernized." Illustrations of Northern Romances, p. 26. But Bouterwek does not seem to think it of so ancient a date; and I believe it is commonly referred to about the year 1200. Schlegel ascribes it to Henry von Offerdingen. Heinsius, iv. 52.

It is highly probable that the "barbara et antiquissima carmina," which — according to Eginhard — Charlemagne caused to be reduced to writing, were no other than the legends of the Nibelungen Lied, and similar traditions of the Gothic and Burgundian time. Weber, p. 6. I will here mention a curious Latin epic poem on the wars of Attila, published by Fischer in 1780. He conceives it to be of the sixth century; but others have referred it to the eighth. [Raynouard (Journal des Savans, August, 1833) places it in the tenth; and my friend, the Hon. and Rev. W. Herbert, in the notes to his poem on Attila (1837), a production displaying an union of acuteness and erudition with great poetical talents, has, probably with no knowledge of Raynouard's judgment, come to the same determination, from the mention of Iceland, under the name of Thile, which was not discovered till 861. "The poem resembles in style and substance the later Scandinavian sagas, and it is probably a Latin version of some such prose narrative; and the spelling of Thule, Thile, seems to have been derived from the Scandinavian orthography Thyle. At the end of the tenth century, the Scandinavians, who were previously illiterate, began to study in Italy; and the discovery of Iceland would have transpired through them. It is probable that this may be the earliest work in which the name Thule has been applied to Iceland, and it is most likely a production of the tenth century. The MS. is said to be of the thirteenth." It appears, however, by M. Raynouard's article, that the MS. in the Royal Library at Paris contains a dedication to an archbishop of Rome near the close of the tenth century; which, in the absence of any presumption to the contrary, may pass for the date of the poem. — 1842.] The heroes are Franks; but the whole is fabulous, except the name of Attila and his Huns. I do not know whether this has any connection with a history of Attila by a writer named Casola, existing in manuscript at Modena, and being probably a translation in prose from Latin into Provençal. A translation of this last into Italian was published by Rossi at Ferrara in 1568: it is a very scarce book; but I have seen two copies of it. Weber's Illustrations, p. 23; Eichhorn, Allg. Gesch., ii. 178; Galvani, Osservazioni sulla Poesia de' Trovatori, p. 16.

The Nibelungen Lied seems to have been less popular in the middle ages than other romances; evidently because it relates to a different state of manners. Bouterwek, p. 141. Heinsius observes that we must consider this poem as the most valuable record of German antiquity; but that to overrate its merit, as some have been inclined to do, can be of no advantage. [The Nibelungen Lied is placed by Gervinus about 1210. It was not liked by the clergy, doubtless on account of its heathenish character; nor by the courtly poets, who thought it too rude; and in fact the style is much behind that of the age. The sources of this poem are unknown: that the author had traditional legends, and probably lays, to guide him, will, of course, hardly be doubted. Little more than a few great names — Attila, Theodoric, Gunther — belong to real history; but the whole complexion of the poem is so different from that of the twelfth century, that we must believe the poet to have imbued himself by some such means with the spirit of times long past. No disparagement, but the reverse, to the genius of him, who in these respects, as well as in his animated and picturesque language, so powerfully reminds us of the father of

and, as far as we can judge, with little or no interpolation of circumstances, from an age anterior to Christianity, to civilization, and to the more refined forms of chivalry. We cannot well think the stories later than the sixth or seventh centuries. The German critics admire the rude grandeur of this old epic; and its fables, marked with a character of barbarous simplicity wholly unlike that of later romance, are become in some degree familiar to ourselves.

Decline of German poetry.

43. The loss of some accomplished princes, and of a near intercourse with the south of France and with Italy, as well as the augmented independence of the German nobility, only to be maintained by unceasing warfare, rendered their manners, from the latter part of the thirteenth century, more rude than before. They ceased to cultivate poetry, or to think it honorable in their rank. Meantime a new race of poets, chiefly burghers of towns, sprang up about the reign of Rodolph of Hapsburg, before the lays of the Minnesingers had yet ceased to resound. These prudent though not inspired votaries of the Muse chose the didactic and moral style, as more salutary than the love-songs, and more reasonable than the romances. They became known in the fourteenth century by the name of Meister-singers, but are traced to the institutions of the twelfth century, called singing-schools, for the promotion of popular music, the favorite recreation of Germany. What they may have done for music, I am unable to say: it was in an evil hour for the art of poetry that they extended their jurisdiction over her. They regulated verse by the most pedantic and minute laws, such as a society with no idea of excellence but conformity to rule would be sure to adopt; though nobler institutions have often done the same, and the Master-burghers were but prototypes of the Italian academicians. The poetry was always moral and serious, but flat. These Meister-singers are said to have originated at Mentz; from which they spread to Augsburg, Strasburg, and other cities, and in none were more renowned than Nuremberg. Charles IV., in 1378, incorporated them by the name of Meistergenoss-schaft, with armorial bearings and peculiar privileges. They became, however, more conspicuous in the sixteenth century. Scarce any names of

poetry. The Nibelungen Lied has been lately modernized in German; and is read perhaps with more pleasure in that form, though it displays less of its original rudeness. — 1853.]

Meister-singers before that age are recorded; nor does it seem that much of their earlier poetry is extant.[1]

Poetry of France and Spain.

44. The French versifiers had by this time, perhaps, become less numerous, though several names in the same style of amatory song do some credit to their age. But the romances of chivalry began now to be written in prose; while a very celebrated poem, the Roman de la Rose, had introduced an unfortunate taste for allegory into verse, from which France did not extricate herself for several generations. Meanwhile the Provençal poets, who, down to the close of the thirteenth century, had flourished in the South, and whose language many Lombards adopted, came to an end. After the re-union of the fief of Toulouse to the crown, and the possession of Provence by a Northern line of princes, their ancient and renowned tongue passed for a dialect, a patois of the people. It had never been much employed in prose, save in the kingdom of Arragon, where, under the name of Valencian, it continued for two centuries to be a legitimate language, till political circumstances of the same kind reduced it, as in Southern France, to a provincial dialect. The Castilian language, which, though it has been traced higher in written fragments, may be considered to have begun, in a literary sense, with the poem of the Cid (not later, as some have thought, than the middle of the twelfth century), was employed by a few extant poets in the next age; and, in the fourteenth, was as much the established vehicle of many kinds of literature in Spain as the French was on the other side of the mountains.[2] The names of Portuguese poets not less early than any in Castile are recorded: fragments are mentioned by Bouterwek as old as the twelfth century; and there exists a collection of lyric poetry, in the style of the Troubadours, which is referred to no late part of the next age.[3] Nothing

[1] Bouterwek, ix. 271–291; Heinsius, iv. 85–98. See also the Biographie Universelle, art. "Folcz;" and a good article in the Retrospective Review, vol. x. p. 113. [See also Gervinus, Poetische Litteratur der Deutschen, p. 112, and *post*.]

[2] Sanchez, Coleccion de Poesias Castellanas anteriores al Siglo 15mo; Velasquez, Historia della Poesia Español, which I only know by the German translation of Dieze (Göttingen, 1769), who has added many notes; Andrès, Origine d' ogni Litteratura, ii. 158; Bouterwek's History of Spanish and Portuguese Literature. I shall quote the English translation of this work.

[3] This very curious fact in literary history has been brought to light by Lord Stuart of Rothesay, who printed at Paris, in 1823, twenty-five copies of a collection of ancient Portuguese songs, from a manuscript in the library of the College of Nobles at Lisbon. An account of this book, by M. Raynouard, will be found in the Journal des Savans for August, 1825; and I have been favored by my noble friend the editor with the loan of a copy, though my ignorance of the language pre-

has been published in the Castilian language of this amatory style older than 1400.

45. Italy came, last of those countries where Latin had been spoken, to the possession of an independent language and literature. No industry has hitherto retrieved so much as a few lines of real Italian till near the end of the twelfth century;[1] and there is not much before the middle of the next. Several poets, however, whose versification is not wholly rude, appeared soon afterwards. The Divine Comedy of Dante seems to have been commenced before his exile from Florence in 1304. The Italian language was much used in prose during the times of Dante and Petrarch, though very little before.

Early Italian language.

46. Dante and Petrarch are, as it were, the morning-stars

vented me from forming an exact judgment of its contents. In the preface, the following circumstances are stated. It consists of seventy-five folios, the first part having been torn off, and the manuscript attached to a work of a wholly different nature. The writing appears to be of the fourteenth century, and in some places older. The idiom seems older than the writing: it may be called, if I understand the meaning of the preface, as old as the beginning of the thirteenth century, and certainly older than the reign of Denis," "pode appellidarse coevo do seculo xiii, e de certo he anterior ao reynado de D. Deniz." Denis, King of Portugal, reigned from 1279 to 1325. It is regular in grammar, and for the most part in orthography, but contains some Gallicisms, which show either a connection between France and Portugal in that age, or a common origin in the Southern tongues of Europe; since certain idioms found in this manuscript are preserved in Spanish, Italian, and Provençal, yet are omitted in Portuguese dictionaries. A few poems are translated from Provençal; but the greater part are strictly Portuguese, as the mention of places, names, and manners, shows. M. Raynouard, however, observes, that the thoughts and forms of versification are similar to those of the Troubadours. The metres employed are usually of seven, eight, and ten syllables, the accent falling on the last: but some lines occur of seven, eight, or eleven syllables, accented on the penultimate; and these are sometimes interwoven, at regular intervals, with the others.

The songs, as far as I was able to judge, are chiefly, if not wholly, amatory: they generally consist of stanzas, the first of which is written (and printed) with intervals for musical notes, and in the form of prose, though really in metre. Each stanza has frequently a burden of two lines. The plan appeared to be something like that of the Castilian glosas of the fifteenth century; the subject of the first stanza being repeated, and sometimes expanded, in the rest. I do not know that this is found in any Provençal poetry. The language, according to Raynouard, resembles Provençal more than the modern Portuguese does. It is a very remarkable circumstance, that we have no evidence, at least from the letter of the Marquis of Santillana early in the fifteenth century, that the Castilians had any of these love-songs till long after the date of this Cancioneiro, and that we may rather collect from it, that the Spanish amatory poets chose the Gallician or Portuguese dialect in preference to their own. Though the very ancient collection to which this note refers seems to have been unknown, I find mention of one by Don Pedro, Count of Barcelos, natural son of King Denis, in Dieze's notes on Velasquez, Gesch. der Span. Dichtkunst, p. 70. This must have been in the first part of the fourteenth century.

[1] Tiraboschi, iii. 323, doubts the authenticity of some inscriptions referred to the twelfth century. The earliest genuine Italian seems to be a few lines by Ciullo d'Alcamo, a Sicilian, between 1187 and 1193, vol. iv. p. 340. [Muratori thinks it probable that Italian might be written sometimes in the twelfth century. "Quando cio precisamente avvenisse, noi nol sappiamo, perchè l' ignoranza e barbarie di que' tempi non ne lasciò memoria, o non compose tale opere, che meritassero di vivere infino ai tempi nostri." Della perfetta Poesia, v. i. p. 6. — 1842.]

of our modern literature. I shall say nothing more of the former in this place: he does not stand in such close connection as Petrarch with the fifteenth century, nor had he such influence over the taste of his age. In this respect, Petrarch has as much the advantage over Dante, as he was his inferior in depth of thought and creative power. He formed a school of poetry, which, though no disciple comparable to himself came out of it, gave a character to the taste of his country. He did not invent the sonnet; but he, perhaps, was the cause that it has continued in fashion for so many ages.[1] He gave purity, elegance, and even stability, to the Italian language, which has been incomparably less changed during near five centuries since his time than it was in one between the age of Guido Guinizzelli and his own; and none have denied him the honor of having restored a true feeling of classical antiquity in Italy, and consequently in Europe.

Dante and Petrarch.

47. Nothing can be more difficult than to determine, except by an arbitrary line, the commencement of the English language; not so much, as in those of the Continent, because we are in want of materials, but rather from an opposite reason, — the possibility of tracing a very gradual succession of verbal changes that ended in a change of denomination. We should probably experience a similar difficulty if we knew equally well the current idiom of France or Italy in the seventh and eighth centuries; for, when we compare the earliest English of the thirteenth century with the Anglo-Saxon of the twelfth, it seems hard to pronounce why it should pass for a separate language, rather than a modification or simplification of the former. We must conform, however, to usage, and say, that the Anglo-Saxon was converted into English, 1. By contracting or otherwise modifying the pronunciation and orthography of words; 2. By omitting many inflections, especially of the noun, and consequently making more use of articles and auxiliaries; 3. By the introduction of French derivatives; 4. By using less inversion and ellipsis, especially in poetry. Of these, the second alone, I think, can be considered as sufficient to describe a new form of language; and this was brought about so gradu-

Change of Anglo-Saxon to English.

[1] Crescimbeni (Storia della vulgar Poesia, vol. ii. p. 269) asserts the claim of Guiton d'Arezzo to the invention of the regular sonnet, or at least the perfection of that in use among the Provençals.

ally, that we are not relieved from much of our difficulty, whether some compositions shall pass for the latest offspring of the mother or the earliest fruits of the daughter's fertility.[1]

48. The Anglo-Norman language is a phrase not quite so unobjectionable as the Anglo-Norman constitution; and, as it is sure to deceive, we might better lay it aside altogether.[2] In the one instance, there was a real fusion of laws and government, to which we can find but a remote analogy, or rather none at all, in the other. It is probable, indeed, that the converse of foreigners might have something to do with those simplifications of the Anglo-Saxon grammar which appear about the reign of Henry II., more than a century after the Conquest; though it is also true, that languages of a very artificial structure, like that of England before that revolution, often became less complex in their forms, without any such violent process as an amalgamation of two different races.[3] What is commonly called the Saxon Chronicle is continued to the death of Stephen in 1154, and in the same language, though with some loss of its purity. Besides the neglect of several grammatical rules, French words now and then obtrude themselves, but not very frequently, in the latter pages of this Chronicle. Peterborough, however, was quite an English monastery; its endowments, its abbots, were Saxon; and the political spirit the Chronicle breathes, in some passages, is that of the indignant subjects, *servi ancor frementi*, of the Norman usurpers. If its last compilers, therefore, gave way to some

[1] It is a proof of this difficulty, that the best masters of our ancient language have lately introduced the word Semi-Saxon, which is to cover every thing from 1150 to 1250. — See Thorpe's preface to Analecta Anglo-Saxonica, and many other recent books.

[2] A popular and pleasing writer has drawn a little upon his imagination in the following account of the language of our forefathers after the Conquest: "The language of the church was Latin; that of the king and nobles, Norman; that of the people, Anglo-Saxon: *the Anglo-Norman jargon was only employed in the commercial intercourse between the conquerors and the conquered.*" Ellis's Specimens of Early English Poets, vol. i. p. 17. What was this jargon? and where do we find a proof of its existence? and what was the commercial intercourse hinted at? I suspect Ellis only meant, what has often been remarked, that the animals which bear a Saxon name in the field acquire a French one in the shambles. But even this is more ingenious than just; for muttons, beeves, and porkers are good old words for the living quadrupeds. [It has, of late years, been more usual to call the French poetry, written in English, Anglo-Norman. — 1842.]

[3] "Every branch of the low German stock, from whence the Anglo-Saxon sprung, displays the same simplification of its grammar." Price's preface to Warton, p. 110. He therefore ascribes little influence to the Norman Conquest or to French connections. [It ought, however, to be observed, that the simplifications of the Anglo-Saxon grammar had begun before the reign of Henry II.: the latter part of the Saxon Chronicle affords full proof of this. — 1847.]

innovations of language, we may presume that these prevailed more extensively in places less secluded, and especially in London.

49. We find evidence of a greater change in Layamon, a translator of Wace's romance of Brut from the French. Layamon's age is uncertain: it must have been after 1155, when the original poem was completed; and can hardly be placed below 1200. His language is accounted rather Anglo-Saxon than English: it retains most of the distinguishing inflections of the mother-tongue, yet evidently differs considerably from that older than the Conquest, by the introduction, or at least more frequent employment, of some new auxiliary forms; and displays very little of the characteristics of the ancient poetry, its periphrases, its ellipses, or its inversions. But, though translation was the means by which words of French origin were afterwards most copiously introduced, very few occur in the extracts from Layamon hitherto published; for we have not yet the expected edition of the entire work. He is not a mere translator, but improves much on Wace. The adoption of the plain and almost creeping style of the metrical French romance, instead of the impetuous dithyrambics of Saxon song, gives Layamon, at first sight, a greater affinity to the new English language than in mere grammatical structure he appears to bear.[1]

50. Layamon wrote in a village on the Severn;[2] and it is agreeable to experience, that an obsolete structure of language should be retained in a distant province, while it has undergone some change among the less rugged inhabitants of a capital. The disuse of Saxon forms crept on by degrees: some metrical lives of saints, apparently written not far from the year 1250,[3] may be deemed English;

Progress of English language.

[1] See a long extract from Layamon in Ellis's Specimens. This writer observes, that "it contains no word which we are under the necessity of referring to a French root." *Duke* and *castle* seem exceptions; but the latter word occurs in the Saxon Chronicle before the Conquest, A.D. 1052

[[2] I believe that Ernley, of which Layamon is said to have been priest, is Over Arley, near Bewdley.—1842.]

[Sir F. Madden says Lower Arley, another village a few miles distant.—1847.]

[3] Ritson's Dissertat. on Romance; Madden's Introduction to Havelok; Notes of Price, in his edition of Warton. Warton himself is of no authority in this matter. Price inclines to put most of the poems quoted by Warton near the close of the thirteenth century.

It should here be observed, that the language underwent its metamorphosis into English by much less rapid gradations in some parts of the kingdom than in others. Not only the popular dialect of many counties, especially in the north, retained long, and still retains, a larger proportion of the Anglo-Saxon peculiarities, but we have evidence that they were not everywhere disused in writing. A manuscript in the Kentish dialect, if that phrase is correct, bearing the date of 1340,

but the first specimen of it that bears a precise date is a proclamation of Henry III., addressed to the people of Huntingdonshire in 1258, but doubtless circular throughout England.[1] A triumphant song, composed, probably in London, on the victory obtained at Lewes by the confederate barons in 1264, and the capture of Richard, Earl of Cornwall, is rather less obsolete in its style than this proclamation, as might naturally be expected. It could not have been written

is more Anglo-Saxon than any of the poems, ascribed to the thirteenth century, which we read in Warton, such as the legends of saints or the Ormulum. This very curious fact was first made known to the public by Mr. Thorpe, in his translation of Cædmon, preface, p. xii.; and an account of the manuscript itself, rather fuller than that of Mr. T., has since been given in the catalogue of the Arundel MSS. in the British Museum.

[The edition of Layamon alluded to in the text has now been published by Sir Frederick Madden, at the expense of the Society of Antiquaries, and will prove an important accession to the history of our language; being by much the most extensive remains of that period denominated Semi-Saxon. The date of this long poem is now referred by the editor to the reign of John, at the beginning of the thirteenth century. A passage formerly quoted by Mr. Sharon Turner, but which had escaped my recollection, manifestly was written after the death of Henry II. in 1189, and probably after that of his queen Eleanor in 1203. Mr. Turner has therefore inclined to the same period as Sir Frederick Madden; and others had acceded to his opinion. The chief objection, and indeed the only one, may be the antiquity of Layamon's language compared with the Ormulum, a well-known but hitherto unpublished poem of a certain Orm; and with another poem, which has been printed, entitled the Owl and the Nightingale. Nothing can exhibit a transitional state of language better than the great work of Layamon, consisting of near 30,000 lines. These are all short, and, though very irregular, coming far nearer to the old Anglo-Saxon than to the octo-syllabic French rhythm. Some of them are rhymed; but, in a much larger proportion, the alliterative euphony of the Northern nations is preferred. The publication of the entire poem enables us to correct some of the judgments founded on mere extracts: thus I should qualify what is said in the text, that Layamon "adopted the plain and almost creeping style of the metrical French romance." His poem has more spirit and fire, in the Scandinavian and Anglo-Saxon style, than had been supposed. Upon the whole, Layamon must be reckoned far more of the older than the newer formation: he is an *eocene*, or at most a *miocene;* while his contemporaries, as they seem to be, belong philologically to a later period.

The poem of the Owl and the Nightingale is supposed by its editor, Mr. Stevenson, to have been written soon after the death of Henry II., who is mentioned in it. But I do not see why the passage leads us to more than that no other king of that name had reigned. We need not, therefore, go higher than the age of John. The Ormulum contains, I believe, no evidence of its date; but the language is very decidedly more English, the versification more borrowed from Norman models, than that of Layamon. Since it is natural to presume that the change of language would not be alike in all parts of England, and even that individuals might continue to preserve forms which were going into comparative disuse, we cannot rely on these varieties as indicating difference of age. The editor of Layamon informs us, that the French words in the older copy of that writer do not amount to fifty. The hypothesis, if we are to use such a word, that the transition of our language from Saxon to English took place more rapidly in some districts than in others, acquires strong confirmation from a few lines preserved in Roger de Hoveden and Benedict Abbas about the year 1190. They seem to be printed inaccurately, and I shall consequently omit them here; but the language is English of Henry III.'s reign. It is possible that it has been a little modernized in the manuscripts of these historians —1847.]

[1] Henry's Hist. of Britain, vol. viii., appendix. "Between 1244 and 1258," says Sir F. Madden, "we know, was written the versification of part of a meditation of St. Augustine, as proved by the age of the prior, who gave the manuscript to the Durham library;" p. 49. This, therefore, will be strictly the oldest piece of English to the date of which we can approach by more than conjecture.

later than that year; because, in the next, the tables were turned on those who now exulted by the complete discomfiture of their party in the battle of Evesham. Several pieces of poetry, uncertain as to their precise date, must be referred to the latter part of this century. Robert of Gloucester, after the year 1297, since he alludes to the canonization of St. Louis,[1] turned the chronicle of Geoffrey of Monmouth into English verse; and on comparing him with Layamon, a native of nearly the same part of England, and a writer on the same subject, it will appear that a great quantity of French had flowed into the language since the loss of Normandy. The Anglo-Saxon inflections, terminations, and orthography had also undergone a very considerable change. That the intermixture of French words was very slightly owing to the Norman Conquest will appear probable by observing at least as frequent an use of them in the earliest specimens of the Scottish dialect, especially a song on the death of Alexander III. in 1285. There is a good deal of French in this, not borrowed, probably, from England, but directly from the original sources of imitation.

English of the fourteenth century. Chaucer. Gower.

51. The fourteenth century was not unproductive of men, both English and Scotch, gifted with the powers of poetry. Laurence Minot, an author unknown to Warton, but whose poems on the wars of Edward III. are referred by their publisher Ritson to 1352, is perhaps the first original poet in our language that has survived; since such of his predecessors as are now known appear to have been merely translators, or, at best, amplifiers, of a French or Latin original. The earliest historical or epic narrative is due to John Barbour, Archdeacon of Aberdeen, whose long poem in the Scots dialect, The Bruce, commemorating the deliverance of his country, seems to have been completed in 1373. But our greatest poet of the middle ages, beyond comparison, was Geoffrey Chaucer; and I do not know that any other country, except Italy, produced his equal in variety of invention, acuteness of observation, or felicity of expression. A vast interval must be made between Chaucer and any other English poet; yet Gower, his contemporary, though not, like him, a poet of Nature's growth, had some effect in rendering the language less rude, and exciting a taste

[1] Madden's Havelok, p. 52.

for verse. If he never rises, he never sinks low: he is always sensible, polished, perspicuous, and not prosaic in the worst sense of the word. Longlands, the supposed author of Piers Plowman's Vision, with far more imaginative vigor, has a more obsolete and unrefined diction.

General disuse of French in England.

52. The French language was spoken by the superior classes of society in England from the Conquest to the reign of Edward III.; though it seems probable that they were generally acquainted with English, at least in the latter part of that period. But all letters, even of a private nature, were written in Latin till the beginning of the reign of Edward I., soon after 1270, when a sudden change brought in the use of French.[1] In grammar-schools, boys were made to construe their Latin into French; and in the statutes of Oriel College, Oxford, we find a regulation so late as 1328, that the students shall converse together, if not in Latin, at least in French.[2] The minutes of the corporation of London, recorded in the town-clerk's office, were in French, as well as the proceedings in Parliament and in the courts of justice; and oral discussions were perhaps carried on in the same language, though this is not a necessary consequence. Hence the English was seldom written, and hardly employed in prose, till after the middle of the fourteenth century. Sir John Mandeville's Travels were written in 1356. This is our earliest English book.[3] Wicliffe's translation of the Bible, a great work that enriched the language, is referred to 1383. Trevisa's version of the Polychronicon of Higden was in 1385, and the Astrolabe of Chaucer in 1392. A few public instruments were drawn up in English under Richard II.; and about the same time, probably, it began to

[1] I am indebted for this fact, which I have ventured to generalize, to the communication of Mr. Stevenson, late sub-commissioner of public records. [I find, however, that letters, even in France, are said to have been written only in Latin to the end of the century. "On n'écrivait encore que très peu de lettres en langue Française." Discours sur l'Etat des Lettres au 13me Siècle, in Hist. Littéraire de la France, vol. xvi. p. 168. It is probable, therefore, that I have used too strong words as to the general usage. — 1842.]

[2] "Si qua inter se proferant, colloquio Latino vel saltem Gallico perfruantur." Warton, i. 6. In Merton-College Statutes, given in 1271, Latin alone is prescribed

[3] [This is only true as to printed books; for there are several copies of a translation of the Psalter and Church Hymns, by Rolle, commonly called the Hermit of Hampole, who has subjoined a comment on each verse. Rolle is said by Mr. Sharon Turner to have died in 1349: we must, therefore, place him a little before Mandeville. Even in him we find a good deal of French and Latin; which indeed he seems to have rather studiously sought, in order "that they that knowes noght the Latyne be the Ynglys may come to many Latyne wordis." Baber's preface to Wicliffe's Translation of New Testament. — 1847.]

be employed in epistolary correspondence of a private nature. Trevisa informs us, that, when he wrote (1385), even gentlemen had much left off to have their children taught French; and names the schoolmaster (John Cornwall), who, soon after 1350, brought in so great an innovation as the making his boys read Latin into English.[1] This change from the common use of French in the upper ranks seems to have taken place as rapidly as a similar revolution has lately done in Germany. By a statute of 1362 (36 E. III., c. 15), all pleas in courts of justice are directed to be pleaded and judged in English, on account of French being so much unknown. But the laws, and, generally speaking, the records of Parliament, continued to be in the latter language for many years; and we learn from Sir John Fortescue, a hundred years afterwards, that this statute itself was not fully enforced.[2] The French language, if we take his words literally, even in the reign of Edward IV., was spoken in affairs of mercantile account, and in many games, the vocabulary of both being chiefly derived from it.[3]

State of European languages about 1400.

53. Thus, by the year 1400, we find a national literature subsisting in seven European languages, — three spoken in the Spanish peninsula, the French, the Italian, the German, and the English; from which last the Scots dialect need not be distinguished. Of these the Italian was the most polished, and had to boast of the greatest writers. The French excelled in their number and variety. Our own tongue, though it had latterly acquired much copiousness in the hands of Chaucer and Wicliffe, both of whom lavishly supplied it with words of French and Latin derivation, was but just growing into a literary existence. The German, as well as that of Valencia, seemed to decline. The former became more precise, more abstract, more intellectual (*geistig*), and less sensible (*sinnlich*) (to use the words of Eichhorn); that is, less full of ideas derived from sense, and, of consequence, less fit for poetry: it fell into the hands of lawyers and mystical theologians. The earliest German prose, a few very ancient fragments excepted, is the collection of Saxon

[1] The passage may be found quoted in Warton, *ubi supra*, or in many other books.

[2] "In the courts of justice, they formerly used to plead in French, till, in pursuance of a law to that purpose, that custom was *somewhat restrained*, but not hitherto quite disused." De Laudibus Legum Angliæ, c. xlviii. I quote from Waterhouse's translation; but the Latin runs "*quam plurimum* restrictus est."

[3] De Laudibus Legum Angliæ, c. xlviii.

laws (Sachsenspiegel), about the middle of the thirteenth century; the next, the Swabian collection (Schwabenspiegel), about 1282.[1] But these forming hardly a part of literature, though Bouterwek praises passages of the latter for religious eloquence, we may deem John Tauler, a Dominican friar of Strasburg, whose influence in propagating what was called the mystical theology gave a new tone to his country, to be the first German writer in prose. "Tauler," says a modern historian of literature, "in his German sermons, mingled many expressions invented by himself, which were the first attempt at a philosophical language, and displayed surprising eloquence for the age wherein he lived. It may be justly said of him, that he first gave to prose that direction in which Luther afterwards advanced so far."[2] Tauler died in 1361. Meantime, as has been said before, the nobility abandoned their love of verse, which the burghers took up diligently, but with little spirit or genius: the common language became barbarous and neglected, of which the strange fashion of writing half-Latin, half-German verses is a proof.[3] This had been common in the darker ages: we have several instances of it in Anglo-Saxon, and also after the Conquest; nor was it rare in France; but it was late to adopt it in the fourteenth century.

54. The Latin writers of the middle ages were chiefly ecclesiastics; but of these, in the living tongues, a large proportion were laymen. They knew, therefore, how to commit their thoughts to writing; and hence the ignorance characteristic of the darker ages must seem to be passing away. This, however, is a very difficult though interesting question, when we come to look nearly at the gradual progress of rudimental knowledge. I can offer but an outline, which those who turn more of their attention towards the subject will be enabled to correct and complete. Before the end of the eleventh century, and especially after the ninth, it was rare to find laymen in France who could read and write.[4] The case was probably not better anywhere else,

Ignorance of reading and writing in darker ages.

[1] Bouterwek, p. 163. There are some novels at the end of the thirteenth or beginning of the fourteenth century. Ib.

[2] Heinsius, iv. 76.

[3] Eichhorn, Allg. Gesch., i. 240.

[4] Hist. Litt. de la France, vii. 2. Some nobles sent their children to be educated in the schools of Charlemagne, especially those of Germany, under Raban, Notker, Bruno, and other distinguished abbots; but they were generally destined for the church. Meiners, ii. 377. The signatures of laymen are often found to deeds of the eighth century, and sometimes of the ninth. Nouv. Traité de la Diplomatique, ii. 422. The ignorance of the laity, ac-

except in Italy. I should incline to except Italy on the authority of a passage in Wippo, a German writer soon after the year 1000, who exhorts the Emperor Henry II. to cause the sons of the nobility to be instructed in letters, using the example of the Italians, with whom, according to him, it was a universal practice.[1] The word "clerks," or "clergymen," became, in this and other countries, synonymous with one who could write, or even read. We all know the original meaning of "benefit of clergy," and the test by which it was claimed. Yet from about the end of the eleventh, or at least of the twelfth century, many circumstances may lead us to believe that it was less and less a conclusive test, and that the laity came more and more into possession of the simple elements of literature.

Reasons for supposing this to have diminished after 1100.

55. I. It will, of course, be admitted, that all who administered or belonged to the Roman law were masters of reading and writing; though we do not find that they were generally ecclesiastics, even in the lowest sense of the word, by receiving the tonsure. Some, indeed, were such. In countries where the feudal law had passed from unwritten custom to record and precedent, and had grown into as much subtlety by diffuseness as the Roman (which was the case of England from the time of Henry II.), the lawyers, though laymen, were unquestionably clerks, or learned. II. The convenience of such elementary knowledge to merchants, who, both in the Mediterranean and in these parts of Europe, carried on a good deal of foreign commerce, and indeed to all traders, may induce us to believe that they were not destitute of it; though it must be confessed that the word "clerk" rather seems to denote that their deficiency was supplied by those employed under them. I do not, however, conceive that the clerks of citizens were ecclesiastics.[2]

cording to this authority, was not strictly parallel to that of the church.

[1] "Tunc fac edictum per terram Teutonicorum
Quilibet ut dives sibi natos instruat omnes
Litterulis, legemque suam persuadeat illis,
Ut cum principibus placitandi venerit usus,
Quisque suis libris exemplum proferat illis.
Moribus his dudum vivebat Roma decenter,
His studiis tantos potuit vincere tyrannos.
Hoc servant Itali post prima crepundia cuncti."

I am indebted for this quotation to Meiners, ii. 344.

[2] The earliest recorded bills of exchange, according to Beckmann (Hist. of Inventions), iii. 430, are in a passage of the jurist Baldus, and bear date in 1328; but they were by no means in common use till the next century. I do not mention this as bearing much on the subject of the text.

III. If we could rely on a passage in Ingulfus, the practice in grammar-schools, of construing Latin into French, was as old as the reign of the Conqueror;[1] and it seems unlikely that this should have been confined to children educated for the English Church. IV. The poets of the north and south of France were often men of princely or noble birth, sometimes ladies: their versification is far too artificial to be deemed the rude product of an illiterate mind; and to these, whose capacity of holding the pen few will dispute, we must surely add a numerous class of readers for whom their poetry was designed. It may be surmised that the itinerant minstrels answered this end, and supplied the ignorance of the nobility; but many ditties of the Troubadours were not so well adapted to the minstrels, who seem to have dealt more with metrical romances. Nor do I doubt that these also were read in many a castle of France and Germany. I will not dwell on the story of Francesca of Rimini, because no one, perhaps, is likely to dispute that a Romagnol lady in the age of Dante would be able to read the tale of Lancelot. But that romance had long been written; and other ladies doubtless had read it, and possibly had left off reading it in similar circumstances, and as little to their advantage. The fourteenth century abounded with books in French prose; nor were they by any means wanting in the thirteenth, when several translations from Latin were made.[2] The extant copies of some are not very few; but no argument against their circulation could have been urged from their scarcity in the present day. It is not, of course, pretended that they were diffused as extensively as printed books have been. V. The fashion of writing private letters in French, instead of Latin, which, as has been mentioned, came in among us soon after 1270, affords perhaps a presumption that they were written in a language intelligible to the correspondent, because he had no longer occasion for assistance in reading them, though they were still generally from the hand of a secretary. But at what time this disuse of Latin began on the continent of Europe, I cannot exactly determine.

56. The art of reading does not imply that of writing: it seems likely that the one prevailed before the other. The latter was difficult to acquire, in consequence of the regularity

[1] "Et pueris etiam in scholis principia literarum Gallicè et non Anglicè traderentur."

[2] Hist. Litt. de la France, xvi. 144. "Notre prose et notre poésie Française existaient avant 1200; mais c'est au treizième siècle qu'elles commencèrent à prendre un caractère national." Id. 254.

of characters preserved by the clerks, and their complex system of abbreviations, which rendered the cursive handwriting introduced about the end of the eleventh century almost as operose, to those who had not much experience of it, as the more stiff characters of older manuscripts. It certainly appears that even autograph signatures are not found till a late period. Philip the Bold, who ascended the French throne in 1272, could not write; though this is not the case with any of his successors. I do not know that equal ignorance is recorded of any English sovereign; though we have, I think, only a series of autographs beginning with Richard II. It is said by the authors of Nouveau Traité de la Diplomatique, Benedictines of laborious and exact erudition, that the art of writing had become rather common among the laity of France before the end of the thirteenth century. Out of eight witnesses to a testament in 1277, five could write their names: at the beginning of that age, it is probable, they think, that not one could have done so.[1] Signatures to deeds of private persons, however, do not begin to appear till the fourteenth, and were not in established use in France till about the middle of the fifteenth century.[2] Indorsements upon English deeds, as well as mere signatures, by laymen of rank, bearing date in the reign of Edward II., are in existence; and there is an English letter from the lady of Sir John Pelham to her husband in 1399, which is probably one of the earliest instances of female penmanship. By the badness of the grammar, we may presume it to be her own.[3]

Increased knowledge of writing in fourteenth century.

[1] Vol. ii. p. 423. Charters in French are rare at the beginning of the thirteenth century, but become common under Philip III. Hist. Litt. de la France, xvi. 155.

[2] Ibid., p. 434 *et post.*

[3] I am indebted for a knowledge of this letter to the Rev. Joseph Hunter, who recollected to have seen it in an old edition of Collins's Peerage. Later editions have omitted it as an unimportant redundancy, though interesting even for its contents, independently of the value it acquires from the language. On account of its scarcity, being only found in old editions now not in request, I shall insert it here; and, till any other shall prefer a claim, it may pass for the oldest private letter in the English language. I have not kept the orthography, but have left several incoherent and ungrammatical phrases as they stand. It was copied by Collins from the archives of the Newcastle Family.

My dear Lord, — I recommend me to your high lordship with heart and body and all my poor might, and with all this I thank you as my dear lord dearest and best beloved of all earthly lords I say for me, and thank you my dear lord with all this that I say before of your comfortable letter that ye sent me from Pontefract that come to me on Mary Magdalene day; for by my troth I was never so glad as when I heard by your letter that ye were strong enough with the grace of God for to keep you from the malice of your enemies. And dear Lord if it like to your high lordship that as soon as ye might that I might hear of your gracious speed; which as God Almighty continue and increase. And my dear lord if it like you for to know of my fare, I am hereby laid in manner of a siege with the county of

57. Laymen, among whom Chaucer and Gower are illustrious examples, received occasionally a learned education; and indeed the great number of gentlemen who studied in the inns of court is a conclusive proof that they were not generally illiterate. The common law required some knowledge of two languages. Upon the whole, we may be inclined to think that in the year 1400, or at the accession of Henry IV., the average instruction of an English gentleman of the first class would comprehend common reading and writing, a considerable familiarity with French, and a slight tincture of Latin; the latter retained or not, according to his circumstances and character, as school learning is at present. This may be rather a favorable statement; but, after another generation, it might be assumed, as we shall see, with more confidence as a fair one.[1]

Average state of knowledge in England.

58. A demand for instruction in the art of writing would increase with the frequency of epistolary correspondence, which, where of a private or secret nature, no one would gladly conduct by the intervention of a secretary. Better education, more refined manners, a closer intercourse of social life, were the primary causes of this increase in private correspondence. But it was greatly facilitated by the invention, or rather extended use, of paper as the vehicle of writing, instead of parchment; a revolution, as it may be called, of high importance, without which both the art of writing would have been much less practised, and the invention of printing less serviceable to mankind. After the subjuga-

Invention of paper.

Sussex, Surrey, and a great parcel of Kent, so that I may nought out no none victuals get me but with much hard. Wherefore my dear if it like you by the advice of your wise counsel for to get remedy of the salvation of your castle and withstand the malice of the shires aforesaid. And also that ye be fully informed of their great malice workers in these shires which that haves so despitefully wrought to you, and to your castle, to your men, and to your tenants for this country have they wasted for a great while. Farewell my dear lord, the Holy Trinity you keep from your enemies, and ever send me good tidings of you. Written at Pevensey in the castle on St. Jacob day last past,

By your own poor
J. PELHAM.

To my true Lord.

[Sir Henry Ellis says, "We have nothing earlier than the fifteenth century which can be called a familiar letter." Original Letters, first series, vol. i. This of Lady Pelham, however, is an exception, and perhaps others will be found; at least, it cannot now be doubtful that some were written, since a lady is not likely to have set the example. Sir H. E., nevertheless, is well warranted in saying, that letters previous to the reign of Henry V. were usually written in French or Latin.—1847.]

[1] It might be inferred from a passage in Richard of Bury, about 1343, that none but ecclesiastics could read at all. He deprecates the putting of books into the hands of *laici*, who do not know one side from another; and, in several places, it seems that he thought they were meant for "the tonsured" alone. But a great change took place in the ensuing half-century; and I do not believe he can be construed strictly even as to his own time.

tion of Egypt by the Saracens, the importation of the papyrus, previously in general use, came, in no long time, to an end: so that, though down to the end of the seventh century all instruments in France were written upon it, we find its place afterwards supplied by parchment; and, under the house of Charlemagne, there is hardly an instrument upon any other material.[1] Parchment, however, a much more durable and useful vehicle than papyrus,[2] was expensive; and its cost not only excluded the necessary waste which a free use of writing requires, but gave rise to the unfortunate practice of erasing manuscripts in order to replace them with some new matter. This was carried to a great extent, and has occasioned the loss of precious monuments of antiquity, as is now demonstrated by instances of their restoration.

Linen paper: when first used.

Cotton paper.

59. The date of the invention of our present paper, manufactured from linen rags, or of its introduction into Europe, has long been the subject of controversy. That paper made from cotton was in use sooner, is admitted on all sides. Some charters written upon that material, not later than the tenth century, were seen by Montfaucon; and it is even said to be found in papal bulls of the ninth.[3] The Greeks, however, from whom the west of Europe is conceived to have borrowed this sort of paper, did not much employ it in manuscript books, according to Montfaucon, till the twelfth century; from which time it came into frequent use among them. Muratori had seen no writing upon this material older than 1100; though, in deference to Montfaucon, he admits its occasional employment earlier.[4] It certainly was not greatly used in Italy before the thirteenth century. Among the Saracens of Spain, on the other hand, as well as those of the East, it was of much greater antiquity. The Greeks called it *charta Damascena;* having been manufactured or sold in the city of Damascus; and Casiri, in his catalogue of the Arabic manuscripts in the Escurial, desires us to understand that they are written on paper

[1] Montfaucon, in Acad. des Inscript., vol. vi. But Muratori says that the papyrus was little used in the seventh century, though writings on it may be found as late as the tenth; Dissert. xliii. This dissertation relates to the condition of letters in Italy as far as the year 1100, as the xlivth does to their subsequent history.

[2] Heeren justly remarks (I do not know that others have done the same), of how great importance the general use of parchment, to which, and afterwards to paper, the whole perishable papyraceous manuscripts were transferred, has been to the preservation of literature. P. 74.

[3] Mém. de l'Acad. des Inscriptions, vi 604; Nouveau Traité de Diplomatique, i. 517; Savigny, Gesch. des Römischen Rechts, iii. 534.

[4] Dissert. xliii.

of cotton or linen, but generally the latter, unless the contrary be expressed.[1] Many in this catalogue were written before the thirteenth, or even the twelfth, century.

60. This will lead us to the more disputed question, as to the antiquity of linen paper. The earliest distinct instance I have found, and which I believe has hitherto been overlooked, is an Arabic version of the Aphorisms of Hippocrates, the manuscript bearing the date of 1100. This, Casiri observes to be on linen paper, not as in itself remarkable, but as accounting for its injury by wet. It does not appear whether it were written in Spain, or, like many in that catalogue, brought from Egypt or the East.[2]

Linen paper as old as 1100.

61. The authority of Casiri must confirm beyond doubt a passage in Peter, Abbot of Clugni, which has perplexed those who place the invention of linen paper very low. In a treatise against the Jews, he speaks of books, "ex pellibus arietum, hircorum, vel vitulorum, sive ex biblis vel juncis Orientalium paludum, aut ex *rasuris veterum pannorum*, seu ex aliâ quâlibet forte viliore materia compactos." A late English writer contends that nothing can be meant by the last words, "unless that all sorts of inferior substances capable of being so applied (among them, perhaps, hemp and the remains of cordage) were used at this period in the manufacture of paper."[3] It certainly at least seems reasonable to interpret the words, "ex rasuris veterum pannorum," of linen rags; and, when I add that Peter Cluniacensis passed a considerable time in Spain about 1141, there can remain, it seems, no rational doubt, that the Saracens of the peninsula were acquainted with that species of paper, though perhaps it was as yet unknown in every other country.

Known to Peter of Clugni.

62. Andrès asserts, on the authority of the Memoirs of the Academy of Barcelona, that a treaty between the kings of Arragon and Castile, bearing the date of 1178, and written upon linen paper, is extant in the archives of that city.[4] He alleges several other instances in

And in 12th and 13th centuries.

[1] "Materiæ, nisi membraneus sit codex, nulla mentio: cæteros bombycinos, ac, maximam partem, chartaceos esse colligas." Præfatio, p. 7.

[2] Casiri, N. 787. Codex anno Christi 1100, chartaceus, &c.

[3] See a memoir on an ancient manuscript of Aratus, by Mr. Ottley, in Archæologia, vol. xxvi

[4] Vol. ii. p. 73. Andrès has gone much at length into this subject, and has collected several important passages which do not appear in my text. The letter of Joinville has been supposed to be addressed to Louis Hutin in 1314; but this seems inconsistent with the writer's age.

the next age; when Mabillon, who denies that paper of linen was then used in charters (which, indeed, no one is likely to maintain), mentions, as the earliest specimen he had seen in France, a letter of Joinville to St. Louis, which must be older than 1270. Andrès refers the invention to the Saracens of Spain, using the fine flax of Valencia and Murcia; and conjectures that it was brought into use among the Spaniards themselves by Alfonso X. of Castile.[1]

Paper of mixed materials.

63. In the opinion of the English writer to whom we have above referred, paper, from a very early period, was manufactured of mixed materials, which have sometimes been erroneously taken for pure cotton. We have in the Tower of London a letter addressed to Henry III. by Raymond, son of Raymond VI., Count of Toulouse, and consequently between 1216 and 1222 (when the latter died), upon very strong paper, and certainly made, in Mr. Ottley's judgment, of mixed materials; while in several of the time of Edward I., written upon genuine cotton paper of no great thickness, the fibres of cotton present themselves everywhere at the backs of the letters so distinctly, that they seem as if they might even now be spun into thread.[2]

Invention of paper placed by some too low.

64. Notwithstanding this last statement, which I must confirm by my own observation, and of which no one can doubt who has looked at the letters themselves, several writers of high authority, such as Tiraboschi and Savigny, persist not only in fixing the invention of linen paper very low, even after the middle of the fourteenth century, but in maintaining that it is undistinguishable from that made of cotton, except by the eye of a manufacturer.[3] Were this indeed true, it would be sufficient for the purpose we have here in view; which is, not to trace the origin of a particular discovery, but the employment of a useful

[1] Vol. ii. p. 84. He cannot mean that it was never employed before Alfonso's time, of which he has already given instances.

[2] Archæologia, ibid. I may, however, observe, that a gentleman as experienced as Mr. Ottley himself inclines to think the letter of Raymond written on paper wholly made of cotton, though of better manufacture than usual.

[3] Tiraboschi, v. 85; Savigny, Gesch. des Römischen Rechts, iii. 534. He relies on a book I have not seen, Wehrs vom Papier, Hall, 1789. This writer, it is said, contends that the words of Peter of Clugny, "ex rasuris veterum pannorum," mean "cotton paper." Heeren, p. 208. Lambinet, on the other hand, translates them, without hesitation, "chiffons de linge." Hist. de l'Origine de l'Imprimerie, i. 93.

Andrès has pointed out, p. 70, that Maffei merely says he has seen no paper of linen earlier than 1300, and no instrument on that material older than one of 1367, which he found among his own family deeds. Tiraboschi, overlooking this distinction, quotes Maffei for his own opinion as to the lateness of the invention.

vehicle of writing. If it be true that cotton paper was fabricated in Italy of so good a texture that it cannot be discerned from linen, it must be considered as of equal utility. It is not the case with the letters on cotton paper in our English repositories; most, if not all, of which were written in France or Spain. But I have seen in the Chapter House at Westminster a letter written from Gascony, about 1315, to Hugh Despencer, upon thin paper, to all appearance made like that now in use, and with a water-mark. Several others of a similar appearance, in the same repository, are of rather later time. There is also one in the King's Remembrancer's Office of the 11th of Edward III. (1337 or 1338), containing the accounts of the king's ambassadors to the Count of Holland, and probably written in that country. This paper has a water-mark; and, if it is not of linen, is at least not easily distinguishable. Bullet declares that he saw at Besançon a deed of 1302 on linen paper. Several are alleged to exist in Germany before the middle of the century; and Lambinet mentions, though but on the authority of a periodical publication, a register of expenses from 1323 to 1354, found in a church at Caen, written on two hundred and eight sheets of that substance.[1] One of the Cottonian manuscripts (Galba, B. I.) is called Codex Chartaceus in the catalogue. It contains a long series of public letters, chiefly written in the Netherlands, from an early part of the reign of Edward III. to that of Henry IV. But upon examination, I find the title not quite accurate: several letters, and especially the earliest, are written on parchment; and paper does not appear at soonest till near the end of Edward's reign.[2] Sir Henry Ellis has said that "very few instances indeed occur, before the fifteenth century, of letters written upon paper."[3] The use of cotton paper was by no means general, or even, I believe, frequent, except in Spain and Italy; perhaps also in the south of France. Nor was it much employed, even in Italy, for books. Savigny tells us there are few manuscripts of law-books, among the multitude that exist, which are not written on parchment.

[1] Lambinet, *ubi supra.* [Linen paper, it is said in Hist. Littéraire de la France, xvi. 38, is used in some proceedings against the Templars in 1309; but the author knows of none earlier. He does not mention cotton paper at all: writing was on vellum or parchment. — 1842.]

[2] Andrès, p. 68, mentions a note, written in 1342, in the Cotton Library, as the earliest English specimen of linen paper. I do not know to what this refers. In the above-mentioned Codex Chartaceus is a letter of 1341; but it is on parchment.

[3] Ellis's Original Letters, i. 1.

65. It will be manifest from what has been said how greatly Robertson has been mistaken in his position, that, "in the eleventh century, the art of making paper, in the manner now become universal, was invented, by means of which not only the number of manuscripts increased, but the study of the sciences was wonderfully facilitated."[1] Even Ginguené, better informed on such subjects than Robertson, has intimated something of the same kind. But paper, whenever or wherever invented, was very sparingly used, and especially in manuscript books, among the French, Germans, or English, or linen paper, even among the Italians, till near the close of the period which this chapter comprehends. Upon the "study of the sciences" it could as yet have had very little effect. The vast importance of the invention was just beginning to be discovered. It is to be added, as a remarkable circumstance, that the earliest linen paper was of very good manufacture, strong and handsome, though perhaps too much like card for general convenience; and every one is aware that the first printed books are frequently beautiful in the quality of their paper.

Not at first very important.

66. III. The application of general principles of justice to the infinitely various circumstances which may arise in the disputes of men with each other is in itself an admirable discipline of the moral and intellectual faculties. Even where the primary rules of right and policy have been obscured in some measure by a technical and arbitrary system, which is apt to grow up, perhaps inevitably, in the course of civilization, the mind gains in precision and acuteness, though at the expense of some important qualities; and a people wherein an artificial jurisprudence is cultivated, requiring both a regard to written authority and the constant exercise of a discriminating judgment upon words, must be deemed to be emerging from ignorance. Such was the condition of Europe in the twelfth century. The feudal customs, long unwritten, though latterly become more steady by tradition, were in some countries reduced into treatises. We have our own Glanvil, in the reign of Henry II.; and, in the next century, much was written upon the national laws in various parts of Europe. Upon these it is not my intention to dwell; but the importance of the civil law in its connection with

Importance of legal studies.

[1] Hist. of Charles V., vol. i. note 10. Heeren inclines to the same opinion; p

ancient learning, as well as with moral and political science, renders it deserving of a place in any general account either of mediæval or modern literature.

67. That the Roman laws, such as they subsisted in the Western Empire at the time of its dismemberment in the fifth century, were received in the new kingdoms of the Gothic, Lombard, and Carlovingian dynasties, as the rule of those who by birth and choice submitted to them, was shown by Muratori and other writers of the last century. This subject has received additional illustration from the acute and laborious Savigny, who has succeeded in tracing sufficient evidence of what had been in fact stated by Muratori, that not only an abridgment of the Theodosian Code, but that of Justinian, and even the Pandects, were known in different parts of Europe long before the epoch formerly assigned for the restoration of that jurisprudence.[1] The popular story, already much discredited, that the famous copy of the Pandects, now in the Laurentian Library at Florence, was brought to Pisa from Amalfi, after the capture of that city by Roger, King of Sicily, with the aid of a Pisan fleet in 1135, and became the means of diffusing an acquaintance with that portion of the law through Italy, is shown by him not only to rest on very slight evidence, but to be unquestionably, in the latter and more important circumstance, destitute of all foundation.[2] It is still indeed an undetermined question, whether other existing manuscripts of the Pandects are not derived from this illustrious copy, which alone contains the entire fifty books, and which has been preserved with a traditional veneration indicating some superiority: but Savigny has shown, that Peter of Valence, a jurist of the eleventh century, made use of an independent manuscript; and it is certain that the Pandects were the subject of legal studies before the siege of Amalfi.

Roman laws never wholly unknown.

68. Irnerius, by universal testimony, was the founder of all

[1] It can be no disparagement to Savigny, who does not claim perfect originality, to say that Muratori, in his 44th dissertation, gives several instances of quotations from the Pandects in writers older than the capture of Amalfi.

[The most decisive proof that Savigny has adduced for the use of the Pandects before the twelfth century is from a work bearing the name of Petrus, called Exceptiones Legum Romanorum, which he supposes to have been written at Valence before the time of Gregory VII. The Pandects are herein cited so copiously, as to leave no doubt that Peter was acquainted with the entire collection. In other instances, it might be doubted whether the quotation implies more than a partial knowledge. Savigny, Gesch. Römisch. Rechts, vol. ii. Appendix. — 1847.]

[2] Savigny, Geschichte des Römischen Rechts in mittel Alter, iii. 83.

learned investigation into the laws of Justinian. He gave lectures upon them at Bologna, his native city, not long, in Savigny's opinion, after the commencement of the century;[1] and, besides this oral instruction, he began the practice of making glosses, or short marginal explanations, on the law-books, with the whole of which he was acquainted. We owe also to him, according to ancient opinion, though much controverted in later times, an epitome, called the Authentica, of what Gravina calls the prolix and difficult ("salebrosis atque garrulis") Novels of Justinian, arranged according to the titles of the Code. The most eminent successors of this restorer of the Roman law, during the same century, were Martinus Gosias, Bulgarus, and Placentinus. They were, however, but a few, among many interpreters, whose glosses have been partly though very imperfectly preserved. The love of equal liberty and just laws in the Italian cities rendered the profession of jurisprudence exceedingly honorable. The doctors of Bologna and other universities were frequently called to the office of *podestà*, or criminal judge, in these small republics: in Bologna itself, they were officially members of the smaller or secret council; and their opinions, which they did not render gratuitously, were sought with the respect that had been shown at Rome to their ancient masters of the age of Severus.

Irnerius: his first successors.

69. A gloss, γλῶσσα, properly meant a word from a foreign language, or an obsolete or poetical word, or whatever requires interpretation. It was afterwards used for the interpretation itself; and this sense, which is not strictly classical, may be found in Isidore, though some have imagined Irnerius himself to have first employed it.[2] In the twelfth century, it was extended from a single word to an entire expository sentence. The first glosses were interlinear; they were afterwards placed in the margin; and extended finally, in some instances, to a sort of running commentary on an entire book. These were called an Apparatus.[3]

Their glosses.

70. Besides these glosses on obscure passages, some lawyers attempted to abridge the body of the law. Placentinus wrote a summary of the Code and Institutes; but this was held inferior to that of Azo, which ap-

Abridgments of law.

[1] Vol. iv. p. 16. Some have erroneously thought Irnerius a German.

[2] Alcuin defines glossa, "unius verbi vel nominis interpretatio." Ducange, præfat. in Glossar., p. 38.

[3] Savigny, iii. 519.

peared before 1220. Hugolinus gave a similar abridgment of the Pandects. About the same time, or a little after, a scholar of Azo, Accursius of Florence, undertook his celebrated work, a collection of the glosses, which, in the century that had elapsed since the time of Irnerius, had grown to an enormous extent, and were, of course, not always consistent. He has inserted little, probably, of his own, but exercised a judgment, not perhaps a very enlightened one, in the selection of his authorities. Thus was compiled his Corpus Juris Glossatum, commonly called Glossa, or Glossa Ordinaria; a work, says Eichhorn, as remarkable for its barbarous style, and gross mistakes in history, as for the solidity of its judgments and practical distinctions. Gravina, after extolling the conciseness, acuteness, skill, and diligence in comparing remote passages, and in reconciling apparent inconsistencies, which distinguished Accursius, or rather those from whom he complied, remarks the injustice of some moderns, who reproach his work with the ignorance inevitable in his age, and seem to think the chance of birth, which has thrown them into more enlightened times, a part of their personal merit.[1]

Accursius's Corpus Glossatum.

71. Savigny has taken still higher ground in his admiration, as we may call it, of the early jurists, — those from the appearance of Irnerius to the publication of the Accursian body of glosses. For the execution of this work, indeed, he testifies no very high respect. Accursius did not sufficient justice to his predecessors; and many of the most valuable glosses are still buried in the dust of unpublished manuscripts.[2] But the men themselves deserve our highest praise. The school of Irnerius rose suddenly; for, in earlier writers, we find no intelligent use or critical interpretation of the passages which they cite. To reflect upon every text, to compare it with every clause or word that might illustrate its meaning in the somewhat chaotic mass of the Pandects and Code, was reserved for these acute and diligent investigators. "Interpretation," says Savigny, "was considered the first and most important object of glossers, as it was of oral instructors. By an unintermitting use of the original law-books, they obtained that full and lively acquaintance with their contents which enabled them to compare different passages with the

Character of early jurists.

[1] Origines Juris, p. 184.

[2] Vol. v. pp. 258-267

utmost acuteness and with much success. It may be reckoned a characteristic merit of many glossers, that they keep the attention always fixed on the immediate subject of explanation, and, in the richest display of comparisons with other passages of the law, never deviate from their point into any thing too indefinite and general; superior often in this to the most learned interpreters of the French and Dutch schools, and capable of giving a lesson even to ourselves. Nor did the glossers by any means slight the importance of laying a sound critical basis for interpretation, but, on the contrary, labored earnestly in the recension and correction of the text."[1]

72. These warm eulogies afford us an instance, to which there are many parallels, of such vicissitudes in literary reputation, that the wheel of Fame, like that of Fortune, seems never to be at rest. For a long time, it had been the fashion to speak in slighting terms of these early jurists; and the passage above quoted from Gravina is in a much more candid tone than was usual in his age. Their trifling verbal explanations of *etsi* by *quamvis*, or *admodum* by *valde;* their strange ignorance in deriving the name of the Tiber from the Emperor Tiberius, in supposing that Ulpian and Justinian lived before Christ, in asserting that Papinian was put to death by Mark Antony, and even interpreting *pontifex* by *papa* or *episcopus*, — were the topics of ridicule to those whom Gravina has so well reproved.[2] Savigny, who makes a similar remark, that we learn, without perceiving it and without any personal merit, a multitude of things which it was impossible to know in the twelfth century, defends his favorite glossers in the best manner he can, by laying part of the blame on the bad selection of Accursius, and by extolling the mental vigor which struggled through so many difficulties.[3] Yet he has the candor to own, that this rather enhances the respect due to the men, than the value of their writings; and, without much acquaintance with the ancient glossers, one may presume to think, that, in explaining the Pandects (a book requiring, beyond any other that has descended to us, an extensive knowledge of the language and antiquities of Rome), their deficiencies, if to be measured by the instances we have given

[1] Vol. v. pp. 199-211.

[2] Gennari, author of Respublica Jurisconsultorum, a work of the last century, who, under color of a fiction, gives rather an entertaining account of the principal jurists, exhibits some curious specimens of the ignorance of the Accursian interpreters, such as those in the text. — See, too, the article "Accursius," in Bayle.

[3] v. 213.

or by the general character of their age, must require a perpetual exercise of our lenity and patience.

73. This great compilation of Accursius made an epoch in the annals of jurisprudence. It put an end, in great measure, to the oral explanations of lecturers which had prevailed before. It restrained, at the same time, the ingenuity of interpretation. The glossers became the sole authorities: so that it grew into a maxim, "No one can go wrong who follows a gloss;" and some said a gloss was worth a hundred texts.[1] In fact, the original was continually unintelligible to a student. But this was accompanied, according to the distinguished historian of mediæval jurisprudence, by a decline of the science. The jurists in the latter part of the thirteenth century are far inferior to the school of Irnerius. It might be possible to seek a general cause, as men are now always prone to do, in the loss of self-government in many of the Italian republics; but Savigny, superior to this affectation of philosophy, admits that this is neither a cause adequate in itself, nor chronologically parallel to the decline of jurisprudence. We must therefore look upon it as one of those revolutions, so ordinary and so unaccountable, in the history of literature, where, after a period fertile in men of great talents, there ensues, perhaps with no unfavorable change in the diffusion of knowledge, a pause in that natural fecundity, without which all our endeavors to check a retrograde movement of the human mind will be of no avail. The successors of Accursius, in the thirteenth century, contented themselves with an implicit deference to the glosses; but this is rather a proof of their inferiority than its cause.[2]

Decline of jurists after Accursius.

74. It has been the peculiar fortune of Accursius, that his name has always stood in a representative capacity, to engross the praise or sustain the blame of the great body of glossers from whom he compiled. One of those proofs of national gratitude and veneration was paid to his memory, which it is the more pleasing to recount, that, from the fickleness and insensibility of mankind, they do not very frequently occur. The city of Bologna was divided into the factions of Lambertazzi and Gieremei. The former, who were Ghibellines, having been wholly overthrown and excluded, according to the practice of Italian republics, from all civil

Respect paid to him at Bologna.

[1] Bayle, *ubi supra;* Eichhorn, Gesch der Litteratur, ii. 461; Savigny, v. 268.
[2] Savigny, v. 320.

power, a law was made in 1306, that the family of Accursius, who had been on the vanquished side, should enjoy all the privileges of the victorious Guelph party, in regard to the memory of one "by whose means the city had been frequented by students, and its fame had been spread through the whole world."[1]

Scholastic jurists. Bartolus.

75. In the next century, a new race of lawyers arose, who, by a different species of talent, almost eclipsed the greatest of their predecessors. These have been called the scholastic jurists; the glory of the schoolmen having excited an emulous desire to apply their dialectic methods in jurisprudence.[2] Of these the most conspicuous were Bartolus and Baldus, especially the former, whose authority became still higher than that of the Accursian glossers. Yet Bartolus, if we may believe Eichhorn, content with the glosses, did not trouble himself about the text, which he was too ignorant of Roman antiquity, and even of the Latin language, unless he is much belied, to expound.[3] "He is so fond of distinctions," says Gravina, "that he does not divide his subject, but breaks it to pieces; so that the fragments are, as it were, dispersed by the wind. But, whatever harm he might do to the just interpretation of the Roman law as a positive code, he was highly useful to the practical lawyer by the number of cases his fertile mind anticipated; for though many of these were unlikely to occur, yet his copiousness, and subtlety of distinction, is such, that he seldom leaves those who consult him quite at a loss."[4] Savigny, who rates Bartolus much below the older lawyers, gives him credit for original thoughts, to which his acquaintance with the practical exercise of justice gave rise. The older jurists were chiefly professors of legal science, rather than conversant with forensic causes; and this has produced an opposition between theory and practice in the Roman law, to which we have not much analogous in our own, but the remains of which are said to be still discernible in the continental jurisprudence.[5]

[1] Savigny, v. 268.

[2] The employment of logical forms in law is not new: instances of it may be found in the earlier jurists. Savigny, v. 330; vi. 6.

[3] Geschichte der Litteratur, ii. 449. Bartolus even said, "*De verbibus* non curat jurisconsultus." Eichhorn gives no authority for this; but Meiners, from whom perhaps he took it, quotes Comnenus, Historia Archigymnasii Patavini; Vergleichung der Sitten, ii. 646. It seems, however, incredible.

[4] Origines Juris, p. 191.

[5] Savigny, vi. 138; v. 201. Of Bartolus and his school, it is said by Grotius, "Temporum suorum infelicitas impedimento sæpe fuit, quo minus recte leges illas in-

76. The later expositors of law, those after the age of Accursius, are reproached with a tedious prolixity, which the scholastic refinements of disputation were apt to produce. They were little more conversant with philological and historical literature than their predecessors, and had less diligence in that comparison of texts by which an acute understanding might compensate the want of subsidiary learning. In the use of language, the jurists, with hardly any exceptions, are uncouth and barbarous. The great school of Bologna had sent out all the earlier glossers. In the fourteenth century, this university fell rather into decline: the jealousy of neighboring states subjected its graduates to some disadvantage; and, while the study of jurisprudence was less efficacious, it was more diffused. Italy alone produced great masters of the science: the professors in France and Germany during the middle ages have left no great reputation.[1]

Inferiority of jurists in fourteenth and fifteenth centuries.

77. IV. The universities, however, with their metaphysics derived from Aristotle through the medium of Arabian interpreters who did not understand him, and with the commentaries of Arabian philosophers who perverted him,[2] the development of the

Classical literature and taste in dark ages.

telligerent; satis solertes alioqui ad indagandam æqui bonique naturam; quo factum ut sæpe optimi sint condendi juris auctores, etiam tunc cum conditi juris mali sunt interpretes. Prolegomena in Jus Belli et Pacis."

1 In this slight sketch of the early lawyers, I have been chiefly guided, as the reader will have perceived, by Gravina and Savigny; and also by a very neat and succinct sketch in Eichhorn, Gesch. der Litteratur, ii. 448–464. The Origines Juris of the first have enjoyed a considerable reputation. But Savigny observes, with severity, that Gravina has thought so much more of his style than his subject, that all he says of the old jurists is perfectly worthless through its emptiness, and want of criticism; iii. 72. Of Terrason's Histoire de la Jurisprudence Romaine he speaks in still lower terms.

2 It has been a subject of controversy, whether the physical and metaphysical writings of Aristotle were made known to Europe, at the beginning of the thirteenth century, through Constantinople, or through Arabic translations. The former supposition rests certainly on what seems good authority, — that of Rigord, a contemporary historian. But the latter is now more generally received, and is said to be proved in a dissertation, which I have not seen, by M. Jourdain. Tennemann, Manuel de l'Hist. de la Philos., i. 355. These Arabic translations were themselves not made directly from the Greek, but from the Syriac. It is thought by Buhle, that the Logic of Aristotle was known in Europe sooner.

[The prize essay of Jourdain, in 1817, entitled Recherches Critiques sur l'Age et l'Origine des Traductions Latines d'Aristote, was republished in 1843 by his son. The three points which he endeavors to establish are: 1. That the Organum of Aristotle alone was known before the thirteenth century. 2. That the other philosophical works were translated in the early part of that age. 3. That some of these translations are from the Greek, others from the Arabic. The last alone, and least important, of these propositions, can be considered as sure. Cousin doubts whether the Analytics and some other parts of the Organum were known to the early schoolmen. But John of Salisbury refers to them, though they were certainly not often quoted. There had been a difference of opinion as to the Greek or Arabic original of all the Aristotelian writings besides the Logic; Muratori and Heeren maintaining the former, Casiri and Buhle the lat-

modern languages with their native poetry, much more the glosses of the civil lawyers, are not what is commonly meant by the revival of learning. In this we principally consider the increased study of the Latin and Greek languages, and, in general, of what we call classical antiquity. In the earliest of the dark ages, as far back as the sixth century, the course of liberal instruction, as has been said above, was divided into the trivium and the quadrivium: the former comprising grammar, logic, and rhetoric; the latter, music, arithmetic, geometry, and astronomy. But these sciences, which seem tolerably comprehensive, were, in reality, taught most superficially, or not at all. The Latin grammar, in its merest rudiments, from a little treatise ascribed to Donatus, and extracts of Priscian,[1] formed the only necessary part of the trivium in ecclesiastical schools. Even this seems to have been introduced afresh by Bede and the writers of the eighth century, who much excel their immediate predecessors in avoiding gross solecisms of grammar.[2] It was natural, that in England, where Latin had never been a living tongue, it should be taught better than in countries which still affected to speak it. From the time of Charlemagne, it was lost on the Continent, in common use, and preserved only through glossaries, of which there were many. The style of Latin in the dark period, independently of its want of verbal purity, is in very bad taste; but no writers seem to have been more inflated and empty than the English.[3]

ter. Jourdain seems, on the whole, to have settled the question; showing by the Greek or Arabic words and idioms in several translations extant in manuscript that they came from different sources. The Greek text of the Metaphysics had been brought to Europe and translated about 1220; but the Physics, the History of Animals, part of the Ethics, and several other works, were first made known through the Arabic (p. 212).

The age of these translations from Aristotle may be judged by their style. In those made before the tenth century, those, *e. gr.*, of Boethius, the Latin is pure, and free from Grecisms: those of the eleventh or later are quite literal, word for word, — rarely the right one chosen; the construction more Greek than Latin. In those immediately from the Arabic, the orthography of Greek words is never correct: sometimes an Arabic word is left.

Writers of the thirteenth century mention translations of the philosophical works by Boethius; but, as this could not be the great Boethius, Jourdain finds some traces of another bearing the name; or it may have been an error in referring a work to a known author.

The quotations from Aristotle in Albertus Magnus show that some were derived from Greek, some from Arabic. He says in one place, "Quod autem hæc vera sint quæ dicta sunt, testatur Aristotelis translatio Arabica quæ sic dicit. . . . Græca autem translatio discordat ab hoc, et, ut puto, est mendosa." Jourdain, p. 38. By "Arabica translatio," he means, of course, a translation from the Arabic.

The translation of Aristotle's Metaphysics, published in 1483, is from the Greek. — 1853.]

[1] Fleury, xvii. 18; Andrès, ix. 284.

[2] Eichhorn, Allg. Gesch., ii. 73. The reader is requested to distinguish, at least if he cares about references, Eichhorn's Allgemeine Geschichte der Cultur from his Geschichte der Litteratur, with which, in future, we shall have more concern.

[3] Fleury, xvii. 23; Ducange, preface to Glossary, p. 10. The Anglo-Saxon charters are distinguished for their pompous absur-

The distinction between the ornaments adapted to poetry and to prose had long been lost, and still more the just sense of moderation in their use. It cannot be wondered at that a vicious rhetoric should have overspread the writings of the ninth and tenth centuries, when there is so much of it in the third and fourth.

Improvement in tenth and eleventh centuries.

78. Eichhorn fixes upon the latter part of the tenth century as an epoch from which we are to deduce, in its beginnings, the restoration of classical taste: it was then that the scholars left the meagre introductions to rhetoric, formerly used, for the works of Cicero and Quintilian.[1] In the school of Paderborn, not long after 1000, Sallust and Statius, as well as Virgil and Horace, appear to have been read.[2] Several writers, chiefly historical, about this period, such as Lambert of Aschaffenburg, Ditmar, Wittikind, are tolerably exempt from the false taste of preceding times; and, if they want a truly classical tone, express themselves with some spirit.[3] Gerbert, who by an uncommon quickness of parts shone in very different provinces of learning, and was beyond question the most accomplished man of the dark ages, displays in his epistles a thorough acquaintance with the best Latin authors, and a taste for their excellences.[4] He writes with the feelings of Petrarch, but in a less auspicious period. Even in England, if we may quote again the famous passage of Ingulfus, the rhetorical works of Cicero, as well as some book which he calls Aristotle, were read at Oxford under Edward the Confessor. But we have no indisputable name in the eleventh century; not even that of John de Garlandiâ, whose Floretus long continued to be a text-book in schools. This is a poor collection of extracts from Latin authors. It is uncertain whether or not the compiler were an Englishman.[5]

dity; and it is the general character of our early historians. One Ethelwerd is the worst; but William of Malmesbury himself, perhaps in some measure by transcribing passages from others, sins greatly in this respect.

[1] Allg. Gesch., ii. 79.

[2] "Viguit Horatius magnus atque Virgilius, Crispus et Sallustius, et Urbanus Statius, ludusque fuit omnibus insudare versibus et dictaminibus jucundisque cantibus." Vita Meinwerci in Leibnitz Script. Brunsvic. apud Eichhorn, ii. 399.

[3] Eichhorn, Gesch. der Litteratur, i. 807; Heeren, p. 157.

[4] Heeren, p. 165. It appears that Cicero de Republicâ was extant in his time.

[5] Hist. Litt. de la France, viii. 84. The authors give very inconclusive reasons for robbing England of this writer, who certainly taught here under William the Conqueror, if not before; but it is possible enough that he came over from France. They say there is no such surname in England as Garland; which happens to be a mistake: but the native English did not often bear surnames in that age.

[In this note, I have been misled by the Histoire Littéraire de la France. John de Garlandiâ, the grammarian, author of the

Lanfranc and his schools.

79. It is admitted on all hands, that a remarkable improvement, both in style and in the knowledge of Latin antiquity, was perceptible towards the close of the eleventh century. The testimony of contemporaries attributes an extensively beneficial influence to Lanfranc. This distinguished person, born at Pavia in 1005, and early known as a scholar in Italy, passed into France, about 1042, to preside over a school at Bec in Normandy. It became conspicuous under his care for the studies of the age, dialectics and theology. It is hardly necessary to add, that Lanfranc was raised by the Conqueror to the primacy of England, and thus belongs to our own history. Anselm, his successor both in the monastery of Bec and the see of Canterbury, far more renowned than Lanfranc for metaphysical acuteness, has shared with him the honor of having diffused a better taste for philological literature over the schools of France. It has, however, been denied by a writer of high authority, that either any knowledge or any love of classical literature can be traced in the works of the two archbishops. They are in this respect, he says, much inferior to those of Lupus, Gerbert, and others of the preceding ages.[1] His contemporaries, who extol the learning of Lanfranc in hyperbolical terms, do so in very indifferent Latin of their own; but it appears indeed more than doubtful, whether the earliest of them meant to praise him for this peculiar species of literature.[2] The Benedictines of St. Maur cannot find much to say for him in this respect. They allege that he and Anselm wrote better than was then usual, — a very moderate compliment; yet they ascribe a great influence to their public lectures, and to the schools which were formed on the model of Bec:[3] and perhaps we

Floretus, lived in the thirteenth century. But there was a writer on arithmetic, named Garland, in the reign of William the Conqueror. See Wright's Biographia Britannica Literaria, vol. ii. p. 16. — 1847.]

The Anglo-Saxon clergy were inconceivably ignorant, "ut cæteris esset stupori qui grammaticam didicisset." Will. Malmesbury, p. 101. This leads us to doubt the Aristotle and Cicero of Ingulfus.

[1] Heeren, p. 185. There seems certainly nothing above the common in Lanfranc's epistles.

[2] Milo Crispinus, Abbot of Westminister, in his Life of Lanfranc, says of him, "Fuit quidam vir magnus Italia oriundus, quem Latinitas in antiquum scientiæ statum ab eo restituta tota supremum debito cum amore et honore agnoscit magistrum, nomine Lanfrancus."

This passage, which is frequently quoted, surely refers to his eminence in dialectics. The words of William of Malmesbury go farther. "Is literatura perinsignis liberales artes quæ jamdudum sorduerant, a Latio in Gallias vocans acumine suo expolivit."

[3] Hist. Litt. de la France, vii. 17, 107; viii. 304. The seventh volume of this long and laborious work begins with an excellent account of the literary condition of France in the eleventh century. At the beginning of the ninth volume, we have a similar view of the twelfth.

could not, without injustice, deprive Lanfranc of the credit he has obtained for the promotion of polite letters. There is at least sufficient evidence that they had begun to revive in France not long after his time.

Italy: Vocabulary of Papias.

80. The signs of gradual improvement in Italy during the eleventh century are very perceptible. Several schools, among which those of Milan and the Convent of Monte Casino are most eminent, were established; and some writers, such as Peter Damiani and Humbert, have obtained praise for rather more elegance and polish of style than had belonged to their predecessors.[1] The Latin vocabulary of Papias was finished in 1053. This is a compilation from the grammars and glossaries of the sixth and seventh centuries; but though many of his words are of very low Latinity, and his etymologies, which are those of his masters, absurd, he shows both a competent degree of learning and a regard to profane literature, unusual in the darker ages, and symptomatic of a more liberal taste.[2]

Influence of Italy upon Europe.

81. It may be said with some truth, that Italy supplied the fire from which other nations in this first, as afterwards in the second, era of the revival of letters, lighted their own torches. Lanfranc; Anselm; Peter Lombard, the founder of systematic theology in the twelfth century; Irnerius, the restorer of jurisprudence; Gratian, the author of the first compilation of canon law; the school of Salerno, that guided medical art in all countries; the first dictionaries of the Latin tongue; the first treatise of algebra; the first great work that makes an epoch in anatomy, — are as truly and exclusively the boast of Italy as the restoration of Greek literature and of classical taste in the fifteenth century.[3] But, if she were the first to propagate an impulse towards intellectual excellence in the rest of Europe, it must be owned that France

[1] Bettinelli, Risorgimento d' Italia dopo il mille; Tiraboschi, iii. 248.

[2] The date of the vocabulary of Papias had been placed by Scaliger, who says he has as many errors as words, in the thirteenth century. But Gaspar Barthius, in his Adversaria, c. i., after calling him "veterum Glossographorum compactor non semper futilis," observes, that Papias mentions an emperor, Henry II., as then living, and thence fixes the era of his book in the early part of the eleventh century; in which he is followed by Bayle, art. "Balbi." It is rather singular that neither of those writers recollected the usage of the Italians to reckon as Henry II. the prince whom the Germans call Henry III., Henry the Fowler not being included by them in the imperial list; and Bayle himself quotes a writer, unpublished in the age of Barthius, who places Papias in the year 1053. This date, I believe, is given by Papias himself. Tiraboschi, iii. 300. A pretty full account of the Latin glossaries, before and after Papias, will be found in the preface to Ducange, p. 38.

[3] Bettinelli, Risorgimento d' Italia, p. 71.

and England, in this dawn of literature and science, went, in many points of view, far beyond her.

Increased copying of manuscripts.

82. Three religious orders, all scions from the great Benedictine stock (that of Clugni, which dates from the first part of the tenth century; the Carthusians, founded in 1084; and the Cistercians, in 1098), contributed to propagate classical learning.[1] The monks of these foundations exercised themselves in copying manuscripts; the arts of calligraphy, and, not long afterwards, of illumination, became their pride; a more cursive handwriting and a more convenient system of abbreviations were introduced; and thus from the twelfth century we find a great increase of manuscripts, though transcribed mechanically as a monastic duty, and often with much incorrectness. The Abbey of Clugni had a rich library of Greek and Latin authors; but few monasteries of the Benedictine rule were destitute of one: it was their pride to collect and their business to transcribe books.[2] These were, in a vast proportion, such as we do not highly value at the present day; yet almost all we do possess of Latin classical literature, with the exception of a small number of more ancient manuscripts, is owing to the industry of these monks. In that age, there was perhaps less zeal for literature in Italy, and less practice in copying, than in France.[3] This shifting of intellectual exertion from one country to another is not peculiar to the middle ages; but, in regard to them, it has not always been heeded by those, who, using the trivial metaphor of light and darkness, which it is not easy to avoid, have too much considered Europe as a single point under a receding or advancing illumination.

John of Salisbury.

83. France and England were the countries where the revival of classical taste was chiefly perceived. In Germany, no sensible improvement in philological literature can be traced, according to Eichhorn and Heeren, before the invention of printing; though I think this must be understood with exceptions, and that Otho of Frisingen, Saxo Grammaticus, and Gunther, author of the poem entitled Ligurinus (who belongs to the first years of the thirteenth century), might stand on an equal footing with any of their contemporaries. But, in the schools which are supposed to have borrowed light from Lanfranc and Anselm, a more keen perception of the

[1] Fleury; Hist. Litt. de la France, ix. 113.
[2] Ibid., p. 139.
[3] Heeren, p. 197.

beauties of the Latin language, as well as an exacter knowledge of its idiom, was imparted. John of Salisbury, himself one of their most conspicuous ornaments, praises the method of instruction pursued by Bernard of Chartres about the end of the eleventh century, who seems indeed to have exercised his pupils vigorously in the rules of grammar and rhetoric. After the first grammatical instruction out of Donatus and Priscian, they were led forward to the poets, orators, and historians of Rome. The precepts of Cicero and Quintilian were studied, and sometimes observed with affectation.[1] An admiration of the great classical writers, an excessive love of philology, and disdain of the studies that drew men from it, shine out in the two curious treatises of John of Salisbury. He is perpetually citing the poets, especially Horace; and had read most of Cicero. Such, at least, is the opinion of Heeren, who bestows also a good deal of praise upon his Latinity.[2] Eichhorn places him at the head of all his contemporaries. But no one has admired his style so much as Meiners, who declares that he has no equal in the writers of the third, fourth, or fifth centuries, except Lactantius and Jerome.[3] In this I cannot but think there is some exaggeration. The style of John of Salisbury, far from being equal to that of Augustin, Eutropius, and a few more of those early ages, does not appear to me by any means elegant. Sometimes he falls upon a good expression; but the general tone is not very classical. The reader may judge from the passage in the note.[4]

84. It is generally acknowledged, that in the twelfth century we find several writers (Abelard, Eloisa, Bernard of Clair-

[1] Hist. Litt. de la France, vii. 16.

[2] P. 203; Hist. Litt. de la France, ix. 47. Peter of Blois also possessed a very respectable stock of classical literature.

[3] Vergleichung der Sitten, ii. 586. He says nearly as much of Saxo Grammaticus and William of Malmesbury. If my recollection of the former does not deceive me, he is a better writer than our monk of Malmesbury.

[4] One of the most interesting passages in John of Salisbury is that above cited, in which he gives an account of the method of instruction pursued by Bernard of Chartres, whom he calls "exundantissimus modernis temporibus fons literarum in Gallia." John himself was taught by some who trod in the steps of this eminent preceptor. "Ad hujus magistri formam præceptores mei in grammatica, Gulielmus de Conchis, et Richardus cognomento Episcopus, officio nunc archidiaconus Constantiensis, vita et conversatione vir bonus, suos discipulos aliquando informaverunt. Sed postmodum ex quo opinio veritati præjudicium fecit, et homines videri quam esse philosophi maluerunt, professoresque artium se totam philosophiam brevius quam triennio aut quadriennio transfusuros auditoribus pollicebantur, impetu multitudinis imperitæ victi cesserunt. Exinde autem minus temporis et diligentiæ in grammaticæ studio impensum est. Ex quo contigit ut qui omnes artes, tam liberales quam mechanicas profitentur, nec primam noverint, sine qua frustra quis progredietur ad reliquas. Licet autem et aliæ disciplinæ ad literaturam proficiant, hæc tamen privilegio singulari facere dicitur literatum." Metalog., lib. i. c. 24.

vaux, Saxo Grammaticus, William of Malmesbury, Peter of Blois), whose style, though never correct (which, in the absence of all better dictionaries than that of Papias, was impossible), and sometimes affected, sometimes too florid and diffuse, is not wholly destitute of spirit, and even of elegance.[1] The Latin poetry, instead of Leonine rhymes, or attempts at regular hexameters almost equally bad, becomes, in the hands of Gunther, Gualterus de Insulis, Gulielmus Brito, and Joseph Iscanus (to whom a considerable number of names might be added), always tolerable, sometimes truly spirited;[2] and, amidst all that still demands the most liberal indulgence, we cannot but perceive the real progress of classical knowledge and the development of a finer taste in Europe.[3]

Improvement of classical taste in twelfth century

85. The vast increase of religious houses in the twelfth century rendered necessary more attention to the rudiments of literature.[4] Every monk, as well as every secular priest, required a certain portion of Latin. In the ruder and darker ages, many illiterate persons had been ordained: there were even kingdoms (as, for example, England) where this is said to have been almost general. But the canons of the church demanded, of course, such a degree of instruction as the continual use of a dead language made indispensable; and, in this first dawn of learning, there can be, I presume, no doubt that none received the higher orders, or became professed in a monastery for which the order of priesthood was necessary, without some degree of grammatical knowledge. Hence this kind of education in the rudiments of Latin was imparted to a greater number of individuals than at present.

Influence of increased number of clergy.

[1] Hist. Litt. de la France, ix. 146. The Benedictines are scarcely fair towards Abelard (xii. 147), whose style, as far as I have seen, which is not much, seems equal to that of his contemporaries.

[The best writers of Latin in England, prose as well as verse, flourished under Henry II. and his sons. William of Malmesbury, who belongs to the reign of Stephen, though not destitute of some skill as well as variety, displays too much of the Anglo-Saxon Latinity, tumid and redundant. But Giraldus Cambrensis and William of Newbury were truly good writers: very few, indeed, even of the fourth century, can be deemed to excel the latter. In verse, John de Hauteville, author of the Architrenius, Nigellus Wireker, and Alexander Neckam, are deserving of praise. Short extracts will be found in Wright. — 1847.]

[2] Warton has done some justice to the Anglo-Latin poets of this century. The Trojan War and Antiocheis of Joseph Iscanus he calls "a miracle in this age of classical composition." The style, he says, is a mixture of Ovid, Statius, and Claudian. Vol. i. p. 163. The extracts Warton gives seem to me a close imitation of the second. The Philippis of William Brito must be of the thirteenth century, and Warton refers the Ligurinus of Gunther to 1206.

[3] Hist. Litt. de la France, vol. ix.; Eichhorn, All. Gesch. der Cultur, ii. 30, 62; Heeren; Meiners.

[4] Hist. Litt. de la France, ix. 11.

Decline of classical literature in 13th century.

86. The German writers to whom we principally refer have expatiated upon the decline of literature after the middle of the twelfth century, unexpectedly disappointing the bright promise of that age; so that, for almost two hundred years, we find Europe fallen back in learning where we might have expected her progress.[1] This, however, is by no means true, in the most limited sense, as to the latter part of the twelfth century, when that purity of classical taste, which Eichhorn and others seem chiefly to have had in their minds, was displayed in better Latin than had been written before. In a general view, the thirteenth century was an age of activity and ardor, though not in every respect the best directed. The fertility of the modern languages in versification; the creation, we may almost say, of Italian and English in this period; the great concourse of students to the universities; the acute, and sometimes profound, reasonings of the scholastic philosophy, which was now in its most palmy state; the accumulation of knowledge, whether derived from original research or from Arabian sources of information, which we find in the geometers, the physicians, the natural philosophers, of Europe, — are sufficient to repel the charge of having fallen back, or even remained altogether stationary, in comparison with the preceding century. But, in politeness of Latin style, it is admitted that we find an astonishing and permanent decline both in France and England. Such complaints are usual in the most progressive times; and we might not rely on John of Salisbury, when he laments the decline of taste in his own age.[2] But, in fact, it would have been rather singular if a classical purity had kept its ground. A stronger party, and one hostile to polite letters, as well as ignorant of them, — that of the theologians and dialecticians, — carried with it the popular voice in the church and the universities. The time allotted by these to philological literature was curtailed, that the professors of logic and philosophy might detain their pupils longer. Grammar continued to be taught in the University of Paris; but rhetoric, another part of the trivium, was given up: by which it is to be understood, as I conceive, that no classical authors were

[1] Meiners, ii. 605; Heeren, p. 228; Eichhorn, Allg. Gesch. der Litteratur, ii. 63-118. The running title of Eichhorn's section, "Die Wissenschaften verfallen in Barbarey," seems much too generally expressed.

[2] Metalogicus, l. i. c. 24. This passage has been frequently quoted He was very inimical to the dialecticians, as philologers generally are.

read, or, if at all, for the sole purpose of verbal explanation.[1] The thirteenth century, says Heeren, was one of the most unfruitful for the study of ancient literature.[2] He does not seem to except Italy; though there, as we shall soon see, the remark is hardly just. But, in Germany, the tenth century, Leibnitz declares, was a golden age of learning, compared with the thirteenth;[3] and France itself is but a barren waste in this period.[4] The relaxation of manners among the monastic orders, which, generally speaking, is the increasing theme of complaint from the eleventh century, and the swarms of worse vermin, the mendicant friars, who filled Europe with stupid superstition, are assigned by Meiners and Heeren as the leading causes of the return of ignorance.[5]

Relapse into barbarism.

87. The writers of the thirteenth century display an incredible ignorance, not only of pure idiom, but of the common grammatical rules. Those who attempted to write verse have lost all prosody, and relapse into Leonine rhymes and barbarous acrostics. The historians use a hybrid jargon intermixed with modern words. The scholastic philosophers wholly neglected their style, and thought it no wrong to enrich the Latin, as in some degree a living language, with terms that seemed to express their meaning. In the writings of Albertus Magnus, of whom Fleury says that he can see nothing great in him but his volumes, the grossest errors of syntax frequently occur, and vie with his ignorance of history and science. Through the sinister example of this man, according to Meiners, the notion that Latin should be written with regard to ancient models was lost in the universities for three hundred years; an evil, however, slight in comparison with what he inflicted on Europe by the credit he gave to astrology, alchemy, and magic.[6]

[1] Crevier, ii. 376.

[2] P. 237.

[3] Introd. in Script. Brunsvic., § lxiii., apud Heeren, et Meiners, ii. 631. No one has dwelt more fully than this last writer on the decline of literature in the thirteenth century, out of his cordial antipathy to the schoolmen. P. 589 *et post.*

Wood, who has no prejudices against Popery, ascribes the low state of learning in England under Edward III. and Richard II. to the misconduct of the mendicant friars, and to the papal provisions that impoverished the church.

[4] [Abelard, Peter of Blois, and others, might pass for models in comparison with Albertus, Aquinas, and the rest of the writers of the thirteeeth century. "La décadence est partout sensible; elle est progressive dans les cours des règnes de St. Louis, de Philippe III., et de Philippe IV.; et quoique le Français restât dans l'enfance, la Latinité déjà si vieille avant l'année 1200 vieillissait et dépérissait encore." Hist. Litt. de la France, xvi. 145.—1842.]

[5] Meiners, ii. 615; Heeren, 235.

[6] Meiners, ii. 692; Fleury, 5me discours in Hist. Ecclés., xvii. 44; Buhle, i. 702. [A far better character of Albertus Magnus is given by Jourdain: "Albert, considéré comme théologien ou philosophe, est sans doute l'un des hommes les plus extraordi-

Duns Scotus and his disciples, in the next century, carried this much farther, and introduced a most barbarous and unintelligible terminology, by which the school metaphysics were rendered ridiculous in the revival of literature.[1] Even the jurists, who more required an accurate knowledge of the language, were hardly less barbarous. Roger Bacon, who is not a good writer, stands at the head in this century.[2] Fortunately, as has been said, the transcribing ancient authors had become a mechanical habit in some monasteries; but it was done in an ignorant and slovenly manner. The manuscripts of these latter ages, before the invention of printing, are by far the most numerous; but they are also the most incorrect, and generally of little value in the eyes of critics.[3]

No improvement in 14th century.

88. The fourteenth century was not in the slightest degree superior to the preceding age. France, England, and Germany were wholly destitute of good Latin scholars in this period. The age of Petrarch and Boccaccio, the age before the close of which classical learning truly revived in Italy, gave no sign whatever of animation throughout the rest of Europe: the genius it produced (and in this it was not wholly deficient) displayed itself in other walks of literature.[4] We may justly praise Richard of Bury for his zeal in collecting books, and still more for his munificence in giving his library to the University of Oxford, with special injunctions that they should be lent to scholars; but his erudition appears crude and uncritical, his style indifferent, and his thoughts superficial.[5] Yet I am not aware that he had any equal in England during this century.

Richard of Bury

Library formed by Charles V. at Paris.

89. The patronage of letters, or collection of books, are not reckoned among the glories of Edward III.; though, if any respect had been attached to learning in his age and country, they might well have suited his mag-

naires de son siècle; je pourrais même dire l'un des génies les plus étonnants des âges passés." P. 302. His History of Animals, "est un monument précieux, qui, présentant l'état des opinions et des connaissances du moyen âge, remplit une longue lacune, et lie l'ancienne histoire de la science à celle des temps modernes." P. 325. His original source in this work was Aristotle's History of Animals, in Michael Scot's translation from the Arabic. The knowledge of Greek possessed by Albertus seems to have been rather feeble. — 1853.]

[1] Meiners, ii. 721.

[2] Heeren, p. 245.

[3] Id., p. 304.

[4] Heeren, p. 300; Andrès, iii. 10.

[5] The Philobiblon of Richard Aungerville, often called Richard of Bury, Chancellor of Edward III., is worthy of being read, as containing some curious illustrations of the state of literature. He quotes a wretched poem, de Vetulâ, as Ovid's; and shows little learning, though he had a great esteem for it. See a note of Warton, History of English Poetry, i. 146, on Aungerville.

nificent disposition. His adversaries, John, and especially Charles V. of France, have more claims upon the remembrance of a literary historian. Several Latin authors were translated into French by their directions;[1] and Charles, who himself was not ignorant of Latin, began to form the Royal Library of the Louvre. We may judge from this of the condition of literature in his time. The number of volumes was about nine hundred. Many of these, especially the missals and psalters, were richly bound and illuminated. Books of devotion formed the larger portion of the library. The profane authors, except some relating to French history, were in general of little value in our sight. Very few classical works are in the list, and no poets except Ovid and Lucan.[2] This library came, during the subsequent English wars, into the possession of the Duke of Bedford; and Charles VII. laid the foundations of that which still exists.[3]

Some improvement in Italy during 13th century.

90. This retrograde condition, however, of classical literature was only perceptible in Cisalpine Europe. By one of those shiftings of literary illumination to which we have alluded, Italy, far lower in classical taste than France in the twelfth century, deserved a higher place in the next. Tiraboschi says that the progress in polite letters was slow; but still some was made: more good books were transcribed; there were more readers; and, of these, some took on them to imitate what they read; so that gradually the darkness which overspread the land began to be dispersed. Thus we find that those who wrote at the end of the thirteenth century were less rude in style than their predecessors at its commencement.[4] A more elaborate account of the state of learning in the thirteenth century will be found in the Life of Ambrogio Traversari, by Mehus; and several names are there mentioned, among whom that of Brunetto Latini is the most celebrated. Latini translated some of the rhetorical treatises of Cicero.[5] And we may per-

[1] Crevier, ii. 424. Warton has amassed a great deal of information, not always very accurate, upon the subject of early French translations. These form a considerable portion of the literature of that country in the fourteenth and fifteenth centuries. History of English Poetry, ii. 414–430. See also De Sade, Vie de Pétrarque, iii. 548; and Crevier, Hist. de l'Univ. de Paris, ii. 424.

[2] Warton adds Cicero to the classical list; and I am sorry to say, that, in my History of the Middle Ages, I have been led wrong by him. Bouvin, his only authority, expressly says, "Pas un seul manuscrit de Cicéron." Mém. de l'Acad. des Inscript., ii. 693.

[3] Id., 701.

[4] Tiraboschi, iv. 420. The Latin versifiers of the thirteenth century were numerous, but generally very indifferent Id., 378.

[5] Mehus, p. 157; Tiraboschi, p. 418.

haps consider as a witness to some degree of progressive learning in Italy at this time the Catholicon of John Balbi, a Genoese monk, more frequently styled Januensis. This book is chiefly now heard of because the first edition, printed by Gutenberg in 1460, is a book of uncommon rarity and price. It is, however, deserving of some notice in the annals of literature. It consists of a Latin grammar, followed by a dictionary, both perhaps superior to what we should expect from the general character of the times. They are at least copious: the Catholicon is a volume of great bulk. Balbi quotes abundantly from the Latin classics, and appears not wholly unacquainted with Greek; though I must own that Tiraboschi and Eichhorn have thought otherwise. The Catholicon, as far as I can judge from a slight inspection of it, deserves rather more credit than it has in modern times obtained. In the grammar, besides a familiarity with the terminology of the old grammarians, he will be found to have stated some questions as to the proper use of words, with *dubitari solet, multum quæritur;* which, though they are superficial enough, indicate that a certain attention was beginning to be paid to correctness in writing. From the great size of the Catholicon, its circulation must have been very limited.[1]

Catholicon of Balbi.

91. In the dictionary, however, of John of Genoa, as in those of Papias and the other glossarists, we find little distinction made between the different gradations of Latinity. The Latin tongue was to them, except so far as the ancient grammarians whom they copied might indicate some to be obsolete, a single body of words; and, ecclesiastics as they were, they could not understand that Ambrose and Hilary were to be proscribed in the vocabulary of a language which was chiefly learned for the sake of reading their works. Nor had they the means of pronouncing

Imperfection of early dictionaries.

[1] "Libellum hunc (says Balbi at the conclusion) ad honorem Dei et gloriosæ Virginis Mariæ, et beati Domini Patris nostri et omnium sanctorum electorum, necnon ad utilitatem meam et ecclesiæ sanctæ Dei, ex diversis majorum meorum dictis multo labore et diligenti studio compilavi. Operis quippe ac studii mei est et fuit multos libros legere et ex plurimis diversos carpere flores."

Eichhorn speaks severely, and, I am disposed to think, unjustly, of the Catholicon, as without order and plan, or any knowledge of Greek, as the author himself confesses (Gesch. der Litteratur, ii. 238). The order and plan are alphabetical, as usual in a dictionary; and, though Balbi does not lay claim to much Greek, I do not think he professes entire ignorance of it. "Hoc difficile est scire et minimè mihi non bene scienti linguam Græcam," — apud Gradenigo, Litteratura Greco-Italiana, p. 104. I have observed that Balbi calls himself *philocalus;* which indeed is no evidence of much Greek erudition.

what it has cost the labor of succeeding centuries to do, that there is no adequate classical authority for innumerable words and idioms in common use. Their knowledge of syntax also was very limited. The prejudice of the church against profane authors had by no means wholly worn away: much less had they an exclusive possession of the grammar-schools, most of the books taught in which were modern. Papias, Uguccio, and other indifferent lexicographers, were of much authority.[1] The general ignorance in Italy was still very great. In the middle of the fourteenth century, we read of a man, supposed to be learned, who took Plato and Cicero for poëts, and thought Ennius a contemporary of Statius.[2]

Restoration of letters due to Petrarch.

92. The first real restorer of polite letters was Petrarch. His fine taste taught him to relish the beauties of Virgil and Cicero; and his ardent praises of them inspired his compatriots with a desire for classical knowledge. A generous disposition to encourage letters began to show itself among the Italian princes. Robert, King of Naples, in the early part of this century, one of the first patrons of Petrarch, and several of the great families of Lombardy, gave this proof of the humanizing effects of peace and prosperity.[3] It has been thought by some, that, but for the appearance and influence of Petrarch at that period, the manuscripts themselves would have perished, as several had done in no long time before, so forgotten and abandoned to dust and vermin were those precious records in the dungeons of monasteries.[4] He was the first who brought in that almost deification of the great ancient writers, which, though carried in following ages to an absurd extent, was the animating sentiment of solitary study, — that through which its fatigues were patiently endured, and its obstacles surmounted. Petrarch tells us himself, that while his comrades at school were reading Æsop's Fables, or a book of one Prosper, a writer of the fifth century, his time was given to the study of Cicero, which delighted his ear, long before he could understand the sense.[5]

[1] Mehus; Muratori, Dissert. 44

[2] Mehus, p. 211; Tiraboschi, v. 82.

[3] Tiraboschi, v. 20 *et post.* Ten universities were founded in Italy during the fourteenth century, some of which did not last long, — Rome and Fermo in 1303; Perugia in 1307; Treviso about 1320; Pisa in 1339; Pavia not long after; Florence in 1348; Siena in 1357; Lucca in 1369; and Ferrara in 1391.

[4] Heeren, 270.

[5] "Et illa quidem ætate nihil intelligere poteram, sola me verborum dulcedo quædam et sonoritas detinebat ut quicquid aliud vel legerem vel audirem, raucum mihi dissonumque videretur." Epist. Seniles, lib. xv., apud De Sade, i. 36.

It was much at his heart to acquire a good style in Latin; and, relatively to his predecessors of the mediæval period, we may say that he was successful. Passages full of elegance and feeling, in which we are at least not much offended by incorrectness of style, are frequent in his writings. But the fastidious scholars of later times contemned these imperfect endeavors at purity. "He wants," says Erasmus, "full acquaintance with the language; and his whole diction shows the rudeness of the preceding age."[1] An Italian writer, somewhat earlier, speaks still more unfavorably. "His style is harsh, and scarcely bears the character of Latinity. His writings are indeed full of thought, but defective in expression, and display the marks of labor without the polish of elegance."[2]

Character of his style.

I incline to agree with Meiners in rating the style of Petrarch rather more highly.[3] Of Boccace, the writer above quoted gives even a worse character. "Licentious and inaccurate in his diction, he has no idea of selection. All his Latin writings are hasty, crude, and unformed. He labors with thought, and struggles to give it utterance; but his sentiments find no adequate vehicle, and the lustre of his native talents is obscured by the depraved taste of the times." Yet his own mother-tongue owes its earliest model of grace and refinement to his pen.

93. Petrarch was more proud of his Latin poem called Africa, the subject of which is the termination of the second Punic war, than of the sonnets and odes which have made his name immortal, though they were not the chief sources of his immediate renown. It is, indeed, written with elaborate elegance, and perhaps superior to any preceding specimen of Latin versification in the middle ages, unless we should think Joseph Iscanus his equal. But it is more to be praised for taste than correctness; and though in the Basle edition of 1554, which I have used, the printer has been excessively negligent, there can be no doubt that the Latin poetry of Petrarch abounds with faults of metre. His eclogues, many of which are covert satires on the court of

His Latin poetry.

[1] Ciceronianus.

[2] "Paulus Cortesius de hominibus doctis." I take the translations from Roscoe's Lorenzo de' Medici, c. vii.

[3] Vergleichung der Sitten, iii. 126. Meiners has expatiated for fifty pages, p. 94–147, on the merits of Petrarch in the restoration of classical literature: he seems unable to leave the subject. Heeren, though less diffuse, is not less panegyrical. De Sade's three quartos are certainly a little tedious.

Avignon, appear to me more poetical than the Africa, and are sometimes very beautifully expressed. The eclogues of Boccaccio, though by no means indifferent, do not equal those of Petrarch.

94. Mehus, whom Tiraboschi avowedly copies, has diligently collected the names, though little more than the names, of Latin teachers at Florence in the fourteenth century.[1] But among the earlier of these there was no good method of instruction, no elegance of language. The first who revealed the mysteries of a pure and graceful style was John Malpaghino, commonly called John of Ravenna, one whom, in his youth, Petrarch had loved as a son; and who, not very long before the end of the century, taught Latin at Padua and Florence.[2] The best scholars of the ensuing age were his disciples; and among them was Gasparin of Barziza, or, as generally called, of Bergamo, justly characterized by Eichhorn as the father of a pure and elegant Latinity.[3] The distinction between the genuine Latin language and that of the Lower Empire was from this generally recognized; and the writers who had been regarded as standards were thrown away with contempt. This is the proper era of the revival of letters, and nearly coincides with the beginning of the fifteenth century.

John of Ravenna.

Gasparin of Barziza.

95. A few subjects, affording less extensive observation, we have postponed to the next chapter, which will contain the literature of Europe in the first part of the fifteenth century. Notwithstanding our wish to preserve in general a strict regard to chronology, it has been impossible to avoid some interruptions of it without introducing a multiplicity of transitions incompatible with any comprehensive views; and which, even as it must inevitably exist in a work of this nature, is likely to diminish the pleasure, and perhaps the advantage, that the reader might derive from it.

[1] Vita Traversari, p. 348.

[2] A life of John Malpaghino of Ravenna is the first in Meiners's Lebensbeschreibungen berühmter Männer, 3 vols., Zurich, 1795; but it is wholly taken from Petrarch's Letters, and from Mehus's Life of Traversari, p. 348. See also Tiraboschi v. 554.

[3] Geschichte der Litteratur, ii. 241.

CHAPTER II.

ON THE LITERATURE OF EUROPE FROM 1400 TO 1440.

Cultivation of Latin in Italy — Revival of Greek Literature — Vestiges of it during the Middle Ages — It is taught by Chrysoloras — his Disciples — and by learned Greeks — State of Classical Learning in other Parts of Europe — Physical Sciences — Mathematics — Medicine and Anatomy — Poetry in Spain, France, and England — Formation of new Laws of Taste in Middle Ages — Their Principles — Romances — Religious Opinions.

1. GINGUÉNÉ has well observed, that the fourteenth century left Italy in the possession of the writings of three great masters of a language formed and polished by them, and of a strong relish for classical learning. But this soon became the absorbing passion, — fortunately, no doubt, in the result, as the same author has elsewhere said; since all the exertions of an age were required to explore the rich mine of antiquity, and fix the standard of taste and purity for succeeding generations. The ardor for classical studies grew stronger every day. To write Latin correctly, to understand the allusions of the best authors, to learn the rudiments at least of Greek, were the objects of every cultivated mind.

Zeal for classical literature in Italy.

2. The first half of the fifteenth century has been sometimes called the age of Poggio Bracciolini, which it expresses not very inaccurately as to his literary life; since he was born in 1381, and died in 1459: but it seems to involve too high a compliment. The chief merit of Poggio was his diligence, aided by good fortune, in recovering lost works of Roman literature that lay mouldering in the repositories of convents. Hence we owe to this one man eight orations of Cicero, a complete Quintilian, Columella, part of Lucretius, three books of Valerius Flaccus, Silius Italicus, Ammianus Marcellinus, Tertullian, and several less important writers: twelve comedies of Plautus were also recovered in Germany through his directions.[1] Poggio, besides this, was

Poggio Bracciolini.

[1] Shepherd's Life of Poggio; Tiraboschi; Corniani; Roscoe's Lorenzo, ch. 1. Fabricius, in his Bibliotheca Latina mediæ et infimæ ætatis, gives a list not quite the

undoubtedly a man of considerable learning for his time, and still greater sense and spirit as a writer, though he never reached a very correct or elegant style.[1] And this applies to all those who wrote before the year 1440, with the single exception of Gasparin, — to Coluccio Salutato, Guarino of Verona, and even Leonard Aretin.[2] Nor is this any disparagement to their abilities and industry. They had neither grammars nor dictionaries in which the purest Latinity was distinguishable from the worst; they had to unlearn a barbarous jargon, made up with scraps of the Vulgate and of ecclesiastical writers, which pervades the Latin of the middle ages; they had great difficulty in resorting to purer models, from the scarcity and high price of

Latin style of that age indifferent.

same; but Poggio's own authority must be the best. The work first above quoted is, for the literary history of Italy in the earlier half of the fifteenth century, what Roscoe's Lorenzo is for the latter. Ginguéné has not added much to what these English authors and Tiraboschi had furnished.

[1] Mr. Shepherd has judged Poggio a little favorably, as became a biographer, but with sense and discrimination. His Italian translator, Tonelli (Firenze, 1825), goes much beyond the mark in extolling Poggio above all his contemporaries, and praising his "vastissima erudizione" in the strain of hyperbole too familiar to Italians. This vast learning, even for that time, Poggio did not possess: we have no reason to believe him equal to Guarino, Filelfo, or Traversari, much less to Valla. Erasmus, however, was led by his partiality to Valla into some injustice towards Poggio, whom he calls "rabula adeo indoctus, ut etiamsi vacaret obscœnitate, tamen indignus esset qui legeretur, adeo autem obscœnus, ut etiamsi doctissimus esset, tamen esset a viris bonis rejiciendus." Epist. ciii. This is said too hastily; but in his Ciceronianus, where we have his deliberate judgment, he appreciates Poggio more exactly. After one of the interlocutors has called him "vividæ cujusdam eloquentiæ virum," the other replies: "Naturæ satis erat, artis et eruditionis non multum; interim impuro sermonis fluxu, si Laurentio Vallæ credimus." Bebel, a German of some learning, rather older than Erasmus, in a letter quoted by Blount (Censura Auctorum in Poggio), praises Poggio very highly for his style, and prefers him to Valla. Paulus Cortesius seems not much to differ from Erasmus about Poggio, though he is more severe on Valla.

It should be added, that Tonelli's notes on the life of Poggio are useful: among other things, he points out that Poggio did not learn Greek of Emanuel Chrysoloras, as all writers on this part of literary history had hitherto supposed, but about 1423, when he was turned of forty.

[2] Coluccio Salutato belongs to the fourteenth century, and was deemed one of its greatest ornaments in learning. "Ma a dir vero," says Tiraboschi, who admits his extensive erudition, relatively to his age, "benchè lo stil di Coluccio abbia non rare volte energia e forza maggiore che quello della maggior parti degli altri scrittori di questi tempi, è certo però, che tanto è diverso da quello di Cicerone nella prosa, e ne' versi da quel di Virgilio, quanto appunto è diversa una scimia da un uomo." v. 537.

Cortesius, in the dialogue quoted above, says of Leonard Aretin, "Hic primus inconditam scribendi consuetudinem ad numerosum quendam sonum inflexit, et attulit hominibus nostris aliquid certe splendidius. . . . . Et ego video hunc nondum satis esse limatum, nec delicatiori fastidio tolerabilem. Atqui dialogi Joannis Ravennatis vix semel leguntur, et Coluccii Epistolæ, quæ tum in honore erant, non apparent; sed Boccaccii Genealogiam legimus, utilem illam quidem, sed non tamen cum Petrarchæ ingenio conferendam. At non videtis quantum his omnibus desit?" p. 12. Of Guarino he says afterwards, "Genus tamen dicendi inconcinnum admodum est et salebrosum; utitur plerumque imprudens verbis poeticis, quod est maxime vitiosum; sed magis est in eo succus, quam color laudandus. Memoria teneo, quendam familiarem meum solitum dicere, melius Guarinum famæ suæ consuluisse, si nihil unquam scripsisset." P. 14.

manuscripts, as well as from their general incorrectness, which it required much attention to set right. Gasparin of Barziza took the right course, by incessantly turning over the pages of Cicero; and thus by long habit gained an instinctive sense of propriety in the use of language, which no secondary means at that time could have given him.

3. This writer, often called Gasparin of Bergamo (his own birthplace being in the neighborhood of that city), was born about 1370, and began to teach before the close of the century. He was transferred to Padua by the Senate of Venice in 1407; and in 1410 accepted the invitation of Filippo Maria Visconti to Milan, where he remained till his death in 1431. Gasparin had here the good fortune to find Cicero de Oratore, and to restore the text of Quintilian by the help of the manuscript brought from St. Gall by Poggio, and another found in Italy by Leonard Aretin. His fame as a writer was acquired at Padua, and founded on his diligent study of Cicero.

Gasparin of Barziza.

4. It is impossible to read a page of Gasparin without perceiving that he is quite of another order of scholars from his predecessors. He is truly Ciceronian in his turn of phrases, and structure of sentences, which never end awkwardly, or with a wrong arrangement of words, as is habitual with his contemporaries. Inexact expressions may of course be found; but they do not seem gross or numerous. Among his works are several orations which probably were actually delivered: they are the earliest models of that classical declamation which became so usual afterwards; and are elegant, if not very forcible. His Epistolæ ad Exercitationem accommodatæ was the first book printed at Paris. It contains a series of exercises for his pupils, probably for the sake of double translation, and merely designed to exemplify Latin idioms.[1]

Merits of his style.

5. If Gasparin was the best writer of this generation, the most accomplished instructor was Victorin of Feltre, to whom the Marquis of Mantua intrusted the education of his own children. Many of the Italian nobility and

Victorin of Feltre.

[1] Morhof, who says, "Primus in Italia aliquid balbutire cœpit Gasparinus," had probably never seen his writings, which are a great deal better in point of language than his own. Cortesius, however, blames Gasparin for too elaborate a style: "Nimia cura attenuabat orationem." He once uses a Greek word in his letters. What he knew of the language does not otherwise appear; but he might have heard Guarino at Venice. He had not seen Pliny's Natural History; nor did he possess a Livy, but was in treaty for one. Epist, p. 200, A.D. 1415.

some distinguished scholars were brought up under the care of Victorin in that city; and, in a very corrupt age, he was still more zealous for their moral than their literary improvement. A pleasing account of his method of discipline will be found in Tiraboschi, or more fully in Corniani, from a life written by one of Victorin's pupils named Prendilacqua.[1] "It could hardly be believed," says Tiraboschi, "that, in an age of such rude manners, a model of such perfect education could be found: if all to whom the care of youth is intrusted would make it theirs, what ample and rich fruits they would derive from their labors!" The learning of Victorin was extensive: he possessed a moderate library; and, rigidly demanding a minute exactness from his pupils in their interpretation of ancient authors as well as in their own compositions, laid the foundations of a propriety in style which the next age was to display. Traversari visited the school of Victorin, for whom he entertained a great regard, in 1433: it had then been for some years established.[2] No writings of Victorin have been preserved.

Leonard Aretin.

6. Among the writers of these forty years, after Gasparin of Bergamo, we may probably assign the highest place in politeness of style to Leonardo Bruni, more commonly called Aretino, from his birthplace, Arezzo. "He was the first," says Paulus Cortesius, "who replaced the rude structure of periods by some degree of rhythm, and introduced our countrymen to something more brilliant than they had known before; though even he is not quite as polished as a fastidious delicacy would require." Aretin's History of the Goths, which, though he is silent on the obligation, is chiefly translated from Procopius, passes for his best work. In the constellation of scholars who enjoyed the sunshine of favor in the palace of Cosmo de' Medici, Leonard Aretin was one of the oldest and most prominent. He died at an advanced age in 1444, and is one of the six illustrious dead who repose in the Church of Santa Croce.[3]

1 Tiraboschi, vii. 306; Corniani, ii. 53; Heeren, p. 235. He is also mentioned with much praise for his mode of education, by his friend Ambrogio Traversari, a passage from whose Hodœporicon will be found in Heeren, p. 237. Victorin died in 1447, and was buried at the public expense; his liberality in giving gratuitous instruction to the poor having left him so.

2 Mehus, p. 421.

3 Madame de Staël unfortunately confounded this respectable scholar, in her Corinne, with Pietro Aretino. I remember well that Ugo Foscolo could never contain his wrath against her for this mistake.

Revival of Greek language in Italy.

7. We come now to a very important event in literary history, — the resuscitation of the study of the Greek language in Italy. During the whole course of the middle ages, we find scattered instances of scholars in the west of Europe, who had acquired some knowledge of Greek; to what extent, it is often a difficult question to determine. In the earlier and darker period, we begin with a remarkable circumstance, already mentioned, of our own ecclesiastical history. The infant Anglo-Saxon churches, desirous to give a national form to their hierarchy, solicited the Pope Vitalian to place a primate at their head. He made choice of Theodore, who not only brought to England a store of Greek manuscripts, but, through the means of his followers, imparted a knowledge of it to some of our countrymen. Bede, half a century afterwards, tells us, of course very hyperbolically, that there were still surviving disciples of Theodore and Adrian who understood the Greek and Latin languages as well as their own.[1] From these he derived, no doubt, his own knowledge, which may not have been extensive; but we cannot expect more, in such very unfavorable circumstances, than a superficial progress in so difficult a study. It is probable that the lessons of Theodore's disciples were not forgotten in the British and Irish monasteries. Alcuin has had credit, with no small likelihood, if not on positive authority, for an acquaintance with Greek;[2] and as

Early Greek scholars of Europe

1 Hist. Eccles., l. v. c. 2. "Usque hodie supersunt ex eorum discipulis, qui Latinam Græcamque linguam æque ac propriam in qua nati sunt, norunt." Bede's own knowledge of Greek is attested by his biographer Cuthbert; "præter Latinam etiam Græcam comparaverat."

[Bede's acquaintance with Greek is attested still better by many proofs which his own works contain. Aldhelm was also a Greek scholar. See Wright's Biograph. Litteraria, vol. i. pp. 40, 51, 275. But when Mr. W. adds, "We might bring many passages together which seem *almost* to prove that Homer continued to be read in the schools till the end of the thirteenth century," I must withhold my assent till the passages have been both produced and well sifted. — 1847.]

A manuscript in the British Museum (Cotton, Galba, i. 18) is of some importance in relation to this, if it be truly referred to the eighth century. It contains the Lord's Prayer in Greek, written in Anglo-Saxon characters, and appears to have belonged to some one of the name of Athelstan. Mr. Turner (Hist. of Anglo-Saxons, vol. iii. p. 396) has taken notice of this manuscript, but without mentioning its antiquity. The manner in which the words are divided shows a perfect ignorance of Greek in the writer; but the Saxon is curious in another respect, as it proves the pronunciation of Greek in the eighth century to have been modern or Romaic, and not what we hold to be ancient.

2 "C'était un homme habile dans le Grec comme dans le Latin.' Hist. Litt. de la Fr., iv. 8.

[M. Jourdain observes that Thomas Aquinas understood Greek, and that he criticises the translations of Aristotle. Recherches Critiques, p. 393. But we ought not to acquiesce in this general position without examining the proofs. I doubt much whether Thomas Aquinas could read Aristotle in the original. — 1853.]

he, and perhaps others from these islands, were active in aiding the efforts of Charlemagne for the restoration of letters, the slight tincture of Greek which we find in the schools founded by that emperor may have been derived from their instruction. It is, however, an equally probable hypothesis, that it was communicated by Greek teachers, whom it was easy to procure. Charlemagne himself, according to Eginhard, could read, though he could not speak, the Greek language. Thegan reports the very same, in nearly the same words, of Louis the Debonair.[1] The former certainly intended that it should be taught in some of his schools;[2] and the Benedictines of St. Maur, in their long and laborious Histoire Littéraire de la France, have enumerated as many as seventeen persons within France, or at least the dominions of the Carlovingian house, to whom they ascribe, on the authority of contemporaries, a portion of this learning.[3] These were all educated in the schools of Charlemagne, except the most eminent in the list, John Scotus Erigena. It is not necessary by any means to suppose that he had acquired by travel the Greek tongue, which he possessed sufficiently to translate, though very indifferently, the works attributed in that age to Dionysius the Areopagite.[4] Most writers of the ninth century, according to the Benedictines, make use of some Greek words. It appears by a letter of the famous Hincmar, Archbishop of Rheims, who censures his nephew Hincmar of Laon for doing this affectedly, that glossaries, from which they picked those exotic flowers, were already in use. Such a glossary in Greek and Latin, compiled under Charles the Bald for the use of the Church of Laon, was, at the date of the publication of the Histoire Littéraire de la France, near the middle

Under Charlemagne and his successors.

[1] The passages will be found in Eichhorn, Allg. Gesch., ii. 265 and 290. That concerning Charlemagne is quoted in many other books. Eginhard says, in the same place, that Charles prayed in Latin as readily as in his own language; and Thegan, that Louis could speak Latin perfectly.

[2] Osnabrug has generally been named as the place where Charlemagne peculiarly designed that Greek should be cultivated. It seems, however, on considering the passage in the Capitularies usually quoted (Baluze, ii. 419), to have been only one out of many. Eichhorn thinks that the existence of a Greek school at Osnabrug is doubtful, but that there is more evidence in favor of Saltzburg and Ratisbon. Allg. Gesch. der Cultur, ii. 383. The words of the Capitulary are, "Græcas et Latinas Scholas in perpetuum manere ordinavimus."

[3] Hist. Litt. de la France, vol. v. Launoy had commenced this enumeration in his excellent treatise on the schools of Charlemagne; but he has not carried it quite so far. See, too, Eichhorn, Allg. Gesch., ii. 420; and Gesch. der Litt., i. 824. Meiners thinks that Greek was better known in the ninth century, through Charlemagne's exertions, than for five hundred years afterwards; ii. 367.

[4] Eichhorn, ii. 227; Brucker; Guizot.

of the last century, in the Library of St. Germain des Prés.[1] We may thus perceive the means of giving the air of more learning than was actually possessed, and are not to infer from these sprinklings of Greek in mediæval writings, whether in their proper characters or Latinized, which is much more frequent, that the poets and profane or even ecclesiastical writers were accessible in a French or English monastery. Neither of the Hincmars seems to have understood the Greek language; and Tiraboschi admits that he cannot assert any Italian writer of the ninth century to be acquainted with it.[2]

In the tenth and eleventh centuries.

8. The tenth century furnishes not quite so many proofs of Greek scholarship. It was, however, studied by some brethren in the Abbey of St. Gall, a celebrated seat of learning for those times, and the library of which, it is said, still bears witness, in its copious collection of manuscripts, to the early intercourse between the scholars of Ireland and those of the Continent. Baldric, Bishop of Utrecht,[3] Bruno of Cologne, and Gerbert, besides a few more whom the historians of St. Maur record, possessed a tolerable acquaintance with the Greek language. They mention a fact that throws light on the means by which it might occasionally be learned. Some natives of that country, doubtless expatriated Catholics, took refuge in the diocese of Toul, under the protection of the bishop, not long before 1000. They formed separate societies, performing divine service in their own language and with their own rites.[4] It is probable, the Benedictines observe, that Humbert, afterwards a cardinal, acquired from them that knowledge of the language by which he distinguished himself in controversy with their countrymen.[5] This great schism of the church, which the Latins deeply felt, might induce some to study a language from which alone they could derive authorities in disputation with these antagonists; but it had also the more unequivocal effect of drawing to the West some of those Greeks who maintained their communion with the Church of Rome. The emigration of these into the diocese of Toul is not a single fact of the kind, and it is probably recorded from the remarkable circumstance of their living

1 Hist. Litt. de la France, vol. iv.; Ducange, præf. in Glossar., p. 40.

2 iii. 206.

3 Baldric lived under Henry the Fowler. His biographer says, "Nullum fuit studiorum liberalium genus in omni Græca et Latina eloquentia quod ingenii sui vivacitatem aufugeret." Launoy, p. 117; Hist Litt., vi. 50.

4 Vol. vi. p. 57.

5 Vol. vii. p. 528.

in community. We find from a passage in Heric, a prelate in the reign of Charles the Bald, that this had already begun,—at the commencement, in fact, of the great schism.[1] Greek bishops and Greek monks are mentioned as settlers in France during the early part of the eleventh century. This was especially in Normandy, under the protection of Richard II., who died in 1028. Even monks from Mount Sinai came to Rouen to share in his liberality.[2] The Benedictines ascribe the preservation of some taste for the Greek and Oriental tongues to these strangers. The list, however, of the learned in them is very short, considering the erudition of these fathers, and their disposition to make the most of all they met with. Greek books are mentioned in the few libraries of which we read in the eleventh century.[3]

In the twelfth.

9. The number of Greek scholars seems not much more considerable in the twelfth century, notwithstanding the general improvement of that age. The Benedictines reckon about ten names, among which we do not find that of Bernard.[4] They are inclined also to deny the pretensions of Abelard;[5] but, as that great man finds a very hostile tribunal in these fathers, we may pause about this, especially as they acknowledge Eloise to have understood both the Greek and Hebrew languages. She established a Greek mass for Whitsunday in the Paraclete convent, which was sung as late as the fifteenth century; and a Greek missal in Latin characters was still preserved there.[6] Heeren speaks more favorably of Abelard's learning, who translated passages from Plato.[7] The pretensions of John of Salisbury are

[1] Ducange, præfat. in Glossar., p. 41.

[2] Hist. Litt. de la France, vii. 69, 124, *et alibi.* A Greek manuscript in the Royal Library at Paris, containing the Liturgy according to the Greek ritual, was written, in 1022, by a monk named *Helie* (they do not give the Latin name), who seems to have lived in Normandy. If this stands for Elias, he was probably a Greek by birth.

[3] Hist. Litt. de la France, vii. p. 48.

[4] Id., pp. 94, 151. Macarius, Abbot of St. Fleury, is said to have compiled a Greek lexicon, which has been several times printed under the name of Beatus Benedictus. [It is one of the glossaries which follow the Thesaurus of Henry Stephens. Journal des Savans, May, 1829. —1842.]

[5] Hist. Litt. de la France, xii. 147. [Mr. Cousin, who has paid more attention than any one to the writings of Abelard, thinks that he was ignorant of Greek beyond a few words: probably Eloise had not much surpassed her preceptor. Fragmens Philosophiques, vol. iv. p. 687; or Introduction aux Œuvres d'Abelard, in Documens Inédits, p. 44. Abelard only says of her, that she was "Græcæ non expers literaturæ:" afterwards, indeed, he uses the words, "peritiam adepta."—1847.]

[6] Id., xii. 642.

[7] P. 204. His Greek was, no doubt, rather scanty, and not sufficient to give him an insight into ancient philosophy. In fact, if his learning had been greater, he could only read such manuscripts as fell into his hands; and there were very few then in France *Vide supra.*

slighter: he seems proud of his Greek, but betrays gross ignorance in etymology.[1]

10. The thirteenth century was a more inauspicious period for learning; yet here we can boast not only of John Basing, Archdeacon of St. Alban's, who returned from Athens about 1240, laden, if we are bound to believe this literally, with Greek books, but of Roger Bacon, and Robert Grostête, Bishop of Lincoln. It is admitted that Bacon had some acquaintance with Greek; and it appears by a passage in Matthew Paris, that a Greek priest, who had obtained a benefice at St. Alban's, gave such assistance to Grostête, as enabled him to translate the Testament of the Twelve Patriarchs into Latin.[2] This is a confirmation of what has been suggested above as the probable means by which a knowledge of that language, in the total deficiency of scholastic education, was occasionally imparted to persons of unusual zeal for learning; and it leads us to another reflection, that by a knowledge of Greek, when we find it asserted of a mediæval theologian like Grostête, we are not to understand an acquaintance with the great classical authors who were latent in Eastern monasteries, but the power of reading some petty treatise of the fathers, or, as in this instance, an apocryphal legend, or at best, perhaps, some of the later commentators on Aristotle. Grostête was a man of considerable merit, but has had his share of applause.

In the thirteenth.

11. The titles of mediæval works are not unfrequently taken from the Greek language, as the Polycraticus and Metalogicus of John of Salisbury, or the Philobiblon of Richard Aungerville of Bury. In this little volume, written about 1343, I have counted five instances of single Greek words; and, what is more important, Aungerville declares that he had caused Greek and Hebrew grammars to be drawn up for students.[3] But we

Little appearance of it in the 14th century.

[1] Ibid. John derives "analytica" from ἀνὰ and λέξις.

[2] Matt. Par., p. 520; see also Turner's History of England, iv. 180. It is said in some books, that Grostête made a translation of Suidas; but this is to be understood merely of a legendary story found in that writer's lexicon. Pegge's Life of Grostête, p. 291. The entire work he certainly could not have translated; nor is it at all credible that he had a copy of it. With respect to the doubt I have hinted in the text as to the great number of manuscripts said to be brought to England by John Basing, it is founded on their subsequent non-appearance. We find very few, if any, Greek manuscripts in England at the end of the fifteenth century.

Michael Scott, the "wizard of dreaded fame," pretended to translate Aristotle; but is charged with having appropriated the labors of one Andrew, a Jew, as his own. Meiners, ii. 664.

[3] C. x

have no other record of such grammars. It would be natural to infer from this passage, that some persons, either in France or England, were occupied in the study of the Greek language; and yet we find nothing to corroborate this presumption. All ancient learning was neglected in the fourteenth century; nor do I know that one man on this side of the Alps, except Aungerville himself, is reputed to have been versed in Greek during that period. I cannot speak positively as to Berchœur, the most learned man in France. The Council of Vienne, indeed, in 1311, had ordered the establishment of professors in the Greek, Hebrew, Chaldaic, and Arabic languages, at Avignon, and in the Universities of Paris, Oxford, Bologna, and Salamanca; but this decree remained a dead letter.

Some traces of Greek in Italy.

12. If we now turn to Italy, we shall find, as is not wonderful, rather more frequent instances of acquaintance with a living language in common use with a great neighboring people. Gradenigo, in an essay on this subject,[1] has endeavored to refute what he supposes to be the universal opinion, that the Greek tongue was first taught in Italy by Chrysoloras and Guarino, at the end of the fourteenth century; contending that, from the eleventh inclusive, there are numerous instances of persons conversant with it; besides the evidence afforded by inscriptions in Greek characters found in some churches, by the use of Greek psalters and other liturgical offices, by the employment of Greek painters in churches, and by the frequent intercourse between the two countries. The latter presumptions have, in fact, considerable weight; and those who should contend for an absolute ignorance of the Greek language, oral as well as written, in Italy, would go too far. The particular instances brought forward by Gradenigo are about thirty. Of these, the first is Papias, who has quoted five lines of Hesiod.[2] Lanfranc had also a considerable acquaintance with the language.[3] Peter Lombard, in his Liber Sententiarum, the systematic basis of scholastic theology, introduces many Greek words, and explains them rightly.[4] But this list is not very long; and when we find the surname Bifarius given to one Ambrose of Bergamo in the eleventh century, on account of his capacity of speaking both

[1] Ragionamento Istorico-critico sopra la Litteratura Greco-Italiana. Brescia, 1759.

[2] P. 37. These are very corruptly given, through the fault of a transcriber; for Papias has translated them into tolerable Latin verse.

[3] Hist. Litt. de la France, vii. 144.

[4] Meiners, iii. 11.

languages, it may be conceived that the accomplishment was somewhat rare. Mehus, in his very learned Life of Traversari, has mentioned two or three names, among whom is the Emperor Frederic II. (not indeed strictly an Italian), that do not appear in Gradenigo;[1] but Tiraboschi conceives, on the other hand, that the latter has inserted some on insufficient grounds. Christine of Pisa is mentioned, I think, by neither: she was the daughter of an Italian astronomer, but lived at the court of Charles V. of France, and was the most accomplished literary lady of that age.[2]

Corruption of Greek language itself.

13. The intercourse between Greece and the west of Europe, occasioned by commerce and by the crusades, had little or no influence upon literature; for, besides the general indifference to it in those classes of society which were thus brought into some degree of contact with the Eastern Empire, we must remember, that although Greek, even to the capture of Constantinople by Mahomet II., was a living language in that city, spoken by the superior ranks of both sexes with tolerable purity, it had degenerated among the common people, and almost universally among the inhabitants of the provinces and islands, into that corrupt form, or rather new language, which we call Romaic.[3] The progress of this innovation went on by steps very similar to those by which the Latin was transformed in the West, though it was not so rapid or complete. A manuscript of the twelfth century, quoted by Du Cange from the Royal Library at Paris, appears to be the oldest written specimen of the modern Greek that has been produced; but the oral change had been gradually going forward for several preceding centuries.[4]

14. The Byzantine literature was chiefly valuable by illus-

[1] Pp. 155, 217, &c. Add to these authorities, Muratori, dissert. 44; Brucker, iii. 644, 647; Tiraboschi, v. 393.

[2] Tiraboschi, v. 388, vouches for Christine's knowledge of Greek. She was a good poetess in French, and altogether a very remarkable person.

[3] Filelfo says, in one of his epistles, dated 1441, that the language spoken in Peloponnesus "adeo est depravata, ut nihil omnino sapiat priscæ illius et eloquentissimæ Greciæ." At Constantinople the case was better: "viri eruditi sunt nonnulli, et culti mores, et sermo etiam nitidus." In a letter of Coluccio Salutato, near the end of the fourteenth century, he says that Plutarch had been translated de Græco in Græcum vulgare. Mehus, p. 294. This seems to have been done at Rhodes. I quote this to remove any difficulty that others may feel; for I believe the Romaic Greek is much older. The progress of corruption in Greek is sketched in the Quarterly Review, vol. xxii., probably by the pen of the Bishop of London. Its symptoms were very similar to those of Latin in the West,—abbreviation of words, and indifference to right inflexions. See also Col. Leake's Researches in the Morea. Eustathius has many Romaic words; yet no one in the twelfth century had more learning.

[4] Du Cange, præfatio in Glossarium mediæ et infimæ Græcitatis.

trating, or preserving in fragments, the historians, philosophers, and in some measure the poets, of antiquity. Constantinople and her empire produced abundantly men of erudition, but few of genius or of taste. But this erudition was now rapidly on the decline. No one was left in Greece, according to Petrarch, after the death of Leontius Pilatus, who understood Homer; words not, perhaps, to be literally taken, but expressive of what he conceived to be their general indifference to the poet: and it seems very probable that some ancient authors, whom we should most desire to recover, especially the lyric poets of the Doric and Æolic dialects, have perished, because they had become unintelligible to the transcribers of the Lower Empire; though this has also been ascribed to the scrupulousness of the clergy. An absorbing fondness for theological subtilties, far more trifling among the Greeks than in the schools of the West, conspired to produce a neglect of studies so remote as heathen poetry. Aurispa tells Ambrogio Traversari that he found they cared little about profane literature. Nor had the Greek learning ever recovered the blow that the capture of Constantinople by the crusaders in 1204, and the establishment for sixty years of a Latin and illiterate dynasty, inflicted upon it.[1] We trace many classical authors to that period, of whom we know nothing later; and the compilations of ancient history by industrious Byzantines came to an end. Meantime the language, where best preserved, had long lost the delicacy and precision of its syntax; the true meaning of the tenses, moods, and voices of the verb was overlooked, or guessed at; a kind of Latinism, or something at least not ancient in structure and rhythm, shows itself in their poetry; and this imperfect knowledge of their once beautiful language is unfortunately too manifest in the grammars of the Greek exiles of the fifteenth century, which have so long been the groundwork of classical education in Europe.

Character of Byzantine literature.

15. We now come to the proper period of the restoration of Greek learning. In the year 1339, Barlaam, a Calabrian by birth, but long resident in Greece, and deemed one of the most learned men of that age, was intrusted by the Emperor Cantacuzenus with a mission to

Petrarch and Boccace learn Greek.

[1] An enumeration — and it is a long one — of the Greek books not wholly lost till this time, will be found in Heeren, p. 125; and also in his Essai sur les Croisades.

Italy.[1] Petrarch, in 1342, as Tiraboschi fixes the time, endeavored to learn Greek from him, but found the task too arduous, or rather had not sufficient opportunity to go on with it.[2] Boccaccio, some years afterwards, succeeded better with the help of Leontius Pilatus, a Calabrian also by birth,[3] who made a prose translation of Homer for his use, and for whom he is said to have procured a public appointment as teacher of the Greek language at Florence in 1361. He remained here about three years: but we read nothing of any other disciples; and the man himself was of too unsocial and forbidding a temper to conciliate them.[4]

Few acquainted with the language in their time.

16. According to a passage in one of Petrarch's letters, fancifully addressed to Homer, there were at that time not above ten persons in Italy who knew how to value the old father of the poets, — five at the most in Florence, one in Bologna, two in Verona, one in Mantua, one in Perugia, but none at Rome.[5] Some pains have been thrown away in attempting to retrieve the names of those to whom he alludes. The letter shows, at least, that there was very little pretension to Greek learning in his age; for I am not convinced that he meant all these ten persons, among whom he seems to reckon himself, to be considered as skilled in that tongue. And we must not be led away by the instances partially collected by Gradenigo out of the whole mass of extant records, to lose sight of the great general fact, that Greek literature was lost in Italy for seven hundred years, in the words of Leonard Aretin, before the arrival of Chrysoloras. The language is one thing, and the learning contained in it is another. For all the purposes of taste and erudition, there was no Greek in Western Europe during the middle ages: if we look only at the knowledge

1 Mehus; Tiraboschi, v. 398; De Sade, i. 406; Biog. Univ., Barlaam.

2 "Incubueram alacri spe magnoque desiderio, sed peregrinæ linguæ novitas et festina præceptoris absentia præciderunt propositum meum." It has been said, and probably with some truth, that Greek, or at least a sort of Greek, was preserved as a living language in Calabria; not because Greek colonies had once been settled in some cities, but because that part of Italy was not lost to the Byzantine Empire till about three centuries before the time of Barlaam and Pilatus. They, however, had gone to a better source: and I should have great doubts as to the goodness of Calabrian Greek in the fourteenth century; which, of course, are not removed by the circumstance, that, in some places, the church service was performed in that language. Heeren, I find, is of the same opinion. P. 287.

3 Many have taken Pilatus for a native of Thessalonica: even Hody has fallen into this mistake; but Petrarch's letters show the contrary.

4 Hody de Græcis illustribus, p. 2; Mehus, p. 273; De Sade, iii. 625. Gibbon has erroneously supposed this translation to have been made by Boccace himself.

5 De Sade, iii. 627; Tiraboschi, v. 371, 400; Heeren, 294.

of bare words, we have seen there was a very slender portion.

It is taught by Chrysoloras about 1395.

17. The true epoch of the revival of Greek literature in Italy, these attempts of Petrarch and Boccace having produced no immediate effect, though they evidently must have excited a desire for learning, cannot be placed before the year 1395,[1] when Emanuel Chrysoloras, previously known as an ambassador from Constantinople to the Western powers in order to solicit assistance against the Turks, was induced to return to Florence as public teacher of Greek. He passed from thence to various Italian universities, and became the preceptor of several early Hellenists.[2] The first, and perhaps the most eminent and useful of these, was Guarino Guarini of Verona, born in 1370. He acquired his knowledge of Greek under Chrysoloras at Constantinople, before the arrival of the latter in Italy. Guarino, upon his return, became professor of rhetoric, first at Venice and other cities of Lombardy, then at Florence, and ultimately at Ferrara, where he closed a long life of unremitting and useful labor in 1460. John Aurispa of Sicily came to the field rather later; but his labors were not less profitable. He brought back to Italy 238 manuscripts from Greece about 1423, and thus put his country in possession of authors hardly known to her by name. Among these were Plato, Plotinus, Diodorus, Arrian, Dio Cassius, Strabo, Pindar, Callimachus, Appian. After teaching Greek at Bologna and Florence, Aurispa also ended a length of days, under the patronage of the house of Este, at

His disciples.

[1] This is the date fixed by Tiraboschi: others refer it to 1391, 1396. 1397 or 1399.

[2] "Literæ per hujus belli intercapedines mirabile quantum per Italiam increvere; accedente tunc primum cognitione literarum Græcarum, quæ septingentis jam annis apud nostros homines desierant esse in usu. Retulit autem Græcam disciplinam ad nos Chrysoloras Byzantinus, vir domi nobilis ac literarum Græcarum peritissimus." Leonard Aretin apud Hody, p. 28. See also an extract from Manetti's Life of Boccace, in Hody, p. 61.

"Satis constat Chrysoloram Byzantinum transmarinam illam disciplinam in Italiam advexisse; quo doctore adhibito primum nostri homines totius exercitationes atque artis ignari, cognitis Græcis literis, vehementer sese ad eloquentiæ studia excitaverunt." P. Cortesius de hominibus doctis, p. 6.

The first visit of Chrysoloras had produced an inclination towards the study of Greek. Coluccio Salutato, in a letter to Demetrius Cydonius, who had accompanied Chrysoloras, says, "Multorum animos ad linguam Helladum accendisti, ut jam videre videar multos fore Græcarum literarum post paucorum annorum curricula non tepide studiosos." Mehus, p 356.

The Erotemata of Chrysoloras, an introduction to Greek grammar, was the first and long the only channel to a knowledge of that language, save oral instruction. It was several times printed, even after the grammars of Gaza and Lascaris had come more into use. An abridgment, by Guarino of Verona, with some additions of his own, was printed at Ferrara in 1509. Ginguéné, iii. 283.

Ferrara. To these may be added, in the list of public instructors in Greek before 1440, Filelfo, a man still more known by his virulent disputes with his contemporaries than by his learning; who, returning from Greece in 1427 laden with manuscripts, was not long afterwards appointed to the chair of rhetoric (that is, of Latin and Greek philology) at Florence; and, according to his own account, excited the admiration of the whole city.[1] But his vanity was excessive, and his contempt of others not less so. Poggio was one of his enemies; and their language towards each other is a noble specimen of the decency with which literary and personal quarrels were carried on.[2] It has been observed, that Gianozzo Manetti, a contemporary scholar, is less known than others, chiefly because the mildness of his character spared him the altercations to which they owe a part of their celebrity.[3]

18. Many of these cultivators of the Greek language devoted their leisure to translating the manuscripts brought into Italy. The earliest of these was Peter Paul Vergerio (commonly called the elder, to distinguish him from a more celebrated man of the same names in the sixteenth century), a scholar of Chrysoloras, but not till he was rather advanced in years. He made, by order of the Emperor Sigismund, and therefore not earlier than 1410, a translation of Arrian, which is said to exist in the Vatican

Translations from Greek into Latin.

1 "Universa in me civitas conversa est; omnes me diligunt, honorant omnes, ac summis laudibus in cœlum efferunt. Meum nomen in ore est omnibus. Nec primarii cives modo, cum per urbem incedo, sed nobilissimæ fœminæ honorandi mei gratiâ loco cedunt, tantumque mihi deferunt, ut me pudeat tanti cultûs. Auditores sunt quotidie ad quadringentos, vel fortassis et amplius; et hi quidem magna in parte viri grandiores et ex ordine senatorio." Phileph. Epist. ad ann., 1428.

2 Shepherd's Life of Poggio, ch. vi. and viii.

3 Hody was, perhaps, the first who threw much light on the early studies of Greek in Italy; and his book, De Græcis illustribus, linguæ Græcæ instauratoribus, will be read with pleasure and advantage by every lover of literature; though Mehus, who came with more exuberant erudition to the subject, has pointed out a few errors. But more is to be found as to its native cultivators; Hody being chiefly concerned with the Greek refugees, in Bayle, Fabricius, Niceron, Mehus, Zeno, Tiraboschi, Meiners, Roscoe, Heeren, Shepherd, Corniani, Ginguéné, and the Biographie Universelle, whom I name in chronological order.

As it is impossible to dwell on the subject within the limits of these pages, I will refer the reader to the most useful of the above writings, some of which, being merely biographical collections, do not give the connected information he would require. The Lives of Poggio and of Lorenzo de' Medici will make him familiar with the literary history of Italy for the whole fifteenth century, in combination with public events, as it is best learned. I need not say that Tiraboschi is a source of vast knowledge to those who can encounter two quarto volumes. Ginguéné's third volume is chiefly borrowed from these, and may be read with great advantage. Finally, a clear, full, and accurate account of those times will be found in Heeren. It will be understood that all these works relate to the revival of Latin as well as Greek

Library; but we know little of its merits.[1] A more renowned person was Ambrogio Traversari, a Florentine monk of the order of Camaldoli, who employed many years in this useful labor. No one of that age has left a more respectable name for private worth: his epistles breathe a spirit of virtue, of kindness to his friends, and of zeal for learning. In the opinion of his contemporaries, he was placed, not quite justly, on a level with Leonard Aretin for his knowledge of Latin; and he surpassed him in Greek.[2] Yet neither his translations, nor those of his contemporaries, Guarino of Verona, Poggio, Leonardo Aretino, Filelfo, who, with several others, rather before 1440, or not long afterwards, rendered the historians and philosophers of Greece familiar to Italy, can be extolled as correct, or as displaying what is truly to be called a knowledge of either language. Vossius, Casaubon, and Huet speak with much dispraise of most of these early translations from Greek into Latin. The Italians knew not enough of the original, and the Greeks were not masters enough of Latin. Gaza, upon the whole, "than whom no one is more successful," says Erasmus, "whether he renders Greek into Latin, or Latin into Greek," is reckoned the most elegant, and Argyropulus the most exact. But George of Trebizond, Filelfo, Leonard Aretin, Poggio, Valla, Perotti, are rather severely dealt with by the sharp critics of later times;[3] for this reproach does not fall only on the scholars of the first generation, but on their successors, except Politian, down nearly

[1] Biogr. Univ.: Vergerio. He seems to have written very good Latin, if we may judge by the extracts in Corniani, ii. 61.

[2] The Hodœporicon of Traversari, though not of importance as a literary work, serves to prove, according to Bayle (Camaldoli, note D), that the author was an honest man, and that he lived in a very corrupt age. It is an account of the visitation of some convents belonging to his order. The Life of Ambrogio Traversari has been written by Mehus very copiously, and with abundant knowledge of the times: it is a great source of the literary history of Italy. There is a pretty good account of him in Niceron, vol. xix.; and a short one in Roscoe: but the fullest biography of the man himself will be found in Meiners, Lebensbeschreibungen berühmter Männer, vol. ii. pp. 222–307.

[3] Baillet, Jugemens des Savans, ii. 376, &c.; Blount, Censura Auctorum, in nominibus nuncupatis: Hody, sæpies; Niceron, vol. ix. in Perotti: see also a letter of Erasmus in Jortin's Life, ii. 425.

Filelfo tells us of a perplexity into which Ambrogio Traversari and Carlo Marsupini, perhaps the two principal Greek scholars in Italy after himself and Guarino, were thrown by this line of Homer: —

Βούλομ' ἐγὼ λαὸν σόον ἔμμεναι, ἢ ἀπόλεσθαι.

The first thought it meant "populum aut salvum esse aut perire;" which Filelfo justly calls "inepta interpretatio et prava." Marsupini said ἢ ἀπόλεσθαι was "aut ipsum perire." Filelfo, after exulting over them, gives the true meaning. Philelph. Epist. ad ann. 1440.

Traversari complains much, in one of his letters, of the difficulty he found in translating Diogenes Laertius, lib. vii. epist. ii.; but Meiners, though admitting many errors, thinks this one of the best among the early translations: ii. 290

to the close of the fifteenth century. Yet, though it is necessary to point out the deficiencies of classical erudition at this time, lest the reader should hastily conclude that the praises bestowed upon it are less relative to the previous state of ignorance, and the difficulties with which that generation had to labor, than they really are, this cannot affect our admiration and gratitude towards men, who, by their diligence and ardor in acquiring and communicating knowledge, excited that thirst for improvement, and laid those foundations of it, which rendered the ensuing age so glorious in the annals of literature.

19. They did not uniformly find any great public encouragement in the early stages of their teaching: on the contrary, Aurispa met with some opposition to philological literature at Bologna.[1] The civilians and philosophers were pleased to treat the innovators as men who wanted to set showy against solid learning. Nor was the state of Italy and of the papacy during the long schism very favorable to their object. Ginguéné remarks that patronage was more indispensable in the fifteenth century than it had been in the last. Dante and Petrarch shone out by a paramount force of genius; but the men of learning required the encouragement of power in order to excite and sustain their industry.

Public encouragement delayed.

20. That encouragement, however it may have been delayed, had been accorded before the year 1440. Eugenius IV. was the first pope who displayed an inclination to favor the learned. They found a still more liberal patron in Alfonso, King of Naples, who, first of all European princes, established the interchange of praise and pension (both, however, well deserved) with Filelfo, Poggio, Valla, Beccatelli, and other eminent men. This seems to have begun before 1440, though it was more conspicuous afterwards until his death in 1458. The earliest literary academy was established at Naples by Alfonso, of which Antonio Beccatelli, more often called Panormita, from his birthplace, was the first president, as Pontano was the second. Nicolas of Este, Marquis of Ferrara, received literary men in his hospitable court. But none were so celebrated or useful in this patronage of letters as Cosmo de' Medici, the Pericles of Florence,

But fully accorded before 1440.

[1] Tiraboschi, vii. 301.

who, at the period with which we are now concerned, was surrounded by Traversari, Niccolo Niccolì, Leonardo Aretino, Poggio; all ardent to retrieve the treasures of Greek and Roman learning. Filelfo alone, malignant and irascible, stood aloof from the Medicean party, and poured his venom in libels on Cosmo and the chief of his learned associates. Niccolì, a wealthy citizen of Florence, deserves to be remembered among these; not for his writings, since he left none; but on account of his care for the good instruction of youth, which has made Meiners call him the Florentine Socrates, and for his liberality as well as diligence in collecting books and monuments of antiquity. The Public Library of St. Mark was founded on a bequest by Niccoli, in 1437, of his own collection of eight hundred manuscripts. It was, too, at his instigation, and that of Traversari, that Cosmo himself, about this time, laid the foundation of that, which, under his grandson, acquired the name of the Laurentian Library.[1]

Emigration of learned Greeks to Italy.

21. As the dangers of the Eastern Empire grew more imminent, a few that had still endeavored to preserve in Greece the purity of their language, and the speculations of ancient philosophy, turned their eyes towards a haven that seemed to solicit the glory of protecting them. The first of these that is well known was Theodore Gaza, who fled from his birthplace, Thessalonica, when it fell under the Turkish yoke in 1430. He rapidly acquired the Latin language by the help of Victorin of Feltre.[2] Gaza became afterwards, but not perhaps within the period to which this chapter is limited, Rector of the University of Ferrara. In this city, Eugenius IV. held a council in 1438, removed next year, on account of sickness, to Florence, in order to reconcile the Greek and Latin churches. Though it is notorious that the appearances of success which attended this hard bargain of the strong with the weak were very fallacious, the presence of several Greeks, skilled in their own language, and even in their ancient philosophy (Pletho, Bessarion, Gaza), stimulated the noble love of truth and science that burned in the bosoms of enlightened Italians. Thus, in 1440, the spirit

[1] I refer to the same authorities, but especially to the Life of Traversari in Meiners, Lebensbeschreibungen, ii. 294. The suffrages of older authors are collected by Baillet and Blount.

[2] Victorin perhaps exchanged instruction with his pupil; for we find by a letter of Traversari (p. 421, edit. Mehus), that he was himself teaching Greek in 1433.

of ancient learning was already diffused on that side the Alps: the Greek language might be learned in at least four or five cities, and an acquaintance with it was a recommendation to the favor of the great; while the establishment of universities at Pavia, Turin, Ferrara, and Florence, since the beginning of the present century or near the close of the last, bore witness to the generous emulation which they served to redouble and concentrate.

Causes of enthusiasm for antiquity in Italy.

22. It is an interesting question, What were the causes of this enthusiasm for antiquity which we find in the beginning of the fifteenth century? — a burst of public feeling that seems rather sudden, but prepared by several circumstances that lie farther back in Italian history. The Italians had for some generations learned more to identify themselves with the great people that had subdued the world. The fall of the house of Swabia, releasing their necks from a foreign yoke, had given them a prouder sense of nationality; while the name of Roman emperor was systematically associated by one party with ancient tradition; and the study of the civil law, barbarously ignorant as its professors often were, had at least the effect of keeping alive a mysterious veneration for antiquity. The monuments of ancient Italy were perpetual witnesses; their inscriptions were read: it was enough that a few men like Petrarch should animate the rest; it was enough that learning should become honorable, and that there should be the means of acquiring it. The story of Rienzi, familiar to every one, is a proof what enthusiasm could be kindled by ancient recollections. Meantime the laity became better instructed: a mixed race, ecclesiastics, but not priests, and capable alike of enjoying the benefices of the church or of returning from it to the world, were more prone to literary than theological pursuits. The religious scruples which had restrained churchmen, in the darker ages, from perusing heathen writers, by degrees gave way, as the spirit of religion itself grew more objective, and directed itself more towards maintaining the outward church in its orthodoxy of profession, and in its secular power, than towards cultivating devout sentiments in the bosom.

Advanced state of society.

23. The principal Italian cities became more wealthy and more luxurious after the middle of the thirteenth century. Books, though still very dear, comparatively with the present value of money, were much

less so than in other parts of Europe.[1] In Milan, about 1300, there were fifty persons who lived by copying them. At Bologna, it was also a regular occupation at fixed prices.[2] In this state of social prosperity, the keen relish of Italy for intellectual excellence had time to develop itself. A style of painting appeared in the works of Giotto and his followers, rude and imperfect, according to the skilfulness of later times, but in itself pure, noble, and expressive, and well adapted to reclaim the taste from the extravagance of romance to classic simplicity. Those were ready for the love of Virgil who had formed their sense of beauty by the figures of Giotto and the language of Dante. The subject of Dante is truly mediæval; but his style, the clothing of poetry, bears the strongest marks of his acquaintance with antiquity. The influence of Petrarch was far more direct, and has already been pointed out.

Exclusive study of antiquity.

24. The love of Greek and Latin absorbed the minds of Italian scholars, and effaced all regard to every other branch of literature. Their own language was nearly silent; few condescended so much as to write letters in it: as few gave a moment's attention to physical science; though we find it mentioned, perhaps as remarkable, in Victorin of Feltre, that he had some fondness for geometry, and had learned to understand Euclid.[3] But even in Latin they wrote very little that can be deemed worthy of remembrance, or even that can be mentioned at all. The ethical dialogues of Francis Barbaro, a noble Venetian, on the married life ("de re uxoria"),[4] and of Poggio on nobility, are

[1] Savigny thinks the price of books in the middle ages has been much exaggerated, and that we are apt to judge by a few instances of splendid volumes, which give us no more notion of ordinary prices than similar proofs of luxury in collectors do at present. Thousands of manuscripts are extant, and the sight of most of them may convince us that they were written at no extraordinary cost. He then gives a long list of law-books, the prices of which he has found recorded. Gesch. des Römischen Rechts, iii. 549. But, unless this were accompanied with a better standard of value than a mere monetary one (which last, Savigny has given very minutely), it can afford little information. The impression left on my mind, without comparing these prices closely with those of other commodities, was that books were in real value very considerably dearer (that is, in the ratio of several units to one) than at present; which is confirmed by many other evidences.

[2] Tiraboschi, iv. 72-80. The price for copying a Bible was eighty Bolognese livres, three of which were equal to two gold florins.

[3] Meiners, Lebensbeschr., ii. 293.

[4] Barbaro was a scholar of Gasparin in Latin. He had probably learned Greek of Guarino; for it is said, that, on the visit of the emperor John Paleologus to Italy in 1423, he was addressed by two noble Venetians, Leonardo Giustiniani and Francesco Barbaro, in as good language as if they had been born in Greece. Andrès, iii. 33. The treatise de re uxoria, which was published about 1417, made a considerable impression in Italy. Some account of it may be found in Shepherd's Life of Poggio, ch. iii.; and in Corniani, ii. 137

almost the only books that fall within this period, except declamatory invectives or panegyrics, and other productions of circumstance. Their knowledge was not yet exact enough to let them venture upon critical philology; though Niccolì and Traversari were silently occupied in the useful task of correcting the text of manuscripts, faulty beyond description in the later centuries. Thus we must consider Italy as still at school,—active, acute, sanguine, full of promise, but not yet become really learned, or capable of doing more than excite the emulation of other nations.

25. But we find very little corresponding sympathy with this love of classical literature in other parts of Europe; not so much owing to the want of intercourse, as to a difference of external circumstances, and still more of national character and acquired habits. Clemangis, indeed, rather before the end of the fourteenth century, is said by Crevier to have restored the study of classical antiquity in France, after an intermission of two centuries;[1] and Eichhorn deems his style superior to that of most contemporary Italians.[2] Even the Latin verses of Clemangis are praised by the same author, as the first that had been tolerably written on this side the Alps for two hundred years. But we do not find much evidence that he produced any effect upon Latin literature in France. The general style was as bad as before. Their writers employed not only the barbarous vocabulary of the schools, but even French words with Latin terminations adapted to them.[3] We shall see that the renovation of polite letters in France must be dated long afterwards. Several universities were established in that kingdom; but even if universities had been always beneficial to literature, which was not the case during the prevalence of scholastic disputation, the civil wars of one unhappy reign, and the English invasions of another, could not but retard the progress of all useful studies. Some Greeks, about 1430, are said to have demanded a stipend, in pursuance of a decree of the Council of Vienne in the preceding century, for teaching their lan-

Classical learning in France low

who thinks it the only work of moral philosophy in the fifteenth century which is not a servile copy of some ancient system. He was grandfather of the more celebrated Hermolaus Barbarus.

[1] Hist. de l'Université de Paris, iii. 189.

[2] Gesch. der Litteratur, ii. 242. Meiners (Vergleich. der Sitten, iii. 33) extols Clemangis in equally high terms. He is said to have read lectures on the rhetoric of Cicero and Aristotle. Id. ii. 647. Was there a translation of the latter so early?

[3] Bulæus, Hist. Univ. Paris, apud Heeren, p. 118.

guage in the University of Paris. The nation of France, one of the four into which that university was divided, assented to this suggestion; but we find no other steps taken in relation to it. In 1455, it is said that the Hebrew language was publicly taught.[1]

Much more so in England.

26. Of classical learning in England, we can tell no favorable story. The Latin writers of the fifteenth century, few in number, are still more insignificant in value. They possess scarce an ordinary knowledge of grammar: to say that they are full of barbarisms, and perfectly inelegant, is hardly necessary. The University of Oxford was not less frequented at this time than in the preceding century, though it was about to decline; but its pursuits were as nugatory and pernicious to real literature as before.[2] Poggio says, more than once, in writing from England about 1420, that he could find no good books, and is not very respectful to our scholars. "Men given up to sensuality we may find in abundance; but very few lovers of learning, and those barbarous, skilled more in quibbles and sophisms than in literature. I visited many convents: they were all full of books of modern doctors, whom we should not think worthy so much as to be heard. They have few works of the ancients, and those are much better with us. Nearly all the convents of this island have been founded within four hundred years: but that was not a period in which either learned men, or such books as we seek, could be expected; for they had been lost before."[3]

Library of Duke of Gloucester.

27. Yet books began to be accumulated in our public libraries. Aungerville, in the preceding century, gave part of his collection to a college at Oxford; and Humphrey, Duke of Gloucester, bequeathed six hundred volumes, as some have said, or one hundred and twenty-nine only, according to another account, to that university.[4]

[1] Crevier, iv. 43; Heeren, p. 121. — [Daunou says (Journal des Savans, May, 1829), that we might find names and books to show that the study of Greek was not totally interrupted in France from 1300 to 1453. — 1842.]

[2] No place was more discredited for bad Latin. "Oxoniensis loquendi mos" became a proverb. This means, that, being disciples of Scotus and Ockham, the Oxonians talked the jargon of their masters.

[3] Pogg. Epist., p. 43 (edit. 1832).

[4] The former number is given by Warton: the latter I find in a short tract on English monastic libraries (1831), by the Rev. Joseph Hunter. In this there is also a catalogue of the library in the Priory of Bretton in Yorkshire, consisting of about 150 volumes, but as late as the middle of the sixteenth century. [The libraries of Aungerville, Cobham, and others, were united at Oxford in 1480 to that of the Duke of Gloucester, and remained till the plunder under Edward VI. This may account for the discrepancy as to the number of books (manuscript) in the latter. — 1842.]

But these books were not of much value in a literary sense, though some may have been historically useful. I am indebted to Heeren for a letter of thanks from the Duke of Gloucester to Decembrio, an Italian scholar of considerable reputation, who had sent him a translation of Plato de Republica. It must have been written before July, 1447, the date of Humphrey's death; and was probably as favorable a specimen of our Latinity as the kingdom could furnish.[1]

Gerard Groot's college at Deventer.

28. Among the Cisalpine nations, the German had the greatest tendency to literary improvement, as we may judge by subsequent events rather than by much that was apparent so early as 1440. Their writers in Latin were still barbarous, nor had they partaken in the love of antiquity which actuated the Italians. But the German nation displayed its best characteristic, — a serious, honest, industrious disposition, loving truth and goodness, and glad to pursue whatever part seemed to lead to them. A proof of this character was given in an institution of considerable influence both upon learning and religion, — the college, or brotherhood, of Deventer, planned by Gerard Groot, but not built and inhabited till 1400, — fifteen years after his death. The associates of this, called by different names, but more usually Brethren of the Life in Common (Gemeineslebens), or Good Brethren and Sisters, were dispersed in different parts of Germany and the Low Countries, but with their head college at Deventer. They bore an evident resemblance to the modern Moravians, by their strict lives, their community (at least a partial one) of goods, their industry in manual labor, their fervent devotion, their tendency to mysticism; but they were as strikingly distinguished from them by the cultivation of knowledge, which was encouraged in brethren of sufficient capacity, and promoted by schools both for primary and for enlarged education. "These schools were," says Eichhorn, "the first genuine nurseries of literature in Germany, so far as it depended on the knowledge of languages; and in them

1 "Hoc uno nos longe felicem judicamus, quod tu totque florentissimi viri Græcis et Latinis literis peritissimi, quot illic apud vos sunt nostris temporibus, habeantur, quibus nesciamus quid laudum digne satis possit excogitari. Mitto quod facundiam priscam illam et priscis viris dignam, quæ prorsus perierat, huic sæculo renovatis; nec id vobis satis fuit, et Græcas literas scrutati estis, ut et philosophos Græcos et vivendi magistros, qui nostris jam obliterati erant et occulti, reseratis, et eos Latinos facientes in propatulum adducitis. Heeren quotes this, p. 135, from Sassi de studiis Mediolanensibus. Warton also mentions the letter; ii. 388. The absurd solecism exemplified in "nos felicem judicamus" was introduced affectedly by the writers of the twelfth century. Hist. Litt. de la France, ix. 146.

was first taught the Latin, and, in the process of time, the Greek and Eastern tongues."[1] It will be readily understood that Latin only could be taught in the period with which we are now concerned; and, according to Lambinet, the brethren did not begin to open public schools till near the middle of the century.[2] These schools continued to flourish till the civil wars of the Low Countries and the progress of the Reformation broke them up. Groningen had also a school, St. Edward's, of considerable reputation. Thomas à Kempis, according to Meiners, whom Eichhorn and Heeren have followed, presided over a school at Zwoll, wherein Agricola, Hegius, Langius, and Dringeberg, the restorers of learning in Germany, were educated. But it seems difficult to reconcile this with known dates, or with other accounts of that celebrated person's history.[3] The brethren Gemeineslebens had forty-five houses in 1430, and in 1460 more than thrice the number. They are said by some to have taken regular vows (though I find a difference in my authorities as to this), and to have professed celibacy. They were bound to live by the labor of their hands, observing the ascetic discipline of monasteries, and not to beg; which made the mendicant orders their enemies. They were protected, however, against these malignant calumniators by the favor of the pope. The passages quoted by Revius, the historian of Deventer, do not quite bear out the reputation for love of literature which Eichhorn has given them; but they were much occupied in copying and binding books.[4] Their house at Bruxelles began to print books, instead of copying them, in 1474.[5]

Physical sciences in middle ages.

29. We have in the first chapter made no mention of the physical sciences, because little was to be said, and it seemed expedient to avoid breaking the subject into unnecessary divisions. It is well known that Europe had more obligations to the Saracens in this than in any other province of research. They indeed had borrowed much from Greece, and much from India; but it was through their language that it came into use among the nations of the West. Gerbert, near the end of the tenth century, was

[1] Meiners, Lebensbeschreibungen berühmter Männer, ii. 311-324. Lambinet, Origines de l'Imprimerie, ii. 170. Eichhorn, Geschichte der Litteratur, ii. 134, iii. 882. Revius, Daventria Illustrata. Mosheim, cent. xv. c. 2, § 22. Biogr. Univ.: Gerard, Kempis

[2] Origines de l'Imprimerie, p. 180.

[3] Meiners, p. 323. Eichhorn, p. 137. Heeren, p. 145. Biog. Univ.: Kempis. Revius, Davent. Illust.

[4] Daventria Illustrata, p. 35.

[5] Lambinet.

the first who, by travelling into Spain, learned something of Arabian science. A common literary tradition ascribes to him the introduction of their numerals, and of the arithmetic founded on them, into Europe. This has been disputed, and again re-asserted, in modern times.[1] It is sufficient to say here, that only a very unreasonable scepticism has questioned the use of Arabic numerals in calculation during the thirteenth century. The positive evidence on this side cannot be affected by the notorious fact, that they were not employed in legal instruments or in ordinary accounts: such an argument, indeed, would be equally good in comparatively modern times. These numerals are found, according to Andrès, in Spanish manuscripts of the twelfth century; and according both to him and Cossali, who speak from actual inspection, in the treatise of arithmetic and algebra by Leonard Fibonacci of Pisa, written in 1220.[2] This has never been printed.[3] It is by far our earliest testimony

Arabian numerals and method.

1 See Andrès, the Archæologia, vol. viii., and the Encyclopædias Britannic and Metropolitan, on one side against Gerbert; Montucla, i. 502, and Kästner, Geschichte der Mathematik, i. 35 and ii. 695, in his favor. The latter relies on a well-known passage in William of Malmesbury concerning Gerbert, "Abacum certe primus a Sarcenis rapiens, regulus dedit, quæ a sudantibus abacistis vix intelliguntur;" upon several expressions in his writings; and upon a manuscript of his Geometry, seen and mentioned by Pez, who refers it to the twelfth century, in which Arabic numerals are introduced. It is answered, that the language of Malmesbury is indefinite; that Gerbert's own expressions are equally so; and that the copyist of the manuscript may have inserted the ciphers.

It is evident that the use of the numeral signs does not of itself imply an acquaintance with the Arabic calculation, though it was a necessary step to it. Signs bearing some resemblance to these (too great for accident) are found in MSS. of Boethius, and are published by Montucla (vol. i. planch. xi.). In one MS. they appear with names written over each of them, not Greek or Latin or Arabic, or in any known anguage. These singular names, and nearly the same forms, are found also in a manuscript well deserving of notice, — No. 343 of the Arundel MSS. in the British Museum, — and which is said to have belonged to a convent at Mentz. This has been referred by some competent judges to the twelfth, and by others to the very beginning of the thirteenth century. It purports to be an introduction to the art of multiplying and dividing numbers; "quicquid ab abacistis excerpere potui, compendiose collegi." The author uses nine digits, but none for ten, or zero; as is also the case in the MS. of Boethius. "Sunt vero integri novem sufficientes ad infinitam multiplicationem, quorum nomina singulis sunt superjecta." A gentleman of the British Museum, who had the kindness, at my request, to give his attention to this hitherto unknown evidence in the controversy, is of opinion that the rudiments, at the very least, of our numeration, are indicated in it; and that the author comes within one step of our present system, which is no other than sup plying an additional character for zero. His ignorance of this character renders his process circuitous, as it does not contain the principle of juxtaposition for the pur pose of summing; but it does contain the still more essential principle, a decuple increase of value for the same sign, in a progressive series of location from right to left. I shall be gratified if this slight notice should cause the treatise, which is very short, to be published, or more fully explained. [This manuscript, as well as that of Boethius, has drawn some attention lately, and is noticed in the publications of Mr. J. O. Halliwell, and of M. Charles at Paris. — 1842.]

2 Montucla, whom several other writers have followed, erroneously places this work in the beginning of the fifteenth century.

3 [(1836.) It has since been published

to the knowledge of algebra in Europe; but Leonard owns that he learned it among the Saracens. "This author appears," says Hutton, or rather Cossali, from whom he borrows, "to be well skilled in the various ways of reducing equations to their final simple state by all the usual methods." His algebra includes the solution of quadratics.

Proofs of them in thirteenth century.

30. In the thirteen century, we find Arabian numerals employed in the tables of Alfonso X., King of Castile, published about 1252. They are said to appear also in the Treatise of the Sphere, by John de Sacro Bosco, probably about twenty years earlier; and a treatise, De Algorismo, ascribed to him, treats expressly of this subject.[1] Algorismus was the proper name for the Arabic notation, and method of reckoning. Matthew Paris, after informing us that John Basing first made Greek numeral figures known in England, observes, that in these any number may be represented by a single figure, which is not the case "in Latin nor in Algorism."[2] It is obvious, that, in some few numbers only, this is true of the Greek; but the passage certainly implies an acquaintance with that notation which had obtained the name of Algorism. It cannot therefore be questioned, that Roger Bacon knew these figures: yet he has, I apprehend, never mentioned them in his writings; for a calendar, bearing the date 1292, which has been blunderingly ascribed to him, is expressly declared to have been framed at Toledo. In the year 1282, we find a single Arabic figure 3 inserted in a public record; not only the first indisputable instance of their employment in England, but the only one of their appearance in so solemn an instrument.[3] But I have

by M. Libri, at Paris, in his Histoire des Sciences Mathématiques en Italie, vol. ii., from a MS. in the Magliobecchi Library. It occupies 170 pages in M. Libri's volume. The editor places Fibonacci at the head of the mathematicians of the middle ages. — 1842.]

[1] Several copies of this treatise are in the British Museum. Montucla has erroneously said that this arithmetic of Sacro Bosco is written in verse. Wallis, his authority, informs us only that some verses, two of which he quotes, are subjoined to the treatise. This is not the case in the manuscripts I have seen. I should add, that only one of them bears the name of Sacro Bosco, and that in a later handwriting. [I have called this an unpublished treatise in my first edition, on the authority of the Biographie Universelle; but Professor De Morgan has informed me that it was printed at Venice in 1523. — 1842.)

[2] "Hic insuper magister Joannes figuras Græcorum numerales, et earum notitiam et significationes in Angliam portavit, et familiaribus suis declaravit. Per quas figuras etiam literæ repræsentantur. De quibus figuris hoc maxime admirandum, quod unica figura quilibet numerus repræsentatur; quod non est in Latino, vel in Algorismo." Mat. Paris, A.D. 1252, p. 721.

[3] Parliamentary Writs, i. 232, edited under the Record Commission by Sir Francis Palgrave. It was probably inserted for want of room; not enough having been left for the word III^um^. It will not be detected with ease, even by the help of this reference.

been informed that they have been found in some private documents before the end of the century. In the following age, though they were still by no means in common use among accountants, nor did they begin to be so till much later, there can be no doubt that mathematicians were thoroughly conversant with them; and instances of their employment in other writings may be adduced.[1]

Mathematical treatises.

31. Adelard of Bath, in the twelfth century, translated the elements of Euclid from the Arabic; and another version was made by Campano in the next age. The first printed editions are of the latter.[2] The writings of Ptolemy became known through the same channel; and the once celebrated treatise on the Sphere, by John de Sacro Bosco (Holywood, or, according to Leland, Halifax), about the beginning of the thirteenth century, is said to be but an abridgment of the Alexandrian geometer.[3] It has been frequently printed, and was even thought worthy of a commentary by Clavius. Jordan of Namur (Nemorarius), near the same time, shows a considerable insight into the properties of numbers.[4] Vitello, a native of Poland, not long afterwards, first made known the principles of optics in a treatise in ten books. several times printed in the sixteenth century, and indicating an extensive acquaintance with the Greek and Arabian geometers. Montucla has charged Vitello with having done no more than compress and arrange a work on the same subject by Alhazen; which Andrès, always partial to the Arabian writers, has not failed to repeat. But the author of an article on Vitello in the Biographie Universelle repels this imputation, which could not, he says, have proceeded from any one who had compared the two writers. A more definite judgment is pronounced by the laborious German historian of mathema-

1 Andrès, ii. 92, gives, on the whole, the best account of the progress of numerals. The article by Leslie in the Encyclopædia Britannica is too dogmatical in denying their antiquity. That in the Encyclopædia Metropolitana, by Mr. Peacock, is more learned. Montucla is but superficial, and Kästner has confined himself to the claims of Gerbert; admitting which, he is too indifferent about subsequent evidence. [Dr. Thomson, in his History of the Royal Society, refers to several papers in their Transactions on the use of Arabic numerals in England, and quotes one in 1741, which asserts that an unquestionable instance of their employment as early as 1011 occurs in the parish church of Romsey (p. 241). But this, I conceive, must be wholly rejected. — 1853.]

2 [M. Charles Jourdain, in his edition of his father's Recherches Critiques sur les Traductions d'Aristote, p. 98, has observed that I have reproduced an error pointed out by Tiraboschi, iv. 151. Campano did not translate Euclid, though he commented upon him. The only translation was by Adelard. — 1853.]

3 Montucla, i. 506. Biogr. Univ.: Kästner.

4 Montucla; Kästner; Drinkwater's Life of Galileo.

ties, Kästner. "Vitello," he says, "has with diligence and judgment collected, as far as lay in his power, what had been previously known; and, avoiding the tediousness of Arabian verbosity, is far more readable, perspicuous, and methodical than Alhazen: he has also gone much farther in the science."[1]

Roger Bacon.

32. It seems hard to determine whether or not Roger Bacon be entitled to the honors of a discoverer in science. That he has not described any instrument analogous to the telescope, is now generally admitted; but he paid much attention to optics, and has some new and important notions on that subject. That he was acquainted with the explosive powers of gunpowder, it seems unreasonable to deny: the mere detonation of nitre in contact with an inflammable substance, which of course might be casually observed, is by no means adequate to his expressions in the well-known passage on that subject. But there is no ground for doubting that the Saracens were already conversant with gunpowder.

His resemblance to Lord Bacon.

33. The mind of Roger Bacon was strangely compounded of almost prophetic gleams of the future course of science, and the best principles of the inductive philosophy, with a more than usual credulity in the superstitions of his own time. Some have deemed him overrated by the nationality of the English;[2] but, if we may have sometimes given him credit for discoveries to which he has only borne testimony, there can be no doubt of the originality of his genius. I have in another place remarked the singular resemblance he bears to Lord Bacon, not only in the character of his philosophy, but in several coincidences of expression. This has since been followed up by a later writer,[3] who plainly charges Lord Bacon with having borrowed much, and with having concealed his obligations. The Opus Majus of Roger Bacon was not published till 1733; but the manuscripts were not uncommon, and Selden had thoughts of printing the work. The quotations from the Franciscan and the Chancellor, printed in parallel columns by Mr. Forster, are sometimes

[1] Gesch. der Mathem., ii. 263. The true name is Vitello, as Playfair has remarked Dissertat. in Encycl. Brit.); but Vitellio is much more common. Kästner is correct, always copying the old editions.

[2] Meiners, of all modern historians of literature, is the least favorable to Bacon, on account of his superstition, and credulity in the occult sciences. Vergleichung der Sitten, ii. 710, and iii. 232. Heeren, p. 244, speaks more candidly of him. It is impossible, I think, to deny that credulity is one of the points of resemblance between him and his namesake.

[3] Hist. of Middle Ages, iii. 539; Forster's Mahometanism Unveiled, ii. 312.

very curiously similar: but he presses the resemblance too far; and certainly the celebrated distinction, in the Novum Organum, of four classes of *Idola* which mislead the judgment, does not correspond, as he supposes, with that of the causes of error assigned by Roger Bacon.

English mathematicians of fourteenth century.

34. The English nation was not at all deficient in mathematicians during the fourteenth century: on the contrary, no other in Europe produced nearly so many. But their works have rarely been published. The great progress of physical science, since the invention of printing, has rendered these imperfect treatises interesting only to the curiosity of a very limited class of readers. Thus Richard Suisset, or Swineshead, author of a book entitled, as is said, the Calculator (of whom Cardan speaks in such language as might be applied to himself), is scarcely known, except by name, to literary historians; and, though it has several times been printed, the book is of great rarity.[1] But the most conspicuous of our English geometers was Thomas Bradwardin, Archbishop of Canterbury; yet more for his rank and for his theological writings than for the arithmetical and geometrical speculations which give him a place in science. Montucla, with a carelessness of which there are too many instances in his valuable work, has placed Bradwardin, who died in 1348, at the beginning of the sixteenth century, though his treatise was printed in 1495.[2]

Astronomy.

35. It is certain that the phenomena of physical astronomy were never neglected: the calendar was known to be erroneous; and Roger Bacon has even been supposed by some to have divined the method of its restoration, which

[1] The character of Suisset's book given by Brucker, iii. 852, who had seen it, does not seem to justify the wish of Leibnitz that it should be republished. It is a strange medley of arithmetical and geometrical reasoning with the scholastic philosophy. Kästner (Geschichte der Mathematik, i. 50) appears not to have looked at Brucker, and, like Montucla, has a very slight notion of the nature of Suisset's book. His suspicion that Cardan had never seen the book he so much extols, because he calls the author the Calculator, which is the title of the work itself, seems unwarrantable. Suisset probably had obtained the name from his book, which is not uncommon; and Cardan was not a man to praise what he had never read. [One of the later editions is in the British Museum, with a manuscript date, 1520; but entered in the catalogue as Venice, 1505. It may be added, that the title in this edition is not the Calculator, though it appears by Brunet to have been so called in the first edition, that of Pavia, 1498; but Subtilissimi Ricardi Suisseti Anglici Calculationes noviter impressæ atque revisæ. I am informed that the work, in one edition or another, is less scarce than, on the authority of Brucker, I had conceived. — 1842.]

[2] It may be considered a proof of the attention paid to geometry in England, that two books of Euclid were read at Oxford about the middle of the fifteenth century. Churton's Life of Smyth, p. 151, from the University Register. We should not have expected to find this

has long afterwards been adopted. The Arabians understood astronomy well, and their science was transfused more or less into Europe. Nor was astrology, the favorite superstition of both the Eastern and Western world, without its beneficial effect upon the observation and registering of the planetary motions. Thus, too, alchemy, which, though the word properly means but chemistry, was generally confined to the mystery that all sought to penetrate, the transmutation of metals into gold, led more or less to the processes by which a real knowledge of the component parts of substances has been attained.[1]

Alchemy.

36. The art of medicine was cultivated with great diligence by the Saracens both of the East and of Spain, but with little of the philosophical science that had immortalized the Greek school. The writings, however, of these masters were translated into Arabic; whether correctly or not, has been disputed among Oriental scholars: and Europe derived her acquaintance with the physic of the mind and body, with Hippocrates as well as Aristotle, through the same channel. But the Arabians had eminent medical authorities of their own (Rhases, Avicenna, Albucazi), who possessed greater influence. In modern times, that is, since the revival of Greek science, the Arabian theories have been in general treated with much scorn. It is admitted, however, that pharmacy owes a long list of its remedies to their experience, and to their intimacy with the products of the East. The school of Salerno, established as early as the eleventh century[2] for the study of medicine, from whence the most considerable writers of the next ages issued, followed the Arabians in their medical theory; but these are deemed rude, and of little utility at present.

Medicine.

37. In the science of anatomy, an epoch was made by the treatise of Mundinus, a professor at Bologna, who died in 1326. It is entitled "Anatome omnium humani corporis interiorum membrorum." This book had one great advantage over those of Galen,—that it was founded on the actual anatomy of the human body: for Galen is sup-

Anatomy.

[1] I refer to Dr. Thomson's History of Chemistry for much curious learning on the alchemy of the middle ages. In a work like the present, it is impossible to follow up every subject; and I think that a general reference to a book of reputation and easy accessibility is better than an attempt to abridge it.

[2] Meiners refers it to the tenth, ii. 413; and Tiraboschi thinks it may be as ancient, iii. 347.

posed to have only dissected apes, and judged of mankind by analogy; and, though there may be reason to doubt whether this were altogether the case, it is certain that he had very little practice in human dissection. Mundinus seems to have been more fortunate in his opportunities of this kind than later anatomists, during the prevalence of a superstitious prejudice, have found themselves. His treatise was long the text-book of the Italian universities; till, about the middle of the sixteenth century, Mundinus was superseded by greater anatomists. The statutes of the University of Padua prescribed that anatomical lecturers should adhere to the literal text of Mundinus. Though some have treated this writer as a mere copier of Galen, he has much, according to Portal, of his own. There were also some good anatomical writers in France during the fourteenth century.[1]

Encyclopedic works of middle ages.

38. Several books of the later middle ages, sometimes of great size, served as collections of natural history, and, in fact, as encyclopædias of general knowledge. The writings of Albertus Magnus belong, in part, to this class. They have been collected, in twenty-one volumes folio, by the Dominican Peter Jammi, and published at Lyons in 1651. After setting aside much that is spurious, Albert may pass for the most fertile writer in the world. He is reckoned by some the founder of the schoolmen; but we mention him here as a compiler, from all accessible sources, of what physical knowledge had been accumulated in his time. A still more comprehensive contemporary writer of this class was Vincent de Beauvais, in the "Speculum naturale, morale, doctrinale, et historiale," written before the middle of the thirteenth century. The second part of this vast treatise in ten volumes folio, usually bound in four, "Speculum morale," seems not to be written by Vincent de Beauvais, and is chiefly a compilation from Thomas Aquinas and other theologians of the same age. The first, or "Speculum naturale," follows the order of creation as an arrangement; and, after pouring out all the author could collect on the heavens and earth, proceeds to the natural kingdoms; and, finally, to the corporeal and mental structure of man. In the third part of this encyclopædia, under the title "Speculum

Vincent of Beauvais.

1 Tiraboschi, v. 209-244, who is very copious for a non-medical writer. Portal, Hist. de l'Anatomie. Biogr. Univ · Mondino, Chauliac. Eichhorn, Gesch. der Lit. ii. 416-447.

doctrinale," all arts and sciences are explained; and the fourth contains an universal history.[1] The sources of this magazine of knowledge are, of course, very multifarious. In the "Speculum naturale," at which alone I have looked, Aristotle's writings (especially the history of animals), those of other ancient authors, of the Arabian physicians, and of all who had treated the same subjects in the middle ages, are brought together in a comprehensive encyclopedic manner, and with vast industry, but with almost a studious desire, as we might now fancy, to accumulate absurd falsehoods. Vincent, like many, it must be owned, in much later times, through his haste to compile, does not give himself the trouble to understand what he copies. But, in fact, he relied on others to make extracts for him, especially from the writings of Aristotle; permitting himself or them, as he tells us, to change the order, condense the meaning, and explain the difficulties.[2] It may be easily believed that neither Vincent of Beauvais, nor his amanuenses, were equal to this work of abridging and transposing their authors. Andrès, accordingly, has quoted a passage from the "Speculum naturale," and another to the same effect from Albertus Magnus, relating no doubt, in the Arabian writer from whom they borrowed, to the polarity of the magnet, but so strangely turned into nonsense, that it is evident they could not have understood in the least what they wrote. Probably, as their language is nearly the same, they copied a bad translation.[3]

Vincent of Beauvais.

39. In the same class of compilation with the Speculum of Vincent of Beauvais, we may place some later works: the Trésor of Brunetto Latini, written in French about 1280; the "Reductorium, Repertorium, et Dictionarium morale" of Berchorius, or Berchœur, a monk, who died at Paris in 1362;[4] and a treatise by Bartholomew Glanvil, "De proprietatibus rerum," soon after that time. Reading all they could find, extracting from all they read, digesting their extracts under some natural, or, at worst, alphabetical classifi-

Berchorius.

[1] Biogr. Univ.: Vincentius Bellovacensis.

[2] "A quibusdam fratribus excerpta susceperam; non eodem penitus verborum schemate, quo in originalibus suis jacent, sed ordine plerumque transposito, nonnunquam etiam mutata perpaululum ipsorum verborum forma, manente tamen auctoris sententia; prout ipsa vel prolixitatis abbreviandæ vel multitudinis in unam colligendæ, vel etiam obscuritatis explanandæ necessitas exigebat."

[3] Andrès, ii. 112. See also xiii. 141.

[4] This book, according to De Sade, Vie de Pétrarque, iii. 550, contains a few good things among many follies. I have never seen it.

cation, these laborious men gave back their studies to the world with no great improvement of the materials, but sometimes with much convenience in their disposition. This, however, depended chiefly on their ability as well as diligence; and, in the mediæval period, the want of capacity to discern probable truth was a very great drawback from the utility of their compilations.

40. It seems to be the better opinion, that few only of the Spanish romances or ballads founded on history or legend, so many of which remain, belong to a period anterior to the fifteenth century. Most of them should be placed still lower. Sanchez has included none in his collection of Spanish poetry, limited by its title to that period; though he quotes one or two fragments which he would refer to the fourteenth century.[1] Some, however, have conceived, perhaps with little foundation, that several in the general collections of romances have been modernized in language from more ancient lays. They have all a highly chivalrous character: every sentiment congenial to that institution — heroic courage, unsullied honor, generous pride, faithful love, devoted loyalty — were displayed in Castilian verse, not only in their real energy, but sometimes with an hyperbolical extravagance to which the public taste accommodated itself, and which long continued to deform the national literature. The ballad of the Conde de Alarcos, which may be found in Bouterwek or in Sismondi, and seems to be ancient, though not before the fifteenth century, will serve as a sufficient specimen.[2]

Spanish ballads.

41. The very early poetry of Spain (that published by Sanchez) is marked by a rude simplicity, a rhythmical and not very harmonious versification, and, especially in the ancient poem of the Cid (written, according to some, before the middle of the twelfth century), by occasional vigor and spirit.[3] This poetry is in that irregular Alexan-

Metres of Spanish poetry.

1 The Marquis of Santillana, early in the fifteenth century, wrote a short letter on the state of poetry in Spain to his own time. Sanchez has published this with ong and valuable notes.

2 Bouterwek's History of Spanish and Portuguese Poetry, i. 55. See also Sismondi, Littérature du Midi, iii. 228, for the romance of the Conde de Alarcos.

Sismondi refers it to the fourteenth century; but perhaps no strong reason for this could be given. I find, however, in the Cancionero General, a "romance viejo," beginning with two lines of the Conde de Alarcos, continued on another subject. It was not uncommon to build romances on the stocks of old ones, taking only the first lines: several other instances occur among those in the Cancionero, which are not numerous.

3 [This has been the opinion of Mr. Southey, and, I believe, of others. But Masdeu, Hist. Critica de España, vol. xx. p. 821, says that the greatest antiquity

drine measure, which, as has been observed, arose out of the Latin pentameter. It gave place in the fifteenth century to a dactylic measure, called *versos de arte mayor*, generally of eleven syllables, the first, fourth, seventh, and tenth being accented; but subject to frequent licenses, especially that of an additional short syllable at the beginning of the line. But the favorite metre in lyric songs and romances was the redon dilla, the type of which was a line of four trochees; requiring, however, alternately, or at the end of a certain number, one deficient in the last syllable, and consequently throwing an emphasis on the close. By this a poem was sometimes divided into short stanzas, the termination of which could not be mistaken by the ear. It is no more, where the lines of eight and seven syllables alternate, than that English metre with which we are too familiar to need an illustration. Bouterwek has supposed that this alternation, which is nothing else than the trochaic verse of Greek and Latin poetry, was preserved traditionally in Spain from the songs of the Roman soldiers; but it seems by some Arabic lines which he quotes, in common characters, that the Saracens had the line of four trochees, which, in all languages where syllables are strongly distinguished in time and emphasis, has been grateful to the ear. No one can fail to perceive the sprightliness and grace of this measure, when accompanied by simple melody. The lighter poetry of the Southern nations is always to be judged with some regard to its dependence upon a sister art. It was not written to be read, but to be heard, and to be heard in the tones of song, and with the notes of the lyre or the guitar. Music is not at all incapable of alliance with reasoning or descriptive poetry; but it excludes many forms which either might assume, and requires a rapidity, as well as intenseness of perception, which language cannot always convey. Hence the poetry designed for musical accompaniment is sometimes unfairly derided by critics, who demand what it cannot pretend to give; but it is still true, that, as it cannot give all which metrical language is able to afford, it is not poetry of the very highest class.

42. The Castilian language is rich in perfect rhymes. But, in their lighter poetry, the Spaniards frequently contented them-

which can be given to the poem of the Cid in the thirteenth century. It is ascribed, according to him, to one Pedro Abad of the church of Seville. — 1842.]

selves with *assonances;* that is, with the correspondence of final syllables, wherein the vowel alone was the same, though with different consonants, as *duro* and *humo*, *boca* and *cosa*. These were often intermingled with perfect or consonant rhymes. In themselves, unsatisfactory as they may seem at first sight to our prejudices, there can be no doubt but that the assonances contained a musical principle, and would soon give pleasure to and be required by the ear. They may be compared to the alliteration so common in the Northern poetry, and which constitutes almost the whole regularity of some of our oldest poems. But, though assonances may seem to us an indication of a rude stage of poetry, it is remarkable that they belong chiefly to the later period of Castilian lyric poetry; and that consonant rhymes, frequently with the recurrence of the same syllable, are reckoned, if I mistake not, a presumption of the antiquity of a romance.[1]

Consonant and assonant rhymes.

43. An analogy between poetry and music, extending beyond the mere laws of sound, has been ingeniously remarked by Bouterwek in a very favorite species of Spanish composition, the *glosa*. In this, a few lines, commonly well known and simple, were glossed, or paraphrased, with as much variety and originality as the poet's ingenuity could give, in a succession of stanzas, so that the leading sentiment should be preserved in each, as the subject of an air runs through its variations. It was often contrived that the chief words of the glossed lines should recur separately in the course of each stanza. The two arts being incapable of a perfect analogy, this must be taken as a general one; but it was necessary that each stanza should be conducted, so as to terminate in the lines, or a portion of them, which form the subject of the gloss.[2] Of these artificial, though doubtless, at the time, very pleasing compositions, there is nothing, as far as I know, to be found beyond the peninsula;[3] though, in a general sense, it may be said, that all lyric poetry, wherein a burthen or repetition of leading verses recurs, must originally be founded on the same principle, less artfully and musically

Nature of the glosa.

[1] Bouterwek's Introduction. Velasquez in Dieze's German translation, p. 288. The assonance is peculiar to the Spaniards. [But it is said by M. Raynouard that assonances are common in the earliest French poetry. Journal des Savans, July, 1833. — 1842.]

[2] Bouterwek, p. 118.

[3] They appear with the name Grosas in the Cancioneiro Geral of Resende; and there seems, as I have observed already, to be something much of the same kind in the older Portuguese collection of the thirteenth century.

developed. The burthen of a song can only be an impertinence, if its sentiment does not pervade the whole.

44. The Cancionero General, a collection of Spanish poetry written between the age of Juan de la Mena, near the beginning of the fifteenth century, and its publication by Castillo in 1517, contains the productions of one hundred and thirty-six poets, as Bouterwek says; and, in the edition of 1520, I have counted one hundred and thirty-nine. There is also much anonymous. The volume is in two hundred and three folios, and includes compositions by Villena, Santillana, and the other poets of the age of John II., besides those of later date. But I find also the name of Don Juan Manuel, which, if it means the celebrated author of the Conde Lucanor, must belong to the fourteenth century, though the preface of Castillo seems to confine his collection to the age of Mena.[1] A small part only are strictly love-songs (*canciones*); but the predominant sentiment of the larger portion is amatory. Several romances occur in this collection: one of them is Moorish, and perhaps older than the capture of Granada; but it was long afterwards that the Spanish romances habitually embellished their fictions with Moorish manners. These romances, as in the above instance, were sometimes glossed; the simplicity of the ancient style readily lending itself to an expansion of the sentiment. Some that are called romances contain no story; as the Rosa Fresca and the Fonte Frida, both of which will be found in Bouterwek and Sismondi.

The Cancionero General.

45. "Love-songs," says Bouterwek, "form by far the principal part of the old Spanish cancioneros. To read them regularly through would require a strong passion for compositions of this class; for the monotony of the authors is interminable. To extend and spin out a theme as long as possible, though only to seize a new modification of the old ideas and phrases, was, in their opinion, essential to the truth and sincerity of their poetic effusions of the heart. That loquacity, which is an hereditary fault of the Italian canzone, must also be endured in perusing the amatory

Bouterwek's character of Spanish songs.

[1] Don Juan Manuel, a prince descended from Ferdinand III., was the most accomplished man whom Spain produced in his age. One of the earliest specimens of Castilian prose, El Conde Lucanor, places him high in the literature of his country. It is a moral fiction, in which, according to the custom of novelists, many other tales are interwoven. "In every passage of the book," says Bouterwek, "the author shows himself a man of the world and an observer of human nature."

flights of the Spanish redondillas, while in them the Italian correctness of expression would be looked for in vain. From the desire, perhaps, of relieving their monotony by some sort of variety, the authors have indulged in even more witticisms, and plays of words, than the Italians; but they also sought to infuse a more emphatic spirit into their compositions than the latter. The Spanish poems of this class exhibit, in general, all the poverty of the compositions of the Troubadours, but blend with the simplicity of these bards the pomp of the Spanish national style in its utmost vigor. This resemblance to the Troubadour songs was not, however, produced by imitation: it arose out of the spirit of romantic love, which at that period, and for several preceding centuries, gave to the south of Europe the same feeling and taste. Since the age of Petrarch, this spirit had appeared in classical perfection in Italy. But the Spanish amatory poets of the fifteenth century had not reached an equal degree of cultivation; and the whole turn of their ideas required rather a passionate than a tender expression. The sighs of the languishing Italians became cries in Spain. Glowing passion, despair, and violent ecstasy, were the soul of the Spanish love-songs. The continually recurring picture of the contest between reason and passion is a peculiar characteristic of these songs. The Italian poets did not attach so much importance to the triumph of reason. The rigidly moral Spaniard was, however, anxious to be wise, even in the midst of his folly. But this obtrusion of wisdom in an improper place frequently gives an unpoetical harshness to the lyric poetry of Spain, in spite of all the softness of its melody." [1]

46. It was in the reign of John II., King of Castile from 1407 to 1454, that this golden age of lyric poetry commenced.[2] A season of peace and regularity, a monarchy well limited, but no longer the sport of domineering families, a virtuous king, a minister too haughty and ambitious, but able and resolute, were encouragements to that light strain of

John II.

[1] Vol. i. p. 109.

[2] Velasquez, pp. 165, 442 (in Dieze), mentions, what has escaped Bouterwek, a more ancient Cancionero than that of Castillo, compiled in the reign of John II., by Juan Alfonso de Baena, and hitherto unpublished. As it is entitled Cancionero di Poetas Antiguos, it may be supposed to contain some earlier than the year 1400. I am inclined to think, however, that few would be found to ascend much higher. I do not find the name of Don Juan Manuel, which occurs in the Cancionero of Castillo. A copy of this manuscript Cancionero of Baena was lately sold (1836) among the MSS. of Mr. Heber, and purchased for £120 by the King of the French.

amorous poetry which a state of ease alone can suffer mankind to enjoy. And Portugal, for the whole of this century, was in as flourishing a condition as Castile during this single reign. But we shall defer the mention of her lyric poetry, as it seems chiefly to be of a later date. In the court of John II. were found three men whose names stand high in the early annals of Spanish poetry, — the Marquises of Villena and Santillana, and Juan de Mena; but, except for their zeal in the cause of letters amidst the dissipations of a court, they have no pretensions to enter into competition with some of the obscure poets to whom we owe the romances of chivalry. A desire, on the contrary, to show needless learning, and to astonish the vulgar by an appearance of profundity, so often the bane of poetry, led them into prosaic and tedious details, and into affected refinements.[1]

Poets of his court.

47. Charles, Duke of Orleans, long prisoner in England after the battle of Agincourt, was the first who gave polish and elegance to French poetry. In a more enlightened age, according to Goujet's opinion, he would have been among their greatest poets.[2] Except a little allegory in the taste of his times, he confined himself to the kind of verse called *rondeaux*, and to slight amatory poems, which, if they aim at little, still deserve the praise of reaching what they aim at. The easy turns of thought and graceful simplicity of style which these compositions require came spontaneously to the Duke of Orleans. Without as much humor as Clement Marot long afterwards displayed, he is much more of a gentleman; and would have been in any times, if not quite what Goujet supposes, a great poet, yet the pride and ornament of the court.[3]

Charles, Duke of Orleans.

48. The English language was slowly refining itself, and growing into general use. That which we sometimes call pedantry and innovation, the forced introduction

English poetry.

[1] Bouterwek, p. 78.

[2] Goujet, Bibliothèque Française, ix. 233.

[3] The following very slight vaudeville will show the easy style of the Duke of Orleans. It is curious to observe how little the manner of French poetry, in such productions, has been changed since the fifteenth century.

"Petit mercier, petit panier:
Pourtant si je n'ai marchandize
Qui soit du tout à votre guise
Ne blamez pour ce mon mestier,
Je gagne denier à denier;
C'est loin du trésor de Vénise.

Petit mercier, petit panier,
Et tandis qu'il est jour, ouvrier,
Le temps perds, quand à vous devise,
Je vais parfaire mon emprise,
Et parmi les rues crier:
Petit mercier, petit panier."

(Recueil des Anciens Poètes Français, i. 196.)

of French words by Chaucer, though hardly more by him than by all his predecessors who translated our neighbors' poetry, and the harsh Latinisms that began to appear soon afterwards, has given English a copiousness and variety which perhaps no other language possesses. But, as yet, there was neither thought nor knowledge sufficient to bring out its capacities. After the death of Chaucer, in 1400, a dreary blank of long duration occurs in our annals. The poetry of Hoccleve is wretchedly bad, abounding with pedantry, and destitute of all grace or spirit.[1] Lydgate, the monk of Bury, nearly of the same age, prefers doubtless a higher claim to respect. An easy versifier, he served to make poetry familiar to the many, and may sometimes please the few. Gray, no light authority, speaks more favorably of Lydgate than either Warton or Ellis, or than the general complexion of his poetry would induce most readers to do.[2] But great poets have often the taste to discern and the candor to acknowledge those beauties which are latent amidst the tedious dulness of their humbler brethren. Lydgate, though probably a man of inferior powers of mind to Gower, has more of the minor qualities of a poet: his lines have sometimes more spirit, more humor, and he describes with more graphic minuteness. But his diffuseness becomes generally feeble and tedious; the attention fails in the schoolboy stories of Thebes and Troy; and he had not the judgment to select and compress the prose narratives from which he commonly derived his subject. It seems highly probable that Lydgate would have been a better poet in satire upon his own times, or delineation of their manners; themes which would have gratified us much more than the fate of princes. The King's Quair, by James I. of Scotland, is a long allegory, polished and imaginative, but with some of the tediousness usual in such productions. It is uncertain whether he, or a later sovereign, James V., were the author of a lively comic poem, Christ's Kirk o' the Green. The style is so provincial, that no Englishman can draw any inference as to its antiquity. It is much more removed from our language than the King's Quair. Whatever else could be mentioned as deserving of praise is anonymous and of uncertain date. It seems to have been early in the fifteenth century

Lydgate.

James I. of Scotland.

1 Warton, ii. 348.

2 Id., 361-407; Gray's Works, by Mathias, ii. 55-73. These remarks on Lydgate show what the history of English poetry would have been in the hands of Gray, as to sound and fair criticism.

that the ballad of our northern minstrels arose; but none of these that are extant could be placed with much likelihood so early as 1440.[1]

Restoration of classical learning due to Italy.

49. We have thus traced in outline the form of European literature as it existed in the middle ages and in the first forty years of the fifteenth century. The result must be to convince us of our great obligations to Italy for her renewal of classical learning. What might have been the intellectual progress of Europe, if she had never gone back to the fountains of Greek and Roman genius, it is impossible to determine: certainly nothing in the fourteenth and fifteenth centuries gave prospect of a very abundant harvest. It would be difficult to find any man of high reputation in modern times who has not reaped benefit, directly or through others, from the revival of ancient learning. We have the greatest reason to doubt, whether, without the Italians of these ages, it would ever have occurred. The trite metaphors of light and darkness, of dawn and twilight, are used carelessly by those who touch on the literature of the middle ages, and suggest by analogy an uninterrupted progression, in which learning, like the sun, has dissipated the shadows of barbarism. But, with closer attention, it is easily seen that this is not a correct representation; that, taking Europe generally, far from being in a more advanced stage of learning at the beginning of the fifteenth century than two hundred years before, she had in many respects gone backwards, and gave little sign of any tendency to recover her ground. There is, in fact, no security, as far as the past history of mankind assures us, that any nation will be uniformly progressive in science, arts, and letters; nor do I perceive, whatever may be the current language, that we can expect this with much greater confidence of the whole civilized world.

50. Before we proceed to a more minute and chronological history, let us consider for a short time some of the prevailing strains of sentiment and opinion which shaped the public mind at the close of the mediæval period.

[1] Chevy Chase seems to be the most ancient of those ballads that has been preserved. It may possibly have been written while Henry VI. was on the throne, though a late critic would bring it down to the reign of Henry VIII. Brydges' British Bibliography, iv. 97. The style is often fiery, like the old war-songs; and much above the feeble, though natural and touching, manner of the later ballads. One of the most remarkable circumstances about this celebrated lay is, that it relates a totally fictitious event with all historical particularity, and with real names. Hence it was probably not composed while many remembered the days of Henry IV., when the fray of Chevy Chase is feigned to have occurred.

51. In the early European poetry, the art sedulously cultivated by so many nations, we are struck by characteristics that distinguish it from the remains of antiquity, and belong to social changes which we should be careful to apprehend. The principles of discernment as to works of imagination and sentiment, wrought up in Greece and Rome by a fastidious and elaborate criticism, were of course effaced in the total oblivion of that literature to which they had been applied. The Latin language, no longer intelligible except to a limited class, lost that adaptation to popular sentiment which its immature progeny had not yet attained. Hence, perhaps, or from some other cause, there ensued, as has been shown in the last chapter, a kind of palsy of the inventive faculties, so that we cannot discern for several centuries any traces of their vigorous exercise.

Character of classical poetry lost.

52. Five or six new languages, however, besides the ancient German, became gradually flexible and copious enough to express thought and emotion with more precision and energy. Metre and rhyme gave poetry its form. A new European literature was springing up, fresh and lively, in gay raiment, by the side of that decrepit Latinity which rather ostentatiously wore its threadbare robes of more solemn dignity than becoming grace. But, in the beginning of the fifteenth century, the revival of ancient literature among the Italians seemed likely to change again the scene, and threatened to restore a standard of critical excellence by which the new Europe would be disadvantageously tried. It was soon felt, if not recognized in words, that what had delighted Europe for some preceding centuries depended upon sentiments fondly cherished, and opinions firmly held, but foreign, at least in the forms they presented, to the genuine spirit of antiquity. From this time we may consider as beginning to stand opposed to each other two schools of criticism, latterly called the classical and romantic; names which should not be understood as absolutely exact, but perhaps rather more apposite in the period to which these pages relate han in the nineteenth century.

New schools of criticism on modern languages.

53. War is a very common subject of fiction, and the warrior's character is that which poets have ever delighted to portray. But the spirit of chivalry, nourished by the laws of feudal tenure and limited monarchy, by the rules of honor, courtesy, and gallantry, by

Effect of chivalry on poetry.

ceremonial institutions and public shows, had rather artificially modified the generous daring which always forms the basis of that character. It must be owned, that the heroic ages of Greece furnished a source of fiction not unlike those of romance; that Perseus, Theseus, or Hercules, answer pretty well to knights-errant; and that many stories in the poets are in the very style of Amadis or Ariosto. But these form no great part of what we call classical poetry; though they show that the word, in its opposition to the latter style, must not be understood to comprise every thing that has descended from antiquity. Nothing could less resemble the peculiar form of chivalry than Greece in the republican times, or Rome in any times.

54. The popular taste had been also essentially affected by changes in social intercourse, rendering it more studiously and punctiliously courteous, and especially by the homage due to women under the modern laws of gallantry. Love, with the ancient poets, is often tender, sometimes virtuous, but never accompanied by a sense of deference or inferiority. This elevation of the female sex through the voluntary submission of the stronger, though a remarkable fact in the philosophical history of Europe, has not, perhaps, been adequately developed. It did not originate, or at least very partially, in the Teutonic manners, from which it has sometimes been derived. The love-songs again, and romances of Arabia, where others have sought its birthplace, display, no doubt, a good deal of that rapturous adoration which distinguishes the language of later poetry, and have perhaps, in some measure, been the models of the Provençal Troubadours; yet this seems rather consonant to the hyperbolical character of Oriental works of imagination, than to a state of manners where the usual lot of women is seclusion, if not slavery. The late editor of Warton has thought it sufficient to call "that reverence and adoration of the female sex, which has descended to our own times, the offspring of the Christian dispensation;"[1] but, until it can be shown that Christianity establishes any such principle, we must look a little farther down for its origin.

Effect of gallantry towards women.

55. Without rejecting, by any means, the influence of these collateral and preparatory circumstances, we might ascribe more direct efficacy to the favor shown to-

Its probable origin.

[1] Preface, p. 123.

wards women in succession to lands, through inheritance or dower, by the later Roman law, and by the customs of the Northern nations; to the respect which the clergy paid them (a subject which might bear to be more fully expanded); but, above all, to the gay idleness of the nobility, consuming the intervals of peace in festive enjoyments. In whatever country the charms of high-born beauty were first admitted to grace the banquet or give brilliancy to the tournament; in whatever country the austere restraints of jealousy were most completely laid aside; in whatever country the coarser, though often more virtuous, simplicity of unpolished ages was exchanged for winning and delicate artifices; in whatever country, through the influence of climate or polish, less boisterousness and intemperance prevailed, — it is there that we must expect to find the commencement of so great a revolution in society.

It is not shown in old Teutonic poetry, but appears in the stories of Arthur.

56. Gallantry, in this sense of a general homage to the fair, a respectful deference to woman, independent of personal attachment, seems to have first become a perceptible element of European manners in the south of France, and probably not later than the end of the tenth century:[1] it was not at all in unison with the rough habits of the Carlovingian Franks or of the Anglo-Saxons. There is little, or, as far as I know, nothing of it in the poem of Beowulf, or in that upon Attila, or in the oldest Teutonic fragments, or in the Nibelungen Lied:[2] love may appear as a natural passion, but not as a

[1] It would be absurd to assign an exact date for that which in its nature must be gradual. I have a suspicion that sexual respect, though not with all the refinements of chivalry, might be traced earlier in the south of Europe than the tenth century; but it would require a long investigation to prove this.

A passage, often quoted, of Radulphus Glaber, on the affected and effeminate manners, as he thought them, of the Southern nobility who came in the train of Constance, daughter of the Count of Toulouse, on her marriage with Robert, King of France, in 999, indicates that the roughness of the Teutonic character, as well perhaps as some of its virtues, had yielded to the arts and amusements of peace. It became a sort of proverb: Franci ad bella, Provinciales ad victualia. Eichhorn, Allg. Gesch., i. Append. 73. The social history of the tenth and eleventh centuries is not easily recovered. We must judge from probabilities founded on single passages, and on the general tone of civil history. The kingdom of Arles was more tranquil than the rest of France.

[2] "Von eigentlicher Galanterie ist in dem Nibelungen Lied wenig zu finden, von Christlichen mysticismus fast gar nichts." Bouterwek, ix. 147. I may observe, that the positions in the text, as to the absence of gallantry in the old Teutonic poetry, are borne out by every other authority; by Weber, Price, Turner, and Eichhorn. The last writer draws rather an amusing inference as to the want of politeness towards the fair sex, from the frequency of abductions in Teutonic and Scandinavian story which he enumerates. Allg. Gesch., i. 37; App., p. 37. [We might appeal also to the very curious old German poems on Hildebrand, perhaps of the

conventional idolatry. It appears, on the other hand, fully developed in the sentiments as well as the usages of Northern France, when we look at the tales of the court of Arthur, which Geoffrey of Monmouth gave to the world about 1128. Whatever may be thought of the foundation of this famous romance, whatever of legendary tradition he may have borrowed from Wales or Brittany, the position that he was merely a faithful translator appears utterly incredible.[1] Besides the numerous allusions to Henry I. of England, and to the history of his times, which Mr. Turner and others have indicated, the chivalrous gallantry, with which alone we are now concerned, is not characteristic of so rude a people as the Welsh or Armoricans. Geoffrey is almost our earliest testimony to these manners; and this gives the chief value to his fables. The crusades were probably the great means of inspiring an uniformity of conventional courtesy into the European aristocracy, which still constitutes the common character of gentlemen; but it may have been gradually wearing away their national peculiarities for some time before.

Romances of chivalry of two kinds.

57. The condition and the opinions of a people stamp a character on its literature; while that literature powerfully re-acts upon and moulds afresh the national temper from which it has taken its distinctive type. This is remarkably applicable to the romances of chivalry. Some have even believed, that chivalry itself, in the fulness of proportion ascribed to it by these works, had never existence beyond their pages; others, with more probability, that it was heightened and preserved by their influence upon a state of society which had given them birth. A considerable difference is perceived between the metrical romances, contemporaneous with, or shortly subsequent to, the crusades, and those in prose after the middle of the fourteenth century. The former are more fierce, more warlike, more full of abhorrence of infidels; they display less of punctilious courtesy, less of submissive deference to woman, less of absorbing and passionate love, less of voluptuousness and luxury; their

eighth century, published by the Grimms at Cassel in 1812. They exhibit chivalry without its gallantry. Some account of them may be found in Roquefort, p. 51; or in Bouterwek. — 1842.]

[1] See in Mr. Turner's History of England, iv. 256-269, two dissertations on the romantic histories of Turpin and of Geoffrey, wherein the relation between the two, and the motives with which each was written, seem irrefragably demonstrated.

superstition has more of interior belief, and less of ornamental machinery, than those to which Amadis de Gaul and other heroes of the later cycles of romance furnished a model. The one reflect, in a tolerably faithful mirror, the rough customs of the feudal aristocracy in their original freedom, but partially modified by the gallant and courteous bearing of France: the others represent to us, with more of licensed deviation from reality, the softened features of society, in the decline of the feudal system through the cessation of intestine war, the increase of wealth and luxury, and the silent growth of female ascendency. This last again was, no doubt, promoted by the tone given to manners through romance: the language of respect became that of gallantry; the sympathy of mankind was directed towards the success of love; and perhaps it was thought that the sacrifices which this laxity of moral opinion cost the less prudent of the fair were but the price of the homage that the whole sex obtained.

Effect of difference of religion upon poetry.

58. Nothing, however, more showed a contrast between the old and the new trains of sentiments, in points of taste, than the difference of religion. It would be untrue to say that ancient poetry is entirely wanting in exalted notions of the Deity; but they are rare in comparison with those which the Christian religion has inspired into very inferior minds, and which, with more or less purity, pervaded the vernacular poetry of Europe. They were obscured in both periods by an enormous superstructure of mythological machinery, but so different in names and associations, though not always in spirit, or even in circumstances, that those who delighted in the fables of Ovid usually scorned the Golden Legend of James de Voragine, whose pages were turned over with equal pleasure by a credulous multitude, little able to understand why any one should relish heathen stories which he did not believe. The modern mythology, if we may include in it the saints and devils, as well as the fairy and goblin armies, which had been retained in service since the days of paganism, is so much more copious, and so much more easily adapted to our ordinary associations, than the ancient, that this has given an advantage to the romantic school in their contention, which they have well known how to employ and to abuse.

59. Upon these three columns — chivalry, gallantry, and religion — repose the fictions of the middle ages, especially

those usually designated as romances. These, such as we now know them, and such as display the characteristics above mentioned, were originally metrical, and chiefly written by natives of the north of France. The English and Germans translated or imitated them. A new era of romance began with the Amadis de Gaul, derived, as some have thought, but upon insufficient evidence, from a French metrical original, but certainly written in Portugal, though in the Castilian language, by Vasco de Lobeyra, whose death is generally fixed in 1325.[1] This romance is in prose; and, though a long interval seems to have elapsed before those founded on the story of Amadis began to multiply, many were written in French during the latter part of the fourteenth and the fifteenth centuries, derived from other legends of chivalry, which became the popular reading, and superseded the old metrical romances, already somewhat obsolete in their forms of language.[2]

General tone of romance.

60. As the taste of a chivalrous aristocracy was naturally delighted with romances, that not only led the imagination through a series of adventures, but presented a mirror of sentiments to which they themselves pretended; so that of mankind in general found its gratification, sometimes in tales of home growth, or transplanted from the East, whether serious or amusing, such as the Gesta Romanorum, the Dolopathos, the Decameron (certainly the most celebrated and best written of these inventions), the Pecorone; sometimes in historical ballads or in moral fables, a favorite style of composition, especially with the Teutonic nations; sometimes again in legends of saints and the popular demonology of the age. The experience and sagacity, the moral sentiments, the invention and fancy, of many obscure centuries, may be discerned more fully and favorably in these various fictions than in their elaborate treatises. No one of the European nations stands so high in this respect as the German: their ancient tales have a raciness and truth which has been only imitated by others. Among the most renowned

Popular moral fictions.

[1] Bouterwek, History of Spanish Literature, p. 48.

[2] The oldest prose romance, which also is partly metrical, appears to be Tristan of Leonois, one of the cycle of the Round Table, written or translated by Lucas de Gast about 1170. Roquefort, Etat de la Poésie Française, p. 147. [Several romances in prose are said in Hist. Litt. de la France, xvi. 170, 177, to be older than the close of the thirteenth century. Those relating to Arthur and the Round Table are esteemed of an earlier date than such as have Charlemagne for their hero. Most of these romances in prose are taken from metrical romances. — 1842.]

of these we must place the story of Reynard the Fox, the origin of which, long sought by literary critics, recedes, as they prolong the inquiry, into greater depths of antiquity. It was supposed to be written, or at least first published, in German rhyme by Henry of Alkmaar, in 1498; but earlier editions, in the Flemish language, have since been discovered.[1] It has been found written in French verse by Jaquemars Gielée, of Lille, near the end, and in French prose by Peter of St. Cloud, near the beginning, of the thirteenth century. Finally the principal characters are mentioned in a Provençal song by Richard Cœur de Lion.[2] But though we thus bring the story to France, where it became so popular as to change the very name of the principal animal, which was always called goupil (*vulpes*) till the fourteenth century, when it assumed, from the hero of the tale, the name of Renard,[3] there seems every reason to believe that it is of German origin; and, according to a conjecture once thought probable, a certain Reinard of Lorraine, famous for his vulpine qualities in the ninth century, suggested the name to some unknown fabulist of the empire. But Raynouard, and, I believe, Grimm, have satisfactorily refuted this hypothesis.[4]

Exclusion of politics from literature.

61. These moral fictions, as well as more serious productions, in what may be called the ethical literature of the middle ages, towards which Germany contributed a large share, speak freely of the vices of the great. But they deal with them as men responsible to God, and subject to natural law, rather than as members of a community. Of political opinions, properly so called, which have in later times so powerfully swayed the conduct of mankind, we find very little to say in the fifteenth century. In so far as they were not merely founded on temporary cir-

[1] [I have been reminded that Caxton's "Historye of Reynard the Foxe," was published in 1481. — 1847.]

[2] Recueil des anciens Poètes, i. 21. M. Raynouard observes that the Troubadours, and, first of all, Richard Cœur de Lion, have quoted the story of Renard, sometimes with allusions not referable to the present romance. Journal des Sav., 1826, p. 340. A great deal has been written about this story; but I shall only quote Bouterwek, ix. 347; Heinsius, iv. 104; and the Biographie Universelle, arts. "Gielée," "Alkmaar."

[3] Something like this nearly happened in England: bears have had a narrow escape of being called only bruins, from their representative in the fable.

[4] [Journal des Savans, July, 1834. Raynouard, in reviewing a Latin poem, Reinardus Vulpis, published at Stutgard in 1832, and referred by its editor to the ninth century, shows that the allegorical meaning ascribed to the story is not in the slightest degree confirmed by real facts, or the characters of the parties supposed to be designed. The poem he places in the twelfth or thirteenth century, rather than the ninth; and there can be no doubt whatever that he is right, with any one who is conversant with the Latin versification of the two periods. — 1842.]

cumstances, or, at most, on the prejudices connected with positive institutions in each country, the predominant associations that influenced the judgment were derived from respect for birth, of which opulence was as yet rather the sign than the substitute. This had long been, and long continued to be, the characteristic prejudice of European society. It was hardly ever higher than in the fifteenth century, when heraldry, the language that speaks to the eye of pride and the science of those who despise every other, was cultivated with all its ingenious pedantry; and every improvement in useful art, every creation in inventive architecture, was made subservient to the grandeur of an elevated class in society. The burghers, in those parts of Europe which had become rich by commerce, emulated in their public distinctions, as they did ultimately in their private families, the ensigns of patrician nobility. This prevailing spirit of aristocracy was still but partially modified by the spirit of popular freedom on one hand, or of respectful loyalty on the other.

Religious opinions.

62. It is far more important to observe the disposition of the public mind in respect of religion, which not only claims to itself one great branch of literature, but exerts a powerful influence over almost every other. The greater part of literature in the middle ages, at least from the twelfth century, may be considered as artillery levelled against the clergy: I do not say against the church, which might imply a doctrinal opposition by no means universal. But if there is one theme upon which the most serious as well as the lightest, the most orthodox as the most heretical, writers are united, it is ecclesiastical corruption. Divided among themselves, the secular clergy detested the regular; the regular monks satirized the mendicant friars; who in their turn, after exposing both to the ill-will of the people, incurred a double portion of it themselves. In this most important respect, therefore, the influence of mediæval literature was powerful towards change; but it rather loosened the associations of ancient prejudice, and prepared mankind for revolutions of speculative opinion, than brought them forward.

Attacks on the church.

Three lines of religious opinion in fifteenth century.

63. It may be said, in general, that three distinct currents of religious opinion are discernible on this side of the Alps in the first part of the fifteenth century. 1. The high pretensions of the Church of Rome to a sort of moral as well as theological infallibility, and to a

paramount authority even in temporal affairs, when she should think fit to interfere with them, were maintained by a great body in the monastic and mendicant orders; and had still, probably, a considerable influence over the people in most parts of Europe. 2. The Councils of Constance and Basle, and the contentions of the Gallican and German churches against the encroachments of the holy see, had raised up a strong adverse party, supported occasionally by the government, and more uniformly by the temporal lawyers and other educated laymen. It derived, however, its greatest force from a number of sincere and earnest persons, who set themselves against the gross vices of the time, and the abuses grown up in the church through self-interest or connivance. They were disgusted also at the scholastic systems, which had turned religion into a matter of subtle dispute, while they labored to found it on devotional feeling and contemplative love. The mystical theology, which, from seeking the illuminating influence and piercing love of the Deity, often proceeded onward to visions of complete absorption in his essence, till that itself was lost, as in the East, from which this system sprang, in an annihilating pantheism, had never wanted, and can never want, its disciples. Some, of whom Bonaventura is the most conspicuous, opposed its enthusiastic emotions to the icy subtilties of the schoolmen. Some appealed to the hearts of the people in their own language. Such was Tauler, whose sermons were long popular, and have often been printed; and another was the unknown author of the German Theology, a favorite work with Luther, and known by the Latin version of Sebastian Castalio. Such, too, were Gerson and Clemangis; and such were the numerous brethren who issued from the College of Deventer.[1] One, doubtless of this class, whenever he may have lived, was author of the celebrated treatise De Imitatione Christi (a title which has been transferred from the first chapter to the entire work), commonly ascribed to Thomas von Kempen, or à Kempis, one of the Deventer Society, but the origin of which has been, and will continue to be, the subject of strenuous controversy. Besides Thomas à Kempis, two candidates have been supported by their respective partisans: John Gerson, the famous Chan-

Treatise De Imitatione Christi.

[1] Eichhorn, vi. 1-136, has amply and well treated the theological literature of the fifteenth century. Mosheim is less satisfactory, and Milner wants extent of learning; yet both will be useful to the English reader. Eichhorn seems well acquainted with the mystical divines, in p. 97 *et post.*

cellor of the University of Paris; and John Gersen, whose name appears in one manuscript, and whom some contend to have been abbot of a monastery at Vercelli in the thirteenth century; while others hold him an imaginary being, except as a misnomer of Gerson. Several French writers plead for their illustrious countryman, and especially M. Gence, one of the last who has revived the controversy; while the German and Flemish writers, to whom the Sorbonne acceded, have always contended for Thomas à Kempis; and Gersen has had the respectable support of Bellarmin, Mabillon, and most of the Benedictine order.[1] The book itself is said to have gone through

[1] I am not prepared to state the external evidence upon this keenly debated question with sufficient precision. In a few words, it may, I believe, be said, that in favor of Thomas à Kempis has been alleged the testimony of many early editions bearing his name, including one about 1471, which appears to be the first; as well as a general tradition from his own time, extending over most of Europe, which has led a great majority, including the Sorbonne itself, to determine the cause in his favor. It is also said that a manuscript of the treatise De Imitatione bears these words at the conclusion, "Finitus et completus per manum Thomæ de Kempis, 1441;" and that in this manuscript are so many erasures and alterations, as give it the appearance of his original autograph. Against Thomas à Kempis it is urged that he was a professed calligrapher or copyist for the College of Deventer; that the Chronicle of St. Agnes, a contemporary work, says of him, "Scripsit Bibliam nostram totaliter, et multos alios libros pro domo et pro pretio;" that the entry above mentioned is more like that of a transcriber than of an author; that the same chronicle makes no mention of his having written the treatise De Imitatione, nor does it appear in an early list of works ascribed to him. For Gerson are brought forward a great number of early editions in France, and still more in Italy, among which is the first that bears a date (Venice, 1483), both in the fifteenth and sixteenth centuries; and some other probabilities are alleged. But this treatise is not mentioned in a list of his writings given by himself. As to Gersen, his claim seems to rest on a manuscript of great antiquity, which ascribes it to him; and indirectly on all those manuscripts which are asserted to be older than the time of Gerson and Thomas à Kempis. But, as I have before observed, I do not profess to give a full view of the external evidence, of which I possess but a superficial knowledge.

From the book itself, two remarks, which I do not pretend to be novel, have suggested themselves to me. 1. The Gallicisms or Italicisms are very numerous, and strike the reader at once; such as "Scientia sine timore Dei quid importat?" — "Resiste in principio inclinationi tuæ" — "Vigilia serotina" — "Homo passionatus" — "Vivere cum nobis contrariantibus" — "Timoratior in cunctis actibus" — "Sufferentia crucis." It seems strange that these barbarous adaptations of French or Italian should have occurred to any one whose native language was Dutch; unless it can be shown, that through St. Bernard, or any other ascetic writer, they had become naturalized in religious style. 2. But, on the other hand, it seems impossible to resist the conviction, that the author was an inhabitant of a monastery; which was not the case with Gerson, originally a secular priest at Paris, and employed for many years in active life as chancellor of the university and one of the leaders of the Gallican Church. The whole spirit breathed by the treatise De Imitatione Christi is that of a solitary ascetic: "Vellem me pluries tacuisse et inter homines non fuisse. — Sed quare tam libenter loquimur, et invicem fabulamur, cum raro sine læsione conscientiæ ad silentium redimus. — Cella continuata dulcescit, et male custodita tædium generat. Si in principio conversionis tuæ bene eam incolueris et custodieris, erit tibi posthac dilecta, amica, et gratissimum solatium."

As the former consideration seems to exclude Thomas à Kempis, so the latter is unfavorable to the claims of Gerson. It has been observed, however, that, in one passage (l. i. c. 24), there is an apparent allusion to Dante, which, if intended, must put an end to Gersen, Abbot of Vercelli, whom his supporters place in the first part of the thirteenth century. But the allusion is not indisputable. Various articles in the Biographie Universelle, from the pen of M. Gence, maintain his favorite

eighteen hundred editions, and has probably been more read than any one work after the Scripture. 3. A third religious party consisted of the avowed or concealed heretics, some disciples of the older sectaries, some of Wicliffe or Huss, resembling the school of Gerson and Gerard Groot in their earnest piety, but drawing a more decided line of separation between themselves and the ruling power, and ripe for a more complete reformation than the others were inclined to desire. It is not possible, however, for us to pronounce on all the shades of opinion that might be secretly cherished in the fifteenth century.

Scepticism. Defences of Christianity.

64. Those of the second class were perhaps comparatively rare at this time in Italy, and those of the third much more so. But the extreme superstition of the popular creed, the conversation of Jews and Mahometans, the unbounded admiration of pagan genius and virtue, the natural tendency of many minds to doubt and to perceive difficulties, which the schoolmen were apt to find everywhere, and nowhere to solve, joined to the irreligious spirit of the Aristotelian philosophy, especially as modified by Averroes, could not but engender a secret tendency towards infidelity, the course of which may be traced with ease in the writings of those ages. Thus the tale of the three rings in Boccace, whether original or not, may be reckoned among the sports of a sceptical philosophy. But a proof, not less decisive, that the blind faith we ascribe to the middle ages was by no means universal, results from the numerous vindications of Christianity written in the fifteenth century. Eichhorn, after referring to several passages in the works of Petrarch, mentions defences of religion by Marsilius Ficinus, Alfonso de Spina (a converted Jew), Savonarola, Æneas Sylvius, Picus of Mirandola. He gives an analysis of the first, which, in its course of argument, differs little from modern apologies of the same class.[1]

hypothesis; and M. Daunou, in the Journal des Savans for 1826, and again in the volume for 1827, espouses the same cause, and even says, "Nous ne nous arrêterons point à ce qui regarde Thomas à Kempis, à qui cet ouvrage n'est plus guère attribué aujourd'hui," p. 631. But *aujourd'hui* must be interpreted rather literally, if this be correct. This is in the review of a defence of the pretensions of Gersen by M. Gregory, who adduces some strong reasons to prove that the work is older than the fourteenth century.

This book contains great beauty and heart-piercing truth in many of its detached sentences, but places its rule of life in absolute seclusion from the world, and seldom refers to the exercise of any social or even domestic duty. It has naturally been less a favorite in Protestant countries, both from its monastic character, and because those who incline towards Calvinism do not find in it the phraseology to which they are accustomed. The translations are very numerous; but there seems to be an inimitable expression in its concise and energetic though barbarous Latin.

[1] Vol. vi. p. 24.

65. These writings, though by men so considerable as most of those he has named, are very obscure at present; but the treatise of Raimond de Sebonde is somewhat better known, in consequence of the chapter in Montaigne entitled an Apology for him. Montaigne had previously translated into French the Theologia Naturalis of this Sebonde, professor of medicine at Barcelona in the early part of the fifteenth century. This has been called by some the first regular system of natural theology; but even if nothing of that kind could be found in the writings of the schoolmen, which is certainly not the case, such an appellation, notwithstanding the title, seems hardly due to Sebonde's book, which is intended, not so much to erect a fabric of religion independent of revelation, as to demonstrate the latter by proofs derived from the order of nature.

Raimond de Sebonde.

66. Dugald Stewart, in his first dissertation prefixed to the Encyclopædia Britannica, observes, that "the principal aim of Sebonde's book, according to Montaigne, is to show that Christians are in the wrong to make human reasoning the basis of their belief, since the object of it is only conceived by faith and by a special inspiration of the divine grace." I have been able to ascertain that the excellent author was misled in this passage by confiding in a translation of Montaigne, which he took in a wrong sense. Far from such being the aim of Sebonde, his book is wholly devoted to the rational proofs of religion; and what Stewart has taken for a proposition of Sebonde himself, is merely an objection, which, according to Montaigne, some were apt to make against his mode of reasoning. The passage is so very clear, that every one who looks at Montaigne (l. ii. c. 12) must instantaneously perceive the oversight which the translator, or rather Stewart, has made; or he may satisfy himself by the article on Sebonde in Bayle.[1]

His views misunderstood.

67. The object of Sebonde's book, according to himself, is to develop those truths as to God and man which are latent in nature, and through which the latter may learn every thing necessary, and especially may understand Scripture, and have an infallible certainty of its truth. This science is incorporate in all the books of the doctors of the

His real object.

1 [The translation used by Stewart may not have been that by Cotton, but one published in 1776, which professes to be original. It must be said, that, if he had been more attentive, the translation could not have misled him. —1842.]

church, as the alphabet is in their words. It is the first science, the basis of all others, and requiring no other to be previously known. The scarcity of the book will justify an extract, which, though in very uncouth Latin, will serve to give a notion of what Sebonde really aimed at; but he labors with a confused expression, arising partly from the vastness of his subject.[1]

68. Sebonde seems to have had floating in his mind, as this extract will suggest, some of those theories as to the correspondence of the moral and material world which were afterwards propounded in their cloudy magnificence by the Theosophists of the next two centuries. He undertakes to prove the Trinity from the analogy of nature. His argument is ingenious enough, if not quite of orthodox tendency; being drawn from the scale of existence, which must lead us to a being immediately derived from the First Cause. He proceeds to derive other doctrines of Christi-

Nature of his arguments.

[1] "Duo sunt libri nobis data a Deo: scilicet liber universitatis creaturarum, sive liber naturæ, et alius est liber sacræ scripturæ. Primus liber fuit datus homini a principio, dum universitas rerum fuit condita, quoniam quælibet creatura non est nisi quædam litera digito Dei scripta, et ex pluribus creaturis sicut ex pluribus literis componitur liber. Ita componitur liber creaturarum, in quo libro etiam continetur homo; et est principalior litera ipsius libri. Et sicut literæ et dictionis factæ ex literis important et includunt scientiam et diversas significationes et mirabiles sententias: ita conformiter ipsæ creaturæ simul conjunctæ et ad invicem comparatæ important et significant diversas significationes et sententias, et continent scientiam homini necessariam. Secundus autem liber scripturæ datus est homini secundo, et hoc in defectu primi libri; eo quia homo nesciebat in primo legere, qui erat cæcus; sed tamen primus liber creaturarum est omnibus communis, quia solum clerici legere sciunt in eo [i.e. secundo].

"Item primus liber, scilicet naturæ, non potest falsificari, nec deleri, neque false interpretari; ideo hæretici non possunt eum false intelligere, nec aliquis potest in eo fieri hæreticus. Sed secundus potest alsificari et falsè interpretari et male ntelligi. Attamen uterque liber est ab eodem, quia idem Dominus et creaturas condidit, et sacram Scripturam revelavit. Et ideo conveniunt ad invicem, et non contradicit unus alteri, sed tamen primus est nobis connaturalis, secundus supernaturalis. Præterea cum homo sit naturaliter rationalis, et susceptibilis disciplinæ et doctrinæ; et cum naturaliter a sua creatione nullam habeat actu doctrinam neque scientiam, sit tamen aptus ad suscipiendum eam; et cum doctrina et scientia sine libro, in quo scripta sit, non possit haberi, convenientissimum fuit, ne frustra homo esset capax doctrinæ et scientiæ, quod divina scientia, homini librum creaverit, in quo per se et sine magistro possit studere doctrinam necessariam; propterea hoc totum istum mundum visibilem sibi creavit, et dedit tanquam librum proprium et naturalem et infallibilem, Dei digito scriptum, ubi singulæ creaturæ quasi literæ sunt, non humano arbitrio sed divino juvante judicio ad demonstrandum homini sapientiam et doctrinam sibi necessariam ad salutem. Quam quidem sapientiam nullus potest videre, neque legere per se in dicto libro semper aperto, nisi fuerit a Deo illuminatus et a peccato originali mundatus. Et ideo nullus antiquorum philosophorum paganorum potest legere hanc scientiam, quia erant excæcati quantum ad propriam salutem, quamvis in dicto libro legerunt aliquam scientiam, et omnem quam habuerunt ab eodem contraxerunt; sed veram sapientiam quæ ducit ad vitam æternam, quamvis fuerat in eo scripta, legere non potuerunt.

"Ista autem scientia non est aliud, nisi cogitare et videre sapientiam scriptam in creaturis, et extrahere ipsam ab illis, et ponere in animâ, et videre significationem creaturarum. Et sic comparando ad aliam et conjungere sicut dictionem dictioni, et ex tali conjunctione resultat sententia et significatio vera, dum tamen sciat homo intelligere et cognoscere."

anity from principles of natural reason; and after this, which occupies about half a volume of 779 closely printed pages, he comes to direct proofs of revelation: first, because God, who does all for his own honor, would not suffer an impostor to persuade the world that he was equal to God, which Mahomet never pretended; and afterwards by other arguments more or less valid or ingenious.

69. We shall now adopt a closer and more chronological arrangement than before; ranging under each decennial period the circumstances of most importance in the general history of literature, as well as the principal books published within it. This course we shall pursue till the channels of learning become so various, and so extensively diffused through several kingdoms, that it will be found convenient to deviate in some measure from so strictly chronological a form, in order to consolidate better the history of different sciences, and diminish in some measure what can never wholly be removed from a work of this nature, — the confusion of perpetual change of subject.

CHAPTER III.

ON THE LITERATURE OF EUROPE FROM 1440 TO THE CLOSE OF THE FIFTEENTH CENTURY.

SECT. I. 1440–1450.

Classical Literature in Italy — Nicolas V. — Laurentius Valla.

1. THE reader is not to consider the year 1440 as a marked epoch in the annals of literature. It has sometimes been treated as such by those who have referred the inventing of printing to this particular era. But it is here chosen as an arbitrary line, nearly coincident with the complete development of an ardent thirst for classical, and especially Grecian, literature in Italy, as the year 1400 was with its first manifestation.

The year 1440 not chosen as an epoch.

2. No very conspicuous events belong to this decennial period. The spirit of improvement, already so powerfully excited in Italy, continued to produce the same effects in rescuing ancient manuscripts from the chances of destruction, accumulating them in libraries, making translations from the Greek, and, by intense labor in the perusal of the best authors, rendering both their substance and their language familiar to the Italian scholar. The patronage of Cosmo de' Medici, Alfonso King of Naples, and Nicolas of Este, has already been mentioned. Lionel, successor of the last prince, was by no means inferior to him in love of letters. But they had no patron so important as Nicolas V. (Thomas of Sarzana), who became pope in 1447; nor has any later occupant of his chair, without excepting Leo X., deserved equal praise as an encourager of learning. Nicolas founded the Vatican Library, and left it, at his death in 1455, enriched with 5,000 volumes, — a treasure far exceeding that of any other collection in Europe. Every scholar who needed maintenance (which was, of course, the

Continual progress of learning.

Nicolas V.

common case) found it at the court of Rome; innumerable benefices all over Christendom, which had fallen into the grasp of the holy see, and frequently required of their incumbents, as is well known, neither residence nor even the priestly character, affording the means of generosity, which have seldom been so laudably applied. Several Greek authors were translated into Latin by direction of Nicolas V.; among which are the history of Diodorus Siculus, and Xenophon's Cyropædia, by Poggio,[1] who still enjoyed the office of apostolical secretary, as he had under Eugenius IV., and with still more abundant munificence on the part of the pope; Herodotus and Thucydides by Valla, Polybius by Perotti, Appian by Decembrio, Strabo by Gregory of Tiferno and Guarino of Verona, Theophrastus by Gaza, Plato de Legibus, Ptolemy's Almagest, and the Præparatio Evangelica of Eusebius by George of Trebizond.[2] These translations, it has been already observed, will not bear a very severe criticism; but certainly there was an extraordinary cluster of learning round the chair of this excellent pope.

Justice due to his character.

3. Corniani remarks, that if Nicolas V., like some popes, had raised a distinguished family, many pens would have been employed to immortalize him; but, not having surrounded himself with relations, his fame has been much below his merits. Gibbon, one of the first to do full justice to Nicolas, has made a similar observation. How striking the contrast between this pope and his famous predecessor Gregory I., who, if he did not burn and destroy heathen authors, was at least anxious to discourage the reading of them! These eminent men, like Michael Angelo's figures of Night and Morning, seem to stand at the two gates of the middle ages, emblems and heralds of the mind's long sleep, and of its awakening.

4. Several little treatises by Poggio, rather in a moral than

[1] This translation of Diodorus has been ascribed by some of our writers, even since the error has been pointed out, to John Free, an Englishman, who had heard the lectures of the younger Guarini in Italy. "Quod opus," Leland observes, "Itali Poggio vanissime attribuunt Florentino." De Scriptoribus Britann., p. 462. But it bears the name of Poggio in the two editions printed in 1472 and 1493; and Leland seems to have been deceived by some one who had put Free's name on a manuscript of the translation. Poggio, indeed, in his preface, declares that he undertook it by command of Nicolas V. See Niceron, ix. 158; Zeno, Dissertazioni Vossiane, i. 41; Ginguéné, iii. 245. Pits follows Leland in ascribing a translation of Diodorus to Free, and quotes the first words: thus, if it still should be suggested that this may be a different work, there are the means of proving it.

[2] Heeren, p. 72.

political strain, display an observing and intelligent mind. Such are those on nobility, and on the unhappiness of princes. For these, which were written before 1440, the reader may have recourse to Shepherd, Corniani, or Ginguéné. A later essay, if we may so call it, on the vicissitudes of fortune, begins with rather an interesting description of the ruins of Rome. It is an enumeration of the more conspicuous remains of the ancient city; and we may infer from it, that no great devastation or injury has taken place since the fifteenth century. Gibbon has given an account of this little tract, which is not, as he shows, the earliest on the subject. Poggio, I will add, seems not to have known some things with which we are familiar, as the Cloaca Maxima, the fragments of the Servian Wall, the Mamertine Prison, the Temple of Nerva, the Giano Quadrifronte; and, by some odd misinformation, believes that the tomb of Cecilia Metella, which he had seen entire, was afterwards destroyed.[1] This leads to a conjecture that the treatise was not finished during his residence at Rome, and consequently not within the present decennium.

Poggio on the ruins of Rome.

5. In the fourth book of this treatise De Varietate Fortunæ, Poggio has introduced a remarkable narration of travels by a Venetian, Nicolo di Conti, who in 1419 had set off from his country, and, after passing many years in Persia and India, returned home in 1444. His account of those regions, in some respects the earliest on which reliance could be placed, will be found, rendered into Italian from a Portuguese version of Poggio, in the first volume of Ramusio. That editor seems not to have known that the original was in print.

Account of the East by Conti.

6. A far more considerable work by Laurentius Valla, on the graces of the Latin language, is rightly, I believe, placed within this period; but it is often difficult to determine the dates of books published before the invention of printing. Valla, like Poggio, had long earned the favor of Alfonso; but, unlike him, had forfeited that of the court of Rome. His character was very irascible and overbearing, — a fault too general with the learned of the fifteenth century: but he may, perhaps, be placed at the head of the literary republic at this time; for if inferior to Poggio, as probably he was, in vivacity and variety of genius, he was

Laurentius Valla.

[1] "Ad calcem postea majore ex parte exterminatum."

undoubtedly above him in what was then most valued and most useful, — grammatical erudition.

His attack on the court of Rome.

7. Valla began with an attack on the court of Rome in his declamation against the donation of Constantine. Some have, in consequence, reckoned him among the precursors of Protestantism; while others have imputed to the Roman see, that he was pursued with its hostility for questioning that pretended title to sovereignty. But neither of these representations is just. Valla confines himself altogether to the temporal principality of the pope; but, as to this, his language must be admitted to have been so abusive, as to render the resentment of the court of Rome not unreasonable.[1]

His treatise on the Latin language.

8. The more famous work of Valla, De Elegantiis Latinæ Linguæ, begins with too arrogant an assumption. "These books," he says, "will contain nothing that has been said by any one else. For many ages past, not only no man has been able to speak Latin, but none have understood the Latin they read: the studious of philosophy have had no comprehension of the philosophers; the advocates, of the orators; the lawyers, of the jurists; the general scholar, of any writers of antiquity." Valla, however, did at least incomparably more than any one who had preceded him; and it would probably appear, that a great part of the distinctions in Latin syntax, inflection, and synonymy, which our best grammars contain, may be traced to his work. It is to be observed, that he made free use of the ancient grammarians; so that his vaunt of originality must be referred to later times. Valla is very copious as to synonymes, on which the delicate, and even necessary, understanding of a language mainly depends. If those have done most for any science who have

[1] A few lines will suffice as a specimen: "O Romani pontifices, exemplum facinorum omnium cæteris pontificibus, et improbissimi scribæ et pharisæi, qui sedetis super cathedram Moysi, et opera Dathan et Abyron facitis, itane vestimenta apparatûs, pompa equitatûs, omnis denique vita Cæsaris, vicarium Christi decebit?" The whole tone is more like Luther's violence than what we should expect from an Italian of the fifteenth century: but it is with the ambitious spirit of aggrandizement as temporal princes that he reproaches the pontiffs; nor can it be denied that Martin and Eugenius had given provocation for his invective. "Nec amplius horrenda vox audiatur, partes contra ecclesiam; ecclesia contra Perusinos pugnat, contra Bononienses. Non contra Christianos pugnat ecclesia, sed papa." Of the papal claim to temporal sovereignty by prescription, Valla writes indignantly: "Præscripsit Romana ecclesia; o imperiti, o divini juris ignari. Nullus quantumvis annorum numerus verum abolere titulum potest. Præscripsit Romana ecclesia. Tace, nefaria lingua. Præscriptionem quæ fit de rebus mutis atque irrationalibus, ad hominem transfers; cujus quo diuturnior in servitute possessio, eo detestabilior."

carried it farthest from the point whence they set out, philology seems to owe quite as much to Valla as to any one who has come since. The treatise was received with enthusiastic admiration; continually reprinted; honored with a paraphrase by Erasmus; commented, abridged, extracted, and even turned into verse.[1]

Its defects.

9. Valla, however, self-confident and of no good temper, in censuring the language of others, fell not unfrequently into mistakes of his own. Vives and Budæus, coming in the next century, and in a riper age of philology, blame the hypercritical disposition of one who had not the means of pronouncing negatively on Latin words and phrases, from his want of sufficient dictionaries: his fastidiousness became what they call superstition, imposing captious scruples and unnecessary observances on himself and the world.[2] And, of this species of superstition, there has been much since his time in philology.

Heeren's praise of it.

10. Heeren, one of the few who have, in modern times, spoken of this work from personal knowledge and with sufficient learning, gives it a high character. "Valla was, without doubt, the best acquainted with Latin of any man in his age; yet, no pedantic Ciceronian, he had studied all the classical writers of Rome. His Elegantiæ is a work on grammar: it contains an explanation of refined turns of expression, especially where they are peculiar to Latin; displaying not only an exact knowledge of that tongue, but often also a really philosophical study of language in general. In an age when nothing was so much valued as a good Latin style, yet when the helps, of which we now possess so many, were all wanting, such a work must obtain a great success, since it relieved a necessity which every one felt."[3]

Valla's annotations on the New Testament

11. We have to give this conspicuous scholar a place in another line of criticism,—that on the text and interpretation of the New Testament. His annotations are the earliest specimen of explanations founded on

[1] Corniani, ii. 221. The editions of Valla de Elegantiis, recorded by Panzer, are twenty-eight in the fifteenth century, beginning in 1471; and thirty-one in the first thirty-six years of the next.

[2] Vives de tradendis disciplinis, i. 478 Budæus observes, "Ego Laurentium Vallensem, egregii spiritus virum, existimo sæculi sui imperitia offensum primum Latine loquendi consuetudinem constituere summa religione instituisse; deinde judicii cerimonia singulari, cum profectus quoque diligentiam æquasset, in eam superstitionem sensim delapsum esse, ut et sese ipse et alios captiosis observationibus scribendique legibus obligaret." Commentar. in Ling. Græc., p. 26 (1529). But sometimes, perhaps, Valla is right, and Budæus wrong in censuring him.

[3] P. 220.

the original language. In the course of these, he treats the Vulgate with some severity. But Valla is said to have had but a slight knowledge of Greek;[1] and it must also be owned, that, with all his merit as a Latin critic, he wrote indifferently, and with less classical spirit than his adversary Poggio. The invectives of these against each other do little honor to their memory, and are not worth recording in this volume, though they could not be omitted in a legitimate history of the Italian scholars.

SECT. II. 1450–1460.

Greeks in Italy — Invention of Printing.

12. THE capture of Constantinople in 1453 drove a few learned Greeks, who had lingered to the last amidst the crash of their ruined empire, to the hospitable and admiring Italy. Among these have been reckoned Argyropulus and Chalcondyles, successively teachers of their own language; Andronicus Callistus, who is said to have followed the same profession both there and at Rome; and Constantine Lascaris, of an imperial family, whose lessons were given for several years at Milan, and afterwards at Messina. It seems, however, to be proved that Argyropulus had been already for several years in Italy.[2]

Fresh arrival of Greeks in Italy.

13. The cultivation of Greek literature gave rise about this time to a vehement controversy, which had some influence on philosophical opinions in Italy. Gemistus Pletho, a native of the Morea, and one of those who attended the Council of Florence in 1439, being an enthusiastic votary of the Platonic theories in metaphysics and natural theology, communicated to Cosmo de' Medici part of his own zeal; and from that time the citizens of Florence formed a scheme of establishing an academy of learned men

Platonists and Aristotelians.

[1] "Annis abhinc ducentis Herodotum et Thucydidem Latinis literis exponebat Laurentius Valla, in ea bene et eleganter dicendi copia, quam totis voluminibus explicavit, inelegans tamen, et pæne barbarus, Græcis ad hoc literis leviter tinctus, ad auctorum sententias parum attentus, oscitans sæpe, et alias res agens, fidem apud eruditos decoxit." Huet de claris Interpretibus, apud Blount. Daunou, however, in the Biographie Universelle, art. "Thucydides," asserts that Valla's translation of that historian is generally faithful. This would show no inconsiderable knowledge of Greek for that age.

[2] Hody; Tiraboschi; Roscoe.

to discuss and propagate the Platonic system. This seems to have been carried into effect early in the present decennial period.

14. Meantime, a treatise by Pletho, wherein he not only extolled the Platonic philosophy, which he mingled, as was then usual, with that of the Alexandrian school, and of the spurious writings attributed to Zoroaster and Hermes, but inveighed without measure against Aristotle and his disciples, had aroused the Aristotelians of Greece, where, as in Western Europe, their master's authority had long prevailed. It seems not improbable that the Platonists were obnoxious to the orthodox party for sacrificing their own church to that of Rome; and there is also some ground for ascribing a rejection of Christianity to Pletho. The dispute, at least, began in Greece, where Pletho's treatise met with an angry opponent in Gennadius, Patriarch of Constantinople.[1] It soon spread to Italy: Theodore Gaza embracing the cause of Aristotle with temper and moderation;[2] and George of Trebizond, a far inferior man, with invectives against the Platonic philosophy and its founder. Others replied in the same tone; and, whether from ignorance or from rudeness, this controversy appears to have been managed as much with abuse of the lives and characters of two philosophers, dead nearly two thousand years, as with any rational discussion of their tenets. Both sides, however, strove to make out, what in fact was the ultimate object, that the doctrine they maintained was more consonant to the Christian religion than that of their adversaries. Cardinal Bessarion, a man of solid and elegant learning, replied to George of Trebizond in a book entitled Adversus Calumniatorem Platonis; one of the first books that appeared from the Roman press in 1470. This dispute may possibly have originated, at least in Greece, before 1450; and it was certainly continued beyond 1460, the

Their controversy.

[1] Pletho's death, in an extreme old age, is fixed by Brucker, on the authority of George of Trebizond, before the capture of Constantinople. A letter, indeed, of Bessarion, in 1462 (Mém. de l'Acad. des Inscript., vol. ii.), seems to imply that he was then living; but this cannot have been the case. Gennadius, his enemy, abdicated the patriarchate of Constantinople in 1458; having been raised to it in 1453. The public burning of Pletho's book was in the intermediate time; and it is agreed that this was done after his death.

[2] Hody, p. 79, doubts whether Gaza's vindication of Aristotle were not merely verbal, in conversation with Bessarion; which is, however, implicitly contradicted by Boivin and Tiraboschi, who assert him to have written against Pletho. The comparison of Plato and Aristotle by George of Trebizond was published at Venice in 1523, as Heeren says on the authority of Fabricius.

writings both of George and Bessarion appearing to be rather of later date.[1]

15. Bessarion himself was so far from being as unjust towards Aristotle as his opponent was towards Plato, that he translated his metaphysics. That philosopher, though almost the idol of the schoolmen, lay still in some measure under the ban of the Church, which had very gradually removed the prohibition she laid on his writings in the beginning of the thirteenth century. Nicolas V. first permitted them to be read without restriction in the universities.[2]

Marsilius Ficinus.

16. Cosmo de' Medici selected Marsilius Ficinus, as a youth of great promise, to be educated in the mysteries of Platonism, that he might become the chief and preceptor of the new academy; nor did the devotion of the young philosopher fall short of the patron's hope. Ficinus declares himself to have profited as much by the conversation of Cosmo as by the writings of Plato; but this is said in a dedication to Lorenzo, and the author has not on other occasions escaped the reproach of flattery. He began as early as 1456, at the age of twenty-three, to write on the Platonic philosophy; but, being as yet ignorant of Greek, prudently gave way to the advice of Cosmo and Landino, that he should acquire more knowledge before he imparted it to the world.[3]

Invention of printing.

17. The great glory of this decennial period is the invention of printing; or at least, as all must allow, its application to the purposes of useful learning. The reader will not expect a minute discussion of so long and unsettled a controversy as that which the origin of this art has furnished. For those who are little conversant with the subject, a very few particulars may be thought necessary.

Block-books.

18. About the end of the fourteenth century, we find a practice of taking impressions from engraved blocks of wood; sometimes for playing-cards, which were not generally used long before that time; sometimes for rude cuts of saints.[4] The latter were frequently accompanied by a few

1 The best account, and that from which later writers have freely borrowed, of this philosophical controversy, is by Boivin, in the second volume of the Memoirs of the Academy of Inscriptions, p. 15. Brucker, iv. 40; Buhle, ii. 107; and Tiraboschi, vi. 303, — are my other authorities.

2 Launoy de varia Aristotelis Fortuna in Academia Parisiensi, p. 44.

3 Brucker, iv. 50; Roscoe.

4 Heinekke and others have proved that playing-cards were known in Germany as early as 1299; but these were probably painted. Lambinet, Origines de l'Imprimerie; Singer's History of Playing-cards. The earliest cards were on parchment.

lines of letters cut in the block. Gradually entire pages were impressed in this manner; and thus began what are called block-books, printed in fixed characters, but never exceeding a very few leaves. Of these there exist nine or ten, often reprinted, as it is generally thought, between 1400 and 1440.[1] In using the word "printed," it is, of course, not intended to prejudice the question as to the real art of printing. These block-books seem to have been all executed in the Low Countries. They are said to have been followed by several editions of the short grammar of Donatus.[2] These also were printed in Holland. This mode of printing from blocks of wood has been practised in China from time immemorial.

Gutenberg and Costar's claims.

19. The invention of printing, in the modern sense, from movable letters, has been referred by most to Gutenberg, a native of Mentz, but settled at Strasburg. He is supposed to have conceived the idea before 1440, and to have spent the next ten years in making attempts at carrying it into effect; which some assert him to have done in short fugitive pieces, actually printed from his movable wooden characters before 1450. But of the existence of these there seems to be no evidence.[3] Gutenberg's priority is disputed by those who deem Lawrence Costar of Haarlem the real inventor of the art. According to a tradition, which seems not to be traced beyond the middle of the sixteenth century, but resting afterwards upon sufficient testimony to prove its local reception, Costar substituted movable for fixed letters as early as 1430; and some have believed that a book called Speculum humanæ Salvationis, of very rude wooden characters, proceeded from the Haarlem press before any other that is generally recognized.[4] The tradition adds, that an unfaithful servant, having fled with the secret, set up for himself at Strasburg or Mentz: and this treachery was originally ascribed to Gutenberg or Fust; but seems, since they have been manifestly cleared of it, to have been laid on one Gensfleisch, reputed to be the brother of Gutenberg.[5] The

[1] Lambinet; Singer; Ottley; Dibdin, &c.

[2] Lambinet.

[3] Mémoires de l'Acad. des Inscript., xvii. 762; Lambinet, p. 113.

[4] In Mr. Ottley's History of Engraving, the claims of Costar are strongly maintained, though chiefly on the authority of Meerman's proofs, which go to establish the local tradition; but the evidence of Ludovico Guicciardini is an answer to those who treat it as a forgery of Hadrian Junius. Santander, Lambinet, and most recent investigators, are for Mentz against Haarlem.

[5] Gensfleisch seems to have been the name of that branch of the Gutenberg Family to which the inventor of printing belonged. Biogr. Univ., art. "Gutenberg."

evidence, however, as to this, is highly precarious; and, even if we were to admit the claims of Costar, there seems no fair reason to dispute that Gutenberg might also have struck out an idea, which surely did not require any extraordinary ingenuity, and left the most important difficulties to be surmounted, as they undeniably were, by himself and his coadjutors.[1]

Progress of the invention.

20. It is agreed by all, that, about 1450, Gutenberg, having gone to Mentz, entered into partnership with Fust, a rich merchant of that city, for the purpose of carrying the invention into effect; and that Fust supplied him with considerable sums of money. The subsequent steps are obscure. According to a passage in the Annales Hirsargienses of Trithemius, written sixty years afterwards, but on the authority of a grandson of Peter Schæffer, their assistant in the work, it was about 1452 that the latter brought the art to perfection by devising an easier mode of casting types.[2] This passage has been interpreted, according to a lax construction, to mean, that Schæffer invented the method of casting types in a matrix; but seems more strictly to intimate, that we owe to him the great improvement in letter-casting; namely, the punches of engraved steel, by which the matrices, or moulds, are struck, and without which, independent of the economy of labor, there could be no perfect uniformity of shape. Upon the former supposition, Schæffer may be reckoned the main inventor of the art of printing; for movable wooden letters, though small books may possibly have been printed by means of them, are so inconvenient, and letters of cut metal so expensive, that few great works were likely to have passed through the press till cast types were employed. Van Praet, however, believes the Psalter of 1457 to have been printed from wooden characters; and some have conceived letters of cut metal to have been employed both in that and in the first Bible. Lambinet, who thinks "the essence of the art of printing is in the engraved punch," naturally gives the chief credit to Schæffer;[3] but this is not the more usual opinion.

[1] Lambinet, p. 315.

[2] "Petrus Opilio de Gernsheim, tunc famulus inventoris primi Joannis Fust, homo ingeniosus et prudens, faciliorem modum fundendi characteras excogitavit, et artem, ut nunc est, complevit. Lambinet, i. 101; see Daunou *contra;* Id., 417.

[3] ii. 213. In another place, he divides the praise better: "Gloire donc à Gutenberg, qui le premier, conçut l'idée de la typographie, en imaginant la mobilité des caractères, qui en est l'âme; gloire à Fust, qui en fit usage avec lui, et sans lequel nous ne jouirions peut-être pas de ce bienfait; gloire à Schæffer, à qui nous devons tout le mécanisme, et toutes les merveilles de l'art;" i. 119.

21. The earliest book, properly so called, is now generally believed to be the Latin Bible, commonly called the Mazarin Bible; a copy having been found, about the middle of the last century, in Cardinal Mazarin's library at Paris.[1] It is remarkable that its existence was unknown before: for it can hardly be called a book of very extraordinary scarcity; nearly twenty copies being in different libraries, half of them in those of private persons in England.[2] No date appears in this Bible; and some have referred its publication to 1452, or even to 1450, which few perhaps would at present maintain; while others have thought the year 1455 rather more probable.[3] In a copy belonging to the Royal Library at Paris, an entry is made, importing that it was completed in binding and illuminating at Mentz, on the Feast of the Assumption (Aug. 15), 1456. But Trithemius, in the passage above quoted, seems to intimate that no book had been printed in 1452; and considering the lapse of time that would naturally be employed in such an undertaking during the infancy of the art, and that we have no other printed book of the least importance to fill up the interval till 1457, and also that the binding and illuminating the above-mentioned copy is likely to have followed the publication at no great length of time, we may not err in placing its appearance in the year 1455, which will secure its hitherto unimpeached priority in the records of bibliography.[4]

First printed Bible.

22. It is a very striking circumstance, that the high-minded inventors of this great art tried at the very outset so bold a flight as the printing an entire Bible, and executed it with astonishing success. It was Minerva leaping on earth in her divine strength and radiant armor, ready at the moment of her nativity to subdue and destroy her enemies.

Beauty of the book.

[1] The Cologne Chronicle says, "Anno Domini 1450, qui jubilæus erat, cœptum est imprimi, primusque liber, qui excudebatur, biblia fuere Latina."

[2] Bibliotheca Sussexiana, i. 293 (1827). The number there enumerated is eighteen; nine in public and nine in private libraries; three of the former, and all the latter, English.

[3] Lambinet thinks it was probably not begun before 1453, nor published till the end of 1455; i. 130. See, on this Bible, an article by Dr. Dibdin in Valpy's Classical Journal, No. 8, which collects the testimonies of his predecessors.

[4] It is very difficult to pronounce on the methods employed in the earliest books, which are almost all controverted. This Bible is thought by Fournier, himself a letter-founder, to be printed from wooden types; by Meerman, from types cut in metal; by Heinekke and Daunou, from cast types, which is most probable. Lambinet, i. 417. Daunou does not believe that any book was printed with types cut either in wood or metal; and that, after block-books, there were none but with cast letters like those now in use, invented by Gutenberg, perfected by Schæffer, and first employed by them and Fust in the Mazarin Bible. Id., p. 423.

The Mazarin Bible is printed, some copies on vellum, some on paper of choice quality, with strong, black, and tolerably handsome characters, but with some want of uniformity; which has led, perhaps unreasonably, to a doubt whether they were cast in a matrix. We may see in imagination this venerable and splendid volume leading up the crowded myriads of its followers, and imploring, as it were, a blessing on the new art, by dedicating its first-fruits to the service of Heaven.

Early printed sheets.

23. A metrical exhortation, in the German language, to take arms against the Turks, dated in 1454, has been retrieved in the present century. If this date unequivocally refers to the time of printing, which does not seem a necessary consequence, it is the earliest loose sheet that is known to be extant. It is said to be in the type of what is called the Bamberg Bible, which we shall soon have to mention. Two editions of Letters of Indulgence from Nicolas V., bearing the date of 1454, are extant in single printed sheets, and two more editions of 1455;[1] but it has justly been observed, that, even if published before the Mazarin Bible, the printing of that great volume must have commenced long before. An almanac for the year 1457 has also been detected; and, as fugitive sheets of this kind are seldom preserved, we may justly conclude that the art of printing was not dormant, so far as these light productions are concerned. A Donatus, with Schæffer's name, but no date, may or may not be older than a Psalter published in 1457 by Fust and Schæffer (the partnership with Gutenberg having been dissolved in November, 1455, and having led to a dispute and litigation), with a colophon, or notice, subjoined in the last page, in these words:—

"Psalmorum codex venustate capitalium decoratus, rubricationibusque sufficienter distinctus, adinventione artificiosa imprimendi ac caracterizandi, absque calami ulla exaratione sic effigiatus, et ad eusebiam Dei industrie est summatus. Per Johannem Fust, civem Moguntinum, et Petrum Schæffer de Gernsheim, anno Domini millesimo ccccl vii. In vigilia Assumptionis."[2]

[1] Brunet, Supplément au Manuel du Libraire. It was not known till lately that more than one edition out of these four was in existence. Santander thinks their publication was after 1460. Dict. Bibliographique du 15me Siècle, i. 92; but this seems improbable, from the transitory character of the subject. He argues from a resemblance in the letters to those used by Fust and Schæffer in the Durandi Rationale of 1459.

[2] Dibdin's Bibliotheca Spenceriana; Biogr. Univ., Gutenberg, &c. In this edition of Donatus, the method of printing is also mentioned: "Explicit Donatus arte nova imprimendi seu caracterizandi per Petrum de Gernsheim in urbe Moguntina effigiatus." Lambinet considers this and

A colophon, substantially similar, is subjoined to several of the Fustine editions; and this seems hard to reconcile with the story that Fust sold his impressions at Paris, as late as 1463, for manuscripts.

Psalter of 1459. Other early books.

24. Another Psalter was printed by Fust and Schæffer with similar characters in 1459; and, in the same year, Durandi Rationale, a treatise on the liturgical offices of the church; of which Van Praet says that it is perhaps the earliest with cast types to which Fust and Schæffer have given their name and a date.[1] The two Psalters he conceives to have been printed from wood; but this would be disputed by other eminent judges.[2] In 1460, a work of considerable size, the Catholicon of Balbi, came out from an opposition press established at Mentz by Gutenberg. The Clementine Constitutions, part of the canon law, were also printed by him in the same year.

Bible of Pfister.

25. These are the only monuments of early typography acknowledged to come within the present decennium. A Bible without a date, supposed by most to have been printed by Pfister at Bamberg, though ascribed by others to Gutenberg himself, is reckoned by good judges certainly prior to 1462, and perhaps as early as 1460. Daunou and others refer it to 1461. The antiquities of typography, after all the pains bestowed upon them, are not unlikely to receive still further elucidation in the course of time.

Greek first taught at Paris.

26. On the 19th of January, 1458, as Crevier, with a minuteness becoming the subject, informs us, the University of Paris received a petition from Gregory, a native of Tiferno in the kingdom of Naples, to be appointed teacher of Greek. His request was granted, and a salary of one hundred crowns assigned to him, on condition that he should teach gratuitously, and deliver two lectures every day, — one on the Greek language, and the other on the art of rhetoric.[3] From this auspicious circumstance, Crevier deduces the restoration of ancient literature in the University of Paris, and consequently in the kingdom of France. For above two hundred years, the scholastic logic and philosophy

the Bible to be the first specimens of typography; for he doubts the Literæ Indulgentiarum, though probably with no cause.

[1] Lambinet, i. 154.

[2] Lambinet, Dibdin. The former thinks the inequality of letters observed in the Psalter of 1457 may proceed from their being cast in a matrix of plaster or clay, instead of metal.

[3] Crevier, Hist. de l'Univ. de Paris, iv. 243.

had crushed polite letters. No mention is made of rhetoric — that is, of the art that instructs in the ornaments of style — in any statute or record of the university since the beginning of the thirteenth century. If the Greek language, as Crevier supposes, had not been wholly neglected, it was at least so little studied, that entire neglect would have been practically the same.

Leave unwillingly granted.

27. This concession was, perhaps, unwillingly made; and, as frequently happens in established institutions, it left the prejudices of the ruling party rather stronger than before. The teachers of Greek and rhetoric were specially excluded from the privileges of regency by the faculty of arts. These branches of knowledge were looked upon as unessential appendages to a good education; but a bigoted adherence to old systems, and a lurking reluctance that the rising youth should become superior in knowledge to ourselves, were no peculiar evil spirits that haunted the University of Paris, though none ever stood more in need of a thorough exorcism. For many years after this time, the Greek and Latin languages were thus taught by permission, and with very indifferent success.

Purbach: his mathematical discoveries.

28. Purbach, or Peurbach, native of a small Austrian town of that name, has been called the first restorer of mathematical science in Europe. Ignorant of Greek, and possessing only a bad translation of Ptolemy, lately made by George of Trebizond,[1] he yet was able to explain the rules of physical astronomy, and the theory of the planetary motions, far better than his predecessors. But his chief merit was in the construction of trigonometrical tables. The Greeks had introduced the sexagesimal division not only of the circle, but of the radius; and calculated chords according to this scale. The Arabians, who, about the ninth century, first substituted the sine, or half-chord of the double arch, in their tables, preserved the same graduation. Purbach made one step towards a decimal scale, which the new notation by Arabic numerals rendered highly convenient, by dividing the radius, or sinus totus, as it was then often called, into 600,000 parts, and gave rules for computing the sines of arcs; which

[1] Montucla, Biogr. Univ. It is, however, certain, and is admitted by Delambre, the author of this article in the Biogr. Univ., that Purbach made considerable progress in abridging and explaining the text of this translation; which, if ignorant of the original, he must have done by his mathematical knowledge. Kästner, ii. 521.

he himself also calculated for every minute of the quadrant, as Delambre and Kästner think, or for every ten minutes, according to Gassendi and Hutton, in parts of this radius. The tables of Albaten, the Arabian geometer, — the inventor, as far as appears, of sines, — had extended only to quarters of a degree.[1]

29. Purbach died young, in 1461, when, by the advice of Cardinal Bessarion, he was on the point of setting out for Italy in order to learn Greek. His mantle descended on Regiomontanus, a disciple, who went beyond his master, though he has sometimes borne away his due credit. A mathematician rather earlier than Purbach was Nicolas Cusanus, raised to the dignity of cardinal in 1448. He was by birth a German, and obtained a considerable reputation for several kinds of knowledge.[2] But he was chiefly distinguished for the tenet of the earth's motion; which, however, according to Montucla, he proposed only as an ingenious hypothesis. Fioravanti, of Bologna, is said, on contemporary authority, to have removed, in 1455, a tower with its foundation to a distance of several feet; and to have restored to the perpendicular, one at Cento, seventy-five feet high, which had swerved five feet.[3]

Other mathematicians.

SECT. III. 1460–1470.

Progress of Art of Printing — Learning in Italy and rest of Europe.

30. THE progress of that most important invention, which illustrated the preceding ten years, is the chief subject of our consideration in the present. Many books, it is to be observed, even of the superior class, were printed, especially in the first thirty years after the invention of the art, without date of time or place; and this was,

Progress of printing in Germany.

[1] Montucla, Hist. des Mathématiques, i. 539. Hutton's Mathematical Dictionary, and his Introduction to Logarithms. Gassendi, Vita Purbachii. Biogr. Univ.: Peurbach (by Delambre). Kästner, Geschichte der Mathematik, i. 529-543, 572; ii. 319. Gassendi twice gives 6,000,000 for the parts of Purbach's radius. None of these writers seem comparable in accuracy to Kästner.

[2] A work upon statics, or rather upon the weight of bodies in water, by Cusanus, seems chiefly remarkable, as it shows both a disposition to ascertain physical truths by experiment, and an extraordinary misapprehension of the results. See Kästner, ii. 122. It is published in an edition of Vitruvius, Strasburg, 1550.

[3] Tiraboschi; Montucla, Biogr. Univ.

of course, more frequently the case with smaller or fugitive pieces. A catalogue, therefore, of books that can be certainly referred to any particular period, must always be very defective. A collection of fables in German was printed at Bamberg in 1461; and another book in 1462, by Pfister, at the same place.[1] The Bible which bears his name has been already mentioned. In 1462, Fust published a Bible, commonly called the Mentz Bible, and which passed for the earliest till that in the Mazarin Library came to light. But in the same year, the city having been taken by Adolphus, Count of Nassau, the press of Fust was broken up; and his workmen, whom he had bound by an oath to secrecy, dispersed themselves into different quarters. Released thus, as they seem to have thought, from their obligation, they exercised their skill in other places. It is certain that the art of printing, soon after this, spread into the towns near the Rhine: not only Bamberg, as before mentioned, but Cologne, Strasburg, Augsburg, and one or two more places, sent forth books before the conclusion of these ten years. Nor was Mentz altogether idle after the confusion occasioned by political events had abated. Yet the whole number of books printed with dates of time and place, in the German Empire, from 1461 to 1470, according to Panzer, was only twenty-four; of which five were Latin, and two German, Bibles. The only known classical works are two editions of Cicero de Officiis, at Mentz, in 1465 and 1466, and another about the latter year at Cologne, by Ulric Zell; perhaps, too, the treatise de Finibus, and that de Senectute, at the same place. There is also reason to suspect that a Virgil, a Valerius Maximus, and a Terence, printed by Mentelin at Strasburg, without a date, are as old as 1470; and the same has been thought of one or two editions of Ovid de Arte Amandi, by Zell of Cologne. One book, Joannis de Turrecremata Explanatio in Psalterium, was printed by Zainer at Cracow in 1465. This is remarkable, as we have no evidence of the Polish press from that time till 1500. Several copies of this book are said to exist in Poland; yet doubts of its authenticity have been entertained. Zainer settled soon afterwards at Augsburg.[2]

31. It was in 1469 that Ulrick Gering, with two more who had been employed as pressmen by Fust at Mentz, were in-

[1] Lambinet.

[2] Panzer, Annales Typographici. Biographie Universelle: Zainer

duced by Fichet and Lapierre, rectors of the Sorbonne, to come to Paris, where several books were printed in 1470 and 1471. The epistles of Gasparin of Barziza appear, by some verses subjoined, to have been the earliest among these.[1] Panzer has increased to eighteen the list of books printed there before the close of 1472.[2]

Introduced into France

32. But there seem to be unquestionable proofs that a still earlier specimen of typography is due to an English printer, the famous Caxton. His Recueil des Histoires de Troye appears to have been printed during the life of Philip, Duke of Burgundy; and consequently before June 15, 1467. The place of publication, certainly within the duke's dominions, has not been conjectured. It is therefore, by several years, the earliest printed book in the French language.[3] A Latin speech by Russell, ambassador of Edward IV. to Charles of Burgundy in 1469, is the next publication of Caxton. This was also printed in the Low Countries.[4]

Caxton's first works.

33. A more splendid scene was revealed in Italy. Sweynheim and Pannartz, two workmen of Fust, set up a press, doubtless with encouragement and patronage, at the Monastery of Subiaco in the Apennines, — a place chosen either on account of the numerous manuscripts it contained, or because the monks were of the German nation; and hence an edition of Lactantius issued in October, 1465, which one, no longer extant, of Donatus's little grammars is said to have preceded. An edition of Cicero de Officiis, without a date, is referred by some to the year 1466. In 1467, after printing Augustin de Civitate Dei, and Cicero de Oratore, the two Germans left Subiaco for Rome, where they sent forth not less than twenty-three editions of ancient Latin authors before the close of 1470. Another German, John of Spire, established a press at Venice in 1469, beginning with Cicero's Epistles. In that and the next year, almost as many classical works were printed at Venice as at Rome, either by John and his brother Vindelin, or by a Frenchman, Nicolas

Printing exercised in Italy.

1 The last four of these lines are the following: —

"Primos ecce libros quos hæc industria finxit
Francorum in terris, ædibus atque tuis.
Michael, Udalricus, Martinusque magistri
Hos impresserunt, et facient alios."

2 See Gresswell's Early Parisian Press.

3 [I am obliged to a correspondent for reminding me that the Recueil des Histoires de Troye, though printed, and afterwards translated, by Caxton, was written by Raoul le Fevre. — 1847.]

4 Dibdin's Typographical Antiquities This is not noticed in the Biographie Universelle, nor in Brunet; an omission hardly excusable.

Jenson. Instances are said to exist of books printed by unknown persons at Milan in 1469; and in 1470, Zarot, a German, opened there a fertile source of typography, though but two Latin authors were published that year. An edition of Cicero's Epistles appeared also in the little town of Foligno. The whole number of books that had issued from the press in Italy, at the close of that year, amounts, according to Panzer, to eighty-two, exclusive of those which have no date, some of which may be referable to this period.

Lorenzo de' Medici.

34. Cosmo de' Medici died in 1464. But the happy impulse he had given to the restoration of letters was not suspended; and, in the last year of the present decade, his wealth and his influence over the republic of Florence had devolved on a still more conspicuous character, his grandson Lorenzo, himself worthy by his literary merits to have done honor to any patron, had not a more prosperous fortune called him to become one.

Italian poetry of fifteenth century.

35. The epoch of Lorenzo's accession to power is distinguished by a circumstance hardly less honorable than the restoration of classical learning,—the revival of native genius in poetry after the slumber of near a hundred years. After the death of Petrarch, many wrote verses, but none excelled in the art; though Muratori has praised the poetry down to 1400, especially that of Giusto di Conti, whom he does not hesitate to place among the first poets of Italy.[1] But that of the fifteenth century is abandoned by all critics as rude, feeble, and ill expressed. The historians of literature scarcely deign to mention a few names, or the editors of selections to extract a few sonnets. The romances of chivalry in rhyme, Buovo d'Antona, la Spagna, l'Ancroja, are only deserving to be remembered as they led in some measure to the great poems of Boiardo and Ariosto. In themselves they are mean and prosaic. It is vain to seek a general cause for this sterility in the cultivation of Latin and Greek literature, which we know did not obstruct the brilliancy of Italian poetry in the next age. There is only one cause for the want of great men in any period: Nature does not think fit to produce them. They are no creatures of education and circumstance.

36. The Italian prose literature of this interval, from the

[1] Muratori della perfetta Poesia, p. 193; Bouterwek, Gesch. der Ital. Poesie, i. 216.

age of Petrarch, would be comprised in a few volumes. Some historical memoirs may be found in Muratori; but far the chief part of his collection is in Latin. Leonard Aretin wrote lives of Dante and Petrarch in Italian, which, according to Corniani, are neither valuable for their information nor for their style. The Vita Civile of Palmieri seems to have been written some time after the middle of the fifteenth century; but of this Corniani says, that having wished to give a specimen, on account of the rarity of Italian in that age, he had abandoned his intention, finding that it was hardly possible to read two sentences in the Vita Civile without meeting some barbarism or incorrectness. The novelists Sacchetti and Ser Giovanni, author of the Pecorone, who belong to the end of the fourteenth century, are read by some: their style is familiar and idiomatic; but Crescimbeni praises that of the former. Corniani bestows some praise on Passavanti and Pandolfini: the first a religious writer, not much later than Boccaccio; the latter a noble Florentine, author of a moral dialogue in the beginning of the fifteenth century. Filelfo, among his voluminous productions, has an Italian commentary on Petrarch, of which Corniani speaks very slightingly. The commentary of Landino on Dante is much better esteemed; but it was not published till 1481.

Italian prose of same age.

37. It was on occasion of a tournament, wherein Lorenzo himself and his brother Julian had appeared in the lists, that poems were composed by Luigi Pulci, and by Politian, then a youth, or rather a boy; the latter of which displayed more harmony, spirit, and imagination than any that had been written since the death of Petrarch.[1] It might thus be seen that there was no real incompatibility between the pursuits of ancient literature and the popular language of fancy and sentiment; and that, if one gave chastity and elegance of style, a more lively and natural expression of the mind could best be attained by the other.

Giostra of Politian.

38. This period was not equally fortunate for the learned

[1] Extracts from this poem will be found n Roscoe's Lorenzo; and in Sismondi, Littérature du Midi, ii. 43, who praises it highly, as the Italian critics have done, and as, by the passages quoted, it seems well to deserve. Roscoe supposes Politian to be only fourteen years old when he wrote the Giostra di Giuliano. But the lines he quotes allude to Lorenzo as chief of the republic; which could not be said before the death of Pietro in December, 1469. If he wrote them at sixteen, it is extraordinary enough; but these two years make an immense difference. Ginguéné is of opinion that they do not allude to the tournament of 1468, but to one in 1473.

in other parts of Italy. Ferdinand of Naples, who came to the throne in 1458, proved no adequate representative of his father Alfonso. But at Rome they encountered a serious calamity. A few zealous scholars, such as Pomponius Lætus, Platina, Callimachus Experiens, formed an academy in order to converse together on subjects of learning, and communicate to each other the results of their private studies. Dictionaries, indexes, and all works of compilation, being very deficient, this was the best substitute for the labor of perusing the whole body of Latin antiquity. They took Roman names,—an innocent folly, long after practised in Europe. The pope, however, Paul II., thought fit, in 1468, to arrest all this society on charges of conspiracy against his life, for which there was certainly no foundation; and of setting up Pagan superstitions against Christianity, of which, in this instance, there seems to have been no proof. They were put to the torture, and kept in prison a twelvemonth; when the tyrant, who is said to have vowed this in his first rage, set them all at liberty: but it was long before the Roman academy recovered any degree of vigor.[1]

Paul II. persecutes the learned.

39. We do not discover as yet much substantial encouragement to literature in any country on this side the Alps, with the exception of one where it was least to be anticipated. Mathias Corvinus, King of Hungary, from his accession in 1458 to his death in 1490, endeavored to collect round himself the learned of Italy, and to strike light into the midst of the depths of darkness that encompassed his country. He determined, therefore, to erect an university, which, by the original plan, was to have been in a distinct city; but the Turkish wars compelled him to fix it at Buda. He availed himself of the dispersion of libraries after the capture of Constantinople to purchase Greek manuscripts; and employed four transcribers at Florence, besides thirty at Buda, to enrich his collection. Thus, at his death, it is said that the Royal Library at Buda contained 50,000 volumes,—a number that appears wholly incredible.[2]

Mathias Corvinus.

His library.

[1] Tiraboschi, vi. 93; Ginguéné; Brucker, Corniani, ii. 280. This writer, inferior to none in his acquaintance with the literature of the fifteenth century, but, though not an ecclesiastic, always favorable to the court of Rome, seems to strive to lay the blame on the imprudence of Platina.

[2] The library collected by Nicolas V. contained only 5,000 manuscripts. The volumes printed in Europe before the death of Corvinus would probably be reckoned highly at 15,000. Heeren suspects the number 50,000 to be hyperbolical; and, in fact, there can be no doubt of it

Three hundred ancient statues are reported to have been placed in the same repository; but, when the city fell into the hands of the Turks in 1527, these noble treasures were dispersed, and in great measure destroyed. Though the number of books, as is just observed, must have been exaggerated, it is possible that neither the burning of the Alexandrian Library by Omar, if it ever occurred, nor any other single calamity recorded in history, except the two captures of Constantinople itself, has been more fatally injurious to literature; and, with due regard to the good intentions of Mathias Corvinus, it is deeply to be regretted that the inestimable relics once rescued from the barbarian Ottomans should have been accumulated in a situation of so little security against their devastating arms.[1]

Slight signs of literature in England.

40. England under Edward IV. presents an appearance, in the annals of publication, about as barren as under Edward the Confessor. There is, I think, neither in Latin nor in English a single book that we can refer to this decennial period.[2] Yet we find a few symptoms, not to be overlooked, of the incipient regard to literature. Leland enumerates some Englishmen who travelled to Italy, perhaps before 1460, in order to become disciples of the younger Guarini at Ferrara,—Robert Fleming, William Gray, Bishop of Ely, John Free, John Gunthorpe, and a very accomplished nobleman, John Tiptoft, Earl of Worcester. It is but fairness to give credit to these men for their love of learning, and to observe that they preceded any whom we could mention on sure grounds either in France or Germany. We trace, however, no distinct fruits from their acquisitions. But, though very few had the means of attaining that on which we set a high value in literature, the mere rudiments of grammatical learning were communicated to many. Nor were munificent patrons, testators, in the words of Burke, to a posterity which they embraced as their own, wanting in this latter period of the middle ages. William of

[1] Brucker; Roscoe; Gibbon. Heeren, p. 173, who refers to several modern books expressly relating to the fate of this library. Part of it, however, found its way to that of Vienna.

[2] The University of Oxford, according to Wood, as well as the church generally, stood very low about this time: the grammar-schools were laid aside; degrees were conferred on undeserving persons for money. A. D. 1455, 1466. He had previously mentioned those schools as kept up in the university under the superintendence of masters of arts. A. D. 1442. But the statutes of Magdalen College, founded in the reign of Edward, provide for a certain degree of learning. Chandler's Life of Waynflete, p. 200.

Wykeham, Chancellor of England under Richard II., and Bishop of Winchester, founded a school in that city, and a college at Oxford in connection with it, in 1373.[1] Henry VI., in imitation of him, became the founder of Eton School, and of King's College, Cambridge, about 1442.[2] In each of these schools seventy boys, and in each college seventy fellows and scholars, are maintained by these princely endowments. It is unnecessary to observe, that they are still the amplest, as they are much the earliest, foundations for the support of grammatical learning in England. What could be taught in these or any other schools at this time, the reader has been enabled to judge: it must have been the Latin language, through indifferent books of grammar, and with the perusal of very few heathen writers of antiquity. In the curious and unique collection of the Paston Letters, we find one from a boy at Eton in 1468, wherein he gives two Latin verses, not very good, of his own composition.[3] I am sensible that the mention of such a circumstance may appear trifling, especially to foreigners: but it is not a trifle to illustrate by any fact the gradual progress of knowledge among the laity, — first in the mere elements of reading and writing, as we did in a former chapter; and now, in the fifteenth century, in such grammatical instruction as could be imparted. This boy of the Paston Family was well born, and came from a distance; nor was he in training for the church, since he seems by this letter to have had marriage in contemplation.

Paston Letters. 41. But the Paston Letters are, in other respects, an important testimony to the progressive condition of society, and come in as a precious link in the chain of the moral history of England, which they alone in this period supply. They stand indeed singly, as far as I know, in Europe; for though it is highly probable that in the archives of Italian families, if not in France or Germany, a series of merely private letters equally ancient may be concealed, I do not recollect that any have been published. They are all written in the reigns of Henry VI. and Edward IV., except

[1] Lowth's Life of Wykeham. He permits in his statutes a limited number of sons of gentlemen (*gentilium*) to be educated in his school. Chandler's Life of Waynflete, p. 5.

[2] Waynflete became the first head-master of Eton in 1442. Chandler, p. 26.

[3] Vol. i. p. 301. Of William Paston, author of these lines, it is said, some years before, that he had "gone to school to a Lombard, called Karol Giles, to learn and to be read in poetry, or else in French. He said that he would be as glad and as fain of a good book of French or of poetry as my master Falstaff would be to pur chase a fair manor." P. 173 (1459).

a few as late as Henry VII., by different members of a wealthy and respectable but not noble family, and are therefore pictures of the life of the English gentry in that age.[1] We are merely concerned with their evidence as to the state of literature; and this, upon the whole, is more favorable, than, from the want of authorship in those reigns, we should be led to anticipate. It is plain that several members of the family, male and female, wrote not only grammatically, but with a fluency and facility, an epistolary expertness, which implies the habitual use of the pen. Their expression is much less formal and quaint than that of modern novelists, when they endeavor to feign the familiar style of ages much later than the fifteenth century. Some of them mix Latin with their English, very bad, and probably for the sake of concealment; and Ovid is once mentioned as a book to be sent from one to another.[2] It appears highly probable, that such a series of letters, with so much vivacity and pertinence, would not have been written by any family of English gentry in the reign of Richard II., and much less before. It is hard to judge from a single case; but the letter of Lady Pelham, quoted in the first chapter of this volume, is ungrammatical and unintelligible. The seed, therefore, was now rapidly germinating beneath the ground; and thus we may perceive that the publication of books is not the sole test of the intellectual advance of a people. I may add, that, although the middle of the fifteenth century was the period in which the fewest books were written, a greater number, in the opinion of experienced judges, were transcribed in that than in any former age; a circumstance easily accounted for by the increased use of linen paper.

Low condition of public libraries.

42. It may be observed here, with reference to the state of learning generally in England down to the age immediately preceding the Reformation, that Leland, in the fourth volume of his Collectanea, has given several lists of books in colleges and monasteries,

[1] This collection is in five quarto volumes, and has become scarce. The length has been doubled by an injudicious proceeding of the editor in printing the original orthography and abbreviations of the letters on each left-hand page, and a more legible modern form on the right. As orthography is of little importance, and abbreviations of none at all, it would have been sufficient to have given a single specimen.

[2] "As to Ovid de Arte Amandi, I shall send him you next week; for I have him not now ready;" iv. 175. This was between 1463 and 1469, according to the editor. We do not know positively of any edition of Ovid de Arte Amandi so early; but Zell of Cologne is supposed to have printed one before 1470, as has been mentioned above. Whether the book to be sent were in print or manuscript must be left to the sagacity of critics.

which do not by any means warrant the supposition of a tolerable acquaintance with ancient literature. We find, however, some of the recent translations made in Italy from Greek authors. The clergy, in fact, were now retrograding, while the laity were advancing; and, when this was the case, the ascendency of the former was near its end.

43. I have said that there was not a new book written within these ten years. In the days of our fathers, it would have been necessary, at least, to mention as a forgery the celebrated poems attributed to Thomas Rowley. But probably no one person living believes in their authenticity; nor should I have alluded to so palpable a fabrication at all, but for the curious circumstance, that a very similar trial of literary credulity has not long since been essayed in France. A gentleman of the name of Surville published a collection of poems, alleged to have been written by Clotilde de Surville, a poetess of the fifteenth century. The muse of the Ardèche warbled her notes during a longer life than the monk of Bristow; and, having sung the relief of Orleans by the Maid of Arc in 1429, lived to pour her swan-like chant on the battle of Fornova in 1495. Love, however, as much as war, is her theme; and it was a remarkable felicity, that she rendered an ode of her prototype Sappho into French verse, many years before any one else in France could have seen it. But having, like Rowley, anticipated too much the style and sentiments of a later period, she has, like him, fallen into the numerous ranks of the dead who never were alive.[1]

Rowley.

Clotilde de Surville.

[1] Auguis, Recueil des Poëtes, vol. ii. Biogr. Univ.: Surville; Villemain, Cours de Littérature, vol. ii.; Sismondi, Hist. des Français, xiii. 593. The forgery is by no means so gross as that of Chatterton; but, as M. Sismondi says, "We have only to compare Clotilde with the Duke of Orleans or Villon." The following lines, quoted by him, will give the reader a fair specimen:—

"Suivons l'amour, tel en soit le danger;
Cy nous attend sur lits charmans de mousse.
A des rigueurs; qui voudroit s'en venger?
Qui (même alors que tout désir s'émousse)
Au prix fatal de ne plus y songer?
Règne sur moi, cher tyran, dont les armes
Ne me sauroient porter coups trop puissans!
Pour m'épargner n'en crois onc à mes larmes;
Sont de plaisir, tant plus auront de charmes
Tes dards aigus, que seront plus cuisans."

It has been justly remarked, that the extracts from Clotilde, in the Recueil des anciens Poëtes, occupy too much space, while the genuine writers of the fifteenth century appear in very scanty specimens.

SECT. IV. 1471–1480.

The same Subjects continued — Lorenzo de' Medici — Physical Controversy — Mathematical Sciences.

44. THE books printed in Italy during these ten years amount, according to Panzer, to 1297; of which, 234 are editions of ancient classical authors. Books without date are of course not included; and the list must not be reckoned complete as to others.

Number of books printed in Italy.

45. A press was established at Florence by Lorenzo, in which Cennini, a goldsmith, was employed; the first printer, except Caxton and Jenson, who was not a German. Virgil was published in 1471. Several other Italian cities began to print in this period. The first edition of Dante issued from Foligno in 1472: it has been improbably, as well as erroneously, referred to Mentz. Petrarch had been published in 1470, and Boccace in 1471. They were reprinted several times before the close of this decade.

46. No one had attempted to cast Greek types in sufficient number for an entire book, though a few occur in the early publications by Sweynheim and Pannartz;[1] while, in those printed afterwards at Venice, Greek words are inserted by the pen; till, in 1476, Zarot of Milan had the honor of giving the Greek grammar of Constantine Lascaris to the world.[2] This was followed in 1480 by Craston's Lexicon, a very imperfect vocabulary; but which, for many years, continued to be the only assistance of the kind to which a student could have recourse. The author was an Italian.

First Greek printed.

47. Ancient learning is to be divided into two great departments: the knowledge of what is contained in the works of Greek and Roman authors; and that of

Study of antiquities.

[1] Greek types first appear in a treatise of Jerome, printed at Rome in 1468. Heeren, from Panzer.

[2] Lascaris Grammatica Græca, Mediolani ex recognitione Demetrii Cretensis per Dionysium Paravisinum, 4to. The characters in this rare volume are elegant and of a moderate size. The earliest specimens of Greek printing consist of detached passages and citations, found in a very few of the first printed copies of Latin authors: such as Lactantius of 1465: the Aulus Gellius and Apuleius of Sweynheim and Pannartz, 1469; and some works of Bessarion about the same time. In all these, it is remarkable that the Greek typography is legibly and creditably executed; whereas the Greek introduced into the Officia et Paradoxa of Cicero, Milan, 1474, by Zarot, is so deformed as to be scarcely legible. I am indebted for the whole of this note to Gresswell's Early Parisian Greek Press, i. 1

the *matériel*, if I may use the word, which has been preserved in a bodily shape, and is sometimes known by the name of antiquities. Such are buildings, monuments, inscriptions, coins, medals, vases, instruments, which, by gradual accumulation, have thrown a powerful light upon ancient history and literature. The abundant riches of Italy in these remains could not be overlooked as soon as the spirit of admiration for all that was Roman began to be kindled. Petrarch himself formed a little collection of coins; and his contemporary Pastrengo was the first who copied inscriptions; but, in the early part of the fifteenth century, her scholars and her patrons of letters began to collect the scattered relics which almost every region presented to them.[1] Niccolo Niccolì, according to the funeral oration of Poggio, possessed a series of medals, and even wrote a treatise in Italian, correcting the common orthography of Latin words, on the authority of inscriptions and coins. The love of collection increased from this time. The Medici and other rich patrons of letters spared no expense in accumulating these treasures of the antiquary. Ciriacus of Ancona, about 1440, travelled into the East in order to copy inscriptions: but he was naturally exposed to deceive himself and to be deceived; nor has he escaped the suspicion of imposture, or at least of excessive credulity.[2]

Works on that subject.

48. The first who made his researches of this kind collectively known to the world was Biondo Flavio, or Flavio Biondo, — for the names may be found in a different order, but more correctly in the first,[3] — secretary to Eugenius IV. and to his successors. His long residence at Rome inspired him with the desire, and gave him the opportunity, of describing her imperial ruins. In a work dedicated to Eugenius IV., who died in 1447, but not printed till 1471, entitled Romæ Instauratæ libri tres, he describes, examines, and explains, by the testimonies of ancient authors, the numerous monuments of Rome. In another, Romæ Triumphantis libri decem, printed about 1472, he treats of the government,

[1] Tiraboschi, vols. v. and vi.; Andrès, ix. 196.

[2] Tiraboschi; Andrès, ix. 199. Ciriaco has not wanted advocates: some of the inscriptions he was accused of having forged have turned out to be authentic; and it is presumed in his favor that others which do not appear may have perished since his time. Biogr. Univ.: Cyriaque. One that rests on his authority is that which is supposed to record the persecution of the Christians in Spain under Nero. See Lardner's Jewish and Heathen Testimonies, vol. i.; who, though by no means a credulous critic, inclines to its genuineness.

[3] Zeno, Dissertazioni Vossiane, i. 229

laws, religion, ceremonies, military discipline, and other antiquities, of the republic. A third work, compiled at the request of Alfonso, King of Naples, and printed in 1474, called Italia Illustrata, contains a description of all Italy, divided into its ancient fourteen regions. Though Biondo Flavio was almost the first to hew his way into the rock, which should cause his memory to be respected, it has naturally happened, that, his works being imperfect and faulty in comparison with those of the great antiquaries of the sixteenth century, they have not found a place in the collection of Grævius, and are hardly remembered by name.[1]

Publications in Germany.

49. In Germany and the Low Countries, the art of printing began to be exercised at Deventer, Utrecht, Louvain, Basle, Ulm, and other places, and, in Hungary, at Buda. We find, however, very few ancient writers; the whole list of what can pass for classics being about thirteen. One or two editions of parts of Aristotle in Latin, from translations lately made in Italy, may be added. Yet it was not the length of manuscripts that discouraged the German printers; for, besides their editions of the Scriptures, Mentelin of Strasburg published in 1473 the great Encyclopædia of Vincent of Beauvais, in ten volumes folio, generally bound in four; and, in 1474, a similar work of Berchorius, or Berchœur, in three other folios. The contrast between these labors and those of his Italian contemporaries is very striking.

In France.

50. Florus and Sallust were printed at Paris early in this decade, and twelve more classical authors at the same place before its termination. An edition of Cicero ad Herennium appeared at Angers in 1476, and one of Horace at Caen in 1480. The press of Lyons also sent forth several works, but none of them classical. It has been said by French writers, that the first book printed in their language is Le Jardin de Dévotion, by Colard Mansion of Bruges, in 1473. This date has been questioned in England; but it is of the less importance, as we have already seen that Caxton's Recueil des Histoires de Troye has the clear prior-

[1] A superior treatise of the same age, on the antiquities of the Roman city, is by Bernard Rucellai (de urbe Româ, in Rer. Ital. Script. Florent., vol. ii.); but it was not published before the eighteenth century. Rucellai wrote some historical works in a very good Latin style, and was distinguished also in the political revolutions of Florence. After the death of Lorenzo, he became the protector of the Florentine Academy, for the members of which he built a palace with gardens. Corniani, iii. 143. Biogr. Univ.: Rucellai.

ity. Le Roman de Baudouin, Comte de Flandres, Lyon, 1474, seems to be the earliest French book printed in France. In 1476, Les Grands Chroniques de St. Denis, an important and bulky volume, appeared at Paris.

In England by Caxton.

51. We come now to our own Caxton, who finished a translation into English of the Recueil des Histoires de Troye, by order of Margaret, Duchess of Burgundy, at Cologne, in September, 1471. It was probably printed there the next year.[1] But, soon afterwards, he came to England with the instruments of his art; and his Game of Chess, a slight and short performance, referred to 1474, though without a date, is supposed to have been the first specimen of English typography.[2] In almost every year from this time to his death in 1483, Caxton continued to publish those volumes which are the delight of our collectors. The earliest of his editions bearing a date in England is the "Dictes and Sayings," a translation by Lord Rivers from a Latin compilation, and published in 1477. In a literary history, it should be observed that the Caxton publications are more adapted to the general than the learned reader, and indicate, upon the whole, but a low state of knowledge in England. A Latin translation, however, of Aristotle's Ethics, was printed at Oxford in 1479.

In Spain.

52. The first book printed in Spain was on the very subject we might expect to precede all others, the Conception of the Virgin. It should be a very curious volume; being a poetical contest on that sublime theme by thirty-six poets, four of whom had written in Spanish, one in Italian, and the rest in Provençal or Valencian. It appeared at Valencia in 1474. A little book on grammar followed in 1475, and Sallust was printed the same year. In that year, printing was also introduced at Barcelona and Saragossa, in 1476 at Seville, in 1480 at Salamanca and Burgos.

53. A translation of the Bible by Malerbi, a Venetian, was ublished in 1471; and two other editions of that, or a different

[1] This book, at the Duke of Roxburghe's famous sale, brought £1,060.

[2] The Expositio Sancti Hieronymi, of which a copy in the Public Library at Cambridge bears the date of Oxford, 1468, on the title-page, is now generally given up. It has been successfully contended by Middleton, and lately by Mr. Singer, that this date should be 1478; the numeral letter x having been casually omitted. Several similar instances occur in which a pretended early book has not stood the keen eye of criticism: as the Decor Puellarum, ascribed to Nicolas Jenson of Venice in 1461, for which we should read 1471; a cosmography of Ptolemy, with the date of 1462; a book appearing to have been printed at Tours in 1467, &c.

version, the same year. Eleven editions are enumerated by Panzer in the fifteenth century. The German translation has already been mentioned; it was several times reprinted in this decade: one in Dutch appeared in 1477; one in the Valencian language, at that city, in 1478.[1] The New Testament was printed in Bohemian, 1475; and in French, 1477. The earliest French translation of the Old Testament seems to be about the same date. The reader will, of course, understand that all these translations were made from the Vulgate Latin. It may naturally seem remarkable, that not only at this period, but down to the Reformation, no attempt was made to render any part of the Scriptures public in English. But, in fact, the ground was thought too dangerous by those in power. The translation of Wicliffe had taught the people some comparisons between the worldly condition of the first preachers of Christianity and their successors, as well as some other contrasts, which it was more expedient to avoid. Long before the invention of printing, it was enacted, in 1408, by a constitution of Archbishop Arundel in convocation, that no one should thereafter "translate any text of Holy Scripture into English, by way of a book, or little book or tract; and that no book should be read that was composed lately in the time of John Wicliffe, or since his death." Scarcely any of Caxton's publications are of a religious nature.

Translations of Scripture.

54. It would have been strange if Spain, placed on the genial shores of the Mediterranean, and intimately connected through the Arragonese kings with Italy, had not received some light from that which began to shine so brightly. Her progress, however, in letters was but slow. Not but that several individuals are named by compilers of literary biography in the first part of the fifteenth century, as well as earlier, who are reputed to have possessed a knowledge of languages, and to have stood at least far above their contemporaries. Alfonsus Tostatus passes for the most considerable. His writings are chiefly theological: but Andrès praises his commentary on the Chronicle of Eusebius, at least as a bold essay;[2] contending also that learning was not de-

Revival of literature in Spain.

[1] This edition was suppressed or destroyed. No copy is known to exist; but there is preserved a final leaf, containing the names of the translator and printer. M'Crie's Reformation in Spain, p. 192. Andrès says (xix. 154) that this translation was made early in the fifteenth century, with the approbation of divines.

[2] ix. 151.

ficient in Spain during the fifteenth century, though he admits that the rapid improvements made at its close, and about the beginning of the next age, were due to Lebrixa's public instructions at Seville and Salamanca. Several translations were made from Latin authors into Spanish; which, however, is not of itself any great proof of peninsular learning. The men to whom Spain chiefly owes the advancement of useful learning, and who should not be defrauded of their glory, were Arias Barbosa, a scholar of Politian, and the more renowned though not more learned or more early propagator of Grecian literature, Antonio of Lebrixa, whose name was Latinized into Nebrissensis, by which he is commonly known. Of Arias, who unaccountably has no place in the Biographie Universelle, Nicolas Antonio gives a very high character.[1] He taught the Greek language at Salamanca probably about this time. But his writings are not at all numerous. For Lebrixa, instead of compiling from other sources, I shall transcribe what Dr. M'Crie has said with his usual perspicuous brevity.

Character of Lebrixa.

55. "Lebrixa, usually styled Nebrissensis, became to Spain what Valla was to Italy, Erasmus to Germany, or Budæus to France. After a residence of ten years in Italy, during which he had stored his mind with various kinds of knowledge, he returned home in 1473, by the advice of the younger Philelphus and Hermolaus Barbarus, with the view of promoting classical literature in his native country. Hitherto the revival of letters in Spain was confined to a few inquisitive individuals, and had not reached the schools and universities, whose teachers continued to teach a barbarous jargon under the name of Latin, into which they initiated the youth by means of a rude system of grammar, rendered unintelligible, in some instances, by a preposterous intermixture of the most abstruse questions in metaphysics. By the lectures which he read in the Universities of Seville, Salamanca, and Alcalá, and by the institutes which he published on Castilian,

[1] "In quo Antonium Nebrissensem socium habuit, qui tamen quicquid usquam Græcarum literarum apud Hispanos esset, ab uno Aria emanâsse in præfatione suarum Introductionum Grammaticarum ingenue affirmavit. His duobus amplissimum illud gymnasium, indeque Hispania tota debet barbariei, quæ longo apud nos bellorum dominatu in immensum creverat, extirpationem, bonarumque omnium disciplinarum divitias. Quas Arias noster ex antiquitatis penu per vicennium integrum auditoribus suis larga et locuplete vena communicavit, in poetica facultate Græcanicaque doctrina Nebrissense melior, a quo tamen in varia multiplicique doctrina superabatur." Bibl. Vetus.

Latin, Greek, and Hebrew grammar, Lebrixa contributed in a wonderful degree to expel barbarism from the seats of education, and to diffuse a taste for elegant and useful studies among his countrymen. His improvements were warmly opposed by the monks, who had engrossed the art of teaching, and who, unable to bear the light themselves, wished to prevent all others from seeing it; but, enjoying the support of persons of high authority, he disregarded their selfish and ignorant outcries. Lebrixa continued to an advanced age to support the literary reputation of his native country."[1]

Library of Lorenzo

56. This was the brilliant era of Florence, under the supremacy of Lorenzo de' Medici. The reader is probably well acquainted with this eminent character by means of a work of extensive and merited reputation. The Laurentian Library, still consisting wholly of manuscripts, though formed by Cosmo, and enlarged by his son Pietro, owed not only its name, but an ample increase of its treasures, to Lorenzo, who swept the monasteries of Greece through his learned agent, John Lascaris. With that true love of letters which scorns the monopolizing spirit of possession, Lorenzo permitted his manuscripts to be freely copied for the use of other parts of Europe.

Classics corrected and explained.

57. It was an important labor of the learned at Florence to correct as well as elucidate the text of their manuscripts, written generally by ignorant and careless monks or trading copyists (though the latter probably had not much concern with ancient writers), and become almost wholly unintelligible through the blunders of these transcribers.[2] Landino, Merula, Calderino, and Politian were the most indefatigable in this line of criticism during the age of Lorenzo. Before the use of printing fixed the text of a whole edition, — one of the most important of its consequences, — the critical amendments of these scholars could only be made useful through their oral lectures; and these appear frequently to have been the foundation of the valuable, though rather prolix, commentaries we find in the old editions. Thus those of Landino accompany many editions of Horace and Virgil, forming, in some measure, the basis of all inter-

1 M'Crie's History of Reformation in Spain, p. 61. It is probable that Lebrixa's exertions were not very effectual in the present decennium, nor perhaps in the next; but his Institutiones Grammaticæ, a very scarce book, were printed at Seville in 1481.

2 Meiners, Vergleich. der Sitten, iii. 108; Heeren, p. 293.

pretative annotations on those poets. Landino in these seldom touches on verbal criticisms; but his explanations display a considerable reach of knowledge. They are founded, as Heeren is convinced, on his lectures, and consequently give us some notion of the tone of instruction. In explaining the poets, two methods were pursued,—the grammatical and the moral; the latter of which consisted in resolving the whole sense into allegory. Dante had given credit to a doctrine, orthodox in this age and long afterwards, that every great poem must have a hidden meaning.[1]

Character of Lorenzo.

58. The notes of Calderino, a scholar of high fame, but infected with the common vice of arrogance, are found with those of Landino in the early editions of Virgil and Horace. Regio commented upon Ovid, Omnibonus Leonicenus upon Lucan, both these upon Quintilian, many upon Cicero.[2] It may be observed for the sake of chronological exactness, that these labors are by no means confined, even principally, to this decennial period. They are mentioned in connection with the name of Lorenzo de' Medici, whose influence over literature extended from 1470 to his death in 1492. Nor was mere philology the soul or the leading pursuit to which so truly noble a mind accorded its encouragement. He sought in ancient learning something more elevated than the narrow though necessary researches of criticism. In a villa overhanging the towers of Florence, on the steep slope of that lofty hill crowned by the mother city, the ancient Fiesole, in gardens which Tully might have envied, with Ficino, Landino, and Politian at his side, he delighted his hours of leisure with the beautiful visions of Platonic philosophy, for which the summer stillness of an Italian sky appears the most congenial accompaniment.

Prospect from his villa at Fiesole.

59. Never could the sympathies of the soul with outward nature be more finely touched; never could more striking suggestions be presented to the philosopher and the statesman. Florence lay beneath them; not with all the magnificence that the later Medici have given her, but, thanks to the piety of former times, presenting almost as varied an outline to the sky. One man, the wonder of Cosmo's age, Brunelleschi, had crowned the beautiful city with the vast dome of its cathedral; a structure unthought of

[1] Heeren, pp. 241, 287.

[2] Id., 297.

in Italy before, and rarely since surpassed. It seemed, amidst clustering towers of inferior churches, an emblem of the catholic hierarchy under its supreme head; like Rome itself, imposing, unbroken, unchangeable, radiating in equal expansion to every part of the earth, and directing its convergent curves to heaven. Round this were numbered, at unequal heights, the Baptistery, with its gates, as Michael Angelo styled them, worthy of Paradise; the tall and richly decorated Belfry of Giotto; the Church of the Carmine, with the frescos of Masaccio; those of Santa Maria Novella (in the language of the same great man), beautiful as a bride; of Santa Croce, second only in magnificence to the Cathedral of St. Mark; and of San Spirito, another great monument of the genius of Brunelleschi; the numerous convents that rose within the walls of Florence, or were scattered immediately about them. From these the eye might turn to the trophies of a republican government that was rapidly giving way before the citizen prince who now surveyed them: the Palazzo Vecchio, in which the signiory of Florence held their councils, raised by the Guelph aristocracy,—the exclusive but not tyrannous faction that long swayed the city; or the new and unfinished palace, which Brunelleschi had designed for one of the Pitti Family, before they fell, as others had already done, in the fruitless struggle against the house of Medici; itself destined to become the abode of the victorious race, and to perpetuate, by retaining its name, the revolutions that had raised them to power.

60. The prospect, from an elevation, of a great city in its silence, is one of the most impressive as well as beautiful we ever behold. But far more must it have brought home thoughts of seriousness to the mind of one, who by the force of events, and the generous ambition of his family and his own, was involved in the dangerous necessity of governing without the right, and, as far as might be, without the semblance of power; one who knew the vindictive and unscrupulous hostility, which, at home and abroad, he had to encounter. If thoughts like these could bring a cloud over the brow of Lorenzo, unfit for the object he sought in that retreat, he might restore its serenity by other scenes which his garden commanded. Mountains bright with various hues, and clothed with wood, bounded the horizon, and, on most sides, at no great distance. But imbosomed in these were other villas and domains of his own; while the level country bore witness to his agricultural improve-

ments, the classic diversion of a statesman's cares. The same curious spirit which led him to fill his garden at Careggi with exotic flowers of the East (the first instance of a botanical collection in Europe) had introduced a new animal from the same regions. Herds of buffaloes, since naturalized in Italy, whose dingy hide, bent neck, curved horns, and lowering aspect, contrasted with the grayish hue and full mild eye of the Tuscan oxen, pastured in the valley, down which the yellow Arno steals silently through its long reaches to the sea.[1]

Platonic academy.

61. The Platonic academy which Cosmo had planned came to maturity under Lorenzo. The academicians were divided into three classes: the patrons (*mecenati*), including the Medici; the hearers (*ascoltatori*, probably from the Greek word ἀκρόαται); and the novices, or disciples, formed of young aspirants to philosophy. Ficino presided over the whole. Their great festival was the 13th of November; being the anniversary of the birth and death of Plato. Much of absurd mysticism, much of frivolous and mischievous superstition, was mingled with their speculations.[2]

Disputationes Camaldulenses of Landino.

62. The Disputationes Camaldulenses of Landino were published during this period, though perhaps written a little sooner. They belong to a class prominent in the literature of Italy in this and the succeeding century; disquisitions on philosophy in the form of dia

1 "Talia Fæsuleo lentus meditabar in antro,
Rure suburbano Medicum, qua mons sacer urbem
Mæoniam, longique volumina despicit Arni:
Qua bonus hospitium felix placidamque quietem
Indulget Laurens."
Politiani Rusticus.

'And let us from the top of Fiesole,
Whence Galileo's glass by night observed
The phases of the moon, look round below
On Arno's vale, where the dove-colored steer
Is ploughing up and down among the vines;
While many a careless note is sung aloud,
Filling the air with sweetness; and on thee,
Beautiful Florence, all within thy walls,
Thy groves and gardens, pinnacles and towers,
Drawn to our feet."

It is hardly necessary to say, that these lines are taken from my friend Mr. Rogers's Italy; a poem full of moral and descriptive sweetness, and written in the chastened tone of fine taste. With respect to the buffaloes, I have no other authority than these lines of Politian, in his poem of Ambra on the farm of Lorenzo at Poggio Cajano: —

"Atque aliud nigris missum, quis credat? ab Indis,
Ruminat insuetas armentum discolor herbas."

But I must own that Buffon tells us, though without quoting any authority, that the buffalo was introduced into Italy as early as the seventh century. I did not take the trouble of consulting Aldrovandus, who would perhaps have confirmed him, —especially as I have a better opinion of my readers than to suppose they would care about the matter.

2 Roscoe; Corniani.

logue, with more solicitude to present a graceful delineation of virtue, and to kindle a generous sympathy for moral beauty, than to explore the labyrinths of theory, or even to lay down clear and distinct principles of ethics. The writings of Plato and Cicero in this manner had shown a track in which their idolaters, with distant and hesitating steps, and more of reverence than emulation, delighted to tread. These Disputations of Landino, in which, according to the beautiful patterns of ancient dialogue, the most honored names of the age appear,—Lorenzo and his brother Julian; Alberti, whose almost universal genius is now best known by his architecture; Ficino, and Landino himself,—turn upon a comparison between the active and contemplative life of man, to the latter of which it seems designed to give the advantage, and are saturated with the thoughtful spirit of Platonism.[1]

63. Landino was not, by any means, the first who had tried the theories of ancient philosophy through the feigned warfare of dialogue. Valla, intrepid and fond of paradox, had vindicated the Epicurean ethics from the calumnious or exaggerated censure frequently thrown upon them; contrasting the true methods by which pleasure should be sought with the gross notions of the vulgar. Several other writings of the same description, either in dialogue or regular dissertation, belong to the fifteenth century, though not always published so early: such as Franciscus Barbarus de re uxoria; Platina de falso et vero bono; the Vita Civile of Palmieri; the moral treatises of Poggio, Alberti, Pontano, and Matteo Bosso, concerning some of which little more than the names are to be learned from literary history, and which it would not, perhaps, be worth while to mention, except as collectively indicating a predilection for this style which the Italians long continued to display.[2]

Philosophical dialogues.

64. Some of these related to general criticism or to that of single authors. My knowledge of them is chiefly limited to the dialogue of Paulus Cortesius de hominibus doctis, written, I conceive, about 1490; no unsuccessful imitation of Cicero de claris oratoribus; from which, indeed, modern Latin writers have always been accustomed to collect

Paulus Cortesius.

[1] Corniani and Roscoe have given this account of the Disputationes Camaldulenses. I have no direct acquaintance with the book.

[2] Corniani is much fuller than Tiraboschi on these treatises. Roscoe seems to have read the ethical writings of Matteo Bosso (Life of Leo X., c. xx.), but hardly adverts to any of the rest I have named. Some of them are very scarce

the discriminating phrases of criticism. Cortesius, who was young at the time of writing this dialogue, uses an elegant if not always a correct Latinity; characterizing agreeably, and with apparent taste, the authors of the fifteenth century. It may be read in conjunction with the Ciceronianus of Erasmus, who, with no knowledge, perhaps, of Cortesius, has gone over the same ground in rather inferior language.

Schools in Germany.

65. It was about the beginning of this decade that a few Germans and Netherlanders, trained in the College of Deventer, or that of Zwoll, or of St. Edward's near Groningen, were roused to acquire that extensive knowledge of the ancient languages which Italy as yet exclusively possessed. Their names should never be omitted in any remembrance of the revival of letters; for great was their influence upon the subsequent times. Wessel of Groningen, one of those who contributed most steadily towards the purification of religion, and to whom the Greek and Hebrew languages are said, but probably on no solid grounds, to have been known, may be reckoned in this class. But others were more directly engaged in the advancement of literature. Three schools, from which issued the most conspicuous ornaments of the next generation, rose under masters learned for that time, and zealous in the good cause of instruction. Alexander Hegius became, about 1475, rector of that at Deventer, where Erasmus received his early education.[1] Hegius was not wholly ignorant of Greek, and imparted the rudiments of it to his illustrious pupil. I am inclined to ascribe the publication of a very rare and curious book, the first endeavor to print Greek on this side of the Alps, to no other person than Hegius.[2] Louis Dringeberg

[1] Heeren, p. 149, says that Hegius began to preside over the school of Deventer in 1480; but I think the date in the text is more probable, as Erasmus left it at the age of fourteen, and was certainly born in 1465. Though Hegius is said to have known but little Greek, I find in Panzer the title of a book by him, printed at Deventer, in 1501, de Utilitate Linguæ Græcæ.

The life of Hegius in Melchior Adam is interesting. "Primus hic in Belgio literas excitavit," says Revius, in Daventria Illustrata, p. 130. "Mihi," says Erasmus, "admodum adhuc puero contigit uti præceptore hujus discipulo Alexandro Hegio Westphalo, qui ludum aliquando celebrem oppidi Daventriensis moderabatur, in quo nos olim admodum pueri utriusque linguæ prima didicimus elementa." Adag. Chil. i. cent. iv. 39. In another place he says of Hegius: "Ne hic quidem Græcarum literarum omnino ignarus est." Epist. 411, in Appendice. Erasmus left Deventer at the age of fourteen; consequently in 1479 or 1480, as he tells us in an epistle, dated 17th April, 1519.

[2] This very rare book, unnoticed by most bibliographers, is of some importance in the history of literature. It is a small quarto tract, entitled Conjugationes verborum Græcæ Daventriæ noviter extremo labore collectæ et impressæ. No date or printer's name appears. A copy is in the British Museum, and another in Lord Spencer's library. It contains nothing but the word τύπτω in all its voices and tenses, with Latin explanations in Gothic

founded, not perhaps before 1480, a still more distinguished seminary at Schelstadt in Alsace. Here the luminaries of Germany in a more advanced stage of learning, Conrad Celtes, Bebel, Rhenanus, Wimpheling, Pirckheimer, Simler, are said to have imbibed their knowledge.[1] The third school was at

letters. The Greek types are very rude, and the characters sometimes misplaced. It must, I should presume, seem probable to every one who considers this book, that it is of the fifteenth century, and consequently older than any known Greek on this side of the Alps, which of itself should render it interesting in the eyes of bibliographers and of every one else; but, fully disclaiming all such acquaintance with the technical science of typographical antiquity as to venture any judgment founded on the appearance of a particular book, or on a comparison of it with others, I would, on other grounds, suggest the probability that this little attempt at Greek grammar issued from the Deventer press about 1480. It appears clear that whoever "collected with extreme labor" these forms of the verb *τύπτω*, had never been possessed of a Greek and Latin grammar. For would it not be absurd to use such expressions about a simple transcription? Besides which, the word is not only given in an arrangement different from any I have ever seen, but with a non-existent form of participle, *τετυψάμενος*, for *τυψάμενος*, which could not surely have been found in any prior grammar. Now the grammar of Lascaris was published, with a Latin translation by Craston, in 1480. It is indeed highly probable that this book would not reach Deventer immediately after its impression; but it does seem as if there could not long have been any extreme difficulty in obtaining a correct synopsis of the verb *τύπτω*.

We have seen that Erasmus, about 1477, acquired a very slight tincture of Greek under Alexander Hegius at Deventer. And here, as he tells us, he saw Agricola, returning probably from Italy to Groningen. "Quem mihi puero, ferme duodecim annos nato, Daventriæ videre contigit, nec aliud contigit." (Jortin, ii. 416.) No one could be so likely as Hegius to attempt a Greek grammar; nor do we find that his successors in that college were men as distinguished for learning as himself. But in fact at a later time it could not have been so incorrect. We might perhaps conjecture that he took down these Greek tenses from the mouth of Agricola, since we must presume oral communication rather than the use of books. Agricola, repeating from memory and not thoroughly conversant with the language, might have given the false participle *τετυψάμενος*. The tract was probably printed by Pafroet, some of whose editions bear as early a date as 1477. It has long been extremely scarce; for Revius does not include it in the list of Pafroet's publications which he has given in Daventria Illustrata, nor will it be found in Panzer. Beloe was the first to mention it in his Anecdotes of Scarce Books; and it is referred by him to the fifteenth century, but apparently without his being aware that there was any thing remarkable in that antiquity. Dr. Dibdin, in Bibliotheca Spenceriana, has given a fuller account; and from him Brunet has inserted it in the Manuel du Libraire. Neither Beloe nor Dibdin seems to have known that there is a copy in the Museum: they speak only of that belonging to Lord Spencer.

If it were true that Reuchlin, during his residence at Orleans, had published, as well as compiled, a Greek grammar, we should not need to have recourse to the hypothesis of this note in order to give the antiquity of the present decade to Greek typography. Such a grammar is asserted by Meiners, in his Life of Reuchlin, to have been printed at Poitiers; and Eichhorn positively says, without reference to the place of publication, that Reuchlin was the first German who published a Greek grammar. (Gesch. der Litt., iii. 275.) Meiners, however, in a subsequent volume (iii. 10), retracts this assertion, and says it has been proved that the Greek Grammar of Reuchlin was never printed. Yet I find in the Bibliotheca Universalis of Gesner: "Joh. Capnio [Reuchlin] scripsit de diversitate quatuor idiomatum Græcæ linguæ lib. i." No such book appears in the list of Reuchlin's works in Niceron, vol. xxv., nor in any of the bibliographies. If it ever existed, we may place it with more probability at the very close of this century, or at the beginning of the next.

[The learned Dr. West, of Dublin, informed me that Reuchlin, in a dedication of a Commentary on the Seven Penitential Psalms in 1512, mentions a work that he had published on the Greek grammar, entitled Micropædia. There seems no reason to suppose that it was earlier than the time at which I have inclined to place it.—1842.]

[1] Eichhorn, iii. 231; Meiners, ii. 369. Eichhorn carelessly follows a bad autho-

Munster; and over this Rodolph Langius presided, — a man not any way inferior to the other two, and of more reputation as a Latin writer, especially as a poet. The school of Munster did not come under the care of Langius till 1483, or perhaps rather later; and his strenuous exertions in the cause of useful and polite literature against monkish barbarians extended into the next century. But his life was long: the first, or nearly such, to awaken his countrymen, he was permitted to behold the full establishment of learning, and to exult in the dawn of the Reformation. In company with a young man of rank and equal zeal, Maurice, Count of Spiegelberg, who himself became the provost of a school at Emmerich, Langius visited Italy, and, as Meiners supposes (though, I think, upon uncertain grounds), before 1460. But, not long afterwards, a more distinguished person than any we have mentioned, Rodolph Agricola of Groningen, sought in that more genial land the taste and correctness which no Cisalpine nation could supply. Agricola passed several years of this decade in Italy. We shall find the effects of his example in the next.[1]

Study of Greek at Paris.

66. Meantime a slight impulse seems to have been given to the University of Paris by the lessons of George Tifernas; for, from some disciples of his, Reuchlin, a young German of great talents and celebrity, acquired, probably about the year 1470, the first elements of the Greek language. This knowledge he improved by the lessons of a native Greek, Andronicus Cartoblacas, at Basle. In that city, he had the good fortune, rare on this side of the Alps, to find a collection of Greek manuscripts, left there at the time of the council by a Cardinal Nicolas of Ragusa. By the advice of Cartoblacas, he taught Greek himself at Basle. After the lapse of some years, Reuchlin went again to Paris, and found a new teacher, George Hermonymus of Sparta, who had settled there about 1472. From Paris he removed to Orleans and Poitiers.[2]

67. The classical literature which delighted Reuchlin and Agricola was disregarded as frivolous by the wise of that day

rity in counting Reuchlin among these pupils of the Schelstadt school.

[1] See Meiners, vol. ii., Eichhorn, and Heeren, for the revival of learning in Germany; or something may be found in Brucker.

[2] Meiners, i. 46. Besides Meiners, Brucker, iv. 358, as well as Heeren, have given pretty full accounts of Reuchlin, and a good life of him will be found in the 25th volume of Niceron; but the Epistolæ ad Reuchlinum throw still more light on the man and his contemporaries.

in the University of Paris; but they were much more keenly opposed to innovation and heterodoxy in their own peculiar line, — the scholastic metaphysics. Most have heard of the long controversies between the Realists and Nominalists concerning the nature of universals, or the genera and species of things. The first, with Plato, and, at least as has been generally held, Aristotle, maintained their objective or external reality; either, as it was called, *ante rem*, as eternal archetypes in the Divine Intelligence; or *in re*, as forms inherent in matter: the second, with Zeno, gave them only a subjective existence as ideas conceived by the mind, and have hence, in later times, acquired the name of Conceptualists.[1] Roscelin, the first of the modern Nominalists, went farther than this, and denied, as Hobbes and Berkeley, with many others, have since done, all universality except to words and propositions. Abelard, who inveighs against the doctrine of Roscelin as false logic and false theology, and endeavors to confound it with the denial of any objective reality even in singular things,[2] may be esteemed the restorer of the Conceptualist school. We do not know his doctrines, however, by his own writings, but by the testimony of John of Salisbury, who seems not well to have understood the subject. The words Realist and Nominalist came into use about the end of the twelfth century. But, in the next, the latter party, by degrees, disappeared; and the great schoolmen, Aquinas and Scotus, in whatever else they might disagree, were united on the Realist side. In the fourteenth century, William Ockham revived the opposite hypothesis with considerable success. Scotus and his disciples were the great maintainers of Realism. If there were no substantial forms, he argued, — that is, nothing real, — which determines the mode of being in each individual, men and brutes would be of the same substance; for they do not differ as to matter, nor can extrinsic

Controversy of Realists and Nominalists.

Scotus.

1 I am chiefly indebted for the facts in the following paragraphs to a dissertation by Meiners, in the Transactions of the Göttingen Academy, vol. xii.

2 "Hic sicut pseudo-dialecticus, ita pseudo-christianus — ut eo loco quo dicitur Dominus partem piscis assi comedisse, partem hujus vocis, quæ est piscis assi, non partem rei intelligere cogatur." — Meiners, p. 27. This may serve to show the cavilling tone of scholastic disputes; and Meiners may well say, "Quicquid Roscelinus peccavit, non adeo tamen insanisse pronuntiandum est, ut Abelardus illum fecisse invidiose fingere sustinuit." [M. Cousin has nevertheless proved, from a passage in some lately discovered manuscripts of Abelard, that he had really learned under Roscelin. This had been asserted by Otho of Frisingen, but doubted on account of a supposed incompatibility of dates. Fragmens Philosophiques, vol. iv. p. 57.—1853.]

accidents make a substantive difference. There must be a substantial form of a horse, another of a lion, another of a man. He seems to have held the immateriality of the soul; that is, the substantial form of man. But no other form, he maintained, can exist without matter naturally, though it may supernaturally by the power of God. Socrates and Plato agree more than Socrates and an ass: they have, therefore, something in common, which an ass has not. But this is not numerically the same: it must, therefore, be something universal; namely, human nature.[1]

68. These reasonings, which are surely no unfavorable specimen of the subtle philosopher (as Scotus was called), were met by Ockham with others which sometimes appear more refined and obscure. He confined reality to objective things; denying it to the host of abstract entities brought forward by Scotus. He defines a universal to be "a particular intention (meaning probably idea, or conception) of the mind itself, capable of being predicated of many things, not for what it properly is itself, but for what those things are: so that, in so far as it has this capacity, it is called universal; but, inasmuch as it is one form really existing in the mind, it is called singular."[2] I have not examined the writings of Ockham, and am unable to determine whether his Nominalism extends beyond that of Berkeley or Stewart, which is generally asserted by the modern inquirers into scholastic philosophy; that is, whether it amounts to Conceptualism. The foregoing definition, as far as I can judge, might have been given by them.[3]

Ockham.

69. The later Nominalists of the scholastic period, Buridan, Biel, and several others mentioned by the historians of philosophy, took all their reasonings from the storehouse of Ockham. His doctrine was prohibited at Paris by Pope John XXII., whose theological opinions, as well as secular encroachments, he had opposed. All masters of arts were bound by oath never to teach Ockhamism. But, after the pope's death, the university condemned a tenet of the Realists, that many truths are eternal, which are not God;

Nominalists in University of Paris.

[1] Meiners, p. 39.

[2] "Unam intentionem singularem ipsius animæ, natam prædicari de pluribus, non pro se, sed pro ipsis rebus; ita quod per hoc, quod ipsa nata est prædicari de pluribus, non pro se sed pro illis pluribus, illa dicitur universalis; propter hoc autem, quod est una forma existens realiter in intellectu, dicitur singulare; p. 42.

[3] [The definition seems hardly such as Berkeley would have given: it plainly recognizes a general conception existing in the mind.—1847.]

and went so far towards the Nominalist theory, as to determine that our knowledge of things is through the medium of words.[1] Peter d'Ailly, Gerson, and other principal men of their age, were Nominalists: the sect was very powerful in Germany, and may be considered, on the whole, as prevalent in this century. The Realists, however, by some management, gained the ear of Louis XI., who, by an ordinance in 1473, explicitly approves the doctrines of the great Realist philosophers, condemns that of Ockham and his disciples, and forbids it to be taught; enjoining the books of the Nominalists to be locked up from public perusal, and all present as well as future graduates in the university to swear to the observation of this ordinance. The prohibition, nevertheless, was repealed in 1481, the guilty books set free from their chains, and the hypothesis of the Nominalists virtually permitted to be held, amidst the acclamations of the university, and especially one of its four nations, that of Germany. Some of their party had, during this persecution, taken refuge in that empire and in England, both friendly to their cause; and this metaphysical contention of the fifteenth century suggests and typifies the great religious convulsion of the next. The weight of ability during this later and less flourishing period of scholastic philosophy was on the Nominalist side; and, though nothing in the Reformation was immediately connected with their principle, this metaphysical sect facilitated in some measure its success.

Low state of learning in England.

70. We should still look in vain to England for either learning or native genius. The reign of Edward IV. may be reckoned one of the lowest points in our literary annals. The universities had fallen in reputation and in frequency of students: where there had been thousands, according to Wood, there was not now one; which must be understood as an hyperbolical way of speaking. But the decline of the universities, frequented as they had been by indigent vagabonds withdrawn from useful labor, and wretched as their pretended instruction had been, was so far from an evil in itself, that it left clear the path for the approaching introduction of real learning. Several colleges were about this time founded at Oxford and Cambridge, which, in the design of their munificent founders, were to become, as they have done, the instruments of a better discipline than the bar-

[1] Meiners, p. 45: "Scientiam habemus de rebus, sed mediantibus terminis."

barous schoolmen afforded. We have already observed, that learning in England was like seed fermenting in the ground through the fifteenth century. The language was becoming more vigorous, and more capable of giving utterance to good thoughts, as some translations from Caxton's press show, such as the Dicts of Philosophers by Lord Rivers. And perhaps the best exercise for a schoolboy people is that of schoolboys. The poetry of two Scotsmen, Henryson and Mercer, which is not without merit, may be nearly referred to the present decade.[1]

71. The progress of mathematical science was regular, though not rapid. We might have mentioned before the gnomon erected by Toscanelli in the cathedral at Florence, which is referred to 1468; a work, it has been said, which, considering the times, has done as much honor to his genius as that so much renowned at Bologna to Cassini.[2] The greatest mathematician of the fifteenth century, Muller, or Regiomontanus, a native of Konigsberg, or Konigshoven, a small town in Franconia, whence he derived his Latinized appellation, died prematurely, like his master Purbach, in 1476. He had begun at the age of fifteen to assist the latter in astronomical observations; and having, after Purbach's death, acquired a knowledge of Greek in Italy, and devoted himself to the ancient geometers, after some years spent with distinction in that country and at the court of Mathias Corvinus, he settled finally at Nuremberg, where a rich citizen, Bernard Walther, both supplied the means of accurate observations, and became the associate of his labors.[3] Regiomontanus died at Rome, whither he had been called to

Mathematics.

Regiomontanus.

1 Campbell's Specimens of British Poets, vol. i.

2 This gnomon of Florence is, by much, the loftiest in Europe. It would be no slight addition to the glory of Toscanelli if we should suppose him to have suggested the discovery of a passage westward to the Indies, in a letter to Columbus, as his article in the Biographie Universelle seems to imply. But the more accurate expressions of Tiraboschi, referring to the correspondence between these great men, leave Columbus in possession of the original idea, at least concurrently with the Florentine astronomer, though the latter gave him strong encouragement to persevere in his undertaking. Toscanelli, however, had, on the authority of Marco Polo, imbibed an exaggerated notion of the distance eastward to China; and consequently believed, as Columbus himself did, that the voyage by the west to that country would be far shorter, than, if the continent of America did not intervene, it could have been. Tiraboschi, vi. 189, 207; Roscoe's Leo X., ch. 20.

3 Walther was more than a patron of science, honorable as that name was. He made astronomical observations worthy of esteem relatively to the age. Montucla, i. 545. It is to be regretted that Walther should have diminished the credit due to his name by withholding from the public the manuscripts of Regiomontanus, which he purchased after the latter's death; so that some were lost by the negligence of his own heirs, and the rest remained unpublished till 1533.

assist in rectifying the calendar. Several of his works were printed in this decade, and among others his ephemerides, or calculations of the places of the sun and moon, for the ensuing thirty years; the best, though not strictly the first, that had been made in Europe.[1] His more extensive productions did not appear till afterwards; and the treatise on triangles, the most celebrated of them, not till 1533. The solution of the more difficult cases, both in plane and spherical trigonometry, is found in this work; and, with the exception of what the science owes to Napier, it may be said that it advanced little for more than two centuries after the age of Regiomontanus.[2] Purbach had computed a table of sines to a radius of 600,000 parts. Regiomontanus, ignorant, as has been thought (which appears very strange), of his master's labors, calculated them to 6,000,000 parts. But, perceiving the advantages of a decimal scale, he has given a second table, wherein the ratio of the sines is computed to a radius of 10,000,000 parts, or as we should say, taking the radius as unity, to seven places of decimals. He subjoined what he calls Canon Fæcundus, or a table of tangents; calculating them, however, only for entire degrees to a radius of 100,000 parts.[3] It has been said that Regiomontanus was inclined to the theory of the earth's motion, which indeed Nicolas Cusanus had already espoused.

Arts of delineation.

72. Though the arts of delineation do not properly come within the scope of this volume, yet, so far as they are directly instrumental to science, they ought not to pass unregarded. Without the tool that presents figures to the eye, not the press itself could have diffused an adequate knowledge either of anatomy or of natural history. As figures cut in wooden blocks gave the first idea of letter-printing, and were for some time associated with it, an obvious invention, when the latter art became improved, was to arrange such blocks together with types in the same page. We find accordingly, about this time, many books adorned or illustrated in this manner; generally with representations of saints, or other ornamental delineations not of much imporance; but, in a few instances, with figures of plants and aninals, or of human anatomy. The Dyalogus creaturarum

[1] Gassendi, Vita Regiomontani. He speaks of them himself, as "quas vulgo vocant almanach;" and Gassendi says that some were extant in Manuscript at Paris, from 1442 to 1472. Those of Regiomontanus contained eclipses, and other matters not in former almanacs.

[2] Hutton's Logarithms, Introduction, p. 3.

[3] Kästner, i. 557.

moralizatus, of which the first edition was published at Gouda, 1480, seems to be nearly, if not altogether, the earliest of these. It contains a series of fables with rude woodcuts in little more than outline. A second edition, printed at Antwerp in 1486, repeats the same cuts, with the addition of one representing a church, which is really elaborate.[1]

73. The art of engraving figures on plates of copper was nearly co-eval with that of printing, and is due either to Thomas Finiguerra about 1460, or to some German about the same time. It was not a difficult step to apply this invention to the representation of geographical maps; and this we owe to Arnold Buckinck, an associate of the printer Sweynheim. His edition of Ptolemy's geography appeared at Rome in 1478. These maps are traced from those of Agathodæmon in the fifth century; and it has been thought that Buckinck profited by the hints of Donis, a German monk, who himself gave two editions of Ptolemy not long afterwards at Ulm.[2] The fifteenth century had already witnessed an increasing attention to geographical delineations. The libraries of Italy contain several unpublished maps, of which that by Fra Mauro, a monk of the order of Camaldoli, now in the Convent of Murano, near Venice, is the most celebrated.[3] Two causes, besides the in-

Maps.

Geography.

[1] Both these editions are in the British Museum. In the same library is a copy of the exceedingly scarce work, Ortus Sanitatus. Mogunt. 1491. The colophon, which may be read in De Bure (Sciences, No. 1554), takes much credit for the carefulness of the delineations. The wooden cuts of the plants, especially, are as good as we usually find in the sixteenth century; the form of the leaves and character of the plant are generally well preserved. The animals are also tolerably figured, though with many exceptions; and, on the whole, fall short of the plants. The work itself is a compilation from the old naturalists, arranged alphabetically.

[2] Biogr. Univ.: Buckinck; Donis.

[3] Andrès, ix. 88; Corniani, iii. 162. [A better account of this celebrated map was given in the seventh volume of the Annales Camaldulenses, p. 252 (1762); and Cardinal Zurla published in 1806 Il Mappamondo di Fra Mauro Camaldolense illustrato. A fine copy of this map, taken from the original at Murano, about forty years since, is in the British Museum: there is also one in a Portuguese convent, supposed to have been made by Fra Mauro himself in 1459, for the use of Alfonso V., king of Portugal. Fra Mauro professes not to have followed Ptolemy in all things, but to have collected information from travellers: "Investigando per molti anni, e practicando cum persone degne di fede, le qual hano veduto ad occhio quelo, que qui suso fedelmente demostro. It appears, however, to me, that he has been chiefly indebted to Marco Polo, who had contributed a vast stock of names to which the geographer was to annex locality in the best manner he could. Very little relating to Asia or Africa will be found in the Murano map which may not be traced to this source. It does not indeed appear manifest that Polo was acquainted with the termination of the African coast; but that had been so often asserted; that we cannot feel surprised when we find, in Fra Mauro's map, the sea rolling round the Cape of Good Hope, though the form of that part of the continent is ill delineated.

The marginal entries of this map are not unworthy of attention. One of them attributes the tides to the attraction of the moon, but not on any philosophical

crease of commerce and the gradual accumulation of knowledge, had principally turned the thoughts of many towards the figure of the earth on which they trod. Two translations, one of them by Emanuel Chrysoloras, had been made early in the century from the cosmography of Ptolemy; and from his maps the geographers of Italy had learned the use of parallels and meridians, which might a little, though inadequately, restrain their arbitrary admeasurements of different countries.[1] But the real discoveries of the Portuguese on the coast of Africa, under the patronage of Don Henry, were of far greater importance in stimulating and directing enterprise. In the academy founded by that illustrious prince, nautical charts were first delineated in a method more useful to the pilot, by projecting the meridians in parallel right lines,[2] instead of curves on the surface of the sphere. This first step in hydrographical science entitles Don Henry to the name of its founder; and, though these early maps and charts of the fifteenth century are to us but a chaos of error and confusion, it was on them that the patient eye of Columbus had rested through long hours of meditation, while strenuous hope and unsubdued doubt were struggling in his soul.

SECT. V. 1480–1490.

Great Progress of Learning in Italy — Italian Poetry — Pulci — Metaphysical Theology — Ficinus — Picus of Mirandola — Learning in Germany — Early European Drama — Alberti and Leonardo da Vinci.

74. THE press of Italy was less occupied with Greek for several years than might have been expected; but the number of scholars was still not sufficient to repay the expenses of impression. The Psalter was

Greek printed in Italy.

principle. He speaks of spring and neap tides as already known, which indeed must have been the case, after the experience of navigators reached beyond the Mediterranean; but says that no one had explained their cause. Zurla, or some one whom he quotes, exaggerates a little the importance of what Fra Mauro has said about the tides, which is mixed up with great error; and loosely talks about an anticipation of Newton. Upon the whole, although this map is curious and interesting, something more has been said of it than it deserves by the author of Annales Camaldulenses: "Mauro itaque Camaldulensi monacho ea gloria jure merito tribuenda erat, ut non parum tabulis suis geographicis juverit ad tentandas expeditiones in terras incognitas, quod postea præstitum erat ab Lusitanis. — 1842.]

[1] Andrès, 86.

[2] Id. 83.

published in Greek twice at Milan in 1481, once at Venice in 1486. Craston's Lexicon was also once printed, and the grammar of Lascaris several times. The first classical work the printers ventured upon was Homer's Battle of Frogs and Mice, published at Venice in 1486, or, according to some, at Milan in 1485; the priority of the two editions being disputed. But in 1488, under the munificent patronage of Lorenzo, and by the care of Demetrius of Crete, a complete edition of Homer issued from the press of Florence. This splendid work closes our catalogue for the present.[1]

75. The first Hebrew book, Jarchi's Commentary on the Pentateuch, had been printed by some Jews, at Reggio in Calabria, as early as 1475. In this period a press was established at Soncino, where the Pentateuch was published in 1482, the greater prophets in 1486, and the whole Bible in 1488; but this was intended for themselves alone. What little instruction in Hebrew had anywhere hitherto been imparted to Christian scholars was only oral. The commencement of Hebrew learning, properly so called, was not till about the end of the century, in the Franciscan monasteries of Tubingen and Basle. Their first teacher, however, was an Italian, by name Raimondi.[2]

Hebrew printed.

76. To enumerate every publication that might scatter a gleam of light on the progress of letters in Italy, or to mention every scholar who deserves a place in biographical collections or in an extended history of literature, would crowd these pages with too many names. We must limit ourselves to those best deserving to be had in remembrance. In 1480, according to Meiners, or, as Heeren says, in 1483, Politian was placed in the chair of Greek and Latin eloquence at Florence; a station perhaps the most conspicuous and the most honorable which any scholar could occupy. It is beyond controversy, that he stands at the head of that class in the fifteenth century. The envy of some of his contemporaries attested his superiority. In 1489, he published his once-celebrated Miscellanea, consisting of one hundred observations illustrating passages of Latin authors, in the desultory manner of Aulus Gellius; which is certainly the easiest, and perhaps the most agreeable, method of conveying information. They are sometimes grammatical, but more

Miscellanies of Politian.

[1] See Maittaire's character of this edition, quoted in Roscoe's Leo X., ch. 21.
[2] Eichhorn, ii. 562.

frequently relate to obscure (at that time) customs or mythological allusions. Greek quotations occur not seldom, and the author's command of classical literature seems considerable. Thus he explains, for instance, the *crambe repetita* of Juvenal by a proverb mentioned in Suidas, δὶς κράμβη θάνατος: κράμβη being a kind of cabbage, which, when boiled a second time, was, of course, not very palatable. This may serve to show the extent of learning which some Italian scholars had reached through the assistance of the manuscripts collected by Lorenzo. It is not improbable that no one in England, at that time, had heard the name of Suidas. Yet the imperfect knowledge of Greek which these early writers possessed is shown when they attempt to write it. Politian has some verses in his Miscellanea, but very bald, and full of false quantities. This remark we may have occasion to repeat; for it is applicable to much greater names in philology than his.[1]

77. The Miscellanies, Heeren says, were then considered an immortal work: it was deemed an honor to be mentioned in them, and those who missed this made it a matter of complaint. If we look at them now, we are astonished at the different measure of glory in the present age. This book probably sprang out of Politian's lectures. He had cleared up in these some difficult passages, which had led him on to further inquiries. Some of his explanations might probably have arisen out of the walks and rides that he was accustomed to take with Lorenzo, who had advised the publication of the Miscellanies. The manner in which these explanations are given, the light yet solid mode of handling the subjects, and their great variety, give, in fact, a charm to the Miscellanies of Politian which few antiquarian works possess. Their success is not wonderful. They were fragments, and chosen fragments, from the lectures of the most celebrated teacher of that age, whom many had heard, but still more had wished to hear. Scarcely had a work appeared in the whole fifteenth century of which so vast expectations had been entertained, and which was received with such curiosity.[2] The very fault of Politian's style, as it

Their character by Heeren.

[1] Meiners has praised Politian's Greek verses, but with very little skill in such matters, p. 214. The compliments he quotes from contemporary Greeks, "non esse tam Atticas Athenas ipsas," may not have been very sincere, unless they meant *esse* to be taken in the present tense. These Greeks, besides, knew but little of their metrical language.

[2] Heeren, p. 263. Meiners, Lebensbeschreibungen, &c., has written the life of Politian, ii. 111–220, more copiously than any one that I have read. His character of the Miscellanies is in p. 136.

was that of Hermolaus Barbarus, his affected intermixture of obsolete words, for which it is necessary in almost every page of his Miscellanies to consult the dictionary, would, in an age of pedantry, increase the admiration of his readers.[1]

His version of Herodian.

78. Politian was the first that wrote the Latin language with much elegance; and, while every other early translator from the Greek has incurred more or less of censure at the hands of judges whom better learning had made fastidious, it is agreed by them that his Herodian has all the spirit of his original, and frequently excels it.[2] Thus we perceive that the age of Poggio, Filelfo, and Valla, was already left far behind by a new generation: these had been well employed as the pioneers of ancient literature; but, for real erudition and taste, we must descend to Politian, Christopher Landino, and Hermolaus Barbarus.[3]

Cornucopia of Perotti.

79. The Cornucopia sive linguæ Latinæ Commentarii, by Nicolas Perotti, Bishop of Siponto, suggests rather more by its title than the work itself seems to warrant. It is a copious commentary upon part of Martial, in which he takes occasion to explain a vast many Latin words, and has been highly extolled by Morhof, and by writers quoted in Baillet and Blount. To this commentary is appended an alphabetical index of words, which rendered it a sort of dictionary for the learned reader. Perotti lived a little before this time; but the first edition seems to have been in 1489. He also wrote a small Latin grammar, frequently reprinted in the fifteenth century; and was an indifferent translator of Polybius.[4]

Latin poetry of Politian.

80. We have not thought it worth while to mention the Latin poets of the fourteenth and fifteenth centuries. They are numerous, and somewhat rude, from Petrarch and Boccace to Maphæus Vegius, the continuator of the Æneid in a thirteenth book, first printed in 1471,

[1] Meiners, pp. 155, 209. In the latter passage, Meiners censures, with apparent justice, the affected words of Politian, some of which he did not scruple to take from such writers as Apuleius and Tertullian, with an inexcusable display of erudition at the expense of good taste.

[2] Huet, apud Blount in Politiano.

[3] Meiners, Roscoe, Corniani, Heeren, and Gresswell's Memoirs of early Italian Scholars, are the best authorities to whom the reader can have recourse for the character of Politian, besides his own works. I think, however, that Heeren has hardly done justice to Politian's poetry. Tiraboschi is unsatisfactory. Blount, as usual, collects the suffrages of the sixteenth century.

[4] Heeren, 272; Morhof, i. 821, who calls Perotti the first compiler of good Latin, from whom those who followed have principally borrowed. See also Baillet and Blount for testimonies to Perotti.

and very frequently afterwards. This is, probably, the best versification before Politian. But his Latin poems display considerable powers of description, and a strong feeling of the beauties of Roman poetry. The style is imbued with these, not too ambitiously chosen, nor in the manner called centonism, but so as to give a general elegance to the composition, and to call up pleasing associations in the reader of taste. This, indeed, is the common praise of good versifiers in modern Latin, and not peculiarly appropriate to Politian, who is inferior to some who followed, though to none, as I apprehend, that preceded in that numerous fraternity. His ear is good, and his rhythm, with a few exceptions, musical and Virgilian. Some defects are nevertheless worthy of notice. He is often too exuberant, and apt to accumulate details of description. His words, unauthorized by any legitimate example, are very numerous, a fault in some measure excusable by the want of tolerable dictionaries; so that the memory was the only test of classical precedent. Nor can we deny that Politian's Latin poetry is sometimes blemished by affected and effeminate expressions, by a too studious use of repetitions, and by a love of diminutives, according to the fashion of his native language, carried beyond all bounds that correct Augustan Latinity could possibly have endured. This last fault, and to a man of good taste it is an unpleasing one, belongs to a great part of the lyrical and even elegiac writers in modern Latin. The example of Catullus would probably have been urged in excuse: but perhaps Catullus went farther than the best judges approved; and nothing in his poems can justify the excessive abuse of that effeminate grace, what the stern Persius would have called "summa delumbe saliva," which pervades the poetry both of Italian and Cisalpine Latinists for a long period. On the whole, Politian, like many of his followers, is calculated to delight and mislead a schoolboy, but may be read with pleasure by a man.[1]

Italian poetry of Lorenzo.

81. Amidst all the ardor for the restoration of classical literature in Italy, there might seem reason to apprehend that native originality would not meet its due reward, and even that the discouraging notion of a degeneracy in the powers of the human mind might come to

[1] The extracts from Politian, and other Latin poets of Italy, by Pope, in the two little volumes entitled Poemata Italorum, are extremely well chosen, and give a just measure of most of them.

prevail. Those who annex an exaggerated value to correcting an unimportant passage in an ancient author, or, which is much the same, interpreting some worthless inscription, can hardly escape the imputation of pedantry; and doubtless this reproach might justly fall on many of the learned in that age, as, with less excuse, it has often done upon their successors. We have already seen, that, for a hundred years, it was thought unworthy a man of letters, even though a poet, to write in Italian; and Politian, with his great patron Lorenzo, deserves no small honor for having disdained the false vanity of the philologers. Lorenzo stands at the head of the Italian poets of the fifteenth century in the sonnet as well as in the light lyrical composition. His predecessors, indeed, were not likely to remove the prejudice against vernacular poetry. Several of his sonnets appear, both for elevation and elegance of style, worthy of comparison with those of the next age. But perhaps his most original claim to the title of a poet is founded upon the Canti Carnascialeschi, or carnival-songs, composed for the popular shows on festivals. Some of these, which are collected in a volume printed in 1558, are by Lorenzo, and display a union of classical grace and imitation with the native raciness of Florentine gayety.[1]

Pulci.

82. But at this time appeared a poet of a truly modern school, in one of Lorenzo's intimate society, — Luigi Pulci. The first edition of his Morgante Maggiore, containing twenty-three cantos, to which five were subsequently added, was published at Venice in 1481. The taste of the Italians has always been strongly inclined to extravagant combinations of fancy, caprices rapid and sportive as the animal from which they take their name. The susceptible and versatile imaginations of that people, and their habitual cheerfulness, enable them to render the serious and terrible instrumental to the ridiculous, without becoming, like some modern fictions, merely hideous and absurd.

Character of Morgante Maggiore.

83. The Morgante Maggiore was evidently suggested by some long romances written within the preceding century in the octave stanza, for which the fabulous chronicle of Turpin, and other fictions wherein the

[1] Corniani; Roscoe. Crescimbeni (della volgar Poesia, ii. 324) strongly asserts Lorenzo to be the restorer of poetry, which had never been more barbarous than in his youth. But certainly the Giostra of Politian was written while Lorenzo was young.

same real and imaginary personages had been introduced, furnished the materials. Under pretence of ridiculing the intermixture of sacred allusions with the romantic legends, Pulci carried it to an excess, which, combined with some sceptical insinuations of his own, seems clearly to display an intention of exposing religion to contempt.[1] As to the heroes of his romance, there can be, as it seems, no sort of doubt, that he designed them for nothing else than the butts of his fancy, that the reader might scoff at those whom duller poets had held up to admiration. It has been a question among Italian critics, whether the poem of Pulci is to be reckoned burlesque.[2] This may seem to turn on the definition, though I do not see what definition could be given, consistently with the use of language, that would exclude it: it is intended as a caricature of the poetical romances, and might even seem by anticipation a satirical, though not ill-natured, parody on the Orlando Furioso. That he meant to excite any other emotion than laughter, cannot, as it seems, be maintained; and a very few stanzas of a more serious character, which may rarely be found, are not enough to make an exception to his general design. The Morgante was to the poetical romances of chivalry what Don Quixote was to their brethren in prose.

1 The story of Meridiana, in the eighth canto, is sufficient to prove Pulci's irony to have been exercised on religion. It is well known to the readers of the Morgante. It has been alleged in the Biographie Universelle, that he meant only to turn into ridicule "ces muses mendiantes du 14me siècle," the authors of La Spagna or Buovo d'Antona, who were in the habit of beginning their songs with scraps of the liturgy, and even of introducing theological doctrines in the most absurd and misplaced style. Pulci has given us much of the latter, wherein some have imagined that he had the assistance of Ficinus.

2 This seems to have been an old problem in Italy (Corniani, ii. 302); and the gravity of Pulci has been maintained of late by such respectable authorities as Foscolo and Panizzi. Ginguéné, who does not go this length, thinks the death of Orlando, and his last prayer, both pathetic and sublime. I can see nothing in it but the systematic spirit of parody which we find in Pulci; but the lines on the death of Forisena, in the fourth canto, are really graceful and serious. The following remarks on Pulci's style come from a more competent judge than myself:—

"There is something harsh in Pulci's manner, owing to his abrupt transition from one idea to another, and to his carelessness of grammatical rules. He was a poet by nature, and wrote with ease; but he never cared for sacrificing syntax to meaning: he did not mind saying any thing incorrectly, if he were but sure that his meaning would be guessed. The rhyme very often compels him to employ expressions, words, and even lines, which frequently render the sense obscure and the passage crooked, without producing any other effect than that of destroying a fine stanza. He has no similes of any particular merit, nor does he stand eminent in description. His verses almost invariably make sense taken singly, and convey distinct and separate ideas. Hence he wants that richness, fulness, and smooth flow of diction, which is indispensable to an epic poet, and to a noble description or comparison. Occasionally, when the subject admits of a powerful sketch which may be presented with vigor and spirit by a few strokes boldly drawn, Pulci appears to a great advantage."—Panizzi on romantic poetry of Italians, in the first volume of his Orlando Innamorato, [illegible]

84. A foreigner must admire the vivacity of the narrative, the humorous gayety of the characters, the adroitness of the satire; but the Italians, and especially the Tuscans, delight in the raciness of Pulci's Florentine idiom, which we cannot equally relish. He has not been without influence on men of more celebrity than himself. In several passages of Ariosto, especially the visit of Astolfo to the moon, we trace a resemblance not wholly fortuitous. Voltaire, in one of his most popular poems, took the dry archness of Pulci, and exaggerated the profaneness, superadding the obscenity from his own stores; but Mr. Frere, with none of these two ingredients in his admirable vein of humor, has come, in the War of the Giants, much closer to the Morgante Maggiore than any one else.

Platonic theology of Ficinus.

85. The Platonic academy, in which the chief of the Medici took so much delight, did not fail to reward his care. Marsilius Ficinus, in his Theologica Platonica (1482), developed a system chiefly borrowed from the later Platonists of the Alexandrian school, full of delight to the credulous imagination, though little appealing to the reason, which, as it seemed remarkably to coincide in some respects with the received tenets of the church, was connived at in a few reveries, which could not so well bear the test of an orthodox standard. He supported his philosophy by a translation of Plato into Latin, executed by the direction of Lorenzo, and printed before 1490. Of this translation Buhle has said, that it has been very unjustly reproached with want of correctness: it is, on the contrary, perfectly conformable to the original, and has even, in some passages, enabled us to restore the text; the manuscripts used by Ficinus, I presume, not being in our hands. It has also the rare merit of being at once literal, perspicuous, and in good Latin.[1]

Doctrine of Averroes on the soul.

86. But the Platonism of Ficinus was not wholly that of the master. It was based on the emanation of the human soul from God, and its capacity of re-union by an ascetic and contemplative life; a theory perpetually reproduced in various modifications of meaning, and far more of words. The nature and immortality of the soul,

[1] Hist. de la Philosophie, vol. ii. The fullest account of the philosophy of Ficinus has been given by Buhle. Those who seek less minute information may have recourse to Brucker or Corniani; or, if they are content with still less, to Tiraboschi, Roscoe Heeren, or the Biographie Universelle.

the functions and distinguishing characters of angels, the being and attributes of God, engaged the thoughtful mind of Ficinus. In the course of his high speculations, he assailed a doctrine, which, though rejected by Scotus and most of the schoolmen, had gained much ground among the Aristotelians, as they deemed themselves, of Italy; a doctrine first held by Averroes, — that there is one common intelligence, active, immortal, indivisible, unconnected with matter, the soul of human kind; which is not in any one man, because it has no material form; but which yet assists in the rational operations of each man's personal soul, and from those operations, which are all conversant with particulars, derives its own knowledge of universals. Thus, if I understand what is meant, which is rather subtle, it might be said, that as, in the common theory, particular sensations furnish means to the soul of forming general ideas; so, in that of Averroes, the ideas and judgments of separate human souls furnish collectively the means of that knowledge of universals, which the one great soul of mankind alone can embrace. This was a theory, built, as some have said, on the bad Arabic version of Aristotle which Averroes used. But, whatever might have first suggested it to the philosopher of Cordova, it seems little else than an expansion of the Realist hypothesis, urged to a degree of apparent paradox. For if the human soul, as an universal, possess an objective reality, it must surely be intelligent; and, being such, it may seem no extravagant hypothesis, though one incapable of that demonstration we now require in philosophy, to suppose that it acts upon the subordinate intelligences of the same species, and receives impressions from them. By this also they would reconcile the knowledge we were supposed to possess of the reality of universals, with the acknowledged impossibility, at least in many cases, of representing them to the mind.

Opposed by Ficinus.

87. Ficinus is the more prompt to refute the Averroists, that they all maintained the mortality of the particular soul; while it was his endeavor, by every argument that erudition and ingenuity could supply, to prove the contrary. The whole of his Platonic Theology appears a beautiful but too visionary and hypothetical system of theism, the groundworks of which lay deep in the meditations of ancient Oriental sages. His own treatise, of which a very copious account will be found in Buhle, soon fell into oblivion; but it belongs to a class of literature, which, in all its exten-

sion, has, full as much as any other, engaged the human mind.

Desire of man to explore mysteries.

88. The thirst for hidden knowledge, by which man is distinguished from brutes, and the superior races of men from savage tribes, burns generally with more intenseness in proportion as the subject is less definitely comprehensible, and the means of certainty less attainable. Even our own interest in things beyond the sensible world does not appear to be the primary or chief source of the desire we feel to be acquainted with them: it is the pleasure of belief itself, of associating the conviction of reality with ideas not presented by sense. It is sometimes the necessity of satisfying a restless spirit, that first excites our endeavor to withdraw the veil that conceals the mystery of our being. The few great truths in religion that reason discovers, or that an explicit revelation deigns to communicate, sufficient as they may be for our practical good, have proved to fall very short of the ambitious curiosity of man. They leave so much imperfectly known, so much wholly unexplored, that, in all ages, he has never been content without trying some method of filling up the void. These methods have often led him to folly and weakness and crime. Yet as those who want the human passions, in their excess the great fountains of evil, seem to us maimed in their nature; so an indifference to this knowledge of invisible things, or a premature despair of attaining it, may be accounted an indication of some moral or intellectual deficiency, some scantness of due proportion in the mind.

Various methods employed.

89. The means to which recourse has been had to enlarge the boundaries of human knowledge in matters relating to the Deity, or to such of his intelligent creatures as do not present themselves in ordinary objectiveness to our senses, have been various, and may be distributed into several classes. Reason itself, as the most valuable, though not the most frequent in use, may be reckoned the first. Whatever deductions have suggested themselves to the acute, or analogies to the observant mind, whatever has seemed the probable interpretation of revealed testimony, is the legitimate province of a sound and rational theology. But so fallible appears the reason of each man to others, and often so dubious are its inferences to himself; so limited is the span of our faculties; so incapable are

Reason and inspiration.

they of giving more than a vague and conjectural probability, where we demand most of definiteness and certainty,—that few, comparatively speaking, have been content to acquiesce even in their own hypotheses upon no other grounds than argument has supplied. The uneasiness that is apt to attend suspense of belief, has required, in general, a more powerful remedy. Next to those who have solely employed their rational faculties in theology, we may place those who have relied on a supernatural illumination. These have nominally been many; but the imagination, like the reason, bends under the incomprehensibility of spiritual things: a few excepted, who have become founders of sects and lawgivers to the rest, the mystics fell into a beaten track, and grew mechanical even in their enthusiasm.

Extended inferences from sacred books.

90. No solitary and unconnected meditations, however, either of the philosopher or the mystic, could furnish a sufficiently extensive stock of theological faith for the multitude, who by their temper and capacities were more prone to take it at the hands of others than choose any tenets for themselves. They looked, therefore, for some authority upon which to repose; and, instead of builders, became, as it were, occupants of mansions prepared for them by more active minds. Among those who acknowledge a code of revealed truths,—the Jews, Christians, and Mahometans,—this authority has been sought in largely expansive interpretations of their sacred books,—either of positive obligation, as the decisions of general councils were held to be; or at least of such weight as a private man's reason, unless he were of great name himself, was not permitted to contravene. These expositions, in the Christian Church as well as among the Jews, were frequently allegorical: a hidden stream of esoteric truth was supposed to flow beneath all the surface of Scripture; and every text germinated, in the hands of the preacher, into meanings far from obvious, but which were presumed to be not undesigned. This scheme of allegorical interpretation began among the earliest fathers, and spread with perpetual expansion through the middle ages.[1] The Reformation swept most of it away; but it has frequently revived in a more partial manner. We mention it here only as one great means of enabling men to believe more than they

[1] Fleury (5me discours), xvii. 37; Mosheim, *passim*.

had done, of communicating to them what was to be received as divine truths, not additional to Scripture, because they were concealed in it, but such as the church could only have learned through her teachers.

Confidence in traditions.

91. Another large class of religious opinions stood on a somewhat different footing. They were, in a proper sense, according to the notions of those times, revealed from God, though not in the sacred writings which were the chief depositories of his word. Such were the received traditions in each of the three great religions, sometimes absolutely infallible; sometimes, as in the former case, of interpretations, resting upon such a basis of authority, that no one was held at liberty to withhold his assent. The Jewish traditions were of this kind; and the Mahometans have trod in the same path. We may add to these the legends of saints: none perhaps were positively enforced as of faith; but a Franciscan was not to doubt the inspiration and miraculous gifts of his founder. Nor was there any disposition in the people to doubt of them: they filled up with abundant measure the cravings of the heart and fancy, till, having absolutely palled both by excess, they brought about a kind of re-action, which has taken off much of their efficacy.

Confidence in individuals as inspired.

92. Francis of Assisi may naturally lead us to the last mode in which the spirit of theological belief manifested itself, — the confidence in a particular man, as the organ of a special divine illumination. But though this was fully assented to by the order he instituted, and probably by most others, it cannot be said that Francis pretended to set up any new tenets, or enlarge, except by his visions and miracles, the limits of spiritual knowledge. Nor would this, in general, have been a safe proceeding in the middle ages. Those who made a claim to such light from heaven as could irradiate what the church had left dark seldom failed to provoke her jealousy. It is, therefore, in later times, and under more tolerant governments, that we shall find the fanatics, or impostors, whom the multitude has taken for witnesses of divine truth, or at least for interpreters of the mysteries of the invisible world.

Jewish Cabala.

93. In the class of traditional theology, or what might be called complemental revelation, we must place the Jewish Cabala. This consisted in a very specific and complex system concerning the nature of the Supreme

Being, the emanation of various orders of spirits in successive links from his essence, their properties and characters. It is evidently one modification of the Oriental philosophy, borrowing little from the Scriptures, at least through any natural interpretation of them; and the offspring of the Alexandrian Jews, not far from the beginning of the Christian era. They referred it to a tradition from Esdras, or some other eminent person, on whom they fixed as a depositary of an esoteric theology communicated by divine authority. The Cabala was received by the Jewish doctors in the first centuries after the fall of their state; and after a period of long duration, as remarkable for the neglect of learning in that people as in the Christian world, it revived again in that more genial season, the eleventh and twelfth centuries, when the brilliancy of many kinds of literature among the Saracens of Spain excited their Jewish subjects to emulation. Many conspicuous men illustrate the Hebrew learning of those and the succeeding ages. It was not till now, about the middle of the fifteenth century, that they came into contact with the Christians in theological philosophy. The Platonism of Ficinus, derived in great measure from that of Plotinus and the Alexandrian school, was easily connected, by means especially of the writings of Philo, with the Jewish Orientalism, sisters as they were of the same family. Several forgeries in celebrated names, easy to effect and sure to deceive, had been committed in the first ages of Christianity by the active propagators of this philosophy. Hermes Trismegistus and Zoroaster were counterfeited in books which most were prone to take for genuine, and which it was not then easy to refute on critical grounds. These altogether formed a huge mass of imposture, or at best of arbitrary hypothesis, which, for more than a hundred years after this time, obtained an undue credence, and consequently retarded the course of real philosophy in Europe.[1]

94. They never gained over a more distinguished proselyte, or one whose credulity was more to be regretted, than a young man who appeared at Florence in 1485, — John Picus of Mirandola. He was then twenty-two years old, the younger son of an illustrious family, which held that little principality as an imperial fief. At the age of four- *Picus of Mirandola.*

[1] Brucker, vol. ii.; Buhle, ii. 316; Meiners, Vergl. der Sitten, iii. 277.

teen, he was sent to Bologna, that he might study the canon law, with a view to the ecclesiastical profession; but, after two years, he felt an inexhaustible desire for more elevated though less profitable sciences. He devoted the next six years to the philosophy of the schools in the chief universities of Italy and France: whatever disputable subtleties the metaphysics and theology of that age could supply became familiar to his mind; but to these he added a knowledge of the Hebrew and other Eastern languages, a power of writing Latin with grace, and of amusing his leisure with the composition of Italian poetry. The natural genius of Picus is well shown, though in a partial manner, by a letter which will be found among those of Politian, in answer to Hermolaus Barbarus. His correspondent had spoken with the scorn, and almost bitterness, usual with philologers of the Transalpine writers, meaning chiefly the schoolmen, for the badness of their Latin. The young scholastic answered, that he had been at first disheartened by the reflection, that he had lost six years' labor; but considered afterwards that the barbarians might say something for themselves; and puts a very good defence in their mouths, — a defence which wants nothing but the truth of what he is forced to assume, that they had been employing their intellects upon things instead of words. Hermolaus found, however, nothing better to reply than the compliment, that Picus would be disavowed by the schoolmen for defending them in so eloquent a style.[1]

His credulity in the Cabala.

95. He learned Greek very rapidly, probably after his coming to Florence; and having been led, through Ficinus, to the study of Plato, he seems to have given up his Aristotelian philosophy for theories more con-

[1] The letter of Hermolaus is dated Apr., 1485. He there says, after many compliments to Picus himself: "Nec enim inter autores Latinæ linguæ numero Germanos istos et Teutonas qui ne viventes quidem vivebant, nedum ut extincti vivant, aut si vivunt, vivunt in pœnam et contumeliam." The answer of Picus is dated in June. A few lines from his pleading for the schoolmen will exhibit his ingenuity and elegance. "Admirentur nos sagaces in inquirendo, circumspectos in explorando, subtiles in contemplando, in judicando graves, implicitos in vinciendo, faciles in enodando. Admirentur in nobis brevitatem styli, fœtam rerum multarum atque magnarum, sub expositis verbis remotissimas sententias, plenas quæstionum, plenas solutionum, quam apti sumus, quam bene instructi ambiguitates tollere, scrupos diluere, involuta evolvere, flexanimis syllogismis et infirmare falsa et vera confirmare. Viximus celebres, o Hermolae, et posthac vivemus, non in scholis grammaticorum et pædagogiis, sed in philosophorum coronis, in conventibus sapientum, ubi non de matre Andromaches, non de Niobes filiis, atque id genus levibus nugis, sed de humanarum divinarumque rerum rationibus agitur et disputatur. In quibus meditandis, inquirendis, et enodandis, ita subtiles acuti acresque fuimus, ut anxii quandoque nimium et morosi fuisse forte videamur, si modo esse morosus quispiam aut curiosus nimio plus in indagando veritate potest." Polit. Epist., lib. 9.

genial to his susceptible and credulous temper. These led him onwards to wilder fancies. Ardent in the desire of knowledge, incapable, in the infancy of criticism, to discern authentic from spurious writings, and perhaps disqualified, by his inconceivable rapidity in apprehending the opinions of others, from judging acutely of their reasonableness, Picus of Mirandola fell an easy victim to his own enthusiasm and the snares of fraud. An impostor persuaded him to purchase fifty Hebrew manuscripts, as having been composed by Esdras, and containing the most secret mysteries of the Cabala. "From this time," says Corniani, "he imbibed more and more such idle fables, and wasted in dreams a genius formed to reach the most elevated and remote truths." In these spurious books of Esdras, he was astonished to find, as he says, more of Christianity than Judaism, and trusted them the more confidently for the very reason that demonstrates their falsity.[1]

96. Picus, about the end of 1486, repaired to Rome, and, with permission of Innocent VIII., propounded his famous nine hundred theses, or questions, logical, ethical, mathematical, physical, metaphysical, theological, magical, and cabalistical, upon every one of which he offered to dispute with any opponent. Four hundred of these propositions were from philosophers of Greece or Arabia, from the schoolmen, or from the Jewish doctors: the rest were announced as his own opinions, which, saving the authority of the church, he was willing to defend.[2] There was some need of this reservation; for several of his theses were ill-sounding, as it was called, in the ears of the orthodox. They raised a good deal of clamor against him; and the high rank, brilliant reputation, and obedient demeanor of Picus were all required to save him from public censure or more serious animadversions. He was compelled, however, to swear that he would adopt such an exposition of his theses as the pope should set forth; but, as this was not done, he published an apology, especially vindicating his employment of cabalistical and magical learning. This excited fresh attacks, which in ome measure continued to harass him, till, on the accession of Alexander VI. to the papal chair, he was finally pronounced free from blamable intention. He had meantime,

His literary performances.

[1] Corniani, iii. 63; Meiners, Lebensbeschreibungen berühmter Männer, ii. 21; Tiraboschi, vii. 325.

[2] Meiners, p. 14

as we may infer from his later writings, receded from some of the bolder opinions of his youth. His mind became more devout, and more fearful of deviating from the church. On his first appearance at Florence, uniting rare beauty with high birth and unequalled renown, he had been much sought by women, and returned their love. But, at the age of twenty-five, he withdrew himself from all worldly distraction; destroying, as it is said, his own amatory poems, to the regret of his friends.[1] He now published several works, of which the Heptaplus is a cabalistic exposition of the first chapter of Genesis. It is remarkable, that, with his excessive tendency to belief, he rejected altogether, and confuted in a distinct treatise, the popular science of astrology, in which men so much more conspicuous in philosophy have trusted. But he had projected many other undertakings of vast extent, — an allegorical exposition of the New Testament, a defence of the Vulgate and Septuagint against the Jews, a vindication of Christianity against every species of infidelity and heresy; and, finally, a harmony of philosophy, reconciling the apparent inconsistencies of all writers, ancient and modern, who deserved the name of wise, as he had already attempted by Plato and Aristotle. In these arduous labors he was cut off by a fever, at the age of thirty-one, in 1494, on the very day that Charles VIII. made his entry into Florence. A man so justly called the phœnix of his age, and so extraordinarily gifted by nature, ought not to be slightly passed over, though he may have left nothing which we could read with advantage. If we talk of the admirable Crichton, who is little better than a shadow, and lives but in panegyric, so much superior and more wonderful a person as John Picus of Mirandola should not be forgotten.[2]

State of learning in Germany

97. If, leaving the genial city of Florence, we are to judge of the state of knowledge in our Cisalpine regions, and look at the books it was thought worth while to publish, which seems no bad criterion, we shall

[1] Meiners, p. 10.

[2] The long biography of Picus in Meiners is in great measure taken from a life written by his nephew, John Francis Picus, Count of Mirandola, himself a man of great literary and philosophical reputation in the next century. Meiners has made more use of this than any one else; but much will be found concerning Picus from this source, and from his own works, in Brucker, Buhle, Corniani, and Tiraboschi. The epitaph on Picus by Hercules Strozza is, I believe, in the Church of St. Mark: —

"Joannes jacet hic Mirandola; cætera nôrunt
Et Tagus et Ganges; forsan et Antipodes."

rate but lowly their proficiency in the classical literature so much valued in Italy. Four editions, and those chiefly of short works, were printed at Deventer, one at Cologne, one at Louvain, five perhaps at Paris, two at Lyons.[1] But a few undated books might, probably, be added. Either, therefore, the love of ancient learning had grown colder, which was certainly not the case, or it had never been strong enough to reward the labor of the too sanguine printers. Yet it was now striking root in Germany. The excellent schools of Munster and Schelstadt were established in some part of this decade; they trained those who were themselves to become instructors; and, the liberal zeal of Langius extending beyond his immediate disciples, scarce any Latin author was published in Germany of which he did not correct the text.[2] The opportunities he had of doing so were not, as has been just seen, so numerous in this period as they became in the next. He had to withstand a potent and obstinate faction. The mendicant friars of Cologne, the head-quarters of barbarous superstition, clamored against his rejection of the old school-books and the entire reform of education. But Agricola addresses his friend in sanguine language: "I entertain the greatest hope from your exertions, that we shall one day wrest from this insolent Italy her vaunted glory of pre-eminent eloquence; and redeeming ourselves from the opprobium of ignorance, barbarism, and incapacity of expression, which she is ever casting upon us, may show our Germany so deeply learned, that Latium itself shall not be more Latin than she will appear."[3] About 1482, Agricola was invited to the court of the elector palatine at Heidelberg. He seems not to have been engaged in public instruction, but passed the remainder of his life, unfortunately too short, for he died in 1485, in diffusing and promoting a taste for literature among his contemporaries. No German wrote in so pure a style, or possessed so large a portion of classical learning. Vives places him, in dignity and grace of language, even above Politian and Hermolaus.[4] The praises of Erasmus, as well as of the

Agricola.

[1] Panzer.

[2] Meiners, Lebensbesch., ii. 328; Eichhorn, iii. 231-239.

[3] "Unum hoc tibi affirmo, ingentem de te concipio fiduciam, summamque in spem adducor, fore aliquando, ut priscam insolenti Italiæ, et propemodum occupatam bene dicendi gloriam extorqueamus; vindicemusque nos, et ab ignavia, qua nos barbaros, indoctosque et elingues, et si quid est his incultius, esse nos jactitant, exsolvamus, futuramque tam doctam et literatam Germaniam nostram, ut non Latinius vel ipsum sit Latium." This is quoted by Heeren, p. 154; and Meiners, ii. 329.

[4] "Vix et hac nostra et patrum memoria fuit unus atque alter dignior, qui multum legeretur, multumque in manibus habere

later critics, if not so marked, are very freely bestowed. His letters are frequently written in Greek, — a fashion of those who could follow it; and, as far as I have attended to them, seem equal in correctness to some from men of higher name in the next age.

Rhenish academy.

98. The immediate patron of Agricola, through whom he was invited to Heidelberg, was John Camerarius of the house of Dalberg, Bishop of Worms, and Chancellor of the Palatinate. He contributed much himself to the cause of letters in Germany, especially if he is to be deemed the founder, as probably he should be, of an early academy, the Rhenish Society, which, we are told, devoted its time to Latin, Greek, and Hebrew criticism, astronomy, music, and poetry, — not scorning to relax their minds with dances and feasts, nor forgetting the ancient German attachment to the flowing cup.[1] The chief seat of the Rhenish Society was at Heidelberg; but it had associate branches in other parts of Germany, and obtained imperial privileges. No member of this academy was more conspicuous than Conrad Celtes, who has sometimes been reckoned its founder, which, from his youth, is hardly probable; and was, at least, the chief instrument of its subsequent extension. He was indefatigable in the vineyard of literature, and, travelling to different parts of Germany, exerted a more general influence than Agricola himself. Celtes was the first from whom Saxony derived some taste for learning. His Latin poetry was far superior to any that had been produced in the empire; and for this, in 1487, he received the laurel crown from Frederick III.[2]

tur, quam Radulphus Agricola Frisius; tantum est in ejus operibus ingenii, artis, gravitatis, dulcedinis, eloquentiæ, eruditionis; at is paucissimis noscitur, vir non minus, qui ab hominibus cognosceretur, dignus quam Politianus, vel Hermolaus Barbarus, quos mea quidem sententia, et majestate et suavitate dictionis non æquat modo, sed etiam vincit." Vives, Comment. in Augustin. (apud Blount, Censura Auctorum, sub nomine Agricola).

"Agnosco virum divini pectoris, eruditionis reconditæ, stylo minime vulgari, solidum, nervosum, elaboratum, compositum. In Italia summus esse poterat, nisi Germaniam prætulisset."—Erasmus in Ciceroniano. He speaks as strongly in many other places. Testimonies to the merits of Agricola from Huet, Vossius, and others, are collected by Bayle, Blount, Baillet, and Niceron. Meiners has written his life, ii. p. 332-363; and several of his letters will be found among those addressed to Reuchlin, Epistolæ ad Reuchlinum; a collection of great importance for this portion of literary history.

[1] "Studebant eximia hæc ingenia Latinorum, Græcorum, Ebræorumque scriptorum lectioni, cum primis criticæ; astronomiam et artem musicam excolebant. Poesin atque jurisprudentiam sibi habebant commendatam; imo et interdum gaudia curis interponebant. Nocturno nimirum tempore, defessi laboribus, ludere solebant, saltare, jocari cum mulierculis, epulari, ac more Germanorum inveterato strenue potare." (Jugler, Hist. Litteraria, p. 1993, vol. iii.) The passage seems to be taken from Ruprecht, Oratio de Societate Litteraria Rhenana, Jenæ, 1752, which I have not seen.

[2] Jugler, *ubi supra;* Eichhorn, ii. 557; Heeren, p. 160; Biogr. Universelle, arts. "Celtes, Dalberg, Trithemius."

Reuchlin.

99. Reuchlin, in 1482, accompanied the Duke of Wirtemberg on a visit to Rome. He thus became acquainted with the illustrious men of Italy, and convinced them of his own pretensions to the name of a scholar. The old Constantinopolitan, Argyropulus, on hearing him translate a passage of Thucydides, exclaimed, "Our banished Greece has now flown beyond the Alps." Yet Reuchlin, though from some other circumstances of his life a more celebrated, was not probably so learned or so accomplished a man as Agricola. He was withdrawn from public tuition by the favor of several princes, in whose courts he filled honorable offices; and, after some years more, he fell unfortunately into the same seducing error as Picus of Mirandola, and sacrificed his classical pursuits for the Cabalistic philosophy.

French language and poetry.

100. Though France contributed little to the philologer, several books were now published in French. In the Cent Nouvelles Nouvelles, 1486, a slight improvement in polish of language is said to be discernible.[1] The poems of Villon are rather of more importance. They were first published in 1489; but many of them had been written thirty years before. Boileau has given Villon credit for being the first who cleared his style from the rudeness and redundancy of the old romancers.[2] But this praise, as some have observed, is more justly due to the Duke of Orleans, a man of full as much talent as Villon, with a finer taste. The poetry of the latter, as might be expected from a life of dissoluteness and roguery, is often low and coarse; but he seems by no means incapable of a moral strain, not destitute of terseness and spirit. Martial d'Auvergne, in his Vigiles de la Mort de Charles VII., which, from its subject, must have been written soon after 1460, though not printed till 1490, displays, to judge from the extracts in Goujet, some compass of imagination.[3] The French poetry of this age was still full of allegorical morality, and had lost a part of its original raciness. Those who desire an acquaintance with it may have recourse to the author just mentioned, or to Bouterwek; and extracts, though not so copious as the title promises, will be found in the Recueil des anciens Poëtes Français.

1 Essai du C. François de Neufchâteau sur les meilleurs ouvrages en prose; prefixed to Œuvres de Pascal (1819), i. p. cxx.

2 "Villon fut le premier dans des siècles grossiers
Débrouiller l'art confus de nos vieux romanciers."
Art Poëtique, l. i. v. 117.

3 Goujet, Bibliothèque Française, vol x.

European drama.

101. The modern drama of Europe is derived, like its poetry, from two sources,—the one ancient or classical, the other mediæval; the one an imitation of Plautus and Seneca, the other a gradual refinement of the rude scenic performances denominated miracles, mysteries, or moralities.

Latin.

Latin plays upon the former model, a few of which are extant, were written in Italy during the fourteenth and fifteenth centuries, and sometimes represented, either in the universities or before an audience of ecclesiastics and others who could understand them.[1] One of these, the Catinia of Secco Polentone, written about the middle of the fifteenth century and translated by a son of the author into the Venetian dialect, was printed in 1482. This piece, however, was confined to the press.[2] Sabellicus, as quoted by Tiraboschi, has given to Pomponius Lætus the credit of having re-established the theatre at Rome, and caused the plays of Plautus and Terence, as well as some more modern, which we may presume to have been in Latin, to be performed before the pope, probably Sixtus IV. And James of Volterra, in a diary published by Muratori, expressly mentions a History of Constantine represented in the papal palace during the carnival of 1484.[3] In imitation of Italy, but perhaps a little after the present decennial period, Reuchlin brought Latin plays of his own composition before a German audience. They were represented by students of Heidelberg. An edition of his Progymnasmata Scenica, containing some of these comedies, was printed in 1498. It has been said that one of them is taken from the French farce Maître Patelin;[4] while another, entitled Sergius, according to Warton, flies a much higher pitch, and is a satire on bad kings and bad ministers; though, from the account of Meiners, it seems rather to fall on the fraudulent arts of the monks.[5] The book is very scarce, and I have never seen it. Conrad Celtes, not long after Reuchlin, produced his own tragedies and comedies in

[1] Tiraboschi, vii. 200.

[2] Id., p. 201.

[3] Id., p. 204.

[4] Gresswell's Early Parisian Press, p. 124; quoting La Monnoye. This seems to be confirmed by Meiners, i. 63. [It has been suggested to me by Dr. West, that the Progymnasmata Scenica is the title of a single comedy, namely, that which is taken from Maître Patelin. Meiners, vol. i. p. 63, seems to confirm this. Some extracts from the Sergius, for which I am indebted to the same obliging correspondent, lead me to conclude that the satire is more general than the account of that play by Meiners had implied; and that priests or monks come in only for a share in it. — 1842.]

[5] Warton, iii. 203; Meiners, i. 62. The Sergius was represented at Heidelberg about 1497.

the public halls of German cities. It is to be remembered, that the oral Latin language might at that time be tolerably familiar to a considerable audience in Germany.

102. The Orfeo of Politian has claimed precedence as the earliest represented drama, not of a religious nature, in a modern language. This was written by him in two days, and acted before the court of Mantua in 1483. Roscoe has called it the first example of the musical drama, or Italian opera; but, though he speaks of this as agreed by general consent, it is certain that the Orfeo was not designed for musical accompaniment, except probably in the songs and choruses.[1] According to the analysis of the fable in Ginguéné, the Orfeo differs only from a legendary mystery by substituting one set of characters for another; and it is surely by an arbitrary definition that we pay it the compliment upon which the modern historians of literature seem to have agreed. Several absurdities which appear in the first edition are said not to exist in the original manuscripts from which the Orfeo has been reprinted.[2] We must give the next place to a translation of the Menæchmi of Plautus, acted at Ferrara in 1486, by order of Ercole I., and, as some have thought, his own production, or to some original plays said to have been performed at the same brilliant court in the following years.[3]

Orfeo of Politian.

103. The less regular, though in their day not less interesting, class of scenical stories, commonly called mysteries, all of which related to religious subjects, were never in more reputation than at this time. It is impossible to fix their first appearance at any single era; and the inquiry into the origin of dramatic representation must be very limited in its subject, or perfectly futile in its scope. All nations probably have at all times, to a certain extent, amused themselves both with pantomimic and oral representation of a feigned story; the sports of children are seldom without both; and the exclusive employment of the

Origin of dramatic mysteries.

[1] Burney (Hist. of Music, iv. 17) seems to countenance this; but Tiraboschi does not speak of musical accompaniment to the Orfeo; and Corniani only says, "Alcuni di essi sembrano dall' autor destinati ad accoppiarsi colla musica. Tali sono i canzoni e i cori alla greca." Probably Roscoe did not mean all that his words imply; for the origin of recitative, in which the essence of the Italian opera consists, more than a century afterwards, is matter of notoriety.

[2] Tiraboschi, vii. 216; Ginguéné, iii. 514. Andrès, v. 125, discussing the history of the Italian and Spanish theatres, gives the precedence to the Orfeo, as a represented play, though he conceives the first act of the Celestina to have been written and well known not later than the middle of the fifteenth century.

[3] Tiraboschi, vii. 203, *et post;* Roscoe, Leo X., ch. ii.; Ginguéné, vi. 18.

former, instead of being a first stage of the drama, as has sometimes been assumed, is rather a variety in the course of its progress.

Their early stage.

104. The Christian drama arose on the ruins of the heathen theatre: it was a natural substitute of real sympathies for those which were effaced and condemned. Hence we find Greek tragedies on sacred subjects almost as early as the establishment of the church, and we have testimonies to their representation at Constantinople. Nothing of this kind being proved with respect to the west of Europe in the dark ages, it has been conjectured, not improbably, though without necessity, that the pilgrims, of whom great numbers repaired to the East in the eleventh century, might have obtained notions of scenical dialogue, with a succession of characters, and with an ornamental apparatus, in which theatrical representation properly consists. The earliest mention of them, it has been said, is in England. Geoffrey, afterwards abbot of St. Alban's, while teaching a school at Dunstable, caused one of the shows vulgarly called miracles, on the story of St. Catherine, to be represented in that town. Such is the account of Matthew Paris, who mentions the circumstance incidentally, in consequence of a fire that ensued. This must have been within the first twenty years of the twelfth century.[1] It is not to be questioned, that Geoffrey, a native of France, had some earlier models in his own country. Le Bœuf gives an account of a mystery written in the middle of the preceding century, wherein Virgil is introduced among the prophets that come to adore the Saviour; doubtless in allusion to the fourth eclogue.

[1] Matt. Paris, p. 1007 (edit. 1684). See Warton's 34th section (iii. 193-233) for the early drama; and Beauchamps, Hist. du Théâtre Français, vol. i., or Bouterwek, v. 95-117, for the French in particular; Tiraboschi, *ubi supra*, or Riccoboni, Hist. du Théâtre Italien, for that of Italy.

[It is not sufficient, in order to prove the continuity of dramatic representation through the dark ages, that we should possess a few poetical dialogues in Latin, or even entire plays, like those of Hroswitha, Abbess of Gandersaen, in the tenth century. A modern French writer calls one of her sacred comedies, "Un des chaînons, le plus brillant, peut-être, et le plus pur de cette série non interrompue d' œuvres dramatiques, jusqu'ici trop peu étudiées, qui lient le théâtre païen, expirant vers le cinquième siècle, au théâtre moderne, renaissant dans presque toutes les contrées de l'Europe vers la fin du treizième siècle." — Quotation in Jubinal, Mystères Inédits du Quinzième Siècle, Paris, 1837, p. 9. But we have no sort of evidence that the dramas of Hroswitha were represented, nor is it by any means probable that they were. Until the new languages, which alone the people understood, were employed in popular writings, the stage must have been silent. In the mystery of the Wise and Foolish Virgins, we find both Latin and Provençal. This, therefore, is an evidence of transition; and, whether as old as the eleventh century, or a little later, may stand at the head of European dramatic literature. Several others, however, are referred by late French antiquaries to the same age, and have been published by M. Monmerqué — 1847.]

Extant English mysteries.

105. Fitz-Stephen, in the reign of Henry II., dwells on the sacred plays acted in London, representing the miracles or passions of martyrs. They became very common, by the names of mysteries or miracles, both in England and on the Continent; and were not only exhibited within the walls of convents, but upon public occasions and festivals for the amusement of the people. It is probable, however, that the performers, for a long time, were always ecclesiastics. The earlier of these religious dramas were in Latin. A Latin farce on St. Nicolas exists, older than the thirteenth century.[1] It was slowly that the modern languages were employed; and perhaps it might hence be presumed that the greater part of the story was told through pantomime. But as this was unsatisfactory, and the spectators could not always follow the fable, there was an obvious inducement to make use of the vernacular language. The most ancient specimens appear to be those which Le Grand d'Aussy found among the compositions of the Trouveurs. He has published extracts from three; two of which are in the nature of legendary mysteries; while the third, which is far more remarkable, and may possibly be of the following century, is a pleasing pastoral drama, of which there seem to be no other instances in the mediæval period.[2] Bouterwek mentions a fragment of a German mystery, near the end of the thirteenth century.[3] Next to this, it seems that we should place an English mystery, called "The Harrowing of Hell." "This," its editor observes, "is believed to be the most ancient production in a dramatic form in our language. The manuscript from which it is now printed is on vellum, and is certainly as old as the reign of Edward III., if not older. It probably formed one of a series of performances of the same kind, founded upon Scripture history." It consists of a prologue, epilogue, and intermediate dialogue of nine persons: Dominus, Sathan, Adam, Eve, &c. Independently of the alleged age of the manuscript itself, the language will hardly be thought

[1] Journal des Savans, 1828, p. 297. These farces, according to M. Raynouard, were the earliest dramatic representations, and gave rise to the mysteries.

[2] Fabliaux, ii. 119.

[3] ix. 265. The "Tragedy of the Ten Virgins" was acted at Eisenach in 1322. This is evidently nothing but a mystery. Weber's Illustrations of Northern Poetry, p. 19. — [A drama of the Wise and Foolish Virgins, written in a mixture of Latin and Romance, and ascribed by Le Bœuf to the eleventh century, has been published by Raynouard. See Journal des Savans, June 1836, p. 366, for this early mystery — 1842.]

later than 1350.[1] This, however, seems to stand at no small distance from any extant work of the kind. Warton having referred the Chester mysteries to 1327, when he supposes them to have been written by Ranulph Higden, a learned monk of that city, best known as the author of the Polychronicon, Roscoe positively contradicts him, and denies that any dramatic composition can be found in England anterior to the year 1500.[2] Two of these Chester mysteries have been since printed; but, notwithstanding the very respectable authorities which assign them to the fourteenth century, I cannot but consider the language in which we now read them not earlier, to say the least, than the middle of the next. It is possible that they have, in some degree, been modernized. Mr. Collier has given an analysis of our own extant mysteries, or, as he prefers to call them, Miracle-plays.[3] There does not seem to be much dramatic merit, even with copious indulgence, in any of them; and some, such as the two Chester mysteries, are in the lowest style of buffoonery: yet they are not without importance in the absolute sterility of English literature during the age in which we presume them to have been written, — the reigns of Henry VI. and Edward IV.

106. The fourteenth and fifteenth centuries were fertile of these religious dramas in many parts of Europe. They were frequently represented in Germany, but more in Latin than the mother-tongue. The French Scriptural theatre, whatever may have been previously exhibited, seems not to be traced in permanent existence beyond the last years of the fourteenth century.[4] It was about 1400, according to Beauchamps, or some years before, as the authorities quoted by Bouterwek imply, that the Confrairie de la

First French theatre.

[1] Mr. Collier has printed twenty-five copies (why veteris tam parcus aceti?) of this very curious record of the ancient drama. I do not know that any other in Europe of that early age has yet been given to the press.

[The Harrowing of Hell has since been published by Mr. Halliwell. In the Théâtre Français du Moyen Age, 1839, M. Michel has published several French mysteries or Miracle-plays of the fourteenth century, or perhaps earlier. — 1847.]

[2] Lorenzo de' Medici, i. 299. Roscoe thinks there is reason to conjecture that the Miracle-play acted at Dunstable was in dumb show; and assumes the same of the "grotesque exhibitions" known by the name of the Harrowing of Hell. In this we have just seen that he was mistaken, and probably in the former.

[3] Hist. of English Dramatic Poetry, vol. ii. The Chester Mysteries were printed for the Roxburghe Club by my friend Mr. Markland; and what are called the Towneley Mysteries are announced for publication. (1836.) — [They have since appeared. — 1842.]

[4] [The mystery of St. Crispin and St. Crispinien, published about 1836, is reviewed by Raynouard in the Journal des Savans for that year. He seems to assign no date to this mystery; but it is clear that similar dramas were represented long before the end of the fourteenth century But not perhaps on a permanent theatre — 1842.]

Passion de N. S. was established as a regular body of actors at Paris.[1] They are said to have taken their name from the mystery of the passion, which in fact represented the whole life of our Lord from his baptism, and was divided into several days. In pomp of show, they far excelled our English mysteries, in which few persons appeared; and the scenery was simple. But, in the mystery of the passion, eighty-seven characters were introduced in the first day; heaven, earth, and hell combined to people the stage; several scenes were written for singing, and some for choruses. The dialogue, of which I have only seen the few extracts in Bouterwek, is rather similar to that of our own mysteries, though less rude, and with more efforts at a tragic tone.[2]

107. The mysteries, not confined to Scriptural themes, embraced those which were hardly less sacred and trustworthy in the eyes of the people, — the legends of saints. These afforded ample scope for the gratification which great part of mankind seem to take in witnessing the endurance of pain. Thus, in one of these Parisian mysteries, St. Barbara is hung up by the heels on the stage; and, after uttering her remonstrances in that unpleasant situation, is torn with pincers, and scorched with lamps, before the audience. The decorations of this theatre must have appeared splendid. A large scaffolding at the back of the stage displayed heaven above and hell below, between which extended the world, with representations of the spot where the scene lay. Nor was the machinist's art unknown. An immense dragon, with eyes of polished steel, sprang out from hell, in a mystery exhibited at Metz in the year 1437, and spread his wings so near to the spectators that they were all in consternation.[3] Many French mysteries, chiefly without date of the year, are in print, and probably belong, typographically speaking, to the present century. One bears, according to Brunet, the date of 1484.[4] These may, however, have been written long before their publication. Beauchamps has given a list of early mysteries and moralities in the French language, beginning near the end of the fourteenth century.

Theatrical machinery.

108. The religious drama was doubtless full as ancient in Italy as in any other country: it was very congenial to a peo-

[1] Beauchamps; Recherches sur le Théâtre Français; Bouterwek, v. 96.

[2] Bouterwek, p. 100.

[3] Id., p. 103-106.

[4] Brunet, Manuel du Libraire.

ple whose delight in sensible objects is so intense. It did not supersede the extemporaneous performances, the mimi and histriones, who had probably never intermitted their sportive license since the days of their Oscan fathers, and of whom we find mention, sometimes with severity, sometimes with toleration, in ecclesiastical writers;[1] but it came into competition with them, and thus may be said to have commenced in the thirteenth century a war of regular comedy against the lawless savages of the stage, which has only been terminated in Italy within very recent recollection. We find a society del Gonfalone, established at Rome in 1264, the statutes of which declare that it is designed to represent the passion of Jesus Christ.[2] Lorenzo de' Medici condescended to publish a drama of this kind on the martyrdom of two saints; and a considerable collection of similar productions during the fifteenth century was in the possession of Mr. Roscoe.[3]

Italian religious dramas.

109. Next to the mysteries came the kindred class, styled moralities. But as these belong more peculiarly to the next century, both in England and France, though they began about the present time, we may better reserve them for that period. There is still another species of dramatic composition, what may be called the farce, not always very distinguishable from comedy, but much shorter; admitting more buffoonery without reproach, and more destitute of any serious or practical end. It may be reckoned a middle link between the extemporaneous effusions of the mimes and the legitimate drama. The French have a diverting piece of this kind, Maître Patelin, ascribed to Pierre Blanchet, and first printed in 1490. It was restored to the stage, with much alteration, under the name of L'Avocat Patelin, about the beginning of the last century; and contains strokes of humor which Molière would not have disdained.[4] Of these productions, there were not a few in Germany, called Fastnachtsspiele, or Carnival-plays, written in the license which

Moralities.

Farces.

[1] Thomas Aquinas mentions the *histrionatûs ars* as lawful if not abused. Antonin of Florence does the same. Riccoboni, i. 23.

[2] Riccoboni. Tiraboschi, however, v. 376, disputes the antiquity of any scenical representations truly dramatic in Italy; in which he seems to be mistaken.

[3] Life of Lorenzo, . 402.

[4] The proverbial expression for quitting a digression, "Revenons à nos moutons," is taken from this farce; which is at least short, and as laughable as most farces are. It seems to have been written not long before its publication. See Pasquier, Recherches de la France, l. viii. c. 59; Biogr. Univ., Blanchet; and Bouterwek, v. 118.

that season has generally permitted. They are scarce, and of little value. The most remarkable is the Apotheosis of Pope Joan, a tragi-comic legend, written about 1480.[1]

110. Euclid was printed for the first time at Venice in 1482; the diagrams in this edition are engraved on copper, and remarkably clear and neat.[2] The translation is that of Campanus from the Arabic. The Cosmography of Ptolemy, which had been already twice published in Italy, appeared the same year at Ulm, with maps by Donis, some of them traced after the plans drawn by Agathodæmon, some modern; and it was reprinted, as well as Euclid, at the same place, in 1486. The tables of Regiomontanus were printed both at Augsburg and Venice in 1490. We may take this occasion of introducing two names which do not exclusively belong to the exact sciences, nor to the present period.

Mathematical works.

111. Leo Baptista Alberti was a man, who, if measured by the universality of his genius, may claim a place in the temple of glory he has not filled; the author of a Latin comedy, entitled Philodoxios, which the younger Aldus Manutius afterwards published as a genuine work of a supposed ancient, Lepidus; a moral writer in the various forms of dialogue, dissertation, fable, and light humor; a poet, extolled by some, though not free from the rudeness of his age; a philosopher of the Platonic school of Lorenzo; a mathematician, and inventor of optical instruments; a painter, and the author of the earliest modern treatise on painting; a sculptor, and the first who wrote about sculpture; a musician, whose compositions excited the applause of his contemporaries; an architect of profound skill, not only displayed in many works, — of which the Church of St. Francis, at Rimini, is the most admired,[3] — but in a theoretical treatise, De re ædificatoriâ, published posthumously in 1485. It has been called the only work on architecture which we can place on a level with that of Vitruvius, and by some has been preferred to it. Alberti had deeply meditated the remains of Roman antiquity, and

Leo Baptista Alberti

[1] Bouterwek, Geschichte der Deutschen Poesie, ix. 357-367; Heinsius, Lehrbuch der Sprachwissenschaft, iv. 125.

[2] A beautiful copy of this edition, presented to Mocenigo, Doge of Venice, is in the British Museum. The diagrams, especially those which represent solids, are better than in most of our modern editions of Euclid. I will take this opportunity of mentioning, that the earliest book in which engravings are found, is the edition of Dante by Landino, published at Florence in 1481. See Brunet, Manuel du Libraire; Dibdin's Bibl.; Spencer, &c.

[3] [Let me add that of St. Andrew at Mantua, worthy of comparison with the best of the sixteenth century, and free from the excessive decoration by which they often lose sight both of pure taste and religious effect. — 1847.]

endeavored to derive from them general theorems of beauty, variously applicable to each description of buildings.[1]

112. This great man seems to have had two impediments to his permanent glory: one, that he came a few years too soon into the world, before his own language was become polished, and before the principles of taste in art had been wholly developed; the other, that, splendid as was his own genius, there were yet two men a little behind, in the presence of whom his star has paled; men not superior to Alberti in universality of mental powers, but in their transcendency and command over immortal fame. Many readers will have perceived to whom I allude, — Leonardo da Vinci, and Michael Angelo.

Leonardo da Vinci.

113. None of the writings of Leonardo were published till more than a century after his death; and, indeed, the most remarkable of them are still in manuscript. We cannot, therefore, give him a determinate place under this, rather than any other decennium; but, as he was born in 1452, we may presume his mind to have been in full expansion before 1490. His Treatise on Painting is known as a very early disquisition on the rules of the art. But his greatest literary distinction is derived from those short fragments of his unpublished writings, that appeared not many years since; and which, according at least to our common estimate of the age in which he lived, are more like revelations of physical truths vouchsafed to a single mind, than the superstructure of its reasoning upon any established basis. The discoveries which made Galileo and Kepler and Mæstlin and Maurolycus and Castelli, and other names, illustrious, the system of Copernicus, the very theories of recent geologers, are anticipated by Da Vinci, within the compass of a few pages, not perhaps in the most precise language, or on the most conclusive reasoning, but so as to strike us with something like the awe of preternatural knowledge. In an age of so much dogmatism, he first laid down the grand principle of Bacon, that experiment and observation must be the guides to just theory in the investigation of nature. If any doubt could be harbored, not as to the right of Leonardo da Vinci to stand as the first name of the fifteenth century, which is beyond all doubt, but as to his originality in so many discoveries, which

[1] Corniani, ii. 160; Tiraboschi, vii. 360.

probably no one man, especially in such circumstances, has ever made, it must be on an hypothesis, not very untenable, that some parts of physical science had already attained a height which mere books do not record. The extraordinary works of ecclesiastical architecture in the middle ages, especially in the fifteenth century, as well as those of Toscanelli and Fioravanti, which we have mentioned, lend some countenance to this opinion. Leonardo himself speaks of the earth's annual motion, in a treatise that appears to have been written about 1510, as the opinion of many philosophers in his age.[1]

[1] The manuscripts of Leonardo da Vinci, now at Paris, are the justification of what has been said in the text. A short account of them was given by Venturi, who designed to have published a part; but, having relinquished that intention, the fragments he has made known are the more important. As they are very remarkable, and not, I believe, very generally known, I shall extract a few passages from his Essai sur les Ouvrages physico-mathématiques de Léonard de Vinci. Paris, 1797.

"En mécanique, Vinci connaissait, entr'autres choses: 1. La théorie des forces appliquées obliquement au bras du levier; 2. La résistance respective des poutres; 3. Les loix du frottement données ensuite par Amontons; 4. L'influence du centre de gravité sur les corps en repos ou en mouvement; 5. L'application du principe des vîtesses virtuelles à plusieurs cas que la sublime analyse a porté de nos jours à sa plus grande généralité. Dans l'optique il décrivit la chambre obscure avant Porta, il expliqua avant Maurolycus la figure de l'image du soleil dans un trou de forme anguleuse; il nous apprend la perspective aérienne, la nature des ombres colorées, les mouvemens de l'iris, les effets de la durée de l'impression visible, et plusieurs autres phénomènes de l'œil qu'on ne rencontre point dans Vitellion. Enfin non seulement Vinci avait remarqué tout ce que Castelli a dit un siècle après lui sur le mouvement des eaux; le premier me paraît même dans cette partie supérieur de beaucoup à l'autre, que l'Italie cependant a regardé comme le fondateur de l'hydraulique.

"Il faut donc placer Léonard à la tête de ceux qui se sont occupés des sciences physico-mathématiques, et de la vraie méthode d'étudier parmi les modernes;" p. 5.

The first extract Venturi gives is entitled, On the descent of heavy bodies combined with the rotation of the earth. He here assumes the latter, and conceives that a body falling to the earth from the top of a tower would have a compound motion, in consequence of the terrestrial rotation. Venturi thinks that the writings of Nicolas de Cusa had set men on speculating concerning this before the time of Copernicus.

Vinci had very extraordinary lights as to mechanical motions. He says plainly that the time of descent on inclined planes of equal height is as their length; that a body descends along the arc of a circle sooner than down the chord; and that a body descending an inclined plane will reascend with the same velocity as if it had fallen down the height. He frequently repeats that every body weighs in the direction of its movement, and weighs the more in the ratio of its velocity; by weight evidently meaning what we call force. He applies this to the centrifugal force of bodies in rotation: "Pendant tout ce temps elle pèse sur la direction de son mouvement.

"Lorsqu'on employe une machine quel conque pour mouvoir un corps grave, toutes les parties de la machine qui ont un mouvement égal à celui du corps grave ont une charge égale au poids entier du même corps. Si la partie qui est le moteur a, dans le même temps, plus de mouvement que le corps mobile, elle aura plus de puissance que le mobile; et cela d'autant plus qu'elle se mouvra plus vîte que les corps même. Si la partie qui est le moteur a moins de vîtesse que le mobile, elle aura d'autant moins de puissance que ce mobile." If in this passage there is not the perfect luminousness of expression we should find in the best modern books, it seems to contain the philosophical theory of motion as unequivocally as any of them.

Vinci had a better notion of geology than most of his contemporaries, and saw that the sea had covered the mountains which contained shells: "Ces coquillages ont vécu dans le même endroit lorsque l'eau de la mer le recouvrait. Les bancs, par la suite des temps, ont été recouverts par d'autres couches de limon de différentes hauteurs; ainsi, les coquilles ont été enclavées sous le bourbier amoncelé au dessus, jusqu'à sortir de l'eau." He seems to have had an idea of the elevation of the

SECT. VI. 1491–1500.

State of Learning in Italy — Latin and Italian Poets — Learning in France and England — Erasmus — Popular Literature and Poetry — Other Kinds of Literature — General Literary Character of Fifteenth Century — Book-trade, its Privileges and Restraints.

114. THE year 1494 is distinguished by an edition of Musæus, generally thought the first work from the press established at Venice by Aldus Manutius, who had settled there in 1489 [1]

continents, though he gives an unintelligible reason for it.

He explained the obscure light of the unilluminated part of the moon by the reflection of the earth, as Mæstlin did long after. He understood the camera obscura, and describes its effect. He perceived that respirable air must support flame: — "Lorsque l'air n'est pas dans un état propre à recevoir la flamme, il n'y peut vivre ni flamme ni aucun animal terrestre ou aérien. Aucun animal ne peut vivre dans un endroit où la flamme ne vit pas."

Vinci's observations on the conduct of the understanding are also very much beyond his time. I extract a few of them.

"Il est toujours bon pour l'entendement d'acquérir des connaissances quelles qu'elles soient; on pourra ensuite choisir les bonnes et écarter les inutiles.

"L'interprète des artifices de la nature, c'est l'expérience. Elle ne se trompe jamais; c'est notre jugement qui quelquefois se trompe lui-même, parcequ'il s'attend à des effets auxquels l'expérience se refuse. Il faut consulter l'expérience, en varier les circonstances jusqu'à ce que nous en ayons tiré des règles générales; car c'est elle qui fournit les vraies règles. Mais à quoi bon ces règles, me direz-vous? Je réponds qu'elles nous dirigent dans les recherches de la nature et les opérations de l'art. Elles empêchent que nous ne nous abusions nous-mêmes ou les autres, en nous promettant des résultats que nous ne saurions obtenir.

"Il n'y a point de certitude dans les sciences où on ne peut pas appliquer quelque partie des mathématiques, ou qui n'en dépendent pas de quelque manière.

"Dans l'étude des sciences qui tiennent aux mathématiques, ceux qui ne consultent pas la nature, mais les auteurs, ne sont pas les enfans de la nature; je dirais qu'ils n'en sont que les petits fils: elle seule, en effet, est le maître des vrais génies. Mais voyez la sottise! on se moque d'un homme qui aimera mieux apprendre de la nature elle-même, que des auteurs, qui n'en sont que les clercs." Is not this the precise tone of Lord Bacon?

Vinci says in another place: "Mon dessein est de citer d'abord l'expérience, et de démontrer ensuite pourquoi les corps sont contraints d'agir de telle manière. C'est la méthode qu'on doit observer dans les recherches des phénomènes de la nature. Il est bien vrai que la nature commence par le raisonnement, et finit par l'expérience; mais n'importe, il nous faut prendre la route opposée: comme j'ai dit, nous devons commencer par l'expérience, et tâcher par son moyen d'en découvrir la raison."

He ascribes the elevation of the equatorial waters above the polar to the heat of the sun: "Elles entrent en mouvement de tous les côtés de cette éminence aqueuse pour rétablir leur sphéricité parfaite." This is not the true cause of the elevation; but by what means could he know the fact?

Vinci understood fortification well, and wrote upon it. Since in our time, he says, artillery has four times the power it used to have, it is necessary that the fortification of towns should be strengthened in the same proportion. He was employed on several great works of engineering. So wonderful was the variety of power in this miracle of nature. For we have not mentioned, that his Last Supper, at Milan, is the earliest of the great pictures in Italy; and that some productions of his easel vie with those of Raphael. His only published work, the Treatise on Painting, does him injustice: it is an ill-arranged compilation from several of his manuscripts. That the extraordinary works, of which this note contains an account, have not been published entire and in their original language, is much to be regretted by all who know how to venerate so great a genius as Leonardo da Vinci.

[1] The Erotemata of Constantine Las-

In the course of about twenty years, with some interruption, he gave to the world several of the principal Greek authors; and though, as we have seen, not absolutely the earliest printer in that language, he so far excelled all others in the number of his editions, that he may be justly said to stand at the head of the list. It is right, however, to mention that Zarot had printed Hesiod and Theocritus in one volume, and also Isocrates, at Milan, in 1493; that the Anthologia appeared at Florence in 1494 Lucian and Apollonius Rhodius in 1496; the Lexicon of Suidas at Milan in 1499. About fifteen editions of Greek works, without reckoning Craston's Lexicon and several grammars, had been published before the close of the century.[1] The most remarkable of the Aldine editions are the Aristotle, in five volumes, the first bearing the date of 1495, the last of 1498; and nine plays of Aristophanes in the latter year. In this Aristophanes, and perhaps in other editions of this time, Aldus had fortunately the assistance of Marcus Musurus, one of the last, but by no means the least eminent, of the Greeks who transported their language to Italy. Musurus was now a public teacher at Padua. John Lascaris, son, perhaps, of Constantine, edited the Anthologia at Florence. It may be doubted whether Italy had as yet produced any scholar, unless it were Varino, more often called Phavorinus, singly equal to the task of superintending a Greek edition. His Thesaurus Cornucopiæ, a collection of thirty-four grammatical tracts in Greek, printed 1496, may be an exception. The Etymologicum Magnum, Venice, 1499, being a lexicon with only Greek explanations, is supposed to be chiefly due to Musurus. Aldus had printed Craston's Lexicon in 1497, with the addition of an index: this has often been mistaken for an original work.[2]

Aldine Greek editions.

115. The state of Italy was not so favorable as it had been to the advancement of philosophy. After the expulsion of the Medici from Florence, in 1494, the Platonic Academy was broken up; and that philosophy

Decline of learning in Italy.

caris, printed by Aldus, bears date Feb., 1494, which seems to mean 1495. But the Musæus has no date, nor the Galeomyomachia, a Greek poem by one Theodorus Prodromus. Renouard, Hist. de l'Imprimerie des Aldes.

[1] The Grammar of Urbano Valeriano was first printed in 1497. It is in Greek and Latin, and of extreme rarity. Roscoe (Leo X., ch. xi.) says, "it was received with such avidity, that Erasmus, on inquiring for it in the year 1499, found that not a copy of this impression remained unsold." I have given, a little below, a different construction to these words of Erasmus.

[2] Renouard; Roscoe's Leo X., ch. xi.

never found again a friendly soil in Italy, though Ficinus had endeavored to keep it up by a Latin translation of Plotinus. Aristotle and his followers began now to regain the ascendant. Perhaps it may be thought that even polite letters were not so flourishing as they had been; no one at least yet appeared to fill the place of Hermolaus Barbarus, who died in 1493, or Politian, who followed him the next year.

116. Hermolaus Barbarus was a noble Venetian, whom Europe agreed to place next to Politian in critical learning, and to draw a line between them and any third name. "No time, no accident, no destiny," says an enthusiastic scholar of the next age, "will ever efface their remembrance from the hearts of the learned."[1] Erasmus calls him a truly great and divine man. He filled many honorable offices for the republic; but lamented that they drew him away from that learning for which he says he was born, and to which alone he was devoted.[2] Yet Hermolaus is but faintly kept in mind at the present day. In his Latin style, with the same fault as Politian, an affectation of obsolete words, he is less flexible and elegant. But his chief merit was in the restoration of the text of ancient writers. He boasts that he had corrected above five thousand passages in Pliny's natural history, and more than three hundred in the very brief geography of Pomponius Mela. Hardouin, however, charges him with extreme rashness in altering passages he did not understand. The pope had nominated Hermolaus to the greatest post in the Venetian Church, the patriarchate of Aquileia; but his mortification at finding that the senate refused to concur in the appointment is said to have hastened his death.[3]

Hermolaus Barbarus.

117. A Latin poet, once of great celebrity, Baptista Mantuan, seems to fall within this period as fitly as any other, though several of his poems had been separately printed before, and their collective publication was not

Mantuan.

[1] "Habuit nostra hæc ætas bonarum literarum proceres duos, Hermolaum Barbarum atque Angelum Politianum: Deum immortalem! quam acri judicio, quanta facundia, quanta linguarum, quanta disciplinarum omnium scientia præditos! Hi Latinam linguam jampridem squalentem et multa barbariei rubigine exesam, ad pristinum revocare nitorem conati sunt, atque illis suus profecto conatus non infeliciter cessit, suntque illi de Latina lingua tam bene meriti, quam qui ante eos optimi meriti fuere. Itaque immortalem sibi gloriam, immortale decus paraverunt, manebitque semper in omnium eruditorum pectoribus consecrata Hermolai et Politiani memoria, nullo ævo, nullo casu, nullo fato abolenda."—Brixeus Erasmo in Erasm., Epist. ccxii.

[2] Meiners, ii. 200.

[3] Bayle; Niceron, vol. xiv.; Tiraboschi, vii. 152; Corniani, iii. 197; Heeren, p. 274.

till 1513. Editions recur very frequently in the bibliography of Italy and Germany. He was, and long continued to be, the poet of schoolrooms. Erasmus says that he would be placed by posterity not much below Virgil;[1] and the Marquis of Mantua, anticipating this suffrage, erected their statues side by side. Such is the security of contemporary compliments! Mantuan has long been utterly neglected, and does not find a place in most selections of Latin poetry. His Eclogues and Silvæ are said to be the least bad of his numerous works. He was among the many assailants of the church, or at least the court of Rome; and this animosity inspired him with some bitter, or rather vigorous, invectives. But he became afterwards a Carmelite friar.[2] Marullus, a Greek by birth, has obtained a certain reputation for his Latin poems, which are of no great value.

Pontanus.

118. A far superior name is that of Pontanus, to whom, if we attend to some critics, we must award the palm above all Latin poets of the fifteenth century. If I might venture to set my own taste against theirs, I should not agree to his superiority over Politian. His hexameters are by no means deficient in harmony, and may perhaps be more correct than those of his rival, but appear to me less pleasing and poetical. His lyric poems are, like too much modern Latin, in a tone of languid voluptuousness; and ring changes on the various beauties of his mistress, and the sweetness of her kisses. The few elegies of Pontanus, among which that addressed to his wife, on the prospect of peace, is the best known, fall very short of the admirable lines of Politian on the death of Ovid. Pontanus wrote some moral and political essays in prose, which are said to be full of just observations and sharp satire on the court of Rome, and written in a style which his contemporaries regarded with admiration. They were published in 1490. Erasmus, though a parsimonious distributor of praise to the Italians, has acknowledged their merit in the Ciceronianus.[3]

1 "Et nisi me fallit augurium, erit, erit aliquando Baptista suo concive gloriâ celebritateque non ita multo inferior, simul invidiam anni detraxerint."—Append. ad Erasm., Epist. cccxcv. (edit. Lugd.). It is not conceivable that Erasmus meant this literally; but the drift of the letter is to encourage the reading of Christian poets.

2 Corniani, iii., 148; Niceron, vol. xxvii. Such of Mantuan's eclogues as are printed in Carmina illustrium Poetarum Italorum, Florent., 1719, are but indifferent. I doubt, however, whether that voluminous collection has been made with much taste; and his satire on the see of Rome would certainly be excluded, whatever might be its merit. Corniani has given an extract, better than what I have seen of Mantuan.

3 Roscoe, Leo X., ch. ii. and xx.; Nice-

119. Pontanus presided at this time over the Neapolitan Academy, a dignity which he had attained upon the death of Beccatelli, in 1471. This was, after the decline of the Roman and the Florentine academies, by far the most eminent re-union of literary men in Italy; and, though it was long conspicuous, seems to have reached its highest point in the last years of this century, under the patronage of the mild Frederic of Aragon, and during that transient calm which Naples was permitted to enjoy between the invasions of Charles VIII. and Louis XII. That city and kingdom offorded many lovers of learning and poetry, some of them in the class of its nobles; each district being, as it were, represented in this academy by one or more of its distinguished residents. But other members were associated from different parts of Italy; and the whole constellation of names is still brilliant, though some have grown dim by time. The House of Este, at Ferrara, were still the liberal patrons of genius; none more eminently than their reigning marquis, Hercules I. And not less praise is due to the families who held the principalities of Urbino and Mantua.[1]

Neapolitan Academy.

120. A poem now appeared in Italy, well deserving of attention for its own sake, but still more so on account of the excitement and direction it gave to one of the most famous poets that ever lived. Matteo Maria Boiardo, Count of Scandiano, a man esteemed and trusted at the court of Ferrara, amused his leisure in the publication of a romantic poem, for which the stories of Charlemagne and his paladins, related by one who assumed the name of Turpin, and already woven into long metrical narrations, current at the end of the fourteenth and during the fifteenth century in Italy, supplied materials, which are almost lost in the original inventions of the author. The first edition of this poem is without date, but probably in 1495. The author, who died the year before, left it unfinished at the ninth canto of the

Boiardo.

ron, vol. viii.; Corniani; Tiraboschi. "Pontanus cum illa quatuor complecti summa cura conatus sit, nervum dico, numeros, candorem, venustatem, profecto est omnia consecutus. Quintum autem illud quod est horum omnium veluti vita quædam, modum intelligo, penitus ignoravit. Aiunt Virgilium cum multos versus matutino calore effudisset, pomeridianis horis novo judicio solitum ad paucorum numerum revocare. Contra quidem Pontano evenisse arbitror. Quæ prima quaque inventione arrisissent, iis plura postea, dum recognosceret, addita, atque ipsis potius carminibus, quam sibi pepercisse." — Scaliger de re poetica (apud Blount).

[1] Roscoe's Leo X., ch. ii. This contains an excellent account of the state of literature in Italy about the close of the century

third book. Agostini, in 1516, published a continuation, indifferently executed, in three more books; but the real complement of the Innamorato is the Furioso.[1] The Orlando Innamorato of Boiardo has hitherto not received that share of renown which seems to be its due: overpowered by the splendor of Ariosto's poem, and almost set aside in its original form by the improved edition or remaking (*rifaccimento*), which Berni afterwards gave, it has rarely been sought or quoted, even in Italy.[2]

Character of his poem.

121. The style is uncouth and hard; but, with great defects of style, which should be the source of perpetual delight, no long poem will be read; and it has been observed by Ginguéné with some justice, that Boiardo's name is better remembered, though his original poem may have been more completely neglected, through the process to which Berni has subjected it. In point of novel invention and just keeping of character, especially the latter, he has not been surpassed by his illustrious follower, Ariosto; and whatever of this we find in the Orlando Innamorato is due to Boiardo alone; for Berni has preserved the sense of almost every stanza. The imposing appearance of Angelica at the court of Charlemagne, in the first canto, opens the poem with a splendor rarely equalled, with a luxuriant fertility of invention, and with admirable art; judiciously presenting the subject in so much singleness, that, amidst all the intricacies and episodes of the story, the reader never forgets the incomparable Princess of Albracca. The latter city, placed in that remote Cathay which Marco Polo had laid open to the range of fancy, and its siege by Agrican's innumerable cavalry, are creations of Boiardo's most inventive mind. Nothing in Ariosto is conceived so nobly, or so much in the true genius of romance. Castelvetro asserts that the names Gradasso, Mandricardo, Sobrino, and others which Boiardo has given to his imaginary characters, belonged to his own peasants of Scandiano; and some have improved upon this by assuring us, that those who take the pains to ascertain the fact may still find the representatives

1 Fontanini, dell' eloquenza Italiana, edit. di Zeno, p. 270.

2 See my friend Mr. Panizzi's excellent introduction to his edition of the Orlando Innamorato. This poem had never been reprinted since 1544; so much was Roscoe deceived in fancying that "the simplicity of the original has caused it to be preferred to the same work, as altered or reformed by Francesco Berni." — Life of Leo X., ch. ii.

of these sonorous heroes at the plough, which, if the story were true, ought to be the case.[1] But we may give him credit for talent enough to invent those appellations; he hardly found an Albracca on his domains; and those who grudge him the rest, acknowledge that, in a moment of inspiration, while hunting, the name of Rodomont occurred to his mind. We know how finely Milton, whose ear pursued, almost to excess, the pleasure of harmonious names, and who loved to expatiate in these imaginary regions, has alluded to Boiardo's poem in the Paradise Regained. The lines are perhaps the most musical he has ever produced:—

> "Such forces met not, nor so wide a camp,
> When Agrican with all his Northern powers
> Besieged Albracca, as romances tell,
> The city of Gallaphron, from thence to win
> The fairest of her sex Angelica,
> His daughter, sought by many prowest knights,
> Both paynim and the peers of Charlemagne." [2]

122. The Mambriano of Francesco Bello, surnamed Il Cieco, another poem of the same romantic class, was published posthumously in 1497. Apostolo Zeno, as quoted by Roscoe, attributes the neglect of the Mambriano to its wanting an Ariosto to continue its subject, or a Berni to reform its style.[3] But this seems a capricious opinion. Bello composed it at intervals to amuse the courtiers of the Marquis of Mantua. The poem, therefore, wants unity. "It is a re-union," says Mr. Panizzi, "of detached tales, without any relation to each other, except in so far as most of the same actors are before us." [4] We may perceive by this how little a series of rhapsodies, not directed by a controlling unity of purpose, even though the work of a single man, are likely to fall into a connected poem. But that a long poem, such as the greatest and most ancient of all, of singular coherence and subordination of parts to an end, should be framed from the random and insulated songs of a great number of persons, is almost as incredible as that the annals of Ennius, to use

Francesco Bello.

[1] Camillo Pellegrino, in his famous controversy with the Academy of Florence on the respective merits of Ariosto and Tasso, having asserted this, they do not deny the fact, but say it stands on the authority of Castelvetro. Opere di Tasso, 4to, ii. 94. The critics held rather a pedantic doctrine, that, though the names of private men may be feigned, the poet has no right to introduce kings unknown to history, as this destroys the probability required for his fiction.

[2] Book iii.

[3] Leo X., ch. ii.

[4] Panizzi's Introduction to Boiardo, p. 360. He does not highly praise the poem, of which he gives an analysis with extracts See, too, Ginguéné. vol. iv.

Cicero's argument against the fortuitous origin of the world, should be formed by shaking together the letters of the alphabet.

Italian poetry near the end of the century.

123. Near the close of the fifteenth century, we find a great increase of Italian poetry, to which the patronage and example of Lorenzo had given encouragement. It is not easy to place within such narrow limits as a decennial period the names of writers whose productions were frequently not published, at least collectively, during their lives. Serafino d'Aquila, born in 1466, seems to fall, as a poet, within this decade; and the same may be said of Tibaldeo and Benivieni. Of these, the first is perhaps the best known: his verses are not destitute of spirit, but extravagance and bad taste deform the greater part.[1] Tibaldeo unites false thoughts with rudeness and poverty of diction. Benivieni, superior to either of these, is reckoned by Corniani a link between the harshness of the fifteenth and the polish of the ensuing century. The style of this age was far from the grace and sweetness of Petrarch; forced in sentiment, low in choice of words, deficient in harmony, it has been condemned by the voice of all Italian critics.[2]

Progress of learning in France and Germany.

124. A greater activity than before was now perceptible in the literary spirit of France and Germany. It was also regularly progressive. The press of Paris gave twenty-six editions of ancient Latin authors, nine of which were in the year 1500. Twelve were published at Lyons. Deventer and Leipsic, especially the latter, which now took a lead in the German press, bore a part in this honorable labor, — a proof of the rapid and extensive influence of Conrad Celtes on that part of Germany. It is to be understood that a very large proportion, or nearly the whole, of the Latin editions printed in Germany were for the use of schools.[3] We should be warranted in drawing an inference as to the progress in literary instruction in these countries from the increase in the number of publications,

[1] Bouterwek, Gesch. der Ital. Poesie, i. 321; Corniani.

[2] Corniani; Muratori, della perfetta Poesia; Crescimbeni, Storia della volgar Poesia.

[3] A proof of this may be found in the books printed at Deventer from 1491 to 1500. They consisted of Virgil's Bucolics three times, Virgil's Georgics twice, and the Eclogues of Galpurnius once, or perhaps twice. At Leipsic, the list is much longer, but, in great measure, of the same kind: single treatises of Seneca or Cicero, or detached parts of Virgil, Horace, Ovid, sometimes very short, as the Culex or the Ibis, form, with not many exceptions, the Cisalpine classical bibliography of the fifteenth century.

small as that number still is, and trifling as some of them may appear. It may be accounted for by the gradual working of the schools at Munster and other places, which had now sent out a race of pupils well fitted to impart knowledge, in their turn to others; and by the patronage of some powerful men, among whom the first place, on all accounts, is due to the Emperor Maximilian. Nothing was so likely to contribute to the intellectual improvement of Germany as the public peace of 1495, which put an end to the barbarous customs of the middle ages, not unaccompanied by generous virtues, but certainly as incompatible with the steady cultivation of literature as with riches and repose. Yet there seems to be no proof that the Greek language had obtained much more attention; no book connected with it is recorded to have been printed; and I do not find mention that it was taught, even superficially, in any university or school, at this time, though it might be conjectured without improbability. Reuchlin had now devoted his whole thoughts to cabalistic philosophy and the study of Hebrew; and Eichhorn, though not unwilling to make the most of early German learning, owns that, at the end of the century, no other person had become remarkable for a skill in Greek.[1]

125. Two men, however, were devoting incessant labor to the acquisition of that language at Paris, for whom was reserved the glory of raising the knowledge of it in Cisalpine Europe to a height which Italy could not attain. These were Erasmus and Budæus. The former, who had acquired as a boy the mere rudiments of Greek under Hegius at Deventer, set himself in good earnest to that study about 1499; hiring a teacher at Paris, old Hermonymus of Sparta,

Erasmus.

[1] Eichhorn, iii. 236. This section in Eichhorn is valuable, but exhibits some want of precision.

Reuchlin had been very diligent in purchasing Greek manuscripts. But these were very scarce, even in Italy. A correspondent of his, Streler by name, one of the young men who went from Germany to Florence for education, tells him, in 1491, "Nullos libros Græcos hic venales reperio;" and again, "De Græcis libris coemendis hoc scias; fui penes omnes hic librarios, nihil horum prorsus reperio." — Epist. ad Reuchl. (1562), fol. 7. In fact, Reuchlin's own library was so large as to astonish the Italian scholars when they saw the catalogue, who plainly owned they could not procure such books themselves. They had, of course, been originally purchased in Italy, unless we suppose some to have been brought by way of Hungary.

It is not to be imagined that the libraries of ordinary scholars were to be compared with that of Reuchlin, probably more opulent than most of them. The early printed books of Italy, even the most indispensable, were very scarce, — at least in France. A Greek grammar was a rarity at Paris in 1499. "Grammaticen Græcam," says Erasmus to a correspondent, "summo studio vestigavi, ut emptam tibi mitterem, sed jam utraque divendita fuerat, et Constantini quæ dicitur, quæque Urbani." — Epist. lix.; see, too, Epist. lxxiii.

of whose extortion he complains: but he was little able to pay any thing; and his noble endurance of privations for the sake of knowledge deserved the high reward of glory that it received. "I have given my whole soul," he says, "to Greek learning; and, as soon as I get any money, I shall first buy Greek books, and then clothes."[1] "If any new Greek book comes to hand, I would rather pledge my cloak than not obtain it; especially if it be religious, such as a Psalter or a Gospel."[2] It will be remembered, that the books of which he speaks must have been frequently manuscripts.

His diligence.

126. Budæus, in his proper name Budé, nearly of the same age as Erasmus, had relinquished every occupation for intense labor in literature. In an interesting letter, addressed to Cuthbert Tunstall in 1517, giving an account of his own early studies, he says that he learned Greek very ill from a bad master at Paris, in 1491. This was certainly Hermonymus, of whom Reuchlin speaks more favorably; but he was not quite so competent a judge.[3] Some years afterwards, Budæus got much better instruction; "ancient literature having derived within a few years great improvement in France by our intercourse with Italy, and by the importation of books in both the learned languages." Lascaris, who now lived at the court of Charles VIII., having returned with him from the Neapolitan expedition, gave Budæus some assistance, though not, according to the latter's biographer, to any great extent.

Budæus: his early studies.

127. France had as yet no writer of Latin who could be endured in comparison with those of Italy. Robert Gaguin praises Fichet, rector of the Sorbonne, as learned and eloquent, and the first who had taught many to employ good language in Latin. The more

Latin not well written in France.

[1] Epist. xxix.

[2] Epist. lviii.

[3] Hody (de Græcis illustribus, p. 238) thinks that the master of Budæus could not have been Hermonymus; probably because the praise of Reuchlin seemed to him incompatible with the contemptuous language of Budæus. But Erasmus is very explicit on this subject: "Ad Græcas literas utcunque puero degustatas jam grandior redii; hoc est, annos natus plus minus triginta, sed tum cum apud nos nulla Græcorum codicum esset copia, neque minor penuria doctorum. Lutetiæ tantum unus Georgius Hermonymus Græcè balbutiebat; sed talis, ut neque potuisset docere si voluisset, neque voluisset si potuisset. Itaque coactus ipse mihi præceptor esse," &c. (A.D. 1524): I transcribe from Jortin, ii. 419. Of Hermonymus, it is said by Beatus Rhenanus, in a letter to Reuchlin, that he was "non tam doctrina quam patria clarus." (Epist. ad Reuchl., fol. 52.) Roy, in his Life of Budæus, says, that the latter, having paid Hermonymus five hundred gold pieces, and read Homer and other books with him, "nihilo doctior est factus"

certain glory of Fichet is to have introduced the art of printing into France. Gaguin himself enjoyed a certain reputation for his style, and his epistles have been printed. He possessed, at least, what is more important, a love of knowledge, and an elevated way of thinking. But Erasmus says of him, that, "whatever he might have been in his own age, he would now scarcely be reckoned to write Latin at all." If we could rely on a panegyrist of Faustus Andrelinus, an Italian who came about 1489 to Paris, and was authorized, in conjunction with one Balbi, and with Cornelio Vitelli, to teach in the university,[1] he was the man who brought polite literature into France, and changed its barbarism for classical purity. But Andrelinus, who is best known as a Latin poet of by no means a high rank, seems not to merit this commendation. Whatever his capacities of teaching may have been, we have little evidence of his success. Yet the number of editions of Latin authors published in France during this decade proves some diffusion of classical learning; and we must admit the circumstance to be quite decisive of the inferiority of England.

Dawn of Greek learning in England.

128. A gleam of light, however, now broke out there. We have seen already, that a few, even in the last years of Henry VI., had overcome all obstacles in order to drink at the fountain-head of pure learning in Italy. One or two more names might be added for the intervening period; Milling, Abbot of Westminster, and Selling, prior of a convent at Canterbury.[2] It is reported by Polydore Virgil, and is proved by Wood, that Cornelio Vitelli, an Italian, came to Oxford, about 1488, in order to give that most barbarous university some notion of what was going forward on the other side of the Alps; and it has been probably conjectured, or rather may be assumed, that he there imparted the rudiments of Greek to William Grocyn.[3] It is

[1] This I find quoted in Bettinelli, Risorgimento d' Italia, i. 250; see also Bayle, and Biogr. Univ., art. "Andrelini." They were only allowed to teach for one hour in the evening, — the jealousy of the logicians not having subsided. Crevier, iv. 439.

[2] Warton, iii. 247; Johnson's Life of Linacre, p. 5. This is mentioned on Selling's monument now remaining in Canterbury Cathedral: —

"Doctor theologus Selling Græca atque Latina
Lingua perdoctus."

Selling, however, did not go to Italy till after 1480, far from returning in 1460, as Warton has said, with his usual indifference to anachronisms.

[3] Polydore says nothing about Vitelli's teaching Greek; though Knight, in his Life of Colet, translates *bonæ literæ*. "Greek and Latin." But the following passages seems decisive as to Grocyn's early studies in the Greek language: "Grocinus, qui prima Græcæ et Latinæ linguæ rudimenta in Britannia hausit, mox solidiorem iisdem operam sub Demetrio Chalcondyle et Politiano præceptoribus in Italia hausit." — Lilly, Elogia Virorum Doctorum, in Knight's Life of

certain, at least, that Grocyn had acquired some insight into that language before he took a better course, and, travelling into Italy, became the disciple of Chalcondyles and Politian. He returned home in 1491, and began to communicate his acquisitions, though chiefly to deaf ears, teaching in Exeter College at Oxford. A diligent emulator of Grocyn, but some years younger, and, like him, a pupil of Politian and Hermolaus, was Thomas Linacre, a physician; but, though a first edition of his translation of Galen has been supposed to have been printed at Venice in 1498, it seems to be ascertained that none preceded that of Cambridge in 1521. His only contribution to literature in the fifteenth century was a translation of the very short mathematical treatise of Proclus on the Sphere, published in a volume of ancient writers on astronomy, by Aldus Manutius, in 1499.[1]

Erasmus comes to England.

129. Erasmus paid his first visit to England in 1497, and was delighted with every thing that he found, especially at Oxford. In an epistle dated Dec. 5th, after praising Grocyn, Colet, and Linacre to the skies, he says of Thomas More, who could not then have been eighteen years old, "What mind was ever framed by nature more gentle, more pleasing, more gifted? — It is incredible what a treasure of old books is found here far and wide. — There is so much erudition, not of a vulgar and ordinary kind, but recondite, accurate, ancient, both Latin and Greek, that you would not seek any thing in Italy but the pleasure of travelling."[2] But this letter is addressed to an Englishman, and the praise is evidently much exaggerated; the scholars were few, and not more than three or four could be found, or at least could now be mentioned, who had any tincture of Greek, — Grocyn, Linacre, William Latimer, who, though an excellent scholar, never published any thing, and More, who had learned

Colet, p. 24. And Erasmus as positively: "Ipse Grocinus, cujus exemplum affers, nonne primum in Anglia Græcæ linguæ rudimenta didicit? Post in Italiam profectus audivit summos viros, sed interim lucro fuit illa prius a qualibuscunque didicisse." — Epist. ccclxiii. Whether the *qualescunque* were Vitelli or any one else, this can leave no doubt as to the existence of some Greek instruction in England before Grocyn; and as no one can be suggested, so far as appears, except Vitelli, it seems reasonable to fix upon him as the first preceptor of Grocyn. Vitelli had returned to Paris in 1489, and taught in the university, as has just been mentioned; so that he could have little time, if Polydore's date of 1488 be right, for giving much instruction at Oxford.

[1] Johnson's Life of Linacre, p. 152.

[2] "Thomæ Mori ingenio quid unquam finxit natura vel mollius, vel dulcius, vel felicius? . . . Mirum est dictu, quam hic passim, quam dense veterum librorum seges efflorescat . . . tantum eruditionis non illius protritæ ac trivialis, sed reconditæ, exactæ, antiquæ, Latinæ Græcæque, ut jam Italiam nisi visendi gratia non multum desideres." — Epist. xiv.

at Oxford under Grocyn.[1] It should here be added, that, in 1497, Terence was printed by Pynson, being the first edition of a strictly classical author in England; though Boethius had already appeared with Latin and English on opposite pages.

He publishes his Adages.

130. In 1500 was printed at Paris the first edition of Erasmus's Adages, doubtless the chief prose work of this century beyond the limits of Italy: but this edition should, if possible, be procured, in order to judge, with chronological exactness, of the state of literature; for, as his general knowledge of antiquity, and particularly of Greek, which was now very slender, increased, he made vast additions. The Adages, which were now about eight hundred, amounted in his last edition to 4151; not that he could find so many which properly deserve that name, but the number is made up by explanations of Latin and Greek idioms, or even of single words. He declares himself, as early as 1504, ashamed of the first edition of his Adages, which already seemed meagre and imperfect.[2] Erasmus had been preceded, in some measure, by Polydore Virgil, best known as the historian of this country, where he resided many years as collector of Papal dues. He published a book of Adages, which must have been rather a juvenile, and is a superficial, production, at Venice in 1498.

Romantic ballads of Spain.

131. The Castilian poets of the fifteenth century have been collectively mentioned on a former occasion. Bouterwek refers to the latter part of this age most of the romances which turn upon Saracen story, and the adventures of "knights of Granada, gentlemen, though Moors." Sismondi follows him without perhaps much reflection, and endeavors to explain what he might have doubted. Fear, he thinks, having long ceased in the bosoms of the Castilian Christians, even before conquest had set its seal to their security, hate, the child of fear, had grown feebler; and the romancers felt themselves at liberty to expatiate in the

[1] A letter of Colet to Erasmus, from Oxford, in 1497, is written in the style of a man who was conversant with the best Latin authors. Sir Thomas More's birth has not been placed by any biographer earlier than 1480.

It has been sometimes asserted, on the authority of Antony Wood, that Erasmus taught Greek at Oxford: but there is no foundation for this; and, in fact, he did not know enough of the language. Knight, on the other hand, maintains that he learned it there under Grocyn and Linacre: but this rests on no evidence; and we have seen that he gives a different account of his studies in Greek. Life of Erasmus, p. 22.

[2] Epist. cii.: "Jejunum atque inops videri cœpit, posteaquam Græcos colui auctores."

rich field of Mohammedan customs and manners. These had already exercised a considerable influence over Spain. But this opinion seems hard to be supported; nor do I find that the Spanish critics claim so much antiquity for the Moorish class of romantic ballads. Most of them, it is acknowledged, belong to the sixteenth, and some to the seventeenth century; and the internal evidence is against their having been written before the Moorish wars had become matter of distant tradition. We shall, therefore, take no notice of the Spanish romance-ballads till we come to the age of Philip II., to which they principally belong.[1]

Pastoral romances.

132. Bouterwek places in this decade the first specimens of the pastoral romance which the Castilian language affords.[2] But the style is borrowed from a neighboring part of the peninsula, where this species of fiction seems to have been indigenous. The Portuguese nation cultivated poetry as early as the Castilian; and we have seen that some is extant of a date anterior to the fourteenth century. But to the heroic romance they seem to have paid no regard: we do not find that it ever existed among them. Love chiefly occupied the Lusitanian muse; and to trace that passion through all its labyrinths, to display its troubles in a strain of languid melancholy, was the great aim of every poet. This led to the invention of pastoral romances, founded on the ancient traditions as to the felicity of shepherds and their proneness to love, and rendered sometimes more interesting for the time by the introduction of real characters and events under a slight disguise.[3] This artificial and effeminate sort of composition, which, if it may now and then be not unpleasing, cannot fail to weary the modern reader by its monotony, is due to Portugal, and, having been adopted in languages better known, became for a long time highly popular in Europe.

Portuguese lyric poetry.

133. The lyrical poems of Portugal were collected by Garcia de Resende, in the Cancioneiro Geral, published in 1516. Some few of these are of the fourteenth century; for we find the name of King Pedro, who died in 1369. Others are by the Infant Don Pedro, son of John I., in the earlier part of the fifteenth. But a greater number belong nearly to the present or preceding decade, or

1 Bouterwek, p. 121; Sismondi, iii. 222; Romances Moriscos, Madr. 1828.

2 P. 123.

3 Bouterwek's Hist. of Portuguese Literature, p. 43.

even to the ensuing age, commemorating the victories of the Portuguese in Asia. This collection is of extreme scarcity: none of the historians of Portuguese literature have seen it. Bouterwek and Sismondi declare that they have caused search to be made in various libraries of Europe without success. There is, however, a copy in the British Museum; and M. Raynouard has given a short account of one that he had seen in the Journal des Savans for 1826. In this article, he observes that the Cancioneiro is a mixture of Portuguese and Spanish pieces. I believe, however, that very little Spanish will be found, with the exception of the poems of the Infante Pedro, which occupy some leaves. The whole number of poets is but one hundred and thirty-two, even if some names do not occur twice; which I mention, because it has been erroneously said to exceed considerably that of the Spanish Cancioneiro. The volume is in folio, and contains two hundred and twenty-seven leaves. The metres are those usual in Spanish; some *versos de arte mayor;* but the greater part in trochaic redondillas. I observed no instance of the assonant rhyme; but there are several glosses, or, in the Portuguese word, *grosas.*[1] The chief part is amatory; but there are lines on the death of kings, and other political events.[2]

German popular books.

134. The Germans, if they did not as yet excel in the higher department of typography, were by no means negligent of their own great invention. The books, if we include the smallest, printed in the empire between 1470 and the close of the century, amount to several thousand editions. A large proportion of these were in their own language. They had a literary public, as we may call it, not merely in their courts and universities, but in their respectable middle class, the burghers of the free cities, and perhaps in the artisans whom they employed. Their reading was almost always with a serious end; but no people so successfully cultivated the art of moral and satirical fable. These, in many instances, spread with great favor through Cisalpine Europe. Among the works of this kind, in the fifteenth century, two deserve mention: the Eulenspiegel, popular after-

1 Bouterwek, p. 30, has observed that the Portuguese employ the *glosa*, calling it *volta*. The word in the Cancioneiro is *grosa*.

2 A manuscript collection of Portuguese lyric poetry of the fifteenth century belonged to Mr. Heber, and was sold to Messrs. Payne and Foss. It would probably be found, on comparison, to contain many of the pieces in the Cancioneiro Geral; but it is not a copy of it

wards in England by the name of Howleglass; and a superior and better known production, the Narrenschiff, or Ship of Fools, by Sebastian Brandt of Strasburg, the first edition of which is referred, by Brunet to the year 1494. The Latin translation, which bears the title of 1488 in an edition printed at Lyons, ought to be placed, according to the same bibliographer, ten years later; a numeral letter having probably been omitted. It was translated into English by Barclay, and published early in 1509. It is a metrical satire on the follies of every class, and may possibly have suggested to Erasmus his Encomium Moriæ. But the idea was not absolutely new: the theatrical company established at Paris, under the name of Enfans de Sans Souci, as well as the ancient office of jester or fool in our courts and castles, implied the same principle of satirizing mankind with ridicule so general, that every man should feel more pleasure from the humiliation of his neighbors than pain from his own. Brandt does not show much poetical talent: but his morality is clear and sound; he keeps the pure and right-minded reader on his side; and, in an age when little better came into competition, his characters of men, though more didactic than descriptive, did not fail to please. The influence such books of simple fiction and plain moral would possess over a people, may be judged by the delight they once gave to children, before we had learned to vitiate the healthy appetite of ignorance by premature refinements and stimulating variety.[1]

135. The historical literature of this century presents very little deserving of notice. The English writers of this class are absolutely contemptible; and, if some annalists of good sense and tolerable skill in narration may be found on the continent, they are not conspicuous enough to arrest our regard in a work which designedly passes over that department of literature, so far as it is merely conversant with particular events. But the memoirs of Philip de Comines, which, though not published till 1529, must have been written before the close of the fifteenth century, are not only of a higher value, but almost make an epoch in historical literature. If Froissart, by his picturesque descriptions and fertility of historical *invention*, may be reckoned the Livy of France, she had her Tacitus in Philip de

Historical works.

Philip de Comines.

[1] Bouterwek, ix. 332-354, v. 113; Heinsius, iv. 113; Warton, iii. 74.

Comines. The intermediate writers, Monstrelet and his continuators, have the merits of neither, certainly not of Comines. He is the first modern writer (or, if there had been any approach to an exception among the Italians, it has escaped my recollection) who in any degree has displayed sagacity in reasoning on the characters of men, and the consequences of their actions, or who has been able to generalize his observation by comparison and reflection. Nothing of this could have been found in the cloister; nor were the philologers of Italy equal to a task which required capacities and pursuits very different from their own. An acute understanding and much experience of mankind gave Comines this superiority: his life had not been spent over books; and he is consequently free from that pedantic application of history which became common with those who passed for political reasoners in the next two centuries. Yet he was not ignorant of former times; and we see the advantage of those translations from antiquity, made during the last hundred years in France, by the use to which he turned them.

136. The earliest printed treatise of algebra, till that of Lionardo Fibonacci was lately given to the press, was published in 1494, by Luca Pacioli di Borgo, a Franciscan, who taught mathematics in the University of Milan. This book is written in Italian, with a mixture of the Venetian dialect, and with many Latin words. In the first part he explains the rules of commercial arithmetic in detail, and is the earliest Italian writer who shows the principles of Italian book-keeping by double entry. Algebra he calls "l'arte maggiore, detta dal volgo la regola de la cosa," over "alghebra e almacabala," which last he explains by "restauratio et oppositio." The known number is called *n*° or *numero; co.* or *cosa* stands for the unknown quantity whence algebra was sometimes called the cossic art. In the early Latin treatises, *Res* is used, or *R.*, which is an approach to literal expression. The square is called *censo* or *ce.;* the cube, *cubo* or *cu.; p.* and *m.* stand for *plus* and *minus.* Thus 3*co. p.* 4*ce. m.* 5*cu. p.* 2*ce.ce. m.* 6*n*° would have been written for what would now be expressed $3x+4x^2-5x^3+2x^4-6$. Luca di Borgo's algebra goes as far as quadratic equations; but, though he had very good notions on the subject, it does not appear that he carried the science much beyond the point where Leonard Fibonacci had left it three centuries before. And its

Algebra.

principles were already familiar to mathematicians; for Regiomontanus, having stated a trigonometrical solution in the form of a quadratic equation, adds, "quod restat, præcepta artis edocebunt." Luca di Borgo perceived, in a certain sense, the applicability of algebra to geometry; observing that the rules as to surd roots are referable to incommensurable magnitudes.[1]

137. This period of ten years, from 1490 to 1500, will ever be memorable in the history of mankind. It is here that we usually close the long interval between the Roman world and this our modern Europe, denominated the Middle Ages. The conquest of Granada, which rendered Spain a Christian kingdom; the annexation of the last great fief of the French crown, Brittany, which made France an entire and absolute monarchy; the public peace of Germany; the invasion of Naples by Charles VIII., which revealed the weakness of Italy, while it communicated her arts and manners to the Cisalpine nations, and opened the scene of warfare and alliances which may be deduced to the present day; the discovery of two worlds by Columbus and Vasco de Gama, — all belong to this decade. But it is not, as we have seen, so marked an era in the progression of literature.

Events from 1490 to 1500.

138. In taking leave of the fifteenth century, to which we have been used to attach many associations of reverence, and during which the desire of knowledge was, in one part of Europe, more enthusiastic and universal than perhaps it has since ever been, it is natural to ask ourselves, what harvest had already rewarded their zeal and labor; what monuments of genius and erudition still receive the homage of mankind?

Close of fifteenth century.

139. No very triumphant answer can be given to this interrogation. Of the books then written, how few are read! Of the men then famous, how few are familiar in our recollection! Let us consider what Italy itself produced of any effective tendency to enlarge the boundaries of knowledge, or to delight the taste and fancy:

Its literature nearly neglected.

[1] Montucla; Kästner; Cossali; Hutton's Mathem. Dict., art. "Algebra." The last writer, and perhaps the first, had never seen the book of Luca Pacioli.

Mr. Colebrooke, in his Indian Algebra, has shown that the Hindoos carried that science considerably farther than either the Greeks or the Arabians (though he thinks they may probably have derived their notions of the science from the former), anticipating some of the discoveries of the sixteenth century.

The treatise of Valla on Latin grammar, the miscellaneous observations of Politian on ancient authors, the commentaries of Landino and some other editors, the Platonic theology of Ficinus, the Latin poetry of Politian and Pontanus, the light Italian poetry of the same Politian and Lorenzo de' Medici, the epic romances of Pulci and Boiardo. Of these, Pulci alone, in an original shape, is still read in Italy, and by some lovers of that literature in other countries; and the Latin poets by a smaller number. If we look on the other side of the Alps, the catalogue is much shorter, or rather does not contain a single book, except Philip de Comines, that enters into the usual studies of a literary man. Froissart hardly belongs to the fifteenth century, his history terminating about 1400. The first undated edition, with a continuation by some one to 1498, was printed between that time and 1509, when the second appeared.

140. If we come to inquire what acquisitions had been made between the years 1400 and 1500, we shall find, that in Italy the Latin language was now written by some with elegance, and by most with tolerable exactness and fluency: while, out of Italy, there had been perhaps a corresponding improvement, relatively to the point from which they started; the flagrant barbarisms of the fourteenth century having yielded before the close of the next to a more respectable, though not an elegant or exact, kind of style. Many Italians had now some acquaintance with Greek, which in 1400 had been hardly the case with any one; and the knowledge of it was of late beginning to make a little progress in Cisalpine Europe. The French and English languages were become what we call more polished, though the difference in the former seems not to be very considerable. In mathematical science, and in natural history, the ancient writers had been more brought to light; and a certain progress had been made by diligent, if not very inventive, philosophers. We cannot say that metaphysical or moral philosophy stood higher than it had done in the time of the schoolmen. The history of Greece and Rome, and the antiquities of the latter, were, of course, more distinctly known after so many years of attentive study bestowed on their principal authors; yet the acquaintance of the learned with those subjects was by no means exact or critical enough to save them from gross errors, or from becoming the dupes of

Summary of its acquisitions.

any forgery. A proof of this was furnished by the impostures of Annius of Viterbo, who, having published large fragments of Megasthenes, Berosus, Manetho, and a great many more lost historians, as having been discovered by himself, obtained full credence at the time, which was not generally withheld for too long a period afterwards, though the forgeries were palpable to those who had made themselves masters of genuine history.[1]

141. We should therefore, if we mean to judge accurately, not over-value the fifteenth century, as one in which the human mind advanced with giant strides in the kingdom of knowledge. General historians of literature are apt to speak rather hyperbolically in respect of men who rose above their contemporaries; language frequently just, in relation to the vigorous intellects and ardent industry of such men, but tending to produce an exaggerated estimate of their absolute qualities. But the question is at present not so much of men, as of the average or general proficiency of nations. The catalogues of printed books in the common bibliographical collections afford, not quite a guage of the learning of any particular period, but a reasonable presumption, which it requires a contrary evidence to rebut. If these present us very few and imperfect editions of books necessary to the progress of knowledge, if the works most in request appear to have been trifling and ignorant productions, it seems as reasonable to draw an inference one way from these scanty and discreditable lists, as on the other hand we hail the progressive state of any branch of knowledge from the redoubled labors of the press, and the multiplication of useful editions. It is true that the deficiency of one country might be supplied by importation from another; and some cities, especially Paris, had acquired a typographical reputation somewhat disproportioned to the local demand for books: but a considerable increase of readers would naturally have created a press, or multiplied its operations, in any country of Europe.

Their imperfection.

142. The bibliographies indeed, even the best and latest, are always imperfect; but the omissions, after the immense pains bestowed on the subject, can hardly be such as to affect our general conclusions. We

Number of books printed.

[1] Annius of Viterbo did not cease to have believers after this time. See Blount; Niceron, vol. ii.; Corniani iii. 131, and his article in Biographie Universelle. Apostolo Zeno and Tiraboschi have imputed less fraud than credulity to Annius, but most have been of another opinion; and it is unimportant for the purpose of the text.

will, therefore, illustrate the literary history of the fifteenth century by a few numbers taken from the typographical annals of Panzer, which might be corrected in two ways: first, by adding editions since brought to light; or, secondly, by striking out some, inserted on defective authority: a kind of mistake which tends to compensate the former. The books printed at Florence down to 1500 are 300; at Milan, 629; at Bologna, 298; at Rome, 925; at Venice, 2,835. Fifty other Italian cities had printing presses in the fifteenth century.[1] At Paris, the number of books is 751; at Cologne, 530; at Nuremberg, 382; at Leipsic, 351; at Basle, 320; at Strasburg, 526; at Augsburg, 256; at Louvain, 116; at Mentz, 134; at Deventer, 169. The whole number printed in England appears to be 141; whereof 130 at London and Westminster; seven at Oxford; four at St. Alban's. Cicero's works were first printed entire by Minutianus, at Milan, in 1498; but no less than 291 editions of different portions appeared in the century. Thirty-seven of these bear date on this side of the Alps; and forty-five have no place named. Of ninety-five editions of Virgil, seventy are complete, twenty-seven are Cisalpine, and four bear no date. On the other hand, only eleven out of fifty-seven editions of Horace contain all his works. It has been already shown, that most editions of classics printed in France and Germany are in the last decennium of the century.

143. The editions of the Vulgate registered in Panzer are ninety-one, exclusive of some spurious or suspected. Next to theology, no science furnished so much occupation to the press as the civil and canon laws. The editions of the Digest and Decretals, or other parts of those systems of jurisprudence, must amount to some hundreds.

Advantages already reaped from printing.

144. But, while we avoid, for the sake of truth, any undue exaggeration of the literary state of Europe at the close of the fifteenth century, we must even more earnestly deprecate the hasty prejudice that no good had been already done by the culture of classical learning, and by the invention of printing. Both were of inestimable value, even where their immediate fruits were not clustering in ripe abundance. It is certain that much more than ten thousand editions of books or pamphlets (a late

[1] I find this in Heeren, p. 127; for I have not counted the number of cities in Panzer.

writer says fifteen thousand[1]) were printed from 1470 to 1500. More than half the number appeared in Italy. All the Latin authors, hitherto painfully copied by the scholar, or purchased by him at inconvenient cost, or borrowed for a time from friends, became readily accessible, and were printed, for the most part, if not correctly, according to our improved criticism, yet without the gross blunders of the ordinary manuscripts. The saving of time which the art of printing has occasioned, can hardly be too highly appreciated. Nor was the Cisalpine press unserviceable in this century, though it did not pour forth so much from the stores of ancient learning. It gave useful food, and such as the reader could better relish and digest. The historical records of his own nation; the precepts of moral wisdom; the regular metre that pleased the ear and supplied the memory; the fictions that warmed the imagination, and sometimes ennobled or purified the heart; the repertories of natural phenomena, mingled as truth was on these subjects, and on all the rest, with error; the rules of civil and canon law that guided the determinations of private right; the subtle philosophy of the scholastics, — were laid open to his choice, while his religious feelings might find their gratification in many a treatise of learned doctrine according to the received creed of the church, in many a legend on which a pious credulity delighted to rely, in the devout aspirations of holy ascetic men; but, above all, in the Scriptures themselves, either in the Vulgate Latin, which had by use acquired the authority of an original text, or in most of the living languages of Europe.

Trade of bookselling.

145. We shall conclude this portion of literary history with a few illustrations of what a German writer calls "the exterior being of books,"[2] for which I do not find an equivalent in English idiom. The trade of bookselling seems to have been established at Paris and at Bologna in the twelfth century; the lawyers and universities called it into life.[3] It is very improbable that it existed in what we properly call the dark ages. Peter of Blois mentions a book which he had bought of a public dealer (*a quodam publico mangone librorum*). But we do not find, I believe, many

[1] Santander. Dict. Bibliogr. du 15me Siècle. I do not think so many would be found in Panzer. I have read somewhere that the library of Munich claims to possess 20,000 Incunabula, or books of the fifteenth century; a word lately so applied in Germany. But, unless this comprehends many duplicates, it seems a little questionable, even understanding it of volumes. Books were not in general so voluminous in that age as at present.

[2] Aüsseres Bücher-wesen; Savigny, iii. 532.

[3] Hist. Litt. de la France, ix. 142.

distinct accounts of them till the next age. These dealers were denominated Stationarii, perhaps from the open stalls at which they carried on their business, though *statio* is a general word for a shop in low Latin.[1] They appear, by the old statutes of the university of Paris, and by those of Bologna, to have sold books upon commission; and are sometimes, though not uniformly, distinguished from the Librarii; a word which, having originally been confined to the copyists of books, was afterwards applied to those who traded in them.[2] They sold parchment and other materials of writing, which with us, though as far as I know, nowhere else, have retained the name of stationery, and naturally exercised the kindred occupations of binding and decorating. They probably employed transcribers: we find at least that there was a profession of copyists in the universities and in large cities; and by means of these, before the invention of printing, the necessary books of grammar, law, and theology were multiplied to a great extent for the use of students; but with much incorrectness, and far more expense than afterwards. That invention put a sudden stop to their honest occupation. But, whatever hatred they might feel towards the new art, it was in vain to oppose its reception: no party could be raised in the public against so manifest and unalloyed a benefit; and the copyists, grown by habit fond of books, frequently employed themselves in the somewhat kindred labor of pressmen.[3]

Books sold by printers.

146. The first printers were always booksellers, and sold their own impressions. These occupations were not divided till the early part of the sixteenth century.[4] But the risks of sale, at a time when learning was by no means general, combined with the great cost of production (paper and other materials being very dear), rendered this a hazardous trade. We have a curious petition of Sweynheim and Pannartz to Sixtus IV. in 1472, wherein they com-

[1] Du Cange, in voc.

[2] The Librarii were properly those who transcribed new books; the Antiquarii, old ones. This distinction is as old as Cassiodorus; but doubtless it was not strictly observed in later times. Muratori, Dissert. 43; Du Cange.

[3] Crevier, ii. 66, 130, *et alibi;* Du Cange, in voc. Stationarii, Librarii; Savigny, iii. 532–548; Chevillier, 302; Eichhorn, ii. 531; Meiners, Vergleich. der Sitten, ii. 539; Gresswell's Parisian Press, p. 8. The Parliament of Paris, on the petition of the copyists, ordered some of the first printed books to be seized. Lambinet calls this superstition: it was more probably false compassion, and regard for existing interests, combined with dislike of all innovation. Louis XI., however, who had the merit of esteeming literature, evoked the process to the council of state, who restored the books. Lambinet, Hist. de l'Imprimerie, p. 172.

[4] Conversations-Lexicon, art. "Buchhandlung."

plain of their poverty, brought on by printing so many works which they had not been able to sell. They state the number of impressions of each edition. Of the classical authors they had generally printed 275; of Virgil and the philosophical works of Cicero, twice that number. In theological publications the usual number of copies had also been 550. The whole number of copies printed was 12,475.[1] It is possible that experience made other printers more discreet in their estimation of the public demand. Notwithstanding the casualties of three centuries, it seems, from the great scarcity of these early editions which has long existed, that the original circulation must have been much below the number of copies printed, as indeed the complaint of Sweynheim and Pannartz shows.[2]

Price of books.

147. The price of books was diminished by four-fifths after the invention of printing. Chevillier gives some instances of a fall in this proportion. But, not content with such a reduction, the university of Paris proceeded to establish a tariff, according to which every edition was to be sold, and seems to have set the prices very low. This was by virtue of the prerogatives they exerted, as we shall soon find, over the book-trade of the capital. The priced catalogues of Colinæus and Robert Stephens are extant, relating, of course, to a later period than the present; but we shall not return to the subject. The Greek Testament of Colinæus was sold for twelve sous, the Latin for six. The folio Latin Bible, printed by Stephens in 1532, might be had for one hundred sous; a copy of the Pandects for forty sous; a Virgil for two sous and six deniers; a Greek grammar of Clenardus for two sous; Demosthenes and Æschines, I know not what edition, for five sous. It would of course be necessary, before we could make any use of these prices, to compare them with that of corn.[3]

1 Maittaire; Lambinet, p. 166. Beckmann, iii. 119, erroneously says that this was the number of volumes remaining in their warehouses.

2 Lambinet says that the number of impressions did not generally exceed three hundred (p. 197). Even this seems large, compared with the present scarcity of books unlikely to have been destroyed by careless use.

3 Chevillier, Origines de l'Imprimerie de Paris, p. 370, *et seqq.* In the preceding pages, he mentions, what I should perhaps have introduced before, that a catalogue of the books in the Sorbonne, in 1292, contains above 1000 volumes, which were collectively valued at 3812 livres, 10 sous, 8 deniers. In a modern English book on literary antiquities, this is set down £3812. 10*s.* 8*d.*; which is a happy way of helping the reader.

Lambinet mentions a few prices of early books which are not trifling. The Mentz Bible, of 1462, was purchased in 1470 by a bishop of Angers for forty gold crowns. An English gentleman paid

148. The more usual form of books printed in the fifteenth century is in folio. But the Psalter of 1457, and the Donatus of the same year, are in quarto; and this size is not uncommon in the early Italian editions of classics. The disputed Oxford book of 1468, Sancti Jeronymi Expositio, is in octavo, and would, if genuine, be the earliest specimen of that size; which may perhaps furnish an additional presumption against the date. It is at least, however, of 1478, when the octavo form, as we shall immediately see, was of the rarest occurrence. Maittaire, in whom alone I have had the curiosity to make this search, which would be more troublesome in Panzer's arrangement, mentions a book printed in octavo at Milan in 1470: but the existence of this and of one or two more that follow seems equivocal; and the first on which we can rely is the Sallust, printed at Valencia in 1475. Another book of that form, at Treviso, occurs in the same year, and an edition of Pliny's epistles at Florence in 1478. They become from this time gradually more common; but, even at the end of the century, form rather a small proportion of editions. I have not observed that the duodecimo division of the sheet was adopted in any instance. But it is highly probable that the volumes of Panzer furnish means of correcting these little notices, which I offer as suggestions to persons more erudite in such matters. The price and convenience of books are evidently not unconnected with their size.

Form of books.

149. Nothing could be less unreasonable than that the printer should have a better chance of indemnifying himself and the author, if in those days the author, as probably he did, hoped for some lucrative return after his exhausting drudgery, by means of an exclusive privilege.

Exclusive privileges.

eighteen gold florins in 1481 for a missal; upon which Lambinet makes a remark: "Mais on a toujours fait payer plus cher aux Anglais qu'aux autres nations" (p. 198). The florin was worth about four francs of present money, equivalent at least to twenty-four in command of commodities. The crown was worth rather more.

Instances of an almost incredible price of manuscripts are to be met with in Robertson and other common authors. It is to be remembered that a particular book might easily bear a monopoly price, and that this is no test of the cost of those which might be multiplied by copying. ["En général nous pourrions dire que le prix moyen d'un volume in folio d'alors [au 14me siècle] équivalent à celui des choses qui coûteraient aujourd'hui quatre à cinq cent francs."—Hist. Litt. de la France, xvi. 39. But this supposes illuminations or other costly ornaments. The price of law-books, such as Savigny has collected, was very much lower; and we may conclude the same of all ordinary manuscripts. Mr. Maitland, in his Letters on the Dark Ages, p. 61, has animadverted with his usual sharpness on Robertson for too hasty a generalization. —1847.]

The senate of Venice granted an exclusive privilege, for five years, to John of Spire in 1469, for the first book printed in the city, — his edition of Cicero's epistles.[1] But I am not aware that this extended to any other work. And this seems to have escaped the learned Beckmann, who says that the earliest instance of protected copyright on record appears to be in favor of a book insignificant enough, — a missal for the Church of Bamberg, printed in 1490. It is probable that other privileges of an older date have not been found. In 1491 one occurs at the end of a book printed at Venice, and five more at the same place within the century, — the Aristotle of Aldus being one of the books: one also is found at Milan. These privileges are always recited at the end of the volume. They are, however, very rare in comparison with the number of books published, and seem not accorded by preference to the most important editions.[2]

Power of universities over bookselling.

150. In these exclusive privileges, the printer was forced to call in the magistrate for his own benefit. But there was often a different sort of interference by the civil power with the press. The destruction of books and the prohibition of their sale had not been unknown to antiquity: instances of it occur in the free republics of Athens and Rome; but it was naturally more frequent under suspicious despotisms, especially when to the jealousy of the state was superadded that of the church, and novelty, even in speculation, became a crime.[3] Ignorance came on with the fall of the empire, and it was unnecessary to guard against the abuse of an art which very few possessed at all. With the first revival of letters in the eleventh and twelfth centuries sprang up the reviving shoots of heretical freedom; but with Berenger and Abelard came also the jealousy of the church, and the usual exertion of the right of the strongest. Abelard was censured by the Council of Soissons, in 1121, for suffering copies of his book to be taken without the approbation of his superiors; and the delinquent volumes were given to the flames. It does not appear, however, that any regulation on this subject had been made.[4] But, when the sale of books became the occupation of a class of traders, it was

[1] Tiraboschi, vi. 139.
[2] Beckmann's Hist. of Inventions, iii.
[3] Beckmann's Hist. of Inventions, iii. 93
[4] Hist. Litt. de la France, ix. 28.

deemed necessary to place them under restraint. Those of Paris and Bologna, the cities doubtless where the greatest business of this kind was carried on, came altogether into the power of the universities. It is proved by various statutes of the university of Paris, originating, no doubt, in some authority conferred by the crown, and bearing date from the year 1275 to 1403, that booksellers were appointed by the university, and considered as its officers, probably matriculated by entry on her roll; that they took an oath, renewable at her pleasure, to observe her statutes and regulations; that they were admitted upon security, and with testimonials to their moral conduct; that no one could sell books in Paris without this permission; that they could expose no book to sale without communication with the university, and without its approbation; that the university fixed the prices, according to the tariff of four sworn booksellers, at which books should be sold or lent to the scholars; that a fine might be imposed for incorrect copies; that the sellers were bound to fix up in their shops a priced catalogue of their books, besides other regulations of less importance. Books deemed by the university unfit for perusal were sometimes burned by its order.[1] Chevillier gives several prices for lending books (*pro exemplari concesso scholaribus*) fixed about 1303. The books mentioned are all of divinity, philosophy, or canon law: on an average, the charge for about twenty pages was a sol. The University of Toulouse exercised the same authority; and Albert III., Archduke of Austria, founding the University of Vienna about 1384, copied the statutes of Paris in this control over bookselling as well as in other respects.[2] The stationarii of Bologna were also bound by oath, and gave sureties to fulfil their duties towards the university: one of these was to keep by them copies of books to the number of one hundred and seventeen, for the hire of which a price was fixed.[3] By degrees, however, a class of booksellers grew up at Paris, who took no oath to the university, and were consequently not admitted to its privileges, being usually poor scholars, who were tolerated in selling books of low price. These were of no importance, till, the privileged or sworn

[1] Chevillier, Origines de l'Imprimerie de Paris, p. 302, *et seqq.* Crevier, ii. 66.

[2] Chevillier, p. 302, *et seqq.*

[3] Savigny, iii. 540.

traders having been reduced by a royal ordinance of 1488 to twenty-four, this lower class silently increased; and at length the practice of taking an oath to the university fell into disuse.[1]

Restraints on sale of printed books.

151. The vast and sudden extension of the means of communicating and influencing opinion which the discovery of printing afforded did not long remain unnoticed. Few have temper and comprehensive views enough not to desire the prevention by force of that which they reckon detrimental to truth and right. Hermolaus Barbarus, in a letter to Merula, recommends that, on account of the many trifling publications which took men off from reading the best authors, nothing should be printed without the approbation of competent judges.[2] The governments of Europe cared little for what seemed an evil to Hermolaus. But they perceived, that, especially in Germany, a country where the principles that were to burst out in the Reformation were evidently germinating in this century, where a deep sense of the corruptions of the church pervaded every class, that incredible host of popular religious tracts, which the Rhine and Neckar poured forth like their waters, were of no slight danger to the two powers, or at least the union of the two, whom the people had so long obeyed. We find, therefore, an instance in 1480 of a book called Nosce teipsum, printed at Heidelberg with the approving testimonies of four persons, who may be presumed, though it is not stated, to have been appointed censors on that occasion.[3] Two others, one of which is a Bible, have been found, printed at Cologne in 1479; in the subscription to which, the language of public approbation by the university is more express. The first known instance, however, of the regular appointment of a censor on books is in the mandate of Berthold, Archbishop of Mentz in 1486. "Notwithstanding," he begins, "the facility given to the acquisition of science by the divine art of printing, it has been found that some abuse this invention, and convert that which was designed for the instruction of mankind to their injury. For books on the duties and doctrines of religion are translated from Latin into German, and circulated among the people, to the disgrace of religion itself; and some

1 Chevillier, 334–351. 2 Beckmann, iii. 98.
3 Beckmann, iii. 99.

have even had the rashness to make faulty versions of the canons of the church into the vulgar tongue, which belong to a science so difficult, that it is enough to occupy the life of the wisest man. Can such men assert that our German language is capable of expressing what great authors have written in Greek and Latin on the high mysteries of the Christian faith, and on general science? Certainly it is not; and hence they either invent new words, or use old ones in erroneous senses, — a thing especially dangerous in Sacred Scripture. For who will admit that men without learning, or women, into whose hands these translations may fall, can find the true sense of the Gospels, or of the Epistles of St. Paul? much less can they enter on questions which, even among catholic writers, are open to subtle discussion. But, since this art was first discovered in this city of Mentz, and we may truly say by divine aid, and is to be maintained by us in all its honor, we strictly forbid all persons to translate, or circulate when translated, any books upon any subject whatever from the Greek, Latin, or any other tongue, into German, until, before printing, and again before their sale, such translations shall be approved by four doctors herein named, under penalty of excommunication and of forfeiture of the books, and of one hundred golden florins to the use of our exchequer."[1]

Effect of printing on the Reformation.

152. I have given the substance of this mandate rather at length, because it has a considerable bearing on the preliminary history of the Reformation; and yet has never, to my knowledge, been produced with that view. For it is obvious, that it was on account of religious translations, and especially those of the Scripture, which had been very early printed in Germany, that this alarm was taken by the worthy archbishop. A bull of Alexander VI., in 1501, reciting that many pernicious books had been printed in various parts of the world, and especially in the provinces of Cologne, Mentz, Treves, and Magdeburg, forbids all printers in these provinces to publish any books without the license of the archbishops or their officials.[2] We here perceive the distinction made between these parts of Germany and the rest of Europe, and can understand their

[1] Beckmann, iii. 101, from the fourth volume of Guden's Codex diplomaticus. The Latin will be found in Beckmann.
[2] Id. 106.

ripeness for the ensuing revolution. We perceive also the vast influence of the art of printing upon the Reformation. Among those who have been sometimes enumerated as its precursors, a place should be left for Schæffer and Gutenberg; nor has this always been forgotten.[1]

[1] Gerdes, in his Hist. Evangel. Reformati, who has gone very laboriously into this subject, justly dwells on the influence of the art of printing.

CHAPTER IV.

ON THE LITERATURE OF EUROPE FROM 1500 TO 1520.

Sect. I. 1501–1510.

Classical Learning of Italy in this period — Of France, Germany, and England — Works of Polite Literature in Languages of Italy, Spain, and England.

Decline of learning in Italy.

1. The new century did not begin very auspiciously for the literary credit of Italy. We may, indeed, consider the whole period between the death of Lorenzo in 1492, and the pontificate of his son in 1513, as less brilliant than the two ages which we connect with their names. But, when measured by the labors of the press, the last ten years of the fifteenth century were considerably more productive than any which had gone before. In the present decade, a striking decline was perceptible. Thus, in comparing the numbers of books printed in the chief towns of Italy, we find —

	1491 — 1500	1501 — 1510
Florence,	179	47
Rome,	460	41
Milan,	228	99
Venice,	1491	536[1]

Such were the fruits of the ambition of Ferdinand and of Louis XII., and the first interference of strangers with the liberties of Italy. Wars so protracted within the bosom of a country, if they do not prevent the growth of original genius, must yet be unfavorable to that secondary but more diffused excellence which is nourished by the wealth of patrons and the tranquillity of universities. Thus, the gymnasium of Rome, founded by Eugenius IV., but lately endowed and regu-

[1] Panzer.

lated by Alexander VI., who had established it in a handsome edifice on the Quirinal Hill, was despoiled of its revenues by Julius II., who, with some liberality towards painters, had no regard for learning; and this will greatly account for the remarkable decline in the typography of Rome. Thus, too, the Platonic school at Florence soon went to decay after the fall of the Medici, who had fostered it; and even the rival philosophy which rose upon its ruins, and was taught at the beginning of this century with much success at Padua by Pomponatius, according to the original principles of Aristotle, and by two other professors of great eminence in their time, Nifo and Achillini, according to the system of Averroes, could not resist the calamities of war. The students of that university were dispersed in 1509, after the unfortunate defeat of Ghiaradadda.

2. Aldus himself left Venice in 1506, his effects in the territory having been plundered; and did not open his press again till 1512, when he entered into partnership with his father-in-law, Andrew Asola. He had been actively employed during the first years of the century. He published Sophocles, Herodotus, and Thucydides in 1502; Euripides and Herodian in 1503; Demosthenes in 1504. These were important accessions to Greek learning, though so much remained behind. A circumstance may be here mentioned, which had so much influence in facilitating the acquisition of knowledge, that it renders the year 1501 a sort of epoch in literary history. He that year not only introduced a new Italian character called Aldine, more easily read perhaps than his Roman letters, which are somewhat rude; but, what was of more importance, began to print in a small octavo or duodecimo form, instead of the cumbrous and expensive folios that had been principally in use. Whatever the great of ages past might seem to lose by this indignity, was more than compensated in the diffused love and admiration of their writings. "With what pleasure," says M. Renouard, "must the studious man, the lover of letters, have beheld these benevolent octavos, these Virgils and Horaces contained in one little volume, which he might carry in his pocket while travelling or in a walk; which, besides, cost him hardly more than two of our francs, so that he could get a dozen of them for the price of one of those folios that had hitherto been the sole furniture of his library! The appearance of these correct and well-printed

Press of Aldus.

octavos ought to be as much remarked as the substitution of printed books for manuscripts itself."[1] We have seen above, that not only small quartos, nearly as portable perhaps as octavos, but the latter form also, had been coming into use towards the close of the fifteenth century, though, I believe, it was sparingly employed for classical authors.

His academy.

3. It was about 1500 that Aldus drew together a few scholars into a literary association, called Aldi Neacademia. Not only amicable discussions, but the choice of books to be printed, of manuscripts and various readings, occupied their time, so that they may be considered as literary partners of the noble-minded printer. This academy was dispersed by the retirement of Aldus from Venice, and never met again.[2]

Dictionary of Calepio.

4. The first edition of Calepio's Latin Dictionary, which, though far better than one or two obscure books that preceded it, and enriched by plundering the stores of Valla and Perotti, was very defective, appeared at Reggio in 1502.[3] It was so greatly augmented by subsequent improvers, that *calepin* has become a name in French for any voluminous compilation. This dictionary was not only of Latin and Italian, but several other languages; and these were extended, in the Basle edition of 1581, to eleven. It is still, if not the best, the most complete polyglott lexicon for the European languages. Calepio, however moderate might be his erudition, has just claim to be esteemed one of the most effective instruments in the restoration of the Latin language, in its purity, to general use; for though some had, by great acuteness and diligence, attained a good style in the fifteenth century, that age was looked upon in Italy itself as far below the subsequent period.[4]

[1] Renouard, Hist. de l'Imprimerie des Aldes; Roscoe's Leo X., ch. ii.

[2] Tiraboschi; Roscoe; Renouard. Scipio Forteguerra, who latinized his name into Carteromachus, was secretary to this society, and among its most distinguished members. He was celebrated in his time for a discourse, De Laudibus Literarum Græcarum, reprinted by Henry Stephens in his Thesaurus. Biogr. Univ., "Forteguerra."

[3] Brunet. Tiraboschi (x. 383) gives some reason to suspect that there may have been an earlier edition.

[4] Calepio is said by Morhof and Baillet to have copied Perotti's Cornucopia almost entire. Sir John Elyot long before had remarked: "Calepin nothing amended, but rather appaired, that which Perottus had studiously gathered." But the Cornucopia was not a complete dictionary. It is generally agreed, that Calepio was an indifferent scholar, and that the first editions of his dictionary are of no great value. Nor have those who have enlarged it done so with exactness, or with selection of good Latinity. Even Passerat, the most learned of them, has not extirpated the unauthorized words of Calepio. Baillet, Jugemens des Savans, ii. 44.

Several bad dictionaries, abridged from

5. We may read in Panzer the titles of three hundred and twenty-five books printed during these ten years at Leipsic, sixty of which are classical, but chiefly, as before, small school-books; fourteen out of two hundred and fourteen at Cologne, ten out of two hundred and eight at Strasburg, one out of eighty-four at Basle, are also classical; but scarcely any books whatever appear at Louvain. One printed at Erfurt in 1501 deserves some attention. The title runs, "Εισαγωγη προς των γραμματων Ἑλλήων, Elementale Introductorium in Idioma Græcanicum," with some more words. Panzer observes: "This Greek grammar, published by some unknown person, is undoubtedly the first which was published in Germany since the invention of printing." In this, however, as has already been shown, he is mistaken; unless we deny to the book printed at Deventer the name of a grammar. But Panzer was not acquainted with it. This seems to be the only attempt at Greek that occurs in Germany during this decade; and it is unnecessary to comment on the ignorance which the gross solecism in the title displays.[1]

Books printed in Germany.

6. Paris contributed in ten years 430 editions, thirty-two being of Latin classics. And, in 1507, Giles Gourmont, a printer of that city, assisted by the purse of Francis Tissard, had the honor of introducing the Greek language on this side, as we may say, of the Alps; for the trifling exceptions we have mentioned scarcely affect his priority. Greek types had been used in a few words by Badius Ascensius, a learned and meritorious Parisian printer, whose publications began about 1498. They occur in his edition (1505) of Valla's Annotations on the Greek Testament.[2] Four little books — namely, a small miscellaneous

First Greek press at Paris.

the Catholicon, appeared near the end of the fifteenth century, and at the beginning of the next. Du Cange, præfat. in Glossar., p. 47.

[1] Panzer, vi. 494. We find, however, a tract by Hegius, De Utilitate Linguæ Græcæ, printed at Deventer in 1501; but whether it contains Greek characters or not must be left to conjecture. Lambinet says that Martens, a Flemish printer, employed Greek types in quotations as early as 1501 or 1502.

[2] Chevillier, Origines de l'Imprimerie de Paris, p. 246; Gresswell's View of Early Parisian Greek Press, i. 15. Panzer, according to Mr. Gresswell, has recorded nearly four hundred editions from the press of Badius. They include almost every Latin classic, usually with notes. He also printed a few Greek authors. See also Bayle and Biogr. Univ. The latter refers the first works from the Parisian press of Badius to 1511, but probably by misprint. Badius had learned Greek at Ferrara. If Bayle is correct, he taught it at Lyons before he set up his press at Paris, which is worthy of notice; but he gives no authority, except for the fact of his teaching in the former city, which might not be the Greek language. It is said, however, that he came to Paris in order to give instruction in Greek about 1499. Bayle,

volume, preceded by an alphabet, the Works and Days of Hesiod, the Frogs and Mice of Homer, and the Erotemata or Greek grammar of Chrysoloras, to which four a late writer has added an edition of Musæus — were the first-fruits of Gourmont's press. Aleander, a learned Italian, who played afterwards no inconsiderable part in the earlier period of the Reformation, came to Paris in 1508, and received a pension from Louis XII.[1] He taught Greek there, and perhaps Hebrew. Through his care, besides a Hebrew and Greek alphabet in 1508, Gourmont printed some of the moral works of Plutarch in 1509.

Early studies of Melanchthon.

7. We learn from a writer of the most respectable authority, Camerarius, that the elements of Greek were already taught to boys in some parts of Germany.[2] About 1508, Reuchlin, on a visit to George Simler, a schoolmaster in Hesse, found a relation of his own, little more than ten years old, who, uniting extraordinary quickness with thirst for learning, had already acquired the rudiments of that language; and presenting him with a lexicon and grammar, precious gifts in those times, changed his German name, Schwartzerd, to one of equivalent meaning and more classical sound, Melanchthon. He had himself set the example of assuming a name of Greek derivation, being almost as much known by the name of Capnio as by his own. And this pedantry, which continued to prevail for a century and a half afterwards, might be excused by the great uncouthness of many German, not to say French and English, sur-

art. "Badius," note H. It is said in the Biographie Universelle that Denys le Fevre taught Greek at Paris in 1504, when only sixteen years old; but the story seems apocryphal.

[1] Aleander was no favorite with Erasmus; and Luther utters many invectives against him. He was a strenuous supporter of all things as they were in the church; and would have presided in the Council of Trent as legate of Paul III., who had given him a cardinal's hat, if he had not been prevented by death.

It is fair to say of Aleander that he was the friend of Sadolet. In a letter of that excellent person to Paul III., he praises Aleander very highly, and requests for him the hat, which the pope, in consequence, bestowed. Sadolet, Epist. l. xii. See, for Aleander, Bayle; Sleidan, Hist. de la Réformation, l. ii. and iii.; Roscoe's Leo X., ch., xxi.; Jortin's Erasmus, *passim.*

[2] "Jam enim pluribus in locis melius quam dudum pueritia institui et doctrina in scholis usurpari politior, quod et bonorum autorum scripta in manus tenerentur, et elementa quoque linguæ Græcæ alicubi proponerentur ad discendum, cum seniorum admiratione maxima, et ardentissima cupiditate juniorum, cujus utriusque tum non tam judicium quam novitas causa fuit. Simlerus, qui postea ex primario grammatico eximius jurisconsultus factus est, initio hanc doctrinam non vulgandam aliquantisper arbitrabatur. Itaque Græcarum literarum scholam explicabat aliquot discipulis suis privatim, quibus dabat hanc operam peculiarem, ut quos summopere diligeret."— Camerarius, Vita Melanchthonis. I find also in one of Melanchthon's own epistles, that he learned the Greek grammar from George Simler. Epist. Melanchth., p. 351 (edit. 1647).

names in their Latinized forms. Melanchthon, the precocity of his youth being followed by a splendid maturity, became not only one of the greatest lights of the Reformation, but, far above all others, the founder of general learning in Germany.[1]

Learning in England.

8. England seems to have been nearly stationary in academical learning during the unpropitious reign of Henry VII.[2] But just hopes were entertained from the accession of his son in 1509, who had received in some degree a learned education. And the small knot of excellent men, united by zeal for improvement, — Grocyn, Linacre, Latimer, Fisher, Colet, More, — succeeded in bringing over their friend Erasmus to teach Greek at Cambridge, in 1510. The students, he says, were too poor to pay him any thing, nor had he many scholars.[3] His instruction was confined to the grammar. In the same year, Colet, Dean of St. Paul's, founded there a school, and published a Latin grammar. Five or six little works of the kind had already appeared in England.[4] These trifling things are mentioned to let the reader take notice that there is nothing more worthy to be named. Twenty-six books were printed at London during this decade: among these, Terence in 1504; but no other Latin author of classical name. The difference in point of learning between Italy and England was at least that of a century; that is, the former was as much advanced in knowledge of ancient literature in 1400 as the latter was in 1500.

9. It is plain, however, that on the Continent of Europe, though no very remarkable advances were made in these ten

[1] Camerarius; Meiners, i. 73. The Biographie Universelle, art. "Melanchthon," calls him nephew of Reuchlin; but this seems not to be the case: Camerarius only says that their families were connected "quadam ognationis necessitudine."

[2] "The schools were much frequented with quirks and sophistry. All things, whether taught or written, seemed to be trite and inane. No pleasant streams of humanity or mythology were gliding among us; and the Greek language, from whence the greater part of knowledge is derived, was at a very low ebb or in a manner forgotten." — Wood's Annals of Oxford, A.D. 1508. The word "forgotten" is improperly applied to Greek, which had never been known. In this reign, but in what part of it does not appear, the university of Oxford hired an Italian, one Caius Auberinus, to compose the public orations and epistles, and to explain Terence in the schools. Warton, ii. 420, from MS. authority.

[3] "Hactenus prælegimus Chrysoloræ grammaticam, sed paucis; fortassis frequentiori auditorio Theodori grammaticam auspicabimur." — Ep. cxxiii. (16th October, 1511.)

[4] Wood talks of Holt's Lac Puerorum, published in 1497, as if it had made an epoch in literature. It might be superior to any grammar we already possessed. [The syntax in Lilly's grammar, which has been chiefly in use with us (under that or other names), was much altered by Erasmus, at Colet's desire: "Sic emendaram, ut pleraque mutarem." It was published anonymously. This syntax is admired for conciseness and perspicuity — 1842.]

years, learning was slowly progressive, and the men were living who were to bear fruit in due season. Erasmus republished his Adages with such great additions as rendered them almost a new work; while Budæus, in his observations upon the Pandects, gave the first example of applying philological and historical literature to the illustration of Roman law, by which others, with more knowledge of jurisprudence than he possessed, were in the next generation signally to change the face of that science.

Erasmus and Budæus.

10. The Eastern languages began now to be studied, though with very imperfect means. Hebrew had been cultivated in the Franciscan monasteries of Tubingen and Basle before the end of the last century. The first grammar was published by Conrad Pellican in 1503. Eichhorn calls it an evidence of the deficiencies of his knowledge, though it cost him incredible pains. Reuchlin gave a better, with a dictionary, in 1506, which, enlarged by Munster, long continued to be a standard book. A Hebrew Psalter, with three Latin translations, and one in French, was published in 1509 by Henry Stephens, the progenitor of a race illustrious in typographical and literary history. Petrus de Alcalá, in 1506, attempted an Arabic vocabulary, printing the words in Roman letter.[1]

Study of Eastern languages.

11. If we could trust an article in the Biographie Universelle, a Portuguese, Gil Vicente, deserves the high praise of having introduced the regular drama into Europe; the first of his pieces having been represented at Lisbon in 1504.[2] But, according to the much superior authority of Bouterwek, Gil Vicente was a writer in the old national style of Spain and Portugal; and his early compositions are Autos, or spiritual dramas, totally unlike any regular plays, and rude both in design and execution. He became, however, a comic writer of great reputation among his countrymen at a later period, but in the same vein of uncultivated genius, and not before Machiavel and Ariosto had estab-

Dramatic works.

[1] Eichhorn, ii. 562, 563, v. 609; Meiners's Life of Reuchlin, in Lebensbeschreibungen berühmter Männer, i. 68. A very few instances of Hebrew scholars in the fifteenth century might be found, besides Reuchlin and Picus of Mirandola. Tiraboschi gives the chief place among these to Giannozzo Manetti, vii. 123.

[2] Biogr. Univ., art. "Gil. Vicente." Another Life of the same dramatist in a later volume, under the title Vicente, seems designed to retract this claim. Bouterwek adverts to this supposed drama of 1504, which is an Auto on the festival of Corpus Christi, and of the simplest kind.

lished their dramatic renown. The Calandra of Bibbiena, afterwards a cardinal, was represented at Venice in 1508, though not published till 1524. An analysis of this play will be found in Ginguéné: it bears only a general resemblance to the Menæchmi of Plautus. Perhaps the Calandra may be considered as the earliest modern comedy, or at least the earliest that is known to be extant; for its five acts and intricate plot exclude the competition of Maître Patelin.[1] But there is a more celebrated piece in the Spanish language, of which it is probably impossible to determine the date,—the tragi-comedy, as it has been called, of Calisto and Meliboea. This is the work of two authors, one generally supposed to be Rodrigo Cota, who planned the story and wrote the first act; the other, Fernando de Rojas, who added twenty more acts to complete the drama. This alarming number does not render the play altogether so prolix as might be supposed, the acts being only what with us are commonly denominated scenes. It is, however, much beyond the limits of representation. Some have supposed Calisto and Meliboea to have been commenced by Juan de la Mena before the middle of the fifteenth century. But this, Antonio tells us, shows ignorance of the style belonging to that author and to his age. It is far more probably of the time of Ferdinand and Isabella; and, as an Italian translation appears to have been published in 1514, we may presume that it was finished and printed in Spain about the present decade.[2]

Calisto and Melibœa.

12. Bouterwek and Sismondi have given some account of this rather remarkable dramatic work. But they hardly do it justice, especially the former, who would lead the reader to expect something very anomalous and extravagant. It appears to me that it is as regular and well contrived as the old comedies generally were: the action is simple and uninterrupted; nor can it be reckoned very extraordinary that what Bouterwek calls the unities of time and

Its character.

[1] Ginguéné, vi. 171. An earlier writer on the Italian theatre is in raptures with this play. "The Greeks, Latins, and moderns have never made, and perhaps never will make, so perfect a comedy as the Calandra. It is, in my opinion, the model of good comedy."—Riccoboni, Hist. du Théâtre Italien, i. 148. This is much to say, and shows an odd taste; for the Calandra neither displays character nor excites interest.

[2] Antonio, Bibl. Hisp. Nova; Andrès, v. 125. "La Celestina," says the latter, "certo contiene un fatto bene svolto, e spiegato con episodj verisimili e naturali, dipinge con verità i caratteri, ed esprime talora con calore gli affetti; e tutto questo à mio giudizio potrà bastare per darli il vanto d' essere stata la prima composizione teatrale scritta con eleganza e regolarità."

place should be transgressed, when for the next two centuries they were never observed. Calisto and Melibœa was at least deemed so original and important an accession to literature, that it was naturalized in several languages. A very early imitation, rather than version, in English, appears to have been printed in 1530.[1] A real translation, with the title Celestina (the name of a procuress who plays the chief part in the drama, and by which it has been frequently known), is mentioned by Herbert under the year 1598. And there is another translation, or second edition, in 1631, with the same title, from which all my acquaintance with this play is derived. Gaspar Barthius gave it in Latin, 1624, with the title Pornobosco-didascalus.[2] It was extolled by some as a salutary exposition of the effects of vice, —

> "Quo modo adolescentulæ
> Lenarum ingenia et mores possent noscere," —

and condemned by others as too open a display of it. Bouterwek has rather exaggerated the indecency of this drama, which is much less offensive, unless softened in the translation, than in most of our old comedies. The style of the first author is said to be more elegant than that of his continuator; but this is not very apparent in the English version. The chief characters throughout are pretty well drawn, and there is a vein of humor in some of the comic parts.

13. The first edition of the works of a Spanish poet, Juan de la Enzina, appeared in 1501, though they were probably written in the preceding century. Some of these are comedies, as one biographer calls them, or rather, perhaps, as Bouterwek expresses it, "sacred and profane eclogues, in the form of dialogues, represented before distinguished persons on festivals." Enzina wrote also a treatise on Castilian poetry, which, according to Bouterwek, is but a short essay on the rules of metre.[3]

Juan de la Enzina.

14. The pastoral romance, as was before mentioned, began a

[1] Dibdin's Typographical Antiquities. Mr. Collier (Hist. of Dramatic Poetry, ii. 408) has given a short account of this production, which he says "is not long enough for a play, and could only have been acted as an interlude." It must, therefore, be very different from the original.

[2] Clement, Bibliothèque Curieuse. This translation is sometimes erroneously named Porno-didascalus; the title of a very different book.

[3] Bouterwek; Biogr. Univ., art. "Enzina." The latter praises this work of Enzina more highly, but whether from equal knowledge I cannot say. The dramatic compositions above mentioned are most scarce.

little before this time in Portugal. An Italian writer of fine genius, Sannazzaro, adopted it in his Arcadia, of which the first edition was in 1502. Harmonious prose intermingled with graceful poetry, and with a fable just capable of keeping awake the attention, though it could never excite emotion, communicate a tone of pleasing sweetness to this volume. But we have been so much used to fictions of more passionate interest, that we hardly know how to accommodate ourselves to the mild languor of these early romances. A recent writer places the Arcadia at the head of Italian prose in that age. "With a less embarrassed construction," he says, "than Boccaccio, and less of a servile mannerism than Bembo, the style of Sannazzaro is simple, flowing, rapid, harmonious. If it should seem now and then too florid and diffuse, this may be pardoned in a romance. It is to him, in short, rather than to Bembo, that we owe the revival of correctness and elegance in the Italian prose of the sixteenth century; and his style in the Arcadia would have been far more relished than that of the Asolani, if the originality of his poetry had not engrossed our attention." He was the first who employed in any considerable degree the *sdrucciolo* verse, though it occurs before; but the difficulty of finding rhymes for it drives him frequently upon unauthorized phrases. He may also be reckoned the first who restored the polished style of Petrarch, which no writer of the fifteenth century had successfully emulated.[1]

Arcadia of Sannazzaro.

15. The Asolani of Peter Bembo, a dialogue, the scene of which is laid at Asola, in the Venetian territory, were published in 1505. They are disquisitions on love, tedious enough to our present apprehension, but in a style so pure and polite, that they became the favorite reading among the superior ranks in Italy, where the coldness and pedantry of such dissertations were forgiven for their classical dignity and moral truth. The Asolani has been thought to make an

Asolani of Bembo.

[1] Salfi, Continuation de Ginguéné, x. 92; Corniani, iv. 12. Roscoe speaks of the Arcadia with less admiration, but perhaps more according to the feelings of the general reader. But I cannot altogether concur in his sweeping denunciation of poetical prose, "that hermaphrodite of literature." In many styles of composition, and none more than such as the Arcadia, it may be read with delight, and without wounding a rational taste. The French language, which is not well adapted to poetry, would have lost some of its most imaginative passages, with which Buffon, St. Pierre, and others have enriched it, if a highly ornamented prose had been wholly proscribed; and we may say the same, with equal truth, of our own. It is another thing to condemn the peculiar style of poetry in writings that from their subject demand a very different tone.

epoch in Italian literature, though the Arcadia is certainly a more original and striking work of genius.

Dunbar.

16. I do not find at what time the poems in the Scottish dialect by William Dunbar were published; but "The Thistle and the Rose," on the marriage of James IV. with Margaret of England in 1503, must be presumed to have been written very little after that time. Dunbar, therefore, has the honor of leading the vanguard of British poetry in the sixteenth century. His allegorical poem, the Golden Targe, is of a more extended range, and displays more creative power. The versification of Dunbar is remarkably harmonious and exact for his age; and his descriptions are often very lively and picturesque. But it must be confessed that there is too much of sunrise and singing-birds in all our mediæval poetry; a note caught from the French and Provençal writers, and repeated to satiety by our own. The allegorical characters of Dunbar are derived from the same source. He belongs, as a poet, to the school of Chaucer and Lydgate.[1]

Anatomy of Zerbi.

17. The first book upon anatomy, since that of Mundinus, was by Zerbi of Verona, who taught in the University of Padua in 1495. The title is Liber anatomiæ corporis humani et singulorum membrorum illius, 1503. He follows in general the plan of Mundinus, and his language is obscure as well as full of inconvenient abbreviations; yet the germ of discoveries that have crowned later anatomists with glory is sometimes perceptible in Zerbi: among others, that of the Fallopian tubes.[2]

Voyages of Cadamosto.

18. We now, for the first time, take relations of voyages into our literary catalogue. During the fifteenth century, though the old travels of Marco Polo had been printed several times and in different languages, and even those of Sir John Mandeville once; though the Cosmography of Ptolemy had appeared in not less than seven editions, and generally with maps, — few if any original descriptions of the kingdoms of the world had gratified the curiosity of modern Europe. But the stupendous discoveries that signalized the last years of that age could not long remain untold. We may, however, give perhaps the first place to the voyages of

[1] Warton, iii. 90. Ellis (Specimens, i. 377) strangely calls Dunbar "the greatest poet that Scotland has produced." Pinkerton places him above Chaucer and Lydgate. Chalmers's Biogr. Dict.

[2] Portal, Hist. de l'Anatomie; Biogr. Univ., art. "Zerbi."

Cadamosto, a Venetian, who, in 1455, under the protection of Prince Henry of Portugal, explored the western coast of Africa, and bore a part in discovering its two great rivers as well as the Cape de Verde islands. "The relation of his voyages," says a late writer, "the earliest of modern travels, is truly a model, and would lose nothing by comparison with those of our best navigators. Its arrangement is admirable, its details are interesting, its descriptions clear and précise."[1] These voyages of Cadamosto do not occupy more than thirty pages in the collection of Ramusio, where they are reprinted. They are said to have first appeared at Vicenza in 1507, with the title Prima navigazione per l' oceano alle terre de' negri della bassa Ethiopa di Luigi Cadamosto. It is supposed, however, by Brunet, that no separate account of Cadamosto's voyage exists earlier than 1519, and that this of 1507 is a confusion with the next book. This was a still more important production, announcing the great discoveries that Americo Vespucci was suffered to wrest, at least in name, from a more illustrious though ill-requited Italian: Mondo nuovo, e pessi nuovamente ritrovati da Alberico Vesputio Florentino intitolati. Vicenza, 1507. But this includes the voyage of Cadamosto. It does not appear that any earlier work on America had been published: but an epistle of Columbus himself, De insulis Indiæ nuper inventis, was twice printed about 1493 in Germany, and probably in other countries; and a few other brief notices of the recent discovery are to be traced. We find also in 1508 an account of the Portuguese in the East, which, being announced as a translation from the native language into Latin, may be presumed to have appeared before.[2]

[1] Biogr. Univ., art. "Cadamosto."

[2] See Brunet, Manuel du Libraire, arts. "Itinerarium, Primo, Vespucci." [Also his Supplément au Manuel du Libraire, art. "Vespucci." This last article corrects the former, and has enabled me to state M. Brunet's opinion more clearly than in my first edition. — 1842.]

SECT. II. 1511–1520.

Age of Leo X. — Italian Dramatic Poetry — Classical Learning, especially Greek, in France, Germany and England — Utopia of More — Erasmus — His Adages — Political Satire contained in them — Opposition of the Monks to Learning — Antipathy of Erasmus to them — Their Attack on Reuchlin — Origin of Reformation — Luther — Ariosto — Character of the Orlando Furioso — Various Works of Amusement in Modern Languages — English Poetry — Pomponatius — Raymond Lully.

Leo X., his patronage of letters.

19. LEO X. became pope in 1513. His chief distinction, no doubt, is owing to his encouragement of the arts, or, more strictly, to the completion of those splendid labors of Raffaelle under his pontificate, which had been commenced by his predecessor. We have here only to do with literature; and, in the promotion of this, he certainly deserves a much higher name than any former pope, except Nicolas V., who, considering the difference of the times and the greater solidity of his own character, as certainly stands far above him. Leo began by placing men of letters in the most honorable stations of his court. There were two, Bembo and Sadolet, who had, by common confession, reached a consummate elegance of style, in comparison of which the best productions of the last age seemed very imperfect. They were made apostolical secretaries. Beroaldo, second of the name, whose father, though a more fertile author, was inferior to him in taste, was intrusted with the Vatican Library. John Lascaris and Marcus Musurus were invited to reside at Rome;[1] and the pope, considering it, he says, no small part of his pontifical duty to promote the Latin literature, caused search to be made everywhere for manuscripts. This expression sounds rather oddly in his mouth; and the less religious character of Transalpine literature is visible in this as in every thing else.

20. The personal taste of Leo was almost entirely directed

[1] John Lascaris, who is not to be confounded with Constantine Lascaris, by some thought to be his father, and to whom we owe a Greek grammar, after continuing for several years under the patronage of Lorenzo at Florence, where he was editor of the Anthologia, or collection of epigrams, printed in 1494, on the fall of the Medici family entered the service of Charles VIII., and lived many years at Paris. He was afterwards employed by Louis XII. as minister at Venice. After a residence of some duration at Rome, he was induced by Francis I. in 1518 to organize the literary institutions designed by the king to be established at Paris. But, these being postponed, Lascaris spent the remainder of his life partly in Paris, partly in Rome; and died in the latter city in 1535. Hody de Græcis illustribus.

towards poetry and the beauties of style. This, Tiraboschi seems to hint, might cause the more serious learning of antiquity to be rather neglected. But there does not seem to be much ground for this charge. We owe to Leo the publication, by Beroaldo, of the first five books of the Annals of Tacitus, which had lately been found in a German monastery. It appears that in 1514 above one hundred professors received salaries in the Roman University or Gymnasium, restored by the pope to its alienated revenues.[1] Leo seems to have founded a seminary distinct from the former, under the superintendence of Lascaris, for the sole study of Greek; and to have brought over young men as teachers from Greece. In this academy a Greek press was established, where the scholiasts on Homer were printed in 1517.[2]

Roman Gymnasium.

21. Leo was a great admirer of Latin poetry; and in his time the chief poets of Italy seem to have written several of their works, though not published till afterwards. The poems of Pontanus, which naturally belong to the fifteenth century, were first printed in 1513 and 1518; and those of Mantuan, in a collective form, about the same time.

Latin poetry.

22. The Rosmunda of Rucellai, a tragedy in the Italian language, on the ancient regular model, was represented before Leo at Florence in 1515. It was the earliest known trial of blank verse; but it is acknowledged by Rucellai himself, that the Sophonisba of his friend Trissino, which is dedicated to Leo in the same year, though not published till 1524, preceded and suggested his own tragedy.[3]

Italian tragedy.

[1] We are indebted to Roscoe for publishing this list. But as the number of one hundred professors might lead us to expect a most comprehensive scheme, it may be mentioned, that they consisted of four for theology, eleven for canon law, twenty for civil law, sixteen for medicine, two for metaphysics, five for philosophy (probably physics), two for ethics, four for logic, one for astrology (probably astronomy), two for mathematics, eighteen for rhetoric, three for Greek, and thirteen for grammar; in all, a hundred and one. The salaries are subjoined in every instance: the highest are among the medical professors; the Greek are also high. Roscoe, ii. 333, and Append. No. 89.

Roscoe remarks that medical botany was one of the sciences taught, and that it was the earliest instance. If this be right, Bonafede of Padua cannot have been the first who taught botany in Europe, as we read that he did in 1533. But in the roll of these Roman professors we only find that one was appointed "ad declarationem simplicium medicinæ." I do not think this means more than the materia medica: we cannot infer that he lectured upon the plants themselves.

[2] Tiraboschi; Hody, p. 247; Roscoe, ch. 11. Leo was anticipated in his Greek editions by Chigi, a private Roman, who, with the assistance of Cornelio Benigno, and with Calliergus, a Cretan, for his printer, gave to the world two good editions of Pindar and Theocritus in 1515 and 1516.

[3] This dedication, with a sort of apology for writing tragedies in Italian, will be found in Roscoe's Appendix, vol. vi. Roscoe quotes a few words from Rucellai's dedication of his poem, L'Api, to Trissino.

The Sophonisba is strictly on the Greek model, divided only by the odes of the chorus, but not into five portions or acts. The speeches in this tragedy are sometimes too long, the style unadorned, the descriptions now and then trivial. But in general there is a classical dignity about the sentiments which are natural, though not novel; and the latter part, which we should call the fifth act, is truly noble, simple, and pathetic. Trissino was thoroughly conversant with the Greek drama, and had imbibed its spirit: seldom has Euripides written with more tenderness, or chosen a subject more fitted to his genius; for that of Sophonisba, in which many have followed Trissino with inferior success, is wholly for the Greek school: it admits, with no great difficulty, of the chorus, and consequently of the unities of time and place. It must, however, always chiefly depend on Sophonisba herself; for it is not easy to make Masinissa respectable, nor has Trissino succeeded in attempting it. The long continuance of alternate speeches in single lines, frequent in this tragedy, will not displease those to whom old associations are recalled by it.

Sophonisba of Trissino.

23. The Rosmunda falls, in my opinion, below the Sophonisba, though it is the work of a better poet; and perhaps in language and description it is superior. What is told in narration, according to the ancient inartificial form of tragedy, is finely told; but the emotions are less represented than in the Sophonisba: the principal character is less interesting, and the story is unpleasing. Rucellai led the way to those accumulations of horrible and disgusting circumstances which deformed the European stage for a century afterwards. The Rosmunda is divided into five acts, but preserves the chorus. It contains imitations of the Greek

Rosmunda of Rucellai.

acknowledging the latter as the inventor of blank verse. "Voi foste il primo, che questo modo di scrivere, in versi materni, liberi delle rime, poneste in luce." — Life of Leo X., ch. 16. See also Ginguéné, vol. vi., and Walker's Memoir on Italian Tragedy, as well as Tiraboschi. The earliest Italian tragedy, which is also on the subject of Sophonisba, by Galeotto del Carretto, was presented to the Marchioness of Mantua in 1502. But we do not find that it was brought on the stage; nor is it clear that it was printed so early as the present decade. But an edition of the Pamphila, a tragedy on the story of Sigismunda, by Antonio da Pistcja was printed at Venice in 1508. Walker, p. 11. Ginguéné has been ignorant of this very curious piece, from which Walker had given a few extracts, in rhymed measures of different kinds. Ginguéné, indeed, had never seen Walker's book; and his own is the worse for it. Walker was not a man of much vigor of mind, but had some taste, and great knowledge of his subject This tragedy is mentioned by Quadrio, iv. 58, with the title Il Filostrato e Panfila, doi amanti.

It may be observed, that, notwithstanding the testimony of Rucellai himself, above quoted, it is shown by Walker (Appendix, No. 3) that blank verse had been occasionally employed before Trissino.

tragedies, especially the Antigone, as the Sophonisba does of the Ajax and the Medea. Some lines in the latter, extolled by modern critics, are simply translated from the ancient tragedians.

Comedies of Ariosto.

24. Two comedies by Ariosto, seem to have been acted about 1512, and were written as early as 1495, when he was but twenty-one years old, which entitles him to the praise of having first conceived and carried into effect the idea of regular comedies, in imitation of the ancient, though Bibbiena had the advantage of first occupying the stage with his Calandra. The Cassaria and Suppositi of Ariosto are, like the Calandra, free imitations of the manner of Plautus, in a spirited and natural dialogue, and with that graceful flow of language which appears spontaneous in all his writings.[1]

Books printed in Italy.

25. The north of Italy still endured the warfare of stranger armies: Ravenna, Novara, Marignan, attest the well-fought contention. Aldus, however, returning to Venice in 1512, published many editions before his death in 1516. Pindar, Plato, and Lysias first appeared in 1513; Athenæus in 1514; Xenophon, Strabo, and Pausanias in 1516; Plutarch's Lives in 1517. The Aldine press then continued under his father-in-law, Andrew Asola, but with rather diminished credit. It appears that the works printed during this period, from 1511 to 1520, were, at Rome 116, at Milan 91, at Florence 133, and at Venice 511. This is, perhaps, less than from the general renown of Leo's age we should have expected. We may select, among the original publications, the Lectiones Antiquæ of Cælius Rhodiginus (1516), and a little treatise on Italian grammar by Fortunio, which has no claim to notice but as the earliest book on the subject.[2] The former, though not the first, appears to have been by far the best and most extensive collection hitherto made from the stores of antiquity. It is now hardly remembered; but obtained almost universal praise, even from severe critics, for the deep erudition of its author,

Cælius Rhodiginus.

[1] Ginguéné, vi. 183, 218, has given a full analysis of these celebrated comedies. They are placed next to those of Machiavel by most Italian critics.

[2] Regole grammaticali della volgar lingua. (Ancona, 1516.) "Questo libro fuor di dubbio è stato il primo che si vidlikesse stampato, a darne insegnamenti d' Italiana, non già eloquenza, ma lingua." Fontanini dell' eloquenza Italiana, p. 5. Fifteen editions were printed within six years; a decisive proof of the importance attached to the subject.

who, in a somewhat rude style, pours forth explanations of obscure and emendations of corrupted passages, with profuse display of knowledge in the customs and even philosophy of the ancients, but more especially in medicine and botany. Yet he seems to have inserted much without discrimination of its value, and often without authority. A more perfect edition was published in 1550, extending to thirty books instead of sixteen.[1]

Greek printed in France and Germany.

26. It may be seen, that Italy, with all the lustre of Leo's reputation, was not distinguished by any very remarkable advance in learning during his pontificate; and I believe it is generally admitted, that the elegant biography of Roscoe, in making the public more familiar with the subject, did not raise the previous estimation of its hero and of his times. Meanwhile the Cisalpine regions were gaining ground upon their brilliant neighbor. From the Parisian press issued, in these ten years, eight hundred books; among which were a Greek Lexicon by Aleander, in 1512, and four more little grammatical works, with a short romance in Greek.[2] This is trifling indeed; but, in the cities on the Rhine, something more was done in that language. A Greek grammar, probably quite elementary, was published at Wittenberg in 1511; one at Strasburg in 1512, — thrice reprinted in the next three years. These were succeeded by a translation of Theodore Gaza's grammar by Erasmus, in 1516; by the Progymnasmata Græcæ Literaturæ of Luscinius, in 1517; and by the Introductiones in Linguam Græcam of Croke, in 1520. Isocrates and Lucian appeared at Strasburg in 1515; the first book of the Iliad next year, besides four smaller tracts:[3] several more followed before the end of the decade. At Basle the excellent printer Frobenius, an intimate friend of Erasmus, had established himself as early as 1491.[4] Besides the great edition of the New Testament by Erasmus, which issued from his press, we find, before the close of 1520, the Works and Days of Hesiod, the Greek Lexicon of Aldus,

1 Blount; Biogr. Univ., art. "Rhodiginus."

2 [It is said in Liron, Singularités Historiques, i. 490, that one Cheradamus taught Greek at Paris about 1517, and published a Greek lexicon there in 1523: "Lexicon Græcum, cæteris omnibus aut in Italia aut Gallia Germaniave, antehac excusis multo locupletius, utpote supra ter mille additiones Basiliensi Lexico, A.D. 1522 apud Carionem impresso, adjectas." I do not find this Lexicon mentioned by Brunet or Watts. — 1842.]

3 These were published by Luscinius (Nachtigall), a native of Strasburg, and one of the chief members of the literary academy established by Wimpheling in that city. Biogr. Univ.

4 Biogr. Univ.

the Rhetoric and Poetics of Aristotle, the first two books of the Odyssey, and several grammatical treatises. At Cologne two or three small Greek pieces were printed in 1517. And Louvain, besides the Plutus of Aristophanes in 1518, and three or four others about the same time, sent forth in the year 1520 six Greek editions, among which were Lucian, Theocritus, and two tragedies of Euripides.[1] We may hence perceive that the Greek language now first became known and taught in Germany and in the Low Countries.

Greek scholars in these countries.

27. It is evident that these works were chiefly designed for students in the universities. But it is to be observed, that Greek literature was now much more cultivated than before. In France there were, indeed, not many names that could be brought forward; but Lefevre of Etaples, commonly called Faber Stapulensis, was equal to writing criticisms on the Greek Testament of Erasmus. He bears a high character among contemporary critics for his other writings, which are chiefly on theological and philosophical subjects: but it appears by his age that he must have come late to the study of Greek.[2] That difficult language was more easily mastered by younger men. Germany had already produced some, deserving of remembrance. A correspondent of Erasmus, in 1515, writes to recommend Œcolampadius as "not unlearned in Greek literature."[3] Melanchthon was, even in his early youth, deemed competent to criticise Erasmus himself. At the age of sixteen, he lectured on the Greek and Latin authors of antiquity. He was the first who printed Terence as verse.[4] The library of this great scholar was in 1835 sold in London, and was proved to be his own by innumerable marginal notes of illustration and correction. Beatus Rhenanus stands perhaps next to him as a scholar: and we may add the names of Luscinius; of Bilibald Pirckheimer, a learned senator of Nuremberg, who made several

[1] The whole number of books, according to Panzer, printed from 1511 to 1520 at Strasburg, was 373; at Basle, 289; at Cologne, 120; at Leipsic, 462; at Louvain, 57. It may be worth while to remind the reader once more, that these lists must be very defective as to the slighter class of publications, which have often perished to every copy. Panzer is reckoned more imperfect after 1500 than before. Biogr. Universelle. In England, we find thirty-six by Pynson, and sixty-six by Wynkyn de Worde, within these ten years.

[2] Jortin's Erasmus, i. 92; Bayle, "Fevre d'Etaples;" Blount; Biogr. Univ., "Febure d'Etaples."

[3] Erasmus himself says afterwards, "Œcolampadius satis novit Græcè, Latini sermonis rudior; quanquam ille magis peccat indiligentia quam imperitia."

[4] Cox's Life of Melanchthon, p. 19. Melanchthon wrote Greek verse indifferently and incorrectly, but Latin with spirit and elegance: specimens of both are given in Dr. Cox's valuable biography

translations; and of Petrus Mosellanus, who became, about 1518, lecturer in Greek at Leipsic.[1] He succeeded our distinguished countryman Richard Croke, a pupil of Grocyn, who had been invited to Leipsic in 1514, with the petty salary of fifteen guilders, but with the privilege of receiving other remuneration from his scholars; and had the signal honor of first imbuing the students of Northern Germany with a knowledge of that language.[2] One or two trifling works on Greek grammar were published by Croke during this decennium. Ceratinus, who took his name, in the fanciful style of the times, from his birthplace, Horn in Holland, was now professor of Greek at Louvain; and in 1525, on the recommendation of Erasmus, became the successor of Mosellanus at Leipsic.[3] William Cop, a native of Basle, and physician to Francis I., published in this period some translations from Hippocrates and Galen.

Colleges at Alcalá and Louvain.

28. Cardinal Ximenez, about the beginning of the century, founded a college at Alcalá, his favorite university, for the three learned languages. This example was followed by Jerome Busleiden, who by his last testament, in 1516 or 1517, established a similar foundation at Louvain.[4] From this source proceeded many men of conspicuous erudition and ability; and Louvain, through its Collegium Trilingue, became, in a still higher degree than Deventer had been in the fifteenth century, not only the chief seat of Belgian learning, but the means of diffusing it over parts

1 The lives and characters of Rhenanus, Pirckheimer, and Mosellanus will be found in Blount, Niceron, and the Biographie Universelle; also in Gerdes's Historia Evangel. Renov., Melchior Adam, and other less common books.

2 "Crocus regnat in Academia Lipsiensi, publicitus Græcas docens litteras." — Erasm. Epist. clvii. 5th June, 1514. Eichhorn says, that Conrad Celtes and others had taught Latin only, iii. 272. Camerarius, who studied for three years under Croke, gives him a very high character: "Qui primus putabatur ita docuisse Græcam linguam in Germania, ut plane perdisci illam posse, et quid momenti ad omnem doctrinæ eruditionem atque cultum hujus cognitio allatura esse videretur, nostri homines sese intelligere arbitrarentur." — Vita Melanchthonis, p. 27; and Vita Eobani Hessi, p. 4. He was received at Leipsic "like a heavenly messenger:" every one was proud of knowing him, of paying whatever he demanded, of attending him at any hour of the day or night, Melancthon *apud* Meiners, i. 163. A pretty good life of Croke is in Chalmers's Biographical Dictionary. Bayle does not mention him. Croke was educated at King's College, Cambridge, to which he went from Eton in 1506, and is said to have learned Greek at Oxford from Grocyn, while still a scholar of King's.

3 Erasmus gives a very high character of Ceratinus: "Græcæ linguæ peritia superat vel tres Mosellanos, nec inferior, ut arbitror, Romanæ linguæ facundia." — Epist. DCCXXXVII. "Ceratinus Græcanicæ literaturæ tam exacte callens, ut vix unum aut alterum habeat Italia quicum dubitem hunc committere. Magnæ doctrinæ erat Mosellanus, spei majoris, et amabam unicè hominis ingenium, nec falso dicunt odiosas esse comparationes; sed hoc ipsa causa me compellit dicere, longe alia res est." — Epist. DCCXXVIII.

4 Bayle, art. "Busleiden."

of Germany. Its institution was resisted by the monks and theologians, unyielding though beaten adversaries of literature.[1]

29. It cannot be said that many yet on this side of the Alps wrote Latin well. Budæus is harsh and unpolished; Erasmus fluent, spirited, and never at a loss to express his meaning; nor is his style much defaced by barbarous words, though by no means exempt from them; yet it seldom reaches a point of classical elegance. Francis Sylvius (probably Dubois), brother of a celebrated physician, endeavored to inspire a taste for purity of style in the university of Paris. He had, however, acquired it himself late; for some of his writings are barbarous. The favorable influence of Sylvius was hardly earlier than 1520.[2] The writer most solicitous about his diction was Longolius (Christopher de Longueil, a native of Malines), the only true Ciceronian out of Italy; in which country, however, he passed so much time, that he is hardly to be accounted a mere Cisalpine. Like others of the Ciceronian denomination, he was more ambitious of saying common things well, than of producing what was intrinsically worthy of being remembered.

Latin style in France.

30. We have the imposing testimony of Erasmus himself, that neither France nor Germany stood so high about this period as England. That country, he says, so distant from Italy, stands next to it in the esteem of the learned. This, however, is written in 1524. About the end of the present decennial period, we can produce a not very small number of persons possessing a competent acquaintance with the Greek tongue, more, perhaps, than could be traced in France, though all together might not weigh as heavy as Budæus alone. Such were Grocyn, the patriarch of English learning, who died in 1519; Linacre, whose translation of Galen, first printed in 1521, is one of the few in that age that escape censure for inelegance or incorrectness; Latimer, beloved and admired by his friends, but of whom we have no memorial in any writings of his own; More, known as a Greek scholar by epigrams of some merit;[3] Lilly, master

Greek scholars in England.

[1] Von der Hardt, Hist. Litt. Reformat.

[2] Bayle, art. "Sylvius."

[3] The Greek verses of More and Lilly, Progymnasmata Mori et Lillii, were published at Basle, 1518. It is in this volume that the distich, about which some curiosity has been shown, is found: "Inveni portum, spes et fortuna valete," &c. But it is a translation from an old Greek epigram.

"Quid tandem non præstitisset admirabilis ista naturæ felicitas, si hoc ingenium

of St. Paul's school, who had acquired Greek at Rhodes, but whose reputation is better preserved by the grammars that bear his name; Lupsett, who is said to have learned from Lilly, and who taught some time at Oxford; Richard Croke, already named; Gerard Lister, a physician, to whom Erasmus gives credit for skill in the three languages; Pace and Tunstall, both men well known in the history of those times; Lee and Stokesley, afterwards bishops, the former of whom published Annotations on the Greek Testament of Erasmus at Basle in 1520,[1] and probably Gardiner; Clement, one of Wolsey's first lecturers at Oxford;[2] Brian, Wakefield, Bullock, Tyndale, and a few more whose names appear in Pits and Wood. We could not of course, without presumption, attempt to enumerate every person who at this time was not wholly unacquainted with the Greek language. Yet it would be an error, on the other hand, to make a large allowance for omissions; much less to conclude that every man who might enjoy some reputation in a learned profession could in a later generation have passed for a scholar. Colet, for example, and Fisher, men as distinguished as almost any of that age, were unacquainted with the Greek tongue; and both made some efforts to attain it at an advanced age.[3] It was not till the

instituisset Italia? si totum Musarum sacris vacasset? si ad justam frugem ac velut autumnum suum maturuisset? Epigrammata lusit adolescens admodum, ac pleraque puer; Britanniam suam nunquam egressus est, nisi semel atque iterum principis sui nomine legatione functus apud Flandros. Præter rem uxoriam, præter curas domesticas, præter publici muneris functionem et causarum undas, tot tantisque regni negotiis distrahitur, ut mireris esse otium vel cogitandi de libris." — Epist. clxix. Aug. 1517. In the Ciceronianus he speaks of More with more discriminating praise, and the passage is illustrative of that just quoted.

[1] Erasmus does not spare Lee. Epist. ccxlviii. "Quo uno nihilunquam adhuc terra produxit, nec arrogantius, nec virulentius, nec stultius." This was the tone of the age towards any adversary who was not absolutely out of reach of such epithets. In another place he speaks of Lee as "nuper Græcæ linguæ rudimentis initiatus." — Ep. cccclxxxxi.

[2] Knight says (*apud* Jortin, i. 45) that Clement was the first lecturer at Oxford in Greek after Linacre, and that he was succeeded by Lupsett. And this seems, as to the fact that they did successively teach, to be confirmed by More. Jortin, ii. 396. But the Biographia Britannica, art., "Wolsey," asserts that they were appointed to the chair of rhetoric or humanity; and that Calpurnius, a native of Greece, was the first professor of the language. No authority is quoted by the editors; but I have found it confirmed by Caius in a little treatise De Pronuntiatione Græcæ et Latinæ Linguæ. "Novit," he says, "Oxoniensis schola quemadmodum ipsa Græcia pronuntiavit, ex Matthæo Calpurnio Græco, quem ex Græciâ Oxoniam Græcarum literarum gratia perduxerat Thomas Wolseus, de bonis literis optime meritus cardinalis, cum non alia ratione pronuntiant illi, quam quâ, nos jam profitemur." — Caius de pronunt. Græc. et Lat. Linguæ, edit. Jebb, p. 228.

[3] "Nunc dolor me tenet," says Colet in 1516, "quod non didicerim Græcum sermonem, sine cujus peritia nihil sumus." From a later epistle of Erasmus, where he says, "Coletus strenue Græcatur," it seems likely that he actually made some progress; but at his age it would not be very considerable. Latimer dissuaded Fisher from the attempt, unless he could procure a master from Italy, which Erasmus thought needless. Epist. ccclxiii. In an edition of his

year 1517 that the first Greek lecture was established at Oxford by Fox, Bishop of Hereford, in his new foundation of Corpus Christi College. Wolsey, in 1519, endowed a regular professorship in the university. It was about the same year that Fisher, chancellor of the university of Cambridge, sent down Richard Croke, lately returned from Leipsic, to tread in the footsteps of Erasmus as teacher of Greek.[1] But this was in advance of our neighbors; for no public instruction in that language was yet given in France.

Mode of teaching in schools.

31. By the statutes of St. Paul's school, dated in 1518, the master is to be "lerned in good and clene Latin literature, and also in Greke, iff such may be gotten." Of the boys he says, "I wolde they were taught always in good literature both Latin and Greke." But it does not follow from hence that Greek was actually taught; and, considering the want of lexicons and grammars, none of which, as we shall see, were published in England for many years afterwards, we shall be apt to think that little instruction could have been given.[2] This, however, is not conclusive, and would lead us to bring down the date of philological learning in our public seminaries much too low. The process of learning without books was tedious and difficult, but not impracticable for the diligent. The teacher provided himself with a lexicon which was in common use among his pupils, and with

Adages, he says, "Joannes Fischerus tres linguas ætate jam vergente non vulgari studio amplectitur."—Chil. iv. cent. v. 1.

[1] Greek had not been neglected at Cambridge during the interval, according to a letter of Bullock (in Latin *Bovillus*) to Erasmus in 1516 from thence. "Hic acriter incumbunt literis Græcis, optantque non mediocriter tuum adventum, et hi magnopere favent tuæ huic in Novum Testamentum editioni." It is probable that Cranmer was a pupil of Croke; for, in the deposition of the latter before Mary's commissioners in 1555, he says that he had known the archbishop thirty-six years, which brings us to his own first lectures at Cambridge. Todd's Life of Cranmer, ii. 449. But Cranmer may have known something of the language before, and is, not improbably, one of those to whom Bullock alludes.

[2] In a letter of Erasmus on the death of Colet in 1522, Epist. ccccxxxv. (and in Jortin's App., ii. 315), though he describes the course of education at St. Paul's school rather diffusely, and in a strain of high panegyric, there is not a syllable of allusion to the study of Greek. Pits, however, in an account of one, William Horman, tells us that he was "ad collegium Etonense studiorum causa missus, ubi avide haustis litteris humanioribus, *perceptisque Græcæ linguæ rudimentis*, dignus habitus est qui Cantabrigiam ad altiores disciplinas destinaretur." Horman became "Græcæ linguæ peritissimus," and returned, as head-master, to Eton; "quo tempore in litteris humanioribus scholares illic insigniter erudivit." He wrote several works, partly grammatical, of which Pits gives the titles, and died *plenus dierum*, in 1535.

If we could depend on the accuracy of all this, we must suppose that Greek was taught at Eton so early, that one who acquired the rudiments of it in that school might die at an advanced age in 1535 But this is not to be received on Pits's authority. And I find in Harwood's Alumni Etonenses, that Horman became head-master as early as 1485; no one will readily believe that he could have learned Greek while at school; and the fact is, that he was not educated at Eton, but at Winchester.

one of the grammars published on the Continent, from which he gave oral lectures, and portions of which were transcribed by each student. The books read in the lecture-room were probably copied out in the same manner, the abbreviations giving some facility to a cursive hand; and thus the deficiency of impressions was in some degree supplied, just as before the invention of printing. The labor of acquiring knowledge strengthened, as it always does, the memory; it excited an industry which surmounted every obstacle, and yielded to no fatigue; and we may thus account for that copiousness of verbal learning which sometimes astonishes us in the scholars of the sixteenth century, and in which they seem to surpass the more exact philologers of later ages.

Few classical works printed here.

32. It is to be observed, that we rather extol a small number of men who have struggled against difficulties, than put in a claim for any diffusion of literature in England, which would be very far from the truth. No classical works were yet printed, except four editions of Virgil's Bucolics, a small treatise of Seneca, the first book of Cicero's Epistles (the latter at Oxford in 1519); all, merely of course, for learners. We do not reckon Latin grammars. And as yet no Greek types had been employed. In the spirit of truth, we cannot quite take to ourselves the compliment of Erasmus: there must evidently have been a far greater diffusion of sound learning in Germany, where professors of Greek had for some time been established in all the universities, and where a long list of men ardent in the cultivation of letters could be adduced.[1] Erasmus had a panegyrical humor towards his friends, of whom there were many in England.

State of learning in Scotland.

33. Scotland had, as might naturally be expected, partaken still less of Italian light than the south of Britain. But the reigning king, contemporary with Henry VII., gave proofs of greater good-will towards letters. A statute of James IV., in 1496, enacts that gentlemen's sons should be sent to school in order to learn Latin. Such provisions were too indefinite for execution, even if the royal authority had been greater than it was; but they serve to display the temper of the sovereign. His natural son,

[1] Such a list is given by Meiners, i. 154, of the supporters of Reuchlin, who comprised all the real scholars of Germany: he enumerates sixty-seven, which might doubtless be enlarged.

Alexander, on whom, at a very early age, he conferred the archbishopric of St. Andrew's, was the pupil of Erasmus in the Greek language. The latter speaks very highly of this promising scion of the house of Stuart in one of his adages.[1] But, at the age of twenty, he perished with his royal father on the disastrous day of Flodden Field. Learning had made no sensible progress in Scotland; and the untoward circumstances of the next twenty years were far from giving it encouragement. The translation of the Æneid by Gawin Douglas, Bishop of Dunkeld, though we are not at present on the subject of poetry, may be here mentioned in connection with Scottish literature. It was completed about 1513, though the earliest edition is not till 1553. "This translation," says Warton, "is executed with equal spirit and fidelity; and is a proof that the Lowland Scotch and English languages were now nearly the same. I mean the style of composition, more especially in the glaring affectation of anglicizing Latin words. The several books are introduced with metrical prologues, which are often highly poetical, and show that Douglas's proper walk was original poetry." Warton did well to explain his rather startling expression, that the Lowland Scotch and English languages were then nearly the same; for I will venture to say, that no Englishman, without guessing at every other word, could understand the long passage which he proceeds to quote from Gawin Douglas. It is true that the differences consisted mainly in pronunciation, and consequently in orthography; but this is the great cause of diversity in dialect. The character of Douglas's original poetry seems to be that of the middle ages in general,—prolix, though sometimes animated, description of sensible objects.[2]

Utopia of More.

34. We must not leave England without mention of the only work of genius that she can boast in this age, the Utopia[3] of Sir Thomas More. Perhaps we scarcely appreciate highly enough the spirit and originality of this fiction, which ought to be considered with regard to the barbarism of the times, and the meagreness of preceding inventions. The Republic of Plato, no doubt, furnished More with the germ of his perfect society:[4] but it would be un-

1 Chil. ii. cent. v. 1.

2 Warton, iii. 111.

3 Utopia is named from a king Utopus. I mention this because some have shown their learning by changing the word to Eutopia.

4 [Perhaps this is at least doubtful; neither the Republic nor the Laws of Plato bear any resemblance to the Utopia.—1847.]

reasonable to deny him the merit of having struck out the fiction of its real existence from his own fertile imagination; and it is manifest, that some of his most distinguished successors in the same walk of romance, especially Swift, were largely indebted to his reasoning as well as inventive talents. Those who read the Utopia in Burnet's translation may believe that they are in Brobdignag; so similar is the vein of satirical humor and easy language. If false and impracticable theories are found in the Utopia (and perhaps he knew them to be such), this is in a much greater degree true of the Platonic Republic; and they are more than compensated by the sense of justice and humanity that pervades it, and his bold censures on the vices of power. These are remarkable in a courtier of Henry VIII.; but, in the first years of Nero, the voice of Seneca was heard without resentment. Nor had Henry much to take to himself in the reprehension of parsimonious accumulation of wealth, which was meant for his father's course of government.

Its inconsistency with his opinions.

35. It is possible that some passages in the Utopia, which are neither philosophical nor compatible with just principles of morals, were thrown out as mere paradoxes of a playful mind; nor is it easy to reconcile his language as to the free toleration of religious worship with those acts of persecution which have raised the only dark cloud on the memory of this great man. He positively, indeed, declares for punishing those who insult the religion of others; which might be an excuse for his severity towards the early reformers. But his latitude as to the acceptability of all religions with God, as to their identity in essential principles, and as to the union of all sects in a common worship, could no more be made compatible with his later writings or conduct, than his sharp satire against the court of Rome for breach of faith, or against the monks and friars for laziness and beggary. Such changes, however, are very common, as we may have abundantly observed, in all seasons of revolutionary commotions. Men provoke these, sometimes in the gayety of their hearts with little design, sometimes with more deliberate intention, but without calculation of the entire consequences, or of their own courage to encounter them. And when such men, like More, are of very quick parts, they are often found to be not over-retentive of their opinions, and have little difficulty in abandoning any

speculative notion, especially when, like those in the Utopia, it can never have had the least influence upon their behavior. We may acknowledge, after all, that the Utopia gives us the impression of its having proceeded rather from a very ingenious than a profound mind; and this, apparently, is what we ought to think of Sir Thomas More. The Utopia is said to have been first printed at Louvain in 1516;[1] it certainly appeared at the close of the preceding year; but the edition of Basle in 1518, under the care of Erasmus, is the earliest that bears a date. It was greatly admired on the Continent: indeed there had been little or nothing of equal spirit and originality in Latin since the revival of letters.

36. The French themselves give Francis I. the credit of having been the father of learning in that country. Galland, in a funeral panegyric on that prince, asks if, at his accession (in 1513), any one man in France could read Greek or write Latin. Now, this is an absurd question, when we recollect the names of Budæus, Longolius, and Faber Stapulensis; yet it shows that there could have been very slender pretensions to classical learning in the kingdom. Erasmus, in his Ciceronianus, enumerates among French scholars, not only Budæus, Faber, and the eminent printer Jodocus Badius (a Fleming by birth), whom, in point of style, he seems to put above Budæus, but John Pin, Nicolas Berald, Francis Deloin, Lazarus Baif, and Ruel. This was, however, in 1529; and the list assuredly is not long. But, as his object was to show that few men of letters were worthy of being reckoned fine writers, he does not mention Longueil, who was one; or whom, perhaps, he might omit as being then dead.

Learning restored in France.

37. Budæus and Erasmus were now at the head of the literary world; and, as the friends of each behaved rather too much like partisans, a kind of rivalry in public reputation began, which soon extended to

Jealousy of Erasmus and Budæus.

[1] Of an undated edition, to which Panzer gives the name of *editio princeps*, there is a copy in the British Museum, and another was in Mr. Heber's library. Dibdin's Utopia, 1808, preface, cxi. It appears from a letter of Montjoy to Erasmus, dated 4th January, 1516, that he had received the Utopia, which must therefore have been printed in 1515; and it was reprinted once at least in 1516 or 1517. Erasm. Epist. cciii. ccv. Append. Ep. xliv. lxxix. ccli. *et alibi.* Panzer mentions one at Louvain in December, 1516. This volume by Dr. Dibdin is a reprint of Robinson's early and almost contemporary translation. That by Burnet, 1685, is more known, and I think it good. Burnet, and I believe some of the Latin editions, omit a specimen of the Utopian language, and some Utopian poetry; which probably was thought too puerile.

to themselves, and lessened their friendship. Erasmus seems to have been, in a certain degree, the aggressor; at least some of his letters to Budæus indicate an irritability which the other, as far as appears, had not provoked. Budæus had published in 1514 an excellent treatise De Asse, the first which explained the denominations and values of Roman money in all periods of history.[1] Erasmus sometimes alludes to this with covert jealousy. It was set up by a party against his Adages, which he justly considered more full of original thoughts and extensive learning. But Budæus understood Greek better; he had learned it with prodigious labor, and probably about the same time with Erasmus, so that the comparison between them was not unnatural. The name of one is at present only retained by scholars, and that of the other by all mankind; so different is contemporary and posthumous reputation, It is just to add, that, although Erasmus had written to Budæus in far too sarcastic a tone,[2] under the smart of that literary sensitiveness which was very strong in his temper; yet, when the other began to take serious offence and to threaten a discontinuance of their correspondence, he made amends by an affectionate letter, which ought to have restored their good understanding. Budæus, however, who seems to have kept his resentments longer than his quick-minded rival, continued to write peevish letters; and fresh circumstances arose afterwards to keep up his jealousy.[3]

[1] "Quod opus ejus," says Vives, in a letter to Erasmus (Ep. DCX.), "Hermolaos omnes, Picos, Politianos, Gazas, Vallas, cunctam Italiam pudefecit."

[2] Epist. cc. I quote the numeration of the Leyden edition.

[3] Erasmi Epistolæ, *passim*. The publication of his Ciceronianus, in 1528, renewed the irritation: in this he gave a sort of preference to Badius over Budæus, in respect to style alone; observing that the latter had great excellences of another kind. The French scholars made this a national quarrel, pretending that Erasmus was prejudiced against their country. He defends himself in his epistles so prolixly and elaborately, as to confirm the suspicion, not of this absurdly imputed dislike to the French, but of some little desire to pique Budæus. Epigrams in Greek were written at Paris against him by Lascaris and Toussain; and thus Erasmus, by an unlucky inability to restrain his pen from sly sarcasm, multiplied the enemies whom an opposite part of his character — its spirit of temporizing and timidity — was always raising up. Erasm. Epist. MVXI. *et alibi*.

This rather unpleasing correspondence between two great men, professing friendship, yet covertly jealous of each other, is not ill described by Von der Hardt, in the Historia Litteraria Reformationis. "Mirum dictu, qui undique aculei, sub mollitissima oratione, inter blandimenta continua. Genius utriusque argutissimus, qui vellendo et acerbe pungendo nullibi videretur referre sanguinem aut vulnus inferre. Possint profecto hæ literæ Budæum inter et Erasmum illustre esse et incomparabile exemplar delicatissimæ sed et perquam aculeatæ concertationis, quæ videretur suavissimo absolvi risu et velut familiarissimo palpo. De alterutrius integritate neuter visus dubitare; uterque tamen semper auceps, tot annis commercio frequentissimo. Dissimulandi artificium inexplicabile, quod attenti lectoris admirationem vehat, eumque præ dissertationum dulcedine subamara in stuporem vertat." P. 46.

Character of Erasmus.

38. Erasmus diffuses a lustre over his age, which no other name among the learned supplies. The qualities which gave him this superiority were his quickness of apprehension, united with much industry, his liveliness of fancy, his wit and good sense. He is not a very profound thinker, but an acute observer; and the age for original thinking was hardly come. What there was of it in More produced little fruit. In extent of learning, no one perhaps was altogether his equal. Budæus, with more accurate scholarship, knew little of theology, and might be less ready perhaps in general literature than Erasmus. Longolius, Sadolet, and several others, wrote Latin fär more elegantly; but they were of comparatively superficial erudition, and had neither his keen wit nor his vigor of intellect. As to theological learning, the great Lutheran divines must have been at least his equals in respect of Scriptural knowledge, and some of them possessed an acquaintance with Hebrew, of which Erasmus knew nothing; but he had probably the advantage in the study of the fathers. It is to be observed, that by far the greater part of his writings are theological. The rest either belong to philology and ancient learning, as the Adages, the Ciceronianus, and the various grammatical treatises, or may be reckoned effusions of his wit, as the Colloquies and the Encomium Moriæ.

His Adages severe on kings.

39. Erasmus, about 1517, published a very enlarged edition of his Adages, which had already grown with the growth of his own erudition. It is impossible to distinguish the progressive accessions they received without a comparison of editions; and some probably belong to a later period than the present. The Adages, as we read them, display a surprising extent of intimacy with Greek and Roman literature.[1] Far the greater portion is illustrative, but Erasmus not unfrequently sprinkles his explanations of ancient phrase with moral or literary remarks of some poignancy. The most remarkable, in every sense, are those which reflect with excessive bitterness and freedom on kings and priests. Jortin has slightly alluded to some of these; but they may deserve more particular notice, as displaying the

[1] In one passage, under the proverb "Herculei labores," he expatiates on the immense labor with which this work, his Adages, had been compiled; mentioning, among other difficulties, the prodigious corruption of the text in all Latin and Greek manuscripts, so that it scarce ever happened that a passage could be quoted from them without a certainty or suspicion of some erroneous reading.

character of the man, and perhaps the secret opinions of his age.

40. Upon the adage, "Frons occipitio prior," meaning that every one should do his own business, Erasmus takes the opportunity to observe, that no one requires more attention to this than a prince, if he will act as a real prince, and not as a robber. But, at present, our kings and bishops are only the hands, eyes, and ears of others, careless of the state, and of every thing but their own pleasure.[1] This, however, is a trifle. In another proverb, he bursts out "Let any one turn over the pages of ancient or modern history, scarcely in several generations will you find one or two princes whose folly has not inflicted the greatest misery on mankind." And after much more of the same kind: "I know not whether much of this is not to be imputed to ourselves. We trust the rudder of a vessel, where a few sailors and some goods alone are in jeopardy, to none but skilful pilots; but the state, wherein the safety of so many thousands is concerned, we put into any hands. A charioteer must learn, reflect upon, and practise his art: a prince need only be born. Yet government, as it is the most honorable, so is it the most difficult, of all sciences. And shall we choose the master of a ship, and not choose him who is to have the care of many cities, and so many souls? But the usage is too long established for us to subvert. Do we not see that noble cities are erected by the people; that they are destroyed by princes? that the community grows rich by the industry of its citizens, —is plundered by the rapacity of its princes? that good laws are enacted by popular magistrates,—are violated by these princes? that the people love peace; that princes excite war?"[2]

Instances in illustration.

41. "It is the aim of the guardians of a prince," he ex-

[1] Chil. i. cent. ii. 19.

[2] "Quin omnes et veterum et ne otericorum annales evolve, nimirum ita comperies, vix sæculis aliquot unum aut alterum extitisse principem, qui non insigni stultitiâ maximam perniciem invexerit rebus humanis. . . . Et haud scio, an nonnulla hujus mali pars nobis ipsis sit imputanda. Clavum navis non committimus nisi ejus rei perito, quod quatuor vectorum aut paucarum mercium sit periculum; et rempublicam, in qua tot hominum millia periclitantur, cuivis committimus. Ut auriga fiat aliquis discit artem, exercet, meditatur; at ut princeps sit aliquis, satis esse putamus natum esse. Atqui rectè gerere principatum, ut est munus omnium longe pulcherrimum, ita est omnium etiam multo difficillimum. Deligis, cui navem committas, non deligis cui tot urbes, tot hominum capita credas? Sed istud receptius est, quam ut convelli possit.

"An non videmus egregia oppida a populo condi, a principibus subverti? rempublicam civium industria ditescere, principum rapacitate spoliari? bonas leges ferri a plebeiis magistratibus, a principibus violari? populum studere paci, principes excitare bellum?"

claims in another passage, "that he may never become a man. The nobility, who fatten on public calamity, endeavor to plunge him into pleasures, that he may never learn what is his duty. Towns are burned, lands are wasted, temples are plundered, innocent citizens are slaughtered, while the prince is playing at dice, or dancing, or amusing himself with puppets, or hunting, or drinking. O race of the Bruti, long since extinct! O blind and blunted thunderbolts of Jupiter! We know, indeed, that those corrupters of princes will render account to Heaven, but not easily to us." He passes, soon afterwards, to bitter invective against the clergy, especially the regular orders.[1]

42. In explaining the adage, "Sileni Alcibiadis," referring to things which, appearing mean and trifling, are really precious, he has many good remarks on persons and things, of which the secret worth is not understood at first sight. But thence passing over to what he calls *inversi Sileni*, those who seem great to the vulgar, and are really despicable, he expatiates on kings and priests, whom he seems to hate with the fury of a philosopher of the last century. It must be owned he is very prolix and declamatory. He here attacks the temporal power of the church with much plainness: we cannot wonder that his Adages required mutilation at Rome.

43. But by much the most amusing and singular of the Adages is "Scarabæus aquilam quærit;" the meaning of which, in allusion to a fable that the beetle, in revenge for an injury, destroyed the eggs of the eagle, is explained to be, that the most powerful may be liable to the resentment of the weakest. Erasmus here returns to the attack upon kings still more bitterly and pointed than before. There is nothing in the Contre un of La Boetie, nothing, we may say, in the most seditious libel of our own time, more indignant and cutting against regal government than this long declamation: "Let any physiognomist, not a blunderer in his trade, consider the look and features of an eagle, those rapacious and wicked eyes, that threatening curve of the beak, those cruel cheeks,

[1] "Miro studio curant tutores, ne unquam vir sit princeps. Adnituntur optimates, ii qui publicis malis saginantur. ut voluptatibus sit quam effœminatissimus, ne quid eorum sciat, quæ maxime decet scire principem. Exuruntur vici, vastantur agri, diripiuntur templa, trucidantur immeriti cives, sacra profanaque miscentur, dum princeps interim otiosus ludit aleam, dum saltitat, dum oblectat se morionibus, dum venatur, dum amat, dum potat. O Brutorum genus jam olim extinctum! o fulmen Jovis aut cæcum aut obtusum! Neque dubium est, quin isti principum corruptores pœnas Deo daturi sint, sed sero nobis."

that stern front, will he not at once recognize the image of a king, a magnificent and majestic king? Add to these a dark, ill-omened color, an unpleasing, dreadful, appalling voice, and that threatening scream, at which every kind of animal trembles. Every one will acknowledge this type, who has learned how terrible are the threats of princes, even uttered in jest. At this scream of the eagle, the people tremble, the senate shrinks, the nobility cringes, the judges concur, the divines are dumb, the lawyers assent, the laws and constitutions give way; neither right nor religion, neither justice nor humanity, avail. And thus, while there are so many birds of sweet and melodious song, the unpleasant and unmusical scream of the eagle alone has more power than all the rest."[1]

44. Erasmus now gives the rein still more to his fancy. He imagines different animals, emblematic, no doubt, of mankind, in relation to his eagle. "There is no agreement between the eagle and the fox, not without great disadvantage to the vulpine race; in which, however, they are perhaps worthy of their fate for having refused aid to the hares when they sought an alliance against the eagle, as is related in the Annals of Quadrupeds, from which Homer borrowed his Battle of the Frogs and Mice."[2] I suppose that the foxes mean the nobility, and the hares the people. Some allusions to animals that follow, I do not well understand. Another is more pleasing: "It is not surprising," he says, "that the eagle agrees ill with the swans, those poetic birds: we may

1 "Age si quis mihi physiognomon non omnino malus vultum ipsum et os aquilæ diligentius contempletur, oculos avidos atque improbos, rictum minacem, genas truculentas, frontem torvam, denique illud quod Cyrum Persarum regem tantopere delectavit in principe γρυπὸν, nonne plane regium quoddam simulacrum agnoscet, magnificum et majestatis plenum. Accedit huc et color ipse funestus, teter et inauspicatus, fusco squalore nigricans. Unde etiam quod fuscum est et subnigrum, aquilum vocamus. Tum vox inamœna, terribilis, exanimatrix, ac minax ille querulusque clangor, quem nullum animantium genus non expavescit. Jam hoc symbolum protinus agnoscit, qui modo periculum fecerit, aut viderit certè, quam sint formidandæ principum minæ, vel joco prolatæ. . . . Ad hanc, inquam, aquilæ stridorem illico pavitat omne vulgus, contrahit sese senatus, observit nobilitas, obsecundant judices, silent theologi, assentantur jurisconsulti, cedunt leges, cedunt instituta; nihil valet fas nec pietas, nec æquitas nec humanitas. Cumque tam multæ sint aves non ineloquentes tam multæ canoræ, tamque variæ sint voces ac modulatus qui vel saxa possint flectere, plus tamen omnibus valet insuavis ille et minime musicus unius aquilæ stridor."

2 "Nihil omnino convenit inter aquilam et vulpem, quanquam id sane non mediocri vulpinæ gentis malo; quo tamen haud scio an dignæ videri debeant, quæ quondam leporibus συμμαχίαν adversus aquilam petentibus auxilium negarint, ut refertur in Annalibus Quadrupedum, a quibus Homerus Βατραχομυομαχίαν mutuatus est. . . . Nequo vero mirum quod illi parum convenit cum oloribus, ave nimirum poetica; illud mirum, ab iis sæpenumero vinci tam pugnacem belluam."

wonder more that so warlike an animal is often overcome by them." He sums up all thus: "Of all birds, the eagle alone has seemed to wise men the apt type of royalty, — not beautiful, not musical, not fit for food; but carnivorous, greedy, plundering, destroying, combating, solitary, hateful to all, the curse of all, and, with its great powers of doing harm, surpassing them in its desire of doing it."[1]

45. But the eagle is only one of the animals in the proverb. After all this bile against those whom the royal bird represents, he does not forget the beetles. These, of course, are the monks, whose picture he draws with equal bitterness and more contempt. Here, however, it becomes difficult to follow the analogy, as he runs a little wildly into mythological tales of the scarabæus, not easily reduced to his purpose. This he discloses at length: "There is a wretched class of men of low degree, yet full of malice, — not less dingy nor less filthy nor less vile than beetles, who, nevertheless by a certain obstinate malignity of disposition, though they can never do good to any mortal, become frequently troublesome to the great. They frighten by their ugliness, they molest by their noise, they offend by their stench; they buzz round us, they cling to us, they lie in ambush for us, so that it is often better to be at enmity with powerful men than to attack these beetles, whom it is a disgrace even to overcome, and whom no one can either shake off or encounter without some pollution."[2]

[1] "Ex universis avibus una aquila viris tam sapientibus idonea visa est, quæ regis imaginem repræsentet, nec formosa, nec canora, nec esculenta, sed carnivora, rapax, prædatrix, populatrix, bellatrix, solitaria, invisa omnibus, pestis omnium; quæ cum plurimum nocere possit, plus tamen velit quam possit."

[2] "Sunt homunculi quidam, infimæ quidem sortis, sed tamen malitiosi, non minus atri quam scarabæi, neque minus putidi, neque minus abjecti; qui tamen pertinaci quadam ingenii malitia, cum nulli omnino mortalium prodesse possint, magnis etiam sæpenumero viris facessunt negotium. Territant nigrore, obstrepunt stridore, obturbant fœtore; circumvolitant, hærent, insidiantur, ut non paulo satius sit cum magnis aliquando viris simultatem suscipere, quam hos lacessere scarabæos, quos pudeat etiam vicisse, quosque nec excutere possis, neque conflictari cum illis queas, nisi discedas contaminatior." — Chil. iii. cent. vii. 1.

In a letter to Budæus, Ep ccli., Erasmus boasts of his παρρησία in the Adages, naming the most poignant of them; but says, "in proverbio ἀετὸν κάνθαρος μαιεύεται, plane lusimus ingenio." This proverb, and that entitled Sileni Alcibiadis, had appeared before 1515, — for they were reprinted in that year by Frobenius, — separately from the other Adages, as appears by a letter of Beatus Rhenanus in Appendice ad Erasm. Epist. Ep. xxviii. Zazius, a famous jurist, alludes to them in another letter, Ep xxvii., praising "fluminosas disserendi undas, amplificationis, immensam ubertatem." And this, in truth, is the character of Erasmus's style. The Sileni Alcibiadis were also translated into English, and published by John Gough: see Dibdin's Typographical Antiquities, article 1433.

There is not a little severity in the remarks which Erasmus makes on princes and nobles in the Moriæ Encomium. But with them he seems through life to have been a privileged person.

46. It must be admitted that this was not the language to conciliate; and we might almost commiserate the sufferance of the poor beetles thus trod upon; but Erasmus knew that the regular clergy were not to be conciliated, and resolved to throw away the scabbard. With respect to his invectives against kings, they proceeded undoubtedly, like those, less intemperately expressed, of his friend More in the Utopia, from a just sense of the oppression of Europe in that age by ambitious and selfish rulers. Yet the very freedom of his animadversions seems to plead a little in favor of these tyrants, who, if they had been as thorough birds of prey as he represents them, might easily have torn to pieces the author of this somewhat outrageous declamation, whom on the contrary they honored and maintained. In one of the passages above quoted, he has introduced, certainly in a later edition, a limitation of his tyrannicidal doctrine, if not a palinodia, in an altered key. "Princes," he says, "must be endured, lest tyranny should give way to anarchy, a still greater evil. This has been demonstrated by the experience of many states; and lately the insurrection of the German boors has taught us, that the cruelty of princes is better to be borne than the universal confusion of anarchy." I have quoted these political ebullitions rather diffusely, as they are, I believe, very little known; and have given the original in my notes, that I may be proved to have no way over-colored the translation, and also that a fair specimen may be presented of the eloquence of Erasmus, who has seldom an opportunity of expressing himself with so much elevation, but whose rapid, fertile, and lively, though not very polished style, is hardly more exhibited in these paragraphs than in the general character of his writings.

47. The whole thoughts of Erasmus began now to be occupied with his great undertaking, — an edition of the Greek Testament with explanatory annotations and a continued paraphrase. Valla, indeed, had led the inquiry as a commentator; and the Greek text without notes was already printed at Alcalá by direction of Cardinal Ximenes, though this edition, commonly styled the Complutensian, did not appear till 1522. That of Erasmus was published at Basle in 1516. It is strictly, therefore, the *princeps editio*. He employed the press of Frobenius, with whom he lived in friendship. Many years of his life were spent at Basle.

His Greek Testament.

48. The public, in a general sense of the word, was hardly

yet recovered enough from its prejudices to give encouragement to letters. But there were not wanting noble patrons, who, besides the immediate advantages of their favor, bestowed a much greater indirect benefit on literature, by making it honorable in the eyes of mankind. Learning, which is held pusillanimous by the soldier, unprofitable by the merchant, and pedantic by the courtier, stands in need of some countenance from those before whom all three bow down, — wherever at least, which is too commonly the case, a conscious self-respect does not sustain the scholar against the indifference or scorn of the prosperous vulgar. Italy was then, and perhaps has been ever since, the soil where literature, if it has not always most flourished, has stood highest in general estimation. But in Germany also, at this time, the Emperor Maximilian, whose character is neither to be estimated by the sarcastic humor of the Italians, nor by the fond partiality of his countrymen, and especially his own, in his self-delineation of Der Weiss Kunig, the White King, but really a brave and generous man of lively talents; Frederic, justly denominated the Wise, Elector of Saxony; Joachim, Elector of Brandenburg; Albert, Archbishop of Mentz, were prominent among the friends of genuine learning. The university of Wittenberg, founded by the second of these princes in 1502, rose, in this decade, to great eminence, not only as the birth-place of the Reformation, but as the chief school of philological and philosophical literature. That of Frankfort on the Oder was established by the Elector of Brandenburg in 1506.

Patrons of letters in Germany.

49. The progress of learning, however, was not to be a march through a submissive country. Ignorance, which had much to lose, and was proud as well as rich; ignorance in high places, which is always incurable, because it never seeks for a cure, — set itself sullenly and stubbornly against the new teachers. The Latin language, taught most barbarously through books whose very titles, Floresta, Mammotrectus, Doctrinale puerorum, Gemma gemmarum, bespeak their style,[1] with the scholastic logic and divinity in

Resistance to learning.

[1] Eichhorn, iii. 273, gives a curious list of names of these early grammars: they were driven out of the schools about this time. Mammotrectus, after all, is a learned word: it means μαμμοθρεπτὸς, that is, a boy taught by his grandmother, and a boy taught by his grandmother means one taught gently.

Erasmus gives a lamentable account of the state of education when he was a boy, and probably later: "Deum immortalem! quale sæculum erat hoc, cum magno

wretched compends, had been held sufficient for all education. Those who had learned nothing else could of course teach nothing else, and saw their reputation and emoluments gone all at once by the introduction of philological literature and real science. Through all the Palaces of Ignorance went forth a cry of terror at the coming light: "A voice of weeping heard and loud lament." The aged giant was roused from sleep, and sent his dark hosts of owls and bats to the war. One man above all the rest, Erasmus, cut them to pieces with irony or invective. They stood in the way of his noble zeal for the restoration of letters.[1] He began his attack

apparatu disticha Joannis Garlandini adolescentibus operosis et prolixis commentariis enarrabantur! cum ineptis versiculis dictandis, repetendis et exigendis magna pars temporis absumeretur; cum disceretur Floresta et Floretus; nam Alexandrum inter tolerabiles numerandum arbitror."

I will take this opportunity of mentioning that Erasmus was certainly born in 1465, not in 1467, as Bayle asserts, whom Le Clerc and Jortin have followed: Burigni perceived this, and it may be proved by many passages in the Epistles of Erasmus. Bayle quotes a letter of February, 1516, wherein Erasmus says, as he transcribes it: "Ago annum undequinquagesimum." But in the Leyden edition, which is the best, I find: "Ego jam annum ago primum et quinquagesimum." Epist. cc. Thus he says also, 15th March, 1528: "Arbitror me nunc ætatem agere, in quo M. Tullius decessit." Some other places I have not taken down. His epitaph at Basle calls him "jam septuagenarius;" and he died in 1536. Bayle's proofs of the birth of Erasmus in 1467 are so unsatisfactory that I wonder how Le Clerc should have so easily acquiesced in them. The Biographie Universelle sets down 1467 without remark.

[1] When the first lectures in Greek were given at Oxford about 1519, a party of students arrayed themselves, by the name of Trojans, to withstand the innovators by dint of clamor and violence, till the king interfered to support the learned side. See a letter of More, giving an account of this, in Jortin's Appendix, p. 662. Cambridge, it is to be observed, was very peaceable at this time, and suffered those who liked it to learn something worth knowing. The whole is so shortly expressed by Erasmus, that his words may be quoted: "Anglia duas habet Academias. In utraque traduntur Græcæ literæ, sed Cantabrigiæ tranquillè, quod ejus scholæ princeps sit Joannes Fischerus, episcopus Roffensis, non eruditione tantum sed et vitâ theologicâ. Verum Oxoniæ cum juvenis quidam non vulgariter doctus satis feliciter Græcè profiteretur, barbarus quispiam in populari concione magnis et atrocibus convitiis debacchari cœpit in Græcas literas. At Rex, ut non indoctus ipse, ita bonis literis favens, qui tum forte in propinquo erat, re per Morum et Pacœum cognitâ, denunciavit ut volentes ac lubentes Græcanicam literaturam amplecterentur. Ita rabulis impositum est silentium."—Appendix, p. 667. See also Erasm. Epist. ccclxxx.

Antony Wood, with rather an excess of academical prejudice, insinuates that the Trojans, who waged war against Oxonian Greek, were "Cambridge men, as it is reported." He endeavors to exaggerate the deficiencies of Cambridge in literature at this time, as if "all things were full of rudeness and barbarousness," which the above letters of More and Erasmus show not to have been altogether the case. On the contrary, More says that even those who did not learn Greek contributed to pay the lecturer.

It may be worth while to lay before the reader part of two orations by Richard Croke, who had been sent down to Cambridge by Bishop Fisher, chancellor of the university. As Croke seems to have left Leipsic in 1518, they may be referred to that, or perhaps more probably the following year. It is evident that Greek was now just incipient at Cambridge.

Maittaire says of these two orations of Richard Croke, "Editio rarissima, cujusque unum duntaxat exemplar inspexisse mihi contigit." The British Museum has a copy, which belonged to Dr. Farmer; but he must have seen another copy, for, the last page of this being imperfect, he has filled it up with his own hand. The book is printed at Paris by Colinæus in 1520.

The subject of Croke's orations, which seem not very correctly printed, is the praise of Greece and of Greek literature,

in his Encomium Moriæ, the Praise of Folly. This was addressed to Sir Thomas More, and published in 1511. Eighteen hundred copies were printed, and speedily sold,

addressed to those who already knew and valued that of Rome, which he shows to be derived from the other. "Quin ipsæ quoque voculationes Romanæ Græcis longe insuaviores, minusque concitatæ sunt, cum ultima semper syllaba rigeat in gravem, contraque apud Græcos et inflectatur nonnunquam et acuatur." Croke, of course, spoke Greek accentually. Greek words, in bad types, frequently occur through this oration.

Croke dwells on the barbarous state of the sciences, in consequence of the ignorance of Greek. Euclid's definition of a line was so ill translated, that it puzzled all the geometers till the Greek was consulted. Medicine was in an equally bad condition: had it not been for the labors of learned men, Linacre, Cop, Ruel, "quorum opera felicissime loquuntur Latinè Hippocrates, Galenus, et Dioscorides, cum summa ipsorum invidia, qui, quod canis in præsepi, nec Græcam linguam discere ipsi voluerunt, nec aliis ut discerent permiserunt." He then urges the necessity of Greek studies for the theologian, and seems to have no respect for the Vulgate above the original.

"Turpe sanè erit, cum mercator sermonem Gallicum, Illyricum, Hispanicum, Germanicum, vel solius lucri causa avide ediscat, vos studiosos Græcum in manus vobis traditum rejicere, quo et divitiæ et eloquentia et sapientia comparari possunt. Imo perpendite rogo viri Cantabrigienses, quo nunc in loco vestræ res sitæ sunt. Oxonienses quos ante hæc in omni scientiarum genere vicistis, ad literas Græcas perfugere, vigilant, jejunant, sudant, et algent; nihil non faciunt ut eas occupent. Quod si contingat, actum est de fama vestra. Erigent enim de vobis tropæum nunquam succumbuturi. Habent duces præter cardinalem Cantuariensem, Wintoniensem, cæteros omnes Angliæ episcopos, excepto uno Roffensi, summo semper fautore vestro, et Eliensi," &c.

"Favet præterea ipsis sancta Grocini et theologo digna severitas, Linacri πολυμάθεια et acre judicium, Tunstali non legibus magis quam utrique linguæ familiaris facundia, Stopleii triplex lingua, Mori candida et eloquentissima urbanitas, Pacei mores doctrina et ingenium, ab ipso Erasmo, optimo eruditionis censore, commendati; quem vos olim habuistis Græcarum literarum professorem, utinamque potuissetis retinere. Succedo in Erasmi locum ego, bone Deus, quam infra illum, et doctrinâ et famâ, quamquam me, ne omnino nihili fiam principes viri, theologici doctores, jurium etiam et medicinæ artium præterea professores innumeri, et præceptorem agnovere, et quod plus est, a scholis ad ædes, ab ædibus ad scholas honorificentissime comitati perduxere. Dii me perdant, viri Cantabrigienses, si ipsi Oxonienses stipendio multorum nobilium præter victum me non invitavere. Sed ego pro mea in hanc academiam et fide et observantia," &c.

In his second oration, Croke exhorts the Cantabrigians not to give up the study of Greek: "Si quisquam omnium sit qui vestræ reipublicæ bene consulere debeat, is ego sum, viri Cantabrigienses. Optime enim vobis esse cupio, et id nisi facerem, essem profecto longe ingratissimus. Ubi enim jacta literarum mearum fundamenta, quibus tantum tum apud nostrates, tum vero apud exteros quoque principes, favoris mihi comparatum est; quibus ea fortuna, ut licet jam olim consanguineorum iniquitate paterna hæreditate sim spoliatus, ita tamen adhuc vivam, ut quibusvis meorum majorum imaginibus videar non indignus." He was probably of the ancient family of Croke. Peter Mosellanus calls him, in a letter among those of Erasmus, "juvenis cum imaginibus."

"Audio ego plerosque vos a litteris Græcis dehortatos esse. Sed vos diligenter expendite, qui sint, et plane non alios fore comperitis, quam qui igitur linguam oderunt Græcam, quia Romanam non norunt. Cæterum jam deprehendo quid facturi sint, qui nostras literas odio prosequuntur, confugiunt videlicet ad religionem, cui uni dicent omnia postponenda. Sentio ego cum illis, sed unde quæso orta religio, nisi è Græciâ? quid enim novum testamentum, excepto Matthæo? quid enim vetus? nunquid Deo auspice a septuaginta Græcè redditum? Oxonia est colonia vestra; uti olim non sine summa laude a Cantabrigia deducta, ita non sine summo vestro nunc dedecore, si doctrina ab ipsis vos vinci patiamini. Fuerunt olim illi discipuli vestri, nunc erunt præceptores? Utinam quo animo hæc a me dicta sunt, eo vos dicta interpretemini; crederetisque, quod est verissimum, si quoslibet alios, certe Cantabrigienses minime decere literarum Græcarum esse desertores."

The great scarcity of this tract will serve as an apology for the length of these extracts, illustrating, as they do, the commencement of classical literature in England.

though the book wanted the attraction that some later editions possess, — the curious and amusing engravings from designs of Holbein. It is a poignant satire against all professions of men, and even against princes and peers; but the chief objects are the mendicant orders of monks. "Though this sort of men," he says, "are so detested by every one, that it is reckoned unlucky so much as to meet them by accident, they think nothing equal to themselves, and hold it a proof of their consummate piety if they are so illiterate as not to be able to read. And when their asinine voices bray out in the churches their psalms, of which they understand the notes but not the words,[1] then it is they fancy that the ears of the saints above are enraptured with the harmony;" and so forth.

Unpopularity of the monks.

50. In this sentence Erasmus intimates, what is abundantly confirmed by other testimony, that the mendicant orders had lost their ancient hold upon the people. There was a growing sense of the abuses prevailing in the church, and a desire for a more scriptural and spiritual religion. We have seen already that this was the case seventy years before. And, in the intermediate period, the exertions of a few eminent men, especially Wessel of Groningen, had not been wanting to purify the doctrines and discipline of the clergy. More popular writers assailed them with satire. Thus every thing was prepared for the blow to be struck by Luther, — better indeed than he was himself; for it is well known that he began his attack on indulgences with no expectation or desire of the total breach with the see of Rome which ensued.[2]

The book excites odium.

51. The Encomium Moriæ was received with applause by all who loved merriment, and all who hated the monks; but grave men, as usual, could not bear to see ridicule employed against grave folly and hypocrisy. A letter of one Dorpius, — a man, it is said, of some merit, — which may be read in Jortin's Life of Erasmus,[3] amusingly complains, that, while the most eminent divines and lawyers were admiring Erasmus, his unlucky Moria had spoiled all, by letting them see that he was mischievously

[1] "Numeratos illos quidem, sed non intellectos." — [I conceive that I have given the meaning rightly. — 1842.]

[2] Seckendorf, Hist. Lutheranismi, p. 226; Gerdes, Hist. Evang. sæc. xvi. renovat., vols. i. and iii.; Milner's Church History, vol. iv.; Mosheim, sæc. xv. et xvi.; Bayle, art. "Wessel." For Wessel's character, as a philosopher who boldly opposed the scholastics of his age, see Brucker, iii. 859.

[3] ii. 336.

fitting asses' ears to their heads. The same Dorpius, who seems, though not an old man, to have been a sworn vassal of the giant Ignorance, objects to any thing in Erasmus's intended edition of the Greek Testament which might throw a slur on the accuracy of the Vulgate.

52. Erasmus was soon in a state of war with the monks; and in his second edition of the New Testament, printed in 1518, the notes, it is said, are full of invectives against them. It must be confessed that he had begun the attack without any motive of provocation, unless zeal for learning and religion is to count for such, which the parties assailed could not be expected to admit, and they could hardly thank him for "spitting on their gaberdine." No one, however, knew better how to pay his court; and he wrote to Leo. X. in a style rather too adulatory, which, in truth, was his custom in addressing the great, and contrasts with his free language in writing about them. The custom of the time affords some excuse for this panegyrical tone of correspondence, as well as for the opposite extreme of severity.

Erasmus attacks the monks.

53. The famous contention between Reuchlin and the German monks, though it began in the preceding decennial period, belongs chiefly to the present. In the year 1509, one Pfeffercorn, a converted Jew, induced the Inquisition at Cologne to obtain an order from the emperor for burning all Hebrew books except the Bible, upon the pretext of their being full of blasphemies against the Christian religion. The Jews made complaints of this injury; but, before it could take place, Reuchlin, who had been consulted by the emperor, remonstrated against the destruction of works so curious and important, which, from his partiality to Cabalistic theories, he rated above their real value. The order was accordingly superseded, to the great indignation of the Cologne inquisitors, and of all that party throughout Germany which resisted the intellectual and religious progress of mankind. Reuchlin had offended the monks by satirizing them in a comedy, perhaps the Sergius, which he permitted to be printed in 1506. But the struggle was soon perceived to be a general one; a struggle between what had been and what was to be. Meiners has gone so far as to suppose a real confederacy to have been formed by the friends of truth and learning through Germany and France, to support Reuchlin

Their contention with Reuchlin.

against the mendicant orders, and to overthrow, by means of this controversy, the embattled legions of ignorance.[1] But perhaps the passages he adduces do not prove more than their unanimity and zeal in the cause. The attention of the world was first called to it about 1513; that is, it assumed about that time the character of a war of opinions, extending, in its principle and consequences, beyond the immediate dispute.[2] Several books were published on both sides; and the party in power employed its usual argument of burning what was written by its adversaries. One of these writings is still known, the Epistolæ Obscurorum Virorum; the production, it is said, of three authors, the principal of whom was Ulric Von Hutten, a turbulent, hot-headed man, of noble birth and quick parts, and a certain degree of learning, whose early death seems more likely to have spared the reformers some degree of shame, than to have deprived them of a useful supporter.[3] Few books have been more eagerly received than these Epistles at their first appearance in 1516,[4] which surely proceeded rather from their suitableness to the time than from much intrinsic merit; though it must be presumed that the spirit of many temporary allusions, which delighted or offended that age, is now lost in a mass of vapid nonsense and bad grammar, which the imaginary writers pour out. Erasmus, though not intimately acquainted with Reuchlin, could not but sympathize in a quarrel with their common enemies in a common cause. In the end, the controversy was referred to the pope: but the pope was Leo; and it was hoped that a pro-

[1] Lebensbeschreib., i. 144, *et seqq.*

[2] Meiners brings many proofs of the interest taken in Reuchlin, as the champion, if not the martyr, of the good cause.

[3] Herder, in his Zerstreute Blätter, v. 329, speaks with unreasonable partiality of Ulric von Hutten; and Meiners has written his Life with an enthusiasm which seems to me quite extravagant. Seckendorf, p. 130, more judiciously observes that he was of little use to the Reformation. And Luther wrote about him in June, 1521, "Quid Huttenus petat vides. Nollem vi et cæde pro evangelio certari, ita scripsi ad hominem." Melanchthon, of course, disliked such friends. Epist. Melanchth., p. 45 (1647), and Camerarius, Vita Melanchth. Erasmus could not endure Hutten; and Hutten, when he found this out, wrote virulently against Erasmus. Jortin, as biographer of Erasmus, treats Hutten perhaps with too much contempt; but this is nearer justice than the veneration of the modern Germans. Hutten wrote Latin pretty well, and had a good deal of wit: his satirical libels, consequently, had great circulation and popularity; which, in respect of such writings, is apt, in all ages, to produce an exaggeration of their real influence. In the mighty movement of the Reformation, the Epistolæ Obscurorum Virorum had about as much effect as the Mariage de Figaro in the French Revolution. A dialogue severely reflecting on Pope Julius II., called Julius Exclusus, of which Jortin suspects Erasmus, in spite of his denial, ii. 595, is given by Meiners to Hutten.

[4] Meiners, in his Life of Hutten, Lebensbesch., iii. 73, inclines to fix the publication of the first part of the Epistles in the beginning of 1517; though he admits an earlier date to be not impossible.

posal to burn books, or to disgrace an illustrious scholar, would not sound well in his ears. But Reuchlin was disappointed, when he expected acquittal, by a mandate to supersede or suspend the process commenced against him by the inquisition of Cologne, which might be taken up at a more favorable time.[1] This dispute has always been reckoned of high importance: the victory in public opinion, though not in judicature, over the adherents to the old system, prostrated them so utterly, that from this time the study of Greek and Hebrew became general among the German youth; and the cause of the Reformation was identified in their minds with that of classical literature.[2]

Origin of the Reformation.

54. We are now brought, insensibly perhaps, but by necessary steps, to the great religious revolution which has just been named. I approach this subject with some hesitation, well aware that impartiality is no protection against unreasonable cavilling; but neither the history of literature, nor of human opinion upon the most important subjects, can dispense altogether with so extensive a portion of its materials. It is not required, however, in a work of this nature, to do much more than state shortly the grounds of dispute, and the changes wrought in the public mind.

55. The proximate cause of the Reformation is well known. Indulgences, or dispensations granted by the pope from the heavy penances imposed on penitents after absolution by the old canons, and also, at least in later ages, from the pains of purgatory, were sold by the papal retailers with the most indecent extortion, and eagerly purchased by the superstitious multitude, for their own sake, or that of their deceased friends. Luther, in his celebrated theses, propounded at Wittenberg, in November, 1517, inveighed against the erroneous views inculcated as to the efficacy of indulgences, and especially against the notion of the pope's power over souls in purgatory. He seems to have believed, that the dealers had exceeded their commission, and would be disavowed by the pope. This, however, was very far from being the case; and the deter-

[1] Meiners, i. 197.

[2] Sleidan, Hist. de la Réformat., l. ii.; Brucker, iv. 366; Mosheim; Eichhorn, iii. 238, vi. 16; Bayle, art. "Hochstrat." None of these authorities are equal in fulness to Meiners, Lebensbeschreibungen berühmter Männer, i 98–212; which I did not consult so early as the rest. But there is also a very copious account of the Reuchlinian controversy, including many original documents, in the second part of Von der Hardt's Historia Litteraria Reformationis.

mination of Leo to persevere in defending all the abusive prerogatives of his see drew Luther on to levy war against many other prevailing usages of the church, against several tenets maintained by the most celebrated doctors, against the divine right of the papal supremacy, and finally to renounce all communion with a power which he now deemed an antichristian tyranny. This absolute separation did not take place till he publicly burned the pope's bull against him, and the volumes of the canon law, at Wittenberg, in November, 1520.

Popularity of Luther.

56. In all this dispute, Luther was sustained by a prodigious force of popular opinion. It was perhaps in the power of his sovereign, Frederic, Elector of Saxony, to have sent him to Rome, in the summer of 1518, according to the pope's direction. But it would have been an odious step in the people's eyes, and, a little later, would have been impossible. Miltitz, an envoy despatched by Leo in 1519, upon a conciliatory errand, told Luther that 25,000 armed men would not suffice to make him a prisoner, so favorable was the impression of his doctrine upon Germany. And Frederic himself, not long afterwards, wrote plainly to Rome, that a change had taken place in his country; the German people were not what they had been; there were many men of great talents and considerable learning among them, and the laity were beginning to be anxious about a knowledge of Scripture; so that, unless Luther's doctrine, which had already taken root in the minds of a great many both in Germany and other countries, could be refuted by better arguments than mere ecclesiastical fulminations, the consequence must be so much disturbance in the empire as would by no means redound to the benefit of the holy see.[1] In fact, the university of Wittenberg was crowded with students and others, who came to hear Luther and Melanchthon. The latter had, at the very beginning, embraced his new master's opinions with a conviction which he did not in all respects afterwards preserve. And, though no overt attempts to innovate on the established ceremonies had begun in this period, before the end of 1520 several preached against them, and the whole north of Germany was full of expectation.

[1] Seckendorf. This remarkable letter will be found also in Roscoe's Leo X., Appendix, No. 185. It bears date April, 1520. See also a letter of Petrus Mosellanus, in Jortin's Erasmus, ii. 353; and Luther's own letter to Leo, of March, 1519.

57. A counterpart to the reformation that Luther was thus effecting in Saxony might be found at the same instant in Switzerland, under the guidance of Zwingle. It has been disputed between the advocates of these leaders, to which the priority in the race of reform belongs. Zwingle himself declares, that in 1516, before he had heard of Luther, he began to preach the gospel at Zurich, and to warn the people against relying upon human authority.[1] But that is rather ambiguous, and hardly enough to substantiate his claim. In 1518, which of course is after Luther's appearance on the scene, the Swiss reformer was engaged in combating the venders of indulgences, though with less attention from the court of Rome. Like Luther, he had the support of the temporal magistrate, the Council of Zurich. Upon the whole, they proceeded so nearly with equal steps, and were so little connected with each other, that it seems difficult to award either any honor of precedence.[2]

Simultaneous reform by Zwingle.

58. The German nation was, in fact, so fully awakened to

[1] Zwingle *apud* Gerdes, i. 103.

[2] Milner, who is extremely partial in the whole of this history, labors to extenuate the claims of Zwingle to independence in the preaching of reformation; and even pretends that he had not separated from the Church of Rome in 1523, when Adrian VI. sent him a civil letter. But Gerdes shows at length that the rupture was complete in 1520. See also the article "Zwingle," in Biogr. Universelle.

The prejudice of Milner against Zwingle throughout is striking, and leads him into much unfairness. Thus, he asserts him, v. 510, to have been consenting to the capital punishment of some Anabaptists at Zurich. But, not to mention that their case was not one of mere religious dissidence, it does not by any means appear that he approved their punishment, which he merely relates as a fact. A still more gross misrepresentation occurs in p. 526. — [Capito says, in a letter to Bullinger (1536), "Antequam Lutherus in lucem emerserit, Zwinglius et ego inter nos communicavimus de pontifice dejiciendo, etiam cum ille vitam degeret in eremitorio. Nam utrique ex Erasmi consuetudine, et lectione bonorum auctorum, qualecunque judicium tum sobolescebat." — Gerdes, p. 117. — 1842.]

[A late writer, as impartial as he is learned and penetrating, thus contrasts the two founders of the Reformation: "If we compare him [Zwingle] with Luther, we find that he had no such tremendous tempests to withstand as those which shook the most secret depths of Luther's soul. As he had never devoted himself with equal ardor to the established church, he had not now to break loose from it with such violent and painful struggles. It was not the profound love of the faith, and of its connection with redemption, in which Luther's efforts originated, that made Zwingle a reformer: he became so chiefly, because, in the course of his study of Scripture in search of truth, he found the church and the received morality at variance with its spirit. Nor was Zwingle trained at an university, or deeply imbued with the prevalent doctrinal opinions. To found a high school, firmly attached to all that was worthy of attachment, and dissenting only on certain most important points, was not his vocation. He regarded it much more as the business and duty of his life to bring about the religious and moral reformation of the republic that had adopted him, and to recall the Swiss Confederation to the principles upon which it was originally founded. While Luther's main object was a reform of doctrine, which, he thought, would be necessarily followed by that of life and morals, Zwingle aimed directly at the improvement of life: he kept mainly in view the practical significancy of Scripture as a whole; his original views were of a moral and political nature; hence his labors were tinged with a wholly peculiar color." — Ranke's Hist. of Reformation, vol. iii. p. 7. — 1847.]

the abuses of the church; the denial of papal sovereignty in the Councils of Constance and Basle had been so effectual in its influence on the public mind, though not on the external policy of church and state, that, if neither Luther nor Zwingle had ever been born, there can be little question that a great religious schism was near at hand. These councils were to the Reformation what the Parliament of Paris was to the French Revolution. Their leaders never meant to sacrifice one article of received faith; but the little success they had in redressing what they denounced as abuses convinced the laity that they must go much farther for themselves. What effect the invention of printing, which in Italy was not much felt in this direction, exerted upon the serious minds of the Teutonic nations, has been already intimated, and must appear to every reflecting person. And, when this was followed by a more extensive acquaintance with the New Testament in the Greek language, nothing could be more natural than that inquisitive men should throw away much of what seemed the novel superstructure of religion, and, what in other times such men had rarely ventured, should be encouraged, by the obvious change in the temper of the multitude, to declare themselves. We find that Pellican and Capito, two of the most learned scholars in Western Germany, had come, as early as 1512, to reject altogether the doctrine of the real presence. We find also that Œcolampadius had begun to preach some of the Protestant doctrines in 1514.[1] And Erasmus, who had so manifestly prepared the way for the new reformers, continued, as it is easy to show from the uniform current of his letters, beyond the year 1520, favorable to their cause. His enemies were theirs; and he concurred in much that they preached, especially as to the exterior practices of religion. Some, however, of Luther's tenets he did not and could not approve; and he was already disgusted by that intemperance of language and conduct which, not long afterwards, led him to recede entirely from the Protestant side.[2]

Reformation prepared beforehand.

[1] Gerdes, i. 117, 124, *et post.* In fact, the precursors of the Reformation were very numerous, and are collected by Gerdes in his first and third volumes, though he has greatly exaggerated the truth by reckoning as such Dante and Petrarch and all opponents of the temporal power of the papacy. Wessel may, upon the whole, be fairly reckoned among the Reformers.

[2] In 1519 and 1520, even in his letters to Albert, Archbishop of Mentz, and others by no means partial to Luther, he speaks of him very handsomely, and with little or no disapprobation, except on account of his intemperance, though professing only a slight acquaintance with his writings. The proofs are too numerous to be cited. He says, in a letter to Zwingle, as late as 1521, "Videor mihi fere omnia

Dangerous tenets of Luther.

59. It would not be just, probably, to give Bossuet credit in every part of that powerful delineation of Luther's theological tenets with which he begins the History of the Variations of Protestant Churches. Nothing, perhaps, in polemical eloquence is so splendid as this chapter. The eagle of Meaux is there truly seen, lordly of form, fierce of eye, terrible in his beak and claws. But he is too determined a partisan to be trusted by those who seek the truth without regard to persons and denominations. His quotations from Luther are short, and in French: I have failed in several attempts to verify the references. Yet we are not to follow the reformer's indiscriminate admirers in dissembling altogether, like Isaac Milner, or in slightly censuring, as others have done, the enormous paradoxes which deform his writings, especially such as fall within the present period. In maintaining salvation to depend on faith as a single condition, he not only denied the importance, in a religious sense, of a virtuous life, but asserted that every one who felt within himself a full assurance that his sins were remitted (which, according to Luther, is the proper meaning of Christian faith), became incapable of sinning at all, or at least of forfeiting the favor of God, so long, but so long only, as that assurance should continue. Such expressions are sometimes said by Seckendorf and Mosheim to have been thrown out hastily, and without precision; but I fear it will be found on examination that they are very definite and clear, the want of precision and perspicuity being rather in those which are alleged as inconsistent with them, and as more consonant to the general doctrine of the Christian church.[1] It must not be supposed for a moment, that Luther, whose soul was penetrated with a fervent piety, and whose integrity as well as purity of life are

docuisse, quæ docet Lutherus, nisi quod non tam atrociter, quodque abstinui a quibusdam ænigmatis et paradoxis." This is quoted by Gerdes, i. 153, from a collection of letters of Erasmus, published by Hottinger, but not contained in the Leyden edition. Jortin seems not to have seen them.

[1] See, in proof of this, Luther's works, vol. i. *passim* (edit. 1554). The first work of Melanchthon, his Loci Communes, — published in 1521, when he followed Luther more obsequiously in his opinions than he did in after-life, — is equally replete with the strongest Calvinism. This word is a little awkward in this place; but I am compelled to use it, as most intelligible to the reader; and I conceive that these two reformers went much beyond the language of Augustin, which the schoolmen thought themselves bound to recognize as authority, though they might elude its spirit. I find the first edition of Melanchthon's Loci Communes in Von der Hardt, Historia Litteraria Reformationis, — a work which contains a great deal of curious matter. It is called by him *opus rarissimum*, not being in the edition of Melanchthon's theological works, which some have ascribed to the art of Peucer, whose tenets were widely different.

unquestioned, could mean to give any encouragement to a licentious disregard of moral virtue; which he valued, as in itself lovely before God as well as man, though, in the technical style of his theology, he might deny its proper obligation. But his temper led him to follow up any proposition of Scripture to every consequence that might seem to result from its literal meaning; and he fancied, that to represent a future state as the motive of virtuous action, or as any way connected with human conduct, for better or worse, was derogatory to the free grace of God, and the omnipotent agency of the Spirit in converting the soul.[1]

[1] I am unwilling to give these pages too theological a cast by proving this statement, as I have the means of doing, by extracts from Luther's own early writings. Milner's very prolix history of this period is rendered less valuable by his disingenuous trick of suppressing all passages in these treatises of Luther which display his Antinomian paradoxes in a strong light. Whoever has read the writings of Luther up to the year 1520 inclusive must find it impossible to contradict my assertion. In treating of an author so full of unlimited propositions as Luther, no positive proof as to his tenets can be refuted by the production of inconsistent passages.

[It was to be expected that what I have here said, and afterwards in Chap. VI., concerning Luther, would grate on the ears of many very respectable persons, whose attachment to the Reformation, and admiration of his eminent character, could not without much reluctance admit that degree of censure which I have felt myself compelled to pass upon him. Two Edinburgh reviewers, for both of whom I feel great respect, have at different times remarked what seemed to them an undue severity; and a late writer, Archdeacon Hare, in his notes to a series of Sermons on the Mission of the Comforter, 1846, has animadverted on it at great length, and with a sufficiently uncompromising spirit. I am unwilling to be drawn on this occasion into controversy, or to follow my prolix antagonist through all his observations upon my short paragraphs, — both because I have in my disposition a good deal of a *stulta clementia*, which leads me to take pity on paper, or rather on myself; and for a better reason, namely, that, notwithstanding what the archdeacon calls my "*aversion* to Luther," I really look upon him as a great man, endowed with many virtues, and an instrument of Providence for a signal good. I am also particularly reluctant, at the present time, to do in any manner the drudgery of the Philistines; and, while those who are not more in my good graces than the archdeacon's, and who had hardly sprouted up when my remarks on Luther were first written, are depreciating the Protestant cause with the utmost animosity, to strengthen any prejudice against it. But I must, as shortly as possible, and perhaps more shortly than an adequate exposition of my defence would require, produce the passages in Luther's own writings which have compelled me to speak out as strongly as I have done.

I may begin by observing, that, in charging Luther, especially in his early writings, with what goes generally by the name of Antinomianism (that is, with representing faith alone as the condition of acceptance with God, not merely for those who for the first time embrace the gospel, but for all who have been baptized and brought up in its profession, and in so great a degree that no sins whatever can exclude a faithful man from salvation), I have maintained no paradox, but what has been repeatedly alleged, not only by Romanist but Protestant theologians. This, however, is not sufficient to prove its truth; and I am therefore under the necessity of quoting a few out of many passages. But I repeat that I have not the remotest intention of charging Luther with wilful encouragement to an immoral life. The Antinomian scheme of religion, which indeed was not called by that name in Luther's age (the word, as applied to the followers of Agricola, involving only a denial of the obligation of the Mosaic law *as such*, moral as well as ceremonial), is only one mode in which the disinterestedness of virtuous actions has been asserted, and may be held by men of the utmost sanctity, though it must be exceedingly dangerous in its general promulgation. Thus we find it substantially, though without

60. Whatever may be the bias of our minds as to the truth of Luther's doctrines, we should be careful, in considering the

intemperance, in some Essays by a highly respected writer, Mr. Thomas Erskine, on the Unconditional Freeness of the Gospel. Nothing is more repugnant to my principles than to pass moral reprobation on persons because I differ, however essentially, from their tenets. Let us leave that to Rome and Oxford, though Luther unfortunately was the last man who could claim this liberty of prophesying for himself on the score of his charity and tolerance for others.

Archdeacon Hare is a man of so much fairness, and so intensely persuaded of being in the right, that he produces himself the leading propositions of Luther, from which others, like myself, have deduced our own very different inferences as to his doctrine.

In the treatise De Captivitate Babylonica, 1520, we find these celebrated words: "Ita vides quam dives sit homo Christianus et baptisatus, qui etiam volens non potest perdere salutem suam quantiscunque peccatis, nisi nolit credere. Nulla enim peccata eum possunt damnare nisi sola incredulitas. Cætera omnia, si redeat vel stet fides in promissionem divinam baptisato factam, in momento absorbentur per eandem fidem, imo veritatem Dei, quia seipsum negare non potest, si tu eum confessus fueris, et promittenti fideliter adhæseris." It may be pretended, that, however paradoxically Luther has expressed himself, he meant to assert the absolute incompatibility of *habitual* sins with a justifying faith. But, even if his language would always bear this meaning, it is to be kept in mind, that faith (πιστις) can never be more than inward persuasion or assurance, whereof, *subjectively*, each man must judge for himself; and, though to the eyes of others a true faith may be wanting, it is not evident that men of enthusiastic minds may not be fully satisfied that they possess it.

Luther, indeed, has, in another position, often quoted, taken away from himself this line of defence: "Si in fide posset fieri adulterium, peccatum non esset." — Disputat. 1520. Archdeacon Hare observes on this that "it is logically true."— P. 794. This appears to me a singular assertion. The hypothesis of Luther is, that a sinful action might be committed in a state of faith; and the consequent of the proposition is, that in such case it would not be a sin at all. Grant that he held the supposition to be impossible, which no doubt he sometimes does, though we should hardly draw that inference from the passage last cited, or from some others, still, in reasoning *ex absurdo*, we are bound to argue rightly upon the assumed hypothesis. But all his notions about sin and merit were so preposterously contradictory to natural morality and religion, that they could not have been permanently received without violating the moral constitution of the human mind. Thus, in the Heidelberg Propositions, 1518, we read: "Opera hominum ut semper speciosa sint, bonaque videantur, probabile tamen est ea esse peccata mortalia. . . . Opera Dei ut semper sint deformia malaque videantur, verè tamen sunt merita immortalia. . . . Non sic sunt opera hominum mortalia (de bonis, ut apparent, loquimur), ut eadem sint crimina. . . . Non sic sunt opera Dei merita (de his quæ per hominem fiunt, loquimur), ut eadem non sint peccata. . . . Justorum opera essent mortalia, nisi pio Dei timore ab ipsismet justis ut mortalia timerentur." Such a series of propositions occasions a sort of bewilderment in the understanding, so unlike are they to the usual tone of moral precept and sentiment.

I am indebted to Archdeacon Hare for another, not at all less singular, passage, in a letter of Luther to Melanchthon in 1521, which I have also found in the very able, though very bitter, Vie de Luther, by M. Audin, Paris, 1839. I do not see the necessity of giving the context, or of explaining on what occasion the letter was written, on the ground, that, where a sentence is complete in itself, and contains a general assertion of an author's own opinion, it is not to be limited by reference to any thing else. "Sufficit," Luther says, "quod agnovimus per divitias gloriæ Dei Agnum, qui tollit peccata mundi; ab hoc non avellet nos peccatum, etiamsi millies millies uno die fornicamur aut occidamus. Putas tam parvum esse pretium et redemtionem pro peccatis nostris factam in tanto et tali agno? Ora fortiter; es enim fortissimus peccator."

It appears that Mr. Ward has translated *uno die* by "every day;" for which the archdeacon animadverts on him: "This mistranslation serves his purpose of blasting Luther's fame, inasmuch as it substitutes a hellish horror — the thought that a continuous life of the most atrocious sin can co-exist with faith and prayer and Christ and righteousness — for that which, justly offensive as it may be, is so mainly from its peculiar Lutheran extravagance of expression."— P. 794. No one will pretend that Mr. Ward ought not to have been more accurate. But I confess that the difference does not strike me as immensely

Reformation as a part of the history of mankind, not to be misled by the superficial and ungrounded representations

great. Luther, I cannot help thinking, would have written *unoquoque die* as readily as *uno*, if the word had suggested itself. He wanted to assert the efficacy of Christ's imputed righteousness in the most forcible terms, by weighing it against an impossible accumulation of offences. It is no more than he had said in the passage quoted above from the treatise De Captivitate Babylonica: "Non potest perdere salutem suam quantiscunque peccatis;" expressed still more offensively.

The real question is, not what interpretation an astute advocate, by making large allowance for warmth of temper, peculiarities of expression, and the necessity of inculcating some truths more forcibly by being silent on others, may put on the writings of Luther (for very few will impute to him either a defective sense of moral duties in himself, or a disposition to set his disciples at liberty from them), but what was the evident tendency of his language. And this, it should be remembered, need not be judged solely by the plain sense of words, though that is surely sufficient. The danger of these exaggerations — the mildest word that I can use, and one not adequate to what I feel — was soon shown in the practical effect of Lutheran preaching. Munzer and Knipperdolling, with the whole rabble of Anabaptist fanatics, were the legitimate brood of Luther's early doctrine. And, even if we set these aside, it is certain that we find no testimonies to any reform of manners in the countries that embraced it. The Swiss Reformation, the English, and the Calvinistic churches generally, make a far better show in this respect.

This great practical deficiency in the Lutheran Reformation is confessed by their own writers. And it is attested by a remarkable letter of Wilibald Pirckheimer, announcing the death of Albert Durer, to a correspondent at Vienna in 1528, which may be found in Reliquien von Albrecht Durer, Nuremberg, 1828, p. 168. In this, he takes occasion to inveigh against the bad conduct of the reformed party at Nuremberg, and seems as indignant at the Lutherans as he had ever been against Popery, though without losing his hatred for the latter. I do not quote the letter, which is long, and in obsolete German; and perhaps it may display too much irritation, natural to an honest man who has been disappointed in his hopes from a revolution: but the witness he bears to the dishonest and dissolute manners which had accompanied the introduction of Lutheranism is not to be slightly regarded, considering the respectability of Pirckheimer, and his known co-operation with the first reform.

I have been thought to speak too disparagingly of Luther's polemical writings, especially that against the bishops, by the expression "bellowing in bad Latin." Perhaps it might be too contemptuous towards a great man; but I had been disgusted by the perusal of them. Those who have taken exception (in the Edinburgh Review) are probably little conversant with Luther's writings. But, independently of the moral censure which his virulence demands, we are surely at liberty to say that it is in the worst taste, and very unlikely to convince or conciliate any man of good sense. One other grave objection to the writings of Luther I have not hitherto been called upon to mention; but I will not wholly omit his scandalous grossness, especially as Archdeacon Hare has entered upon an elaborate apology for it. We all know quite as well as he does, that the manners of different ages, different countries, and different conditions of life, are not alike; and that what is universally condemned in some periods has been tolerated in others. Such an excuse may often be made with great fairness; but it cannot be made for Luther. We have writings of his contemporaries, we have writings of grave men in ages less polished than his own. No serious author of the least reputation will be found who defiles his pages, I do not say with such indelicacy, but with such disgusting filthiness, as Luther. He resembles Rabelais alone in this respect, and absolutely goes beyond him. Audin, whose aim is to destroy as far as possible the moral reputation of Luther, has collected a great deal more than Bossuet would have deigned to touch; and, considering this object, in the interests of his own religion, I do not know how he can be blamed; though I think that he should have left more passages untranslated. Those taken from the Colloquia Mensalia might perhaps be forgiven, and the blame thrown on the gossiping retailer of his table-talk; but, in all his attacks on popes and cardinals, Luther disgraces himself by a nasty and stupid brutality The great cause, also, of the marriage of priests ceases to be holy and honorable in his advocacy.

And I must express my surprise that Archdeacon Hare should vindicate, against Mr. Ward, the Sermo de Matrimonio, preached at Wittenberg, 1522; for, though he says there are four sermons with this title in Luther's works, I have little doubt

which we sometimes find in modern writers. Such is this, that Luther, struck by the absurdity of the prevailing superstitions, was desirous of introducing a more rational system of religion; or that he contended for freedom of inquiry, and the boundless privileges of individual judgment; or, what others have been pleased to suggest, that his zeal for learning and ancient philosophy led him to attack the ignorance of the monks, and the crafty policy of the church, which withstood all liberal studies.

61. These notions are merely fallacious refinements, as every man of plain understanding, who is acquainted with the writings of the early reformers, or has considered their history, must acknowledge. The doctrines of Luther, taken altogether, are not more rational, that is, more conformable to what men, *à priori*, would expect to find in religion, than those of the Church of Rome; nor did he ever pretend that they were so. As to the privilege of free inquiry, it was of course exercised by those who deserted their ancient altars, but certainly not upon any theory of a right in others to judge amiss, that is, differently from themselves. Nor, again, is there any foundation for imagining that Luther was concerned for the interests of literature. None had he himself, save theological; nor are there, as I apprehend, many allusions to profane studies, or any proof of his regard to them, in all his works. On the contrary, it is probable that both the principles of this great founder of the Reformation, and the natural tendency of so intense an application to theological controversy, checked, for a time, the progress of philological and philosophical literature on this side of the Alps.[1] Every solution of the conduct of the

Real explanation of them.

that Mr. Ward was led to this by Audin, who makes many quotations from it. "The date of this sermon, 1522, when many of the inmates of the convents were quitting them, and when the errors of the Anabaptists were beginning to spread, shows that there was urgent need for the voice of wisdom to set forth the true idea, relations, and obligations of marriage; nor could this be done without an exposition and refutation of the manifold scandalous errors and abuses concerning it, bred and propagated by the papacy."—P. 771. A very rational sentence! but utterly unlike Luther's sermon, which is far more in the tone of the Anabaptists than against them. But, without dwelling on this, and referring to Audin, vol. ii. p. 34, whose quotations cannot be forgeries, or to the shorter extracts in Bossuet, Hist. des Variations, c. 6, § 11, I shall only observe, that, if the voice was that of wisdom, it was not that of Christianity. But here I conclude a note far longer than I wished to make it: the discussion being akin to the general subject of these volumes, and forced upon me by a direct attack of many pages. For Archdeacon Hare himself, I have all the respect which his high character, and an acquaintance of long duration, must naturally have created. —1847.]

[1] Erasmus, after he had become exasperated with the reformers, repeatedly charges them with ruining literature. "Ubicunque regnat Lutheranismus, ibi literarum est interitus." — Epist. MVI.

reformers must be nugatory, except one,—that they were men absorbed by the conviction that they were fighting the battle of God. But, among the population of Germany or Switzerland, there was undoubtedly another predominant feeling; the sense of ecclesiastical oppression, and scorn for the worthless swarm of monks and friars. This may be said to have divided the propagators of the Reformation into such as merely pulled down, and such as built upon the ruins. Ulric von Hutten may pass for the type of the one; and Luther himself, of the other. And yet it is hardly correct to say of Luther, that he erected his system on the ruins of Popery. For it was rather the growth and expansion in his mind of one positive dogma, justification by faith, in the sense he took it (which can be easily shown to have preceded the dispute about indulgences [1]), that broke down and crushed successively the various doctrines of the Romish Church; not because he had originally much objection to them, but because there was no longer room for them in a consistent system of theology.[2]

62. The laws of synchronism, which we have hitherto obeyed, bring strange partners together, and we may pass at once from Luther to Ariosto. The Orlando

Orlando Furioso.

(1528). "Evangelicos istos, cum multis aliis, tum hoc nomine præcipue odi, quod per eos ubique languent, frigent, jacent, intereunt bonæ literæ, sine quibus quid est hominum vita? Amant viaticum et uxorem, cætera pili non faciunt. Hos fucos longissime arcendos censeo a vestro contubernio."—Ep. DCCCCXLVI. (eod. ann.) There were, however, at this time, as well as afterwards, more learned men on the side of the Reformation than on that of the church.

[1] See his disputations at Wittenberg, 1516; and the sermons preached in the same and the subsequent year.

[2] The best authorities for the early history of the Reformation are Seckendorf, Hist. Lutheranismi, and Sleidan, Hist. de la Réformation, in Courayer's French translation; the former being chiefly useful for the ecclesiastical, the latter for political history. But, as these confine themselves to Germany, Gerdes (Hist. Evangel. Reformat.) is necessary for the Zwinglian history, as well as for that of the Northern kingdoms. The first sections of Father Paul's History of the Council of Trent are also valuable. Schmidt, Histoire des Allemands, vols. vi. and vii., has told the story on the side of Rome speciously and with some fairness; and Roscoe has vindicated Leo X. from the imputation of unnecessary violence in his proceeding against Luther. Mosheim is always good, but concise; Milner, far from concise, but highly prejudiced, and in the habit of giving his quotations in English, which is not quite satisfactory to a lover of truth.

The essay on the influence of the Reformation, by Villers, which obtained a prize from the French Institute, and has been extolled by a very friendly but better-informed writer in the Biographie Universelle, appears to me the production of a man who had not taken the pains to read any one work contemporaneous with the Reformation, or even any compilation which contains many extracts. No wonder that it does not represent, in the slightest degree, the real spirit of the times, or the tenets of the reformers. Thus, e. gr., "Luther," he says, "exposed the abuse of the traffic of indulgences, and the danger of believing that heaven and the remission of all crimes could be bought with money; while a sincere repentance and an amended life were the only means of appeasing the divine justice."—(P. 65, Engl. transl.) This, at least, is not very like Luther's Antinomian contempt for repentance, and amendment of life: it might come near to the notions of Erasmus.

Furioso was first printed at Ferrara in 1516. This edition contained forty cantos, to which the last six were added in 1532. Many stanzas, chiefly of circumstance, were interpolated by the author from time to time.

63. Ariosto has been, after Homer, the favorite poet of Europe. His grace and facility; his clear and rapid stream of language; his variety and beauty of invention; his very transitions of subject, so frequently censured by critics, but artfully devised to spare the tediousness that hangs on a protracted story,—left him no rival in general popularity. Above sixty editions of the Orlando Furioso were published in the sixteenth century. "There was not one," says Bernardo Tasso, "of any age or sex or rank, who was satisfied after more than a single perusal." If the change of manners and sentiments have already in some degree impaired this attraction; if we cease to take interest in the prowess of Paladins, and find their combats a little monotonous,—this is perhaps the necessary lot of all poetry, which, as it can only reach posterity through the medium of contemporary reputation, must accommodate itself to the fleeting character of its own time. This character is strongly impressed on the Orlando Furioso: it well suited an age of war and pomp and gallantry; an age when chivalry was still recent in actual life, and was reflected in concentrated brightness from the mirror of romance.

Its popularity.

64. It has been sometimes hinted, as an objection to Ariosto, that he is not sufficiently in earnest, and leaves a little suspicion of laughing at his subject. I do not perceive that he does this in a greater degree than good sense and taste permit. The poets of knight-errantry might, in this respect, be arranged in a scale, of which Pulci and Spenser would stand at the extreme points: the one mocking the absurdities he coolly invents; the other, by intense strength of conception, full of love and faith in his own creations. Between these, Berni, Ariosto, and Boiardo take successively their places; none so deeply serious as Spenser, none so ironical as Pulci. It was not easy in Italy, especially after the Morgante Maggiore had roused the sense of ridicule, to keep up at every moment the solemn tone which Spain endured in the romances of the sixteenth century; nor was this consonant to the gayety of Ariosto. It is the light carelessness of his manner which constitutes a great part of its charm.

Want of seriousness.

A continuation of Boiardo.

65. Castelvetro has blamed Ariosto for building on the foundations of Boiardo.[1] He seems to have had originally no other design than to carry onward, a little better than Agostini, that very attractive story; having written, it is said, at first, only a few cantos to please his friends.[2] Certainly, it is rather singular that so great and renowned a poet should have been little more than the continuator of one who had so lately preceded him; though Salviati defends him by the example of Homer; and other critics, with whom we shall perhaps not agree, have thought this the best apology for writing a romantic instead of an heroic poem. The story of the Orlando Innamorato must be known before we can well understand that of the Furioso. But this is nearly what we find in Homer; for who can reckon the Iliad any thing but a fragment of the tale of Troy? It was indeed less felt by the compatriots of Homer, already familiar with that legendary cyclus of heroic song, than it is by the readers of Ariosto, who are not, in general, very well acquainted with the poem of his precursor. Yet experience has even here shown that the popular voice does not echo the complaint of the critic. This is chiefly owing to the want of a predominant unity in the Orlando Furioso, which we commonly read in detached parcels. The principal unity that it does possess, distinct from the story of Boiardo, consists in the loves and announced nuptials of Rogero and Bradamante, the imaginary progenitors of the house of Este; but Ariosto does not gain by this condescension to the vanity of a petty sovereign.

In some points inferior.

66. The inventions of Ariosto are less original than those of Boiardo, but they are more pleasing and various. The tales of old mythology and of modern romance furnished him with those delightful episodes we all admire, with his Olimpia and Bireno, his Ariodante and Geneura, his Cloridan and Medoro, his Zerbino and Isabella. He is more conversant with the Latin poets, or has turned them to better account, than his predecessor. For the sudden transitions in the middle of a canto, or even a stanza, with which every reader of Ariosto is familiar, he is indebted to

[1] Poetica d'Aristotele (1570). It violates, he says, the rule of Aristotle, ἄσχη ἐστὶν ὁ ἐξ ἀνάγκης μὴ μετ' ἀλλό ἐστι. Camillo Pellegrini, in his famous controversy with the Academicians of Florence repeats the same censure.

[2] Quadrio, Storia d' ogni Poesia, vi. 606

Boiardo, who had himself imitated in them the metrical romancers of the preceding age. From them also, that justice may be rendered to those nameless rhymers, Boiardo drew the individuality of character by which their heroes were distinguished, and which Ariosto has not been so careful to preserve. His Orlando has less of the honest simplicity, and his Astolfo less of the gay boastfulness, that had been assigned to them in the cyclus.

67. Corniani observes of the style of Ariosto, what we may all perceive on attending to it to be true, that he is sparing in the use of metaphors, contenting himself generally with the plainest expression; by which, if he loses something in dignity, he gains in perspicuity. It may be added, that he is not very successful in figurative language, which is sometimes forced and exaggerated. Doubtless this transparency of phrase, so eminent in Ariosto, is the cause that he is read and delighted in by the multitude, as well as by the few; and it seems also to be the cause that he can never be satisfactorily rendered into any language less musical, and consequently less independent upon an ornamental dress in poetry, than his own, or one which wants the peculiar advantages by which conventional variations in the form of words, and the liberty of inversion, as well as the frequent recurrence of the richest and most euphonious rhymes, elevate the simplest expression in Italian verse above the level of discourse. Galileo, being asked by what means he had acquired the remarkable talent of giving perspicuity and grace to his philosophical writings, referred it to the continual study of Ariosto. His similes are conspicuous for their elaborate beauty; they are familiar to every reader of this great poet; imitated, as they usually are, from the ancients, they maintain an equal strife with their models, and occasionally surpass them. But even the general strain of Ariosto, natural as it seems, was not unpremeditated, or left to its own felicity: his manuscript at Ferrara, part of which is shown to strangers, bears numerous alterations; the *pentimenti*, if I may borrow a word from a kindred art, of creative genius.

Beauties of its style.

68. The Italian critics love to expatiate in his praise, though they are often keenly sensible to his defects. The variety of style and of rhythm in Ariosto, it is remarked by Gravina, is suitable to that of his subject. His rhymes, the same author observes, seem to

Accompanied with faults.

spring from the thoughts, and not from the necessities of metre. He describes minutely, but with much felicity, and gives a clear idea of every part; like the Farnesian Hercules, which seems greater by the distinctness of every vein and muscle.[1] Quadrio praises the correspondence of the sound to the sense. Yet neither of these critics is blindly partial. It is acknowledged, indeed, by his warmest advocates, that he falls sometimes below his subject, and that trifling and feeble lines intrude too frequently in the Orlando Furioso. I can hardly regret, however, that, in the passages of flattery towards the house of Este, such as that long genealogy which he deduces in the third canto, his genius has deserted him, and he degenerates, as it were wilfully, into prosaic tediousness. In other allusions to contemporary history, he is little better. I am hazarding a deviation from the judgment of good critics when I add, that in the opening stanza of each canto, where the poet appears in his own person, I find generally a deficiency of vigor and originality, a poverty of thought and of emotion, which is also very far from unusual in the speeches of his characters. But these introductions have been greatly admired.

69. Many faults of language in Ariosto are observed by his countrymen. They justly blame also his inobservance of propriety, his hyperbolical extravagance, his harsh metaphors, his affected thoughts. These are sufficiently obvious to a reader of reflecting taste: but the enchantment of his pencil redeems every failing; and his rapidity, like that of Homer, leaves us little time to censure before we are hurried forward to admire. The Orlando Furioso, as a great single poem, has been very rarely surpassed in the living records of poetry. He must yield to three, and only three, of his predecessors. He has not the force, simplicity, and truth to nature of Homer, the exquisite style and sustained majesty of Virgil, nor the originality and boldness of Dante. The most obvious parallel is Ovid, whose metamorphoses, however, are far excelled by the Orlando Furioso, not in fertility of invention, or variety of images and sentiments, but in purity of taste, in grace of language, and harmony of versification.

Its place as a poem.

70. No edition of Amadis de Gaul has been proved to

[1] Ragion Poetica, p. 104.

exist before that printed at Seville in 1519, which yet is suspected of not being the first.[1] This famous romance, which in its day was almost as popular as the Orlando Furioso itself, was translated into French by Herberay between 1540 and 1557, and into English by Munday in 1619. The four books by Vasco de Lobeyra grew to twenty by successive additions, which have been held by lovers of romance far inferior to the original. They deserve at least the blame, or praise, of making the entire work unreadable by the most patient or the most idle of mankind. Amadis de Gaul can still perhaps impart pleasure to the susceptible imagination of youth; but the want of deep or permanent sympathy leaves a naked sense of unprofitableness in the perusal, which must, it should seem, alienate a reader of mature years. Amadis at least obtained the laurel at the hands of Cervantes, speaking through the barber and curate, while so many of Lobeyra's unworthy imitators were condemned to the flames.

Amadis de Gaul.

71. A curious dramatic performance, if it may deserve such an appellation, was represented at Paris in 1511, and published in 1516. It is entitled Le Prince des Sots et la Mère sotte, by one Peter Gringore, who had before produced some other pieces of less note, and bordering more closely on the moralities. In the general idea there was nothing original. A prince of fools had long ruled his many-colored subjects on the theatre of a joyous company, *les Enfans sans Souci*, who had diverted the citizens of Paris with their buffoonery, under the name, perhaps, of moralities, while their graver brethren represented the mysteries of Scripture and legend. But the chief aim of La Mère sotte was to turn the pope and court of Rome into ridicule during the sharp contest of Louis XII. with Julius II. It consists of four parts, all in verse. The first of these is called The Cry, and serves as a sort of prologue, summoning all fools of both sexes to see the prince of fools play on Shrove Tuesday. The second is The Folly. This is an irregular dramatic piece, full of poignant satire on the clergy, but especially on the pope. A third part is entitled The Morality of the Obstinate Man; a dialogue in allusion to the same dispute. Finally comes an indecent farce, unconnected with the preceding subject. Gringore, who represented the character of La

Gringore.

1 Brunet, Man. du Libraire.

Mère sotte, was generally known by that name, and assumed it in his subsequent publications.[1]

72. Gringore was certainly at a great distance from the Italian stage, which had successfully adapted the plots of Latin comedies to modern stories. But, among the *barbarians*, a dramatic writer, somewhat younger than he, was now beginning to earn a respectable celebrity, though limited to a yet uncultivated language, and to the inferior class of society. Hans Sachs, a shoemaker of Nuremberg, born in 1494, is said to have produced his first carnival play (Fastnacht-spiel) in 1517. He belonged to the fraternity of poetical artisans, the Meister-singers of Germany, who, from the beginning of the fourteenth century, had a succession of mechanical (in every sense of the word) rhymers to boast, for whom their countrymen felt as much reverence as might have sufficed for more genuine bards. In a spirit which might naturally be expected from artisans, they required a punctual observance of certain arbitrary canons, the by-laws of the corporation Muses, to which the poet must conform. These, however, did not diminish the fecundity, if they repressed the excursiveness of our Meister-singers, and least of all that of Hans Sachs himself, who poured forth, in about forty years, fifty-three sacred and seventy-eight profane plays, sixty-four farces, fifty-nine fables, and a large assortment of other poetry. These dramatic works are now scarce, even in Germany: they appear to be ranked in the same class as the early fruits of the French and English theatres. We shall mention Hans Sachs again in another chapter.[2]

Hans Sachs.

73. No English poet, since the death of Lydgate, had arisen whom it could be thought worth while to mention.[3] Many, perhaps, will not admit that Stephen Hawes, who now meets us, should be reckoned in that honorable list. His "Pastime of Pleasure, or the Historie of Graunde Amour and La bel Pucel," finished in 1506, was printed by Wynkyn de Worde in 1517. From this title we might hardly expect

Stephen Hawes.

[1] Beauchamps, Recherches sur le Théâtre Français; Goujet, Bibl. Française, xi. 212; Niceron, vol. xxxiv.; Bouterwek, Gesch. der Französischen Poesie, v. 113; Biogr. Univers. The works of Gringore, says the last authority, are rare, and sought by the lovers of our old poetry because they display the state of manners at the beginning of the sixteenth century.

[2] Biogr. Univ.; Eichhorn, iii. 948; Bouterwek, ix. 381; Heinsius, iv. 150; Retrospective Review, vol. x.

[3] I have adverted in another place to Alexander Barclay's translation of the Ship of Fools from Sebastian Brandt; and I may here observe, that he has added many original strokes on his own countrymen, especially on the clergy.

a moral and learned allegory, in which the seven sciences of the trivium and quadrivium, besides a host of abstract virtues and qualities, play their parts, in living personality, through a poem of about six thousand lines. Those who require the ardent words or the harmonious grace of poetical diction will not frequently be content with Hawes. Unlike many of our older versifiers, he would be judged more unfavorably by extracts than by a general view of his long work. He is rude, obscure, full of pedantic Latinisms, and probably has been disfigured in the press; but learned and philosophical, reminding us frequently of the school of James I. The best, though probably an unexpected parallel for Hawes, is John Bunyan: their inventions are of the same class, various and novel, though with no remarkable pertinence to the leading subject, or naturally consecutive order; their characters, though abstract in name, have a personal truth about them, in which Phineas Fletcher, a century after Hawes, fell much below him; they render the general allegory subservient to inculcating a system, the one of philosophy, the other of religion. I do not mean that the Pastime of Pleasure is equal in merit, as it certainly has not been in success, to the Pilgrim's Progress. Bunyan is powerful and picturesque from his concise simplicity; Hawes has the common failings of our old writers, a tedious and languid diffuseness, an expatiating on themes of pedantry in which the reader takes no interest, a weakening of every picture and every reflection by ignorance of the touches that give effect. But, if we consider the "Historie of Graunde Amour" less as a poem to be read than as a measure of the author's mental power, we shall not look down upon so long and well-sustained an allegory. In this style of poetry, much was required that no mind ill-stored with reflection, or incapable of novel combination, could supply, — a clear conception of abstract modes, a familiarity with the human mind, and with the effects of its qualities on human life, a power of justly perceiving and vividly representing the analogies of sensible and rational objects. Few that preceded Hawes have possessed more of these gifts than himself.

74. This poem was little known till Mr. Southey reprinted it in 1831: the original edition is very rare. Warton had given several extracts, which, as I have observed, are disadvantageous to Hawes, and an analysis of the whole;[1] but,

[1] Hist. of Engl. Poetry, iii. 54.

though he praises the author for imagination, and admits that the poem has been unjustly neglected, he has not dwelt enough on the erudition and reflection it displays. Hawes appears to have been educated at Oxford, and to have travelled much on the Continent. He held also an office in the court of Henry VII. We may reckon him, therefore, among the earliest of our learned and accomplished gentlemen; and his poem is the first-fruits of that gradual ripening of the English mind, which must have been the process of the laboratory of time, in the silence and darkness of the fifteenth century. It augured a generation of grave and stern thinkers, and the omen was not vain.

Change in English language.

75. Another poem, the Temple of Glass, which Warton had given to Hawes, is now by general consent restored to Lydgate. Independently of external proof, which is decisive,[1] it will appear that the Temple of Glass is not written in the English of Henry VII.'s reign. I mention this only for the sake of observing, that, in following the line of our writers in verse and prose, we find the old obsolete English to have gone out of use about the accession of Edward IV. Lydgate and Bishop Pecock, especially the latter, are not easily understood by a reader not habituated to their language: he requires a glossary, or must help himself out by conjecture.[2] In the Paston Letters, on the contrary,

[1] See note in Price's edition of Warton, *ubi supra;* to which I add, that the Temple of Glass is mentioned in the Paston Letters, ii. 90, long before the time of Hawes.

[2] [The language of Bishop Pecock is more obsolete than that of Lydgate, or any other of his contemporaries; and this may also be observed with respect to Wicliffe's translation of the Bible. Yet even he has many French and Latin words, though in a smaller proportion than Chaucer and Gower, or even Mandevile and Trevisa. In a passage of Mandevile, quoted by Burnet (Specimens of Early English Writers, vol. i. p. 16), I counted 41 French and 53 Saxon words, omitting particles and a few common pronouns, which of course belong to the latter. But this is not in the usual ratio; and in Trevisa I found the Saxon to be as two to one. The form *ben* for *be* occurs more often in Trevisa than in Mandevile, which may probably be owing to ancient or modern transcribers. Both these writers seem to have undergone some repairs as to orthography and antique terminations. In Wicliffe's translation, made about 1380, the preponderance of Saxon, counting only nouns, verbs, and adverbs, is considerably greater, probably nearly three to one: those who have included pronouns and particles (all which are notoriously Teutonic) have brought forward a much higher ratio of Saxon even in modern books; especially if, like Mr. Sharon Turner and Sir James Mackintosh, they reckon each word as often as it occurs. I have never counted a single word, in any of these experiments, more than once; and my results have certainly given a much greater proportion of French and Latin than these writers have admitted. But this is in reference to later periods of the language than that with which we have to do.

Pecock, and probably Wicliffe before him, was apparently studious of a sort of archaism. He preserves the old terminations which were going into disuse, perhaps from a tenaciousness of purity in language, which we often find in literary men. Hence we have in him, as in Wicliffe, *schulen* for *shall*, *wolden* for *would*, *tho* for *them*, and *her* for *their;* and this almost invariably. Now we possess hardly any

in Harding the metrical chronicler, or in Sir John Fortescue's Discourse on the difference between an absolute and limited monarchy, he finds scarce any difficulty: antiquated words and forms of termination frequently occur; but he is hardly sensible that he reads these books much less fluently than those of modern times. These were written about 1470 But in Sir Thomas More's History of Edward V., written about 1509, or in the beautiful ballad of the Nut-brown Maid, which we cannot place very far from the year 1500, but which, if nothing can be brought to contradict the internal evidence, I should incline to refer to this decennium, there is not only a diminution of obsolete phraseology, but a certain modern turn and structure, both in the verse and prose, which denotes the commencement of a new era, and the establishment of new rules of taste in polite literature. Every one will understand that a broad line cannot be traced for the beginning of this change: Hawes, though his English is very different from that

prose exactly of Pecock's age, about 1440, with the exception of the Rolls of Parliament. These would be of material authority for the progress of our language, if we could be sure that they have been faithfully transcribed; but I have been informed that this is not altogether the case. It is possible, therefore, that modern forms of language have been occasionally substituted for the more ancient. I should not conceive that this has very frequently occurred, as there has evidently been a general intention to preserve the original with accuracy: there is no designed modernization, even of orthography. But in the Rolls of Parliament, during the reign of Henry VI., we rarely find the termination *en* to the infinitive mood; though I have observed it twice about 1459, and probably it occurs oftener. In the participle it continued longer, even to the 16th century; as in Fabian, who never employs this termination in the infinitive. And, in the present tense, we find *usen* in Fortescue; *ben* for *be*, and a few more plurals, in Caxton. Some inferior writers adopt this plural down to the reign of Henry VIII.

Caxton republished the translation of Higden's Polychronicon by Trevisa, made about a hundred years before, in the new English of his own age. "Certainly," he says, "our language now used varyeth far from that which was spoken *when I was born;* for we English men *ben* born under the domination of the moon, which is never stedfast, but ever wavering; waxing one season, and waneth and decreaseth another season. And common English that is spoken in one shire varyeth from another." He then tells a story of one *axing* for eggs in Kent, when the good wife replied she could speak no French: at last, the word *eyren* being used, she understood it. Caxton resolved to employ a mean between the common and the ancient English, "not over rude ne curious, but in such terms as should be understood." The difference between the old copy of Trevisa and Caxton's modernization is perhaps less than from the above passage we might expect; but possibly we have not the former in its perfect purity of text. Trevisa was a parson in Cornwall; and Caxton tells us that he himself learned his English in the Weald of Kent, "where I doubt not is spoken as brode and rude English as is in any place in England."

Caxton has a fluent and really good style: he is even less obsolete than Fortescue, an older man and a lawyer, who for both reasons might adhere to antiquity. Yet in him we have *eyen* for *eyes*, *syn* for *afterwards*, and a few more marks of antiquity. In Lord Rivers's preface to his Dictionary of Philosophers, 1477, as quoted in the introduction to Todd's edition of Johnson's Dictionary, there is no archaism at all. But the first book that I have read through without detecting any remnant of obsolete forms (excepting of course the termination of the third person singular in *eth*, which has not been wholly disused for a hundred years, and may indeed be found in Reid's Inquiry into the Human Mind, published in 1764, and later) is Sir Thomas More's History of Edward V — 1847.]

of Lydgate, seems to have had a great veneration for him, and has imitated the manner of that school, to which, in a marshalling of our poets, he unquestionably belongs. Skelton, on the contrary, though ready enough to coin words, has comparatively few that are obsolete.

Skelton. 76. The strange writer, whom we have just mentioned, seems to fall well enough within this decade; though his poetical life was long, if it be true that he received the laureate crown at Oxford in 1483, and was also the author of a libel on Sir Thomas More, ascribed to him by Ellis, which, alluding to the Nun of Kent, could hardly be written before 1533.[1] But, though this piece is somewhat in Skelton's manner, we find it said that he died in 1529; and it is probably the work of an imitator. Skelton is certainly not a poet, unless some degree of comic humor, and a torrent-like volubility of words in doggrel rhyme, can make one; but this uncommon fertility, in a language so little copious as ours was at that time, bespeaks a mind of some original vigor. Few English writers come nearer, in this respect, to Rabelais, whom Skelton preceded. His attempts in serious poetry are utterly contemptible; but the satirical lines on Cardinal Wolsey were probably not ineffective. It is impossible to determine whether they were written before 1520. Though these are better known than any poem of Skelton's, his dirge on Philip Sparrow is the most comic and imaginative.[2]

Oriental languages. 77. We must now take a short survey of some other departments of literature during this second decade of the sixteenth century. The Oriental languages become a little more visible in bibliography than before. An Ethiopic, that is, Abyssinian grammar, with the Psalms in the same language, was published at Rome by Potken in 1513; a short treatise in Arabic at Fano in 1514, being the first time those characters had been used in type; a Psalter in 1516, by Giustiniani at Genoa, in Hebrew, Chaldee, Arabic, and Greek;[3] and a Hebrew Bible, with the

[1] Ellis's Specimens, vol. ii. [Skelton was laureate at Oxford in 1490: it does not appear how long before. But he had written an Elegy on Edward IV. in 1483. —1853.]

[2] This last poem is reprinted in Southey's Selections from the older Poets. Extracts from Skelton occur also in Warton, and one in the first volume of the Somers Tracts. Mr. Dyce has published a collective edition of Skelton's works.

[3] It is printed in eight columns, which Gesner, *apud* Bayle, Justiniani, Note D, thus describes: "Quarum prima habet Hebræam editionem, secunda Latinam interpretationem respondentem Hebrææ de verbo in verbum, tertia Latinam communem, quarta Græcam, quinta Arabi-

Chaldee paraphrase and other aids, by Felice di Prato, at Venice in 1519. The Book of Job in Hebrew appeared at Paris in 1516. Meantime, the magnificent polyglott Bible of Alcalá proceeded under the patronage of Cardinal Ximenez, and was published in five volumes folio, between the years 1514 and 1517. It contains, in triple columns, the Hebrew, the Septuagint Greek, and Latin Vulgate; the Chaldee paraphrase of the Pentateuch, by Onkelos, being also printed at the foot of the page.[1] Spain, therefore, had found men equal to superintend this arduous labor. Lebrixa was still living, though much advanced in years; Stunica and a few other now obscure names were his coadjutors. But that of Demetrius Cretensis appears among these in the titlepage, to whom the principal care of the Greek was doubtless intrusted; and it is highly probable that all the early Hebrew and Chaldee publications demanded the assistance of Jewish rabbis.

Pomponatius.

78. The school of Padua, renowned already for its medical science as well as for the cultivation of the Aristotelian philosophy, labored under a suspicion of infidelity, which was considerably heightened by the work of Pomponatius, its most renowned professor, on the immortality of the soul, published in 1516. This book met with several answers, and was publicly burned at Venice: but the patronage of Bembo sustained Pomponatius at the court of Leo; and he was permitted by the Inquisition to reprint his treatise with some corrections. He defended himself by declaring that he merely denied the validity of philosophical arguments for the soul's immortality, without doubting in the least the authority of revelation, to which and to that of the church he had expressly submitted. This, however, is the current language of philosophy in the sixteenth and seventeenth centuries, which must be judged by other presumptions. Brucker and Ginguéné are clear as to the real disbelief of Pomponatius in the doctrine, and bring some proofs from his other writings, which seem more unequivocal than any that the treatise De Immortalitate affords. It is certainly possible

cam, sexta paraphrasim, sermone quidem Chaldæo, sed literis Hebraicis conscriptam; septima Latinam respondentem Chaldeæ, ultima vero, id est octava, continet scholia, hoc est, annotationes sparsas et intercisas."

[1] Andrès, xix. 35. An observation in the preface to the Complutensian edition has been often animadverted upon, that they print the Vulgate between the Hebrew and the Greek, like Christ between two thieves. The expression, however it may have been introduced, is not to be wholly defended; but at that time it was generally believed that the Hebrew text had been corrupted by the Jews.

and not uncommon for men to deem the arguments on that subject inconclusive, so far as derived from reason, while they assent to those that rest on revelation. It is, on the other hand, impossible for a man to believe inconsistent propositions, when he perceives them to be so. The question, therefore, can only be, as Buhle seems to have seen, whether Pomponatius maintained the rational arguments for a future state to be repugnant to known truths, or merely insufficient for conviction; and this a superficial perusal of his treatise hardly enables me to determine: though there is a presumption, on the whole, that he had no more religion than the philosophers of Padua generally kept for a cloak. That university was for more than a century the focus of atheism in Italy.[1]

Raymond Lully.

79. We may enumerate among the philosophical writings of this period, as being first published in 1516, a treatise full two hundred years older, by Raymond Lully, a native of Majorca,—one of those innovators in philosophy, who, by much boasting of their original discoveries in the secrets of truth, are taken by many at their word, and gain credit for systems of science which those who believe in them seldom trouble themselves to examine, or even understand. Lully's principal treatise is his Ars Magna; being, as it professes, a new method of reasoning on all subjects. But this method appears to be only an artificial disposition, readily obvious to the eye, of subjects and predicables, according to certain distinctions, which, if it were meant for any thing more than a topical arrangement, such as the ancient orators employed to aid their invention, could only be compared to the similar scheme of using machinery instead of mental labor, devised by the philosophers of Laputa. Leibnitz is of opinion that the method might be convenient in extemporary speaking, which is the utmost limit that can be assigned to its usefulness. Lord Bacon has truly said of this, and of such idle or fraudulent attempts to substitute trick for science, that they are "not a lawful method, but a method of imposture, which is to deliver knowledges in such

His method.

[1] Tiraboschi, vol. viii.; Corniani; Ginguéné; Brucker; Buhle; Niceron; Biogr. Universelle. The two last of these are more favorable than the rest to the intentions of the Paduan philosopher.

Pomponatius, or Peretto, as he was sometimes called, on account of his diminutive stature, which he had in common with his predecessor in philosophy, Marsilius Ficinus, was ignorant of Greek, though he read lectures on Aristotle. In one of Sperone's dialogues (p. 120, edit. 1596), he is made to argue, that, if all books were read in translations, the time now consumed in learning languages might be better employed.

manner as men may speedily come to make a show of learning who have it not;" and that they are "nothing but a mass of words of all arts, to give men countenance, that those which use the terms might be thought to understand them."

80. The writings of Lully are admitted to be very obscure and those of his commentators and admirers, among whom the meteors of philosophy, Cornelius Agrippa and Jordano Bruno, were enrolled, are hardly less so. But, as is usual with such empiric medicines, it obtained a great deal of celebrity, and much ungrounded praise, not only for the two centuries which intervened between the author's age and that of its appearance from the press, but for a considerable time afterwards, till the Cartesian philosophy drove that to which the art of Lully was accommodated from the field; and even Morhof, near the end of the seventeenth century, avows that, though he had been led to reckon it a frivolous method, he had very much changed his opinion on fuller examination.[1] The few pages which Brucker has given to Lully do not render his art very intelligible;[2] but they seem sufficient to show its uselessness for the discovery of truth. It is utterly impossible, as I conceive, for those who have taken much pains to comprehend this method, which is not the case with me, to give a precise notion of it in a few words, even with the help of diagrams, which are indispensably required.[3]

81. The only geographical publication which occurs in this

[1] Morhof, Polyhistor, l. ii. c. 5. But, if I understand the ground on which Morhof rests his favorable opinion of Lully's art, it is merely for its usefulness in suggesting middle terms to a syllogistic disputant.

[2] Brucker, iv. 9-21. Ginguéné, who observes that Brucker's analysis, *à sa manière accoutumée*, may be understood by those who have learned Lully's method, but must be very confused to others, has made the matter a great deal more unintelligible by his own attempt to explain it. Hist. Litt. de l'Italie, vii. 497. I have found a better development of the method in Alstedius, Clavis Artis Lullianæ (Argentor. 1633), a stanch admirer of Lully. But his praise of the art, when examined, is merely as an aid to the memory and to disputation, "de quavis quæstione utramque in partem disputandi." This is rather an evil than a good; and though mnemonical contrivances are not without utility, it is probable that much better could be found than that of Lully.

[3] Buhle has observed that the favorable reception of Lully's method is not surprising, since it really is useful in the association of ideas, like all other topical contrivances, and may be applied to any subject, though often not very appropriately, suggesting materials in extemporary speaking, and, notwithstanding its shortness, professing to be a complete system of topics; but whoever should try it, must be convinced of its inefficacy in reasoning. Hence he thinks that such men as Agrippa and Bruno kept only the general principle of Lully's scheme, enlarging it by new contrivances of their own. Hist. de Philos., ii. 612. See also an article on Lully in the Biographie Universelle. — Tennemann calls the Ars Magna a logical machine to let men reason about every thing without study or reflection. Manuel de la Philos., i. 380. But this seems to have been much what Lully reckoned its merit.

period is an account of the recent discoveries in America by Peter Martyr, of Anghiera, a Milanese, who passed great part of his life in the court of Madrid. The title is, De Rebus Oceanicis decades tres; but it is, in fact, a series of epistles, thirty in number, written, or feigned to be written, at different times, as fresh information was received, — the first bearing date a few days only after the departure of Columbus in 1493; while the two last decades are addressed to Leo X. An edition is said to have appeared in 1516, which is certainly the date of the author's dedication to Charles V.; yet this edition seems not to have been seen by bibliographers. Though Peter Martyr's own account has been implicitly believed by Robertson and many others, there seems strong internal presumption against the authenticity of these epistles in the character they assume. It appears to me evident, that he threw the intelligence he had obtained into that form many years after the time. Whoever will take the trouble of comparing the two first letters in the decades of Peter Martyr with any authentic history, will, I should think, perceive that they are a negligent and palpable imposture; every date being falsified, even that of the year in which Columbus made his great discovery. It is a strange instance of oversight in Robertson, that he has uniformly quoted them as written at the time; for the least attention must have shown him the contrary. And it may here be mentioned, that a similar suspicion may be reasonably entertained with respect to another collection of epistles by the same author, rather better known than the present. There is a folio volume with which those who have much attended to the history of the sixteenth century are well acquainted, purporting to be a series of letters from Anghiera to various friends between the years 1488 and 1522. They are full of interesting facts, and would be still more valuable than they are, could we put our trust in their genuineness as strictly contemporary documents. But though Robertson has almost wholly relied upon them in his account of the Castilian insurrection, and even in the Biographie Universelle no doubt is raised as to their being truly written at their several dates, yet La Monnoye (if I remember right, — certainly some one) long since charged the author with imposture, on the ground that the letters, into which he wove the history of his times, are so full of anachronisms as to render it evident that

Peter Martyr's epistles.

they were fabricated afterwards. It is several years since I read these epistles; but I was certainly struck with some palpable errors in chronology, which led me to suspect that several of them were wrongly dated,—the solution of their being feigned not occurring to my mind, as the book is of considerable reputation.[1] A ground of suspicion hardly less striking is, that the letters of Peter Martyr are too exact for verisimilitude: he announces events with just the importance they ought to have, predicts nothing but what comes to pass, and must in fact be either an impostor (in an innocent sense of the word), or one of the most sagacious men of his time. But, if not exactly what they profess to be, both these works of Anghiera are valuable as contemporary history; and the first mentioned, in particular, De Rebus Oceanicis, is the earliest account we possess of the settlement of the Spaniards in Darien, and of the whole period between Columbus and Cortes.

82. It would be embarrassing to the reader, were we to pursue any longer that rigidly chronological division by short decennial periods, which has hitherto served to display the regular progress of European literature, and especially of classical learning. Many other provinces were now culti vated; and the history of each is to be traced separately from the rest, though frequently with mutual reference, and with regard, as far as possible, to their common unity. In the period immediately before us, that unity was chiefly preserved by the diligent study of the Latin and Greek languages: it was to the writers in those languages that the theologian, the civil lawyer, the physician, the geometer and philosopher, even the poet for the most part, and dramatist, repaired for

[1] The following are specimens of anachronism, which seem fatal to the genuineness of these epistles, and are only selected from others. In the year 1489, he writes to a friend (Arias Barbosa): "In peculiarem te nostræ tempestatis morbum, qui appellatione Hispanâ Bubarum dicitur, ab Italis morbus Gallicus, medicorum Elephantiam alii, alii aliter appellant, incidisse præcipitem, libero ad me scribis pede."—Epist. 68. Now, if we should even believe that this disease was known some years before the discovery of America and the siege of Naples, is it probable that it could have obtained the name of *morbus Gallicus* before the latter era? In February, 1511, he communicates the absolution of the Venetians by Julius II., which took place in February, 1510. Epist. 451. In a letter dated at Brussels, Aug. 31, 1520 (Epist. 689), he mentions the burning of the canon law at Wittenberg by Luther, which is well known to have happened in the ensuing November.—[Mr. Prescott, in his excellent History of Ferdinand and Isabella, vol. ii. p. 78, has expressed his dissent from this suspicion that P. Martyr's letters were written after the time, and ascribes the anachronisms to the misplacing of some letters by the original editor. This will probably account for some of them; but my suspicion is not wholly removed.—1842.]

the materials of their knowledge and the nourishment of their minds. We shall begin, therefore, by following the further advances of philological literature; and some readers must here, as in other places, pardon what they will think unnecessary minuteness in so general a work as the present, for the sake of others who set a value on precise information.

CHAPTER V.

HISTORY OF ANCIENT LITERATURE IN EUROPE FROM 1520 TO 1550.

Classical Taste of the Italians — Ciceronians — Erasmus attacks them — Writings on Roman Antiquity — Learning in France — Commentaries of Budæus — Progress of Learning in Spain, Germany, England — State of Cambridge and Oxford — Advance of Learning still slow — Encyclopedic Works.

Superiority of Italy in taste.

1. ITALY, the genial soil where the literature of antiquity had been first cultivated, still retained her superiority in the fine perception of its beauties and in the power of retracing them by spirited imitation. It was the land of taste and sensibility, — never surely more so than in the age of Raffaelle as well as Ariosto. Far from the clownish ignorance so long predominant in the Transalpine aristocracy, the nobles of Italy, accustomed to a city life and to social festivity, more than to war or the chase, were always conspicuous for their patronage, and, what is more important than mere patronage, their critical skill in matters of art and elegant learning. Among the ecclesiastical order, this was naturally still more frequent. If the successors of Leo X. did not attain so splendid a name, they were perhaps, after the short reign of Adrian VI., — which, if we may believe the Italian writers, seemed to threaten an absolute return of barbarism,[1] — not less munificent or sedulous in encouraging

[1] Valerianus, in his treatise De Infelicitate Litteratorum, — a melancholy series of unfortunate authors, in the manner, though not quite with the spirit and interest, of Mr. D'Israeli, — speaks of Adrian VI. as of another Paul II. in hatred of literature. "Ecce adest musarum et eloquentiæ, totiusque nitoris hostis acerrimus, qui literatis omnibus inimicitias minitatur, quoniam, ut ipse dictitabat, Terentiani essent, quos cum odisse atque etiam persequi cœpisset, voluntarium alii exilium, alias atque alias alii latebras quærentes, tamdiu latuere, quoad Dei beneficio, altero imperii anno decessit, qui si aliquanto diutius vixisset, Gotica illa tempora adversus bonas literas videbatur suscitaturus." — Lib. ii. p. 34. It is but fair to a ld, that Erasmus ascribes to Adrian the protection of letters in the Low Countries. "Vix nostra phalanx sustinuisset hostium conjurationem, ni Adrianus tum Cardinalis, postea Romanus pontifex, hoc edidisset oraculum: Bonas literas non damno, hæreses et schismata damno." — Epist. MCLXXVI. There is not indeed much in this; but the Biographie Universelle (Suppl., art. "Busleiden") informs us that this pope was compelled to interfere, in order to remove the impediments to the foundation of Busleiden's Collegium Trilingue at Louvain. It is

polite and useful letters. The first part, indeed, of this period of thirty years was very adverse to the progress of learning, especially in that disastrous hour when the lawless mercenaries of Bourbon's army were led on to the sack of Rome. In this and in other calamities of the same kind, it happened that universities and literary academies were broken up; that libraries were destroyed or dispersed. That of Sadolet, having been with difficulty saved in the pillage of Rome, was dispersed, in consequence of shipwreck during its transport to France.[1] A better era commenced with the pacification of Italy in 1531. The subsequent wars were either transient or partial in their effects. The very extinction of all hope for civil freedom, which characterized the new period, turned the intellectual energies of an acute and ardent people towards those tranquil pursuits which their rulers would both permit and encourage.

2. The real excellence of the ancients in literature as well as art gave rise to an enthusiastic and exclusive admiration of antiquity, not unusual indeed in other parts of Europe, but in Italy a sort of national pride which all partook. They went back to the memory of past ages for consolation in their declining fortunes, and conquered their barbarian masters of the north in imagination with Cæsar and Marius. Every thing that reminded them of the slow decay of Rome, sometimes even their religion itself, sounded ill in their fastidious ears. Nothing was so much at heart with the Italian scholars as to write a Latin style, not only free from barbarism, but conformable to the standard of what is sometimes called the Augustan age, that is, of the period from Cicero to Augustus. Several of them affected to be exclusively Ciceronian.

Admiration of antiquity.

3. Sadolet, one of the apostolic secretaries under Leo X. and Clement VII., and raised afterwards to the purple by Paul III., stood in as high a rank as any

Sadolet.

well known that Adrian VI. was inclined to reform some abuses in the church, enough to set the Italians against him. See his Life, in Bayle, Note D.

1 "Cum enim direptis rebus cæteris, libri soli superstites ab hostium injuria intacti, in navim conjecti, ad Galliæ littus jam pervecti essent, incidit in vectores, et in ipsos familiares meos pestilentia. Quo metu ii permoti, quorum ad littora navis appulsa fuerat, onera in terram exponi non permisere. Ita asportati sunt in alienas et ignotas terras; exceptisque voluminibus paucis, quæ deportavi mecum huc proficiscens, mei reliqui illi tot labores quos impenderamus, Græcis præsertim codicibus conquirendis undique et colligendis, mei tanti sumptus, meæ curæ, omnes iterum jam ad nihilum reciderunt." — Sadolet, Epist. lib. i p. 23. (Colon. 1554.)

for purity of language without affectation, though he seems to have been reckoned of the Ciceronian school. Except his Epistles, however, none of Sadolet's works are now read, or even appear to have been very conspicuous in his own age, though Corniani has given an analysis of a treatise on education.[1] A greater name, in point of general literary reputation, was Peter Bembo, a noble Venetian, secretary with Sadolet to Leo, and raised, like him, to the dignity of a cardinal by Paul III. Bembo was known in Latin and in Italian literature; and, in each language, both as a prose writer and a poet. We shall thus have to regard four claims which he prefers to a niche in the temple of fame, and we shall find none of them ungrounded. In pure Latin style he was not perhaps superior to Sadolet, but would not have yielded to any competitor in Europe. It has been told, in proof of Bembo's scrupulous care to give his compositions the utmost finish, that he kept forty portfolios, into which every sheet entered successively, and was only taken out to undergo his corrections before it entered into the next limbo of this purgatory. Though this may not be quite true, it is but an exaggeration of the laborious diligence by which he must often have reduced his sense to feebleness and vacuity. He was one of those exclusive Ciceronians, who, keenly feeling the beauties of their master's eloquence, and aware of the corruption which, after the age of Augustus, came rapidly over the purity of style, rejected with scrupulous care not only every word or phrase which could not be justified by the practice of what was called the golden age, but even insisted on that of Cicero himself, as the only model they thought absolutely

Bembo.

[1] Niceron says of Sadolet's Epistles, which form a very thick volume, "Il y a plusieurs choses dignes d'être remarquées dans les lettres de Sadolet: mais elles sont quelquefois trop diffuses, et par conséquent ennuyeuses à lire." I concur in this: yet it may be added, that the Epistles of Cicero would sometimes be tedious, if we took as little interest in their subjects as we commonly do in those of Sadolet. His style is uniformly pure and good; but he is less fastidious than Bembo, and does not use circuity to avoid a theological expression. They are much more interesting, at least, than the ordinary Latin letters of his contemporaries, such as those of Paulus Manutius. An uniform goodness of heart and love of right prevail in the epistles of Sadolet. His desire of ecclesiastical reformation in respect of morals has caused him to be suspected of a bias towards Protestantism; and a letter in the most flattering terms, which he wrote to Melanchthon, but which that learned man did not answer, has been brought in corroboration of this; yet the general tenor of his letters refutes this surmise: his theology, which was wholly semi-Pelagian, must have led him to look with disgust on the early Lutheran school (Epist. l. iii. p. 121, and l. ix. p. 410); and, after Paul III. bestowed on him the purple, he became a stanch friend of the court of Rome, though never losing his wish to see a reform of its abuses. This will be admitted by every one who takes the trouble to run over Sadolet's epistles.

perfect. Paulus Manutius, one of the most rigorous, though of the most eminent among these, would not employ the words of Cicero's correspondents, though as highly accomplished and polite as himself. This fastidiousness was, of course, highly inconvenient in a language constantly applicable to the daily occurrences of life in epistles or in narration; and it has driven Bembo, according to one of his severest critics, into strange affectation and circuity in his Venetian history. It produced also, what was very offensive to the more serious reader, and is otherwise frigid and tasteless, an adaptation of heathen phrases to the usages and even the characters of Christianity.[1] It has been remarked also, that, in his great solicitude about the choice of words, he was indifferent enough to the value of his meaning, — a very common failing of elegant scholars when they write in a foreign language. But if some praise is due, as surely it is, to the art of reviving that consummate grace and richness which enchants every successive generation in the periods of Cicero, we must place Bembo, had we nothing more than this to say of him, among the ornaments of literature in the sixteenth century.

Ciceronianus of Erasmus.

4. The tone which Bembo and others of that school were studiously giving to ancient literature provoked one of the most celebrated works of Erasmus, — the dialogues entitled Ciceronianus. The primary aim of these was to ridicule the fastidious purity of that sort of writers who would not use a case or tense for which they could not find authority in the works of Cicero. A whole winter's night, they thought, was well spent in composing a single sentence; but even then it was to be revised over and over again. Hence they wrote little except elaborated epistles. One of their rules, he tells us, was never to speak Latin, if they could help it, which must have seemed extraordinary in an age when it was the common language of scholars from different countries. It is certain, indeed, that the practice cannot be favorable to very pure Latinity.

[1] This affectation had begun in the preceding century, and was carried by Campano in his Life of Braccio di Montone to as great an extreme as by Bembo, or any Ciceronian of his age. Bayle (Bembus, Note B) gives some odd instances of it in the latter. Notwithstanding his laborious scrupulosity as to language, Bembo is reproached by Lipsius, and others of a more advanced stage of critical knowledge with many faults of Latin, especially in his letters. Ibid. Sturm says of the letters of Bembo, "Ejus epistolæ scriptæ mihi magis quam missæ esse videntur. Indicia sunt hominis otiosi et imitatoris speciem magis rerum quam res ipsas consectantis." — Ascham, Epist. cccxci.

[The origin of the Ciceronian controversy will have some light thrown on it by the Epistles of Politian, lib. v. 1-4. — 1842.]

5. Few books of that age give us more insight into its literary history and the public taste than the Ciceronianus. In a short retrospect, Erasmus characterizes all the considerable writers in Latin since the revival of letters, and endeavors to show how far they wanted this Ciceronian elegance for which some were contending. He distinguishes, in a spirit of sound taste, between a just imitation which leaves free scope for genius, and a servile following of a single writer. "Let your first and chief care," he says, "be to understand thoroughly what you undertake to write about. That will give you copiousness of words, and supply you with true and natural sentiments. Then will it be found how your language lives and breathes, how it excites and hurries away the reader, and how it is a just image of your own mind. Nor will that be less genuine which you add to your own by imitation."

6. The Ciceronianus, however, goes, in some passages, beyond the limited subject of Latin style. The controversy had some reference to the division between the men of learning and the men of taste, between the lovers of the solid and of the brilliant; in some measure also to that between Christianity and Paganism, a garb which the incredulity of the Italians affected to put on. All the Ciceronian party, except Longolius, were on the other side of the Alps.[1] The object of the Italian scholars was to write pure Latin, to glean little morsels of Roman literature, to talk a heathenish philosophy in private, and leave the world to its own abuses. That of Erasmus was to make men wiser and better by wit, sense, and learning.

Scaliger's invective against it.

7. Julius Cæsar Scaliger wrote against the Ciceronianus with all that unmannerly invective which is the disgrace of many scholars, and very much his own. His vanity blinded him to what was then obvious to Europe, that, with considerable learning and still better parts, he was totally unworthy of being named with the first man in the literary republic. Nor in fact had he much right to take

[1] Though this is generally said, on the authority of Erasmus himself, Peter Bunel is asserted by some French scholars of great name, and particularly by Henry Stephens, to have equalled in Ciceronian purity the best of the Italians; and Paulus Manutius owns him as his master, in one of his epistles: "Ego ab illo maximum habebam beneficium, quod me cum Politianis et Erasmis nescio quibus miserè errantem, in hanc rectè scribendi viam primus in duxerat." In a later edition, for *Politianis et Erasmis*, it was thought more decent to introduce *Philelphis et Campanis*. Bayle, art. "Bunel," Note A. The letters of Bunel, written with great purity, were published in 1551. It is to be observed that he had lived much in Italy. Erasmus does not mention him in the Ciceronianus.

up the cause of the Ciceronian purists, with whom he had no pretension to be reckoned, though his reply to Erasmus is not ill-written. It consists chiefly in a vindication of Cicero's life and writings against some passages in the Ciceronianus which seem to affect them, scarcely touching the question of Latin style. Erasmus made no answer, and thus escaped the danger of retaliating on Scaliger in his own phrases.

Editions of Cicero.

8. The devotedness of the Italians to Cicero was displayed in a more useful manner than by this close imitation. Pietro Vettori (better known as Victorius), professor of Greek and Roman literature at Florence, published an entire edition of the great orator's writings in 1534. But this was soon surpassed by a still more illustrious scholar, Paulus Manutius, son of Aldus, and his successor in the printing-house at Venice. His edition of Cicero appeared in 1540,—the most important which had hitherto been published of any ancient author. In fact, the notes of Manutius, which were subsequently very much augmented,[1] form at this day in great measure the basis of interpretation and illustration of Cicero, as what are called the Variorum editions will show. A further accession to Ciceronian literature was made by Nizolius in his Observationes in M. Tullium Ciceronem, 1535. This title hardly indicates that it is a dictionary of Ciceronian words, with examples of their proper senses. The later and improved editions bear the title of Thesaurus Ciceronianus. I find no critical work, in this period, of greater extent and labor than that of Scaliger De Causis Latinæ Linguæ,—by *causis* meaning its principles. It relates much to the foundations of the language, or the rules by which its various peculiarities have been formed. He corrects many alleged errors of earlier writers, and sometimes of Valla himself; enumerating, rather invidiously, 634 of such errors in an index. In this book he shows much acuteness and judgment.

Alexander ab Alexandro.

9. The Geniales Dies of Alexander ab Alexandro, a Neapolitan lawyer, published in 1522, are on the model of Aulus Gellius, a repertory of miscellaneous learning, thrown together without arrangement, on every subject of Roman philology and antiquities. The author had lived with the scholars of the fifteenth century, and even remembered Philelphus; but his own reputation seems not to have been extensive, at least through Europe. "He has

[1] Renouard, Imprimerie des Aldes

known every one," says Erasmus, in a letter: "no one knows who he is."[1] The Geniales Dies has had better success in later ages than most early works of criticism; a good edition having appeared, with Variorum notes, in 1673. It gives, like the Lectiones Antiquæ of Cælius Rhodiginus, an idea of the vast extent to which the investigation of Latin antiquity had been already carried.

10. A very few books of the same class belong to this period; and may deserve mention, although long since superseded by the works of those to whom we have just alluded, and who filled up and corrected their outline. Marlianus on the Topography of Rome, 1534, is admitted, though with some hesitation, by Grævius into his Thesaurus Antiquitatum Romanarum, while he absolutely sets aside the preceding labors of Blondus Flavius and Pomponius Lætus. The Fasti Consulares were first published by Marlianus in 1549; and a work on the same subject in 1550 was the earliest production of the great Sigonius. Before these, the memorable events of Roman history had not been critically reduced to a chronological series. A treatise by Raphael of Volterra, De Magistratibus et Sacerdotibus Romanorum, is very inaccurate and superficial.[2] Mazochius, a Roman bookseller, was the first who, in 1521, published a collection of inscriptions. This was very imperfect, and full of false monuments. A better appeared in Germany by the care of Apianus, professor of mathematics at Ingoldstadt, in 1534.[3]

Works on Roman antiquities.

11. It could not be expected that the elder and more copious fountain of ancient lore, the Greek language, would slake the thirst of Italian scholars as readily as the Latin. No local association, no patriotic sentiment, could attach them to that study. Greece itself no longer sent out a Lascaris or a Musurus: subdued, degraded, barbarous in language and learning; alien, above all, by insuperable enmity, from the church,—she had ceased to be a liv-

Greek less studied in Italy.

1 "Demiror quis sit ille Alexander ab Alexandro. Novit omnes celebres Italiæ viros, Philelphum, Pomponium Lætum, Hermolaum, et quos non? Omnibus usus est familiariter; tamen nemo novit illum." —Appendix, ad Erasm. Epist. ccclxxiii. (1533.) Bayle also remarks that Alexander is hardly mentioned by his contemporaries. Tiraqueau, a French lawyer of considerable learning, undertook the task of writing critical notes on the Geniales Dies about the middle of the century, correcting many of the errors which they contained.

2 It is published in Sallengre, Novus Thesaurus Antiquit., vol. iii.

3 Burmann, præfat. in Gruter, Corpus Inscriptionum.

ing guide to her own treasures. Hence we may observe, even already, not a diminution, but a less accelerated increase, of Greek erudition in Italy. Two, however, among the most considerable editions of Greek authors, in point of labor, that the century produced, are the Galen by Andrew of Asola in 1525, and the Eustathius from the press of Bladus at Rome in 1542.[1] We may add, as first editions of Greek authors, Epictetus, at Venice, in 1528, and Arrian in 1535; Ælian, at Rome, in 1545. The Etymologicum Magnum of Phavorinus, whose real name was Guarino, published at Rome in 1523, was of some importance while no lexicon but the very defective one of Craston had been printed. The Etymologicum of Phavorinus, however, is merely a compilation from Hesychius, Suidas, Phrynichus, Harpocration, Eustathius, the Etymologica, the lexicon of Philemon, some treatises of Trypho, Apollonius, and other grammarians and various scholiasts. It is valuable as furnishing several important corrections of the authors from whom it was collected, and not a few extracts from unpublished grammarians.[2]

Schools of classical learning.

12. Of the Italian scholars, Vettori, already mentioned, seems to have earned the highest reputation for his skill in Greek. But there was no considerable town in Italy, besides the regular universities, where public instruction in the Greek as well as Latin tongue was not furnished, and in many cases by professors of fine taste and recondite learning, whose names were then eminent; such as Bonamico, Nizzoli, Parrhasio, Corrado, and Maffei, commonly called Raphael of Volterra. Yet, according to Tiraboschi, something was still wanting to secure these schools from the too frequent changes of teachers, which the hope of better salaries produced, and to give the students a more vigorous emulation and a more uniform scheme of discipline.[3] This was to be supplied by the followers of Ignatius Loyola. But their interference with education in Italy did not begin in quite so early a period as the present.

13. If we cross the Alps, and look at the condition of learning in countries which we left in 1520 rapidly advancing

[1] Gresswell's Early Parisian Greek Press, p. 14.

[2] Quarterly Review, vol. xxii.; Roscoe's Leo, ch. xi. Stephens is said to have inserted many parts of this lexicon of Guarino in his Thesaurus. Niceron, xxii. 141.

[3] Vol. viii. 114; x. 319. Ginguéné, vii. 232, has copied Tiraboschi's account of these accomplished teachers with little addition, and probably with no knowledge of the original sources of information.

on the footsteps of Italy, we shall find, that, except in purity of Latin style, both France and Germany were now capable of entering the lists of fair competition. France possessed, by general confession, the most profound Greek scholar in Europe, Budæus. If this could before have been in doubt, he raised himself to a pinnacle of philological glory by his Commentarii Linguæ Græcæ, Paris, 1529. The publications of the chief Greek authors by Aldus, which we have already specified, had given a compass of reading to the scholars of this period which those of the fifteenth century could not have possessed. But, with the exception of the Etymologicum of Phavorinus, just mentioned, no attempt had been made by a native of Western Europe to interpret the proper meaning of Greek words even he had confined himself to compiling from the grammarians. In this large and celebrated treatise, Budæus has established the interpretation of a great part of the language. All later critics write in his praise. There will never be another Budæus in France, says Joseph Scaliger, the most envious and detracting, though the most learned, of the tribe.[1] But, referring to what Baillet and Blount have collected from older writers,[2] we will here insert the character of these commentaries, which an eminent living scholar has given.

Budæus: his Commentaries on Greek.

14. "This great work of Budæus has been the text-book and common storehouse of succeeding lexicographers. But a great objection to its general use was its want of arrangement. His observations on the Greek language are thrown together in the manner of a commonplace-book, an inconvenience which is imperfectly remedied by an alphabetical index at the end. His authorities and illustrations are chiefly drawn from the prose writers of Greece, the historians, orators, and fathers. With the poets he seems to have had a less intimate acquaintance. His interpretations are mostly correct, and always elegantly expressed; displaying an union of Greek and Latin literature which renders his Commentaries equally useful to the students of both languages. The peculiar value of this work consists in the full and exact account which it gives of the Greek legal and forensic terms, both by literal interpretation and by a comparison with the corresponding terms in Roman jurisprudence. So copious

Its character.

[1] Scaligerana, i. 33.
[2] Baillet, Jugemens des Savans, ii. 328 (Amst. 1725); Blount, in Budæo.

and exact is this department of the work, that no student can read the Greek orators to the best advantage, unless he consults the Commentaries of Budæus. It appears from the Greek epistle subjoined to the work, that the illustration of the forensic language of Athens and Rome was originally all that his plan embraced; and that, when circumstances tempted him to extend the limits of his work, this still continued to be his chief object."[1]

Greek grammars and lexicons.

15. These Commentaries of Budæus stand not only far above any thing else in Greek literature before the middle of the sixteenth century, but are alone in their class. What comes next, but at a vast interval, is the Greek grammar of Clenardus, printed at Louvain in 1530. It was, however, much beyond Budæus in extent of circulation, and probably, for this reason, in general utility. This grammar was continually reprinted with successive improvements, and defective as, especially in its original state, it must have been, was far more perspicuous than that of Gaza, though not, perhaps, more judicious in principle. It was for a long time commonly used in France, and is in fact the principal basis of those lately or still in use among us, such as the Eton Greek grammar. The proof of this is, that they follow Clenardus in most of his innovations, and, too frequently for mere accident, in the choice of instances.[2] The

[1] Quarterly Review, vol. xxii., an article ascribed to the Bishop of London. The Commentaries of Budæus are written in a very rambling and desultory manner, passing from one subject to another as a casual word may suggest the transition. "Sic enim," he says, "hos commentarios scribere instituimus, ut quicquid in ordinem seriemque scribendi incurreret, vel ex diverticulo quasi obviam se offerret, ad id digredi." A large portion of what is valuable in this work has been transferred by Stephens to his Thesaurus. The Latin criticisms of Budæus have also doubtless been borrowed.

Budæus and Erasmus are fond of writing Greek in their correspondence. Others had the same fancy; and it is curious that they ventured upon what has wholly gone out of use since the language has been so well understood. But probably this is the reason that later scholars have avoided it. Neither of these great men shines much in elegance or purity. One of Budæus, Aug. 15, 1519 (in Erasm. Epist. cccclv.), seems often incorrect, and in the mere style of a schoolboy.

[2] Clenardus seems first to have separated simple from contracted nouns, thus making ten declensions. Wherever he differs from Gaza, our popular grammars seem, in general, to have followed him. He tells us that he had drawn up his own for the use of his private pupils. Baillet observes that the grammar of Clenardus, notwithstanding the mediocrity of his learning, has had more success than any other; those who have followed having mostly confined themselves to correcting and enlarging it. Jugemens des Savans, ii. 164. This is certainly true, as far as England is concerned, though the Eton grammar is in some degree an improvement on Clenardus.

[This was stated rather too strongly in my first edition. A learned person at the head of one of our public schools, in a communication with which he has favored me, does not think, on a comparison of the two works, that the Eton Greek grammar owes very much to that of Clenardus, though there is, no doubt, much that may have been borrowed from him; and is inclined to believe that it was formed upon one published by the university of Padua.

account of syntax in this grammar, as well as that of Gaza, is very defective. A better treatise, in this respect, is by Varenius of Malines, Syntaxis Linguæ Græcæ, printed at Louvain about 1532. Another Greek grammar by Vergara, a native of Spain, has been extolled by some of the older critics, and depreciated by others.[1] A Greek lexicon, of which the first edition was printed at Basle in 1537, is said to abound in faults and inaccuracies of every description. The character given of it by Henry Stephens, even when it had been enlarged, if not improved, does not speak much for the means that the scholars of this age had possessed in laboring for the attainment of Greek learning.[2]

16. The most remarkable editions of Greek authors from the Parisian press were those of Aristophanes in 1528, and of Sophocles in 1529, — the former printed by Gourmont, the latter by Colinæus; the earliest edition of Dionysius Halicarnassensis in 1546, and of Dio Cassius in 1548, — both by Robert Stephens. The first Greek edition of the Elements of Euclid appeared at Basle in 1533, of Diogenes Laertius the same year, of five books of Diodorus in 1539, of Josephus in 1544; the first of Polybius in 1530, at Haguenau. Besides these editions of classical authors, Basil, and other of the Greek fathers, occupied the press of Frobenius, under the superintendence of Erasmus. The publications of Latin authors by Badius Ascensius con-

Editions of Greek authors.

which contains the Eton grammar *totidem verbis*, and a great deal of other matter.

Of this Paduan grammar I am wholly ignorant: if published before that of Clenardus, it must be of some interest in literary history. But certainly the grammar of Clenardus differs considerably from that of Gaza, by distinguishing contracted from simple nouns, as separate declensions, surely a great error; and by dividing the conjugations of verbs into thirteen, which Gaza makes but four, ending in ω, and one in μι. The choice of words for examples with Clenardus is very often the same as in our modern grammars, though not so constantly as I had at first supposed. It would be easy to point out rules in that grammarian which have been copied verbatim by his successors. — 1842.]

[1] Vergara, De omnibus Græcæ linguæ grammaticæ partibus, 1573; rather 1537, for "deinde Parisiis, 1550," follows in Antonio, Bibl. Nova.

[2] H. Stephanus, De typographiæ suæ statu. Gesner himself says of this lexicon, which sometimes bore his name: "Circa annum 1537, lexicon Græco-Latinum, quod jam ante a diversis et innominatis nescio quibus miserè satis consarcinatum erat, ex Phavorini Camertis Lexico Græco ita auxi, ut nihil in eo extaret, quod non ut singulari fide, ita labore maximo adjicerem; sed typographus me inscio, et præter omnem expectationem meam, exiguam duntaxat accessionis meæ partem adjecit, reservans sibi forte auctarium ad sequentes etiam editiones." He proceeds to say, that he enlarged several other editions down to 1556, when the last that had been enriched by his additions appeared at Basle. "Cæterum hoc anno, quo hæc scribo, 1562, Genevæ prodiisse audio longe copiosissimum emendatissimumque Græcæ linguæ thesaurum a Rob. Constantino incomparabilis doctrinæ viro, ex Joannis Crispini officinâ." — Vide Gesneri Biblioth. Universalis, art. "Conrad Gesner:" this is part of a long account given here by Gesner of his own works.

tinued till his death in 1535. Colinæus began to print his small editions of the same class at Paris about 1521. They are in that cursive character which Aldus had first employed.[1] The number of such editions, both in France and Germany, became far more considerable than in the preceding age. They are not, however, in general, much valued for correctness of text; nor had many considerable critics even in Latin philology yet appeared on this side of the Alps. Robert Stephens stands almost alone, who, by the publication of his Thesaurus in 1535, augmented in a subsequent edition of 1543, may be said to have made an epoch in this department of literature. The preceding dictionaries of Calepio and other compilers had been limited to an interpretation of single words, sometimes with reference to passages in the authors who had employed them. This produced, on the one hand, perpetual barbarisms and deviations from purity of idiom, while it gave rise in some to a fastidious hypercriticism, of which Valla had given an example.[2] Stephens first endeavored to exhibit the proper use of words, not only in all the anomalies of idiom, but in every delicate variation of sense to which the pure taste and subtle discernment of the best writers had adapted them. Such an analysis is perhaps only possible with respect to a language wherein the extant writers, and especially those who have acquired authority, are very limited in number; and even in Latin, the most extensive dictionary, such as has grown up, long since the days of Robert Stephens, under the hands of Gesner, Forcellini, and Facciolati, or such as might still improve upon their labor, could only approach an unattainable perfection. What Stephens himself achieved would now be deemed far too defective for general use; yet it afforded the means of more purity in style than any could, in that age, have reached without unwearied exertion. Accordingly it is to be understood, that, while a very few scholars, chiefly in Italy, had acquired a facility and exactness of language which has seldom been surpassed, the general style retained a great deal of barbarism, and neither in single words, nor always in mere grammar, can bear a critical eye. Erasmus

Latin Thesaurus of R. Stephens.

[1] Gresswell's History of the Early Parisian Greek Press.

[2] Vives, De causis corrupt. art. (Opera Lud. Vives, edit. Basle, 1555, i. 358). He observes in another work, that there was no full and complete dictionary of Latin. Id., p. 475.

is often incorrect, especially in his epistles, and says modestly of himself in the Ciceronianus, that he is hardly to be named among writers at all, unless blotting a great deal of paper with ink is enough to make one. He is, however, among the best of his contemporaries, if a vast command of Latin phrase, and a spirited employment of it, may compensate for some want of accuracy. Budæus, as has been already said, is hard and unpolished. Vives assumes that he has written his famous and excellent work on the corruption of the sciences, with some elegance; but this he says in language which hardly warrants the boast.[1] In fact he is by no means a good writer. But Melanchthon excelled Erasmus by far in purity of diction, and correctness of classical taste. With him we may place Calvin in his Institutes, and our countryman Sir John Cheke, as distinguished from most other Cisalpine writers by the merit of what is properly called style. The praise, however, of writing pure Latin, or the pleasure of reading it, is dearly bought when accompanied by such vacuity of sense as we experience in the elaborate epistles of Paulus Manutius, and the Ciceronian school in Italy.

Progress of learning in France.

17. Francis I. has obtained a glorious title, the father of French literature. The national propensity (or what once was such) to extol kings may have had something to do with this; for we never say the same of Henry VIII. In the early part of his reign, he manifested a design to countenance ancient literature by public endowments. War, an unsuccessful war, sufficiently diverted his mind from this scheme. But in 1531, a season of peace, he established the royal college of three languages in the university of Paris, which did not quite deserve its name till the foundation of a Latin professorship in 1534. Vatable was the first professor of Hebrew, and Danes of Greek. In 1545 it appears that there were three professors of Hebrew in the royal college, three of Greek, one of Latin, two of mathematics, one of medicine, and one of philosophy. But this college had to encounter the jealousy of the university, tenacious of its ancient privileges, which it fancied to be trampled upon, and stimulated by the hatred of the pretended philosophers, the

1 "Nitorem præterea sermonis addidi aliquem, et quod non expediret res pulcherrimas sordidè ac spuriè vestiri, et ut studiosi elegantiarum [orum?] literarum non perpetuo in vocum et sermonis cognitione adhærescerent; quod hactenus fere accidit, tædio nimirum infrugiferæ ac horridæ molestiæ, quæ in percipiendis artibus diutissimè erat devorata."—i. 324.

scholastic dialecticians, against philological literature. They tried to get the parliament on their side; but that body, however averse to innovation, of which it gave in this age, and long afterwards, many egregious proofs, was probably restrained by the king's known favor to learning from obstructing the new college as much as the university desired.[1] Danes had a colleague and successor as Greek professor in a favorite pupil of Budæus, and a good scholar, Toussain, who handed down the lamp in 1547 to one far more eminent, Turnebus. Under such a succession of instructors, it may be naturally presumed that the knowledge of Greek would make some progress in France. And no doubt the great scholars of the next generation were chiefly trained under these men. But the opposition of many, and the coldness almost of all, in the ecclesiastical order, among whom that study ought principally to have flourished, impeded in the sixteenth century, as it has perhaps ever since, the diffusion of Grecian literature in all countries of the Romish communion. We do not find much evidence of classical, at least of Greek, learning in any university of France, except that of Paris, to which students repaired from every quarter of the kingdom.[2] But a few once distinguished names of the age of Francis I. deserve to be mentioned, — William Cop, physician to the king, and John Ruel, one of the earliest promoters of botanical science, the one translator of Galen, the other of Dioscorides; Lazarus Baif, a poet of some eminence in that age, who rendered two Greek tragedies into French verse; with a few rather more obscure, such as Petit, Pin, Deloin, De Chatel, who are cursorily mentioned in literary history, or to whom Erasmus sometimes alludes. Let us not forget John Grollier, a gentleman who, having filled with honor some public employments, became the first perhaps on this side of the Alps who formed a very ex-

1 The faculty of theology in 1530 condemned these propositions: 1. Scripture cannot be well understood without Greek and Hebrew. 2. A preacher cannot explain the Epistle and Gospel without these languages. In the same year, they summoned Danes and Vatable with two more to appear in parliament, that they might be forbidden to explain Scripture by the Greek and Hebrew without permission of the university; or to say the Hebrew or the Greek is so and so, lest they should injure the credit of the Vulgate. They admitted, however, that the study of Hebrew and Greek was praiseworthy in skilful and orthodox theologians, disposed to maintain the inviolable authority of the Vulgate. Contin. de Fleury, Hist. Ecclésiast., xxvii. 233. See also Gaillard, Hist. de François I., vi. 289.

2 We find, however, that a Greek and Latin school was set up in the diocese of Sadolet (Carpentras), about 1533: he endeavored to procure a master from Italy, and seems, by a letter of the year 1540, to have succeeded. Sadol. Epist., lib. ix. and xvi.

tensive library and collection of medals. He was the friend and patron of the learned during a long life; a character little affected in that age by private persons of wealth on the less sunny side of the Alps. Grollier's library was not wholly sold till the latter part of the seventeenth century.[1]

Learning in Spain.

18. In Spain the same dislike of innovation stood in the way. Greek professorships existed, however, in the universities; and Nunnes, usually called Pincianus (from the Latin name for the city of Valladolid), a disciple of Lebrixa, whom he surpassed, taught the language at Alcalá, and afterwards at Salamanca. He was the most learned man whom Spain had possessed; and his edition of Seneca, in 1536, has obtained the praise of Lipsius.[2] Resende, the pupil of Arias Barbosa and Lebrixa in Greek, has been termed the restorer of letters in Portugal. None of the writings of Resende, except a Latin grammar, published in 1540, fall within the present period; but he established, about 1531, a school at Lisbon, and one afterwards at Evora, where Estaço, a man rather better known, was educated.[3] School divinity and canon law over-rode all liberal studies throughout the Peninsula, of which the catalogue of books at the end of Antonio's Bibliotheca Nova is a sufficient witness.

Effects of Reformation on learning.

19. The first effects of the great religious schism in Germany were not favorable to classical literature.[4] An all-absorbing subject left neither relish nor leisure for human studies. Those who had made the greatest advances in learning were themselves generally involved in theological controversy; and, in some countries, had to encounter either personal suffering on account of their opinions, or, at least, the jealousy of a church that hated the advance of knowledge. The knowledge of Greek and Hebrew was always liable to the suspicion of heterodoxy. In Italy, where classical antiquity was the chief object, this dread of learning could not subsist. But few learned much of Greek in these parts of Europe, without some reference to theology,[5] especially to the grammatical interpretation of the Scriptures In those parts which embraced the Reformation, a still more threatening danger arose from the distempered fanaticism of its adherents. Men who interpreted the Scripture by the

1 Biog. Univ., "Grollier."

2 Antonio, Bibl. Nova.; Biogr. Univ.

3 Biogr. Univ.

4 Erasm. Epist. *passim.*

5 Erasm. Adag., chil. iv. c. v. § 1; Vives *apud* Meiners, Vergl. der Sitten, ii. 737.

Spirit could not think human learning of much value in religion; and they were as little likely to perceive any other advantage it could possess. There seemed, indeed, a considerable peril that through the authority of Carlostadt, or even of Luther, the lessons of Crocus and Mosellanus would be totally forgotten.[1] And this would very probably have been the case, if one man, Melanchthon, had not perceived the necessity of preserving human learning, as a bulwark to theology itself, against the wild waves of enthusiasm. It was owing to him that both the study of the Greek and Latin languages, and that of the Aristotelian philosophy, were maintained in Germany.[2] Nor did his activity content itself with animating the universities. The schools of preparatory instruction, which had hitherto furnished merely the elements of grammar, throwing the whole burthen of philological learning on the universities, began before the middle of the century to be improved by Melanchthon, with the assistance of a friend, even superior to him, probably, in that walk of literature, Joachim Camerarius. "Both these great men," says Eichhorn, "labored upon one plan, upon the same principle, and with equal zeal: they were, in the strictest sense, the fathers of that pure taste and solid learning by which the next generation was distinguished." Under the names of Lycæum or Gymnasium, these German schools gave a more complete knowledge of the two languages, and sometimes the elements of philosophy.[3]

Sturm's account of German schools.

20. We derive some acquaintance with the state of education in this age from the writings of John Sturm, than whom scarce any one more contributed to the cause of letters in Germany. He became in 1538, and continued for above forty years, rector of a celebrated school at Strasburg. Several treatises on education, especially one, De Literarum Ludis rectè instituendis, bear witness to his assiduity. If the scheme of classical instruction which he has here laid down may be considered as one actually in use, there was a solid structure of learning erected in the early years of life, which none of our modern academies would pretend to emulate. Those who feel any curiosity

[1] Seckendorf, p. 198.

[2] [It is said by Melchior Adam, Vitæ Philosophorum, p. 87, that when Melanchthon first lectured on the Philippics of Demosthenes, in 1524, he had but four hearers, and these were obliged to transcribe from their teacher's copy. — 1842.]

[3] Eichhorn, iii. 254, *et post.*

about the details of this course of education, which seems almost too rigorous for practice, will find the whole in Morhof's Polyhistor.[1] It is sufficient to say that it occupies the period of life between the ages of six and fifteen, when the pupil is presumed to have acquired a very extensive knowledge of the two languages. Trifling as it may appear to take notice of this subject, it serves at least as a test of the literary pre-eminence of Germany. For we could, as I conceive, trace no such education in France, and certainly not in England.

21. The years of the life of Camerarius correspond to those of the century. His most remarkable works fall partly into the succeeding period; but many of the editions and translations of Greek authors, which occupied his laborious hours, were published before 1550. He was one of the first who knew enough of both languages and of the subjects treated to escape the reproach which has fallen on the translators of the fifteenth century. His Thucydides, printed in 1540, was superior to any preceding edition. The universities of Tubingen and Leipsic owed much of their prosperity to his superintending care. Next to Camerarius among the German scholars, we may place Simon Grynæus, professor of Greek at Heidelberg in 1523, and translator of Plutarch's Lives. Micyllus, his successor in this office, and author of a treatise De re metricâ, of which Melanchthon speaks in high terms of praise, was more celebrated than most of his countrymen for Latin poetry. Yet in this art he fell below Eobanus Hessus, whose merit is attested by the friendship of Erasmus, Melanchthon, and Camerarius, as well as by the best verses that Germany had to boast. It would be very easy to increase the list of scholars in that empire; but we should find it more difficult to exhaust the enumeration. Germany was not only far elevated in literary progress above France, but on a level, as we may fairly say, with Italy herself. The University of Marburg was founded in 1526, that of Copenhagen in 1539, of Konigsberg in 1544, of Jena in 1548.

Learning in Germany.

22. We come now to investigate the gradual movement of learning in England, the state of which about 1520 we have already seen. In 1521 the first Greek

In England: Linacre.

[1] Lib. ii. c. 10.

characters appear in a book printed at Cambridge,—Linacre's Latin translation of Galen de Temperamentis,—and in the titlepage, but there only, of a treatise περὶ Διψάδων, by Bullock. They are employed several times for quotations in Linacre de Emendata Structura Orationis, 1524.[1] This treatise is chiefly a series of grammatical remarks relating to distinctions in the Latin language now generally known. It must have been highly valuable, and produced a considerable effect in England, where nothing of that superior criticism had been attempted. In order to judge of its proper merit, it should be compared with the antecedent works of Valla and Perotti. Every rule is supported by authorities; and Linacre, I observe, is far more cautious than Valla in asserting what is not good Latin, contenting himself for the most part with showing what is. It has been remarked, that, though Linacre formed his own style on the model of Quintilian, he took most of his authorities from Cicero. This treatise, the first-fruits of English erudition, was well received, and frequently printed on the Continent. Melanchthon recommended its use in the schools of Germany. Linacre's translation of Galen has been praised by Sir John Cheke, who in some respects bears rather hardly on his learned precursor.[2]

Lectures in the universities.

23. Croke, who became tutor to the Duke of Richmond, son of Henry VIII., did not remain at Cambridge long after the commencement of this period. But in 1524, Robert Wakefield, a scholar of some reputation, who had been professor in a German university, opened a public lecture there in Greek, endowed with a salary by the king. We know little individually of his hearers; but, notwithstanding the confident assertions of Antony Wood, there can be no doubt that Cambridge was, during the whole of this reign, at least on a level with the sister university, and indeed, to speak plainly, above it. Wood enumerates several persons educated at Oxford about this time, sufficiently skilled in Greek to write in that language, or to translate from it, or to comment upon Greek authors. The list might be enlarged by the help of Pits; but he is less of a scholar than Wood.

[1] The author begins by bespeaking the reader's indulgence for the Greek printing. "Pro tuo candore, optime lector, æquo animo feras, si quæ literæ in exemplis Hellenismi vel tonis, vel spiritibus, vel affectionibus careant. Iis enim non sátis erat instructus typographus, videlicet recens ab eo fusis characteribus Græcis, nec parata ea copia quæ ad hoc agendum opus est."

[2] Johnson's Life of Linacre.

This much, after all, appears, that the only editions of classical authors published in England before 1540, except those already mentioned, are five of Virgil's Bucolics, two of a small treatise of Seneca, with one of Publius Syrus; all evidently for the mere use of schoolboys. We may add one of Cicero's Philippics, printed for Pinson in 1521; and the first book of his epistles at Oxford in 1529. Lectures in Greek and Latin were, however, established in a few colleges at Oxford.

Greek perhaps taught to boys.

24. If Erasmus, writing in 1528, is to be believed, the English boys were wont to disport in Greek epigrams.[1] But this must be understood as only applicable to a very few, upon whom some extraordinary pains had been bestowed. Thus Sir Thomas Elyot, in his Governor, first published in 1531, points out a scheme of instruction which comprehends the elements of the Greek language. There is no improbability in the supposition, and some evidence to support it, that the masters of our great schools, a Lily, a Cox, an Udal, a Nowell, did not leave boys of quick parts wholly unacquainted with the rudiments of a language they so much valued.[2] It tends to confirm this supposition, that, in the statutes of the new cathedrals established by Henry in 1541, it is provided that there shall be a grammar-school for each, with a head-master "learned in Latin and Greek." Such statutes, however, are not conclusive evidences that they were put in force.[3] In the statutes of Wolsey's intended foundation at Ipswich, some years earlier, though the course of instruction is amply detailed, we do not find it extend to the merest elements of Greek.[4] It is curious to compare this with the course prescribed by Sturm for the German schools.

25. But English learning was chiefly indebted for its more

1 "An tu credidisses unquam fore, ut apud Britannos aut Batavos pueri Græcè garrirent, Græcis epigrammatiis non infeliciter luderent?" — Dial. de Pronuntiatione, p. 48, edit. 1528.

2 Churton, in his Life of Nowell, says that the latter taught the Greek Testament to the boys at Westminster School; referring for authority to a passage in Strype, which I have not been able to find. There is nothing at all improbable in the fact. These inquiries will be deemed too minute by some in this age. But they are not unimportant in their bearing on the history of literature; and an exaggerated estimate of English learning in the age of the Reformation generally prevails. Sir Thomas Pope, founder of Trinity College, Oxford, observes, in a letter to Cardinal Pole in 1556, that, when he was "a young scholar at Eton, the Greek tongue was growing apace; the study of which is now alate much decayed." — Warton, iii. 279. I do not think this implies more than a reference to the time, which was about 1520: he means that Greek was beginning to be studied in England.

3 Warton, iii. 265.

4 Strype's Ecclesiastical Memorials, Appendix, No. 35.

Teaching of Smith at Cambridge.

rapid advance to two distinguished members of the university of Cambridge, — Smith, afterwards secretary of state to Elizabeth, and Cheke. The former began to read the Greek lecture in 1533; and both of them soon afterwards combined to bring in the true pronunciation of Greek, upon which Erasmus had already written. The early students of that language, receiving their instructions from natives, had acquired the vicious uniformity of sounds belonging to the corrupted dialect. Reuchlin's school, of which Melanchthon was one, adhered to this, and were called Itacists, from the continual recurrence of the sound of Iota in modern Greek; being thus distinguished from the Etists of Erasmus's party.[1] Smith and Cheke proved, by testimonies of antiquity, that the latter were right; and "by this revived pronunciation," says Strype, "was displayed the flower and plentifulness of that language, the variety of vowels, the grandeur of diphthongs, the majesty of long letters, and the grace of distinct speech."[2] Certain it is, that about this time some Englishmen began to affect a knowledge of Greek. Sir Ralph Sadler, in his embassy to the king of Scotland in 1540, had two or three Greek words embroidered on the sleeves of his followers, which led to a ludicrous mistake on the part of the Scotch bishops. Scotland, however, herself was now beginning to receive light: the Greek language was first taught in 1534 at Montrose, which continued for many years to be what some called a flourishing school.[3] But the whole number of books printed in Scotland before the middle of the century has been asserted to be only seven. No classical author, or even a grammar, is among these.[4]

[1] Eichhorn, iii. 217. Melancthon, in his Greek grammar, follows Reuchlin: Luscinius is on the side of Erasmus. Ibid. In very recent publications I observe that attempts have been made to set up again the "lugubres sonos, et illud flebile iota" of the modern Greeks. To adopt their pronunciation, even if right, would be buying truth very dear.

[2] Strype's Life of Smith, p. 17. "The strain I heard was of a higher mood." I wonder what author honest John Strype has copied or translated in this sentence; for he never leaves the ground so far in his own style.

[3] M'Crie's Life of Knox, i. 6, and Note C, p. 342.

[4] The list in Herbert's History of Printing, iii. 468, begins with the breviary of the church of Aberdeen; the first part printed at Edinburgh in 1509, the second in 1510. A poem without date, addressed to James V., De suscepto regni regimine, which seems to be in Latin, and must have been written about 1528, comes the nearest to a learned work. Two editions of Lindsay's poems, two of a translation of Hector Boece's chronicles, two of a temporary pamphlet called Scotland's Complaint, with one of the statutes of the kingdom, printed in pursuance of an act of Parliament, passed in 1540, and a religious tract by one Balnaves, — compose the rest. [But this list appears to be not quite accurate. A collection of pamphlets in the Scottish dialect has been discovered, printed at Edinburgh in 1508, and therefore older than the breviary in the foregoing enu-

26. Cheke, successor of Smith as lecturer in Greek at Cambridge, was appointed the first royal professor of that language in 1540, with a respectable salary. He carried on Smith's scheme, if indeed it were not his own, for restoring the true pronunciation, in spite of the strenuous opposition of Bishop Gardiner, chancellor of the university. This prelate, besides a literary controversy in letters between himself and Cheke, published at Basle in 1555, interfered, in a more orthodox way, by prohibiting the new style of speech in a decree which, for its solemnity, might relate to the highest articles of faith. Cheke, however, in this, as in greater matters, was on the winning side; and the corrupt pronunciation was soon wholly forgotten.

Succeeded by Cheke.

27. Among the learned men who surrounded Cheke at Cambridge, none was more deserving than Ascham; whose knowledge of ancient languages was not shown in profuse quotation, or enveloped in Latin phrase, but served to enrich his mind with valuable sense, and taught him to transfer the firmness and precision of ancient writers to our own English, in which he is nearly the first that deserves to be named, or that is now read. He speaks in strong terms of his university. "At Cambridge also, in St. John's College, in my time, I do know that not so much the good statutes as two gentlemen of worthy memory, Sir John Cheke and Dr. Redman, by their own example of excellency in learning, of godliness in living, of diligence in studying, of counsel in exhorting, by good order in all things, did breed up so many learned men in that one college of St. John's at one time as I believe the whole university of Louvain in many years was never able to afford."[1] Lectures

Ascham's character of Cambridge.

meration. Pinkerton's Scottish Poems, 1792, vol. i. p. 22. On the other hand, it is contended that no edition of Lindsay's poems, printed in Scotland, is older than 1568. Pinkerton's Ancient Scottish Poems (a different publication from the former), 1786, vol. i. p. 104. — 1842.]

[1] Ascham's Schoolmaster. In the Life of Ascham, by Grant, prefixed to the former's epistles, he enumerates the learned of Cambridge about 1530. Ascham was himself under Pember, "homini Græcæ linguæ admirabili facultate excultissimo." The others named are Day, Redman, Smith, Cheke, Ridley, Grindal (not the archbishop), Watson, Haddon, Pilkington, Horn, Christopherson, Wilson, Seton, *et infiniti alii excellenti doctrinâ præditi.* Most of these are men afterwards distinguished in the church on one side or the other. This is a sufficient refutation of Wood's idle assertion of the superiority of Oxford: the fact seems to have been wholly otherwise. Ascham himself, in a letter without date, but evidently written about the time that the controversy of Cheke and Gardiner began, praises thus the learning of Cambridge: "Aristoteles nunc et Plato, quod factum est etiam apud nos hic quinquennium, in sua lingua a pueris leguntur Sophocles et Euripides sunt hic familiariores, quam olim Plautus fuerat, cum tu hic eras. Herodotus, Thucydides, Xenophon, magis in ore et manibus omnium tenentur, quam tum Titus Livius, &c." — Ibid., p. 74. What,

in humanity, that is, in classical literature, were, in 1535, established by the king's authority in all colleges of the university of Oxford where they did not already exist; and in the royal injunctions at the same time, for the reformation of academical studies, a regard to philological learning is enforced.[1]

Wood's account of Oxford.

28. Antony Wood, though he is by no means always consistent, gives rather a favorable account of the state of philological learning at Oxford in the last years of Henry VIII. There can, indeed, be no doubt that it had been surprisingly increasing in all England through his reign. More grammar schools, it is said by Knight, were founded in thirty years before the Reformation, meaning, I presume, the age of Henry, than in three hundred years preceding. But the suddenness with which the religious establishment was changed on the accession of Edward, and still more the rapacity of the young king's council, who alienated or withheld the revenues designed for the support of learning, began to cloud the prospect before the year 1550.[2] Wood, in reading whom allowance is to be made for a strong, though not quite avowed, bias towards the old system of ecclesiastical and academical government, inveighs against the visitors of the university appointed by the crown in 1548, for burning and destroying valuable books. And this seems to be confirmed by other evidence. It is true that these books, though it was a vile act to destroy them, would have been more useful to the English antiquary than to the classical student. Ascham, a contemporary Protestant, denies that the university of Cambridge declined at all before the accession of Mary in 1553.

Education of Edward and his sisters.

29. Edward himself received a learned education, and, according to Ascham, read the Ethics of Aristotle in Greek. Of the Princess Elizabeth, his favorite pupil, we have a similar testimony.[3] Mary was not by any means illiterate. It is hardly necessary to

then, can be thought of Antony Wood when he says, "Cambridge was, in the said king's reign, overspread with barbarism and ignorance, as 'tis often mentioned by several authors"?—Hist. and Antiq. of Oxford, A.D. 1545.

1 Warton, iii. 272.

2 Strype, ii. 258; Todd's Cranmer, ii. 33.

3 Of the king he says: "Dialecticam didicit, et nunc Græcè discit Aristotelis Ethica. Eo progressus est in Græca lingua, ut in philosophia Ciceronis ex Latinis Græca facillime faciat."—December, 1550. Ascham, Epist. iv. Elizabeth spoke French and Italian as well as English; Latin fluently and correctly; Greek tolerably. She began every day by reading the Greek Testament, and afterwards the orations of Isocrates and tragedies of Sophocles. Some years afterwards, in 1555,

mention Jane Grey and the wife of Cecil. Their proficiency was such as to excite the admiration of every one, and is no measure of the age in which they lived. And their names carry us on a little beyond 1550, though Ascham's visit to the former was in that year.

The progress of learning is still slow.

30. The reader must be surprised to find, that, notwithstanding these high and just commendations of our scholars, no Greek grammars or lexicons were yet printed in England, and scarcely any works in that or the Latin language. In fact, there was no regular press in either university at this time, though a very few books had been printed in each about 1520; nor had they one till near the end of Elizabeth's reign. Reginald Wolfe, a German printer, obtained a patent, dated April 19, 1541, giving him the exclusive right to print in Latin, Greek, and Hebrew, and also Greek and Latin grammars, though mixed with English, and charts and maps. But the only productions of his press before the middle of the century are two homilies of Chrysostom, edited by Cheke in 1543. Elyot's Latin and English Dictionary, 1538, was the first, I believe, beyond the mere vocabularies of schoolboys; and it is itself but a meagre performance.[1] Latin grammars were of course so frequently published, that it has not been worth while to take notice of them. But the Greek and Latin lexicon of Hadrian Junius, though dedicated to Edward VI., and said to have been compiled in England (I know not how this could be the case), being the work of a foreigner, and printed at Basle in 1548, cannot be reckoned as part of our stock.[2]

he writes of her to Sturm: "Domina Elizabeth et ego una legimus Græcè orationes Æschinis et Demosthenis περὶ στεφάνου. Illa prælegit mihi, et primo aspectu tam scienter intelligit non solum proprietatem linguæ et oratoris sensum, sed totam causæ contentionem, populi scita, consuetudinem et mores illius urbis, ut summopere admireris." — P. 53. In 1560, he asserts that there are not four persons, in court or college (*in aula, in academia*), who know Greek better than the queen.

"Habemus Angliæ reginam," says Erasmus, long before of Catherine, "feminam egregiè doctam, cujus filia Maria scribit bene Latinas epistolas. Thomæ Mori domus nihil aliud quam musarum est domicilium." — Epist. MXXXIV.

[1] Elyot boasts that this "contains a thousand more Latin words than were together in any one dictionary published in this realm at the time when I first began to write this commentary." Though far from being a good, or even, according to modern notions, a tolerable dictionary, it must have been of some value at the time. It was afterwards much augmented by Cooper.

[2] Wood ascribes to one Tolley or Tolleius a sort of Greek grammar, Progymnasmata Linguæ Græcæ, dedicated to Edward VI. And Pits, in noticing also other works of the same kind, says of this: "Habentur Monachii in Bavaria in bibliotheca ducali." As no mention is made of such a work by Herbert or Dibdin, I had been inclined to think its existence apocryphal. It is certainly foreign.

[I have, since my first edition, seen this

Want of books and public libraries.

31. It must appear, on the whole, that under Edward VI. there was as yet rather a commendable desire of learning, and a few vigorous minds at work for their own literary improvement, than any such diffusion of knowledge as can entitle us to claim for that age an equality with the chief continental nations. The means of acquiring true learning were not at hand. Few books, as we have seen, useful to the scholar, had been published in England: those imported were, of course, expensive. No public libraries of any magnitude had yet been formed in either of the universities: those of private men were exceedingly few. The king had a library, of which honorable mention is made; and Cranmer possessed a good collection of books at Lambeth, but I do not recollect any other person of whom this is recorded.

Destruction of monasteries no injury to learning.

32. The progress of philological literature in England was connected with that of the Reformation. The learned of the earlier generation were not all Protestants; but their disciples were zealously such. They taunted the adherents of the old religion with ignorance; and, though by that might be meant ignorance of the Scriptures, it was by their own acquaintance with languages that they obtained their superiority in this respect. And here I may take notice that we should be deceived by acquiescing in the strange position of Warton, that the dissolution of the monasteries in 1536 and the next two years gave a great temporary check to the general state of letters in England.[1] This writer is inconsistent with himself; for no one had a greater contempt for the monastic studies, dialectics, and theology. But as a desire to aggravate, in every possible respect, the supposed mischiefs of the dissolution of monasteries is abundantly manifest in many writers later than Warton, I shall briefly observe, that men are

book in the British Museum. Its title is Progymnasmata Græcæ grammatices autore David Tavelego medico. Antwerp, 1547. It is dedicated to Edward VI.; and the dedication is dated at Oxford, Kal. Jul. 1546; but the privilege to print is at Bruxelles, Nov. 13, 1546. The author says it had been written eight years, as well as a Latin grammar already printed. "Græca vero rudimenta nondum prodiere in publicum." It does not appear that Tavelegus, called Tolley and Taulæus by others, was preceptor to the young prince. The grammar is very short, and seems to be a compendium of Clenardus. It is remarkable that in this copy, which appears to have been presented to Edward, he is called VI. while his father was still living. Κύριε σῶσον τὸν Ἐδούαρδον ἕκτον πρωτόγονον τοῦ βασίλεως. This is on an illuminated page adorned with the prince's feather, and the lines subscribed:

"Principis Edwardi sunt hæc insignia sexti,
Cujus honos nomenque precor subsistat in ævum."

— 1842.]

[1] History of Engl. Poetry, iii. 268.

deceived, or deceive others, by the equivocal use of the word learning. If good learning, *bonæ literæ*, which for our present purpose means a sound knowledge of Greek and Latin, was to be promoted, there was no more necessary step in doing so than to put down bad learning, which is worse than ignorance, and which was the learning of the monks, so far as they had any at all. What would Erasmus have thought of one who should in his days have gravely intimated that the abolition of monastic foundations would retard the progress of literature? In what Protestant country was it accompanied with such a consequence? and from whom, among the complaints sometimes made, do we hear this cause assigned? I am ready to admit, that, in the violent courses pursued by Henry VIII., many schools attached to monasteries were broken up; and I do not think it impossible that the same occurred in other parts of Europe. It is also to be fully stated, and kept in mind, that by the Reformation the number of ecclesiastics, and consequently of those requiring what was deemed a literate education, was greatly reduced. The English universities, as we are well aware, do not contain by any means the number of students that frequented them in the thirteenth century. But are we therefore a less learned nation than our fathers of the thirteenth century? Warton seems to lament, that "most of the youth of the kingdom betook themselves to mechanical or other illiberal employments; the profession of letters being now supposed to be without support or reward." Doubtless many who would have learned the Latin accidence, and repeated the breviary, became useful mechanics. But is this to be called not rewarding the profession of letters? and are tho deadliest foes of the Greek and Roman muses to be thus confounded with their worshippers? The loss of a few schools in the monasteries was well compensated by the foundation of others on a more enlightened plan, and with much better instructors; and, after the lapse of some years, the communication of substantial learning came in the place of that tincture of Latin which the religious orders had supplied. Warton, it should be remarked, has been able to collect the names of not more than four or five abbots and other regulars, in the time of Henry VIII., who either possessed some learning themselves or encouraged it in others.

33. We may assist our conception of the general state of learning in Europe, by looking at some of the books which

were then deemed most usefully subsidiary to its acquisition.

Ravisius Textor. Besides the lexicons and grammatical treatises that have been mentioned, we have a work first published about 1522, but frequently reprinted, and in much esteem, — the Officina of Ravisius Textor. Of this book, Peter Danes, a man highly celebrated in his day for erudition, speaks as if it were an abundant storehouse of knowledge; admirable for the manner of its execution, and comparable to any work of antiquity. In spite of this praise, it is no more than a common-place-book from Latin authors and from translations of the Greek, and could deserve no regard except in a half-informed generation.

34. A far better evidence of learning was given by Conrad Gesner, a man of prodigious erudition, in a continuation of his Bibliotheca Universalis (the earliest general catalogue of books with an estimate of their merits), to which he gave the rather ambitious title of Pandectæ Universales, as if it were to hold the same place in general science that the Digest of Justinian does in civil law. It is a sort of index to all literature, containing references only, and therefore less generally useful, though far more learned and copious in instances, than the Officina of Ravisius. It comprehends, besides all ancient authors, the schoolmen and other writers of the middle ages. The references are sometimes very short, and more like hints to one possessed of a large library than guides to the general student. In connection with the Bibliotheca Universalis, it forms a literary history or encyclopædia, of some value to those who are curious to ascertain the limits of knowledge in the middle of the sixteenth century.

Conrad Gesner.

CHAPTER VI.

HISTORY OF THEOLOGICAL LITERATURE IN EUROPE FROM 1520 TO 1550.

Advance of the Reformation — Differences of Opinion — Erasmus — The Protestant Opinions spread farther — Their Prevalence in Italy — Reaction of Church of Rome — Theological Writings — Luther — Spirit of the Reformation — Translations of Scripture.

1. THE separation of part of Europe from the Church of Rome is the great event that distinguishes these thirty years. But, as it is not our object to traverse the wide field of civil or ecclesiastical history, it will suffice to make a few observations rather in reference to the spirit of the times than to the public occurrences that sprung from it. The new doctrine began to be freely preached, and with immense applause of the people, from the commencement of this period, or, more precisely, from the year 1522, in many parts of Germany and Switzerland: the Duke of Deuxponts in that year, or, according to some authorities, in 1523, having led the way in abolishing the ancient ceremonies; and his example having been successively followed in Saxony, Hesse, Brandenburg, Brunswick, many imperial cities, and the kingdoms of Denmark and Sweden, by the disciples of Luther: while those who adhered to Zwingle made similar changes in Zurich and in several other cantons of Switzerland.[1]

Progress of the Reformation.

2. The magistrates generally proceeded, especially at the outset, with as great caution and equity as were practicable in so momentous a revolution; though perhaps they did not always respect the laws of the empire. They commonly began by allowing freedom of preaching, and forbade that any one should be troubled about his religion. This, if steadily acted upon, repressed the tumultuous populace, who were eager for demolishing images, the memorials of the old religion, as much as it did the episcopal courts, which, had they been strong enough, might have

Interference of civil power

[1] Seckendorf; Gerdes.

molested those who so plainly came within their jurisdiction. The Reformation depended chiefly on zealous and eloquent preachers; the more eminent secular clergy, as well as many regulars, having espoused its principles. They encountered no great difficulty in winning over the multitude; and when thus a decisive majority was obtained, — commonly in three or four years from the first introduction of free preaching, — the government found it time to establish, by a general edict, the abolition of the mass and of such ceremonies as they did not deem it expedient to retain. The conflict between the two parties in Germany seems to have been less arduous than we might expect. It was usually accompanied by an expulsion of the religious of both sexes from their convents, — a measure, especially as to women, unjust and harsh,[1] — and sometimes by an alienation of ecclesiastical revenues to the purposes of the state; but this was not universal in Germany, nor was it countenanced by Luther. I cannot see any just reason to charge the Protestant princes of the empire with having been influenced generally by such a motive. In Sweden, however, the proceedings of Gustavus Vasa, who confiscated all ecclesiastical estates, subject only to what he might deem a sufficient maintenance for the possessors, have very much the appearance of arbitrary spoliation.[2]

3. But while these great innovations were brought in by the civil power, and sometimes with too despotic a contempt of

[1] Wilibald Pirckheimer wrote to Melanchthon, complaining that a convent of nuns at Nuremberg, among whom were two of his sisters, had been molested and insulted because they would not accept confessors appointed by the senate. "Res eo deducta est ut quicunque miserandas illas offendere et incessere audet, obsequium Deo se præstitisse arbitretur. Idque non solum a viris agitur, sed et a mulieribus; et illis mulieribus, quarum liberis omnem exhibuere caritatem. Non solum enim viris, qui alios docere contendunt, se ipsos vero minime emendant, urbs nostra referta est, sed et mulieribus curiosis, garrulis et otiosis, quæ omnia potius quam domum propriam gubernare satagunt."—Pirckheimer, Opera, Frankf. 1610, p. 375. He was a moderate man, concurring with the Lutherans in most of their doctrine, but against the violation of monastic vows. Several letters passed between him and Erasmus. The latter, though he could not approve the hard usage of women, hated the monks so much that he does not greatly disapprove what was done towards them. "In Germaniâ multa virginum ac monachorum monasteria crudeliter direpta sunt. Quidam magistratus agunt moderatius. Ejecerunt eos duntaxat, qui illic non essent professi, et vetuerunt novitios recipi; ademerunt illis curam virginum, et jus alibi concionandi quam in suis monasteriis. Breviter, absque magistratus permissu nihil licet illis agere. Videntur huc spectare, ut ex monasteriis faciant parochias. Existimant enim hos conjuratos phalangas et tot privilegiis armatos diutius ferri non posse." (Basil. Aug. 1525.)—Epist. DCCCLIV. "Multis in locis durè tractati sunt monachi; verum plerique cum sint intolerabiles, alia tamen ratione corrigi non possunt."—Epist. DCCLVII.

[2] Gerdes, Hist. Evangel. Reform.; Seckendorf, *et alii supra nominati*. The best account I have seen of the Reformation in Denmark and Sweden is in the third volume of Gerdes, p. 279, &c.

legal rights, the mere breaking-up of old settlements had so disturbed the minds of the people, that they became inclined to further acts of destruction and more sweeping theories of revolution. It is one of the fallacious views of the Reformation, to which we have adverted in a former page, to fancy that it sprang from any notions of political liberty, in such a sense as we attach to the word. But, inasmuch as it took away a great deal of coercive jurisdiction exercised by the bishops, without substituting much in its place, it did unquestionably relax the bonds of laws not always unnecessary; and, inasmuch as the multitude were in many parts instrumental in destroying by force the exterior symbols of the Roman worship, it taught them a habit of knowing and trying the efficacy of that popular argument. Hence the insurrection of the German peasants in 1525 may, in a certain degree, be ascribed to the influence of the new doctrine; and, in fact, one of their demands was the establishment of the gospel. But as the real cause of that rebellion was the oppressive yoke of their lords, which, in several instances before the Reformation was thought of, had led to similar efforts at relief, we should not lay too much stress on this additional incitement.[1]

Excitement of revolutionary spirit.

4. A more immediate effect of overthrowing the ancient system was the growth of fanaticism, to which, in its worst shape, the Antinomian extravagances of Luther yielded too great encouragement. But he was the first to repress the pretences of the Anabaptists:[2] and, when he saw the danger of general licentiousness which he had unwarily promoted, he listened to the wiser counsels of Melanchthon, and permitted his early doctrine upon justification to be so far modified or mitigated in expression, that it ceased to give apparent countenance to immorality; though his differences with the Church of Rome, as to the very question from which he had started, thus became of less practical importance and less tangible to ordinary minds than before.[3] Yet, in his own

Growth of fanaticism.

[1] Seckendorf.

[2] Id. Melanchthon was a little staggered by the first Anabaptists, who appeared during the concealment of Luther in the Castle of Wartburg. "Magnis rationibus," he says, "adducor certè ut contemnere eos nolim, nam esse in iis spiritus quosdam multis argumentis apparet, sed de quibus judicare præter Martinum nemo facile possit." As to infant baptism, he seemed to think it a difficult question. But the elector observed that they passed for heretics already, and it would be unwise to moot a new point. Luther, when he came back, rejected the pretences of the Anabaptists at once.

[3] See two remarkable passages in Seckendorf, part ii. p 90 and p. 106. The era

writings, we may find to the last such language as to the impossibility of sin in the justified man, who was to judge solely by an internal assurance as to the continuance of his own justification, as would now be universally condemned in all our churches, and is hardly to be heard from the lips of the merest enthusiast.

Differences of Luther and Zwingle.

5. It is well known, that Zuinglius, unconnected with Luther in throwing off his allegiance to Rome, took in several respects rather different theological views, but especially in the article of the real presence, asserted by the Germans as vigorously as in the Church of Rome, though with a modification sufficient, in the spirit of uncompromising orthodoxy, to separate them entirely from her communion, but altogether denied by the Swiss and Belgian reformers. The attempts made to disguise this division of opinion, and to produce a nominal unanimity by ambiguous and incoherent jargon, belong to ecclesiastical history, of which they form a tedious and not very profitable portion.[1]

of what may be called the palinodia of early Lutheranism was in 1527, when Melanchthon drew up instructions for the visitation of the Saxon churches. Luther came into this; but it produced that jealousy of Melanchthon among the rigid disciples, such as Amsdorf and Justus Jonas, which led to the molestation of his latter years. In 1537, Melanchthon writes to a correspondent: "Scis me quædam minus horridè dicere, de prædestinatione, de assensu voluntatis, de necessitate obedientiæ nostræ, de peccato mortali. De his omnibus scio re ipsa Lutherum sentire eadem, sed ineruditi quædam ejus φορτικώτερα dicta, cum non videant quo pertineant, nimium amant." — Epist., p. 445 (edit. 1647).

I am not convinced that this apology for Luther is sufficient. Words are, of course, to be explained, when ambiguous, by the context and scope of the argument. But when single detached aphorisms, or even complete sentences in a paragraph, bear one obvious sense, I do not see that we can hold the writer absolved from the imputation of that meaning because he may somewhere else have used a language inconsistent with it. If the Colloquia Mensalia are to be fully relied upon, Luther continued to talk in the same Antinomian strain as before, though he grew sometimes more cautious in writing. See chap. xii. of that work.

[1] [The Zuinglian doctrine, which denies the real, in the sense of literal and substantial, presence of Christ's body and blood in the symbols of bread and wine, was apparently in opposition to the usual language of the church. It had been, however, remarkably supported in the ninth century by one Bertram, or Ratramn, abbot of Corvey; and there is no reason to think that he was advancing a novel and heterodox opinion, though certainly it was not one to which all were ready to accede. The history of his book is well known: but it seems as if the book itself were not; when some, with Dr. Lingard, pretend that he believed in transubstantiation; and others, with Mr. Alexander Knox, suppose him to have held the unintelligible middle hypothesis which they prefer. Bertram writes with more candor and clearness than some Protestants of the school of Bucer and Calvin, and states the question tersely thus: — "Utrum quod in cœna Domini fidelium ore sumitur, corpus et sanguis Christi in mysterio sive figura fiat, an in veritate;" determining for the former.

Erasmus would, as he tells us, have assented to the Zuinglian tenets, if he could have believed the church to have remained so long in a portentous error. "Nisi me moveret tantus ecclesiæ consensus, possim in Œcolampadii sententiam pedibus dis cedere; nunc in eo persisto, quod mihi tradit scripturarum interpres ecclesia." — Ep. MLIII. And some time before, in a letter to Pirckheimer, he intimates his preference of the doctrine of Œcolampadius

6. The Lutheran princes, who the year before had acquired the name of Protestants by their protest against the resolutions of the majority in the diet of Spire, presented in 1530 to that held at Augsburg the celebrated Confession, which embodies their religious creed. It has been said that there are material changes in subsequent editions; but this is denied by the Lutherans. Their denial can only be as to the materiality; for the fact is clear.[1]

Confession of Augsburg.

7. Meantime it was not all the former opponents of abuses in the church who now served under the banner of either Luther or Zwingle. Some few, like Sir Thomas More, went violently back to the extreme of maintaining the whole fabric of superstition: a greater number, without abandoning their own private sentiments, shrunk, for various reasons, from an avowed separation from the church. Such we may reckon Faber Stapulensis, the most learned Frenchman of that age, after Budæus; such perhaps was Budæus himself;[2] and such were Bilibaldus Pirckheimer,[3] Petrus Mosellanus, Beatus Rhenanus, and Wimpfeling, all men of just renown in their time. Such, above all, we may say, was Erasmus, the precursor of bolder prophets than himself, who, in all his latter years, stood in a very unenviable state, exposed to the shafts of two parties who forgave no man that moderation which was a reproach to themselves. At the beginning of this period, he had certainly an esteem for Melanchthon, Œcolampadius, and other reformers; and though already shocked by the violence of Luther, which he expected

Conduct of Erasmus.

above that of Luther, if both were private opinions; but prefers the authority of the church to either. "Mihi non displiceret Œcolampadii sententia, nisi obstaret consensus ecclesiæ. Nec enim video quid agat corpus insensibile nec utilitatem allaturum si sentiretur, modo adsit in symbolis gratia spiritualis. Et tamen ab ecclesiæ consensu non possum discedere, nec unquam discessi. Tu sic dissentis ab Œcolampadio, ut cum Luthero sentire malis, quam cum ecclesia." — Ep. DCCCXXIII. Sadolet thought, like Erasmus, that the whole church could not have been in so great an error as the corporal presence would be, if false, for so many ages. Sadoleti Epistolæ, p. 161. — 1842.]

[1] Bossuet, Variations des Eglises Protestantes, vol. i.; Seckendorf, p. 170; Clement, Bibliothèque Curieuse, vol. ii. In the editions of 1531, we read: "De cœna Domini docent, quod corpus et sanguis Christi vere adsint, et distribuantur vescentibus in cœna Domini et improbant secus docentes." In those of 1540, it runs thus: "De cœna Domini docent, quod cum pane et vino vere exhibeantur corpus et sanguis Christi vescentibus in cœna Domini."

[2] Budæus was suspected of Protestantism, and disapproved many things in his own church; but the passages quoted from him by Gerdes, i. 186, prove that he did not mean to take the leap.

[3] Gerdes, vol. i. § 66–83. We have seen above the moderation of Pirckheimer in some respects. I am not sure, however, that he did not comply with the Reformation after it was established at Nuremberg.

to ruin the cause altogether, had not begun to speak of him with disapprobation.[1] In several points of opinion he professed to coincide with the German reformers; but his own temper was not decisive. He was capable of viewing a subject in various lights; his learning, as well as natural disposition, kept him irresolute; and it might not be easy to determine accurately the tenets of so voluminous a theologian. One thing was manifest, that he had greatly contributed to the success of the Reformation. It was said that Erasmus had laid the egg, and Luther had hatched it. Erasmus afterwards, when more alienated from the new party, observed that he had laid a hen's egg, but Luther had hatched a crow's.[2] Whatever was the bird, it pecked still at the church. In 1522 came out the Colloquies of Erasmus, a book even now much read, and deserving to be so. It was professedly designed for the instruction and amusement of youth; but both are conveyed at the expense of the prevalent usages in religion. The monkish party could not be blind to its effect. The faculty of theology at Paris, in 1526, led by one Beda, a most bigoted enemy of Erasmus, censured the Colloquies for slighting the fasts of the church, virginity, monkery, pilgrimages, and other established parts of the religious system. They incurred of course the displeasure of Rome, and have several times been forbidden to be read in schools. Erasmus pretended that in his Ἰχθυοφαγία he only turned into ridicule the abuse of fasting, and not the ordinances of the church. It would be difficult, however, to find out this distinction in the dialogue, or indeed any thing favorable to the ecclesiastical cause in the whole book of Colloquies. The clergy are everywhere represented as idle and corrupt. No one who desired to render established institutions odious could set about it in a shorter or surer way; and it would be strange if Erasmus had not done the church more harm by such publications than he could compensate by a few sneers at the reformers in his pri-

[1] "Male metuo misero Luthero; sic undique fervet conjuratio; sic undique irritantur in illum principes, ac præcipuè Leo pontifex. Utinam Lutherus meum secutus consilium, ab odiosis illis ac seditiosis abstinuisset. Plus erat fructûs et minus invidiæ. Parum esset unum hominem perire; si res hæc illis succedit, nemo feret illorum insolentiam. Non conquiescent donec linguas ac bonas literas omnes subverterint." — Epist. DLXVIII., Sept. 1520. "Lutherus, quod negari non potest, optimam fabulam susceperat, et Christi pene aboliti negotium summo cum orbis applausu cœperat agere. Sed utinam rem tantam gravioribus ac sedatioribus egisset consiliis, majoreque cum animi calamique moderatione; atque utinam in scriptis illius non essent tam multa bona, aut sua bona non vitiâsset malis haud ferendis.' — Epist. DCXXXV., 3d Sept. 1521.

[2] Epist. DCCXIX., Dec. 1524.

vate letters. In the single year 1527, Colinæus printed 24,000 copies of the Colloquies, all of which were sold.

8. But, about the time of this very publication, we find Erasmus growing by degrees more averse to the radical innovations of Luther. He has been severely blamed for this by most Protestants; and doubtless, so far as an undue apprehension of giving offence to the powerful, or losing his pensions from the emperor and king of England, might influence him, no one can undertake his defence. But it is to be remembered, that he did not by any means espouse all the opinions either of Luther or Zwingle; that he was disgusted at the virulent language too common among the reformers, and at the outrages committed by the populace; that he anticipated great evils from the presumptuousness of ignorant men in judging for themselves in religion; that he probably was sincere in what he always maintained as to the necessity of preserving the communion of the Catholic Church, which he thought consistent with much latitude of private faith; and that, if he had gone among the reformers, he must either have concealed his real opinions more than he had hitherto done, or lived, as Melanchthon did afterwards, the victim of calumny and oppression. He had also to allege that the fruits of the Reformation had by no means shown themselves in a more virtuous conduct, and that many heated enthusiasts were depreciating both all profane studies and all assistance of learning in theology.[1]

Estimate of it.

[1] The letters of Erasmus, written under the spur of immediate feelings, are a perpetual commentary on the mischiefs with which the Reformation, in his opinion, was accompanied. "Civitates aliquot Germaniæ implentur erroribus, desertoribus monasteriorum, sacerdotibus conjugatis, plerisque famelicis ac nudis. Nec aliud quam saltatur, editur, bibitur ac subatur; nec docent nec discunt; nulla vitæ sobrietas, nulla sinceritas. Ubicunque sunt, ibi jacent omnes bonæ disciplinæ cum pietate." — (1527.) Epist. DCCCCII. "Satis jam diu audivimus, Evangelium, Evangelium, Evangelium; mores Evangelicos desideramus." — Epist. DCCCCXLVI. "Duo tantum quærunt, censum et uxorem. Cætera prestat illis Evangelium, hoc est, potestatem vivendi ut volunt." — Epist. MVI. "Tales vidi mores (Basileæ) ut etiamsi minus displicuissent dogmata, non placuisset tamen cum hujusmodi [sic] fœdus inire." — Epist. MLXVI. Both these last are addressed to Pirckheimer, who was rather more a Protestant than Erasmus; so that there is no fair suspicion of temporizing. The reader may also look at the 788th and 793d Epistles, on the wild doctrines of the Anabaptists and other reformers; and at the 731st, on the effects of Farel's first preaching at Basle in 1525. See also Bayle, "Farel," note B.

It is become very much the practice with our English writers to censure Erasmus for his conduct at this time. Milner rarely does justice to any one who did not servilely follow Luther. And Dr. Cox, in his Life of Melanchthon, p. 35, speaks of a third party, "at the head of which the learned, witty, vacillating, avaricious, and artful Erasmus is unquestionably to be placed." I do not deny his claim to this place, but why the last three epithets? Can Erasmus be shown to have vacillated in his tenets? If he had done so, it might be no great reproach; but his religious creed was nearly that of the moderate members of the Church of Rome, nor have

His controversy with Luther.

9. In 1524, Erasmus, at the instigation of those who were resolved to dislodge him from a neutral station his timidity rather affected, published his Diatribe de libero arbitrio; selecting a topic upon which Luther, in the opinion of most reasonable men, was very open to attack. Luther answered in a treatise, De servo arbitrio; flinching not, as suited his character, from any tenet because it seemed paradoxical, or revolting to general prejudice. The controversy ended with a reply of Erasmus, entitled Hyperaspistes.[1] It is not to be understood, from the titles of these

I observed any proof of a change in it. But vacillation, some would reply, may be imputed to his conduct. I hardly think this word is applicable; though he acted from particular impulses, which might make him seem a little inconsistent in spirit, and certainly wrote letters not always in the same tone, according to his own temper at the moment, or that of his correspondent. Nor was he avaricious: at least I know no proof of it; and as to the epithet "artful," it ill applies to a man who was perpetually involving himself by an unguarded and imprudent behavior. Dr. Cox proceeds to charge Erasmus with seeking a cardinal's hat. But of this there is neither proof nor probability: he always declared his reluctance to accept that honor; and I cannot think, that in any part of his life he went the right way to obtain it.

Those who arraign Erasmus so severely (and I am not undertaking the defence of every passage in his voluminous Epistles) must proceed either on the assumption that no man of his learning and ability could honestly remain in the communion of the Church of Rome, which is the height of bigotry and ignorance; or that, according to his own religious opinions, it was impossible for him to do so. This is somewhat more tenable, inasmuch as it can only be answered by a good deal of attention to his writings. But, from various passages in them, it may be inferred, that, though his mind was not made up on several points, and perhaps for that reason, he thought it right to follow, in assent as well as conformity, the catholic tradition of the church; and, above all, not to separate from her communion. The reader may consult, for Erasmus's opinions on some chief points of controversy, his Epistles, Dccccxxiii., Dcccclxxvii. (which Jortin has a little misunderstood), Mxxxv., Mliii., Mxciii. And see Jortin's own fair statement of the case, i. 274.

Melanchthon had doubtless a sweeter temper and a larger measure of human charities than Erasmus, nor would I wish to vindicate one great man at the expense of another. But I cannot refrain from saying, that no passage in the letters of Erasmus is read with so much pain as that in which Melanchthon, after Luther's death, and writing to one not very friendly, says of his connection with the founder of the Reformation, "Tuli servitutem pæne deformem," &c. — Epist. Melanchthon, p. 21 (edit. 1647). But the characters of literary men are cruelly tried by their correspondence, especially in an age when more conventional dissimulation was authorized by usage than at present.

[1] Seckendorf took hold of a few words in a letter of Erasmus, to insinuate that he had taken a side against his conscience in writing his treatise, De libero arbitrio. Jortin, acute as he was, seems to have understood the passage the same way, and endeavors to explain away the sense, as if he meant only that he had undertaken the task unwillingly. Milner, of course, repeats the imputation; though it must be owned, that, perceiving the absurdity of making Erasmus deny what in all his writings appears to have been his real opinion, he adopts Jortin's solution. I am persuaded that they are all mistaken, and that Erasmus was no more referring to his treatise against Luther than to the Trojan war. The words occur in an answer to a letter of Vives, written from London, wherein he had blamed some passages in the Colloquies on the usual grounds of their freedom as to ecclesiastical practices. Erasmus, rather piqued at this, after replying to the observations, insinuates to Vives that the latter had not written of his own free-will, but at the instigation of some superior. "Verum, ut ingenuè dicam, perdidimus liberum arbitrium. Illic mihi aliud dictabat animus, aliud scribebat calamus." By a figure of speech far from unusual, he delicately suggests his own suspicion as Vives's apology. And the next letter of Vives leaves no room for doubt: "Liberum arbitrium non perdidimus, quod tu asserueris," — words that could have no possible meaning, upon the hypo-

tracts, that the question of free-will was discussed between Luther and Erasmus in a philosophical sense; though Melanchthon in his Loci Communes, like the modern Calvinists, had combined the theological position of the spiritual inability of man with the metaphysical tenet of general necessity. Luther on most occasions, though not uniformly, acknowledged the freedom of the will as to indifferent actions, and also as to what they called the works of the law. But he maintained, that, even when regenerated and sanctified by faith and the Spirit, man had no spiritual free-will; and as before that time he could do no good, so after it he had no power to do ill; nor indeed could he, in a strict sense, do either good or ill, God always working in him, so that all his acts were properly the acts of God, though, man's will being of course the proximate cause, they might, in a secondary sense, be ascribed to him. It was this that Erasmus denied, in conformity with the doctrine afterwards held by the Council of Trent, by the Church of England, and, if we may depend on the statements of writers of authority, by Melanchthon and most of the later Lutherans. From the time of this controversy, Luther seems to have always spoken of Erasmus with extreme ill-will; and, if the other was a little more measured in his expressions, he fell not a jot behind in dislike.[1]

Character of his epistles.

10. The epistles of Erasmus, which occupy two folio volumes in the best edition of his works, are a vast treasure for the ecclesiastical and literary history of his times.[2] Morhof advises the student to commonplace them; a task which, even in his age, few would have

thesis of Seckendorf. There is nothing in the context that can justify it; and it is equally difficult to maintain the interpretation Jortin gives of the phrase, "aliud dictabat animus, aliud scribebat calamus," which can mean nothing but that he wrote what he did not think. The letters are DCCCXXIX., DCCLXXI., DCCLXXVI. in Erasmus's Epistles; or the reader may turn to Jortin, i. 413.

[1] Many of Luther's strokes at Erasmus occur in the Colloquia Mensalia, which I quote from the translation: "Erasmus can do nothing but cavil and flout: he cannot confute." "I charge you in my will and testament, that you hate and loathe Erasmus, that viper."—ch. xliv. "He called Erasmus an epicure and ungodly creature, for thinking, that, if God dealed with men here on earth as they deserved, it would not go so ill with the good, or so well with the wicked."—ch. vii "Lutherus," says the other, "sic respondit (diatribæ de libero arbitrio) ut antehac in neminem virulentius; et homo suavis post editum librum per literas dejerat se in me esse animo candidissimo, ac propemodum postulat, ut ipsi gratias agam, quod me tam civiliter tractavit, longe aliter scripturus si cum hoste fuisset res."—Ep. DCCCXXXVI.

[2] [Many of the epistles of Erasmus were published by Rhenanus from the press of Frovenius about 1519. He pretended to be angry, and that Frobenius had done this against his will; which even Jortin perceives to be untrue. Epist. DVII. This was a little like Voltaire, to whose physiognomy that of Erasmus has often been observed to bear some resemblance; and he has been suspected of other similar tricks. —1842.]

spared leisure to perform, and which the good index of the Leyden edition renders less important. Few men carry on so long and extensive a correspondence without affording some vulnerable points to the criticism of posterity. The failings of Erasmus have been already adverted to: it is from his own letters that we derive our chief knowledge of them. An extreme sensibility to blame in his own person, with little regard to that of others; a genuine warmth of friendship towards some, but an artificial pretence of it too frequently assumed; an inconsistency of profession both as to persons and opinions, partly arising from the different character of his correspondence, but in a great degree from the varying impulses of his ardent mind, — tend to abate that respect which the name of Erasmus at first excites, and which, on a candid estimate of his whole life, and the tenor even of this correspondence, it ought to retain. He was the first conspicuous enemy of ignorance and superstition; the first restorer of Christian morality on a Scriptural foundation; and, notwithstanding the ridiculous assertion of some moderns that he wanted theological learning, the first who possessed it in its proper sense, and applied it to its proper end.

His alienation from the reformers increases.

11. In every succeeding year, the letters of Erasmus betray increasing animosity against the reformers. He had long been on good terms with Zwingle and Œcolampadius, but became so estranged by these party differences, that he speaks of their death with a sort of triumph.[1] He still, however, kept up some intercourse with Melanchthon. The latter years of Erasmus could not have been happy: he lived in a perpetual irritation from the attacks of adversaries on every side; his avowed dislike of the

[1] "Bene habet, quod duo Coryphæi perierint, Zuinglius in acie, Œcolampadius paulo post febri et apostemate. Quod si illis favisset ενυαλιος, actum fuisset de nobis."— Epist. MCCV. It is, of course, to be regretted that Erasmus allowed this passage to escape him, even in a letter. With Œcolampadius he had long carried on a correspondence. In some book the latter had said, "Magnus Erasmus noster." This was at a time when much suspicion was entertained of Erasmus, who writes rather amusingly, in February, 1525, to complain; telling Œcolampadius that it was best neither to be praised nor blamed by his party, but, if they must speak of him, he would prefer their censure to being styled *noster*. Epist. DCCXXVIII. Milner quotes this, leaving poor Erasmus to his reader's indignation for what he would insinuate to be a piece of the greatest baseness. But, in good truth, what right had Œcolampadius to use the word *noster*, if it could be interpreted as claiming Erasmus to his own side? He was not theirs, as Œcolampadius well knew, in exterior profession, nor theirs in the course they had seen fit to pursue.

It is just towards Erasmus to mention, that he never dissembled his affection for Lewis Berquin, the first martyr to Protestantism in France, who was burned in 1528, even in the time of his danger. Epist. DCCCCLXXVI. Erasmus had no more inveterate enemies than in the university of Paris.

reformers by no means assuaging the virulence of his original foes in the church, or removing the suspicion of lukewarmness in the orthodox cause. Part of this should fairly be ascribed to the real independence of his mind in the formation of his opinions, though not always in their expression, and to their incompatibility with the extreme doctrines of either side. But an habitual indiscretion, the besetting sin of literary men, who seldom restrain their wit, rendered this hostility far more general than it need have been; and, accompanied as it was with a real timidity of character, exposed him to the charge of insincerity, which he could better palliate by the example of others than deny to have some foundation. Erasmus died in 1536, having returned to Basle, which, on pretence of the alterations in religion, he had quitted for Friburg in Brisgau a few years before. No differences of opinion had abated the pride of the citizens of Basle in their illustrious visitor. Erasmus lies interred in their cathedral, the earliest, except Œcolampadius, in the long list of the literary dead which have rendered that cemetery conspicuous in Europe.

Appeal of the reformers to the ignorant.

12. The most striking effect of the first preaching of the Reformation was that it appealed to the ignorant; and though political liberty, in the sense we use the word, cannot be reckoned the aim of those who introduced it, yet there predominated that revolutionary spirit which loves to witness destruction for its own sake, and that intoxicated self-confidence which renders folly mischievous. Women took an active part in religious dispute; and, though in some respects the Roman Catholic religion is very congenial to the female sex, we cannot be surprised that many ladies might be good Protestants against the right of any to judge better than themselves. The translation of the New Testament by Luther in 1522, and of the Old a few years later, gave weapons to all disputants: it was common to hold conferences before the burgomasters of German and Swiss towns, who settled the points in controversy, one way or other, perhaps as well as the learned would have done.

Parallel of those times with the present.

13. We cannot give any attention to the story of the Reformation, without being struck by the extraordinary analogy it bears to that of the last fifty years. He who would study the spirit of this mighty age may see it reflected as in a mirror from the days of Luther and Erasmus. Man, who, speaking of him collectively,

has never reasoned for himself, is the puppet of impulses and prejudices, be they for good or for evil. These are, in the usual course of things, traditional notions and sentiments, strengthened by repetition, and running into habitual trains of thought. Nothing is more difficult, in general, than to make a nation perceive any thing as true, or seek its own interest in any manner, but as its forefathers have opined or acted. Change in these respects has been, even in Europe, where there is most of flexibility, very gradual; the work, not of argument or instruction, but of exterior circumstances slowly operating through a long lapse of time. There have been, however, some remarkable exceptions to this law of uniformity, or, if I may use the term, of *secular variation.* The introduction of Christianity seems to have produced a very rapid subversion of ancient prejudices, a very conspicuous alteration of the whole channel through which moral sentiments flow, in nations that have at once received it. This has also not unfrequently happened through the influence of Mohammedism in the East. Next to these great revolutions in extent and degree, stand the two periods we have begun by comparing; that of the Reformation in the sixteenth century, and that of political innovation wherein we have long lived. In each the characteristic features are a contempt for antiquity, a shifting of prejudices, an inward sense of self-esteem leading to an assertion of private judgment in the most uninformed, a sanguine confidence in the amelioration of human affairs, a fixing of the heart on great ends, with a comparative disregard of all things intermediate. In each there has been so much of alloy in the motives, and, still more, so much of danger and suffering in the means, that the cautious and moderate have shrunk back, and sometimes retraced their own steps rather than encounter evils which at a distance they had not seen in their full magnitude. Hence we may pronounce with certainty what Luther, Hutten, Carlostadt, what again More, Erasmus, Melanchthon, Cassander, would have been in the nineteenth century, and what our own contemporaries would have been in their times. But we are too apt to judge others, not as the individualities of personal character and the varying aspects of circumstances rendered them, and would have rendered us, but according to our opinion of the consequences, which, even if estimated by us rightly, were such as they could not determinately have foreseen.

14. In 1531, Zwingle lost his life on the field of battle. It was the custom of the Swiss that their pastors should attend the citizens in war to exhort the combatants and console the dying. But the Reformers soon acquired a new chief in a young man superior in learning and probably in genius, John Calvin, a native of Noyon in Picardy. His Institutions, published in 1536, became the text-book of a powerful body, who deviated in some few points from the Helvetic school of Zwingle. They are dedicated to Francis I., in language good, though not perhaps as choice as would have been written in Italy, temperate, judicious, and likely to prevail upon the general reader, if not upon the king. This treatise was the most systematic and extensive defence and exposition of the Protestant doctrine which had appeared. Without the overstrained phrases and wilful paradoxes of Luther's earlier writings, the Institutes of Calvin seem to contain most of his predecessor's theological doctrine, except as to the corporal presence. He adopted a middle course as to this, and endeavored to distinguish himself from the Helvetic divines. It is well known that he brought forward the predestinarian tenets of Augustin more fully than Luther, who seems, however, to have maintained them with equal confidence. They appeared to Calvin, as doubtless they are, clearly deducible from their common doctrine as to the sinfulness of all natural actions, and the arbitrary irresistible conversion of the passive soul by the power of God. The city of Geneva, throwing off subjection to its bishop, and embracing the reformed religion in 1536, invited Calvin to an asylum, where he soon became the guide and legislator, though never the ostensible magistrate, of the new republic.

Calvin.

His Institutes.

15. The Helvetian reformers at Zurich and Bern were now more and more separated from the Lutherans; and, in spite of frequent endeavors to reconcile their differences, each party, but especially the latter, became as exclusive and nearly as intolerant as the church which they had quitted. Among the Lutherans themselves, those who rigidly adhered to the spirit of their founder's doctrine grew estranged, not externally, but in language and affection, from the followers of Melanchthon.[1]

Increased differences among reformers

1 "Amsdorfius Luthero scripsit, viperam eum in sinu alere, me significans, omitto alia multa." — Epist. Melanchthon, p. 450 (edit. 1647). Luther's temper seems to have grown more impracticable as he advanced in life. Melanchthon threatened

Luther himself, who never withdrew his friendship from the latter, seems to have been alternately under his influence and that of inferior men. The Anabaptists, in their well-known occupation of Munster, gave such proof of the tremendous consequences of fanaticism, generated in great measure by the Lutheran tenet of assurance, that the paramount necessity of maintaining human society tended more to silence these theological subtleties than any arguments of the same class. And, from this time, that sect itself, if it did not lose all its enthusiasm, learned how to regulate it in subordination to legal and moral duties.

Reformed tenets spread in England.

16. England, which had long contained the remnants of Wicliffe's followers, could not remain a stranger to this revolution. Tyndale's New Testament was printed at Antwerp in 1526; the first translation that had been made into English. The cause of this delay has been already explained, and great pains were taken to suppress the circulation of Tyndale's version. But England was then inclined to take its religion from the nod of a capricious tyrant. Persecution would have long repressed

to leave him. Amsdorf and that class of men flattered his pride. See the following letters. In one, written about 1549, he says: "Tuli etiam antea servitutem pæne deformem cum sæpe Lutherus magis suæ naturæ, in qua φιλονεικία erat haud exigua, quam vel personæ suæ, vel utilitati communi serviret." — p. 21. This letter is too apologetical and temporizing. "Nec movi has controversias quæ distraxerunt rempublicam; sed incidi in motas, quæ cum et multæ essent et inexplicatæ, quodam simplici studio quærendæ veritatis, præsertim cum multi docti et sapientes initio applauderent, considerare eas cœpi. Et quanquam materias quasdam horridiores autor initio miscuerat, tamen alia vera et necessaria non putavi rejicienda esse. Hæc cum excerpta amplecterer, paulatim aliquas absurdas opiniones vel sustuli vel lenii." Melanchthon should have remembered that no one had laid down these opinions with more unreserve, or in a more "horrid" way of disputation, than himself in the first edition of his Loci Communes. In these and other passages, he endeavors to strike at Luther for faults which were equally his own, though doubtless not so long persisted in.

Melanchthon, in the first edition of the Loci Communes, which will scarcely be found except in Von der Hardt, sums up the free-will question thus: —

"Si ad prædestinationem referas humanam voluntatem, nec in externis, nec in internis operibus ulla est libertas, sed eveniunt omnia juxta destinationem divinam.

"Si ad opera externa referas voluntatem, quædam videtur esse, judicio naturæ, libertas.

"Si ad affectus referas voluntatem, nulla plane libertas est, etiam naturæ judicio." This proves what I have said in another place, that Melanchthon held the doctrine of strict philosophical necessity. Luther does the same, in express words, once at least in the treatise De servo arbitrio, vol. ii. fol. 429 (edit. Wittenberg, 1554).

In an epistle often quoted by others, Melanchthon wrote: "Nimis horridæ fuerunt apud nostros disputationes de fato, et disciplinæ nocuerunt." But a more thoroughly ingenuous man might have said *nostræ* for *apud nostros*. Certain it is, however, that he had changed his opinions considerably before 1540, when he published his Moralis Philosophiæ Epitome, which contains evidence of his holding the synergism, or activity, and co-operation with divine grace of the human will. See p. 39.

The animosity excited in the violent Lutherans by Melanchthon's moderation in drawing up the Confession of Augsburg is shown in Camerarius, Vita Melanchthon, p. 124 (edit. 1696). From this time it continued to harass him till his death.

the spirit of free judgment, and the king, for Henry's life at least, have retained his claim to the papal honor conferred on him as defender of the faith, if "gospel light," as Gray has rather affectedly expressed it, had not "flashed from Boleyn's eyes." But we shall not dwell on so trite a subject. It is less familiar to every one, that in Italy the seeds of the Reformation were early and widely sown. A translation of Melanchthon's Loci Communes, under the name of Ippofilo da Terra Nigra, was printed at Venice in 1521, the very year of its appearance at Wittenberg: the works of Luther, Zwingle, and Bucer were also circulated under false names.[1] The Italian translations of Scripture made in the fifteenth century were continually reprinted; and, in 1530, a new version was published at Venice by Brucioli, with a preface written in a Protestant tone.[2] The great intercourse of Italy with the Cisalpine nations through war and commerce, and the partiality of Renée of France, Duchess of Ferrara, to the new doctrines, whose disciples she encouraged at her court, under the pretext of literature, contributed to spread an active spirit of inquiry. In almost every considerable city, between 1525 and 1540, we find proofs of a small band of Protestants, not in general abandoning the outward profession of the church, but coinciding in most respects with Luther or Zwingle. It has lately been proved that a very early proselyte to the Reformation, and one whom we should least expect to find in that number, was Berni, before the completion, if not the commencement, of his labor on the Orlando Innamorato; which he attempted to render in some places the vehicle of his disapprobation of the church. This may account for the freedom from indecency which distinguishes that poem, and contrasts with the great licentiousness of Berni's lighter and earlier productions.[3]

In Italy.

1 M'Crie's Hist. of Reformation in Italy. Epigrams were written in favor of Luther as early as 1521; p. 32.

2 Id., p. 53, 55.

3 This curious and unexpected fact was brought to light by Mr. Panizzi, who found a short pamphlet of extreme scarcity, and unnoticed, I believe, by Zeno or any other bibliographer (except Niceron, xxxviii. 76), in the library of Mr. Grenville. It is written by Peter Paul Vergerio, and printed at Basle in 1554. This contains eighteen stanzas, intended to have been prefixed by Berni to the twentieth canto of the Orlando Innamorato. They are of a decidedly Protestant character. For these stanzas others are substituted in the printed editions much inferior, and, what is remarkable, almost the only indecent passage in the whole poem. Mr. Panizzi is of opinion that great liberties have been taken with the Orlando Innamorato, which is a posthumous publication; the earliest edition being at Venice, 1541, five years after the author's death. Vergerio, in this tract, the whole of which has been reprinted by Mr. P. in iii. 361 of his Boiardo, says of Berni: "Costui quasi agli ultimi suoi anni

17. The Italians are an imaginative, but not essentially a superstitious people, or liable, nationally speaking, to the gloomy prejudices that master the reason. Among the classes whose better education had strengthened and developed the acuteness and intelligence so general in Italy, a silent disbelief of the popular religion was far more usual than in any other country. In the majority, this has always taken the turn of a complete rejection of all positive faith; but, at the era of the Reformation especially, the substitution of Protestant for Romish Christianity was an alternative to be embraced by men of more serious temperaments. Certain it is, that we find traces of this aberration from orthodoxy, in one or the other form, through much of the literature of Italy; sometimes displaying itself only in censures of the vices of the clergy, — censures from which, though in other ages they had been almost universal, the rigidly Catholic party began now to abstain. We have already mentioned Pontanus and Mantuan. Trissino, in his Italia Liberata, introduces a sharp invective against the Church of Rome.[1] The Zodiachus Vitæ of Manzolli, whose assumed Latin name, by which he is better known, was Palingenius Stellatus, teems with invectives against the monks, and certainly springs from a Protestant source.[2] The

Italian heterodoxy.

non fù altro che carne e mondo; di che ci fanno ampia fede alcuni suoi capitoli e poesie, delle quali egli molti fogli inbrattò. Ma perchè il nome suo era scritto nel libro della vita, ne era possibile ch' egli potesse fuggire delle mani del celeste padre, &c. Veggendo egli che questo gran tiranno non permittea onde alcuno potesse comporre all' aperta di quei libri, per li quali altri possa penetrare nella cognizione del vero, andando attorno per le man d' ognuno un certo libro profano chiamato innamoramento d' Orlando, che era inetto e mal composto, il Berna [sic] s' immaginò di fare un bel trattato; e ciò fù ch' egli si pose a racconciare le rime e le altre parti di quel libro, di che esso n' era ottimo artefice, e poi aggiungendovi di suo alcune stanze, pensò di entrare con questa occasione e con quel mezzo (insin che d' altro migliore ne avesse potuto avere) ad insegnare la verità dell' Evangelio," &c. Whether Vergerio is wholly to be trusted in all this account, more of which will be found on reference to Panizzi's edition of the Orlando Innamorato, I must leave to the competent reader. The following expressions of Mr. P., though, I think, rather strong, will show the opinion of one conversant with the literature and history of those times: "The more we reflect on the state of Italy at that time, the more have we reason to suspect that the reforming tenets were as popular among the higher classes in Italy in those days as liberal notions in ours." — p. 361.

[1] This passage, which is in the sixteenth canto, will be found in Roscoe's Leo X., Append. No. 164; but the reader would be mistaken in supposing, as Roscoe's language seems to imply, that it is only contained in the first edition of 1548. The fact is, that Trissino cancelled these lines in the unsold copies of that edition, so that very few are found to contain them; but they are restored in the edition of the Italia Liberata printed at Verona in 1729.

[2] The Zodiacus Vitæ is a long moral poem, the books of which are named from the signs of the zodiac. It is not very poetical, but by no means without strong passages of sense and spirit in a lax Horatian metre. The author has said more than enough to incur the suspicion of Lutheranism.

first edition is of 1537, at Basle. But no one writer is more indignantly severe than Alamanni.[1]

18. This rapid, though rather secret, progress of heresy among the more educated Italians, could not fail to alarm their jealous church. They had not won over the populace to their side; for, though censures on the superior clergy were listened to with approbation in every country, there was little probability that the Italians would generally abjure modes of worship so congenial to their national temper, as to have been devised, or retained from heathen times, in compliance with it. Even of those who had associated with the reformers, and have been in consequence reckoned among them, some were far from intending to break off from a church which had been identified with all their prejudices and pursuits. Such was Flaminio, one of the most elegant of poets and best of men; and such was the accomplished and admirable Vittoria Colonna.[2] But those who had drunk deeper of the cup of free thought had no other resource, when their private assemblies had been detected, and their names proscribed, than to fly beyond the Alps. Bernard Ochino, a Capuchin preacher of great eminence, being summoned to Rome, and finding his death resolved upon, fled to Geneva. His apostasy struck his admirers with astonishment, and possibly put the Italians more on their guard against others. Peter Martyr, well known afterwards in England, soon followed him; the academy of Modena, a literary society highly distinguished, but long suspected of heresy, was compelled, in 1542, to sub-

Its progress in the literary classes.

I have observed several proofs of this: the following will suffice: —

"Sed tua præsertim non intret limina quisquam
Frater, nec monachus, vel quavis lege sacerdos.
Hos fuge; pestis enim nulla hac immanoir; hi sunt
Fæx hominum, fons stultitiæ, sentina malorum,
Agnorum sub pelle lupi, mercede colentes,
Non pietate, Deum; falsa sub imagine vecti
Decipiunt stolidos, ac religionis in umbra
Mille actus vetitos, et mille piacula condunt," &c.
Leo (lib. v.).

I could find, probably, more decisive Lutheranism in searching through the poem, but have omitted to make notes in reading it.

[1] "Ahi cieca gente, che l' hai troppo 'n pregio;
Tu credi ben, che questa ria semenza
Habbian più d' altri gratia e privilegio;
Ch' altra trovi hoggi in lei vera scienza,
Che dissimulazion, menzogne e frodi.
Beato 'l mondo, che sarà mai senza," &c.
Satir. i.

The twelfth Satire concludes with a similar execration, in the name of Italy, against the Church of Rome.

[2] M'Crie discusses at length the opinions of these two, p. 164-177, and seems to leave those of Flaminio in doubt; but his letters, published at Nuremberg in 1571, speak in favor of his orthodoxy.

scribe a declaration of faith; and, though Lombardy was still full of secret Protestants, they lived in continual terror of persecution during the rest of this period. The small reformed church of Ferrara was broken up in 1550: many were imprisoned, and one put to death.[1]

19. Meantime the natural tendency of speculative minds to press forward, though checked at this time by the inflexible spirit of the leaders of the Reformation, gave rise to some theological novelties. A Spanish physician, Michael Reves, commonly called Servetus, was the first to open a new scene in religious innovation. The ancient controversies on the Trinity had long subsided: if any remained whose creed was not unlike that of the Arians, we must seek for them among the Waldenses, or other persecuted sects. But even this is obscure; and Erasmus, when accused of Arianism, might reply with apparent truth, that no heresy was more extinct. Servetus, however, though not at all an Arian, framed a scheme, not probably quite novel, which is a difficult matter, but sounding very unlike what was deemed orthodoxy. Being an imprudent and impetuous man, he assailed the fundamental doctrines of reformers as much as of the Catholic Church with none of the management necessary in such cases, as the title of his book, printed in 1531, De Trinitatis erroribus, is enough to show. He was so little satisfied with his own performance, that in a second treatise, called Dialogues on the Trinity, he retracts the former as ill-written, though without having changed any of his opinions. These works are very scarce and obscurely worded; but the tenets seem to be nearly what are called Sabellian.[2]

Servetus.

20. The Socinian writers derive their sect from a small knot of distinguished men, who met privately at Vicenza about 1540; including Lælius Socinus, at that time too young to have had any influence, Ochino, Gentile, Alciati, and some others. This fact has been doubted by Mosheim and M'Crie, and does not rest on much evidence; while some of the above names are rather improbable.[3] It is

Arianism in Italy.

[1] Besides Dr. M'Crie's History of the Reformation in Italy, which has thrown a collected light upon a subject interesting and little familiar, I have made use of his predecessor, Gerdes, Specimen Italiæ reformatæ; of Tiraboschi, viii. 150; of Giannone, iv. 108, *et alibi;* and of Galluzzi, Istoria del Gran Ducato, ii. 292, 369.

[2] The original editions of the works of Servetus very rarely occur; but there are reprints of the last century, which themselves are by no means common.

[3] Lubienecius, Hist. Reformat. Polonicæ; M'Crie's Hist. of Reformation in Italy, p. 154.

certain, however, that many of the Italian reformers held anti-Trinitarian opinions, chiefly of the Arian form. M'Crie suggests that these had been derived from Servetus; but it does not appear that they had any acquaintance, or concurred, in general, with him, who was very far from Arianism; and it is much more probable that their tenets originated among themselves. If, indeed, it were necessary to look for an heresiarch, a Spanish gentleman, resident at Naples, by name Valdes, is far more likely than Servetus. It is agreed that Valdes was one of the chief teachers of the Reformation in Italy; and he has also been supposed to have inclined towards Arianism.[1]

Protestants in Spain and Low Countries.

21. Even in Spain, the natural soil of tenacious superstition, and the birthplace of the Inquisition, a few seeds of Protestantism were early sown. The first writings of Luther were translated into Spanish soon after their appearance: the Holy Office began to take alarm about 1530. Several suspected followers of the new creed were confined in monasteries, and one was burnt at Valladolid in 1541.[2] But in no country where the Reformation was severely restrained by the magistrate did it spread so extensively as in the Netherlands. Two Augustine monks were burned at Brussels in 1523; and their death had the effect, as Erasmus tells us, of increasing prodigiously the number of heretics.[3] From that time a bitter persecution was carried on both by destroying books, and punishing their readers; but most of the seventeen provinces were full of sectaries.

Order of Jesuits.

22. Deeply shaken by all this open schism and lurking disaffection, the Church of Rome seemed to have little hope but in the superstition of the populace, the pre-

[1] Dr. M'Crie is inclined to deny the Arianism of Valdes, and says it cannot be found in his writings (p. 122); others have been of a different opinion. See Chalmers's Dictionary, art. "Valdesso," and "Bayle." His Considerations were translated into English in 1638. I can find no evidence as to this point one way or the other in the book itself, which betrays a good deal of fanaticism, and confidence in the private teaching of the Spirit. The tenets are high Lutheranism as to human action, and derived perhaps from the Loci Communes of Melanchthon. Beza condemned the book.

[2] M'Crie's Hist. of Reformation in Spain.

[3] "Cœpta est carnificina. Tandem Bruxellæ tres Augustinenses [duo?] publicitus affecti sunt supplicio. Quæris exitum? Ea civitas antea purissima cœpit habere Lutheri discipulos, et quidem non paucos. Sævitum est et in Hollandiâ. Quid multis? Ubicunque fumos excitavit nuncius, ubicunque sævitiam exercuit Carmelita, ibi diceres fuisse factam hæresion sementem." — Ep. MCLXIII. The history of the Reformation in the Low Countries has been copiously written by Gerard Brandt, to whose second and third books I refer the reader.

carious support of the civil power, or the quarrels of her adversaries. But she found an unexpected source of strength in her own bosom; a green shoot from the yet living trunk of an aged tree. By a bull, dated the 27th of September, 1540, Paul III. established the order of Jesuits, planned a few years before by Ignatius Loyola. The leading rules of this order were, that a general should be chosen for life, whom every Jesuit was to obey as he did God; and that besides the three vows of the regulars, poverty, chastity, and obedience, he should promise to go wherever the pope should command. They were to wear no other dress than the clergy usually did: no regular hours of prayer were enjoined; but they were bound to pass their time usefully for their neighbors, in preaching, in the direction of consciences, and the education of youth. Such were the principles of an institution which has, more effectually than any other, exhibited the moral power of a united association in moving the great unorganized mass of mankind.

Their popularity.

23. The Jesuits established their first school in 1546, at Gandia in the kingdom of Valencia, under the auspices of Francis Borgia, who derived the title of duke from that city. It was erected into a university by the pope, and king of Spain.[1] This was the commencement of that vast influence they were speedily to acquire by the control of education. They began about the same time to scatter their missionaries over the East. This had been one of the great objects of their foundation. And when news was brought, that thousands of barbarians had flocked to the preaching of Francis Xavier, that he had poured the waters of baptism on their heads, and raised the cross over the prostrate idols of the East, they had enough, if not to silence the envy of competitors, at least to secure the admiration of the Catholic world. Men saw in the Jesuits courage and self-devotion, learning and politeness; qualities the want of which had been the disgrace of monastic fraternities. They were formidable to the enemies of the church; and those who were her friends cared little for the jealousy of the secular clergy, or for the technical opposition of lawyers. The mischiefs and dangers that might attend the institution were too remote for popular alarm.

24. In the external history of Protestant churches, two

[1] Fleury, Hist. Ecclés., xxix. 221.

events, not long preceding the middle of the sixteenth century, served to compensate each other, — the unsuccessful league of the Lutheran princes of Germany, ending in their total defeat, and the establishment of the reformed religion in England by the council of Edward VI. It admits, however, of no doubt, that the principles of the Reformation were still progressive, not only in those countries where they were countenanced by the magistrate, but in others, like France and the Low Countries, where they incurred the risk of martyrdom. Meantime Paul III. had, with much reluctance, convoked a general council at Trent. This met on the 13th of December, 1545; and after determining a large proportion of the disputed problems in theology, especially such as related to grace and original sin, was removed by the pope, in March, 1547, to his own city of Bologna, where they sat but a short time before events occurred which compelled them to suspend their sessions. They did not re-assemble till 1551.

Council of Trent.

25. The greatest difficulties which embarrassed the Council of Trent appear to have arisen from the clashing doctrines of scholastic divines, especially the respective followers of Thomas Aquinas and Duns Scotus, embattled as rival hosts of Dominicans and Franciscans.[1] The fathers endeavored, as far as possible, to avoid any decision which might give too unequivocal a victory to either; though it has generally been thought, that the former, having the authority of Augustin, as well as their own great champion, on their side, have come off, on the whole, superior in the decisions of the council.[2] But we must avoid these subtilties, into which it is difficult not to slide when we touch on such topics.

Its chief difficulties.

26. In the history of the Reformation, Luther is incomparably the greatest name. We see him, in the skilful composition of Robertson, the chief figure of a group of gownsmen, standing in contrast on the canvas with

Character of Luther.

[1] Fleury, xxix. 154, *et alibi;* F. Paul, lib. ii. and iii. *passim.*

[2] It is usual for Protestant writers to inveigh against the Tridentine fathers. I do not assent to their decisions, which is not to the purpose, nor vindicate the intrigues of the papal party. But I must presume to say, that, reading their proceedings in the pages of that very able and not very lenient historian to whom we have generally recourse, an adversary as decided as any that could have come from the reformed churches, I find proofs of much ability, considering the embarrassments with which they had to struggle, and of an honest desire of reformation, among a large body, as to those matters which, in their judgment, ought to be reformed. The notes of Courayer on Sarpi's history, though he is not much less of a Protestant than his original, are more candid, and generally very judicious. Pallavicini I have not read; but what is valuable in him will doubtless be found in the continuation of Fleury, vol. xxix. *et alibi*

the crowned rivals of France and Austria, and their attendant warriors; but blended in the unity of that historic picture. This amazing influence on the revolutions of his own age, and on the opinions of mankind, seems to have produced, as is not unnatural, an exaggerated notion of his intellectual greatness. It is admitted on all sides, that he wrote his own language with force and purity; and he is reckoned one of its best models. The hymns in use with the Lutheran church, many of which are his own, possess a simple dignity and devoutness, never probably excelled in that class of poetry, and alike distinguished from the poverty of Sternhold or Brady, and from the meretricious ornament of later writers. But from the Latin works of Luther, few readers, I believe, will rise without disappointment. Their intemperance, their coarseness, their inelegance, their scurrility, their wild paradoxes, that menace the foundations of religious morality, are not compensated, so far at least as my slight acquaintance with them extends, by much strength or acuteness, and still less by any impressive eloquence. Some of his treatises, and we may instance his reply to Henry VIII., or the book "against the falsely-named order of bishops," can be described as little else than bellowing in bad Latin. Neither of these books display, as far as I can judge, any striking ability. It is not to be imagined that a man of his vivid parts fails to perceive any advantage which may offer itself in that close grappling, sentence by sentence, with an adversary, which fills most of his controversial writings; and in scornful irony he had no superior. His epistle to Erasmus, prefixed to the treatise De servo arbitrio, is bitterly insolent in terms as civil as he could use. But the clear and comprehensive line of argument, which enlightens the reader's understanding, and resolves his difficulties, is always wanting. An unbounded dogmatism, resting on an absolute confidence in the infallibility, practically speaking, of his own judgment, pervades his writings; no indulgence is shown, no pause allowed, to the hesitating; whatever stands in the way of his decisions, the fathers of the church, the schoolmen and philosophers, the canons and councils, are swept away in a current of impetuous declamation; and as every thing contained in Scripture, according to Luther, is easy to be understood,[1] and can only be understood

[1] [This, however, is only for those who are illuminated by the Spirit. "Spiritus enim requiritur ad totam Scripturam, et ad quamlibet ejus partem intelligendam." Vol. ii. fol. 428, edit. Wittenberg, 1554. — 1842.]

in his sense, every deviation from his doctrine incurs the anathema of perdition. Jerome, he says, far from being rightly canonized, must, but for some special grace, have been damned for his interpretation of St. Paul's Epistle to the Romans.[1] That the Zuinglians, as well as the whole Church of Rome and the Anabaptists, were shut out by their tenets from salvation, is more than insinuated in numerous passages of Luther's writings. Yet he had passed himself through several changes of opinion. In 1518, he rejected auricular confession; in 1520, it was both useful and necessary; not long afterwards, it was again laid aside. I have found it impossible to reconcile, or to understand, his tenets concerning faith and works; and can only perceive, that, if there be any reservation in favor of the latter, not merely sophistical, of which I am hardly well convinced, it consists in distinctions too subtle for the people to apprehend. These are not the oscillations of the balance in a calm understanding, conscious of the difficulty which so often attends the estimate of opposite presumptions, but alternate gusts of dogmatism, during which, for the time, he was as tenacious of his judgment as if it had been uniform.

27. It is not impossible that some offence will be taken at this character of his works by those who have thought only of the man; extraordinary as he doubtless was in himself, and far more so as the instrument of mighty changes on earth. Many of late years, especially in Germany, without holding a single one of Luther's more peculiar tenets, have thought it necessary to magnify his intellectual gifts. Frederic Schlegel is among these; but in his panegyric there seems a little wish to insinuate that the reformer's powerful understanding had a taint of insanity. This has not unnaturally occurred to others, from the strange tales of diabolical visions Luther very seriously recounts, and from the inconsistencies as well as the extravagance of some passages. But the total absence of self-restraint, with the intoxicating effects of presumptuousness, is sufficient to account for aberrations, which men of regular minds construe into actual madness. Whether Luther were perfectly in earnest as to his personal interviews with the devil, may be doubtful: one of them he seems to represent as internal.

[1] "Infernum potius quam cœlum Hieronymus meruit; tantum abest ut ipsum canonizare aut sanctum esse audeam dicere." — Id. fol. 478.

Theological writings. Erasmus.

28. Very little of theological literature published between 1520 and 1550, except such as bore immediately on the great controversies of the age, has obtained sufficient reputation to come within our researches, which, upon this most extensive portion of ancient libraries, do not extend to disturb the slumbers of forgotten folios. The Paraphrase of Erasmus was the most distinguished work in Scriptural interpretation. Though not satisfactory to the violent of either party, it obtained the remarkable honor of being adopted in the infancy of our own Protestantism. Every parish church in England, by an order of council in 1547, was obliged to have a copy of this Paraphrase. It is probable, or rather obviously certain, that this order was not complied with.[1]

Melancthon. Romish writers.

29. The Loci Communes of Melancthon have already been mentioned. The writings of Zwingle, collectively published in 1544, did not attain equal reputation: with more of natural ability than erudition, he was left behind in the general advance of learning. Calvin stands on higher ground. His Institutes are still in the hands of that numerous body who are usually denominated from him. The works of less conspicuous advocates of the Reformation which may fall within this earlier period of controversy will not detain us; nor is it worth while to do more on this occasion than mention the names of a few once celebrated men in the communion of Rome, — Vives, Cajetan, Melchior, Cano, Soto, and Catharin.[2] The two latter were prominent in the Council of Trent: the first being of the Dominican party, or that of Thomas Aquinas, which was virtually that of Augustin; the second, a Scotist, and in some points deviating a little from what passed for the more orthodox tenets either in the Catholic or Protestant Churches.[3]

This literature nearly forgotten.

30. These elder champions of a long war, especially the Romish, are, with a very few exceptions, known only by their names and lives. These are they, and many more there were down to the middle of the seventeenth century, at whom, along the shelves of

[1] Jortin says, that, "taking the Annotations and the Paraphrase of Erasmus together, we have an interpretation of the New Testament as judicious and exact as could be made in his time, and to which very few deserve to be preferred of those which have since been published." — ii. 91.

[2] Eichhorn, vi. 210-226; Andrès, xviii. 236.

[3] Sarpi and Fleury, *passim.*

an ancient library, we look, and pass by. They belong no more to man, but to the worm, the moth, and the spider. Their dark and ribbed backs, their yellow leaves, their thousand folio pages, do not more repel us than the unprofitableness of their substance. Their prolixity; their barbarous style; the perpetual recurrence, in many, of syllogistic forms; the reliance, by way of proof, on authorities that have been abjured; the temporary and partial disputes, which can be neither interesting nor always intelligible at present,—must soon put an end to the activity of the most industrious scholar.[1] Even the coryphæi of the Reformation are probably more quoted than read, more praised than appreciated; their works, though not scarce, are voluminous and expensive; and it may not be invidious to surmise that Luther and Melanchthon serve little other purpose, at least in England, than to give an occasional air of erudition to a theological paragraph, or to supply its margin with a reference that few readers will verify. It will be unnecessary to repeat this remark hereafter; but it must be understood as applicable, with such few exceptions as will from time to time appear, throughout at least the remainder of the sixteenth century.

31. No English treatise on a theological subject, published before the end of 1550, seems to deserve notice in the general literature of Europe, though some may be reckoned interesting in the history of our Reformation. The sermons of Latimer, however, published in 1548, are read for their honest zeal and lively delineation of manners. They are probably the best specimens of a style then prevalent in the pulpit, and which is still not lost in Italy, nor among some of our own sectaries; a style that came at once home to the vulgar; animated and effective, picturesque and intelligible, but too unsparing both of ludicrous associations and commonplace invective. The French have some preachers, earlier than Latimer, whose great fame was obtained in this manner,—Maillard and Menot. They belong to the reign of Louis XII. I am but slightly acquainted with the former, whose sermons, printed if not preached in Latin, with sometimes a sort of almost macaronic intermixture of French, appeared to me very much inferior to those of Latimer. Henry Stephens, in his Apologie pour Herodote, has culled many passages from these preachers, in proof of

Sermons.

[1] Eichhorn.

the depravity of morals in the age before the Reformation. In the little I have read of Maillard, I did not find many ridiculous, though some injudicious passages; but those who refer to the extracts of Niceron, both from him and Menot, will have as much gratification as consummate impropriety and bad taste can furnish.[1]

Spirit of the Reformation.

32. The vital spirit of the Reformation, as a great working in the public mind, will be inadequately discerned in the theological writings of this age. Two controversies overspread their pages, and almost efface more important and more obvious differences between the old and the new religions. Among the Lutherans, the tenet of justification or salvation by faith alone, called, in the barbarous jargon of polemics, solifidianism, was always prominent: it was from that point their founder began; it was there that, long afterwards, and when its original crudeness had been mellowed, Melanchthon himself thought the whole principle of the contest was grounded.[2] In the disputes again of the Lutherans with the Helvetic reformers, as well as in those of the latter school, including the Church of England, with that of Rome, the corporal or real presence (which are generally synonymous with the writers of that century) in the Lord's supper was the leading topic of debate. But in the former of these doctrines, after it had been purged from the Antinomian extravagances of Luther, there was found, if not absolutely a verbal, yet rather a subtle, and by no means practical, difference between themselves and the Church of Rome;[3] while, in the Eucharistic controversy, many of the reformers bewildered themselves, and strove to perplex their antagonists, with incompatible and unintelligible propositions, to which the mass of the people paid as little regard as they deserved. It was not for these trials of metaphysical acuteness that the ancient cathedrals shook in their inmost shrines; and though it would be very erroneous to deny, that many not merely of the learned laity, but of the inferior ranks, were apt to tread in such thorny paths, we must look

[1] Niceron, vols. xxiii and xxiv. If these are the original sermons, it must have been the practice in France, as it was in Italy, to preach in Latin; but Eichhorn tells us, that the sermons of the fifteenth century, published in Germany, were chiefly translated from the mother-tongue. vi 113. Tauler certainly preached in German; yet Eichhorn, in another place, iii. 282, seems to represent Luther and his Protestant associates as the first who used that language in the pulpit.

[2] Melancth., Epist., p. 290, ed. Peucer, 1570.

[3] Burnet on Eleventh Article.

to what came closer to the apprehension of plain men for their zeal in the cause of reformed religion, and for the success of that zeal. The abolition of saint-worship; the destruction of images; the sweeping-away of ceremonies, of absolutions, of fasts and penances; the free circulation of the Scriptures; the communion in prayer by the native tongue; the introduction, if not of a good, yet of a more energetic and attractive style of preaching than had existed before; and, besides this, the eradication of monkery which they despised, the humiliation of ecclesiastical power which they hated, the immunity from exactions which they resented,—these are what the north of Europe deemed its gain by the public establishment of the Reformation, and to which the common name of Protestantism was given. But it is rather in the history than in the strictly theological literature of this period, that we are to seek for the character of that revolution in religious sentiment, which ought to interest us from its own importance, and from its analogy to other changes in human opinion.

Limits of private judgment.

33. It is often said, that the essential principle of Protestantism, and that for which the struggle was made, was something different from all we have mentioned; a perpetual freedom from all authority in religious belief, or what goes by the name of the right of private judgment. But, to look more nearly at what occurred, this permanent independence was not much asserted, and still less acted upon. The Reformation was a change of masters; a voluntary one, no doubt, in those who had any choice; and in this sense, an exercise, for the time, of their personal judgment. But no one having gone over to the Confession of Augsburg, or that of Zurich, was deemed at liberty to modify those creeds at his pleasure. He might of course become an Anabaptist or an Arian; but he was not the less a heretic in doing so, than if he had continued in the Church of Rome. By what light a Protestant was to steer, might be a problem which at that time, as ever since, it would perplex a theologian to decide; but, in practice, the law of the land, which established one exclusive mode of faith, was the only safe, as, in ordinary circumstances, it was, upon the whole, the most eligible guide.

34. The adherents to the Church of Rome have never failed to cast two reproaches on those who left them: one, that the reform was brought about by intemperate and calumni-

ous abuse, by outrages of an excited populace, or by the tyranny of princes; the other, that, after stimulating the most ignorant to reject the authority of their church, it instantly withdrew this liberty of judgment, and devoted all who presumed to swerve from the line drawn by law, to virulent obloquy, or sometimes to bonds and death. These reproaches, it may be a shame for us to own, "can be uttered, and cannot be refuted." But, without extenuating what is morally wrong, it is permitted to observe, that the Protestant religion could, in our human view of consequences, have been established by no other means. Those who act by calm reason are always so few in number, and often so undeterminate in purpose, that, without the aid of passion and folly, no great revolution can be brought about. A persuasion of some entire falsehood, in which every circumstance converges to the same effect on the mind; an exaggerated belief of good or evil disposition in others; a universal inference peremptorily derived from some particular case, — these are what sway mankind, not the simple truth with all its limits and explanations, the fair partition of praise and blame, or the measured assent to probability that excludes not hesitation. That condition of the heart and understanding which renders men cautious in their judgment, and scrupulous in their dealings, unfits them for revolutionary seasons. But of this temper there is never much in the public. The people love to be told that they can judge; but they are conscious that they can act. Whether a saint in sculpture ought to stand in the niches of their cathedrals, it was equally tedious and difficult to inquire: that he could be defaced, was certain; and this was achieved. It is easy to censure this as precipitancy; but it was not a mere act of the moment: it was, and much more was of the same kind, the share that fell naturally to the multitude in a work which they were called to fulfil, and for which they sometimes encountered no slight danger.

Passions instrumental in Reformation.

35. But if it were necessary, in the outset of the Reformation, to make use of that democratic spirit of destruction by which the populace answered to the bidding of Carlostadt or of Knox; if the artisans of Germany and Switzerland were to be made arbiters of controversy, it was not desirable that this reign of religious anarchy should be more than temporary. Protestantism, whatever,

Establishment of new dogmatism.

from the generality of the word, it may since be considered, was a positive creed; more distinctly so in the Lutheran than in the Helvetic churches; but in each, after no great length of time, assuming a determinate and dogmatic character. Luther himself, as has been already observed, built up before he pulled down; but the Confession of Augsburg was the first great step made in giving the discipline and subordination of regular government to the rebels against the ancient religion. In this, however, it was taken for granted, that their own differences of theological opinion were neither numerous nor inevitable: a common symbol of faith, from which no man could dissent without criminal neglect of the truth or blindness to it, seemed always possible, though never attained; the pretensions of Catholic infallibility were replaced by a not less uncompromising and intolerant dogmatism, availing itself, like the other, of the secular power, and arrogating to itself, like the other, the assistance of the Spirit of God. The mischiefs that have flowed from this early abandonment of the right of free inquiry are as evident as its inconsistency with the principles upon which the reformers had acted for themselves: yet, without the Confession of Augsburg and similar creeds, it may be doubtful whether the Protestant churches would have possessed a sufficient unity to withstand their steady, veteran adversaries, either in the war of words, or in those more substantial conflicts to which they were exposed for the first century after the Reformation. The schism of the Lutheran and Helvetic Protestants did injury enough to their cause: a more multitudinous brood of sectaries would, in the temper of those times, have been such a disgrace as it could not have overcome. It is still very doubtful whether the close phalanx of Rome can be opposed, in ages of strong religious zeal, by any thing except established or at least confederate churches.

36. We may conclude this section with mentioning the principal editions or translations of Scripture published between 1520 and 1550. The Complutensian edition of the New Testament, suspended since the year 1514, when the printing was finished, became public in 1522. The Polyglott of the Old Testament, as has been before mentioned, had appeared in 1517. An edition of the Greek Testament was published at Strasburg by Cephalæus in 1524, and of the Septuagint in 1526. The New Testament appeared at

Editions of Scripture.

Haguenau in 1521, and from the press of Colinæus at Paris in 1534; another at Venice in 1538. But these, which have become very scarce, were eclipsed in reputation by the labors of Robert Stephens, who printed three editions in 1546, 1549, and 1550; the two former of a small size, the last in folio. In this he consulted more manuscripts than any earlier editor had possessed; and his margin is a register of their various readings. It is therefore, though far from the most perfect, yet the first endeavor to establish the text on critical principles.

Translations of Scripture.

37. The translation of the Old and New Testament by Luther is more renowned for the purity of its German idiom than for its adherence to the original text. Simon has charged him with ignorance of Hebrew; and when we consider how late he came to the study of either that or the Greek language, and the multiplicity of his employments, it may be believed that his knowledge of them was far from extensive.[1] From this translation, however, and from the Latin Vulgate, the English one of Tyndale and Coverdale, published in 1535 or 1536, is avowedly taken.[2] Tyndale had printed his version of the New Testament in 1526. That of 1537, commonly called Matthews's Bible, from the name of the printer, though in substance the same as Tyndale's, was superintended by Rogers, the first martyr in the persecution of Mary, who appears to have had some skill in the original languages. The Bible of 1539, more usually called Cranmer's Bible, was certainly revised by comparison with the original. It is, however, questionable whether there was either sufficient leisure, or adequate knowledge of the Hebrew and Greek languages,

English.

[1] Simon, Hist. Critique V. T., p. 432; Andrès, xix. 169. Eichhorn, however, says that Luther's translation must astonish any impartial judge, who reflects on the lamentable deficiency of subsidiary means in that age. iii. 317. The Lutherans have always highly admired this work on account of its pure Germanism: it has been almost as ill spoken of among Calvinists as by the Catholics themselves. St. Aldegonde says it is farther from the Hebrew than any one he knows; "ex qua manavit nostra, ex vitiosa Germanicâ facta vitiosior Belgico-Teutonica." — Gerdes, iii. 60.

[2] Tyndale's translation of the Pentateuch had been published in 1530. It has been much controverted of late years whether he were acquainted or not with Hebrew.

[Tyndale's translation of the Greek Testament, so far as it is made from the Latin at all, is from that of Erasmus, not from the Vulgate. But it is said that he frequently adheres to the original where Erasmus departs from it; so that he must be reckoned sufficiently acquainted with Greek. See Historical Accounts of English Versions of the Scriptures, prefixed to the English Hexapla, printed in 1841.

Coverdale had other versions to assist him besides that of Luther, and the Vulgate. But his own was executed with a rapidity absolutely incompatible with deliberate consideration, even if his learning had been greater than it was. — 1847.]

in the reign of Henry VIII., to consummate so arduous a task as the thorough censure of the Vulgate text.

38. Brucioli, of Venice, published a translation of the Scriptures into Italian, which he professes to have formed upon the original text.[1] It was retouched by Marmocchini, and printed as his own in 1538. Zaccarias, a Florentine monk, gave another version in 1542, taken chiefly from his two predecessors. The earlier translation of Malerbi passed through twelve editions in this century.[2] The Spanish New Testament, by Francis de Enzina, was printed at Antwerp in 1543; as the Pentateuch, in the same language, was by some Jews at Constantinople in 1547.[3] Olaus Petri, the chief ecclesiastical adviser of Gustavus Vasa, translated the Scriptures into Swedish, and Palladius into Danish, before the middle of the century. But in no language were so many editions of Scripture published as in that of Flanders or Holland; the dialects being still more slightly different, I believe, at that time than they are now. The old translation from the Vulgate, first printed at Delft in 1497, appeared several times before the Reformation from the presses of Antwerp and Amsterdam. A Flemish version of the New Testament from that of Luther came out at Antwerp in 1522, the very year of its publication at Wittenberg; and twelve times more in the next five years. It appears from the catalogue of Panzer that the entire Bible was printed in the Flemish or Dutch language, within the first thirty-six years of the sixteenth century, in fifteen editions; one of which was at Louvain, one at Amsterdam, and the rest at Antwerp. Thirty-four editions of the New Testament alone in that language appeared within the same period; twenty-four of them at Antwerp.[4] Most of these were taken from Luther, but some from the Vulgate. There can be no sort of

In Italy and Low Countries.

[1] The truth of this assertion is denied by Andrès, xix. 188.

[2] M'Crie's Reformation in Italy, p. 43.

[3] This translation, which could have been of little use, was printed in Hebrew characters, with the original, and with a version in modern Greek, but in the same characters. It was reprinted in 1553 by some Italian Jews, in the ordinary letter. This Spanish translation is of considerable antiquity, appearing by the language to be of the twelfth century: it was made for the use of the Spanish Jews, and preserved privately in their synagogues and schools. This is one out of several translations of Scripture that were made in Spain during the middle ages; one of them, perhaps, by order of Alfonso X. Andrès, xix. 151. But in the sixteenth century, even before the alarm about the progress of heresy began in Spain, a stop was put to their promulgation, partly through the suspicions entertained of the half-converted Jews. Id. 183. The translation of Enzina, a suspected Protestant, was, of course, not well received, and was nearly suppressed Id. ibid. M'Crie's Hist. of the Reformation in Spain.

[4] Panzer, Annales Typographici, Index

comparison between the number of these editions, and consequently the eagerness of the people of the Low Countries for Biblical knowledge, considering the limited extent of their language, and any thing that could be found in the Protestant states of the empire.

Latin translations.

39. Notwithstanding the authority given to the Vulgate by the Church of Rome, it has never been forbidden either to criticise the text of that version, or to publish a new one. Sanctes Pagninus, an oriental scholar of some reputation, published a translation of the Old and New Testament at Lyons in 1528. This has been reckoned too literal, and consequently obscure and full of solecisms. That of Sebastian Munster, a more eminent Hebraist, printed at Basle in 1534, though not free from oriental idioms, which indeed very few translations have been, or perhaps rightly can be, and influenced, according to some, by the false interpretations of the rabbins, is more intelligible. Two of the most learned and candid Romanists, Huet and Simon, give it a decided preference over the version of Pagninus. Another translation by Leo Juda and Bibliander, at Zurich in 1543, though more elegant than that of Munster, deviates too much from the literal sense. This was reprinted at Paris in 1545 by Robert Stephens, with notes attributed to Vatable.[1]

French translations.

40. The earliest Protestant translation in French is that by Olivetan at Neufchâtel in 1535. It has been said, that Calvin had some share in this edition, which, however, is of little value, except from its scarcity, if it be true that the text of the version from the Vulgate by Faber Stapulensis has been merely retouched. Faber had printed this, in successive portions, some time before, — at first in France; but the Parliament of Paris, in 1525, having prohibited his translation, he was compelled to have recourse to the press of Antwerp. This edition of Faber appeared several times during the present period. The French Bible of Louvain, which is that of Faber, revised by the command of Charles V., appeared as a new translation in 1550.[2]

[1] Simon, Hist. Crit. du V. T.; Biogr. Univ.; Eichhorn, v. 565, *et post*; Andrès, xix. 165.

[2] Simon, Hist. Crit. du V. T.; Biogr Univ.; Eichhorn, v 565, *et post*; Andrès xix. 165.

CHAPTER VII.

HISTORY OF SPECULATIVE, MORAL, AND POLITICAL PHILOSOPHY, AND OF JURISPRUDENCE, IN EUROPE, FROM 1520 TO 1550.

SECT. I. 1520–1550.

Speculative Philosophy.

1. UNDER this head we shall comprehend not only what passes by the loose, yet not unintelligible appellation, metaphysics, but those theories upon the nature of things, which, resting chiefly upon assumed dogmas, could not justly be reduced to the division of physical science. The distinction may sometimes be open to cavil; but every man of a reflecting mind will acknowledge the impossibility of a rigorous classification of books. The science of logic, not only for the sake of avoiding too many partitions, but on account of its peculiar connection, in this period of literature, with speculative philosophy, will be comprised in the same department.

Logic included under this head.

2. It might be supposed, that the old scholastic philosophy, the barbarous and unprofitable disputations which occupied the universities of Europe for some hundred years, would not have endured much longer against the contempt of a more enlightened generation. Wit and reason, learning and religion, combined their forces to overthrow the idols of the schools. They had no advocates able enough to say much in their favor; but established possession, and that inert force which ancient prejudices retain, even in a revolutionary age, especially when united with civil and ecclesiastical authority, rendered the victory of good sense and real philosophy very slow.

Slow defeat of scholastic philosophy.

3. The defenders of scholastic disputation availed them-

selves of the commonplace plea, that its abuses furnished no conclusion against its use. The barbarousness of its terminology might be in some measure discarded; the questions which had excited ridicule might be abandoned to their fate: but it was still contended, that too much of theology was involved in the schemes of school philosophy erected by the great doctors of the church to be sacrificed for heathen or heretical innovations. The universities adhered to their established exercises; and though these, except in Spain, grew less active, and provoked less emulation, they at least prevented the introduction of any more liberal course of study. But the chief supporters of scholastic philosophy, which became, in reality or in show, more nearly allied to the genuine authority of Aristotle than it could have been while his writings were unknown or ill-translated, were found, after the revival of letters, among the Dominican or Franciscan orders, to whom the Jesuits, inferior to none in acuteness, lent, in process of time, their own very powerful aid.[1] Spain was, above all countries, and that for a very long time, the asylum of the schoolmen; and this seems to have been one among many causes which have excluded, as we may say, the writers of that kingdom, with but few exceptions, from the catholic communion of European literature.

It is sustained by the universities and regulars.

4. These men, or many of them, at least towards the middle of the century, were acquainted with the writings of Aristotle. But, commenting upon the Greek text, they divided it into the smallest fragments, gave each a syllogistic form, and converted every proposition into a complex series of reasonings, till they ended, says Buhle, in an endless and insupportable verbosity. "In my own labors upon Aristotle," he proceeds, "I have sometimes had recourse, in a difficult passage, to these scholastic commentators, but never gained any thing else by my trouble than an unpleasant confusion of ideas; the little there is of value being scattered and buried in a chaos of endless words."[2]

Commentators on Aristotle.

5. The scholastic method had the reformers both of religion and literature against it. One of the most strenuous of the latter was Ludovicus Vives, in his great work, De corruptis artibus et tradendis disciplinis. Though

Attack of Vives on scholastics.

[1] Brucker, iv. 117, *et post.* Buhle has drawn copiously from his predecessor, ii. 448
[2] ii. 417.

the main object of this is the restoration of what were called the studies of humanity (*humaniores literæ*), which were ever found incompatible with the old metaphysics, he does not fail to lash the schoolmen directly in parts of this long treatise, so that no one, according to Brucker, has seen better their weak points, or struck them with more effect. Vives was a native of Valencia, and at one time preceptor to the Princess Mary in England.[1]

Contempt of them in England.

6. In the report of the visitation of Oxford, ordered by Henry VIII. in 1535, contempt for the scholastic philosophy is displayed in the triumphant tone of conquerors. Henry himself had been an admirer of Thomas Aquinas. But the recent breach with the see of Rome made it almost necessary to declare against the schoolmen, its steadiest adherents; and the lovers of ancient learning, as well as the favorers of the Reformation, were gaining ground in the English government.[2]

Veneration for Aristotle.

7. But, while the subtle though unprofitable ingenuity of the Thomists and Scotists was giving way, the ancient philosophy, of which that of the scholastic doctors was a corruption, restored in its genuine lineaments, kept possession of the field with almost redoubled honor. What the doctors of the middle ages had been in theology, that was Aristotle in all physical and speculative science; and the church admitted him into an alliance of dependency for her own service. The Platonic philosophy, to which the patronage of the Medici and the writings of Ficinus had given countenance in the last century, was much fallen, nor had, at this particular time, any known supporters in Europe. Those who turned their minds to physical knowledge, while they found little to their purpose in Plato, were furnished by the rival school with many confident theories and some useful truth. Nor was Aristotle without adherents among the conspicuous cultivators of polite literature, who

[1] Brucker, iv. 87. Meiners (Vergleich. der Sitten, ii. 730-755) has several extracts from Vives as to the scholasticism of the beginning of this century. He was placed by some of his contemporaries in a triumvirate with Erasmus and Budæus. [This treatise of Vives is in seven books. The first is general; the second treats of the corrupt teaching of grammar; the third, of logic; the fourth, of rhetoric; the fifth, of medicine and mathematics; the sixth, of ethics; the last, of the civil law. Thus, on every side, except theology, which he certainly did not mean to represent as standing in no need of correction, he wages war against the universities and their system. — 1842.]

[2] Wood's Hist. of University of Oxford. The passage wherein Antony Wood deplores the "setting Duns in Bocardo" has been often quoted by those who make merry with the lamentations of ignorance.

willingly paid that deference to a sage of Greece, which they blushed to show for a barbarian dialectician of the thirteenth century. To them, at least, he was indebted for appearing in a purer text, and in more accurate versions; nor was the criticism of the sixteenth century more employed on any other writer. By the help of philology, as her bounden handmaid, philosophy trimmed afresh her lamp. The true peripatetic system, according to so competent a judge as Buhle, was first made known to the rest of Europe in the sixteenth century; and the new disciples of Aristotle, endeavoring to possess themselves of the spirit as well as literal sense of his positions, prepared the way for a more advanced generation to poise their weight in the scale of reason.[1]

Melanchthon countenances him.

8. The name of Aristotle was sovereign in the continental universities; and the union between his philosophy, or what bore that title, and the church, appeared so long established, that they must stand or fall together. Luther accordingly, in the commencement of the Reformation, inveighed against the Aristotelian logic and metaphysics, or rather against those sciences themselves; nor was Melanchthon at that time much behind him. But time ripened in this, as it did in theology, the disciple's excellent understanding; and he even obtained influence enough over the master to make him retract some of that invective against philosophy, which at first threatened to bear down all human reason. Melanchthon became a strenuous advocate of Aristotle, in opposition to all other ancient philosophy. He introduced into the university of Wittenberg, to which all Protestant Germany looked up, a scheme of dialectics and physics, founded upon the peripatetic school, but improved, as Buhle tells us, by his own acuteness and knowledge. Thus, in his books, logic is taught with a constant reference to rhetoric; and the physical science of antiquity is enlarged by all that had been added in astronomy and physiology. It need hardly be said, that the authority of Scripture was always resorted to as controlling a philosophy which had been considered unfavorable to natural religion.[2]

His own philosophical treatises

9. I will not contend, after a very cursory inspection of this latter work of Melanchthon, against the elaborate panegyric of Buhle; but I cannot think the Initia Doctrinæ Physicæ much calculated to ad-

[1] Buhle, ii. 462.

[2] Buhle, ii. 427.

ance the physical sciences. He insists very fully on the nfluence of the stars in producing events which we call ortuitous, and even in moulding the human character, — a rejudice under which this eminent man is well known to ave labored. Melanchthon argues, sometimes from the dogas of Aristotle, sometimes from a literal interpretation of cripture, so as to arrive at strange conclusions. Another reatise, entitled De animâ, which I have not seen, is extolled y Buhle as comprehending, not only the psychology, but the hysiology also, of man; and as having rendered great service the age for which it was written. This universality of alents, and we have not yet adverted to the ethics and diaectics of Melanchthon, enhanced his high reputation; nor is surprising that the influence of so great a name should have ecured the preponderance of the Aristotelian philosophy in he Protestant schools of Germany for more than a cenury.

Aristotelians of Italy.

10. The treatise of the most celebrated Aristotelian of his ge, Pomponatius, on the immortality of the soul, as been already mentioned. In 1525, he published wo books; one on incantations, the other on fate nd free-will. They are extremely scarce, but, according to he analysis of Brucker, indicate a scheme of philosophy by o means friendly to religion.[1] I do not find any other of the ristotelian school, who falls within the present thirty years, f sufficient celebrity to deserve mention in this place. But he Italian Aristotelians were divided into two classes, — ne, to which Pomponatius belonged, following the interpretaion of the ancient Greek scholiasts, especially Alexander of phrodisea; the other, that of the famous Spanish philosoher of the twelfth century, Averroes, who may rather be onsidered an heresiarch in the peripatetic church than a enuine disciple of its founder. The leading tenet of Averoism was the numerical unity of the soul of mankind, notithstanding its partition among millions of living individuals.[2] his proposition, which it may seem difficult to comprehend, nd which Buhle deems a misapprehension of a passage in ristotle, natural enough to one who read him in a bad rabic version, is so far worthy of notice, that it contains the erm of an atheistical philosophy, which spread far, as we

[1] Brucker, iv. 166.

[2] See Bayle, "Averroes," note E, to which I omitted to refer on a former mention of the subject, p. 201.

shall hereafter see, in the latter part of this century, and i the seventeenth.

University of Paris.

11. Meantime, the most formidable opposition to the autho rity of Aristotle sprang up in the very centre of hi dominions, — a conspiracy against the sovereign i his court itself. For, as no university had been equal in re nown for scholastic acuteness to that of Paris, there was non so tenacious of its ancient discipline. The very study o Greek and Hebrew was a dangerous innovation in the eye of its rulers, which they sought to restrain by the interventio of the civil magistrate. Yet here, in their own schools, th ancient routine of dialectics was suddenly disturbed by a audacious hand.

New logic of Ramus.

12. Peter Ramus (Ramée), a man of great natural acute ness, an intrepid though too arrogant a spirit, and sincere lover of truth, having acquired a considerabl knowledge of languages as well as philosophy in the univer sity, where he originally filled, it is said, a menial office i one of the colleges, began publicly to attack the Aristotelia method of logic, by endeavoring to substitute a new system o his own. He had been led to ask himself, he tells us, afte three years passed in the study of logic, whether it had ren dered him more conversant with facts, more fluent in speec more quick in poetry, wiser, in short, any way than it ha found him; and, being compelled to answer all this in th negative, he was put on considering whether the fault were i himself or in his course of study. Before he could be quit satisfied as to this question, he fell accidentally upon readin some dialogues of Plato, in which, to his infinite satisfactio he found a species of logic very unlike the Aristotelian, an far more apt, as it appeared, to the confirmation of trut From the writings of Plato, and from his own ingenious min Ramus framed a scheme of dialectics, which immediatel shook the citadel of the Stagirite; and, though in itself it di not replace the old philosophy, contributed very powerfully t its ultimate decline. The Institutiones Dialecticæ of Ramu were published in 1543.

It meets with unfair treatment.

13. In the first instance, however, he met with the strenu ous opposition which awaits such innovators. Th university laid their complaint before the Parliame of Paris: the king took it out of the hands of th Parliament, and a singular trial was awarded as to the meri

f the rival systems of logic; two judges being nominated by Goveanus, the prominent accuser of Ramus, two by himelf, and a fifth by the king. Francis, it seems, though favorable to the classical scholars, whose wishes might generally go against the established dialectics, yet, perhaps from connecting this innovation with those in religion, took the side of the university; and after a regular hearing, though, as is alleged, a very partial one, the majority of the judges pronouncing an unfavorable decision, Ramus was prohibited from teaching, and his book was suppressed. This prohibition, however, was taken off a few years afterwards, and his popularity as a lecturer in rhetoric gave umbrage to the university. It was not till some time afterwards that his system spread over part of the Continent.[1]

14. Ramus has been once mentioned by Lord Bacon, certainly no bigot to Aristotle, with much contempt, and another time with limited praise.[2] It is, however, generally admitted by critical historians of philosophy, that he conferred material obligations on science by decrying the barbarous logic of the schoolmen. What are the merits of his own method is a different question. It seems evidently to have been more popular and convenient than that in use. He treated logic as merely the art of arguing to others, *ars disserendi*; and, not unnaturally from this definition, comprehended in it much that the ancients had placed in the province of rhetoric, — the invention and disposition of proofs in discourse.

Its merits and character.

15. "If we compare," says Buhle, "the logic of Ramus with that which was previously in use, it is impossible not to recognize its superiority. If we judge of it by comparison with the extent of the science itself, and the degree of perfection it has attained in the hands of modern

Buhle's account of it.

1 Launoy, De variâ Aristot. fortuna in Acad. Paris. The sixth stage of Aristotle's fortune, Launoy reckons to be the Ramean controversy, and the victory of the Greek philosopher. He quotes a passage from Omer Talon, which shows that the trial was conducted with much unfairness and violence, p. 112. See also Brucker, v. 548-583, for a copious account of Ramus; and Buhle, ii. 579-602; also Bayle.

2 Hooker also says with severe irony: "In the poverty of that other new-devised aid, two things there are, notwithstanding, singular. Of marvellous quick despatch it is, and doth show them that have it as much almost in three days as if it had dwelt threescore years with them," &c. Again: "Because the curiosity of man's wit doth many times with peril wade farther in the search of things than were convenient, the same is thereby restrained unto such generalities as, everywhere offering themselves, are apparent unto men of the weakest conceit that need be; so as, following the rules and precepts thereof, we may find it to be an art, which teacheth the way of speedy discourse, and restraineth the mind of man, that it may not wax overwise." — Eccles. Pol., i. § 6.

writers, we shall find but an imperfect and faulty attempt.' Ramus neglected, he proceeds to say, the relation of the reason to other faculties of the mind, the sources of error, and the best means of obviating them, the precautions necessary in forming and examining our judgments. His rules display the pedantry of system as much as those of the Aristotelians.[1]

16. As the logic of Ramus appears to be of no more direct utility than that of Aristotle in assisting us to determine the absolute truth of propositions, and consequently could not satisfy Lord Bacon; so perhaps it does not interfere with the proper use of syllogisms, which indeed, on a less extended scale than in Aristotle, form part of the Ramean dialectics. Like all those who assailed the authority of Aristotle, he kept no bounds in depreciating his works; aware, no doubt, that the public, and especially younger students, will pass more readily from admiration to contempt, than to a qualified estimation, of any famous man.

17. While Ramus was assaulting the stronghold of Aristotelian despotism, the syllogistic method of argumentation, another province of that extensive empire, its physical theory, was invaded by a still more audacious, and, we must add, a much more unworthy innovator, Theophrastus Paracelsus. Though few of this extraordinary person's writings were published before the middle of the century, yet, as he died in 1541, and his disciples began very early to promulgate his theories, we may introduce his name more appropriately in this than in any later period. The system, if so it may be called, of Paracelsus had a primary regard to medicine, which he practised with the boldness of a wandering empiric. It was not unusual in Germany to carry on this profession; and Paracelsus employed his youth in casting nativities, practising chiromancy, and exhibiting chemical tricks. He knew very little Latin, and his writings are as unintelligible from their style as their substance. Yet he was not without acuteness in his own profession; and his knowledge of pharmaceutic chemistry was far beyond that of his age. Upon this real advantage he founded those extravagant theories which attracted many ardent minds in the sixteenth century, and were afterwards woven into new schemes of fanciful philosophy. His own models were the oriental reveries of the

Paracelsus.

[1] Buhle, ii. 593, 595.

Cabala, and the theosophy of the mystics. He seized hold of a notion which easily seduces the imagination of those who do not ask for rational proof, — that there is a constant analogy between the macrocosm, as they called it, of external nature, and the microcosm of man. This harmony and parallelism of all things, he maintains, can only be made known to us by divine revelation; and hence all heathen philosophy has been erroneous. The key to the knowledge of nature is in the Scriptures only, studied by means of the Spirit of God communicating an interior light to the contemplative soul. So great an obscurity reigns over the writings of Paracelsus, which, in Latin at least, are not originally his own, for he had but a scanty acquaintance with that language, that it is difficult to pronounce upon his opinions, especially as he affects to use words in senses imposed by himself: the development of his physical system consisted in an accumulation of chemical theorems, none of which are conformable to sound philosophy.[1]

18. A mixture of fanaticism and imposture is very palpable in Paracelsus, as in what he calls his Cabalistic art, which produces by imagination and natural faith, *per fidem naturalem ingenitam*, all magical operations, and counterfeits by these means whatever we see in the external world. Man has a sidereal as well as material body, an astral element, which all do not partake in equal degrees; and therefore the power of magic, which is in fact the power of astral properties, or of producing those effects which the stars naturally produce, is not equally attainable by all. This astral element of the body survives, for a time, after death, and explains the apparition of dead persons; but in this state it is subject to those who possess the art of magic, which is then called necromancy.

His impostures.

19. Paracelsus maintained the animation of every thing: all minerals both feed and render their food. And, besides this life of every part of nature, it is peopled with spiritual beings, inhabitants of the four elements, subject to disease and death like man. These are the silvains (sylphs), undines, or nymphs, gnomes, and salamanders. It is thus observable that he first gave these names, which rendered

And extravagances.

[1] Brucker, iv. 646–684, has copiously descanted on the theosophy of Paracelsus; and a still more enlarged account of it will be found in the third volume of Sprengel's Geschichte der Arzneykunste, which I use in the French translation. Buhle is very brief in this instance, though he has a general partiality to mystical rhapsodies.

afterwards the Rosicrucian fables so celebrated. These live with man, and sometimes, except the salamanders, bear children to him; they know future events. and reveal them to us; they are also guardians of hidden treasures, which may be obtained by their means.[1] I may perhaps have said too much about paradoxes so absurd and mendacious: but literature is a garden of weeds as well as flowers; and Paracelsus forms a link in the history of opinion, which should not be overlooked.

Cornelius Agrippa.

20. The sixteenth century was fertile in men, like Paracelsus, full of arrogant pretensions, and eager to substitute their own dogmatism for that they endeavored to overthrow. They are, compared with Aristotle, like the ephemeral demagogues who start up to a power they abuse as well as usurp on the overthrow of some ancient tyranny. One of these was Cornelius Agrippa, chiefly remembered by the legends of his magical skill. Agrippa had drunk deep at the turbid streams of cabalistic philosophy, which had already intoxicated two men of far greater merit, and born for greater purposes, Picus of Mirandola and Reuchlin. The treatise of Agrippa on occult philosophy is a rhapsody of wild theory and juggling falsehood. It links, however, the theosophy of Paracelsus and the later sect of Behmenists with an oriental lore, venerable in some measure for its antiquity, and full of those aspirations of the soul to break her limits, and withdraw herself from the dominion of sense, which soothed, in old time, the reflecting hours of many a solitary sage on the Ganges and the Oxus. The Jewish doctors had borrowed much from this Eastern source, and especially the leading principle of their Cabala, — the emanation of all finite being from the infinite. But this philosophy was, in all its successive stages, mingled with arbitrary, if not absurd, notions as to angelic and demoniacal intelligences, till it reached a climax in the sixteenth century.

His pretended philosophy.

21. Agrippa, evidently the precursor of Paracelsus, builds his pretended philosophy on the four elements, by whose varying forces the phenomena of the world are chiefly produced; yet not altogether, since there are occult forces of greater efficacy than the elementary, and which are derived from the soul of the world, and from the influence of the stars. The mundane spirit actuates every being, but in different degrees, and gives life and form to each;

[1] Sprengel, iii. 305.

form being derived from the ideas which the Deity has empowered his intelligent ministers, as it were by the use of his seal, to impress. A scale of being, that fundamental theorem of the emanative philosophy, connects the higher and lower orders of things: and hence arises the power of magic; for all things have, by their concatenation, a sympathy with those above and below them, as sound is propagated along a string. But besides these natural relations, which the occult philosophy brings to light, it teaches us also how to propitiate and influence the intelligences, mundane, angelic, or demoniacal, which people the universe. This is best done by fumigations, with ingredients corresponding to their respective properties. They may even thus be subdued, and rendered subject to man. The demons are clothed with a material body, and attached to the different elements; they always speak Hebrew, as the oldest tongue.[1] It would be trifling to give one moment's consideration to this gibberish, were it not evidently connected with superstitious absurdities. that enchained the mind of Europe for some generations. We see the credence in witchcraft and spectral appearances, in astrology and magical charms, in demoniacal possessions,—those fruitful springs of infatuation, wretchedness, and crime,—sustained by an impudent parade of metaphysical philosophy. The system of Agrippa is the mere creed of magical imposture, on which Paracelsus, and still more Jacob Behmen, grafted a sort of religious mysticism. But, in their general influence, these theories were still more pernicious than the technical pedantry of the schools. A Venetian monk, Francis Georgius, published a scheme of blended Cabalistic and Platonic or Neo-Platonic philosophy in 1525; but having no collateral pretensions to fame, like some other worshippers of the same phantom, he can only be found in the historians of obsolete paradoxes.[2]

His sceptical treatise.

22. Agrippa has left, among other forgotten productions, a treatise on the uncertainty of the sciences, which served in some measure to promote a sceptical school of philosophy; no very unnatural result of such theories as he had proposed. It is directed against the imperfections sufficiently obvious in most departments of science, but contains nothing which has not been said more ably since that time. It is remarkable that he contradicts much that he had advanced

[1] Brucker, iv. 410; Sprengel, iii. 226; Buhle, ii. 368.
[2] Brucker, iv. 374–386; Buhle, ii. 367.

in favor of the occult philosophy, and of the art of Raymond Lully.[1]

23. A man far superior to both Agrippa and Paracelsus was Jerome Cardan: his genius was quick, versatile, fertile, and almost profound; yet no man can read the strange book on his own life, wherein he describes, or pretends to describe, his extraordinary character, without suspecting a portion of insanity, — a suspicion which the hypothesis of wilful falsehood would, considering what the book contains, rather augment than diminish. Cardan's writings are extremely voluminous: the chief that relate to general philosophy are those entitled De subtilitate et varietate rerum. Brucker praises these for their vast erudition, supported by innumerable experiments and observations on nature, which furnish no trifling collection of facts to readers of judgment; while his incoherence of ideas, his extravagance of fancy, and confused method, have rendered him of little service to philosophy. Cardan professed himself a stanch enemy of Aristotle.[2]

Cardan.

SECT. II. 1520–1550.

On Moral and Political Philosophy.

24. BY moral philosophy, we are to understand not only systems of ethics, and exhortations to virtue, but that survey of the nature or customs of mankind, which men of reflecting minds are apt to take, and by which they become qualified to guide and advise their fellows. The influence of such men, through the popularity of their writings, is not the same in all periods of society; it has sensibly abated in modern times, and is chiefly exercised through fiction, or at least a more amusing style than was

Influence of moral writers.

[1] Brucker; Buhle.

[2] Brucker, v. 85. Cardan had much of the same kind of superstition as Paracelsus and Agrippa. He admits, as the basis of his physical philosophy, a sympathy between the heavenly bodies and our own; not only general but distributive; the sun being in harmony with the heart, the moon with the animal juices. All organized bodies he held to be animated, so that there is no principle which may not be called nature. All is ruled by the properties of numbers. Heat and moisture are the only real qualities in nature; the first being the formal, the second the material, cause of all things. Sprengel, iii. 278.

found sufficient for our forefathers; and from this change of fashion, as well as from the advance of real knowledge and the greater precision of language, many books once famous have scarcely retained a place in our libraries, and never lie on our tables.

25. In this class of literature, good writing, such at least as at the time appears to be good, has always been the condition of public esteem. They form a large portion of the classical prose in every language. And it is chiefly in this point of view that several of the most distinguished can deserve any mention at present. None was more renowned in Italy than the Cortegiano of Castiglione, the first edition of which is in 1528. We here find both the gracefulness of the language, in this, perhaps its best age, and the rules of polished life in an Italian court. These, indeed, are rather favorably represented, if we compare them with all we know of the state of manners from other sources; but it can be no reproach to the author that he raised the standard of honorable character above the level of practice. The precepts, however, are somewhat trivial, and the expression diffuse; faults not a little characteristic of his contemporaries. A book of this kind that is serious without depth of thought, or warmth of feeling, cannot be read through with pleasure.

Cortegiano of Castiglione.

26. At some distance below Castiglione in merit, and equally in reputation, we may place the dialogues of Sperone Speroni, a writer whose long life embraced two ages of Italian literature. These dialogues belong to the first, and were published in 1544. Such of them as relate to moral subjects, which he treats more theoretically than Castiglione, are solemn and dry: they contain good sense in good language; but the one has no originality, and the other no spirit.

27. A Spanish prelate in the court of Charles obtained an extraordinary reputation in Europe by a treatise so utterly forgotten at present, that Bouterwek has even omitted his name. This was Guevara, author of Marco Aurelio, or the Golden Book. It contains several feigned letters of the Emperor Marcus Aurelius, which probably in a credulous age passed for genuine, and gave vogue to the book. It was continually reprinted in different languages for more than a century: scarce any book except the Bible, says Casaubon, has been so much translated or so

Marco Aurelio of Guevara.

frequently printed.[1] It must be owned that Guevara is dull; but he wrote in the infancy of Spanish literature.[2] It is fair

[1] [This was afterwards greatly enlarged by the author; and the title, Relox de principes, the watch or dial of princes, added to the former. The counterfeited letters are in this second work interspersed amidst a farrago of trite moral and religious reflections. — 1842.]

Bayle speaks of Guevara's Marco Aurelio with great contempt: its reputation had doubtless much declined before that time.

[2] [The account of Guevara in the former edition, though conformable to the bibliographers, stood in need of some correction, which the learned Dr. W. West, of Dublin, has enabled me to give: "There are some circumstances connected with the Relox not generally known, which satisfactorily account for various erroneous statements that have been made on the subject by writers of high authority. The fact is that Guevara, about the year 1518, commenced a life and letters of M. Aurelius, which purported to be a translation of a Greek work he found at Florence. Having some time afterwards lent this in MS. to the emperor, it was surreptitiously copied, and printed, as he informs us himself, first in Seville, and afterwards in Portugal. This was the famous *Libro aureo*, or Golden Book, which for more than a century afterwards was so very popular, and which was so often translated. Guevara himself subsequently published it (1529), with considerable additions, under the title mentioned by you, but still, as I have already stated, forming but one treatise. An Italian translation of this was published in Venice in 1606, and there is also a Latin translation; but it was never so popular, nor so often reprinted, as the Golden Book, its original form. I have a copy of this letter in the original Spanish, printed at Antwerp in 1529, and have seen another, printed at Toledo in 1554; so that, even after the author published it in an enlarged and altered form, it was apparently preferred. The English translation of the 'Golden Boke of Marcus Aurelius, Emperour and eloquent Oratour,' was made from the French in 1532, by Lord Berners, the translator of Froissart. According to Lowndes, it was first printed by Berthelet in 1534, in octavo. My edition, by the same printer, is in quarto, 1539. I cannot discover from what French translation the English was made, the earliest mentioned by Brunet being 1535. It must, however, have been very accurate; as the English, though taken from the Spanish only at second hand, through the French, follows it so closely as to have the appearance of a literal translation made directly from it. I have likewise the Aldine edition of the Italian version with additions (Venice, 1546). Antonio, Watts, and Lowndes, all seem to have been unaware of the literary history of the two works."

In a subsequent letter, Dr. West observes, that the evidence of his statement is easily given from the language of Guevara himself, towards the conclusion of the prologue to the Relox de principes.

The following passage at the beginning of an edition of this work in the British Museum, without a titlepage, but referred by a pencil note in the fly-leaf to the date of Seville, 1540, will confirm Dr. West's assertion: —

"Comienca el primero libro del famosissimo emperador Marco Aurelio con el Relox de principes nuevamente añadido, compuesto por el muy reverendo y magnifico señor Don Antonio de Guevara, obispo de Guadix, predicador y coronista del emperador y rey Don Carlos quinto deste nombre; á cuya imperial celsitad se dirige la presente obra. En la qual son añadidas ciertas cartas del emperador Marco Aurelio, que si quitaron en otras impressiones que se hizieron antes desta, y tractase en este primero libro quanta excelencia es en el principe ser buen christiano, y quantos males se sigue de ser tyrano."

The second book is announced as follows: "Comienca el segundo libro llamado Relox de principes, en el qual va encorporado otro muy famoso libro llamado Marco Aurelio; trata el autor en el presente libro della manera que los principes y grandes señores se han de aver con sus mujeres, y de como han de criar á sus hijos."

I have not searched for the numerous editions of the Golden Book; but one in Spanish (Antwerp, 1529), which I have seen, contains only the original fiction of Marcus Aurelius, without the Dial of Princes. Dr. West is probably right in supposing that the former was the celebrated work which was so often printed throughout Europe; but there are several editions of the second in different languages. One in Italian, Venice, 1584, contains a fourth book, purporting to be the genuine work of Guevara, and translated from the Spanish in 1562. But whether this appears in any Spanish edition I do not know.

The account given of Guevara in the Biographie Universelle is plainly written in ignorance of the facts for which I am indebted to my learned correspondent. — 1842.]

to observe, that Guevara seems uniformly a friend to good and just government, and that he probably employs Roman stories as a screen to his satire on the abuses of his time. Antonio and Bayle censure this as a literary forgery more severely than is quite reasonable. Andrès extols the style very highly.[1]

28. Guevara wrote better, or more pleasingly, in some other moral essays. One of them, Menosprecio di corte y alabanza d'aldea, indifferently translated into English by Thomas Tymme in 1575, contains some eloquent passages; and, being dictated apparently by his own feelings instead of the spirit of bookmaking, is far superior to the more renowned Marco Aurelio. Antonio blames Guevara for affectation of antithesis, and too studious a desire to say every thing well. But this sententious and antithetical style of the Spanish writers is worthy of our attention; for it was imitated by their English admirers, and formed a style much in vogue in the reigns of Elizabeth and James. Thus, to take a very short specimen from Tymme's translation: "In the court," says Guevara, "it profits little to be wise, forasmuch as good service is soon forgotten, friends soon fail, and enemies augment, the nobility doth forget itself, science is forgotten, humility despised, truth cloaked and hid, and good counsel refused." This elaborately condensed antithetical manner cannot have been borrowed from the Italians, of whom it is by no means a distinguishing feature.

His Menosprecio di corte.

29. Bouterwek has taken notice of a moral writer contemporary with Guevara, though not so successful in his own age, Perez d'Oliva. Of him Andrès says, that the slight specimen he has left in his dialogue on the dignity of man displays the elegance, politeness, and vigor of his style. "It is written," says Bouterwek, "in a natural and easy manner; the ideas are for the most part clearly and accurately developed; and the oratorical language, particularly where it is appropriately introduced, is powerful and picturesque."[2]

Perez d'Oliva.

30. The writings of Erasmus are very much dedicated to the inculcation of Christian ethics. The Enchiridion Militis Christiani, the Lingua, and, above all, the Colloquies, which

[1] vii. 148. In 1541 Sir Thomas Elyot published "The image of government compiled of the acts and sentences of Alexander Severus," as the work of Encolpius, an imaginary secretary to that emperor. Some have thought this genuine, or at least no forgery of Elyot's; but I see little reason to doubt that he imitated Guevara Fabric. Bibl. Lat. and Herbert.

[2] Bouterwek, p. 309; Andrès, vii. 149.

have this primary object in view, may be distinguished from the rest. The Colloquies are, from their nature, the most sportive and amusing of his works; the language of Erasmus has no prudery, nor his moral code, though strict, any austerity; it is needless to add, that his piety has no superstition. The dialogue is short and pointed; the characters display themselves naturally; the ridicule falls, in general, with skill and delicacy; the moral is not forced, yet always in view; the manners of the age in some of the Colloquies, as in the German Inn, are humorously and agreeably represented. Erasmus, perhaps, in later times, would have been successful as a comic writer. The works of Vives breathe an equally pure spirit of morality. But it is unnecessary to specify works of this class, which, valuable as they are in their tendency, form too much the staple literature of every generation to be enumerated in its history. The treatise of Melanchthon, Moralis Philosophiæ Epitome, stands on different grounds. It is a compendious system of ethics, built in great measure on that of Aristotle, but with such variation as the principles of Christianity, or his own judgment, led him to introduce. Hence, though he exhorts young students, as the result of his own long reflection on the subject, to embrace the Peripatetic theory of morals, in preference to those of the Stoic or Epicurean school;[1] and contends for the utility of moral philosophy, as part of the law of God, and the exposition of that of nature, he admits that the reason is too weak to discern the necessity of perfect obedience, or the sinfulness of natural appetite.[2] In this epitome, which is far from servilely

Ethical writings of Erasmus and Melanchthon.

[1] "Ego vero qui has sectarum controversias diu multumque agitavi, ἄνω καὶ κάτω στρέφων, ut Plato facere præcipit, valde adhortor adolescentulos, ut repudiatis Stoicis et Epicureis, amplectantur Peripatetica." — Præfat. ad Mor. Philos. Epist. (1549).

[2] Id., p. 4. The following passage, taken nearly at random, may serve as a fair specimen of Melanchthon's style:—

"Primum cum necesse sit legem Dei, item magistratuum leges nosse, ut disciplinam teneamus ad coercendas cupiditates, facile intelligi potest, hanc philosophiam etiam prodesse, quæ est quædam domestica disciplina, quæ cum demonstrat fontes et causas virtutum, accendit animos ad earum amorem; abeunt enim studia in mores, atque hoc magis invitantur animi, quia quo propius aspicimus res bonas, eo magis ipsas et admiramur et amamus. Hic autem perfecta notitia virtutis quæritur. Neque vero dubium est, quin, ut Plato ait, sapientia, si quod ejus simulacrum manifestum in oculos incurreret, acerrimos amores excitaret. Nulla autem fingi effigies potest, quæ propius exprimat virtutem et clarius ob oculos ponat spectantibus, quam hæc doctrina. Quare ejus tractatio magnam vim habet ad excitandos animos ad amorem rerum honestarum, præsertim in bonis ac mediocribus ingeniis." — p. 6.

He tacitly retracts in this treatise all he had said against free-will in the first edition of the Loci Communes: "In hac quæstione moderatio adhibenda est, ne quas amplectamur opiniones immoderatas in utramque partem, quæ aut moribus officiant, aut beneficia Christi obscurent." — p. 34.

following the Aristotelian dogmas, he declares wholly against usury, less wise in this than Calvin, and asserts the magistrate's right to punish heretics.

Sir T. Elyot's Governor.

31. Sir Thomas Elyot's Governor, published in 1531, though it might also find a place in the history of political philosophy or of classical literature, seems best to fall under this head; education of youth being certainly no insignificant province of moral science. The author was a gentleman of good family, and had been employed by the king in several embassies. The Biographia Britannica pronounces him "an excellent grammarian. poet, rhetorician, philosopher, physician, cosmographer, and historian." For some part of this sweeping eulogy we have no evidence; but it is a high praise to have been one of our earliest English writers of worth, and, though much inferior in genius to Sir Thomas More, equal perhaps in learning and sagacity to any scholar of the age of Henry VIII. The plan of Sir Thomas Elyot in his Governor, as laid down in his dedication to the king, is bold enough. It is "to describe in our vulgar tongue the form of a just public weal, which matter I have gathered as well of the sayings of most noble authors, Greek and Latin, as by mine own experience; I being continually pained in some daily affairs of the public weal of this most noble realm almost from my childhood." But it is far from answering to this promise. After a few pages on the superiority of regal over every other government, he passes to the subject of education, not of a prince only, but any gentleman's son, with which he fills up the rest of his first book.

Severity of education.

32. This contains several things worthy of observation. He advises that children be used to speak Latin from their infancy, and either learn Latin and Greek together, or begin with Greek. Elyot deprecates "cruel and *yrous* schoolmasters, by whom the wits of children be dulled, whereof we need no better author to witness than daily experience."[1] All testimonies concur to this savage ill-treatment of boys in the schools of this period. The fierceness of the Tudor government, the religious intolerance, the polemical brutality, the rigorous justice, when justice it was, of our laws, seem to have engendered a hardness of character, which displayed itself in severity of discipline, when it did not even reach the point of arbitrary or malignant cruelty. Every one

[1] Chap. x.

knows the behavior of Lady Jane Grey's parents towards their accomplished and admirable child, — the slave of their temper in her brief life, — the victim of their ambition in death. The story told by Erasmus of Colet is also a little too trite for repetition. The general fact is indubitable; and I think we may ascribe much of the hypocrisy and disingenuousness, which were so unfortunately too much displayed in this and the first part of the next century, to the rigid scheme of domestic discipline so frequently adopted; though I will not say but that we owe some part of the firmness and power of self-command, which were equally manifest in the English character, to the same cause.

He seems to avoid politics.

33. Elyot dwells much and justly on the importance of elegant arts, such as music, drawing, and carving, by which he means sculpture, and of manly exercises, in liberal education; and objects with reason to the usual practice of turning mere boys at fifteen to the study of the laws.[1] In the second book, he seems to come back to his original subject, by proposing to consider what qualities a governor ought to possess. But this soon turns to long commonplace ethics, copiously illustrated out of ancient history, but perhaps, in general, little more applicable to kings than to private men, at least those of superior station. It is plain that Elyot did not venture to handle the political part of his subject as he wished to do. He seems worthy, upon the whole, on account of the solidity of his reflections, to hold a higher place than Ascham, to whom, in some respects, he bears a good deal of resemblance.

Nicolas Machiavel.

34. Political philosophy was not yet a common theme with the writers of Europe, unless so far as the moral duties of princes may have been vaguely touched touched by Guevara or Elyot, or their faults strongly but incidentally adverted to by Erasmus and More. One great luminary, however, appeared at this time, though, as he has been usually deemed, rather a sinister meteor than a benignant star. It is easy to anticipate the name of Nicolas Machiavel. His writings are posthumous, and were first published at Rome early in 1532, with an approbation of the pope. It is certain, however, that the treatise called The Prince was written in 1513, and the Discourses on

[1] Chap. xiv.

Livy about the same time.[1] Few are ignorant that Machiavel filled, for nearly fifteen years, the post of secretary to that government of Florence which was established between the expulsion of the Medici in 1494 and their return in 1512. This was, in fact, the remnant of the ancient oligarchy, which had yielded to the ability and popular influence of Cosmo and Lorenzo de' Medici. Machiavel, having served this party, over which the gonfalonier Pietro Soderini latterly presided with great talents and activity, was naturally involved in their ruin, and, having undergone imprisonment and torture on a charge of conspiracy against the new government, was living in retired poverty when he set himself down to the composition of his two political treatises. The strange theories that have been brought forward to account for The Prince of Machiavel could never be revived after the publication of Ginguéné's history of Italian literature, and the article on Machiavel in the Biographie Universelle, if men had not sometimes a perverse pleasure in seeking refinements after the simple truth has been laid before them.[2] His own language may assure us of what certainly is not very improbable, that his object was to be employed in the service of Julian de' Medici, who was at the head of the state in Florence, almost in the situation of a prince, though without the title; and that he wrote this treatise to recommend himself in his eyes. He had been faithful to the late powers: but these powers were dissolved; and in a republic, a dissolved government, itself the recent creature of force and accident, being destitute of the prejudice in favor of legitimacy, could have little chance of reviving again. It is probable, from the general tenor of Machiavel's writings, that he would rather have lived under a republic than under a prince; but the choice was not left; and it was better, in his judgment, to serve a master usefully for the state, than to waste his life in poverty and insignificance.

His motives in writing The Prince.

35. We may also in candor give Machiavel credit for sincerity in that animated exhortation to Julian which concludes the last chapter of The Prince, where he calls him forth to the noble enterprise of rescuing

[1] There are mutual references in each of these books to the other, from which Ginguéné has reasonably inferred that they were in progress at the same time. Hist. Litt. de l'Italie, viii. 46.

[2] Ginguéné has taken great pains with his account of Machiavel, and I do not know that there is a better. The Biographie Universelle has a good anonymous article. Tiraboschi had treated the subject in a most slovenly manner.

Italy from the barbarians. Twenty years that beautiful land had been the victim of foreign armies, before whom in succession every native state had been humiliated or overthrown. His acute mind easily perceived that no republican institutions would possess stability or concert enough to cast off this yoke. He formed, therefore, the idea of a prince; one raised newly to power, for Italy furnished no hereditary line; one sustained by a native army, for he deprecates the employment of mercenaries; one loved, but feared also, by the many; one to whom, in so magnanimous an undertaking as the liberation of Italy, all her cities would render a willing obedience. It might be, in part, a strain of flattery in which he points out to Julian of Medici a prospect so disproportionate, as we know historically, to his opportunities and his character; yet it was one also perhaps of sanguine fancy and unfeigned hope.

Some of his rules not immoral.

36. None of the explanations assigned for the motives of Machiavel in The Prince is more groundless than one very early suggested, that, by putting the house of Medici on schemes of tyranny, he was artfully luring them to their ruin. Whether this could be reckoned an excuse, may be left to the reader; but we may confidently affirm that it contradicts the whole tenor of that treatise. And, without palliating the worst passages, it may be said that few books have been more misrepresented. It is very far from true that he advises a tyrannical administration of government, or one likely to excite general resistance, even to those whom he thought or rather knew from experience to be placed in the most difficult position for retaining power, by having recently been exalted to it. The prince, he repeatedly says, must avoid all that will render him despicable or odious, especially injury to the property of citizens, or to their honor.[1] This will leave him nothing to guard against but the ambition of a few. Conspiracies, which are of little importance while the people are well affected, become unspeakably dangerous as soon as they are hostile.[2] Their love, therefore, or at least the absence of their hatred, is the basis of the governor's security, and far better than any fortresses.[3] A wise prince will honor the nobility, at the same time that he gives content to the people.[4] If the observance of these maxims is likely to sub-

[1] c. xvii. and xix.

[2] c. xix.

[3] c. xx.: "La miglior fortezza che sia è non essere odiato de' popoli."

[4] c. xix.

vert a ruler's power, he may be presumed to have designed the ruin of the Medici. The first duke in the new dynasty of that house, Cosmo I., lived forty years in the practice of all that Machiavel would have advised, for evil as well as good; and his reign was not insecure.

37. But much of a darker taint is found in The Prince. Good faith, justice, clemency, religion, should be ever in the mouth of the ideal ruler; but he must learn not to fear the discredit of any actions which he finds necessary to preserve his power.[1] In a new government, it is impossible to avoid the charge of cruelty; for new states are always exposed to dangers. Such cruelties perpetrated at the outset and from necessity, "if we may be permitted to speak well of what is evil," may be useful; though, when they become habitual and unnecessary, they are incompatible with the continuance of this species of power.[2] It is best to be both loved and feared; but, if a choice must be made, it should be of the latter. For men are naturally ungrateful, fickle, dissembling, cowardly, and will promise much to a benefactor, but desert him in his need, and will break the bonds of love much sooner than those of fear. But fear does not imply hatred; nor need a prince apprehend that, while he abstains from the properties and the lives of his subjects. Occasions to take the property of others never cease, while those of shedding blood are rare; and, besides, a man will sooner forgive the death of his father than the loss of his inheritance.[3]

But many dangerous.

38. The eighteenth chapter, on the manner in which princes should observe faith, might pass for a satire on their usual violations of it, if the author did not too seriously manifest his approbation of them. The best palliation of this, and of what else has been justly censured in Machiavel, is to be derived from his life and times. These led him to consider every petty government as in a continual state of self-defence against treachery and violence, from its ill-affected citizens, as well as from its ambitious neighbors. It is very difficult to draw the straight line of natural right in such circumstances; and neither perhaps the cool reader of a remote age, nor the secure subject of a well-organized community, is altogether a fair arbiter of what has been done or counselled in days of peril and necessity; relatively, I mean,

Its only palliation.

[1] c xvi, xviii [2] c. viii. [3] c. xvii.

to the persons, not to the objective character of actions. There is certainly a steadiness of moral principle and Christian endurance which tells us that it is better not to exist at all than to exist at the price of virtue; but few indeed of the countrymen and contemporaries of Machiavel had any claim to the practice, whatever they might have to the profession, of such integrity. His crime in the eyes of the world, and it was truly a crime, was to have cast away the veil of hypocrisy, the profession of a religious adherence to maxims which at the same moment were violated.[1]

His Discourses on Livy.

39. The Discourses of Machiavel upon the first books of Livy, though not more celebrated than The Prince, have been better esteemed. Far from being exempt from the same bias in favor of unscrupulous politics, they abound with similar maxims, especially in the third book: but they contain more sound and deep thinking on the spirit of small republics, than could be found in any preceding writer that has descended to us; more, probably, in a practical sense, than the Politics of Aristotle, though they are not so comprehensive. In reasoning upon the Roman government, he is naturally sometimes misled by confidence in Livy; but his own acquaintance with modern Italy was in some measure the corrective that secured him from the errors of ordinary antiquaries.

Their leading principles.

40. These discourses are divided into three books, and contain 143 chapters, with no great regard to arrangement; written probably as reflections occasionally presented themselves to the author's mind. They are built upon one predominant idea, — that, the political and military annals of early Rome having had their counterparts in a great variety of parallel instances which the recent history of Italy furnished, it is safe to draw experimental principles from them, and to expect the recurrence of similar consequences in the same circumstances. Though this reasoning may easily mislead us from an imperfect estimate of the conditions, and does not give a high probability to our anticipations, it is such as those entrusted with the safety of com-

[1] Morhof has observed that all the arts of tyranny which we read in Machiavel had been unfolded by Aristotle; and Ginguéné has shown this, in some measure, from the eleventh chapter of the fifth book of the latter's Politics. He might also have quoted the Œconomics; the second book, however, of which, full of the stratagems and frauds of Dionysius, though nearly of the age of Aristotle, is not genuine. Mitford, with his usual partiality to tyrants (chap. xxxi sect. 8), seems to think them all laudable

nonwealths ought not to neglect. But Machiavel sprinkles hese discourses with thoughts of a more general cast, and often applies a comprehensive knowledge of history, and a ong experience of mankind.

41. Permanence, according to Machiavel, is the great aim of government.[1] In this very common sentiment among writers accustomed to republican forms, although experience of the mischiefs generally attending upon change might lead o it, there is, no doubt, a little of Machiavel's original taint, he reference of political ends to the benefit of the rulers rather than that of the community. But the polity which he seems for the most part to prefer, though he does not speak explicitly, nor always perhaps consistently, is one wherein the people should at least have great weight. In one passage he recommends, like Cicero and Tacitus, the triple form, which endeavors to conciliate the power of a prince with that of a nobility and a popular assembly; as the best means of preventing that cycle of revolutions through which, as he supposes, the simpler institutions would naturally, if not necessarily, pass; from monarchy to aristocracy, from that to democracy, and finally to monarchy again; though, as he observes, it rarely happens that there is time given to complete this cycle, which requires a long course of ages; the community itself, as an independent state, being generally destroyed before the close of the period.[2] But, with his predilection for a republican polity, he yet saw its essential weakness in difficult circumstances; and hence observes that there is no surer way to ruin a democracy than to set it on bold undertakings, which it is sure to misconduct.[3] He has made also the profound and important remark, that states are rarely either formed or reformed, except by one man.[4]

Their use and influence.

42. Few political treatises can even now be read with more advantage than the Discourses of Machiavel; and in proportion as the course of civil society tends farther towards democracy, and especially if it should lead to what seems the inevitable consequence of democracy, a considerable subdivision of independent states, they may acquire an additional value. The absence of all passion; the

[1] l. i. c. ii.

[2] c. ii and vi.

[3] c. liii.

[4] c. 9. Corniani, iv. 70, has attempted to reduce into system the Discourses of Machiavel, which have no regular arrangement, so that nearly the same thoughts recur in different chapters.

continual reference of every public measure to a distinct end; the disregard of vulgar associations with names or persons, render him, though too cold of heart for a very generous reader, a sagacious and useful monitor for any one who can employ the necessary methods of correcting his theorems. He formed a school of subtle reasoners upon political history, which, both in Italy and France, was in vogue for two centuries; and, whatever might be its errors, has hardly been superseded for the better by the loose declamation that some dignify with the name of philosophical politics, and in which we continually find a more flagitious and undisguised abandonment of moral rules for the sake of some idol of a general principle than can be imputed to The Prince of Machiavel.

His History of Florence.

43. Besides these two works, the History of Florence is enough to immortalize the name of Nicolas Machiavel. Seldom has a more giant stride been made in any department of literature than by this judicious, clear, and elegant history: for the preceding historical works, whether in Italy or out of it, had no claims to the praise of classical composition; while this has ranked among the greatest of that order. Machiavel was the first who gave at once a general and a luminous development of great events in their causes and connections, such as we find in the first book of his History of Florence. That view of the formation of European societies, both civil and ecclesiastical, on the ruins of the Roman Empire, though it may seem now to contain only what is familiar, had never been attempted before, and is still, for its conciseness and truth, as good as any that can be read.

Treatises on Venetian government.

44. The little treatises of Giannotti and Contarini on the republic of Venice, being chiefly descriptive of actual institutions, — though the former, a Florentine by birth, sometimes reasons upon and even censures them, — would not deserve notice, except as they display an attention to the workings of a most complicated, and at the same time a most successful, machine. The wonderful permanency, tranquillity, and prosperity of Venice became the admiration of Europe, and especially, as was most natural, of Italy; where she stood alone, without internal usurpation, or foreign interference, strong in wisdom more than in arms, the survivor of many lines of petty princes, and many revolutions of turbulent democracy, which had, on either side of the

Apennine, run their race of guilt and sorrow for several preceding centuries.[1]

45. Calvin alone, of the reformers in this period, has touched upon political government as a theme of rational discussion; though he admits that it is needless to dispute which is the best form of polity, since private men have not the right of altering that under which they live. The change from monarchy to despotism, he says, is easy; nor is that from aristocracy to the dominion of a few much more difficult; but nothing is so apt to follow as sedition from a popular regimen. But, upon the whole, he considers an aristocratic form to be far better than the other two, on account of the vices and infirmity of human nature.[2]

Calvin's political principles.

SECT. III. 1501–1510.

Jurisprudence.

46. UNDER the name jurisprudence, we are not yet to seek for writings on that high department of moral philosophy, which treats of the rules of universal justice, by which positive legislation and courts of judicature ought to be directed. Whatever of this kind may appear in works of this period arises incidentally out of their subject, and does not constitute their essence. According to the primary and established sense of the word, especially on the Continent, jurisprudence is the science of the Roman law, and is seldom applied to any other positive system, but least of all to the law of nature. Yet the application of this study has been too extensive in Europe, and the renown of its chief writers too high, to admit of our passing wholly over this department of literature, as we do some technical and professional subjects.

Jurisprudence confined to Roman law.

47. The civil or Roman law is comprehended in four leading divisions (besides some later than the time of Justinian), very unequal in length, but altogether

The laws not well arranged.

[1] These are both published in Grævius, Thesaur. Antiq. Italiæ. See, too, Ginguéné, viii. 186.

[2] Calv. Inst., l. iv. c. 20, § 8.

forming that multifarious collection usually styled the Corpus Juris Civilis. As this has sometimes been published in a single, though a vast and closely printed volume, it may seem extraordinary, that by means of arranged indexes, marginal references, and similar resources, it was not, soon after it came into use as a standard authority, or, at least, soon after the invention of printing, reduced into a less disorderly state than its present disposition exhibits. But the labors of the older jurists, in accumulating glosses or short marginal interpretations, were more calculated to multiply than to disentangle the intricacies of the Pandects.

Adoption of the entire system.

48. It is at first sight more wonderful, that many nations of Europe, instead of selecting the most valuable portion of the civil law, as directory to their own tribunals, should have bestowed decisive authority on that entire unwieldy body which bore the name of Justinian; laws which they could not understand, and which, in great measure, must, if understood, have been perceived to clash with the new order of human society. But the homage paid to the Roman name; the previous reception of the Theodosian code in the same countries; the vague notion of the Italians, artfully encouraged by one party, that the Conrads and Frederics were really successors of the Theodosii and Justinians; the frequent clearness, acuteness, and reasonableness of the decisions of the old lawyers which fill the Pandects; the immense difficulty of separating the less useful portion, and of obtaining public authority for a new system; the deference, above all, to great names, which cramped every effort of the human mind in the middle ages, — will sufficiently account for the adoption of a jurisprudence so complicated, uncertain, unintelligible, and ill-fitted to the times.

Utility of general learning to lawyers.

49. The portentous ignorance of the earlier jurists in every thing that could aid their textual explanations has been noticed in the first chapter of this volume. This could not hold out long after the revival of learning. Budæus, in his Observations on the Pandects, was the first to furnish better verbal interpretations; but his philological erudition was not sustained by that knowledge of the laws themselves which nothing but long labor could impart.[1] Such a knowledge of the Latin language as,

[1] Gravina, Origines Jur. Civ., p. 211.

even after the revival of letters, was given in the schools, or, we may add, as is now obtained by those who are counted learned among us, is by no means sufficient for the understanding those Roman lawyers, whose short decisions, or, as we should call them, opinions, occupy the fifty books of the Pandects. They had not only a technical terminology, as is perhaps necessary in professional usage, but many words and phrases not merely technical occur, as to the names and notions of things, which the classical authors, especially such as are commonly read, do not contain. Yet these writers of antiquity, when diligently pursued, throw much light upon jurisprudence; they assist conjecture, if they do not afford proof, as to the meaning of words; they explain allusions; they connect the laws with their temporary causes or general principles; and if they seem a little to lead us astray from the great object of jurisprudence, the adjudication of right, it was still highly important, in the conditions that Europe had imposed upon herself, to ascertain what it was that she had chosen to obey.

Alciati: his reform of law.

50. Ulric Zasius, a professor at Friburg, and Garcia d'Erzilla, whose Commentaries were printed in 1515, should have the credit, according to Andrès, of leading the way to a more elegant jurisprudence.[1] The former of these is known, in some measure, as a scholar and a correspondent of Erasmus: for the latter, I have to depend on the testimony of his countryman. But the general voice of Europe has always named Andrew Alciati, of Milan, as the restorer of the Roman law. He taught, from the year 1518 to his death in 1550, in the universities of Avignon, Milan, Bourges, Paris, and Bologna. Literature became with him the handmaid of law: the historians of Rome, her antiquaries, her orators and poets, were called upon to elucidate the obsolete words and obscure allusions of the Pandects; to which — the earlier as well as the more valuable and extensive portion of the civil law — this method of classical interpretation is chiefly applicable. Alciati had another advantage, denied to his predecessors of the middle ages, in the possession of the Byzantine jurists; with whom, says Gravina, the learn-

1 Andrès, xvi. 143. Savigny agrees with Andrès as to the merits of Zazius, and observes that the revival of the study of the laws in their original sources, instead of the commentators, had been announced by several signs before the sixteenth century. Ambrogio Traversari had recommended this, and Lebrixa wrote against the errors of Accursius, though in a superficial manner. Gesch. des Römischen Rechts, vi. 364.

ing of Roman law had been preserved in a more perfect state amidst other vestiges of the empire, and, while almost extinquished in Italy by the barbarians, had been in daily usage at Constantinople down to its capture. Alciati was the first who taught the lawyers to write with purity and elegance. Erasmus has applied to him the eulogy of Cicero on Scævola, that he was the most jurisprudent of orators, and the most eloquent of lawyers. But he deserved also the higher praise of sweeping away the rubbish of conflicting glosses, which had so confounded the students by their contrary subtilties, that it had become a practice to count, instead of weighing, their authorities. It has been regretted, that he made little use of philosophy in the exposition of law; but this could not have been attempted in the sixteenth century without the utmost danger of misleading the interpreter.[1]

Opposition to him.

51. The practical lawyers, whose prejudices were nourished by their interests, conspired with the professors of the old school to clamor against the introduction of literature into jurisprudence. Alciati was driven sometimes from one university to another by their opposition; but more frequently his restless disposition, and his notorious desire of gain, were the causes of his migrations. They were the means of diffusing a more liberal course of studies in France as well as Italy, and especially in the great legal university of Bourges. He stood not, however, alone in scattering the flowers of polite literature over the thorny brakes of jurisprudence. An eminent Spaniard, Antonio Agustino, might perhaps be placed almost on a level with him. The first work of Agustino, Emendationes Juris Civilis, was published in 1544. Andrès, seldom deficient in praising his compatriots, pronounces such an eulogy on the writings of Agustino, as to find no one but Cujacius worthy of being accounted his equal, if indeed he does not give the preference in genius and learning to the older writer.[2] Gravina is less diffusely panegyrical; and in fact it is certain that Agustino, though a lawyer of great erudition and intelligence, has been eclipsed by those for whom he prepared the way.

Agustino.

[1] Bayle, art. "Alciati;" Gravina, p. 206; Tiraboschi, ix 115; Corniani, v. 57.
[2] Vol. xvi. p. 148.

CHAPTER VIII.

HISTORY OF THE LITERATURE OF TASTE IN EUROPE FROM 1520 TO 1550.

SECT. I. 1520–1550.

Poetry in Italy — In Spain and Portugal — In France and Germany — In England — Wyatt and Surrey — Latin Poetry.

1. THE singular grace of Ariosto's poem had not less distinguished it than his fertility of invention, and brilliancy of language. For the Italian poetry, since the days of Petrarch, with the exception of Lorenzo and Politian, the boasts of Florence, had been very deficient in elegance; the sonnets and odes of the fifteenth century, even those written near its close, by Tibaldeo, Serafino d'Aquila, Benivieni, and other now obscure names, though the list of poets in Crescimbeni will bè found very long, are hardly mentioned by the generality of critics but for the purpose of censure; while Boiardo, who deserved most praise for bold and happy inventions, lost much of it through an unpolished and inharmonious style. In the succeeding period, the faults of the Italian school were entirely opposite; in Bembo, and those who, by their studious and servile imitation of one great master, were called Petrarchists, there was an elaborate sweetness, a fastidious delicacy, a harmony of sound, which frequently served as an excuse for coldness of imagination, and poverty of thought. "As the too careful imitation of Cicero," says Tiraboschi, "caused Bembo to fall into an affected elegance in his Latin style; so in his Italian poetry, while he labors to restore the manner of Petrarch, he displays more of art than of natural genius. Yet by banishing the rudeness of former poetry, and pointing out the right path, he was of

Poetry of Bembo.

no small advantage to those who knew how to imitate his excellences, and avoid his faults."[1]

Its beauties and defects.

2. The chief care of Bembo was to avoid the unpolished lines which deformed the poetry of the fifteenth century in the eyes of one so exquisitely sensible to the charms of diction. It is from him that the historians of Italian literature date the revival of the Petrarcan elegance; of which a foreigner, unless conversant with the language in all its varieties, can hardly judge; though he may perceive the want of original conception, and the monotony of conventional phrases, which is too frequently characteristic of the Italian sonnet. Yet the sonnets of Bembo on the death of his Morosina, the mother of his children, display a real tenderness not unworthy of his master; and the canzone on that of his brother has obtained not less renown; though Tassoni, a very fastidious critic, has ridiculed its centonism, or studious incorporation of lines from Petrarch; a practice which the habit of writing Latin poetry, wherein it should be sparingly employed, but not wholly avoided, would naturally encourage.[2]

Character of Italian poetry.

3. The number of versifiers whom Italy produced in the sixteenth century was immensely great. Crescimbeni gives a list of eighty earlier than 1550, whom he selects from many hundred ever-forgotten names. By far the larger proportion of these confined themselves to the sonnet and the canzone or ode; and the theme is generally love, though they sometimes change it to religion. A conventional phraseology, an interminable repetition of the beauties and coldness of perhaps an ideal, certainly to us an unknown, mistress, run through these productions; which so much resemble each other as sometimes to suggest to any one who reads the Sceltas, which bring together many extracts from these poets, no other parallel than that of the hooting of owls in concert: a sound melancholy and not unpleasing to all ears in its way; but monotonous, unintellectual, and manifesting as little real sorrow or sentiment in the bird as these compositions do in the poet.[3]

4. A few exceptions may certainly be made. Alamanni,

[1] Vol. x. p. 3.

[2] Tiraboschi, ibid.; Corinani, iv. 102.

[3] Muratori himself observes the tantalizing habit in which sonneteers indulge themselves, of threatening to die for love, which never comes to any thing; "quella volgare smania che mostrano gl' amanti di voler morire, e che tante volte s' ode bocca loro, ma non mai viene ad effetto."

though the sonnet is not his peculiar line of strength, and though he often follows the track of Petrarch with almost servile imitation, could not, with his powerful genius, but raise himself above the common level. His Lygura Pianta, a Genoese lady, the heroine of many sonnets, is the shadow of Laura; but, when he turns to the calamities of Italy and his own, that stern sound is heard again that almost reminds us of Dante and Alfieri. The Italian critics, to whom we must of course implicitly defer as to the grace and taste of their own writers, speak well of Molza, and some other of the smaller poets, though they are seldom exempt from the general defects above mentioned. But none does Crescimbeni so much extol as a poetess, in every respect the most eminent of her sex in Italy, the widow of the Marquis of Pescara, Vittoria Colonna, surnamed, he says, by the public voice, the divine. The rare virtues and consummate talents of this lady were the theme of all Italy, in that brilliant age of her literature; and her name is familiar to the ordinary reader at this day. The canzone dedicated to the memory of her illustrious husband is worthy of both.[1]

Alamanni.

Vittoria Colonna.

5. The satires of Ariosto, seven in number, and composed in the Horatian manner, were published after his death in 1534. Tiraboschi places them at the head of that class of poetry. The reader will find an analysis of these satires, with some extracts, in Ginguéné.[2] The twelve satires of Alamanni, one of the Florentine exiles, of which the first edition is dated in 1532, though of earlier publication than those of Ariosto, indicate an acquaintance with them. They are to one another as Horace and Juvenal, and as their fortunes might lead us to expect: one gay, easy, full of the best form of Epicurean philosophy, cheerfulness, and content in the simpler enjoyments of life; the other ardent, scornful, unsparing, declamatory, a hater of vice, and no great lover of mankind, pouring forth his moral wrath in no feeble strain. We have seen in another place his animadversions on the court of Rome; nor does any thing in Italy

Satires of Ariosto and Alamanni.

1 Crescimbeni della volgar Poesia, vols. ii. and iii. For the character of Vittoria Colonna, see ii. 350. Roscoe (Leo X., iii. 314) thinks her canzone on her husband in no respect inferior to that of Bembo on his brother. It is rather by a stretch of chronology that this writer reckons Vittoria, Berni, and several more, among the poets of Leo's age.

2 ix. 100-129; Corniani, iv. 55. In one passage of the second satire, Ariosto assumes a tone of higher dignity than Horace ever ventured, and inveighs against the Italian courts in the spirit of his rival, Alamanni.

escape his resentment.[1] The other poems of Alamanni are of a very miscellaneous description; eclogues, little else than close imitations of Theocritus and Virgil, elegies, odes, hymns, psalms, fables, tragedies, and what were called *selve*, a name for all unclassed poetry.

Alamanni. 6. Alamanni's epic, or rather romantic poem, the Avarchide, is admitted by all critics to be a work of old age, little worthy of his name. But his poem on agriculture, La Coltivazione, has been highly extolled. A certain degree of languor seems generally to hang on Italian blank verse, and in didactic poetry it is not likely to be overcome.

Rucellai. The Bees of Rucellai is a poem written with exquisite sweetness of style; but the critics have sometimes forgotten to mention that it is little else than a free translation from the fourth Georgic.[2] No one has ever pretended to rescue from the charge of dulness and insipidity

Trissino. the epic poem of the father of blank verse, Trissino, on the liberation of Italy from the Goths by Belisarius. It is, of all long poems that are remembered at all, the most unfortunate in its reputation.

Berni. 7. A very different name is that of Berni, partly known by his ludicrous poetry, which has given that style the appellation of Poesia Bernesca, rather on account of his excellence than originality, for nothing is so congenial to the Italians,[3] but far more by his *ri-faccimento*, or remoulding of the poem of Boiardo. The Orlando Innamorato, an ill-written poem, especially to Tuscan ears, had been encumbered by the heavy continuation of Agostini. Yet, if its own intrinsic beauties of invention would not have secured it from oblivion, the vast success of the Orlando Furioso, itself only a continuation, and borrowing most of its characters from Boiardo's poem, must have made it impossible for Italians of any curiosity to neglect the primary source of so much delight.

[1] The following lines, which conclude the twelfth and last satire, may serve as a specimen of Alamanni's declamatory tone of invective, and his bitter attacks on Rome, whom he is addressing:—

"O chi vedesse il ver, vedrebbe come
Più disnor tu, che 'l tuo Luther Martino
Porti a te stessa, e piu gravose some;
Non la Germania, nò; ma l' ocio, il vino,
Avarizia, ambition, lussuria e gola,
Ti mena al fin, che già veggiam vicino.
Non pur questo dico io non Francia sola,
Non pur la Spagna, tutta Italia ancora
Che ti tien d' heresia, di vizi scuola.
E che nol crede, ne dimandi ogn' ora
Urbin, Ferrara, l' Orso, et la Colonna,
La Marca, il Romagnuol, ma più che plora
Per te servendo, che fù d'altri donna."

[2] Roscoe's Leo, iii. 351; Tiraboschi, x. 85. Algarotti and Corniani (v. 116), who quotes him, do not esteem the poem of Rucellai highly.

[3] Corniani, iv. 252; Roscoe, iii. 323.

Berni, therefore, undertook the singular office of writing over again the Orlando Innamorato; preserving the sense of almost every stanza, though every stanza was more or less altered, and inserting nothing but a few introductory passages, in the manner of Ariosto, to each canto.[1] The genius of Berni, playful, satirical, flexible, was admirably fitted to perform this labor: the rude Lombardisms of the lower Po gave way to the racy idiom of Florence; and the Orlando Innamorato has descended to posterity as the work of two minds, remarkably combined in this instance: the sole praise of invention, circumstance, description, and very frequently that of poetical figure and sentiment, belonging to Boiardo; that of style, in the peculiar and limited use of the word, to Berni. The character of the poem, as thus adorned, has sometimes been misconceived. Though Berni is almost always sprightly, he is not, in this romance, a burlesque or buffoon poet.[2] I once heard Foscolo prefer him to Ariosto. A foreigner, not so familiar with the peculiarities of language, would probably think his style less brilliant and less pellucid; and it is in execution alone that he claims to be considered as an original poet. The Orlando Innamorato was also remoulded by Domenichi in 1545; but the excellence of Berni has caused this feeble production to be nearly passed over by the Italian critics.[3]

[1] The first edition of the Rifaccimento is in 1541, and the second in 1542. In that of 1545, the first eighty-two stanzas are very different from those that correspond in former editions: some that follow are suspected not to be genuine. It seems that we have no edition on which we can wholly depend. No edition of Berni appeared from 1545 to 1725, though Domenichi was printed several times. This reformer of Boiardo did not alter the text nearly so much as Berni. Panizzi, vol. ii.

[2] Tiraboschi, vii. 195, censures Berni for "motti e racconti troppo liberi ed empi, che vi ha inseriti." Ginguéné exclaims, as well he may, against this imputation. Berni has inserted no stories; and, unless it were the few stanzas against monastic hypocrisy that remain at the head of the twentieth canto, it is hard to say what Tiraboschi meant by impieties. But though Tiraboschi must have read Berni, he has here chosen to copy Zeno, who talks of "il poema di Boiardo, rifatto dal Berni, e di serio trasformato in ridicolo, e di onesto in iscandoloso, e però giustamente dannato dalla chiesa." — (Fontanini, p. 273.) Zeno, even more surely than Tiraboschi, was perfectly acquainted with Berni's poem: how could he give so false a character of it? Did he copy some older writer? and why? It seems hard not to think that some suspicion of Berni's bias towards Protestantism had engendered a prejudice against his poem, which remained when the cause had been forgotten, as it certainly was in the days of Zeno and Tiraboschi.

[3] "The ingenuity," says Mr. Panizzi, "with which Berni finds a resemblance between distant objects, and the rapidity with which he suddenly connects the most remote ideas; the solemn manner in which he either alludes to ludicrous events or utters an absurdity; the air of innocence and naiveté with which he presents remarks full of shrewdness, and knowledge of the world; that peculiar *bonhommie* with which he seems to look kindly and at the same time unwillingly on human errors or wickedness; the keen irony which he uses with so much appearance of simplicity, and aversion to bitterness; the seeming singleness of heart with which he appears anxious to excuse men and actions, at the very moment that he is most inveterate in exposing them, — these are the chief elements of Berni's poetry. Add to this the style, the loftiness of the verse contrasting

8. Spain now began to experience one of those revolutions in fashionable taste which await the political changes of nations. Her native poetry, whether Castilian or Valencian, had characteristics of its own, that placed it in a different region from the Italian. The short heroic, amatory, or devotional songs, which the Peninsular dialects were accustomed to exhibit, were too ardent, too hyperbolical for a taste which, if not correctly classical, was at least studious of a grace not easily compatible with extravagance. But the continual intercourse of the Spaniards with Italy, partly subject to their sovereign, and the scene of his wars, accustomed their nobles to relish the charms of a sister language, less energetic, but more polished, than their own. Two poets, Boscan and Garcilasso de la Vega, brought from Italy the softer beauties of amorous poetry, embodied in the regular sonnet, which had hitherto been little employed in the Peninsula. These poems seem not to have been printed till 1543, when both Boscan and Garcilasso were dead, and their new school had already met with both support and opposition at the court of Valladolid. The national character is not entirely lost in these poets: love still speaks with more impetuous ardor, with more plaintive sorrow, than in the contemporary Italians; but the restraints of taste and reason are perceived to control his voice. An eclogue of Garcilasso, called Salicio and Nemoroso, is pronounced by the Spanish critics to be one of the finest works in their language. It is sadder than the lament of saddest nightingales. We judge of all such poetry differently in the progressive stages of life.

Spanish poets.

Boscan. Garcilasso.

9. Diego Mendoza, one of the most remarkable men for variety of talents whom Spain has produced, ranks with Boscan and Garcilasso as a reformer of Castilian poetry. His character as a soldier, as the severe governor of Siena, as the haughty minister of Charles at the

Mendoza.

with the frivolity of the argument, the gravest conception expressed in the most homely manner; the seasonable use of strange metaphors and of similes sometimes sublime, and for this very reason the more laughable, when considered with relation to the subject which they are intended to illustrate, form the most remarkable features of his style." — p. 120.

"Any candid Italian scholar who will peruse the Rifaccimento of Berni with attention will be compelled to admit, that, although many parts of the poem of Boiardo have been improved in that work, such has not always been the case; and will, moreover, be convinced that some parts of the Rifaccimento, besides those suspected in former times, are evidently either not written by Berni, or have not received from him, if they be his, such corrections as to be worthy of their author." — p. 141. Mr. P. shows in several passages his grounds for this suspicion.

court of Rome and the council of Trent, is notorious in history.[1] His epistles, in an Horatian style, full of a masculine and elevated philosophy, though deficient in harmony and polish, are preferred to his sonnets; a species of composition where these faults are more perceptible; and for which, at least in the style then popular, the stern understanding of Mendoza seems to have been ill adapted. "Though he composed," says Bouterwek, "in the Italian manner, with less facility than Boscan and Garcilasso, he felt more correctly than they or any other of his countrymen the difference between the Spanish and Italian languages, with respect to their capabilities for versification. The Spanish admits of none of those pleasing elisions, which, particularly when terminating vowels are omitted, render the mechanism of Italian versification so easy, and enable the poet to augment or diminish the number of syllables according to his pleasure; and this difference in the two languages renders the composition of a Spanish sonnet a difficult task. Still more does the Spanish language seem hostile to the soft termination of a succession of feminine rhymes; for the Spanish poet, who adopts this rule of the Italian sonnet, is compelled to banish from his rhymes all infinitives of verbs, together with a whole host of sonorous substantives and adjectives. Mendoza, therefore, availed himself of the use of masculine rhymes in his sonnets; but this metrical license was strongly censured by all partisans of the Italian style. Nevertheless, had he given to his sonnets more of the tenderness of Petrarch, it is probable that they would have found imitators. Some of them, indeed, may be considered as successful productions; and, throughout all, the language is correct and noble."[2]

10. The lyric poems of Mendoza, written in the old national style, tacitly improved and polished, are preferred by the Spaniards to his other works. Many of them are printed in the Romancero General. Saa di Miranda, though a Portuguese, has written much in Castilian, as well as in his own language. Endowed by nature with the melancholy temperament akin to poetic sensibility, he fell readily into the pastoral strain, for which his own language is said to be peculiarly formed. The greater and better part of

Saa di Miranda.

[1] Sadolet, in one of his epistles dated 1532 (lib. vi p. 309, edit. 1554), gives an interesting character of Mendoza, then young, who had visited him at Carpentras on his way to Rome; a journey undertaken solely for the sake of learning.

[2] P. 198.

his eclogues, however, are in Castilian. He is said to have chosen the latter language for imagery, and his own for reflection.[1] Of this poet, as well as of his Castilian contemporaries, the reader will find a sufficient account in Bouterwek and Sismondi.

Ribeyro.

11. Portugal, however, produced one who did not abandon her own soft and voluptuous dialect, Ribeyro; the first distinguished poet she could boast. His strains are chiefly pastoral, the favorite style of his country, and breathe that monotonous and excessive melancholy, with which it requires some congenial emotion of our own to sympathise. A romance of Ribeyro, Menina e Moça, is one of the earliest among the few specimens of noble prose which we find in that language. It is said to be full of obscure allusions to real events in the author's life, and cannot be read with much interest; but some have thought that it is the prototype of the Diana of Montemayor, and the whole school of pastoral romance, which was afterwards admired in Europe for an entire century. We have, however, seen that the Arcadia of Sannazzaro has the priority; and I am not aware that there is any specific distinction between that romance and this of Ribeyro. It may be here observed, that Ribeyro should, in strictness, have been mentioned before; his eclogues seem to have been written, and possibly published, before the death of Emanuel in 1521. The romance, however, was a later production.[2]

French poetry.

12. The French versifiers of the age of Francis I. are not few. It does not appear that they rise above the level of the three preceding reigns, Louis XI., Charles VIII., and Louis XII.; some of them mistaking insipid allegory for the creations of fancy, some tamely describing the events of their age; others, with rather more spirit, satirizing the vices of mankind, and especially of the clergy; while many, in little songs, expressed their ideal love with more perhaps of conventional gallantry than passion or tenderness,[3] yet with some of those light and graceful touches which distinguish this style of French poetry. Clement Marot ranks far higher.

Marot.

The psalms of Marot, though famous in their day, are among his worst performances. His distinguishing

[1] Bouterwek, p. 240; Sismondi.

[2] Bouterwek, Hist. of Portuguese Liter., p. 24; Sismondi, iv. 280.

[3] Goujet, Bibliothèque Française, vols. x. and xi. *passim;* Auguis, Recueil des anciens Poètes Français, vols. ii. and iii.

xcellence is a *naïveté*, or pretended simplicity, of which it is ıe highest praise to say that it was the model of La Fontaine. 'his style of humor, than which nothing is more sprightly r diverting, seems much less indigenous among ourselves, if e may judge by our older literature, than either among the 'rench or Italians.

Their metrical structure.

13. In the days of Marot, French poetry had not put on all s chains. He does not observe the regular alternaon of masculine and feminine rhymes, nor scruple use the open vowel, the suppression of a mute *e* efore a consonant in scanning the verse, the carrying on the nse without a pause to the middle of the next line. These emishes, as later usage accounts them, are common to Marot ith all his contemporaries. In return, they dealt much in tificial schemes of recurring words or lines, as the chant oyal, where every stanza was to be in the same rhyme and to onclude with the same verse; or the rondeau, a very popular pecies of metre long afterwards, wherein two or three initial ords were repeated at the refrain or close of every stanza.[1]

German poetry

14. The poetical and imaginative spirit of Germany, subıed as it had long been, was never so weak as in ıis century. Though we cannot say that this overty of genius was owing to the Reformation, it is certain ıat the Reformation aggravated very much in this sense the ational debasement. The controversies were so scholastic their terms, so sectarian in their character, so incapable of liance with any warmth of soul, that, so far as their influıce extended, and that was to a large part of the educated asses, they must have repressed every poet, had such apeared, by rendering the public insensible to his superiority. 'he Meister-singers were sufficiently prosaic in their original onstitution: they neither produced, nor perhaps would have ıffered to exhibit itself, any real excellence in poetry. But ıey became in the sixteenth century still more rigorous in ıeir requisitions of a mechanical conformity to rule; while the same time they prescribed a new code of law to the ersifier, — that of theological orthodoxy. Yet one man, of ıore brilliant fancy and powerful feeling than the est, Hans Sachs, the shoemaker of Nuremberg, ands out from the crowd of these artisans. Most conspicu-

Hans Sachs.

[1] Goujet, Bibl. Française, xi. 36; Gailrd, Vie de François I., vii. 20; Pasquier, Recherches de la France, l. vii. c. 5; Auguis, vol. iii.

ous as a dramatic writer, his copious muse was silent in r line of verse. Heinsius accounts the bright period of Ha Sachs's literary labors to have been from 1530 to 153 though he wrote much both sooner and after that time. H poems of all kinds are said to have exceeded six thousan but not more than one fourth of them are in print. In th facility of composition, he is second only to Lope de Veg and it must be presumed, that, uneducated, unread, accustom to find his public in his own class, so wonderful a fluency w accompanied by no polish, and only occasionally by gleams c vigor and feeling. The German critics are divided concer ing the genius of Hans Sachs: Wieland and Goethe ga him lustre at one time by their eulogies; but, these havi been as exaggerated as the contempt of a former generatio the place of the honest and praiseworthy shoemaker seems n likely to be fixed very high; and there has not been demar enough for his works, some of which are very scarce, to e courage their republication.[1]

German hymns.

15. The Germans, constitutionally a devout people, we never so much so as in this first age of Protestantis And this, in combination with their musical temper ment, displayed itself in the peculiar line of hymns. No oth nation has so much of this poetry. At the beginning of t eighteenth century, the number of religious songs was reckon at 33,000, and that of their authors at 500. Those of Luth have been more known than the rest; they are hard and rud but impressive and deep. But this poetry, essentially r strained in its flight, could not develop the creative powe of genius.[2]

Theuerdanks of Pfintzing.

16. Among the few poems of this age, none has been celebrated as the Theuerdanks of Melchior Pfintzin secretary to the Emperor Maximilian; a poem at o time attributed to the master, whose praises it recor instead of the servant. This singular work, published o ginally in 1517, with more ornament of printing and de neation than was usual, is an allegory, with scarce any spi of invention or language; wherein the knight Theuerdank and his adventures in seeking the marriage of the Prince Ehrreich, represent the memorable union of Maximilian wi the heiress of Burgundy. A small number of German poe

[1] Heinsius, iv 150; Bouterwek, ix. 381; Retrospective Review, vol. x.
[2] Bouterwek; Heinsius.

e commemorated by Bouterwek and Heinsius, superioı no ubt in ability to Pfintzing, but so obscure in our eyes, and little extolled by their countrymen, that we need only refer their pages.

English poetry: Lyndsay.

17. In the earlier part of this period of thirty years, we can d very little English poetry. Sir David Lyndsay, accomplished gentleman and scholar of Scotland, cels his contemporary Skelton in such qualities, not in fertility of genius. Though inferior to Dunbar in vidness of imagination and in elegance of language, he shows more reflecting and philosophical mind; and certainly his tire upon James V. and his court is more poignant than the her's panegyric upon the Thistle. But, in the ordinary style his versification, he seems not to rise much above the prosaic ıd tedious rhymers of the fifteenth century. His descriptions e as circumstantial without selection as theirs; and his nguage, partaking of a ruder dialect, is still more removed om our own. The poems of Lyndsay are said by Herbert have been printed in 1540, and would be among the first-uits of the Scottish press; but one of these, the Complaint the Papingo, had appeared in London two years before.[1] yndsay's poetry is said to have contributed to the Reforma-on in Scotland; in which, however, he is but like many poets his own and preceding times. The clergy were an inex-austible theme of bitter reproof.

Wyatt and Surrey.

18. "In the latter end of King Henry VIII.'s reign," says uttenham in his Art of Poesie, "sprung up a new ompany of courtly makers, of whom Sir Thomas Vyatt the elder, and Henry, Earl of Surrey, were the two hieftains, who having travailed into Italy, and there tasted the weet and stately measures and style of the Italian poesie, as ovices newly crept out of the schools of Dante, Ariosto, and etrarch, they greatly polished our rude and homely manner f vulgar poesie, from that it had bene before, and for that ause may justly be sayd the first reformers of our English neeteı and stile. In the same time or not long after was the ord Nicolas Vaux, a man of much facilitie in vulgar ma-ings."[2] The poems of Sir Thomas Wyatt, who died in 1544, nd of the Earl of Surrey, executed in 1547, were first pub-

1 [Pinkerton, however, denies that there s any genuine Scots edition before 1568.— 842.]

2 Puttenham, book i. ch. 31.

lished in 1557, with a few by other hands, in a scarce litt book called Tottel's Miscellanies. They were, however, in a probability, known before; and it seems necessary to mentic them in this period, as they mark an important epoch in Eng lish literature.

19. Wyatt and Surrey — for we may best name them in th order of time, rather than of civil or poetical rank — have ha recently the good fortune to be recommended by an editor c extensive acquaintance with literature, and of still superic taste. It will be a gratification to read the following compariso of the two poets, which I extract the more willingly that it found in a publication somewhat bulky and expensive for th mass of readers.

20. "They were men whose minds may be said to hav been cast in the same mould; for they differ only i those minuter shades of character which always mus exist in human nature; shades of difference so infi nitely varied, that there never were and never will be two per sons in all respects alike. In their love of virtue and thei instinctive hatred and contempt of vice, in their freedom fron personal jealousy, in their thirst after knowledge and intellec tual improvement, in nice observation of nature, promptitud to action, intrepidity and fondness for romantic enterprise, in magnificence and liberality, in generous support of others an high-spirited neglect of themselves, in constancy in friendship and tender susceptibility of affections of a still warmer nature and in every thing connected with sentiment and principle they were one and the same; but, when those qualities branch out into particulars, they will be found in some respects to differ.

Dr. Nott's character of them.

21. "Wyatt had a deeper and more accurate penetration into the characters of men than Surrey had; hence arises the difference in their satires. Surrey, in his satire against the citizens of London, deals only in reproach; Wyatt, in his abounds with irony, and those nice touches of ridicule which make us ashamed of our faults, and therefore often silently effect amendment.[1] Surrey's observation of nature was minute

[1] Wyatt's best poem in this style, the Epistle to John Poins, is a very close imitation of the tenth satire of Alamanni: it is abridged, but every thought and every verse in the English is taken from the Italian. Dr. Nott has been aware of this; but it certainly detracts a leaf from the laurel of Wyatt, though he has translated well.

The lighter poems of Wyatt are more unequal than those of Surrey; but his Ode to his Lute does not seem inferior to any production of his noble competitor. The sonnet in which he intimates his se-

but he directed it towards the works of nature in general, and the movements of the passions, rather than to the foibles and characters of men; hence it is that he excels in the description of rural objects, and is always tender and pathetic. In Wyatt's Complaint we hear a strain of manly grief which commands attention, and we listen to it with respect for the sake of him that suffers. Surrey's distress is painted in such natural terms that we make it our own, and recognize in his sorrows emotions which we are conscious of having felt ourselves.

22. "In point of taste and perception of propriety in composition, Surrey is more accurate and just than Wyatt: he therefore seldom either offends with conceits or wearies with repetition; and, when he imitates other poets, he is original as well as pleasing. In his numerous translations from Petrarch, he is seldom inferior to his master; and he seldom improves upon him. Wyatt is almost always below the Italian, and frequently degrades a good thought by expressing it so that it is hardly recognizable. Had Wyatt attempted a translation of Virgil, as Surrey did, he would have exposed himself to unavoidable failure."[1]

23. To remarks so delicate in taste and so founded in knowledge, I should not venture to add much of my own. Something, however, may generally be admitted to modify the ardent panegyrics of an editor. Those who, after reading this brilliant passage, should turn for the first time to the poems either of Wyatt or of Surrey, might think the praise too unbounded, and, in some respects perhaps, not appropriate. It seems to be now ascertained, after sweeping away a host of foolish legends and traditionary prejudices, that the Geraldine of Surrey, Lady Elizabeth Fitzgerald, was a child of thirteen, for whom his passion, if such it is to be called, began several years after his own marriage.[2] But in fact there is more of the conventional tone of amorous songs, than of real emotion, in Surrey's poetry. The

Perhaps rather exaggerated.

"Easy sighs, such as men draw in love,"

cret passion for Anne Boleyn, whom he describes under the allegory of a doe bearing on her collar, —

"Noli me tangere: I Cæsar's am,"

is remarkable for more than the poetry, though that is pleasing. It may be doubtful whether Anne were yet queen: but, in one of Wyatt's latest poems, he seems to allude penitentially to his passion for her.

1 Nott's edition of Wyatt and Surrey, ii. 156.

2 Surrey was born about 1518; married Lady Frances Vere in 1535; fell in love, if so it was, in 1541, with Geraldine, who was born in 1528.

are not like the deep sorrows of Petrarch, or the fiery transports of the Castilians.

24. The taste of this accomplished man is more striking than his poetical genius. He did much for his own country and his native language. The versification of Surrey differs very considerably from that of his predecessors. He introduced, as Dr. Nott says, a sort of involution into his style, which gives an air of dignity, and remoteness from common life. It was, in fact, borrowed from the license of Italian poetry, which our own idiom has rejected. He avoids pedantic words, forcibly obtruded from the Latin, of which our earlier poets, both English and Scots, had been ridiculously fond. The absurd epithets of Hoccleve, Lydgate, Dunbar, and Douglas, are applied equally to the most different things, so as to show that they annexed no meaning to them. Surrey rarely lays an unnatural stress on final syllables, merely as such, which they would not receive in ordinary pronunciation; another usual trick of the school of Chaucer. His words are well chosen and well arranged.

Surrey improves our versification.

25. Surrey is the first who introduced blank verse into our English poetry. It has been doubted whether it had been previously employed in Italian, save in tragedy; for the poems of Alamanni and Rucellai were not published before many of our noble poet's compositions had been written. Dr. Nott, however, admits that Boscan and other Spanish poets had used it. The translation by Surrey of the second book of the Æneid, in blank verse, is among the chief of his productions. No one had, before his time, known how to translate or imitate with appropriate expression. But the structure of his verse is not very harmonious, and the sense is rarely carried beyond the line.

Introduces blank verse.

26. If we could rely on a theory, advanced and ably supported by his editor, Surrey deserves the still more conspicuous praise of having brought about a great revolution in our poetical numbers. It had been supposed to be proved by Tyrwhitt, that Chaucer's lines are to be read metrically, in ten or eleven syllables, like the Italian, and, as I apprehend, the French of his time. For this purpose it is necessary to presume that many terminations, now mute, were syllabically pronounced; and, where verses prove refractory after all our endeavors, Tyrwhitt has no scruple in declaring them corrupt. It may be added, that

Dr. Nott's hypothesis as to his metre.

Gray, before the appearance of Tyrwhitt's essay on the versification of Chaucer, had adopted, without hesitation, the same hypothesis.[1] But, according to Dr. Nott, the verses of Chaucer, and of all his successors down to Surrey, are merely rhythmical, to be read by cadence, and admitting of considerable variety in the number of syllables, though ten may be the more frequent. In the manuscripts of Chaucer, the line is always broken by a cæsura in the middle, which is pointed out by a virgule; and this is preserved in the early editions down to that of 1532. They come near, therefore, to the short Saxon line, differing chiefly by the alternate rhyme, which converts two verses into one. He maintains that a great many lines of Chaucer cannot be read metrically, though harmonious as verses of cadence. This rhythmical measure he proceeds to show in Hoccleve, Lydgate, Hawes, Barclay, Skelton, and even Wyatt; and thus concludes that it was first abandoned by Surrey, in whom it very rarely occurs.[2]

27. This hypothesis, it should be observed, derives some additional plausibility from a passage in Gascoyne's "Notes of instruction concerning the making of verse or rhyme in English," printed in 1575. "Whosoever do peruse and well consider his (Chaucer's) works, he shall find that, although his lines are not always of one self-same number of syllables, yet, being read by one that hath understanding, the longest verse, and that which hath most syllables in it, will fall (to the ear) correspondent unto that which hath fewest syllables; and likewise that which hath fewest syllables shall be found yet to consist of words that have such natural sound as may seem equal in length to a verse which hath many more syllables of lighter accents."

But seems too extensive.

28. A theory so ingeniously maintained, and with so much induction of examples, has naturally gained a good deal of credit. I cannot, however, by any means concur in the extension given to it. Pages may be read in Chaucer, and still more in Dunbar, where every line is regularly and harmoniously decasyllabic; and, though the cæsura may perhaps fall rather more uniformly than it does in modern verse, it would be very easy to find exceptions, which could not acquire a rhythmical cadence by any artifice of the reader.[3]

[1] Gray's Works (edit. Mathias), ii. 1.

[2] Nott's Dissertation, subjoined to the second volume of his Wyatt and Surrey.

[3] Such as these among multitudes more:—

"A lover, and a lusty bachelor."

Chaucer

The deviations from the normal type, or decasyllable line, were they more numerous than, after allowance for the license of pronunciation, as well as the probable corruption of the text, they appear to be, would not, I conceive, justify us in concluding that it was disregarded. For these aberrant lines are much more common in the dramatic blank verse of the seventeenth century. They are, doubtless, vestiges of the old rhythmical forms; and we may readily allow that English versification had not, in the fifteenth or even sixteenth centuries, the numerical regularity of classical or Italian metre. In the ancient ballads, Scots and English, the substitution of the anapæst for the iambic foot is of perpetual recurrence, and gives them a remarkable elasticity and animation; but we never fail to recognize a uniformity of measure, which the use of nearly equipollent feet cannot, on the strictest metrical principles, be thought to impair.

29. If we compare the poetry of Wyatt and Surrey with that of Barclay or Skelton, about thirty or forty years before, the difference must appear wonderful. But we should not, with Dr. Nott, attribute this wholly to superiority of genius. It is to be remembered that the later poets wrote in a court, and in one which, besides the aristocratic manners of chivalry, had not only imbibed a great deal of refinement from France and Italy, but a considerable tinge of ancient literature. Their predecessors were less educated men, and they addressed a more vulgar class of readers. Nor was this polish of language peculiar to Surrey and his friend. In the short poems of Lord Vaux, and of others about the same time, even in those of Nicolas Grimoald, a lecturer at Oxford, who was no courtier, but had acquired a classical taste, we find a rejection of obsolete and trivial phrases, and the beginnings of what we now call the style of our older poetry.

Politeness of Wyatt and Surrey.

30. No period since the revival of letters has been so con-

"But reason, with the shield of gold so shene." *Dunbar.*

"The rock, again the river resplendent." *Id.*

Lydgate apologizes for his own lines, —

"Because I know the verse therein is wrong,
As being some too short, and some too long," —

in Gray, ii. 4. This seems at once to exclude the rhythmical system, and to account for the imperfection of the metrical. Lydgate has, perhaps, on the whole, more aberrations from the decasyllable standard than Chaucer.

Puttenham, in his Art of Poesie (1586), book ii. ch. 3, 4, though he admits the licentiousness of Chaucer, Lydgate, and other poets, in occasionally disregarding the cæsura, does not seem to doubt that they wrote by metrical rules, which indeed is implied in this censure. Dr. Nott's theory does not admit a disregard of cæsura.

spicuous for Latin poetry as the present. Three names of great reputation adorn it, Sannazarius, Vida, Fracastorius. The first of these, Sannazarius, or San Nazaro, or Actius Sincerus, was a Neapolitan, attached to the fortunes of the Aragonese line of kings; and, following the last of their number, Frederic, after his unjust spoliation, into France, remained there till his master's death. Much of his poetry was written under this reign, before 1503; but his principal work, De Partu Virginis, did not appear till 1522. This has incurred not unfair blame for the intermixture of classical mythology, at least in language, with the Gospel story; nor is the latter very skilfully managed. But it would be difficult to find its equal for purity, elegance, and harmony of versification. The unauthorized word, the doubtful idiom, the modern turn of thought, so common in Latin verse, scarce ever appear in Sannazarius: a pure taste enabled him to diffuse a Virgilian hue over his language; and a just ear, united with facility in command of words, rendered his versification melodious and varied beyond any competitor. The Piscatory Eclogues of Sannazarius, which are perhaps better known, deserve, at least, equal praise: they seem to breathe the beauty and sweetness of that fair bay they describe. His elegies are such as may contend with Tibullus. If Sannazarius does not affect sublimity, he never sinks below his aim: the sense is sometimes inferior to the style, as he is not wholly free from conceits;[1] but it would perhaps be more difficult to find cold and prosaic passages in his works than in those of any other Latin poet in modern times.

Latin poetry.

Sannazarius.

31. Vida of Cremona is not by any means less celebrated than Sannazarius: his poem on the Art of Poetry, and that on the Game of Chess, were printed in 1527; the Christiad, an epic poem, as perhaps it deserves to be called, in 1535; and that on Silk Worms, in 1537. Vida's precepts are clear and judicious; and we admire, in his Game of Chess especially, and the poem on Silk Worms, the skill with which the dry rules of art, and descriptions the most apparently irreducible to poetical conditions, fall into his elegant and classical language. It has been observed, that he is

Vida

[1] The following lines, on the constellation Taurus, are more puerile than any I have seen in this elegant poet:—

"Torva bovi facies; sed qua non altera coelo
Dignior, imbriferum quæ cornibus inchoet annum,
Nec *quæ tam claris mugitibus ast cessat.*"

the first who laid down rules for imitative harmony, illustrating them by his own example. The Christiad shows not so much, I think, of Vida's great talents, at least in poetical language; but the subject is better managed than by Sannazarius. Yet, notwithstanding some brilliant passages, among which the conclusion of the second book De Arte Poetica is prominent, Vida appears to me far inferior to the Neapolitan poet. His versification is often hard and spondaic, the elisions too frequent, and the cæsura too much neglected. The language, even where the subject bests admits of it, is not always so elevated as we should desire.

Fracastorius.

32. Fracastorius has obtained his reputation by the Syphilis, published in 1530; and certainly, as he thought fit to make choice of the subject, there is no reader but must admire the beauty and variety of his digressions, the vigor and nobleness of his style. Once only has it been the praise of genius to have delivered the rules of practical art in all the graces of the most delicious poetry, without inflation, without obscurity, without affectation, and generally, perhaps, with the precision of truth. Fracastorius, not emulous in this of the author of the Georgics, seems to have made Manilius, rather, I think, than Lucretius, his model in the didactic portion of his poem.

Latin verse not to be disdained.

33. Upon a fair comparison, we should not err much, in my opinion, by deciding that Fracastorius is the greater poet, and Sannazarius the better author of Latin verses. In the present age, it is easy to anticipate the supercilious disdain of those who believe it ridiculous to write Latin poetry at all, because it cannot, as they imagine, be written well. I must be content to answer, that those who do not know when such poetry is good, should be as slow to contradict those who do, as the ignorant in music to set themselves against competent judges. No one pretends that Sannazarius was equal to Ariosto. But it may be truly said, that his poetry, and a great deal more that has been written in Latin, beyond comparison excels most of the contemporary Italian: we may add, that its reputation has been more extended and European.

Other Latin poets in Italy.

34. After this famous triumvirate, we might reckon several in different degrees of merit. Bembo comes forward again in these lists. His Latin poems are not numerous: that upon the lake Benacus is the best known.

He shone more, however, in elegiac than hexameter verse. This is a common case in modern Latin, and might be naturally expected of Bembo, who had more of elegance than of vigor. Castiglione has left a few poems; among which the best is in the archaic lapidary style, on the statue of Cleopatra in the Vatican. Molza wrote much in Latin: he is the author of the epistle to Henry VIII., in the name of Catherine, which has been ascribed to Joannes Secundus. It is very spirited and Ovidian. These poets were, perhaps, surpassed by Naugerius and Flaminius; both, but especially the latter, for sweetness and purity of style, to be placed in the first rank of lyric and elegiac poets in the Latin language. In their best passages, they fall not by any means short of Tibullus or Catullus. Aonius Palearius, though his poem on the Immortality of the Soul is equalled by Sadolet himself to those of Vida and Sannazarius, seems not entitled to any thing like such an eulogy. He became afterwards suspected of Lutheranism, and lost his life on the scaffold at Rome. We have in another place mentioned the Zodiacus Vitæ of Palingenius Stellatus, whose true name was Manzolli. The Deliciæ Poetarum Italorum present a crowd of inferior imitations of classical models; but I must repeat, that the volumes published by Pope, and entitled Poemata Italorum, are the best evidences of the beauties of these poets.

35. The Cisalpine nations, though at a vast distance from Italy, cannot be reckoned destitute, in this age, of respectable Latin poets. Of these, the best known, and perhaps upon the whole the best, is Joannes Secundus, who found the doves of Venus in the dab-chicks of Dutch marshes. The Basia, however, are far from being superior to his elegies, many of which, though not correct, and often sinning by false quantity, a fault pretty general with these early Latin poets, especially on this side of the Alps, are generally harmonious, spirited, and elegant. Among the Germans, Eobanus Hessus, Micyllus, professor at Heidelberg, and Melanchthon, have obtained considerable praise.

In Germany.

SECT. II. 1520–1550.

State of Dramatic Representation in Italy — Spain and Portugal — France — Germany — England.

36. We have already seen the beginnings of the Italian comedy, founded in its style, and frequently in its subjects, upon Plautus. Two of Ariosto's comedies have been mentioned, and two more belong to this period. Some difference of opinion has existed with respect to their dramatic merit. But few have hesitated to place above them the Mandragola and Clitia of a great contemporary genius, Machiavel. The Mandragola was probably written before 1520, but certainly in the fallen fortunes of its author, as he intimates in the prologue. Ginguéné, therefore, forgot his chronology when he supposes Leo X. to have been present, as cardinal, at its representation.[1] It seems, however, to have been acted before this pope at Rome. The story of the Mandragola, which hardly bears to be told, though Ginguéné has done it, is said to be founded on a real and recent event at Florence, — one of its striking resemblances to the Athenian comedy. It is admirable for its comic delineations of character, the management of the plot, and the liveliness of its idiomatic dialogue. Peter Aretin, with little of the former qualities, and inferior in all respects to Machiavel, has enough of humorous extravagance to amuse the reader. The licentiousness of the Italian stage in its contempt of morality, and even, in the comedies of Peter Aretin, its bold satire on the great, remind us rather of Athens than of Rome: it is more the effrontery of Aristophanes than the pleasant freedom of Plautus. But the depravity which had long been increasing in Italy gained, in this first part of the sixteenth century, a zenith which it could not surpass, and from which it has very gradually receded. These comedies are often very satirical on the clergy; the bold strokes of Machiavel surprise us at present; but the Italian stage had something like the license of a masquerade; it was a tacit agreement that men should laugh at things sacred within

Italian comedy.

Machiavel.

Aretin.

[1] Ginguéné, vi. 222.

those walls, but resume their veneration for them at the door.[1]

37. Those who attempted the serious tone of tragedy were less happy in their model: Seneca generally represented to them the ancient buskin. The Canace of Sperone Speroni; the Tullia of Martelli, and the Orbecche of Giraldi Cinthio, esteemed the best of nine tragedies he has written, are within the present period. They are all works of genius. But Ginguéné observes how little advantage the first of these plays afforded for dramatic effect; most of the action passing in narration. It is true, that he could hardly have avoided this without aggravating the censures of those who, as Crescimbeni tells us, thought the subject itself unfit for tragedy.[2] The story of the Orbecche is taken by Cinthio from a novel of his own invention, and is remarkable for its sanguinary and disgusting circumstances. This became the characteristic of tragedy in the sixteenth century; not by any means peculiarly in England, as some half-informed critics of the French school used to pretend. The Orbecche, notwithstanding its passages in the manner of Titus Andronicus, is in many parts an impassioned and poetical tragedy. Riccoboni, though he censures the general poverty of style, prefers one scene in the third act to any thing on the stage: "If one scene were sufficient to decide the question, the Orbecche would be the finest play in the world."[3] Walker observes that this is the first tragedy wherein the prologue is separated from the play, of which, as is very well known, it made a part on the ancient theatre. But in Cinthio, and in other tragic writers long afterwards, the prologue continued to explain and announce the story.[4]

Tragedy.

Sperone.
Cinthio.

38. Meantime, a people very celebrated in dramatic literature was forming its national theatre. A few attempts were made in Spain to copy the classical model. But these seem not to have gone beyond translation, and had little effect on the public taste. Others, in imitation of the Celestina, which passed for a moral example, produced

Spanish drama.

[1] Besides the plays themselves, see Ginguéné, vol. vi., who gives more than a hundred pages to the Calandra, and to the comedies of Ariosto, Machiavel, and Aretin. Many of the old comedies are reprinted in the great Milan collection of Classici Italiani. Those of Machiavel and Ariosto are found in most editions of their works.

[2] Della volgar Poesia, ii. 391. Alfieri went still farther than Sperone in his Mirra. Objections of a somewhat similar kind were made to the Tullia of Martelli.

[3] Hist. du Théâtre Italien, vol. i.

[4] Walker, Essay on Italian Tragedy; Ginguéné, vi. 61, 69.

tedious scenes, by way of mirrors of vice and virtue, without reaching the fame of their original. But a third class was far more popular, and ultimately put an end to competition. The founders of this were Torres Naharro, in the first years of Charles, and Lope de Rueda, a little later. "There is very little doubt," says Bouterwek, "that Torres Naharro was the real inventor of the Spanish comedy. He not only wrote his eight comedies in redondillas in the romance style, but he also endeavored to establish the dramatic interest solely on an ingenious combination of intrigues, without attaching much importance to the development of character, or the moral tendency of the story. It is besides probable that he was the first who divided plays into three acts, which, being regarded as three days' labor in the dramatic field, were called *jornadas*. It must, therefore, be unreservedly admitted that these dramas, considered both with respect to their spirit and their form, deserve to be ranked as the first in the history of the Spanish national drama; for, in the same path which Torres Naharro first trod, the dramatic genius of Spain advanced to the point attained by Calderon, and the nation tolerated no dramas except those which belonged to the style which had thus been created."[1]

Torres Naharro.

39. Lope de Rueda, who is rather better known than his predecessor, was at the head of a company of players, and was limited in his inventions by the capacity of his troop and of the stage upon which they were to appear. Cervantes calls him the great Lope de Rueda, even when a greater Lope was before the world. "He was not," to quote again from Bouterwek, "inattentive to general character, as is proved by his delineation of old men, clowns, &c., in which he was particularly successful. But his principal aim was to interweave in his dramas a succession of intrigues; and, as he seems to have been a stranger to the art of producing stage effect by striking situations, he made complication the great object of his plots. Thus, mistakes, arising from personal resemblances, exchanges of children, and such-like commonplace subjects of intrigue, form the groundwork of his stories; none of which are remarkable for ingenuity of invention. There is usually a multitude of characters in his dramas, and jests and witticisms are freely introduced; but these in general

Lope de Rueda.

[1] P. 285. Andrès thinks Naharro low, insipid, and unworthy of the praise of Cervantes, v. 136.

consist of burlesque disputes, in which some clown is engaged."[1]

Gil Vicente.

40. The Portuguese Gil Vicente may perhaps contend with Torres Naharro for the honor of leading the dramatists of the Peninsula. His Autos, indeed, as has been observed, do not, so far as we can perceive, differ from the mysteries, the religious dramas of France and England. Bouterwek, strangely forgetful of these, seems to have assigned a character of originality, and given a precedence to the Spanish and Portuguese Autos which they do not deserve. The specimen of one of these by Gil Vicente, given in the History of Portuguese Literature, is far more extravagant and less theatrical than our John Parfre's contemporary mystery of Candlemas Day. But a few comedies, or, as they are more justly styled, farces, remain; one of which, mentioned by the same author, is superior in choice and management of the fable to most of the rude productions of that time. Its date is unknown. Gil Vicente's dramatic compositions of various kinds were collectively published in 1562: he had died in 1557, at a very advanced age.

41. "These works," says Bouterwek of the dramatic productions of Gil Vicente in general, "display a true poetic spirit, which, however, accommodated itself entirely to the age of the poet, and which disdained cultivation. The dramatic genius of Gil Vicente is equally manifest from his power of invention, and from the natural turn and facility of his imitative talent. Even the rudest of these dramas is tinged with a certain degree of poetic feeling."[2] The want of complex intrigue, such as we find afterwards in the Castilian drama, ought not to surprise us in these early compositions.

Mysteries and moralities in France.

42. We have no record of any original dramatic composition belonging to this age in France, with the exception of mysteries and moralities, which are very abundant. These were considered, and perhaps justly, as types of the regular drama. "The French morality," says an author of that age, "represents, in some degree, the tragedy of the Greeks and Romans; particularly because it treats of serious and important subjects; and, if it

[1] P. 282

[2] Hist. of Portuguese Lit., p. 83-111. It would be vain to look elsewhere for so copious an account of Gil Vicente, and very difficult probably to find his works. See, too, Sismondi, Hist. de la Litt. du Midi, iv. 448.

[A much fuller account of Gil Vicente has since been given in the Quarterly Review for January, 1847.]

were contrived in French that the conclusion of the morality should be always unfortunate, it would become a tragedy. In the morality, we treat of noble and virtuous actions, either true, or at least probable; and choose what makes for our instruction in life."[1] It is evident, from this passage and the whole context, that neither tragedy nor comedy were yet known. The circumstance is rather remarkable, when we consider the genius of the nation, and the politeness of the court. But, from about the year 1540, we find translations from Latin and Italian comedies into French. These probably were not represented. Les Amours d'Erostrate, by Jacques Bourgeois, published in 1545, is taken from the Suppositi of Ariosto. Sibilet translated the Iphigenia of Euripides in 1549; Bouchetel, the Hecuba in 1550; and Lazarus Baif, two other plays about the same time. But a great dramatic revolution was now prepared by the strong arm of the state. The first theatre had been established at Paris about 1400, by the Confrairie de la Passion de N.S., for the representation of Scriptural mysteries. This was suppressed by the parliament in 1547, on account of the scandal which this devout buffoonery had begun to give. The company of actors purchased next year the Hôtel de la Bourgogne, and were authorized by the parliament to represent profane subjects, "lawful and decent" (*licites et honnêtes*), but enjoined to abstain from "all mysteries of the passion, or other sacred mysteries."[2]

German theatre. Hans Sachs.

43. In Germany, meantime, the pride of the Meistersingers, Hans Sachs, was alone sufficient to pour forth a plenteous stream for the stage. His works, collectively printed at Nuremberg in five folio volumes, 1578, and reprinted in five quartos at Kempten, 1606, contain 197 dramas among the rest. Many of his comedies in one act, called Schwanken, are coarse satires on the times. Invention, expression, and enthusiasm, if we may trust his admirers, are all united in Hans Sachs.[3]

[1] Sibilet, Art. "Poétique" (1548), *apud* Beauchamps, Recherches sur le Théâtre Français, i. 82.

In the Jardin de Plaisance, an anonymous undated poem, printed at Lyons probably before the end of the fifteenth century, we have rules given for composing moralities. Beauchamps (p. 86) extracts some of these; but they seem not worth copying.

[2] Beauchamps, i. 91.

[3] Hans Sachs has met with a very laudatory critic in the Retrospective Review x. 113, who even ventures to assert that Goethe has imitated the old shoemaker in Faust.

The Germans had many plays in this age. Gesner says, in his Pandectæ Universales: "Germanicæ fabulæ multæ extant. Fabula decem ætatum et Fusio stultorum Colmariæ actæ sunt. Fusio edita est 1537, chartis quatuor. Qui volet hoc loco plures ascribat in vulgaribus linguis, nos ad alia festinamus."

44. The mysteries founded upon Scriptural or legendary histories, as well as the moralities, or allegorical dramas, which, though there might be an intermixture of human character with abstract personification, did not aim at that illusion which a possible fable affords, continued to amuse the English public. Nor were they confined, as perhaps they were before, to churches and monasteries. We find a company of players in the establishment of Richard III. while Duke of Gloucester; and in the subsequent reigns, especially under Henry VIII., this seems to have been one of the luxuries of the great. The frugal Henry VII. maintained two distinct sets of players; and his son was prodigally sumptuous in every sort of court-exhibition, bearing the general name of revels, and superintended by a high-priest of jollity, styled the Abbot of Misrule. The dramatic allegories, or moral plays, found a place among them. It may be presumed, that from their occasionality, or want of merit, far the greater part have perished.[1] Three or four, which we may place before 1550, are published in Hawkins's Ancient Drama and Dodsley's Old Plays; one is extant, written by Skelton, the earliest that can be referred to a known author.[2] A late writer, whose diligence seems to have almost exhausted our early dramatic history, has retrieved the titles of a few more. The most ancient of these moral plays he traces to the reign of Henry VI. They became gradually more complicated, and approached nearer to a regular form. It may be observed that a line is not easily defined between the Scriptural mysteries and the legitimate drama: the choice of the story, the succession of incidents, are those of tragedy; even the intermixture of buffoonery belongs to all our ancient stage; and it is only by the meanness of the sentiments and diction that we exclude the Candlemas Day, which is one of the most perfect of the mysteries, or even those of the fifteenth century, from our tragic series.[3] Nor were the moralities, such as we find them in the reign of Henry VIII., at a prodigious distance from the regular stage: deviations from the original structure of these, as Mr. Collier has well observed, "by the relinquishment of abstract for individual character,

Moralities and similar plays in England.

[1] Collier's Annals of the Stage, i. 34, &c.

[2] Warton, iii. 188.

[3] Candlemas Day, a mystery, on the murder of the Innocents, is published in Hawkins's Early English Drama. It is by John Parfre, and may be referred to the first years of Henry VIII.

paved the way, by a natural and easy gradation, for tragedy and comedy, the representations of real life and manners."[1]

They are turned to religious satire.

45. The moralities were, in this age, distinguished by the constant introduction of a witty, mischievous, and profligate character, denominated the Vice. This seems originally to have been an allegorical representation of what the word denotes; but the Vice gradually acquired a human individuality, in which he came very near to our well-known Punch. The devil was generally introduced in company with the Vice, and had to endure many blows from him. But the moralities had another striking characteristic in this period. They had always been religious, but they now became theological. In the crisis of that great revolution then in progress, the stage was found a ready and impartial instrument for the old or the new faith. Luther and his wife were satirized in a Latin morality represented at Gray's Inn in 1529. It was easy to turn the tables on the clergy. Sir David Lyndsay's satire of the Three Estatis, a direct attack upon them, was played before James V. and his queen at Linlithgow, in 1539;[2] and in 1543 an English statute was made prohibiting all plays and interludes which meddle with the interpretation of Scripture. In 1549, the council of Edward VI. put a stop by proclamation to all kinds of stage-plays.[3]

Latin plays.

46. Great indulgence, or a strong antiquarian prejudice, is required to discover much genius in these moralities and mysteries. There was, however, a class of dramatic productions that appealed to a more instructed audience. The custom of acting Latin plays prevailed in our universities at this time, as it did long afterwards. Whether it were older than the fifteenth century seems not to be proved; and the presumption is certainly against it. "In an original draught," says Warton, "of the statutes of Trinity College at Cambridge, founded in 1546, one of the chapters is entitled 'De Præfecto ludorum qui imperator dicitur,' under whose direction and authority Latin comedies and tragedies are to be exhibited in the hall at Christmas."[4] It is probable that Christopherson's

[1] Hist. of English Dramatic Poetry, ii. 260. This I quote by its proper title; but it is in fact the same work as the Annals of the Stage, so far as being incorporated and sold together renders it the same.

[2] Warton, iv. 23.

[3] Collier, i. 144.

[4] Hist. of Engl. Poetry, iii. 205.

tragedy of Jephthah, and another by Grimoald on John the Baptist, both older than the middle of the century, were written for academical representation. Nor was this confined to the universities. Nicolas Udal, head-master of Eton, wrote several plays in Latin to be acted in the long nights of winter by his boys.[1] And, if we had to stop here, it might seem an unnecessary minuteness to take notice of the diversions of school-boys, especially as the same is recorded of other teachers besides Udal. But there is something more in this. Udal has lately become known in a new and more brilliant light, as the father of English comedy. It was mentioned by Warton, but without any comment, that Nicolas Udal wrote some English plays to be represented by his scholars; a passage from one of which is quoted by Wilson in his Art of Logic, dedicated to Edward VI.[2] It might have been conjectured, by the help of this quotation, that these plays were neither of the class of moralities or mysteries, nor mere translations from Plautus and Terence, as it would not have been unnatural at first to suppose. Within a few years, however, the comedy from which Wilson took his extract has been discovered. It was printed in 1565, but probably written not later than 1540. The title of this comedy is Ralph Roister Doister, a name uncouth enough, and from which we should expect a very barbarous farce. But Udal, an eminent scholar, knew how to preserve comic spirit and humor without degenerating into licentious buffoonery. Ralph Roister Doister, in spite of its title, is a play of some merit, though the wit may seem designed for the purpose of natural merriment rather than critical glory. We find in it, what is of no slight value, the earliest lively picture of London manners among the gallants and citizens, who furnished so much for the stage down to the civil wars. And perhaps there is no striking difference in this respect between the dramatic manners under Henry VIII. and James I. This comedy, for there seems no kind of reason why it should be refused that honorable name, is much

First English comedy

[1] Udal was not the first, if we could trust Harwood's Alumni Etonenses, who established an Eton theatre. Of Rightwise, who succeeded Lily as master of St. Paul's, it is said by him, that he was "a most eminent grammarian, and wrote the tragedy of Dido from Virgil, which was acted before Cardinal Wolsey with great applause by himself and other scholars of Eton." But, as Rightwise left Eton for King's College in 1508, this cannot be true, at least so far as Wolsey is concerned. It is said afterwards, in the same book, of one Hallewill, who went to Cambridge in 1532, that he wrote "the tragedy of Dido." Which should we believe, or were there two Didos? But Harwood's book is not reckoned of much authority beyond the mere records which he copied.

[2] Hist. of Engl. Poetry, iii. 213.

superior to Gammar Gurton's Needle, written twenty years afterwards, from which it has wrested a long established precedence in our dramatic annals.[1]

SECT. III. 1520–1550.

Romances and Novels — Rabelais.

Romances of chivalry.

47. THE popularity of Amadis de Gaul gave rise to a class of romances, the delight of the multitude in the sixteenth century, though since chiefly remembered by the ridicule and ignominy that has attached itself to their name, — those of knight-errantry. Most of these belong to Spanish or Portuguese literature. Palmerin of Oliva, one of the earliest, was published in 1525. Palmerin, less fortunate than his namesake of England, did not escape the penal flame to which the barber and curate consigned many also of his younger brethren. It has been observed by Bouterwek, that every respectable Spanish writer, as well as Cervantes, resisted the contagion of bad taste which kept the prolix mediocrity of these romances in fashion.[2]

Novels.

48. A far better style was that of the short novel, which the Italian writers, especially Boccaccio, had rendered popular in Europe. But, though many of these were probably written within this period of thirty years, none of much distinction come within it, as the date of their earliest publication, except the celebrated Belphegor of Machiavel.[3]

[1] See an analysis, with extracts of Ralph Roister Doister, in Collier's Hist. of Dram. Poetry, ii. 445–460.

["The plot," Mr. C. observes, "of Ralph Roister Doister is amusing and well conducted, with an agreeable intermixture of serious and comic dialogue, and a variety of character to which no other piece of a similar date can make any pretension. When we recollect that it was perhaps written in the reign of Henry VIII., we ought to look upon it as a masterly production. Had it followed Gammar Gurton's Needle by as many years as it preceded it, it would have been entitled to our admiration on its own separate merits, independent of any comparison with other pieces. The character of Matthew Merrygreeke here and there savors a little of the Vice of the moralities; but his humor never depends upon the accidents of dress and accoutrements." — 1842.]

[2] Hist. of Spanish Literature, p. 304; Dunlop's Hist. of Fiction, vol. ii.

[3] I cannot make another exception for Il Pellegrino by Caviceo of Parma, the first known edition of which, published at Venice in 1526, evidently alludes to one earlier: "Diligentemente in lingua tosca corretto, e novamente stampato et historiato." The editor speaks of the book as obsolete in orthography and style. It is probably, however, not older than the last years of the fifteenth century, being dedicated to Lucrezia Borgia. It is a very prolix and tedious romance, in three books and two hundred and nineteen chapters, written in a semi-poetical, diffuse style, and much

The amusing story of Lazarillo de Tormes was certainly written by Mendoza in his youth. But it did not appear in print within our present period.[1] This is the first known specimen in Spain of the *picaresque*, or rogue style, in which the adventures of the low and rather dishonest part of the community are made to furnish amusement for the great. The Italian novelists are by no means without earlier instances; but it became the favorite and almost peculiar class of novel with the Spanish writers about the end of the century.

49. But the most celebrated, and certainly the most brilliant, performance in the path of fiction, that belongs to this age, is that of Rabelais. Few books are less likely to obtain the praise of a rigorous critic; but few have more the stamp of originality, or show a more redundant fertility, always of language, and sometimes of imagination. He bears a slight resemblance to Lucian, and a considerable one to Aristophanes. His reading is large, but always rendered subservient to ridicule; he is never serious in a single page, and seems to have had little other aim, in his first two volumes, than to pour out the exuberance of his animal gayety. In the latter part of Pantagruel's history, that is the fourth and fifth books, one published in 1552, the other after the author's death in 1561, a dislike to the Church of Rome, which had been slightly perceived in the first volumes, is not at all disguised; but the vein of merriment becomes gradually less fertile, and weariness steals on before the close of a work which had long amused while it disgusted us. Allusions to particular characters are frequent, and in general transparent enough, with the aid of a little information about contemporaneous history, in several parts of Rabelais; but much of what has been taken for political and religious satire cannot, as far as I perceive, be satisfactorily traced beyond the capricious imagination of the

Rabelais.

in the usual manner of love-stories. Ginguéné and Tiraboschi do not mention it: the Biographie Universelle does.

Mr. Dunlop has given a short account of a French novel, entitled, Les Aventures de Lycidas et de Cleorithe, which he considers as the earliest and best specimen of what he calls the spiritual romance, unmixed with chivalry or allegory. Hist. of Fiction, iii. 51. It was written in 1529 by Basire, Archdeacon of Sens. I should suspect that there had been some of this class already in Germany: they certainly became common in that country afterwards.

[1] [Nicolas Antonio tells us that the first edition of Lazarillo de Tormes was in 1586 But Brunet mentions one printed at Burgos in 1554, and three at Antwerp in 1553 and 1555. Supplément au Manuel du Libraire, art. "Hurtado." The following early edition also is in the British Museum, of which I transcribe the titlepage: "La Vida de Lazarillo de Tormes y de sus fortunas y adversidades, nuevamente impressa, corregida, y de nuevo añadida ex este segunda impression. Vendense en Alcalá de Henares en casa de Salzedo librero año de N.D. 1554." A colophon recites the same date and place of impression.—1842.]

author. Those who have found Montluc, the famous Bishop of Valence, in Panurge, or Antony of Bourbon, father of Henry IV., in Pantagruel, keep no measures with chronology. Panurge is so admirably conceived that we may fairly reckon him original; but the germ of the character is in the *gracioso*, or clown, of the extemporaneous stage; the roguish, selfish, cowardly, cunning attendant, who became Panurge in the plastic hands of Rabelais, and Sancho in those of Cervantes. The French critics have not in general done justice to Rabelais, whose manner was not that of the age of Louis XIV. The Tale of a Tub appears to me by far the closest imitation of it, and to be conceived altogether in a kindred spirit; but in general those who have had reading enough to rival the copiousness of Rabelais have wanted his invention and humor, or the riotousness of his animal spirits.

SECT. IV. 1520–1550.

Struggle between Latin and Italian Languages — Italian and Spanish Polite Writers — Criticism in Italy — In France and England.

Contest of Latin and Italian languages.

50. AMONG the polished writers of Italy, we meet on every side the name of Bembo; great in Italian as well as in Latin literature, in prose as in verse. It is now the fourth time that it occurs to us; and in no instance has he merited more of his country. Since the fourteenth century, to repeat what has been said before, so absorbing had become the love of ancient learning, that the natural language, beautiful and copious as it really was, and polished as it had been under the hands of Boccaccio, seemed to a very false-judging pedantry scarce worthy of the higher kinds of composition. Those, too, who with enthusiastic diligence had acquired the power of writing Latin well, did not brook so much as the equality of their native language. In an oration delivered at Bologna in 1529 before the emperor and pope, by Romolo Amaseo, one of the good writers of the sixteenth century, he not only pronounced a panegyric upon the Latin tongue, but contended that the Italian should be reserved for shops and markets, and the conversation of the

vulgar;[1] nor was this doctrine, probably in rather a less degree, uncommon during that age. A dialogue of Sperone relates to this debated question, whether the Latin or Italian language should be preferred; one of the interlocutors (probably Lazaro Buonamici, an eminent scholar) disdaining the latter as a mere corruption. It is a very ingenious performance, well conducted on both sides, and may be read with pleasure. The Italians of that age are as clever in criticism as they are wearisome on the commonplaces of ethics. It purports to have been written the year after the oration of Romolo Amaseo, to which it alludes.

Influence of Bembo in this.

51. It is an evidence of the more liberal spirit that generally accompanies the greatest abilities, that Bembo, superior even to Amaseo in fame as a Latin writer, should have been among the first to retrieve the honor of his native language by infusing into it that elegance and selection of phrase which his taste had taught him in Latin, and for which the Italian is scarcely less adapted. In the dialogue of Sperone, quoted above, it is said that "it was the general opinion no one would write Italian who could write Latin; a prejudice in some measure lightened by the poem of Politian on the tournament of Julian de' Medici, but not taken away till Bembo, a Venetian gentleman, as learned in the ancient languages as Politian, showed that he did not disdain his maternal tongue."[2]

Apology for Latinists.

52. It is common in the present age to show as indiscriminating a disdain of those who wrote in Latin as they seem to have felt towards their own literature. But the taste and imagination of Bembo are not given to every one; and we must remember, in justice to such men as Amaseo, who, though they imitate well, are yet but imitators in style, that there was really scarce a book in Italian prose written with any elegance, except the Decamerone of Boccaccio; the manner of which, as Tiraboschi justly observes, however suitable to those sportive fictions, was not very well adapted to serious eloquence.[3] Nor has the Italian language,

[1] Tiraboschi, x. 389.

[2] P. 430 (edit. 1596).

[3] x. 402. [Bettinelli speaks not very favorably of the style of the Decameron. "Certo è, che il costumare, il dipingere, l' arte del dialogo, la grazia de' motti, la verità e varietà di caratteri nel Decamerone fanno un' opera molto eloquente. Ma certo è non meno, che affettata è la sua rotondità di periodo, faticosa la costruzione, dure e spiacevoli le trasposizioni, etc. L' altre opere sue di fatti non sono autorevoli fuorchè in Crusca." — Risorgimento d' Italia dopo il Millesimo, vol. i p. 192. — 1842.]

we may add, in its very best models, attained so much energy and condensation as will satisfy the ear or the understanding of a good Latin scholar; and there can be neither pedantry nor absurdity in saying that it is an inferior organ of human thought. The most valid objection to the employment of Latin in public discourses or in moral treatises is its exclusion of those whose advantage we are supposed to seek, and whose sympathy we ought to excite. But this objection, though not much less powerful in reality than at present, struck men less sensibly in that age, when long use of the ancient language, in which even the sermons of the clergy were frequently delivered, had taken away the sense of its impropriety.[1]

Character of the controversy.

53. This controversy points out some degree of change in public opinion, and the first stage of that struggle against the aristocracy of erudition which lasted more or less for nearly two centuries, till, like other struggles of still more importance, it ended in the victory of the many. In the days of Poggio and Politian, the native Italian no more claimed an equality than the plebeians of Rome demanded the consulship in the first years of the republic. These are the revolutions of human opinion, bearing some analogy and parallelism to those of civil society, which it is the business of an historian of literature to indicate.

Life of Bembo.

54. The life of Bembo was spent, after the loss of his great patron, Leo X., in literary elegance at Padua. Here he formed an extensive library, and collection of medals; and here he enjoyed the society of the learned, whom that university supplied, or who visited him from other parts of Italy and Europe. Far below Sadolet in the solid virtues of his character, and not probably his superior in learning, he has certainly left a greater name, and contributed more to the literary progress of his native country. He died at an advanced age in 1547; having a few years before obtained a cardinal's hat on the recommendation of Sadolet.[2]

55. The style of some other Italian and Spanish writers,

[1] Sadolet himself had rather discouraged Bembo from writing Italian, as appears from one of his epistles, thanking his friend for the present of a book, perhaps Le Prose. "Sed tu fortasse conjicis ex eo, illa mihi non placere, quod te avocare solebam ab illis literis. Faciebam ego id quidem, sed consilio, ut videbar, bono. Cum enim in Latinis major multo inesset dignitas, tuque in ea facultate princeps mihi longe viderere, non tam abstrahebam te illinc, quam huc vocabam. Nec studium reprehendebam in illis tuum, sed te majora quædam spectare debere arbitrabar." — Epist., lib. ii. p. 55.

[2] Tiraboschi, ix. 296; Corniani, iv. 99 Sadolet. Epist., lib. xii. p. 555.

Castiglione, Sperone, Machiavel. Guevara, Oliva, has been already adverted to when the subject of their writings was before us; and it would be tedious to dwell upon them again in this point of view. The Italians have been accustomed to associate almost every kind of excellence with the word *cinquecento*. They extol the elegant style and fine taste of those writers. But Andrès has remarked, with no injustice, that if we find purity, correctness, and elegance of expression, in the chief prose writers of this century, we cannot but also acknowledge an empty prolixity of periods, a harsh involution of words and clauses, a jejune and wearisome circuity of sentences, with a striking deficiency of thought. "Let us admit the graces of mere language in the famous authors of this period; but we must own them to be far from models of eloquence, so tedious and languid as they are."[1] The Spanish writers of the same century, he says afterwards, nourished as well as the Italian with the milk of antiquity, transfused the spirit and vigor of these ancients into their own compositions, not with the servile imitation of the others, nor seeking to arrange their phrases and round their periods, the source of languor and emptiness, so that the best Spanish prose is more flowing and harmonious than the contemporary Italian.[2]

Character of Italian and Spanish style.

56. The French do not claim, I believe, to have produced at the middle of the sixteenth century any prose writer of a polished or vigorous style, Calvin excepted, the dedication of whose Institutes in French to Francis I is a model of purity and elegance for the age.[3] Sir Thomas More's Life of Edward V., written about 1509, appears to me the first example of good English language; pure and perspicuous, well-chosen, without vulgarisms or pedantry.[4] His polemical tracts are inferior, but not ill-written. We have seen that Sir Thomas Elyot had some vigor of style. Ascham, whose Toxophilus, or Dialogue on Archery, came out in 1544, does not excel him. But his works have been reprinted in modern times, and are consequently better known than those of Elyot. The early English writers are seldom select enough in their phrases

English writers.

More.

Ascham.

1 Andrès, vii. 68.

2 Id. 72.

3 Neufchâteau, Essai sur les meilleurs ouvrages dans la langue Française, p. 135.

4 This has been reprinted entire in Hollingshed's Chronicle; and the reader may find a long extract in the preface to Todd's edition of Johnson's Dictionary. I should name the account of Jane Shore as a model of elegant narration

to bear such a critical judgment as the academicians of Italy were wont to exercise.

Italian criticism.

57. Next to the models of style, we may place those writings which are designed to form them. In all sorts of criticism, whether it confines itself to the idioms of a single language, or rises to something like a general principle of taste, the Italian writers had a decided priority in order of time as well as of merit. We have already mentioned the earliest work, that of Fortunio, on Italian grammar. Liburnio, at Venice, in 1521, followed with his Volgari Eleganzie. But this was speedily eclipsed by a work of Bembo, published in 1525, with the rather singular title, Le Prose. These observations on the native language, commenced more than twenty years before, are written in dialogue, supposed to originate in the great controversy of that age, whether it were worthy of a man of letters to employ his mother-tongue instead of Latin.

Bembo.

Bembo well defended the national cause, and by judicious criticism on the language itself and the best writers in it, put an end to the most specious argument under which the advocates of Latin sheltered themselves,—that the Italian, being a mere assemblage of independent dialects, varying not only in pronunciation and orthography, but in their words and idioms, and having been written with unbounded irregularity and constant adoption of vulgar phrases, could afford no certain test of grammatical purity or graceful ornament. It was thought necessary by Bembo to meet this objection by the choice of a single dialect; and, though a Venetian, he had no hesitation to recognize the superiority of that spoken in Florence. The Tuscan writers of that century proudly make use of his testimony in aid of their pretensions to dictate the laws of Italian idiom. Varchi says, "The Italians cannot be sufficiently thankful to Bembo, for having not only purified their language from the rust of past ages, but given it such regularity and clearness, that it has become what we now see." This early work, however, as might be expected, has not wholly escaped the censure of a school of subtle and fastidious critics, in whom Italy became fertile.[1]

58. Several other treatises on the Italian language appeared even before the middle of the century, though few comparatively with the more celebrated and elaborate labors of criti-

[1] Ginguéné, vii 390; Corniani, iv. 111.

cism in its latter portion. None seem to deserve mention, unless it be the Observations of Lodovico Dolce (Venice, 1550), which were much improved in subsequent editions. Of the higher kind of criticism, which endeavors to excite and guide our perceptions of literary excellence, we find few or no specimens, even in Italy, within this period, except so far as the dialogues of Bembo furnish instances.

Grammarians and critics in France.

59. France was not destitute of a few obscure treatises at this time, enough to lay the foundations of her critical literature. The complex rules of French metre were to be laid down; and the language was iregular in pronunciation, accent, and orthography. These meaner, but necessary, elements of correctness occupied three or four writers, of whom Goujet has made brief mention: Sylvius, or Du Bois, who seems to have been the earliest writer on grammar;[1] Stephen Dolet, better known by his unfortunate fate than by his essay on French punctuation;[2] and, though Goujet does not name him, we may add an Englishman, Palsgrave, who published a French grammar in English as early as 1530.[3] An earlier production than any of these is the Art de plaine Rhétorique, by Peter Fabry, 1521; in which, with the help of some knowledge of Cicero, he attempted, but with little correctness, and often in absurd expressions, to establish the principles of oratory. If his work is no better than Goujet represents it to be, its popularity must denote a low condition of literature in France.[4] The first who aspired to lay down any thing like laws of taste in poetry was Thomas Sibilet, whose Art Poétique appeared in 1548. This is in two books; the former relating to the metrical rules of French verse, the latter giving precepts, short and judicious, for different kinds of composition. It is not, however, a work of much importance.[5]

Orthography of Meigret.

60. A more remarkable grammarian of this time was Louis Meigret, who endeavored to reform orthography by adapting it to pronunciation. In a language where these had come to differ so prodigiously as they did in French, something of this kind would be silently effected by the printers: but the bold scheme of Meigret went beyond their ideas of reformation; and he complains that he could not

[1] [The Sylvius here mentioned was, as I have been informed, James Du Bois, the physician, brother of Francis, who is recorded, p. 271.—1842.]

[2] Goujet, Biblioth. Française, i. 42, 81

[3] Biogr. Univ., "Palsgrave."

[4] Goujet, i. 361.

[5] Goujet, iii. 92.

prevail to have his words given to the public in the form he preferred. They were ultimately less rigid; and the new orthography appears in some grammatical treatises of Meigret, published about 1550. It was not, as we know, very successful; but he has credit given him for some improvements which have been retained in French printing. Meigret's French Grammar, it has been said, is the first that contains any rational or proper principles of the language. It has been observed, I know not how correctly, that he was the first who denied the name of case to those modifications of sense in nouns which are not marked by inflection; but the writer to whom I am indebted for this adds, what all will not alike admit, that this limited meaning of the word "case," which the modern grammars generally adopt, is rather an arbitrary deviation from their predecessors.[1]

61. It would have been strange, if we could exhibit a list of English writers on the subject of our language in the reign of Henry VIII., when it has at all times been the most neglected department of our literature. The English have ever been as indocile in acknowledging the rules of criticism, even those which determine the most ordinary questions of grammar, as the Italians and French have been voluntarily obedient. Nor had they as yet drunk deep enough of classical learning to discriminate, by any steady principle, the general beauties of composition. Yet, among the scanty rivulets that the English press furnished, we find "The Art or Craft of Rhetoryke," dedicated by Leonard Cox to Hugh Faringdon, Abbot of Reading. This book, which, though now very scarce, was translated into Latin, and twice printed at Cracow, in the year 1526,[2] is the work of a schoolmaster and man of reputed learning. The English edition has no date, but was probably published about 1524. Cox says: "I have partly translated out of a work of rhetoric written in the Latin tongue, and partly compiled of my own, and so made a little treatise in manner of an introduction into this aforesaid science, and that in the English tongue; remembering that every good thing, after the saying of the philosopher, the more common the better it is." His Art of Rhetoric follows the usual distribution of the ancients, both as to the kinds of oration and their parts;

Cox's Art of Rhetoric.

[1] Biogr. Univ., "Meigret," a good article; Goujet, i. 83.
[2] Panzer.

with examples, chiefly from Roman history, to direct the choice of arguments. It is hard to say how much may be considered as his own. The book is in duodecimo, and contains but eighty-five pages: it would of course be unworthy of notice in a later period.

CHAPTER IX.

ON THE SCIENTIFIC AND MISCELLANEOUS LITERATURE OF EUROPE, FROM 1520 TO 1550.

SECTION I.

On Mathematical and Physical Science.

Geometrical treatises.

1. THE first translation of Euclid from the Greek text was made by Zamberti of Venice, and appeared in 1505. It was republished at Basle in 1537. The Spherics of Theodosius and the Conics of Apollonius were translated by men, it is said, more conversant with Greek than with geometry. A higher praise is due to Werner of Nuremberg, the first who aspired to restore the geometrical analysis of the ancients. The treatise of Regiomontanus on triangles was first published in 1533. It may be presumed that its more important contents were already known to geometers. Montucla hints that the editor Schæner may have introduced some algebraic solutions which appear in this work; but there seems no reason to doubt that Regiomontanus was sufficiently acquainted with that science. The treatise of Vitello on optics, which belongs to the thirteenth century, was first printed in 1533.[1]

Fernel.

2. Oronce Finée, with some reputation in his own times, has, according to Montucla, no pretension to the name of a geometer; and another Frenchman, Fernel, better known as a physician, who published a Cosmotheoria in 1527, though he first gave the length of a degree of the meridian, and came not far from the truth, arrived at it by so unscientific a method, being in fact no other than counting the revolutions of a wheel along the main road, that he cannot be reckoned much higher.[2] These are obscure

Rhœticus.

[1] Montucla, Kästner.

[2] Montucla, ii. 316; Kästner, ii. 329. [It has lately been shown by Professor de Morgan (Philosophical Magazine for December, 1841), that Montucla, Delambre, and others have made an egregious error about Fernel's measurement, which they have reduced to French toises, in direct

names in comparison with Joachim, surnamed Rhœticus, from his native country. After the publication of the work of Regiomontanus on trigonometry, he conceived the project of carrying those labors still farther, and calculated the sines, tangents, and secants, the last of which he first reduced to tables, for every minute of the quadrant, to a radius of unity followed by fifteen ciphers; one of the most remarkable monuments, says Montucla, of human patience, or rather of a devotion to science, the more meritorious that it could not be attended with much glory. But this work was not published till 1594, and then not so complete as Rhœticus had left it.[1]

3. Jerome Cardan is, as it were, the founder of the higher algebra; for, whatever he may have borrowed from others, we derive the science from his Ars Magna, published in 1545. It contains many valuable discoveries; but that which has been most celebrated is the rule for the solution of cubic equations, generally known by Cardan's name, though he had obtained it from a man of equal genius in algebraic science, Nicolas Tartaglia. The original inventor appears to have been Scipio Ferreo, who, about 1505, by some unknown process, discovered the solution of a single case; that of $x^3 + p\,x = q$. Ferreo imparted the secret to one Fiore, or Floridus, who challenged Tartaglia to a public trial of skill, not unusual in that age. Before he heard of this, Tartaglia, as he assures us himself, had found out the solution of two other forms of cubic equation; $x^3 + p\,x^2 = q$, and $x^3 - p\,x^2 = q$. When the day of trial arrived, Tartaglia was able, not only to solve the problems offered by Fiore, but to baffle him entirely by others which resulted in the forms of equation, the solution of which had been discovered by himself. This was in 1535; and, four years afterwards, Cardan obtained the secret from Tartaglia under an oath of secrecy. In his Ars Magna, he did not hesitate to violate this engagement; and, though he gave Tartaglia the credit of the discovery, revealed the process to the world.[2]

Cardan and Tartaglia.

Cubic equations.

opposition to what he has said himself. He estimates the degree of latitude at 68.096 Italian miles (equal to 63 or 64 English), and consequently falls very short of the truth.—1842.]

[1] Montucla, i. 582; Biogr. Univ., art. "Joachim;" Kästner, i. 561.

[2] Playfair, in his second dissertation in the Encyclopædia Britannica, though he cannot but condemn Cardan, seems to think Tartaglia rightly treated for having concealed his discovery; and others have echoed this strain. Tartaglia himself says, in a passage I have read in Cossali, that he meant to have divulged it ultimately; but, in that age, money as well as credit was to be got by keeping the secret; and those who censure him wholly forget that the solution of cubic equations was, in the actual state of algebra, perfectly devoid of any utility to the world.

He has said himself, that by the help of Ferrari, a very good mathematician, he extended his rule to some cases not comprehended in that of Tartaglia; but the best historian of early algebra seems not to allow this claim.[1]

Beauty of the discovery.

4. This writer, Cossali, has ingeniously attempted to trace the process by which Tartaglia arrived at this discovery;[2] one which, when compared with the other leading rules of algebra, where the invention, however useful, has generally lain much nearer the surface, seems an astonishing effort of sagacity. Even Harriott's beautiful generalization of the composition of equations was prepared by what Cardan and Vieta had done before, or might have been suggested by observation in the less complex cases.[3]

Cardan's other discoveries.

5. Cardan, though not entitled to the honor of this discovery, nor even equal, perhaps, in mathematical genius to Tartaglia, made a great epoch in the science of algebra; and, according to Cossali and Hutton, has a claim to much that Montucla has unfairly or carelessly attributed to his favorite Vieta. "It appears," says Dr. Hutton, "from this short chapter (lib. x. cap. 1 of the

[1] Cossali, Storia Critica d' Algebra (1797), ii. 96, &c.; Hutton's Mathematical Dictionary; Montucla, i. 591; Kästner, i. 152.

[2] Ibid., p. 145. Tartaglia boasts of having discovered, by a geometrical construction, that the cube of $p+q=p^3+p^2q+pq^2+q^3$. I give the modern formula; but literal algebra was unknown to him.

[3] Cardan strongly expresses his sense of this recondite discovery. And as the passage in which he retraces the early progress of algebra is short, and is quoted from Cardan's works, which are scarce in England, by Kästner, who is himself not very commonly known here, I shall transcribe the whole passage as a curiosity for our philomaths. "Hæc ars olim a Mahomete Mosis Arabis filio initium sumpsit. Etenim hujus rei locuples testis Leonardus Pisanus. Reliquit autem capitula quatuor, cum suis demonstrationibus quas nos locis suis ascribemus. Post multa vero temporum intervalla tria capitula derivativa addita illis sunt, incerto autore, quæ tamen cum principalibus a Luca Paciolo posita sunt. Demum etiam ex primis, alia tria derivativa, a quodam ignoto viro inventa legi, hæc tamen minimè in lucem prodierant, cum essent aliis longe utiliora, nam cubi et numeri et cubi quadrati æstimationem docebant. Verum temporibus nostris Scipio Ferreus Bononiensis, capitulum cubi et rerum numero æqualium [$x^3+px=q$] invenit, rem sane pulchram et admirabilem: *cum omnem humanam subtilitatem, omnis ingenii mortalis claritatem ars hæc superet. donum profecto cæleste, experimentum autem virtutis animorum, atque adeo illustre, ut qui hæc attigerit nihil non intelligere posse se credat.* Hujus æmulatione Nicolaus Tartalea Brixellensis, amicus noster, cum in certamen cum illius discipulo Antonio Maria Florido venisset, capitulum idem ne vinceretur invenit, qui mihi ipsum multis precibus exoratus tradidit. Deceptus enim ego verbis Lucæ Pacioli, qui ultra sua capitula generale ullum aliud esse posse negat (quanquam tot jam antea rebus a me inventis sub manibus esset), desperabam tamen invenire quod quærere non audebam.* Inde autem illo habito demonstrationem venatus, intellexi complura alia posse haberi. Ac eo studio, auctaque jam confidentia, per me partim, ac etiam aliqua per Ludovicum Ferrarium, olim alumnum nostrum, inveni. Porro quæ ab his inventa sunt, illorum nominibus decorabuntur, cætera quæ nomine carent nostra sunt. At etiam demonstrationes, præter tres Mahometis, et duas Ludovici, omnes nostræ sunt, singulæ que capitibus suis præponentur, inde regula addita, subjicietur experimentum." — Kästner, p. 152. The passage in Italics is also quoted by Cossali, p. 159.

* [This was very erroneously printed in the first edition; in consequence, as I believe, of a mistake I had made in transcription. — 1842.]

Ars Magna), that he had discovered most of the principal roperties of the roots of equations, and could point out the umber and nature of the roots, partly from the signs of he terms, and partly from the magnitude and relations of the o-efficients." Cossali has given the larger part of a quarto olume to the algebra of Cardan; his object being to establish he priority of the Italian's claim to most of the discoveries scribed by Montucla to others, and especially to Vieta. Cardan knew how to transform a complete cubic equation nto one wanting the second term; one of the flowers which Montucla has placed on the head of Vieta; and this he explains so fully, that Cossali charges the French historian of nathématics with having never read the Ars Magna.[1] Leoard of Pisa had been aware, that quadratic equations might ave two positive roots; but Cardan first perceived, or at east first noticed, the negative roots, which he calls *fictæ adices*.[2] In this, perhaps, there is nothing extraordinary: he algebraic language must early have been perceived by uch acute men as exercised themselves in problems to give a ouble solution of every quadratic equation; but, in fact, the onditions of these problems, being always numerical, were uch as to render a negative result practically false, and imertinent to the question. It is therefore, perhaps, without nuch cause that Cossali triumphs in the ignorance shown of egative values by Vieta, Bachet, and even Harriott, though Cardan had pointed them out;[3] since we may better say, that hey did not trouble themselves with what, in the actual appliation of algebra, could be of no utility. Cardan also is said o have discovered, that every cubic equation has one or three eal roots, and (what seems hardly probable in the state of cience at that time) that there are as many positive or true oots as changes of sign in the equation; that the co-efficient of the second term is equal to the sum of the roots; so that, vhere it is wanting, the positive and negative values must compensate each other;[4] and that the known term is the product of all the roots. Nor was he ignorant of a method of extracting roots by approximation; but in this again the defi-

[1] P. 164.

[2] Montucla gives Cardan the credit due or this; at least in his second edition 1799), p. 595.

[3] i. 23.

[4] It must, apparently, have been through his knowledge of this property of the coefficient of the second term, that Cardan recognized the existence of equal roots, even when affected by the same sign (Cossali, ii. 362), which, considered in relation to the numerical problems then in use, would seem a kind of absurdity.

niteness of solution, which numerical problems admit and re quire, would prevent any great progress from being made. The rules are not perhaps all laid down by him very clearly and it is to be observed, that he confined himself chiefly to equations not above the third power; though he first pub lished the method of solving biquadratics, invented by hi co-adjutor Ferrari. Cossali has also shown, that the applica tion of algebra to geometry, and even to the geometrical con struction of problems, was known in some cases by Tartagli and Cardan; thus plucking another feather from the wing of Vieta or of Descartes. It is a little amusing to see, that after Montucla had labored with so much success to despoi Harriott of the glory which Wallis had, perhaps with too national a feeling, bestowed upon him for a long list of dis coveries contained in the writings of Vieta, a claimant by an older title started up in Jerome Cardan; who, if we may trus his accomplished advocate, seems to have established his righ at the expense of both.

Imperfections of algebraic language.

6. These anticipations of Cardan are the more truly won derful when we consider that the symbolical languag of algebra, that powerful instrument not only in ex pediting the processes of thought, but in suggestin general truths to the mind, was nearly unknown i his age. Diophantus, Fra Luca, and Cardan make use occa sionally of letters to express indefinite quantities besides th *res* or *cosa*, sometimes written shortly, for the assumed un known number of an equation. But letters were not ye substituted for known quantities. Michael Stifel, in his Arith metica Integra, Nuremberg, 1544, is said to have first use the signs + and —, and numeral exponents of powers.[2] It is very singular that discoveries of the greatest convenience, an apparently not above the ingenuity of a parish schoolmaster should have been overlooked by men of extraordinary acute ness, like Tartaglia, Cardan, and Ferrari, and hardly less so that by dint of this acuteness they dispensed with the aid of these contrivances, in which we suppose that so much of the utility of algebraic expression consists.

[1] Kästner, p. 161. In one place, Cossali shows that Cardan had transported all the quantities of an equation to one side, making the whole equal to zero, which Wallis has ascribed to Harriott as his leading discovery, p. 324. Yet in another passage we find Cossali saying: "Una somma di quantità uguale al zero avea un' ari mostruosa, e non sapeasi di equazion s fatta concepire idea." — p. 159.

[2] Hutton; Kästner.

7. But the great boast of science during this period is the reatise of Copernicus on the revolutions of the eavenly bodies, in six books, published at Nuremerg in 1543.[1] This founder of modern astronomy was born t Thorn, of a good family, in 1473; and, after receiving the est education his country furnished, spent some years in Italy, endering himself master of all the mathematical and astroomical science at that time attainable. He became possessed fterwards of an ecclesiastical benefice in his own country. It ppears to have been about 1507, that, after meditating on arious schemes besides the Ptolemaic, he began to adopt and onfirm in writing that of Pythagoras, as alone capable of xplaining the planetary motions with that simplicity which ives a presumption of truth in the works of nature.[2] Many ears of exact observation confirmed his mind in the persuaion that he had solved the grandest problem which can occuy the astronomer. He seems to have completed his treatise bout 1530; but perhaps dreaded the bigoted prejudices which afterwards oppressed Galileo. Hence he is careful o propound his theory as an hypothesis, though it is sufficintly manifest that he did not doubt of its truth. It was first ublicly announced by his disciple Joachim Rhœticus, already nentioned for his trigonometry, in the Narratio de Revoluionibus Copernici, printed at Dantzic in 1540. The treatise f Copernicus himself, three years afterwards, is dedicated to he pope, Paul III., as if to shield himself under that sacred nantle. But he was better protected by the common safeuard against oppression. The book reached him on the day f his death; and he just touched with his hands the great egacy he was to bequeath to mankind. But many years vere to elapse before they availed themselves of the wisdom

Copernicus.

[1] The titlepage and advertisement of so mous a work, and which so few of my eaders will have seen, are worth copying om Kästner, ii. 595. "Nicolai Copernici orinensis de revolutionibus orbium cœlesum libri vi.

"Habes in hoc opere jam recens nato et dito, studiose lector, motus stellarum tam xarum quam erraticarum, cum ex veteibus tum etiam ex recentibus observaonibus restitutos; et novis insuper ac dmirabilibus hypothesibus ornatos. Haes etiam tabulas expeditissimas, ex quibus osdem ad quodvis tempus quam facillime alculare poteris. Igitur eme, lege, fruere. Αγεωμετρητος ουδεις εισιτω." Noribergæ, *apud* Joh. Petreium, anno MDxliii.

[2] This is the proper statement of the Copernican argument, as it then stood: it rested on what we may call a metaphysical probability, founded upon its beauty and simplicity; for it is to be remembered that the Ptolemaic hypothesis explained all the phenomena then known. Those which are only to be solved by the supposition of the earth's motion were discovered long afterwards. This excuses the slow reception of the new system, interfering as it did with so many prejudices, and incapable of that kind of proof which mankind generally demand

of Copernicus. The progress of his system, even amon astronomers, as we shall hereafter see, was exceeding slow We may just mention here, that no kind of progress wa made in mechanical or optical science during the first part o the sixteenth century.

SECTION II.

On Medicine and Anatomy.

8. THE revival of classical literature had an extensiv influence where we might not immediately anticipate it, — o the science of medicine. Jurisprudence itself, thoug nominally and exclusively connected with the law of Rome, was hardly more indebted to the restorer of ancient learning than the art of healing, which seems t own no mistress but nature, no code of laws but those whic regulate the human system. But the Greeks, among their othe vast superiorities above the Arabians, who borrowed so much and so much perverted what they borrowed, were not onl the real founders, but the best teachers, of medicine, — a science which in their hands seems, more than any other, t have anticipated the Baconian philosophy; being founded o an induction proceeding by select experience, always obser vant, always cautious, and ascending slowly to the generalitie of theory. But, instead of Hippocrates and Galen, the Ara bians brought in physicians of their own, men, doubtless, of considerable though inferior merit; and substituted arbitrar or empirical precepts for the enlarged philosophy of th Greeks. The scholastic subtilty also obtruded itself even int medicine; and the writings of the middle ages on these sub jects are alike barbarous in style and useless in substance Pharmacy owes much to this oriental school; but it has

Revival of Greek medicine.

[1] Gassendi, Vita Copernici; Biogr. Univ.; Montucla; Kästner; Playfair. Gassendi, p. 14–22, gives a short analysis of the great work of Copernicus, De orbium cœlestium revolutionibus, p. 22. The hypothesis is generally laid down in the first of the six books. One of the most remarkable passages in Copernicus is his conjecture, that gravitation was not a central tendency, as had been supposed, but an attraction common to matter, and probably extending t the heavenly bodies, though it does no appear that he surmised their mutual influences in virtue of it: "Gravitatem ess affectionem non terræ totius, sed partium ejus propriam, qualem soli etiam et lunæ cæterisque astris convenire credibile est." These are the words of Copernicus himself quoted by Gassendi, p. 19.

retained no reputation in physiological or pathological science.

9. Nicolas Leonicenus, who became professor at Ferrara before 1470, was the first restorer of the Hippocratic method of practice. He lived to a very advanced age, and was the first translator of Galen from the Greek.[1] Our excellent countryman, Linacre, did almost as much for medicine. The College of Physicians, founded by Henry VIII. in 1518, venerates him as its original president. His primary object was to secure a learned profession, to rescue the art of healing from mischievous ignorance, and to guide the industrious student in the path of real knowledge, which at that time lay far more through the regions of ancient learning than at present. It was important, not for the mere dignity of the profession, but for its proper ends, to encourage the cultivation of the Greek language or to supply its want by accurate versions of the chief medical writers.[2] Linacre himself, and several eminent physicians on the Continent, Cop, Ruel, Gonthier, Fuchs, by such labors in translation, restored the school of Hippocrates. That of the Arabians rapidly lost ground, though it preserved through the sixteenth century an ascendency in Spain; and some traces of its influence, especially the precarious empiricism of judging diseases by the renal secretion, without sight of the patient, which was very general in that age, continued long afterwards in several parts of Europe.[3]

Linacre and other physicians.

10. The study of Hippocrates taught the medical writers of this century to observe and describe like him. Their works, chiefly indeed after the period with which we are immediately concerned, are very numerous; and some of them deserve much praise, though neither the theory of the science, nor the power of judiciously observing and describing, was yet in a very advanced state. The besetting sin of all who should have labored for truth, an undue respect for authority, made Hippocrates and Galen, especially the former, as much the idols of the medical world as Augustin and Aristotle were of theology and metaphysics. This led to a pedantic erudition, and contempt of opposite experience, which rendered the professors of medicine an inexhaustible

Medical innovators.

[1] Biogr. Univ.; Sprengel, Hist. de la Médecine (traduite par Jourdan), vol. ii.

[2] Johnson's Life of Linacre, p. 207, 279; Biogr. Britann.

[3] Sprengel, vol iii. *passim*

theme of popular ridicule. Some, however, even at an early time, broke away from the trammels of implicit obedience to the Greek masters. Fernel, one of the first physicians in France, rejecting what he could not approve in their writings, gave an example of free inquiry. Argentier of Turin tended to shake the influence of Galen by founding a school which combated many of his leading theories.[1] But the most successful opponent of the orthodox creed was Paracelsus. Of his speculative philosophy, or rather the wild chimeras which he borrowed or devised, enough has been said in former pages. His reputation was originally founded on a supposed skill in medicine; and it is probable, that independently of his real merit in the application of chemistry to medicine, and in the employment of very powerful agents, such as antimony, the fanaticism of his pretended philosophy would exercise that potency over the bodily frame, to which disease has, in recent experience, so often yielded.[2]

Paracelsus.

11. The first important advances in anatomical knowledge since the time of Mundinus were made by Berenger of Carpi, in his commentary upon that author, printed at Bologna in 1521, which it was thought worth while to translate into English as late as 1664, and in his Isagogæ breves in Anatomiam, Bologna, 1522. He followed the steps of Mundinus in human dissection, and thus gained an advantage over Galen. Hence we owe to him the knowledge of several specific differences between the human structure and that of quadrupeds. Berenger is asserted to have discovered two of the small bones of the ear, though this is contested on behalf of Achillini. Portal observes, that, though some have regarded Berenger as the restorer of the science of anatomy, it is hard to strip one so much superior to him as Vesalius of that honor.[3]

Anatomy. Berenger.

12. Every early anatomist was left far behind when Vesalius, a native of Brussels, who acquired in early youth an extraordinary reputation on this side of the Alps, and in 1540 became professor of the science at Pavia, published at Basle, in 1543, his great work De Corporis humani Fabrica. If Vesalius was not quite to anatomy what

Vesalius.

[1] Id. 204. "Argentier," he says, "was the first to lay down a novel and true principle, that the different faculties of the soul are not inherent in certain distinct parts of the brain."

[2] Sprengel, vol. iii.

[3] Hist. de l'Anatomie, i. 277.

Copernicus was to astronomy, he has yet been said, a little hyperbolically, to have discovered a new world. A superstitious prejudice against human dissection had confined the ancient anatomists in general to pigs and apes, though Galen, according to Portal, had some experience in the former. Mundinus and Berenger, by occasionally dissecting the human body, had thrown much additional light on its structure; and the superficial muscles, those immediately under the integuments, had been studied by Da Vinci and others for the purposes of painting and sculpture. Vesalius first gave a complete description of the human body, with designs, which, at the time, were ascribed to Titian. We have here, therefore, a great step made in science: the precise estimation of Vesalius's discoveries must be sought, of course, in anatomical history.[1]

Portal's account of him.

13. "Vesalius," says Portal, in the rapturous strain of one devoted to his own science, "appears to me one of the greatest men who ever existed. Let the astronomers vaunt their Copernicus, the natural philosophers their Galileo and Torricelli, the mathematicians their Pascal, the geographers their Columbus, — I shall always place Vesalius above all their heroes. The first study for man is man. Vesalius has had this noble object in view, and has admirably attained it: he has made on himself and his fellows such discoveries as Columbus could only make by travelling to the extremity of the world. The discoveries of Vesalius are of direct importance to man: by acquiring fresh knowledge of his own structure, man seems to enlarge his existence; while discoveries in geography or astronomy affect him but in a very indirect manner." He proceeds to compare him with Winslow, more than a century later, in order to show how little had been done in the intermediate time. Vesalius seems not to have known the osteology of the ear. His account of the teeth is not complete; but he first clearly described the bones of the feet. He has given a full account of the muscles, but with some mistakes; and was ignorant of a very few. In his account of the sanguineous and nervous systems, the errors seem more numerous. He describes the intestines better than his predecessors, and the heart very well; the organs of generation not better than they, and some

[1] Portal, i. 394–433.

times omits their discoveries; the brain admirably, little having since been added.

14. The zeal of Vesalius and his fellow-students for anatomical science led them to strange scenes of adventure. Those services which have since been thrown on the refuse of mankind, they voluntarily undertook.

His human dissections.

"Entire affection scorneth nicer hands."

They prowled by night in charnel-houses; they dug up the dead from the grave; they climbed the gibbet, in fear and silence, to steal the mouldering carcass of the murderer, — the risk of ignominious punishment, and the secret stings of superstitious remorse, exalting, no doubt, the delight of these useful but not very enviable pursuits.[1]

15. It may be mentioned here, that Vesalius, after living for some years in the court of Charles and Philip as their physician, met with a strange reverse, characteristic enough of such a place. Being absurdly accused of having dissected a Spanish gentleman before he was dead, Vesalius only escaped capital punishment, at the instance of the Inquisition, by undertaking a pilgrimage to Jerusalem; during which he was shipwrecked, and died of famine in one of the Greek islands.[2]

Fate of Vesalius.

16. The best anatomists were found in Italy. But Francis I. invited one of these, Vidus Vidius, to his royal college at Paris; and, from that time, France had several of respectable name. Such were Charles Etienne, one of the great typographical family, Sylvius, and Gonthier.[3] A French writer about 1540, Levasseur, has been thought to have known, at least, the circulation of the blood through the lungs, as well as the valves of the arteries and veins, and their direction, and its purpose; treading closely on an anticipation of Harvey.[4] But this seems to be too hastily inferred. Portal has erroneously supposed the celebrated passage of Servetus on the circulation of the blood to be contained in his book De Trinitatis erroribus, published in 1531;[5] whereas it is

Other anatomists.

[1] Portal, p. 395.

[2] Portal; Tiraboschi, ix. 34; Biogr. Univ. [Sprengel, Hist. de la Médecine, vol. iv. p. 6, treats the cause of the pilgrimage of Vesalius, assigned by these writers, as a fable. — 1842.]

[3] Portal, i. 330, *et post.*

[4] Portal, p. 373, quotes the passage, which at first seems to warrant this inference, but is rather obscurely worded. We shall return to this subject when we arrive at Harvey.

[5] P. 300.

really found in the Christianismi Restitutio, which did not appear till 1553.

17. The practice of trusting to animal dissection, from which it was difficult for anatomists to extricate themselves, led some men of real merit into errors. They seem also not to have profited sufficiently by the writings of their predecessors. Massa of Venice, one of the greatest of this age, is ignorant of some things known to Berenger. Many proofs occur in Portal how imperfectly the elder anatomists could yet demonstrate the more delicate parts of the human body.

Imperfection of the science.

SECTION III.

On Natural History.

18. THE progress of natural history, in all its departments, was very slow, and should of course be estimated by the additions made to the valuable materials collected by Aristotle, Theophrastus, Dioscorides, and Pliny The few botanical treatises that had appeared before this time were too meagre and imperfect to require mention. Otto Brunfels of Strasburg was the first who published, in 1530, a superior work, Herbarum vivæ Eicones, in three volumes folio, with 238 wooden cuts of plants.[1] Euricius Cordus, of Marburg, in his Botanilogicon, or dialogues on plants, displays, according to the Biographie Universelle, but little knowledge of Greek, and still less observation of nature. Cordus has deserved more praise (though this seems better due to Lorenzo de' Medici), as the first who established a botanical garden. This was at Marburg in 1530.[2] But the fortunes of private physicians were hardly

Botany.

Botanical gardens.

[1] Biogr. Univ.

[2] Id.; Andrès, xiii. 80; Eichhorn, iii. 304. See, too, Roscoe's Leo X., iv. 125, for some pleasing notices of the early studies in natural history. Pontanus was fond of it; and his poem on the cultivation of the lemon, orange, and citron (De hortis Hesperidum) shows an acquaintance with some of the operations of horticulture. The garden of Bembo was also celebrated. Theophrastus and Dioscorides were published in Latin before 1500. But it was not till about the middle of the sixteenth century that botany, through the commentaries of Matthioli on Dioscorides, began to assume a distinct form, and to be studied as a separate branch.

equal to the cost of an useful collection. The University of Pisa led the way by establishing a public garden in 1545, according to the date which Tiraboschi has determined: that of Padua had founded a professorship of botany in 1533.[1]

19. Ruel, a physician of Soissons, an excellent Greek scholar, had become known by a translation of Dioscorides in 1516, upon which Huet has bestowed high praise. His more celebrated treatise, De Natura Stirpium, appeared at Paris in 1536, and is one of the handsomest offspring of that press. It is a compilation from the Greek and Latin authors on botany, made with taste and judgment. His knowledge, however, derived from experience, was not considerable, though he has sometimes given the French names of species described by the Greeks, so far as his limited means of observation and the difference of climate enabled him. Many later writers have borrowed from Ruel their general definitions and descriptions of plants, which he himself took from Theophrastus.[2]

Ruel.

20. Ruel, however, seems to have been left far behind by Leonard Fuchs, professor of medicine in more than one German university, who has secured a verdant immortality in the well-known Fuchsia. Besides many works on his own art, esteemed in their time, he published at Basle in 1542 his Commentaries on the History of Plants, containing above 500 figures, a botanical treatise frequently reprinted, and translated into most European languages. "Considered as a naturalist, and especially as a botanist, Fuchs holds a distinguished place; and he has thrown a strong light on that science. His chief object is to describe exactly the plants used in medicine; and his prints, though mere outlines, are generally faithful. He shows that the plants and vegetable products mentioned by Theophrastus, Dioscorides, Hippocrates, and Galen, had hitherto been ill known."[3]

Fuchs.

21. Matthioli, an Italian physician, in a peaceful retreat near Trent, accomplished a laborious repertory of medical botany in his Commentaries on Dioscorides, published originally, 1544, in Italian, but translated by himself into Latin, and frequently reprinted throughout Europe. Notwithstanding a bad arrangement, and the author's proneness

Matthioli.

[1] ix. 10. [2] Biogr. Univ. (by M. du Petit Thouars) [3] Id

to credulity, it was of great service at a time when no good work on that subject was in existence in Italy; and its reputation seems to have been not only general, but of long duration.[1]

22. It was not singular that much should have been published, imperfect as it might be, on the natural history of plants, while that of animal nature, as a matter of science, lay almost neglected. The importance of vegetable products in medicine was far more extensive and various; while the ancient treatises, which formed substantially the chief knowledge of nature possessed in the sixteenth century, are more copious and minute on the botanical than the animated kingdom. Hence we find an absolute dearth of books relating to zoölogy. That of P. Jovius de Piscibus Romanis is rather one of a philologer and a lover of good cheer than a naturalist, and treats only of the fish eaten at the Roman tables.[2] Gillius de vi et natura animalium is little else than a compilation from Ælian and other ancient authors, though Niceron says that the author has interspersed some observations of his own.[3] No work of the least importance, even for that time, can perhaps be traced in Europe on any part of zoölogy, before the Avium præcipuarum historia of our countryman Turner, published at Cologne in 1548, though this is confined to species described by the ancients. Gesner, in his Pandects, which bear date in the same year, several times refers to it with commendation.[4]

Low state of zoölogy.

23. Agricola, a native of Saxony, acquired a perfect knowledge of the processes of metallurgy from the miners of Chemnitz, and perceived the immense resources that might be drawn from the abysses of the earth. "He is the first mineralogist," says Cuvier, "who appeared after the revival of science in Europe. He was to mineralogy what Gesner was to zoölogy: the chemical part of metallurgy, and especially what relates to assaying, is treated with great care, and has been little improved down to the end of the eighteenth century. It is plain that he was acquainted with the classics,

Agricola.

[1] Tiraboschi, ix. 2; Andrès, xiii. 85; Corniani, vi. 5.

[2] Andrès, xiii. 143; Roscoe's Leo X., *ubi supra*.

[3] Vol. xxiii.; Biogr. Univ.; Andrès, xiii. 144.

[4] Pandect. Univers., lib. 14. Gesner may be said to make great use of Turner; a high compliment from so illustrious a naturalist. He quotes also a book on quadrupeds lately printed in German by Michael Herr. Turner, whom we shall find again as a naturalist, became afterwards Dean of Wells, and was one of the early Puritans. See Chalmers's Dictionary.

the Greek alchemists, and many manuscripts. Yet he believed in the goblins to whom miners ascribe the effects of mephitic exhalations."[1]

SECTION IV.

On Oriental Literature.

24. THE study of Hebrew was naturally one of those which flourished best under the influence of Protestantism. It was exclusively connected with Scriptural interpretation, and could neither suit the polished irreligion of the Italians nor the bigotry of those who owned no other standard than the Vulgate translation. Sperone observes in one of his dialogues, that as much as Latin is prized in Italy, so much do the Germans value the Hebrew language.[2] We have anticipated in another place the translations of the Old Testament by Luther, Pagninus, and other Hebraists of this age. Sebastian Munster published the first grammar and lexicon of the Chaldee dialect in 1527. His Hebrew Grammar had preceded in 1525. The Hebrew Lexicon of Pagninus appeared in 1529, and that of Munster himself in 1543. Elias Levita, the learned Jew who has been already mentioned, deserves to stand in this his natural department above even Munster. Among several works that fall within this period, we may notice the Masorah (Venice, 1538, and Basle, 1539), wherein he excited the attention of the world by denying the authority and antiquity of vowel-points, and a Lexicon of the Chaldee and Rabbinical dialects, in 1541. "Those," says Simon, "who would thoroughly understand Hebrew should read the Treatises of Elias Levita, which are full of important observations necessary for the explanation of the sacred text."[3] Pellican, one of the first who embraced the principles of the Zuinglian reform, has merited a warm eulogy from Simon for his Commentarii Bibliorum (Zurich, 1531–1536, five volumes in folio), especially for avoiding that display of rabbinical learning which the German Hebraists used to affect.[4]

Hebrew.

Elias Levita.

Pellican.

[1] Biogr. Univ.
[2] P. 102 (edit. 1596).
[3] Biogr. Univ.
[4] Id.

25. Few endeavors were made in this period towards the cultivation of the other Oriental languages. Pagnino printed an edition of the Koran at Venice in 1530; but it was immediately suppressed, a precaution hardly required while there was no one able to read it. But it may have been supposed, that the leaves of some books, like that recorded in the Arabian Nights, contain an active poison that does not wait for the slow process of understanding their contents. Two crude attempts at introducing the Eastern tongues were made soon afterwards. One of these was by William Postel, a man of some parts and more reading, but chiefly known, while he was remembered at all, for mad reveries of fanaticism, and an idolatrous veneration for a saint of his own manufacture, La Mère Jeanne, the Joanna Southcote of the sixteenth century. We are only concerned at present with his collection of alphabets, twelve in number, published at Paris in 1538. The greater part of these are Oriental. An Arabic Grammar followed the same year; but the types are so very imperfect that it would be difficult to read them. A polyglott alphabet on a much larger scale appeared at Pavia the next year, through the care of Teseo Ambrogio, containing those of forty languages. Ambrogio gave also an introduction to the Chaldee, Syriac, and Armenian, but very defective, at least as to the two latter. Such rude and incorrect publications hardly deserve the name of beginnings. According to Andrès, Arabic was publicly taught at Paris by Giustiniani, and at Salamanca by Clenardus. The Ethiopic version of the New Testament was printed at Rome in 1548.

Arabic and Oriental literature.

SECTION V.

On Geography and History.

26. THE curiosity natural to mankind had been gratified by various publications since the invention of printing, containing either the relations of ancient travellers, such as Marco Polo, or of those under the Spanish or Portuguese flags, who had laid open two new worlds to the European reader. These were for the first time collected, to the number

Geography of Grynæus.

of seventeen, by Simon Grynæus, a learned professor at Basle, in Novus orbis regionum et insularum veteribus incognitarum, printed at Paris in 1532. We find in this collection, besides an introduction to cosmography by Sebastian Munster, a map of the world bearing the date 1531. The Cosmography of Apianus, professor at Ingoldstadt, published in 1524, contains also a map of the four quarters of the world. In this of Grynæus's collection, a rude notion of the eastern regions of Asia appears. Sumatra is called Taprobane, and placed in the 150th meridian. A vague delineation of China and the adjacent sea is given; but Catay is marked farther north. The island of Gilolo, which seems to be Japan, is about 240° east longitude. South America is noted as *Terra Australis recenter inventa, sed nondum plane cognita;* and there is as much of North America as Sebastian Cabot had discovered, a little enlarged by lucky conjecture. Magellan, by circumnavigating the world, had solved a famous problem. We find accordingly in this map an attempt to divide the globe by the 360 meridians of longitude. The best account of his voyage, that by Pigafetta, was not published till 1556; but the first, Maximilianus de insulis Moluccis, appeared in 1523.

Apianus.

27. The Cosmography of Apianus, above mentioned, was reprinted with additions by Gemma Frisius in 1533 and 1550. It is, however, as a work of mere geography, very brief and superficial, though it may exhibit as much of the astronomical part of the science as the times permitted. **Munster.** That of Sebastian Munster, published in 1546, notwithstanding its title, extends only to the German Empire.[1] The Isolario of Bordone (Venice, 1528) contains a description of all the islands of the world, with maps.[2]

Voyages

28. A few voyages were printed before the middle of the century, which have, for the most part, found their way into the collection of Ramusio. The most con-

[1] Eichhorn, iii. 294.

[2] Tiraboschi, ix. 179. [The best map, probably, of this period is one in the British Museum, executed in France before 1536, as is inferred from the form of the French king's crown, which was altered in that year. This map is generally superior to some which were engraved at a later time, and represents the figure of the African continent. It has excited some attention in consequence of an apparent delineation of Australia, under the name of Java Grande. But this, which seems to come immediately from some Italian work, may be traced to Marco Polo, the great father of geographical conjecture in the middle ages. He gives an account, such as he picked up in China, of two islands, Java Major and Java Minor. The continent delineated in this French map is only the island of Java, vastly enlarged. —1842.]

iderable is the History of the Indies, that is, of the Spanish lominions in America, by Gonzalo Hernandez, some- **Oviedo.** imes called Oviedo, by which name he is recorded in he Biographie Universelle. The author had resided for some ears in St. Domingo. He published a summary of the geneal and natural history of the Indies in 1526, and twenty books f this entire work in 1535. The remaining thirty did not ppear till 1783. In the long list of geographical treatises iven by Ortelius, a small number belong to this earlier period f the century. But it may be generally said, that the acuaintance of Europe with the rest of the world could as yet e only obtained orally from Spanish and Portuguese sailors r adventurers, and was such as their falsehood and blundering vould impart.

29. It is not my design to comprehend historical literature, xcept as to the chief publications, in these volumes; **Historical works.** nd it is hitherto but a barren field: for, though Guicciardini died in 1540, his great history did not appear till 564. Some other valuable histories, those of Nardi, Segni, Varchi, were also kept back, through political or other causes, ill a comparatively late period. That of Paulus Jovius, which s not in very high estimation, appeared in 1550, and may be eckoned, perhaps, after that of Machiavel, the best of this ge. Upon this side of the Alps, several works of this class, o which the historical student has recourse, might easily be numerated, but none of a philosophical character, or remarkable for beauty of style. I should, however, wish to make an exception for the Memoirs of the Chevalier Bayard, written by his secretary, and known by the title of Le Loyal Serviteur: hey are full of warmth and simplicity. A chronicle bearing he name of Carion, but really written by Melanchthon, and published in the German language, 1532, was afterwards translated into Latin, and became the popular manual of universal history.[1] But ancient and mediæval history was as yet very imperfectly made known to those who had no access to its original sources. Even in Italy, little had yet been done with critical or even extensive erudition.

1 Bayle, art. "Carion;" Eichhorn, iii 285.

Italian academies.

30. Italy in the sixteenth century was remarkable for the number of her literary academies; institutions which, though by no means peculiar to her, have in no other country been so general or so conspicuous. We have already taken notice of that established by Aldus Manutius at Venice early in this century, and of those of older date, which had enjoyed the patronage of princes at Florence and Naples, as well as of that which Pomponius Lætus and his associates, with worse auspices, had endeavored to form at Rome. The Roman academy, after a long season of persecution or neglect, revived in the genial reign of Leo X. "Those were happy days," says Sadolet in 1529, writing to Angelo Colocci, a Latin poet of some reputation, "when in your suburban gardens, or mine on the Quirinal, or in the Circus, or by the banks of the Tiber, we held those meetings of learned men, all recommended by their own virtues and by public reputation. Then it was, that, after a repast, which the wit of the guests rendered exquisite, we heard poems or orations recited to our great delight, — productions of the ingenious Casanuova, the sublime Vida, the elegant and correct Beroaldo, and many others still living or now no more."[1] Corycius, a wealthy German, encouraged the good-humored emulation of these Roman luminaries.[2] But the miserable reverse that not long after the death of Leo befell Rome put an end to this academy, which was afterwards replaced by others of less fame.

They pay regard to the language.

31. The first academies of Italy had chiefly directed their attention to classical literature: they compared manuscripts, they suggested new readings or new interpretations, they deciphered inscriptions and coins, they sat in judgment on a Latin ode, or debated the propriety of a phrase. Their own poetry had, perhaps, never been neglected; but it was not till the writings of Bembo founded a new code of criticism in the Italian language that they began to study it minutely, and judge of compositions with that fastidious scrupulousness which they had been used to exercise upon modern Latinity. Several academies were established with a view to this purpose, and became the self-appointed censors of their native literature. The reader will remember what has been already mentioned, that there was a peculiar

[1] Sadolet, Epist., p. 225 (edit. 1554). Roscoe has quoted this interesting letter.
[2] Roscoe, iii. 480.

source of verbal criticism in Italy, from the want of a recognized standard of idiom. The very name of the language was long in dispute. Bembo maintained that Florentine was the proper appellation. Varchi and other natives of the city have adhered to this very restrictive monopoly. Several, with more plausibility, contended for the name Tuscan; and this, in fact, was so long adopted, that it is hardly yet, perhaps, altogether out of use. The majority, however, were not Tuscans; and, while it is generally agreed that the highest purity of their language is to be found in Tuscany, the word Italian has naturally prevailed as its denomination.

Their fondness for Petrarch.

32. The academy of Florence was instituted in 1540 to illustrate and perfect the *Tuscan* language, especially by a close attention to the poetry of Petrarch. Their admiration of Petrarch became an exclusive idolatry: the critics of this age would acknowledge no defect in him, nor excellence in any different style. Dissertations and commentaries on Petrarch, in all the diffuseness characteristic of the age and the nation, crowd the Italian libraries. We are, however, anticipating a little in mentioning them; for few belong to so early a period as the present. But, by dint of this superstitious accuracy in style, the language rapidly acquired a purity and beauty which has given the writers of the sixteenth century a value in the eyes of their countrymen not always so easily admitted by those who, being less able to perceive the delicacy of expression, are at leisure to yawn over their frequent tediousness and inanity.

They become numerous.

33. The Italian academies which arose in the first half of the century, and we shall meet with others hereafter, are too numerous to be reckoned in these pages. The most famous were the Intronati of Siena, founded in 1525, and devoted, like that of Florence, to the improvement of their language; the Infiammati of Padua, founded by some men of high attainments in 1534; and that of Modena, which, after a short career of brilliancy, fell under such suspicions of heresy, and was subjected to such inquisitorial jealousy about 1542, that it never again made any figure in literary history.[1]

34. Those academies have usually been distinguished by little peculiarities, which border sometimes on the ridiculous,

[1] Tiraboschi, viii. ch. 4, is my chief authority about the Italian academies of this period.

but serve probably, at least in the beginning, to keep up the spirit of such societies. They took names humorously quaint; they adopted devices and distinctions which made them conspicuous and inspired a vain pleasure in belonging to them. The Italian nobility, living a good deal in cities, and restrained from political business, fell willingly into these literary associations. They have, perhaps, as a body, been better educated, or, at least, better acquainted with their own literature and with classical antiquity, than men of equal rank in other countries. This was more the case in the sixteenth century than at present. Genius and erudition have been always honored in Italy; and the more, probably, that they have not to stand the competition of overpowering wealth or of political influence.

Their distinctions.

35. Academies of the Italian kind do not greatly favor the vigorous advances in science, and much less the original bursts of genius, for which men of powerful minds are designed by nature. They form an oligarchy, pretending to guide the public taste, as they are guided themselves, by arbitrary maxims and close adherence to precedents The spirit of criticism which they foster is a salutary barrier against bad taste and folly, but is too minute and scrupulous in repressing the individualities that characterize real talents, and ends by producing an unblemished mediocrity, without the powers of delight or excitement, for which alone the literature of the imagination is desired.

Evils connected with them.

36. In the beginning of this century, several societies were set on foot in Germany for the promotion of ancient learning, besides that already mentioned, of the Rhine, established by Camerarius of Dalberg and Conrad Celtes in the preceding age. Wimpfeling presided over one at Strasburg in 1514; and we find another at Augsburg in 1518. It is probable that the religious animosities which followed stood in the way of similar institutions; or they may have existed without obtaining much celebrity.[1]

They succeed less in Germany.

37. Italy was rich, far beyond any other country, in public and private libraries. The Vatican, first in dignity, in antiquity, and in number of books, increased under almost every successive pope, except Julius II., the least favorable to learning of them all. The Laurentian library, pur-

Libraries.

[1] Jugler, in his Hist. Litteraria, mentions none between that of the Rhine, and one established at Weimar in 1617, p. 1994.

chased by Leo X. before his accession to the papacy, from a monastery at Florence, which had acquired the collection after the fall of the Medici in 1494, was restored to that city by Clement VII., and placed in the newly erected building which still contains it. The public libraries of Venice and Ferrara were conspicuous; and even a private citizen of the former, the Cardinal Grimani, is said to have left one of eight thousand volumes; at that time, it appears, a remarkable number.[1] Those of Heidelberg and Vienna, commenced in the fifteenth century, were still the most distinguished in Germany; and Cardinal Ximenes founded one at Alcalá.[2] It is unlikely that many private libraries of great extent existed in the empire; but the trade of bookselling, though not yet, in general, separated from that of printing, had become of considerable importance.

1 Tiraboschi, viii. 197-219.

2 Jugler, Hist. Litteraria, p. 206, *et alibi*.

END OF VOL. I.

INTRODUCTION

TO THE

LITERATURE OF EUROPE

IN THE

FIFTEENTH, SIXTEENTH, AND SEVENTEENTH CENTURIES.

By HENRY HALLAM, LL.D., F.R.A.S.,

FOREIGN ASSOCIATE OF THE INSTITUTE OF FRANCE.

VOLUME II.

CONTENTS

OF

THE SECOND VOLUME.

PART II.

ON THE LITERATURE OF THE LATTER HALF OF THE SIXTEENTH CENTURY.

CHAPTER I.

HISTORY OF ANCIENT LITERATURE IN EUROPE FROM 1550 TO 1600.

CONTENTS

OF

THE SECOND VOLUME.

PART II.

ON THE LITERATURE OF THE LATTER HALF OF THE SIXTEENTH CENTURY.

CHAPTER I.

HISTORY OF ANCIENT LITERATURE IN EUROPE FROM 1550 TO 1600.

CHAPTER II.

HISTORY OF THEOLOGICAL LITERATURE IN EUROPE FROM 1550 TO 1600.

CHAPTER III.

HISTORY OF SPECULATIVE PHILOSOPHY FROM 1550 TO 1600.

CHAPTER IV.

HISTORY OF MORAL AND POLITICAL PHILOSOPHY, AND OF JURISPRUDENCE, FROM 1550 TO 1600.

CHAPTER V.

HISTORY OF POETRY FROM 1550 TO 1600.

CHAPTER VI.

HISTORY OF DRAMATIC LITERATURE FROM 1550 TO 1600.

CHAPTER VII.

HISTORY OF POLITE LITERATURE IN PROSE FROM 1550 TO 1600.

CHAPTER VIII.

HISTORY OF PHYSICAL AND MISCELLANEOUS LITERATURE FROM 1500 TO 1600.

PART III.

ON THE LITERATURE OF THE FIRST HALF OF THE SEVENTEENTH CENTURY.

CHAPTER I.

HISTORY OF ANCIENT LITERATURE IN EUROPE FROM 1600 TO 1650.

CHAPTER II.

HISTORY OF THEOLOGICAL LITERATURE IN EUROPE FROM 1600 TO 1650.

INTRODUCTION

TO THE

LITERATURE OF EUROPE

IN THE FIFTEENTH, SIXTEENTH, AND SEVENTEENTH CENTURIES.

PART II.

ON THE LITERATURE OF THE LATTER HALF OF THE SIXTEENTH CENTURY.

CHAPTER I.

HISTORY OF ANCIENT LITERATURE IN EUROPE FROM 1550 TO 1600.

Section I.

Progress of Classical Learning — Principal Critical Scholars — Editions of ancient Authors — Lexicons and Grammars — Best Writers of Latin — Muretus — Manutius — Decline of Taste — Scaliger — Casaubon — Classical Learning in England under Elizabeth.

1. In the first part of the sixteenth century, we have seen hat the foundations of a solid structure of classical earning had been laid in many parts of Europe; the superiority of Italy had generally become far less conspicuous, or might perhaps be wholly denied; in all the German Empire, in France, and even in England, the study of ancient iterature had been almost uniformly progressive. But it was he subsequent period of fifty years which we now approach, hat more eminently deserved the title of an age of scholars, and filled our public libraries with immense fruits of literary abor. In all matters of

Progress of philology.

INTRODUCTION

TO THE

LITERATURE OF EUROPE

IN THE FIFTEENTH, SIXTEENTH, AND SEVENTEENTH CENTURIES.

PART II.

ON THE LITERATURE OF THE LATTER HALF OF THE SIXTEENTH CENTURY.

CHAPTER I.

HISTORY OF ANCIENT LITERATURE IN EUROPE FROM 1550 TO 1600.

SECTION I.

'rogress of Classical Learning — Principal Critical Scholars — Editions of ancient Au thors — Lexicons and Grammars — Best Writers of Latin — Muretus — Manutius — Decline of Taste — Scaliger — Casaubon — Classical Learning in England under Elizabeth.

Progress of philology.

1. IN the first part of the sixteenth century, we have seen hat the foundations of a solid structure of classical earning had been laid in many parts of Europe; he superiority of Italy had generally become far less conspi- uous, or might perhaps be wholly denied; in all the German Empire, in France, and even in England, the study of ancient iterature had been almost uniformly progressive. But it was he subsequent period of fifty years, which we now approach, hat more eminently deserved the title of an age of scholars, and filled our public libraries with immense fruits of literary abor. In all matters of criticism and philology, what was

written before the year 1550 is little in comparison with what the next age produced.

First editions of Classics.

2. It may be useful in this place to lay before the reader at one view the dates of the first editions of Greek and Latin authors, omitting some of inconsiderable reputation or length. In this list I follow the authority of Dr. Dibdin, to which no exception will probably be taken:—

Ælian	1545.	*Rome.*
Æschylus	1518.	*Venice, Aldus*
Æsop	1480?	*Milan.*
Ammianus	1474.	*Rome.*
Anacreon	1554.	*Paris.*
Antoninus	1558.	*Zurich.*
Apollonius Rhodius	1496.	*Florence.*
Appianus	1551.	*Paris.*
Apuleius	1469.	*Rome.*
Aristophanes	1498.	*Venice.*
Aristoteles	1495–8.	*Venice.*
Arrian	1535.	*Venice.*
Athenæus	1514.	*Venice.*
Aulus Gellius	1469.	*Rome.*
Ausonius	1472.	*Venice.*
Boethius	Absque anno; circ. **1470.**	
Cæsar	1469.	*Rome.*
Callimachus	Absque anno.	*Florence.*
Catullus	1472.	*Venice.*
Ciceronis Opera	1498.	*Milan.*
Cicero de Officiis	1465.	*Mentz.*
—— Epistolæ Famil.	1467.	*Rome.*
—— Epistolæ ad Attic.	1469.	*Rome.*
—— de Oratore	1465.	*Mentz and Subiaco.*
—— Rhetorica	1490.	*Venice.*
—— Orationes	1471.	*Rome.*
—— Opera Philosoph.	1469. 1471.	*Rome.*
Claudian	Absque anno.	*Brescia.*
Demosthenes	1504.	*Venice.*
Diodorus, v. lib.	1539.	*Basle.*
—— xv. lib.	1559	*Paris.*
Diogenes Laertius	1533.	*Basle.*
Dio Cassius	1548.	*Paris.*
Dionysius Halicarn.	1546.	*Paris.*
Epictetus	1528.	*Venice.*
Euripides	1503.	*Venice.*
Euclid	1533.	*Basle.*
Florus	1470.	*Paris.*
Herodian	1503.	*Venice.*
Herodotus	1502.	*Venice.*
Hesiod. Op. et Dies	1493.	*Milan.*
—— Op. omnia	1495.	*Venice.*
Homer	1488.	*Florence.*
Horatius	Absque anno.	
Isocrates	1493.	*Milan.*

Josephus	1544.	*Basle.*
Justin	1470.	*Venice.*
Juvenal	Absque anno.	*Rome.*
Livius	1469.	*Rome.*
Longinus	1554.	*Basle.*
Lucan	1469.	*Rome.*
Lucian	1496.	*Florence.*
Lucretius	1473.	*Brescia.*
Lysias	1513.	*Venice.*
Macrobius	1472.	*Venice.*
Manilius	Ante 1474.	*Nuremberg.*
Martialis	1471.	*Ferrara.*
Oppian	1515.	*Florence.*
Orpheus	1500.	*Florence.*
Ovid	1471.	*Bologna.*
Pausanias	1516.	*Venice.*
Petronius	1476?	
Phædrus	1596.	*Troyes.*
Photius	1601.	*Augsburg.*
Pindar	1513.	*Venice.*
Plato	1513.	*Venice.*
Plautus	1472.	*Venice.*
Plinii Nat. Hist.	1469.	*Venice.*
—— Epist.	1471.	
Plutarch Op. Moral.	1509.	*Venice.*
——— Vitæ	1517.	*Venice.*
Polybius	1530.	*Haguenow.*
Quintilian	1470.	*Rome.*
Quintus Curtius	Absque anno.	*Rome.*
Sallust	1470.	*Paris.*
Seneca	1475.	*Naples.*
Senecæ Tragediæ	1484.	*Ferrara.*
Silius Italicus	1471.	*Rome.*
Sophocles	1502.	*Venice.*
Statius	1472?	
Strabo	1516.	*Venice.*
Suetonius	1470.	*Rome.*
Tacitus	1468?	*Venice.*
Terence	Ante 1470?	*Strasburg.*
Theocritus	1493.	*Milan.*
Thucydides	1502.	*Venice.*
Valerius Flaccus	1474.	*Rome.*
Valerius Maximus	Ante 1470?	*Strasburg.*
Velleius Paterculus	1520.	*Basle.*
Virgil	1469.	*Rome.*
Xenophon	1516.	*Florence.*

Change in character of learning.

3. It will be perceived, that, even in the middle of this century, some far from uncommon writers had not yet been given to the press. But most of the rest had gone through several editions, which it would be tedious to enumerate; and the means of acquiring an extensive, though not in all respects very exact, erudition might perhaps be nearly as copious as at present. In consequence, probably, among other reasons, of these augmented stores of

classical literature, its character underwent a change. It became less polished and elegant, but more laborious and profound. The German or Cisalpine type, if I may use the word, prevailed over the Italian, the school of Budæus over that of Bembo; nor was Italy herself exempt from its ascendency. This advance of erudition at the expense of taste was perhaps already perceptible in 1550, for we cannot accommodate our arbitrary divisions to the real changes of things; yet it was not hitherto so evident in Italy as it became in the latter part of the century. The writers of this age, between 1550 and 1600, distinguish themselves from their predecessors not only by a disregard for the graces of language, but by a more prodigal accumulation of quotations, and more elaborate efforts to discriminate and to prove their positions. Aware of the censors whom they may encounter in an increasing body of scholars, they seek to secure themselves in the event of controversy, or to sustain their own differences from those who have gone already over the same ground. Thus, books of critical as well as antiquarian learning often contain little of original disquisition, which is not interrupted at every sentence by quotation, and in some instances are hardly more than the *adversaria*, or commonplace-books, in which the learned were accustomed to register their daily observations in study. A late German historian remarks the contrast between the Commentary of Paulus Cortesius on the scholastic philosophy, published in 1503, and the Mythologia of Natalis Comes, in 1551. The first, in spite of its subject, is classical in style, full of animation and good sense; the second is a tedious mass of quotations, the materials of a book rather than a book, without a notion of representing any thing in its spirit and general result.[1] This is, in great measure, a characteristic of the age, and grew worse towards the end of the century. Such a book as the Annals of Baronius, the same writer says, so shapeless, so destitute of every trace of eloquence, could not have appeared in the age of Leo. But it may be added, that, with all the defects of Baronius, no one, in the age of Leo, could have put the reader in the possession of so much knowledge.

Cultivation of Greek.

4. We may reckon, among the chief causes of this diminution of elegance in style, the increased culture of the Greek language; not certainly that the great writers

[1] Ranke, Die Päpste des 16ten und 17ten Jahrhunderts, i. 484.

n Greek are inferior models to those in Latin, but because he practice of composition was confined to the latter. Nor vas the Greek really understood, in its proper structure and yntax, till a much later period. It was, however, a sufficiently aborious task, with the defective aids then in existence, to earn even the single words of that most copious tongue; and n this some were eminently successful. Greek was not very nuch studied in Italy: we may perhaps say, on the contrary, hat no one native of that country, after the middle of the entury, except Angelus Caninius and Æmilius Portus, both of whom lived wholly on this side of the Alps, acquired any emarkable reputation in it; for Petrus Victorius had been listinguished in the earlier period. It is to France and Germany that we should look for those who made Grecian literature the domain of scholars. It is impossible to mention every name, but we must select the more eminent; not, however, distinguishing the laborers in the two vineyards of ancient learning, since they frequently lent their service alternately to each.

Principal scholars: Turnebus.

5. The university of Paris, thanks to the encouragement given by Francis I., stood in the first rank for philological learning; and, as no other in France could pretend to vie with her, she attracted students from every part. Toussain, Danes, and Dorat were conspicuous professors of Greek. The last was also one of the celebrated pleiad of French poets, but far more distinguished in the dead tongues than in his own. But her chief boast was Turnebus, so called by the gods, but by men Tournebœuf, and, as some have said, of a Scots family, who must have been denominated Turnbull.[1] Turnebus was one of those industrious scholars who did not scorn the useful labor of translating Greek authors into Latin, and is among the best of that class. But his reputation is chiefly founded on the Adversaria, the first part of which appeared in 1564, the second in 1565, the third, posthumously, in 1580. It is wholly miscellaneous, divided into chapters, merely as resting-places to the reader; for the contents of each are mostly a collection of unconnected notes. Such books, truly *adversaria* or commonplaces, were not

1 Biogr. Univ. The penultimate of Turnebus is made both short and long by the Latin poets of the age, but more commonly the latter, which seems contrary to what we should think right. Even Greek will not help us, for we find him called both τουρνεβος and τουρνηβος Maittaire, Vitæ Stephanor., vol. iii.

unusual; but can, of course, only be read in a desultory manner, or consulted upon occasion. The Adversaria of Turnebus contains several thousand explanations of Latin passages. They are eminent for conciseness; few remarks exceeding half a page, and the greater part being much shorter. He passes without notice from one subject to another the most remote, and has been so much too rapid for his editor, that the titles of each chapter, multifarious as they are, afford frequently but imperfect notions of its contents. The phrases explained are generally difficult; so that this miscellany gives a high notion of the erudition of Turnebus, and it has furnished abundant materials to later commentators. The best critics of that and the succeeding age, Gesner, Scaliger, Lipsius, Barthius, are loud in his praises; nor has he been blamed, except for his excess of brevity and rather too great proneness to amend the text of authors, wherein he is not remarkably successful.[1] Montaigne has taken notice of another merit in Turnebus, that, with more learning than any who had gone before for a thousand years, he was wholly exempt from the pedantry characteristic of scholars, and could converse upon topics remote from his own profession, as if he had lived continually in the world.

Petrus Victorius.

6. A work very similar in its nature to the Adversaria of Turnebus was the Variæ Lectiones of Petrus Victorius (Vettori), professor of Greek and Latin rhetoric at Florence during the greater part of a long life, which ended in 1585. Thuanus has said, with some hyperbole, that Victorius saw the revival and almost the extinction of learning in Italy.[2] No one, perhaps, deserved more praise in the restoration of the text of Cicero; no one, according to Huet, translated better from Greek; no one was more accurate in observing the readings of manuscripts, or more cautious in his own corrections. But his Variæ Lectiones, in 38 books, of which the first edition appeared in 1583, though generally

[1] Blount; Baillet. The latter begins his collection of these testimonies by saying that Turnebus has had as many admirers as readers, and is almost the only critic whom envy has not presumed to attack. Baillet, however, speaks of his correction of *Greek* and Latin passages. I have not observed any of the former in the Adversaria: the book, if I am not mistaken, relates wholly to Latin criticism. Muretus calls Turnebus, "Homo immensa quadam doctrinæ copia instructus, sed interdum nimis propere, et nimis cupidè amplexari solitus est ea quæ in mentem venerant." — Variæ Lectiones, l. x. c. 18. Muretus, as usual with critics, *vineta cædit sua:* the same charge might be brought against himself.

[2] "Petrus Victorius longæva ætate id consecutus est, ut literas in Italia renascentes et pæne extinctas viderit." — Thuanus ad ann. 1585, *apud* Blount.

extolled, has not escaped the severity of Scaliger, who says that there is less of valuable matter in the whole work than in one book of the Adversaria of Turnebus.[1] Scaliger, however, had previously spoken in high terms of Victorius: there had been afterwards, as he admits, some ill-will between them; and the tongue or pen of this great scholar was never guided by candor towards an opponent. I am not acquainted with the Variæ Lectiones of Victorius except through my authorities.

7. The same title was given to a similar miscellany by Marc Antony Muretus, a native of Limoges. The first part of this, containing eight books, was published in 1559, seven more books in 1586, the last four in 1600. This great classical scholar of the sixteenth century found in the eighteenth one well worthy to be his editor, Ruhnkenius of Leyden, who has called the Variæ Lectiones of Muretus "a work worthy of Phidias;" an expression rather amusingly characteristic of the value which verbal critics set upon their labors. This book of Muretus contains only miscellaneous illustrations of passages which might seem obscure, in the manner of those we have already mentioned. Sometimes he mingles conjectural criticisms; and, in many chapters, only points out parallel passages, or relates incidentally some classical story. His emendations are frequently good and certain, though at other times we may justly think him too bold.[2] Muretus is read with far more pleasure than Turnebus: his illustrations relate more to the attractive parts of Latin criticism, and may be compared to the miscellaneous remarks of Jortin.[3] But in depth of erudition he is probably

Muretus.

[1] Scaligerana Secunda.

[2] The following will serve as an instance. In the speech of Galgacus (Taciti Vita Agricolæ), instead of "libertatem non in præsentia laturi," which indeed is unintelligible enough, he would read, "in libertatem, non in populi Romani servitium nati." Such a conjecture would not be endured in the present state of criticism. Muretus, however, settles it in the current style: "vulgus quid probet, quid non probet, nunquam laboravi."

[3] The following titles of chapters, from the eighth book of the Variæ Lectiones, will show the agreeable diversity of Muretus's illustrations: —

1. Comparison of poets to bees, by Pindar, Horace, Lucretius. Line of Horace —

"Necte meo Lamiæ coronam;" illustrated by Euripides.

2. A passage in Aristotle's Rhetoric, lib. ii., explained differently from P. Victorius.

3. Comparison of a passage in the Phædrus of Plato, with Cicero's translation.

4. Passage in the Apologia Socratis, corrected and explained.

5. Line in Virgil, shown to be imitated from Homer.

6. Slips of memory in P. Victorius, noticed.

7. Passage in Aristotle's Rhetoric explained from his Metaphysics.

8. Another passage in the same book explained.

much below the Parisian professor. Muretus seems to take pleasure in censuring Victorius.

Gruter's Thesaurus Criticus.

8. Turnebus, Victorius, Muretus, with two who have been mentioned in the first part of this work, Cœlius Rhodiginus and Alexander ab Alexandro, may be reckoned the chief contributors to this general work of literary criticism in the sixteenth century. But there were many more, and some of considerable merit, whom we must pass over. At the beginning of the next century, Gruter collected the labors of preceding critics in six very thick and closely printed volumes, to which Paræus, in 1623, added a seventh, entitled "Lampas, sive Fax Liberalium Artium," but more commonly called Thesaurus Criticus. A small portion of these belong to the fifteenth century, but none extend beyond the following. Most of the numerous treatises in this ample collection belong to the class of Adversaria, or miscellaneous remarks. Though not so studiously concise as those of Turnebus, each of these is generally contained in a page or two, and their multitude is consequently immense. Those who now by glancing at a note obtain the result of the patient diligence of these men, should feel some respect for their names, and some admiration for their acuteness and strength of memory. They had to collate the whole of antiquity, they plunged into depths which the indolence of modern philology, screening itself under the garb of fastidiousness, affects to deem unworthy to be explored; and thought themselves bound to become lawyers, physicians, historians, artists, agriculturists, to elucidate the difficulties which ancient writers present. It may be doubted also, whether our more recent editions of the

9. Passage in Cicero pro Rabirio, corrected.

10. Imitation of Æschines in two passages of Cicero's 3d Catilinarian oration.

11. Imitation of Æschines and Demosthenes in two passages of Cicero's Declamation against Sallust. [Not genuine.]

12. *Inficetus* is the right word, not *infacetus*.

13. Passage in 5th book of Aristotle's Ethics corrected.

14. The word διαψευδεσθαι, in the 2d book of Aristotle's Rhetoric, not rightly explained by Victorius.

15. The word *asinus*, in Catullus (Carm. 95), does not signify an ass, but a millstone.

16. Lines of Euripides, ill translated by Cicero.

17. Passage in Cicero's Epistles misunderstood by Politian and Victorius.

18. Passage in the Phædrus explained.

19 Difference between accusation and invective, illustrated from Demosthenes and Cicero.

20. Imitation of Æschines by Cicero. Two passages of Livy amended.

21. "Mulieres eruditas plerumque libidinosas esse," from Juvenal and Euripides.

22. Nobleness of character displayed by Iphicrates.

23. That Hercules was a physician, who cured Alcestis when given over.

24. Cruelty of king Dejotarus, related from Plutarch.

25. Humane law of the Persians.

classics have preserved all the important materials which the indefatigable exertions of the men of the sixteenth century accumulated. In the present state of philology, there is incomparably more knowledge of grammatical niceties, at least in the Greek language, than they possessed, and more critical acuteness perhaps in correction, though in this they were not always deficient; but, for the exegetical part of criticism, — the interpretation and illustration of passages, not corrupt, but obscure, — we may not be wrong in suspecting that more has been lost than added in the eighteenth and present centuries to the *savans in us*, as the French affect to call them, whom we find in the bulky and forgotten volumes of Gruter.

Editions of Greek and Latin authors.

9. Another and more numerous class of those who devoted themselves to the same labor, were the editors of Greek and Roman authors. And here again it is impossible to do more than mention a few, who seem, in the judgment of the best scholars, to stand above their contemporaries. The early translations of Greek, made in the fifteenth century, and generally very defective through the slight knowledge of the language that even the best scholars then possessed, were replaced by others more exact; the versions of Xenophon by Leunclavius, of Plutarch by Xylander, of Demosthenes by Wolf, of Euripides and Aristides by Canter, — are greatly esteemed. Of the first, Huet says, that he omits or perverts nothing, his Latin often answering to the Greek, word for word, and preserving the construction and arrangement, so that we find the original author complete, yet with a purity of idiom, and a free and natural air, not often met with.[1] Stephens, however, according to Scaliger, did not highly esteem the learning of Leunclavius.[2] France, Germany, and the Low Countries, beside Basle and Geneva, were the prolific parents of new editions, in many cases very copiously illustrated by erudite commentaries.

Tacitus of Lipsius.

10. The Tacitus of Lipsius is his best work, in the opinion of Scaliger, and in his own. So great a master was he of this favorite author, that he offered to repeat any passage with a dagger at his breast, to be used against him on a failure of memory.[3] Lipsius, after residing several years at Leyden, in the profession of the reformed religion, went to Louvain, and discredited himself by writing in favor

1 Baillet; Blount; Niceron, vol. xxvi.
2 Scaligerana Secunda
3 Niceron, xxiv. 119

of the legendary miracles of that country, losing sight of all his critical sagacity. The Protestants treated his desertion, and these later writings, with a contempt which has perhaps sometimes been extended to his productions of a superior character. The article on Lipsius, in Bayle, betrays some of this spirit; and it appears in other Protestants, especially Dutch critics. Hence they undervalue his Greek learning, as if he had not been able to read the language, and impute plagiarism, when there seems to be little ground for the charge. Casaubon admits that Lipsius has translated Polybius better than his predecessors, though he does not rate his Greek knowledge very high.[1]

11. Acidalius, whose premature death robbed philological literature of one from whom much had been expected,[2] Paulus Manutius, and Petrus Victorius, are to be named with honor for the criticism of Latin authors; and the Lucretius of Giffen or Giphanius, published at Antwerp, 1566, is still esteemed.[3] But we may select the Horace of Lambinus as a conspicuous testimony to the classical learning of this age. It appeared in 1561. In this, he claims to have amended the text, by the help of ten manuscripts, most of them found by him in Italy, whither he had gone in the suite of Cardinal Tournon. He had previously made large collections for the illustration of Horace, from the Greek philosophers and poets, from Athenæus, Stobæus, and Pausanias, and other sources with which the earlier interpreters had been less familiar. Those commentators, however, among whom Hermannus Figulus, Badius Ascensius, and Antonius Mancinellus, as well as some who had confined themselves to the Ars Poetica, namely, Grisolius, Achilles Statius (in his real name Estaço, one of the few good scholars of Portugal), and Luisinius, are the most considerable, had not left unreaped a very abundant harvest of mere explanation. But Lambinus contributed much to a more elegant criticism, by pointing out parallel passages, and by displaying the true spirit and feeling of his author. The text acquired a new aspect, we may almost say, in the hands of Lambinus, — at

Horace of Lambinus.

[1] Casaub. Epist. xxi A long and elaborate critique on Lipsius will be found in Baillet, vol. ii (4to edit.) art. 437. See also Blount, Bayle, and Niceron.

[2] The notes of Acidalius (who died at the age of 28, in 1595) on Tacitus, Plautus, and other Latin authors, are much esteemed. He is a bold corrector of the text. The Biographie Universelle has a better article than that in the 34th volume of Niceron.

[3] Biogr. Univ.

least when we compare it with the edition of Landino in 1482; but some of the gross errors in this had been corrected by intermediate editors. It may be observed, that he had far less assistance from prior commentators in the Satires and Epistles than in the Odes. Lambinus, who became professor of Greek at Paris in 1561, is known also by his editions of Demosthenes, of Lucretius, and of Cicero.[1] That of Plautus is in less esteem. He has been reproached with a prolixity and tediousness which has naturalized the verb *lambiner* in the French language. But this imputation is not, in my opinion, applicable to his commentary upon Horace, which I should rather characterize as concise. It is always pertinent and full of matter. Another charge against Lambinus is for rashness in conjectural[2] emendation; no unusual failing of ingenious and spirited editors.

12. Cruquius (de Crusques), of Ypres, having the advantage of several new manuscripts of Horace, which he discovered in a convent at Ghent, published an edition with many notes of his own, besides an abundant commentary, collected from the glosses he found in his manuscripts, usually styled the Scholiast of Cruquius. The Odes appeared at Bruges, 1565; the Epodes at Antwerp, 1569; the Satires in 1575: the whole together was first published in 1578. But the Scholiast is found in no edition of Cruquius's Horace before 1595.[3] Cruquius appears to me inferior as a critic to Lambinus; and, borrowing much from him as well as Turnebus, seldom names him except for censure. An edition of Horace at Basle, in 1580, sometimes called that of the forty commentators, including a very few before the extinction of letters, is interesting in philological history, by the

Of Cruquius.

[1] This edition by Lambinus is said to mark the beginning of one of the seven ages in which those of the great Roman orator have been arranged. The first comprehends the early editions of separate works. The second begins with the earliest entire edition, that of Milan, in 1498. The third is dated from the first edition which contains copious notes, that of Venice, by Petrus Victorius, in 1534. The fourth from the more extensive annotations given not long afterwards by Paulus Manutius. The fifth, as has just been said, from this edition by Lambinus, in 1566, which has been thought too rash in correction of the text. A sixth epoch was made by Gruter, in 1618; and this period is reckoned to comprehend most editions of that and the succeeding century; for the seventh and last age dates, it seems, only from the edition of Ernesti, in 1774. Biogr. Univ., art. "Cicero." See Blount, for discrepant opinions expressed by the critics about the general merits of Lambinus.

[2] Henry Stephens says that no one had been so audacious in altering the text by conjecture as Lambinus. "In Manutio non tantam quantam in Lambino audaciam, sed valde tamen periculosam et citam." — Maittaire, Vitæ Stephanorum, p. 401. It will be seen that Scaliger finds exactly the same fault with Stephens himself.

[3] Biogr. Univ.

light it throws on the state of criticism in the earlier part of the century, for it is remarkable that Lambinus is not included in the number; and it will, I think, confirm what has been said above in favor of those older critics.

Henry Stephens.

13. Henry Stephens, thus better known among us than by his real surname Etienne, the most illustrious (if indeed he surpassed his father) of a family of great printers, began his labors at Paris in 1554, with the *princeps editio* of Anacreon.[1] He had been educated in that city under Danes, Toussain, and Turnebus;[2] and, though equally learned in both languages, devoted himself to Greek, as being more neglected than Latin.[3] The press of Stephens might be called the central point of illumination to Europe. In the year 1557 alone, he published, as Maittaire observes, more editions of ancient authors than would have been sufficient to make the reputation of another scholar. His publications, as enumerated by Niceron (I have not counted them in Maittaire), amount to a hundred and three; of which by far the greater part are classical editions, more valuable than his original works. Baillet says of Henry Stephens, that he was second only to Budæus in Greek learning, though he seems to put Turnebus and Camerarius nearly on the same level. But perhaps the majority of scholars would think him superior, on the whole, to all the three; and certainly Turnebus, whose Adversaria are confined to Latin interpretation, whatever renown he might deserve by his oral lectures, has left nothing that could warrant our assigning him an equal place.[4] Scaliger, however, accuses Henry Stephens of spoiling all the authors he edited, by wrong alterations of the text.[5] This

[1] Almeloveen, Vitæ Stephanorum, p. 60; Maittaire, p. 200. An excellent life of Henry Stephens, as well as others of the rest of his family, was written by Maittaire, but which does not supersede those formerly published by Almeloveen. These together are among the best illustrations of the philological history of the 16th century that we possess. They have been abridged, with some new matter, by Mr. Greswell, in his Early History of the Parisian Greek Press.

[2] Almeloveen, p. 70. His father made him learn Greek before he had acquired Latin. Maittaire, p. 198.

[3] The life of Stephens, in the 36th volume of Niceron, is long and useful. That in the Biographie Universelle is not bad, but enumerates few editions published by this most laborious scholar, and thus reduces the number of his works to twenty-six. Huet says (whom I quote from Blount) that Stephens may be called "The Translator par excellence;" such is his diligence and accuracy, so happy his skill in giving the character of his author, so great his perspicuity and elegance.

[4] [The works of Turnebus, 3 vols. folio, bound in one, contain, 1. his commentaries on Latin authors; 2. his translations from Greek; 3. his miscellaneous writings, including the Adversaria. Turnebus did comparatively little for Greek except in the way of translation. — 1842.]

[5] "Omnes quotquot edidit, editve libros, etiam meos, suo arbitrio jam corrupit et deinceps corrumpet." — Scaliger. Prima,

charge is by no means unfrequently brought against the critics of this age.

14. The year 1572 is an epoch in Greek literature, by the publication of Stephens's Thesaurus. A lexicon had been published at Basle in 1562, by Robert Constantin, who, though he made use of that famous press, lived at Caen, of which he was a native. Scaliger speaks in a disparaging tone both of Constantin and his lexicon. But its general reputation has been much higher. A modern critic observes, that "a very great proportion of the explanations and authorities in Stephens's Thesaurus are borrowed from it."[1] We must presume that this applies to the first edition; for the second, enlarged by Æmilius Portus, which is more common, did not appear till 1591.[2] "The principal defects of Constantin," it is added, "are, first, the confused and ill-digested arrangement of the interpretation of words; and, secondly, the absence of all distinction between primitives and derivatives." It appears by a Greek letter of Constantin, prefixed to the first edition, that he had been assisted in his labors by Gesner, Henry Stephens, Turnebus, Camerarius, and other learned contemporaries. He gives his authorities, if not so much as we should desire, very far more than the editors of the former Basle lexicon. This lexicon, as was mentioned in another place, is extremely defective, and full of errors; though a letter of Grynæus, prefixed to the edition of 1539, is nothing but a strain of unqualified eulogy, little warranted by the suffrage of later scholars. I found, however, on a loose calculation, the number of words in this edition to be not much less than 50,000.[3]

Lexicon of Constantin.

p. 96. Against this sharp, and perhaps rash, judgment, we may set that of Maittaire, a competent scholar, though not like Scaliger, and without his arrogance and scorn of the world. "Henrici editiones ideo miror, quod eas, quam posset accuratissime aut ipse aut per alios, quos complures noverat, viros eruditos, ad omnium tum manuscriptorum tum impressorum codicum fidem, non sine maximo delectu et suo (quo maximè in Græcis præsertim pollebat) aliorumque judicio elaboravit." Vitæ Stephanorum, t. ii. p. 284. No man perhaps ever published so many editions as Stephens, nor was any other printer of so much use to letters; for he knew much more than the Aldi or the Juntas. Yet he had planned many more publications, as Maittaire has collected from what he has dropped in various places, p. 469.

[1] Quarterly Review, vol. xxvii.

[2] The first edition of this Lexicon sometimes bears the name of Crespin, the printer at Basle; and both Baillet and Bayle have fallen into the mistake of believing that there were two different works. See Niceron, vol. xxvii.

[3] Henry Stephens, in an epistle, De suæ Typographiæ Statu ad quosdam Amicos, gives an account of his own labors on the Thesaurus. The following passage on the earlier lexicons may be worth reading: "Iis quæ circumferuntur lexicis Græco-Latinis primam imposuit manum monachus quidam, frater Johannes Crastonus, Placentinus, Carmelitanus; sed cum is

Thesaurus of Stephens.

15. Henry Stephens had devoted twelve years of his laborious life to his own immense work, large materials for which had been collected by his father. In comprehensive and copious interpretation of words, it not only left far behind every earlier dictionary, but is still the single Greek lexicon; one which some have ventured to abridge or enlarge, but none have presumed to supersede. Its arrangement, as is perhaps scarce necessary to say, is not according to an alphabetical but a radical order; that is, the supposed roots following each other alphabetically, every derivative or compound, of whatever initial letter, is placed after the primary word. This method is certainly not very convenient to the uninformed reader; and perhaps, even with a view to the scientific knowledge of the language, it should have been deferred for a more advanced stage of etymological learning. The Thesaurus embodies the critical writings of Budæus and Camerarius, with whatever else had been contributed by the Greek exiles of the preceding age and by their learned disciples. Much, no doubt, has since been added to what we find in the Thesaurus of Stephens, as to the nicety of idiom and syntax, or to the principles of formation of words, but not perhaps in copiousness of explanation, which is the proper object of a dictionary. "The leading defects conspicuous in Stephens," it is said by the critic already quoted, "are inaccurate or falsified quotations, the deficiency of several thousand words, and a wrong classification both of primitives and derivatives. At the same time we ought rather

jejunis expositionibus, in quibus vernaculo etiam sermone interdum, id est Italico, utitur, contentus fuisset, perfunctoriè item constructiones verborum indicasset, nullos autorum lccos proferens ex quibus illæ pariter et significationes cognosci possent; multi postea certatim multa hinc inde sine ullo delectu ac judicio excerpta inseruerunt. Donec tandem indoctis typographis de augenda lexicorum mole inter se certantibus, et præmia iis qui id præstarent proponentibus, quæ jejunæ, et, si ita loqui licet, macilentæ antea erant expositiones, adeo pingues et crassæ redditæ sunt, ut in illis passim nihil aliud quam Bœoticam suem agnoscamus. Nam pauca ex Budæo, aliisque idoneis autoribus, et ea quidem parum fideliter descripta, utpote parum intellecta, multa contra ex Lapo Florentino, Leonardo Aretino, aliisque ejusdem farinæ interpretibus, ut similes habent labra lactucas, in opus illud transtulerunt. Ex iis quidem certe locis in quorum interpretatione felix fuit Laurentius Valla, paucissimos protulerunt; sed pro perverso suo judicio, perversissimas quasque ejus interpretationes, quales prope innumeras a me annotatas in Latinis Herodoti et Thucydidis editionibus videbis, delegerunt egregii illi lexicorum seu consarcinatores seu interpolatores, quibus, tamquam gemmis, illa insignirent. Quod si non quam multa, sed duntaxat quam multorum generum errata ibi sint, commemorare velim, merito certe exclamabo, τί πρῶτον, τί δ' ἔπειτα, τί δ' ὑστάτιον καταλέξω; vix enim ullum vitii genus posse a nobis cogitari aut fingi existimo, cujus ibi aliquod exemplum non extat." — p. 156. He produces afterwards some gross instances of error.

to be surprised, that, under existing disadvantages, he accomplished so much even in this last department, than that he left so much undone."

16. It has been questioned among bibliographers whether there are two editions of the Thesaurus; the first in 1572, the second without a date, and probably after 1580. The affirmative seems to be sufficiently proved.[1] The sale, however, of so voluminous and expensive a work did not indemnify its author; and it has often been complained of, that Scapula, who had been employed under Stephens, injured his superior by the publication of his well-known abridgment in 1579. The fact, however, that Scapula had possessed this advantage rests on little evidence; and his preface, if it were true, would be the highest degree of effrontery:[2] it was natural that some one would abridge so voluminous a lexicon. Literature, at least, owes an obligation to Scapula.[3] The temper of Henry Stephens, restless and uncertain, was not likely to retain riches: he passed several years in wandering over Europe, and, having wasted a considerable fortune amassed by his father, died in a public hospital at Lyons in 1598,[4] "opibus," says his biographer, "atque etiam ingenio destitutus in nosocomio."

Abridged by Scapula.

1 Niceron (vol. xxvi.) contends that the supposed second edition differs only by a change in the title-page, wherein we find rather an unhappy attempt at wit, in the following distich aimed at Scapula:—

"Quidam επιτεμνων me capulo tenus abdidit ensem:
Æger eram a scapulis; sanus at huc redeo."

But it seems that Stephens, in his Palæstra de Justi Lipsii Latinitate, mentions this second edition, which is said by those who have examined it to have fewer typographical errors than the other, though it is admitted that the leaves might be intermixed without inconvenience, so close is the resemblance. Vide Maittaire, p. 356-360. Brunet, Man. du Libr. Gresswell, vol. ii. p. 289.

2 ["Incidi forte in Thesaurum ab Henrico Stephano conscriptum."—Gresswell's Greek press, ii. 284. —1842.]

3 Maittaire says that Scapula's lexicon is as perfidious to the reader as its author was to his master, and that Dr. Busby would not suffer his boys to use it, p. 358. But this has hardly been the general opinion. See Quarterly Review, *ubi suprà.*

4 Casaubon writes frequently to Scaliger about the strange behavior of his father-in-law, and complains that he had not even leave to look at the books in the latter's library, which he himself scarce ever visited. "Nôsti hominem, nôsti mores, nôsti quid apud eum possim, hoc est, quam nihil possim, qui videtur in suam perniciem conspirâsse."—Epist. 21. And, still more severely, Epist. 41. "Nam noster, etsi vivens valensque, pridem numero hominum, certe doctorum, eximi meruit; eà est illius inhumanitas, et, quod invitus dico, delirium; qui libros quoslibet veteres, ut Indici gryphi aurum, aliis invidet, sibi perire sinit, sed quid ille habeat aut non, juxta scio ego cum ignavissimo." After Stephens's death, he wrote in kinder terms than he had done before; but regretting some publications, by which the editor of Casaubon's letters thinks he might mean the Apologie pour Hérodote, and the Palæstra de Justi Lipsii Latinitate; the former of which, a very well-known book, contains a spirited attack on the Romish priesthood, but with less regard either for truth or decorum in the selection of his stories than became the character of Stephens; and the latter is of little pertinence to its avowed subject. Henry Stephens had long been subject to a disorder natural enough to laborious

17. The Hellenismus of Angelus Caninius, a native of the Milanese, is merely a grammar. Tanaquil Faber prefers it not only to that of Clenardus, but to all which existed even in his own time. It was published at Paris in 1555. Those who do not express themselves so strongly, place him above his predecessors. Caninius is much fuller than Clenardus, — the edition by Crenius (Leyden, 1700) containing 380 pages. The syntax is very scanty; but Caninius was well conversant with the mutations of words, and is diligent in noting the differences of dialects, in which he has been thought to excel. He was acquainted with the digamma, and with its Latin form. I will take this opportunity of observing, that the Greek grammar of Vergara, mentioned in the first part of this work (page 335), and of which I now possess the Paris edition of 1557, printed by William Morel (*ad Complutensem editionem excusum et restitutum*), appears superior to those of Clenardus or Varenius. This book is doubtless very scarce: it is plain that Tanaquil Faber, Baillet, Morhof, and, I should add, Nicolas Antonio, had never seen it;[1] nor is it mentioned by Brunet or Watts.[2] There is, however, a copy in the British Museum. Scaliger says that it is very good, and that Caninius has borrowed from it the best parts.[3] Vergara had, of course, profited by the commentaries of Budæus, the great source of Greek philology in Western Europe; but he displays, as far as I can judge by recollection more than comparison, an ampler knowledge of the rules of Greek than any of his other contemporaries. This grammar contains 438 pages, more than 100 of

Hellenismus of Caninius.

Vergara's grammar.

men, "quædam actionum consuetarum satietas et fastidium." — Maittaire, p. 248.

Robert Stephens had carried with him to Geneva in 1550, the punches of his types, made at the expense of Francis I., supposing that they were a gift of the king. On the death, however, of Henry Stephens, they were claimed by Henry IV.; and the senate of Geneva restored them. They had been pledged for 400 crowns; and Casaubon complains, as of a great injury, that the estate of Stephens was made answerable to the creditor when the pledge was given up to the king of France. See Le Clerc's remarks on this in Bibliothèque Choisie, vol. xix. p. 219. Also a vindication of Stephens by Maittaire from the charge of having stolen them (Vitæ Stephanorum, i. 34); and again in Gresswell's Parisian Press, i. 399. He seems above the suspicion of theft; but, whether he had just cause to think the punches were his own, it is now impossible to decide.

[1] Blount; Baillet.

[2] Antonio says it was printed at Alcalá, 1573; *deinde Parisiis*, 1550. The first is of course a false print; if the second is not so likewise, he had never seen the book.

[3] Scaligerana Secunda. "F. Vergara, Espagnol, a composé une bonne grammaire Grecque, mais Caninius a pris tout le meilleur de tous, et a mis du sien aussi quelque chose dans son Hellenismus." This, as Bayle truly observes, reduces the eulogies Scaliger has elsewhere given Caninius to very little. Scaliger's loose expressions are not of much value. Yet he who had seen Vergara's grammar might better know what was original in others, than Tanaquil Faber, who had never seen it

which are given to the syntax. A small grammar by Nunnez, or Pincianus, published at Valencia in 1555, seems chiefly borrowed from Clenardus or Vergara.

Grammars of Ramus and Sylburgius.

18. Peter Ramus, in 1557, gave a fresh proof of his acuteness and originality, by publishing a Greek grammar, with many important variances from his precursors. Scaliger speaks of it with little respect; but he is habitually contemptuous towards all but his immediate friends.[1] Lancelot, author of the Port Royal grammar, praises highly that of Ramus, though he reckons it too intricate. This grammar I have not seen in its original state; but Sylburgius published one in 1582, which he professes to have taken from the last edition of the Ramean grammar. It has been said, that Laurence Rhodomann was the first who substituted the partition of the declensions of Greek nouns into three for that of Clenardus, who introduced or retained the prolix and unphilosophical division into ten.[2] But Ramus is clearly entitled to this credit. It would be doubted whether he is equally to be praised, as he certainly has not been equally followed, in making no distinction of conjugations, nor separating the verbs in μι from those in ω, on the ground that their general flection is the same. Much has been added to this grammar by Sylburgius himself, a man in the first rank of Greek scholars; "especially," as he tells us, "in the latter books; so that it may be called rather a supplement than an abridgment of the grammar of Ramus." The

[1] Scaligerana. Casaubon, it must be owned, who had more candor than Scaliger, speaks equally ill of the grammar of Ramus. Epist. 878.

[2] Morhof, l. iv. c. 6. Preface to translation of Matthiæ's Greek Grammar. The learned author of this preface has not alluded to Ramus, and, though he praises Sylburgius for his improvements in the mode of treating grammar, seems unacquainted with that work which I mention in the text. Two editions of it are in the British Museum, 1582 and 1600; but, upon comparison, I believe that there is no difference between them.

The best of these grammars of the 16th century bear no sort of comparison with those which have been latterly published in Germany. And it seems strange at first sight, that the old scholars, such as Budæus, Erasmus, Camerarius, and many more, should have written Greek, which they were fond of doing, much better than from their great ignorance of many fundamental rules of syntax we could have anticipated. But reading continually and thinking in Greek, they found comparative accuracy by a secret tact, and by continual imitation of what they read. Language is always a mosaic work, made up of associated fragments, not of separate molecules: we repeat, not the simple words, but the phrases and even the sentences we have caught from others. Budæus wrote Greek without knowing its grammar, that is, without a distinct notion of moods or tenses, as men speak their own language tolerably well without having ever attended to a grammatical rule. Still many faults must be found in such writing on a close inspection. The case was partly the same in Latin during the middle ages, except that Latin was at that time better understood than Greek was in the sixteenth century; not that so many words were known, but those who wrote it best had more correct notions of the grammar.

syntax in this grammar is much better than in Clenardus, from whom some have erroneously supposed Sylburgius to have borrowed; but I have not compared him with Vergara.[1] The Greek grammar of Sanctius is praised by Lancelot; yet, from what he tells us of it, we may infer that Sanctius, though a great master of Latin, being comparatively unlearned in Greek, displayed such temerity in his hypotheses as to fall into very great errors. The first edition was printed at Antwerp in 1581.

Camerarius; Canter; Robortellus.

19. A few more books of a grammatical nature, falling within the present period, may be found in Morhof, Baillet, and the bibliographical collections; but neither in number nor importance do they deserve much notice.[2] In a more miscellaneous philology, the Commentaries of Camerarius, 1551, are superior to any publication of the kind since that of Budæus in 1529. The Novæ Lectiones of William Canter, though the work of a very young man, deserve to be mentioned as almost the first effort of an art which has done much for ancient literature,—that of restoring a corrupt text, through conjecture, not loose and empirical, but guided by a skilful sagacity, and upon principles which we may without impropriety not only call scientific, but approximating sometimes to the logic of the Novum Organum. The earlier critics, not always possessed of many manuscripts, had recourse, more indeed in Latin than in Greek, to conjectural emendation; the prejudice against which, often carried too far by those who are not sufficiently aware of the enormous ignorance and carelessness which ordinary manuscripts display, has also been heightened by the random and sometimes very improbable guesses of editors. Canter, besides the practice he showed in his Novæ Lectiones, laid down the principles of his theory in a Syntagma de Ratione emendandi Græcos Auctores, reprinted in the second volume of Jebb's edition of Aristides. He here shows what letters are apt to be changed into others by error of transcrip-

[1] Vossius says of the grammarians in general, "ex quibus doctrinæ et industriæ laudem maxime mihi meruisse videntur Angelus Caninius et Fridericus Sylburgius."—Aristarchus, p. 6. It is said that, in his own grammar, which is on the basis of Clenardus, Vossius added little to what he had taken from the two former. Baillet, in Caninio.

[2] In the British Museum is a book by one Guillon, of whom I find no account in biography, called Gnomon, on the quantity of Greek syllables. This seems to be the earliest work of the kind; and he professes himself to write against those who think "quidvis licere in quantitate syllabarum." It is printed at Paris, 1556; and it appears by Watts that there are other editions.

tion, or through a source not perhaps quite so obvious, — the uniform manner of pronouncing several vowels and diphthongs among the later Greeks, which they were thus led to confound, especially when a copyist wrote from dictation. But, besides these corruptions, it appears by the instances Canter gives, that almost any letters are liable to be changed into almost any others. The abbreviations of copyists are also great causes of corruption, and require to be known by those who would restore the text. Canter, however, was not altogether the founder of this school of criticism. Robortellus, whose vanity and rude contempt of one so much superior to himself as Sigonius has perhaps caused his own real learning to be undervalued, had already written a treatise entitled De Arte sive Ratione corrigendi Antiquorum Libros Disputatio; in which he claims to be the first who devised this art, *nunc primum à me excogitata.* It is not a bad work, though probably rather superficial according to our present views. He points out the general characters of manuscripts and the different styles of hand-writing; after which, he proceeds to the rules of conjecture, making good remarks on the causes of corruption and consequent means of restoration. It is published in the second volume of Gruter's Thesaurus Criticus. Robortellus, however, does not advert to Greek manuscripts; a field upon which Canter first entered. The Novæ Lectiones of William Canter are not to be confounded with the Variæ Lectiones of his brother Theodore, a respectable but less eminent scholar. Canter, it may be added, was the first, according to Boissonade, who, in his edition of Euripides, restored some sort of order and measure to the choruses.[1]

Editions by Sylburgius.

20. Sylburgius, whose grammar has been already praised, was of great use to Stephens in compiling the Thesaurus: it has even been said, but perhaps with German partiality, that the greater part of its value is due to him.[2] The editions of Sylburgius, especially those of Aris-

[1] Biogr. Univ. The Life of Canter in Melchior Adam is one of the best his collection contains: it seems to be copied from one by Miræus. Canter was a man of great moral as well as literary excellence: the account of his studies and mode of life in this biography is very interesting. The author of it dwells justly on Canter's skill in exploring the text of manuscripts, and in observing the variations of orthography. See also Blount; Baillet; Niceron, vol. xxix.; and Chalmers.

[2] Melchior Adam, p. 193. In the article of the Quarterly Review, several times already quoted, it is said that the Thesaurus "bears much plainer marks of the sagacity and erudition of Sylburgius than of the desultory and hasty studies of his master, than whom he was more clear-sighted;" a compliment at the expense of Stephens, not perhaps easily reconcilable with the eulogy a little before passed by the reviewer on the latter, as the greatest of Greek scholars except Casaubon. Stephens says

totle and Dionysius of Halicarnassus, are among the best of that age: none, indeed, containing the entire works of the Stagirite, is equally esteemed.[1] He had never risen above the station of a schoolmaster in small German towns, till he relinquished the employment for that of superintendent of classical editions in the press of Wechel, and afterwards in that of Commelin. But the death of this humble and laborious man, in 1596, was deplored by Casaubon as one of the heaviest blows that learning could have sustained.

21. Michael Neander, a disciple of Melanchthon and Camerarius, who became rector of a flourishing school at Isfeld in Thuringia soon after 1550, and remained there till his death in 1595, was certainly much inferior to Sylburgius; yet to him Germany was chiefly indebted for keeping alive, in the general course of study, some little taste for Grecian literature, which towards the end of the century was rapidly declining. The "Erotemata Græcæ Linguæ" of Neander, according to Eichhorn, drove the earlier grammars out of use in the schools.[2] But the publications of Neander appear to be little more than such extracts from the Greek writers as he thought would be useful in education.[3] Several of them are gnomologies, or collections of moral sentences, from the poets; a species of compilation not uncommon in the sixteenth and seventeenth centuries, but neither exhibiting much learning nor favorable to the acquisition of a true feeling for ancient poetry. The Thesaurus of Basilius Faber, another work of the same class, published in 1571, is reckoned by Eichhorn among the most valuable school-books of this period, and continued to be used and reprinted for two hundred years.[4]

Neander.

22. Conrad Gesner belongs almost equally to the earlier and later periods of the sixteenth century. Endowed with unwearied diligence, and with a mind

Gesner.

of himself, "quem habuit (Sylburgius), novo quodam more, dominum simul ac præceptorem, quod ille beneficium pro sua ingenuitate agnoscit."—(*apud* Maittaire, p. 421). But it has been remarked that Stephens was not equally ingenuous, and never acknowledges any obligation to Sylburgius, p. 583. Scaliger says, "Stephanus non solus fecit Thesaurum; plusieurs y ont mis la main;" and in another place, "Sylburgius a travaillé au Trésor de H. Etienne." But it is impossible for us to apportion the disciple's share in this great work; which might be more than Stephens owned, and less than the Germans have claimed. Niceron, which is remarkable, has no life of Sylburgius.

1 The Aristotle of Sylburgius is properly a series of editions of that philosopher's separate works, published from 1584 to 1596. It is in great request when found complete, which is rarely the case. It has no Latin translation.

2 Geschichte der Cultur, iii. 277.

3 Niceron, vol. xxx.

4 Eichhorn, 274.

capacious of omnifarious erudition, he was probably the most comprehensive scholar of the age. Some of his writings have been mentioned in another place. His Mithridates, sive de Differentiis Linguarum, is the earliest effort on a great scale to arrange the various languages of mankind by their origin and analogies. He was deeply versed in Greek literature, and especially in the medical and physical writers; but he did not confine himself to that province. It may be noticed here, that, in his Stobæus, published in 1543, Gesner first printed Greek and Latin in double columns.[1] He was followed by Turnebus, in an edition of Aristotle's Ethics (Paris, 1555); and the practice became gradually general, though some sturdy scholars, such as Stephens and Sylburgius, did not comply with it. Gesner seems to have had no expectation that the Greek text would be much read, and only recommends it as useful in conjunction with the Latin.[2] Scaliger, however, deprecates so indolent a mode of study, and ascribes the decline of Greek learning to these unlucky double columns.[3]

Decline of taste in Germany.

23. In the beginning of the century, as has been shown in the first part of this work, the prospects of classical literature in Germany seemed most auspicious. Schools and universities, the encouragement of liberal princes, the instruction of distinguished professors, the formation of public libraries, had given an impulse, the progressive effects of which were manifest in every Protestant state of the empire. Nor was any diminution of this zeal and taste discernible for a few years. But after the death of Melanchthon in 1560, and of Camerarius in 1574, a literary decline commenced, slow but uniform and permanent, during which Germany had to lament a strange eclipse of that lustre which had distinguished the preceding age. This was first shown in an inferiority of style, and in a neglect of the best standards of good writing. The admiration of Melanchthon himself led in some measure to this; and to copy his manner (*genus dicendi Philippicum*, as it was called) was more the fashion than to have recourse to his masters, Cicero and Quin-

1 This I give only on the authority of Chevillier, Origines de l'Imprimerie de Paris.

2 Chevillier, Origines de l'Imprimerie de Paris. — p. 240.

3 Scalig. Secunda. Accents on Latin words, it is observed by Scaliger (in the Scaligerana Prima), were introduced within his memory; and, as he says, which would be more important, the points called comma and semicolon, of which Paulus Manutius was the inventor. But in this there must be some mistake; for the comma is frequent in books much older than any edited by Manutius.

tilian.[1] But this, which would have kept up a very tolerable style, gave way, not long afterwards, to a tasteless and barbarous turn of phrase, in which all feeling of propriety and elegance was lost. This has been called *Apuleianismus*, as if that indifferent writer of the third century had been set up for imitation, though probably it was the mere sympathy of bad taste and incorrect expression. The scholastic philosophy came back about the same time into the German universities, with all its technical jargon, and triumphed over the manes of Erasmus and Melanchthon. The disciples of Paracelsus spread their mystical rhapsodies far and wide, as much at the expense of classical taste as of sound reason. And when we add to these untoward circumstances the dogmatic and polemical theology, studious of a phraseology certainly not belonging to the Augustan age, and the necessity of writing on many other subjects almost equally incapable of being treated in good language, we cannot be much astonished that a barbarous and slovenly Latinity should become characteristic of Germany, which, even in later ages, very few of its learned men have been able to discard.[2]

German learning.

24. In philological erudition, we have seen that Germany long maintained her rank, if not quite equal to France in this period, yet nearer to her than to any third nation. We have mentioned several of the most distinguished; and to these we might add many names from Melchior Adam, the laborious biographer of his learned countrymen; such as Oporinus, George Fabricius, Frischlin, and Crusius, who first taught the Romaic Greek in Germany. One, rather more known than these, was Laurence Rhodomann. He was the editor of several authors; but his chief claim to a niche in the temple seems to rest upon his Greek verses, which have generally been esteemed superior to any of his generation. The praise

Greek verses of Rhodomann.

[1] Eichhorn, iii. 268. The Germans usually said Philippus for Melanchthon.

[2] Melchior Adam, after highly praising Wolf's translation of Demosthenes, proceeds to boast of the Greek learning of Germany, which, rather singularly, he seems to ascribe to this translation: "Effecit ut ante ignotus plerisque Demosthenes nunc familiariter nobiscum versetur in scholis et academiis. Est sanè quod gratulemur Germaniæ nostræ, quod per Wolfium tantorum fluminum eloquentiæ particeps facta est. Fatentur ipsi Græci, qui reliqui sunt hodie Constantinopoli, præ cæteris eruditi, et Christianæ religionis amantes, totum musarum chorum, relicto Helicone, in Germaniam transmigrâsse." —(Vitæ Philosophorum.) Melchior Adam lived in the early part of the seventeenth century, when this high character was hardly applicable to Germany; but his panegyric must be taken as designed for the preceding age, in which the greater part of his eminent men flourished. Besides this, he is so much a compiler that this passage may not be his own.

does not imply much positive excellence; for in Greek composition, and especially in verse, the best scholars of the sixteenth century make but an indifferent figure. Rhodomann's Life of Luther is written in Greek hexameters. It is also a curious specimen of the bigotry of his church. He boasts that Luther predicted the deaths of Zuingle, Carlostadt, and Œcolampadius as the punishment of their sacramentarian hypothesis. The lines will be found in a note,[1] and may serve as a fair specimen of as good Greek as could perhaps be written in that age of celebrated erudition. But some other poems of Rhodomann, which I have not seen, are more praised by the critics.

Learning declines;

25. But, at the expiration of the century, few were left, besides Rhodomann, of the celebrated philologers of Germany; nor had a new race arisen to supply their place. Æmilius Portus, who taught with reputation at Heidelberg, was a native of Ferrara, whose father, a Greek by origin, emigrated to Genoa on account of religion. The state of literature, in a general sense, had become sensibly deteriorated in the empire. This was most perceptible, or perhaps only perceptible, in its most learned provinces, those which had embraced the Reformation. In the opposite quarter there had been little to lose, and something was gained. In the first period of the Reformation, the Catholic universities, governed by men whose prejudices were insuperable even by appealing to their selfishness, had kept still in the same track, educating their students in the barbarous logic and literature of the middle ages, careless that every method was employed in Protestant education to develop and direct the talents of youth; and this had given the manifest intellectual superiority, which taught the

Except in Catholic Germany.

[1] Καὶ τὰ μὲν ὡς τετέλεστο μετὰ χρόνον, ὡς μεμόρητο·
ὡς γὰρ δωδεκάμηνος ἕλιξ τρίτος ἔτρεχε Φοίβου
δὴ τότε μοῖρα, θεοῦ κρυφίην πρησσοῦσα μενοινὴν,
μαντοσύναις ἐπέθηκε θεοφραδέεσσι τελευτὴν
ἀνδρὸς, ὃς οὔτιν' ἄπρηκτον ἀπὸ κραδίης βάλε μῦθον.
ἄμφω γὰρ στυγεροῦ πλαγξήνορε δογματος ἀρχῷ
Οἰκιολαμπάδιον καὶ Κίγκλιον ἔφθασεν ἄτη
πότμου δακρυόεντος' ἵνα φρίξειε καὶ ἄλλος
ἀτρεκίης πρὸς κέντρον ἀναίδεια ταρσὸν ἰαψαι.
οὐδὲ μὲν ὀξυμόρους Καρολοστάδιος φύγε ποινὰς,
τὸν δὲ γὰρ ἀντιβολῶν κρυερῷ μετα φάσματι δαίμων
ἐξαπίνης ἐτάραξε, καὶ ἥρπασεν οὗ χρέος ἦεν.

disciples and contemporaries of the first reformers a scorn for the stupidity and ignorance of the Popish party, somewhat exaggerated, of course, as such sentiments generally are, but dangerous above measure to its influence. It was, therefore, one of the first great services which the Jesuits performed to get possession of the universities, or to found other seminaries for education. In these, they discarded the barbarous school-books then in use; put the rudimentary study of the languages on a better footing; devoted themselves, for the sake of religion, to those accomplishments which religion had hitherto disdained; and by giving a taste for elegant literature, with as much solid and scientific philosophy as the knowledge of the times and the prejudices of the church would allow, both wiped away the reproach of ignorance, and drew forth the native talents of their novices and scholars. They taught gratuitously, which threw, however unreasonably, a sort of discredit upon salaried professors:[1] it was found that boys learned more from them in six months than in two years under other masters; and, probably for both these reasons, even Protestants sometimes withdrew their children from the ordinary gymnasia, and placed them in Jesuit colleges. No one will deny, that in their classical knowledge, particularly of the Latin language, and in the elegance with which they wrote it, the order of Jesuits might stand in competition with any scholars of Europe. In this period of the sixteenth century, though not perhaps in Germany itself, they produced several of the best writers whom it could boast.[2]

Philological works of Stephens.

26. It is seldom that an age of critical erudition is one also of fine writing: the two have not perhaps a natural incompatibility with each other; but the bond-woman too often usurps the place of the free-woman, and the auxiliary science of philology controls, instead of adorning and ministering to, the taste and genius of original minds. As the study of the Latin language advanced, as better editions were published, as dictionaries and books of criticism were more carefully drawn up, we naturally expect to find it

1 "Mox, ubi paululum firmitatis accessit, pueros sine mercede docendos et erudiendos susceperunt; quo artificio non vulgarem vulgi favorem emeruere, criminandis præsertim aliis doctoribus, quorum doctrina venalis esset, et scholæ nulli sine mercede paterent, et interdum etiam doctrina peregrina personarent. Incredibile dictu est, quantum hæc criminatio valuerit." — Hospinian, Hist. Jesuitarum, l. ii. c. 1, fol. 84; see also l. i. fol. 59.

2 Ranke, ii. 32; Eichhorn, iii. 266. The latter scarcely does justice to the Jesuits as promoters of learning in their way.

written with more correctness, but not with more force and truth. The Expostulation of Henry Stephens de Latinitate Falso Suspecta, 1576, is a collection of classical authorities for words and idioms, which seem so like French, that the reader would not hesitate to condemn them. Some among these, however, are so familiar to us as good Latin, that we can hardly suspect the dictionaries not to have contained them. I have not examined any earlier edition than that of Calepin's dictionary, as enlarged by Paulus Manutius, of the date of 1579, rather after this publication by Henry Stephens; and certainly it does not appear to want these words, or to fail in sufficient authority for them.

Style of Lipsius

27. In another short production by Stephens, De Latinitate Lipsii Palæstra, he turns into ridicule the affected style of that author, who ransacked all his stores of learning to perplex the reader. A much later writer, Scioppius, in his Judicium de Stylo Historico, points out several of the affected and erroneous expressions of Lipsius. But he was the founder of a school of bad writers, which lasted for some time, especially in Germany. Seneca and Tacitus were the authors of antiquity whom Lipsius strove to emulate. "Lipsius," says Scaliger, "is the cause that men have now little respect for Cicero, whose style he esteems about as much as I do his own. He once wrote well; but his third century of epistles is good for nothing."[1] But a style of point and affected conciseness will always have its admirers, till the excess of vicious imitation disgusts the world.[2]

Minerva of Sanctius.

28. Morhof, and several authorities quoted by Baillet, extol the Latin grammar of a Spaniard, Emanuel Alvarez, as the first in which the fancies of the ancient grammarians had been laid aside. Of this work I know nothing farther. But the Minerva of another native of Spain, Sanchez, commonly called Sanctius, the first edition of which

1 Scaligerana Secunda.

2 Miræus, quoted in Melchior Adam's Life of Lipsius, praises his eloquence, with contempt of those who thought their own feeble and empty writing like Cicero's. See also Eichhorn, iii. 299; Baillet, who has a long article on the style of Lipsius and the school it formed (Jugemens des Savans, vol. ii. p. 192, 4to edition); and Blount; also the note M, in Bayle's article on Lipsius. The following passage of Scioppius I transcribe from Blount: "In Justi Lipsii stylo, scriptoris ætate nostra clarissimi, istæ apparent dotes; acumen, venustas, delectus, ornatus vel nimius, cum vix quicquam proprie dictum ei placeat, tum schemata nullo numero, tandem verborum copia; desunt autem perspicuitas, puritas, æquabilitas, collocatio, junctura et numerus oratorius. Itaque oratio ejus est obscura, non paucis barbarismis et solœcismis, pluribus vero archaismis et idiotismis, innumeris etiam neoterismis inquinata, comprehensio obscura, compositio fracta et in particulas concisa, vocum similium aut ambiguarum puerilis captatio."

appeared at Salamanca in 1587, far excelled any grammatical treatise that had preceded it, especially as to the rules of syntax, which he has reduced to their natural principles by explaining apparent anomalies. He is called the prince of grammarians, a divine man, the Mercury and Apollo of Spain, the father of the Latin language, the common teacher of the learned, in the panegyrical style of the Lipsii or Scioppii.[1] The Minerva, enlarged and corrected at different times by the most eminent scholars, Scioppius, Perizonius, and others more recent, still retains a leading place in philology. "No one among those," says its last editor, Bauer, "who have written well upon grammar, has attained such reputation and even authority as the famous Spaniard whose work we now give to the press." But Sanctius has been charged with too great proneness to censure his predecessors, especially Valla, and with an excess of novelty in his theoretical speculations.

29. The writers who in this second moiety of the sixteenth century appear to have been most conspicuous for purity of style, were Muretus, Paulus Manutius, Perpinianus, Osorius, Maphæus, to whom we may add our own Buchanan, and perhaps Haddon. Muretus is celebrated for his Orations, published by Aldus Manutius in 1576. Many of these were delivered a good deal earlier. Ruhnkenius, editor of the works of Muretus, says that he at once eclipsed Bembo, Sadolet, and the whole host of Ciceronians; expressing himself so perfectly in that author's style that we should fancy ourselves to be reading him, did not the subject betray a modern hand. "In learning," he says, "and in knowledge of the Latin language, Manutius was not inferior to Muretus: we may even say that his zeal in imitating Cicero was still stronger, inasmuch as he seemed to have no other aim all his life than to bear a perfect resemblance to that model. Yet he rather followed than overtook his master, and in this line of imitation cannot be compared with Muretus. The reason of this was, that Nature had bestowed on Muretus the same kind of genius that she had given to Cicero, while that of Manutius was very different. It was from this similarity of temperament that Muretus acquired such felicity of expression, such grace in narration, such wit in raillery, such perception of what would gratify the ear in

Orations of Muretus.

Panegyric of Ruhnkenius.

[1] Baillet.

the structure and cadence of his sentences. The resemblance of natural disposition made it a spontaneous act of Muretus to fall into the footsteps of Cicero; while, with all the efforts of Manutius, his dissimilar genius led him constantly away: so that we should not wonder when the writings of one so delight us that we cannot lay them down, while we are soon wearied with those of the other, correct and polished as they are, on account of the painful desire of imitation which they betray. No one, since the revival of letters," Ruhnkenius proceeds, "has written Latin more correctly than Muretus; yet, even in him, a few inadvertencies may be discovered."[1]

30. Notwithstanding the panegyric of so excellent a scholar, I cannot feel this very close approximation of Muretus to the Ciceronian standard; and it even seems to me that I have not rarely met with modern Latin of a more thoroughly classical character. His style is too redundant and florid, his topics very trivial. Witness the whole oration on the battle of Lepanto, where the greatness of his subject does not raise them above the level of a schoolboy's exercise. The celebrated eulogy on the St. Bartholomew Massacre, delivered before the pope, will serve as a very fair specimen to exemplify the Latinity of Muretus.[2] Scaliger, invidious for the most part in his characters of contemporary scholars, declares that no one since Cicero had written so well as Muretus, but that he adopted the Italian diffuseness, and says little in many words. This observation seems perfectly just.

Defects of his style.

[1] Mureti opera, cura Ruhnkenii, Lugd. 1789.

[2] "O noctem illam memorabilem et in fastis eximiæ alicujus notæ adjectione signandam, quæ paucorum seditiosorum interitu regem a præsenti cædis periculo, regnum a perpetua bellorum civilium formidine liberavit! Qua quidem nocte stellas equidem ipsas luxisse solito nitidius arbitror, et flumen Sequanam malores undas volvisse, quo citius illa impurorum hominum cadavera evolveret et exoneraret in mare. O felicissimam mulierem Catharinam, regis matrem, quæ cum tot annos admirabili prudentia parique sollicitudine regnum filio, filium regno conservasset, tum demum secura regnantem filium adspexit! O regis fratres ipsos quoque beatos! quorum alter cum, qua ætate cæteri vix adhuc arma tractare incipiunt, eâ ipse quater commisso prælio fraternos hostes fregisset ac fugasset, hujus quoque pulcherrimi facti præcipuam gloriam ad se potissimum voluit pertinere; alter, quamquam ætate nondum ad rem militarem idonea erat, tanta tamen est ad virtutem indole, ut neminem nisi fratrem in his rebus gerendis æquo animo sibi passurus fuerit anteponi. O diem denique illum plenum lætitiæ et hilaritatis, quo tu, beatissime pater, hoc ad te nuncio allato, Deo immortali, et Divo Ludovico regi, cujus hæc in ipso pervigilio evenerant, gratias acturus, indictas a te supplicationes pedes obiisti! Quis optabilior ad te nuncius adferri poterat? aut nos ipsi quod felicius optare poteramus principium pontificatus tui, quam ut primis illis mensibus tetram illam caliginem, quasi exorto sole, discussam cerneremus?" — Vol. i p. 177, edit. Ruhnken.

Epistles of Manutius.

31. The epistles of Paulus Manutius are written in what we may call a gentleman-like tone, without the virulence or querulousness that disgusts too often in the compositions of literary men. Of Panvinius, Robortellus, Sigonius, his own peculiar rivals, he writes in a friendly spirit and tone of eulogy. His letters are chiefly addressed to the great classical scholars of his age. But, on the other hand, though exclusively on literary subjects, they deal chiefly in generalities; and the affectation of copying Cicero in every phrase gives a coldness and almost an air of insincerity to the sentiments. They have but one note, the praise of learning; yet it is rarely that they impart to us much information about its history and progress. Hence they might serve for any age, and seem like pattern-forms for the epistles of a literary man. In point of mere style, there can be no comparison between the letters of a Sadolet or Manutius on the one hand, and those of a Scaliger, Lipsius, or Casaubon on the other. But, while the first pall on the reader by their monotonous elegance, the others are full of animation and pregnant with knowledge. Even in what he most valued, correct Latin, Manutius, as Scioppius has observed, is not without errors. But the want of perfect dictionaries made it difficult to avoid illegitimate expressions which modern usage suggested to the writer.[1]

Care of the Italian Latinists.

32. Manutius, as the passage above quoted has shown, is not reckoned by Ruhnkenius quite equal to Muretus, at least in natural genius. Scioppius thinks him consummate in delicacy and grace. He tells us that Manutius could hardly speak three words of Latin, so that the Germans who came to visit him looked down on his deficiency. But this, Scioppius remarks, as Erasmus had done a hundred years before, was one of the rules observed by the Italian scholars to preserve the correctness of their style. They perceived that the daily use of Latin in speech must bring in a torrent of barbarous phrases, which, "claiming afterwards the privileges of acquaintance" (*quodam familiaritatis jure*), would obtrude their company during composition, and render it difficult for the most accurate writer to avoid them.[2]

1 Scioppius, Judicium de Stylo Historico.

2 Id., p. 65. This was so little understood in England, that, in some of our colleges, and even schools, it was the regulation for the students to speak Latin when within hearing of their superiors. Even Locke was misled into recommending this preposterous barbarism.

33. Perpinianus, a Valencian Jesuit, wrote some orations, hardly remembered at present; but Ruhnkenius has placed him along with Muretus, as the two Cisalpines (if that word may be so used for brevity) who have excelled the Italians in Latinity. A writer of more celebrity was Osorius, a Portuguese bishop, whose treatise on Glory, and, what is better known, his History of the Reign of Emanuel, have placed him in a high rank among the imitators of the Augustan language. Some extracts from Osorius de Gloria will be found in the first volume of the Retrospective Review. This has been sometimes fancied to be the famous work of Cicero with that title, which Petrarch possessed and lost, and which Petrus Alcyonius has been said to have transferred to his own book De Exilio. But for this latter conjecture there is, I believe, neither evidence nor presumption; and certainly Osorius, if we may judge from the passages quoted, was no Cicero. Lord Bacon has said of him, that "his vein was weak and waterish," which these extracts confirm. They have not elegance enough to compensate for their verbosity and emptiness. Dupin, however, calls him the Cicero of Portugal.[1] Nor is less honor due to the Jesuit Maffei (Maphæus), whose chief work is the History of India, published in 1586. Maffei, according to Scioppius, was so careful of his style, that he used to recite the breviary in Greek, lest he should become too much accustomed to bad Latin.[2] This may perhaps be said in ridicule of such purists. Like Manutius, he was tediously elaborate in correction: some have observed that his History of India has scarce any value except for its style.[3]

Perpinianus; Osorius; Maphæus.

34. The writings of Buchanan, and especially his Scottish history, are written with strength, perspicuity, and neatness.[4] Many of our own critics have extolled the Latinity of Walter Haddon. His Orations were published in 1567. They belong to the first years of this period. But they seem hardly to deserve any high praise. Haddon had certainly labored at an imitation of Cicero, but without catching his manner, or getting rid of the florid, semi-poetical tone of the fourth century. A specimen, taken much at

Buchanan; Haddon.

[1] Niceron, vol. ii.

[2] De Stylo Hist., p. 71.

[3] Tiraboschi; Niceron, vol. v.; Biogr. Univ.

[4] Le Clerc, in an article of the Bibliothèque Choisie, vol. viii., pronounces a high eulogy on Buchanan, as having written better than any one else in verse and prose; that is, as I understand him, having written prose better than any one who has written verse so well, and the converse.

random, but rather favorable than otherwise, from his oration on the death of the young brothers of the house of Suffolk, at Cambridge, in 1550, is given in a note.[1] Another work of a different kind, wherein Haddon is said to have been concerned jointly with Sir John Cheke, is the Reformatio Legum Ecclesiasticarum, the proposed code of the Anglican Church, drawn up under Edward VI. It is, considering the subject, in very good language.

Sigonius De Consolatione.

35. These are the chief writers of this part of the sixteenth century who have attained reputation for the polish and purity of their Latin style. Sigonius ought, perhaps, to be mentioned in the same class, since his writings exhibit not only perspicuity and precision, but as much elegance as their subjects would permit. He is also the acknowledged author of the treatise De Consolatione, which long passed with many for a work of Cicero. Even Tiraboschi was only undeceived of this opinion by meeting with some unpublished letters of Sigonius, wherein he confesses the forgery.[2] It seems, however, that he had inserted some authentic fragments. Lipsius speaks of this counterfeit with the utmost contempt, but, after all his invective, can scarcely detect any bad Latinity.[3] The Consolatio is, in fact, like many other imitations of the philosophical writings of Cicero, resembling their original in his faults of verbosity and want of depth, but flowing and graceful in language. Lipsius, who affected the other extreme, was not likely to value that which deceived the Italians into a belief that Tully himself was before them. It

[1] "O laboriosam et si non miseram certe mirabiliter exercitam, tot cumulatam funeribus Cantabrigiam! Gravi nos vulnere percussit hyems, æstas saucios ad terram afflixit. Calendæ Martiæ stantem adhuc Academiam nostram et erectam vehementer impulerunt, et de priori statu suo depresserunt. Idus Juliæ nutantem jam et inclinatam oppresserunt. Cum magnus ille fidei magister et excellens noster in vera religione doctor, Martinus Bucerus, frigoribus hybernis conglaciavisset, tantam in ejus occasu plagam accepisse videbamur, ut majorem non solum ullam expectaremus, sed ne posse quidem expectari crederemus. Verum postquam inundantes, et in Cantabrigiam effervescentes æstivi sudores, illud præstans et aureolum par Suffolciensium fratrum tum quidem peregrinatum a nobis, sed tamen plane nostrum obruerunt, sic ingemuimus, ut infinitus dolor vix ullam tanti mali levationem invenire possit. Perfectus omni scientia pater, et certe senex incomparabilis, Martinus Bucerus, licet nec reipublicæ nec nostro, tamen suo tempore mortuus est, nimirum ætate, et annis et morbo affectus. Suffolcienses autem, quos ille florescentes ad omnem laudem. tanquam alumnos disciplinæ reliquit suæ, tam repente sudorum fluminibus absorpti sunt, ut prius mortem illorum audiremus, quam morbum animadverteremus."

[2] Biogr. Univ., art. "Sigonio."

[3] Lipsii Opera Critica. His stylo is abusive, as usual in this age. "Quis autem ille suaviludius qui latere se posse censuit sub illâ personâ? Male mehercule de seculo nostro judicavit. Quid enim tam dissimile ab illo auro, quam hoc plumbum? ne simia quidem Ciceronis esse potest, nedum ut ille. . . . Habes judicium meum, in quo si aliqua asperitas, ne mirere. Fatua enim hæc superbia tanto nomini se inserendi dignissima insectatione fuit."

was, at least, not every one who could have done this like Sigonius.

36. Several other names, especially from the Jesuit colleges, might, I doubt not, be added to the list of good Latin writers by any competent scholar, who should prosecute the research through public libraries by the aid of the biographical dictionaries. But more than enough may have been said for the general reader. The decline of classical literature in this sense, to which we have already alluded, was the theme of complaint towards the close of the century, and above all in Italy. Paulus Manutius had begun to lament it long before. But Latinus Latinius himself, one of the most learned scholars of that country, states positively, in 1584, that the Italian universities were forced to send for their professors from Spain and France.[1] And this abandonment by Italy of her former literary glory was far more striking in the next age, an age of science, but not of polite literature. Ranke supposes that, the attention of Italy being more turned towards mathematics and natural history, the study of the ancient writers, which do not contribute greatly to these sciences, fell into decay. But this seems hardly an adequate cause, nor had the exact sciences made any striking progress in the period immediately under review. The rigorous orthodoxy of the church, which in some measure revived an old jealousy of heathen learning, must have contributed far more to the effect. Sixtus V. notoriously disliked all profane studies, and was even kept with difficulty from destroying the antiquities of Rome, several of which were actually demolished by his bigoted and barbarous zeal.[2] No other pope, I believe, has been guilty of what the Romans always deemed sacrilege. In such discouraging circumstances, we could hardly wonder at what is reported, that Aldus Manutius, having been made professor of rhetoric at Rome about 1589, could only get one or two hearers. But this, perhaps, does not rest on very good authority.[3] It is agreed that the Greek language was almost wholly neglected at the end of the century, and there was no one in Italy distinguished for a knowledge of it. Baronius must be reckoned a man of

Decline of taste and learning in Italy.

[1] Tiraboschi, x. 387.

[2] Ranke, i. 476.

[3] Id., 482. Renouard, Imprimerie des Aldes, iii. 197, doubts the truth of this story which is said to come on the authority alone of Rossi, a writer who took the name of Erythræus, and has communicated a good deal of literary miscellaneous information, but not always such as deserves confidence.

laborious erudition, yet he wrote his annals of the ecclesiastical history of twelve centuries without any acquintance with that tongue.

Joseph Scaliger.

37. The two greatest scholars of the sixteenth century, being rather later than most of the rest, are yet unnamed, — Joseph Scaliger and Isaac Casaubon. The former, son of Julius Cæsar Scaliger, and, in the estimation at least of some, his inferior in natural genius, though much above him in learning and judgment, was perhaps the most extraordinary master of general erudition that has ever lived. His industry was unremitting through a length of life; his memory, though he naturally complains of its failure in latter years, had been prodigious; he was, in fact, conversant with all ancient, and very extensively with modern, literature. The notes of his conversations, taken down by some of his friends, and well known by the name of Scaligerana, though full of vanity and contempt of others, and though not always perhaps faithful registers of what he said, bear witness to his acuteness, vivacity, and learning.[1] But his own numerous

[1] The Scaligerana Prima, as they are called, were collected by Francis Vertunien, a physician of Poitiers; the Secunda, which are much the longest, by two brothers, named De Vassan, who were admitted to the intimacy of Scaliger at Leyden. They seem to have registered all his table-talk in commonplace-books alphabetically arranged. Hence, when he spoke at different times of the same person or subject, the whole was published in an undigested, incoherent, and sometimes self-contradictory paragraph. He was not strict about consistency, as men of his temper seldom are in their conversation; and one would be slow in relying on what he has said: but the Scaligerana, with its many faults, deserves perhaps the first place among those amusing miscellanies known by the name of Ana.

It was little to the honor of the Scaligers, father and son, that they lay under the strongest suspicions of extreme credulity, to say nothing worse, in setting up a descent from the Scala princes of Verona; though the world could never be convinced that their proper name was not Burden, of a plebeian family, and known as such in that city. Joseph Scaliger took as his device, *Fuimus Troes;* and his letters, as well as the Scaligerana, bear witness to the stress he laid on this pseudo-genealogy. Lipsius observes on this, with the true spirit which a man of letters ought to feel, that it would have been a great honor for the Scalas to have descended from the Scaligers, who had more real nobility than the whole city of Verona. (Thuana, p. 14.) But, unfortunately, the vain, foolish, and vulgar part of mankind cannot be brought to see things in that light; and both the Scaligers knew that such princes as Henry II. and even Henry IV. would esteem them more for their ancestry than for their learning and genius.

The epitaph of Daniel Heinsius on Joseph Scaliger, pardonably perhaps on such an occasion, mingles the real and fabulous glories of his friend.

"Regius a Brenni deductus sanguine sanguis
Qui dominos rerum tot numerabat avos,
Cui nihil indulsit sors, nil natura negavit,
Et jure imperii conditor ipse sui,
Invidiæ scopulus, sed cœlo proximus illa,
Illa Juliades conditur, hospes, humo.
Centum illic proavos et centum pone triumphos,
Sceptraque Veronæ sceptrigerosque Deos;
Mastinosque, Canesque, et totam ab origine gentem,
Et quæ præterea non bene nota latent.
Illic stent aquilæ priscique insignia regni,
Et ter Cæsareo munere fulta domus.

nd laborious publications are the best testimonies to these ualities. His name will occur to us more than once again. n the department of philology, he was conspicuous as an xcellent critic both of the Latin and Greek languages; hough Bayle, in his own paradoxical but acute and truly udicious spirit, has suggested that Scaliger's talents and earning were too great for a good commentator, — the one naking him discover in authors more hidden sense than they ossessed, the other leading him to perceive a thousand llusions which had never been designed. He frequently ltered the text in order to bring these more forward; and in is conjectures is bold, ingenious, and profound, but not always very satisfactory.[1] His critical writings are chiefly on the Latin poets: but his knowledge of Greek was eminent; and, perhaps, it may not be too minute to notice as a proof of it, that his verses in that language, if not good according to our present standard, are at least much better than those of Casaubon. The latter, in an epistle to Scaliger, extols his correspondent as far above Gaza or any modern Greek in poetry, and worthy to have lived in Athens with Aristophanes and Euripides. This cannot be said of his own attempts, in which their gross faultiness is as manifest as their general want of spirit.

38. This eminent person, a native of Geneva,[2] — that little city, so great in the annals of letters, — and the son-in-law of Henry Stephens, rose above the horizon in 1583, when his earliest work, the Annotations on Diogenes Laertius, was published, — a performance of which he was afterwards ashamed, as being unworthy of his riper studies. Those on Strabo, an author much neglected before, followed in 1587. For more than twenty years, Casaubon employed himself upon editions of Greek writers, many of which, as that of Theophrastus, in 1593, and that of Athenæus, in 1600, deserve particular mention. The latter, especially,

Isaac Casaubon.

Plus tamen invenies quicquid sibi contulit ipse,
Et minimum tantæ nobilitatis eget.
Aspice tot linguas, totumque in pectore mundum;
Innumeras gentes continet iste locus.
Crede illic Arabas, desertaque nomina Pœnos,
Et crede Armenios Æthiopasque tegi.
Terrarum instar habes; et quam natura negavit
Laudem uni populo, contigit illa viro.

1 Niceron, vol. xxiii.; Blount, Biogr. Univ.

2 The father of Casaubon was from the neighborhood of Bordeaux. He fled to Geneva during a temporary persecution of the Huguenots, but returned home afterwards. Casaubon went back to Geneva in his nineteenth year for the sake of education. See his Life by his son Meric, prefixed to Almeloveen's edition of his epistles.

which he calls *molestissimum, difficillimum et tædii plenissimum opus*, has always been deemed a noble monument of critical sagacity and extensive erudition. In conjectural emendation of the text, no one hitherto had been equal to Casaubon. He may probably be deemed a greater scholar than his father-in-law Stephens, or even, in a critical sense, than his friend Joseph Scaliger. These two lights of the literary world, though it is said that they had never seen each other,[1] continued, till the death of the latter, in regular correspondence and unbroken friendship. Casaubon, querulous but not envious, paid freely the homage which Scaliger was prepared to exact, and wrote as to one superior in age, in general celebrity, and in impetuosity of spirit. Their letters to each other, as well as to their various other correspondents, are highly valuable for the literary history of the period they embrace; that is, the last years of the present, and the first of the ensuing, century.

General result.

39. Budæus, Camerarius, Stephens, Scaliger, Casaubon, appear to stand out as the great restorers of ancient learning, and especially of the Greek language. I do not pretend to appreciate them by deep skill in the subject, or by a diligent comparison of their works with those of others, but from what I collect to have been the more usual suffrage of competent judges. Canter, perhaps, or Sylburgius, might be rated above Camerarius; but the last seems, if we may judge by the eulogies bestowed upon him, to have stood higher in the estimation of his contemporaries. Their labors restored the integrity of the text in the far greater part of the Greek authors, — though they did not yet possess as much metrical knowledge as was required for that of the poets, — explained most dubious passages, and nearly exhausted the copiousness of the language. For another century, mankind was content, in respect to Greek philology, to live on the accumulations of the sixteenth; and it was not till after so long a period had elapsed that new scholars arose, more exact, more philosophical, more acute in "knitting up the ravelled sleeve" of speech, but not, to say the least, more abundantly stored with erudition, than those who had cleared the way, and upon whose foundations they built.

40. We come, in the last place, to the condition of ancient

[1] Morhof, l. i. c. xv. s. 57.

learning in this island, — a subject which it may be interesting to trace with some minuteness, though we can offer no splendid banquet, even from the reign of the Virgin Queen. Her accession was indeed a happy epoch in our literary as well as civil annals. She found a great and miserable change in the state of the universities since the days of her father. Plunder and persecution, the destroying spirits of the last two reigns, were enemies against which our infant muses could not struggle.[1] Ascham, however, denies that there was much decline of learning at Cambridge before the time of Mary. The influence of her reign was, not indirectly alone, but by deliberate purpose, injurious to all useful knowledge.[2] It was in contemplation, he tells us (and surely it was congenial enough to the spirit of that government), that the ancient writers should give place in order to restore Duns Scotus and the scholastic barbarians.

Learning in England under Edward and Mary.

41. It is indeed impossible to restrain the desire of noble minds for truth and wisdom. Scared from the banks of Isis and Cam, neglected or discountenanced by power, learning found an asylum in the closets of private men, who laid up in silence stores for future use. And some of course remained out of those who had listened to Smith and Cheke, or the contemporary teachers of Oxford. But the mischief was effected, in a general sense, by breaking up the course of education in the universities. At the beginning of the new queen's reign, but few of the clergy, to which-

Revival under Elizabeth.

1 The last editor of Wood's Athenæ Oxonienses bears witness to having seen chronicles and other books mutilated, as he conceives, by the Protestant visitors of the university under Edward. "What is most," he says, "to the discredit of Cox (afterwards Bishop of Ely), was his unwearied diligence in destroying the ancient manuscripts and other books in the public and private libraries at Oxford. The savage barbarity with which he executed this hateful office can never be forgotten," &c., p. 468. One book only of the famous library of Humphrey, Duke of Gloucester, bequeathed to Oxford, escaped mutilation. This is a Valerius Maximus. But, as Cox was really a man of considerable learning, we may ask whether there is evidence to lay these Vandal proceedings on him rather than on his colleagues.

2 "And what was the fruit of this seed? Verily, judgment in doctrine was wholly altered; order in discipline very much changed; the love of good learning began suddenly to wax cold: the knowledge of the tongues, in spite of some that therein had flourished, was manifestly contemned, and so the way of right study manifestly perverted; the choice good authors of malice confounded; old sophistry, I say not well, not old, but that new rotten sophistry, began to beard and shoulder logic in their own tongue; yea, I know that heads were cast together, and counsel devised, that Duns, with all the rabble of barbarous questionists, should have dispossessed, of their places and room, Aristotle, Plato, Tully, and Demosthenes; whom good Mr. Redman, and those two worthy stars of the university, Mr. Cheke and Mr. Smith, with their scholars, had brought to flourish as notably in Cambridge, as ever they did in Greece and in Italy; and for the doctrine of those four, the four pillars of learning, Cambridge then giving no place to no university, neither in France, Spain, Germany, nor Italy." — p. 317.

ever mode of faith they might conform, had the least tincture of Greek learning; and the majority did not understand Latin. The Protestant exiles, being far the most learned men of the kingdom, brought back a more healthy tone of literary diligence The universities began to revive. An address was delivered in Greek verses to Elizabeth at Cambridge in 1564, to which she returned thanks in the same language.[2] Oxford would not be outdone. Lawrence, regius professor of Greek, as we are told by Wood, made an oration at Carfax, a spot often chosen for public exhibition, on her visit to the city in 1566; when her majesty, thanking the university in the same tongue, observed "it was the best Greek speech she had ever heard."[3] Several slight proofs of classical learning appear from this time in the History and Antiquities of Oxford, — marks of a progress, at first slow and silent, which I only mention because nothing more important has been recorded.

42. In 1575, the queen having been now near twenty years on the throne, we find, on positive evidence, that lectures on Greek were given in St. John's College, Cambridge, — which, indeed, few would be disposed to doubt, reflecting on the general character of the age and the length of opportunity that had been afforded. It is said in the life of Mr. Bois, or Boyse, one of the revisers of the translation of the Bible under James, that "his father was a great scholar, being learned in the Hebrew and Greek excellently well, which, considering the manners, that I say not, the looseness of the times of his education, was almost a miracle." The son was admitted at St. John's in 1575. "His father had well educated him in the Greek tongue before his coming, which caused him to be taken notice of in the college. For, besides himself, there was but one there who could write Greek. Three lectures in that language were read in the college. In the first, grammar was taught, as is commonly now done in schools. In the second, an easy author was explained in the grammatical way. In the third was read somewhat which might seem fit for their capacities who had passed over the other two. A year was usually spent in the first, and two in the second."[4] It will be perceived that the course of instruction was still elementary; but it is well known

Greek lectures at Cambridge.

1 Hallam's Constit. Hist. of Eng., i. 187.
2 Peck's Desiderata Curiosa, p. 270.
3 Wood, Hist. and Antiq. of Oxford.
4 Peck's Desiderata Curiosa, p. 327. Chalmers.

that many, or rather most, students entered the universities at an earlier age than is usual at present.[1]

43. We come very slowly to books, even subsidiary to education, in the Greek language. And since this cannot be conveniently carried on to any great extent without books, though I am aware that some contrivances were employed as substitutes for them, and since it was as easy to publish either grammars or editions of ancient authors in England as on the Continent, we can, as it seems, draw no other inference from the want of them than the absence of any considerable demand. I shall therefore enumerate all the books instrumental to the study of Greek, which appeared in England before the close of the century.

Few Greek editions in England.

44. It has been mentioned in another place that two alone had been printed before 1550. In 1553 a Greek version of the second Æneid, by George Etherege, was published. Two editions of the Anglican liturgy in Latin and Greek, by Whitaker, one of our most learned theologians, appeared in 1569;[2] a short catechism in both languages, 1573 and 1578. We find also in 1578 a little book entitled *χριστιανισμου στοιχειωσις εις την παιδων ωφελειαν ἑλληνιστι και λατινιστι εκτεθεισα.* This is a translation, made also by Whitaker, from Nowell's Christianæ Pietatis Prima Institutio, ad Usum Scholarum Latine scripta. The Biographia Britannica puts the first edition of this Greek version in 1575, and informs us also that Nowell's lesser Catechism was published in Latin and Greek, 1575; but I do not find any confirmation of this in Herbert or Watts. In 1575, Grant, master of Westminster School, published Græcæ Linguæ Spicilegium, intended

School-books enumerated.

[1] It is probable that Cambridge was at this time better furnished with learning than Oxford. Even Wood does not give us a favorable notion of the condition of that university in the first part of the queen's reign. Oxford was for a long time filled with Popish students, that is, with conforming partisans of the former religion; many of whom, from time to time, went off to Douay. Leicester, as chancellor of the university, charged it, in 1582, and in subsequent years, with great neglect of learning; the disputations had become mere forms, and the queen's lecturers in Greek and Hebrew seldom read. It was as bad in all the other sciences. Wood's Antiquities and Athenæ, *passim.* The colleges of Corpus Christi and Merton were distinguished beyond the rest in the reign of Elizabeth; especially the former, where Jewell read the lecture in rhetoric (at an earlier time, of course), Hooker in logic, and Raynolds in Greek. Leicester succeeded in *puritanizing*, as Wood thought, the university, by driving off the old party, and thus rendering it a more effective school of learning.

Harrison, about 1586, does not speak much better of the universities: "The quadrivials, I mean arithmetic, music, geometry, and astronomy, are now small regarded in either of them." — Description of Britain, p. 252. Few learned preachers were sent out from them, which he ascribes, in part, to the poor endowments of most livings.

[2] Scaliger says of Whitaker, "O qu'il étoit bien docte!" — Scalig Secunda

evidently for the use of his scholars; and, in 1581, the same Grant superintended an edition of Constantin's Lexicon, probably in the abridgment under the name of the Basle printer Crespin, enriching it with four or five thousand new words, which he most likely took from Stephens's Thesaurus. A Greek, Latin, French, and English lexicon, by John Barret or Baret, in 1580,[1] and another by John Morel (without the French), in 1583, are recorded in bibliographical works; but I do not know whether any copies have survived.

Greek taught in schools.

45. It appears, therefore, that, before even the middle of the queen's reign, the rudiments of the Greek language were imparted to boys at Westminster School, and no doubt also at those of Eton, Winchester, and St. Paul's.[2] But probably it did not yet extend to many others. In Ascham's Schoolmaster, a posthumous treatise, published in 1570, but evidently written some years after the accession of Elizabeth, while very detailed, and, in general, valuable rules are given for the instruction of boys in the Latin language, no intimation is found that Greek was designed to be taught. In the statutes of Witton School in Cheshire, framed in 1558, the founder says: "I will there were always taught good literature, both Latin and Greek."[3] But this seems to be only an aspiration after an hopeless excellence; for he proceeds to enumerate the Latin books intended to be used, without any mention of Greek. In the statutes of Merchant Taylors' School, 1561, the high-master is required to be "learned in good and clean Latin literature, and also in Greek, if such may be gotten."[4] These words are copied from those of Colet, in the foundation of St. Paul's School. But in the regulations of Hawkshead School in Lancashire, 1588, the master is directed "to teach grammar and the principles of the Greek tongue."[5] The little tracts, indeed, above mentioned, do not lead us to believe that

[1] Chalmers mentions an earlier edition of this dictionary in 1573, but without the Greek.

[2] Harrison mentions, about the year 1586, that at the great collegiate schools of Eton, Winchester, and Westminster, boys "are well entered in the knowledge of the Latin and Greek tongues and rules of versifying." — Description of England, prefixed to Hollingshed's Chronicles, p. 254 (4to edition). He has just before taken notice of "the great number of grammar-schools throughout the realm, and those very liberally endowed for the relief of poor scholars, so that there are not many corporate towns now under the queen's dominion that have not one grammar-school at the least, with a sufficient living for a master and usher appointed for the same."

[3] Carlisle's Endowed Schools, vol. i. p 129.

[4] Id., vol. ii. p. 49.

[5] Carlisle's Endowed Schools, vol. i. p. 656.

the instruction, even at Westminster, was of more than the slightest kind. They are but verbal translations of known religious treatises, wherein the learner would be assisted by his recollection at almost every word. But in the rules laid down by Mr. Lyon, founder of Harrow School, in 1590, the books designed to be taught are enumerated, and comprise some Greek orators and historians, as well as the poems of Hesiod.[1]

46. We have now, however, descended very low in the century. The twilight of classical learning in England had yielded to its morning. It is easy to trace many symptoms of enlarged erudition after 1580. Scot, in his Discovery of Witchcraft, 1584, and doubtless many other writers, employ Greek quotations rather freely; and the use of Greek words, or adaptation of English forms to them, is affected by Webb and Puttenham in their treatises on poetry. Greek titles are not infrequently given to books: it was a pedantry that many affected. Besides the lexicons above mentioned, it was easy to procure, at no great price, those of Constantin and Scapula. We may refer to the ten years after 1580, the commencement of that rapid advance which gave the English nation, in the reign of James, so respectable a place in the republic of letters. In the last decennium of the century, the Ecclesiastical Polity of Hooker is a monument of real learning, in profane as well as theological antiquity. But certainly the reading of our scholars in this period was far more generally among the Greek fathers than the classics. Even this, however, required a competent acquaintance with the language.

Greek better known after 1580.

47. The two universities had abandoned the art of printing since the year 1521. No press is known to have existed afterwards at Cambridge till 1584, or at Oxford till 1586, when six homilies of Chrysostom in Greek were published at a press erected by Lord Leicester at his own expense.[2] The first book of Herodotus came out at the same place in 1591; the treatise of Barlaam on the Papacy, in 1592; Lycophron, in the same year; the Knights of Aris-

Editions of Greek.

[1] Id., ii. 133. I have not discovered any other proofs of Greek education in Mr. Carlisle's work. In the statutes or regulations of Bristol School, founded in the sixteenth century, it is provided that the head-master should be "well learned in the Latin, Greek, and Hebrew." But these must be modern, as appears, *inter alia*, by the words, "well affected to the Constitution in Church and State."

[2] Herbert.

tophanes, in 1593; fifteen orations of Demosthenes, in 1593 and 1597; Agatharcides, in the latter year. One oration of Lysias was printed at Cambridge in 1593. The Greek Testament appeared from the London press in 1581, in 1587, and again in 1592; a treatise of Plutarch, and three orations of Isocrates, in 1587; the Iliad in 1591. These, if I have overlooked none, or if none have been omitted by Herbert, are all the Greek publications (except grammars, of which there are several, one by Camden, for the use of Westminster School, in 1597,[1] and one in 1600, by Knolles, author of the History of the Turks) that fall within the sixteenth century; and all, apparently, are intended for classes in the schools and universities.[2]

And of Latin Classics.

48. It must be expected that the best Latin writers were more honored than those of Greece. Besides grammars and dictionaries, which are too numerous to mention, we find not a few editions, though principally for the purposes of education: Cicero de Officiis (in Latin and English), 1553; Virgil, 1570; Sallust, 1570 and 1571; Justin, 1572; Cicero de Oratore, 1573; Horace and Juvenal, 1574. It is needless to proceed lower, when they become more frequent. The most important classical publication was a complete edition of Cicero, which was, of course,

[1] This grammar by Camden was probably founded on that of Grant, above mentioned, — "cujus rudimenta," says Smith, the author of Camden's life, "cum multa ex parte laborarent deficerentque, non tam reformanda, quam de novo instituenda censens, observationibus quas ex Græcis omne genus scriptoribus acri judicio et longo usu collegerat, sub severum examen revocatis, grammaticam novam non soli scholæ cui præerat, sed universis per Angliam scholis deinceps inservituram, eodem anno edidit." — p. 19, edit. 1691.

[I have since been informed by the learned correspondent to whom I have alluded in vol. i. p. 334, that, "after some search and inquiry, I feel no doubt the author of the Eton Grammar was Camden, and that it was originally compiled by him when he was head-master of Westminster School, for the use of that school, in 1595. Thence it was very likely to have been adopted at Eton by his friend Sir Henry Savile, who was made provost the year after Camden's grammar appeared. I have an edition before me, bearing date 1595, *in usum Regiæ Scholæ Westmonasteriensis.* It is what is now called the Eton Grammar *totidem verbis.* But Camden's grammar was superseded by Busby's at Westminster about 1650, having gone through more than thirty editions." — 1842.]

The excessive scarcity of early schoolbooks makes it allowable to mention the Progymnasma Scholasticum of John Stockwood, an edition of which, with the date of 1597, is in the Inner-Temple Library. It is merely a selection of epigrams from the Anthologia of H. Stephens, and shows but a moderate expectation of proficiency from the studious youth for whom it was designed; the Greek being written in interlinear Latin characters over the original, *ad faciliorem eorundem lectionem.* A literal translation into Latin follows, and several others in metre. Stockwood had been master of Tunbridge School: *Scholæ Tunbridgiensis olim ludimagister;* so that there may possibly have been earlier editions of this little book.

[2] The arrangement of editions recorded in Herbert, following the names of the printers, does not afford facilities for any search. I may, therefore, have omitted one or two trifles, and it is likely that I have; but the conclusion will be the same. "Angli," says Scaliger, "nunquam excuderunt bonos libros veteres, tantum vulgares."

more than a school-book. This appeared at London in 1585, from the press of Ninian Newton. It is said to be a reprint from the edition of Lambinus.

Learning lower than in Spain.

49. It is obvious that foreign books must have been largely imported, or we should place the learning of the Elizabethan period as much too low as it has ordinarily been exaggerated. But we may feel some surprise that so little was contributed by our native scholars. Certain it is, that, in most departments of literature, they did not yet occupy a distinguished place. The catalogue, by Herbert, of books published down to the end of the century, presents no favorable picture of the queen's reign. Without instituting a comparison with Germany or France, we may easily make one with the classed catalogue of books printed in Spain, which we find at the close of the Bibliotheca Nova of Nicolas Antonio. Greek appears to have been little studied in Spain, though we have already mentioned a few grammatical works: but the editions of Latin authors, and the commentators upon them, are numerous; and upon the whole it is undeniable, that in most branches of erudition, so far as we can draw a conclusion from publications, Spain, under Philip II., held a higher station than England under Elizabeth. The poverty of the English church, the want of public libraries, and the absorbing influence of polemical theology, will account for much of this; and I am not by any means inclined to rate our English gentlemen of Elizabeth's age for useful and even classical knowledge below the hidalgos of Castile. But this class were not the chief contributors to literature. It is, however, in consequence of the reputation for learning acquired by some men distinguished in civil life, such as Smith, Sadler, Raleigh, and even by ladies, among whom the queen herself, and the accomplished daughters of Sir Antony Cooke, Lady Cecil, and Lady Russell, are particularly to be mentioned, that the general character of her reign has been, in this point of view, considerably over-rated. No Englishman ought, I conceive, to suppress this avowal, or to feel any mortification in making it: with the prodigious development of wisdom and genius that illustrated the last years of Elizabeth, we may well spare the philologers and antiquaries of the Continent.

50. There had arisen, however, towards the conclusion of the century, a very few men of such extensive learning as entitled them to an European reputation. Sir Henry Savile

stood at the head of these: we may justly deem him the most learned Englishman, in profane literature, of the reign of Elizabeth. He published, in 1581, a translation of part of Tacitus, with annotations not very copious or profound, but pertinent, and deemed worthy to be rendered into Latin in the next century by the younger Gruter, and reprinted on the Continent.[1] Scaliger speaks of him with personal ill-will, but with a respect he seldom showed to those for whom he entertained such sentiments. Next to Savile we may rank Camden, whom all foreigners name with praise for the Britannia. Hooker has already been mentioned; but I am not sure that he could be said to have much reputation beyond our own shores. I will not assert that no other was extensively known even for profane learning: in our own biographical records, several may be found, at least esteemed at home. But our most studious countrymen long turned their attention almost exclusively to theological controversy, and toiled over the prolix volumes of the fathers; a labor not to be defrauded of its praise, but to which we are not directing our eyes on this occasion.[2]

Improvement at the end of the century.

51. Scotland had hardly as yet partaken of the light of letters; the very slight attempts at introducing an enlarged scheme of education, which had been made thirty years before, having wholly failed in consequence of the jealous spirit that actuated the chiefs of the old religion, and the devastating rapacity that disgraced the partisans of the new. But, in 1575, Andrew Melville was appointed principal of the university of Glasgow, which he found almost broken up and abandoned. He established so solid and extensive a system of instruction, wherein the best Greek authors were included, that Scotland, in some years' time, instead of sending her own natives to foreign universities, found students from other parts of Europe repairing to her own.[3] Yet Ames has observed, that no Greek characters appear in any book printed in Scotland before 1599. This assertion has been questioned by Herbert. In the treatise of Buchanan, De Jure Regni (Edinburgh, 1580), I have remarked that the Greek quotations are

Learning in Scotland.

[1] They are contained in a small volume, 1649, with Savile's other treatise on the Roman Militia.

[2] It is remarkable, that in Jewell's Defence of the Apology, by far the most learned work in theological erudition which the age produced, he quotes the Greek fathers in Latin; and there is a scanty sprinkling of Greek characters throughout this large volume.

[3] M'Crie's Life of Melville, vol. i. p. 72.

inserted with a pen. It is at least certain that no book in that language was printed north of the Tweed within this century; nor any Latin classic, nor dictionary, nor any thing of a philological nature, except two or three grammars. A few Latin treatises by modern authors on various subjects appeared. It seems questionable whether any printing-press existed in Ireland: the evidence to be collected from Herbert is precarious; but I know not whether any thing more satisfactory has since been discovered.

Latin little used in writing.

52. The Latin language was by no means so generally employed in England as on the Continent. Our authors have, from the beginning, been apt to prefer their mother-tongue, even upon subjects which, by the usage of the learned, were treated in Latin; though works relating to history, and especially to ecclesiastical antiquity, such as those of Parker and Goodwin, were sometimes written in that language. It may be alleged that very few books of a philosophical class appeared at all in the far-famed reign of Elizabeth. But probably such as Scot's Discovery of Witchcraft, Rogers's Anatomy of the Mind, and Hooker's Ecclesiastical Polity, would have been thought to require a learned dress in any other country. And we may think the same of the great volumes of controversial theology; as Jewell's Defence of the Apology, Cartwright's Platform, and Whitgift's Reply to it. The free spirit, not so much of our government, as of the public mind itself, and the determination of a large portion of the community to choose their religion for themselves, rendered this descent from the lofty grounds of learning indispensable. By such a deviation from the general laws of the republic of letters, which, as it is needless to say, was by no means less practised in the ensuing age, our writers missed some part of that general renown they might have challenged from Europe: but they enriched the minds of a more numerous public at home; they gave their own thoughts with more precision, energy, and glow; they invigorated and amplified their native language, which became in their hands more accommodated to abstract and philosophical disquisition, though, for the same reason, more formal and pedantic than any other in Europe. This observation is as much intended for the reigns of James and Charles as for that of Elizabeth.

SECTION II.

Principal Writers on Antiquities — Manutius; Sigonius; Lipsius — Numismatics — Mythology — Chronology of Scaliger.

Early works on antiquities.

53. THE attention of the learned had been frequently directed, since the revival of letters, to elucidate the antiquities of Rome, her customs, rites, and jurisprudence. It was more laborious than difficult to commonplace all extant Latin authors; and, by this process of comparison, most expressions, perhaps, in which there was no corruption of the text, might be cleared up. This seems to have produced the works already mentioned, of Cælius Rhodiginus and Alexander ab Alexandro, which afford explanations of many hundred passages that might perplex a student. Others had devoted their time to particular subjects; as Pomponius Lætus, and Raphael of Volterra, to the distinctions of magistrates; Marlianus, to the topography of ancient Rome; and Robortellus, to family names. It must be confessed that most of these early pioneers were rather praiseworthy for their diligence and good-will, than capable of clearing away the more essential difficulties that stood in the way: few treatises, written before the middle of the sixteenth century, have been admitted into the collections of Grævius and Sallengre. But, soon afterwards, an abundant light was thrown upon the most interesting part of Roman antiquity, the state of government and public law, by four more eminent scholars than had hitherto explored that field, — Manutius, Panvinius, and Sigonius in Italy; Gruchius (or Grouchy) in France.

P. Manutius on Roman Laws.

54. The first of these published in 1558 his treatise De Legibus Romanorum; and, though that De Civitate did not appear till 1585, Grævius believes it to have been written about the same time as the former. Manutius has given a good account of the principal laws made at Rome during the republic; not many of the empire. Augustinus, however, Archbishop of Tarragona, had preceded him with considerable success; and several particular laws were better illustrated afterwards by Brisson, Balduin, and Gothofred. It will be obvious to any one, very slightly familiar with the Roman law, that this subject, as far as it relates to

he republican period, belongs much more to classical antiquity han to jurisprudence.

55. The second Treatise of Manutius, De Civitate, discusses he polity of the Roman republic. Though among he very first scholars of his time, he will not always ear the test of modern acuteness. Even Grævius, who imself preceded the most critical age, frequently corrects his rrors. Yet there are marks of great sagacity in Manutius; nd Niebuhr, who has judged the antiquaries of the sixteenth entury as they generally deserve, might have found the germ f his own celebrated hypothesis, though imperfectly devel-ped, in what this old writer has suggested; that the *populus Romanus* originally meant the inhabitants of Rome *intra omœria*, as distinguished from the *cives Romani*, who dwelt eyond that precinct in the territory.[1]

Manutius, De Civitate.

56. Onuphrius Panvinius, a man of vast learning and in-lustry, but of less discriminating judgment, and who lid not live to its full maturity, fell short, in his reatise De Civitate Romana, of what Manutius (from whom, owever, he could have taken nothing) has achieved on the ame subject; and his writings, according to Grævius, would rield a copious harvest to criticism.[2] But neither of the two vas comparable to Sigonius of Modena,[3] whose works on the

Panvinius; Sigonius.

[1] The first paragraph of the preface to Niebuhr's History deserves to be quoted. ' The History of Rome was treated dur-ng the first two centuries after the revival f letters, with the same prostration of he understanding and judgment to the vritten letter that had been handed down, nd with the same fearfulness of going be-ond it, which prevailed in all the other ranches of knowledge. If any one had sserted a right of examining the cred-bility of the ancient writers, and the alue of their testimony, an outcry would ave been raised against his atrocious pre-umption. The object aimed at was, in pite of all internal evidence, to combine vhat was related by them: at the utmost, ne authority was, in some one particular nstance, postponed to another as gently s possible, and without inducing any fur-her results. Here and there, indeed, a ree-born mind, such as Glareanus, broke hrough these bonds; but infallibly a sen-ence of condemnation was forthwith pro-ounced against him: besides, such men vere not the most learned, and their bold ttempts were only partial, and were want-ng in consistency. In this department, s in others, men of splendid talents and the most copious learning conformed to the narrow spirit of their age; their la-bors extracted from a multitude of in-sulated details what the remains of ancient literature did not afford united in any sin-gle work, a systematic account of Roman antiquities. What they did in this respect is wonderful; and this is sufficient to earn for them an imperishable fame."

[2] "In Onuphrio Panvinio fuerunt multæ literæ, multa industria, sed tanta ingenii vis non erat, quanta in Sigonio et Manutio, quorum scripta longe sunt limatiora."

Paulus Manutius calls Panvinius, "ille antiquitatis helluo, spectatæ juvenis in-dustriæ . . . sæpe litigat obscuris de rebus cum Sigonio nostro, sed utriusque bonitas, mutuus amor, excellens ad cognoscendam veritatem judicium facit ut inter eos facile conveniat." — Epist., lib. ii. p. 81.

[3] It appears from some of the Lettere Volgari of Manuzio, that the proper name of Sigonius was not Sigonio, but Sigone. Corniani (vol. vi. p. 151) has made the same observation on the authority of Si-gone's original unpublished letters. But the biographers, as well as Tiraboschi, though himself an inhabitant of the same city, do not advert to it.

Roman government not only form an epoch in this department of ancient literature, but have left, in general, but little for his successors. Mistakes have of course been discovered, where it is impossible to reconcile, or to rely upon, every ancient testimony; and Sigonius, like the other scholars of his age might confide too implicitly in his authorities. But his treatises, De Jure Civium Romanorum, 1560, and De Jure Italiæ, 1562, are still the best that can be read in illustration of the Roman historians and the orations of Cicero. Whoever, says Grævius, sits down to the study of these orations, without being acquainted with Sigonius, will but lose his time. In another treatise, published in 1574, De Judiciis Romanorum, he goes through the whole course of judicial proceedings, more copiously than Heineccius, the most celebrated of his successors, and with more exclusive regard to writers of the republican period. The Roman Antiquities of Grævius contain several other excellent pieces by Sigonius, which have gained him the indisputable character of the first antiquary, both for learning and judgment, whom the sixteenth century produced. He was engaged in several controversies: one with Robortellus;[1] another with a more considerable antagonist, Gruchius, a native of Rouen, and professor of Greek at Bordeaux, who, in his treatise De Comitiis Romanorum, 1555, was the first that attempted to deal with a difficult and important subject. Sigonius and he interchanged some thrusts, with more urbanity and mutual respect than was usual in that age. An account of this controversy, which chiefly related to a passage in Cicero's oration, De Lege Agraria, as to the confirmation of popular elections by the *comitia curiata*, will be found in the preface to the second volume of Grævius, wherein the treatises themselves are published. Another contemporary writer, Latino Latini, seems to have solved the problem much better than either Grouchy or Sigone. But both parties were misled by the common source of error in the most learned men of the sixteenth century, an excess of confidence in the truth of ancient testimony. The words of Cicero, who often

Gruchius.

[1] The treatises of Robortellus, republished in the second volume of Gruter's Lampas, are full of vain-glory and affected scorn of Sigonius. Half the chapters are headed, Error Sigonii. One of their controversies concerned female *prænomina*, which Robortellus denied to be ancient, except in the formula of Roman marriage, "Ubi tu Cajus, ego Caja;" though he admits that some appear in late inscriptions. Sigonius proved the contrary by instances from republican times. It is evident that they were unusual; but several have been found in inscriptions. See Grævius, vol. ii., *in præfatione*.

spoke for an immediate purpose; those of Livy and Dionysius, who knew but imperfectly the primitive history of Rome; those even of Gellius or Pomponius, to whom all the republican institutions had become hardly intelligible,—were deemed a sort of infallible text, which a modern might explain as best he could, but must not be presumptuous enough to reject.

Sigonius on Athenian polity

57. Besides the works of these celebrated scholars, one by Zamoscius, a young Pole, De Senatu Romano (1563), was so highly esteemed, that some have supposed him to have been assisted by Sigonius. The latter, among his other pursuits, turned his mind to the antiquities of Greece, which had hitherto, for obvious reasons, attracted far less attention than those of ancient Italy. He treated the constitution of the Athenian republic so fully, that, according to Gronovius, he left little for Meursius and others who trod in his path.[1] He has, however, neglected to quote the very words of his authorities, which alone can be satisfactory to a diligent reader, translating every passage, so that hardly any Greek words occur in a treatise expressly on the Athenian polity. This may be deemed a corroboration of what has been said above, as to the decline of Greek learning in Italy.

Patrizzi and Lipsius on Roman militia.

58. Francis Patrizzi was the first who unfolded the military system of Rome. He wrote in Italian a treatise Della Milizia Romana, 1583, of which a translation will be found in the tenth volume of Grævius.[2] It is divided into fifteen parts, which seem to comprehend the whole subject: each of these again is divided into sections; and each section explains a text from the sixth book of Polybius, or from Livy. But he comes down no lower in history than those writers extend, and is consequently not aware of, or but slightly alludes to, the great military changes that ensued in later times. On Polybius he comments sentence by sentence. He had been preceded by

1 "Nonnulla quidem variis locis attigit Meursius et alii, sed teretiore prorsus et rotundo magis ore per omnia Sigonius."—Thesaur. Antiq. Græc., vol. v.

2 "Primus Romanæ rei militaris præstantiam Polybium secutus detexit, cui quantum debeant qui post illum in hoc argumento elaborarunt, non nesciunt viri docti qui Josephi Scaligeri epistolas, aut Nicii Erythræi Pinacothecam legerunt. Nonnulli quidem rectius et explicatius sunt tradita de hac doctrina post Patricium a Justo Lipsio et aliis, qui in hoc stadio cucurrerunt; ut non difficulter inventis aliquid additur aut in iis emendatur, sed præclare tamen fractæ glaciei laus Patricio est tribuenda."—Grævius, in præfat. ad decimum volumen. This book has been confounded by Blount and Ginguéné with a later work of Patrizzi, entitled Paralleli Militari, Rome, 1594, in which he compared the military art of the ancients with that of the moderns, exposing, according to Tiraboschi (viii. 494), his own ignorance of the subject.

Robortellus, and by Francis, Duke of Urbino, in endeavoring to explain the Roman castrametation from Polybius. Their plans differ a little from his own.[1] Lipsius, who some years afterwards wrote on the same subject, resembles Patrizzi in his method of a running commentary on Polybius. Scaliger, who disliked Lipsius very much, imputes to him plagiarism from the Italian antiquary.[2] But I do not perceive, on a comparison of the two treatises, much pretence for this insinuation. The text of Polybius was surely common ground; and I think it possible that the work of Patrizzi, which was written in Italian, might not be known to Lipsius. But, whether this were so or not, he is much more full and satisfactory than his predecessor, who, I would venture to hint, may have been a little over-praised. Lipsius, however, seems to have fallen into the same error of supposing that the whole history of the Roman militia could be explained from Polybius.

Lipsius and other antiquaries.

59. The works of Lipsius are full of accessions to our knowledge of Roman antiquity, and he may be said to have stood as conspicuous on this side of the Alps as Sigonius in Italy. His treatise on the amphitheatre, 1584, completed what Panvinius, De Ludis Circensibus, had begun. A later work, by Peter Fabre, president in the parliament of Toulouse, entitled Agonisticon, sive de Re Athletica, 1592, relates to the games of Greece as well as Rome, and has been highly praised by Gronovius. It will be found in the eighth volume of the Thesaurus Antiquitatum Græcarum. Several antiquaries traced the history of Roman families and names; such as Fulvius Ursinus, Sigonius, Panvinius, Pighius, Castalio, Golzius.[3] A Spaniard of immense erudition, Petrus Ciaconius (Chacon), besides many illustrations of ancient monuments, especially the rostral column of Duilius, has left a valuable treatise, De Triclinio Romano, 1588.[4] He is not to be confounded with Alfonsus Ciaconius,

[1] All these writers err, in common, I believe, with every other before General Roy, in his Military Antiquities of the Romans in Britain (1793), in placing the *prætorium*, or tent of the general, near the front gate of the camp, called Porta Prætoria, instead of the opposite, Porta Decumana. Lipsius is so perplexed by the assumption of this hypothesis, that he struggles to alter the text of Polybius.

[2] Scalig. Secunda. In one of Casaubon's epistles to Scaliger, he says: "Franciscus Patritius solus mihi videtur digitum ad fontes intendisse, quem ad verbum alii, qui hoc studium tractarunt, cum sequuntur tamen ejus nomen ne semel quidem memorarunt. Quod equidem magis miratus sum in illis de quorum candore dubitare piaculum esse putassem."

[3] Grævius, vol. vii.

[4] Blount; Niceron, vol. xxxvi.

a native also of Spain, but not of the same family, who wrote an account of the column of Trajan. Pancirollus, in his Notitia Dignitatum, or rather his commentary on a public document of the age of Constantine so entitled, threw light on that later period of imperial Rome.

60. The first contribution that England made to ancient literature in this line was the View of Certain Military Matters, or Commentaries concerning Roman Warfare, by Sir Henry Savile, in 1598. This was translated into Latin, and printed at Heidelberg as early as 1601. It contains much information in small compass, extending only to about 130 duodecimo pages. Nor is it borrowed, as far as I could perceive, from Patrizzi or Lipsius, but displays an independent and extensive erudition.

Savile on Roman militia.

61. It would encumber the reader's memory, were these pages to become a register of books. Both in this and the succeeding periods, we can only select such as appear, by the permanence, or, at least, the immediate lustre of their reputation, to have deserved of the great republic of letters better than the rest. And, in such a selection, it is to be expected that the grounds of preference or of exclusion will occasionally not be obvious to all readers, and possibly would not be deemed, on reconsideration, conclusive to the author. In names of the second or third class, there is often but a shadow of distinction.

62. The foundations were laid, soon after the middle of the century, of an extensive and interesting science,— that of ancient medals. Collections of these had been made from the time of Cosmo de' Medici, and perhaps still earlier; but the rules of arranging, comparing, and explaining them were as yet unknown, and could be derived only from close observation, directed by a profound erudition. Eneas Vico of Venice, in 1555, published Discorsi sopra le Medaglie degl' Antichi; "in which he justly boasts," says Tiraboschi, "that he was the first to write in Italian on such a subject; but he might have added that no one had yet written upon it in any language."[1] The learning of Vico was the more remarkable in that he was by profession an engraver. He afterwards published a series of imperial medals, and another of the empresses; adding to each a life of the person,

Numismatics.

[1] Tiraboschi, ix. 226; Ginguéné, vii. 292; Biogr. Univ.

and explanation of the reverse. But in the latter he was excelled by Sebastian Erizzo, a noble Venetian, who, four years after Vico, published a work with nearly the same title. This is more fully comprehensive than that of Vico: medallic science was reduced in it to fixed principles; and it is particularly esteemed for the erudition shown by the author in explaining the reverses.[1] Both Vico and Erizzo have been sometimes mistaken; but what science is perfect in its commencement? It has been observed, that the latter, living at the same time, in the same city, and engaged in the same pursuit, makes no mention of his precursor; a consequence, no doubt, of the jealous humor so apt to prevail with the professors of science, especially when they do not agree in their opinions. This was the case here: Vico having thought ancient coins and medals identical; while Erizzo made a distinction between them, in which modern critics in numismatic learning have generally thought him in the wrong. The medallic collections, published by Hubert Golzius, a Flemish engraver, who had examined most of the private cabinets in Europe, from 1557 to 1579, acquired great reputation, and were long reckoned the principal repertory of that science. But it seems that suspicions entertained by many of the learned have been confirmed, and that Golzius has published a great number of spurious and even of imaginary medals; his own good faith being also much implicated in these forgeries.[2]

63. The ancient mythology is too closely connected with all classical literature to have been neglected so long as numismatic antiquity. The compilations of Rhodiginus and Alexander ab Alexandro, besides several other works, and indeed all annotations on Greek and Latin authors, had illustrated it. But this was not done systematically; and no subject more demands a comparison of authorities, which will not always be found consistent or intelligible. Boccaccio had long before led the way in his Genealogiæ Deorum; but the erudition of the fourteenth century could clear away but little of the cloud that still in some measure hangs over the religion of the ancient world. In the first decade of the present period, we find a work of considerable merit for the times, by Lilio Gregorio Giraldi, one of the

Mythology.

[1] Biogr. Univ. [2] Idem.

most eminent scholars of that age, entitled Historia de Diis Gentium. It had been preceded by one of inferior reputation, the Mythologia of Natalis Comes. "Giraldi," says the Biographie Universelle, "is the first who has treated properly this subject, so difficult on account of its extent and complexity. He made use not only of all Greek and Latin authors, but of ancient inscriptions, which he has explained with much sagacity. Sometimes the multiplicity of his quotations renders him obscure, and sometimes he fails in accuracy, through want of knowing what has since been brought to light. But the Historia de Diis Gentium is still consulted."

Scaliger's Chronology.

64. We can place in no other chapter but the present a work, to which none published within this century is superior, and perhaps none is equal, in originality, depth of erudition, and vigorous encountering of difficulty, — that of Joseph Scaliger, De Emendatione Temporum. The first edition of this appeared in 1583; the second, which is much enlarged and amended, in 1598; and a third, still better, in 1609. Chronology, as a science, was hitherto very much unknown: all ancient history, indeed, had been written in a servile and uncritical spirit, copying dates, as it did every thing else, from the authorities immediately under the compiler's eye, with little or no endeavor to reconcile discrepancies, or to point out any principles of computation. Scaliger perceived that it would be necessary to investigate the astronomical schemes of ancient calendars, not always very clearly explained by the Greek and Roman writers, and requiring much attention and acuteness, besides a multifarious erudition, oriental as well as classical, of which he alone in Europe could be reckoned master. This work, De Emendatione Temporum, is, in the first edition, divided into eight books. The first relates to the lesser equal year, as he denominates it, or that of 360 days, adopted by some Eastern nations, and founded, as he supposes, on the natural lunar year, before the exact period of a lunation was fully understood; the second book is on the true lunar year, and some other divisions connected with it; the third, on the greater equal year, so called, or that of 365 days; the fourth, on the more accurate schemes of the solar period. In the fifth and sixth books, he comes to particular epochs, determining in both many important dates in profane and sacred history. The seventh and eighth discuss the modes of computation, and the terminal epochs used in different na-

tions, with miscellaneous remarks, and critical emendations of his own. In later editions these two books are thrown into one. The great intricacy of many of these questions, which cannot be solved by testimonies often imperfect and inconsistent, without much felicity of conjecture, serves to display the surprising vigor of Scaliger's mind, who grapples like a giant with every difficulty. Le Clerc has censured him for introducing so many conjectures, and drawing so many inferences from them, that great part of his chronology is rendered highly suspicious.[1] But, whatever may be his merit in the determination of particular dates, he is certainly the first who laid the foundations of the science. He justly calls it "Materia intacta et a nobis nunc primum tentata." Scaliger in all this work is very clear, concise, and pertinent, and seems to manifest much knowledge of physical astronomy, though he was not a good mathematician, and did little credit to his impartiality by absolutely rejecting the Gregorian calendar.

65. The chronology of Scaliger has become more celebrated through his invention of the Julian period; a name given, in honor of his father,[2] to a cycle of 7980 years, beginning 4713 before Christ, and consequently before the usual date of the creation of the world. He was very proud of this device: "It is impossible to describe," he says, "its utility; chronologers and astronomers cannot extol it too much." And, what is more remarkable, it was adopted for many years afterwards, even by the opponents of Scaliger's chronology, and is almost as much in favor with Petavius as with the inventor.[3] This Julian period is formed by multiplying together the years of three cycles, once much in use, — the solar of twenty-eight, according to the old calendar; the lunar or Metonic of nineteen; and the indiction, an arbitrary and political division, introduced about the time of Constantine, and common both in the church and empire, consisting of fifteen years. Yet I confess myself unable to perceive the great advantage of this scheme. It affords, of course, a fixed terminus from which all dates may be reckoned in progressive numbers, better than the era of the creation, on ac-

Julian period.

[1] Parrhasiana, ii. 363.

[2] [This, though commonly said, appears to be an erroneous supposition. Scaliger himself gives a different reason, and one much more natural: "Periodum Julianam vocavimus, quia ad annum Julianum accommodata est." For this I am indebted to the Etudes Historiques of Daunou, vol. iii. p. 336. — 1847.]

[3] "Usus illius opinione major est in chronicis, quæ ab orbe condito vel alio quovis initio ante æram Christianam inchoantur." — Petav. Rationarium Temporum, part ii. lib. i. c. 14.

count of the uncertainty attending that epoch; but the present method of reckoning them in a retrograde series from the birth of Christ, which seems never to have occurred to Scaliger or Petavius, is not found to have much practical inconvenience. In other respects, the only real use that the Julian period appears to possess is, that dividing any year in it by the numbers 28, 19, or 15, the remainder above the quotient will give us the place such year holds in the cycle, by the proper number of which it has been divided. Thus, if we desire to know what place in the Metonic cycle the year of the Julian period 6402, answering to the year of our Lord 1689, held, or, in other words, what was the Golden Number, as it is called, of that year, we must divide 6402 by 19, and we shall find in the quotient a remainder 18; whence we perceive that it was the eighteenth year of a lunar or Metonic cycle. The adoption of the Gregorian calendar, which has greatly protracted the solar cycle by the suppression of one bissextile year in a century, as well as the general abandonment of the indiction, and even of the solar and lunar cycles, as divisions of time, have diminished whatever utility this invention may have originally possessed.

CHAPTER II.

HISTORY OF THEOLOGICAL LITERATURE IN EUROPE FROM 1550 TO 1600.

Progress of Protestantism — Re-action of the Catholic Church — The Jesuits — Causes of the Recovery of Catholicism — Bigotry of Lutherans — Controversy on Free-will — Trinitarian Controversy — Writings on Toleration — Theology in England — Bellarmin — Controversy on Papal Authority — Theological Writers — Ecclesiastical Histories — Translations of Scripture.

Diet of Augsburg in 1555.

1. In the arduous struggle between prescriptive allegiance to the Church of Rome and rebellion against its authority, the balance continued, for some time after the commencement of this period, to be strongly swayed in favor of the reformers. A decree of the Diet of Augsburg in 1555, confirming an agreement made by the emperor three years before, called the Pacification of Passau, gave the followers of the Lutheran confession for the first time an established condition; and their rights became part of the public law of Germany. No one, by this decree, could be molested for following either the old or the new form of religion; but those who dissented from that established by their ruler were only to have the liberty of quitting his territories, with time for the disposal of their effects. No toleration was extended to the Helvetic or Calvinistic, generally called the Reformed party; and by the Ecclesiastical Reservation, a part of the decree to which the Lutheran princes seem not to have assented, every Catholic prelate of the empire quitting his religion was declared to forfeit his dignity.

Progress of Protestantism.

2. This treaty, though incapable of warding off the calamities of a future generation, might justly pass, not only for a basis of religious concord, but for a signal triumph of the Protestant cause; such as, a few years before, it would have required all their steadfast faith in the arm of Providence to anticipate. Immediately after its enactment, the principles of the Confession of Augsburg, which had been restrained by fear of the imperial laws against

heresy, spread rapidly to the shores of the Danube, the Drave, and the Vistula. Those half-barbarous nations, who might be expected, by a more general analogy, to remain longest in their ancient prejudices, came more readily into the new religion than the civilized people of the south. In Germany itself, the progress of the Reformation was still more rapid: most of the Franconian and Bavarian nobility, and the citizens of every considerable town, though subjects of Catholic princes, became Protestant; while in Austria it has been said that not more than one thirtieth part of the people continued firm in their original faith. This may probably be exaggerated; but a Venetian ambassador in 1558 (and the reports of the envoys of that republic are remarkable for their judiciousness and accuracy) estimated the Catholics of the German Empire at only one tenth of the population.[1] The universities produced no defenders of the ancient religion. For twenty years, no student of the University of Vienna had become a priest. Even at Ingolstadt, it was necessary to fill with laymen, offices hitherto reserved for the clergy. The prospect was not much more encouraging in France. The Venetian ambassador in that country (Micheli, whom we know by his reports of England under Mary) declares, that in 1561 the common people still frequented the churches: but all others, especially the nobility, had fallen off; and this defection was greatest among the younger part.

Its causes.

3. This second burst of a revolutionary spirit in religion was as rapid, and perhaps more appalling, to its opponents, than that under Luther and Zwingle about 1520. It was certainly prepared by long working in the minds of a part of the people; but most of its operation was due to that generous sympathy which carries mankind along with any pretext of common interest in the redress of wrong. A very few years were sufficient to make millions desert their altars, abjure their faith, loathe, spurn, and insult their gods; words hardly too strong, when we remember how the saints and the Virgin had been honored in their images, and how they and those were now despised. It is to be observed, that the Protestant doctrines had made no sensible progress in the south of Germany before the Pacification of Passau in 1552, nor much in France before the death of Henry II. in 1559.

[1] Ranke, vol. ii. p. 125, takes a general survey of the religious state of the empire about 1563

The spirit of reformation, suppressed under his severe administration, burst forth when his weak and youthful son ascended the throne, with an impetuosity that threatened for a time the subversion of that profligate despotism by which the house of Valois had replaced the feudal aristocracy. It is not for us here to discriminate the influences of ambition and oligarchical factiousness from those of high-minded and strenuous exertion in the cause of conscience.

Wavering of Catholic princes.

4. It is not surprising that some Catholic governments wavered for a time, and thought of yielding to a storm which might involve them in ruin. Even as early as 1556, the Duke of Bavaria was compelled to make concessions which would have led to a full introduction of the Reformation. The emperor Ferdinand I. was tolerant in disposition, and anxious for some compromise that might extinguish the schism: his successor, Maximilian II., displayed the same temper so much more strongly, that he incurred the suspicion of a secret leaning towards the reformed tenets. Sigismund Augustus, King of Poland, was probably at one time wavering which course to adopt; and, though he did not quit the Church of Rome, his court and the Polish nobility became extensively Protestant: so that, according to some, there was a very considerable majority at his death who professed that creed. Among the Austrian and Hungarian nobility, as well as the burghers in the chief cities, it was held by so preponderating a body that they obtained a full toleration and equality of privileges. England, after two or three violent convulsions, became firmly Protestant; the religion of the court being soon followed with sincere good-will by the people. Scotland, more unanimously and impetuously, threw off the yoke of Rome. The Low Countries very early caught the flame, and sustained the full brunt of persecution at the hands of Charles and Philip.

Extinguished in Italy.

5. Meantime, the infant Protestantism of Italy had given some signs of increasing strength, and began more and more to number men of reputation; but, unsupported by popular affection, or the policy of princes, it was soon wholly crushed by the arm of power. The reformed church of Locarno was compelled in 1554 to emigrate in the midst of winter, and took refuge at Zurich. That of Lucca was finally dispersed about the same time. A fresh storm of persecution arose at Modena in 1556; many

ost their lives for religion in the Venetian States before 1560; thers were put to death at Rome. The Protestant countries vere filled with Italian exiles, many of them highly gifted nen, who, by their own eminence, and by the distinction which as in some instances awaited their posterity, may be compared vith those whom the revocation of the Edict of Nantes long fterwards dispersed over Europe. The tendency owards Protestantism in Spain was of the same kind, ut less extensive, and certainly still less popular, than in taly. The Inquisition took it up, and applied its usual remelies with success. But this would lead us still farther from iterary history than we have already wandered.

And Spain.

6. This prodigious increase of the Protestant party in Europe after the middle of the century did not continue nore than a few years. It was checked and fell ack, not quite so rapidly or so completely as it came n, but so as to leave the antagonist church in perfect security. Though we must not tread closely on the ground of political history, nor discuss too minutely any revolutions of opinion which do not distinctly manifest themselves in literature, it seems not quite foreign from the general purpose of these volumes, or at least a pardonable digression, to dwell a little on the leading causes of this retrograde movement of Protestantism; a fact as deserving of explanation as the previous excitement of the Reformation itself, though, from its more negative nature, it has not drawn so much of the attention of mankind. Those who behold the outbreaking of great revolutions in civil society or in religion, will not easily believe that the rush of waters can be stayed in its course; that a pause of indifference may come on, perhaps, very suddenly, or a re-action bring back nearly the same prejudices and passions as those which men had renounced. Yet this has occurred not very rarely in the annals of mankind, and never on a larger scale than in the history of the Reformation.

Re-action of Catholicity;

7. The Church of Rome, and the prince whom it most strongly influenced, Philip II., acted on an unremitting, uncompromising policy of subduing, instead of making terms with, its enemies. In Spain and Italy, the Inquisition soon extirpated the remains of heresy. The fluctuating policy of the French court, destitute of any strong religious zeal, and therefore prone to expedients, though always desirous of one end, is well known. It was, in fact, impossible

Especially in Germany.

to conquer a party so prompt to resort to arms and so skilful in their use as the Huguenots. But in Bavaria Albert V. with whom about 1564 the re-action began, in the Austrian dominions Rodolph II., in Poland Sigismund III., by shutting up churches, and by discountenancing in all respects their Protestant subjects, contrived to change a party once exceedingly powerful into an oppressed sect. The decrees of the Council of Trent were received by the spiritual princes of the empire in 1566; "and from this moment," says the excellent historian who has thrown most light on this subject "began a new life for the Catholic Church in Germany."[1] The profession of faith was signed by all orders of men; no one could be admitted to a degree in the universities nor keep a school without it. Protestants were in some places excluded from the court; a penalty which tended much to bring about the reconversion of a poor and proud nobility.

Discipline of the clergy.

8. That could not, however, have been effected by any efforts of the princes against so preponderating a majority as the Protestant Churches had obtained, if the principles that originally actuated them had retained their animating influence, or had not been opposed by more efficacious resistance. Every method was adopted to revive an attachment to the ancient religion, insuperable by the love of novelty or the force of argument. A stricter discipline and subordination was introduced among the clergy: they were early trained in seminaries, apart from the sentiments and habits, the vices and virtues, of the world. The monastic orders resumed their rigid observances. The Capucins, not introduced into France before 1570, spread over the realm within a few years, and were most active in getting up processions and all that we call foolery, but which is not the less stimulating to the multitude for its folly. It is observed by Davila, that these became more frequent after the accession of Henry III. in 1574.

Influence of Jesuits.

9. But, far above all the rest, the Jesuits were the instruments of regaining France and Germany to the church they served. And we are the more closely concerned with them here, that they are in this age among the links between religious opinion and literature. We have seen, in the last chapter, with what spirit they took the lead in polite letters and classical style; with what dexterity they

[1] Ranke, ii. 46. [I quote the German; but this valuable work has now been translated. — 1842.]

made the brightest talents of the rising generation, which the church had once dreaded and checked, her most willing and effective instruments. The whole course of liberal studies, however deeply grounded in erudition or embellished by eloquence, took one direction, one perpetual aim, — the propagation of the Catholic faith. They availed themselves, for this purpose, of every resource which either human nature or prevalent opinion supplied. Did they find Latin versification highly prized? their pupils wrote sacred poems. Did they observe the natural taste of mankind for dramatic representations, and the repute which that species of literature had obtained? their walls resounded with sacred tragedies. Did they perceive an unjust prejudice against stipendiary instruction? they gave it gratuitously. Their endowments left them in the decent poverty which their vows required, without the offensive mendicancy of the friars.

Their progress.

10. In 1551 Ferdinand established a college of Jesuits at Vienna; in 1556 they obtained one, through the favor of the Duke of Bavaria, at Ingolstadt, and in 1559 at Munich. They spread rapidly into other Catholic states of the empire, and, some time later, into Poland. In France, their success was far more equivocal; the Sorbonne declared against them as early as 1554, and they had always to encounter the opposition of the parliament of Paris. But they established themselves at Lyons in 1569, and afterwards at Bordeaux, Toulouse, and other cities. Their three duties were preaching, confession, and education; the most powerful levers that religion could employ. Indefatigable and unscrupulous, as well as polite and learned, accustomed to consider veracity and candor, when they weakened an argument, in the light of treason against the cause (language which might seem harsh, were it not almost equally applicable to so many other partisans), they knew how to clear their reasonings from scholastic pedantry and tedious quotation, for the simple and sincere understandings whom they addressed; yet, in the proper field of controversial theology, they wanted nothing of sophistical expertness or of erudition. The weak points of Protestantism they attacked with embarrassing ingenuity; and the reformed churches did not cease to give them abundant advantage by inconsistency, extravagance, and passion.[1]

[1] Hospinian. Hist. Jesuitarum; Ranke, vol. ii. p. 32, *et post*. Tiraboschi, viii. 116. The first of these works is entirely on one side, and gives no credit to the Jesuits for

11. At the death of Ignatius Loyola in 1556, the order that he had founded was divided into thirteen provinces, besides the Roman; most of which were in the Spanish peninsula or its colonies. Ten colleges belonged to Castile, eight to Aragon, five to Andalusia. Spain was for some time the fruitful mother of the disciples, as she had been of the master. The Jesuits who came to Germany were called "Spanish priests." They took possession of the universities; "they conquered us," says Ranke, "on our own ground, in our own homes, and stripped us of a part of our country." This, the acute historian proceeds to say, sprang certainly from the want of understanding among the Protestant theologians, and of sufficient enlargement of mind to tolerate unessential differences. The violent opposition among each other left the way open to these cunning strangers, who taught a doctrine not open to dispute.

Their colleges.

12. But, though Spain for a time supplied the most active spirits in the order, its central point was always at Rome. It was there that the general to whom they had sworn resided; and from thence issued to the remotest lands the voice, which, whatever secret counsels might guide it, appeared that of a single, irresponsible irresistible will. The Jesuits had three colleges at Rome; one for their own novices, another for German, and a third for English students. Possevin has given us an account of the course of study in Jesuit seminaries, taking that of Rome as a model. It contained nearly 2000 scholars, of various descriptions. "No one," he says, "is admitted without a foundation of grammatical knowledge. The abilities, the dispositions, the intentions for future life, are scrupulously investigated in each candidate; nor do we open our doors to any who do not come up in these respects to what so eminent a school of all virtue requires. They attend divine service daily; they confess every month. The professors are numerous; some teaching the exposition of Scripture, some scholastic theology, some the science of controversy with heretics, some casuistry: many instruct in logic and philosophy, in mathematics, or rhetoric, polite literature, and poetry; the Hebrew and Greek, as well as Latin, tongues are taught. Three years are given

Jesuit seminary at Rome.

their services to literature. The second is of a very different class, philosophical and profound, and yet with much more learning, that is, with a more extensive range of knowledge, than any writer of Hospinian's age could possess.

to the course of philosophy, four to that of theology. But if any are found not so fit for deep studies, yet likely to be useful in the Lord's vineyard, they merely go through two years of practical, that is, casuistical theology. These seminaries are for youths advanced beyond the inferior classes or schools; but, in the latter also, religious and grammatical learning go hand in hand."[1]

Patronage of Gregory XIII.

13. The popes were not neglectful of such faithful servants. Under Gregory XIII., whose pontificate began in 1572, the Jesuit college at Rome had twenty lecture-rooms and 360 chambers for students; a German college was restored after a temporary suspension; and an English one founded by his care; perhaps there was not a Jesuit seminary in the world which was not indebted to his liberality. Gregory also established a Greek college (not of Jesuits) for the education of youths, who there learned to propagate the Catholic faith in their country.[2] No earlier pope had been more alert and strenuous in vindicating his claims to universal allegiance; nor, as we may judge from the well-known pictures of Vasari in the vestibule of the Sistine Chapel, representing the Massacre of St. Bartholomew, more ready to sanction any crime that might be serviceable to the church.

Conversions in Germany and France.

14. The resistance made to this aggressive warfare was for some time considerable. Protestantism, so late as 1578, might be deemed preponderant in all the Austrian dominions except the Tyrol.[3] In the Polish diets, the dissidents, as they were called, met their opponents with vigor and success. The ecclesiastical principalities were full of Protestants; and, even in the chapters, some of them might be found. But the contention was unequal, from the different character of the parties: religious zeal and devotion, which fifty years before had overthrown the ancient rites in Northern Germany, were now more invigorating sentiments in those who rescued them from further innovation. In religious struggles, where there is any thing like an equality of forces, the question soon comes to be which party will make the greatest sacrifice for its own faith. And, while the Catholic self-devotion had grown far stronger, there was much more of

[1] Possevin, Bibliotheca Selecta, lib. i. c. 39.
[2] Ranke, i. 419, *et post;* Ginguéné, vii. 12; Tiraboschi, viii. 34.
[3] Ranke, ii. 78

secular cupidity, lukewarmness, and formality in the Lutheran Church. In a very few years, the effects of this were distinctly visible. The Protestants of the Catholic principalities went back into the bosom of Rome. In the bishopric of Wurtzburg alone, 62,000 converts are said to have been received in the year 1586.[1] The Emperor Rodolph and his brother archdukes, by a long series of persecutions and banishment, finally, though not within this century, almost outrooted Protestantism from the hereditary provinces of Austria. It is true that these violent measures were the proximate cause of so many conversions; but, if the reformed had been ardent and united, they were much too strong to have been thus subdued. In Bohemia, accordingly, and Hungary, where there was a more steady spirit, they kept their ground. The reaction was not less conspicuous in other countries. It is asserted that the Huguenots had already lost more than two-thirds of their number in 1580;[2] comparatively, I presume, with twenty years before: and the change in their relative position is manifest from all the histories of this period. In the Netherlands, though the Seven United Provinces were slowly winning their civil and religious liberties at the sword's point, yet West Flanders, once in great measure Protestant, became Catholic before the end of the century; while the Walloon provinces were kept from swerving by some bishops of great eloquence and excellent lives, as well as by the influence of the Jesuits planted at St. Omer and Douay. At the close of this period of fifty years, the mischief done to the old church in its first decennium was very nearly repaired; the proportions of the two religions in Germany coincided with those which had existed at the Pacification of Passau. The Jesuits, however, had begun to encroach a little on the proper domain of the Lutheran Church: besides private conversions, which, on account of the rigor of the laws, not certainly less intolerant than in their own communion, could not be very prominent, they had sometimes hopes of the Protestant princes, and had once, in 1578, obtained the promise of John, King of Sweden, to embrace openly the Romish faith, as he had already done in secret to Possevin, an emissary despatched by the pope on this important errand. But the symptoms of an opposition, very formidable in a country which has never allowed its kings

[1] Ranke, p. 147.
[2] Ranke, ii. p. 121. The number seems rather startling.

to trifle with it, made this wavering monarch retrace his steps. His successor, Sigismund, went farther, and fell a victim to his zeal by being expelled from the kingdom.

15. This great revival of the Papal religion, after the shock it had sustained in the first part of the sixteenth century, ought for ever to restrain that temerity of prediction so frequent in our ears. As women sometimes believe the fashion of last year in dress to be wholly ridiculous, and incapable of being ever again adopted by any one solicitous about her beauty, so those who affect to pronounce on future events are equally confident against the possibility of a resurrection of opinions which the majority have for the time ceased to maintain. In the year 1560, every Protestant in Europe doubtless anticipated the overthrow of Popery: the Catholics could have found little else to warrant hope than their trust in Heaven. The late rush of many nations towards democratical opinions has not been so rapid and so general as the change of religion about that period. It is important and interesting to inquire what stemmed this current. We readily acknowledge the prudence, firmness, and unity of purpose, that for the most part distinguished the court of Rome, the obedience of its hierarchy, the severity of intolerant laws, and the searching rigor of the Inquisition, the resolute adherence of great princes to the Catholic faith, the influence of the Jesuits over education; but these either existed before, or would at least not have been sufficient to withstand an overwhelming force of opinion. It must be acknowledged that there was a principle of vitality in that religion, independent of its external strength. By the side of its secular pomp, its relaxation of morality, there had always been an intense flame of zeal and devotion. Superstition it might be in the many, fanaticism in a few; but both of these imply the qualities which, while they subsist, render a religion indestructible. That revival of an ardent zeal, through which the Franciscans had, in the thirteenth century, with some good and much more evil effect, spread a popular enthusiasm over Europe, was once more displayed in counteraction of those new doctrines, that themselves had drawn their life from a similar development of moral emotion.

Causes of this revival.

16. Even in the court of Leo X., soon after the bursting forth of the Reformation in Saxony, a small body was

formed by men of rigid piety, and strenuous for a different species of reform. Sadolet, Caraffa (afterwards Paul IV.), Cajetan, and Contareni, both the latter eminent in the annals of the church, were at the head of this party.[1] Without dwelling on what belongs strictly to ecclesiastical history, it is sufficient to say that they acquired much weight; and, while adhering generally to the doctrine of the church (though Contareni held the Lutheran tenets on justification), aimed steadily at a restoration of moral discipline, and the abolition of every notorious abuse. Several of the regular orders were reformed, while others were instituted, more active in sacerdotal duties than the rest. The Jesuits must be considered as the most perfect type of the rigid party. Whatever may be objected, perhaps not quite so early, to their system of casuistry, whatever want of scrupulousness may have been shown in their conduct, they were men who never swerved from the path of labor, and, it might be, suffering, in the cause which they deemed that of God. All self-sacrifice in such circumstances, especially of the highly-gifted and accomplished, though the bigot steels his heart and closes his eyes against it, excites the admiration of the unsophisticated part of mankind.

A rigid party in the church.

17. The Council of Trent, especially in its later sessions, displayed the antagonistic parties in the Roman Church; one struggling for lucrative abuses, one anxious to overthrow them. They may be called the Italian and Spanish parties: the first headed by the pope's legates, dreading above all things both the reforming spirit of Constance and Basle, and the independence either of princes or of national churches; the other actuated by much of the spirit of those councils, and tending to confirm that independence. The French and German prelates usually sided with the Spanish; and they were together strong enough to establish as a rule, that in every session a decree for reformation should accompany the declaration of doctrine. The council, interrupted in 1547 by the measure that Paul III. found it necessary for his own defence against these reformers to adopt, the translation of its sittings to Bologna, with which the Imperial prelates refused to comply, was opened again by Julius III. in 1552; and, having been once more suspended

Its efforts at Trent.

[1] Ranke, i. 133.

in the same year, resumed its labor for the last time under Pius IV. in 1562. It terminated in 1564, when the court of Rome, which, with the Italian prelates, had struggled hard to obstruct the redress of every grievance, compelled the more upright members of the council to let it close, after having effected such a reformation of discipline as they could obtain. The court was certainly successful in the contest, so far as it might be called one, of prerogative against liberty, and partially successful in the preservation of its lesser interests and means of influence. Yet it seems impossible to deny, that the effects of the Council of Trent were on the whole highly favorable to the church for whose benefit it was summoned. The Reformation would never have roused the whole north of Europe, had the people seen nothing in it but the technical problems of theology. It was against ambition and cupidity, sluggish ignorance and haughty pomp, that they took up arms. Hence the abolition of many long-established abuses by the honest zeal of the Spanish and Cisalpine fathers in that council took away much of the ground on which the prevalent disaffection rested.

No compromise in doctrine.

18. We should be inclined to infer from the language of some contemporaries, that the council might have proceeded farther with more advantage than danger to their church, by complying with the earnest and repeated solicitations of the emperor, the Duke of Bavaria, and even the court of France, that the sacramental cup should be restored to the laity, and that the clergy should not be restrained from marriage. Upon this, however, it is not here for us to dilate. The policy of both concessions, but especially of the latter, was always questionable, and has not been demonstrated by the event. In its determinations of doctrine, the council was generally cautious to avoid extremes, and left, in many momentous questions of the controversy, such as the invocation of saints, no small latitude for private opinion. It has been thought by some, that they lost sight of this prudence in defining transubstantiation so rigidly as they did in 1551, and thus opposed an obstacle to the conversion of those who would have acquiesced in a more equivocal form of words. But, in truth, no alternative was left upon this point. Transubstantiation had been asserted by a prior council, the Fourth Lateran, in 1215, so positively, that to recede would have surrendered the main principle of the Catholic Church.

And it is also to be remembered, when we judge of what might have been done, as we fancy, with more prudence, that, if there was a good deal of policy in the decisions of the Council of Trent, there was no want also of conscientious sincerity; and that, whatever we may think of this doctrine, it was one which seemed of fundamental importance to the serious and obedient sons of the church.[1]

Consultation of Cassander.

19. There is some difficulty in proving for the Council of Trent that universality to which its adherents attach an infallible authority. And this was not held to be a matter of course by the great European powers. Even in France, the Tridentine decrees, in matters of faith, have not been formally received, though the Gallican Church has never called any of them in question: those relating to matters of discipline are distinctly held not obligatory. The Emperor Ferdinand seems to have hesitated about acknowledging the decisions of a council which had at least failed in the object for which it was professedly summoned,—

[1] A strange notion has been started of late years in England, that the Council of Trent made important innovations in the previously established doctrines of the Western Church; an hypothesis so paradoxical in respect to public opinion, and, it must be added, so prodigiously at variance with the known facts of ecclesiastical history, that we cannot but admire the facility with which it has been taken up. It will appear, by reading the accounts of the sessions of the council, either in Father Paul or in any more favorable historian, that, even in certain points, such as justification, which had not been clearly laid down before, the Tridentine decrees were mostly conformable with the sense of the majority of those doctors who had obtained the highest reputation; and that upon what are more usually reckoned the distinctive characteristics of the Church of Rome, namely, transubstantiation, purgatory, and invocation of the saints and the Virgin, they assert nothing but what had been so ingrafted into the faith of this part of Europe as to have been rejected by no one without suspicion or imputation of heresy. Perhaps Erasmus would not have acquiesced with good will in *all* the decrees of the council; but was Erasmus deemed orthodox? It is not impossible that the great hurry with which some controversies of considerable importance were despatched in the last sessions may have had as much to do with the short and vague phrases employed in respect to them as the prudence I have attributed to the fathers; but the facts will remain the same on either supposition. — 1839. [The persons alluded to in this note have since changed their ground, and discovered that the Council of Trent has not been quite so great an innovator as they had imagined. — 1842.]

No general council ever contained so many persons of eminent learning and ability as that of Trent; nor is there ground for believing that any other ever investigated the questions before it with so much patience, acuteness, temper, and desire of truth. The early councils, unless they are greatly belied, would not bear comparison in these characteristics. Impartiality, and freedom from prejudice, no Protestant will attribute to the fathers of Trent; but where will he produce these qualities in an ecclesiastical synod? But it may be said that they had only one leading prejudice, — that of determining theological faith according to the tradition of the Catholic Church, as handed down to their own age. This one point of authority conceded, I am not aware that they can be proved to have decided wrong, or at least against all reasonable evidence. Let those who have imbibed a different opinion ask themselves whether they have read Sarpi through with any attention, especially as to those sessions of the Tridentine Council which preceded its suspension in 1547.

the conciliation of all parties to the church. For we find, that, even after its close, he referred the chief points in controversy to George Cassander, a German theologian of very moderate sentiments and temper. Cassander wrote, at the emperor's request, his famous Consultation, wherein he passes in review every article in the Confession of Augsburg, so as to give, if possible, an interpretation consonant to that of the Catholic Church. Certain it is, that between Melanchthon's desire of concord in drawing up the Confession, and that of Cassander in judging of it, no great number of points seem to be left for dispute. In another treatise of Cassander, De Officio Pii Viri in hoc Dissidio Religionis (1561), he holds the same course that Erasmus had done before; blaming those who, on account of the stains in the church, would wholly subvert it, as well as those who erect the pope into a sort of deity, by setting up his authority as an infallible rule of faith. The rule of controversy laid down by Cassander is, Scripture explained by the tradition of the ancient church, which is best to be learned from the writings of those who lived from the age of Constantine to that of Gregory I.; because, during that period, the principal articles of faith were most discussed. Dupin observes, that the zeal of Cassander for the re-union and peace of the church made him yield too much to the Protestants, and advance some propositions that were too bold. But they were by no means satisfied with his concessions. This treatise was virulently attacked by Calvin, to whom Cassander replied. No one should hesitate to prefer the spirit of Cassander to that of Calvin; but it must be owned, that the practical consequence of his advice would have been to check the profession of the reformed religion, leaving amendment to those who had little disposition to amend any thing. Nor is it by any means unlikely that this conciliatory scheme, by extenuating disagreements, had a considerable influence in that cessation of the advance of Protestantism, or rather that recovery of lost ground by the opposite party, to which we have lately adverted, and of which more proofs were afterwards given.

Bigotry of Protestant churches.

20. We ought to reckon also among the principal causes of this change, those perpetual disputes, those irreconcilable animosities, that bigotry, above all, and persecuting spirit, which were exhibited in the Lutheran and Calvinistic Churches. Each began with a common prin-

ciple, — the necessity of an orthodox faith. But this orthodoxy meant evidently nothing more than their own belief, as opposed to that of their adversaries, — a belief acknowledged to be fallible, yet maintained as certain, rejecting authority in one breath, and appealing to it in the next, and claiming to rest on sure proofs of reason and Scripture, which their opponents were ready with just as much confidence to invalidate.

Tenets of Melanchthon.

21. The principle of several controversies which agitated the two great divisions of the Protestant name was still that of the real presence. The Calvinists, as far as their meaning could be divined through a dense mist of nonsense which they purposely collected,[1] were little, if at all, less removed from the Romish and Lutheran parties than the disciples of Zwingle himself, who spoke out more perspicuously. Nor did the orthodox Lutherans fail to perceive this essential discrepancy. Melanchthon, incontestably the most eminent man of their church after the death of Luther, had obtained a great influence over the younger students of theology. But his opinions, half concealed as they were, and perhaps unsettled, had long been tending to a very different line from those of Luther. The deference exacted by the latter, and never withheld, kept them from any open dissension. But some, whose admiration for the founder of their church was not checked by any scruples at his doctrine, soon began to inveigh against the sacrifice of his favorite tenets, which Melanchthon seemed ready to make through timidity, as they believed, or false judgment. To the Romanists he was willing to concede the primacy of the pope and the jurisdiction of bishops; to the Helvetians he was suspected of leaning on the great controversy of the real presence; while, on the still more important questions of faith and works, he not only rejected the Antinomian exaggerations of the high Lutherans, but introduced a doctrine said to be nearly similar to that called Semi-Pelagian; according to which, the grace communicated to adult persons so as to draw them to God required a correspondent action of their own free will in order to become effectual. Those who held this tenet were called Synergists.[2] It appears to be the same, or nearly

[1] See some of this in Bossuet, Variations des Eglises Protestantes, l. ix. I do not much trust to Bossuet; but it would be too easy to find similar evidence from our own writers.

[2] Mosheim; Bayle, art. "Synergistes."

so, as that adopted by the Arminians in the next century, but was not, perhaps, maintained by any of the schoolmen; nor does it seem consonant to the decisions of the Council of Trent, nor probably to the intention of those who compiled the articles of the English Church. It is easy, however, to be mistaken as to these theological subtilties, which those who write of them with most confidence do not really discriminate by any consistent or intelligible language.

A party hostile to him.

22. There seems good reason to suspect, that the bitterness manifested by the rigid Lutherans against the new school was aggravated by some political events of this period; the university of Wittenberg, in which Melanchthon long resided, being subject to the elector Maurice, whose desertion of the Protestant confederacy and unjust acquisition of the electorate at the expense of the best friends of the Reformation, though partly expiated by his subsequent conduct, could never be forgiven by the adherents and subjects of the Ernestine line. Those first protectors of the reformed faith, now become the victims of his ambition, were reduced to the duchies of Weimar and Gotha, within the former of which the university of Jena, founded in 1559, was soon filled with the sternest zealots of Luther's school. Flacius Illyricus, most advantageously known as the chief compiler of the Centuriæ Magdeburgenses, was at the head of this university, and distinguished by his animosity against Melanchthon, whose gentle spirit was released by death from the contentions he abhorred, in 1560. Bossuet exaggerates the indecision of Melanchthon on many disputable questions, which, as far as it existed, is rather perhaps a matter of praise; but his want of firmness makes it not always easy to determine his real sentiments, especially in his letters, and somewhat impaired the dignity and sincerity of his mind.

Form of Concord, 1576.

23. After the death of Melanchthon, a controversy, begun by one Brentius, relating to the ubiquity, as it was called, of Christ's body, proceeded with much heat. It is sufficient to mention that it led to what is denominated the Formula Concordiæ, a declaration of faith on several matters of controversy, drawn up at Torgau in 1576, and subscribed by the Saxon and most other Lutheran Churches of Germany, though not by those of Brunswick, or of the Northern kingdoms. It was justly considered as a com-

plete victory of the rigid over the moderate party. The strict enforcement of subscription to this creed gave rise to a good deal of persecution against those who were called Crypto-Calvinists, or suspected of a secret bias towards the proscribed doctrine. Peucer, son-in-law of Melanchthon, and editor of his works, was kept for eleven years in prison. And a very narrow spirit of orthodoxy prevailed for a century and a half afterwards in Lutheran theology. But, in consequence of this spirit, that theology has been almost entirely neglected and contemned in the rest of Europe, and not many of its books during that period are remembered by name.[1]

Controversy raised by Baius.

24. Though it may be reckoned doubtful whether the Council of Trent did not repel some wavering Protestants by its unqualified re-enactment of the doctrine of transubstantiation, it prevented, at least, those controversies on the real presence which agitated the Protestant communions. But, in another more extensive and important province of theology, the decisions of the council, though cautiously drawn up, were far from precluding such differences of opinion as ultimately gave rise to a schism in the Church of Rome, and have had no small share in the decline of its power. It is said that some of the Dominican order, who could not but find in their most revered authority, Thomas Aquinas, a strong assertion of Augustin's scheme of divinity, were hardly content with some of the decrees at Trent, as leaving a door open to Semi-Pelagianism.[2] The controversy, however, was first raised by Baius, professor of divinity at Louvain, now chiefly remarkable as the precursor of Jansenius. Many propositions attributed to Baius were censured by the Sorbonne in 1560, and by a bull of Pius V. in 1567. He submitted to the latter; but his tenets, which are hardly distinguishable from those of Calvin, struck root, especially in the Low Countries, and seem to have passed from the disciples of Baius to the famous bishop of Ypres in the next century. The bull of Pius apparently goes much farther from the Calvinistic hypothesis than the Council of Trent had done. The Jansenist party,

[1] Hospinian, Concordia Discors, is my chief authority. He was a Swiss Calvinist, and of course very hostile to the Lutheran party. But Mosheim does not vindicate very strongly his own church. See also several articles in Bayle; and Eichhorn, vi. part i. 234.

[2] Du Chesne, Histoire du Baianisme, vol. i. p. 8. This opinion is ascribed to Peter Soto, confessor to Charles V., who took a part in the reconversion of England under Mary. He is not to be confounded with the more celebrated Dominic Soto. Both these divines were distinguished ornaments of the Council of Trent.

in later times, maintained that it was not binding upon the church.[1]

25. These disputes, after a few years, were revived and inflamed by the treatise of Molina, a Spanish Jesuit, in 1588, on free-will. In this he was charged with swerving as much from the right line on one side as Baius had been supposed to do on the other. His tenets, indeed, as usually represented, do not appear to differ from those maintained afterwards by the Arminians in Holland and England. But it has not been deemed orthodox in the Church of Rome to deviate ostensibly from the doctrine of Augustin in this controversy; and Thomas Aquinas, though not quite of equal authority in the church at large, was held almost infallible by the Dominicans, a powerful order, well stored with learning and logic, and already jealous of the rising influence of the Jesuits. Some of the latter did not adhere to the Semi-Pelagian theories of Molina; but the spirit of the order was roused, and they all exerted themselves successfully to screen his book from the condemnation which Clement VIII. was much inclined to pronounce upon it. They had before this time been accused of Pelagianism by the Thomists, and especially by the partisans of Baius, who procured from the universities of Louvain and Douay a censure of the tenets that some Jesuits had promulgated.[2]

Treatise of Molina on Free-will

26. The Protestant theologians did not fail to entangle themselves in this intricate wilderness. Melanchthon drew a large portion of the Lutherans into what was afterwards called Arminianism; but the reformed churches, including the Helvetian, which, after the middle of the century, gave up many at least of those points of difference which

Protestant tenets.

[1] Some of the tenets asserted in the articles of the Church of England are condemned in this bull, especially the 13th. Du Chesne, p. 78, *et post.* See Biogr. Univ., art. "Baius and Bayle." Du Chesne is reckoned an unfair historian by those who favor Baius.

[2] Du Chesne; Biogr. Univ., art. "Molina." The controversy had begun before the publication of Molina's treatise; and the faculty of Louvain censured thirty-one propositions of the Jesuits in 1587. Paris, however, refused to confirm the censure. Bellarmin, in 1588, drew up an abstract of the dispute by command of Sixtus V. In this he does not decide in favor of either side; but the pope declared the Jesuit propositions to be *sanæ doctrinæ articuli*, p. 258. The appearance of Molina's book, which was thought to go much farther towards Pelagianism, renewed the flame. Clement VIII. was very desirous to condemn Molina; but Henry IV., who now favored the Jesuits, interfered for their honor. Cardinal Perron took the same side, and told the pope that a Protestant might subscribe the Dominican doctrine. Ranke, ii. 295, *et post.* Paul V. was also rather inclined against the Jesuits; but it would have been hard to mortify such good friends, and in 1607 he issued a declaration postponing the decision *sine die.* The Jesuits deemed themselves victorious, as in fact they were. Id., p. 353.

had distinguished them from that of Geneva, held the doctrine of Augustin on absolute predestination, on total depravity, and arbitrary irresistible grace.

27. A third source of intestine disunion lay deep in recesses beyond the soundings of human reason. The doctrine of the Trinity, which theologians agree to call inscrutable, but which they do not fail to define and analyze with the most confident dogmatism, had already, as we have seen in a former passage, been investigated by some bold spirits with little regard to the established faith. They had soon, however, a terrible proof of the danger that still was to wait on such momentous aberrations from the prescribed line. Servetus, having, in 1553, published, at Vienne in Dauphiné, a new treatise, called Christianismi Restitutio, and escaping from thence, as he vainly hoped, to the Protestant city of Geneva, became a victim to the bigotry of the magistrates, instigated by Calvin, who had acquired an immense ascendency over that republic.[1] He did not leave, as far as we know,

Trinitarian controversy.

[1] This book is among the scarcest in the world, *ipsa raritate rarior*, as it is called by Schelhorn. "Il est reconnu," says De Bure, "pour le plus rare de tous les livres." It was long supposed that no copy existed except that belonging to Dr. Mead, afterwards to the Duke de la Valière, and now in the Royal Library at Paris. But a second is said to be in the Imperial Library at Vienna; and Brunet observes, "On connoît à peine trois exemplaires," which seems to hint that there may be a third. Allwoerden, in his life of Servetus, published in 1727, did not know where any printed copy could be found; several libraries having been named by mistake. But there were at that time several manuscript copies, one of which he used himself. It had belonged to Samuel Crellius, and afterwards to La Croze, from whom he had borrowed it, and was transcribed from a printed copy belonging to an Unitarian minister in Transylvania, who had obtained it in England between 1660 and 1670.

This celebrated book is a collection of several treatises, with the general title, Christianismi Restitutio. But that of the first and most remarkable part has been differently given. According to a letter from the Abbé Rive, librarian to the Duke de la Valière, to Dutens, which the latter has published in the second edition of his Origines des Découvertes attribuées aux Modernes, vol. ii. p. 359, all former writers on the subject have been incorrect. The difference, however, is but in one word. In Sandius, Niceron, Allwoerden, and, I suppose, others, the title runs: "De Trinitate Divina, quod in ea non sit *indivisibilium* trium rerum illusio, sed vera substantiæ Dei manifestatio in verbo, et communicatio in spiritu, libri vii." The Abbé Rive gives the word *invisibilium;* and this I find also in the additions of Simler to the Bibliotheca Universalis of Gesner, to which M. Rive did not advert. In Allwoerden, however, a distinct heading is given to the 6th and 7th dialogues, wherein the same title is repeated, with the word *invisibilium* instead of *indivisibilium*. It is remarked in a note, by Rive or Dutens, that it was a gross error to put *indivisibilium*, as it makes Servetus say the contrary of what his system requires. I am not entirely of this opinion; and if I understand the system of Servetus at all, the word *indivisibilium* is very intelligible. De Bure, who seems to write from personal inspection of the same copy, which he supposed to be unique, gives the title with *indivisibilium*. The Christianismi Restitutio was reprinted at Nuremberg, about 1790, in the same form as the original edition: but I am not aware which word is used in the titlepage; nor would the evidence of a modern reprint, possibly not taken immediately from a printed copy, be conclusive.

The Life of Servetus by Allwoerden, Helmstadt, 1727, is partly founded on materials collected by Mosheim, who put them into the author's hands. Barbier is much mistaken in placing it among pseu

ny peculiar disciples. Many, however, among the German ιnabaptists, held tenets not unlike those of the ancient Arians. ›everal persons, chiefly foreigners, were burned for such eresies in England under Edward VI., Elizabeth, and James. 'hese Anabaptists were not very learned or conspicuous ad-ocates of their opinions; but some of the Italian confessors f Protestantism were of more importance. Several of these ·ere reputed to be Arians. None, however, became so cele-rated as Lælius Socinus, a young man of considerable ability,

onymous works, as if Allwoerden had een a fictitious denomination of Mosheim. ictionnaire des Anonymes (1824), iii. 555. he book contains, even in the titlepage, ll possible vouchers for its authenticity. losheim himself says, in a letter to All-oerden, "Non dubitavi negotium hoc bi committere, atque Historiam Serveti oncinnandam et apte construendam tra-ere." But it appears that Allwoerden dded much from other sources, so that cannot reasonably be called the work of ny one else The Biographie Universelle scribes to Mosheim a Latin History of ervetus, Helmstadt, 1737; but, as I be-eve, by confusion with the former. They lso mention a German work by Mosheim n the same subject in 1748. See Biogr. Jniv., arts. "Mosheim and Servetus."

The analysis of the Christianismi Resti-utio, given by Allwoerden, is very meagre; ut he promises a fuller account, which ever appeared. It is a far more extensive cheme of theology than had been pro-nulgated by Servetus in his first treatises; he most interesting of his opinions being, f course, those which brought him to the take. He distinctly held the divinity of Christ. "Dialogus secundus modum generationis Christi docet, quod ipse non it creatus nec finitæ potentiæ, sed vere dorandus verusque Deus." — Allwoerden,). 214. He probably ascribed this divinity o the presence of the Logos, as a manifes-ation of God by that name, but denied its listinct personality in the sense of an in-elligent being different from the Father. Many others may have said something of he same kind, but in more cautious lan-guage, and respecting more the conven-tional phraseology of theologians. "Ille rucem, hic diadema." Servetus, in fact, was burned, not so much for his heresies, as for some personal offence he had several years before given to Calvin. The latter wrote to Bolsec in 1546, "Servetus cupit huc venire, sed a me accersitus. Ego autem nunquam committam, ut fidem meam eatenus obstrictam habeat. Jam enim constitutum habeo, si veniat, nun-quam pati ut salvus exeat." — Allwoerden, p. 43. A similar letter to Farel differs in some phrases, and especially by the word *vivus* for *salvus*. The latter was published by Wytenbogart, in an ecclesiastical histo-ry written in Dutch. Servetus had, in some printed letters, charged Calvin with many errors, which seems to have exaspe-rated the great reformer's temper, so as to make him resolve on what he afterwards executed.

The death of Servetus has perhaps as many circumstances of aggravation as any execution for heresy that ever took place. One of these, and among the most striking, is, that he was not the subject of Geneva, nor domiciled in the city; nor had the Christianismi Restitutio been published there, but at Vienne. According to our laws, and those, I believe, of most civilized nations, he was not amenable to the tri-bunals of the republic.

The tenets of Servetus are not easily ascertained in all respects, nor very in-teresting to the reader. Some of them were considered infidel, and even panthe-istical; but there can be little ground for such imputations, when we consider the tenor of his writings, and the fate which he might have escaped by a retractation. It should be said in justice to Calvin, that he declares himself to have endeavored to obtain a commutation of the sentence for a milder kind of death. "Genus mortis conati sumus mutare, sed frustra." — All-woerden, p. 106. But he has never re-covered, in the eyes of posterity, the blow this gave to his moral reputation, which the Arminians, as well as Socinians, were always anxious to depreciate. "De Serve-to," says Grotius, "ideo certi aliquid pro-nuntiare ausus non sum, quia causam ejus non bene didici; neque Calvino ejus hosti capitali credere audeo, cum sciam quam inique et virulente idem ille Calvi-nus tractaverit viros multo se meliores Cassandrum, Balduinum, Castellionem." —Grot. Op. Theolog., iv. 639. Of Servetus and his opinions, he says, in another place, very fairly, "Est in illo negotio difficilli-mo facilis error." — p. 655.

who is reckoned the proper founder of that sect which take its name from his family. Prudently shunning the fate o Servetus, he neither published any thing, nor permitted hi tenets to be openly known. He was, however, in Poland no long after the commencement of this period; and there seem reason to believe that he left writings, which, coming into th hands of some persons in that country who had already adopted the Arian hypothesis, induced them to diverge still farthe from the orthodox line. The Anti-Trinitarians became numerous among the Polish Protestants; and in 1565, having separated from the rest, they began to appear as a distinc society. Faustus, nephew of Lælius Socinus, joined them about 1578; and, acquiring a great ascendency by his talents gave a name to the sect, though their creed was already conformable to his own. An university, or rather academy, for it never obtained a legal foundation, established at Racow, a small town belonging to a Polish nobleman of their persuasion, about 1570, sent forth men of considerable eminence and great zeal in the propagation of their tenets. These, indeed, chiefly belong to the ensuing century; but, before the termination of the present, they had begun to circulate books in Holland.[1]

28. As this is a literary, rather than an ecclesiastical history, we shall neither advert to the less learned sectaries, nor speak of controversies which had chiefly a local importance, such as those of the English Puritans with the established church. Hooker's Ecclesiastical Polity will claim attention in a subsequent chapter.

29. Thus, in the second period of the Reformation, those ominous symptoms which had appeared in its earlier stage, disunion, virulence, bigotry, intolerance, far from yielding to any benignant influence, grew more inveterate and incurable. Yet some there were, even in this century, who laid the foundations of a more charitable and rational indulgence to diversities of judgment, which the principle of the Reformation itself had in some measure sanctioned. It may be said that this tolerant spirit rose out of the ashes of Servetus. The right of civil magistrates to punish heresy with death had been already impugned by some Protestant theologians as well as by Erasmus. Luther had declared

Religious intolerance.

[1] Lubienecius, Hist. Reformat. Polonicæ; Rees, History of Racovian Catechism; Bayle, art. "Socinus;" Mosheim; Dupin; Eichhorn.

gainst it; and though Zwingle, who had maintained the same rinciple as Luther, has been charged with having afterwards pproved the drowning of some Anabaptists in the Lake of urich, it does not appear that his language requires such an nterpretation. The early Anabaptists, indeed, having been editious and unmanageable to the greatest degree, it is not asy to show that they were put to death simply on account f their religion. But the execution of Servetus, with cir- umstances of so much cruelty, and with no possible pretext ut the error of his opinions, brought home to the minds of erious men the importance of considering whether a mere ersuasion of the truth of our own doctrines can justify the nfliction of capital punishment on those who dissent from hem; and how far we can consistently reprobate the perse- utions of the Church of Rome, while acting so closely after er example. But it was dangerous to withstand openly the ancor of the ecclesiastics domineering in the Protestant Churches, or the usual bigotry of the multitude. Melanch- hon himself, tolerant by nature, and knowing enough of the pirit of persecution which disturbed his peace, was yet un- ortunately led by timidity to express, in a letter to Beza, his pprobation of the death of Servetus, though he admits that ome saw it in a different light. Calvin, early in 1554, pub- ished a dissertation to vindicate the magistrates of Geneva in heir dealings with this heretic. But Sebastian Cas- alio, under the name of Martin Bellius, ventured to eply in a little tract, entitled De Hæreticis quomodo cum is agendum sit variorum Sententiæ. This is a collation f different passages from the fathers and modern authors in avor of toleration, to which he prefixed a letter of his own to he Duke of Wirtemberg, more valuable than the rest of the work; and, though written in the cautious style required by he times, containing the pith of those arguments which have ltimately triumphed in almost every part of Europe. The mpossibility of forcing belief, the obscurity and insignificance of many disputed questions, the sympathy which the fortitude of heretics produced, and other leading topics, are well touched in this very short tract; for the preface does not exceed twenty- eight pages in 16mo.[1]

Castalio.

[1] This little book has been attributed by some to Lælius Socinus; I think Castalio more probable. Castalio entertained very different sentiments from those of Beza on some theological points, as appears by his dialogues on predestination and free-will, which are opposed to the Augustinian system then generally prevalent. He seems

30. Beza answered Castalio, whom he perfectly knew unde the mask of Bellius, in a much longer treatise, D Hæreticis a Civili Magistratu Puniendis. It is un necessary to say that his tone is that of a man who is sure o having the civil power on his side. As to capital punishment for heresy, he acknowledges that he has to contend not onl with such sceptics as Castalio, but with some pious and learne men.[1] He justifies their infliction, however, by the magnitud of the crime, and by the Mosaic law, as well as by prece dents in Jewish and Christian history. Calvin, he positivel asserts, used his influence that the death of Servetus migh not be by fire, for the truth of which he appeals to the Senate but, though most lenient in general, they had deemed no les expiation sufficient for such impiety.[2]

Answered by Beza.

31. A treatise written in a similar spirit to that of Castalio by Aconcio, one of the numerous exiles from Italy De Stratagematibus Satanæ, Basle, 1565, deserve some notice in the history of opinions, because it is, per haps, the first wherein the limitation of fundamental article of Christianity, to a small number, is laid down at consider able length. He instances, among doctrines which he doe not reckon fundamental, those of the real presence and of the Trinity; and, in general, such as are not either expressed in Scripture or deducible from it by unequivocal reasoning. Aconcio inveighs against capital punishments for heresy; but his argument, like that of Castalio, is good against every minor penalty. "If the clergy," he says, "once get the upper hand, and carry this point, that, as soon as one opens his mouth the executioner shall be called in to cut all knots with his knife, what will become of the study of Scripture? They will think it very little worth while to trouble their heads with it; and, if I may presume to say so, will set up every fancy of their own for truth. O unhappy times! O wretched poste- rity! if we abandon the arms by which alone we can subdue our adversary." Aconcio was not improbably an Arian: this may be surmised, not only because he was an Italian Protes-

Aconcio.

also to have approximated to the Sabellian theories of Servetus on the Trinity. See p. 144, edit. 1613.

[1] "Non modo cum nostris academicis, sed etiam cum piis alioqui et eruditis hominibus mihi negotium fore prospicio."— p. 208. Bayle has an excellent remark (Beza, note F.) on this controversy.

[2] "Sed tanta erat ejus hominis rabies, tam execranda tamque horrenda impietas, ut Senatus alioqui clementissimus solis flammis expiari posse existimarit."— p. 91.

[3] The account given of this book in the Biographie Universelle is not accurate: a better will be found in Bayle.

ant, and because he seems to intimate it in some passages of is treatise, but on the authority of Strype, who mentions him s reputed to be such while belonging to a small congregation f refugees in London.[1] This book attracted a good deal of otice: it was translated both into French and English; and, n one language or another, went through several editions. n the next century, it became of much authority with the Arminians of Holland.

Minus Celsus; Koornhert

32. Mino Celso, of Siena, and another of the same class of efugees, in a long and elaborate argument against ersecution, De Hæreticis Capitali Supplicio non Afficiendis, quotes several authorities from writers of he sixteenth century in his favor.[2] We should add to these dvocates of toleration the name of Theodore Koornhert, who ourageously stood up in Holland against one of the most ncroaching and bigoted hierarchies of that age. Koornhert, verse in other points to the authority of Calvin and Beza, eems to have been a precursor of Arminius; but he is chiefly nown by a treatise against capital punishment for heresy, ublished in Latin after his death. It is extremely scarce; nd I have met with no author, except Bayle and Brandt, who peaks of it from direct knowledge.[3] Thus, at the end of the ixteenth century, the simple proposition, that men for holding r declaring heterodox opinions in religion ought not to be urned alive, or otherwise put to death, was itself little else han a sort of heterodoxy; and, though many privately must ave been persuaded of its truth, the Protestant churches vere as far from acknowledging it as that of Rome. No one ad yet pretended to assert the general right of religious worhip, which, in fact, was rarely or never conceded to the Romanists in a Protestant country, though the Huguenots

[1] Strype's Life of Grindal, p. 42; see lso Bayle. Elizabeth gave him a pension or a book on fortification.

[2] Celso was formerly supposed to be a ctitious person; but the contrary has een established. The book was pubished in 1584, but without name of lace. He quotes Aconcio frequently. The following passage seems to refer to Servetus: "Superioribus annis, ad hæetici cujusdam in flammis constantiam, t ex fide dignis accepi, plures ex astantius sanæ doctrinæ viri, non posse id sine Dei spiritu fieri persuasum habentes, ac ropterea hæreticum martyrem esse plane redentes, ejus hæresin pro veritate complexi, in fide naufragium fecerunt." — fol. 109.

[3] Bayle, Biogr. Univ.; Brandt, Hist. de la Réformation des Provinces Unies, i. 435. Lipsius had, in his Politica, inveighed against the toleration of more religions than one in a commonwealth. "Ure, seca, ut membrum potius aliquod, quam totum corpus intereat." Koornhert answered this, dedicating his answer to the magistrates of Leyden, who, however, thought fit to publish that they did not accept the dedication, and requested that those who read Koornhert would read also the reply of Lipsius, ibid. This was in 1590, and Koornhert died the same year

shed oceans of blood to secure the same privilege for them selves.

33. In the concluding part of the century, the Protestan cause, though not politically unprosperous, but rathe manifesting some additional strength through th great energies put forth by England and Holland, wa less and less victorious in the conflict of opinion. It might perhaps, seem to a spectator that it gained more in Franc by the dissolution of the League and the establishment of a perfect toleration, sustained by extraordinary securities in the Edict of Nantes, than it lost by the conformity of Henr IV. to the Catholic religion. But, if this is considered mor deeply, the advantage will appear far greater on the othe side; for this precedent, in the case of a man so conspi cuous, would easily serve all who might fancy they had any public interest to excuse them, from which the transitio would not be long to the care of their own. After this time accordingly, we find more numerous conversions of the Hu guenots, especially the nobler classes, than before. They were furnished with a pretext by an unlucky circumstance In a public conference, held at Fontainebleau in 1600, befor Henry IV., from which great expectation had been raised Du Plessis Mornay, a man of the noblest character, but though very learned as a gentleman, more fitted to maintai his religion in the field than in the schools, was signally worst ed, having been supplied with forged or impertinent quota tions from the fathers, which his antagonist, Perron, easily exposed. Casaubon, who was present, speaks with shame, bu without reserve, of his defeat; and it was an additional morti fication that the king pretended ever afterwards to have been more thoroughly persuaded by this conference that he ha embraced the truth, as well as gained a crown, by abandonin the Protestant side.[1]

Decline of Protestantism.

34. The men of letters had another example, about th same time, in one of the most distinguished of their fraternity

[1] Scaliger, it must be observed, praises very highly the book of Du Plessis Mornay on the Mass, and says that no one after Calvin and Beza had written so well; though he owns that he would have done better not to dispute about religion before the king. Scaligerana Secunda, p. 461. Du Plessis himself, in a publication after the conference of Fontainebleau, retaliated the charge of falsified quotations on Perron. I shall quote hereafter what Casaubon has said on the subject. See the articl "Mornay" in the Biographie Universelle in which, though the signature seems t indicate a descendant or relation, the in accuracy of the quotations is acknow ledged.

Justus Lipsius. He left Leyden on some pretence in 1591, for the Spanish Low Countries, and soon afterwards embraced the Romish faith. Lest his conversion should be suspected, Lipsius disgraced a name, great at least in literature, by writing in favor of the local superstitions of those bigoted provinces. It is true, however, that some, though the lesser, portion of his critical works were published after his change of religion.

Desertion of Lipsius.

35. The controversial divinity poured forth during this period is now little remembered. In England it may be thought necessary to mention Jewell's celebrated Apology. This short book is written with spirit; the style is terse, the arguments pointed, the authorities much to the purpose, so that its effects are not surprising. This treatise is written in Latin; his Defence of the Apology, a much more diffuse work, in English. Upon the merits of the controversy of Jewell with the Jesuit Harding, which this defence embraces, I am not competent to give any opinion: in length and learning, it far surpasses our earlier polemical literature.

Jewell's Apology.

36. Notwithstanding the high reputation which Jewell obtained by his surprising memory and indefatigable reading, it cannot be said that many English theologians of the reign of Elizabeth were eminent for that learning which was required for ecclesiastical controversy. Their writings are neither numerous nor profound. Some exceptions ought to be made. Hooker was sufficiently versed in the fathers; and he possessed also a far more extensive know ledge of the philosophical writers of antiquity than any others could pretend. The science of morals, according to Mosheim, or rather of casuistry, which Calvin had left in a rude and imperfect state, is confessed to have been first reduced into some kind of form, and explained with some accuracy and precision, by Perkins, whose works, however, were not published before the next century.[1] Hugh Broughton was deep in Jewish erudition. Whitaker and Nowell ought also to be mentioned. It would not be difficult to extract a few more names from biographical collections, but names so obscure that we could not easily bring their merit as scholars to any sufficient test. Sandys's sermons may be called perhaps good, but certainly not very distinguished.

English theologians.

[1] Mosheim; Chalmers.

The most eminently learned man of the queen's reign seems to have been Dr. John Rainolds; and a foreign author of the last century, Colomies, places him among the first six in copiousness of erudition whom the Protestant churches had produced.[1] Yet his works are, I presume, read by nobody, nor am I aware that they are ever quoted; and Rainolds himself is chiefly known by the anecdote, that, having been educated in the Church of Rome, as his brother was in the Protestant communion, they mutually converted each other in the course of disputation. Rainolds was on the Puritan side, and took a part in the Hampton-Court conference.

37. As the century drew near its close, the Church of Rome brought forward her most renowned and formidable champion, Bellarmin, a Jesuit, and afterwards a cardinal. No one had entered the field on that side with more acuteness, no one had displayed more skill in marshalling the various arguments of controversial theology, so as to support each other, and serve the grand purpose of church authority. "He does not often," says Dupin, "employ reasoning, but relies on the textual authority of Scripture, of the councils, the fathers, and the consent of the theologians,—seldom quitting his subject or omitting any passage useful to his argument,—giving the objections fairly, and answering them in few words. His style is not so elegant as that of writers who have made it their object, but clear, neat, and brief, without dryness or barbarism. He knew well the tenets of Protestants, and states them faithfully, avoiding the invective so common with controversial writers." It is, nevertheless, alleged by his opponents, and will not seem incredible to those who know what polemical theology has always been, that he attempts to deceive the reader, and argues only in the interests of his cause.[2]

Bellarmin.

[1] Colomesiana. The other five are Usher, Gataker, Blondel, Petit, and Bochart. See also Blount, Baillet, and Chalmers, for testimonies to Rainolds, who died in 1607. Scaliger regrets his death, as a loss to all Protestant churches, as well as that of England. Wood admits that Rainolds was "a man of infinite reading, and of a vast memory;" but laments that, after he was chosen divinity-lecturer at Oxford in 1586, the face of the university was much changed towards Puritanism. Hist. and Antiq. In the Athenæ, ii. 14, he gives a very high character of Rainolds, on the authority of Bishop Hall and others; and a long list of his works. But, as he wanted a biographer, he has become obscure in comparison with Jewell, who probably was not at all his superior.

[2] [Casaubon, in one of his epistles, which I quote from Blount, not having observed the passage, says with great acrimony: "Est tamen Baronius Bellarmino melior homine ad strophas, sophismata, mendacia apto, nulli alii rei idoneo. Norma illius viri non est sacra scriptura, sed libido papæ quem ut deum in terris consistat, quam sceleste, quam sæpe mentitur! — 1842.]

38. Bellarmin, if we may believe Du Perron, was not unlearned in Greek;[1] but it is positively asserted, on the other side, that he could hardly read it, and that he quotes the writers in that language only from translations. Nor has his critical judgment been much esteemed. But his abilities are best testified by Protestant theologians, not only in their terms of eulogy, but indirectly in the peculiar zeal with which they chose him as their worthiest adversary. More than half a dozen books in the next fifty years bear the title of Anti-Bellarminus: it seemed as if the victory must remain with those who should bear away the *spolia opima* of this hostile general. The Catholic writers, on the other hand, borrow every thing, it has been said, from Bellarmin, as the poets do from Homer.[2]

Topics of controversy changed.

39. In the hands of Bellarmin, and other strenuous advocates of the church, no point of controversy was neglected. But, in a general view, we may justly say that the heat of battle was not in the same part of the field as before. Luther and his immediate disciples held nothing so vital as the tenet of justification by faith alone, while the arguments of Eckius and Cajetan were chiefly designed to maintain the modification of doctrine on that subject which had been handed down to them by the fathers and schoolmen. The differences of the two parties, as to the mode of corporeal presence in the eucharist, though quite sufficient to keep them asunder, could hardly bear much controversy; inasmuch as the primitive writers, to whom it was usual to appeal, have not, as is universally agreed, drawn these metaphysical distinctions with much preciseness. But when the Helvetic churches, and those bearing the general name of Reformed, became, after the middle of the century, as prominent, to say the least, in theological literature as the Lutheran, this controversy acquired much greater importance; the persecutions in England and the Netherlands were principally directed against this single heresy of denying the real presence, and the disputes of the press turned so generally upon no other topic.

It turns on Papal power.

40. In the last part of the century, through the influence of some political circumstances, we find a new theme of polemical discussion, more peculiarly characteristic

1 Perroniana.

2 Dupin; Bayle; Blount; Eichhorn, vi. part ii. p. 30; Andrès, xviii. 243; Niceron, vol. xxxi.

of the age. Before the appearance of the early reformers, a republican or aristocratic spirit in ecclesiastical polity, strengthened by the decrees of the Councils of Constance and Basle, by the co-operation, in some instances, of the national church with the state in redressing or demanding the redress of abuses, and certainly also both by the vices of the court of Rome, and its diversion to local politics, had fully counterbalanced, or even in a great measure silenced, the bold pretensions of the school of Hildebrand. In such a lax notion of Papal authority, prevalent in Cisalpine Europe, the Protestant Reformation had found one source of its success. But for this cause the theory itself lost ground in the Catholic Church. At the Council of Trent, the aristocratic or episcopal party, though it seemed to display itself in great strength, comprising the representatives of the Spanish and Gallican churches, was for the most part foiled in questions that touched the limitations of Papal supremacy. From this time, the latter power became lord of the ascendant. "No Catholic," says Schmidt, "dared after the Reformation to say one hundredth part of what Gerson, Peter d' Ailly, and many others, had openly preached." The same instinct, of which we may observe the workings in the present day, then also taught the subjects of the church that it was no time to betray jealousy of their own government, when the public enemy was at their gates.

This upheld by the Jesuits.

41. In this resuscitation of the court of Rome, that is, of the Papal authority, in contradistinction to the general doctrine and discipline of the Catholic Church, much, or rather most, was due to the Jesuits. Obedience, not to that abstraction of theologians, the Catholic Church, a shadow eluding the touch and vanishing into emptiness before the inquiring eye, but to its living, acting centre, the one man, was their vow, their duty, their function. They maintained, therefore, if not quite for the first time, yet with little countenance from the great authorities of the schools, his personal infallibility in matters of faith. They asserted his superiority to general councils, his prerogative of dispensing with all the canons of the church, on grounds of spiritual expediency, whereof he alone could judge. As they grew bolder, some went on to pronounce even the divine laws subject to this control; but it cannot be said that a principle, which seemed so paradoxical, though per-

haps only a consequence from their assumptions, was generally received.

42. But the most striking consequence of this novel position of the Papacy was the renewal of its claims to temporal power, or, in stricter language, to pronounce the forfeiture of it by lawful sovereigns for offences against religion. This pretension of the Holy See, though certainly not abandoned, had in a considerable degree lain dormant in that period of comparative weakness which followed the great schism of the fourteenth century. Paul III. deprived Henry VIII. of his dominions, as far as a bull could have that effect: but the deposing power was not generally asserted with much spirit against the first princes who embraced the Reformation. In this second part of the century, however, the see of Rome was filled by men of stern zeal and intrepid ambition, aided by the Jesuits and other regulars with an energy unknown before, and favored also by the political interests of the greatest monarch in Christendom. Two circumstances of the utmost importance gave them occasion to scour the rust away from their ancient weapons, — the final prostration of the Romish faith in England by Elizabeth, and the devolution of the French crown on a Protestant heir. Incensed by the former event, Pius V., the representative of the most rigid party in the church, issued in 1570 his famous bull, releasing English Catholics from their allegiance to the queen, and depriving her of all right and title to the throne. Elizabeth and her parliament retaliated by augmented severities of law against these unfortunate subjects, who had little reason to thank the Jesuits for announcing maxims of rebellion which it was not easy to carry into effect. Allen and Persons, secure at St. Omer and Douay, proclaimed the sacred duty of resisting a prince who should break his faith with God and the people; especially when the supreme governor of the church, whose function it is to watch over its welfare, and separate the leprous from the clean, has adjudged the cause.

Claim to depose Princes.

Bull against Elizabeth

43. In the war of the League, men became still more familiar with this tenet. Those who fought under that banner did not all acknowledge, or at least would not in other circumstances have admitted, the pope's deposing power; but no faction will reject a false principle that adds strength to its side. Philip II., though ready enough to treat

And Henry IV.

the see of Rome as sharply and rudely as the Italians do their saints when refractory, found it his interest to encourage a doctrine so dangerous to monarchy, when it was directed against Elizabeth and Henry. For this reason, we may read with less surprise in Balthazar Ayala, a layman, a lawyer, and judge-advocate in the armies of Spain, the most unambiguous and unlimited assertion of the deposing theory: "Kings abusing their power may be variously compelled," he says, "by the sovereign pontiff to act justly; for he is the earthly vicegerent of God, from whom he has received both swords, temporal as well as spiritual, for the peace and preservation of the Christian commonwealth. Nor can he only control, if it is for the good of this commonwealth, but even depose kings; as God, whose delegate he is, deprived Saul of his kingdom, and as Pope Zachary released the Franks from their allegiance to Childeric."[1]

Deposing power owned in Spain.

44. Bellarmin, the brilliant advocate of whom we have already spoken, amidst the other disputes of the Protestant quarrel, did not hesitate to sustain the Papal authority in its amplest extension. His treatise, De Summo Pontifice, Capite Totius Militantis Ecclesiæ, forms a portion, and by no means the least important, of those entitled The Controversies of Bellarmin; and first appeared separately in 1586. The pope, he asserts, has no direct temporal authority in the dominions of Christian princes: he cannot interfere with their merely civil affairs, unless they are his feudal vassals; but indirectly, that is, for the sake of some spiritual advantage, all things are submitted to his disposal. He cannot depose these princes, even for a just cause, as their immediate superior, unless they are feudally his vassals; but he can take away and give to others their kingdoms, if the salvation of souls require it.[2] We shall observe hereafter how artfully this Papal scheme was combined with the more captivating tenets of popular sovereignty; each designed for the special case, that of Henry IV., whose legitimate rights, established by the constitution of France, it was expected by this joint effort to overthrow.

Asserted by Bellarmin.

45. Two methods of delivering theological doctrine had prevailed in the Catholic Church for many ages. The one,

[1] Ayala, De Jure et Officiis Bellicis (Antwerp, 1597), p. 32.
[2] Ranke, ii. 182.

called positive, was dogmatic rather than argumentative, deducing its tenets from immediate authorities of Scripture or of the fathers, which it interpreted and explained for its own purpose. It was a received principle, conveniently for this system of interpretation, that most parts of Scripture had a plurality of meaning; and that the allegorical or analogical senses were as much to be sought as the primary and literal. The scholastic theology, on the other hand, which acquired its name because it was frequently heard in the schools of divinity, and employed the weapons of dialectics, was a scheme of inferences drawn, with all the subtilty of reasoning, from the same fundamental principles of authority, the Scriptures, the fathers, the councils of the church. It must be evident upon reflection, that where many thousand propositions, or sentences easily convertible into them, had acquired the rank of indisputable truths, it was not difficult to raise a specious structure of connected syllogisms; and hence the theology of the schools was a series of inferences from the acknowledged standards of orthodoxy, as their physics were from Aristotle, and their metaphysics from a mixture of the two.

Methods of theological doctrine.

46. The scholastic method, affecting a complete and scientific form, led to the compilation of theological systems, generally called Loci Communes. These were very common in the sixteenth and seventeenth centuries, both in the Church of Rome, and, after some time, in the two Protestant communions. But Luther, though at first he bestowed immense praise upon the Loci Communes of Melanchthon, grew unfavorable to all systematic theology. His own writings belong to that class we call positive. They deal with the interpretation of Scripture and the expansion of its literal meaning. Luther rejected, except in a very sparing application, the search after allegorical senses. Melanchthon also, and in general the divines of the Augsburg confession, adhered chiefly to the principle of single interpretation.[1]

Loci Communes.

47. The Institutes of Calvin, which belong to the preceding part of the century, though not entitled Loci Communes, may be reckoned a full system of deductive theology. Wolfgang Musculus published a treatise with the usual title. It should be observed, that, in the Lutheran

In the Protestant

[1] Eichhorn, Gesch. der Cultur, vi. part i. p. 175; Mosheim, cent. 16, sect. 3, part ii.

Church, the ancient method of scholastic theology revived after the middle of this century, especially in the divines of Melanchthon's party; one of whose characteristics was a greater deference to ecclesiastical usage and opinion than the more rigid Lutherans would endure to pay. The Loci Theologici of Chemnitz and those of Strigelius were, in their age, of great reputation; the former, by one of the compilers of the Formula Concordiæ, might be read without risk of finding those heterodoxies of Melanchthon which the latter was supposed to exhibit.[1]

48. In the Church of Rome, the scholastic theology retained an undisputed respect: it was for the heretical Protestants to dread a method of keen logic, by which their sophistry was cut through. The most remarkable book of this kind, which falls within the sixteenth century, is the Loci Theologici of Melchior Canus, published at Salamanca in 1563, three years after the death of the author, a Dominican, and professor in that university. It is, of course, the theology of the reign and country of Philip II.; but Canus was a man acquainted with history, philosophy, and ancient literature. Eichhorn, after giving several pages to an abstract of this volume, pronounces it worthy to be still read. It may be seen by his analysis, how Canus, after the manner of the schoolmen, incorporated philosophical with theological science. Dupin, whose abstract is rather different in substance, calls this an excellent work, and written with all the elegance we could desire.[2]

And Catholic Church.

49. Catharin, one of the theologians most prominent in the Council of Trent, though he seems not to have incurred the charge of heresy, went farther from the doctrine of Augustin and Aquinas than was deemed strictly orthodox in the Catholic Church. He framed a theory to reconcile predestination with the universality of grace, which has since been known in this country by the name of Baxterianism, and is, I believe, adopted by many divines at this day. Dupin, however, calls it a new invention, unknown to the ancient fathers, and never received in the schools. It has been followed, he adds, by nobody.

Catharin.

50. In the critical and expository department of theological literature, much was written during this period, forming

[1] Eichhorn, 236; Mosheim.
[2] Eichhorn, p. 216-227; Dupin, cent. 16, book 5.

no small proportion of the great collection called Critici Sacri. In the Romish Church we may distinguish the Jesuit Maldonat, whose commentaries on the evangelists have been highly praised by theologians of the Protestant side; and among these we may name Calvin and Beza, who occupy the highest place,[1] while below them are ranked Bullinger, Zanchius, Musculus, Chemnitz, and several more. But I believe, that, even in the reviving appetite for obsolete theology, few of these writers have yet attracted much attention. A polemical spirit, it is observed by Eichhorn, penetrated all theological science, not only in dogmatical writings, but in those of mere interpretation: in catechisms, in sermons, in ecclesiastical history, we find the author armed for combat, and always standing in imagination before an enemy.

Critical and expository writings.

51. A regular and copious history of the church, from the primitive ages to the Reformation itself, was first given by the Lutherans under the title, Centuriæ Magdeburgenses, from the name of the city where it was compiled. The principal among several authors concerned, usually called Centuriatores, was Flacius Illyricus, a most inveterate enemy of Melanchthon. This work has been more than once reprinted, and is still, in point of truth and original research, the most considerable ecclesiastical history on the Protestant side. Mosheim, or his translator, calls this an immortal work;[2] and Eichhorn speaks of it in strong terms of admiration for the boldness of the enterprise, the laboriousness of the execution, the spirit with which it cleared away a mass of fable, and placed ecclesiastical history on an authentic basis. The faults, both those springing from the imperfect knowledge and from the prejudices of the compilers, are equally conspicuous.[3] Nearly forty years afterwards, between the

Ecclesiastical historians.

[1] "Literas sacras," says Scaliger of Calvin, "tractavit ut tractandæ sunt, vere inquam et pure ac simpliciter sine ullis argutationibus scholasticis, et divino vir præditus ingenio multa divinavit quæ non nisi a linguæ Hebraicæ peritissimis (cujusmodi tamen ipse non erat), divinari possunt." — Scaligerana Prima. A more detailed, and apparently a not uncandid, statement of Calvin's character as a commentator on Scripture, will be found in Simon, Hist. Critique du Vieux Testament. He sets him, in this respect, much above Luther. See also Blount, art. "Calvin." Scaliger does not esteem much the learning of Beza, and blames him for affecting to despise Erasmus as a commentator. I have named Beza in the text as superior to Zanchius and others, in deference to common reputation; for I am wholly ignorant of the writings of all.

[2] Cent. 16, sect. 3, part ii. c. 9. This expression is probably in the original; but it is difficult to quote Maclaine's translation with confidence, on account of the liberties which he took with the text.

[3] Vol. vi. part ii. p. 149.

years 1588 and 1609, the celebrated Annals of Cardinal Baronius, in twelve volumes, appeared. These were brought down by him only to the end of the twelfth century: their continuation by Rainaldus, published between 1646 and 1663, goes down to 1566. It was the object of Protestant learning in the seventeenth century to repel the authority and impugn the allegations of Baronius. Those of his own communion, in a more advanced stage of criticism, have confessed his mistakes; many of them, arising from a want of acquaintance with the Greek language, indispensable, as we should now justly think, for one who undertook a general history of the church, but not sufficiently universal in Italy, at the end of the sixteenth century, to deprive those who did not possess it of a high character for erudition. Eichhorn speaks far less favorably of Baronius than of the Centuriators.[1] But of these two voluminous histories, written with equal prejudice on opposite sides, an impartial and judicious scholar has thus given his opinion: —

Le Clerc's character of them.

52. "An ecclesiastical historian," Le Clerc satirically observes, "ought to adhere inviolably to this maxim, that whatever can be favorable to heretics is false, and whatever can be said against them is true; while, on the other hand, all that does honor to the orthodox is unquestionable, and every thing that can do them discredit is surely a lie. He must suppress, too, with care, or at least extenuate as far as possible, the errors and vices of those whom the orthodox are accustomed to respect, whether they know any thing about them or no; and must exaggerate, on the contrary, the mistakes and faults of the heterodox to the utmost of his power. He must remember that any orthodox writer is a competent witness against a heretic, and is to be trusted implicitly on his word; while a heretic is never to be believed against the orthodox, and has honor enough done him in allowing him to speak against his own side, or in favor of our own. It is thus that the Centuriators of Magdeburg, and thus that Cardinal Baronius have written; each of their works having by this means acquired an immortal glory with its own party. But it must be owned that they are not the earliest, and that they have only imitated most of their predecessors in this plan of writing. For many ages, men had only sought

[1] Id., p. 180

ecclesiastical antiquity, not what was really to be found here, but what they conceived ought to be there for the good of their own party."[1]

Deistical writers.

53. But in the midst of so many dissentients from each other, some resting on the tranquil bosom of the church, some fighting the long battle of argument, some catching at gleams of supernatural light, the very truths of natural and revealed religion were called in question by a different party. The proofs of this, before the middle of the sixteenth century, are chiefly to be derived from Italy. Pomponatius has already been mentioned, and some other Aristotelian philosophers might be added. But these, whose scepticism extended to natural theology, belong to the class of metaphysical writers, whose place is in the next chapter. If we limit ourselves to those who directed their attacks against Christianity, it must be presumed, that in an age when the tribunals of justice visited, even with the punishment of death, the denial of any fundamental doctrine, few books of an openly irreligious tendency could appear.[2] A short pamphlet by one Vallée cost him his life in 1574. Some others were clandestinely circulated in France before the end of the century; and the list of men suspected of infidelity, if we could trust all private anecdotes of the time, would be by no means short. Bodin, Montaigne, Charron, have been reckoned among the rejecters of Christianity. The first I conceive to have acknowledged no revelation but the Jewish; the second is free, in my opinion, from all reasonable suspicion of infidelity; the principal work of the third was not published till 1601. His former treatise, Des Trois Vérités, is an elaborate vindication of the Christian and Catholic religion.[3]

Wierus, De Præstigiis.

54. I hardly know how to insert, in any other chapter than the present, the books that relate to sorcery and demoniacal possessions, though they can only in a very lax sense be ranked with theological literature. The greater

[1] Parrhasiana, vol. i. p. 168.

[2] The famous Cymbalum Mundi, by Bonaventure des Periers, published in 1538, which, while it continued extremely scarce, had the character of an irreligious work, has proved, since it was reprinted, in 1711, perfectly innocuous, though there are a few malicious glances at priests and nuns. It has always been the habit of the literary world, as much as at present, to speak of books by hearsay The Cymbalum Mundi is written in dialogue, somewhat in the manner of Lucian, and is rather more lively than books of that age generally are.

[3] "Des Trois Vérités contre les Athées, Idolâtres, Juifs, Mahumétans, Hérétiques, et Schismatiques." — Bourdeaux, 1593. Charron has not put his name to this book; and it does not appear that he has taken any thing from himself in his subsequent work, De la Sagesse.

part are contemptible in any other light than as evidences o the state of human opinion. Those designed to rescue th innocent from sanguinary prejudices, and chase the real demo of superstition from the mind of man, deserve to be comme morated. Two such works belong to this period. Wierus, physician of the Netherlands, in a treatise, De Præstigiis Basle, 1564, combats the horrible prejudice by which thos accused of witchcraft were thrown into the flames. He show a good deal of credulity as to diabolical illusions, but take these unfortunate persons for the devil's victims rather tha his accomplices. Upon the whole, Wierus destroys mor superstition than he seriously intended to leave behind.

Scot on Witchcraft.

55. A far superior writer is our countryman Reginald Scot whose object is the same, but whose views are incomparably more extensive and enlightened. He denies altogether to the devil any power of controlling the course of nature. It may be easily supposed that this solid and learned person, for such he was beyond almost all the English of that age, did not escape in his own time, or long afterwards, the censure of those who adhered to superstition. Scot's Discovery of Witchcraft was published in 1584.[1] Bodin, on the other hand, endeavored to sustain the vulgar notions of witchcraft in his Démonomanie des Sorciers. It is not easy to conceive a more wretched production; besides his superstitious absurdities, he is guilty of exciting the magistrate against Wierus, by representing him as a real confederate of Satan.

Authenticity of Vulgate.

56. We may conclude this chapter by mentioning the principal versions and editions of Scripture. No edition of the Greek Testament, worthy to be specified, appeared after that of Robert Stephens, whose text was invariably followed. The Council of Trent declared the Vulgate translation of Scripture to be authentic, condemning all that should deny its authority. It has been a commonplace with Protestants to inveigh against this decree, even while they have virtually maintained the principle upon which it is founded,— one by no means peculiar to the Church of Rome, — being no other than that it is dangerous to unsettle the minds of the ignorant, or partially learned in religion; a proposition not easily disputable by any man of sense, but when

[1] It appears by Scot's book that not only the common, but the more difficult, tricks of conjurers were practised in his time: he shows how to perform some of them.

ted upon, as incompatible as any two contraries can be with e free and general investigation of truth.

57. Notwithstanding this decision in favor of the Vulgate, ere was room left for partial uncertainty. The ouncil of Trent, declaring the translation itself to be ıthentic, pronounced nothing in favor of any manuript or edition; and, as it would be easier to put ɔwn learning altogether than absolutely to restrain the search-g spirit of criticism, it was soon held that the council's decree ent but to the general fidelity of the version, without warınting every passage. Many Catholic writers, accordingly, ıve put a very liberal interpretation on this decree, suggestıg such emendations of particular texts as the original seemed demand. They have even given new translations: one by rias Montanus is chiefly founded on that of Pagninus; and n edition of the Vulgate, by Isidore Clarius, is said to semble a new translation, by his numerous corrections of the xt from the Hebrew.[1] Sixtus V. determined to put a stop a license which rendered the Tridentine provisions almost ugatory. He fulfilled the intentions of the council by ausing to be published in 1590 the Sistine Bible; an authoritive edition to be used in all churches. This was, however, ıperseded by another, set forth only two years afterwards by lement VIII., which is said to differ more than any other om that which his predecessor had published as authentic; circumstance not forgotten by Protestant polemics. The istine edition is now very scarce. The same pope had pubshed a standard edition of the Septuagint in 1587.[2]

Latin versions and editions by Catholics.

58. The Latin translations made by Protestants in this eriod were that by Sebastian Castalio, which, in earch of more elegance of style, deviates from the implicity as well as sense of the original, and fails therefore f obtaining that praise at the hands of men of taste for which ıore essential requisites have been sacrificed;[3] and that by 'remellius and Junius, published at Frankfort in 1575 and ubsequent years. It was retouched some time afterwards by

By Protestants.

[1] Andrès, xix. 40; Simon, 358.

[2] Andrès, xix. 44; Schelhorn, Amœnit. iterar., vol. ii. 359, and vol. iv. 439.

[3] Andrès, xix 166. Castalio, according o Simon (Hist. Critique du V. T. p. 363), ffects politeness to an inconceivable degree f bad taste, especially in such phrases as these in his translation of the Canticles: "Mea columbula, ostende mihi tuum vulticulum; fac ut audiam tuam voculam." &c. He was, however, Simon says, tolerably acquainted with Hebrew, and spoke modestly of his own translation.

Junius, after the death of his coadjutor. This translation w better esteemed in Protestant countries, especially at firs than by the Catholic critics. Simon speaks of it with litt respect. It professedly adheres closely to the Hebrew idiom Beza gave a Latin version of the New Testament. It doubtful whether any of these translations have much improve upon the Vulgate.

Versions into modern languages.

59. The new translations of the Scriptures into moder languages were naturally not so numerous as at a earlier period. Two in English are well known: th Geneva Bible of 1560, published in that city b Coverdale, Whittingham, and other refugees; an the Bishop's Bible of 1568. Both of these, or at least th latter, were professedly founded upon the prior version but certainly not without a close comparison with the origina text. The English Catholics published a translation of th New Testament from the Vulgate at Rheims in 1582. Th Polish translation, commonly ascribed to the Socinians, wa printed under the patronage of Prince Radzivil in 156; before that sect could be said to exist, though Lismanin an Blandrata, both of heterodox tenets, were concerned in it This edition is of the greatest rarity. The Spanish Bible o Ferrara, 1553, and the Sclavonian of 1581, are also ver scarce. The curious in bibliography are conversant wit other versions and editions of the sixteenth century, chiefl of rare occurrence.[2]

[1] Bayle, art. "Radzivil."

[2] Brunet, &c.

CHAPTER III.

HISTORY OF SPECULATIVE PHILOSOPHY, FROM 1550 TO 1600.

Aristotelian Philosophers — Cesalpin — Opposite Schools of Philosophy — Telesio — Jordano Bruno — Sanchez — Aconcio — Nizolius — Logic of Ramus.

Predominance of Aristotelian philosophy.

1. THE authority of Aristotle, as the great master of dogmatic philosophy, continued generally predominant through the sixteenth century. It has been already observed, that besides the strenuous support of the Catholic clergy, and especially of the Sorbonne, who regarded all innovation with abhorrence, the Aristotelian philosophy had been received, through the influence of Melanchthon, in the Lutheran universities. The reader must be reminded, that, under the name of speculative philosophy, we comprehend not only the logic and what was called ontology of the schools, but those physical theories of ancient or modern date, which, appealing less to experience than to assumed hypotheses, cannot be mingled, in a literary classification, with the researches of true science, such as we shall hereafter have to place under the head of natural philosophy.

Scholastic and genuine Aristotelians.

2. Brucker has made a distinction between the scholastic and the genuine Aristotelians: the former being chiefly conversant with the doctors of the middle ages, adopting their terminology, their distinctions, their dogmas, and relying with implicit deference on Scotus or Aquinas, though, in the progress of learning, they might make some use of the original master; while the latter, throwing off the yoke of the schoolmen, prided themselves on an equally complete submission to Aristotle himself. These were chiefly philosophers and physicians, as the former were theologians; and the difference of their objects suffices to account for the different lines in which

they pursued them, and the lights by which they were guided.[1]

3. Of the former class, or successors and adherents of the old schoolmen, it might be far from easy, were it worth while, to furnish any distinct account. Their works are mostly of considerable scarcity; and none of the historians of philosophy, except perhaps Morhof profess much acquaintance with them. It is sufficient to repeat that among the Dominicans, Franciscans, and Jesuits, especially in Spain and Italy, the scholastic mode of argumentation was retained in their seminaries, and employed in prolix volumes, both upon theology and upon such parts of metaphysics and natural law as are allied to it. The reader may find some more information in Brucker, whom Buhle, saying the same things in the same order, may be presumed to have silently copied.[2]

The former class little remembered.

4. The second class of Aristotelian philosophers, devoting themselves to physical science, though investigating it with a very unhappy deference to mistaken dogmas, might seem to offer a better hope of materials for history; and in fact we meet here with a very few names of men once celebrated and of some influence over the opinions of their age. But even here their writings prove to be not only forgotten, but incapable, as we may say, on account of their rare occurrence, and the improbability of their republication, of being ever again known.

The others not much better known.

5. The Italian schools, and especially those of Pisa and Padua, had long been celebrated for their adherence to Aristotelian principles, not always such as could justly be deduced from the writings of the Stagirite himself, but opposing a bulwark against novel speculation, as well as against the revival of the Platonic, or any other ancient philosophy. Simon Porta of the former university, and Cæsar Cremonini of the latter, stood at the head of the rigid Aristotelians; the one near the commencement of this period, the other about its close. Both these philosophers have been reproached with the tendency to atheism, so common in the Italians of this period. A similar imputation has fallen on another professor of the university of Pisa, Cesalpini, who is said to have deviated from the strict

Schools of Pisa and Padua.

Cesalpini.

1 Brucker, Hist. Philos., iv. 117, *et post.*
2 Ibid.; Buhle, ii. 448.

system of Aristotle towards that of Averroes, though he did not altogether coincide even with the latter. The real merits of Cesalpin, in very different pursuits, it was reserved for a later age to admire. His Quæstiones Peripateticæ, published in 1575, is a treatise on metaphysics, or the first philosophy, founded professedly upon Aristotelian principles, but with considerable deviation. This work is so scarce that Brucker had never seen it; but Buhle has taken much pains to analyze its very obscure contents. Paradoxical and unintelligible as they now appear, Cesalpin obtained a high reputation in his own age, and was denominated, by excellence, the Philosopher. Nicolas Taurellus, a professor at Altdorf, denounced the Quæstiones Peripateticæ in a book to which, in allusion to his adversary's name, he gave the puerile title of Alpes Cæsæ.

Sketch of his system

6. The system of Cesalpin is one modification of that ancient hypothesis, which, losing sight of all truth and experience in the love of abstraction, substitutes the barren unity of pantheism for religion, and a few incomprehensible paradoxes for the variety of science. Nothing, according to him, was substance which was not animated; but the particular souls which animate bodies are themselves only substances, because they are parts of the first substance, a simple, speculative, but not active intelligence, perfect and inmovable, which is God. The reasonable soul, however, of mankind is not numerically one; for matter being the sole principle of plurality, and human intelligences being combined with matter, they are plural in number. He differed also from Averroes in maintaining the separate immortality of human souls; and, while the philosopher of Cordova distinguished the one soul which he ascribed to mankind from the Deity, Cesalpin considered the individual soul as a portion, not of this common human intelligence, which he did not admit, but of the first substance, or Deity. His system was therefore more incompatible with theism, in any proper sense, than that of Averroes himself, and anticipated in some measure that of Spinoza, who gave a greater extension to his one substance, by comprehending all matter as well as spirit within it. Cesalpin also denied, and in this he went far from his Aristotelian creed, any other than a logical difference between substances and accidents. I have no knowledge of the writings of Cesalpin except through Buhle; for though I

confess that the Quæstiones Peripateticæ may be found in the British Museum,[1] it would scarce repay the labor to examine what is both erroneous and obscure.

Cremonini.

7. The name of Cremonini, professor of philosophy for above forty years at Padua, is better known than his writings. These have become of the greatest scarcity. Brucker tells us he had not been able to see any of them; and Buhle had met with but two or three.[2] Those at which I have looked are treatises on the Aristotelian physics: they contain little of any interest; nor did I perceive that they countenance, though they may not repel, the charge of atheism sometimes brought against Cremonini, but which, if at all well-founded, seems rather to rest on external evidence. Cremonini, according to Buhle, refutes the Averroistic notion of an universal human intelligence. Gabriel Naudé, both in his letters, and in the records of his conversation called Naudæana, speaks with great admiration of Cremonini.[3] He had himself passed some years at Padua, and was at that time a disciple of the Aristotelian school in physics, which he abandoned after his intimacy with Gassendi.

Opponents of Aristotle.

8. Meantime the authority of Aristotle, great in name and respected in the schools, began to lose more and more of its influence over speculative minds. Cesalpin, an Aristotelian by profession, had gone wide in some points from his master. But others waged an open war as philosophical reformers. Francis Patrizzi, in his Discussiones Peripateticæ (1571 and 1581), appealed to prejudice with the arms of calumny, raking up the most unwarranted aspersions against the private life of Aristotle, to prepare the way for assailing his philosophy; a warfare not the less unworthy that it is often successful. In the case of Patrizzi, it was otherwise: his book was little read; and his own notions of philosophy, borrowed from the later Platonists, and that rabble of spurious writers who had misled Ficinus and Picus of Mirandola, dressed up by Patrizzi with a fantastic terminology, had little chance of subverting

Patrizzi

[1] Buhle, ii, 525. Brucker (iv. 222) laments that he had never seen this book. It seems that there were few good libraries in Germany in Brucker's age, or at least that he had no access to them; for it is surprising how often he makes the same complaint. He had, however, seen a copy of the Alpes Cæsæ of Taurellus, and gives rather a long account both of the man and of the book. Ibid. and p. 300.

[2] Buhle, ii. 519.

[3] Some passages in the Naudæana tend to confirm the suspicion of irreligion, both with respect to Cremonini and Naudé himself.

well-established and acute a system as that of Aristo-
.[1]

9. Bernard Telesio, a native of Cosenza, had greater success, and attained a more celebrated name. The st two books of his treatise, De Natura Rerum ixta Propria Principia, appeared at Rome in 1565; the st was published in 1586. These contain an hypothesis ore intelligible than that of Patrizzi, and less destitute of a rtain apparent correspondence with the phenomena of nare. Two active incorporeal principles, heat and cold, cond with perpetual opposition for the dominion over a third, hich is passive matter. Of these three, all nature consists. he region of pure heat is in the heavens, in the sun and ars, where it is united with the most subtle matter; that of old in the centre of the earth, where matter is most conensed; all between is their battle-field, in which they continally struggle, and alternately conquer. These principles are ot only active, but intelligent, so far at least as to perceive eir own acts and mutual impressions. Heat is the cause of otion: cold is by nature immovable, and tends to keep all ings in repose.[2]

System of Telesio.

10. Telesio has been generally supposed to have borrowed his theory from that of Parmenides, in which the antagonist rinciples of heat and cold had been employed in a similar anner. Buhle denies the identity of the two systems, and onsiders that of Telesio as more nearly allied to the Aristoelian, except in substituting heat and cold for the more bstract notions of form and privation. Heat and cold, it night rather perhaps be said, seem to be merely ill-chosen ames for the hypothetical causes of motion and rest; and he real laws of nature, with respect to both of these, were as ittle discoverable in the Telesian as in the more established heory. Yet its author perceived that the one possessed an xpansive, the other a condensing power; and his principles of heat and cold bear a partial analogy to repulsion and ttraction, the antagonist forces which modern philosophy employs. Lord Bacon was sufficiently struck with the system of Telesio to illustrate it in a separate fragment of the Instauratio Magna, though sensible of its inadequacy to solve th mysteries of nature; and a man of eccentric genius, Campa-

[1] Buhle, ii. 548; Brucker, iv. 422.
[2] Brucker, iv. 449; Buhle, ii. 563; Ginguéné, vii. 501.

nella, to whom we shall come hereafter, adopted it as th basis of his own wilder speculations. Telesio seems to hav ascribed a sort of intelligence to plants, which his last-mei tioned disciple carried to a strange excess of paradox.

Jordano Bruno.

11. The name of Telesio is perhaps hardly so well know at present as that of Jordano Bruno. It was fa otherwise formerly; and we do not find that th philosophy of this singular and unfortunate man attracte much further notice than to cost him his life. It may b doubted, indeed, whether the Inquisition at Rome did nc rather attend to his former profession of Protestantism an invectives against the church, than to the latent atheism i pretended to detect in his writings, which are at least a innocent as those of Cesalpin. The self-conceit of Brunc his contemptuous language about Aristotle and his followers the paradoxical strain, the obscurity and confusion in man places of his writings, we may add his poverty and frequen change of place, had rendered him of little estimation in th eyes of the world. But, in the last century, the fate of Brun excited some degree of interest about his opinions. Whethe his hypotheses were truly atheistical became the subject o controversy: his works, by which it should have been decided were so scarce that few could speak with knowledge of thei contents; and Brucker, who inclines to think there was n sufficient ground for the imputation, admits that he had only seen one of Bruno's minor treatises. The later Germar philosophers, however, have paid more attention to these obscure books, from a similarity which they sometimes founc in Bruno's theories to their own. Buhle has devoted above a hundred pages to this subject.[1] The Italian treatises have within a few years been reprinted in Germany, and it is no uncommon in modern books to find an eulogy on the philo- sopher of Nola. I have not made myself acquainted with his Latin writings, except through the means of Buhle, who has taken a great deal of pains to explain them. The three

His Italian works.

principal Italian treatises are entitled, La Cena de li Ceneri; Della Causa, Principio, ed Uno; and Dell' Infinito Universo. Each of these is in five dialogues.

Cena de li Ceneri.

The Cena de li Ceneri contains a physical theory of the world, in which the author makes some show

[1] Vol. ii. p. 604–730

of geometrical diagrams, but deviates so often into rhapsodies of vanity and nonsense, that it is difficult to pronounce whether he had much knowledge of the science. Copernicus, to whose theory of the terrestrial motion Bruno entirely adheres, he praises as superior to any former astronomer; but intimates that he did not go far beyond vulgar prejudices, being more of a mathematician than a philosopher. The gravity of bodies he treats as a most absurd hypothesis; all natural motion, as he fancies, being circular. Yet he seems to have had some dim glimpse of what is meant by the composition of motions, asserting that the earth has four simple motions, out of which one is compounded.[1]

Della Causa, Principio, ed Uno

12. The second, and much more important treatise, Della Causa, Principio, ed Uno, professes to reveal the metaphysical philosophy of Bruno, a system which, at least in pretext, brought him to the stake at Rome, and the purport of which has been the theme of much controversy. The extreme scarcity of his writings has, no doubt, contributed to this variety of judgment; but though his style, strictly speaking, is not obscure, and he seems by no means inclined to conceal his meaning, I am not able to resolve with certainty the problem that Brucker and those whom he quotes have discussed.[2] Yet the system of Bruno, so far as I understand it from what I have read of his writings, and from Buhle's analysis of them, may be said to contain a sort of double pantheism. The world is animated by an omnipresent intelligent soul, the first cause of every form that matter can assume, but not of matter itself. This soul of the universe is the only physical agent, the interior artist that works in the vast whole, that calls out the plant from the seed and matures the fruit, that lives in all things, though they may not seem to live, and in fact do not, when unorganized, live separately considered, though they all partake of the universal life, and in their component parts may be rendered living. A table as a table, a coat as a coat, are not alive; but, inasmuch as they derive their substance from nature, they are composed of living particles.[3] There is nothing so small or so unimportant,

[1] Dial. v. p. 120 (1830). These dialogues were written, or purport to have been written, in England. He extols Leicester, Walsingham, and especially Sidney.

[2] Brucker, vol. v. 52.

[3] Thus Buhle, or at least his French translator; but the original words are different. "Dico dunque che la tavola come tavola non è animata, nè la veste, nè il cuojo come cuojo, nè il vetro come vetro, ma *come cose naturali e composte*

but that a portion of spirit dwells in it; and this spiritu substance requires but a proper subject to become a plant c an animal. Forms particular are in constant change; but th first form, being the source of all others, as well as the firs matter, are eternal. The soul of the world is the constituer principle of the universe and of all its parts. And thus w have an intrinsic, eternal, self-subsistent principle of form, fa better than that which the sophists feigned, whose substance are compounded and corruptible, and, therefore, nothing els than accidents.[1] Forms in particular are the accidents o matter, and we should make a divinity of matter like som Arabian peripatetics, if we did not recur to the living fountai of form,—the eternal soul of the world. The first matter i neither corporeal nor sensible; it is eternal and unchangeabl the fruitful mother of forms and their grave. Form an matter, says Bruno, pursuing this fanciful analogy, may b compared to male and female. Form never errs, is neve imperfect, but through its conjunction with matter; it migh adopt the words of the father of the human race: "Mulie quam mihi dedisti (la materia, la quale mi hai dato consorte) me decepit (lei è cagione d' ogni mio peccato)." The specu lations of Bruno now become more and more subtle, and h admits that our understandings cannot grasp what he pretend to demonstrate,—the identity of a simply active and simpl

hanno in se la materia e la forma. Sia pur cosa quanto piccola e minima si voglia, ha in se parte di sustanza spirituale, la quale, se trova il soggetto disposto, si stende ad esser pianta, ad esser animale, e riceve membri de qual si voglia corpo, che comunemente si dice animato; per chè spirto si trova in tutte le cose, e non è minimo corpusculo, che non contegna cotal porzione in se, che non inanimi."—p. 241. Buhle seems not to have understood the words in Italics, which certainly are not remarkably plain, and to have substituted what he thought might pass for meaning.

The recent theories of equivocal generation, held by some philosophers, more on the Continent than in England, according to which all matter, or at least all matter susceptible of organization by its elements, may become organized and living under peculiar circumstances, seem not very dissimilar to this system of Bruno.

1 "Or, quanto a la causa effettrice, dico l' efficiente fisico universale esser l' intelletto universale, ch' è la prima e princi pial facultà dell' anima del mondo, l qual è forma universale di quello. . . . L' intelletto universale è l' intima pi reale e propria facultà, e parte potenzial dell' anima del mondo. Questo è un medesimo ch' empie il tutto, illumina l universo, e indrizza la natura à produrr le sue specie, come si conviene, e cosi h rispetto à la produzione di cose naturali come il nostro intelletto è la congrua pro duzione di specie razionali. . . . Questo nominato da Platonici fabbro del mondo." —p. 235.

"Dunque abbiamo un principio intrin seco formale eterno e sussistente, incom parabilmente migliore di quello, che ha finto li sophisti, che versano circa gl' ac cidenti, ignoranti de la sustanza de l cose, e che vengono a ponere le sustanz corrottibili, perchè quello chiamano mas simamente, primamente e principalment sustanza, che risulta da la composizione il che non è altro, ch' uno accidente, ch non contiene in se nulla stabilità e verit e si risolve in nulla."—p. 242.

passive principle; but the question really is, whether we can see any meaning in his propositions.

13. We have said that the system of Bruno seems to involve a double pantheism. The first is of a simple kind, the hylozoism, which has been exhibited in the preceding paragraph: it excludes a creative deity, in the strict sense of creation, but, leaving an active provident intelligence, cannot be reckoned by any means chargeable with positive atheism. But to this soul of the world Bruno appears not to have ascribed the name of divinity.[1] The first form and the first matter, and all the forms generated by the two, make, in his theory, but one being, the infinite unchangeable universe, in which is every thing, both in power and in act, and which, being all things collectively, is no one thing separately: it is form and not form, matter and not matter, soul and not soul. He expands this mysterious language much farther, resolving the whole nature of the Deity into an abstract, barren, all-embracing unity.[2]

Pantheism of Bruno.

[1] "Son tre sorti d' intelletto; il divino, ch' è tutto; questo mondano, che fà tutto; gli altri particulari, che si fanno tutte. . . . È vera causa efficiente (l' intelletto mondano) non tanto estrinseca, come anco intrinseca di tutte cose naturali. . . . Mi par, che detrahano à la divina bontà e à l' eccellenza di questo grande animale e simulacro del primo principio quelli, che non vogliano intendere, nè affirmare, il mondo con li suoi membri essere animato." — p. 239.

[2] "È dunque l' universo uno, infinito, immobile. Uno dico è la possibilità assoluta, uno l' atto, una la forma o anima, una la materia o corpo, una la cosa, uno lo ente, uno il massimo e ottimo, il quale non deve posser essere compreso, e però infinibile e interminabile, e per tanto infinito e interminato, e per conseguenza immobile. Questo non si muove localmente; per chè non ha cosa fuor di sè, ove si trasporte, atteso chè sia il tutto. Non si genera; per chè non è altro essere, che lui possa desiderare o aspettare, atteso che abbia tutto lo essere. Non si corrompe; per chè non è altra cosa, in cui si cangi, atteso che lui sia ogni cosa. Non può sminuire o crescere, atteso ch' è infinito, a cui come non si può aggiungere, cosi è da cui non si può sottrarre, per ciò che lo infinito non ha parti proporzionali. Non è alterabile in altra disposizione, per chè non ha esterno, da cui patisca, e per cui venga in qualche affezione. Oltre chè per comprender tutte contrarietadi nell' esser suo, in unità e convenienza, e nessuna inclinazione posser avere ad altro e novo essere, o pur ad altro e altro modo d' essere, non può esser soggetto di mutazione secundo qualità alcuna, nè può aver contrario o diverso, che l' alteri, per chè in lui è ogni cosa concorde. Non è materia, per chè non è figurato, nè figurabile non è terminato, nè terminabile. Non è forma, per chè non informa, nè figura altro, atteso che è tutto, è massimo, è uno, è universo. Non è misurabile, nè misura. Non si comprende; per chè non è maggior di sè. Non sì è compreso; per chè non è minor di se. Non si agguaglia; per chè non è altro e altro, ma uno e medesimo. Essendo medesimo ed uno, non ha essere ed essere; et per chè non ha essere ed essere, non ha parti e parti; e per ciò che non ha parte e parte, non è composto. Questo è termine di sorte, chè non è termine; è talmente forma, chè non è forma; è talmente materia, chè non è materia; è talmente anima, chè non è anima; per chè è il tutto indifferentemente, e però è uno, l' universo è uno." — p. 280.

"Ecco, come non è possibile, ma necessario, che l' ottimo, massimo incomprensibile è tutto, è par tutto, è in tutto, per chè come simplice ed indivisible può esser tutto, esser per tutto, essere in tutto. E così non è stato vanamente detto, che Giove empie tutte le cose, inabita tutte le parti dell' universo, è centro di ciò, che ha l' essere uno in tutto, e per cui uno è tutto. Il quale, essendo tutte le cose, e comprendendo tutto l' essere in se, viene a far, che ogni cosa sia in ogni cosa. Ma mi direste, per chè dunque le cose si cangiano, la ma

Bruno's other writings.

14. These bold theories of Jordano Bruno are chiefly contained in the treatise Della Causa, Principio, ed Uno. In another, entitled Dell' Infinito Universo e Mondi, which, like the former, is written in dialogue, he asserts the infinity of the universe, and the plurality of worlds. That the stars are suns, shining by their own light; that each has its revolving planets, now become the familiar creed of children, — were then among the enormous paradoxes and capital offences of Bruno. His strong assertion of the Copernican theory was, doubtless, not quite so singular; yet this had but few proselytes in the sixteenth century. His other writings, of all which Buhle has furnished us with an account, are numerous; some of them relate to the art of Raymond Lully, which Bruno professed to esteem very highly; and in these mnemonical treatises he introduced much of his own theoretical philosophy. Others are more exclusively metaphysical, and designed to make his leading principles, as to unity, number, and form, more intelligible to the common reader. They are full, according to what we find in Brucker and Buhle, of strange and nonsensical propositions, such as men, unable to master their own crude fancies on subjects above their reach, are wont to put forth. None, however, of his productions has been more often mentioned than the Spaccio della Bestia Trionfante, alleged by some to be full of his atheistical impieties, while others have taken it for a mere satire on the Roman Church. This diversity was very natural in those who wrote of a book they had never seen. It now appears that this famous work is a general moral satire in an allegorical form, with little that could excite attention, and less that could give such offence as to provoke the author's death.[1]

teria particolare si forza ad altre forme? vi rispondo, che non è mutazione, che cerca altro essere, ma altro modo di essere. E questa è la differenza tra l' universo e le cose dell' universo; per chè nullo comprende tutto l' essere e tutti modi di essere; di queste ciascuna ha tutto l' essere, ma non tutti i modi di essere." — p. 282.

The following sonnet by Bruno is characteristic of his mystical imagination; but we must not confound the personification of an abstract idea with theism: —

"Causa, Principio, ed Uno sempiterno,
Onde l' esser, la vita, il moto pende,
E a lungo, a largo, e profondo si stende
Quanto si dice in ciel, terra ed inferno;
Con senso, con ragion, con mente scerno
Ch' atto, misura e conto non comprende,
Quel vigor, mole e numero, che tende
Oltre ogni inferior, mezzo e superno.
Cieco error, tempo avaro, ria fortuna,
Sorda invidia, vil rabbia, iniquo zelo,
Crudo cor, empio ingegno, strano ardire,
Non basteranno a farmi l' aria bruna,
Non mi porrann' avanti gl' occhi il velo.
Non faran mai, ch' il mio bel Sol non mire."

If I have quoted too much from Jordano Bruno, it may be excused by the great rarity of his works, which has been the cause that some late writers have not fully seen the character of his speculations.

[1] Ginguéné, vol. vii., has given an analysis of the Spaccio della Bestia.

General character of his philosophy.

15. Upon the whole, we may probably place Bruno in this province of speculative philosophy, though not high, yet above Cesalpin, or any of the school of Averroes. He has fallen into great errors; but they seem to have perceived no truth. His doctrine was not original: it came from the Eleatic philosophers, from Plotinus and the Neo-Platonists,[1] and in some measure from Plato himself; and it is ultimately, beyond doubt, of Oriental origin. What seems most his own, and I must speak very doubtfully as to this, is the syncretism of the tenet of a pervading spirit, an Anima Mundi, which in itself is an imperfect theism, with the more pernicious hypothesis of an universal Monad, to which every distinct attribute, except unity, was to be denied. Yet it is just to observe, that, in one passage already quoted in a note, Bruno expressly says, "There are three kinds of intelligence: the divine, which is every thing; the mundane, which does every thing; and the particular intelligences, which are all made by the second." The inconceivableness of ascribing intelligence to Bruno's universe, and yet thus distinguishing it as he does from the mundane intelligence, may not perhaps be a sufficient reason for denying him a place among theistic philosophers. But it must be confessed, that the general tone of these dialogues conveys no other impression than that of a pantheism, in which every vestige of a supreme intelligence, beyond his soul of the world, is effaced.[2]

Sceptical theory of Sanchez.

16. The system, if so it may be called, of Bruno was essentially dogmatic, reducing the most subtle and incomprehensible mysteries into positive aphorisms of science. Sanchez, a Portuguese physician, settled as a public instructor at Toulouse, took a different course: the preface of his treatise, Quod Nihil Scitur, is dated from

[1] See a valuable analysis of the philosophy of Plotinus in Degerando's Histoire Comparée des Systèmes, iii. 357 (edit. 1823). It will be found that his language with respect to the mystic supremacy of unity is that of Bruno himself. Plotin, however, was not only theistic, but intensely religious, and, if he had come a century later, would, instead of a heathen philosopher, have been one of the first names among the saints of the church. It is probable that his influence, as it is, has not been small in modelling the mystic theology. Scotus Erigena was of the same school; and his language about the first Monad is similar to that of Bruno. Degerando, vol. iv. p. 372.

[2] I can hardly agree with Mr. Whewell in supposing that Jordano Bruno "probably had a considerable share in introducing the new opinions (of Copernicus) into England."—Hist. of Inductive Sciences, i. 385. Very few in England seem to have embraced these opinions; and those who did so, like Wright and Gilbert, were men who had somewhat better reasons than the *ipse dixit* of a wandering Italian.

that city in 1576; but no edition is known to have existed before 1581.[1] This work is a mere tissue of sceptical fallacies, propounded, however, with a confident tone not unusual in that class of sophists. He begins abruptly with these words: "Nec unum hoc scio, me nihil scire, conjector tamen nec me nec alios. Hæc mihi vexillum propositio sit, hæc sequenda venit, Nihil Scitur. Hanc si probare scivero, merito concludam nihil sciri; si nescivero, hoc ipso melius; id enim asserebam." A good deal more follows in the same sophistical style of cavillation. "Hoc unum semper maxime ab aliquo expetivi, quod modo facio, ut vere diceret an aliquid perfecte sciret; nusquam tamen inveni, præterquam in sapiente illo proboque viro Socrate (licet et Pyrrhonii, Academici et Sceptici vocati, cum Favorino id etiam assererent) quod hoc unum sciebat quod nihil sciret. Quo solo dicto mihi doctissimus indicatur; quanquam nec adhuc omnino mihi explêrit mentem; cum et illud unum, sicut alia, ignoraret."[2]

17. Sanchez puts a few things well; but his scepticism, as we perceive, is extravagant. After descanting on Montaigne's favorite topic, the various manners and opinions of mankind, he says, "Non finem faceremus si omnes omnium mores recensere vellemus. An tu his eandem rationem, quam nobis, omnino putes? Mihi non verisimile videtur. Nihil tamen ambo scimus. Negabis forsan tales aliquos esse homines. Non contendam; sic ab aliis accepi."[3] Yet, notwithstanding his sweeping denunciation of all science in the boldest tone of Pyrrhonism, Sanchez comes at length to admit the possibility of a limited or probable knowledge of truth; and, as might perhaps be expected, conceives that he had himself attained it. "There are two modes," he observes, "of discovering truth, by neither of which do men learn the real nature of things, but yet obtain some kind of insight into them. These are experiment and reason, neither being sufficient alone; but experiments, however well conducted, do not show us the nature of things, and reason can only conjecture them. Hence there can be no such thing as perfect science; and books have been employed to eke out the deficiencies of our own experience: but their confusion, prolixity, multitude,

[1] Brucker, iv. 541, with this fact before his eyes, strangely asserts Sanchez to have been born in 1562. Buhle and Cousin copy him without hesitation. Antonio is ignorant of any edition of Quod Nihil Scitur, except that of Rotterdam in 1649; and ignorant also that the book contains any thing remarkable.

[2] P. 10.

[3] P. 39.

and want of trustworthiness, prevent this resource from being of much value; nor is life long enough for so much study. Besides, this perfect knowledge requires a perfect recipient of it, and a right disposition of the subject of knowledge; which two I have never seen. Reader, if you have met with them, write me word." He concludes this treatise by promising another, "in which we shall explain the method of knowing truth, as far as human weakness will permit;" and, as his self-complacency rises above his affected scepticism, adds, "Mihi in animo est firmam et facilem quantum possim scientiam fundare."

18. This treatise of Sanchez bears witness to a deep sense of the imperfections of the received systems in science and reasoning, and to a restless longing for truth, which strikes us in other writers of this latter period of the sixteenth century. Lord Bacon, I believe, has never alluded to Sanchez; and such paradoxical scepticism was likely to disgust his strong mind: yet we may sometimes discern signs of a Baconian spirit in the attacks of our Spanish philosopher on the syllogistic logic, as being built on abstract and not significant terms, and in his clear perception of the difference between a knowledge of words and one of things.

19. What Sanchez promised, and Bacon gave, a new method of reasoning, by which truth might be better determined than through the common dialectics, had been partially attempted already by Aconcio, mentioned in the last chapter as one of those highly-gifted Italians who fled for religion to a Protestant country. Without openly assailing the authority of Aristotle, he endeavored to frame a new discipline of the faculties for the discovery of truth. His treatise, De Methodo, sive Recta Investigandarum Tradendarumque Scientiarum Ratione, was published at Basle in 1558, and was several times reprinted; till later works, those especially of Bacon and Des Cartes, caused it to be forgotten. Aconcio defines logic, the right method of thinking and teaching, *recta contemplandi docendique ratio*. Of the importance of method, or right order in prosecuting our inquiries, he thinks so highly, that, if thirty years were to be destined to intellectual labor, he would allot two-thirds of the time to acquiring dexterity in this art; which seems to imply that he did not consider it very easy. To know any thing, he tells us, is to know what it is, or what are its causes and effects.

Logic of Aconcio.

All men have the germs of knowledge latent in them, as to matters cognizable by human faculties; it is the business of logic to excite and develop them: "Notiones illas seu scintillas sub cinere latentes detegere aptèque ad res obscuras illustrandas applicare."[1]

20. Aconcio next gives rules at length for constructing definitions, by attending to the genus and differentia. These rules are good, and might very properly find a place in a book of logic; but, whether they contain much that would vainly be sought in other writers, we do not determine. He comes afterwards to the methods of distributing a subject. The analytic method is by all means to be preferred for the investigation of truth, and, contrary to what Galen and others have advised, even for communicating it to others; since a man can learn that of which he is ignorant, only by means of what is better known, whether he does this himself, or with help of a teacher: the only process being, *a notioribus ad minus nota*. In this little treatise of Aconcio, there seem to be the elements of a sounder philosophy and a more steady direction of the mind to discover the reality of things than belonged to the logic of the age, whether as taught by the Aristotelians or by Ramus. It has not, however, been quoted by Lord Bacon, nor are we sure that he has profited by it.

Nizolius on the principles of philosophy.

21. A more celebrated work than this by Aconcio is one by the distinguished scholar, Marius Nizolius,—De Veris Principiis et Vera Ratione Philosophandi contra Pseudo-Philosophos. (Parma, 1553.) It owes, however, what reputation it possesses to Leibnitz, who reprinted it in 1670, with a very able preface, one of his first contributions to philosophy. The treatise itself, he says, was almost strangled in the birth; and certainly the invectives of Nizolius against the logic and metaphysics of Aristotle could have had little chance of success in a country like Italy, where that authority was more undoubted and durable than in any other. The aim of Nizolius was to set up the best authors of Greece and Rome and the study of philology against the scholastic terminology. But it must be owned, that this polite literature was not sufficient for the discovery of truth; nor does the book keep up to the promise

[1] P. 30.

of its title, though, by endeavoring to eradicate barbarous sophistry, he may be said to have labored in the interests of real philosophy. The preface of Leibnitz animadverts on what appeared to him some metaphysical errors of Nizolius, especially an excess of nominalism, which tended to undermine the foundations of certainty, and his presumptuous scorn of Aristotle.[1] His own object was rather to recommend the treatise as a model of philosophical language without barbarism, than to bestow much praise on its philosophy. Brucker has spoken of it rather slightingly, and Buhle with much contempt. I am not prepared, by a sufficient study of its contents, to pass any judgment; but Buhle's censure has appeared to me somewhat unfair. Dugald Stewart, who was not acquainted with what the latter has said, thinks Nizolius deserving of more commendation than Brucker has assigned to him.[2] He argues against all dialectics, and therefore differs from Ramus; concluding with two propositions as the result of his whole book: That as many logicians and metaphysicians as are any where found, so many capital enemies of truth will then and there exist; and that, so long as Aristotle shall be supreme in the logic and metaphysics of the schools, so long will error and barbarism reign over the mind. There is nothing very deep or pointed in this summary of his reasoning.

[1] Nizolius maintained that universal terms were only particulars, — *collectivè sumpta*. Leibnitz replies that they are particulars, — *distributivè sumpta*; as, "Omnis homo est animal" means that every one man is an animal; not that the genus man, taken collectively, is an animal. "Nec vero Nizolii error hic levis est; habet enim magnum aliquid in recessu. Nam si universalia nihil aliud sunt quam singularium collectiones, sequitur, scientiam nullam haberi per demonstrationem, quod et infra colligit Nizolius, sed collectionem singularium seu inductionem. Sed ea ratione prorsus evertuntur scientiæ, ac Sceptici vicere. Nam nunquam constitui possunt ea ratione propositiones perfecte universales, quia inductione nunquam certus es, omnia individue a te tentata esse; sed semper intra hanc propositionem subsistes; omnia illa quæ expertus sum sunt talia; cum vero non possit esse ulla ratio universalis, semper manebit possibile innumera quæ tu non sis expertus esse diversa. Hinc jam patet inductionem per se nihil producere, ne certitudinem quidem moralem, sine adminiculo propositionum non ab inductione, sed ratione universali prudentium; nam si essent et adminicula ab inductione, indigerent novis adminiculis, nec haberetur certitudo moralis in infinitum. Sed certitudo moralis ab inductione sperari plane non potest, additis quibuscunque adminiculis, et propositionem hanc, totum magis esse sua parte, sola inductione nunquam perfecte sciemus. Mox enim prodibit, qui negabit ob peculiarem quondam rationem in aliis nondum tentatis veram esse, quemadmodum ex facto scimus Gregorium a Sancto Vincentio negasse totum esse majus sua parte, in angulis saltem contactûs, alios in infinito; et Thomam Hobbes (at quem virum!) cœpisse dubitare de propositione illa geometrica a Pythagora demonstrata, et hecatombæ sacrificio digna habita; quod ego non sine stupore legi." This extract is not very much to the purpose of the text, but it may please some of those who take an interest in such speculations.

[2] Dissertation on Progress of Philosophy, p. 88.

Margarita Antoniana of Pereira.

22. The Margarita Antoniana, by Gomez Pereira, published at Medina del Campo in 1554, has been chiefly remembered as the ground of one of the many charges against Des Cartes for appropriating unacknowledged opinions of his predecessors. The book is exceedingly scarce, which has been strangely ascribed to the efforts of Des Cartes to suppress it.[1] There is, however, a copy of the original edition in the British Museum, and it has been reprinted in Spain. It was an unhappy theft, if theft it were; for what Pereira maintained was precisely the most untenable proposition of the great French philosopher, — the absence of sensation in brutes. Pereira argues against this with an extraordinary disregard of common phenomena, on the assumption of certain maxims which cannot be true, if they contradict inferences from our observation far more convincing than themselves. We find him give a curious reason for denying that we can infer the sensibility of brutes from their outward actions: namely, that this would prove too much, and lead us to believe them rational beings; instancing among other stories, true or false, of apparent sagacity, the dog in pursuit of a hare, who coming where two roads meet, if he traces no scent on the first, takes the other without trial.[2] Pereira is a rejecter of Aristotelian despotism; and observes that, in matters of speculation and not of faith, no authority is to be respected.[3] Notwithstanding this assertion of freedom, he seems to be wholly enchained by the metaphysics of the schools; nor should I have thought the book worthy of notice, but for its scarcity and the circumstance above mentioned about Des Cartes.

23. These are, as far as I know, the only works deserving of commemoration in the history of speculative philosophy. A few might easily be inserted from the catalogues of libraries, or from biographical collections, as well as from the learned labors of Morhof, Brucker, Tennemann, and Buhle. It is also not to be doubted, that in treatises of a different character, theological, moral, or medical, very many passages, worthy of remembrance for their truth, their ingenuity, or

[1] Biogr. Univ.; Brunet, Manuel du Libraire. Bayle has a long article on Pereira; but, though he says the book had been shown to him, he wanted probably the opportunity to read much of it.

According to Brunet, several copies have been sold in France, some of them at no great price. The later edition, of 1749, is of course cheaper.

[2] Fol. 18. This is continually told of dogs; but does any sensible sportsman confirm it by his own experience? I ask for information only.

[3] Fol. 4.

originality, might be discovered, that bear upon the best methods of reasoning, the philosophy of the human mind, the theory of natural religion, or the general system of the material world.

Logic of Ramus: its success.

24. We should not, however, conclude this chapter without adverting to the dialectical method of Ramus, whom we left at the middle of the century, struggling against all the arms of orthodox logic in the University of Paris. The reign of Henry II. was more propitious to him than that of Francis. In 1551, through the patronage of the Cardinal of Lorraine, Ramus became royal professor of rhetoric and philosophy; and his new system, which, as has been mentioned, comprehended much that was important in the art of rhetoric, began to make numerous proselytes. Omer Talon, known for a treatise on eloquence, was among the most ardent of these; and to him we owe our most authentic account of the contest of Ramus with the Sorbonne. The latter were not conciliated, of course, by the success of their adversary; and, Ramus having adhered to the Huguenot party in the civil feuds of France, it has been ascribed to the malignity of one of his philosophical opponents that he perished in the massacre of St. Bartholomew. He had, however, already, by personally travelling and teaching in Germany, spread the knowledge of his system over that country. It was received in some of the German universities with great favor, notwithstanding the influence which Melanchthon's name retained, and which had been entirely thrown into the scale of Aristotle. The Ramists and Anti-Ramists contended in books of logic through the rest of this century, as well as afterwards; but this was the principal period of Ramus's glory. In Italy he had few disciples; but France, England, and still more Scotland and Germany, were full of them. Andrew Melville introduced the logic of Ramus at Glasgow. It was resisted for some time at St. Andrew's, but ultimately became popular in all the Scottish universities.[1] Scarce any eminent public school, says Brucker, can be named in which the Ramists were not teachers. They encountered an equally zealous militia under the Aristotelian standard; while some, with the spirit of compromise which always takes possession of a few minds, though it is rarely very successful, endeavored

[1] M'Crie's Life of Melville, ii. 306

to unite the two methods, which in fact do not seem essentially exclusive of each other. It cannot be required of me to give an account of books so totally forgotten and so uninteresting in their subjects as these dialectical treatises on either side. The importance of Ramus in philosophical history is not so much founded on his own deserts as on the effect he produced in loosening the fetters of inveterate prejudice, and thus preparing the way, like many others of his generation, for those who were to be the restorers of genuine philosophy.[1]

[1] Brucker, v. 576; Buhle, ii. 601.

CHAPTER IV.

HISTORY OF MORAL AND POLITICAL PHILOSOPHY AND OF JURISPRUDENCE, FROM 1550 TO 1600.

SECT. I.—ON MORAL PHILOSOPHY.

Soto—Hooker—Essays of Montaigne—Their Influence on the Public—Italian and English Moralists.

1. It must naturally be supposed, that by far the greater part of what was written on moral obligations in the sixteenth century will be found in the theological quarter of ancient libraries. The practice of auricular confession brought with it an entire science of casuistry, which had gradually been wrought into a complicated system. Many, once conspicuous writers in this province, belong to the present period; but we shall defer the subject till we arrive at the next, when it had acquired a more prominent importance.

2. The first original work of any reputation in ethical philosophy since the revival of letters, and which, being apparently designed in great measure for the chair of the confessional, serves as a sort of link between the class of mere casuistry and the philosophical systems of morals which were to follow, is by Dominic Soto, a Spanish Dominican, who played an eminent part in the deliberations of the Council of Trent, in opposition both to the Papal court and to the theologians of the Scotist, or, as it was then reckoned by its adversaries, the Semi-Pelagian school. This folio volume, entitled De Justitia et Jure, was first published, according to the Biographie Universelle, at Antwerp, in 1568. It appears to be founded on the writings of Thomas Aquinas, the polar star of every true Dominican. Every question is discussed

Soto, De Justitia.

with that remarkable observation of distinctions, and that unremitting desire both to comprehend and to distribute a subject, which is displayed in many of these forgotten folios, and ought to inspire us with reverence for the zealous energy of their authors, even when we find it impossible, as must generally be the case, to read so much as a few pages consecutively, or when we light upon trifling and insufficient arguments in the course of our casual glances over the volume.

3. Hooker's Ecclesiastical Polity might seem more properly to fall under the head of theology; but, the first book of this work being by much the best, Hooker ought rather to be reckoned among those who have weighed the principles, and delineated the boundaries, of moral and political science. I have, on another occasion,[1] done full justice to the wisdom and eloquence of this earliest among the great writers of England, who, having drunk at the streams of ancient philosophy, has acquired from Plato and Tully somewhat of their redundancy and want of precision, with their comprehensiveness of observation and their dignity of soul. The reasonings of Hooker, though he bore in the ensuing century the surname of Judicious, are not always safe or satisfactory, nor, perhaps, can they be reckoned wholly clear or consistent; his learning, though beyond that of most English writers in that age, is necessarily uncritical; and his fundamental principle, the mutability of ecclesiastical government, has as little pleased those for whom he wrote as those whom he repelled by its means.[2] But he stood out at a vast height

Hooker.

[1] Constitut. Hist. Engl., chap. iv.

[2] [The phrase, "fundamental principle," may appear too strong to those who have not paid much attention to the subject, especially when a man of so much ability as the last editor of the Ecclesiastical Polity has labored to persuade his readers that Hooker maintained the divine right of episcopal government. By a fundamental principle, I mean a leading theorem which determines the character of a book, and gives it its typical form, as distinguished from others which may have the same main object in view. Thus, to take a very different instance, the main object of Homer was to celebrate the prowess of the Greeks in the war of Troy; but the mode in which he presented this, the typical character of the Iliad, was the illustration of one memorable portion of that contest, the quarrel of Achilles with Agamemnon. What the wrath of Achilles was to Homer, that was the mutability of positive laws to Hooker; a leading idea, which gave its peculiar form to his work, and through which his ultimate end, the defence of the ecclesiastical constitution of his country, was to be effected. It may be inquired of those who think otherwise, why the first book of the Ecclesiastical Polity was written at all? Was it merely to display his reasoning or eloquence upon a subject far more appertaining to philosophy than to theology? Surely this would have been idle ostentation, especially in the very outset of his work. But those who read it can hardly fail to perceive that it is the broad basis of what is to follow in the second and third books; that in laying down the distinction between natural and positive law, and affirming the former alone to be immutable, he prepares the way for denying the main position of his Puritan antagonists, that all things con-

above his predecessors and contemporaries in the English Church, and was perhaps the first of our writers who had any considerable acquaintance with the philosophers of Greece, not merely displayed in quotation, of which others may have sometimes set an example, but in a spirit of reflection and comprehensiveness which the study of antiquity alone could have infused. The absence of minute ramifications of argument, in which the schoolmen loved to spread out, distinguishes Hooker from the writers who had been trained in those arid dialectics, such as Soto or Suarez; but, as I have hinted, considering the depth and difficulty of several questions that he deals with in the first book of the Polity, we might wish for a little less of the expanded palm of rhetoric, and somewhat of more dialectical precision in the reasoning.[1]

tained in Scripture are of perpetual obligation. It is his doctrine, that, where God has not declared a positive command to be perpetual, it may be dispensed with by lawful human authority; and, in the third book, he in express words asserts this of ecclesiastical government. Whether he is right or no, we do not here inquire; but those who prefer an honest avowal of truth to that small party interest which is served by counting all names as on our side, cannot feel any hesitation about his opinion on this point. I repeat, that it may be called his fundamental principle.

I do not, however, deny that in the seventh book of the Ecclesiastical Polity, written several years after the former, there are signs that Hooker had in some degree abandoned the broad principle of indifferency; and that he occasionally seems to contend for episcopal government as always best, though not always indispensable. Whether this were owing to the natural effects of controversy, in rendering the mind tenacious of every point it has to maintain, or rather to the bolder course of defence which Saravia and Bancroft had latterly taught the advocates of the church to take, I do not determine. But, even in this book, we shall not find that he ever asserts in terms the perpetual obligation of episcopacy: nor does he, I believe, so much as allude to what is commonly called the apostolical succession, or transmission of spiritual power from one bishop to another; a question wholly distinct from that of mere ecclesiastical government, though perpetually confounded with it. — 1842.]

[1] It has been shown with irresistible proof by the last editor of Hooker, that the sixth book of the Ecclesiastical Polity has been lost; that which we read as such being, with the exception of a few paragraphs at the beginning, altogether a different production, though bearing marks of the same author. This is proved, not only by its want of relation to the general object of the work, and to the subject announced in the title of this very book, but by the remarkable fact that a series of observations, by two friends of Hooker, on the sixth book are extant, and published in the last edition, which were obviously designed for a totally different treatise from that which has always passed for the sixth book of the Ecclesiastical Polity. This can only be explained by the confusion in which Hooker's manuscripts were left at his death, and upon which suspicions of interpolation have been founded. Such suspicions are not reasonable; and, notwithstanding the exaggerated language which has sometimes been used, I think it very questionable whether any more perfect manuscript was ever in existence. The reasoning in the seventh and eighth books appears as elaborate, the proofs as full, the grammatical structure as perfect, as in the earlier books; and the absence of those passages of eloquence, which we occasionally find in the former, cannot afford even a presumption that the latter were designed to be written over again. The eighth book is manifestly incomplete, wanting some discussions which the author had announced; but this seems rather adverse to the hypothesis of a more elaborate copy. The more probable inference is, that Hooker was interrupted by death before he had completed his plan. It is possible also that the conclusion of the eighth book has been lost like the sixth. All the stories on this sub-

4. Hooker, like most great moral writers both of antiquity and of modern ages, rests his positions on one solid basis, the eternal obligation of natural law. A small number had been inclined to maintain an arbitrary power of the Deity, even over the fundamental principles of right and wrong; but the sounder theologians seem to have held, that, however the will of God may be the proper source of moral obligation in mankind, concerning which they were not more agreed then than they have been since, it was impossible for him to deviate from his immutable rectitude and holiness. They were unanimous also in asserting the capacity of the human faculties to discern right from wrong, little regarding what they deemed the prejudices or errors that had misled many nations, and more or less influenced the majority of mankind.

His theory of natural law.

5. But there had never been wanting those who, struck by the diversity of moral judgments and behavior among men, and especially under circumstances of climate, manners, or religion, different from our own, had found it hard to perceive how reason could be an unerring arbiter, when there was so much discrepancy in what she professed to have determined. The relations of travellers, continually pressing upon the notice of Europe in the sixteenth century, and perhaps rather more exaggerated than at present, in describing barbarous tribes, afforded continual aliment to the suspicion. It was at least evident, without any thing that could be called unreasonable scepticism, that these diversities ought to be well explained and sifted before we acquiesced in the pleasant conviction that we alone could be in the right.

Doubts felt by others.

6. The Essays of Montaigne, the first edition of which appeared at Bordeaux in 1580,[1] make in several respects an epoch in literature, less on account of their real importance, or the novel truths they contain, than of their influence upon the taste and the opinions of Europe. They are the first *provocatio ad populum*, the first appeal from the porch and the academy to the haunts of busy and of idle men, the first book that taught the unlearned reader to

Essays of Montaigne.

ject in the Life of Hooker by Walton, who seems to have been a man always too credulous of anecdote, are unsatisfactory to any one who exacts real proof.

[1] This edition contains only the first and second books of the Essays: the third was published in that of Paris, 1588.

observe and reflect for himself on questions of moral philosophy. In an age when every topic of this nature was treated systematically, and in a didactic form, he broke out without connection of chapters, with all the digressions that levity and garrulous egotism could suggest, with a very delightful, but at that time most unusual, rapidity of transition from seriousness to gayety. It would be to anticipate much of what will demand attention in the ensuing century, were we to mention here the conspicuous writers who, more or less directly, and with more or less of close imitation, may be classed in the school of Montaigne: it embraces, in fact, a large proportion of French and English literature, and especially of that which has borrowed his title of Essays. No prose writer of the sixteenth century has been so generally read, nor probably has given so much delight. Whatever may be our estimate of Montaigne as a philosopher, a name which he was far from arrogating, there will be but one opinion of the felicity and brightness of his genius.

Their characteristics.

7. It is a striking proof of these qualities, that, in reading his Essays, we can hardly help believing him to have struck out all his thoughts by a spontaneous effort of his mind, and to have fallen afterwards upon his quotations and examples by happy accident. I have little doubt but that the process was different; and that, either by dint of memory, though he absolutely disclaims the possessing a good one, or by the usual method of commonplacing, he had made his reading instrumental to excite his own ingenious and fearless understanding. His extent of learning was by no means great for that age, but the whole of it was brought to bear on his object; and it is a proof of Montaigne's independence of mind, that, while a vast mass of erudition was the only regular passport to fame, he read no authors but such as were most fitted to his own habits of thinking. Hence he displays an unity, a self-existence, which we seldom find so complete in other writers. His quotations, though they perhaps make more than one-half of his Essays, seem parts of himself, and are like limbs of his own mind, which could not be separated without laceration. But over all is spread a charm of a fascinating simplicity, and an apparent abandonment of the whole man to the easy inspiration of genius, combined with a good nature, though rather too epicurean, and destitute of moral energy, which, for that very reason,

made him a favorite with men of similar dispositions, for whom courts and camps, and country mansions, were the proper soil.

8. Montaigne is superior to any of the ancients in liveliness, in that careless and rapid style where one thought springs naturally, but not consecutively, from another, by analogical rather than deductive connection; so that, while the reader seems to be following a train of arguments, he is imperceptibly hurried to a distance by some contingent association. This may be observed in half his Essays, the titles of which often give us little insight into their general scope. Thus the apology for Raymond de Sebonde is soon forgotten in the long defence of moral Pyrrhonism, which occupies the twelfth chapter of the second book. He sometimes makes a show of coming back from his excursions; but he has generally exhausted himself before he does so. This is what men love to practise (not advantageously for their severer studies) in their own thoughts; they love to follow the casual associations that lead them through pleasant labyrinths, — as one, riding along the high road, is glad to deviate a little into the woods, though it may sometimes happen that he will lose his way, and find himself far remote from his inn. And such is the conversational style of lively and eloquent old men. We converse with Montaigne, or rather hear him talk; it is almost impossible to read his Essays without thinking that he speaks to us; we see his cheerful brow, his sparkling eye, his negligent but gentlemanly demeanor; we picture him in his arm-chair, with his few books round the room, and Plutarch on the table.

9. The independence of his mind produces great part of the charm of his writing: it redeems his vanity, without which it could not have been so fully displayed, or, perhaps, so powerfully felt. In an age of literary servitude, when every province into which reflection could wander was occupied by some despot, — when, to say nothing of theology, men found Aristotle or Ulpian or Hippocrates, at every turning, to dictate their road, it was gratifying to fall in company with a simple gentleman, who, with much more reading than generally belonged to his class, had the spirit to ask a reason for every rule.

10. Montaigne has borrowed much, besides his quotations, from the few ancient authors whom he loved to study. In

one passage he even says that his book is wholly compiled from Plutarch and Seneca; but this is evidently intended to throw the critics off their scent. "I purposely conceal the authors from whom I borrow," he says in another place, "to check the presumption of those who are apt to censure what they find in a modern. I am content that they should lash Seneca and Plutarch through my sides."[1] These were his two favorite authors; and, in order to judge of the originality of Montaigne in any passage, it may often be necessary to have a considerable acquaintance with their works. "When I write," he says, "I care not to have books about me; but I can hardly be without a Plutarch."[2] He knew little Greek; but most editions at that time had a Latin translation: he needed not for Plutarch to go beyond his own language. Cicero he did not much admire, except the epistles to Atticus. He esteemed the moderns very slightly in comparison with antiquity, though praising Guicciardini and Philip de Comines. Dugald Stewart observes, that Montaigne cannot be suspected of affectation, and therefore must himself have believed what he says of the badness of his memory; forgetting, as he tells us, the names of the commonest things, and even of those he constantly saw. But his vanity led him to talk perpetually of himself; and, as often happens to vain men, he would rather talk of his own failings than of any foreign subject. He could not have had a very defective memory so far as it had been exercised, though he might fall into the common mistake of confounding his inattention to ordinary objects with weakness of the faculty.

11. Montaigne seldom defines or discriminates; his mind had great quickness, but little subtilty: his carelessness and impatience of labor rendered his views practically one-sided; for, though he was sufficiently free from prejudice to place the objects of consideration in different lights, he wanted the power, or did not use the diligence, to make that comparative appreciation of facts which is necessary to distinguish the truth. He appears to most advantage in matters requiring good sense and calm observation, as in the education of children. The twenty-fourth and twenty-eighth chapters of the first book, which relate to this subject, are among the best in the collection. His excellent temper made him an enemy

[1] L. ii. c. 32.

[2] L. ii. c 10.

to the harshness and tyranny so frequent at that time in the management of children, as his clear understanding did to the pedantic methods of overloading and misdirecting their faculties. It required some courage to argue against the grammarians who had almost monopolized the admiration of the world. Of these men Montaigne observes, that, though they have strong memories, their judgment is usually very shallow; making only an exception for Turnebus, who, though in his opinion the greatest scholar that had existed for a thousand years, had nothing of the pedant about him but his dress. In all the remarks of Montaigne on human character and manners, we find a liveliness, simplicity, and truth. They are such as his ordinary opportunities of observation or his reading suggested; and, though several writers have given proofs of deeper reflection or more watchful discernment, few are so well calculated to fall in with the apprehension of the general reader.

12. The scepticism of Montaigne, concerning which so much has been said, is not displayed in religion, for he was a steady Catholic, though his faith seems to have been rather that of acquiescence than conviction; nor in such subtilties of metaphysical Pyrrhonism as we find in Sanchez, which had no attraction for his careless nature. But he had read much of Sextus Empiricus, and might perhaps have derived something from his favorite Plutarch. He had also been forcibly struck by the recent narratives of travellers, which he sometimes received with a credulity as to evidence not rarely combined with theoretical scepticism, and which is too much the fault of his age to bring censure on an individual. It was then assumed that all travellers were trustworthy, and, still more, that none of the Greek and Roman authors have recorded falsehoods. Hence he was at a loss to discover a general rule of moral law, as an implanted instinct, or necessary deduction of common reason, in the varying usages and opinions of mankind. But his scepticism was less extravagant and unreasonable at that time than it would be now. Things then really doubtful have been proved; and positions, entrenched by authority which he dared not to scruple, have been overthrown:[1] Truth, in retiring from her outposts, has become more unassailable in her citadel.

[1] Montaigne's scepticism was rightly exercised on witchcraft and other supernatural stories; and he had probably some weight in discrediting those superstitions See l. iii. c. 11.

13. It may be deemed a symptom of wanting a thorough love of truth, when a man overrates, as much as when he overlooks, the difficulties he deals with. Montaigne is perhaps not exempt from this failing. Though sincere and candid in his general temper, he is sometimes more ambitious of setting forth his own ingenuity than desirous to come to the bottom of his subject. Hence he is apt to run into the fallacy common to this class of writers, and which La Mothe le Vayer employed much more, — that of confounding the variations of the customs of mankind in things morally indifferent, with those which affect the principles of duty; and hence the serious writers on philosophy in the next age, Pascal, Arnauld, Malebranche, animadvert with much severity on Montaigne. They considered him, not perhaps unjustly, as an enemy to the candid and honest investigation of truth, both by his sceptical bias and by the great indifference of his temperament; scarcely acknowledging, so much as was due, the service he had done by chasing away the servile pedantry of the schools, and preparing the road for closer reasoners than himself. But the very tone of their censures is sufficient to prove the vast influence he had exerted over the world.

14. Montaigne is the earliest classical writer in the French language, the first whom a gentleman is ashamed not to have read. So long as an unaffected style and an appearance of the utmost simplicity and good nature shall charm, so long as the lovers of desultory and cheerful conversation shall be more numerous than those who prefer a lecture or a sermon, so long as reading is sought by the many as an amusement in idleness, or a resource in pain, so long will Montaigne be among the favorite authors of mankind. I know not whether the greatest blemish of his Essays has much impeded their popularity: they led the way to the indecency too characteristic of French literature, but in no writer on serious topics, except Bayle, more habitual than in Montaigne. It may be observed, that a larger portion of this quality distinguishes the third book, published after he had attained a reputation, than the two former. It is also more overspread by egotism; and it is not agreeable to perceive that the two leading faults of his disposition became more unrestrained and absorbing as he advanced in life.

15. The Italians have a few moral treatises of this period, but chiefly scarce and little read. The Instituzioni Morali

of Alexander Piccolomini; the Instituzioni di Tutta la Vita dell' Uomo Nato Nobile e in città Libera, by the same author; the Latin treatise of Mazzoni de Triplici Vita, which, though we mention it here as partly ethical, seems to be rather an attempt to give a general survey of all science, — are among the least obscure, though they have never been of much reputation in Europe.[1] But a more celebrated work, relating indeed to a minor department of ethics, the rules of polite and decorous behavior, is the Galateo of Casa, Bishop of Benevento, and an elegant writer of considerable reputation. This little treatise is not only accounted superior in style to most Italian prose, but serves to illustrate the manners of society in the middle of the sixteenth century. Some of the improprieties which he censures are such as we should hardly have expected to find in Italy, and almost remind us of a strange but graphic poem of one Dedekind, on the manners of Germany in the sixteenth century, called Grobianus. But his own precepts in other places, though hardly striking us as novel, are more refined, and relate to the essential principles of social intercourse, rather than to its conventional forms.[2] Casa wrote also a little book on the duties to be observed between friends of unequal ranks. The inferior, he advises, should never permit himself to jest upon his patron; but, if he is himself stung by any unpleasing wit or sharp word, ought to receive it with a smiling countenance, and to answer so as to conceal his resentment. It is probable that this art was understood in an Italian palace without the help of books.

Writers on morals in Italy.

16. There was never a generation in England which, for worldly prudence and wise observation of mankind, stood higher than the subjects of Elizabeth. Rich in men of strong mind, that age had given them a discipline unknown to ourselves; the strictness of the Tudor government, the suspicious temper of the queen, the spirit not only of intolerance, but of inquisitiveness as to religious dissent, the uncertainties of the future, produced a caution rather foreign to the English character, accompanied by a closer attention to

In England.

[1] For these books, see Tiraboschi, Corniani, and Ginguené. Niceron, vol. xxiii., observes of Piccolomini, that he was the first who employed the Italian language in moral philosophy. This must, however, be taken very strictly; for, in a general sense of the word, we have seen earlier instances than his Instituzioni Morali in 1575.

[2] Casa inveighs against the punctilious and troublesome ceremonies, introduced, as he supposes, from Spain, making distinctions in the mode of addressing different ranks of nobility.

ie workings of other men's minds, and their exterior signs. his, for similar reasons, had long distinguished the Italians; ut it is chiefly displayed perhaps in their political writings. Ve find it, in a larger and more philosophical sense, near the nd of Elizabeth's reign, when our literature made its first rong shoot, prompting the short condensed reflections of Burleigh and Raleigh, or saturating with moral observation ie mighty soul of Shakspeare.

17. The first in time, and we may justly say the first in xcellence, of English writings on moral prudence, re the Essays of Bacon. But these as we now ead them, though not very bulky, are greatly enlarged since heir first publication in 1597. They then were but ten in umber, — entitled, 1. Of Studies; 2. Of Discourse; 3. Of Ceremonies and Respects; 4. Of Followers and Friends; 5. Of Suitors; 6. Of Expense; 7. Of Regiment of Health; 8. Of Honor and Reputation; 9. Of Faction; 10. Of Negoiating. And even these few have been expanded in later editions to nearly double their extent. The rest were added chiefly in 1612, and the whole were enlarged in 1625. The pith indeed of these ten Essays will be found in the edition of 1597; the additions being merely to explain, correct, or illustrate. But, as a much greater number were incorporated with them in the next century, we shall say no more of Bacon's Essays for the present.

Bacon's Essays.

Sect. II.—On Political Philosophy.

Freedom of Writing on Government at this Time — Its Causes — Hottoman — Languet — La Boetie — Buchanan — Poynet — Rose — Mariana — The Jesuits — Botero and Paruta — Bodin — Analysis of his Republic.

18. The present period, especially after 1570, is far more fruitful than the preceding in the annals of political science. It produced several works both of tempo- rary and permanent importance. Before we come to Bodin, who is its most conspicuous ornament, it may be fit to mention some less considerable books, which, though belonging partly to the temporary class, have in several

Number of political writers.

instances survived the occasion which drew them forth, an indicate a state of public opinion not unworthy of notice.

Oppression of governments,

19. A constant progress towards absolute monarchy, sometimes silent, at other times attended with violence had been observable in the principal kingdoms of Europe for the last hundred years. This had been brought about by various circumstances which belong to civil history; but, among others, by a more skilful management, and a more systematic attention to the maxims of statecraft, which had sometimes assumed a sort of scientific form as in The Prince of Machiavel, but were more frequently inculcated in current rules familiar to the counsellors of kings. The consequence had been not only many flagrant instances of violated public right, but in some countries, especially France, an habitual contempt for every moral as well as political restraint on the ruler's will. But oppression is always felt to be such, and the breach of known laws cannot be borne without resentment, though it may without resistance; nor were there wanting several causes that tended to generate a spirit of indignation against the predominant despotism. Independent of those of a political nature, which varied according to the circumstances of kingdoms, there were three that belonged to the sixteenth century as a learned and reflecting age, which, if they did not all exercise a great influence over the multitude, were sufficient to affect the complexion of literature, and to indicate a somewhat novel state of opinion in the public mind.

And spirit generated by it.

Derived from classic history.

20. I. From the Greek and Roman poets, orators, or historians, the scholar derived the principles, not only of equal justice, but of equal privileges: he learned to reverence free republics, to abhor tyranny, to sympathize with a Timoleon or a Brutus. A late English historian, who carried to a morbid excess his jealousy of democratic prejudices, fancied that these are perceptible in the versions of Greek authors by the learned of the sixteenth century, and that Xylander or Rhodomann gratified their spite against the sovereigns of their own time by mistranslating their text, in order to throw odium on Philip or Alexander. This is probably unfounded; but it may still be true that men, who had imbibed notions, perhaps as indefinite as exaggerated, of the blessings of freedom in ancient Rome and Greece,

ould draw no advantageous contrast with the palpable outges of arbitrary power before their eyes. We have seen, ty years before, a striking proof of almost mutinous indigtion in the Adages of Erasmus; and I have little doubt at further evidence of it might be gleaned from the letters d writings of the learned.

21. II. In proportion as the antiquities of the existing uropean monarchies came to be studied, it could t but appear that the royal authority had outown many limitations that primitive usage or tablished law had imposed upon it; and the farther back ese researches extended, the more they seemed, according to me inquirers, to favor a popular theory of constitutional lity. III. Neither of these considerations, which affected ly the patient scholar, struck so powerfully on the public ind as the free spirit engendered by the Reformation, and pecially the Judaizing turn of the early Protestants, those least of the Calvinistic school, which sought for precedents d models in the Old Testament, and delighted to recount ow the tribes of Israel had fallen away from Rehoboam, how e Maccabees had repelled the Syrian, how Eglon had been nitten by the dagger of Ehud. For many years the Protstants of France had made choice of the sword, when their ternative was the stake; and amidst defeat, treachery, and assacre, sustained an unequal combat with extraordinary eroism, and a constancy that only a persuasion of acting ccording to conscience could impart. That persuasion it was e business of their ministers and scholars to encourage by rgument. Each of these three principles of liberty was sserted by means of the press in the short period between 570 and 1580.

From their own and the Jewish.

22. First in order of publication is the Franco-Gallia of 'rancis Hottoman, one of the most eminent lawyers f that age. This is chiefly a collection of passages rom the early French historians, to prove the share f the people in government, and especially their right of lecting the kings of the first two races. No one in such nquiries would now have recourse to the Franco-Gallia, which has certainly the defect of great partiality, and an nwarrantable extension of the author's hypothesis. But t is also true that Hottoman revealed some facts, as to the ncient monarchy of France, which neither the later histo-

Franco-Gallia of Hottoman.

rians, flatterers of the court, nor the lawyers of the parliame of Paris, against whom he is prone to inveigh, had suffered transpire.

23. An anonymous treatise, Vindiciæ contra Tyranno Auctore Stephano Junio Bruto Celta, 1579, com monly ascribed to Hubert Languet, the friend of S Philip Sidney, breathes the stern spirit of Judaical Huguen tism.[1] Kings, that lay waste the church of God, and suppo idolatry; kings, that trample upon their subjects' privilege may be deposed by the states of their kingdom, who indee are bound in duty to do so, though it is not lawful for privat men to take up arms without authority. As kings derive thei pre-eminence from the will of the people, they may be co sidered as feudally vassals of their subjects, so far that the may forfeit their crown by felony against them. Thoug Languet speaks honorably of ancient tyrannicides, it seem as if he could not mean to justify assassination, since he re fuses the right of resistance to private men.

Vindiciæ of Languet.

24. Hottoman and Languet were both Protestants, and the latter especially, may have been greatly influ enced by the perilous fortunes of their religion. A short treatise, however, came out in 1578, written probabl near thirty years before, by Stephen de la Boetie, best know to posterity by the ardent praises of his friend Montaigne and an adherent to the church. This is called Le Contr'Un ou Discours de la Servitude Volontaire. It well deserves it title. Roused by the flagitious tyranny of many contemporary rulers, and few were worse than Henry II., under whose reig it was probably written, La Boetie pours forth the vehemen indignation of a youthful heart, full of the love of virtue and of the brilliant illusions which a superficial knowledge of an cient history creates, against the voluntary abjectness of man kind, who submit as slaves to one no wiser, no braver, no stronger than any of themselves. "He who so plays the master over you has but two eyes, has but two hands, has bu one body, has nothing more than the least among the vast num ber who dwell in our cities; nothing has he better than you save the advantage that you give him, that he may ruin you. Whence has he so many eyes to watch you, but that you

Contr'Un of Boetie.

[1] [Le Clerc has a dissertation printed at the end of the English translation of Bayle's Dictionary, to prove that Du Plessis Mornay wrote the Vindiciæ contra Tyrannos. But the majority have continued to ascribe it to Languet. — 1853.]

give them to him? How has he so many hands to strike you, but that he employs your own? How does he come by the feet which trample on your cities, but by your means? How can he have any power over you, but what you give him? How could he venture to persecute you, if he had not an understanding with yourselves? What harm could he do you, if you were not receivers of the robber that plunders you, accomplices of the murderer who kills you, and traitors to your own selves? You, you sow the fruits of the earth, that he may waste them; you furnish your houses that he may pillage them; you rear your daughters, that they may glut his wantonness, and your sons, that he may lead them at the best to his wars, or that he may send them to execution, or make them the instruments of his concupiscence, the ministers of his revenge. You exhaust your bodies with labor, that he may revel in luxury, or wallow in base and vile pleasures; you weaken yourselves, that he may become more strong, and better able to hold you in check. And yet from so many indignities, that the beasts themselves, could they be conscious of them, would not endure, you may deliver yourselves, if you but make an effort, not to deliver yourselves, but to show the will to do it. Once resolve to be no longer slaves, and you are already free. I do not say that you should assail him, or shake his seat; merely support him no longer, and you will see, that like a great Colossus, whose basis has been removed from beneath him, he will fall by his own weight, and break to pieces."[1]

25. These bursts of a noble patriotism, which no one who is in the least familiar with the history of that period will think inexcusable, are much unlike what we generally expect from the French writers. La Boetie, in fact, is almost a single instance of a thoroughly republican character till nearly the period of the Revolution. Montaigne, the staunchest supporter of church and state, excuses his friend, "the greatest man, in my opinion, of our age," assuring us that he was always a loyal subject, though, if he had been permitted his own choice, "he would rather have been born at Venice than at Sarlat." La Boetie died young, in 1561; and his Discourse was written some years before: he might have lived to perceive how much more easy it is to inveigh against the abuses of government than to bring about any thing better by rebellion.

[1] Le Contr'Un of La Boetie is published at the end of some editions of Montaigne

Buchanan, De Jure Regni.

26. The three great sources of a free spirit in politics, admiration of antiquity, zeal for religion, and persuasion of positive right, which separately had animated La Boetie, Languet, and Hottoman, united their streams to produce, in another country, the treatise of George Buchanan (De Jure Regni apud Scotos), a scholar, a Protestant, and the subject of a very limited monarchy. This is a dialogue elegantly written, and designed, first, to show the origin of royal government from popular election; then, the right of putting tyrannical kings to death, according to Scripture, and the conditional allegiance due to the crown of Scotland, as proved by the coronation oath, which implies that it is received in trust from the people. The following is a specimen of Buchanan's reasoning, which goes very materially farther than Languet had presumed to do: "Is there, then," says one of the interlocutors, "a mutual compact between the king and the people? M. Thus it seems. — B. Does not he who first violates the compact, and does any thing against his own stipulations, break his agreement? M. He does. — B. If, then, the bond which attached the king to the people is broken, all rights he derived from the agreement are forfeited? M. They are forfeited. — B. And he who was mutually bound becomes as free as before the agreement? M. He has the same rights and the same freedom as he had before. — B. But if a king should do things tending to the dissolution of human society, for the preservation of which he has been made, what name should we give him? M. We should call him a tyrant. — B. But a tyrant not only possesses no just authority over his people, but is their enemy? M. He is surely their enemy. — B. Is there not a just cause of war against an enemy who has inflicted heavy and intolerable injuries upon us? M. There is. — B. What is the nature of a war against the enemy of all mankind, that is, against a tyrant? M. None can be more just. — B. Is it not lawful in a war justly commenced, not only for the whole people, but for any single person, to kill an enemy? M. It must be confessed. — B. What, then, shall we say of a tyrant, a public enemy, with whom all good men are in eternal warfare? may not any one of all mankind inflict on him every penalty of war? M. I observe that all nations have been of that opinion; for Theba is extolled for having killed her husband, and Timoleon for his brother's and Cassius for his son's death."[1]

[1] P. 96.

27. We may include among political treatises of this class some published by the English and Scottish exiles during the persecution of their religion by the two Marys. They are, indeed prompted by circumstances, and in some instances have too much of a temporary character to deserve a place in literary history. I will, however, give an account of one, more theoretical than the rest, and characteristic of the bold spirit of these early Protestants, especially as it is almost wholly unknown except by name. This is in the titlepage, "A Short Treatise of Politique Power, and of the true obedience which subjects owe to kings and other civil governors, being an answer to seven questions: '1. Whereof politique power groweth, wherefore it was ordained, and the right use and duty of the same? 2. Whether kings, princes, and other governors have an absolute power and authority over their subjects? 3. Whether kings, princes, and other politique governors be subject to God's laws, or the positive laws of their countries? 4. In what things, and how far, subjects are bound to obey their princes and governors? 5. Whether all the subject's goods be the emperor's or king's own, and that they may lawfully take them for their own? 6. Whether it be lawful to depose an evil governor, and kill a tyrant? 7. What confidence is to be given to princes and potentates?'"

Poynet, on Politique Power.

28. The author of this treatise was John Poynet, or Ponnet, as it is spelled in the last edition, Bishop of Winchester under Edward VI., and who had a considerable share in the Reformation.[1] It was first published in 1558, and reprinted in 1642, "to serve," says Strype, "the turn of those times." "This book," observes truly the same industrious person, "was not over favorable to princes." Poynet died very soon afterwards, so that we cannot determine whether he would have thought it expedient to speak as fiercely under the reign that was to come. The place of publication of the first edition I do not know, but I presume it was at Geneva or Frankfort. It is closely and vigorously written; deserving, in many parts, a high place among the English prose of that age, though not entirely free from the usual fault, — vulgar and ribaldrous invective. He determines all the questions stated in the titlepage on principles

Its liberal theory.

[1] Chalmers; Strype's Memorials.

adverse to royal power; contending, in the sixth chapter, that "the manifold and continual examples that have been, from time to time, of the deposing of kings and killing of tyrants, do most certainly confirm it to be most true, just, and consonant to God's judgment. The history of kings in the Old Testament is full of it; and, as Cardinal Pole truly citeth, England lacketh not the practice and experience of the same; for they deprived King Edward II., because, without law, he killed the subjects, spoiled them of their goods, and wasted the treasures of the realm. And upon what just causes Richard II. was thrust out, and Henry IV. put in his place, I refer it to their own judgment. Denmark also now, in our days, did nobly the like act, when they deprived Christiern the tyrant, and committed him to perpetual prison.

Argues for tyrannicide.

29. "The reasons, arguments, and laws, that serve for the deposing and displacing of an evil governor, will do as much for the proof that it is lawful to kill a tyrant, if they may be indifferently heard. As God hath ordained magistrates to hear and determine private men's matters, and to punish their vices, so also willeth he, that the magistrates' doings be called to account and reckoning, and their vices corrected and punished by the body of the whole congregation or commonwealth: as it is manifest by the memory of the ancient office of the High Constable of England, unto whose authority it pertained, not only to summon the king personally before the parliament, or other courts of judgment, to answer and receive according to justice, but also upon just occasion to commit him unto ward.[1] Kings, princes, and governors have their authority of the people, as all laws, usages, and policies do declare and testify. For in some places and countries they have more and greater authority; in some places less; and in some the people have not given this authority to any other, but retain and exercise it themselves. And is any man so unreasonable to deny that the whole may do as much as they have permitted one member to do, or those that have appointed an office upon trust have not authority upon just occasion (as the abuse of it) to take away what they gave? All laws do agree that men may revoke their proxies and letters of attorney when it pleaseth them, much more when they see their proctors and attorneys abuse it.

[1] It is scarcely necessary to observe, that this is an impudent falsehood.

30. "But now, to prove the latter part of this question affirmatively, that it is lawful to kill a tyrant, there is no man can deny, but that the Ethnics, albeit they had not the right and perfect true knowledge of God, were endued with the knowledge of the law of nature, — for it is no private law to a few, or certain people, but common to all, — not written in books, but grafted in the hearts of men; not made by men, but ordained of God, which we have not learned, received, or read, but have taken, sucked, and drawn it out of nature, whereunto we are not taught, but made; not instructed, but seasoned;[1] and, as St. Paul saith, 'Man's conscience bearing witness of it,'" &c. He proceeds in a strain of some eloquence (and this last passage is not ill translated from Cicero) to extol the ancient tyrannicides, accounting the first nobility to have been "those who had revenged and delivered the oppressed people out of the hands of their governors. Of this kind of nobility was Hercules, Theseus, and such like."[2] It must be owned the worthy bishop is a bold man in assertions of fact. Instances from the Old Testament, of course, follow, wherein Jezebel and Athalia are not forgotten, for the sake of our bloody queen.

The tenets of parties swayed by circumstances.

31. If too much space has been allowed to so obscure a production, it must be excused on account of the illustration it gives to our civil and ecclesiastical history, though of little importance in literature. It is also well to exhibit an additional proof that the tenets of most men, however general and speculative they may appear, are espoused on account of the position of those who hold them, and the momentary consequences that they may produce. In a few years' time, the Church of England, strong in the protection of that royalty which Poynet thus assailed in his own exile, enacted the celebrated homily against rebellion which denounces every pretext of resistance to governors. It rarely happens, that any parties, even the best and purest, will, in the strife to retain or recover their ascendency, weaken themselves by a scrupulous examination of the reasoning or the testimony which is to serve their purpose. Those have lived and read to little advantage who have not discovered this.

32. It might appear that there was some peculiar associa-

[1] Sic · the Latin in Cic. pro Mil. is *imbuti*.

[2] P. 49.

tion between these popular theories of resistance and the Protestant faith. Perhaps, in truth, they had a degree of natural connection; but circumstances, more than general principles, affect the opinions of mankind. The rebellion of the League against Henry III., their determination not to acknowledge Henry IV., reversed the state of parties, and displayed, in an opposite quarter, the republican notions of Languet and Buchanan as fierce and as unlimited as any Protestants had maintained them. Henry of Bourbon could only rely upon his legitimate descent, upon the indefeasible rights of inheritance. If France was to choose for herself, France demanded a Catholic king: all the topics of democracy were thrown into that scale; and, in fact, it is well known that Henry had no prospect whatever of success but by means of a conversion, which, though not bearing much semblance of sincerity, the nation thought fit to accept. But, during that struggle of a few years, we find, among other writings of less moment, one ascribed by some to Rose, Bishop of Senlis, a strenuous partisan of the League, which may perhaps deserve to arrest our attention.[1]

Similar tenets among the Leaguers.

33. This book, De Justa Reipublicæ Christianæ in Reges Potestate, published in 1590, must have been partly written before the death of Henry III. in the preceding year. He begins with the origin of human society, which he treats with some eloquence, and on the principle of an election of magistrates by the community, that they might live peaceably, and in enjoyment of their possessions. The different forms and limitations of government have sprung from the choice of the people, except where they have been imposed by conquest. He exhibits many instances of this variety: but there are two dangers, one of limiting too much the power of kings, and letting the populace change the dynasty at their pleasure; the other, that of ascrib-

Rose on the Authority of Christian States over Kings.

[1] The author calls himself Rossæus, and not, as has been asserted, Bishop of Senlis. But Pits attributes this book to Rainolds (brother of the more celebrated Dr. John Rainolds), who is said to have called himself Rossæus. The Biographie Universelle (art. Rose) says this opinion has not gained ground: but it is certainly favored by M. Barbier, in the Dictionnaire des Anonymes; and some grounds for it are alleged. From internal evidence, it seems rather the work of a Frenchman than a foreigner; but I have not paid much attention to so unimportant a question. Jugler, in his Historia Literaria, c. 9, does not even name Rose. By a passage in Schelhorn, viii. 465, the book seems to have been sometimes ascribed to Genebrard. [Herbert names Rainolds as the author, and says that it is supposed to have been printed at Edinburgh; but I cannot think this at all probable. — 1842.]

ing a sort of divinity to kings, and taking from the nation all the power of restraining them in whatever crimes they may commit. The Scottish Calvinists are an instance of the first error; the modern advocates of the house of Valois, of the other. The servile language of those who preach passive obedience has encouraged not only the worst Roman emperors, but such tyrants as Henry VIII., Edward VI., and Elizabeth of England.

34. The author goes, in the second chapter, more fully into a refutation of this doctrine, as contrary to the practice of ancient nations, who always deposed tyrants; to the principles of Christianity; and to the constitution of European communities, whose kings are admitted under an oath to keep the laws and to reign justly. The subject's oath of allegiance does not bind him, unless the king observe what is stipulated from him; and this right of withdrawing obedience from wicked kings is at the bottom of all the public law of Europe. It is also sanctioned by the church. Still more has the nation a right to impose laws and limitations on kings, who have certainly no superiority to the law, so that they can transgress it at pleasure.

35. In the third chapter, he inquires who is a tyrant; and, after a long discussion, comes to this result, that a tyrant is one who despoils his subjects of their possessions, or offends public decency by immoral life, but, above all, who assails the Christian faith, and uses his authority to render his subjects heretical. All these characters are found in Henry of Valois. He then urges in the two following chapters, that all Protestantism is worse than Paganism, inasmuch as it holds out less inducement to a virtuous life, but that Calvinism is much the worst form of the Protestant heresy. The Huguenots, he proceeds to prove, are neither parts of the French Church nor commonwealth. He infers, in the seventh chapter, that the King of Navarre, being a heretic of this description, is not fit to rule over Christians. The remainder of the book is designed to show, that every king, being schismatic or heretical, may be deposed by the pope, of which he brings many examples; nor has any one deserved this sentence more than Henry of Navarre. It has always been held lawful that an heretical king should be warred upon by his own subjects and by all Christian sovereigns; and he maintains that a real tyrant, who, after being deposed by the wiser part of his

subjects, attempts to preserve his power by force, may be put to death by any private person. He adds that Julian was probably killed by a Christian soldier, and quotes several fathers and ecclesiastical historians who justify and commend the act. He concludes by exhorting the nobility and other orders of France, since Henry is a relapsed heretic, who is not to be believed for any oaths he may make, to rally round their Catholic king, Charles of Bourbon.

Treatise of Boucher in the same spirit.

36. The principles of Rose, if he were truly the author, both as to rebellion and tyrannicide, belonged naturally to those who took up arms against Henry III., and who applauded his assassin. They were adopted, and perhaps extended, by Boucher, a leaguer still more furious, if possible, than Rose himself, in a book published in 1589, De Justa Henrici III. Abdicatione à Francorum Regno. This book is written in the spirit of Languet, asserting the general right of the people to depose tyrants, rather than confining it to the case of heresy. The deposing power of the pope, consequently, does not come much into question. He was answered, as well as other writers of the same tenets, by a Scottish Catholic residing at Paris, William Barclay, father of the more celebrated author of the Argenis, in a treatise De Regno et Regali Potestate adversus Buchananum, Brutum, Boucherum et Reliquos Monarchomachos, 1600. Barclay argues, on the principles current in France, that the king has no superior in temporals; that the people are bound in all cases to obey him; that the laws owe their validity to his will. The settlement of France by the submission of the League on the one hand, and by the Edict of Nantes on the other, naturally put a stop to the discussion of questions which, theoretical and universal as they might seem, would never have been brought forward but through the stimulating influence of immediate circumstances.

Answered by Barclay.

The Jesuits adopt these tenets.

37. But while the war was yet raging, and the fate of the Catholic religion seemed to hang upon its success, many of the Jesuits had been strenuous advocates of the tyrannicidal doctrine; and the strong spirit of party attachment in that order renders it hardly uncandid to reckon among its general tenets whatever was taught by its most conspicuous members. The boldest and most celebrated assertion of these maxims was by Ma-

Mariana, De Rege.

riana, in a book, De Rege et Regis Institutione. The first edition of this remarkable book, and which is of considerable scarcity, was published at Toledo in 1599, dedicated to Philip III., and sanctioned with more than an approbation, with a warm eulogy, by the censor (one of the same order, it may be observed), who by the king's authority had perused the manuscript. It is, however, not such as in an absolute monarchy we should expect to find countenance. Mariana, after inquiring what is the best form of government, and deciding for hereditary monarchy, but only on condition that the prince shall call the best citizens to his councils, and administer all affairs according to the advice of a senate, comes to show the difference between a king and a tyrant. His invectives against the latter prepare us for the sixth chapter, which is entitled, Whether it be lawful to overthrow a tyrant? He begins by a short sketch of the oppression of France under Henry III., which had provoked his assassination. Whether the act of James Clement, "the eternal glory of France, as most reckon him,"[1] were in itself warrantable, he admits to be a controverted question, stating the arguments on both sides, but placing last those in favor of the murder, to which he evidently leans. All philosophers and theologians, he says, agree that an usurper may be put to death by any one. But in the case of a lawful king, governing to the great injury of the commonwealth or of religion (for we ought to endure his vices so long as they do not reach an intolerable height), he thinks that the states of the realm should admonish him, and, on his neglect to reform his life, may take up arms, and put to death a prince whom they have declared to be a public enemy; and any private man may do the same. He concludes, therefore, that it is only a question of fact who is a tyrant; but not one of right, whether a tyrant may be killed. Nor does this maxim give a license to attempts on the lives of good princes; since it can never be applied till wise and experienced men have conspired with the public voice in declaring the prince's tyranny. "It is a wholesome thing," he proceeds, "that sovereigns should be convinced, that if they oppress the state, and become intolerable by their wickedness, their assassination will not only be lawful but glorious to the perpe-

[1] These words, *æternum Galliæ decus* are omitted in the subsequent editions; but, as far as I have compared them, there is very little other alteration: yet the first alone is in request.

trator."[1] This language, whatever indignation it might excite against Mariana and his order, is merely what we have seen in Buchanan.

38. Mariana discusses afterwards the question, whether the power of the king or of the commonwealth be the greater; and after intimating the danger of giving offence, and the difficulty of removing the blemishes which have become inveterate by time (with allusion, doubtless, to the change of the Spanish constitution under Charles and Philip), declares in strong terms for limiting the royal power by laws. In Spain, he asserts, the king cannot impose taxes against the will of the people "He may use his influence, he may offer rewards, sometimes he may threaten, he may solicit with promises and bribes (we will not say whether he may do this rightly); but, if they refuse, he must give way; and it is the same with new laws, which require the sanction of the people. Nor could they preserve their right of deposing and putting to death a tyrant, if they had not retained the superior power to themselves when they delegated a part to the king. It may be the case in some nations, who have no public assemblies of the states, that of necessity the royal prerogative must compel obedience, — a power too great, and approaching to tyranny; but we speak (says Mariana) not of barbarians, but of the monarchy which exists, and ought to exist among us, and of that form of polity which of itself is the best." Whether any nation has a right to surrender its liberties to a king, he declines to inquire; observing only that it would act rashly in making such a surrender, and the king almost as much so in accepting it.

39. In the second book, Mariana treats of the proper education of a prince; and, in the third, on the due administration of his government, inveighing vehemently against excessive taxation, and against debasement of the coin, which he thinks ought to be the last remedy in a public crisis. The whole work, even in its reprehensible exaggerations, breathes a spirit of liberty, and regard to the common good. Nor does Mariana, though a Jesuit, lay any stress on the Papal power to depose princes, which, I believe, he has never once intimated through the whole volume. It is absolutely on political

[1] "Est salutaris cognitio, ut sit principibus persuasum, si rempublicam oppresserint, si vitiis et fœditate intolerandi erunt, ea conditione vivere, ut non jure tantum sed cum laude et gloria perire possint." — p. 77.

principles that he reasons, unless we except that he considers impiety as one of the vices which constitute a tyrant.[1]

Popular theories in England.

40. Neither of the conflicting parties in Great Britain had neglected the weapons of their contemporaries: the English Protestants under Mary, the Scots under her unfortunate namesake, the Jesuits and Catholic priests under Elizabeth, appealed to the natural rights of men, or to those of British citizens. Poynet, Goodman, Knox, are of the first description; Allen and Persons, of the second. Yet this was not done, by the latter at least, so boldly, and so much on broad principles, as it was on the Continent; and Persons, in his celebrated Conference, under the name of Doleman, tried the different and rather inconsistent path of hereditary right. The throne of Elizabeth seemed to stand in need of a strongly monarchical sentiment in the nation. Yet we find, that the popular origin of government, and the necessity of popular consent to its due exercise, are laid down by Hooker in the first and eighth books of the Ecclesiastical Polity, with a boldness not very usual in her reign, and, it must be owned, with a latitude of expression that leads us forward to the most unalloyed democracy. This theory of Hooker, which he endeavored in some places to qualify, with little success or consistency, though it excited, perhaps, not much attention at the time, became the basis of Locke's more celebrated Essay on Government, and, through other stages, of the political creed which actuates at present, as a possessing spirit, the great mass of the civilized world.[2]

Hooker.

Political Memoirs.

41. The bold and sometimes passionate writers, who possibly will be thought to have detained us too long, may be contrasted with another class more cool and prudent, who sought rather to make the most of what they found established in civil polity than to amend or subvert it. The condition of France was such as to force men into think-

[1] Bayle, art. "Mariana," notes G, H, and I, has expatiated upon this notable treatise, which did the Jesuits infinite mischief, though they took pains to disclaim any participation in the doctrine.

[2] Bilson, afterwards Bishop of Winchester, in his Difference between Christian Subjection and Unchristian Rebellion, published in 1585, argues against the Jesuits, that Christian subjects may not bear arms against their princes for any religious quarrel; but admits, "if a prince should go about to subject his kingdom to a foreign realm, or change the form of the commonwealth from impery to tyranny, or neglect the laws established by common consent of prince and people, to execute his own pleasure, in these and other cases which might be named, if the nobles and commons join together to defend their ancient and accustomed liberty, regiment, and laws, they may not well be counted rebels." — p. 520.

ing, where nature had given them the capacity of it. In some of the memoirs of the age, such as those of Castelnau or Tavannes, we find an habitual tendency to reflect, to observe the chain of causes, and to bring history to bear on the passing time. De Comines had set a precedent; and the fashion of studying his writings and those of Machiavel conspired with the force of circumstances to make a thoughtful generation. The political and military discourses of La Noue, being thrown into the form of dissertation, come more closely to our purpose than merely historical works. They are full of good sense, in a high moral tone, without pedantry or pretension; and throw much light on the first period of the civil wars. The earliest edition is referred by the Biographie Universelle to 1587, which I believe should be 1588; but the book seems to have been finished long before.

La Noue.

42. It would carry us beyond the due proportions of this chapter, were I to seek out every book belonging to the class of political philosophy; and we are yet far from its termination. The Politica of Justus Lipsius deserve little regard: they are chiefly a digest of Aristotle, Tacitus, and other ancient writers. Charron has incorporated or abridged the greater part of this work in his own. In one passage, Lipsius gave great and just offence to the best of the Protestant party, whom he was about to desert, by recommending the extirpation of heresy by fire and sword. A political writer of the Jesuit school was Giovanni Botero, whose long treatise, Ragione di Stato, 1589, while deserving of considerable praise for acuteness, has been extolled by Guinguéné, who had never read it, for some merits it is far from possessing.[1] The tolerant spirit, the maxims of good faith, the enlarged philosophy, which, on the credit of a Piedmontese panegyrist, he ascribes to Botero, will be sought in vain. This Jesuit justifies the Massacre of St. Bartholomew, and all other atrocities of that age; observing that the Duke of Alba made a mistake in the public execution of Horn and Egmont, instead of getting rid of them privately.[2] Conservation is with him, as with Machiavel, the great end of government, which is to act so as neither to deserve nor per-

Lipsius.

Botero.

[1] Vol. viii. p. 210.

[2] "Poteva contentarsi di sbrigarsene con dar morte quanto si può segretamente fosse possibile." This is in another treatise by Botero, Relazioni Universali de' Capitani Illustri.

ait opposition. The immediate punishment of the leaders of edition, with as much silence and secrecy as possible, is the est remedy where the sovereign is sufficiently powerful. In ases of danger, it is necessary to conquer by giving way, and o wait for the cooling of men's tempers, and the disunion hat will infallibly impair their force; least of all should he bsent himself, like Henry III., from the scene of tumult, and hus give courage to the seditious, while he diminishes their espect for himself.

43. Botero had thought and observed much: he is, in extent of reading, second only to Bodin, and his views are sometimes luminous. The most remarkable passage that has occurred to me is on the subject of population. No encouragement to matrimony, he observes, will increase the numbers of the people without providing also the means of subsistence, and without due care for breeding children up. If this be wanting, they either die prematurely, or grow up of little service to their country.[1] Why else, he asks, did the human race reach, three thousand years ago, as great a population as exists at present? Cities begin with a few inhabitants, increase to a certain point, but do not pass it, as we see at Rome, at Naples, and in other places. Even if all the monks and nuns were to marry, there would not, he thinks, be more people in the world than there are; two things being requisite for their increase,—generation and education (or what we should perhaps rather call rearing), and if the multiplication of marriages may promote the one, it certainly hinders the other.[2] Botero must here have meant, though he does not fully express it, that the poverty attending upon improvident marriages is the great impediment to rearing their progeny.

His remarks on population.

44. Paolo Paruta, in his Discorsi Politici, Venice, 1599, is perhaps less vigorous and acute than Botero; yet he may be reckoned among judicious writers on general politics. The first book of these discourses relates to Roman, the second chiefly to modern, history. His turn of thinking is

Paruta.

1 "Concio sia cosa chè se bene senza il congiungimento dell' uomo e della donna non si può il genere umano moltiplicarsi, non dimeno la moltitudine di congiungimenti non è sola causa della moltiplicazione; si ricerca oltre di ciò, la cura d'allevarli, e la commodità di sustentarli; senza la quale o muojono innanzi tempo, o riescono inutili, e di poco giovimento alla patria."—Lib. viii. p. 284.

2 Ibid. "Ricercandosi due cose per la propagazione de popoli, la generazione e l'educazione, se bene la moltitudine de matrimonj ajuta forte l'una, impedisce però del sicuro l' altro."

independent, and unprejudiced by the current tide of opinion as when he declares against the conduct of Hannibal in invading Italy. Paruta generally states both sides of a political problem very fairly, as in one of the most remarkable of his discourses, where he puts the famous question on the usefulness of fortified towns. His final conclusion is favorable to them. He was a subject of Venice, and, after holding considerable offices, was one of those historians employed by the Senate, whose writings form the series entitled Istorici Veneziani.

45. John Bodin, author of several other less valuable works, acquired so distinguished a reputation by his Republic, published in French in 1577, and in Latin, with many additions, by himself in 1586,[1] and has in fact so far outstripped the political writers of his own period, that I shall endeavor to do justice to his memory by something like an analysis of this treatise, which is far more known by name than generally read. Many have borne testimony to his extraordinary reach of learning and reflection. "I know of no political writer of the same period," says Stewart, "whose extensive and various and discriminating reading appears to me to have contributed more to facilitate and guide the researches of his successors, or whose references to ancient learning have been more frequently transcribed without acknowledgment."[2]

Bodin.

46. What is the object of political society? Bodin begins by inquiring. The greatest good, he answers, of every citizen, which is that of the whole state. And this he places in the exercise of the virtues proper to man, and in the knowledge of things natural, human,

Analysis of his treatise called The Republic.

[1] This treatise, in its first edition, made so great an impression, that, when Bodin came to England in the service of the Duke of Alençon, he found it explained by lecturers both in London and Cambridge, but not, as has sometimes been said, in the public schools of the university. This put him upon translating it into Latin himself, to render its fame more European. See Bayle, who has a good article on Bodin. I am much inclined to believe, that the perusal of Bodin had a great effect in England. He is not perhaps very often quoted, and yet he is named with honor by the chief writers of the next age; but he furnished a store, both of arguments and of examples, which were not lost on the thoughtful minds of our countrymen.

Grotius, who is not very favorable to Bodin, though of necessity he often quotes the Republic, imputes to him an incorrectness as to facts, which in some cases raises a suspicion of ill-faith. Epist. ccclii. It would require a more close study of Bodin than I have made, to judge of the weight of this charge.

[2] Dissertation on Progress of Philosophy, p. 40. Stewart, however, thinks Bodin become so obscure that he makes an apology for the space he has allotted to the Republic, though not exceeding four pages. He was better known in the seventeenth century than at present.

nd divine. But as all have not agreed as to the chief good f a single man, nor whether the good of individuals be also hat of the state, this has caused a variety of laws and customs according to the humors and passions of rulers. This rst chapter is in a more metaphysical tone than we usually nd in Bodin. He proceeds in the next to the rights of amilies (*jus familiare*), and to the distinction between a amily and a commonwealth. A family is the right government of many persons under one head, as a commonwealth is hat of many families.[1] Patriarchal authority he aises high, both marital and paternal; on each subject pouring out a vast stream of knowledge: nothing that sacred and profane history, the accounts of travellers, or the Roman lawyers could supply, ever escapes the omprehensive researches of Bodin.[2] He intimates his opinion in favor of the right of repudiation, one of the many roofs that he paid more regard to the Jewish than the Christian law,[3] and vindicates the full extent of the paternal ower in the Roman republic, deducing the decline of the mpire from its relaxation.

Authority of heads of families.

47. The patriarchal government includes the relation of master to servant, and leads to the question whether lavery should be admitted into a well-constituted commonwealth. Bodin, discussing this with many arguments n both sides, seems to think that the Jewish law, with its imitations as to time of servitude, ought to prevail; since the

Domestic servitude.

[1] "Familia est plurium sub unius ac jusdem patris familias imperium subditoum, earumque rerum quæ ipsius propria unt, recta moderatio." He has an odd heory, that a family must consist of five persons, in which he seems to have been nfluenced by some notions of the jurists, hat three families may constitute a republic, and that fifteen persons are also the minimum of a community.

[2] Cap. iii. 34. Bodin here protests against the stipulation sometimes made before marriage, that the wife shall not be in the power of the husband; "agreements so contrary to divine and human laws, that they cannot be endured, nor are they to be observed even when ratified by oath, since no oath in such circumstances can be binding."

[3] It has often been surmised, that Bodin, though not a Jew by nativity, was such by conviction. This seems to be confirmed by his Republic, wherein he quotes the Old Testament continually and with great deference, but seldom or never the New. Several passages might be alleged in proof, but I have not noted them all down. In one place, lib. i. c. 6. he says, "Paulus, Christianorum sæculi sui facile princeps," which is at least a singular mode of expression. In another, he states the test of true religion so as to exclude all but the Mosaic. An unpublished work of Bodin, called the Heptaplomeres, is said to exist in many manuscripts, both in France and Germany; in which, after debating different religions in a series of dialogues, he gives the advantage to Deism or Judaism, — for those who have seen it seem not to have determined which. No one has thought it worth while to print this production. Jugler, Hist. Literaria, p. 1740 · Biogr. Univ.; Niceron, xvii 264.

A posthumous work of Bodin, published in 1596, Universæ Naturæ Theatrum, has been called by some a disguised Pantheism. This did not appear, from what I have read of it, to be the case.

divine rules were not laid down for the boundaries of Pale tine, but being so wise, so salutary, and of such authorit ought to be preferred above the constitutions of men. Sla very, therefore, is not to be permanently established; bu where it already exists, it will be expedient that emancipa tion should be gradual.[1]

Origin of common-wealths.

48. These last are the rights of persons in a state of natur to be regulated but not created by the law. "Be fore there was either city or citizen, or any form o a commonwealth amongst men (I make use in thi place of Knolles's very good translation), every master of family was master in his own house, having power of life an death over his wife and children: but after that force, vio lence, ambition, covetousness, and desire of revenge, had arme one against another, the issues of wars and combats, givin victory unto the one side, made the other to become unto then slaves; and, amongst them that overcame, he that was chose chief and captain, under whose conduct and leading they ha obtained the victory, kept them also in his power and com mand as his faithful and obedient servants, and the other a his slaves. Then that full and entire liberty, by nature give to every man to live as himself best pleased, was altogethe taken from the vanquished, and in the vanquishers themselve in some measure also diminished in regard of the conqueror for that now it concerned every man in private to yield hi obedience unto his chief sovereign; and he that would no abate any thing of his liberty, to live under the laws and com mandments of another, lost all. So the words of lord and servant, of prince and subject, before unknown to the world were first brought into use. Yea, reason, and the very ligh of nature, leadeth us to believe very force and violence to have given cause and beginning unto commonwealths."[2]

Privileges of citizens.

49. Thus, therefore, the patriarchal simplicity of govern ment was overthrown by conquest, of which Nimrod seems to have been the earliest instance; and now fathers of families, once sovereign, are become citizens. A citizen is a free man under the supreme government of an other.[3] Those who enjoy more privileges than others are not citizens more than they. "It is the acknowledgment of the

[1] c. 5. [2] c. 6.

[3] "Est civis nihil aliud quam liber homo, qui summa alterius potestate obligatur."

sovereign by his free subject, and the protection of the sovereign towards him, that makes the citizen." This is one of the fundamental principles, it may be observed by us in passing, which distinguish a monarchical from a republican spirit in constitutional jurisprudence. Wherever mere subjection, or even mere nativity, is held to give a claim to citizenship, there is an abandonment of the republican principle. This, always reposing on a real or imaginary contract, distinguishes the nation, the successors of the first community, from alien settlers, and, above all, from those who are evidently of a different race. Length of time must, of course, ingraft many of foreign origin upon the native tree; but to throw open civil privileges at random to new-comers, is to convert a people into a casual aggregation of men. In a monarchy, the hereditary principle maintains an unity of the commonwealth; which may better permit, though not entirely without danger, an equality of privileges among all its subjects. Thus under Caracalla, but in a period in which we should not look for good precedents, the great name, as once it had been, of Roman citizen was extended, east and west, to all the provinces of the empire.

Nature of sovereign power.

50. Bodin comes next to the relation between patron and client, and to those alliances among states which bear an analogy to it. But he is careful to distinguish patronage or protection from vassalage. Even in unequal alliances, the inferior is still sovereign; and, if this be not reserved, the alliance must become subjection.[1] Sovereignty, of which he treats in the following chapter, he defines a supreme and perpetual power, absolute and subject to no law.[2] A limited prince, except so far as the limitation is confined to the laws of nature, is not sovereign. A sovereign cannot bind his successor, nor can he be bound by his own laws, unless confirmed by oath; for we must not confound the laws and contracts of princes: the former depend upon his will, but the latter oblige his conscience. It is convenient to call parliaments or meetings of states-general for advice and consent; but the king is not bound by them: the contrary notion has done much harm. Even in England, where laws made in parliament cannot be repealed without its consent, the king may reject any new one without regard to the desire

[1] c. 7.
[2] "Majestas est summa in cives ac subditos legibusque soluta potestas."

of the nation.[1] And, though no taxes are imposed in England without consent of parliament, this is the case also in other countries, if necessity does not prevent the meeting of the states. He concludes that the English parliament may have a certain authority, but that the sovereignty and legislative power are solely in the king. Whoever legislates is sovereign, for this power includes all other. Whether a vassal or tributary prince is to be called sovereign, is a question that leads Bodin into a great quantity of feudal law and history he determines it according to his own theory.[2]

Forms of government.

51. The second book of the Republic treats of the different species of civil government. These, according to Bodin, are but three; no mixed form being possible, since sovereignty or the legislative power is indivisible. A democracy he defines to be a government where the majority of the citizens possess the sovereignty. Rome he holds to have been a democratic republic, in which, however, he is not exactly right; and he is certainly mistaken in his general theory, by arguing as if the separate definition of each of the three forms must be applicable after their combination.[3]

Despotism and monarchy.

In his chapter on despotic monarchy, he again denies that governments were founded on original contract. The power of one man, in the origin of political society, was absolute; and Aristotle was wrong in supposing a fabulous golden age, in which kings were chosen by suffrage.[4] Despotism is distinguished from monarchy by the subjects being truly slaves, without a right over their properties; but, as the despot may use them well, even this is not necessarily a tyranny.[5] Monarchy, on the other hand, is the rule of one man according to the law of nature, who maintains the liberties and properties of others as much as his own.[6] As this definition does not imply any other restraint than the will of the prince imposes on him-

[1] "Hoc tamen singulare videri possit, quod, quæ leges populi rogatione ac principis jussu feruntur, non aliter quam populi comitiis abrogari possunt. Id enim Dellus Anglorum in Gallia legatus mihi confirmavit; idem tamen confitetur legem probari aut respui consuevisse contra populi voluntatem utcunque principi placuerit."

[2] c. 9 and 10.

[3] lib. ii. c. 1.

[4] In the beginning of states, "quo societas hominum coalescere cœpit, ac reipublicæ forma quædam constitui, unius imperio ac dominatu omnia tenebantur. Fallit enim Aristoteles, qui aureum illud genus hominum fabulis poeticis quam re-ipsa illustrius, reges heroas suffragio creasse prodidit; cum omnibus persuasum sit ac perspicuum monarchiam omnium primam in Assyria fuisse constitutam Nimrodo principe," &c.

[5] c. 2.

[6] c. 3.

self, Bodin labors under the same difficulty as Montesquieu. Every English reader of the Esprit des Loix has been struck by the want of a precise distinction between despotism and monarchy. Tyranny differs, Bodin says, from despotism, merely by the personal character of the prince; but severity towards a seditious populace is not tyranny: and here he censures the lax government of Henry II. Tyrannicide he justifies in respect of an usurper who has no title except force, but not as to lawful princes, or such as have become so by prescription.[1]

Aristocracy.

52. An aristocracy he conceives always to exist where a smaller body of the citizens governs the greater.[2] This definition, which has been adopted by some late writers, appears to lead to consequences hardly compatible with the common use of language. The electors of the House of Commons in England are not a majority of the people. Are they, therefore, an aristocratical body? The same is still more strongly the case in France, and in most representative governments of Europe. We might better say, that the distinguishing characteristic of an aristocracy is the enjoyment of privileges which are not communicable to other citizens simply by any thing they can themselves do to obtain them. Thus no government would be properly aristocratical where a pecuniary qualification is alone sufficient to confer political power; nor did the ancients ever use the word in such a sense.

Senates and councils of state.

53. Sovereignty resides in the supreme legislative authority; but this requires the aid of other inferior and delegated ministers, to the consideration of which the third book of Bodin is directed. A senate he defines, "a lawful assembly of counsellors of state, to give advice to them who have the sovereignty in every commonwealth; we say, to give advice, that we may not ascribe any power of command to such a senate." A council is necessary in a monarchy; for much knowledge is generally mischievous in a king. It is rarely united with a good disposition and with a moral discipline of mind. None of the emperors were so illiterate as Trajan, none more learned than Nero. The counsellors should not be too numerous; and he advises that they should retain their offices for life. It would be dan-

[1] c. 4.

[2] "Ego statum semper aristocraticum esse judico, si minor pars civium cæteris imperat."—c. 1.

gerous as well as ridiculous to choose young men for such a post, even if they could have wisdom and experience; since neither older persons, nor those of their own age, would place confidence in them. He then expatiates, in his usual manner, upon all the councils that have existed in ancient or modern states.[1]

Duties of magistrates.

54. A magistrate is an officer of the sovereign, possessing public authority.[2] Bodin censures the usual definitions of magistracy, distinguishing from magistrates both those officers who possess no right of command, and such commissioners as have only a temporary delegation. In treating of the duty of magistrates towards the sovereign, he praises the rule of the law of France, that the judge is not to regard private letters of the king against the justice of a civil suit.[3] But after stating the doubt, whether this applies to matters affecting the public, he concludes that the judge must obey any direction he receives, unless contrary to the law of nature, in which case he is bound not to forfeit his integrity. It is, however, better, as far as we can, to obey all the commands of the sovereign than to set a bad example of resistance to the people. This has probably a regard to the frequent opposition of the parliament of Paris to what it deemed the unjust or illegal ordinances of the court. Several questions, discussed in these chapters on magistracy, are rather subtle and verbal; and, in general, the argumentative part of Bodin is almost drowned in his erudition.

Corporations.

55. A state cannot subsist without colleges and corporations; for mutual affection and friendship is the necessary bond of human life. It is true that mischiefs have sprung from these institutions, and they are to be regulated by good laws; but as a family is a community natural, so a college is a community civil, and a commonwealth is but a community governed by a sovereign power; and thus the word "community" is common unto all three.[4] In this chapter, we have a full discussion of the subject; and, in adverting to the Spanish Cortes and English House of Commons as a sort of colleges in the state, he praises them as useful institutions, observing, with somewhat more boldness than is ordinary to him, that, in several provinces in France, there

[1] c. 1. [2] c. 3. [3] c. 4. [4] c. 7.

had been assemblies of the states, which had been abolished by those who feared to see their own crimes and peculations brought to light.

56. In the last chapter of the third book, on the degrees and orders of citizens, Bodin seems to think that slaves, being subjects, ought to be reckoned parts of the state.[1] This is, as has been intimated, in conformity with his monarchical notions. He then enters upon the different modes of acquiring nobility, and inveighs against making wealth a passport to it; discussing also the derogation to nobility by plebeian occupation. The division into three orders is useful in every form of government.

Slaves, part of the state.

57. Perhaps the best chapter in the Republic of Bodin is the first in the fourth book, on the rise, progress, and stationary condition, revolutions, decline, and fall of states. A commonwealth is said to be changed when its form of polity is altered; for its identity is not to be determined by the long standing of the city walls; but when popular government becomes monarchy, or aristocracy is turned to democracy, the commonwealth is at an end. He thus uses the word *respublica* in the sense of polity or constitution, which is not, perhaps, strictly correct, though sanctioned by some degree of usage, and leaves his proposition a tautological truism. The extinction of states may be natural or violent, but in one way or the other it must happen; since there is a determinate period to all things, and a natural season in which it seems desirable that they should come to an end. The best revolution is that which takes place by a voluntary cession of power.

Rise and fall of states.

58. As the forms of government are three, it follows that the possible revolutions from one to another are six. For anarchy is the extinction of a government, not a revolution in it. He proceeds to develop the causes of revolutions with great extent of historical learning and with judgment, if not with so much acuteness or so much vigor of style as Machiavel. Great misfortunes in war, he observes, have a tendency to change popular rule to aristocracy; and success has an opposite effect: the same seems applicable to all public adversity and prosperity. Democracy, however,

Causes of revolutions.

1 "Si mihi tabellæ ac jura suffragiorum in hac disputatione tribuantur, servos æque ac liberos homines civitate donari cupiam." By this he may only mean that he would desire to emancipate them.

more commonly ends in monarchy, as monarchy does in democracy, especially when it has become tyrannical; and such changes are usually accompanied by civil war or tumult. Nor can aristocracy, he thinks, be changed into democracy without violence, though the converse revolution sometimes happens quietly, as when the laboring classes and traders give up public affairs to look after their own: in this manner, Venice, Lucca, Ragusa, and other cities, have become aristocracies. The great danger for an aristocracy is, that some ambitious person, either of their own body or of the people, may arm the latter against them: and this is most likely to occur when honors and magistracy are conferred on unworthy men, which affords the best topic to demagogues, especially where the plebeians are wholly excluded; which, though always grievous to them, is yet tolerable so long as power is intrusted to deserving persons; but, when bad men are promoted, it becomes easy to excite the minds of the people against the nobility, above all, if there are already factions among the latter, a condition dangerous to all states, but mostly to an aristocracy. Revolutions are more frequent in small states, because a small number of citizens is easily split into parties: hence we shall find in one age more revolutions among the cities of Greece or Italy than have taken place during many in the kingdoms of France or Spain. He thinks the ostracism of dangerous citizens itself dangerous, and recommends rather to put them to death, or to render them friends. Monarchy, he observes, has this peculiar to it, that, if the king be a prisoner, the constitution is not lost; whereas, if the seat of government in a republic be taken, it is at an end, the subordinate cities never making resistance. It is evident that this can only be applicable to the case, hitherto the more common one, of a republic, in which the capital city entirely predominates. "There is no kingdom which shall not, in continuance of time, be changed, and at length also be overthrown. But it is best for them who least feel their changes by little and little made, whether from evil to good, or from good to evil."

Astrological fancies of Bodin.

59. If this is the best, the next is the worst chapter in Bodin. It professes to inquire, whether the revolutions of states can be foreseen. Here he considers whether the stars have such an influence on human affairs that political changes can be foretold by their means, and declares entirely against it, with such expressions as would

seem to indicate his disbelief in astrology. If it were true, he says, that the conditions of commonwealths depended on the heavenly bodies, there could be yet no certain prediction of them; since the astrologers lay down their observations with such inconsistency, that one will place the same star in direct course at the moment that another makes it retrograde. It is obvious that any one who could employ this argument must have perceived, that it destroys the whole science of astrology. But, after giving instances of the blunders and contradictions of these pretended philosophers, he so far gives way as to admit, that, if all the events from the beginning of the world could be duly compared with the planetary motions, some inferences might be deduced from them; and thus, giving up his better reason to the prejudices of his age, he acknowledges astrology as a theoretical truth. The hypothesis of Copernicus he mentions as too absurd to deserve refutation; since, being contrary to the tenets of all theologians and philosophers and to common sense, it subverts the foundations of every science. We now plunge deeper into nonsense; Bodin proceeding to a long arithmetical disquisition founded on a passage in Plato, ascribing the fall of states to want of proportion.[1]

Danger of sudden changes

60. The next chapter, on the danger of sudden revolutions in the entire government, asserts that even the most determined astrologers agree in denying that a wise man is subjugated by the starry influences, though they may govern those who are led by passion like wild beasts. Therefore a wise ruler may foresee revolutions and provide remedies. It is doubtful whether an established law ought to be changed, though not good in itself, lest it should bring others into contempt, especially such as affect the form of polity. These, if possible, should be held immutable; yet it is to be remembered that laws are only made for the sake of the community, and public safety is the supreme law of laws. There is, therefore, no law so sacred that it may not be changed through necessity. But, as a general rule, whatever change is to be made should be effected gradually.[2]

Judicial power of the sovereign.

61. It is a disputed question whether magistrates should be temporary or perpetual. Bodin thinks it essential that the council of state should be permanent, but high civil commands ought to be temporary.[3] It

[1] c. 2. [2] c. 3. [3] c. 4.

is in general important that magistrates shall accord i their opinions; yet there are circumstances in which thei emulation or jealousy may be beneficial to a state.[1] Whethe the sovereign ought to exercise judicial functions may seem he says, no difficult question to those who are agreed tha kings were established for the sake of doing justice. This however, is not his theory of the origin of government; an after giving all the reasons that can be urged in favor of a monarch-judge, including as usual all historical precedents, h decides that it is inexpedient for the ruler to pronounce th law himself. His reasons are sufficiently bold, and grounde on an intimate knowledge of the vices of courts, which he doe not hesitate to pour out.[2]

Toleration of religions.

62. In treating of the part to be taken by the prince, or b a good citizen, in civil factions, after a long detai from history of conspiracies and seditions, he come to disputes about religion, and contends against th permission of reasonings on matters of faith. What can b more impious, he says, than to suffer the eternal laws of God which ought to be implanted in men's minds with the utmos certainty, to be called in question by probable reasonings? For there is nothing so demonstrable which men will no undermine by argument. But the principles of religion d not depend on demonstrations and arguments, but on faith alone; and whoever attempts to prove them by a train of reasoning, tends to subvert the foundations of the whole fabric. Bodin in this sophistry was undoubtedly insincere. He goes on, however, having purposely sacrificed this cock to Æsculapius, to contend, that, if several religions exist in a state, the prince should avoid violence and persecution; the natural tendency of man being to give his assent voluntarily, but never by force.[3]

Influence of climate on government.

63. The first chapter of the fifth book, on the adaptation of government to the varieties of race and climate, has excited more attention than most others, from its being supposed to have given rise to a theory of Montesquieu. In fact, however, the general principle is more ancient; but no one had developed it so fully as Bodin. Of this he seems to be aware. No one, he says, has hitherto treated on this important subject, which should always be kept in mind, lest we establish institutions not suitable to the

[1] c. 5. [2] c. 6 [3] c. 7.

people, forgetting that the laws of nature will not bend to the fancy of man. He then investigates the peculiar characteristics of the northern, middle, and southern nations, as to physical and moral qualities. Some positions he has laid down erroneously; but, on the whole, he shows a penetrating judgment and comprehensive generalization of views. He concludes that bodily strength prevails towards the poles, mental power towards the tropics; and that the nations lying between partake in a mixed ratio of both. This is not very just; but he argues from the great armies that have come from the north, while arts and sciences have been derived from the south. There is certainly a considerable resemblance to Montesquieu in this chapter; and like him, with better excuse, Bodin accumulates inaccurate stories. Force prevails most with northern nations, reason with the inhabitants of a temperate or middle climate, superstition with those of the south: thus astrology, magic, and all mysterious sciences, have come from the Chaldeans and Egyptians. Mechanical arts and inventions, on the other hand, flourish best in northern countries; and the natives of the south hardly know how to imitate them, their genius being wholly speculative, nor have they so much industry, quickness in perceiving what is to be done, or worldly prudence. The stars appear to exert some influence over national peculiarities; but, even in the same latitudes, great variety of character is found, which arises from a mountainous or level soil, and from other physical circumstances. We learn by experience that the inhabitants of hilly countries and the northern nations generally love freedom, but, having less intellect than strength, submit readily to the wisest among them. Even winds are not without some effect on national character. But the barrenness or fertility of the soil is more important; the latter producing indolence and effeminacy, while one effect of a barren soil is to drive the people into cities, and to the exercise of handicrafts for the sake of commerce, as we see at Athens and Nuremberg, the former of which may be contrasted with Bœotia.

64. Bodin concludes, after a profusion of evidence drawn from the whole world, that it is necessary not only to consider the general character of the climate as affecting an entire region, but even the peculiarities of single districts, and to inquire what effects may be wrought on the dispositions of the inhabitants by the air, the water, the mountains and valleys,

or prevalent winds, as well as those which depend on their religion, their customs, their education, their form of government: for whoever should conclude alike as to all who live in the same climate would be frequently deceived; since, in the same parallel of latitude, we may find remarkable differences even of countenance and complexion. This chapter abounds with proofs of the comprehension as well as patient research which distinguishes Bodin from every political writer who had preceded him.

Means of obviating inequality.

65. In the second chapter, which inquires how we may avoid the revolutions which an excessive inequality of possessions tends to produce, he inveighs against a partition of property, as inconsistent with civil society, and against an abolition of debts, because there can be no justice where contracts are not held inviolable; and observes that it is absurd to expect a division of all possessions to bring about tranquillity. He objects also to any endeavor to limit the number of the citizens, except by colonization. In deference to the authority of the Mosaic law, he is friendly to a limited right of primogeniture, but disapproves the power of testamentary dispositions, as tending to inequality, and the admission of women to equal shares in the inheritance, lest the same consequence should come through marriage. Usury he would absolutely abolish, to save the poorer classes from ruin.

Confiscations: rewards.

66. Whether the property of condemned persons shall be confiscated is a problem, as to which, having given the arguments on both sides, he inclines to a middle course, that the criminal's own acquisitions should be forfeited, but what has descended from his ancestors should pass to his posterity. He speaks with great freedom against unjust prosecutions, and points out the dangers of the law of forfeiture.[1] In the next, being the fourth chapter of this book, he treats of rewards and punishments. All states depend on the due distribution of these; but, while many books are full of the latter, few have discussed the former, to which he here confines himself. Triumphs, statues, public thanks, offices of trust and command, are the most honorable; exemptions from service or tribute, privileges, and the like, the most beneficial. In a popular government, the former are more readily conceded than the latter; in a mo-

[1] c. 3.

narchy, the reverse. The Roman triumph gave a splendor to the republic itself. In modern times, the sale of nobility and of public offices renders them no longer so honorable as they should be. He is here again very free-spoken as to the conduct of the French, and of other governments.[1]

67. The advantage of warlike habits to a nation, and the utility of fortresses, are then investigated. Some have objected to the latter as injurious to the courage of the people, and of little service against an invader; and also as furnishing opportunities to tyrants and usurpers, or occasionally to rebels. Bodin, however, inclines in their favor, especially as to those on the frontier, which may be granted as feudal benefices, but not in inheritance. The question of cultivating a military spirit in the people depends on the form of polity: in popular states it is necessary; in an aristocracy, unsafe. In monarchies, the position of the state with respect to its neighbors is to be considered. The capital city ought to be strong in a republic, because its occupation is apt to carry with it an entire change in the commonwealth. But a citadel is dangerous in such a state. It is better not to suffer castles, or strongholds of private men, as is the policy of England; unless when the custom is so established, that they cannot be dismantled without danger to the state.[2]

Fortresses.

68. Treaties of peace and alliance come next under review. He points out with his usual prolixity the difference between equal and unequal compacts of this kind. Bodin contends strongly for the rigorous maintenance of good faith, and reprobates the civilians and canonists who induced the Council of Constance to break their promise towards John Huss. No one yet, he exclaims, has been so consummately impudent as to assert the right of violating a fair promise: but one alleges the deceit of the enemy; another, his own mistake; a third, the change of circumstances, which has rendered it impossible to keep his word; a fourth, the ruin of the state which it would entail. But no excuse, according to Bodin, can be sufficient, save the unlawfulness of the promise, or the impossibility of fulfilling it. The most difficult terms to keep are between princes and their subjects, which generally require the guarantee of other states. Faith, however, ought to be kept in such cases; and

Necessity of good faith.

[1] c 4

[2] c. 5.

he censures, though under an erroneous impression of the fact, as a breach of engagement, the execution of the Duke of York in the reign of Henry VI.; adding, that he prefers to select foreign instances rather than those at home, which he would wish to be buried in everlasting oblivion. In this he probably alludes to the day of St. Bartholomew.[1]

69. The first chapter of the sixth book relates to a periodical census of property, which he recommends as too much neglected. The Roman censorship of manners he extols, and thinks it peculiarly required, when all domestic coercion is come to an end. But he would give no coercive jurisdiction to his censors, and plainly intimates his dislike to a similar authority in the church.[2] A more important disquisition follows on public revenues. These may be derived from seven sources: namely, national domains; confiscation of enemy's property; gifts of friendly powers; tributes from dependent allies; foreign trade carried on by the state; tolls and customs on exports and imports; or, lastly, taxes directly levied on the people. The first of these is the most secure and honorable; and here we have abundance of ancient and modern learning, while of course the French principle of inalienability is brought forward. The second source of revenue is justified by the rights of war, and practice of nations; the third has sometimes occurred; and the fourth is very frequent. It is dishonorable for a prince to be a merchant, and thus gain a revenue in the fifth mode, yet the kings of Portugal do not disdain this; and the mischievous usage of selling offices in some other countries seems to fall under this head. The different taxes on merchandise, or, in our language, of customs and excise, come in the sixth place. Here Bodin advises to lower the import duties on articles with which the people cannot well dispense, but to lay them heavily on manufactured goods, that they may learn to practise these arts themselves.

Census of property.

Public revenues.

70. The last species of revenue, obtained from direct taxation, is never to be chosen but from necessity; and, as taxes are apt to be kept up when the necessity is passed, it is better that the king should borrow money of subjects than impose taxes upon them. He then enters on

Taxation.

[1] c. 6. "Externa libentius quam domestica recordor, quæ utinam sempiterna oblivione sepulta jacerent."

[2] Lib. vi. c. 1.

the history of taxation in different countries, remarking it as peculiar to France, that the burthen is thrown on the people to the ease of the nobles and clergy, which is the case nowhere except with the French, among whom, as Cæsar truly wrote, nothing is more despised than the common people. Taxes on luxuries, which serve only to corrupt men, are the best of all; those also are good which are imposed on proceedings at law, so as to restrain unnecessary litigation. Borrowing at interest, or by way of annuity, as they do at Venice, is ruinous. It seems, therefore, that Bodin recommends loans without interest, which must be compulsory. In the remainder of this chapter, he treats of the best mode of expending the public revenue, and advises that royal grants should be closely examined, and, if excessive, be rescinded, at least after the death of the reigning king.[1]

Adulteration of coin.

71. Every adulteration of coin, to which Bodin proceeds, and every change in its value, is dangerous, as it affects the certainty of contracts, and renders every man's property insecure. The different modes of alloying coin are then explained according to practical metallurgy; and, assuming the constant ratio of gold to silver as twelve to one, he advises that coins of both metals should be of the same weight. The alloy should not be above one in twenty-four; and the same standard should be used for plate. Many curious facts in monetary history will be found collected in this chapter.[2]

Superiority of monarchy.

72. Bodin next states fully, and with apparent fairness, the advantages and disadvantages both of democracy and aristocracy, and, admitting that some evils belong to monarchy, contends that they are all much less than in the two other forms. It must be remembered, that he does not acknowledge the possibility of a mixed government; a singular error, which, of course, vitiates his reasonings in this chapter. But it contains many excellent observations on democratical violence and ignorance, which history had led him duly to appreciate.[3] The best form of polity he holds to be a monarchy by agnatic succession, such as, in contradiction to Hottoman, he maintains to have been always established in France, pointing out also the mischiefs that have ensued in other countries for want of a Salic law.[4]

1 c. 2. 2 c. 8. 3 c. 4. 4 c. 5.

73. In the concluding chapter of the work, Bodin, with too much parade of mathematical language, descants on what he calls arithmetical, geometrical, and harmonic proportions as applied to political regimen. As the substance of all this appears only to be, that laws ought sometimes to be made according to the circumstances and conditions of different ranks in society, sometimes to be absolutely equal, it will probably be thought by most rather incumbered by this philosophy, which, however, he borrowed from the ancients, and found conformable to the spirit of learned men in his own time. Several interesting questions in the theory of jurisprudence are incidentally discussed in this chapter, such as that of the due limits of judicial discretion.

Conclusion of the work.

74. It must appear, even from this imperfect analysis, in which much has been curtailed of its fair proportion, and many both curious and judicious observations omitted, that Bodin possessed a highly philosophical mind, united with the most ample stores of history and jurisprudence. No former writer on political philosophy had been either so comprehensive in his scheme or so copious in his knowledge; none, perhaps, more original, more independent and fearless in his inquiries. Two names alone, indeed, could be compared with his, — Aristotle and Machiavel. Without, however, pretending that Bodin was equal to the former in acuteness and sagacity, we may say, that the experience of two thousand years, and the maxims of reason and justice, suggested or corrected by the gospel and its ministers, by the philosophers of Greece and Rome, and by the civil law, gave him advantages, of which his judgment and industry fully enabled him to avail himself. Machiavel, again, has discussed so few, comparatively, of the important questions in political theory, and has seen many things so partially, according to the narrow experience of Italian republics, that, with all his superiority in genius, and still more in effective eloquence, we can hardly say that his Discourses on Livy are a more useful study than the Republic of Bodin.

Bodin compared with Aristotle and Machiavel,

75. It has been often alleged, as we have mentioned above, that Montesquieu owed something, and especially his theory of the influence of climate, to Bodin. But, though he had unquestionably read the Republic with that advantage which the most fertile minds derive from

And with Montesquieu.

others, this ought not to detract in our eyes from his real originality. The Republic and the Spirit of Laws bear, however, a more close comparison than any other political systems of celebrity. Bodin and Montesquieu are, in this province of political theory, the most philosophical of those who have read so deeply, the most learned of those who have thought so much. Both acute, ingenious, little respecting authority in matters of opinion, but deferring to it in established power, and hence apt to praise the fountain of waters whose bitterness they exposed: both in advance of their age; but one so much that his genius neither kindled a fire in the public mind, nor gained its own due praise; the other more fortunate in being the immediate herald of a generation which he stimulated, and which repaid him by its admiration: both conversant with ancient and mediæval history, and with the Roman as well as national law: both just, benevolent, and sensible of the great object of civil society, but displaying this with some variation according to their times: both sometimes seduced by false analogies, but the one rather through respect to an erroneous philosophy, the other through personal thirst of praise and affectation of originality: both aware that the basis of the philosophy of man is to be laid in the records of his past existence; but the one prone to accumulate historical examples without sufficient discrimination, and to overwhelm, instead of convincing, the reader by their redundancy; the other aiming at an induction from select experience, but hence appearing sometimes to reason generally from particular premises, or dazzling the student by a proof that does not satisfy his reason.[1]

[1] This account of Bodin's Republic will be found too long by many readers; and I ought, perhaps, to apologize for it on the score that M. Lerminier, in his brilliant and agreeable Introduction à l' Historie Générale du Droit (Paris, 1829), has preoccupied the same ground. This, however, had escaped my recollection (though I was acquainted with the work of M. L.) when I made my own analysis, which has not been borrowed in a single line from his. The labors of M. Lerminier are not so commonly known in England as to render it unnecessary to do justice to a great French writer of the sixteenth century.

As I have mentioned M. Lerminier, I would ask whether the following is a fair translation of the Latin of Bodin: "Eo nos ipsa ratio deducit, imperia scilicet ac respublicas vi primum coaluisse, *etiam si ab historia deseramur;* quamquam pleni sunt libri, plenæ leges, plena antiquitas. En établissant la théorie de l'origine des sociétés, il déclare qu'il y persiste, *quand même les faits iraient à l'encontre.*"—Hist. du Droit, pp. 62 and 67.

SECT. III.—ON JURISPRUDENCE.

Golden Age of Jurisprudence — Cujacius — Other Civilians — Anti-Tribonianus of Hottoman — Law of Nations — Franciscus a Victoria — Balthazar Ayala — Albericus Gentilis.

76. THE latter part of the sixteenth century, denominated by Andrès the golden age of jurisprudence, produced the men who completed what Alciat and Augustinus had begun in the preceding generation, by elucidating, and reducing to order, the dark chaos which the Roman law, enveloped in its own obscurities and those of its earlier commentators, had presented to the student. The most distinguished of these, Cujacius, became professor at Bourges, the chief scene of his renown, and the principal seminary of the Roman law in France, about the year 1555. His works, of which many had been separately published, were collected in 1577; and they make an epoch in the annals of jurisprudence. This greatest of all civil lawyers pursued the track that Alciat had so successfully opened, avoiding all scholastic subtleties of interpretation, for which he substituted a general erudition, that rendered the science at once more intelligible and more attractive. Though his works are voluminous, Cujacius has not the reputation of diffuseness: on the contrary, the art of lucid explanation with brevity is said to have been one of his great characteristics. Thus, in the Paratitla on the Digest, a little book which Hottoman, his rival and enemy, advised his own son to carry constantly about with him, we find a brief exposition, in very good Latin, of every title in order, but with little additional matter. And it is said, that he thought nothing requisite for the Institutes but short, clear notes, which his thorough admirers afterwards contrasted with the celebrated but rather verbose commentaries of Vinnius.

Golden age of jurisprudence.

Cujacius.

77. Notwithstanding this conciseness, his works extend to a formidable length. For the civil law itself is, for the most part, very concisely written, and stretches to such an extent, that his indefatigable diligence in illustrating every portion of it could not be satisfied within narrow bounds. "Had Cujacius been born sooner," in the

Eulogies bestowed upon him.

words of the most elegant of his successors, "he would have sufficed instead of every other interpreter. For neither does he permit us to remain ignorant of any thing, nor to know any thing which he has not taught. He alone instructs us on every subject, and what he teaches is always his own. Hence, though the learned style of jurisprudence began with Alciat, we shall call it Cujacian."[1] "Though the writings of Cujacius are so voluminous," says Heineccius, "that scarce any one seems likely to read them all, it is almost peculiar to him, that, the longer any of his books is, the more it is esteemed. Nothing in them is trivial, nothing such as might be found in any other; every thing so well chosen that the reader can feel no satiety; and the truth is seen of what he answered to his disciples, when they asked for more diffuse commentaries, that his lectures were for the ignorant, his writings for the learned."[2] A later writer, Gennari, has given a more fully elaborate character of this illustrious lawyer, who might seem to have united every excellence without a failing.[3] But without listening to the enemies whom his own eminence, or the polemical fierceness of some disputes in which he was engaged, created among the jurists of that age, it has since been observed, that in his writings may be detected certain inconsistencies, of which whole books have been invidiously compiled, and that he was too prone to abuse his acuteness by conjectural emendations of the text; a dangerous practice, as Bynkershoek truly remarks, when it may depend upon a single particle whether the claim of Titius or of Marius shall prevail.[4]

78. Such was the renown of Cujacius, that, in the public schools of Germany, when his name was mentioned, every one took off his hat.[5] The continual bickerings of his contempo-

[1] Gravina, Origines Juris Civilis, p. 219.

[2] Heineccii Opera, xiv. 203. He prefers the Observationes atque Emendationes of Cujacius to all his other works. These contain twenty-eight books, published, at intervals, from the year 1556. They were designed to extend to forty books.

[3] Respublica Jurisconsultorum, p. 237. "Intactum in jurisprudentia reliquit nihil, et quæ scribit, non tam ex aliis excerpta, quam a se inventa, sane fatentur omnes; ita omnia suo loco posita, non nimis protracta, quæ nauseam creant, non arcte ac jejune tractata, quæ explicationis paullo diffusioris pariunt desiderium. Candida perspicuitate brevis, elegans sub amabili simplicitate, caute eruditus, quantum patitur occasio, ubique docens, ne aliqua parte arguatur otiosus, tam nihil habet inane, nihil inconditum, nihil curtum, nihil claudicans, nihil redundans, amœnus in Observationibus, subtilis in Tractatibus, uber ac planus in Commentariis, generosus in refellendis objectis, accuratus in confingendis notis, in Paratitlis brevis ac succi plenus, rectus prudensque in Consultationibus."

[4] Heinecc., xiv. 209; Gennari, p. 199.

[5] Gennari, p. 246; Biogr. Univ.

raries, not only of the old Accursian school, among whom Albericus Gentilis was prominent in disparaging him but of those who had been trained in the steps of Alciat like himself, did not affect this honest admiration of the general student.[1] But we must not consider Cujacius exactly in the light of what we now call a great lawyer. He rejected all modern forensic experience with scorn, declaring that he had misspent his youth in such studies. We have, indeed, fifty of his consultations which appear to be actual cases. But, in general, it is observed by Gravina, that both he and the greatest of his disciples "are but ministers of ancient jurisprudence, hardly deigning to notice the emergent questions of modern practice. Hence, while the elder jurists of the school of Bartolus, deficient as they are in expounding the Roman laws, yet apply them judiciously to new cases, these excellent interpreters hardly regard any thing modern, and leave to the others the whole honor of advising and deciding rightly." Therefore he recommends that the student who has imbibed the elements of Roman jurisprudence in all their purity from the school of Cujacius, should not neglect the interpretations of Accursius in obscure passages; and, above all, should have recourse to Bartolus and his disciples for the arguments, authorities, and illustrations which ordinary forensic questions will require.[2]

Cujacius an interpreter of law rather than a lawyer.

79. At some distance below Cujacius, but in places of honor, we find, among the great French interpreters of the civil law in this age, Duaren, as devoted to ancient learning as Cujacius, but differing from him by inculcating the necessity of forensic practice to form a perfect lawyer;[3] Govea, who, though a Portuguese, was always resident in France, whom some have set even above Cujacius for ability, and of whom it has been said that he is the only jurist who ought to have written more;[4] Brisson, a man of various learning, who became in the seditions of Paris an unfortunate victim of his own weak ambition; Balduin, a strenuous advocate for uniting the study

French lawyers below Cujacius: Govea and others.

[1] Heineccius, ibid.; Gennari, p. 242.

[2] Gravina, pp. 222, 230.

[3] "Duarenus . . . sine forensis exercitationis præsidio nec satis percipi, nec recte commodeque doceri jus civile existimat." — Gennari, p. 179.

[4] "Goveanus . . . vir, de quo uno desideretur, plura scripsisse, de cæteris vero, pauciora . . . quia felix ingenio, naturæ viribus tantum confideret, ut diligentiæ laudem sibi non necessariam, minus etiam honorificam putare videatur." — Gennari, p. 281.

of ancient history with that of law; Godefroi, whose Corpus Juris Civilis makes an epoch in jurisprudence, being the text-book universally received; and Connan, who is at least much quoted by the principal writers on the law of nature and nations. The boast of Germany was Gifanius.

Opponents of the Roman law.

80. These "ministers of ancient jurisprudence" seemed to have no other office than to display the excellences of the old masters in their original purity. Ulpian and Papinian were to them what Aristotle and Aquinas were to another class of worshippers. But the jurists of the age of Severus have come down to us through a compilation in that of Justinian; and Alciat himself had begun to discover the interpolations of Tribonian, and the corruption which, through ignorance or design, had penetrated the vast reservoir of the Pandects. Augustinus, Cujacius, and other French lawyers of the school of Bourges, followed in this track, and endeavored not only to restore the text from errors introduced by the carelessness of transcribers, a necessary and arduous labor, but from such as had sprung out of the presumptuousness of the lawgiver himself, or of those whom he had employed. This excited a vehement opposition, led by some of the chief lawyers of France, jealous of the fame of Cujacius. But, while they pretended to rescue the orthodox vulgate from the innovations of its great interpreter, another sect rose up, far bolder than either, which assailed the law itself. Of these, the most determined were Faber and Hottoman.

Faber of Savoy.

81. Antony Faber, or Fabre, a lawyer of Savoy, who became president of the court of Chamberi in 1610, acquired his reputation in the sixteenth century. He waged war against the whole body of commentators, and even treated the civil law itself as so mutilated and corrupt, so inapplicable to modern times, that it would be better to lay it altogether aside. Gennari says, that he would have been the greatest of lawyers, if he had not been too desirous to appear such:[1] his temerity and self-confidence diminished the effect of his ability. His mind was ardent, and unappalled by difficulties; no one had more enlarged views of jurisprudence, but in his interpretations he was prone to make the laws rather what they ought to have been than what they were. His love of paradox is hardly a greater

[1] P. 97.

fault than the perpetual carping at his own master Cujacius, as if he thought the reform of jurisprudence should have been reserved for himself.[1]

Anti-Tribonianus of Hottoman.

82. But the most celebrated production of this party is the Anti-Tribonianus of Hottoman. This was written in 1567, and though not published in French till 1609, nor in the original till 1647, seems properly to belong to the sixteenth century. He begins by acknowledging the merit of the Romans in jurisprudence, but denies that the compilation of Justinian is to be confounded with the Roman law. He divides his inquiry into two questions: first, whether the study of these laws is useful in France; and secondly, what are their deficiencies. These laws, he observes by the way, contain very little instruction about Roman history or antiquities, so that in books on those subjects we rarely find them cited. He then adverts to particular branches of the civil law, and shows that numberless doctrines are now obsolete, such as the state of servitude, the right of arrogation, the ceremonies of marriage, the peculiar law of guardianship, while for matters of daily occurrence they give us no assistance. He points out the useless distinctions between things *mancipi* and *non mancipi*, between the *dominium quiritarium* and *bonitarium;* the modes of acquiring property by mancipation, *cessio in jure*, *usucapio*, and the like, the unprofitable doctrines about *fidei commissa* and the *jus accrescendi*. He dwells on the folly of keeping up the old forms of stipulation in contracts, and those of legal process, from which no one can depart a syllable without losing his suit. And on the whole he concludes that not a twentieth part of the Roman law survives, and of that not one-tenth can be of any utility. In the second part, Hottoman attacks Tribonian himself for suppressing the genuine works of great lawyers, for barbarous language, for perpetually mutilating, transposing, and interpolating the passages which he inserts, so that no cohesion or consistency is to be found in these fragments of materials, nor is it possible to restore them. The evil has been increased by the herd of commentators and

[1] Heineccius, p. 236. "Fabre," says Ferrière, as quoted by Terrasson, Hist. de la Jurisprudence, "est celui des jurisconsultes modernes qui a porté le plus loin les idées sur le droit. C'étoit un esprit vaste qui ne se rebutoit par de plus grandes difficultés. Mais on l'accuse avec raison d'avoir décidé un peu trop hardiment contre les opinions communes, et de s'être donné souvent trop de liberté de retrancher ou d'ajouter dans les lois." See, too, the article "Favre," in Biographie Universelle.

interpreters since the twelfth century; those who have lately appeared and applied more erudition rarely agreeing in their conjectural emendations of the text, which yet frequently varies in different manuscripts so as to give rise to endless disputes. He ends by recommending that some jurisconsults and advocates should be called together, in order to compile a good code of laws; taking whatever is valuable in the Roman system, and adding whatever from other sources may seem worthy of reception, drawing them up in plain language, without too much subtilty, and attending chiefly to the principles of equity. He thinks that a year or two would suffice for the instruction of students in such a code of laws, which would be completed afterwards, as was the case at Rome, by forensic practice.

Civil law not countenanced in France.

83. These opinions of Hottoman, so reasonable in themselves, as to the inapplicability of much of the Roman law to the actual state of society, were congenial to the prejudices of many lawyers in France. That law had in fact to struggle against a system already received, the feudal customs which had governed the greater part of the kingdom. And this party so much prevailed, that by the ordinance of Blois, in 1579, the University of Paris was forbidden to give lectures or degrees in civil law. This was not wholly regarded; but it was not till a century afterwards that public lectures in that science were re-established in the university, on account of the uncertainty which the neglect of the civil law was alleged to have produced.

Turamini.

84. France now stood far pre-eminent in her lawyers. But Italy was not wanting in men once conspicuous, whom we cannot afford time to mention. One of them, Turamini, professor at Ferrara, though his name is not found in Tiraboschi, or even in Gravina, seems to have had a more luminous conception of the relation which should subsist between positive laws and those of nature, as well as of their distinctive provinces, than was common in the great jurists of that generation. His commentary on the title De Legibus, in the first book of the Pandects, gave him an opportunity for philosophical illustration. An account of his writings will be found in Corniani.[1]

85. The canon law, though by no means a province sterile

[1] Vol. vi. p. 197

in the quantity of its produce, has not deserved to arrest our attention. It was studied conjointly with that of Rome, from which it borrows many of its principles and rules of proceeding, though not servilely, nor without such variations as the independence of its tribunals, and the different nature of its authorities might be expected to produce. Covarruvias and other Spaniards were the most eminent canonists; Spain was distinguished in this line of jurisprudence.

Canon law.

86. But it is of more importance to observe, that in this period we find a foundation laid for the great science of international law, the determining authority in questions of right between independent states. Whatever had been delivered in books on this subject, had rested too much on theological casuistry, or on the analogies of positive and local law, or on the loose practice of nations, and precedents rather of arms than of reason. The fecial law, or rights of ambassadors, was that which had been most respected. The customary code of Europe, in military and maritime questions, as well as in some others, to which no state could apply its particular jurisprudence with any hope of reciprocity, grew up by degrees to be administered, if not upon solid principles, yet with some uniformity. The civil jurists, as being conversant with a system more widely diffused, and of which the equity was more generally recognized than any other, took into their hands the adjudication of all these cases. In the fifteenth and sixteenth centuries, the progress of international relations, and, we may add, the frequency of wars, though it did not at once create a common standard, showed how much it was required. War itself, it was perceived, even for the advantage of the belligerents, had its rules; an enemy had his rights: the study of ancient history furnished precedents of magnanimity and justice, which put the more recent examples of Christendom to shame; the spirit of the gospel could not be wholly suppressed, at least in theory; the strictness of casuistry was applied to the duties of sovereigns; and perhaps the scandal given by the writings of Machiavel was not without its influence in dictating a nobler tone to the morality of international law.

Law of nations. Its early state.

87. Before we come to works strictly belonging to this kind of jurisprudence, one may be mentioned which connects it with theological casuistry. The Relec-

Francis a Victoria.

tiones Theologicæ of Francis a Victoria, a professor in Salamanca, and one on whom Nicolas Antonio and many other Spanish writers bestow the highest eulogy, as the restorer of theological studies in their country, is a book of remarkable scarcity, though it has been published at least in four editions. Grotius has been supposed to have made use of it in his own great work; but some of those who since his time have mentioned Victoria's writings on this subject lament that they are not to be met with. Dupin, however, has given a short account of the Relectiones; and there are at least two copies in England,—one in the Bodleian Library, and another in that of Dr. Williams in Redcross Street. The edition I have used is of Venice, 1626, being probably the latest: it was published first at Lyons in 1557, at Salamanca in 1565, and again at Lyons in 1587, but had become scarce before its republication at Venice.[1] It consists of thirteen relections, as Victoria calls them, or dissertations on different subjects, related in some measure to theology, at least by the mode in which he treats them. The fifth, entitled De Indis, and the sixth, De Jure Belli, are the most important.

His opinions on public law.

88. The third is entitled, De Potestate Civili. In this he derives government and monarchy from divine institution, and holds that, as the majority of a state may choose a king whom the minority are bound to obey, so the majority of Christians may bind the minority by the choice of an universal monarch. In the chapter concerning the Indians. he strongly asserts the natural right of those nations to dominion over their own property and to sovereignty, denying the argument to the contrary founded on their infidelity or vices. He treats this question methodically, in a scholastic manner, giving the reasonings on both sides. He denies that the emperor or the pope is lord of the whole world, or that the pope has any power over the barbarian Indians or other infidels. The right of sovereignty in the King of Spain over these people he rests on such grounds as he can find; namely, the refusal of permission to trade, which he holds to be a just cause of war, and the cessions made to him

[1] This is said on the authority of the Venetian edition. But Nicolas Antonio mentions an edition at Ingoldstadt in 1580, and another at Antwerp in 1604. He is silent about those of 1587 and 1626. He also says that the Relectiones are twelve in number. Perhaps he had never seen the book, but he does not advert to its scarcity. Morhof, who calls it *Prælectiones*, names the two editions of Lyons, and those of Ingoldstadt and Antwerp. Brunet, Watts, and the Biographie Universelle, do not mention Victoria at all.

by allies among the native powers. In the sixth relection on the right of war, he goes over most of the leading questions, discussed afterwards by Albericus Gentilis and Grotius. His dissertation is exceedingly condensed, comprising sixty sections in twenty-eight pages; wherein he treats of the general right of war, the difference between public war and reprisal, the just and unjust causes of war, its proper ends, the right of subjects to examine its grounds, and many more of a similar kind. He determines that a war cannot be just on both sides, except through ignorance; and also that subjects ought not to serve their prince in a war which they reckon unjust. Grotius has adopted both these tenets. The whole relection, as well as that on the Indians, displays an intrepid spirit of justice and humanity, which seems to have been rather a general characteristic of the Spanish theologians. Dominic Soto, always inflexibly on the side of right, had already sustained by his authority the noble enthusiasm of Las Casas.

Ayala on the rights of war.

89. But the first book, so far as I am aware, that systematically reduced the practice of nations in the conduct of war to legitimate rules, is a treatise by Balthazar Ayala, judge-advocate (as we use the word) to the Spanish army in the Netherlands, under the Prince of Parma, to whom it is dedicated. The dedication bears date 1581; and the first edition is said to have appeared the next year. I have only seen that of 1597, and I apprehend every edition to be very scarce. For this reason, and because it is the opening of a great subject, I shall give the titles of his chapters in a note.[1] It will appear, that the second book of

[1] Balth. Ayalæ, J. C. et exercitus regii apud Belgas supremi juridici, de jure et officiis bellicis et disciplina militari, libri tres. Antw. 1597. 12mo, p. 405.

Lib. i.
c. 1. De Ratione Belli Indicendi, aliisque Cæremoniis Bellicis.
2. De Bello Justo.
3. De Duello, sive Singulari Certamine.
4. De Pignerationibus, quas vulgo Represalias vocant.
5. De Bello Captis et Jure Postliminii.
6. De Fide Hosti Servanda.
7. De Fœderibus et Induciis.
8. De Insidiis et Fraude Hostili.
9. De Jure Legatorum.

Lib. ii.
c. 1 De Officiis Bellicis.
2. De Imperatore vel Duce Exercitus.

Lib. ii.
c. 3. Unum non Plures Exercitui Præfici debere.
4. Utrum Lenitate et Benevolentia, an Severitate et Sævitia, plus proficiet Imperator.
5. Temporum Rationem præcipue in Bello Habendam.
6. Contentiosas et Lentas de Rebus Bellicis Deliberationes admodum Noxias esse.
7. Dum Res sunt Integræ ne minimum quidem Regi vel Reipublicæ de Majestate sua Concedendum esse; et errare eos qui Arrogantiam Hostium Modestia et Patientia vinci posse existimant.
8. An præstet Bellum Domi excipere, an vero in Hostilem Agrum inferre.

Ayala relates more to politics and to strategy than to international jurisprudence; and that, in the third, he treats entirely of what we call martial law. But, in the first, he aspires to lay down great principles of public ethics; and Grotius, who refers to Ayala with commendation, is surely mistaken in saying that he has not touched the grounds of justice and injustice in war.[1] His second chapter is on this subject, in thirty-four pages; and, though he neither sifts the matter so exactly nor limits the right of hostility so much as Grotius, he deserves the praise of laying down the general principle without subtilty or chicanery. Ayala positively denies, with Victoria, the right of levying war against infidels, even by authority of the pope, on the mere ground of their religion: for their infidelity does not deprive them of their right of dominion; nor was that sovereignty over the earth given originally to the faithful alone, but to every reasonable creature. And this, he says, has been shown by Covarruvias to be the sentiment of the majority of doctors.[2] Ayala deals abundantly in examples from ancient history, and in authorities from the jurists.

90. We find, next in order of chronology, a treatise by Albericus Gentilis, De Legationibus, published in 1583.

Lib. ii.
c. 9. An præstet Initio Prœlii Magno Clamore et Concitato Cursu in Hostes pergere, an vero Loco manere.
10. Non esse Consilii invicem Infensos Civilibus Dissensionibus Hostes Sola Discordia Fretum invadere.
11. Necessitatem Pugnandi Magno Studio Imponendam esse Militibus et Hostibus Remittendam.
12. In Victoria potissimum de Pace Cogitandum.
13. Devictis Hostibus qua potissimum Ratione Perpetua Pace Quieti obtineri possint [sic].

Lib. iii.
c. 1. De Disciplina Militari.
2. De Officio Legati et aliorum qui Militibus præsunt.
3. De Metatoribus sive Mensoribus.
4. De Militibus, et qui Militare possunt.
5. De Sacramento Militari.
6. De Missione.
7. De Privilegiis Militum
8. De Judiciis Militaribus.
9 De Pœnis Militum.
10. De Contumacibus et Ducum Dicto non Parentibus

Lib. iii.
c. 11. De Emansoribus.
12. De Desertoribus.
13. De Transfugis et Proditoribus.
14. De Seditiosis.
15. De Iis qui in Acie Loco cedunt aut Victi Se dedunt.
16. De Iis qui Arma alienant vel amittunt.
17. De Iis qui Excubias deserunt vel minus recte agunt.
18. De Eo qui Arcem vel Oppidum cujus Præsidio impositus est, amittit vel Hostibus dedit.
19. De Furtis et aliis Delictis Militaribus.
20. De Præmiis Militum.

1 "Causas unde bellum justum aut injustum dicitur Ayala non tetigit." — De Jure B. et P. Prolegom., § 38.

2 "Bellum adversus infideles ex eo solum quod infideles sunt, ne quidem auctoritate imperatoris vel summi pontificis indici potest; infidelitas enim non privat infideles dominio quod habent jure gentium; nam non fidelibus tantum rerum dominia, sed omni rationabili creaturæ data sunt. . . . Et hæc sententia plerisque probatur, ut ostendit Covarruvias."

Gentilis was an Italian Protestant, who, through the Earl of Leicester, obtained the chair of civil law at Oxford in 1582. His writings on Roman jurisprudence are numerous, but not very highly esteemed. This work on the Law of Embassy is dedicated to Sir Philip Sidney, the patron of so many distinguished strangers. The first book contains an explanation of the different kinds of embassies, and of the ceremonies anciently connected with them. His aim, as he professes, is to elevate the importance and sanctity of ambassadors, by showing the practice of former times. In the second book, he enters more on their peculiar rights. The envoys of rebels and pirates are not protected. But difference of religion does not take away the right of sending ambassadors. He thinks that civil suits against public ministers may be brought before the ordinary tribunals. On the delicate problem as to the criminal jurisdiction of these tribunals over ambassadors conspiring against the life of the sovereign, Gentilis holds that they can only be sent out of the country, as the Spanish ambassador was by Elizabeth. The civil law, he maintains, is no conclusive authority in the case of ambassadors, who depend on that of nations, which in many respects is different from the other. The second book is the most interesting; for the third chiefly relates to the qualifications required in a good ambassador. His instances are more frequently taken from ancient than modern history.

Albericus Gentilis on Embassies.

91. A more remarkable work by Albericus Gentilis is his treatise, De Jure Belli, first published at Lyons, 1589. Grotius acknowledges his obligations to Gentilis, as well as to Ayala, but in a greater degree to the former. And that this comparatively obscure writer was of some use to the eminent founder, as he has been deemed, of international jurisprudence, were it only for mapping his subject, will be evident from the titles of his chapters, which run almost parallel to those of the first and third books of Grotius.[1] They embrace, as the reader will

His treatise on the Rights of War.

[1] Lib. i.
c. 1. De Jure Gentium Bellico.
2. Belli Definitio.
3. Principes Bellum gerunt.
4. Latrones Bellum non gerunt.
5. Bella juste geruntur.
6. Bellum juste geri utrinque.
7. De Caussis Bellorum.
8. De Caussis Divinis Belli Faciendi.

Lib. i.
c. 9. An Bellum Justum sit pro Religione.
10. Si Princeps Religionem Bello apud suos juste tuetur.
11. An Subditi bellent contra Principem ex Caussa Religionis.
12. Utrum sint Caussæ Naturales Belli Faciendi.

perceive, the whole field of public faith, and of the rights both of war and victory. But I doubt whether the obligation has been so extensive as has sometimes been insinuated. Grotius does not, as far as I have compared them, borrow many quotations from Gentilis, though he cannot but sometimes allege the same historical examples. It will also be found in almost every chapter, that he goes deeper into the subject, reasons much more from ethical principles, relies less on the authority of precedent, and is in fact a philosopher where the other is a compiler.

92. Much that bears on tne subject of international law may probably be latent in the writings of the jurists Baldus, Covarruvias, Vasquez, especially the two latter, who seem to have combined the science of casuistry with that of the civil law. Gentilis, and even Grotius, refer much to them; and

Lib. i.
c. 13. De Necessaria Defensione.
14. De Utili Defensione.
15. De Honesta Defensione.
16. De Subditis Alienis contra Dominum Defendendis.
17. Qui Bellum necessarie inferunt.
18 Qui utiliter Bellum inferunt.
19. De Naturalibus Caussis Belli inferendi.
20. De Humanis Caussis Belli inferendi.
21. De Malefactis Privatorum.
22. De Vetustis Caussis non Excitandis.
23. De Regnorum Eversionibus.
24. Si in Posteros movetur Bellum.
25. De Honesta Caussa Belli inferendi.

Lib. ii.
c. 1. De Bello Indicendo.
2. Si quando Bellum non indicitur.
3. De Dolo et Stratagematis.
4. De Dolo Verborum.
5. De Mendaciis.
6. De Veneficiis.
7. De Armis et Mentitis Armis.
8. De Scævola, Juditha, et Similibus.
9. De Zopiro et aliis Transfugis.
10. De Pactis Ducum.
11. De Pactis Militum.
12 De Induciis.
13. Quando contra Inducias fiat.
14. De Salvo Conductu.
15. De Permutationibus et Liberationibus.
16. De Captivis, et non necandis.
17. De His qui se Hosti tradunt

Lib. ii.
c. 18. In Deditos, et Captos sæviri.
19. De Obsidibus.
20. De Supplicibus.
21. De Pueris et Fœminis.
22. De Agricolis, Mercatoribus, Peregrinis, aliis Similibus
23. De Vastitate et Incendiis.
24. De Cæsis sepeliendis.

Lib. iii.
c. 1. De Belli Fine et Pace.
2. De Ultione Victoris.
3. De Sumptibus et Damnis Belli.
4. Tributis et Agris multari Victos.
5. Victoris Acquisitio Universalis.
6. Victos Ornamentis Spoliari.
7. Urbes diripi, dirui.
8. De Ducibus Hostium Captis.
9. De Servis.
10. De Statu Mutando.
11. De Religionis aliarumque Rerum Mutatione.
12. Si Utile cum Honesto pugnet.
13. De Pace Futura Constituenda.
14. De Jure Conveniendi.
15. De Quibus cavetur in Fœderibus et in Duello.
16. De Legibus et Libertate.
17. De Agris et Postliminio.
18. De Amicitia et Societate.
19. Si Fœdus recte contrahitur cum Diversæ Religionis Hominibus.
20. De Armis et Classibus.
21. De Arcibus et Præsidiis.
22. Si Successores Fœderatorum tenentur.
23. De Ratihabitione, Privatis, Piratis, Exulibus, Adhærentibus.
24. Quando Fœdus violatur.

the former, who is no great philosopher, appears to have borrowed from that source some of his general principles. It is honorable to these men, as we have already seen in Soto, Victoria, and Ayala, that they strenuously defended the maxims of political justice.

CHAPTER V.

HISTORY OF POETRY FROM 1550 TO 1600.

Sect. I.—On Italian Poetry.

Character of the Italian Poets of this Age — Some of the best enumerated — Bernardino Rota — Gaspara Stampa — Bernardo Tasso—Gierusalemme Liberata of Torquato Tasso.

General character of Italian poets in this age.

1. The school of Petrarch, restored by Bembo, was prevalent in Italy at the beginning of this period. It would demand the use of a library, formed peculiarly for this purpose, as well as a great expenditure of time, to read the original volumes which this immensely numerous class of poets, the Italians of the sixteenth century, filled with their sonnets. In the lists of Crescimbeni, they reach the number of 661. We must, therefore, judge of them chiefly through selections, which, though they may not always have done justice to every poet, cannot but present to us an adequate picture of the general style of poetry. The majority are feeble copyists of Petrarch. Even in most of those who have been preferred to the rest, an affected intensity of passion, a monotonous repetition of customary metaphors, of hyperboles reduced to commonplaces by familiarity, of mythological allusions pedantic without novelty, cannot be denied incessantly to recur. But, in observing how much they generally want of that which is essentially the best, we might be in danger of forgetting that there is a praise due to selection of words, to harmony of sound, and to skill in overcoming metrical impediments, which it is for natives alone to award. The authority of Italian critics should, therefore, be respected, though not without keeping in mind both their national prejudice, and that which

Their usual faults.

the habit of admiring a very artificial style must always generate.

Their beauties.

2. It is perhaps hardly fair to read a number of these compositions in succession. Every sonnet has its own unity, and is not, it might be pleaded, to be charged with tediousness or monotony, because the same structure of verse, or even the same general sentiment, may recur in an equally independent production. Even collectively taken, the minor Italian poetry of the sixteenth century may be deemed a great repertory of beautiful language, of sentiments and images, that none but minds finely tuned by nature produce, and that will ever be dear to congenial readers, presented to us with exquisite felicity and grace, and sometimes with an original and impressive vigor. The sweetness of the Italian versification goes far towards their charm; but are poets forbidden to avail themselves of this felicity of their native tongue, or do we invidiously detract, as we might on the same ground, from the praise of Theocritus and Bion?

Character given by Muratori.

3. "The poets of this age," says one of their best critics, "had, in general, a just taste; wrote with elegance; employed deep, noble, and natural sentiments; and filled their compositions with well-chosen ornaments. There may be observed, however, some difference between the authors who lived before the middle of the century and those who followed them. The former were more attentive to imitate Petrarch, and, unequal to reach the fertility and imagination of this great master, seemed rather dry, with the exception, always, of Casa and Costanzo, whom, in their style of composition, I greatly admire. The later writers, in order to gain more applause, deviated in some measure from the spirit of Petrarch, seeking ingenious thoughts, florid conceits, splendid ornaments, of which they became so fond, that they fell sometimes into the vicious extreme of saying too much."[1]

Poetry of Casa.

4. Casa and Costanzo, whom Muratori seems to place in the earlier part of the century, belong, by the date of publication at least, to this latter period. The former was the first to quit the style of Petrarch, which Bembo had rendered so popular. Its smoothness evidently

[1] Muratori, della Perfetta Poesia, i. 22.

wanted vigor; and it was the aim of Casa to inspire a more masculine tone into the sonnet, at the expense of a harsher versification. He occasionally ventured to carry on the sense without pause from the first to the second tercet; an innovation praised by many, but which, at that time, few attempted to imitate, though in later ages it has become common, not much perhaps to the advantage of the sonnet. The poetry of Casa speaks less to the imagination, the heart, or the ear, than to the understanding.[1]

Of Costanzo.

5. Angelo di Costanzo, a Neapolitan, and author of a well-known history of his country, is highly extolled by Crescimbeni and Muratori: perhaps no one of these lyric poets of the sixteenth century is so much in favor with the critics. Costanzo is so regular in his versification, and so strict in adhering to the unity of subject, that the Society of Arcadians, when, towards the close of the seventeenth century, they endeavored to rescue Italian poetry from the school of Marini, selected him as the best model for imitation. He is ingenious, but perhaps a little too refined; and by no means free from that coldly hyperbolical tone in addressing his mistress, which most of these sonneteers assume. Costanzo is not to me, in general, a pleasing writer; though sometimes he is very beautiful, as in the sonnet on Virgil, "Quella cetra gentil," justly praised by Muratori, and which will be found in most collections; remarkable, among higher merits, for being contained in a single sentence. Another, on the same subject, "Cigni felici," is still better. The poetry of Camillo Pellegrini much resembles that of Costanzo.[2] The sonnets of Baldi, especially a series on the ruins and antiquities of Rome, appear to me deserving of a high place among those of the age. They may be read among his poems; but few have found their way into the collections by Gobbi and Rubbi, which are not made with the best taste. Caro, says Crescimbeni, is less rough than Casa, and more original than Bembo. Salfi extols the felicity of his

Baldi.

Caro.

[1] "Casa . . . per poco deviando dalla dolcezza del Petrarca, a un novello stile diede principio, col quale le sue rime compose, intendendo sopra il tutto alla gravità; per conseguir la quale, si valse spezialmente del carattere aspro, e de' raggirati periodi e rotondi, insino a condurre uno stesso sentimento d' uno in altro quadernario, e d' uno in altro terzetto; cosa in prima da alcuno non più tentata; perlochè somma lode ritrasse de chiunque coltivò in questi tempi la toscana poesia. Ma perche si fatto stile era proprio, e adattato all' ingegno del suo inventore, molto difficile riuscì il seguitarlo." — Crescimbeni, della Volgar Poesia, ii. 410. See also Ginguéné, ix. 329; Tiraboschi, x. 22. Casa is generally, to my apprehension, very harsh and prosaic.

[2] Crescimbeni, vol. iv. p. 25

style, and the harmony of his versification; while he owns that his thoughts are often forced and obscure.[1]

Odes of Celio Magno.

6. Among the canzoni of this period, one by Celio Magno on the Deity stands in the eyes of foreigners, and I believe of many Italians, prominent above the rest. It is certainly a noble ode.[2] Rubbi, editor of the Parnaso Italiano, says that he would call Celio the greatest lyric poet of his age, if he did not dread the clamor of the Petrarchists. The poetry of Celio Magno, more than one hundred pages extracted from which will be found in the thirty-second volume of that collection, is not in general amatory, and displays much of that sonorous rhythm and copious expression which afterwards made Chiabrera and Guidi famous. Some of his odes, like those of Pindar, seem to have been written for pay, and have somewhat of that frigid exaggeration which such conditions produce. Crescimbeni thinks that Tansillo, in the ode, has no rival but Petrarch.[3] The poetry in general of Tansillo, especially La Balia, which contains good advice to mothers about nursing their infants very prosaically delivered, seems deficient in spirit.[4]

Coldness of the amatory sonnets.

7. The amatory sonnets of this age, forming the greater number, are very frequently cold and affected. This might possibly be ascribed in some measure to the state of manners in Italy, where, with abundant licentiousness, there was still much of jealousy; and public sentiment applauded alike the successful lover and the vindictive husband. A respect for the honor of families, if not for virtue, would impose on the poet who felt or assumed a passion for any distinguished lady, the conditions of Tasso's Olindo, — to desire much, to hope for little, and to ask nothing. It is also at least very doubtful whether much of the amorous sorrow of the sonneteers were not purely ideal.

[1] Crescimbeni, ii. 429. Ginguéné (continuation par Salfi), ix. 12. Caro's sonnets on Castelvetro, written during their quarrel, are full of furious abuse with no wit. They have the ridiculous particularity, that the last line of each is repeated so as to begin the next.

[2] This will be found in the Componimenti Lirici of Mathias, — a collection good on the whole, yet not perhaps the best that might have been made; nor had the editor at that time so extensive an acquaintance with Italian poetry as he afterwards acquired. Crescimbeni reckons Celio the last of the good age in poetry: he died in 1612. He praises also Scipio Gaetano (not the painter of that name). whose poems were published, but posthumously, in the same year.

[3] Della Volgar Poesia, ii. 436.

[4] Roscoe republished La Balia, which was very little worth while. The following is an average specimen: —

"Questo degenerar, ch' ognor si vede,
Sendo voi caste, donne mie, vi dico,
Che d' altro che dal latte non procede.
L' altrui latte oscurar fa 'l pregio antico
Degli avi illustri e adulterar le razze,
E s' infetta talor sangue pudico."

8. Lines and phrases from Petrarch are as studiously introduced as we find those of classical writers in modern Latin poetry. It cannot be said that this is unpleasing; and to the Italians, who knew every passage of their favorite poet, it must have seemed at once a grateful homage of respect, and an ingenious artifice to bespeak attention. They might well look up to him as their master, but could not hope that even a foreigner would ever mistake the hand through a single sonnet. He is to his disciples, especially those towards the latter part of the century, as Guido is to Franceschini or Elisabetta Serena: an effeminate and mannered touch enfeebles the beauty which still lingers round the pencil of the imitator. If they produce any effect upon us beyond sweetness of sound and delicacy of expression, it is from some natural feeling, some real sorrow, or from some occasional originality of thought in which they cease for a moment to pace the banks of their favorite Sorga. It would be easy to point out not a few sonnets of this higher character among those especially of Francesco Coppetta, of Claudio Tolomei, of Ludovico Paterno, or of Bernardo Tasso.

Studied imitation of Petrarch.

9. A school of poets, that has little vigor of sentiment, falls readily into description, as painters of history or portrait that want expression of character endeavor to please by their landscape. The Italians, especially in this part of the sixteenth century, are profuse in the song of birds, the murmur of waters, the shade of woods; and, as these images are always delightful, they shed a charm over much of their poetry, which only the critical reader, who knows its secret, is apt to resist, and that to his own loss of gratification. The pastoral character, which it became customary to assume, gives much opportunity for these secondary, yet very seducing, beauties of style. They belong to the decline of the art, and have something of the voluptuous charm of evening. Unfortunately they generally presage a dull twilight, or a thick darkness of creative poetry. The Greeks had much of this in the Ptolemaic age, and again in that of the first Byzantine emperors. It is conspicuous in Tansillo, Paterno, and both the Tassos.

Their fondness for description

10. The Italian critics, Crescimbeni, Muratori, and Quadrio, have given minute attention to the beauties of particular sonnets culled from the vast stores of the sixteenth century.

Judgment of Italian critics.

But as the development of the thought, the management of the four constituent clauses of the sonnet, especially the last, the propriety of every line, for nothing digressive or merely ornamental should be admitted constitute in their eyes the chief merit of these short compositions, they extol some which in our eyes are not so pleasing as what a less regular taste might select. Without presuming to rely on my own judgment, defective both as that of a foreigner, and of one not so extensively acquainted with the minor poetry of this age, I will mention two writers, well known, indeed, but less prominent in the critical treatises than some others, as possessing a more natural sensibility and a greater truth of sorrow than most of their contemporaries, — Bernardino Rota and Gaspara Stampa.

Bernardino Rota.

11. Bernardino Rota, a Neapolitan of ancient lineage and considerable wealth, left poems in Latin as well as Italian; and among the latter his eclogues are highly praised by his editor. But he is chiefly known by a series of sonnets, intermixed with canzoni, upon a single subject, Portia Capece, his wife, whom, "what is unusual among our Tuscan poets (says his editor), he loved with an exclusive affection." But be it understood, lest the reader should be discouraged, that the poetry addressed to Portia Capece is all written before their marriage, or after her death. The earlier division of the series, "Rime in Vita," seems not to rise much above the level of amorous poetry. He wooed, was delayed, complained, and won, — the natural history of an equal and reasonable love. Sixteen years intervened of that tranquil bliss which contents the heart without moving it, and seldom affords much to the poet in which the reader can find interest. Her death in 1559 gave rise to poetical sorrows, as real, and certainly full as rational, as those of Petrarch, to whom some of his contemporaries gave him the second place; rather probably from the similarity of their subject, than from the graces of his language. Rota is by no means free from conceits, and uses sometimes affected and unpleasing expressions, as *mia dolce guerra*, speaking of his wife, even after her death; but his images are often striking:[1] and, above all,

[1] Muratori blames a line of Rota as too bold, and containing a false thought: —

"Feano i begl' occhi a se medesmi giorno."

It seems to me not beyond the limits of poetry, nor more hyperbolical than many others which have been much admired. It is, at least, *Petrarchesque* in a high degree.

he resembles Petrarch, with whatever inferiority, in combining the ideality of a poetical mind with the naturalness of real grief. It has never again been given to man, nor will it probably be given, to dip his pen in those streams of ethereal purity which have made the name of Laura immortal; but a sonnet of Rota may be not disadvantageously compared with one of Milton, which we justly admire for its general feeling, though it begins in pedantry and ends in conceit.[1] For my own part, I would much rather read again the collection of Rota's sonnets than those of Costanzo.

Gaspara Stampa. Her love for Collalto

12. The sorrows of Gaspara Stampa were of a different kind, but not less genuine than those of Rota. She was a lady of the Paduan territory, living near the small river Anaso, from which she adopted the poetical name of Anasilla. This stream bathes the foot of certain lofty hills, from which a distinguished family, the counts of Collalto, took their appellation. The representative of this house, himself a poet as well as soldier, and, if

[1] This sonnet is in Mathias, iii. 256. That of Milton will be remembered by most readers.

" In lieto e pien di riverenza aspetto,
Con veste di color bianco e vermiglio,
Di doppia luce serenato il ciglio,
Mi viene in sonno il mio dolce diletto.
Io me l' inchino, e con cortese affetto
Seco ragiono e seco mi consiglio.
Com' abbia a governarmi in quest' esiglio,
E piango intanto, e la risposta aspetto.
Ella m' ascolta fiso, e dice cose
Veramente celesti, ed io l' apprendo,
E sèrbo ancor nella memoria ascose.
Mi lascia al fine e parte, e va spargendo
Per l' aria nel partir viole e rose;
Io le porgo la man; poi mi reprendo."

In one of Rota's sonnets we have the thought of Pope's epitaph on Gay: —

" Questo cor, questa mente e questo petto
Sia 'l tuo sepolcro e non la tomba o 'l sasso;
Ch' io t' apparecchio qui doglioso e lasso;
Non si deve a te, donna, altro ricetto."

He proceeds very beautifully: —

' Ricca sia la memoria e l' intelletto,
Del ben per cui tutt' altro a dietro io lasso;
E mentre questo mar di pianto passo,
Vadami sempre innanzi il caro objetto.
Alma gentil, dov' abitar solei
Donna e reina, in terren fascio avvolta,
Ivi regnar celeste immortal dei.
Vantisi pur la morte averti tolta
Al mondo, a me non già; ch' a pensier miei
Una sempre sarai viva e sepolta."

The poems of Rota are separately published in two volumes. Naples, 1726. They contain a mixture of Latin. Whether Milton intentionally borrowed the sonnet on his wife's death,

"Methought I saw my last espousèd saint,"

from that above quoted, I cannot pretend to say: certainly his resemblances to the Italian poets often seem more than accidental. Thus two lines in an indifferent writer, Girolamo Preti (Mathias, iii. 329), are exactly like one of the sublimest flights in the Paradise Lost.

" Tu per soffrir della cui luce i rai
Si fan con l' ale i serafini un velo."

" Dark with excessive light thy skirts appear;
Yet dazzle Heaven, that brightest seraphim
Approach not, but with both wings veil their eyes."

[But it has been suggested to me that both poets must have alluded to Isa. vi. 2. Thus, too, the language of the Jewish liturgies represents the seraphim as veiling their eyes with wings in the presence of God. — 1842.]

we believe his fond admirer, endowed with every virtue except constancy, was loved by Gaspara with enthusiastic passion. Unhappily, she learned only by sad experience the want of generosity too common to man; and sacrificing, not the honor, but the pride, of her sex, by submissive affection, and finally by querulous importunity, she estranged a heart never so susceptible as her own. Her sonnets, which seem arranged nearly in order, begin with the delirium of sanguine love: they are extravagant effusions of admiration, mingled with joy and hope; but soon the sense of Collalto's coldness glides in and overpowers her bliss.[1] After three years' expectation of seeing his promise of marriage fulfilled, and when he had already caused alarm by his indifference, she was compelled to endure the pangs of absence by his entering the service of France. This does not seem to have been of long continuance; but his letters were infrequent, and her complaints, always vented in a sonnet, become more fretful. He returned; and Anasilla exults with tenderness, yet still timid in the midst of her joy.

> "Oserò io, con queste fide braccia,
> Cingerli il caro collo, ed accostare
> La mia tremante alla sua viva faccia?"

But jealousy, not groundless, soon intruded; and we find her doubly miserable. Collalto became more harsh, avowed his indifference, forbade her to importune him with her complaints, and, in a few months, espoused another woman. It is said by the historians of Italian literature, that the broken heart of Gaspara sunk very soon under these accumulated sorrows into the grave.[2] And such, no doubt, is what my readers expect, and (at least the gentler of them) wish to find. But inexorable truth, to whom I am the sworn vassal, compels me to say that the poems of the lady herself contain unequivocal proofs that she avenged herself better on Collalto, — by falling in love again. We find the acknowledgment of another incipient passion, which speedily comes to maturity; and, while declaring that her present flame is much stronger than the last, she

Is ill requited.

Her second love.

[1] In an early sonnet, she already calls Collato, "il Signor, *ch' io amo, e ch' io pavento;*" an expression descriptive enough of the state in which poor Gaspara seems to have lived several years.

[2] She anticipated her epitaph, on this hypothesis of a broken heart; which did not occur.

> "Per amar molto, ed esser poco amata
> Visse e morì infelice; ed or quì giace
> La più fedel amante che sia stata.
> Pregale, viator, riposo e pace,
> Ed impara da lei si mal trattata
> A non seguire un cor crudo e fugace."

dismisses her faithless lover with the handsome compliment, that it was her destiny always to fix her affections on a noble object. The name of her second choice does not appear in her poems; nor has any one hitherto, it would seem, made the very easy discovery of his existence. It is true that she died young, "but not of love."[1]

13. The style of Gaspara Stampa is clear, simple, graceful: the Italian critics find something to censure in the versification. In purity of taste, I should incline to set her above Bernardino Rota, though she has less vigor of imagination. Corniani has applied to her the well-known lines of Horace upon Sappho.[2] But the fires of guilt and shame, that glow along the strings of the Æolian lyre, ill resemble the pure sorrows of the tender Anasilla. Her passion for Collalto, ardent and undisguised, was ever virtuous; the sense of gentle birth, though so inferior to his as perhaps to make a proud man fear disparagement, sustained her against dishonorable submission.

Style of Gaspara Stampa.

"E ben ver, che 'l desio, con che amo voi,
E tutto d' onestà pieno, e d' amore;[3]
Perchè altrimente non convien tra noi."[4]

But, not less in elevation of genius than in dignity of character, she is very far inferior to Vittoria Colonna, or even to Veronica Gambar, a poetess, who, without equalling Vittoria,

[1] It is impossible to dispute the evidence of Gaspara herself in several sonnets, so that Corniani, and all the rest, must have read her very inattentively. What can we say to these lines? —

"Perchè mi par vedere a certi segni
Ch' ordisci (Amor) nuovi lacci e nuove faci,
E di ritrarme al giogo tuo t' ingegni."

And afterwards more fully: —

"Qual darai fine, Amor, alle mie pene,
Se dal cinere estinto d' uno ardore
Rinasce l' altro, tua mercè, maggiore,
E si vivace a consumar mi viene?
Qual nelle più felici e calde arene
Nel nido acceso sol di vario odore
D' una fenice estinta esce poi fuore
Un verme, che fenice altra diviene.
In questo io debbo à tuoi cortesi strali
Che sempre è degno, ed onorato oggetto
Quello, onde mi ferisci, onde m' assali.
Ed ora è tale, e tanto, e sì perfetto,
Ha tante doti alla bellezza eguali,
Ch' ardor per lui m' è sommo alto diletto."

[2] ". . . spirat adhuc amor
Vivuntque commissi calores
Æoliæ fidibus puellæ."

Corniani, v. 212, and Salfi in Ginguéné, ix. 406, have done some justice to the poetry of Gaspara Stampa, though by no means more than it deserves. Bouterwek, ii. 150, observes only, "Viel Poesie zeigt sich nicht in diesen Sonetten;" which, I humbly conceive, shows that either he had not read them, or was an indifferent judge; and, from his general taste, I prefer the former hypothesis.

[3] *Sic.* Leg. onore?

[4] I quote these lines on the authority of Corniani, v. 215. But I must own, that they do not appear in the two editions of the Rime della Gaspara Stampa which I have searched. I must also add, that, willing as I am to believe all things in favor of a lady's honor, there is one very awkward sonnet among those of poor Gaspara, upon which it is by no means easy to put such a construction as we should wish.

had much of her noblenesss and purity. We pity the Gasparas: we should worship, if we could find them, the Vittorias.

14. Among the longer poems which Italy produced in this period, two may be selected. The Art of Navigation, La Nautica, published by Bernardino Baldi in 1590, is a didactic poem in blank verse, too minute sometimes and prosaic in its details, like most of that class, but neither low nor turgid nor obscure, as many others have been. The descriptions, though never very animated, are sometimes poetical and pleasing. Baldi is diffuse; and this conspires with the triteness of his matter to render the poem somewhat uninteresting. He by no means wants the power to adorn his subject, but does not always trouble himself to exert it, and is tame where he might be spirited. Few poems bear more evident marks that their substance had been previously written down in prose.

La Nautica of Baldi.

15. Bernardo Tasso, whose memory has almost been effaced with the majority of mankind by the splendor of his son, was not only the most conspicuous poet of the age wherein he lived, but was placed by its critics, in some points of view, above Ariosto himself. His minor poetry is of considerable merit.[1] But that to which he owed most of his reputation is an heroic romance on the story of Amadis, written about 1540, and first published in 1560. L'Amadigi is of prodigious length, containing 100 cantos, and about 57,000 lines. The praise of facility, in the best sense, is fully due to Bernardo. His narration is fluent, rapid, and clear; his style not in general feeble or low, though I am not aware that many brilliant passages will be found. He followed Ariosto in his tone of relating the story: his lines perpetually remind us of the Orlando; and I believe it would appear, on close examination, that much has been borrowed with slight change. My own acquaintance, however,

Amadigi of Bernardo Tasso.

[1] "The character of his lyric poetry is a sweetness and abundance of expressions and images, by which he becomes more flowing and full (*più morbido e più pastoso*, metaphors not translatable by single English words) than his contemporaries of the school of Petrarch." — Corniani, v. 127.

A sonnet of Bernardo Tasso, so much admired at the time, that almost every one, it is said, of a refined taste had it by heart, will be found in Panizzi's edition of the Orlando Innamorato, vol. i. p. 376, with a translation by a lady well known for the skill with which she has transferred the grace and feeling of Petrarch into our language. The sonnet, which begins "Poichè la parte men perfetta e bella," is not found in Gobbi or Mathias. It is distinguished from the common crowd of Italian sonnets in the sixteenth century by a novelty, truth, and delicacy of sentiment, which is comparatively rare in them.

vith the Amadigi is not sufficient to warrant more than a ;eneral judgment. Ginguéné, who rates this poem very ighly, praises the skill with which the disposition of the riginal romance has been altered and its canvas enriched by ew insertions, the beauty of the images and sentiments, the 'ariety of the descriptions, the sweetness, though not always ree from languor, of the style; and finally recommends its erusal to all lovers of romantic poetry, and to all who would ppreciate that of Italy.[1] It is evident, however, that the hoice of a subject become frivolous in the eyes of mankind, ot less than the extreme length of Bernardo Tasso's poem, nust render it almost impossible to follow this advice.

Satirical and burlesque poetry: Aretin.

16. The satires of Bentivoglio, it is agreed, fall short of hose by Ariosto, though some have placed them bove those of Alamanni.[2] But all these are satires n the regular model, assuming at least a half-seri-us tone. A style more congenial to the Italians vas that of burlesque poetry, sometimes poignantly satirical, ut as destitute of any grave aim, as it was light and familiar, ven to popular vulgarity, in its expression, though capable f grace in the midst of its gayety, and worthy to employ the est masters of Tuscan language.[3] But it was disgraced by ome of its cultivators, and by none more than Peter Aretin. The character of this profligate and impudent person is well nown: it appears extraordinary, that, in an age so little scru-ulous as to political or private revenge, some great princes, vho had never spared a worthy adversary, thought it not nbecoming to purchase the silence of an odious libeller, who alled himself their scourge. In a literary sense, the writings f Aretin are unequal; the serious are for the most part reck-ned wearisome and prosaic; in his satires a poignancy and pirit, it is said, frequently breaks out; and though his opularity, like that of most satirists, was chiefly founded on he ill-nature of mankind, he gratified this with a neatness nd point of expression, which those who cared nothing for he satire might admire.[4]

[1] Vol. v. pp. 61–108. Bouterwek (vol. . 159) speaks much less favorably of the madigi, and, as far as I can judge, in too isparaging a tone. Corniani, a great dmirer of Bernardo, owns that his *mor-idezza* and fertility have rendered him o frequently diffuse and flowery. See lso Panizzi, p. 393, who observes that the madigi wants interest, but praises its imaginative descriptions as well as its delicacy and softness.

[2] Ginguéné, ix. 198; Biogr. Univ.; Tiraboschi, x. 66.

[3] A canzon by Coppetta on his cat, in the twenty-seventh volume of the Parnaso Italiano, is rather amusing.

[4] Bouterwek, ii. 207. His authority does not seem sufficient; and Ginguéné,

17. Among the writers of satirical, burlesque, or licentiou

Other burlesque writers.

poetry, after Aretin, the most remarkable are Firen zuola, Casa (one of whose compositions passed s much all bounds as to have excluded him from th purple, and has become the subject of a sort of a literary con troversy, to which I can only allude),[1] Franco, and Grazzin surnamed Il Lasca. I must refer to the regular historian of Italian literature for accounts of these, as well as fo the styles of poetry called *macaronica* and *pedantesca*, whic

Attempts at Latin metres.

appear wholly contemptible, and the attempts t introduce Latin metres, a folly with which ever nation has been inoculated in its turn.[2] Claudi Tolomei, and Angelo Costanzo himself, by writing sapphic and hexameters, did more honor to so strange a pedantr than it deserved.

18. The translation of the Metamorphoses of Ovid b

Poetical translations.

Anguillara seems to have acquired the highest nam with the critics;[3] but that of the Æneid by Caro i certainly the best known in Europe. It is not, however, ver faithful, though written in blank verse, which leaves a trans lator no good excuse for deviating from his original: the styl is diffuse, and, upon the whole, it is better that those who rea it should not remember Virgil. Many more Italian poet ought, possibly, to be commemorated; but we must haste forward to the greatest of them all.

19. The life of Tasso is excluded from these pages by th

Torquato Tasso.

rule I have adopted; but I cannot suppose an reader to be ignorant of one of the most interestin and affecting stories that literary biography presents. It wa

ix. 212, gives a worse character of the style of Aretin. But Muratori (Della Perfetta Poesia, ii. 284) extols one of his sonnets as deserving a very high place in Italian poetry.

[1] A more innocent and diverting capitolo of Casa turns on the ill luck of being named John.

"S' io avessi manco quindici o vent' anni,
Messer Gandolfo, io mi sbattezzerei,
Per non aver mai più nome Giovanni.
Perch' io non posso andar pe' fatti miei,
Nè partirmi di quì per ir si presso
Ch' io nol senta chiamar da cinque e sei."

He ends by lamenting that no alteration mends the name

"Mutalo, o sminuiscil, se tu sai,
O Nanni, o Gianni, o Giannino, o Giannozzo,
Come più tu lo tocchi, peggio fai,
Che gli è cattivo intero, e peggior mozzo."

[2] Macaronic verse was invented by on Folengo, in the first part of the century This worthy had written an epic poem which he thought superior to the Æneid A friend, to whom he showed the manu script, paid him the compliment, as h thought, of saying that he had *equalle* Virgil. Folengo, in a rage, threw his poem into the fire, and sat down for the rest of his life to write Macaronics. Journal de Savans, December, 1831.

[3] Salfi (continuation de Ginguéné), x 180; Corniani, vi. 113.

in the first stages of a morbid melancholy, almost of intellectual derangement, that the Gierusalemme Liberata was finished: it was during a confinement, harsh in all its circumstances, though perhaps necessary, that it was given to the world. Several portions had been clandestinely published, in consequence of the author's inability to protect his rights; and even the first complete edition, in 1581, seems to have been without his previous consent. In the later editions of the same year, he is said to have been consulted; but his disorder was then at a height, from which it afterwards receded, leaving his genius undiminished, and his reason somewhat more sound, though always unsteady. Tasso died at Rome in 1595, already the object of the world's enthusiastic admiration, rather than of its kindness and sympathy.

The Jerusalem excellent in choice of subject.

20. The Jerusalem is the great epic poem, in the strict sense, of modern times. It was justly observed by Voltaire, that, in the choice of his subject, Tasso is superior to Homer. Whatever interest tradition might have attached among the Greeks to the wrath of Achilles and the death of Hector, was slight to those genuine recollections which were associated with the first crusade. It was not the theme of a single people, but of Europe; not a fluctuating tradition, but certain history; yet history so far remote from the poet's time, as to adapt itself to his purpose with almost the flexibility of fable. Nor could the subject have been chosen so well in another age or country; it was still the holy war, and the sympathies of his readers were easily excited for religious chivalry: but, in Italy, this was no longer an absorbing sentiment; and the stern tone of bigotry, which perhaps might still have been required from a Castilian poet, would have been dissonant amidst the soft notes that charmed the court of Ferrara.

Superior to Homer and Virgil in some points.

21. In the variety of occurrences, the change of scenes and images, and of the trains of sentiment connected with them in the reader's mind, we cannot place the Iliad on a level with the Jerusalem. And again, by the manifest unity of subject, and by the continuance of the crusading army before the walls of Jerusalem, the poem of Tasso has a coherence and singleness, which is comparatively wanting to that of Virgil. Every circumstance is in its place: we expect the victory of the Christians, but

acknowledge the probability and adequacy of the events that delay it. The episodes, properly so to be called, are few and short; for the expedition of those who recall Rinaldo from the arms of Armida, though occupying too large a portion of the poem, unlike the fifth and sixth, or even the second and third books of the Æneid, is an indispensable link in the chain of its narrative.

Its characters.

22. In the delineation of character, at once natural, distinct, and original, Tasso must give way to Homer, perhaps to some other epic and romantic poets. There are some indications of the age in which he wrote; some want of that truth to nature, by which the poet, like the painter, must give reality to the conceptions of his fancy. Yet here also the sweetness and nobleness of his mind, and his fine sense of moral beauty, are displayed. The female warrior had been an old invention; and few, except Homer, had missed the opportunity of diversifying their battles with such a character. But it is of difficult management: we know not how to draw the line between the savage virago, from whom the imagination revolts, and the gentler fair one, whose feats in arms are ridiculously incongruous to her person and disposition. Virgil first threw a romantic charm over his Camilla; but he did not render her the object of love. In modern poetry, this seemed the necessary compliment to every lady; but we hardly envy Rogero the possession of Bradamante, or Arthegal that of Britomart. Tasso alone, with little sacrifice of poetical probability, has made his readers sympathize with the enthusiastic devotion of Tancred for Clorinda. She is so bright an ideality, so heroic, and yet, by the enchantment of verse, so lovely, that no one follows her through the combat without delight, or reads her death without sorrow. And how beautiful is the contrast of this character with the tender and modest Erminia! The heroes, as has been hinted, are drawn with less power. Godfrey is a noble example of calm and faultless virtue; but we find little distinctive character in Rinaldo. Tancred has seemed to some rather too much enfeebled by his passion; yet this may be justly considered as part of the moral of the poem.

Excellence of its style.

23. The Jerusalem is read with pleasure in almost every canto. No poem, perhaps, if we except the Æneid, has so few weak or tedious pages: the worst passages

are the speeches, which are too diffuse. The native melancholy of Tasso tinges all his poem: we meet with no lighter strain, no comic sally, no effort to relieve for an instant the tone of seriousness that pervades every stanza. But it is probable that some become wearied by this uniformity, which his metre serves to augment. The *ottava rima* has its inconveniences: even its intricacy, when once mastered, renders it more monotonous; and the recurrence of marked rhymes, the breaking of the sense into equal divisions, while they communicate to it a regularity that secures the humblest verse from sinking to the level of prose, deprive it of that variety which the hexameter most eminently possesses. Ariosto lessened this effect by the rapid flow of his language, and perhaps by its negligence and inequality: in Tasso, who is more sustained at a high pitch of elaborate expression than any great poet except Virgil, and in whom a prosaic or feeble stanza will rarely be found, the uniformity of cadence may conspire with the lusciousness of style to produce a sense of satiety in the reader. This is said rather to account for the injustice, as it seems to me, with which some speak of Tasso, than to express my own sentiments; for there are few poems of great length which I so little wish to lay aside as the Jerusalem.

24. The diction of Tasso excites perpetual admiration: it is rarely turgid or harsh; and, though more figurative than that of Ariosto, it is so much less than that of most of our own or the ancient poets, that it appears simple in our eyes. Virgil, to whom we most readily compare him, is far superior in energy, but not in grace. Yet his grace is often too artificial, and the marks of the file are too evident in the exquisiteness of his language. Lines of superior beauty occur in almost every stanza: pages after pages may be found, in which, not pretending to weigh the style in the scales of the Florentine Academy, I do not perceive one feeble verse or improper expression.

Some faults in it.

25. The conceits so often censured in Tasso, though they bespeak the false taste that had begun to prevail, do not seem quite so numerous as his critics have been apt to insinuate; but we find sometimes a trivial or affected phrase, or, according to the usage of the times, an idle allusion to mythology, when the verse or stanza requires to be filled up. A striking instance may be given from the admirable

passage where Tancred discovers Clorinda in the warrior on whom he has just inflicted a mortal blow

> "La vide, e la conobbe; e restò senza
> E moto e senso" ——

The effect is here complete, and here he would have desired to stop. But the necessity of the verse induced him to finish it with feebleness and affectation. *Ahi vista! Ahi conoscenza!* Such difficult metres as the ottava rima demand these sacrifices too frequently. Ariosto has innumerable lines of necessity.

Defects of the poem.

26. It is easy to censure the faults of this admirable poem. The supernatural machinery is perhaps somewhat in excess; yet this had been characteristic of the romantic school of poetry, which had moulded the taste of Europe, and is seldom displeasing to the reader. A still more unequivocal blemish is the disproportionate influence of love upon the heroic crusaders, giving a tinge of effeminacy to the whole poem, and exciting something like contempt in the austere critics, who have no standard of excellence in epic song but what the ancients have erected for us. But, while we must acknowledge that Tasso has indulged too far the inspirations of his own temperament, it may be candid to ask ourselves, whether a subject so grave, and by necessity so full of carnage, did not require many of the softer touches which he has given it. His battles are as spirited and picturesque as those of Ariosto, and perhaps more so than those of Virgil; but, to the taste of our times, he has a little too much of promiscuous slaughter. The Iliad had here set an unfortunate precedent, which epic poets thought themselves bound to copy. If Erminia and Armida had not been introduced, the classical critic might have censured less in the Jerusalem; but it would have been far less also the delight of mankind.

It indicates the peculiar genius of Tasso.

27. Whatever may be the laws of criticism, every poet will best obey the dictates of his own genius. The skill and imagination of Tasso made him equal to descriptions of war; but his heart was formed for that sort of pensive voluptuousness which most distinguishes his poetry, and which is very unlike the coarser sensuality of Ariosto. He lingers around the gardens of Armida, as though he had been himself her thrall. The

Florentine critics vehemently attacked her final reconciliation with Rinaldo in the twentieth canto, and the renewal of their loves; for the reader is left with no other expectation. Nor was their censure unjust; since it is a sacrifice of what should be the predominant sentiment in the conclusion of the poem. But Tasso seems to have become fond of Armida, and could not endure to leave in sorrow and despair the creature of his ethereal fancy, whom he had made so fair and so winning. It is probable that the majority of readers are pleased with this passage; but it can never escape the condemnation of severe judges.

Tasso compared to Virgil;

28. Tasso, doubtless, bears a considerable resemblance to Virgil. But independently of the vast advantages which the Latin language possesses in majesty and vigor, and which render exact comparison difficult as well as unfair, it may be said that Virgil displays more justness of taste, a more extensive observation, and, if we may speak thus in the absence of so much poetry which he may have imitated, a more genuine originality. Tasso did not possess much of the self-springing invention which we find in a few great poets, and which, in this higher sense, I cannot concede to Ariosto: he not only borrows freely, and perhaps studiously, from the ancients, but introduces frequent lines from earlier Italian poets, and especially from Petrarch. He has also some favorite turns of phrase, which serve to give a certain mannerism to his stanzas.

To Ariosto;

29. The Jerusalem was no sooner published than it was weighed against the Orlando Furioso; and neither Italy nor Europe have yet agreed which scale inclines. It is indeed one of those critical problems that admit of no certain solution, whether we look to the suffrage of those who feel acutely and justly, or to the general sense of mankind. We cannot determine one poet to be superior to the other, without assuming premises which no one is bound to grant. Those who read for a stimulating variety of circumstances, and the enlivening of a leisure hour, must prefer Ariosto; and he is probably, on this account, a poet of more universal popularity. It might be said perhaps by some, that he is more a favorite of men, and Tasso of women. And yet, in Italy, the sympathy with tender and graceful poetry is so general, that the Jerusalem has hardly been less in favor with the people than its livelier rival; and its fine stanzas may

still be heard by moonlight from the lips of a gondolier, floating along the calm bosom of the Venetian waters.[1]

30. Ariosto must be placed much more below Homer than Tasso falls short of Virgil. The Orlando has not the impetuosity of the Iliad: each is prodigiously rapid, but Homer has more momentum by his weight; the one is a hunter, the other a war-horse. The finest stanzas in Ariosto are fully equal to any in Tasso; but the latter has by no means so many feeble lines. Yet his language, though never affectedly obscure, is not so pellucid, and has a certain refinement which makes us sometimes pause to perceive the meaning. Whoever reads Ariosto slowly, will probably be offended by his negligence: whoever reads Tasso quickly, will lose something of the elaborate finish of his style.

To the Bolognese painters.

31. It is not easy to find a counterpart among painters for Ariosto. His brilliancy and fertile invention might remind us of Tintoret; but he is more natural, and less solicitous of effect. If indeed poetical diction be the correlative of coloring in our comparison of the arts, none of the Venetian school can represent the simplicity and averseness to ornament of language which belong to the Orlando Furioso; and it would be impossible, for other reasons, to look for a parallel in Roman or Tuscan pencil. But with Tasso the case is different; and, though it would be an affected expression to call him the founder of the Bolognese school, it is evident that he had a great influence on its chief painters, who came but a little after him. They imbued themselves with the spirit of a poem so congenial to their age, and so much admired in it. No one, I think, can consider their works, without perceiving both the analogy of the place

[1] The following passages may perhaps be naturally compared, both as being celebrated, and as descriptive of sound. Ariosto has, however, much the advantage; and I do not think the lines in the Jerusalem, though very famous, are altogether what I should select as a specimen of Tasso.

"Aspri concenti, orribile armonia
D' alte querele, d' ululi, e di strida
Della misera gente, che peria
Nel fondo per cagion della sua guida,
Istranamente concordar s' udia
Col fiero suon della fiamma omicida."
Orland. Fur., c. 14.

"Chiama gli abitator dell' ombre eterne
Il rauco suon della tartarea tromba;
Treman le spaziose atre caverne,
E l' aer cieco a quel rumor rimbomba.
Nè si stridendo mai dalle superne
Regioni del cielo il folgor piomba;
Nè si scossa giammai trema la terra
Quando i vapori in sen gravida serra."
Gierus. Lib., c. 4.

In the latter of these stanzas, there is rather too studied an effort at imitative sound: the lines are grand and nobly expressed; but they do not hurry along the reader like those of Ariosto. In his, there is little attempt at vocal imitation; yet we seem to hear the cries of the suffering, and the crackling of the flames.

each hold in their respective arts, and the traces of a feeling, caught directly from Tasso as their prototype and model. We recognize his spirit in the sylvan shades and voluptuous forms of Albano and Domenichino; in the pure beauty that radiates from the ideal heads of Guido; in the skilful composition, exact design, and noble expression, of the Caracci. Yet the school of Bologna seems to furnish no parallel to the enchanting grace and diffused harmony of Tasso; and we must, in this respect, look back to Correggio as his representative.

SECT. II.—ON SPANISH POETRY.

Luis de Leon — Herrera — Ercilla — Camoens — Spanish Ballads.

Poetry cultivated under Charles and Philip.

32. THE reigns of Charles and his son have long been reckoned the golden age of Spanish poetry; and if the art of verse was not cultivated in the latter period by any quite so successful as Garcilasso and Mendoza, who belonged to the earlier part of the century, the vast number of names that have been collected by diligent inquiry show, at least, a national taste which deserves some attention. The means of exhibiting a full account of even the most select names in this crowd are not readily at hand. In Spain itself, the poets of the age of Philip II., like those who lived under his great enemy in England, were, with very few exceptions, little regarded till after the middle of the eighteenth century. The Parnaso Español of Sedano, the first volumes of which were published in 1768, made them better known; but Bouterwek observes, that it would have been easy to make a superior collection, as we do not find several poems of the chief writers, with which the editor seems to have fancied the public to be sufficiently acquainted. An imperfect knowledge of the language, and a cursory view of these volumes, must disable me from speaking confidently of Castilian poetry; so far as I feel myself competent to judge, the specimens

chosen by Bouterwek do no injustice to the compilation.[1]

33. The best lyric poet of Spain in the opinion of many, with whom I venture to concur, was Fra Luis Ponce de Leon, born in 1527, and whose poems were probably written not very long after the middle of the century. The greater part are translations; but his original productions are chiefly religious, and full of that soft mysticism which allies itself so well to the emotions of a poetical mind. One of his odes, De la Vida del Cielo, which will be found entire in Bouterwek, is an exquisite piece of lyric poetry, which, in its peculiar line of devout aspiration, has perhaps never been excelled.[2] But the warmth of his piety was tempered by a classical taste, which he had matured by the habitual imitation of Horace. "At an early age," says Bouterwek, "he became intimately acquainted with the odes of Horace; and the elegance and purity of style which distinguish those compositions made a deep impression on his imagination. Classical simplicity and dignity were the models constantly present to his creative fancy. He, however, appropriated to himself the character of Horace's poetry too naturally ever to incur the danger of servile imitation. He discarded the prolix style of the canzone, and imitated the brevity of the strophes of Horace in romantic measures of syllables and rhymes: more just feeling for the imitation of the ancients was never evinced by any modern poet. His odes have, however, a character totally different from those of Horace, though the sententious air which marks the style of both authors imparts to them a deceptive resemblance. The religious austerity of Luis de Leon's life was not to be reconciled with the epicurism of the Latin poet: but, notwithstanding this very different disposition of the mind, it is not surprising that they should have adopted the same form of poetic expression; for each possessed a fine imagination, subordinate to the control of a sound understanding. Which of the two is

Luis de Leon.

1 "The merit of Spanish poems," says a critic equally candid and well-informed, "independently of those intended for representation, consists chiefly in smoothness of versification and purity of language, and in facility rather than strength of imagination."—Lord Holland's Lope de Vega, vol. i. p. 107. He had previously observed, that these poets were generally voluminous; "it was not uncommon even for the nobility of Philip IV.'s time to converse for some minutes in extemporaneous poetry; and in carelessness of metre, as well as in commonplace images, the verses of that time often remind us of the *improvisatori* of Italy."—p. 106.

2 P. 248.

the superior poet, in the most extended sense of the word, it would be difficult to determine; as each formed his style by free imitation, and neither overstepped the boundaries of a certain sphere of practical observation. Horace's odes exhibit a superior style of art, and, from the relationship between the thoughts and images, possess a degree of attraction which is wanting in those of Luis de Leon; but, on the other hand, the latter are the more rich in that natural kind of poetry which may be regarded as the overflowing of a pure soul, elevated to the loftiest regions of moral and religious idealism."[1] Among the fruits of these Horatian studies of Luis de Leon, we must place an admirable ode suggested by the prophecy of Nereus, wherein the genius of the Tagus, rising from its waters to Rodrigo, the last of the Gothic kings, as he lay encircled in the arms of Cava, denounces the ruin which their guilty loves were to entail upon Spain.[2]

34. Next to Luis de Leon in merit, and perhaps above him in European renown, we find Herrera, surnamed the Divine. He died in 1578; and his poems seem to have been first collectively published in 1582 He was an innovator in poetical language, whose boldness was sustained by popularity, though it may have diminished his fame. "Herrera was a poet," says Bouterwek, "of powerful talent, and one who evinced undaunted resolution in pursuing the new path which he had struck out for himself. The novel style, however, which he wished to introduce into Spanish poetry, was not the result of a spontaneous essay, flowing from immediate inspiration, but was theoretically constructed on artificial principles. Thus, amidst traits of real beauty, his poetry everywhere presents marks of affectation. The great fault of his language is too much singularity; and his expression, where it ought to be elevated, is merely far-fetched."[3] Velasquez observes, that, notwithstanding the genius and spirit of Herrera, his extreme care to polish his versification has rendered it sometimes unpleasing to those who require harmony and ease.[4]

Herrera.

35. Of these defects in the style of Herrera, I cannot

[1] P. 243.

[2] This ode I first knew many years since by a translation in the poems of Russell, which are too little remembered, except by a few good judges. It has been surmised by some Spanish critics to have suggested the famous vision of the Spirit of the Cape to Camoens; but the resemblance is not sufficient, and the dates rather incompatible.

[3] P. 229.

[4] Geschichte der Spanischen Dichtkunst, p. 207.

judge: his odes appear to possess a lyric elevation and richness of phrase, derived in some measure from the study of Pindar, or still more perhaps of the Old Testament, and worthy of comparison with Chiabrera. Those on the battle of Lepanto are most celebrated: they pour forth a torrent of resounding song, in those rich tones which the Castilian language so abundantly supplies. I cannot so thoroughly admire the ode addressed to Sleep, which Bouterwek as well as Sedano extol. The images are in themselves pleasing and appropriate, the lines steal with a graceful flow on the ear; but we should desire to find something more raised above the commonplaces of poetry.

General tone of Castilian poetry.

36. The poets of this age belong generally, more or less, to the Italian school. Many of them were also translators from Latin. In their odes, epistles, and sonnets, the resemblance of style, as well as that of the languages, make us sometimes almost believe that we are reading the Italian instead of the Spanish Parnaso. There seem, however, to be some shades of difference even in those who trod the same path. The Castilian amatory verse is more hyperbolical, more full of extravagant metaphors, but less subtle, less prone to ingenious trifling, less blemished by verbal conceits, than the Italian. Such at least is what has struck me, in the slight acquaintance I have with the former. The Spanish poets are also more redundant in descriptions of Nature, and more sensible to her beauties. I dare not assert that they have less grace and less power of exciting emotion: it may be my misfortune to have fallen rarely on passages that might repel my suspicion.

Castillejo.

37. It is at least evident that the imitation of Italy, propagated by Boscan and his followers, was not the indigenous style of Castile. And of this some of her most distinguished poets were always sensible. In the Diana of Montemayor, — a romance which, as such, we shall have to mention hereafter, — the poetry, largely interspersed, bears partly the character of the new, partly that of the old or native, school. The latter is esteemed superior. Castillejo endeavored to restore the gay rhythm of the redondilla, and turned into ridicule the imitators of Petrarch. Bouterwek speaks rather slightingly of his general poetic powers, though some of his canciones have a considerable share of elegance.

His genius, playful and witty, rather than elegant, seemed not ill-fitted to revive the popular poetry.[1] But those who claimed the praise of superior talents did not cease to cultivate the polished style of Italy. The most conspicuous, perhaps, before the end of the century, were Gil Polo, Espinel, Lope de Vega, Barahona de Soto, and Figueroa.[2] Several other names, not without extracts, will be found in Bouterwek.

Araucana of Ercilla.

38. Voltaire, in his early and very defective essay on epic poetry, made known to Europe the Araucana of Ercilla, which has ever since enjoyed a certain share of reputation, though condemned by many critics as tedious and prosaic. Bouterwek depreciates it in rather more sweeping a manner than seems consistent with the admissions he afterwards makes.[3] A talent for lively description and for painting situations, a natural and correct diction, which he ascribes to Ercilla, if they do not constitute a claim to a high rank among poets, are at least as much as many have possessed. An English writer of good taste has placed him in a triumvirate with Homer and Ariosto for power of narration.[4] Raynouard observes that Ercilla has taken Ariosto as his model, especially in the opening of his cantos. But the long digressions and episodes of the Araucana, which the poet has not had the art to connect with his subject, render it fatiguing. The first edition, in 1569, contains but fifteen books; the second part was published in 1578; the whole together in 1590.[5]

Many epic poems in Spain.

39. The Araucana is so far from standing alone in this class of poetry, that not less than twenty-five epic poems appeared in Spain within little more than half a century. These will be found enumerated, and, as far as possible, described and characterized, in Velasquez's History of Spanish Poetry, which I always quote in

P. 267.

Lord Holland has given a fuller account of the poetry of Lope de Vega than either Bouterwek or Velasquez and Dieze; and the extracts in his Lives of Lope de Vega and Guillen de Castro will not, I believe, be found in the Parnaso Español, which is contrived on a happy plan of excluding what is best. Las Lagrimas de Angelica, by Barahona de Soto, Lord H. says, "has always been esteemed one of the best poems in the Spanish language" — vol. i. p. 33. Bouterwek says he has never met with the book. It is praised by Cervantes in Don Quixote.

The translation of Tasso's Aminta, by Jauregui, has been preferred by Menage as well as Cervantes to the original. But there is no extraordinary merit in turning Italian into Spanish, even with some improvement of the diction.

3 P. 407.

4 Pursuits of Literature.

5 Journal des Savans, September, 1824.

the German translation with the valuable notes of Dieze.[1] Bouterwek mentions but a part of the number; and a few of them may be conjectured by the titles not to be properly epic. It is denied by these writers, that Ercilla excelled all his contemporaries in heroic song. I find, however, a different sentence in a Spanish poet of that age, who names him as superior to the rest.[2]

Camoens.

40. But in Portugal there had arisen a poet, in comparison of whose glory that of Ercilla is as nothing. The name of Camoens has truly an European reputation; but the Lusiad is written in a language not generally familiar. From Portuguese critics it would be unreasonable to demand want of prejudice in favor of a poet so illustrious, and of a poem so peculiarly national. The Æneid reflects the glory of Rome as from a mirror: the Lusiad is directly and exclusively what its name, "The Portuguese" (Os Lusiadas), denotes, the praise of the Lusitanian people. Their past history chimes in, by means of episodes, with the great event of Gama's voyage to India. The faults of Camoens, in the management of his fable and the choice of machinery, are sufficiently obvious: it is, nevertheless, the first successful attempt in modern Europe to construct an epic poem on the ancient model; for the Gierusalemme Liberata, though incomparably superior, was not written or published so soon. In consequence perhaps of this epic form, which, even when imperfectly delineated, long obtained, from the general veneration for antiquity, a greater respect at the hands of critics than perhaps it deserved, the celebrity of Camoens has always been considerable. In point of fame, he ranks among the poets of the South immediately after the first names of Italy; nor is the distinctive character that belongs to the poetry of the southern languages anywhere more fully perceived than in the Lusiad. In a general estimate of its

Defects of the Lusiad.

1 Pp. 376–407; Bouterwek, p. 413.

2 "Oye el estilo grave, el blando acento,
Y altos concentos del varon famoso
Que en el heroyco verso fue el primero
Que honró a su patria, y aun quiza el postrero.
Del fuerte Arauco el pecho altivo espanta
Don Alonso de Ercilla con el mano,
Con ella lo derriba y lo levanta,
Vence y honra venciendo al Araucano;
Calla sus hechos, los agenos canta,
Con tal estilo que eclipsó al Toscano:
Virtud que el cielo para sí reserva
Que en el furor de Marte esté Minerva."

La Casa de la Memoria, por Vicente Espinel, in Parnaso Español, viii. 352.

Antonio, near the end of the seventeenth century, extols Ercilla very highly, but intimates that some did not relish his simple perspicuity. "Ad hunc usque diem ab iis omnibus avidissime legitur, qui facile dicendi genus atque perspicuum admittere vim suam et nervos, nativaque sublimitate quadam attolli posse, cothurnatumque ire non ignorant."

merits, it must appear rather feeble and prosaic; the geographical and historical details are insipid and tedious; a skilful use of poetical artifice is never exhibited; we are little detained to admire an ornamented diction, or glowing thoughts, or brilliant imagery; a certain negligence disappoints us in the most beautiful passages; and it is not till a second perusal that their sweetness has time to glide into the heart. The celebrated stanzas on Inez de Castro are a proof of this.

41. These deficiencies, as a taste formed in the English school, or in that of classical antiquity, is apt to account them, are greatly compensated, and doubtless far more to a native than they can be to us, by a freedom from all that offends, — for he is never turgid nor affected nor obscure; by a perfect ease and transparency of narration; by scenes and descriptions, possessing a certain charm of coloring, and perhaps not less pleasing from the apparent negligence of the pencil; by a style kept up at a level just above common language; by a mellifluous versification; and, above all, by a kind of soft languor which tones, as it were, the whole poem, and brings perpetually home to our minds the poetical character and interesting fortunes of its author. As the mirror of a heart so full of love, courage, generosity, and patriotism, as that of Camoens, the Lusiad can never fail to please us, whatever place we may assign to it in the records of poetical genius.[1]

Its excellences.

42. The Lusiad is best known in England by the translation of Mickle, who has been thought to have done something more than justice to his author, both by the unmeasured eulogies he bestows upon him, and by the more substantial service of excelling the original in his unfaithful delineation. The style of Mickle is certainly more poetical, according to our standard, than that of Camoens; that is, more figurative and emphatic: but it seems to me replenished with commonplace phrases, and wanting in the facility and sweetness of the original; in which it is well known that he has interpolated a great deal without a pretence.[2]

Mickle's translation.

1 "In every language," says Mr. Southey, probably, in the Quarterly Review, xxvii. 38, "there is a magic of words as untranslatable as the Sesame in the Arabian tale: you may retain the meaning; but, if the words be changed, the spell is lost. The magic has its effect only upon those to whom the language is as familiar as their mother-tongue; hardly, indeed, upon any but those to whom it is really such. Camoens possesses it in perfection: it is his peculiar excellence."

2 Several specimens of Mickle's infidelity in translation, which exceed all liberties ever taken in this way, are mentioned in the Quarterly Review.

43. The most celebrated passage in the Lusiad is that wherein the Spirit of the Cape, rising in the midst of his stormy seas, threatens the daring adventurer that violates their unploughed waters. In order to judge fairly of this conception, we should endeavor to forget all that has been written in imitation of it. Nothing has become more commonplace in poetry than one of its highest flights, — supernatural personification; and, as children draw notable monsters when they cannot come near the human form, so every poetaster, who knows not how to describe one object in nature, is quite at home with a goblin. Considered by itself. the idea is impressive and even sublime. Nor am I aware of any evidence to impeach its originality, in the only sense which originality of poetical invention can bear: it is a combination which strikes us with the force of novelty, and which we cannot instantly resolve into any constituent elements. The prophecy of Nereus, to which we have lately alluded, is much removed in grandeur and appropriateness of circumstance from this passage of Camoens, though it may contain the germ of his conception. It is, however, one that seems much above the genius of its author. Mild, graceful, melancholy, he has never given in any other place signs of such vigorous imagination; and, when we read these lines on the Spirit of the Cape, it is impossible not to perceive, that, like Frankenstein, he is unable to deal with the monster he has created. The formidable Adamastor is rendered mean by particularity of description, descending even to yellow teeth. The speech put into his mouth is feeble and prolix; and it is a serious objection to the whole, that the awful vision answers no purpose but that of ornament, and is impotent against the success and glory of the navigators. A spirit of whatever dimensions, that can neither overwhelm a ship, nor even raise a tempest, is incomparably less terrible than a real hurricane.

Celebrated passage in the Lusiad.

44. Camoens is still, in his shorter poems, esteemed the chief of Portuguese poets in this age, and possibly in every other: his countrymen deem him their model, and judge of later verse by comparison with his. In every kind of composition then used in Portugal, he has left proofs of excellence. "Most of his sonnets," says Bouterwek, "have love for their theme, and they are of very unequal merit; some are full of Petrarchic tenderness and grace, and moulded with classical correctness; others are im-

Minor poems of Camoens.

petuous and romantic, or disfigured by false learning, or full of tedious pictures of the conflicts of passion with reason. Upon the whole, however, no Portuguese poet has so correctly seized the character of the sonnet as Camoens. Without apparent effort, merely by the ingenious contrast of the first eight with the last six lines, he knew how to make these little effusions convey a poetic unity of ideas and impressions, after the model of the best Italian sonnets, in so natural a manner, that the first lines or quartets of the sonnet excite a soft expectation, which is harmoniously fulfilled by the tercets or last six lines."[1] The same writer praises several other of the miscellaneous compositions of Camoens.

45. But, though no Portuguese of the sixteenth century has come near to this illustrious poet, Ferreira endeavored with much good sense, if not with great elevation, to emulate the didactic tone of Horace, both in lyric poems and epistles, of which the latter had been most esteemed.[2] The classical school formed by Ferreira produced other poets in the sixteenth century; but it seems to have been little in unison with the national character. The reader will find as full an account of these as, if he is unacquainted with the Portuguese language, he is likely to desire, in the author on whom I have chiefly relied.

Ferreira.

46. The Spanish ballads or romances are of very different ages. Some of them, as has been observed in another place, belong to the fifteenth century; and there seems sufficient ground for referring a small number to even an earlier date. But by far the greater portion is of the reign of Philip II., or even that of his successor. The Moorish romances in general, and all those on the Cid, are reckoned by Spanish critics among the most modern. Those published by Depping and Duran have rarely an air of the raciness and simplicity which usually distinguish the poetry of the people, and seem to have been written by poets of Valladolid or Madrid, the contemporaries of Cervantes, with a good deal of elegance, though not much vigor. The Moors of romance, the chivalrous gentlemen of Granada, were displayed by these Castilian poets in attractive colors;[3] and much more

Spanish ballads.

[1] Hist. of Portuguese Literature, p. 187.

[2] Id., p. 111.

[3] Bouterwek, Sismondi, and others have quoted a romance, beginning "Tanta Zayda v Adalifa," as the effusion of an orthodox zeal, which had taken offence at these encomiums on infidels. Whoever reads this little poem, which may be found in Depping's collection, will see that it is written more as a humorous ridicule on con-

did the traditions of their own heroes, especially of the Cid, the bravest and most noble-minded of them all, furnish materials for their popular songs. Their character, it is observed by the latest editor, is unlike that of the older romances of chivalry, which had been preserved orally, as he conceives, down to the middle of the sixteenth century, when they were inserted in the Cancionero de Romances at Antwerp, 1555.[1] I have been informed, that an earlier edition, printed in Spain, has lately been discovered. In these there is a certain prolixity and hardness of style, a want of connection, a habit of repeating verses or entire passages from others. They have nothing of the marvellous, nor borrow any thing from Arabian sources. In some others of the more ancient poetry, there are traces of the oriental manner, and a peculiar tone of wild melancholy. The little poems scattered through the prose romance, entitled, Las Guerras de Granada, are rarely, as I should conceive, older than the reign of Philip II. These Spanish ballads are known to our public, but generally with inconceivable advantage, by the very fine and animated translations of Mr. Lockhart.[2]

temporary poets than a serious reproof. It is much more lively than the answer, which these modern critics also quote. Both these poems are of the end of the sixteenth century. Neither Bouterwek nor Sismondi have kept in mind the recent date of the Moorish ballads.

[1] Duran, in the preface to his Romancero of 1832. These Spanish collections of songs and ballads, called Cancioneros and Romanceros, are very scarce; and there is some uncertainty among bibliographers as to their editions. According to Duran, this of Antwerp contains many romances unpublished before, and far older than those of the fifteenth century, collected in the Cancionero General of 1516. It does not appear, perhaps, that the number which can be referred with probability to a period anterior to 1400 is considerable; but they are very interesting. Among these are Los Fronterizos, or songs which the Castilians used in their incursions on the Moorish frontier. These were preserved orally, like other popular poetry. We find in these early pieces, he says, some traces of the Arabian style, rather in the melancholy of its tone than in any splendor of imagery; giving, as an instance, some lines quoted by Sismondi, beginning "Fonte frida, fonte frida, Fonte frida y con amor," which are evidently very ancient. Sismondi says (Littérature du Midi, iii. 240) that it is difficult to explain the charm of this little poem, but "by the tone of truth, and the absence of all object;" and Bouterwek calls it very nonsensical. It seems to me that some real story is shadowed in it under images in themselves of very little meaning, which may account for the tone of truth and pathos it breathes.

The older romances are usually in alternate verses of eight and seven syllables; and the rhymes are *consonant*, or real rhymes. The *assonance* is, however, older than Lord Holland supposes, who says (Life of Lope de Vega, vol. ii. p. 12) that it was not introduced till the end of the sixteenth century. It occurs in several that Duran reckons ancient.

The romance of the Conde Alarcos is probably of the fifteenth century. This is written in octosyllable consonant rhymes, without division of strophes. The Moorish ballads, with a very few exceptions, belong to the reigns of Philip II. and Philip III.; and those of the Cid, about which so much interest has been taken, are the latest, and among the least valuable of all. All these are, I believe, written on the principle of assonances.

[2] An admirable romance on a bull-fight, in Mr. Lockhart's volume, is faintly to be traced in one introduced in Las Guerras de Granada; but I have since found it much more at length in another collection. It is still, however, far less poetical than the English imitation.

SECT. III.—ON FRENCH AND GERMAN POETRY.

French Poetry—Ronsard—His Followers—German Poetry.

French poets numerous.

47. THIS was an age of verse in France; and perhaps in no subsequent period do we find so long a catalogue of her poets. Goujet has recorded not merely the names, but the lives, in some measure, of nearly two hundred, whose works were published in this half-century. Of this number, scarcely more than five or six are much remembered in their own country. It is possible, indeed, that the fastidiousness of French critics, or their idolatry of the age of Louis XIV., and of that of Voltaire, may have led to a little injustice in their estimate of these early versifiers. Our own prejudices are apt, of late, to take an opposite direction.

Change in the tone of French poetry.

48. A change in the character of French poetry, about the commencement of this period, is referable to the general revolution of literature. The allegorical personifications which, from the era of the Roman de la Rose, had been the common field of verse, became far less usual, and gave place to an inundation of mythology and classical allusion. The *Désir* and *Reine d' Amour* of the older school became Cupid with his arrows, and Venus with her doves; the theological and cardinal virtues, which had gained so many victories over *Sensualité* and *Faux Semblant*, vanished themselves from a poetry which had generally enlisted itself under the enemy's banner. This cutting off of an old resource rendered it necessary to explore other mines. All antiquity was ransacked for analogies; and, where the images were not wearisomely commonplace, they were absurdly far-fetched. This revolution was certainly not instantaneous; but it followed the rapid steps of philological learning, which had been nothing at the accession of Francis I., and was every thing at his death.[1] In his court, and in

[1] [Sainte-Beuve, in his learned Tableau de la Poésie Française au seizième Siècle, Paris, 1828, speaks of this revolution in taste, which substituted a classical school for that of the middle ages, kept up as it had been by Marot and his contemporaries, as almost sudden: "Tout enfin semble promettre à Marot une postérité d'admirations encore plus que de rivaux et à la poésie un perfectionnement paisible et con-

that of his son, if business or gallantry rendered learning impracticable, it was at least the mode to affect an esteem for it. Many names in the list of French poets are conspicuous for high rank, and a greater number are among the famous scholars of the age. These, accustomed to writing in Latin, sometimes in verse, and yielding a superstitious homage to the mighty dead of antiquity, thought that they ennobled their native language by destroying her idiomatic purity.

49. The prevalence, however, of this pedantry was chiefly owing to one poet, of great though short-lived renown, Pierre Ronsard. He was the first of seven contemporaries in song under Henry II., then denominated the French Pleiad; the others were Jodelle, Bellay, Baif, Thyard, Dorat, and Belleau. Ronsard, well acquainted with the ancient languages, and full of the most presumptuous vanity, fancied that he was born to mould the speech of his fathers into new forms more adequate to his genius.

Ronsard.

> "Je fis des nouveaux mots,
> J'en condamnai les vieux." [1]

His style, therefore, is as barbarous, if the continual adoption of Latin and Greek derivatives renders a modern language barbarous, as his allusions are pedantic. They are more ridiculously such in his amatory sonnets: in his odes these faults are rather less intolerable, and there is a spirit and grandeur which show him to have possessed a poetical mind.[2] The popularity of Ronsard was extensive; and, though he sometimes complained of the neglect of the great, he wanted not the approbation of those whom poets are most ambitious to please. Charles IX. addressed some lines to Ronsard, which are really elegant, and at least do more honor to that prince than any thing else recorded of him; and the verses of this poet are said to have lightened the weary hours of Mary Stuart's imprisonment. On his death, in 1586, a funeral service was performed in Paris, with the best music that the

tinu, lorsqu'à l'improviste la génération nouvelle réclame contre une admiration jusque là unanime, et, le détachant brusquement du passé, déclare qu'il est temps de s'ouvrir par d'autres voies un avenir de gloire. *L'Illustration de la Langue Française*, par Joachim Dubellay, est comme le manifeste de cette insurrection soudaine, qu'on peut dater de 1549." The extracts which he proceeds to give from this work of Dubellay prove that it was at least intended to recommend the cultivation of style in the native language through a careful study of classical models. — 1847.]

[1] Goujet, Bibliothèque Française, xii. 199.

[2] Id., 216.

king could command: it was attended by the Cardinal de Bourbon and an immense concourse; eulogies in prose and verse were recited in the university; and in those anxious moments, when the crown of France was almost in its agony, there was leisure to lament that Ronsard had been withdrawn. How differently attended was the grave of Spenser![1]

50. Ronsard was capable of conceiving strongly and bringing his conceptions in clear and forcible, though seldom in pure or well-chosen language, before the mind. The poem entitled Promesse, which will be found in Auguis's Recueil des Anciens Poëtes, is a proof of this, and excels what little besides I have read of this poet.[2] Bouterwek, whose criticism on Ronsard appears fair and just, and who gives him, and those who belonged to his school, credit for perceiving the necessity of elevating the tone of French verse above the creeping manner of the allegorical rhymers, observes that, even in his errors, we discover a spirit striving upwards, disdaining what is trivial, and restless in the pursuit of excellence.[3] But such a spirit may produce very bad and tasteless poetry. La Harpe, who admits Ronsard's occasional beauties and his poetic fire, is repelled by his scheme of versification, full of *enjambemens*, as disgusting to a correct French ear as they are, in a moderate use, pleasing to our own. After the appearance of Malherbe, the poetry of Ronsard fell into contempt; and the pure correctness of Louis XIV.'s age was not likely to endure his barbarous innovations and false taste.[4] Balzac, not long afterwards, turns his pedantry into ridicule, and, admitting the abundance of the stream, adds that it was turbid.[5] In later times, more justice has been done to the spirit and imagination of this poet, without repealing the sentence against his style.[6]

1 Id., 207.

2 Vol. iv. p. 135.

3 Geschichte der Poesie, v. 214.

4 Goujet, 245. Malherbe scratched out about half from his copy of Ronsard, giving his reasons in the margin. Racan, one day looking over this, asked whether he approved what he had not effaced. "Not a bit more," replied Malherbe, "than the rest."

5 "Encore aujourd'hui il est admiré par les trois quarts du parlement de Paris, et généralement par les autres parlemens de France. L'université et les Jésuites tiennent encore son part contre la cour, et contre l'académie. . . Ce n'est pas un poëte bien entier, c'est le commencement et la matière d'un poëte. On voit, dans ses œuvres, des parties naissantes, et à demi animées, d'un corps qui se forme et qui se fait, mais qui n'a garde d' estre achevé. C'est une grande source, il faut l'avouer; mais c'est une source troublée et boueuse; une source, où non seulement il y a moins d'eau que de limon, mais où l'ordure empêche de couler l'eau." — Œuvres de Balzac, i. 670; and Goujet, *ubi supra*.

6 La Harpe; Biogr. Univ.

[M. Sainte-Beuve has devoted a whole volume to a selection from Ronsard, Paris, 1828, to whom, without undue praise, he has restored a more honorable place than

51. The remaining stars of the Pleiad, except perhaps Bellay, sometimes called the French Ovid, and whose "Regrets," or lamentations for his absence from France during a residence at Rome, are almost as querulous, if not quite so reasonable, as those of his prototype on the Ister,[1] seem scarce worthy of particular notice; for Jodelle, the founder of the stage in France, has deserved much less credit as a poet, and fell into the fashionable absurdity of making French out of Greek. Raynouard bestows some eulogy on Baif.[2] Those who came afterwards were sometimes imitators of Ronsard, and, like most imitators of a faulty manner, far more pedantic and far-fetched than himself. An unintelligible refinement, which every nation in Europe seems in succession to have admitted into its poetry, has consigned much then written in France to oblivion. As large a proportion of the French verse in this period seems to be amatory as of the Italian; and the Italian style is sometimes followed. But a simpler and more lively turn of language, though without the naïveté of Marot, often distinguishes these compositions. These pass the bounds of decency not seldom; a privilege which seems in Italy to have been reserved for certain Fescennine metres, and is not indulged to the solemnity of the sonnet or canzone. The Italian language is ill adapted to the epigram, in which the French succeed so well.[3]

Other French poets.

52. A few may be selected from the numerous versifiers under the sons of Henry II. Amadis Jamyn, the pupil of Ronsard, was reckoned by his contemporaries almost a rival, and is more natural, less inflated and emphatic, than his master.[4] This praise is by no means due to a more celebrated poet, Du Bartas. His numerous productions, unlike those of his contemporaries, turn mostly upon sacred history; but his poem on the Creation, called La Se-

Du Bartas.

Malherbe and those who took their tone from him had assigned him. The extracts are chiefly from his lighter poetry, in which the pedantry of his more pompous style does not much appear. Though with little invention,—and indeed a large proportion of these selections is taken from Latin or Greek poets,—Ronsard is often more happy in expression, and more spirited as well as gay in sentiment, than we should expect to find after reading his labored poems.—1847.]

[1] Goujet, xiii. 128; Auguis.

[2] "Baif is one of the poets, who, in my opinion, have happily contributed by their example to fix the rules of our versification."—Journal des Savans, Feb. 1825.

[3] Goujet devotes three volumes, the twelfth, thirteenth, and fourteenth of his Bibliothèque Française, to the poets of these fifty years. Bouterwek and La Harpe have touched only on a very few names. In the Recueil des Anciens Poëtes, the extracts from them occupy about a volume and a half.

[4] Goujet, xiii. 229; Biogr. Univ.

maine, is that which obtained most reputation, and by which alone he is now known. The translation by Silvester has rendered it in some measure familiar to the readers of our old poetry; and attempts have been made, not without success, to show that Milton had been diligent in picking jewels from this mass of bad taste and bad writing. Du Bartas, in his style, was a disciple of Ronsard: he affects words derived from the ancient languages, or, if founded on analogy, yet without precedent, and has as little naturalness or dignity in his images as purity in his idiom. But his imagination, though extravagant, is vigorous and original.[1]

Pibrac: Desportes

53. Pibrac, a magistrate of great integrity, obtained an extraordinary reputation by his quatrains; a series of moral tetrastichs in the style of Theognis. These first appeared in 1574, fifty in number, and were augmented to 126 in later editions. They were continually republished in the seventeenth century, and translated into many European and even oriental languages. It cannot be wonderful, that, in the change of taste and manners, they have ceased to be read.[2] An imitation of the sixth satire of Horace, by Nicolas Rapin, printed in the collection of Auguis, is good and in very pure style.[3] Philippe Desportes, somewhat later, chose a better school than that of Ronsard: he rejected its pedantry and affectation, and by the study of Tibullus, as well as by his natural genius, gave a tenderness and grace to the poetry of love which those pompous versifiers had never sought. He has been esteemed the precursor of a better era; and his versification is rather less lawless,[4] according to La Harpe, than that of his predecessors.

French metre and versification.

54. The rules of metre became gradually established. Few writers of this period neglect the alternation of masculine and feminine rhymes;[5] but the open vowel will be found in several of the earlier. Du

[1] Goujet, xiii. 304. The Semaine of Du Bartas was printed thirty times within six years, and translated into Latin, Italian, German, and Spanish, as well as English. Id., 312, on the authority of La Croix du Maine.

Du Bartas, according to a French writer of the next century, used methods of exciting his imagination which I recommend to the attention of young poets. "L'on dit en France que Du Bartas, auparavant que de faire cette belle description de cheval où il a si bien rencontré, s'enfermoit quelquefois dans une chambre, et se mettant à quatre pattes, souffloit, hennissoit, gambadoit, tiroit des ruades, alloit l'amble, le trot, le galop, à courbette, et tâçhoit par toutes sortes de moyens à bien contrefaire le cheval." — Naudé, Considérations sur les Coups d'Estat, p. 47.

[2] Goujet, xii. 266; Biogr. Univ.

[3] Recueil des Poëtes, v. 361.

[4] Goujet, xiv. 63; La Harpe; Auguis, v. 343-377.

[5] Grevin, about 1558, is an exception. Goujet, xii. 159.

Bartas almost affects the *enjambement*, or continuation of the sense beyond the couplet; and even Desportes does not avoid it. Their metres are various: the Alexandrine, if so we may call it, or verse of twelve syllables, was occasionally adopted by Ronsard, and in time displaced the old verse of ten syllables, which became appropriated to the lighter style. The sonnets, as far as I have observed, are regular; and this form, which had been very little known in France, after being introduced by Jodelle and Ronsard, became one of the most popular modes of composition.[1] Several attempts were made to naturalize the Latin metres; but this pedantic innovation could not long have success. Specimens of it may be found in Pasquier.[2]

General character of French poetry.

55. It may be said, perhaps, of French poetry in general, but at least in this period, that it deviates less from a certain standard than any other. It is not often low, as may be imputed to the earlier writers, because a peculiar style, removed from common speech, and supposed to be classical, was a condition of satisfying the critics: it is not often obscure, at least in syntax, as the Italian sonnet is apt to be, because the genius of the language and the habits of society demanded perspicuity. But it seldom delights us by a natural sentiment, or unaffected grace of diction, because both one and the other were fettered by conventional rules. The monotony of amorous song is more wearisome, if that be possible, than among the Italians.

56. The characteristics of German verse impressed upon it

[1] Bouterwek, v. 212.

[2] Recherches de la France, l. vii. c. 11. Baif has passed for the inventor of this foolish art in France, which was more common there than in England. But Prosper Marchand ascribes a translation of the Iliad and Odyssey into regular French hexameters to one Mousset, of whom nothing is known; on no better authority, however, than a vague passage of D'Aubigné, who "remembered to have seen such a book sixty years ago." Though Mousset may be imaginary, he furnishes an article to Marchand, who brings together a good deal of learning as to the Latinized French metres of the sixteenth century. Dictionnaire Historique.

Passerat, Ronsard, Nicolas Rapin, and Pasquier tried their hands in this style. Rapin improved upon it by rhyming in Sapphics. The following stanzas are from his ode on the death of Ronsard:—

"Vous que les ruisseaux d'Hélicon fréquentez,
Vous que les jardins solitaires hantez,
Et le fonds des bois, curieux de choisir
L'ombre et le loisir.

"Qui vivant bien loin de la fange et du bruit,
Et de ces grandeurs que le peuple poursuit,
Estimez les vers que la muse après vous
Trempe de miel doux.

"Notre grand Ronsard, de ce monde sorti,
Les efforts derniers de la Parque a senti;
Ses faveurs n'ont pu le garantir enfin
Contre le destin," &c. &c.

PASQUIER, *ubi sup. a.*

by the Meister-singers still remained, though the songs of those fraternities seem to have ceased. It was chiefly didactic or religious, often satirical, and employing the veil of apologue. Luther, Hans Sachs, and other more obscure names, are counted among the fabulists; but the most successful was Burcard Waldis, whose fables, partly from Æsop, partly original, were first published in 1548. The Froschmauseler of Rollenhagen, in 1545, is in a similar style of political and moral apologue with some liveliness of description. Fischart is another of the moral satirists, but extravagant in style and humor, resembling Rabelais, of whose romance he gave a free translation. One of his poems, Die Gluckhafte Schiff, is praised by Bouterwek for beautiful descriptions and happy inventions; but in general he seems to be the Skelton of Germany. Many German ballads belong to this period, partly taken from the old tales of chivalry: in these the style is humble, with no poetry except that of invention, which is not their own; yet they are true-hearted and unaffected, and better than what the next age produced.[1]

German poetry.

SECT. IV.—ON ENGLISH POETRY.

Paradise of Dainty Devices — Sackville — Gascoyne — Spenser's Shepherd's Kalendar — Improvement in Poetry — England's Helicon — Sidney — Shakspeare's Poems — Poets near the close of the Century — Translations — Scots and English Ballads — Spenser's Faery Queen.

57. THE poems of Wyatt and Surrey, with several more, first appeared in 1557, and were published in a little book, entitled Tottel's Miscellanies. But, as both of these belonged to the reign of Henry VIII., their poetry has come already under our review. It is probable that Lord Vaux's short pieces, which are next to those of Surrey and Wyatt in merit, were written before the middle of the century. Some of these are published in Tottel, and others in a scarce collection; the first edition of which

Paradise of Dainty Devices.

1 Bouterwek, vol. ix.; Heinsius, vol. iv.

was, in 1576, quaintly named, The Paradise of Dainty Devices. The poems in this volume, as in that of Tottel are not coeval with its publication: it has been supposed to represent the age of Mary, full as much as that of Elizabeth; and one of the chief contributors, if not framers, of the collection, Richard Edwards, died in 1566. Thirteen poems are by Lord Vaux, who certainly did not survive the reign of Mary.

Character of this collection.

58. We are indebted to Sir Egerton Brydges for the republication, in his British Bibliographer, of the Paradise of Dainty Devices; of which, though there had been eight editions, it is said that not above six copies existed.[1] The poems are almost all short, and by more nearly thirty than twenty different authors. "They do not, it must be admitted," says their editor, "belong to the higher classes: they are of the moral and didactic kind. In their subject there is too little variety, as they deal very generally in the commonplaces of ethics, such as the fickleness and caprices of love, the falsehood and instability of friendship, and the vanity of all human pleasures. But many of these are often expressed with a vigor which would do credit to any era. . . . If my partiality does not mislead me, there is in most of these short pieces some of that indescribable attraction which springs from the coloring of the heart. The charm of imagery is wanting; but the precepts inculcated seem to flow from the feelings of an overloaded bosom." Edwards he considers, probably with justice, as the best of the contributors, and Lord Vaux the next. We should be inclined to give as high a place to William Hunnis, were his productions all equal to one little poem;[2] but too often he falls into trivial morality and a ridiculous excess of alliteration. The amorous poetry is the best in this Paradise; it is not imaginative or very graceful, or exempt from the false taste of antithetical conceits, but sometimes natural and pleasing; the serious pieces are in general very heavy, yet there

[1] Beloe's Anecdotes of Literature, vol. v.

[2] This song is printed in Campbell's Specimens of English Poets, vol. i. p. 117. It begins, —

"When first mine eyes did view and mark."

The little poem of Edwards, called Amantium Iræ, has often been reprinted in modern collections, and is reckoned by Brydges one of the most beautiful in the language. But hardly any light poem of this early period is superior to some lines addressed to Isabella Markham by Sir John Harrington, bearing the date of 1564. If these are genuine, and I know not how to dispute it, they are as polished as any written at the close of the queen's reign. These are not in the Paradise of Dainty Devices.

is a dignity and strength in some of the devotional strains. They display the religious earnestness of that age with a kind of austere philosophy in their views of life. Whatever indeed be the subject, a tone of sadness reigns through this misnamed Paradise of Daintiness, as it does through all the English poetry of this particular age. It seems as if the confluence of the poetic melancholy of the Petrarchists with the reflective seriousness of the Reformation overpowered the lighter sentiments of the soul; and some have imagined, I know not how justly, that the persecutions of Mary's reign contributed to this effect.

59. But at the close of that dark period, while bigotry might be expected to render the human heart torpid, and the English nation seemed too fully absorbed in religious and political discontent to take much relish in literary amusements, one man shone out for an instant in the higher walks of poetry. This was Thomas Sackville, many years afterwards Lord Buckhurst, and high treasurer of England, thus withdrawn from the haunts of the Muses to a long and honorable career of active life. The Mirrour of Magistrates, published in 1559, is a collection of stories by different authors, on the plan of Boccaccio's prose work, De Casibus Virorum Illustrium, recounting the misfortunes and reverses of men eminent in English history. It was designed to form a series of dramatic soliloquies united in one interlude.[1] Sackville, who seems to have planned the scheme, wrote an Induction, or prologue, and also one of the stories, that of the first Duke of Buckingham. The Induction displays best his poetical genius: it is, like much earlier poetry, a representation of allegorical personages, but with a fertility of imagination, vividness of description, and strength of language, which not only leave his predecessors far behind, but may fairly be compared with some of the most poetical passages in Spenser. Sackville's Induction forms a link which unites the school of Chaucer and Lydgate to the Faery Queen. It would certainly be vain to look in Chaucer, wherever Chaucer is original, for the grand creations of Sackville's fancy; yet we should never find any one who would rate Sackville

Sackville's Induction.

[1] Warton, iv. 40. A copious account of the Mirrour for Magistrates occupies the forty-eighth and three following sections of the History of Poetry, pp. 33-105. In this, Warton has introduced rather a long analysis of the Inferno of Dante, which he seems to have thought little known to the English public; as in that age, I believe, was the case.

above Chaucer. The strength of an eagle is not to be measured only by the height of his place, but by the time that he continues on the wing. Sackville's Induction consists of a few hundred lines; and even in these there is a monotony of gloom and sorrow which prevents us from wishing it to be longer. It is truly styled by Campbell a landscape on which the sun never shines. Chaucer is various, flexible, and observant of all things in outward nature, or in the heart of man. But Sackville is far above the frigid elegance of Surrey; and, in the first days of Elizabeth's reign, is the herald of that splendor in which it was to close.

Inferiority of poets in early years of Elizabeth.

60. English poetry was not speedily animated by the example of Sackville. His genius stands absolutely alone in the age to which as a poet he belongs. Not that there was any deficiency in the number of versifiers: the Muses were honored by the frequency, if not by the dignity, of their worshippers. A different sentence will be found in some books; and it has become common to elevate the Elizabethan age in one undiscriminating panegyric. For wise counsellors, indeed, and acute politicians, we could not perhaps extol one part of that famous reign at the expense of another. Cecil and Bacon, Walsingham, Smith, and Sadler, belong to the earlier days of the queen. But, in a literary point of view, the contrast is great between the first and second moiety of her four-and-forty years. We have seen this already in other subjects than poetry; and in that we may appeal to such parts of the Mirrour of Magistrates as are not written by Sackville, to the writings of Churchyard, or to those of Gouge and Turberville. These writers scarcely venture to leave the ground, or wander in the fields of fancy. They even abstain from the ordinary commonplaces of verse, as if afraid that the reader should distrust or misinterpret their images. The first who deserves to be mentioned as an exception is George Gascoyne, whose

Gascoyne.

Steel Glass, published in 1576, is the earliest instance of English satire, and has strength and sense enough to deserve respect. Chalmers has praised it highly. "There is a vein of sly sarcasm in this piece which appears to me to be original; and his intimate knowledge of mankind enabled him to give a more curious picture of the dress, manners, amusements, and follies of the times, than we meet with in almost any other author. His Steel Glass is among the first specimens of blank verse in our language." This blank verse, however, is but indifferently constructed. Gascoyne's long poem, called the Fruits of War, is in the doggerel style of his age; and the general commendations of Chalmers on this poet seem rather hyperbolical. But his minor poems, especially one called The Arraignment of a Lover, have much spirit and gayety;[1] and we may leave him a respectable place among the Elizabethan versifiers.

Spenser's Shepherd's Kalendar.

61. An epoch was made, if we may draw an inference from the language of contemporaries, by the publication of Spenser's Shepherd's Kalendar, in 1579.[2] His primary idea, that of adapting a pastoral to every month of the year, was pleasing and original, though he has frequently neglected to observe the season, even when it was most abundant in appropriate imagery. But his Kalendar is, in another respect, original, at least when compared with the pastoral writings of that age. This species of composition had become so much the favorite of courts, that no language was thought to suit it but that of courtiers, which, with all its false beauties of thought and expression, was transferred to the mouths of shepherds. A striking instance of this had lately been shown in the Aminta; and it was a proof of Spenser's judgment, as well as genius, that he struck out a new line of pastoral, far more natural, and therefore more pleasing, so far as imitation of nature is the source of poetical pleasure, instead of vying, in our more harsh and uncultivated language, with the consummate elegance of Tasso. It must be admitted, however, that he fell too much into the opposite extreme, and gave a Doric rudeness to his dialogue, which is a little repulsive to our taste. The dialect of Theocritus is musical to our ears, and free from vulgarity; praises which we cannot bestow on the uncouth provincial rusticity of Spenser. He has been less justly censured on another account, for intermingling allusions to the political history and religious differences of his own times; and an ingenious critic has asserted that the description of the grand and beautiful objects of nature, with well-selected scenes of rural life, real but not coarse, constitute the only proper materials of pastoral poetry.

1 Ellis's Specimens; Campbell's Specimens, ii. 146.

2 The Shepherd's Kalendar was printed anonymously. It is ascribed to Sidney by Whetstone in a monody on his death, in 1586. But Webbe, in his Discourse of English Poetry, published the same year, mentions Spenser by name.

These limitations, however, seem little conformable to the practice of poets or the taste of mankind; and, if Spenser has erred in the allegorical part of his pastorals, he has done so in company with most of those who have tuned the shepherd's pipe. Several of Virgil's Eclogues, and certainly the best, have a meaning beyond the simple songs of the hamlet; and it was notorious that the Portuguese and Spanish pastoral romances, so popular in Spenser's age, teemed with delineations of real character, and sometimes were the mirrors of real story. In fact, mere pastoral must soon become insipid, unless it borrows something from active life or elevated philosophy. The most interesting parts of the Shepherd's Kalendar are of this description; for Spenser has not displayed the powers of his own imagination, so strongly as we might expect, in pictures of natural scenery. This poem has spirit and beauty in many passages; but is not much read in the present day, nor does it seem to be approved by modern critics. It was otherwise formerly. Webbe, in his Discourse of English Poetry, 1586, calls Spenser "the rightest English poet he ever read," and thinks he would have surpassed Theocritus and Virgil, "if the coarseness of our speech had been no greater impediment to him, than their pure native tongues were to them." And Drayton says, "Master Edmund Spenser had done enough for the immortality of his name, had he only given us his Shepherd's Kalendar, a masterpiece, if any."[1]

Sidney's character of contemporary poets.

62. Sir Philip Sidney, in his Defence of Poesie, which may have been written at any time between 1581 and his death in 1586, laments that "poesy, thus embraced in all other places, should only find in our time a bad welcome in England;" and, after praising Sackville, Surrey, and Spenser for the Shepherd's Kalendar, does not "remember to have seen many more that have poetical sinews in them. For proof whereof, let but most of the verses be put into prose, and then ask the meaning, and it will be found that one verse did but beget another, without ordering at the first what should be at the last; which becomes a confused mass of words, with a tinkling sound of rhyme, barely accompanied with reason. . . . Truly many of such writings as come under the banner of irresistible love, if I were a

[1] Preface to Drayton's Pastorals.

mistress, would never persuade me they were in love; so coldly they apply fiery speeches, as men that had rather read lovers' writings, and so caught up certain swelling phrases than that in truth they feel those passions."

Improvement soon after this time.

63. It cannot be denied that some of these blemishes are by no means unusual in the writers of the Elizabethan age, as in truth they are found also in much other poetry of many countries. But a change seems to have come over the spirit of English poetry soon after 1580. Sidney, Raleigh, Lodge, Breton, Marlowe, Greene, Watson, are the chief contributors to a collection called England's Helicon, published in 1600, and comprising many of the fugitive pieces of the last twenty years. Davison's Poetical Rhapsody, in 1602,[1] is a miscellany of the same class. A few other collections are known to have existed, but are still more scarce than these. England's Helicon, by far the most important, has been reprinted in the same volume of the British Bibliographer as the Paradise of Dainty Devices. In this juxtaposition, the difference of their tone is very perceptible. Love occupies by far the chief portion of the latter miscellany; and love no longer pining and melancholy, but sportive and boastful. Every one is familiar with the beautiful song of Marlowe, "Come live with me, and be my love;" and with the hardly less beautiful answer ascribed to Raleigh. Lodge has ten pieces in this collection, and Breton eight. These are generally full of beauty, grace, and simplicity; and while, in reading the productions of Edwards and his coadjutors, every sort of allowance is to be made, — and we can only praise a little at intervals, — these lyrics, twenty or thirty years later, are among the best in our language. The conventional tone is that of pastoral; and thus, if they have less of the depth sometimes shown in serious poetry, they have less also of obscurity and false refinement.[2]

Relaxation of moral austerity

64. We may easily perceive, in the literature of the later period of the queen, what our biographical knowledge confirms, that much of the austerity characteristic of her earlier years had vanished away. The

[1] [It was much enlarged in 1608 and 1621, and is not now scarce, having been reprinted by Sir Harris Nicolas in 1826. — 1847.]

[2] Ellis, in the second volume of his Specimens of English Poets, has taken largely from this collection. It must be owned, that his good taste in selection gives a higher notion of the poetry of this age, than, on the whole, it would be found to deserve; yet there is so much of excellence in England's Helicon, that he has been compelled to omit many pieces of great merit.

course of time, the progress of vanity, the prevalent dislike, above all, of the Puritans, avowed enemies of gayety, concurred to this change. The most distinguished courtiers, Raleigh, Essex, Blount, and we must add Sidney, were men of brilliant virtues, but not without license of morals; while many of the wits and poets, such as Nash, Greene, Peele, Marlowe, were notoriously of very dissolute lives.

Serious poetry.

65. The graver strains, however, of religion and philosophy were still heard in verse. The Soul's Errand, printed anonymously in Davison's Rhapsody, and ascribed by Ellis, probably without reason, to Silvester, is characterized by strength, condensation, and simplicity.[1] And we might rank in a respectable place among these English poets, though I think he has been lately overrated, one whom the jealous law too prematurely deprived of life, — Robert Southwell, executed as a seminary priest in 1591, under one of those persecuting statutes which even the traitorous restlessness of the English Jesuits cannot excuse. Southwell's poetry wears a deep tinge of gloom, which seems to presage a catastrophe too usual to have been unexpected. It is, as may be supposed, almost wholly religious: the shorter pieces are the best.[2]

Poetry of Sidney.

66. Astrophel and Stella, a series of amatory poems by Sir Philip Sidney, though written nearly ten years before, was published in 1591. These songs and sonnets recount the loves of Sidney and Lady Rich, sister of Lord Essex; and it is rather a singular circumstance, that, in her own and her husband's life-time, this ardent courtship of a married woman should have been deemed fit for publication. Sidney's passion seems indeed to have been unsuc-

1 Campbell reckons this, and I think justly, among the best pieces of the Elizabethan age. Brydges gives it to Raleigh without evidence, and, we may add, without probability. It is found in manuscripts, according to Mr. Campbell, of the date of 1593. Such poems as this could only be written by a man who had seen and thought much; while the ordinary Latin and Italian verses of this age might be written by any one who had a knack of imitation and a good ear. [It was published in the second edition of Davison, 1608, with the title, The Lie. In Silvester's works it bears the present title. Its publication therein would of course be presumptive evidence that he was the author, were it not weakened, as Sir Harris Nicolas observes, by the circumstance that it is also published among the poems of the Earl of Pembroke. If it is really found, as Campbell tells us, in a manuscript of 1593, Pembroke's claim must be out of the question. — 1847.]

2 I am not aware that Southwell has gained any thing by a republication of his entire poems in 1817. Headley and Ellis had culled the best specimens. St. Peter's Complaint, the longest of his poems, is wordy and tedious; and, in reading the volume, I found scarce any thing of merit which I had not seen before.

cessful, but far enough from being Platonic.[1] Astrophel and Stella is too much disfigured by conceits, but is in some places very beautiful; and it is strange, that Chalmers, who reprinted Turberville and Warner, should have left Sidney out of his collection of British poets. A poem by the writer just mentioned, Warner, with the quaint title, Albion's England, 1586, has at least the equivocal merit of great length. It is rather legendary than historical: some passages are pleasing; but it is not a work of genius, and the style, though natural, seldom rises above that of prose.

Epithalamium of Spenser.

67. Spenser's Epithalamium on his own marriage, written perhaps in 1594, is of a far higher mood than any thing we have named. It is a strain redolent of a bridegroom's joy, and of a poet's fancy. The English language seems to expand itself with a copiousness unknown before, while he pours forth the varied imagery of this splendid little poem. I do not know any other nuptial song, ancient or modern, of equal beauty. It is an intoxication of ecstasy, ardent, noble, and pure. But it pleased not Heaven that these day-dreams of genius and virtue should be undisturbed.

Poems of Shakspeare.

68. Shakspeare's Venus and Adonis appears to have been published in 1593, and his Rape of Lucrece the following year. The redundance of blossoms in these juvenile effusions of his unbounded fertility obstructs the reader's attention, and sometimes almost leads us to give him credit for less reflection and sentiment than he will be found to display. The style is flowing, and in general more perspicuous than the Elizabethan poets are wont to be. But I am not sure that they would betray themselves for the works of Shakspeare, had they been anonymously published.

Daniel and Drayton.

69. In the last decade of this century, several new poets came forward. Samuel Daniel is one of these. His Complaint of Rosamond, and probably many of his minor poems, belong to this period; and it was also that of his greatest popularity. On the death of Spenser, in 1598,

[1] Godwin having several years since made some observations on Sidney's amour with Lady Rich, — a circumstance which such biographers as Dr. Zouch take good care to suppress, — a gentleman who published an edition of Sidney's Defence of Poetry thought fit to indulge in recriminating attacks on Godwin himself. It is singular that men of sense and education should persist in fancying that such arguments are likely to convince any dispassionate reader

he was thought worthy to succeed him as poet-laureate; and some of his contemporaries ranked him in the second place; an eminence due rather to the purity of his language than to its vigor.[1] Michael Drayton, who first tried his shepherd's pipe with some success in the usual style, published his Barons' Wars in 1598. They relate to the last years of Edward II., and conclude with the execution of Mortimer under his son. This poem, therefore, seems to possess a sufficient unity, and, tried by rules of criticism, might be thought not far removed from the class of epic, — a dignity, however, to which it has never pretended. But, in its conduct, Drayton follows history very closely; and we are kept too much in mind of a common chronicle. Though not very pleasing, however, in its general effect, this poem, The Barons' Wars, contains several passages of considerable beauty, which men of greater renown, especially Milton, who availed himself largely of all the poetry of the preceding age, have been willing to imitate.

Nosce Teipsum of Davies.

70. A more remarkable poem is that of Sir John Davies, afterwards chief-justice of Ireland, entitled Nosce Teipsum, published in 1599, usually, though rather inaccurately, called, On the Immortality of the Soul. Perhaps no language can produce a poem, extending to so great a length, of more condensation of thought, or in which fewer languid verses will be found. Yet, according to some definitions, the Nosce Teipsum is wholly unpoetical, inasmuch as it shows no passion and little fancy. If it reaches the heart at all, it is through the reason. But, since strong argument in terse and correct style fails not to give us pleasure in prose, it seems strange that it should lose its effect when it gains the aid of regular metre to gratify the ear and assist the memory. Lines there are in Davies which far outweigh much of the descriptive and imaginative poetry of the last two centuries, whether we estimate them by the pleasure they impart to us, or by the intellectual vigor they display. Experience has shown that the faculties peculiarly deemed poetical are frequently exhibited in a considerable degree; but very few have been able to preserve a perspicuous brevity without stiffness or pedantry (allowance

[1] British Bibliographer, vol. ii. Headley remarks that Daniel was spoken of by contemporary critics as the polisher and purifier of the English language

made for the subject and the times), in metaphysical reasoning, so successfully as Sir John Davies.

Satires of Hall, Marston, and Donne.

71. Hall's Satires are tolerably known, partly on account of the subsequent celebrity of the author in a very different province, and partly from a notion, to which he gave birth by announcing the claim, that he was the first English satirist. In a general sense of satire, we have seen that he had been anticipated by Gascoyne; but Hall has more of the direct Juvenalian invective, which he may have reckoned essential to that species of poetry. They are deserving of regard in themselves. Warton has made many extracts from Hall's Satires: he praises in them "a classical precision, to which English poetry had yet rarely attained;" and calls the versification "equally energetic and elegant."[1] The former epithet may be admitted; but elegance is hardly compatible with what Warton owns to be the chief fault of Hall, — "his obscurity, arising from a remote phraseology, constrained combinations, unfamiliar allusions, elliptical apostrophes, and abruptness of expression." Hall is in fact not only so harsh and rugged, that he cannot be read with much pleasure, but so obscure in very many places, that he cannot be understood at all; his lines frequently bearing no visible connection in sense or grammar with their neighbors. The stream is powerful, but turbid and often choked.[2] Marston and Donne may be added to Hall in this style of poetry, as belonging to the sixteenth century; though the satires of the latter were not published till long afterwards. With as much obscurity as Hall, he has a still more inharmonious versification, and not nearly equal vigor.

Modulation of English verse.

72. The roughness of these satirical poets was perhaps studiously affected; for it was not much in unison with the general tone of the age. It requires a good deal of care to avoid entirely the combinations of consonants that clog our language; nor have Drayton or Spenser always escaped this embarrassment. But, in the lighter poetry of the queen's last years, a remarkable sweetness of modulation has always been recognized. This

[1] Hist. of English Poetry, iv. 383.

[2] Hall's Satires are praised by Campbell, as well as Warton, full as much in my opinion as they deserve. Warton has compared Marston with Hall, and concludes that the latter is more "elegant, exact, and elaborate." More so than his rival, he may by possibility be esteemed; but these three epithets cannot be predicated of his satires in any but a relative sense.

has sometimes been attributed to the general fondness for music. It is at least certain, that some of our old madrigals are as beautiful in language as they are in melody. Several collections were published in the reign of Elizabeth.[1] And it is evident, that the regard to the capacity of his verse for marriage with music, that was before the poet's mind, would not only polish his metre, but give it grace and sentiment; while it banished also the pedantry, the antithesis, the prolixity, which had disfigured the earlier lyric poems. Their measures became more various: though the quatrain, alternating by eight and six syllables, was still very popular, we find the trochaic verse of seven, sometimes ending with a double rhyme, usual towards the end of the queen's reign. Many of these occur in England's Helicon, and in the poems of Sidney.

Translation of Homer by Chapman.

73. The translations of ancient poets by Phaier, Golding, Stanyhurst, and several more, do not challenge our attention; most of them in fact being very wretched performances.[2] Marlowe, a more celebrated name, did not, as has commonly been said, translate the poem of Hero and Leander ascribed to Musæus, but expanded it into what he calls six Sestiads on the same subject; a paraphrase, in every sense of the epithet, of the most licentious kind. This he left incomplete, and it was finished by Chapman.[3] But the most remarkable productions of this kind are the Iliad of Chapman, and the Jerusalem of Fairfax, both printed in 1600; the former, however, containing in that edition but fifteen books, to which the rest was subsequently added. Pope, after censuring the haste, negligence, and fustian language of Chapman, observes, "that which is to be allowed him, and which very much contributed to cover his defects, is a free, daring spirit that animates his translation, which is something like what one might imagine Homer himself would have written before he arrived at years of discretion." He might have added, that Chapman's translation, with all its defects, is often exceedingly Homeric; a praise which Pope himself seldom attained. Chapman deals abundantly in com-

[1] Morley's Musical Airs, 1594, and another collection in 1597, contain some pretty songs. British Bibliographer, i. 342. A few of these madrigals will also be found in Mr. Campbell's Specimens.

[2] Warton, chap. liv., has gone very laboriously into this subject.

[3] Marlowe's poem is republished in the Restituta of Sir Egerton Brydges. It is singular that Warton should have taken it for a translation of Musæus.

pound epithets, some of which have retained their place: his verse is rhymed, of fourteen syllables, which corresponds to the hexameter better than the decasyllable couplet: he is often uncouth, often unmusical, and often low; but the spirited and rapid flow of his metre makes him respectable to lovers of poetry. Waller, it is said, could not read him without transport. It must be added, that he is an unfaithful translator, and interpolated much, besides the general redundancy of his style.[1]

Tasso, Fairfax.

74. Fairfax's Tasso has been more praised, and is better known. Campbell has called it, in rather strong terms, "one of the glories of Elizabeth's reign." It is not the first version of the Jerusalem, one very literal and prosaic having been made by Carew in 1594.[2] That of Fairfax, if it does not represent the grace of its original, and deviates also too much from its sense, is by no means deficient in spirit and vigor. It has been considered as one of the earliest works, in which the obsolete English, which had not been laid aside in the days of Sackville, and which Spenser affected to preserve, gave way to a style not much differing, at least in point of single words and phrases, from that of the present age. But this praise is equally due to Daniel, to Drayton, and to others of the later Elizabethan poets. The translation of Ariosto by Sir John Harrington, in 1591, is much inferior.

Employment of ancient measures.

75. An injudicious endeavor to substitute the Latin metres for those congenial to our language met with no more success than it deserved; unless it may be called success, that Sidney, and even Spenser, were for a moment seduced into approbation of it. Gabriel Harvey, best now remembered as the latter's friend, recommended the adoption of hexameters in some letters which passed between them; and Spenser appears to have concurred. Webbe, a few years afterwards, a writer of little taste or ear for poetry, supported the same scheme, but may be said to have avenged the wrong of English verse upon our great

1 Warton, iv. 269. Retrospective Review, vol. iii. See also a very good comparison of the different translations of Homer, in Blackwood's Magazine for 1831 and 1832, where Chapman comes in for his due.

2 In the third volume of the Retrospective Review, these translations are compared; and it is shown that Carew is far more literal than Fairfax, who has taken great liberties with his original. Extracts from Carew will also be found in the British Bibliographer, i. 30. They are miserably bad. [Carew translated only the first five books of Tasso. — 1847.]

poet, by travestying the Shepherd's Kalendar into Sapphics.[1] Campion, in 1602, still harps upon this foolish pedantry; many instances of which may be found during the Elizabethan period. It is well known that in German the practice has been in some measure successful, through the example of a distinguished poet, and through translations from the ancients in measures closely corresponding with their own. In this there is doubtless the advantage of presenting a truer mirror of the original. But as most imitations of Latin measures, in German or English, begin by violating their first principle, which assigns an invariable value in time to the syllables of every word, and produce a chaos of false quantities, it seems as if they could only disgust any one acquainted with classical versification. In the early English hexameters of the period before us, we sometimes perceive an intention to arrange long and short syllables according to the analogies of the Latin tongue. But this would soon be found impracticable in our own, which, abounding in harsh terminations, cannot long observe the law of position.

76. It was said by Ellis, that nearly one hundred names of poets belonging to the reign of Elizabeth might be enumerated, besides many that have left no memorial except their songs. This, however, was but a moderate computation. Drake has made a list of more than two hundred, some few of whom, perhaps, do not strictly belong to the Elizabethan period.[2] But many of these are only known by short pieces in such miscellaneous collections as have been mentioned. Yet, in the entire bulk of poetry, England could not perhaps bear comparison with Spain or France, to say nothing of Italy. She had come, in fact, much later to cultivate poetry as a general accomplishment. And, consequently, we find much less of the mechanism of style, than in the contemporaneous verse of other languages. The English sonneteers deal less in cus-

Number of poets in this age.

[1] Webbe's success was not inviting to the Latinists. Thus in the second Eclogue of Virgil, for the beautiful lines, —

"At mecum raucis, tua dum vestigia lustro,
Sole sub ardenti resonant arbusta cicadis," —

we have this delectable hexametric version. —

"But by the scorched bank-sides i' thy footsteps still I go plodding:
Hedge-rows hot do resound with grasshops mournfully squeaking."

[2] Shakspeare and his Times, i. 674. Even this catalogue is probably incomplete: it includes, of course, translators

tomary epithets and conventional modes of expression. Every thought was to be worked out in new terms, since the scanty precedents of early versifiers did not supply them. This was evidently the cause of many blemishes in the Elizabethan poetry; of much that was false in taste, much that was either too harsh and extravagant or too humble, and of more that was so obscure as to defy all interpretation. But it saved also that monotonous equability that often wearies us in more polished poetry. There is more pleasure, more sense of sympathy with another mind, in the perusal even of Gascoyne or Edwards, than in that of many French and Italian versifiers whom their contemporaries extolled. This is all that we can justly say in their favor; for any comparison of the Elizabethan poetry, save Spenser's alone, with that of the nineteenth century, would show an extravagant predilection for the mere name or dress of antiquity.

Scots and English ballads.

77. It would be a great omission to neglect, in any review of the Elizabethan poetry, that extensive though anonymous class, the Scots and English ballads. The very earliest of these have been adverted to in our account of the fifteenth century. They became much more numerous in the present. The age of many may be determined by historical or other allusions; and from these, availing ourselves of similarity of style, we may fix, with some probability, the date of such as furnish no distinct evidence. This, however, is precarious, because the language has often been modernized; and, passing for some time by oral tradition, they are frequently not exempt from marks of interpolation. But, upon the whole, the reigns of Mary and James VI., from the middle to the close of the sixteenth century, must be reckoned the golden age of the Scottish ballad; and there are many of the corresponding period in England.

78. There can be, I conceive, no question as to the superiority of Scotland in her ballads. Those of an historic or legendary character, especially the former, are ardently poetical: the nameless minstrel is often inspired with an Homeric power of rapid narration, bold description, lively or pathetic touches of sentiment. They are familiar to us through several publications, but chiefly through the Minstrelsy of the Scottish Border, by one whose genius these indigenous lays had first excited, and whose own writings, when the whole

civilized world did homage to his name, never ceased to bear the indelible impress of the associations that had thus been generated. The English ballads of the northern border, or perhaps of the northern counties, come near in their general character and cast of manners to the Scottish, but, as far as I have seen, with a manifest inferiority. Those again which belong to the south, and bear no trace either of the rude manners or of the wild superstitions which the bards of Ettrick and Cheviot display, fall generally into a creeping style, which has exposed the common ballad to contempt. They are sometimes, nevertheless, not devoid of elegance, and often pathetic. The best are known through Percy's Reliques of Ancient Poetry; a collection singularly heterogeneous, and very unequal in merit, but from the publication of which, in 1765, some of high name have dated the revival of a genuine feeling for true poetry in the public mind.

The Faery Queen.

79. We have reserved to the last the chief boast of this period, the Faery Queen. Spenser, as is well known, composed the greater part of his poem in Ireland, on the banks of his favorite Mulla. The first three books were published in 1590: the last three did not appear till 1596. It is a perfectly improbable supposition, that the remaining part, or six books required for the completion of his design, have been lost. The short interval before the death of this great poet was filled up by calamities sufficient to wither the fertility of any mind.

Superiority of the first book.

80. The first book of the Faery Queen is a complete poem, and, far from requiring any continuation, is rather injured by the useless re-appearance of its hero in the second. It is generally admitted to be the finest of the six. In no other is the allegory so clearly conceived by the poet, or so steadily preserved, yet with a disguise so delicate, that no one is offended by that servile setting-forth of a moral meaning we frequently meet with in allegorical poems; and the reader has the gratification which good writing in works of fiction always produces,—that of exercising his own ingenuity without perplexing it. That the red-cross knight designates the militant Christian, whom Una, the true church, loves; whom Duessa, the type of Popery, seduces; who is reduced almost to despair, but rescued by the intervention of Una, and the assistance of Faith, Hope, and Charity,—is what no one feels any difficulty in acknowledging, but what

every one may easily read the poem without perceiving or remembering. In an allegory conducted with such propriety, and concealed or revealed with so much art, there can surely be nothing to repel our taste; and those who read the first book of the Faery Queen without pleasure, must seek (what others perhaps will be at no loss to discover for them) a different cause for their insensibility than the tediousness or insipidity of allegorical poetry. Every canto of this book teems with the choicest beauties of imagination: he came to it in the freshness of his genius, which shines throughout with an uniformity it does not always afterwards maintain, unsullied as yet by flattery, unobstructed by pedantry, and unquenched by languor.

The succeeding books.

81. In the following books, we have much less allegory; for the personification of abstract qualities, though often confounded with it, does not properly belong to that class of composition: it requires a covert sense beneath an apparent fable, such as the first book contains. But of this I do not discover many proofs in the second or third, the legends of Temperance and Chastity: they are contrived to exhibit these virtues and their opposite vices, but with little that is not obvious upon the surface. In the fourth and sixth books, there is still less; but a different species of allegory, the historical, which the commentators have, with more or less success, endeavored to trace in other portions of the poem, breaks out unequivocally in the legend of Justice, which occupies the fifth. The friend and patron of Spenser, Sir Arthur Grey, Lord Deputy of Ireland, is evidently portrayed in Arthegal; and the latter cantos of this book represent, not always with great felicity, much of the foreign and domestic history of the times. It is sufficiently intimated by the poet himself, that his Gloriana, or Faery Queen, is the type of Elizabeth; and he has given her another representative in the fair huntress Belphœbe. Spenser's adulation of her beauty (at some fifty or sixty years of age) may be extenuated, we can say no more, by the practice of wise and great men, and by his natural tendency to clothe the objects of his admiration in the hues of fancy; but its exaggeration leaves the servility of the Italians far behind.

Spenser's sense of beauty.

82. It has been justly observed by a living writer of the most ardent and enthusiastic genius, whose eloquence is as the rush of mighty waters, and has left it for

others almost as invidious to praise in terms of less rapture, as to censure what he has borne along in the stream of unhesitating eulogy, that "no poet has ever had a more exquisite sense of the beautiful than Spenser."[1] In Virgil and Tasso, this was not less powerful; but even they, even the latter himself, do not hang with such a tenderness of delight, with such a forgetful delay, over the fair creations of their fancy. Spenser is not averse to images that jar on the mind by exciting horror or disgust, and sometimes his touches are rather too strong; but it is on love and beauty, on holiness and virtue, that he reposes with all the sympathy of his soul. The slowly sliding motion of his stanza, "with many a bout of linked sweetness long drawn out," beautifully corresponds to the dreamy enchantment of his description, when Una or Belphœbe or Florimel or Amoret is present to his mind. In this varied delineation of female perfectness, no earlier poet had equalled him; nor, excepting Shakspeare, has he had, perhaps, any later rival.

Compared to Ariosto.

83. Spenser is naturally compared with Ariosto. "Fierce wars and faithful loves did moralize the song" of both poets. But in the constitution of their minds, in the character of their poetry, they were almost the reverse of each other. The Italian is gay, rapid, ardent; his pictures shift like the hues of heaven: even while diffuse, he seems to leave in an instant what he touches, and is prolix by the number, not the duration, of his images. Spenser is habitually serious; his slow stanza seems to suit the temper of his genius; he loves to dwell on the sweetness and beauty which his fancy portrays. The ideal of chivalry, rather derived from its didactic theory than from the precedents of romance, is always before him; his morality is pure and even stern, with nothing of the libertine tone of Ariosto. He worked with far worse tools than the bard of Ferrara, with a language not quite formed, and into which he rather injudiciously poured an unnecessary archaism, while the style of his contemporaries was undergoing a rapid change in the opposite direction. His stanza of nine lines is particularly inconvenient and languid in narration, where the Italian octave is sprightly and vigorous; though even this becomes ultimately

[1] I allude here to a very brilliant series of papers on the Faery Queen, published in Blackwood's Magazine during the years 1834 and 1835. [They are universally ascribed to Professor Wilson. —1842.]

monotonous by its regularity, — a fault from which only the ancient hexameter and our blank verse are exempt.

84. Spenser may be justly said to excel Ariosto in originality of invention, in force and variety of character, in strength and vividness of conception, in depth of reflection, in fertility of imagination, and, above all, in that exclusively poetical cast of feeling, which discerns in every thing what common minds do not perceive. In the construction and arrangement of their fable, neither deserves much praise; but the siege of Paris gives the Orlando Furioso, spite of its perpetual shiftings of the scene, rather more unity in the reader's apprehension than belongs to the Faery Queen. Spenser is, no doubt, decidedly inferior in ease and liveliness of narration, as well as clearness and felicity of language. But, upon thus comparing the two poets, we have little reason to blush for our countryman. Yet the fame of Ariosto is spread through Europe, while Spenser is almost unknown out of England; and even in this age, when much of our literature is so widely diffused, I have not observed proofs of much acquaintance with him on the Continent.

Style of Spenser.

85. The language of Spenser, like that of Shakspeare, is an instrument manufactured for the sake of the work it was to perform. No other poet had written like either, though both have had their imitators. It is rather apparently obsolete by his partiality to certain disused forms, such as the *y* before the participle, than from any close resemblance to the diction of Chaucer or Lydgate.[1] The enfeebling expletives *do* and *did*, though certainly very common in our early writers, had never been employed with such an unfortunate predilection as by Spenser. Their everlasting recurrence is among the great blemishes of his style. His versification is in many passages beautifully harmonious; but he has frequently permitted himself, whether for the sake of variety or from some other cause, to balk the ear in the conclusion of a stanza.[2]

1 "Spenser," says Ben Jonson, "in affecting the ancients, writ no language; yet I would have him read for his matter, but as Virgil read Ennius." This is rather in the sarcastic tone attributed to Jonson.

2 Coleridge, who had a very strong perception of the beauty of Spenser's poetry, has observed his alternate alliteration, — "which, when well used, is a great secret in melody; as '*sad* to see her *sorrowful* constraint;' — 'on the grass her *dainty* limbs *did* lay.'" But I can hardly agree with him when he proceeds to say, "It never strikes any unwarned ear as artificial, or other than the result of the necessary movement of the verse." The artifice seems often very obvious. I do not also quite understand, or, if I do, cannot acquiesce in what follows, that "Spenser's descriptions are not in the true sense of

Inferiority of the latter books.

86. The inferiority of the last three books to the former is surely very manifest. His muse gives gradual signs of weariness, the imagery becomes less vivid, the vein of poetical description less rich, the digressions more frequent and verbose. It is true that the fourth book is full of beautiful inventions, and contains much admirable poetry; yet, even here, we perceive a comparative deficiency in the quantity of excelling passages, which becomes far more apparent as we proceed; and the last book falls very short of the interest which the earlier part of the Faery Queen had excited. There is, perhaps, less reason than some have imagined, to regret that Spenser did not complete his original design. The Faery Queen is already in the class of longest poems. A double length, especially if, as we may well suspect, the succeeding parts would have been inferior, might have deterred many readers from the perusal of what we now possess. It is felt already in Spenser, as it is perhaps even in Ariosto, when we read much of either, that tales of knights and ladies, giants and salvage men, end in a satiety which no poetical excellence can overcome. Ariosto, sensible of this intrinsic defect in the epic romance, has enlivened it by great variety of incidents, and by much that carries us away from the peculiar tone of chivalrous manners. The world he lives in is before his eyes, and to please it is his aim. He plays with his characters as with puppets that amuse the spectator and himself. In Spenser, nothing is more remarkable than the steadiness of his apparent faith in the deeds of knighthood. He had little turn for sportiveness; and in attempting it, as in the unfortunate instance of Malbecco, and a few shorter passages, we find him dull as well as coarse. It is in the ideal world of pure and noble virtues that his spirit, wounded by neglect, and weary of trouble, loved to refresh itself without reasoning or mockery: he forgets the reader, and cares little for his taste, while he can indulge the dream of his own delighted fancy. It may be here also observed, that the elevated and religious morality of Spenser's poem would secure it, in the eyes of every man of just taste, from the ridicule which the mere romances of knight-errantry must incur, and against which Ariosto evidently guarded himself by the gay tone of his narration. The Orlando Furioso and the Faery Queen are each in the spirit of its age; but

the word picturesque, but are *composed* *dreams*." — Coleridge's Remains, vol. I p. 93. *of a wondrous series of images, as in our*

the one was for Italy in the days of Leo, the other for England under Elizabeth, before, though but just before, the severity of the Reformation had been softened away. The lay of Britomart, in twelve cantos, in praise of chastity, would have been received with a smile at the court of Ferrara, which would have had almost as little sympathy with the justice of Arthegal.

87. The allegories of Spenser have been frequently censured. One of their greatest offences, perhaps, is that they gave birth to some tedious and uninteresting poetry of the same kind. There is usually something repulsive in the application of an abstract or general name to a person, in which, though with some want of regard, as I have intimated above, to the proper meaning of the word, we are apt to think that allegorical fiction consists. The French and English poets of the middle ages had far too much of this; and it is to be regretted that Spenser did not give other appellations to his Care and Despair, as he has done to Duessa and Talus. In fact, Orgoglio is but a giant, Humiltà a porter, Obedience a servant. The names, when English, suggest something that perplexes us; but the beings exhibited are mere persons of the drama, men and women, whose office or character is designated by their appellation.

Allegories of the Faery Queen.

88. The general style of the Faery Queen is not exempt from several defects besides those of obsoleteness and redundancy. Spenser seems to have been sometimes deficient in one attribute of a great poet, the continual reference to the truth of nature, so that his fictions should be always such as might exist on the given conditions. This arises in great measure from copying his predecessors too much in description, not suffering his own good sense to correct their deviations from truth. Thus, in the beautiful description of Una, where she first is introduced to us, riding —

Blemishes in the diction

"Upon a lowly ass more white than snow;
Herself much whiter."

This absurdity may have been suggested by Ovid's *Brachia Sithonia candidiora nive;* but the image in this line is not brought so distinctly before the mind as to be hideous as well as untrue: it is merely a hyperbolical parallel.[1] A similar

[1] Vincent Bourne, in his translation of William and Margaret, has one of the most elegant lines he ever wrote: — "Candidior nivibus, frigidiorque manus." But this is said of a ghost.

objection lies to the stanza enumerating as many kinds of trees as the poet could call to mind in the description of a forest.

> "The sailing pine, the cedar proud and tall,
> The vine-prop elm, the poplar never dry,
> The builder oak, sole king of forests all,
> The aspine good for staves, the cypress funeral," —

with thirteen more in the next stanza. Every one knows that a natural forest never contains such a variety of species; nor indeed could such a medley as Spenser, treading in the steps of Ovid, has brought together from all soils and climates, exist long if planted by the hands of man. Thus also, in the last canto of the second book, we have a celebrated stanza, and certainly a very beautiful one, if this defect did not attach to it; where winds, waves, birds, voices, and musical instruments, are supposed to conspire in one harmony. A good writer has observed upon this, that, "to a person listening to a concert of voices and instruments, the interruption of singing birds, winds, and waterfalls, would be little better than the torment of Hogarth's enraged musician."[1] But perhaps the enchantment of the Bower of Bliss, where this is feigned to have occurred, may in some degree justify Spenser in this instance, by taking it out of the common course of nature. The stanza is translated from Tasso, whom our own poet has followed with close footsteps in these cantos of the second book of the Faery Queen, — cantos often in themselves beautiful, but which are rendered stiff by a literal adherence to the original, and fall very short of its ethereal grace and sweetness. It would be unjust not to relieve these strictures, by observing that very numerous passages might be brought from the Faery Queen of admirable truth in painting, and of indisputable originality. The cave of Despair, the hovel of Corceca, the incantation of Amoret, are but a few among those that will occur to the reader of Spenser.

Admiration of the Faery Queen.

89. The admiration of this great poem was unanimous and enthusiastic. No academy had been trained to carp at his genius with minute cavilling; no recent popularity, no traditional fame (for Chaucer was rather venerated than much in the hands of the reader), interfered with the immediate recognition of his supremacy. The Faery

[1] Twining's Translation of Aristotle's Poetics, p. 14.

Queen became at once the delight of every accomplished gentleman, the model of every poet, the solace of every scholar. In the course of the next century, by the extinction of habits derived from chivalry, and the change both of taste and language, which came on with the civil wars and the Restoration, Spenser lost something of his attraction, and much more of his influence over literature; yet, in the most phlegmatic temper of the general reader, he seems to have been one of our most popular writers. Time, however, has gradually wrought its work; and, notwithstanding the more imaginative cast of poetry in the present century, it may be well doubted whether the Faery Queen is as much read or as highly esteemed as in the days of Anne. It is not perhaps very difficult to account for this: those who seek the delight that mere fiction presents to the mind (and they are the great majority of readers) have been supplied to the utmost limit of their craving by stores accommodated to every temper, and far more stimulant than the legends of Faeryland. But we must not fear to assert, with the best judges of this and of former ages, that Spenser is still the third name in the poetical literature of our country; and that he has not been surpassed, except by Dante, in any other.[1]

General parallel of Italian and English poetry.

90. If we place Tasso and Spenser apart, the English poetry of Elizabeth's reign will certainly not enter into competition with that of the corresponding period in Italy. It would require not only much national prejudice, but a want of genuine *æsthetic* discernment, to put them on a level. But it may still be said that our own muses had their charms; and even that, at the end of the century, there was a better promise for the future than beyond the Alps. We might compare the poetry

[1] Mr. Campbell has given a character of Spenser, not so enthusiastic as that to which I have alluded, but so discriminating, and, in general, sound, that I shall take the liberty of extracting it from his Specimens of the British Poets, i. 125. "His command of imagery is wide, easy, and luxuriant. He threw the soul of harmony into our verse, and made it more warmly, tenderly, and magnificently descriptive than it ever was before, or, with a few exceptions, than it has ever been since. It must certainly be owned that in description he exhibits nothing of the brief strokes and robust power which characterize the very greatest poets; but we shall nowhere find more airy and expansive images of visionary things, a sweeter tone of sentiment, or a finer flush in the colors of language, than in this Rubens of English poetry. His fancy teems exuberantly in minuteness of circumstances, like a fertile soil sending bloom and verdure through the utmost extremities of the foliage which it nourishes. On a comprehensive view of the whole work, we certainly miss the charm of strength, symmetry, and rapid or interesting progress; for, though the plan which the poet designed is not completed, it is easy to see that no additional cantos could have rendered it less perplexed."

of one nation to a beauty of the court, with noble and regular features, a slender form, and grace in all her steps, but wanting a genuine simplicity of countenance, and with somewhat of sickliness in the delicacy of her complexion, that seems to indicate the passing-away of the first season of youth; while that of the other would rather suggest a country maiden, newly mingling with polished society, not of perfect lineaments, but attracting beholders by the spirit, variety, and intelligence of her expression, and rapidly wearing off the traces of rusticity, which are still sometimes visible in her demeanor.

SECT. V.—ON LATIN POETRY.

In Italy—Germany—France—Great Britain.

Decline of Latin poetry in Italy

91. THE cultivation of poetry in modern languages did not as yet thin the ranks of Latin versifiers. They are, on the contrary, more numerous in this period than before. Italy, indeed, ceased to produce men equal to those who had flourished in the age of Leo and Clement. Some of considerable merit will be found in the great collection, Carmina Illustrium Poetarum (Florentiæ, 1719); one too, which, rigorously excluding all voluptuous poetry, makes some sacrifice of genius to scrupulous morality. The brothers Amaltei are perhaps the best of the later period. It is not always easy, at least without more pains than I have taken, to determine the chronology of these poems, which are printed in the alphabetical order of the authors' names. But a considerable number must be later than the middle of the century. It cannot be denied that most of these poets employ trivial images, and do not much vary their forms of expression. They often please, but rarely make an impression on the memory. They are generally, I think, harmonious; and perhaps metrical faults, though not uncommon, are less so than among the Cisalpine Latinists. There appears, on the whole, an evident decline since the preceding age.

92. This was tolerably well compensated in other parts of Europe. One of the most celebrated authors is a native

of Germany, Lotichius, whose poems were first published in 1551, and with much amendment in 1561. They are written in a strain of luscious elegance, not rising far above the customary level of Ovidian poetry, and certainly not often falling below it. The versification is remarkably harmonious and flowing, but with a mannerism not sufficiently diversified: the first foot of each verse is generally a dactyle, which adds to the grace, but, so continually repeated, somewhat impairs the strength.[1] Lotichius is, however, a very elegant and classical versifier, and perhaps equal in elegy to Joannes Secundus, or any Cisalpine writer of the sixteenth century.[2] One of his elegies, on the siege of Magdeburg, gave rise to a strange notion, — that he predicted, by a sort of divine enthusiasm, the calamities of that city in 1631. Bayle has spun a long note out of this fancy of some Germans.[3] But those who take the trouble, which these critics seem to have spared themselves, of attending to the poem itself, will perceive that the author concludes it with prognostics of peace instead of capture. It was evidently written on the siege of Magdeburg by Maurice in 1550. George Sabinus, son-in-law of Melanchthon, ranks second in reputation to Lotichius among the Latin poets of Germany during this period.

Compensated in other countries. Lotichius.

93. But France and Holland, especially the former, became the more favored haunts of the Latin muse. A collection in three volumes by Gruter, under the fictitious name of Ranusius Gherus, Deliciæ Poetarum Gallorum, published in 1609, contains the principal writers of the former country, some entire, some in selection. In these volumes there are about 100,000 lines: in the Deliciæ Poetarum Belgarum, a similar publication by Gruter, I find about as many: his third collection, Deliciæ Poetarum Italorum, seems not so long; but I have not seen more than one volume. These poets are disposed alphabetically: few, comparatively speaking, of the Italians seem to

Collections of Latin poetry by Gruter.

1 [It is not worth while to turn again to Lotichius; but the first foot in elegiac metre ought to be *generally* a dactyle, though there may be a possible excess. In Ovid's Epistles, the first foot is a dactyle in four cases out of five, especially in the pentameter. In the second book, De Arte Amandi, out of 746 lines, only 105 begin with a spondee. In the fourth of the Fasti, out of the first 400 lines, only 65 to 335.—1847.]

2 Baillet calls him the best poet of Germany after Eobanus Hessus.

3 Morhof, l. i. c. 19. Bayle, art. "Lotichius," note G. This seems to have been agitated after the publication of Bayle; for I find in the catalogue of the British Museum a disquisition, by one Krusike, Utrum Petrus Lotichius secundam obsidionem Urbis Magdeburgensis prædixerit; published as late as 1703.

belong to the latter half of the century, but very much the larger proportion of the French and Dutch. A fourth collection, Deliciæ Poetarum Germanorum, I have never seen. All these bear the fictitious name of Gherus. According to a list in Baillet, the number of Italian poets selected by Gruter is 203; of French, 108; of Dutch or Belgic, 129; of German, 211.

Characters of some Gallo-Latin poets.

94. Among the French poets, Beza, who bears in Gruter's collection the name of Adeodatus Seba, deserves high praise, though some of his early pieces are rather licentious.[1] Bellay is also an amatory poet: in the opinion of Baillet, he has not succeeded so well in Latin as in French. The poems of Muretus are perhaps superior. Joseph Scaliger seemed to me to write Latin verse tolerably well; but he is not rated highly by Baillet and the authors whom he quotes.[2] The epigrams of Henry Stephens are remarkably prosaic and heavy. Passerat is very elegant: his lines breathe a classical spirit, and are full of those fragments of antiquity with which Latin poetry ought always to be inlaid; but in sense they are rather feeble.[3] The epistles, on the contrary, of the Chancellor de l'Hospital, in an easy Horatian versification, are more interesting than such insipid effusions, whether of flattery or feigned passion, as the majority of modern Latinists present. They are unequal, and fall too often into a creeping style: but sometimes we

[1] Baillet, n. 1366, thinks Beza an excellent Latin poet. The Juvenilia first appeared in 1548. The later editions omitted several poems.

[2] Jugemens des Savans, n. 1295. One of Scaliger's poems celebrates that immortal flea, which, on a great festival at Poitiers, having appeared on the bosom of a learned, and doubtless beautiful, young lady, Mademoiselle des Roches, was the theme of all the wits and scholars of the age. Some of their lines, and those of Joe Scaliger among the number, seem designed, by the freedom they take with the fair pucelle, to beat the intruder himself in impudence. See Œuvres de Pasquier, ii. 950.

[3] Among the epigrams of Passerat, I have found one which Amaltheus seems to have shortened and improved, retaining the idea, in his famous lines on Acona and Leonilla. I do not know whether this has been observed.

"Cætera formosi, dextro est orbatus ocello
Frater, et est lævo lumine capta soror.
Frontibus adversis ambo si jungitis ora,
Bina quidem facies, vultus at unus erit.
Sed tu, Carle, tuum lumen transmitte sorori,
Continuo ut vestrûm fiat uterque Deus.
Plena hæc fulgebit fraterna luce Diana,
Hujus frater eris tu quoque, cæcus Amor."

This is very good, and Passerat ought to have credit for the invention; but the other is better. Though most know the lines by heart, I will insert them here:—

"Lumine Acon dextro, capta est Leonilla sinistro,
Et potis est forma vincere uterque Deos.
Blande puer, lumen quod habes, concede sorori,
Sic tu cæcus Amor, sic erit illa Venus."

[I now believe, on the authority of a friend, that this epigram, published in 1576, preceded that of Passerat.—1842.]

find a spirit and nervousness of strength and sentiment worthy of his name; and, though keeping in general to the level of Horatian satire, he rises at intervals to a higher pitch, and wants not the skill of descriptive poetry.

95. The best of Latin poets whom France could boast was Sammarthanus (Sainte Marthe), known also, but less favorably, in his own language. His Latin poems are more classically elegant than any others which met my eye in Gruter's collection; and this, I believe, is the general suffrage of critics.[1] Few didactic poems, probably, are superior to his Pædotrophia, on the nurture of children: it is not a little better, which indeed is no high praise, than the Balia of Tansillo on the same subject.[2] We may place Sammarthanus, therefore, at the head of the list; and, not far from the bottom of it, I should class Bonnefons, or Bonifonius, a French writer of Latin verse in the very worst taste, whom it would not be worth while to mention, but for a certain degree of reputation he has acquired. He might almost be suspected of designing to turn into ridicule the effeminacy which some Italians had introduced into amorous poetry. Bonifonius has closely imitated Secundus, but is much inferior to him in every thing but his faults. The Latinity is full of gross and obvious errors.[3]

Sammarthanus.

1 Baillet, n. 1401. Some did not scruple to set him above the best Italians; and one went so far as to say, that Virgil would have been envious of the Pædotrophia.

2 The following lines are a specimen of the Pædotrophia, taken much at random:—

"Ipsæ etiam Alpinis villosæ in cautibus ursæ,
Ipsæ etiam tigres, et quicquid ubique ferarum est,
Debita servandis concedunt ubera natis.
Tu, quam miti animo natura benigna creavit,
Exuperes feritate feras? nec te tua tangant
Pignora, nec querulos puerili e gutture planctus,
Nec lacrymas miserêris, opemque injusta recuses,
Quam præstare tuum est, et quæ te pendet ab unâ.
Cujus onus teneris hærebit dulce lacertis
Infelix puer, et molli se pectore sternet?
Dulcia quis primi captabit gaudia risûs
Et primas voces et blæsæ murmura linguæ?
Tune fruenda alii potes illa relinquere demens,
Tantique esse putas teretis servare papillæ
Integrum decus, et juvenilem in pectore florem?" — Lib. i. (*Gruter*, iii. 266.)

3 The following lines are not an unfair specimen of Bonifonius:—

"Nympha bellula, nympha mollicella,
Cujus in roseis latent labellis
Meæ deliciæ, meæ salutes, &c.
* * * *
Salvete aureolæ meæ puellæ
Crines aureolique crispulique,
Salvete et mihi vos puellæ ocelli,
Ocelli improbuli protervulique;
Salvete et Veneris pares papillis
Papillæ teretesque turgidæque;
Salvete æmula purpuræ labella;
Tota denique Pancharilla salve.
* * * *
Nunc te possideo, alma Pancharilla,
Turturilla mea et columbililla."

Bonifonius has been thought worthy of several editions, and has met with more favorable judges than myself.

Belgic poets.

96. The Deliciæ Poetarum Belgarum appeared to me, on rather a cursory inspection, inferior to the French. Secundus outshines his successors. Those of the younger Dousa, whose premature death was lamented by all the learned, struck me as next in merit. Dominic Baudius is harmonious and elegant, but with little originality or vigor. These poets are loose and negligent in versification, ending too often a pentameter with a polysyllable and with feeble effect: they have also little idea of several common rules of Latin composition.

Scots poets: Buchanan.

97. The Scots, in consequence of receiving very frequently a continental education, cultivated Latin poetry with ardor. It was the favorite amusement of Andrew Melville, who is sometimes a mere scribbler, at others tolerably classical and spirited. His poem on the Creation, in Deliciæ Poetarum Scotorum, is very respectable. One by Hercules Rollock, on the marriage of Anne of Denmark, is better, and equal, a few names withdrawn, to any of the contemporaneous poetry of France. The Epistolæ Heroidum of Alexander Bodius, or Boyd, are also good. But the most distinguished among the Latin poets of Europe in this age was George Buchanan, of whom Joseph Scaliger and several other critics have spoken in such unqualified terms, that they seem to place him even above the Italians at the beginning of the sixteenth century.[1] If such were their meaning, I should crave the liberty of hesitating. The best poem of Buchanan, in my judgment, is that on the Sphere, than which few philosophical subjects could afford better opportunities for ornamental digression. He is not, perhaps, in hexameters inferior to Vida, and certainly far superior to Palearius. In this poem, Buchanan descants on the absurdity of the Pythagorean system, which supposes the motion of the earth. Many good passages occur in his elegies, though we may not reckon him equal in this metre to several of the Italians. His celebrated translation of the Psalms I must also presume to think overpraised:[2] it is difficult, perhaps, to find

[1] "Buchananus unus est in tota Europa omnes post se relinquens in Latina poesi." — Scaligerana Prima.

Henry Stephens, says Maittaire, was the first who placed Buchanan at the head of all the poets of his age; and all France, Italy, and Germany have since subscribed to the same opinion, and conferred that title upon him. Vitæ Stephanorum, ii. 258. I must confess that Sainte Marthe appears to me not inferior to Buchanan. The latter is very unequal: if we frequently meet with a few lines of great elegance, they are compensated by others of a different description.

[2] Baillet thinks it impossible that those

one, except the 137th, with which he has taken particular pains, that can be called truly elegant or classical Latin poetry. Buchanan is now and then incorrect in the quantity of syllables, as indeed is common with his contemporaries.

98. England was far from strong, since she is not to claim Buchanan, in the Latin poetry of this age. A poem in ten books, De Republica Instauranda, by Sir Thomas Chaloner, published in 1579, has not perhaps received so much attention as it deserves, though the author is more judicious than imaginative, and does not preserve a very good rhythm. It may be compared with the Zodiacus Vitæ of Palingenius, rather than any other Latin poem I recollect, to which, however, it is certainly inferior. Some lines relating to the English constitution, which, though the title leads us to expect more, forms only the subject of the last book, the rest relating chiefly to private life, will serve as a specimen of Chaloner's powers,[1] and also display the principles of our government as an experienced statesman understood them. The Anglorum Prœlia, by Ockland, which was directed by an order of the

who wish for what is solid as well as what is agreeable in poetry can prefer any other Latin verse of Buchanan to his Psalms. Jugemens des Savans, n. 1328. But Baillet and several others exclude much poetry of Buchanan on account of its reflecting on Popery. Baillet and Blount produce abundant testimonies to the excellence of Buchanan's verses. Le Clerc calls his translation of the Psalms incomparable, Bibl. Choisie, viii. 127, and prefers it much to that by Beza, which I am not prepared to question. He extols also all his other poetry, except his tragedies and the poem of the Sphere, which I have praised above the rest. So different are the humors of critics! But as I have fairly quoted those who do not quite agree with myself, and by both number and reputation ought to weigh more with the reader, he has no right to complain that I mislead his taste.

[1] "Nempe tribus simul ordinibus jus esse sacratas
Condendi leges patrio pro more vetustas
Longo usu sic docta tulit, modus iste rogandi
Haud secus ac basis hanc nostram sic constituit rem,
Ut si inconsultis reliquis pars ulla superbo
Imperio quicquam statuat, seu tollat, ad omnes
Quod spectat, posthac quo nomine læsa vocetur
Publica res nobis, nihil amplius ipse laboro.
* * * * *
Plebs primum reges statuit; jus hoc quoque nostrûm est
Cunctorum, ut regi faveant popularia vota;
(Si quid id est, quod plebs respondet rite rogata)
Nam neque ab invitis potuit vis unica multis
Extorquere datos concordi munere fasces;
Quin populus reges in publica commoda quondam
Egregios certa sub conditione paravit,
Non reges populum; namque his antiquior ille est.
* * * * *
Nec cupiens nova jura ferat, seu condita tollat,
Non prius ordinibus regni de more vocatis,
Ut procerum populique rato stent ordine vota,
Omnibus et positum sciscat conjuncta voluntas."
De Rep. Inst., l. 10.

Privy Council to be read exclusively in schools, is an hexameter poem, versified from the chronicles, in a tame strain, not exceedingly bad, but still farther from good. I recollect no other Latin verse of the queen's reign worthy of notice.

CHAPTER VI.

HISTORY OF DRAMATIC LITERATURE FROM 1550 TO 1600.

Italian Tragedy and Comedy — Pastoral Drama — Spanish Drama — Lope de Vega — French Dramatists — Early English Drama — Second Era: of Marlowe and his Contemporaries — Shakspeare — Character of several of his Plays written within this Period.

1. MANY Italian tragedies are extant, belonging to these fifty years, though not very generally known; nor can I speak of them except through Ginguéné and Walker, the latter of whom has given a few extracts. The Marianna and Didone of Lodovico Dolce, the Œdipus of Anguillara, the Merope of Torelli, the Semiramis of Manfredi, are necessarily bounded, in the conduct of their fable, by what was received as truth. But others, as Cinthio had done, preferred to invent their story, in deviation from the practice of antiquity. The Hadriana of Groto, the Acripanda of Decio da Orto, and the Torrismond of Tasso, are of this kind. In all these we find considerable beauties of language, a florid and poetic tone, but declamatory and not well adapted to the rapidity of action, in which we seem to perceive the germ of that change from common speech to recitative, which, fixing the attention of the hearer on the person of the actor, rather than on his relation to the scene, destroyed, in great measure, the character of dramatic representation. The Italian tragedies are deeply imbued with horror: murder and cruelty, with all attending circumstances of disgust, and every pollution of crime, besides a profuse employment of spectral agency, seem the chief weapons of the poet's armory to subdue the spectator. Even the gentleness of Tasso could not resist the contagion in his Torrismond. These tragedies still retain the chorus at the termination of every act. Of the Italian comedies, little can be added to what has been said before: no comic writer of this period is comparable in reputation to Machiavel,

Italian tragedy.

Ariosto, or even Aretin.[1] They are rather less licentious; and, in fact, the profligacy of Italian manners began, in consequence, probably, of a better example in the prelates of the church, to put on some regard for exterior decency in the latter part of the century.

Pastoral Drama.

2. These regular plays, though possibly deserving of more attention than they have obtained, are by no means the most important portion of the dramatic literature of Italy in this age. A very different style of composition has, through two distinguished poets, contributed to spread the fame of Italian poetry, and the language itself, through Europe. The fifteenth and sixteenth centuries were abundantly productive of pastoral verse; a style pleasing to those who are not severe in admitting its conventional fictions. The pastoral dialogue had not much difficulty in expanding to the pastoral drama. In the Sicilian gossips of Theocritus, and in some other ancient eclogues, new interlocutors supervene, which is the first germ of a regular action. Pastorals of this kind had been written, and possibly represented, in Spain, such as the Mingo Rebulgo, in the middle of the fifteenth century.[2] Ginguéné has traced the progress of similar representations, becoming more and more dramatic, in Italy.[3] But it is admitted, that the honor of giving the first example of a true pastoral fable to the theatre was due to Agostino Beccari of Ferrara. This piece, named Il Sagrifizio, was acted at that court in 1554. Its priority in a line which was to become famous appears to be its chief merit. In this, as in earlier and more simple attempts at pastoral dialogue, the choruses were set to music.[4]

Aminta of Tasso.

3. This pleasing, though rather effeminate, species of poetry was carried, more than twenty years afterwards, one or two unimportant imitations of Beccari having intervened, to a point of excellence which perhaps it has never surpassed, in the Aminta of Tasso. Its admirable author was then living at the court of Ferrara, yielding up his heart to those seductive illusions of finding happiness in the favor of the great, and even in ambitious and ill-assorted love, which his sounder judgment already saw through, the Aminta bearing witness to both states of mind. In the character of

[1] Ginguéné, vol. vi.

[2] Bouterwek's Spanish Literature, i 129.

[3] vi. 327, *et post.*

[4] Id., vi. 332

Tirsi, he has drawn himself; and seems once (though with the proud consciousness of genius) to hint at that eccentric melancholy, which soon increased so fatally for his peace.

> "Ne già cose scrivea degne di riso,
> Se ben cose facea degne di riso."

The language of all the interlocutors in the Aminta is alike, nor is the satyr less elegant or recondite than the learned shepherds. It is in general too diffuse and florid, too uniform and elaborate, for passion; especially if considered dramatically, in reference to the story and the speakers. But it is to be read as what it is, — a beautiful poem; the delicacy and gracefulness of many passages rendering them exponents of the hearer's or reader's feelings, though they may not convey much sympathy with the proper subject. The death of Aminta, however, falsely reported to Sylvia, leads to a truly pathetic scene. It is to be observed that Tasso was more formed by classical poetry, and more frequently an imitator of it, than any earlier Italian. The beauties of the Aminta are in great measure due to Theocritus, Virgil, Ovid, Anacreon, and Moschus.

4. The success of Tasso's Aminta produced the Pastor Fido of Guarini, himself long in the service of the Duke of Ferrara, where he had become acquainted with Tasso; though, in consequence of some dissatisfaction at that court, he sought the patronage of the Duke of Savoy. The Pastor Fido was first represented at Turin in 1585, but seems not to have been printed for some years afterwards. It was received with general applause; but the obvious resemblance to Tasso's pastoral drama could not fail to excite a contention between their respective advocates, which long survived the mortal life of the two poets. Tasso, it has been said, on reading the Pastor Fido, was content to observe, that, if his rival had not read the Aminta, he would not have excelled it. If his modesty induced him to say no more than this, very few would be induced to dispute his claim: the characters, the sentiments, are evidently imitated; and, in one celebrated instance, a whole chorus is parodied with the preservation of every rhyme.[1] But it is far more questionable whether the palm of superior merit, independent of

Pastor Fido of Guarini

[1] This is that beginning, "O bella età dell' oro"

originality, should be awarded to the later poet. More elegance, and purity of taste, belong to the Aminta, more animation and variety to the Pastor Fido. The advantage, in point of morality, which some have ascribed to Tasso, is not very perceptible: Guarini may transgress rather more in some passages; but the tone of the Aminta, in strange opposition to the pure and pious life of its author, breathes nothing but the avowed laxity of an Italian court. The Pastor Fido may be considered, in a much greater degree than the Aminta, a prototype of the Italian opera; not that it was spoken in recitative; but the short and rapid expressions of passion, the broken dialogue, the frequent changes of personages and incidents, keep the effect of representation and of musical accompaniment continually before the reader's imagination. Any one who glances over a few scenes of the Pastor Fido will, I think, perceive that it is the very style which Metastasio, and inferior coadjutors of musical expression, have rendered familiar to our ears.

Italian opera.

5. The great invention, which, though chiefly connected with the history of music and of society, was by no means without influence upon literature, the melodrame, usually called the Italian opera, belongs to the very last years of this century. Italy, long conspicuous for such musical science and skill as the middle ages possessed, had fallen, in the first part of the sixteenth century, very short of some other countries, and especially of the Netherlands; from which the courts of Europe, and even of the Italian princes, borrowed their performers and their instructors. But a revolution in church music, which had become particularly dry and pedantic, was brought about by the genius of Palestrina about 1560; and the art, in all its departments, was cultivated with an increased zeal for all the rest of the century.[1] In the splendor that environed the houses of Medici and Este, in the pageants they loved to exhibit, music, carried to a higher perfection by

[1] Ranke, with the musical sentiment of a German, ascribes a wonderful influence in the revival of religion after the middle of the century to the compositions of Palestrina. Church music had become so pedantic and technical, that the Council of Trent had some doubts whether it should be retained. Pius IV. appointed a commission to examine this question, who could arrive at no decision. The artists said it was impossible to achieve what the church required, a co-incidence of expression between the words and the music. Palestrina appeared at this time, and composed the mass of Marcellus, which settled the dispute for ever. Other works by himself and his disciples followed, which elevated sacred music to the highest importance among the accessories of religious worship. Die Päpste, vol. i. p. 498. But a large proportion of the performers, I apprehend, were Germans, especially in theatrical music.

foreign artists, and by the natives who came forward to emulate them, became of indispensable importance; it had already been adapted to dramatic representation in choruses; interludes and pieces written for scenic display were now given with a perpetual accompaniment, partly to the songs, partly to the dance and pantomime which intervened between them.[1] Finally, Ottavio Rinuccini, a poet of considerable genius, but who is said to have known little of musical science, by meditating on what is found in ancient writers on the accompaniment to their dramatic dialogue, struck out the idea of recitative. This he first tried in the pastoral of Dafne, represented privately in 1594; and its success led him to the composition of what he entitled a tragedy for music, on the story of Eurydice. This was represented at the festival on the marriage of Mary of Medicis in 1600. "The most astonishing effects," says Ginguéné, "that the theatrical music of the greatest masters has produced, in the perfection of the science, are not comparable to those of this representation, which exhibited to Italy the creation of a new art."[2] It is, however, a different question whether this immense enhancement of the powers of music, and consequently of its popularity, has been favorable to the development of poetical genius in this species of composition; and in general it may be said, that if music has, on some occasions, been a serviceable handmaid, and even a judicious monitress, to poetry, she has been apt to prove but a tyrannical mistress. In the melodrame, Corniani well observes, poetry became her vassal, and has been ruled with a despotic sway.

The national taste revives in the Spanish drama.

6. The struggle that seemed arduous in the earlier part of this century between the classical and national schools of dramatic poetry in Spain proved of no long duration. The latter became soon decisively superior; and, before the end of the present period, that kingdom was in possession of a peculiar and extensive literature, which has attracted the notice of Europe, and has enriched both the French theatre and our own. The spirit of the Spanish drama is far different from that which animated the Italian writers: there is not much of Machiavel in their comedy, and still less of Cinthio in their tragedy. They

[1] Ginguéné, vol. vi., has traced the history of the melodrame with much pains.

[2] P. 474. Corniani, vii. 31, speaks highly of the poetical abilities of Rinuccini. See also Galluzzi, Storia del Gran Ducato, v. 547.

abandoned the Greek chorus, which still fettered their contemporaries, and even the division into five acts, which later poets, in other countries, have not ventured to renounce. They gave more complication to the fable, sought more unexpected changes of circumstance, were not solicitous in tragedy to avoid colloquial language or familiar incidents, showed a preference to the tragi-comic intermixture of light with serious matter, and cultivated grace in poetical diction more than vigor. The religious mysteries, once common in other parts of Europe, were devoutly kept up in Spain; and, under the name of Autos Sacramentales, make no inconsiderable portion of the writings of their chief dramatists.[1]

7. Andrès, favorable as he is to his country, is far from enthusiastic in his praises of the Spanish theatre. Its exuberance has been its ruin: no one, he justly remarks, can read some thousand plays in the hope of finding a few that are tolerable. Andrès, however, is not exempt from a strong prejudice in favor of the French stage. He admits the ease and harmony of the Spanish versification, the purity of the style, the abundance of the thoughts, and the ingenious complexity of the incidents. This is peculiarly the merit of the Spanish comedy; as its great defect, in his opinion, is the want of truth and delicacy in the delineation of the passions, and of power to produce a vivid impression on the reader. The best work, he concludes rather singularly, of the comic poets of Spain has been the French theatre.[2]

Lope de Vega.

8. The most renowned of these is Lope de Vega, so many of whose dramas appeared within the present century, that although, like Shakspeare, he is equally to be claimed by the next, we may place his name, once for all, in this period. Lope de Vega is called by Cervantes a prodigy of nature; and such he may justly be reckoned: not that we can ascribe to him a sublime genius, or a mind abounding with fine original thought; but his fertility of invention and readiness of versifying are beyond competition. It was said foolishly, if meant as praise, of Shakspeare, and we may be sure untruly, that he never blotted a line. This may almost be presumed of Vega. "He required," says Bouterwek, "no more than four and twenty hours to write a versified drama of three acts in redondillas,

His extraordinary fertility:

[1] Bouterwek.

[2] Vol. v. p. 138.

interspersed with sonnets, tercets, and octaves, and, from beginning to end, abounding in intrigues, prodigies, or interesting situations. This astonishing facility enabled him to supply the Spanish theatre with upwards of 2,000 original dramas, of which not more than 300 have been preserved by printing. In general, the theatrical manager carried away what he wrote before he had even time to revise it; and immediately a fresh applicant would arrive to prevail on him to commence a new piece. He sometimes wrote a play in the short space of three or four hours." . . . "Arithmetical calculations have been employed in order to arrive at a just estimate of Lope de Vega's facility in poetic composition. According to his own testimony, he wrote, on an average, five sheets a day; it has therefore been computed that the number of sheets which he composed during his life must have amounted to 133,225; and that, allowing for the deduction of a small portion of prose, Lope de Vega must have written upwards of 21,300,000 verses. Nature would have overstepped her bounds, and have produced the miraculous, had Lope de Vega, along with this rapidity of invention and composition, attained perfection in any department of literature."[1]

His versification.

9. This peculiar gift of rapid composition will appear more extraordinary when we attend to the nature of Lope's versification, very unlike the irregular lines of our old drama, which it is not perhaps difficult for one well practised to write or utter extemporaneously. "The most singular circumstance attending his verse," says Lord Holland, "is the frequency and difficulty of the tasks which he imposes on himself. At every step, we meet with acrostics, echoes, and compositions of that perverted and laborious kind, from attempting which another author would be deterred by the trouble of the undertaking, if not by the little real merit attending the achievement. They require no genius, but they exact much time; which one should think that such a voluminous poet could little afford to waste. But Lope made a parade of his power over the vocabulary: he was not contented with displaying the various order in which he could dispose the syllables and marshal the rhymes of his language; but he

[1] Pp. 361, 363. Montalvan, Lope's friend, says that he wrote 1800 plays and 400 autos. In a poem of his own, written in 1609, he claims 483 plays; and he continued afterwards to write for the stage. Those that remain and have been collected in twenty-five volumes are about 300.

also prided himself upon the celerity with which he brought them to go through the most whimsical but the most difficult evolutions. He seems to have been partial to difficulties, for the gratification of surmounting them." This trifling ambition is usual among second-rate poets, especially in a degraded state of public taste; but it may be questionable whether Lope de Vega ever performed feats of skill more surprising in this way than some of the Italian *improvvisatori*, who have been said to carry on at the same time three independent sonnets, uttering, in their unpremeditated strains, a line of each in separate succession. There is reason to believe that their extemporaneous poetry is as good as any thing in Lope de Vega.

His popularity. 10. The immense popularity of this poet, not limited, among the people itself, to his own age, bespeaks some attention from criticism. "The Spaniards who affect fine taste in modern times," says Schlegel, "speak with indifference of their old national poets; but the people retain a lively attachment to them, and their productions are received on the stage, at Madrid or at Mexico, with passionate enthusiasm." It is true that foreign critics have not in general pronounced a very favorable judgment of Lope de Vega. But a writer of such prodigious fecundity is ill appreciated by single plays: the whole character of his composition manifests that he wrote for the stage, and for the stage of his own country, rather than for the closet of a foreigner. His writings are divided into spiritual plays; heroic and historical comedies, most of them taken from the annals and traditions of Spain; and, lastly, comedies of real life, or, as they were called, "of the cloak and sword" (*capa y espada*), a name answering to the *comœdia togata* of the Roman stage. These have been somewhat better known than the rest, and have, in several instances, found their way to our own theatre, by suggesting plots and incidents to our older writers. The historian of Spanish literature, to whom I am so much indebted, has given a character of these comedies, in which the English reader will perhaps recognize much that might be said also of Beaumont and Fletcher.

Character of his comedies. 11. "Lope de Vega's comedies De Capa y Espada, or those which may properly be denominated his dramas of intrigue, though wanting in the delineation of character, are romantic pictures of manners, drawn from real life. They present, in their peculiar style, no less interest with respect to situations than his heroic comedies, and the same irregularity in the composition of the scenes. The language, too, is alternately elegant and vulgar, sometimes highly poetic, and sometimes, though versified, reduced to the level of the dullest prose. Lope de Vega seems scarcely to have bestowed a thought on maintaining probability in the succession of the different scenes: ingenious complication is with him the essential point in the interest of his situations. Intrigues are twisted and entwined together, until the poet, in order to bring his piece to a conclusion, without ceremony cuts the knots he cannot untie; and then he usually brings as many couples together as he can, by any possible contrivance, match. He has scattered through his pieces occasional reflections, and maxims of prudence: but any genuine morality, which might be conveyed through the stage, is wanting; for its introduction would have been inconsistent with that poetic freedom on which the dramatic interest of the Spanish comedy is founded. His aim was to paint what he observed, not what he would have approved, in the manners of the fashionable world of his age; but he leaves it to the spectator to draw his own inferences."[1]

Tragedy of Don Sancho Ortiz.

12. An analysis of one of these comedies from real life is given by Bouterwek, and another by Lord Holland. The very few that I have read appear lively and diversified, not unpleasing in the perusal, but exciting little interest, and rapidly forgotten. Among the heroic pieces of Lope de Vega, a high place appears due to the Estrella de Sevilla, published, with alterations by Triquero, under the name of Don Sancho Ortiz.[2] It resembles the Cid in its subject. The king, Sancho the brave, having fallen in love with Estrella, sister of Don Bustos Tabera, and being foiled by her virtue,[3] and by the vigilance of her brother, who had drawn his sword upon him, as in disguise he was attempting to penetrate into her apartment, resolves to have him murdered; and persuades Don Sancho Ortiz, a soldier full of courage and loyalty, by describing the attempt made on his

[1] Bouterwek, p. 375.

[2] In Lord Holland's Life of Lope de Vega, a more complete analysis than what I have offered is taken from the original play. I have followed the *rifaccimento* of Triquero, which is substantially the same.

[3] Lope de Vega has borrowed for Estrella the well-known answer of a lady to a king of France, told with several variations of names, and possibly true of none.

"Soy (she says)
Para esposa vuestra poco
Para dama vuestra mucho."

person, to undertake the death of one whose name is contained in a paper he gives him. Sancho is the accepted lover of Estrella, and is on that day to espouse her with her brother's consent. He reads the paper, and after a conflict which is meant to be pathetic, but in our eyes is merely ridiculous, determines, as might be supposed, to keep his word to his sovereign. The shortest course is to contrive a quarrel with Bustos, which produces a duel, wherein the latter is killed. The second act commences with a pleasing scene of Estrella's innocent delight in her prospect of happiness: but the body of her brother is now brought in; and the murderer, who had made no attempt to conceal himself, soon appears in custody. His examination before the judges, who endeavor in vain to extort one word from him in his defence, occupies part of the third act. The king, anxious to save his life, but still more so to screen his own honor, requires only a pretext to pardon the offence. But the noble Castilian disdains to save himself by falsehood, and merely repeats that he had not slain his friend without cause, and that the action was atrocious, but not criminal.

"Dice que fue atrocidad,
Pero que no delito."

13. In this embarrassment, Estrella appears, demanding, not the execution of justice on her brother's murderer, but that he should be delivered up to her. The king, with his usual feebleness, consents to this request; observing that he knows by experience it is no new thing for her to be cruel. She is, however, no sooner departed with the royal order, than the wretched prince repents, and determines to release Sancho, making compensation to Estrella by marrying her to a *rico-hombre* of Castile. The lady meantime reaches the prison, and, in an interview with her unfortunate lover, offers him his liberty; which, by the king's concession, is in her power. He is not to be outdone in generous sentiments, and steadily declares his resolution to be executed. In the fifth act, this heroic emulation is reported, by one who had overheard it, to the king. All the people of this city, he replies, are heroes, and outstrip nature herself by the greatness of their souls. The judges now enter, and with sorrow report their sentence that Sancho must suffer death. But the king is at length roused, and publicly acknowledges that the death of Bustos

had been perpetrated by his command. The president of the tribunal remarks, that, as the king had given the order, there must doubtless have been good cause. Nothing seems to remain but the union of the lovers. Here, however, the high Castilian principle once more displays itself. Estrella refuses to be united to one she tenderly loves, but who has brought such a calamity into her family; and Sancho himself, willingly releasing her engagement, admits that their marriage under such circumstances would be a perpetual torment. The lady therefore chooses, what is always at hand in Catholic fiction, the dignified retirement of a nunnery; and the lover departs to dissipate his regrets in the Moorish war.

14. Notwithstanding all in the plan and conduct of this piece, which neither our own state of manners nor the laws of any sound criticism can tolerate, it is very conceivable, that, to the factitious taste of a Spanish audience in the age of Lope de Vega, it would have appeared excellent. The character of Estrella is truly noble, and much superior in interest to that of Chimène. Her resentment is more genuine, and free from that hypocrisy, which, at least in my judgment, renders the other almost odious and contemptible. Instead of imploring the condemnation of him she loves, it is as her own prisoner that she demands Sancho Ortiz, and this for the generous purpose of setting him at liberty. But the great superiority of the Spanish play is at the close. Chimène accepts the hand stained with her father's blood, while Estrella sacrifices her own wishes to a sentiment which the manners of Spain, and, we may add, the laws of natural decency, required.

His spiritual plays.

15. The spiritual plays of Lope de Vega abound with as many incongruous and absurd circumstances as the mysteries of our forefathers. The Inquisition was politic enough to tolerate, though probably the sternness of Castilian orthodoxy could not approve, these strange representations, which, after all, had the advantage of keeping the people in mind of the devil, and of the efficacy of holy water in chasing him away. But the regular theatre, according to Lord Holland, has always been forbidden in Spain by the church; nor do the kings frequent it.

Numancia of Cervantes.

16. Two tragedies by Bermudez, both on the story of Inez de Castro, are written on the ancient model, with a chorus, and much simplicity of fable. They are, it is said, in a few scenes impressive and pathetic, but

interrupted by passages of flat and tedious monotony.[1] Cervantes was the author of many dramatic pieces, some of which are so indifferent as to have been taken for intentional satires upon the bad taste of his times, so much of it do they display. One or two, however, of his comedies have obtained some praise from Schlegel and Bouterwek. But his tragedy of Numancia stands apart from his other dramas, and, as I conceive, from any thing on the Spanish stage. It is probably one of his earlier works, but was published for the first time in 1784. It is a drama of extraordinary power, and may justify the opinion of Bouterwek, that, in different circumstances, the author of Don Quixote might have been the Æschylus of Spain. If terror and pity are the inspiring powers of tragedy, few have been for the time more under their influence than Cervantes in his Numancia. The story of that devoted city, its long resistance to Rome, its exploits of victorious heroism, that foiled repeatedly the consular legions, are known to every one. Cervantes has opened his tragedy at the moment when Scipio Æmilianus, enclosing the city with a broad trench, determines to secure its reduction by famine. The siege lasted five months, when the Numantines, exhausted by hunger, but resolute never to yield, setting fire to a pile of their household goods, after slaying their women and children, cast themselves into the flame. Every circumstance that can enhance horror, the complaints of famished children, the desperation of mothers, the sinister omens of rejected sacrifice, the appalling incantations that re-animate a recent corpse to disclose the secrets of its prison-house, are accumulated with progressive force in this tremendous drama. The love-scenes of Morando and Lira, two young persons whose marriage had been frustrated by the public calamity, though some incline to censure them, contain nothing beyond poetical truth, and add, in my opinion, to its pathos, while they somewhat relieve its severity.

17. Few, probably, would desire to read the Numancia a second time. But it ought to be remembered, that the historical truth of this tragedy, though, as in the Ugolino of Dante, it augments the painfulness of the impression, is the legitimate apology of the author. Scenes of agony, and images of unspeakable sorrow, when idly accumulated by an inventor at his ease, as in many of our own older tragedies, and in much of modern fiction, give offence to a reader of just

[1] Bouterwek, 296.

taste, from their needlessly trespassing upon his sensibility. But in that which excites an abhorrence of cruelty and oppression, or which, as the Numancia, commemorates ancestral fortitude, there is a moral power, for the sake of which the sufferings of sympathy must not be flinched from.

18. The Numancia is divided into four jornadas or acts, each containing changes of scene, as on our own stage. The metre, by a most extraordinary choice, is the regular octave stanza, ill adapted as that is to the drama, intermixed with the favorite redondilla. The diction, though sometimes what would seem tame and diffuse to us, who are accustomed to a bolder and more figurative strain in tragedy than the Southern nations require, rises often with the subject to nervous and impressive poetry. There are, however, a few sacrifices to the times. In a finely imagined prosopopœia, where Spain, crowned with towers, appears on the scene to ask the Duero what hope there could be for Numancia, the river-god, rising with his tributary streams around him, after bidding her despair of the city, goes into a tedious consolation, in which the triumphs of Charles and Philip are specifically, and with as much tameness as adulation, brought forward as her future recompense. A much worse passage occurs in the fourth act, where Lira, her brother lying dead of famine, and her lover of his wounds before her, implores death from a soldier who passes over the stage. He replies that some other hand must perform that office; he was born only to adore her.[1] This frigid and absurd line, in such a play by such a poet, is an almost incredible proof of the mischief which the Provençal writers, with their hyperbolical gallantry, had done to European poetry. But it is just to observe that this is the only faulty passage, and that the language of the two lovers is simple, tender, and pathetic. The material accompaniments of representation on the Spanish theatre seem to have been full as defective as on our own. The Numancia is printed with stage directions, almost sufficient to provoke a smile in the midst of its withering horrors.

French theatre: Jodelle.

19. The mysteries which had delighted the Parisians for a century and a half were suddenly forbidden by the parliament as indecent and profane in 1548. Four years only elapsed before they were replaced, though

1 "Otra mano, otro hierro ha de acabaros,
Que yo solo nació por adoraros."

not on the same stage, by a different style of representation. Whatever obscure attempts at a regular dramatic composition may have been traced in France at an earlier period, Jodelle was acknowledged by his contemporaries to be the true father of their theatre. His tragedy of Cléopatre, and his comedy of La Rencontre, were both represented for the first time before Henry II. in 1552. Another comedy, Eugène, and a tragedy on the story of Dido, were published about the same time. Pasquier, who tells us this, was himself a witness of the representation of the two former.[1] The Cléopatre, according to Fontenelle, is very simple, without action or stage effect, full of long speeches, and with a chorus at the end of every act. The style is often low and ludicrous, which did not prevent this tragedy, the first-fruits of a theatre which was to produce Racine, from being received with vast applause. There is, in reality, amidst these raptures that frequently attend an infant literature, something of an undefined presage of the future, which should hinder us from thinking them quite ridiculous. The comedy of Eugène is in verse, and, in the judgment of Fontenelle, much superior to the tragedies of Jodelle. It has more action, a dialogue better conceived, and some traits of humor and nature. This play, however, is very immoral and licentious; and it may be remarked, that some of its satire falls on the vices of the clergy.[2]

Garnier.

20. The Agamemnon of Toutain, published in 1557, is taken from Seneca; and several other pieces about the same time, or soon afterwards, seem also to be translations.[3] The Jules César of Grevin was represented in 1560.[4] It contains a few lines that La Harpe has extracted,

[1] "Cette comédie et la Cléopatre furent représentées devant le roi Henri à Paris en l'Hostel de Rheims, avec un grand applaudissement de toute la compagnie; et depuis encore au collège de Boncourt, où toutes les fenestres estoient tapissées d'une infinité de personnages d'honneur, et la cour si pleine d'escoliers que les portes du collège en regorgeoient. Je le dis comme celuy qui y estois présent, avec le grand Tornebus en une mesme chambre. Et les entreparleurs estoient tous hommes de nom. Car même Remy Belleau et Jean de la Peruse jouoient les principaux roullets." Suard tells us that the whole troop of performers, the Confrères de la Passion, whose mysteries had been interdicted, availed themselves of an exclusive privilege granted to them by Charles VI., in 1400, to prevent the representation of the Cléopatre by public actors. Jodelle was, therefore, forced to have it performed by his friends. See Recherches de la France, l. vii. c. 6; Fontenelle, Hist. du Théâtre François (in Œuvres de Font., edit. 1776), vol. iii. p. 52; Beauchamps, Recherches sur les Théâtres de France; Suard, Mélanges de Littérature, vol. iv. p. 59. The last writer, in what he calls Coup-d'Œil sur l'Histoire de l'Ancien Théâtre Français (in the same volume), has given an amusing and instructive sketch of the French drama down to Corneille.

[2] Fontenelle, p. 61.

[3] Beauchamps; Suard.

[4] Suard, p. 73; La Harpe, Cours de Littérature. Grevin also wrote comedies which were very licentious, as those of the

as not without animation. But the first tragedian that deserves much notice after Jodelle was Robert Garnier, whose eight tragedies were collectively printed in 1580. They are chiefly taken from mythology or ancient history, and are evidently framed according to a standard of taste which has ever since prevailed on the French stage. But they retain some characteristics of the classical drama which were soon afterwards laid aside: the chorus is heard between every act; and a great portion of the events is related by messengers. Garnier makes little change in the stories he found in Seneca or Euripides; nor had love yet been thought essential to tragedy. Though his speeches are immeasurably long, and overladen with pompous epithets; though they have often much the air of bad imitations of Seneca's manner, from whom probably, if any one should give himself the pains to make the comparison, some would be found to have been freely translated, we must acknowledge that in many of his couplets the reader perceives a more genuine tone of tragedy, and the germ of that artificial style which reached its perfection in far greater men than Garnier. In almost every line there is some fault, either against taste or the present rules of verse; yet there are many which a good poet would only have had to amend and polish. The account of Polyxena's death in La Troade is very well translated from the Hecuba. But his best tragedy seems to be Les Juives, which is wholly his own, and displays no inconsiderable powers of poetical description. In this I am confirmed by Fontenelle, who says that this tragedy has many noble and touching passages; wherein he has been aided by taking much from Scripture, the natural sublimity of which cannot fail to produce an effect.[1] We find, however, in Les Juives a good deal of that propensity to exhibit cruelty, by which the Italian and English theatres were at that time distinguished. Pasquier says, that every one gave the prize

16th century generally were in France and Italy, and were not in England, or, I believe, in Spain.

[1] P. 71. Suard, who dwells much longer on Garnier than either Fontenelle or La Harpe has done, observes, as I think, with justice: "Les ouvrages de Garnier méritent de faire époque dans l'histoire du théâtre, non par la beauté de ses plans; il n'en faut chercher de bons dans aucune des tragédies du seizième siècle; mais les sentimens qu'il exprime sont nobles, son style a souvent de l'élévation sans enflure et beaucoup de sensibilité; sa versification est facile et souvent harmonieuse. C'est lui qui a fixé d'une manière invariable la succession alternative des rimes masculines et féminines. Enfin c'est le premier des tragiques Français dont la lecture pût être utile à ceux qui voudraient suivre la même carrière; on a même prétendu que son Hyppolite avait beaucoup aidé Racine dans la composition de Phèdre. Mais s'il l'a aidé, c'est comme l'Hyppolite de Sénèque, dont celui de Garnier n'est qu'une imitation." — p. 81

to Garnier above all who had preceded him, and, after enumerating his eight plays, expresses his opinion that they would be admired by posterity.[1]

21. We may consider the comedies of Larivey, published in 1579, as making a sort of epoch in the French drama. This writer, of whom little is known but that he was a native of Champagne, prefers a claim to be the first who chose subjects for comedy from real life in France (forgetting in this those of Jodelle), and the first who wrote original dramas in prose. His comedies are six in number, to which three were added in a subsequent edition, which is very rare.[2] These six are Le Laquais, La Veuve, Les Esprits, Le Morfondu, Les Jaloux, and Les Ecoliers. Some of them are partly borrowed from Plautus and Terence; and in general they belong to that school, presenting the usual characters of the Roman stage, with no great attempt at originality. But the dialogue is conducted with spirit; and in many scenes, especially in the play called Le Laquais, which, though the most free in all respects, appears to me the most comic and amusing, would remind any reader of the minor pieces of Molière, being conceived, though not entirely executed, with the same humor. All these comedies of Larivey are highly licentious both in their incidents and language. It is supposed in the Biographie Universelle, that Molière and Regnard borrowed some ideas from Larivey; but both the instances alleged will be found in Plautus.

Larivey.

22. No regular theatre was yet established in France. These plays of Garnier, Larivey, and others of that class, were represented either in colleges or in private houses. But the Confrères de la Passion, and another company, the Enfans de Sans Souci, whom they admitted into a participation of their privilege, used to act gross and stupid farces, which few respectable persons witnessed. After some unsuccessful attempts, two companies of regular actors appeared near the close of the century: one, in 1598, having purchased the exclusive right of the Confrères de la Passion, laid the foundations of the Comédie Française, so celebrated

Theatres in Paris.

[1] Suard.

[2] The first edition itself, I conceive, is not very common; for few writers within my knowledge have mentioned Larivey. Fontenelle, I think, could not have read his plays, or he would have given him a place in his brief sketch of the early French stage, as the father of comedy in prose. La Harpe was too superficial to know any thing about him. Beauchamps, vol. ii. p. 68, acknowledges his pretensions; and he has a niche in the Biographie Universelle. Suard has also done him some justice

and so permanent; the other, in 1600, established by its permission a second theatre in the Marais. But the pieces they represented were still of a very low class.[1]

23. England, at the commencement of this period, could boast of little besides the Scripture mysteries, already losing ground, but which have been traced down to the close of the century, and the more popular moral plays, which furnished abundant opportunities for satire on the times, for ludicrous humor, and for attacks on the old or the new religion. The latter, however, were kept in some restraint by the Tudor government. These moralities gradually drew nearer to regular comedies, and sometimes had nothing but an abstract name given to an individual, by which they could be even apparently distinguished from such. We have already mentioned Ralph Royster Doyster, written by Udal in the reign of Henry VIII., as the earliest English comedy in a proper sense, so far as our negative evidence warrants such a position. Mr. Collier has recovered four acts of another, called Misogonus, which he refers to the beginning of Elizabeth's reign.[2] It is, like the former, a picture of London life. A more celebrated piece is Gammar Gurton's Needle, commonly ascribed to John Still, afterwards Bishop of Bath and Wells. No edition is known before 1575; but it seems to have been represented in Christ's College at Cambridge, not far from the year 1565.[3] It is impossible for any thing to be meaner in subject and characters than this strange farce; but the author had some vein of humor, and writing neither for fame nor money, but to make light-hearted boys laugh, and to laugh with them, and that with as little grossness as the story would admit, is not to be judged with severe criticism. He comes, however, below Udal, and perhaps below the writer of Misogonus. The Supposes of George Gascoyne, acted at Gray's Inn in 1566, is but a translation in prose from the Suppositi of Ariosto. It seems to have been published in the same year.[4]

English stage.

Gammar Gurton's Needle.

1 Suard.

2 Hist. of Dramatic Poetry, ii. 464.

3 Mr. Collier agrees with Malone in assigning this date; but it is merely conjectural, as one rather earlier might be chosen with equal probability. Still is said in the biographies to have been born in 1543; but this date seems to be too low. He became Margaret's professor of divinity in 1570 Gammar Gurton's Needle must have been written while the Protestant establishment, if it existed, was very recent; for the parson is evidently a Papist.

4 Warton, iv. 304; Collier. iii. 6. The original had been first published in prose, 1525; and, from this, Gascoyne took his translation, adopting some of the changes Ariosto had introduced when he turned it into verse; but he has inserted little of his own. Ib

24. But the progress of literature soon excited in one person an emulation of the ancient drama. Sackville has the honor of having led the way. His tragedy of Gorboduc was represented at Whitehall before Elizabeth in 1562.[1] It is written in what was thought the classical style, like the Italian tragedies of the same age, but more inartificial and unimpassioned. The speeches are long and sententious; the action, though sufficiently full of incident, passes chiefly in narration; a chorus, but in the same blank-verse measure as the rest, divides the acts; the unity of place seems to be preserved, but that of time is manifestly transgressed. The story of Gorboduc, which is borrowed from our fabulous British legends, is as full of slaughter as was then required for dramatic purposes: but the characters are clearly drawn and consistently sustained; the political maxims grave and profound; the language not glowing or passionate, but vigorous; and, upon the whole, it is evidently the work of a powerful mind, though in a less poetical mood than was displayed in the Induction to the Mirror of Magistrates. Sackville, it has been said, had the assistance of Norton in this tragedy; but Warton has decided against this supposition from internal evidence.[2]

Gorboduc of Sackville.

25. The regular form adopted in Gorboduc, though not wholly without imitators, seems to have had little success with the public.[3] An action passing visibly on the stage, instead of a frigid narrative, a copious intermixture of comic buffoonery with the gravest story, were requisites with which no English audience would dispense. Thus Edwards treated the story of Damon and Pythias, which, though according to the notions of those times, it was too bloodless to be called a tragedy at all, belonged to the elevated class of dramatic compositions.[4] Several other subjects were taken from ancient history: this indeed became an

Preference given to the irregular form.

[1] The 18th of January, 1561, to which date its representation is referred by Mr. Collier, seems to be 1562, according to the modern style; and this tallies best with what is said in the edition of 1571, that it had been played about nine years before. See Warton, iv 179.

[2] Hist. of Engl. Poetry, iv. 194. Mr. Collier supports the claim of Norton to the first three acts, which would much reduce Sackville's glory, ii. 481. I incline to Warton's opinion, grounded upon the identity of style, and the superiority of the whole tragedy to any thing we can certainly ascribe to Norton, a coadjutor of Sternhold in the old version of the Psalms, and a contributor to the Mirror of Magistrates.

[3] The Jocasta of Gascoyne, translated with considerable freedom, in adding, omitting, and transposing, from the Phœnissæ of Euripides, was represented at Gray's Inn in 1563. Warton, iv. 196; Collier, iii. 7. Gascoyne had the assistance of two obscure poets in this play.

[4] Collier, iii. 2.

usual source of the fable; but, if we may judge from those few that have survived, they were all constructed on the model which the mysteries had accustomed our ancestors to admire.

First theatres.

26. The office of Master of the Revels, in whose province it lay to regulate, among other amusements of the court, the dramatic shows of various kinds, was established in 1546. The inns of court vied with the royal palace in these representations, and Elizabeth sometimes honored the former with her presence. On her visits to the universities, a play was a constant part of the entertainment. Fifty-two names, though nothing more, of dramas acted at court under the superintendence of the Master of the Revels, between 1568 and 1580, are preserved.[1] In 1574 a patent was granted to the Earl of Leicester's servants to act plays in any part of England; and in 1576 they erected the first public theatre in Blackfriars. It will be understood that the servants of the Earl of Leicester were a company under his protection; as we apply the word, Her Majesty's Servants, at this day, to the performers of Drury Lane.[2]

Plays of Whetstone and others

27. As we come down towards 1580, a few more plays are extant. Among these may be mentioned the Promos and Cassandra of Whetstone, on the subject which Shakspeare, not without some retrospect to his predecessor, so much improved in Measure for Measure.[3] But in these early dramas there is hardly any thing to praise; or, if they please us at all, it is only by the broad humor of their comic scenes. There seems little reason, therefore, for regretting the loss of so many productions, which no one contemporary has thought worthy of commendation. Sir Philip Sidney, writing about 1583, treats our English stage with great disdain. His censures, indeed, fall chiefly on the ne-

[1] Collier, i. 193, *et post;* iii. 24. Of these fifty-two plays, eighteen were upon classical subjects, historical or fabulous; twenty-one taken from modern history or romance; seven may by their titles, which is a very fallible criterion, be comedies or farces from real life; and six may, by the same test, be moralities. It is possible, as Mr. C. observes, that some of these plays, though no longer extant in their integrity, may have formed the foundation of others; and the titles of a few in the list countenance this supposition.

[2] See Mr. Collier's excellent History of Dramatic Poetry to the Time of Shakspeare, vol. i., which, having superseded the earlier works of Langbaine, Reid, and Hawkins, so far as this period is concerned, it is superfluous to quote them.

[3] Promos and Cassandra is one of the Six Old Plays reprinted by Steevens. Shakspeare found in it not only the main story of Measure for Measure, which was far from new, and which he felicitously altered by preserving the chastity of Isabella, but several of the minor circumstances and names, unless even these are to be found in the novels, from which all the dramatists ultimately derived their plot

glect of the classical unities, and on the intermixture of kings with clowns.[1] It is amusing to reflect, that this contemptuous reprehension of the English theatre (and he had spoken in as disparaging terms of our general poetry) came from the pen of Sidney, when Shakspeare had just arrived at manhood. Had he not been so prematurely cut off, what would have been the transports of that noble spirit which the ballad of Chevy Chase could "stir as with the sound of a trumpet," in reading the Faery Queen or Othello!

Marlowe and his contemporaries.

28. A better era commenced not long after, nearly coincident with the rapid development of genius in other departments of poetry. Several young men of talent appeared, Marlowe, Peele, Greene, Lilly, Lodge, Kyd, Nash, the precursors of Shakspeare, and real founders, as they may in some respects be called, of the English drama. Sackville's Gorboduc is in blank verse, though of bad and monotonous construction; but his first followers wrote, as far as we know, either in rhyme or in prose.[2] In the tragedy of Tamburlaine, referred by Mr. Collier to 1586, and the production wholly or principally of Marlowe,[3] a better kind of blank verse is first employed; the lines are interwoven; the occasional hemistich and redundant syllables break the monotony of the measure, and give more of a colloquial spirit to the dialogue. Tamburlaine was ridiculed on account of its inflated style. The bombast, however, which is not so excessive as has been alleged, was thought appropriate to such oriental tyrants. This play has more spirit and poetry than any which, upon clear grounds, can be shown to have preceded it. We find also more action on the stage, a shorter and more dramatic dialogue, a more figurative style, with a far more varied and skilful versification.[4] If Marlowe did not re-estab-

Tamburlaine.

Blank verse of Marlowe.

[1] "Our tragedies and comedies, not without cause, are cried out against, observing rules neither of honest civility nor skilful poetry;" and proceeds to ridicule their inconsistencies and disregard to time and place. Defence of Poesy.

[2] It may be a slight exception to this, that some portions of the second part of Whetstone's Promos and Cassandra are in blank verse. This play is said never to have been represented. Collier, iii. 64.

[3] Nash has been thought the author of Tamburlaine by Malone; and his inflated style, in pieces known to be his, may give some countenance to this hypothesis. It is mentioned, however, as Marlowe's Tamburlaine in the contemporary diary of Henslow, a manager or proprietor of a theatre, which is preserved at Dulwich College. Marlowe and Nash are allowed to have written Dido, Queen of Carthage, in conjunction. Mr. Collier has produced a body of evidence to show that Tamburlaine was written, at least principally, by the former, which leaves no room, as it seems, for further doubt. Vol. iii. p. 113.

[4] Shakspeare having turned into ridicule a passage or two in Tamburlaine, the

lish blank verse, which is difficult to prove, he gave it at least a variety of cadence, and an easy adaptation of the rhythm to the sense; by which it instantly became in his hands the finest instrument that the tragic poet has ever employed for his purpose, less restricted than that of the Italians, and falling occasionally almost into numerous prose, lines of fourteen syllables being very common in all our old dramatists, but regular and harmonious at other times as the most accurate ear could require.

Marlowe's Jew of Malta,

29. The savage character of Tamburlaine, and the want of all interest as to every other, render this tragedy a failure in comparison with those which speedily followed from the pen of Christopher Marlowe. The first two acts of the Jew of Malta are more vigorously conceived, both as to character and circumstance, than any other Elizabethan play, except those of Shakspeare; and perhaps we may think that Barabas, though not the prototype of Shylock, a praise of which he is unworthy, may have suggested some few ideas to the inventor. But the latter acts, as is usual with our old dramatists, are a tissue of uninteresting crimes and slaughter.[1] Faustus is better known: it contains nothing, perhaps, so dramatic as the first part of the Jew of Malta; yet the occasional glimpses of repentance, and struggles of alarmed conscience in the chief character, are finely brought in. It is full of poetical beauties; but an intermixture of buffoonery weakens the effect, and leaves it, on the whole, rather a sketch by a great genius than a finished performance. There is an awful melancholy about Marlowe's Mephistopheles, perhaps more impressive than the malignant mirth of that fiend in the renowned work of Goethe. But the fair form of Margaret is wanting; and Marlowe has hardly earned the credit of having breathed a few casual inspirations into a greater mind than his own.[2]

And Faustus.

30. Marlowe's Life of Edward II., which was entered on the books of the Stationers' Company in 1593, has been

critics have concluded it to be a model of bad tragedy. Mr. Collier, iii. 115–126, has elaborately vindicated its dramatic merits, though sufficiently aware of its faults.

1 "*Blood*," says a late witty writer, "is made as light of in some of these old dramas as *money* in a modern sentimental comedy; and, as *this* is given away till it reminds us that it is nothing but counters, so *that* is spilt till it affects us no more than its representative, the paint of the property-man in the theatre." — Lamb's Specimens of Early Dramatic Poets, i. 19.

2 The German story of Faust is said to have been published for the first time in 1587. It was rapidly translated into most languages of Europe. We need hardly name the absurd supposition, that Fust, the great printer, was intended.

deemed by some the earliest specimen of the historical play founded upon English chronicles. Whether this be true or not, and probably it is not, it is certainly by far the best after those of Shakspeare.[1] And it seems probable that the old plays of the Contention of Lancaster and York, and the True Tragedy of Richard, Duke of York, which Shakspeare remodelled in the second and third parts of Henry VI., were in great part by Marlowe, though Greene seems to put in for some share in their composition.[2] These plays claim certainly a very low rank among those of Shakspeare: his original portion is not inconsiderable; but it is fair to observe, that some of the passages most popular, such as the death of Cardinal Beaufort, and the last speech of the Duke of York, seem not to be by his hand.

His Edward II.

Plays whence Henry VI. was taken.

31. No one could think of disputing the superiority of Marlowe to all his contemporaries of this early school of the English drama. He was killed in a tavern fray in 1593. There is more room for difference of tastes as to the second place. Mr. Campbell has bestowed high praises upon Peele: "His David and Bethsabe is the earliest fountain of pathos and harmony that can be traced in our dramatic poetry. His fancy is rich, and his feeling

Peele.

[1] Collier observes, that "the character of Richard II. in Shakspeare seems modelled in no slight degree upon that of Edward II. But I am reluctant to admit, that Shakspeare modelled his *characters* by those of others; and it is natural to ask whether there were not an extraordinary likeness in the dispositions as well as fortunes of the two kings."

[2] These old plays were reprinted by Steevens in 1766. Malone, on a laborious comparison of them with the second and third parts of Henry VI., has ascertained that 1771 lines in the latter plays were taken from the former unaltered, 2373 altered by Shakspeare, while 1899 were altogether his own. It remains to inquire who are to claim the credit of these other plays, so great a portion of which has passed with the world for the genuine work of Shakspeare. The solution seems to be given, as well as we can expect, in a passage often quoted from Robert Greene's Groat's Worth of Wit, published not long before his death in September, 1592. "Yes," says he, addressing himself to some one who has been conjectured to be Peele, but more probably Marlowe, "trust them (the players) not; for there is an upstart crow, beautified with our feathers, that, with his tiger's heart wrapped in a player's hide, supposes he is as well able to bombast out a blank verse as the best of you; and, being an absolute Johannes factotum, is, in his own conceit, the only *Shakescene* in a country." An allusion is here manifest to the "tiger's heart, wrapt in a woman's hide," which Shakspeare borrowed from the old play, The Contention of the Houses, and which is here introduced to hint the particular subject of plagiarism that prompts the complaint of Greene. The bitterness he displays must lead us to suspect that he had been one himself of those who were thus preyed upon. But the greater part of the plays in question is, in the judgment, I conceive, of all competent critics, far above the powers either of Greene or Peele, and exhibits a much greater share of the spirited versification, called by Jonson the "mighty line," of Christopher Marlowe. Malone, upon second thoughts, gave both these plays to Marlowe, having, in his dissertation on the three parts of Henry VI., assigned one to Greene, the other to Peele. None of the three parts have any resemblance to the manner of Peele.

tender; and his conceptions of dramatic character have no inconsiderable mixture of solid veracity and ideal beauty. There is no such sweetness of versification and imagery to be found in our blank verse anterior to Shakspeare."[1] I must concur with Mr. Collier in thinking these compliments excessive. Peele has some command of imagery, but in every other quality it seems to me that he has scarce any claim to honor; and I doubt if there are three lines together in any of his plays that could be mistaken for Shakspeare's. His Edward I. is a gross tissue of absurdity, with some facility of language, but nothing truly good. It has also the fault of grossly violating historic truth, in a hideous misrepresentation of the virtuous Eleanor of Castile; probably from the base motive of rendering the Spanish nation odious to the vulgar. This play, which is founded on a ballad equally false, is referred to the year 1593. The versification of Peele is much inferior to that of Marlowe; and, though sometimes poetical, he seems rarely dramatic.

32. A third writer for the stage in this period is Robert Greene, whose "Friar Bacon and Friar Bungay" may probably be placed about the year 1590. This comedy, though savoring a little of the old school, contains easy and spirited versification, superior to Peele, and, though not so energetic as that of Marlowe, reminding us perhaps more frequently of Shakspeare.[2] Greene succeeds pretty well in that florid and gay style, a little redundant in images, which Shakspeare frequently gives to his princes and courtiers, and which renders some unimpassioned scenes in his historic plays effective and brilliant. There is great talent shown, though upon a very strange canvas, in Greene's

Greene.

[1] Specimens of English Poetry, i. 140. Hawkins says of three lines in Peele's David and Bethsabe, that they contain a metaphor worthy of Æschylus:—

"At him the thunder shall discharge his bolt,
And his fair spouse with bright and fiery wings
Sit ever burning on his hateful bones."

It may be rather Æschylean, yet I cannot much admire it. Peele seldom attempts such flights. "His genius was not boldly original; but he had an elegance of fancy, a gracefulness of expression, and a melody of versification, which, in the earlier part of his career, was scarcely approached."—Collier, iii. 191

[2] "Greene, in facility of expression and in the flow of his blank verse, is not to be placed below his contemporary Peele. His usual fault, more discoverable in his plays than in his poems, is an absence of simplicity; but his pedantic classical references, frequently without either taste or discretion, he had in common with the other scribbling scholars of the time. It was Shakspeare's good fortune to be in a great degree without the knowledge, and therefore, if on no other account, without the defect."—Collier, iii. 153. Tieck gives him credit for "a happy talent, a clear spirit, and a lively imagination, which characterize all his writings."—Collier, iii. 148.

"Looking Glass for London and England." His angry allusion to Shakspeare's plagiarism is best explained by supposing that he was himself concerned in the two old plays which had been converted into the second and third parts of Henry VI.[1] In default of a more probable claimant, I have sometimes been inclined to assign the first part of Henry VI. to Greene. But those who are far more conversant with the style of our dramatists do not suggest this; and we are evidently ignorant of many names, which might have ranked not discreditably by the side of these tragedians. The first part, however, of Henry VI. is, in some passages, not unworthy of Shakspeare's earlier days, nor, in my judgment, unlike his style; nor in fact do I know any one of his contemporaries who could have written the scene in the Temple Garden. The light touches of his pencil have ever been still more inimitable, if possible, than its more elaborate strokes.[2]

33. We can hardly afford time to dwell on several other writers anterior to Shakspeare. Kyd, whom Mr. Collier places, as a writer of blank verse, next to Marlowe,[3] Lodge,[4] Lilly, Nash, Hughes, and a few

Other writers of this age.

[1] Mr. Collier says, iii. 146, Greene may possibly have had a hand in the True History of Richard, Duke of York. But why possibly? when he claims it, if not in express words, yet so as to leave no doubt of his meaning. See the note in p. 377.

In a poem written on Greene in 1594 are these lines:—

"Green is the pleasing object of an eye;
Greene pleased the eyes of all that look'd upon him:
Green is the ground of every painter's die;
Greene gave the ground to all that wrote upon him:
Nay, more, the men that so eclipsed his fame
Purloin'd his plumes; can they deny the same?"

This seems an allusion to Greene's own metaphor, and must be taken for a covert attack on Shakspeare, who had by this time pretty well eclipsed the fame of Greene.

[2] "These three gifted men" (Peele, Greene, and Marlowe), says their late editor, Mr. Dyce (Peele's Works, preface, xxxv.), "though they often present to us pictures that in design and coloring outrage the truth of nature, are the earliest of our tragic writers who exhibit any just delineation of the workings of passion; and their language, though now swelling into bombast, and now sinking into meanness, is generally rich with poetry, while their versification, though somewhat monotonous, is almost always flowing and harmonious. They as much excel their immediate predecessors as they are themselves excelled by Shakspeare." Not quite as much.

[3] Collier, iii. 207. Kyd is author of Jeronymo, and of the Spanish Tragedy, a continuation of the same story. Shakspeare has selected some of their absurdities for ridicule, and has left an abundant harvest for the reader. Parts of the Spanish Tragedy, Mr. C. thinks, "are in the highest degree pathetic and interesting." This perhaps may be admitted, but Kyd is not, upon the whole, a pleasing dramatist.

[4] Lodge, one of the best poets of the age, was concerned, jointly with Greene, in the Looking Glass for London. In this strange performance, the prophet Hosea is brought to Nineveh; and the *dramatis personæ*, as far as they are serious, belong to that city: but all the farcical part relates to London. Of Lodge, Mr. C. says that he is "second to Kyd in vigor and boldness of conception; but as a drawer of character, so essential a part of dramatic poetry, he unquestionably has the advantage." — iii. 214.

more, have all some degree of merit. Nor do the anonymous tragedies, some of which were formerly ascribed to Shakspeare, and which even Schlegel, with less acuteness of criticism than is usual with him, has deemed genuine, always want a forcible delineation of passion, and a vigorous strain of verse, though not kept up for many lines. Among these are specimens of the domestic species of tragic drama, drawn probably from real occurrences, such as Arden of Feversham and the Yorkshire Tragedy; the former of which especially has very considerable merit. Its author, I believe, has not been conjectured; but it may be referred to the last decade of the century.[1] Another play of the same kind, A Woman killed with Kindness, bears the date of 1600, and is the earliest production of a fertile dramatist, Thomas Heywood. The language is not much raised above that of comedy; but we can hardly rank a tale of guilt, sorrow, and death, in that dramatic category. It may be read with interest and approbation at this day; being quite free from extravagance either in manner or language, the besetting sin of our earlier dramatists, and equally so from buffoonery. The subject resembles that of Kotzebue's drama, The Stranger, but is managed with a nobler tone of morality. It is true that Mrs. Frankfort's immediate surrender to her seducer, like that of Beaumelé in the Fatal Dowry, makes her contemptible; but this, though it might possibly have originated in the necessity created by the narrow limits of theatrical time, has the good effect of preventing that sympathy with her guilt which is reserved for her penitence.

Heywood's Woman killed with Kindness.

34. Of William Shakspeare,[2] whom, through the mouths of

[1] The murder of Arden of Feversham occurred under Edward VI.; but the plan was published in 1592. The impression made by the story must have been deep, to produce a tragedy so long afterwards. It is said by Mr. Collier, that Professor Tieck has inclined to think Arden of Feversham a genuine work of Shakspeare. I cannot but venture to suspect, that, if this distinguished critic were a native, he would discern such differences of style as render this hypothesis improbable. The speeches in Arden of Feversham have spirit and feeling; but there is none of that wit, that fertility of analogical imagery, which the worst plays of Shakspeare display. The language is also more plain and perspicuous than we ever find in him, especially on a subject so full of passion. Mr. Collier discerns the hand of Shakspeare in the Yorkshire Tragedy, and thinks that "there are some speeches which could scarcely have proceeded from any other pen." — Collier, iii. 51. It was printed with his name in 1608; but this, which would be thought good evidence in most cases, must not be held sufficient. It is impossible to explain the grounds of internal persuasion in these nice questions of æsthetic criticism; but I cannot perceive the hand of Shakspeare in any of the anonymous tragedies.

[2] Though I shall not innovate in a work of this kind, not particularly relating to Shakspeare, I must observe, that Sir Frederick Madden has offered very specious reasons (in the Archæologia, vol. xxvi.) for believing that the poet and his

those whom he has inspired to body forth the modifications of his immense mind, we seem to know better than any human writer, it may be truly said that we scarcely know any thing. We see him, so far as we do see him, not in himself, but in a reflex image from the objectivity in which he was manifested: he is Falstaff and Mercutio and Malvolio and Jaques and Portia and Imogen and Lear and Othello; but to us he is scarcely a determined person, a substantial reality of past time, the man Shakspeare. The two greatest names in poetry are to us little more than names. If we are not yet come to question his unity, as we do that of "the blind old man of Scio's rocky isle," an improvement in critical acuteness doubtless reserved for a distant posterity, we as little feel the power of identifying the young man who came up from Stratford, was afterwards an indifferent player in a London theatre, and retired to his native place in middle life, with the author of Macbeth and Lear, as we can give a distinct historic personality to Homer. All that insatiable curiosity and unwearied diligence have hitherto detected about Shakspeare serves rather to disappoint and perplex us than to furnish the slightest illustration of his character. It is not the register of his baptism, or the draft of his will, or the orthography of his name, that we seek. No letter of his writing, no record of his conversation, no character of him drawn with any fulness by a contemporary, has been produced.[1]

William Shakspeare.

35. It is generally supposed that he settled in London about 1587, being then twenty-three years old. For some time afterwards, we cannot trace him distinctly. Venus and Adonis, published in 1593, he describes, in his dedication to Lord Southampton, as "the first

His first writings for the stage.

family spelt their name *Shakspere*, and that there are, at least, no exceptions in his own autographs, as has commonly been supposed. A copy of Florio's translation of Montaigne, a book which he had certainly read (see Malone's note on Tempest, act ii. scene 1), has been lately discovered with the name *W. Shakspere* clearly written in it; and there seems no reason to doubt that it is a genuine signature. This book has, very properly, been placed in the British Museum, among the choice κειμηλια of that repository.

1 [I am not much inclined to qualify this paragraph in consequence of the petty circumstances relating to Shakspeare which have been lately brought to light, and which rather confirm than otherwise what I have said. But I laud the labors of Mr. Collier, Mr. Hunter, and other collectors of such crumbs; though I am not sure that we should not venerate Shakspeare as much, if they had left him undisturbed in his obscurity. To be told that he played a trick to a brother-player in a licentious amour, or that he died of a drunken frolic, as a stupid vicar of Stratford recounts (long after the time) in his diary, does not exactly inform us of the man who wrote Lear. If there was a Shakspeare of earth, as I suspect, there was also one of heaven; and it is of him that we desire to know something. -- 1842.]

heir of his invention." It is, however, certain that it must have been written some years before, unless we take these words in a peculiar sense: for Greene, in his Groat's Worth of Wit, 1592, alludes, as we have seen, to Shakspeare as already known among dramatic authors. It appears by this passage, that he had converted the two plays on the wars of York and Lancaster into what we read as the second and third parts of Henry VI. What share he may have had in similar repairs of the many plays then represented cannot be determined. It is generally believed that he had much to do with the tragedy of Pericles, which is now printed among his works, and which external testimony, though we should not rely too much on that as to Shakspeare, has assigned to him; but the play is full of evident marks of an inferior hand.[1] Its date is unknown: Drake supposes it to have been his earliest work, rather from its inferiority than on any other ground. Titus Andronicus is now by common consent denied to be, in any sense, a production of Shakspeare: very few passages, I should think not one, resemble his manner.[2]

Comedy of Errors.

36. The Comedy of Errors may be presumed, by an allusion it contains, to have been written before the submission of Paris to Henry IV. in 1594, which nearly put an end to the civil war.[3] It is founded on a very popular subject. This furnishes two extant comedies of Plautus; a translation from one of which, the Menæchmi, was represented in Italy earlier than any other play. It had been already, as Mr. Collier thinks, brought upon the stage in England; and another play, later than the Comedy of Errors, has been reprinted by Steevens. Shakspeare himself was so well pleased with the idea, that he has returned to it in Twelfth Night. Notwithstanding the opportunity which these mistakes of identity furnish for ludicrous situations, and for carrying on a complex plot, they are

[1] Malone, in a dissertation on the tragedy of Pericles, maintained that it was altogether an early work of Shakspeare. Steevens contended that it was a production of some older poet, improved by him; and Malone had the candor to own that he had been wrong. The opinion of Steevens is now general. Drake gives the last three acts, and part of the former, to Shakspeare; but I can hardly think his share is by any means so large.

[2] Notwithstanding this internal evidence, Meres, so early as 1598, enumerates Titus Andronicus among the plays of Shakspeare, and mentions no other but what is genuine. Drake, ii. 287 But, in criticism of all kinds, we must acquire a dogged habit of resisting testimony, when *res ipsa per se vociferatur* to the contrary.

[3] Act iii. scene 2. Some have judged the play from this passage to be written as early as 1591, but on precarious grounds

not very well adapted to a dramatic effect, not only from the manifest difficulty of finding performers quite alike, but because, were this overcome, the audience must be in as great embarrassment as the represented characters themselves. In the Comedy of Errors there are only a few passages of a poetical vein, yet such perhaps as no other living dramatist could have written: but the story is well invented and well managed; the confusion of persons does not cease to amuse; the dialogue is easy and gay beyond what had been hitherto heard on the stage; there is little buffoonery in the wit, and no absurdity in the circumstances.

Two Gentlemen of Verona.

37. The Two Gentlemen of Verona ranks above the Comedy of Errors, though still in the third class of Shakspeare's plays. It was probably the first English comedy in which characters are drawn from social life, at once ideal and true: the cavaliers of Verona and their lady-loves are graceful personages, with no transgression of the probabilities of nature; but they are not exactly the real men and women of the same rank in England. The imagination of Shakspeare must have been guided by some familiarity with romances before it struck out this comedy. It contains some very poetical lines. Though these two plays could not give the slightest suspicion of the depth of thought which Lear and Macbeth were to display, it was already evident that the names of Greene, and even Marlowe, would be eclipsed without any necessity for purloining their plumes.

Love's Labor Lost.

38. Love's Labor Lost is generally placed, I believe, at the bottom of the list. There is indeed little interest in the fable, if we can say that there is any fable at all; but there are beautiful coruscations of fancy, more original conception of character than in the Comedy of Errors, more lively humor than in the Gentlemen of Verona, more symptoms of Shakspeare's future powers as a comic writer than in either. Much that is here but imperfectly developed came forth again in his later plays, especially in As you Like It, and Much Ado about Nothing. The Taming of the Shrew is the only play, except Henry VI., in which Shakspeare has been very largely a borrower. The best parts are certainly his; but it must be confessed that several passages for which we give him credit, and which are very amusing, belong to his unknown predecessor. The ori-

Taming of the Shrew.

ginal play, reprinted by Steevens, was published in 1594.[1] I do not find so much genius in the Taming of the Shrew as in Love's Labor Lost; but, as an entire play, it is much more complete.

39. The beautiful play of Midsummer Night's Dream is placed by Malone as early as 1592: its superiority to those we have already mentioned affords some presumption that it was written after them. But it evidently belongs to the earlier period of Shakspeare's genius; poetical, as we account it, more than dramatic; yet rather so because the indescribable profusion of imaginative poetry in this play overpowers our senses till we can hardly observe any thing else, than from any deficiency of dramatic excellence. For in reality the structure of the fable, consisting as it does of three if not four actions, very distinct in their subjects and personages, yet wrought into each other without effort or confusion, displays the skill, or rather instinctive felicity, of Shakspeare, as much as in any play he has written. No preceding dramatist had attempted to fabricate a complex plot; for low comic scenes, interspersed with a serious action upon which they have no influence, do not merit notice. The Menæchmi of Plautus had been imitated by others as well as by Shakspeare; but we speak here of original invention.

Midsummer Night's Dream.

40. The Midsummer Night's Dream is, I believe, altogether original in one of the most beautiful conceptions that ever visited the mind of a poet,—the fairy machinery. A few before him had dealt in a vulgar and clumsy manner with popular superstitions; but the sportive, beneficent, invisible population of the air and earth, long since established in the creed of childhood, and of those simple as children, had never for a moment been blended with "human mortals" among the personages of the drama. Lilly's Maid's Metamorphosis is probably later than this play of Shakspeare, and was not published till 1600.[2] It is unnecessary to observe, that the fairies of Spenser, as he has dealt with them, are wholly of a different race.

Its machinery.

[1] Mr. Collier thinks that Shakspeare had nothing to do with any of the scenes where Katherine and Petruchio are not introduced. The underplot resembles, he says, the style of Haughton, author of a comedy called Englishmen for my Money, iii. 78.

[2] Collier, iii. 185. Lilly had, however, brought fairies, without making them speak, into some of his earlier plays. Ibid.

41. The language of Midsummer Night's Dream is equally novel with the machinery. It sparkles in perpetual brightness with all the hues of the rainbow, yet there is nothing overcharged or affectedly ornamented. Perhaps no play of Shakspeare has fewer blemishes, or is from beginning to end in so perfect keeping; none in which so few lines could be erased, or so few expressions blamed. His own peculiar idiom, the dress of his mind, which began to be discernible in the Two Gentlemen of Verona, is more frequently manifested in the present play. The expression is seldom obscure; but it is never in poetry, and hardly in prose, the expression of other dramatists, and far less of the people. And here, without reviving the debated question of Shakspeare's learning, I must venture to think that he possessed rather more acquaintance with the Latin language than many believe. The phrases, unintelligible and improper, except in the sense of their primitive roots, which occur so copiously in his plays, seem to be unaccountable on the supposition of absolute ignorance. In the Midsummer Night's Dream these are much less frequent than in his later dramas. But here we find several instances. Thus, "things base and vile, holding no *quantity*," for value; rivers, that "have overborn their *continents*," the *continente ripa* of Horace; "*compact* of imagination;" "something of great *constancy*," for consistency; "sweet Pyramus *translated* there;" "the law of Athens, which by no means we may *extenuate*." I have considerable doubts whether any of these expressions would be found in the contemporary prose of Elizabeth's reign, which was less overrun by pedantry than that of her successor; but, could authority be produced for Latinisms so forced, it is still not very likely that one who did not understand their proper meaning would have introduced them into poetry. It would be a weak answer, that we do not detect in Shakspeare any imitations of the Latin poets. His knowledge of the language may have been chiefly derived, like that of schoolboys, from the dictionary, and insufficient for the thorough appreciation of their beauties. But, if we should believe him well acquainted with Virgil or Ovid, it would be by no means surprising that his learning does not display itself in imitation. Shakspeare seems now and then to have a tinge on his imagination from former passages; but he never designedly imitates, though, as we have seen, he has sometimes adopted.

Its language.

The streams of invention flowed too fast from his own mind to leave him time to accommodate the words of a foreign language to our own. He knew that to create would be easier and pleasanter and better.[1]

Romeo and Juliet.

42. The tragedy of Romeo and Juliet is referred by Malone to the year 1596. Were I to judge by internal evidence, I should be inclined to date this play before the Midsummer Night's Dream: the great frequency of rhymes; the comparative absence of Latinisms; the want of that thoughtful philosophy, which, when it had once germinated in Shakspeare's mind, never ceased to display itself; and several of the faults that juvenility may best explain and excuse, — would justify this inference.

Its plot.

43. In one of the Italian novels to which Shakspeare had frequently recourse for his fable, he had the good fortune to meet with this simple and pathetic subject. What he found he has arranged with great skill. The incidents in Romeo and Juliet are rapid, various, unintermitting in interest, sufficiently probable, and tending to the catastrophe. The most regular dramatist has hardly excelled one writing for an infant and barbarian stage. It is certain that the observation of the unity of time, which we find in this tragedy, unfashionable as the name of unity has become in our criticism, gives an intenseness of interest to the story, which is often diluted and dispersed in a dramatic history. No play of Shakspeare is more frequently represented, or honored with more tears.

Its beauties and blemishes.

44. If, from this praise of the fable, we pass to other considerations, it will be more necessary to modify our eulogies. It has been said above of the Midsummer Night's Dream, that none of Shakspeare's plays have fewer blemishes. We can by no means repeat this commendation of Romeo and Juliet. It may be said, rather, that few, if any, are more open to reasonable censure; and we are almost equally struck by its excellences and its defects.

1 The celebrated essay by Farmer on the learning of Shakspeare put an end to such notions as we find in Warburton and many of the older commentators, that he had imitated Sophocles, and I know not how many Greek authors. Those indeed who agree with what I have said in a former chapter, as to the state of learning under Elizabeth, will not think it probable that Shakspeare could have acquired any knowledge of Greek. It was not a part of such education as he received. The case of Latin is different: we know that he was at a grammar school, and could hardly have spent two or three years there without bringing away a certain portion of the language.

45. Madame de Staël has truly remarked, that in Romeo and Juliet we have, more than in any other tragedy, the mere passion of love; love, in all its vernal promise, full of hope and innocence, ardent beyond all restraint of reason, but tender as it is warm. The contrast between this impetuosity of delirious joy, in which the youthful lovers are first displayed, and the horrors of the last scene, throws a charm of deep melancholy over the whole. Once alone, each of them, in these earlier moments, is touched by a presaging fear: it passes quickly away from them, but is not lost on the reader. To him there is a sound of despair in the wild effusions of their hope, and the madness of grief is mingled with the intoxication of their joy. And hence it is, that, notwithstanding its many blemishes, we all read and witness this tragedy with delight. It is a symbolic mirror of the fearful realities of life, where "the course of true love" has so often "not run smooth," and moments of as fond illusion as beguiled the lovers of Verona have been exchanged, perhaps as rapidly, not indeed for the dagger and the bowl, but for the many-headed sorrows and sufferings of humanity.

46. The character of Romeo is one of excessive tenderness. His first passion for Rosaline, which no vulgar poet would have brought forward, serves to display a constitutional susceptibility. There is indeed so much of this in his deportment and language, that we might be in some danger of mistaking it for effeminacy, if the loss of his friend had not aroused his courage. It seems to have been necessary to keep down a little the other characters, that they might not overpower the principal one; and though we can by no means agree with Dryden, that, if Shakspeare had not killed Mercutio, Mercutio would have killed him, there might have been some danger of his killing Romeo. His brilliant vivacity shows the softness of the other a little to a disadvantage. Juliet is a child, whose intoxication in loving and being loved whirls away the little reason she may have possessed. It is, however, impossible, in my opinion, to place her among the great female characters of Shakspeare's creation.

The characters.

47. Of the language of this tragedy what shall we say? It contains passages that every one remembers, that are among the nobler efforts of Shakspeare's poetry, and many short and beautiful touches of his proverbial sweet-

The language.

ness. Yet, on the other hand, the faults are in prodigious number. The conceits, the phrases that jar on the mind's ear, if I may use such an expression, and interfere with the very emotion the poet would excite, occur at least in the first three acts without intermission. It seems to have formed part of his conception of this youthful and ardent pair, that they should talk irrationally. The extravagance of their fancy, however, not only forgets reason, but wastes itself in frigid metaphors and incongruous conceptions: the tone of Romeo is that of the most bombastic commonplace of gallantry, and the young lady differs only in being one degree more mad. The voice of virgin love has been counterfeited by the authors of many fictions: I know none who have thought the style of Juliet would represent it. Nor is this confined to the happier moments of their intercourse. False thoughts and misplaced phrases deform the whole of the third act. It may be added, that, if not dramatic propriety, at least the interest of the character, is affected by some of Juliet's allusions. She seems, indeed, to have profited by the lessons and language of her venerable guardian; and those who adopt the edifying principle of deducing a moral from all they read, may suppose that Shakspeare intended covertly to warn parents against the contaminating influence of such domestics. These censures apply chiefly to the first three acts; as the shadows deepen over the scene, the language assumes a tone more proportionate to the interest: many speeches are exquisitely beautiful; yet the tendency to quibbles is never wholly eradicated.

Second period of Shakspeare.

48. The plays we have hitherto mentioned, to which one or two more might be added, belong to the earlier class, or, as we might say, to his first manner. In the second period of his dramatic life, we should place his historical plays, and such others as were written before the end of the century, or perhaps before the death of Elizabeth. The Merchant of Venice, As You Like It, and Much Ado about Nothing, are among these. The versification in these is more studied; the pauses more artificially disposed; the rhymes, though not quite abandoned, become less frequent; the language is more vigorous and elevated; the principal characters are more strongly marked, more distinctly conceived, and framed on a deeper insight into mankind. Nothing in the earlier plays can be compared, in

this respect, with the two Richards, or Shylock or Falstaff or Hotspur.

49. Many attempts had been made to dramatize the English chronicles, but, with the single exception of Marlowe's Edward II., so unsuccessfully, that Shakspeare may be considered as almost an original occupant of the field. He followed historical truth with considerable exactness; and in some of his plays, as in that of Richard II., and generally in Richard III. and Henry VIII., admitted no imaginary personages, nor any scenes of amusement. The historical plays have had a great effect on Shakspeare's popularity. They have identified him with English feelings in English hearts, and are very frequently read more in childhood, and consequently better remembered, than some of his superior dramas. And these dramatic chronicles borrowed surprising liveliness and probability from the national character and form of government. A prince and a courtier and a slave are the stuff on which the historic dramatist would have to work in some countries; but every class of freemen, in the just subordination without which neither human society, nor the stage, which should be its mirror, can be more than a chaos of huddled units, lay open to the selection of Shakspeare. What he invented is as truly English, as truly historical, in the large sense of moral history, as what he read.

The historical plays.

50. The Merchant of Venice is generally esteemed the best of Shakspeare's comedies. This excellent play is referred to the year 1597.[1] In the management of the plot, which is sufficiently complex without the slightest confusion or incoherence, I do not conceive that it has been surpassed in the annals of any theatre. Yet there are those who still affect to speak of Shakspeare as a barbarian; and others who, giving what they think due credit to his genius, deny him all judgment and dramatic taste. A comparison of his works with those of his contemporaries — and it is surely to them that we should look — will prove that his judgment is

Merchant of Venice.

[1] Meres, in his Palladis Tamia, or Wit's Treasury, 1598, has a passage of some value in determining the age of Shakspeare's plays, both by what it contains and by what it omits. "As Plautus and Seneca are accounted the best for comedy and tragedy among the Latins, so Shakspeare among the English is the most excellent in both kinds for the stage: for comedy, witness his Gentlemen of Verona, his Errors, his Love's Labor Lost, his Love's Labor Won [the original appellation of All's Well that Ends Well], his Midsummer Night's Dream, and his Merchant of Venice; for tragedy, his Richard II., his Richard III., Henry IV., King John, *Titus Andronicus*, and his Romeo and Juliet." — Drake, ii. 287.

by no means the least of his rare qualities. This is not so remarkable in the mere construction of his fable, though the present comedy is absolutely perfect in that point of view; and several others are excellently managed, as in the general keeping of the characters, and the choice of incidents. If Shakspeare is sometimes extravagant, the Marstons and Middletons are seldom otherwise. The variety of characters in the Merchant of Venice, and the powerful delineation of those upon whom the interest chiefly depends, the effectiveness of many scenes in representation, the copiousness of the wit, and the beauty of the language, it would be superfluous to extol; nor is it our office to repeat a tale so often told as the praise of Shakspeare. In the language there is the commencement of a metaphysical obscurity which soon became characteristic; but it is perhaps less observable than in any later play.

51. The sweet and sportive temper of Shakspeare, though it never deserted him, gave way to advancing years, and to the mastering force of serious thought. What he read we know but very imperfectly; yet, in the last years of this century, when five and thirty summers had ripened his genius, it seems that he must have transfused much of the wisdom of past ages into his own all-combining mind. In several of the historical plays, in the Merchant of Venice, and especially in As You Like It, the philosophic eye, turned inward on the mysteries of human nature, is more and more characteristic; and we might apply to the last comedy the bold figure that Coleridge has less appropriately employed as to the early poems, that "the creative power and the intellectual energy wrestle as in a war-embrace." In no other play, at least, do we find the bright imagination and fascinating grace of Shakspeare's youth so mingled with the thoughtfulness of his maturer age. This play is referred with reasonable probability to the year 1600. Few comedies of Shakspeare are more generally pleasing, and its manifold improbabilities do not much affect us in perusal. The brave, injured Orlando, the sprightly but modest Rosalind, the faithful Adam, the reflecting Jaques, the serene and magnanimous Duke, interest us by turns, though the play is not so well managed as to condense our sympathy, and direct it to the conclusion.

As You Like It.

52. The comic scenes of Shakspeare had generally been

drawn from novels, and laid in foreign lands. But several of our earliest plays, as has been partly seen, delineate the prevailing manners of English life. None had acquired a reputation which endured beyond their own time, till Ben Jonson, in 1596, produced, at the age of twenty-two, his first comedy, Every Man in his Humor; an extraordinary monument of early genius, in what is seldom the possession of youth, a clear and unerring description of human character, various, and not extravagant beyond the necessities of the stage. He had learned the principles of comedy, no doubt, from Plautus and Terence; for they were not to be derived from the moderns at home or abroad: but he could not draw from them the application of living passions and manners; and it would be no less unfair, as Gifford has justly observed, to make Bobadil a copy of Thraso, than to deny the dramatic originality of Kitely.

Jonson's Every Man in his Humor.

53. Every Man in his Humor is perhaps the earliest of European domestic comedies that deserves to be remembered; for even the Mandragora of Machiavel shrinks to a mere farce in comparison.[1] A much greater master of comic powers than Jonson was indeed his contemporary, and, as he perhaps fancied, his rival; but, for some reason, Shakspeare had never yet drawn his story from the domestic life of his countrymen. Jonson avoided the common defect of the Italian and Spanish theatre, the sacrifice of all other dramatic objects to one only, a rapid and amusing succession of incidents: his plot is slight and of no great complexity; but his excellence is to be found in the variety of his characters, and in their individuality, very clearly defined, with little extravagance.

[1] This would not have been approved by a modern literary historian. "Quelle était, avant que Molière parût et même de son temps, la comédie moderne comparable à la Calandria, à la Mandragore, aux meilleures pièces de l'Arioste, à celles de l'Aretin, du Cecchi, du Lasca, du Bentivoglio, de Francesco D'Ambra, et de tant d'autres?"—Ginguéné, vi. 316. This comes of deciding before we know any thing of the facts. Ginguéné might possibly be able to read English, but certainly had no sort of acquaintance with the English theatre. I should have no hesitation in replying, that we could produce at least forty comedies, before the age of Molière, superior to the best of those he has mentioned, and perhaps three times that number as good as the worst.

CHAPTER VII.

HISTORY OF POLITE LITERATURE IN PROSE, FROM 1550 TO 1600.

SECTION I.

Style of best Italian Writers — Those of France — England.

1. I AM not aware that we can make any great distinction in the character of the Italian writers of this and the preceding period, though they are more numerous in the present. Some of these have been already mentioned on account of their subjects. In point of style, to which we now chiefly confine ourselves, Casa is esteemed among the best.[1] The Galateo is certainly diffuse, but not so languid as some contemporary works; nor do we find in it, I think, so many of the inversions which are common blemishes in the writings of this age. The prose of Tasso is placed by Corniani almost on a level with his poetry for beauty of diction. "We find in it," he says, "dignity, rhythm, elegance, and purity without affectation, and perspicuity without vulgarity. He is never trifling or verbose, like his contemporaries of that century, but endeavors to fill every part of his discourses with meaning."[2] These praises may be just; but there is a tediousness in the moral essays of Tasso, which, like many other productions of that class, assert what the reader has never seen denied, and distinguish what he is in no danger of confounding.

Italian writers.

Casa.

Tasso.

2. Few Italian writers, it is said by the editors of the voluminous Milan collection, have united equally with Firenzuola the most simple naïveté to a delicate sweetness, that diffuses itself over the heart of the reader. His dialogue on the Beauty of Women

Firenzuola. Character of Italian prose.

[1] Corniani, v. 174. Parini called the Galateo, "Capo d'opera di nostra lingua.'
[2] Corniani, vi. 240.

is reckoned one of the best of his works. It is diffuse, but seems to deserve the praise bestowed upon its language. His translation of the Golden Ass of Apuleius is read with more pleasure than the original. The usual style of Italian prose in this, accounted by some its best age, is elaborate, ornate, yet not to excess, with a rhythmical structure apparently much studied, very rhetorical, and for the most part trivial, as we should now think, in its matter. The style of Machiavel, to which perhaps the reader's attention was not sufficiently called while we were concerned with his political philosophy, is eminent for simplicity, strength, and clearness. It would not be too much to place him at the head of the prose writers of Italy. But very few had the good taste to emulate so admirable a model. "They were apt to presume," says Corniani, "that the spirit of good writing consisted in the artificial employment of rhetorical figures. They hoped to fertilize a soil barren of argument by such resources. They believed that they should become eloquent by accumulating words upon words, and phrases upon phrases, hunting on every side for metaphors, and exaggerating the most trifling theme by frigid hyperboles."[1]

Italian letter-writers.

3. A treatise on Painting, by Raffaelle Borghino, published in 1584, called Il Riposo, is highly praised for its style by the Milan editors; but it is difficult for a foreigner to judge so correctly of these delicacies of language, as he may of the general merits of composition. They took infinite pains with their letters, great numbers of which have been collected. Those of Annibal Caro are among the best known;[2] but Pietro Aretino, Paolo Manuzio, and Bonfàdio are also celebrated for their style. The appearance of labor and affectation is still less pleasing in epistolary correspondence than in writings more evidently designed for the public eye; and there will be found abundance of it in these

[1] Corniani, vi. 52.

[2] It is of no relevancy to the history of literature; but in one of Caro's letters to Bernardo Tasso, about 1544, he censures the innovation of using the third person in addressing a correspondent. "Tutto questo secolo (dice Monsignor de la Casa) è adulatore; ognuno che scrive dà de le signorie; ognuno, a chi si scrive, le vuole; e non pure i grandi, ma i mezzani e i plebei quasi aspirano a questi gran nomi, e si tengono anco per affronto, se non gli hanno, e d' errore son notati quelli, che non gli danno. Cosa, che a me pare stranissima e stomachosa, che habbiamo a parlar con uno, come se fosse un altro, e tutta via in astratto, quasi con la idea di colui, con chi si parla, non con la persona sua propria. Pure l' abuso è gia fatto, ed è generale," &c. — lib. i. p. 122 (edit. 1581). I have found the third person used as early as a letter of Paolo Manuzio to Castelvetro in 1543: but, where there was any intimacy with an equal rank, it is not much employed; nor is it always found in that age in letters to men of very high rank from their inferiors.

Italian writers, especially in addressing their superiors. Cicero was a model perpetually before their eyes, and whose faults they did not perceive. Yet perhaps the Italian writings of this period, with their flowing grace, are more agreeable than the sententious antitheses of the Spaniards. Both are artificial; but the efforts of the one are bestowed on diction and cadence, those of the other display a constant strain to be emphatic and profound. What Cicero was to Italy, Seneca became to Spain.

Davanzati's Tacitus.

4. An exception to the general character of diffuseness is found in the well-known translation of Tacitus by Davanzati. This, it has often been said, he has accomplished in fewer words than the original. No one, for the most part, inquires into the truth of what is confidently said, even where it is obviously impossible. But whoever knows the Latin and Italian languages must know that a translation of Tacitus into Italian cannot be made in fewer words. It will be found, as might be expected, that Davanzati has succeeded by leaving out as much as was required to compensate the difference that articles and auxiliary verbs made against him. His translation is also censured by Corniani,[1] as full of obsolete terms and Florentine vulgarisms.

Jordano Bruno.

5. We can place under no better head than the present that lighter literature, which, without taking the form of romance, endeavors to amuse the reader by fanciful invention and gay remark. The Italians have much of this; but it is beyond our province to enumerate productions of no great merit or renown. Jordano Bruno's celebrated Spaccio della Bestia Trionfante is one of this class. Another of Bruno's light pieces is entitled La Cabala del Cavallo Pegaseo, con l' Aggiunta de l' Asino Cillenico. This has more profaneness in it than the Spaccio della Bestia. The latter, as is well known, was dedicated to Sir Philip Sidney; as was also another little piece, Gli Eroici Furori. In this he has a sonnet addressed to the English ladies: "Dell' Inghilterra o Vaghe Ninfe e Belle;" but ending, of course, with a compliment, somewhat at the expense of these beauties, to "l' unica Diana, Qual' è trà voi quel, che trà gl' astri il sole." It had been well for Bruno if he had kept himself under the protection of Diana. The "chaste beams of that watery

[1] vi. 58.

moon" were less scorching than the fires of the Inquisition.

6. The French generally date the beginning of an easy and natural style in their own language from the publication of James Amyot's translation of Plutarch in 1559. Some earlier writers, however, have been mentioned in another place, and perhaps some might have been added. The French style of the sixteenth century is for the most part diffuse, endless in its periods, and consequently negligent of grammar: but it was even then lively and unaffected, especially in narration; the memoirs of that age being still read with pleasure. Amyot, according to some, knew Greek but indifferently, and was perhaps on that account a better model of his own language; but, if he did not always render the meaning of Plutarch, he has made Plutarch's reputation, and that, in some measure, of those who have taken Plutarch for their guide. It is well known how popular, more perhaps than any other ancient, this historian and moralist has been in France; but it is through Amyot that he has been read. The style of his translator, abounding with the native idiom, and yet enriching the language, not at that time quite copious enough for its high vocation in literature, with many words which usage and authority have recognized, has always been regarded with admiration, and by some, in the prevalence of a less natural taste, with regret. It is in French prose what that of Marot is in poetry; and suggests, not an uncultivated simplicity, but the natural grace of a young person, secure of appearing to advantage, but not at bottom indifferent to doing so. This *naïveté*, a word which, as we have neither naturalized in orthography nor translated it, I must adopt, has ever since been the charm of good writing in France. It is, above all, the characteristic of one who may justly be called the disciple of Amyot, and who extols him above all other writers in the language,—Montaigne. The fascination of Montaigne's manner is acknowledged by all who read him; and with a worse style, or one less individually adapted to his character, he would never have been the favorite of the world.[1]

French writers: Amyot.

7. In the Essays of Montaigne, a few passages occur of striking though simple eloquence. But it must be admitted,

[1] See the articles on Amyot in Baillet, iv. 428; Bayle; La Harpe; Biogr. Universelle; Préface aux Œuvres de Pascal, par Neufchâteau.

that the familiar idiomatic tone of Amyot was better fitted to please than to awe, to soothe the mind than to excite it, to charm away the cares of the moment than to impart a durable emotion. It was also so remote from the grand style which the writings of Cicero and the precepts of rhetoric had taught the learned world to admire, that we cannot wonder to find some who sought to model their French by a different standard. The only one of these, so far as I am aware, that falls within the sixteenth century, is Du Vair, a man not less distinguished in public life than in literature; having twice held the seals of France under Louis XIII. "He composed," says a modern writer, "many works, in which he endeavored to be eloquent; but he fell into the error, at that time so common, of too much wishing to Latinize our mother-tongue. He has been charged with fabricating words, such as *sponsion*, *cogitation*, *contumélie*, *dilucidité*, *contemnement*,"[1] &c. Notwithstanding these instances of bad taste, which, when collected, seem more monstrous than as they are dispersed in his writings, Du Vair is not devoid of a flowing eloquence, which, whether perfectly congenial to the spirit of the language or not, has never wanted its imitators and admirers, and those very successful and brilliant, in French literature.[2] It was, of course, the manner of the bar and of the pulpit, after the pulpit laid aside its buffoonery, far more than that of Amyot and Montaigne.

Montaigne; Du Vair.

8. It is not in my power to communicate much information

[1] Neufchâteau, in Préface à Pascal, p. 181. Bouterwek, v. 326, praises Du Vair; but he does not seem a favorite with his compatriot critics.

[2] "Du Vair's Essay de la Constance et Consolations ès Malheurs Publiques, of which the first edition is in 1594, furnishes some eloquent declamation in a style unlike that of Amyot. "Repassez en votre memorie l'histoire de toute l'antiquité; et quand vous trouverez un magistrat qui aura eu grand crédit envers un peuple, ou auprès d'un prince, et qui se sera voulu comporter vertueusement, dites hardiment: Je gage que cestui-ci a été banni, que cestui-ci a été tué, que cestui-ci a été empoisonné. A Athènes, Aristidès, Themistoclès, et Phocion; à Rome, infinis desquels je laisse les noms pour n'emplir le papier, me contentant de Camille, Scipion, et Ciceron pour l'antiquité, de Papinien pour les temps des empereurs Romains, et de Boece sous les Gots. Mais pourquoi le prenons-nous si haut? Qui avons-nous vu de notre siècle tenir les sceaux de France, qui n'ait été mis en cette charge, pour en être déjetté avec contumélie? Celui qui auroit vu M. le Chancelier Olivier, ou M. le Chancelier de l'Hospital, partir de la cour pour se retirer en leurs maisons, n'auriot jamais envié de tels honneurs, ni de tels charges. Imaginez vous ces braves et vénérables vieillards, esquels reluisoient toutes sortes de vertus, et esquels entre une infinité de grandes parties vous n'eussiez sçu que choisir, remplis d'érudition, consommez ès affaires, amateurs de leur patrie, vraiment dignes de telles charges, si le siècle eust été digne d'eux. Après avoir longuement et fidèlement servis la patrie, on leur dresse des querelles d'Allemans, et de fausses accusations pour les bannir des affaires, ou plutôt pour en priver les affaires; comme un navire agité de la conduite de si sages et experts pilotes, afin de le faire plus aisément briser." — p. 76 (edit. 1604).

as to the minor literature of France. One book may be named as being familiarly known, the Satire Menippée. The first edition bears the date of 1593, but is said not to have appeared till 1594, containing some allusions to events of that year. It is a ridicule on the proceedings of the League, who were then masters of Paris; and has commonly been ascribed to Leroy, canon of Rouen, though Passerat, Pithou, Rapin, and others are said to have had some share in it. This book is historically curious; but I do not perceive that it displays any remarkable degree of humor or invention. The truth appears so much throughout, that it cannot be ranked among works of fiction.[1]

Satire Menippée.

9. In the scanty and obscure productions of the English press under Edward and Mary, or in the early years of Elizabeth, we should search, I conceive, in vain for any elegance or eloquence in writing. Yet there is an increasing expertness and fluency; and, the language insensibly rejecting obsolete forms, the manner of our writers is less uncouth, and their sense more pointed and perspicuous, than before. Wilson's Art of Rhetorique is at least a proof that some knew the merits of a good style, if they did not yet bring their rules to bear on their own language. In Wilson's own manner there is nothing remarkable. The first book which can be worth naming at all is Ascham's Schoolmaster, published in 1570, and probably written some years before. Ascham is plain and strong in his style, but without grace or warmth: his sentences have no harmony of structure. He stands, however, as far as I have seen, above all other writers in the first half of the queen's reign. The best of these, like Reginald Scot, express their meaning well, but with no attempt at a rhythmical structure or figurative language: they are not bad writers, because their solid sense is aptly conveyed to the mind; but they are not good, because they have little selection of words, and give no pleasure by means of style. Puttenham is perhaps the first who wrote a well-measured prose: in his Art of English Poesie, published in 1586, he is elaborate, studious of elevated and chosen expression, and rather diffuse, in the manner of the Italians of the sixteenth century, who affected that fulness of style, and whom he probably

English writers.

Ascham.

[1] Biogr. Univ. art. "Leroy;" Vigneul-Marville, i. 197.

meant to imitate. But in these later years of the queen, when almost every one was eager to be distinguished for sharp wit or ready learning, the want of good models of writing in our own language gave rise to some perversion of the public taste. Thoughts and words began to be valued, not as they were just and natural, but as they were removed from common apprehension, and most exclusively the original property of those who employed them. This in poetry showed itself in affected conceits, and in prose led to the pedantry of recondite mythological allusion, and of a Latinized phraseology.

Euphues of Lilly.

10. The most remarkable specimen of this class is the Euphues of Lilly; a book of little value, but which deserves notice on account of the influence it is recorded to have had upon the court of Elizabeth; an influence also over the public taste, which is manifested in the literature of the age.[1] It is divided into two parts, having separate titles: the first, "Euphues, the Anatomy of wit;" the second, "Euphues and his England." This is a very dull story of a young Athenian, whom the author places at Naples in the first part, and brings to England in the second: it is full of dry commonplaces. The style, which obtained celebrity, is antithetical and sententious to affectation; a perpetual effort, with no adequate success, rendering the book equally disagreeable and ridiculous, though it might not be difficult to find passages rather more happy and ingenious than the rest. The following specimen is taken at random; and, though sufficiently characteristic, is perhaps rather unfavorable to Lilly, as a little more affected and empty than usual:—

11. "The sharpest north-east wind, my good Euphues, doth never last three days; tempests have but a short time; and the more violent the thunder is, the less permanent it is. In the like manner, it falleth out with jars and carpings of friends, which, begun in a moment, are ended in a moment. Necessary it is, that among friends there should be some thwarting; but, to continue in anger, not convenient: the camel first troubleth the water before he drink; the frankincense is burned before it smell; friends are tried before they be

[1] [Euphues, Mr. Collier thinks, was published early in 1579: Malone had a copy of that year, which he took to be the second edition. Watts refers the first edition to 1580.—1842.]

trusted, lest, shining like the carbuncle, as though they had fire, they be found, being touched, to be without fire. Friendship should be like the wine which Homer, much commending, called Maroneum, whereof one pint being mingled with five quarts of water, yet it keepeth his old strength and virtue, not to be qualified by any discourtesy. Where salt doth grow, nothing else can breed; where friendship is built, no offence can harbor. Then, Euphues, let the falling-out of friends be the renewing of affection, that in this we may resemble the bones of the lion, which, lying still and not moved, begin to rot; but, being stricken one against another, break out like fire, and wax green."

12. "The lords and gentlemen in that court (of Elizabeth) are also an example," he says in a subsequent passage, "for all others to follow, — true types of nobility, the only stay and staff of honor; brave courtiers, stout soldiers, apt to revel in peace, and ride in war. In fight fierce, not dreading death; in friendship firm, not breaking promise; courteous to all that deserve well, cruel to none that deserve ill. Their adversaries they trust not, — that showeth their wisdom; their enemies they fear not, — that argueth their courage. They are not apt to proffer injuries, not fit to take any; loath to pick quarrels, but longing to revenge them." Lilly pays great compliments to the ladies for beauty and modesty, and overloads Elizabeth with panegyric. "Touching the beauty of this prince, her countenance, her majesty, her personage, I cannot think that it may be sufficiently commended, when it cannot be too much marvelled at: so that I am constrained to say, as Praxiteles did when he began to paint Venus and her son, who doubted whether the world could afford colors good enough for two such fair faces, and I whether my tongue can yield words to blaze that beauty, the perfection whereof none can imagine; which, seeing it is so, I must do like those that want a clear sight, who, being not able to discern the sun in the sky, are enforced to behold it in the water."

Its popularity.

13. It generally happens, that a style devoid of simplicity, when first adopted, becomes the object of admiration for its imagined ingenuity and difficulty; and that of Euphues was well adapted to a pedantic generation, who valued nothing higher than far-fetched allusions and sententious precepts. All the ladies of the time, we are told, were Lilly's scholars; "she who spoke not Euphuism

being as little regarded at court as if she could not speak French." "His invention," says one of his editors, who seems well worthy of him, "was so curiously strung, that Elizabeth's court held his notes in admiration."[1] Shakspeare has ridiculed this style in Love's Labor Lost, and Jonson in Every Man out of his Humor; but, as will be seen on comparing the extracts I have given above with the language of Holofernes and Fastidious Brisk, a little in the tone of caricature, which Sir Walter Scott has heightened in one of his novels, till it bears no great resemblance to the real Euphues. I am not sure that Shakspeare has never caught the Euphuistic style, when he did not intend to make it ridiculous, especially in some speeches of Hamlet.

14. The first good prose-writer, in any positive sense of the word, is Sir Philip Sidney. The Arcadia appeared in 1590. It has been said of the author of this famous romance, to which, as such, we shall have soon to revert, that "we may regard the whole literary character of that age as in some sort derived and descended from him, and his work as the fountain from which all the vigorous shoots of that period drew something of their verdure and strength. It was, indeed, the Arcadia which first taught to the contemporary writers that inimitable interweaving and contexture of words, that bold and unshackled use and application of them, that art of giving to language, appropriated to objects the most common and trivial, a kind of acquired and adventitious loftiness, and to diction in itself noble and elevated a sort of superadded dignity, that power of ennobling the sentiments by the language, and the language by the sentiments, which so often excites our admiration in perusing the writers of the age of Elizabeth."[2] This panegyric appears a good deal too strongly expressed; and perhaps the Arcadia had not this great influence over the writers of the latter years of Elizabeth, whose *age* is, in the passage quoted, rather too indefinitely mentioned. We are sometimes apt to mistake an improvement, springing from the general condition of the public mind, for imitation of the one writer who has first displayed the effects of it. Sidney is, as

Sidney's Arcadia.

[1] In Biogr. Britannica, art. "Lilly."

[2] Retrospective Review, vol. ii. p. 42.

I have said, our earliest good writer; but, if the Arcadia had never been published, I cannot believe that Hooker or Bacon would have written worse.

His Defence of Poesie.

15. Sidney's Defence of Poesie, as has been surmised by his last editor, was probably written about 1581. I should incline to place it later than the Arcadia;[1] and he may perhaps allude to himself where he says, "Some have mingled matters heroical and pastoral." This treatise is elegantly composed, with perhaps too artificial a construction of sentences: the sense is good; but the expression is very diffuse, which gives it too much the air of a declamation. The great praise of Sidney in this treatise is, that he has shown the capacity of the English language for spirit, variety, gracious idiom, and masculine firmness. It is worth notice, that, under the word "poesy," he includes such works as his own Arcadia, or, in short, any fiction. "It is not rhyming and versing that maketh poesy: one may be a poet without versing, and a versifier without poetry."

Hooker.

16. But the finest, as well as the most philosophical, writer of the Elizabethan period is Hooker. The first book of the Ecclesiastical Polity is at this day one of the masterpieces of English eloquence. His periods, indeed, are generally much too long and too intricate, but portions of them are often beautifully rhythmical; his language is rich in English idiom without vulgarity, and in words of a Latin source without pedantry; he is more uniformly solemn than the usage of later times permits, or even than writers of that time, such as Bacon, conversant with mankind as well as books, would have reckoned necessary: but the example of ancient orators and philosophers upon themes so grave as those which he discusses may justify the serious dignity from which he does not depart. Hooker is perhaps the first of such, in England, who adorned his prose with the images of poetry: but this he has done more judiciously and with more moderation than others of great name; and we must be bigots in Attic severity before we can object to some of his grand figures of speech. We may praise him also for avoiding the superfluous luxury of quotation; a rock on which the writers of the succeeding age were so frequently wrecked.

[1] [Zouch, quoted in Nicolas's edition of Davison's Rhapsody, says the Arcadia was written in 1580; and the Defence of Poesie, in 1582. — 1847.]

Character of Elizabethan writers.

17. It must be owned, however, by every one not absolutely blinded by a love of scarce books, that the prose literature of the queen's reign, taken generally, is but very mean. The pedantic Euphuism of Lilly overspreads the productions which aspire to the praise of politeness; while the common style of most pieces of circumstance, like those of Martin Mar-prelate and his answerers (for there is little to choose in this respect between parties), or of such efforts at wit and satire as came from Greene, Nash, and other worthies of our early stage, is low, and, with few exceptions, very stupid ribaldry. Many of these have a certain utility in the illustration of Shakspeare and of ancient manners, which is neither to be overlooked in our contempt for such trash, nor to be mistaken for intrinsic merit. If it is alleged that I have not read enough of the Elizabethan literature to censure it, I must reply, that, admitting my slen der acquaintance with the numberless little books that some years since used to be sold at vast prices, I may still draw an inference from the inability of their admirers, or at least purchasers, to produce any tolerable specimens. Let the labors of Sir Egerton Brydges, the British Bibliographer, the Censura Literaria, the Restituta, — collections so copious, and formed with so much industry, — speak for the prose of the queen's reign. I would again repeat, that good sense in plain language was not always wanting upon serious subjects: it is to polite writing alone that we now refer.[1] Spenser's dialogue upon the State of Ireland, the Brief Conceit of English Policy, and several other tracts, are written as such treatises should be written; but they are not to be counted in the list of eloquent or elegant compositions.

[1] It is not probable that Brydges, a man of considerable taste and judgment, whatever some other pioneers in the same track may have been, would fail to select the best portions of the authors he has so carefully perused. And yet I would almost defy any one to produce five passages in prose from his numerous volumes, so far as the sixteenth century is concerned, which have any other merit than that of illustrating some matter of fact, or of amusing by their oddity. I have only noted, in traversing that long desert, two sermons by one Edward Dering, preached before the queen (British Bibliographer, i. 260 and 560), which show considerably more vigor than was usual in the style of that age.

SECT. II. — ON CRITICISM.

State of Criticism in Italy — Scaliger — Castelvetro — Salviati — In other Countries — England.

18. IN the earlier periods with which we have been conversant, criticism had been the humble handmaid of the ancient writers, content to explain, or sometimes aspiring to restore, but seldom presuming to censure, their text, or even to justify the superstitious admiration that modern scholars felt for it. There is, however, a different and far higher criticism, which excites and guides the taste for truth and beauty in works of imagination, — a criticism to which even the great masters of language are responsible, and from which they expect their reward. But, of the many who have sat in this tribunal, a small minority have been recognized as rightful arbiters of the palms they pretend to confer; and an appeal to the public voice has as often sent away the judges in dishonor as confirmed their decision.

State of Criticism.

19. It is a proof at least of the talents and courage which distinguished Julius Cæsar Scaliger, that he, first of all the moderns (or, if there are exceptions, they must be partial and inconsiderable), undertook to reduce the whole art of verse into system, illustrating and confirming every part by a profusion of poetical literature. His Poetics form an octavo of about 900 pages, closely printed. We can give but a slight sketch of so extensive a work. In the first book, he treats of the different species of poems; in the second, of different metres; the third is more miscellaneous, but relates chiefly to figures and turns of phrase; the fourth proceeds with the same subject, but these two are very comprehensive. In the fifth, we come to apply these principles to criticism; and here we find a comparison of various poets one with another, especially of Homer with Virgil. The sixth book is a general criticism on all Latin poets, ancient and modern. The seventh is a kind of supplement to the rest, and seems to contain all the miscellaneous matter that he found himself to have omitted, together with some questions purposely reserved, as he tells us, on account of their difficulty. His comparison of Homer with Virgil is very ela

Scaliger's Poetics.

borate, extending to every simile or other passage wherein a resemblance or imitation can be observed, as well as to the general management of their epic poems. In this comparison, he gives an invariable preference to Virgil, and declares that the difference between these poets is as great as between a lady of rank and the awkward wife of a citizen. Musæus he conceives to be far superior to Homer, according to the testimony of antiquity; and the poem of Hero and Leander, which it does not occur to him to suspect, is the only one in Greek that can be named in competition with Virgil, as he shows by comparison of the said poem with the very inferior effusions of Homer. If Musæus had written on the same subject as Homer, Scaliger does not doubt but that he would have left the Iliad and Odyssey far behind.[1]

His preference of Virgil to Homer.

20. These opinions will not raise Scaliger's taste very greatly in our eyes. But it is not, perhaps, surprising that an Italian, accustomed to the polished effeminacy of modern verse, both in his language and in Latin, should be delighted with the poem of Hero and Leander, which has the sort of charm that belongs to the statues of Bacchus, and soothes the ear with voluptuous harmony, while it gratifies the mind with elegant and pleasing imagery. It is not, however, to be taken for granted, that Scaliger is always mistaken in his judgments on particular passages in these greatest of poets. The superiority of the Homeric poems is rather incontestable in their general effect, and in the vigorous originality of his verse, than in the selection of circumstance, sentiment, or

1 "Quod si Musæus, ea, quæ Homerus scripsit, scripsisset, longè melius eum scripturum fuisse judicamus."

The following is a specimen of Scaliger's style of criticism, chosen rather for its shortness than any other cause:—

"Ex vicesimo tertio Iliadis transtulit versus illos in comparationem:—

μάστιγι δ' αἰὲν ἔλαυνε κατωμαδόν· οἱ δέ οἱ ἵπποι
ὑψόσ' ἀειρέσθην ῥίμφα πρήσσοντε κέλευθον.

ἰσχνολογία multa; at in nostro animata ratio;

"Non tam præcipites bijugo certamine campum
Corripuere, ruuntque effusi carcere currus," &c.

Cum virtutibus horum carminum non est conferenda jejuna illa humilitas; audent præferre tamen grammatici temerarii. Principio, nihil infelicius quam *μάστιγι αἰὲν ἔλαυνεν*. Nam continuatio et equorum diminuit opinionem, et contemptum facit verberum. Frequentibus intervallis stimuli plus proficiunt. Quod vero admirantur Græculi, pessimum est, *ὑψόσ' ἀειρέσθην*. Extento namque, et, ut milites loquantur, clauso cursu non subsilientes opus est. Quare divinus vir, *undantia lora;* hoc enim pro flagro, et *præcipites*, et *corripuere campum;* idque in præterito, ad celeritatem. Et *ruunt*, quasi in diversa, adeo celeres sunt. Illa vero supra omnem Homerum, *proni in verbera pendent.*"—l. v. c. 3.

expression. It would be a sort of prejudice almost as tasteless as that of Scaliger, to refuse the praise of real poetic superiority to many passages of Virgil, even as compared with the Iliad, and far more with the Odyssey. If the similes of the older poet are more picturesque and animated, those of his imitator are more appropriate and parallel to the subject. It would be rather whimsical to deny this to be a principal merit in a comparison. Scaliger sacrifices Theocritus as much as Homer at the altar of Virgil; and, of course, Apollonius has little chance with so partial a judge. Horace and Ovid, at least the latter, are also held by Scaliger superior to the Greeks, whenever they come into competition.

His critique on modern Latin poets.

21. In the fourth chapter of the sixth book, Scaliger criticises the modern Latin poets, beginning with Marullus; for, what is somewhat remarkable, he says that he had been unable to see the Latin poems of Petrarch. He rates Marullus low, though he dwells at length on his poetry; and thinks no better of Augurellus. The continuation of the Æneid by Maphæus he highly praises; Augerianus, not at all; Mantuan has some genius, but no skill; and Scaliger is indignant that some ignorant schoolmasters should teach from him rather than from Virgil. Of Dolet he speaks with great severity; his unhappy fate does not atone for the badness of his verses in the eyes of so stern a critic: "The fire did not purify him, but rather he polluted the fire." Palingenius, though too diffuse, he accounts a good poet; and Cotta, as an imitator of Catullus. Palearius aims rather to be philosophical than poetical. Castiglione is excellent: Bembus wants vigor, and sometimes elegance; he is too fond, as many others are, of trivial words. Of Politian, Scaliger does not speak highly: he rather resembles Statius, has no grace, and is careless of harmony. Vida is reckoned, he says, by most, the first poet of our time: he dwells, therefore, long on the Ars Poetica, and extols it highly, though not without copious censure. Of Vida's other poems, the Bombyx is the best. Pontanus is admirable for every thing, if he had known where to stop. To Sannazarius and Fracastorius he assigns the highest praise of universal merit, but places the last at the head of the whole band.

22. The Italian language, like those of Greece and Rome, had been hitherto almost exclusively treated by grammarians; the superior criticism having little place even in the

writings of Bembo. But, soon after the middle of the century, the academies established in many cities, dedicating much time to their native language, began to point out beauties, and to animadvert on defects, beyond the province of grammar. The enthusiastic admiration of Petrarch poured itself forth in tedious commentaries upon every word of every sonnet; one of which, illustrated with the heavy prolixity of that age, would sometimes be the theme of a volume. Some philosophical or theological pedants spiritualized his meaning, as had been attempted before: the absurd paradox of denying the real existence of Laura is a known specimen of their refinements. Many wrote on the subject of his love for her; and a few denied its Platonic purity, which, however, the Academy of Ferrara thought fit to decree. One of the heretics, by name Cresci, ventured also to maintain that she was married; but this probable hypothesis had not many followers.[1]

Critical influence of the academies.

23. Meantime, a multitude of new versifiers, chiefly close copyists of the style of Petrarch, lay open to the malice of their competitors, and the strictness of these self-chosen judges of song. A critical controversy that sprang up about 1558 between two men of letters, very prominent in their age, — Annibal Caro and Ludovico Castelvetro, — is celebrated in the annals of Italian literature. The former had published a canzone in praise of the King of France, beginning, —

Dispute of Caro and Castelvetro.

"Venite all' ombra de' gran gigli d' oro."

Castelvetro made some sharp animadversions on this ode, which seems really to deserve a good deal of censure; being in bad taste, turgid, and foolish. Caro replied with the bitterness natural to a wounded poet. In this there might be nothing unpardonable, and even his abusive language might be extenuated at least by many precedents in literary story; but it is imputed to Caro, that he excited the Inquisition against his suspected adversary. Castelvetro had been of the celebrated Academy of Modena, whose alleged inclination to Protestantism had proved, several years before, the cause of its dissolution, and of the persecution which some of its members suffered. Castelvetro, though he had avoided censure at

1 Crescimbeni, Storia della Volgar Poesia, ii. 295-309.

that time, was now denounced about 1560, when the persecution was hottest, to the Inquisition at Rome. He obeyed its summons, but soon found it prudent to make his escape; and reached Chiavenna, in the Grison dominions. He lived several years afterwards in safe quarters, but seems never to have made an open profession of the reformed faith.[1]

Castelvetro on Aristotle's Poetics.

24. Castelvetro himself is one of the most considerable among the Italian critics; but his taste is often lost in subtlety, and his fastidious temper seems to have sought nothing so much as occasion for censure. His greatest work is a commentary upon the Poetics of Aristotle; and it may justly claim respect, not only as the earliest exposition of the theory of criticism, but for its acuteness, erudition, and independence of reasoning, which disclaims the Stagirite as a master, though the diffuseness usual in that age, and the microscopic subtlety of the writer's mind, may render its perusal tedious. Twining, one of the best critics on the Poetics, has said, in speaking of the Commentaries of Castelvetro, and of a later Italian, Beni, that "their prolixity, their scholastic and trifling subtlety, their useless tediousness of logical analysis, their microscopic detection of difficulties invisible to the naked eye of common sense, and their waste of confutation upon objections made only by themselves, and made on purpose to be confuted, — all this, it must be owned, is disgusting and repulsive. It may sufficiently release a commentator from the duty of reading their works throughout, but not from that of examining and consulting them: for in both these writers, but more especially in Beni, there are many remarks equally acute and solid; many difficulties will be seen clearly stated, and sometimes successfully removed; many things usefully illustrated and clearly explained; and, if their freedom of censure is now and then disgraced by a little disposition to cavil, this becomes almost a virtue when compared with the servile and implicit admiration of Dacier."[2]

Severity of Castelvetro's criticism.

25. Castelvetro, in his censorious humor, did not spare the greatest shades that repose in the laurel groves of Parnassus, nor even those whom national pride had elevated to a level with them. Homer is less blamed than any other; but frequent shafts are levelled at

[1] Muratori, Vita del Castelvetro, 1727; Crescimbeni, ii. 431; Tiraboschi, x. 31; Ginguéné, vii 365; Corniani, vi. 61.

[2] Twining's Aristotle's Poetics, preface, p. 13.

Virgil, and not always unjustly, if poetry of real genius could ever bear the extremity of critical rigor, in which a monotonous and frigid mediocrity has generally found refuge.[1] In Dante, he finds fault with the pedantry that has filled his poems with terms of science, unintelligible and unpleasing to ignorant men, for whom poems are chiefly designed.[2] Ariosto he charges with plagiarism; laying unnecessary stress on his borrowing some stories, as that of Zerbino, from older books: and even objects to his introduction of false names of kings; since we may as well invent new mountains and rivers, as violate the known truths of history.[3] This punctilious cavil is very characteristic of Castelvetro. Yet he sometimes reaches a strain of philosophical analysis, and can by no means be placed in the ranks of criticism below La Harpe; to whom, by his attention to verbal minuteness, as well as by the acrimony and self-confidence of his character, he may in some measure be compared.

Ercolano of Varchi.

26. The Ercolano of Varchi, a series of dialogues, belongs to the inferior but more numerous class of critical writings, and, after some general observations on speech and language as common to men, turns to the favorite theme of his contemporaries, their native idiom. He is one, who, with Bembo, contends that the language should not be called Italian, or even Tuscan, but Florentine; though admitting, what might be expected, that few agree to this except the natives of the city. Varchi had written on the side of Caro, against Castelvetro; and though, upon the whole, he does not speak of the latter, in the Ercolano, with incivility, cannot restrain his wrath at an assertion of the stern critic of Modena, that there were as famous writers in the Spanish and French

1 One of his censures falls on the minute particularity of the prophecy of Anchises in the sixth Æneid: "Peccando Virgilio nella convenevolezza della profetia, la quale non suole condescendere a nomi proprj, ne a cose tanto chiare e particolari, ma, tacendo i nomi, suole manifestare le persone, e le loro azioni con figure di parlare alquanto oscure, si come si vede nelle profetie della scrittura sacra e nell' Alessandra di Licophrone," p 219 (edit. 1576). This is not unjust in itself; but Castelvetro wanted the candor to own, or comprehensiveness to perceive, that a prophecy of the Roman history, couched in allegories, would have had much less effect on Roman readers.

2 "Rendendola massimamente per questa via difficile ad intendere e meno piacente a uomini idioti, per gli quali principalmente si fanno i poemi." — p. 597. But the Comedy of Dante was about as much written for *gl' idioti*, as the Principia of Newton.

3 Castelvetro, p. 212. He objects, on the same principle, to Giraldi Cinthio, that he had chosen a subject for tragedy which never had occurred, nor had been reported to have occurred, and this of royal persons unheard of before: "Il qual peccato di prendere soggetto tale per la tragedie non è da perdonare." — p. 103

as in the Italian language. Varchi even denies that there was any writer of reputation in the first of these, except Juan de la Mena, and the author of Amadis de Gaul. Varchi is now chiefly known as the author of a respectable history, which, on account of its sincerity, was not published till the last century. The prejudice that, in common with some of his fellow-citizens, he entertained in favor of the popular idiom of Florence, has affected the style of his history, which is reckoned both tediously diffuse, and deficient in choice of phrase.[1]

Controversy about Dante.

27. Varchi, in a passage of the Ercolano, having extolled Dante even in preference to Homer, gave rise to a controversy, wherein some Italian critics did not hesitate to point out the blemishes of their countryman. Bulgarini was one of these. Mazzoni undertook the defence of Dante, in a work of considerable length; and seems to have poured out, still more abundantly than his contemporaries, a torrent of philosophical disquisition. Bulgarini replied again to him.[2] Crescimbeni speaks of these discussions as having been advantageous to Italian poetry.[3] The good effects, however, were not very sensibly manifested in the next century.

Academy of Florence.

28. Florence was the chief scene of these critical wars. Cosmo I., the most perfect type of the Prince of Machiavel, sought by the encouragement of literature in this its most innocuous province, as he did by the arts of embellishment, both to bring over the minds of his subjects a forgetfulness of liberty, and to render them unapt for its recovery. The Academy of Florence resounded with the praises of Petrarch. A few seceders from this body established the more celebrated academy, Della Crusca, of the *sieve*, whose appellation bespoke the spirit in which they meant to sift all they undertook to judge. They were soon engaged, and with some loss to their fame, in a controversy upon the Gierusalemme Liberata. Camillo Pellegrino, a Neapolitan, had published, in 1584, a dialogue on epic poetry, entitled Il Caraffa, wherein he gave the preference to Tasso above Ariosto. Though Florence had no peculiar interest in this question, the academicians thought themselves guardians of the elder bard's renown; and Tasso had offended the

[1] Corniani, vi. 43.

[2] Id., vi. 260; Ginguéné, vii. 491.

[3] Hist. della Volgar Poesia, ii. 282.

citizens by some reflections in one of his dialogues. The Academy permitted themselves, in a formal reply, to place even Pulci and Boiardo above Tasso. It was easier to vindicate Ariosto from some of Pellegrino's censures, which are couched in the pedantic tone of insisting with the reader that he ought not to be pleased. He has followed Castelvetro in several criticisms. The rules of epic poetry so long observed, he maintains, ought to be reckoned fundamental principles, which no one can dispute without presumption. The Academy answer this well on behalf of Ariosto. Their censures on the Jerusalem apply in part to the characters and incidents, wherein they are sometimes right, in part to the language; many phrases, according to them, being bad Italian, as *pietose* for *pie* in the first line.[1]

Salviati's attack on Tasso.

29. Salviati, a verbose critic, who had written two quarto volumes on the style of Boccaccio, assailed the new epic in two treatises, entitled L' Infarinato. Tasso's Apology followed very soon; but it has been sometimes thought that these criticisms, acting on his morbid intellect, though he repelled them vigorously, might have influenced him to that waste of labor, by which, in the last years of his life, he changed so much of his great poem for the worse. The obscurer insects whom envy stirred up against its glory are not worthy to be remembered. The chief praise of Salviati himself is that he laid the foundations of the first classical dictionary of any modern language, — the Vocabulario della Crusca.[2]

Pinciano's Art of Poetry.

30. Bouterwek has made us acquainted with a treatise, in Spanish, on the art of poetry, which he regards as the earliest of its kind in modern literature. It could not be so, according to the date of its publication, which is in 1596: but the author, Alonzo Lopez Pinciano, was physician to Charles V.; and it was therefore

[1] In the second volume of the edition of Tasso at Venice, 1735, the Caraffa of Pellegrino, the Defence of Ariosto by the Academy, Tasso's Apology, and the Infarinato of Salviati, are cut into sentences, placed to answer each other like a dialogue. This produces an awkward and unnatural effect, as passages are torn from their context to place them in opposition.

The criticism on both sides becomes infinitely wearisome; yet not more so than much that we find in our modern reviews, and with the advantage of being more to the purpose, less ostentatious, and with less pretence to eloquence or philosophy. An account of the controversy will be found in Crescimbeni, Ginguéné, or Corniani, and more at length in Serassi's Life of Tasso.

[2] Corniani, vi. 204. The Italian literature would supply several more works on criticism, rhetoric, and grammar. Upon all these subjects it was much richer, at this time, than the French or English.

written, in all probability, many years before it appeared from the press. The title is rather quaint, Philosophia Antigua Poetica; and it is written in the form of letters. Pinciano is the first who discovered the Poetics of Aristotle, which he had diligently studied, to be a fragment of a larger work, as is now generally admitted. "Whenever Lopez Pinciano," says Bouterwek, "abandons Aristotle, his notions respecting the different poetic styles are as confused as those of his contemporaries; and only a few of his notions and distinctions can be deemed of importance at the present day. But his name is deserving of honorable remembrance; for he was the first writer of modern times who endeavored to establish a philosophic art of poetry; and, with all his veneration for Aristotle, he was the first scholar who ventured to think for himself, and to go somewhat farther than his master."[1] The Art of Poetry, by Juan de la Cueva, is a poem of the didactic class, containing some information as to the history of Spanish verse.[2] The other critical treatises which appeared in Spain about this time seem to be of little importance; but we know by the writings of Cervantes, that the poets of the age of Philip were, as usual, followed by the animal for whose natural prey they are designed, the sharp-toothed and keen-scented critic.

French treatises of criticism.

31. France produced very few books of the same class. The Institutiones Oratoriæ of Omer Talon is an elementary and short treatise of rhetoric.[3] Baillet and Goujet give some praise to the Art of Poetry by Pelletier, published in 1555.[4] The treatise of Henry Stephens, on the Conformity of the French Language with the Greek, is said to contain very good observations.[5] But it must be (for I do not recollect to have seen it) rather a book of grammar than of superior criticism. The Rhetorique Française of Fouquelin (1555) seems to be little else than a summary of rhetorical figures.[6] That of Courcelles, in 1557, is not much better.[7] All these relate rather to prose than to poetry. From the number of versifiers in France, and the popularity of Ronsard and his school, we might have expected a larger

[1] Hist. of Span. Lit., p. 323.

[2] It is printed entire in the eighth volume of Parnaso Español.

[3] Gibert, Maîtres de l'Eloquence, printed in Baillet, viii. 181.

[4] Baillet, iii. 351; Goujet, iii. 97. Pelletier had previously rendered Horace's Art of Poetry into French verse, id., 66.

[5] Baillet, iii. 353.

[6] Gibert, p. 184

[7] Ibid., p. 366.

harvest of critics. Pasquier, in his valuable miscellany, Les Recherches de la France, has devoted a few pages to this subject, but not on an extensive or systematic plan; nor can the two Bibliothèques Françaises, by La Croix du Maine and Verdier, both published in 1584, though they contain a great deal of information as to the literature of France, with some critical estimates of books, be reckoned in the class to which we are now adverting.

Wilson's Art of Rhetorique.

32. Thomas Wilson, afterwards secretary of state, and much employed under Elizabeth, is the author of an Art of Rhetorique, dated, in the preface, January, 1553. The rules in this treatise are chiefly from Aristotle, with the help of Cicero and Quintilian; but his examples and illustrations are modern. Warton says that it is the first system of criticism in our language.[1] But, in common use of the word, it is no criticism at all, any more than the treatise of Cicero de Oratore: it is what it professes to be, a system of rhetoric in the ancient manner; and, in this sense, it had been preceded by the work of Leonard Cox, which has been mentioned in another place. Wilson was a man of considerable learning, and his Art of Rhetorique is by no means without merit. He deserves praise for censuring the pedantry of learned phrases, or, as he calls them, "strange *inkhorn* terms," advising men "to speak as is commonly received;" and he censures also, what was not less pedantic, the introduction of a French or Italian idiom, which the travelled English affected in order to show their politeness, as the scholars did the former to prove their erudition. Wilson had before published an Art of Logic.

Gascoyne; Webbe.

33. The first English criticism, properly speaking, that I find, is a short tract by Gascoyne, doubtless the poet of that name, published in 1575: "Certain Notes of Instruction concerning the Making of Verse or Rhyme in English." It consists only of ten pages; but the observations are judicious. Gascoyne recommends that the sentence should, as far as possible, be finished at the close of two lines in the couplet measure.[2] Webbe, author of a Discourse of English Poetry (1586), is copious in comparison with Gascoyne, though he stretches but to seventy pages. His taste is better

[1] Hist. of Engl. Poetry, iv. 157.

[2] Gascoyne, with all the other early English critics, was republished in a collection by Mr. Haslewood in two volumes 1811 and 1815.

shown in his praise of Spenser for the Shepherd's Kalendar, than of Gabriel Harvey for his "reformation of our English verse;" that is, by forcing it into uncouth Latin measures, which Webbe has himself most unhappily attempted.

Puttenham's Art of Poesie.

34. A superior writer to Webbe was George Puttenham, whose Art of English Poesie, published in 1589, is a small quarto of 258 pages in three books. It is in many parts very well written, in a measured prose, rather elaborate and diffuse. He quotes occasionally a little Greek. Among the contemporary English poets, Puttenham extols, "for eclogue and pastoral poetry, Sir Philip Sidney and Master Chaloner, and that other gentleman who wrote the late Shepherd's Kalendar. For ditty and amorous ode, I find Sir Walter Rawleigh's vein most lofty, insolent [uncommon], and passionate; Master Edward Dyer for elegy most sweet, solemn, and of high conceit; Gascon [Gascoyne] for a good metre and for a plentiful vein; Phaer and Golding for a learned and well-connected verse, specially in translation, clear, and very faithfully answering their author's intent. Others have also written with much facility, but more commendably perhaps, if they had not written so much nor so popularly. But last in recital, and first in degree, is the queen, our sovereign lady, whose learned, delicate, noble muse easily surmounteth all the rest that have written before her time or since, for sense, sweetness, and subtilty, be it in ode, elegy, epigram, or any other kind of poem, heroic or lyric, wherein it shall please her majesty to employ her pen, even by so much odds as her own excellent estate and degree exceedeth all the rest of her most humble vassals."[1] On this it may be remarked, that the only specimen of Elizabeth's poetry, which, as far as I know, remains, is prodigiously bad.[2] In some passages of Puttenham, we find an approach to the higher province of philosophical criticism.

Sidney's Defence of Poesy.

35. These treatises of Webbe and Puttenham may have been preceded in order of writing, though not of publication, by the performance of a more illustrious author, Sir Philip Sidney. His Defence of Poesy was not published till 1595. The Defence of Poesy has already been reckoned among the polite writings of the Elizabethan age, to which class it rather belongs than to that of

[1] Puttenham, p. 51 of Haslewood's edition; or in Censura Literaria, i. 348.

[2] Ellis's Specimens, ii 162.

criticism; for Sidney rarely comes to any literary censure, and is still farther removed from any profound philosophy. His sense is good, but not ingenious; and the declamatory tone weakens its effect.

SECT. III.—ON WORKS OF FICTION.

Novels and Romances in Italy and Spain—Sidney's Arcadia

36. THE novels of Bandello, three parts of which were published in 1554, and a fourth in 1573, are perhaps the best known and the most admired in that species of composition after those of Boccaccio. They have been censured as licentious, but are far less so than any of preceding times; and the reflections are usually of a moral cast. These, however, as well as the speeches, are very tedious. There is not a little predilection in Bandello for sanguinary stories. Ginguéné praises these novels for just sentiments, adherence to probability, and choice of interesting subjects. In these respects, we often find a superiority in the older novels above those of the nineteenth century; the golden age, as it is generally thought, of fictitious story. But, in the management of these subjects, the Italian and Spanish novelists show little skill; they are worse cooks of better meat; they exert no power over the emotions beyond what the intrinsic nature of the events related must produce; they sometimes describe well, but with no great imagination; they have no strong conception of character, no deep acquaintance with mankind, not often much humor, no vivacity, and spirit of dialogue.

Novels of Bandello;

37. The Hecatomithi, or Hundred Tales, of Giraldi Cinthio have become known in England by the recourse that Shakspeare has had to them in two instances, Cymbeline and Measure for Measure, for the subjects of his plays. Cinthio has also borrowed from himself in his own tragedies. He is still more fond of dark tales of blood than Bandello. He seems consequently to have possessed an unfortunate influence over the stage; and to him, as well as his brethren of the Italian novel, we trace those scenes of improbable and disgusting horror, from which, though the native taste

Of Cinthio;

and gentleness of Shakspeare for the most part disdained such helps, we recoil in almost all the other tragedians of the old English school. Of the remaining Italian novelists that belong to this period, it is enough to mention Erizzo, better known as one of the founders of medallic science. His Sei Giornate contain thirty-six novels, called Avvenimenti. They are written with intolerable prolixity, but in a pure and even elevated tone of morality. This character does not apply to the novels of Lasca.

Of the Queen of Navarre.

38. The French novels, ascribed to Margaret, Queen of Navarre, and first published in 1558, with the title Histoire des Amans fortunés, are principally taken from the Italian collections or from the fabliaux of the trouveurs. Though free in language, they are written in a much less licentious spirit than many of the former, but breathe throughout that anxiety to exhibit the clergy, especially the regulars, in an odious or ridiculous light, which the principles of their illustrious authoress might lead us to expect. Belleforest translated, perhaps with some variation, the novels of Bandello into French.[1]

Spanish romances of chivalry.

39. Few probably will now dispute that the Italian novel, a picture of real life, and sometimes of true circumstances, is perused with less weariness than the Spanish romance, — the alternative then offered to the lovers of easy reading. But this had very numerous admirers in that generation; nor was the taste confined to Spain. The popularity of Amadis de Gaul, and Palmerin of Oliva, with their various continuators, has been already mentioned.[2] One of these, Palmerin of England, appeared in French

[1] Bouterwek, v. 286, mentions by name several other French novelists of the sixteenth century: I do not know any thing of them.

[2] La Noue, a severe Protestant, thinks them as pernicious to the young as the writings of Machiavel had been to the old. This he dwells upon in his sixth discourse. "De tout temps," this honest and sensible writer says, "il y a eu des hommes qui ont esté diligens d'escrire et mettre en lumière des choses vaines. Ce qui plus les y a conviez est, que ils sçavoient que leurs labeurs seroient agréables à ceux de leurs siècles, dont la plus part a toujours heimé [aimé] la vanité, comme le poisson fait l'eau. Les vieux romans dont nous voyons encor les fragmens par-ci et par-là, à savoir de Lancelot du Lac, de Perceforest, Tristan, Giron le courtois, et autres, font foy de ceste vanité antique. On s'en est repeu l'espace de plus de cinq cens ans, jusques à ce que nostre langage estant devenu plus orné et nostres esprits plus frétillans, il a fallu inventer quelque nouveauté pour les égayer. Voilà comment les livres d'Amadis sont venus en évidence parmi nous en ce dernier siècle. Mais pour en parler au vrai, l'Espagne les a engendrez, et la France les a seulement revêtus de plus beaux habillemens. Sous le règne du roy Henry Second, ils ont eu leur principale vogue; et croy qui si quelqu'un les eust voulu alors blasmer, en luy eust craché au visage," &c. — p. 153, edit. 1558

at Lyons in 1555. It is uncertain who was the original author, or in what language it was first written. Cervantes has honored it with a place next to Amadis. Mr. Southey, though he condescended to abridge Palmerin of England, thinks it inferior to that Iliad of romantic adventure. Several of the tales of knight-errantry that are recorded to have stood on the unfortunate shelves of Don Quixote belong to this latter part of the century, among which Don Bellianis of Greece is better known by name than any other. These romances were not condemned by Cervantes alone. "Every poet and prose writer," says Bouterwek, "of cultivated talent, labored to oppose the contagion."[1]

Diana of Montemayor.

40. Spain was the parent of a romance in a very different style; but, if less absurd and better written, not perhaps much more interesting to us than those of chivalry, the Diana of Montemayor. Sannazaro's beautiful model of pastoral romance, the Arcadia, and some which had been written in Portugal, take away the merit of originality from this celebrated fiction. It formed, however, a school in this department of literature, hardly less numerous, according to Bouterwek, than the imitators of Amadis.[2] The language of Montemayor is neither labored nor affected, and though sometimes of rather too formal a solemnity, especially in what the author thought philosophy, is remarkably harmonious and elevated; nor is he deficient in depth of feeling, or fertility of imagination. Yet the story seems incapable of attracting any reader of this age. The Diana, like Sannazaro's Arcadia, is mingled with much lyric poetry, which Bouterwek thinks is the soul of the whole composition. Cervantes, indeed, condemns all the longer of these poems to the flames, and gives but limited praise to the Diana. Yet this romance, and a continuance of it by Gil Polo, had inspired his own youthful genius in the Galatea. The chief merit of the Galatea, published in 1584, consists in the poetry which the story seems intended to hold together. In the Diana of Montemayor, and even in the Galatea, it has been supposed that real adventures and characters were generally

[1] In the opinion of Bouterwek (v. 282), the taste for chivalrous romance declined in the latter part of the century, through the prevalence of a classical spirit in literature which exposed the mediæval fictions to derision. The number of shorter and more amusing novels might probably have more to do with it: the serious romance has a terrible enemy in the lively. But it revived with a little modification in the next age.

[2] Hist. Span. Lit., p. 305.

shadowed, — a practice not already without precedent, and which, by the French especially, was carried to a much greater length in later times.

Novels in the picaresque style.

41. Spain became celebrated about the end of this century for her novels in the *picaresque* style, of which Lazarillo de Tormes is the oldest extant specimen. The continuation of this little work is reckoned inferior to the part written by Mendoza himself; but both together are amusing and inimitably short.[1] The first edition of the most celebrated romance of this class, Guzman d'Alfarache, falls within the sixteenth century. It was written by Matthew Aleman, who is said to have lived long at court. He might there have acquired, not a knowledge of the tricks of common rogues, but an experience of mankind, which is reckoned one of the chief merits of his romance. Many of his stories also relate to the manners of a higher class than that of his hero. Guzman d'Alfarache is a sort of prototype of Gil Blas; though, in fact, Le Sage has borrowed very freely from all the Spanish novels of this school. The adventures are numerous and diversified enough to amuse an idle reader; and Aleman has displayed a great deal of good sense in his reflections, which are expressed in the pointed, condensed style affected by most writers of Spain. Cervantes has not hesitated to borrow from him one of Sancho's celebrated adjudications, in the well-known case of the lady, who was less pugnacious in defence of her honor, than of the purse awarded by the court as its compensation. This story is, however, if I am not mistaken, older than either of them.[2]

Guzman d'Alfarache.

[1] Though the continuation of Lazarillo de Tormes is reckoned inferior to the original, it contains the only story in the whole novel which has made its fortune, — that of the man who was exhibited as a sea-monster.

[2] The following passage, which I extract from the Retrospective Review, vol. v. p. 199, is a fair and favorable specimen of Aleman as a moralist; who is, however, apt to be tedious, as moralists usually are: —

"The poor man is a kind of money that is not current, the subject of every idle housewife's chat, the offscum of the people, the dust of the street, first trampled under foot, and then thrown on the dunghill; in conclusion, the poor man is the rich man's ass. He dineth with the last, fareth with the worst, and payeth dearest; his sixpence will not go so far as the rich man's threepence; his opinion is ignorance, his discretion foolishness, his suffrage scorn, his stock upon the common abused by many, and abhorred by all. If he come into company, he is not heard; if any chance to meet him, they seek to shun him; if he advise, though never so wisely, they grudge and murmur at him; if he work miracles, they say he is a witch; if virtuous, that he goeth about to deceive: his venial sin is a blasphemy; his thought is made treason; his cause, be it never so just, is not regarded; and, to have his wrongs righted, he must appeal to that other life. All men crush him; no man favoreth him. There is no man that will relieve his wants; no man that will bear him company when he is alone and

42. It may require some excuse that I insert in this place Las Guerras de Granada, a history of certain Moorish factions in the last days of that kingdom, both because it has been usually referred to the seventeenth century, and because many have conceived it to be a true relation of events. It purports to have been translated by Gines Perez de la Hita, an inhabitant of the city of Murcia, from an Arabic original of one Aben Hamili. Its late English translator seems to entertain no doubt of its authenticity; and it has been sagaciously observed, that no Christian could have known the long genealogies of Moorish nobles which the book contains. Most of those, however, who read it without credulity, will feel, I presume, little difficulty in agreeing with Antonio, who ranks it "among Milesian fables, though very pleasing to those who have nothing to do." The Zegris and Abencerrages, with all their romantic exploits, seem to be mere creations of Castilian imagination: nor has Conde, in his excellent history of the Moors in Spain, once deigned to notice them even as fabulous; so much did he reckon this famous production of Perez de la Hita below the historian's regard. Antonio mentions no edition earlier than that of Alcalá in 1604; the English translator names 1601 for the date of its publication, an edition of which year is in the Museum: nor do I find that any one has been aware of an earlier, published at Saragoça in 1595, except Brunet, who mentions it as rare and little known. It appears by the same authority that there is another edition of 1598.

Las Guerras de Granada.

43. The heroic and pastoral romance of Spain contributed something, yet hardly so much as has been supposed, to Sir Philip Sidney's Arcadia, the only original production of this kind worthy of notice which our older literature can boast. The Arcadia was published in 1590; having been written, probably, by its highly accomplished author about ten years before.

Sidney's Arcadia.

44. Walpole, who thought fit to display the dimensions of

oppressed with grief. None help him, all hinder him; none give him, all take from him; he is debtor to none, and yet must make payment to all. O the unfortunate and poor condition of him that is poor, to whom even the very hours are sold which the clock striketh, and payeth custom for the sunshine in August!"

This is much in the style of our English writers in the first part of the seventeenth century, and confirms what I have suspected, that they formed it in a great measure on the Spanish school. Guzman d'Alfarache was early translated into English, as most other Spanish books were; and the language itself was more familiar in the reigns of James and Charles than it became afterwards.

his own mind by announcing that he could perceive nothing remarkable in Sir Philip Sidney (as if the suffrage of Europe in what he admits to be an age of heroes were not a decisive proof that Sidney himself overtopped those sons of Anak), says of the Arcadia, that it is "a tedious, lamentable, pedantic, pastoral romance, which the patience of a young virgin in love cannot now wade through." We may doubt whether Walpole could altogether estimate the patience of a reader so extremely unlike himself; and his epithets, except perhaps the first, are inapplicable. The Arcadia is more free from pedantry than most books of that age; and though we are now so accustomed to a more stimulant diet in fiction, that few would read it through with pleasure, the story is as sprightly as most other romances, sometimes indeed a little too much so: for the Arcadia is not quite a book for "young virgins," of which some of its admirers by hearsay seem not to have been aware. By the epithet "pastoral," we may doubt whether Walpole knew much of this romance beyond its name; for it has far less to do with shepherds than with courtiers, though the idea might probably be suggested by the popularity of the Diana. It does not appear to me that the Arcadia is more tiresome and uninteresting than the generality of that class of long romances, proverbially among the most tiresome of all books; and, in a less fastidious age, it was read, no doubt, even as a story, with some delight.[1] It displays a superior mind, rather complying with a temporary taste than affected by it; and many pleasing passages occur, especially in the tender and innocent loves of Pyrocles and Philoclea. I think it, nevertheless, on the whole, inferior in sense, style, and spirit to the Defence of Poesy. The following passage has some appearance of having suggested a well-known poem in the next age to the lover of Sacharissa: we may readily believe that Waller had turned over, in the glades of Penshurst, the honored pages of her immortal uncle:[2]—

Its character.

45. "The elder is named Pamela, by many men not

[1] "It appears," says Drake, "to have been suggested to the mind of Sir Philip by two models of very different ages, and to have been built, in fact, on their admixture: these are the Ethiopic History of Heliodorus, Bishop of Tricca in Thessaly, and the Arcadia of Sannazaro."—p. 549. A translation of Heliodorus had been published a short time before.

[2] The poem I mean is that addressed to Amoret, "Fair! that you may truly know," drawing a comparison between her and Sacharissa.

deemed inferior to her sister. For my part, when I marked them both, methought there was (if at least such perfections may receive the word of more) more sweetness in Philoclea, but more majesty in Pamela: methought love played in Philoclea's eyes, and threatened in Pamela's: methought Philoclea's beauty only persuaded, but so persuaded as all hearts must yield; Pamela's beauty used violence, and such violence as no heart could resist; and it seems that such proportion is between their minds. Philoclea so bashful, as if her excellences had stolen into her before she was aware; so humble, that she will put all pride out of countenance; in sum, such proceeding as will stir hope, but teach hope good manners: Pamela, of high thoughts, who avoids not pride with not knowing her excellences, but by making that one of her excellences to be void of pride; her mother's wisdom, greatness, nobility, but, if I can guess aright, knit with a more constant temper."

Inferiority of other English fictions.

46. The Arcadia stands quite alone among English fictions of this century. But many were translated in the reign of Elizabeth from the Italian, French, Spanish, and even Latin; among which Painter's Palace of Pleasure, whence Shakspeare took several of his plots, and the numerous labors of Antony Munday, may be mentioned. Palmerin of England in 1580, and Amadis of Gaul in 1592, were among these; others of less value were transferred from the Spanish text by the same industrious hand; and since these, while still new, were sufficient to furnish all the gratification required by the public, our own writers did not much task their invention to augment the stock. They would not have been very successful, if we may judge by such deplorable specimens as Breton and Greene, two men of considerable poetical talent, have left us.[1] The once famous story of the Seven Champions of Christendom, by one Johnson, is of rather a superior class: the adventures are not original; but it is by no means a translation from

[1] The Mavillia of Breton, the Dorastus and Fawnia of Greene, will be found in the collections of the indefatigable Sir Egerton Brydges. The first is below contempt; the second, if not quite so ridiculous, is written with a quaint, affected, and empty euphuism. British Bibliographer, i. 508. But, as truth is generally more faithful to natural sympathies than fiction, a little tale, called Never too Late, in which Greene has related his own story, is unaffected and pathetic. Drake's Shakspeare and his Times, i. 489.

any single work.[1] Mallory's famous romance, La Morte d'Arthur, is of much earlier date, and was first printed by Caxton. It is, however, a translation from several French romances, though written in very spirited language.

[1] Drake, i. 529.

CHAPTER VIII.

HISTORY OF PHYSICAL AND MISCELLANEOUS LITERATURE FROM 1500 TO 1600

SECT. I.—ON MATHEMATICAL AND PHYSICAL SCIENCE.

Algebraists of this Period—Vieta—Slow Progress of Copernican Theory—Tycho Brahe—Reform of Calendar—Mechanics—Stevinus—Gilbert.

Tartaglia and Cardan.

1. THE breach of faith towards Tartaglia, by which Cardan communicated to the world the method of solving cubic equations, having rendered them enemies, the injured party defied the aggressor to a contest, wherein each should propose thirty-one problems to be solved by the other. Cardan accepted the challenge, and gave a list of his problems, but devolved the task of meeting his antagonist on his disciple Ferrari. The problems of Tartaglia are so much more difficult than those of Cardan, and the latter's representative so frequently failed in solving them, as to show the former in a high rank among algebraists, though we have not so long a list of his discoveries.[1] This is told by himself in a work of miscellaneous mathematical and physical learning, Quesiti ed Invenzioni Diverse, published in 1546. In 1555 he put forth the first part of a treatise, entitled Trattato di Numeri e Misure; the second part appearing in 1560.

Algebra of Pelletier.

2. Pelletier of Mans, a man advantageously known both in literature and science, published a short treatise on algebra in 1554. He does not give the method of solving cubic equations; but Hutton is mistaken in supposing that he was ignorant of Cardan's work, which he quotes. In fact, he promises a third book, this treatise being divided into two, on the higher parts of algebra; but I do not know

[1] Montucla, p. 568.

whether this be found in any subsequent edition. Pelletier does not employ the signs + and —, which had been invented by Stifelius, using *p* and *m* instead; but we find the sign √ of irrationality. What is perhaps the most original in this treatise is, that its author perceived, that in a quadratic equation, where the root is rational, it must be a divisor of the absolute number.[1]

Record's Whetstone of Wit.

3. In the Whetstone of Wit, by Robert Record, in 1557, we find the signs + and —, and for the first time that of equality =, which he invented.[2] Record knew that a quadratic equation has two roots. The scholar (for it is in dialogue) having been perplexed by this as a difficulty, the master answers, "That variety of roots doth declare that one equation in number may serve for two several questions. But the form of the question may easily instruct you which of these two roots you shall take for your purpose. Howbeit, sometimes you may take both."[3] He says nothing of cubic equations; having been prevented by an interruption, the nature of which he does not divulge, from continuing his algebraic lessons. We owe, therefore, nothing to Record but his invention of a sign. As these artifices not only abbreviate, but clear up the process of reasoning, each successive improvement in notation deserves, even in the most concise sketch of mathematical history, to be remarked; but certainly they do not exhibit any peculiar ingenuity, and might have occurred to the most ordinary student.

1 Pelletier seems to have arrived at this not by observation, but in a scientific method. "Comme $x^2 = 2x + 15$" (I substitute the usual signs for clearness), "il est certain que x que nous cherchons doit estre contenu également en 15, puisque x^2 est égal à deux x, et 15 davantage, et que tout nombre *censique* (quarré) contient les racines également et précisément. Maintenant puisque $2x$ font certain nombre de racines, il faut donc que 15 fasse l'achèvement des racines qui sont nécessaires pour accomplir x^2." — p. 40. (Lyon, 1554.)

2 "And to avoid the tedious repetition of these words, 'is equal to,' I will set, as I do often in work use, a pair of parallels, *gemowe* lines of one length thus =, because no two things can be more equal. The word *gemowe*, from the French *gemeau*, twin (Cotgrave), is very uncommon: it was used for a double ring, a *gemel* or *gemou* ring."— Todd's Johnson's Dictionary.

3 This general mode of expression might lead us to suppose that Record was acquainted with negative as well as positive roots, the *fictæ radices* of Cardan. That a quadratic equation of a certain form has two positive roots, had long been known. In a very modern book, it is said that Mohammed ben Musa, an Arabian of the reign of Almamon, whose algebra was translated by the late Dr. Rosen in 1831, observes that there are two roots in the form $ax^2 + b = cx$, but that this cannot be in the other three cases. Libri, Hist. des Sciences Mathématiques en Italie, vol. ii. (1838.) Leonard of Pisa had some notion of this, but did not state it, according to M. Libri, so generally as Ben Musa. Upon reference to Colebrooke's Indian Algebra, it will appear that the existence of two positive roots in some cases, though the conditions of the problem will often be found to exclude the application of one of them, is clearly laid down by the Hindoo algebraists. But one of them says, "People do not approve a negative absolute number."

4. The great boast of France, and indeed of algebraical science generally, in this period, was Francis Viète, oftener called Vieta; so truly eminent a man, that he may well spare laurels which are not his own. It has been observed in another place, that after Montucla had rescued from the hands of Wallis, who claims every thing for Harriott, many algebraical methods indisputably contained in the writings of his own countryman, Cossali has come forward, with an equal cogency of proof, asserting the right of Cardan to the greater number of them. But the following steps in the progress of algebra may be justly attributed to Vieta alone: 1. We must give the first place to one less difficult in itself than important in its results. In the earlier algebra, alphabetical characters were not generally employed at all, except that the Res, or unknown quantity, was sometimes set down R. for the sake of brevity. Stifelius, in 1544, first employed a literal notation, A. B. C., to express unknown quantities; while Cardan, and, according to Cossali, Luca di Borgo, to whom we may now add Leonard of Pisa himself, make some use of letters to express indefinite numbers.[1] But Vieta first applied them as general symbols of quantity, and, by thus forming the scattered elements of spe-

Vieta.

His discoveries.

[1] Vol. i. p. 54. A modern writer has remarked that Aristotle employs letters of the alphabet to express indeterminate quantities, and says it has never been observed before. He refers to the Physics, in Aristot. Opera, i. 543, 550, 565, &c., but without mentioning any edition. The letters α, β, γ, &c., express force, mass, space, or time. Libri, Hist. des Sciences Mathématiques en Italie, i. 104. Upon reference to Aristotle, I find many instances in the sixth book of the Physicæ Auscultationes, and in other places.

Though I am reluctant to mix in my text, which is taken from established writers, any observations of my own on a subject wherein my knowledge is so very limited as in mathematics, I may here remark, that although Tartaglia and Cardan do not use single letters as symbols of known quantity, yet, when they refer to a geometrical construction, they employ in their equations double letters, the usual signs of lines. Thus we find, in the Ars Magna, AB*m*AC, where we should put $a - b$. The want of a good algorithm was doubtless a great impediment; but it was not quite so deficient as from reading modern histories of algebraical discovery, without reference to the original writers, we might be led to suppose.

The process by which the rule for solving cubic equations was originally discovered seems worthy, as I have intimated in another place (vol. i. p. 449), of exciting our curiosity. Maseres has investigated this in the Philosophical Transactions for 1780, reprinted in his Tracts on Cubic and Biquadratic Equations, p. 55–69; and in Scriptores Logarithmici, vol. ii. It is remarkable that he does not seem to have been aware of what Cardan has himself told us on the subject in the sixth chapter of the Ars Magna; yet he has nearly guessed the process which Tartaglia pursued; that is, by a geometrical construction. It is manifest, by all that these algebraists have written on the subject, that they had the clearest conviction they were dealing with continuous or geometrical, not merely with discrete or arithmetical, quantity. This gave them an insight into the fundamental truth, which is unintelligible so long as algebra passes for a specious *arithmetic*, that *every* value which the conditions of the problem admit may be assigned to unknown quantities, without distinction of rationality and irrationality. To abstract number itself, irrationality is inapplicable.

cious analysis into a system, has been justly reckoned the founder of a science, which, from its extensive application, has made the old problems of mere numerical algebra appear elementary and almost trifling. "Algebra," says Kästner, "from furnishing amusing enigmas to the Cossists," as he calls the first teachers of the art, "became the logic of geometrical invention."[1] It would appear a natural conjecture, that the improvement, towards which so many steps had been taken by others, might occur to the mind of Vieta simply as a means of saving the trouble of arithmetical operations in working out a problem. But those who refer to his treatise entitled De Arte Analytica Isagoge, or even the first page of it, will, I conceive, give credit to the author for a more scientific view of his own invention. He calls it *logistice speciosa*, as opposed to the *logistice numerosa* of the older analysis:[2] his theorems are all general, the given quantities being considered as indefinite; nor does it appear that he substituted letters for the known quantities in the investigation of particular problems. Whatever may have suggested this great invention to the mind of Vieta, it has altogether changed the character of his science.

5. Secondly, Vieta understood the transformation of equations, so as to clear them from co-efficients or surd roots, or to eliminate the second term. This, however, is partly claimed by Cossali for Cardan. Yet it seems that the process employed by Cardan was much less neat and short than that of Vieta, which is still in use.[3] 3. He obtained a solution of cubic equations in a different method from that of Tartaglia. 4. "He shows," says Montucla, "that, when the unknown quantity of any equation may have several positive values (for it must be admitted that it is only these that he considers), the second term has for its co-efficient the sum of these values with the sign —; the third has the sum of the products

[1] Geschichte der Mathematik, i. 63.

[2] "Forma autem Zetesin ineundi ex arte propria est, non jam in numeris suam logicam exercente, quæ fuit oscitantia veterum analystarum, sed per logisticen sub specie noviter inducendam, feliciorem multo et potiorem numerosa, ad comparandum inter se magnitudines, proposita primum homogeniorum lege," &c. — p. i., edit. 1646.

A profound writer on algebra, Mr. Peacock, has lately defined it, "the science of general reasoning by symbolical language." In this sense there was very little algebra before Vieta; and it would be improper to talk of its being known to the Greeks, Arabs, or Hindoos. The definition would also include the formulæ of logic. The original definition of algebra seems to be the science of finding an equation between known and unknown quantities, *per oppositionem et restaurationem*.

[3] It is fully explained in his work, De Recognitione Æquationum, cap. 7.

of these values multiplied in pairs; the fourth, the sum of such products multiplied in threes, and so forth; finally, that the absolute term is the product of all the values. Here is the discovery of Harriott pretty nearly made." It is at least no small advance towards it.[1] Cardan is said to have gone some way towards this theory, but not with much clearness, nor extending it to equations above the third degree. 5. He devised a method of solving equations by approximation, analogous to the process of extracting roots, which has been superseded by the invention of more compendious rules.[2] 6. He has been regarded by some as the true author of the application of algebra to geometry; giving copious examples of the solution of problems by this method, though all belonging to straight lines. It looks like a sign of the geometrical relation under which he contemplated his own science, that he uniformly denominates the first power of the unknown quantity *latus*. But this will be found in older writers.[3]

[1] Some theorems given by Vieta very shortly, and without demonstration, show his knowledge of the structure of equations. I transcribe from Maseres, who has expressed them in the usual algebraic language. "Si $a + b \times x - x^2$ æquetur ab, x explicabilis est de qualibet illarum duarum a vel b." The second theorem is: "Si $x^3 - \left.\begin{matrix} a \\ b \\ c \end{matrix}\right\} x + \left.\begin{matrix} ab \\ ac \\ bc \end{matrix}\right\} x$ æquetur abc, x explicabilis est de qualibet illarum trium a, b, vel c." The third and fourth theorems extend this to higher equations.

[2] Montucla, i. 600; Hutton's Mathematical Dictionary; Biogr. Univers. art. "Viète."

[3] It is certain that Vieta perfectly knew the relation of algebra to magnitude as well as number, as the first pages of his In Artem Analyticam Isagoge fully show. But it is equally certain, as has been observed before, that Tartaglia and Cardan, and much older writers, Oriental as well as European, knew the same: it was by help of geometry, which Cardan calls *via regia*, that the former made his great discovery of the solution of cubic equations. Cossali, ii. 147; Cardan, Ars Magna, ch. xi.

Latus and *radix* are used indifferently for the first power of the unknown quantity in the Ars Magna. Cossali contends that Fra Luca had applied algebra to geometry. Vieta, however, it is said, was the first who taught how to construct geometrical figures by means of algebra. Montucla, p. 604. But compare Cossali, p. 427

A writer lately quoted, and to whose knowledge and talents I bow with deference, seems, as I would venture to suggest, to have overrated the importance of that employment of letters to signify quantities, known or unknown, which he has found in Aristotle, and in several of the moderns, and in consequence to have depreciated the real merit of Vieta. Leonard of Pisa, it seems, whose algebra this writer has for the first time published, to his own honor and the advantage of scientific history, makes use of letters as well as lines to represent quantities. "Quelquefois il emploie des lettres pour exprimer des quantités indéterminées, connues ou inconnues, sans les représenter par des lignes. On voit ici comment les modernes ont été amenés à se servir des lettres d'alphabet (même pour exprimer des quantités connues) long temps avant Viète, à qui on a attribué à tort une notation qu'il faudrait peut-être faire remonter jusqu'à Aristote, et que tant d'algebraistes modernes ont employée avant le géomètre Français. Car outre Leonard de Pise, Paciolo, et d'autres géomètres Italiens firent usage des lettres pour indiquer les quantités connues, et c'est d'eux plutôt que d'Aristote que les modernes ont appris cette notation." — Libri, vol. ii. p. 34. But there is surely a wide interval between the use of a short symbolic expression for particular quantities, as M. Libri has remarked in Aristotle, or even the *partial* employment of letters to designate known quantities, as in the Italian algebraists, and the method of stating general relations by the exclusive use of letters, which Vieta first

6. "Algebra," says a philosopher of the present day, "was still only an ingenious art, limited to the investigation of numbers: Vieta displayed all its extent, and instituted general expressions for particular results. Having profoundly meditated on the nature of algebra, he perceived that the chief characteristic of the science is to express relations. Newton, with the same idea, defined algebra an universal arithmetic. The first consequences of this general principle of Vieta were his own application of his specious analysis to geometry, and the theory of curve lines, which is due to Descartes; a fruitful idea, from which the analysis of functions, and the most sublime discoveries, have been deduced. It has led to the notion that Descartes is the first who applied algebra to geometry: but this invention is really due to Vieta; for he resolved geometrical problems by algebraic analysis, and constructed figures by means of these solutions. These investigations led him to the theory of angular sections, and to the general equations which express the values of chords."[1] It has been observed above, that this requires a slight limitation as to the solution of problems.

7. The Algebra of Bombelli, published in 1589, is the only other treatise of the kind, during this period, that seems worthy of much notice. Bombelli saw better than Cardan the nature of what is called the irreducible case in cubic equations. But Vieta, whether after Bombelli or not is not certain, had the same merit.[2] It is remarkable that Vieta seems to have paid little regard to the discoveries of his predecessors. Ignorant, probably, of the writings of Record, and perhaps even of those of Stifelius, he neither uses the sign = of equality, employing instead the clumsy word Æquatio, or rather Æquetur,[3] nor numeral exponents; and Hutton observes, that Vieta's algebra has, in consequence, the appearance of being older than it is. He mentions, however, the signs + and —, as usual in his own time.

introduced. That Tartaglia and Cardan, and even, as it now appears, Leonard of Pisa, went a certain way towards the invention of Vieta, cannot much diminish his glory; especially when we find that he entirely apprehended the importance of his own *logistice speciosa* in science. I have mentioned above, that, as far as my observation has gone, Vieta does not work particular problems by the specious algebra.

[1] M. Fourier, quoted in Biographie Universelle.

[2] Cossali; Hutton.

[3] Vieta uses =, but it is to denote that the proposition is true both of + and —; where we put ±. It is almost a presumption of copying one from another, that several modern writers say Vieta's word is *æquatio*. I have always found it *æquetur;* a difference not material in itself.

8. Amidst the great progress of algebra through the sixteenth century, the geometers, content with what the ancients had left them, seem to have had little care but to elucidate their remains. Euclid was the object of their idolatry: no fault could be acknowledged in his elements; and to write a verbose commentary upon a few propositions was enough to make the reputation of a geometer. Among the almost innumerable editions of Euclid that appeared, those of Commandin and Clavius, both of them in the first rank of mathematicians for that age, may be distinguished. Commandin, especially, was much in request in England, where he was frequently reprinted; and Montucla calls him the model of commentators, for the pertinence and sufficiency of his notes. The commentary of Clavius, though a little prolix, acquired a still higher reputation. We owe to Commandin editions of the more difficult geometers, Archimedes, Pappus, and Apollonius; but he attempted little, and that without success, beyond the province of a translator and a commentator. Maurolycus of Messina had no superior among contemporary geometers. Besides his edition of Archimedes, and other labors on the ancient mathematicians, he struck out the elegant theory, in which others have followed him, of deducing the properties of the conic sections from those of the cone itself. But we must refer the reader to Montucla, and other historical and biographical works, for the less distinguished writers of the sixteenth age.[1]

Geometers of this period.

9. The extraordinary labor of Joachim Rhæticus in his trigonometrical calculations has been mentioned in our first volume. His Opus Palatinum de Triangulis was published from his manuscript, by Valentine Otho, in 1594. But the work was left incomplete, and the editor did not accomplish what Joachim had designed. In his tables, the sines, tangents, and secants are only calculated to ten instead of fifteen places of decimals. Pitiscus, in 1613, not only completed Joachim's intention, but carried the minuteness of calculation a good deal farther.[2]

Joachim Rhæticus.

10. It can excite no wonder, that the system of Copernicus, simple and beautiful as it is, met with little encouragement for a long time after its promulgation, when we reflect upon the natural obstacles to its re-

Copernican theory.

[1] Montucla; Kästner; Hutton; Biogr. Univ.

[2] Montucla, p. 581.

ception. Mankind can, in general, take these theories of the celestial movements only upon trust from philosophers; and, in this instance, it required a very general concurrence of competent judges to overcome the repugnance of what called itself common sense, and was in fact a prejudice as natural, as universal, and as irresistible, as could influence human belief. With this was united another, derived from the language of Scripture; and though it might have been sufficient to answer, that phrases implying the rest of the earth, and motion of the sun, are merely popular, and such as those who are best convinced of the opposite doctrine must employ in ordinary language, this was neither satisfactory to the vulgar, nor recognized by the church. Nor were the astronomers in general much more favorable to the new theory than either the clergy or the multitude. They had taken pains to familiarize their understandings with the Ptolemaic hypothesis; and it may be often observed, that those who have once mastered a complex theory are better pleased with it than with one of more simplicity. The whole weight of Aristotle's name, which, in the sixteenth century, not only biassed the judgment, but engaged the passions, connected as it was with general orthodoxy and the preservation of established systems, was thrown into the scale against Copernicus. It was asked, what demonstration could be given of his hypothesis; whether the movements of the heavenly bodies could not be reconciled to the Ptolemaic; whether the greater quantity of motion, and the complicated arrangement which the latter required, could be deemed sufficient objections to a scheme proceeding from the Author of nature, to whose power and wisdom our notions of simplicity and facility are inapplicable; whether the moral dignity of man, and his peculiar relations to the Deity, unfolded in Scripture, did not give the world he inhabits a better claim to the place of honor in the universe, than could be pretended, on the score of mere magnitude, for the sun. It must be confessed, that the strongest presumptions in favor of the system of Copernicus were not discovered by himself.

11. It is easy, says Montucla, to reckon the number of adherents to the Copernican theory during the sixteenth century. After Rhæticus, they may be nearly reduced to Reinhold, author of the Prussian tables; Rothman, whom Tycho drew over afterwards to his own system; Christian Wursticius (Ursticius), who made some proselytes in Italy; finally,

Mæstlin, the illustrious master of Kepler. He might have added Wright and Gilbert, for the credit of England. Among the Italian proselytes made by Wursticius, we may perhaps name Jordano Bruno, who strenuously asserts the Copernican hypothesis; and two much greater authorities in physical science, — Benedetti, and Galileo himself. It is evident that the preponderance of valuable suffrages was already on the side of truth.[1]

12. The predominant disinclination to contravene the apparent testimonies of sense and Scripture had, perhaps, more effect than the desire of originality in suggesting the middle course taken by Tycho Brahe. He was a Dane of noble birth, and early drawn, by the impulse of natural genius, to the study of astronomy. Frederic III., his sovereign, after Tycho had already obtained some reputation, erected for him the observatory of Uraniburg in a small isle of the Baltic. In this solitude he passed above twenty years, accumulating the most extensive and accurate observations which were known in Europe before the discovery of the telescope and the improvement of astronomical instruments. These, however, were not published till 1606, though Kepler had previously used them in his Tabulæ Rodolphinæ. Tycho himself did far more in this essential department of the astronomer than any of his predecessors; his resources were much beyond those of Copernicus; and the latter years of this century may be said to make an epoch in physical astronomy. Frederic, Landgrave of Hesse, was more than a patron of the science. The observations of that prince have been deemed worthy of praise long after his rank had ceased to avail them. The Emperor Rodolph, when Tycho had been driven by envy from Denmark, gave him an asylum and the means of carrying on his observations at Prague, where he died in 1601. He was the first in modern times who made a catalogue of stars, registering their positions as well as his instruments permitted him. This catalogue, published in his Progymnasmata in 1602, contained 777; to which, from Tycho's own manuscripts, Kepler added 223 stars.[2]

Tycho Brahe.

13. In the new mundane system of Tycho Brahe, which, though first regularly promulgated to the world in his Progymnasmata, had been communicated in his

His system.

[1] Montucla, p. 638.

[2] Id., pp 653-659.

epistles to the Landgrave of Hesse, he supposes the five planets to move round the sun, but carries the sun itself with these five satellites, as well as the moon, round the earth. Though this, at least at the time, might explain the known phenomena as well as the two other theories, its want of simplicity always prevented its reception. Except Longomontanus, the countryman and disciple of Tycho, scarce any conspicuous astronomer adopted an hypothesis, which, if it had been devised some time sooner, would perhaps have met with better success. But, in the seventeenth century, the wise all fell into the Copernican theory, and the many were content without any theory at all.

14. A great discovery in physical astronomy may be assigned to Tycho. Aristotle had pronounced comets to be meteors generated below the orbit of the moon. But, a remarkable comet in 1577 having led Tycho to observe its path accurately, he came to the conclusion that these bodies are far beyond the lunar orbit, and that they pass through what had always been taken for a solid firmament, environing the starry orbs, and which plays no small part in the system of Ptolemy. He was even near the discovery of their elliptic revolution; the idea of a curve round the sun having struck him, though he could not follow it by observation.[1]

15. The acknowledged necessity of reforming the Julian calendar, gave, in this age, a great importance to astronomy. It is unnecessary to go into the details of this change, effected by the authority of Gregory XIII., and the skill of Lilius and Clavius, the mathematicians employed under him. The new calendar was immediately received in all countries acknowledging the Pope's supremacy; not so much on that account, though a discrepancy in the ecclesiastical reckoning would have been very inconvenient, as of its real superiority over the Julian. The Protestant countries came much more slowly into the alteration; truth being no longer truth when promulgated by the pope. It is now admitted that the Gregorian calendar is very nearly perfect, at least as to the computation of the solar year, though it is not quite accurate for the purpose of finding Easter. In that age, it had to encounter the opposition of Mæstlin, an astronomer of deserved reputation; and of Scaliger, whose knowledge

Gregorian calendar.

[1] Montucla, p. 662.

of chronology ought to have made him conversant with the subject, but who, by a method of squaring the circle, which he announces with great confidence as a demonstration, showed the world that his genius did not guide him to the exact sciences.[1]

16. The science of optics, as well as all other branches of the mixed mathematics, fell very short of astronomy in the number and success of its promoters. It was carried not much farther than the point where Alhazen, Vitello, and Roger Bacon left it. Maurolycus of Messina, in a treatise published in 1575, though written, according to Montucla, fifty years before, entitled Theoremata de Lumine et Umbra, has mingled a few novel truths with error. He explains rightly the fact that a ray of light, received through a small aperture of any shape, produces a circular illumination on a body intercepting it at some distance; and points out why different defects of vision are remedied by convex or concave lenses. He had, however, mistaken notions as to the visual power of the eye, which he ascribed, not to the retina, but to the crystalline humor; and, on the whole, Maurolycus, though a very distinguished philosopher in that age, seems to have made few considerable discoveries in physical science.[2] Baptista Porta, who invented, or at least made known, the camera obscura, though he dwells on many optical phenomena in his Magia Naturalis, sometimes making just observations, had little insight into the principles that explain them.[3] The science of perspective has been more frequently treated, especially in this period, by painters and architects than by mathematicians. Albert Durer, Serlio, Vignola, and especially Peruzzi, distinguished themselves by practical treatises; but the geometrical principles were never well laid down before the work of Guido Ubaldi in 1600.[4]

Optics.

17. This author, of a noble family in the Apennines, ranks high also among the improvers of theoretical mechanics. This great science, checked, like so many others, by the erroneous principles of Aristotle, made scarce any progress till near the end of the century. Cardan and Tartaglia wrote upon the subject; but their acuteness in abstract mathematics did not compensate for a want of accurate observation and a strange looseness of reasoning. Thus,

Mechanics.

[1] Montucla, pp. 674–686.
[2] Id., p. 695.
[3] Id., p. 698.
[4] Id., p. 708.

Cardan infers that the power required to sustain a weight on an inclined plane varies in the exact ratio of the angle, because it vanishes when the plane is horizontal, and becomes equal to the weight when the plane is perpendicular. But this must be the case if the power follows any other law of direct variation, as that of the sine of inclination, that is, the height, which it really does.[1] Tartaglia, on his part, conceived that a cannon-ball did not, indeed, describe two sides of a parallelogram, as was commonly imagined, even by scientific writers; but, what is hardly less absurd, that its point-blank direction and line of perpendicular descent are united by a circular arch, to which they are tangents. It was generally agreed, till the time of Guido Ubaldi, that the arms of a lever charged with equal weights, if displaced from the horizontal position, would recover it when set at liberty. Benedetti of Turin had juster notions than his Italian contemporaries: he ascribed the centrifugal force of bodies to their tendency to move in a straight line; he determined the law of equilibrium for the oblique lever, and even understood the composition of motions.[2]

18. If, indeed, we should give credit to the sixteenth century for all that was actually discovered, and even reduced to writing, we might now proceed to the great name of Galileo; for it has been said that his treatise Della Scienza Meccanica was written in 1592, though not published for more than forty years afterwards.[3] But as it has been our rule, with not many exceptions, to date books from their publication, we must defer any mention of this remarkable work to the next period. The experiments, however, made by Galileo, when lecturer in mathematics at Pisa, on falling bodies, come strictly within our limits. He was appointed to this office in 1589, and left it in 1592. Among the many unfounded assertions of Aristotle in physics, it was one, that the velocity of falling bodies was proportionate to their weights: Galileo took advantage of the leaning tower of Pisa to prove the contrary. But this important though obvious experiment, which laid open much of the theory of motion, displeased the adherents of Aristotle so highly, that they compelled him to

[1] Montucla, p. 690.

[2] Id., p. 693.

[3] Playfair has fallen into the mistake of supposing that this treatise was *published* in 1592; and those who, on second thoughts, would have known better, have copied him.

leave Pisa. He soon obtained a chair in the University of Padua.

19. But, on the same principle that we exclude the work of Galileo on mechanics from the sixteenth century, it seems reasonable to mention that of Simon Stevinus of Bruges; since the first edition of his Statics and Hydrostatics was printed in Dutch as early as 1585, though we can hardly date its reception among the scientific public before the Latin edition in 1608. Stevinus has been chiefly known by his discovery of the law of equilibrium on the inclined plane, which had baffled the ancients, and, as we have seen, was mistaken by Cardan. Stevinus supposed a flexible chain of uniform weight to descend down the sides of two connected planes, and to hang in a sort of festoon below. The chain would be in equilibrio, because, if it began to move, there would be no reason why it should not move for ever, the circumstances being unaltered by any motion it could have; and thus there would be a perpetual motion, which is impossible. But the part below, being equally balanced, must, separately taken, be in equilibrio; consequently, the part above, lying along the planes, must also be in equilibrio; and hence the weight of the two parts of the chain must be equal; or, if that lying along the shorter plane be called the power, it will be to the other as the lengths; or if there be but one plane, and the power hang perpendicularly, as the height to the length.

Statics of Stevinus

20. The first discovery made in hydrostatics, since the time of Archimedes, is due to Stevinus. He found that the vertical pressure of fluids on a horizontal surface is as the product of the base of the vessel by its height, and showed the law of pressure even on the sides.[1]

Hydrostatics.

21. The year 1600 was the first in which England produced a remarkable work in physical science; but this was one sufficient to raise a lasting reputation for its author. Gilbert, a physician, in his Latin treatise on the magnet, not only collected all the knowledge which others had possessed on that subject, but became at once the father of experimental philosophy in this island, and, by a singular felicity and acuteness of genius, the founder of theories which have been revived after the lapse of ages, and

Gilbert on the magnet.

[1] Montucla, ii. 180.

are almost universally received into the creed of the science. The magnetism of the earth itself, his own original hypothesis, *nova illa nostra et inaudita de tellure sententia*, could not, of course, be confirmed by all the experimental and analogical proof which has rendered that doctrine accepted in recent philosophy; but it was by no means one of those vague conjectures that are sometimes unduly applauded, when they receive a confirmation by the favor of fortune. He relied on the analogy of terrestrial phenomena to those exhibited by what he calls a *terrella*, or artificial spherical magnet. What may be the validity of his reasonings from experiment, it is for those who are conversant with the subject to determine; but it is evidently by the torch of experiment that he was guided. A letter from Edward Wright, whose authority as a mathematician is of some value, admits the terrestrial magnetism to be proved. Gilbert was also one of our earliest Copernicans, at least as to the rotation of the earth;[1] and, with his usual sagacity, inferred, before the invention of the telescope, that there are a multitude of fixed stars beyond the reach of our vision.[2]

[1] Mr. Whewell thinks that Gilbert was more doubtful about the annual than the diurnal motion of the earth, and informs us that in a posthumous work he seems to hesitate between Tycho and Copernicus. Hist. of Inductive Sciences, i. 389. Gilbert's argument for the diurnal motion would extend to the annual. "Non probabilis modo sed manifesta videtur terræ diurna circumvolutio, cum natura semper agit per pauciora magis quam plura, atque rationi magis consentaneum videtur unum exiguum corpus telluris diurnam volutationem efficere quam mundum totum circumferri."

[2] l. 6, c. 3. The article on Gilbert in the Biographie Universelle is discreditable to that publication. If the author was so very ignorant as not to have known any thing of Gilbert, he might at least have avoided the assumption that nothing was to be known.

Sarpi, who will not be thought an incompetent judge, names Gilbert with Vieta as the only original writers among his contemporaries. "Non ho veduto in questo secolo uomo quale abbia scritto cosa sua propria, salvo Vieta in Francia e Gilberti in Inghilterra." — Lettere di Fra Paolo, p. 31.

[Griselini, who published some memoirs of Father Paul in 1760, and had seen his manuscripts, thinks fit to claim for him the priority as to all the magnetic observations of Gilbert. "Ora io dico che nel trattato del Gilbert non v' è cosa che non sia stata prima osservata ed esperimentata dal Sarpi. Le medesime sono le sue viste; e riguardo a' fenomeni, tutta la varietà si riduce al modo di esporli, o ne' ragguagli. Frà Paolo è semplice, conciso, e non fa deduzioni sistematiche, e segue la massima inculcata dappoi da Bacone di Verulamio, cioè storia, osservazioni e sperienze." — Cited in Vita di F. Paolo Sarpi, per Bianchi Giovini. Bruxelles, 1836. It is for the reader to consider whether Sarpi would have praised Gilbert's originality as he has done without a hint that he had made the same discoveries.

It may be added that Griselini was no great master of scientific subjects, as appears in Biogr. Universelle, art. "Sarpi."

This is not said to depreciate the physical science of Sarpi, who was a wonderful man upon almost every subject, and had, I have no doubt, collected much as to magnetism. — 1847.]

SECT. II.—ON NATURAL HISTORY.

Zoölogy — Gesner; Aldrovandus. Botany — Lobel; Cæsalpin; and others.

22. ZOÖLOGY and botany, in the middle of the sixteenth century, were as yet almost neglected fields of knowledge: scarce any thing had been added to the valuable history of animals by Aristotle, and those of plants by Theophrastus and Dioscorides. But in the year 1551 was published the first part of an immense work, the History of Animals, by that prodigy of general erudition, Conrad Gesner. This treats of viviparous quadrupeds; the second, which appeared in 1554, of the oviparous; the third, in 1555, of birds; the fourth, in the following year, of fishes and aquatic animals; and one, long afterwards, published in 1587, relates to serpents. The first part was reprinted with additions in 1560; and a smaller work of woodcuts and shorter descriptions, called Icones Animalium, appeared in 1553.

Gesner's Zoölogy.

23. This work of the first great naturalist of modern times is thus eulogized by one of the latest: "Gesner's History of Animals," says Cuvier, "may be considered as the basis of all modern zoölogy; copied almost literally by Aldrovandus, abridged by Jonston, it has become the foundation of much more recent works; and more than one famous author has borrowed from it silently most of his learning: for those passages of the ancients, which have escaped Gesner, have scarce ever been observed by the moderns. He deserved their confidence by his accuracy, his perspicuity, his good faith, and sometimes by the sagacity of his views. Though he has not laid down any natural classification by genera, he often points out very well the true relations of beings."[1]

Its character by Cuvier.

24. Gesner treats of every animal under eight heads or chapters: — 1. Its name in different languages; 2. Its external description and usual place of habitation; 3. Its natural actions, length of life, diseases, &c.; 4. Its disposition, or, as we may say, moral charac-

Gesner's arrangement.

[1] Biogr. Universelle, art. "Gesner."

ter; 5. Its utility, except for food and medicine; 6. Its use as food; 7. Its use in medicine; 8. The philological relations of the name and qualities, their proper and figurative use in language, which is subdivided into several sections. So comprehensive a notion of zoölogy displays a mind accustomed to encyclopedic systems, and loving the labors of learning for their own sake. Much, of course, would have a very secondary value in the eyes of a good naturalist. His method is alphabetical: but it may be reckoned an alphabet of genera; for he arranges what he deems cognate species together. In the Icones Animalium, we find somewhat more of classification. Gesner divides quadrupeds into Animalia Mansueta and Animalia Fera; the former in two, the latter in four, orders. Cuvier, in the passage above cited, writing probably from memory, has hardly done justice to Gesner in this respect. The delineations in the History of Animals and in the Icones are very rude; and it is not always easy, with so little assistance from engraving, to determine the species from his description.

His additions to known quadrupeds.

25. Linnæus, though professing to give the synonymes of his predecessors, has been frequently careless, and unjust towards Gesner; his mention of several quadrupeds (the only part of the latter's work at which I have looked) having been unnoticed in the Systema Naturæ. We do not find, however, that Gesner had made very considerable additions to the number of species known to the ancients; and it cannot be reckoned a proof of his acuteness in zoölogy, that he placed the hippopotamus among aquatic animals, and the bat among birds. In the latter extraordinary error, he was followed by all other naturalists till the time of Ray. Yet he shows some judgment in rejecting plainly fabulous animals. In the edition of 1551, I find but few quadrupeds, except those belonging to the countries round the Mediterranean, or mentioned by Pliny and Ælian.[1] The Reindeer, which it is doubtful whether the ancients knew, though there seems reason to believe that it was formerly an inhabitant of Poland and Germany, he found in Albertus Magnus; and from him, too, Gesner had

[1] In Cardan, De Subtilitate, lib. 10, published in 1550, I find the ant-eater, *ursus formicarius*, which, if I am not mistaken, Gesner has omitted, though it is in Hernando d'Oviedo; also a *cercopithecus*, as large as man, which persists long in standing erect, "amat pueros et mulieres, conaturque concumbere, quod nos vidimus." This was probably one of the large baboons of Africa.

got some notion of the Polar Bear. He mentions the Musk-deer, which was known through the Arabian writers, though unnoticed by the ancients. The new world furnished him with a scanty list. Among these is the Opossum, or Simi-Vulpa (for which Linnæus has not given him credit), an account of which he may have found in Pinzon or Peter Martyr;[1] the Manati, of which he found a description in Hernando's History of the Indies; and the Guinea pig, Cuniculus Indus, which he says was, within a few years, first brought to Europe from the New World, but was become everywhere common. In the edition of 1560, several more species are introduced. Olaus Magnus had, in the mean time, described the Glutton; and Belon had found an Armadillo among itinerant quacks in Turkey, though he knew that it came from America.[2] Belon had also described the Axis-deer of India. The Sloth appears, for the first time, in this edition of Gesner, and the Sagoin, or Ouistiti, as well as what he calls *Mus Indicus alius*, which Linnæus refers to the Raccoon, but seems rather to be the Nasua, or Coati Mondi. Gesner has given only three cuts of monkeys, but was aware that there were several kinds, and distinguishes them in description. I have not presumed to refer his cuts to particular species, which, probably, on account of their rudeness, a good naturalist would not attempt. The Simia Inuus, or Barbary ape, seems to be one, as we might expect.[3] Gesner was not very diligent in examining the histories of the New World. Peter Martyr

[1] In the voyage of Pinzon, the companion of Columbus in his last voyage, when the continent of Guiana was discovered, which will be found in the Novus Orbis of Grynæus, a specimen of the genus Didelphis is mentioned with the astonishment which the first appearance of the marsupial type would naturally excite in an European. "Conspexere etiamnum ibi animal quadrupes, prodigiosum quidem; nam pars anterior vulpem, posterior vero simiam præsentabat, nisi quod pedes effingit humanos; aures autem habet noctuæ, et infra consuetam alvum aliam habet instar crumenæ, in qua delitescunt catuli ejus tantisper, donec tuto prodire queant, et absque parentis tutela cibatum quærere, nec unquam exeunt crumenam, nisi cum sugunt. Portentosum hoc animal cum catulis tribus Sibiliam delatum est; et ex Sibilia Illiberim, id est Granatam, in gratiam regum, qui novis semper rebus oblectantur." — p. 116, edit. 1532. In Peter Martyr, De Rebus Oceanicis, dec. i., lib. 9, we find a longer account of the "monstrosum illud animal vulpino rostro, cercopithecea cauda, vespertilioneis auribus, manibus humanius, pedibus simiam æmulans; quod natos jam filios alio gestat quocunque proficiscatur utero exteriore in modum magnæ crumenæ." This animal, he says, lived some months in Spain, and was seen by him after its death. Several species are natives of Guiana.

[2] *Tatus, quadrupes peregrina.* The species figured in Gesner is *Dasypus novemcinctus.* This animal, however, is mentioned by Hernando d'Oviedo under the name Bardati.

[3] "Sunt et cynocephalorum diversa genera, nec unum genus caudatorum." I think he knew the leading characteristics founded on the tail, but did not attend accurately to subordinate distinctions, though he knew them to exist.

and Hernando would have supplied him with several he has overlooked, as the Tapir, the Peccary, the Ant-eater, and the fetid Polecat.[1]

Belon.

26. Less acquainted with books, but with better opportunities of observing nature, than Gesner, his contemporary Belon made greater accessions to zoölogy. Besides his excellent travels in the Levant and Egypt, we have from him a history of fishes in Latin, printed in 1553, and translated by the author into French, with alterations and additions; and one of birds, published in French in 1555, written with great learning, though not without fabulous accounts, as was usual in the earlier period of natural history. Belon was perhaps the first, at least in modern times, who had glimpses of a great typical conformity in nature. In one of his works, he places the skeletons of a man and a bird in apposition, in order to display their essential analogy. He introduced also many exotic plants into France. Every one knows, says a writer of the last century, that our gardens owe all their beauty to Belon.[2] The same writer has satisfactorily cleared this eminent naturalist from the charge of plagiarism, to which credit had been hastily given.[3] Belon may, on the whole, be placed by the side of Gesner.

Salviani and Rondelet's Ichthyology.

27. Salviani published, in 1558, a history of fishes (Animalium Aquatilium Historia), with figures well executed, but by no means numerous. He borrows most of his materials from the ancients, and, having frequently failed in identifying the species they describe, cannot be read without precaution.[4] But Rondelet (De Piscibus Marinis, 1554) was far superior as an ichthyologist, in the judgment of Cuvier, to any of his contemporaries, both by the number of fishes he has known, and the accuracy of his figures, which exceed three hundred for fresh-water and marine species. His knowledge of those which inhabit the Mediterranean Sea was so extensive, that little has been added since his time. "It is the work," says the same great authority, "which has supplied almost every thing which we find on that subject in Gesner, Aldrovandus, Willoughby,

[1] The Tapir is mentioned by Peter Martyr, the rest in Hernando.

[2] Liron, Singularités Historiques, i. 456.

[3] Liron, Singularités Historiques, i. 438. It had been suspected that the manuscripts of Gilles, the author of a compilation from Ælian, who had himself travelled in the East, fell into the hands of Belon, who published them as his own. Gesner has been thought to insinuate this; but Liron is of opinion that Belon was not meant by him.

[4] Biogr. Univ. (Cuvier).

Artedi, and Linnæus; and even Lacepede has been obliged, in many instances, to depend on Rondelet." The text, however, is far inferior to the figures, and is too much occupied with an attempt to fix the ancient names of the several species.[1]

28. The very little book of Dr. Caius on British Dogs, published in 1570, the whole of which, I believe, has been translated by Pennant in his British Zoölogy, is hardly worth mentioning; nor do I know that zoölogical literature has any thing more to produce till almost the close of the century, when the first and second volumes of Aldrovandus's vast natural history were published. These, as well as the third, which appeared in 1603, treat of birds; the fourth is on insects; and these alone were given to the world by the laborious author, a professor of natural history at Bologna. After his death in 1605, nine more folio volumes, embracing with various degrees of detail most other parts of natural history, were successively published by different editors. "We can only consider the works of Aldrovandus," says Cuvier, "as an immense compilation, without taste or genius; the very plan and materials being in a great measure borrowed from Gesner; and Buffon has had reason to say, that it would be reduced to a tenth part of its bulk by striking out the useless and impertinent matter."[2] Buffon, however, which Cuvier might have gone on to say, praises the method of Aldrovandus and his fidelity of description, and even ranks his work above every other natural history.[3] I am not acquainted with its contents; but, according to Linnæus, Aldrovandus, or the editors of his posthumous volumes, added only a very few species of quadrupeds to those mentioned by Gesner, among which are the Zebra, the Jerboa, the Musk-rat of Russia, and the Manis or Scaly Ant-eater.[4]

Aldrovandus.

29. A more steady progress was made in the science of Botany, which commemorates, in those living memorials with

1 Biogr. Univ. (Cuvier).

2 Id.

3 Hist. Naturelle, Premier Discours. The truth is, that all Buffon's censures on Aldrovandus fall equally on Gesner, who is not less accumulative of materials not properly bearing on natural history, and not much less destitute of systematic order. The remarks of Buffon on this waste of learning are very just, and applicable to the works of the sixteenth century on almost every subject as well as zoölogy.

4 Collections of natural history seem to have been formed by all who applied themselves to the subject in the sixteenth century; such as Cordus, Mathiolus, Mercati, Gesner, Agricola, Belon, Rondelet, Ortelius, and many others. Hakluyt mentions the cabinets of some English collectors from which he had derived assistance. Beckman's Hist. of Inventions ii. 57.

which she delights to honor her cultivators, several names still respected, and several books that have not lost their utility. Our countryman, Dr. Turner, published the first part of a New Herbal in 1551: the second and third did not appear till 1562 and 1568. "The arrangement," says Pulteney, "is alphabetical according to the Latin names; and, after the description, he frequently specifies the places and growth. He is ample in his discrimination of the species, as his great object was to ascertain the Materia Medica of the ancients, and of Dioscorides in particular, throughout the vegetable kingdom. He first gives names to many English plants; and allowing for the time when specifical distinctions were not established, when almost all the small plants were disregarded, and the Cryptogamia almost wholly overlooked, the number he was acquainted with is much beyond what could easily have been imagined in an original writer on his subject." [1]

Botany: Turner.

30. The work of Maranta, published in 1559, on the method of understanding medicinal plants, is, in the judgment of a late writer of considerable reputation, nearly at the head of any in that age. The author is independent, though learned; extremely acute in discriminating plants known to the ancients; and has discovered many himself, ridiculing those who dared to add nothing to Dioscorides.[2] Maranta had studied in the private garden formed by Pinelli at Naples. But public gardens were common in Italy. Those of Pisa and Padua were the earliest, and perhaps the most celebrated. One established by the Duke of Ferrara was peculiarly rich in exotic plants procured from Greece and Asia.[3] And perhaps the generous emulation, in all things honorable, between the houses of Este and Medici, led Ferdinand of Tuscany, some time afterwards, near the end of the century, to enrich the gardens of Pisa with the finest plants of Asia and America. The climate of France was less favorable: the first public garden seems to have been formed at Montpellier; and there was none at Paris in 1558.[4] Meantime, the vegetable productions of newly discovered countries became familiar to Europe. Many are described in the excellent History of the Indies by Hernando d'Oviedo;

Maranta: Botanical gardens.

[1] Pulteney's Historical Sketch of the Progress of Botany in England, p. 68.

[2] Sprengel, Historia Rei Herbariæ (1807), i. 345

[3] Id., 360.

[4] Id., 363.

such as the Cocos, the Cactus, the Guiacum. Another Spanish author, Carate, first describes the Solanum Tuberosum, or Potato, under the name of Papas.[1] It has been said that Tobacco is first mentioned, or at least first well described, by Benzoni, in Nova Novi Orbis Historia (Geneva, 1578).[2] Belon went to the Levant soon after the middle of the century, on purpose to collect plants: several other writers of voyages followed before its close. Among these was Prosper Alpinus, who passed several years in Egypt; but his principal work, De Plantis Exoticis, is posthumous, and did not appear till 1627. He is said to be the first European author who has mentioned coffee.[3]

31. The critical examination of the ancients, the establishment of gardens, the travels of botanists, thus furnished a great supply of plants: it was now required to compare and arrange them. Gesner first undertook this: he had formed a garden of his own at Zurich, and has the credit of having discovered the true system of classifying plants according to the organs of fructification; which, however, he does not seem to have made known, nor were his botanical writings published till the last century. Gesner was the first who mentions the Indian sugar-cane and the tobacco, as well as many indigenous plants. It is said that he was used to chew and smoke tobacco; "by which he rendered himself giddy, and, in a manner, drunk."[4] As Gesner died in 1564, this carries back the knowledge of tobacco in Europe several years beyond the above-mentioned treatise of Benzoni.

Gesner.

32. Dodoens, or Dodonæus, a Dutch physician, in 1553, translated into his own language the history of plants by Fuchs, to which he added 133 figures. These, instead of using the alphabetical order of his predecessor, he arranged according to a method which he thought more natural. "He explains," says Sprengel, "well and learnedly, the ancient botanists, and described many plants for the first time:" among these are the Ulex Europæus and

Dodoens.

[1] Sprengel, 378.

[2] Id., 373.

[3] Id., 384; Corniani, vi. 25; Biogr. Univ Yet, in the article on Rauwolf, a German naturalist, who published an account of his travels in the Levant as early as 1581, he is mentioned as one of the first "qui ait parlé de l'usage de boire du café, et en ait décrit la préparation avec exactitude." It is possible, that, this book of Rauwolf being written in German, and the author being obscure in comparison with Prosper Alpinus his prior claim has been, till lately, overlooked.

[4] Sprengel, 373, 390.

the Hyacinthus non scriptus. The great aim of rendering the modern Materia Medica conformable to the ancient seems to have made the early botanists a little inattentive to objects before their eyes. Dodoens himself is rather a physician than a botanist, and is more diligent about the uses of plants than their characteristics. He collected all his writings, under the title Stirpium Historiæ Pemptades Sex, at Antwerp in 1583, with 1,341 figures; a greater number than had yet been published.

Lobel.

33. The Stirpium Adversaria, by Pena and Lobel, the latter of whom is best known as a botanist, was published at London in 1570. Lobel indeed, though a native of Lille, having passed most of his life in England, may be fairly counted among our botanists. He had previously travelled much over Europe. "In the execution of this work," says Pulteney, "there is exhibited, I believe, the first sketch, rude as it is, of a natural method of arrangement; which, however, extends no farther than throwing the plants into large tribes, families, or orders, according to the external appearance or habit of the whole plant or flower, without establishing any definitions or characters. The whole forms forty-four tribes. Some contain the plants of one or two modern genera, others many, and some, it must be owned, very incongruous to each other. On the whole, they are much superior to Dodoens's divisions."[1] Lobel's Adversaria contains descriptions of 1,200 or 1,500 plants, with 272 engravings: the former are not clear or well expressed, and in this he is inferior to his contemporaries; the latter are on copper, very small, but neat.[2] In a later work, the Plantarum Historia, Antwerp, 1576, the number of figures is very considerably greater; but the book has been less esteemed, being a sort of complement to the other. Sprengel speaks more highly of Lobel than the Biographie Universelle.

Clusius.

34. Clusius, or Lecluse, born at Arras, and a traveller, like many other botanists, over Europe, till he settled at Leyden as professor of botany in 1593, is generally reckoned the greatest master of his science whom the age produced. His descriptions are remarkable for their exactness, precision, elegance, and method, though he seems to have had little regard to natural classification. He has added

[1] Historical Sketch, p. 102

[2] Sprengel, 399

a long list to the plants already known. Clusius began by a translation of Dodoens into Latin: he published several other works within the century.[1]

35. Cæsalpin was not only a botanist, but greater in this than in any other of the sciences he embraced. He was the first (the writings of Gesner, if they go so far, being in his time unpublished) who endeavored to establish a natural order of classification on philosophical principles. He founded it on the number, figure, and position of the fructifying parts, observing the situation of the calix and flower relatively to the germen, the divisions of the former, and, in general, what has been regarded in later systems as the basis of arrangement. He treats of trees and of herbs separately, as two grand divisions; but, under each, follows his own natural system. The distinction of sexes he thought needless in plants, on account of their simplicity; though he admits it to exist in some, as in the hemp and the juniper. His treatise on Plants, in 1583, is divided into sixteen books; in the first of which, he lays down the principles of vegetable anatomy and physiology. Many ideas, says Du Petit Thouars, are found there, of which the truth was long afterwards recognized. He analyzed the structure of seeds, which he compares to the eggs of animals; an analogy, however, which had occurred to Empedocles among the ancients. "One page alone," the same writer observes, "in the dedication of Cæsalpin to the Duke of Tuscany, concentrates the principles of a good botanical system so well, that, notwithstanding all the labors of later botanists, nothing material could be added to his sketch; and, if this one page out of all the writings of Cæsalpin remained, it would be enough to secure him an immortal reputation."[2] Cæsalpin, unfortunately, gave no figures of plants, which may have been among the causes that his system was so long overlooked.

Cæsalpin.

36. The Historia Generalis Plantarum by Dalechamps, in 1587, contains 2,731 figures; many of which, however, appear to be repetitions. These are divided into eighteen classes, according to their form and size, but with no natural method. His work is imperfect and faulty:

Dalechamps; Bauhin.

[1] Sprengel, 407; Biogr. Univ.; Pulteney.

[2] Biogr. Univ. Sprengel, after giving an analysis of the system of Cæsalpin, concludes: "En primi systematis carpologici specimen, quod licet imperfectum sit, ingenii tamen summi monumentum et aliorum omnium ad Gærtnerium usque exemplar est." — p. 430.

most of the descriptions are borrowed from his predecessors.[1] Tabernæmontanus, in a book in the German language, has described 5,800 species, and given 2,480 figures.[2] The Phytopinax of Gerard Bauhin (Basle, 1596) is the first important work of one, who, in conjunction with his brother John, labored for forty years in the advancement of botanical knowledge. It is a catalogue of 2,460 plants, including, among about 250 others that were new, the first accurate description of the potato, which, as he informs us, was already cultivated in Italy.[3]

Gerard's Herbal.

37. Gerard's Herbal, published in 1597, was formed on the basis of Dodoens, taking in much from Lobel and Clusius: the figures are from the blocks used by Tabernæmontanus. It is not now esteemed at all by botanists, at least in this first edition; "but," says Pulteney, "from its being well timed, from its comprehending almost the whole of the subjects then known, by being written in English, and ornamented with a more numerous set of figures than had ever accompanied any work of the kind in this kingdom, it obtained great repute."[4]

SECT. III.—ON ANATOMY AND MEDICINE.

Fallopius, Eustachius, and other Anatomists—State of Medicine.

Anatomy: Fallopius.

38. FEW sciences were so successfully pursued in this period as that of anatomy. If it was impossible to snatch from Vesalius the pre-eminent glory that belongs to him as almost its creator, it might still be said that two men now appeared, who, had they lived earlier, would probably have gone as far, and who, by coming later, were enabled to go beyond him. These were Fallopius and Eustachius, both Italians. The former is, indeed, placed by Sprengel even above Vesalius, and reckoned the first anatomist of the sixteenth century. No one had understood that delicate part of the human structure, the organ of hearing, so well as Fallopius, though even he left much for others. He added

[1] Sprengel, 432.
[2] Id., 496.
[3] Sprengel, 451.
[4] Hist. Sketch, p. 122.

several to the list of muscles, and made some discoveries in the intestinal and generative organs.[1]

39. Eustachius, though on the whole inferior to Fallopius, went beyond him in the anatomy of the ear; in which a canal, as is well known, bears his name. One of his biographers has gone so far as to place him above every anatomist for the number of his discoveries. He has treated very well of the teeth, a subject little understood before; and was the first to trace the vena azygos through all its ramifications. No one, as yet, had exhibited the structure of the human kidneys; Vesalius having examined them only in dogs.[2] The scarcity of human subjects was, in fact, an irresistible temptation to take upon trust the identity between quadrupeds and man, which misled the great anatomists of the sixteenth century.[3] Comparative anatomy was therefore not yet promoted to its real dignity, both as an indispensable part of natural history, and as opening the most conclusive and magnificent views of teleology. Coiter, an anatomist born in Holland, but who passed his life in Italy, Germany, and France, was perhaps the first to describe the skeletons of several animals; though Belon, as we have seen, had views far beyond his age in what is strictly comparative anatomy. Coiter's work bears the date of 1575: in 1566 he had published one on human osteology, where that of the fœtus is said to be first described, though some attribute this merit to Fallopius. Coiter is called in the Biographie Universelle one of the creators of pathological anatomy.

Eustachius.

Coiter.

40. Columbus (De Re Anatomica, Venice, 1559), the successor of Vesalius at Padua, and afterwards professor at Pisa and Rome, has announced the discovery of several muscles, and given the name of *vomer* to the small bone which sustains the cartilage of the nose, and which Vesalius had taken for a mere process of the sphenoid. Columbus, though too arrogant in censuring his great predecessor, generally follows him.[4] Arantius, in 1571, is among the first who made known the anatomy of the gravid uterus and the struc-

Columbus.

[1] Portal; Sprengel, Hist. de la Médecine.

[2] Portal.

[3] The church had a repugnance to permit the dissection of dead bodies; but Fallopius tells us that the Duke of Tuscany was sometimes obliging enough to send a living criminal to the anatomists, *quem interficimus nostro modo et anatomisamus*. Sprengel suggests that "nostro modo" meant by opium; but this seems to be merely a conjecture. Hist. de la Médecine, iv. 11.

[4] Portal, i. 541.

ture of the fœtus.[1] He was also conversant, as Vidius, a professor at Paris, of Italian birth, as early as 1542, had already been, with the anatomy of the brain. But this was much improved by Varoli in his Anatomia, published in 1573, who traced the origin of the optic nerves, and gave a better account than any one before him of the eye and of the voice. Piccolomini (Anatomiæ Prælectiones, 1586) is one of the first who described the cellular tissue, and, in other respects, has made valuable observations. Ambrose Paré, a French surgeon, is deemed the founder of chirurgic science, at least in that country. His works were first collected in 1561; but his treatise on gunshot-wounds is as old as 1545. Several other names are mentioned with respect by the historians of medicine and anatomy; such as those of Alberti, Benivieni, Donatus, and Schank. Never, says Portal, were anatomy and surgery better cultivated, with more emulation or more encouragement, than about the end of the sixteenth century. A long list of minor discoveries in the human frame are recorded by this writer and by Sprengel. It will be readily understood, that he gives these names, which of itself it is rather an irksome labor to enumerate, with no other object, than that none of those, who by their ability and diligence carried forward the landmarks of human knowledge, should miss, in a history of general literature, of their meed of remembrance. We reserve to the next period those passages in the anatomists of this age which have seemed to anticipate the great discovery that immortalizes the name of Harvey.

Circulation of the blood.

41. These continual discoveries in the anatomical structure of man tended to guide and correct the theory of medicine. The observations of this period became more acute and accurate. Those of Plater and Foresti, especially the latter, are still reputed classical in medical literature. Prosper Alpinus may be deemed the father, in modern times, of diagnostic science.[2] Plater, in his Praxis Medica, made the first, though an imperfect, attempt at a classification of diseases. Yet the observations made in this age, and the whole practical system, are not exempt from considerable faults: the remedies were too topical; the symptoms of disease were more regarded than its cause; the theory was too simple

Medicinal science.

[1] Portal, vol ii. p. 3.

[2] Sprengel, iii 173.

and general; above all, a great deal of credulity and superstition prevailed in the art.[1] Many among the first in science believed in demoniacal possessions and sorcery, or in astrology. This was most common in Germany, where the school of Paracelsus, discreditably to the national understanding, exerted much influence. The best physicians of the century were either Italian or French.

42. Notwithstanding the bigoted veneration for Hippocrates that most avowed, several physicians, not at all adhering to Paracelsus, endeavored to set up a rational experience against the Greek school, when they thought them at variance. Joubert of Montpellier, in his Paradoxes (1566), was a bold innovator of this class; but many of his paradoxes are now established truths. Botal of Asti, a pupil of Fallopius, introduced the practice of venesection on a scale before unknown, but prudently aimed to show that Hippocrates was on his side. The faculty of medicine, however, at Paris, condemned it as erroneous and very dangerous. His method, nevertheless, had great success, especially in Spain.[2]

SECT. IV. — ON ORIENTAL LITERATURE.

Syriac version of New Testament.

43. THIS is a subject over which, on account of my total ignorance of Eastern languages, I am glad to hasten. The first work that appears after the middle of the century is a grammar of the Syriac, Chaldee, and Rabbinical, compared with the Arabic and Ethiopic languages, which Angelo Canini, a man as great in Oriental as in Grecian learning, published at Paris in 1554. In the next year, Widmandstadt gave, from the press of Vienna, the first edition of the Syriac version of the New Testament.[3] Several lexicons and grammars of this tongue, which is in fact only a dialect not far removed from the Chaldee, though in a different alphabetical character, will be found in the

[1] Sprengel, 156.
[2] Id., iii. p. 215.
[3] Schelhorn, Amœnitates Literariæ, xiii. 234; Biogr. Universelle; Andrès, xix. 45; Eichhorn, v. 435. In this edition the Syriac text alone appeared: Henry Stephens reprinted it with the Greek and with two Latin translations.

bibliographical writers. The Syriac may be said to have been now fairly added to the literary domain. The Antwerp Polyglot of Arias Montanus, besides a complete Chaldee paraphrase of the Old Testament, the Complutensian having only contained the Pentateuch, gives the New Testament in Syriac, as well as Pagnini's Latin translation of the Old.[1]

Hebrew critics.

44. The Hebrew language was studied, especially among the German Protestants, to a considerable extent, if we may judge from the number of grammatical works published within this period. Among these, Morhof selects the Erotemata Linguæ Hebrææ by Neander, printed at Basle in 1567. Tremellius, Chevalier, and Drusius among Protestants, Masius and Clarius in the Church of Rome, are the most conspicuous names. The first, an Italian refugee, is chiefly known by his translation of the Bible into Latin, in which he was assisted by Francis Junius. The second, a native of France, taught Hebrew at Cambridge, and was there the instructor of Drusius, whose father had emigrated from Flanders, on the ground of religion. Drusius himself, afterwards professor of Hebrew at the University of Franeker, has left writings of more permanent reputation than most other Hebraists of the sixteenth century: they relate chiefly to biblical criticism and Jewish antiquity, and several of them have a place in the Critici Sacri and in the collection of Ugolini.[2] Clarius is supposed to have had some influence on the decree of the Council of Trent, asserting the authenticity of the Vulgate.[3] Calasio was superior probably to them all; but his principal writings do not belong to this period. No large proportion of the treatises published by Ugolini ought, so far as I know their authors, to be referred to the sixteenth century.

Its study in England.

45. The Hebrew language had been early studied in England, though there has been some controversy as to the extent of the knowledge which the first translators of the Bible possessed. We find that both Chevalier

[1] Andrès, xix. 49. The whole edition is richer in materials than that of Ximenes.

[2] Drusius is extolled by all critics except Scaliger (Scaligerana Secunda), who seems to have conceived one of his personal prejudices against the Franeker professor, and depreciates his moral character. Simon thinks Drusius the most learned and judicious writer we find in the Critici Sacri. Hist. Critique du V. T., p. 498; Biogr. Univ.; Blount.

[3] Clarius, according to Simon, knew Hebrew but indifferently, and does little more than copy Munster, whose observations are too full of Judaism, as he consulted no interpreters but the rabbinical writers. Masius, the same author says, is very learned, but has the like fault of dealing in rabbinical expositions. — p. 499.

read lectures on Hebrew at Cambridge not long after the queen's accession, and his disciple Drusius at Oxford, from 1572 to 1576.[1] Hugh Broughton was a deeply learned rabbinical scholar. I do not know that we could produce any other name of marked reputation; and we find that the first Hebrew types, employed in any considerable number, appear in 1592. These are in a book not relating directly to Hebrew, Rheses Institutiones Linguæ Cambro-Britannicæ. But a few Hebrew characters, very rudely cut in wood, are found in Wakefield's Oration, printed as early as 1524.[2]

Arabic begins to be studied.

46. The Syriac and Chaldee were so closely related to Hebrew, both as languages and in the theological purposes for which they were studied, that they did not much enlarge the field of Oriental literature. The most copious language, and by far the most fertile of books, was the Arabic. A few slight attempts at introducing a knowledge of this had been made before the middle of the century. An Arabic as well as Syriac press at Vienna was first due to the patronage of Ferdinand I., in 1554; but, for a considerable time, no fruit issued from it. But the increasing zeal of Rome for the propagation of its faith, both among infidels and schismatics, gave a larger sweep to the cultivation of Oriental languages. Gregory XIII. founded a Maronite college at Rome, in 1584, for those Syrian Christians of Libanus who had united themselves to the Catholic Church; the Cardinal Medici, afterwards Grand Duke of Florence, established an Oriental press, about 1580, under the superintendence of John Baptista Raimondi; and Sixtus V., in 1588, that of the Vatican, which, though principally designed for early Christian literature, was possessed of types for the chief Eastern languages. Hence the Arabic, hitherto almost neglected, began to attract more attention; the Gospels in that language were published at Rome in 1590 or 1591; some works of Euclid and Avicenna had preceded; one or two elementary books on grammar appeared in Germany; and several other publications belong to the last years of the century.[3] Scaliger now entered upon the study of Arabic with all his indefatigable activity. Yet, at the end of the

[1] Wood's Hist. and Antiquities. In 1574 he was appointed to read publicly in Syriac.

[2] Preface to Herbert's Typographical Antiquities.

[3] Eichhorn, v. 641, *et alibi;* Tiraboschi, viii. 195; Ginguéné, vol. vii. p. 258.

century, few had penetrated far into a region so novel and extensive, and in which the subsidiary means of knowledge were so imperfect. The early grammars are represented by Eichhorn as being very indifferent; and, in fact, very few Arabic books had been printed. The edition of the Koran by Pagninus, in 1529, was unfortunately suppressed, as we have before mentioned, by the zeal of the court of Rome. Casaubon, writing to Scaliger in 1597, declares that no one within his recollection had even touched with the tips of his fingers that language, except Postel in a few rhapsodies; and that neither he nor any one else had written any thing on the Persic.[1] Gesner, however, in his Mithridates, 1558, had given the Lord's Prayer in twenty-two languages; to which Rocca at Rome, in 1591, added three more; and Megiser increased the number, in a book published next year at Frankfort, to forty.[2]

SECT. V.—ON GEOGRAPHY.

Voyages in the Indies — Those of the English — Of Ortelius and others.

47. A MORE important accession to the knowledge of Europe as to the rest of the world, than had hitherto been made through the press, is due to Ramusio, a Venetian, who had filled respectable offices under the republic. He published, in 1550, the first volume of his well-known collection of Travels; the second appeared in 1559; and the third, in 1565. They have been reprinted several times, and all the editions are not equally complete. No general collection of travels had hitherto been published, except the Novus Orbis of Grynæus; and though the greater part, perhaps, of those included in Ramusio's three volumes had appeared separately, others came forth for the first time. The Africa of Leo Africanus, a baptized Moor, with which

Collection of voyages by Ramusio.

1 "Nostra autem memoria, qui eas linguas vel ακρῳ, quod aiunt, δακτυλῳ attigerit, novi neminem, nisi quod Postellum nescio quid muginatum esse de lingua Arabica memini. Sed illa quam tenuia, quam exilia! de Persicâ, quod equidem memini neque ille, neque alius quisquam vel γρυ το λεγομενον." — Epist. ciii.

2 Biogr. Univ., arts. "Megiser" and "Rocca."

3 Biogr. Univ.

Ramusio begins, is among these; and it is upon this work that such knowledge as we possessed, till very recent times, as to the interior of that continent, was almost entirely founded. Ramusio, in the remainder of this volume, gives many voyages in Africa, the East Indies, and Indian Archipelago, including two accounts of Magellan's circumnavigation of the world, and one of Japan, which had very lately been discovered. The second volume is dedicated to travels through Northern Europe and Asia, beginning with that of Marco Polo, including also the curious, though very questionable, voyage of the Zeni brothers, about 1400, to some unknown region north of Scotland. In the third volume, we find the conquests of Cortes and Pizarro, with all that had already been printed of the excellent work of Hernando d'Oviedo on the Western World. Few subsequent collections of voyages are more esteemed for the new matter they contain than that of Ramusio.[1]

48. The importance of such publications as that of Ramusio was soon perceived, not only in the stimulus they gave to curiosity or cupidity towards following up the paths of discovery, but in calling the attention of reflecting minds, such as Bodin and Montaigne, to so copious a harvest of new facts illustrating the physical and social character of the human species. But from the want of a rigid investigation, or more culpable reasons, these early narratives are mingled with much falsehood, and misled some of the more credulous philosophers almost as often as they enlarged their knowledge.

Curiosity they awakened.

49. The story of the Portuguese conquests in the East, more varied and almost as wonderful as romance, was recounted in the Asia of Joam de Barros (1552), and in that of Castanheda in the same and two ensuing years: these have never been translated. The great voyage of Magellan had been written by one of his companions, Pigafetta. This was first published in Italian in 1556. The History of the Indies, by Acosta, in 1590, may perhaps belong more strictly to other departments of literature than to geography.

Other voyages

50. The Romish missionaries, especially the Jesuits, spread themselves with intrepid zeal during this period over infidel nations. Things strange to European

Accounts of China.

[1] Biogr. Univ.

prejudice, the books, the laws, the rites, the manners, the dresses, of those remote people, were related by them on their return, for the most part orally, but sometimes through the press. The vast empire of China, the Cathay of Marco Polo, over which an air of fabulous mystery had hung, and which is delineated in the old maps with much ignorance of its position and extent, now first was brought within the sphere of European knowledge. The Portuguese had some traffic to Canton; but the relations they gave were uncertain, till, in 1577, two Augustine friars persuaded a Chinese officer to take them into the country. After a residence of four months, they returned to Manilla; and, in consequence of their reports, Philip II. sent, in 1580, an embassy to the court of Pekin. The History of China by Mendoza, as it is called, contains all the knowledge that the Spaniards were able to collect by these means; and it may be said, on comparison with later books on the same subject, to be as full and ample an account of China as could have been given in such circumstances. This book was published in 1585; and from that time, but no earlier, do we date our acquaintance with that empire.[1] Maffei, in his History of India, threw all the graces of a pure Latin style over his description of the East. The first part of a scarce and curious collection of voyages to the two Indies, with the names of De Bry and Merian as its editors, appeared at Frankfort in 1590. Six other volumes were published at intervals down to 1634. Possevin, meantime, told us more of a much nearer state, Muscovy, than was before familiar to Western Europe, though the first information had been due to England.

India and Russia.

51. The spirit of lucre vied with that of religion in penetrating unknown regions. In this, the English have most to boast: they were the first to pass the Icy Cape, and anchor their ships in the White Sea. This was in the famous voyage of Chancellor in 1553. Anthony Jenkinson soon afterwards, through the heart of Russia, found his way to Bokhara and Persia. They followed up the discoveries of Cabot in North America; and, before the end of the century, had ascertained much of the coasts about Labrador and Hudson's Bay, as well as those of Virginia, the first colony. These English voyages were recorded

English discoveries in the Northern seas.

[1] Biogr. Univ. This was translated into English by R Parke in 1588; at least I believe it to be the same work, but have never seen the original.

in the three parts of the Collection of Voyages, by Hakluyt, published in 1598, 1599, and 1600. Drake, second to Magellan in that bold enterprise, traversed the circumference of the world; and the reign of Elizabeth, quite as much as any later age, bears witness to the intrepidity and skill, if not strictly to the science, of our sailors. For these undaunted navigators, traversing the unexplored wildernesses of ocean in small ill-built vessels, had neither any effectual assistance from charts, nor the means of making observations themselves, or of profiting by those of others. Hence, when we come to geographical knowledge, in the proper sense of the word, we find it surprisingly scanty, even at the close of the sixteenth century.

Geographical books: Ortelius.

52. It had not, however, been neglected, so far as a multiplicity of books could prove a regard to it. Ortelius, in his Theatrum Orbis Terrarum (the first edition of which was in 1570, augmented afterwards by several maps of later dates), gives a list of about 150 geographical treatises, most of them subsequent to 1560. His own work is the first general atlas since the revival of letters, and has been justly reckoned to make an epoch in geography; being the basis of all collections of maps since formed, and deserving, it is said, even yet to be consulted, notwithstanding the vast progress of our knowledge of the earth.[1] The maps in the later editions of the sixteenth century bear various dates. That of Africa is of 1590; and, though the outline is tolerably given, we do not find the Mauritius Isles; while the Nile is carried almost to the Cape of Good Hope, and made to issue from a great lake. In the map of America, dated 1587, the outline on the N. E. side contains New France, with the *city* of Canada; the St. Lawrence traverses the country, but without lakes; Florida is sufficiently distinguished, but the intervening coast is loosely laid down. Estotiland, the supposed discovery of the Zeni, appears to the north, and Greenland beyond. The outline of South America is worse, the southern parts covering nearly as much longitude as the northern,—an error which was in some measure diminished in a map of 1603. An immense solid land, as in all the older maps, connects Terra del Fuego with New Guinea. The delineation of the southern coasts of Asia

[1] Biogr. Univ.

is not very bad, even in the earlier maps of Ortelius; but some improvement is perceived in his knowledge of China and the adjacent seas in that of the world, given in the edition of 1588. The maps of Europe in Ortelius are chiefly defective as to the countries on the Baltic Sea and Russia; but there is a general incorrectness of delineation, which must strike the eye at once of any person slightly experienced in geography.

53. Gerard Mercator, a native of the Duchy of Juliers, where he passed the greater part of his life, was perhaps superior to Ortelius. His fame is most diffused by the invention of a well-known mode of delineating hydrographical charts, in which the parallels and meridians intersect each other at right angles. The first of these was published in 1569; but the principle of the method was not understood till Edward Wright, in 1599, explained it in his Correction of Errors in Navigation.[1] The Atlas of Mercator, in an edition of 1598, which contains only part of Europe, is superior to that of Ortelius; and as to England, of which there had been maps published by Lluyd in 1569, and by Saxton in 1580, it may be reckoned very tolerably correct. Lluyd's map, indeed, is published in the Atlas of Ortelius. But, in the northern regions of Europe, we still find a mass of arbitrary, erroneous conjecture.

54. Botero, the Piedmontese Jesuit mentioned in another place, has given us a cosmography, or general description of as much of the world as was then known, entitled Relazioni Universali: the edition I have seen is undated, but he mentions the discovery of Nova Zembla in 1594. His knowledge of Asia is very limited, and chiefly derived from Marco Polo. China, he says, extends from 17° to 52° of latitude, and has 22° of longitude. Japan is 60 leagues from China, and 150 from America. The coasts, Botero observes, from Bengal to China, are so dangerous, that two or three are lost out of every four ships; but the master who succeeds in escaping these perils is sure to make his fortune.

55. But the best map of the sixteenth century is one of uncommon rarity, which is found in a very few copies of the first edition of Hakluyt's Voyages. This contains Davis's Straits (Fretum Davis), Virginia by name, and the Lake Ontario. The coast of Chili is placed more correctly than

[1] Montucla, ii. 651; Biogr. Univ., art. "Mercator."

in the prior maps of Ortelius; and it is noticed in the margin, that this trending of the coast, less westerly than had been supposed, was discovered by Drake in 1577, and confirmed by Sarmiento and Cavendish. The huge Terra Australis of the old geography is left out. Corea is represented near its place, and China with some degree of correctness; even the north coast of New Holland is partially traced. The Strait of Anian, which had been presumed to divide Asia from America, has disappeared; while a marginal note states that the distance between those two continents in latitude 38° is not less than 1,200 leagues. The Ultra-Indian region is inaccurate; the Sea of Aral is still unknown; and little pains have been tâken with Central and Northern Asia. But, upon the whole, it represents the utmost limit of geographical knowledge at the close of the sixteenth century, and far excels the maps in the edition of Ortelius at Antwerp in 1588.[1]

SECT. VI. — ON HISTORY.

56. THE history of Italy by Guicciardini, though it is more properly a work of the first part of the century, was not published till 1564. It is well known for the solidity of the reflections, the gravity and impartiality with which it is written, and the prolixity of the narration; a fault, however, frequent and not unpardonable in historians contemporary and familiar with the events they relate. If the siege of Pisa in 1508 appeared so uninteresting a hundred years afterwards, as to be the theme of ridicule with Boccalini, it was far otherwise to the citizens of Florence soon after the time. Guicciardini has generally held the first place among Italian historians, though he is by no means equal in literary merit to Machiavel. Adriani, whose continuation of Guicciardini extends to 1574, is little read; nor does he seem to be much recommended by style. No other historian of that country need be mentioned for works published within the sixteenth century.

Guicciardini.

[1] [This map is in the British Museum. — 1842.]

57. The French have ever been distinguished for those personal memoirs of men more or less conversant with public life, to which Philip de Comines led the way. Several that fell within this period are deserving of being read, not only for their relation of events, with which we do not here much concern ourselves, but for a lively style, and occasionally for good sense and acute thinking. Those of Montluc may be praised for the former. Spain had a considerable historian in Mariana, twenty books of whose history were published in Latin in 1592, and five more in 1595: the concluding five books do not fall within the century. The style is vigorous and classical, the thoughts judicious. Buchanan's History of Scotland has already been praised for the purity of its language. Few modern histories are more redolent of an antique air. We have nothing to boast in England: our historical works of the Elizabethan age are mere chronicles, and hardly good even as such. Nor do I know any Latin historians of Germany or the Low Countries who, as writers, deserve our attention.

French memoirs.

SECT. VII. — GENERAL STATE OF LITERATURE.

58. THE great Italian universities of Bologna, Padua, Pisa, and Pavia, seem to have lost nothing of their lustre throughout the century. New colleges, new buildings in that stately and sumptuous architecture which distinguishes this period, bore witness to a continual patronage, and a public demand for knowledge. It is true that the best days of classical literature had passed away in Italy. But the revival of theological zeal, and of those particular studies which it fostered, might perhaps more than compensate, in its effect on the industry of the learned, for this decline of philology. The sciences also of medicine and mathematics attracted many more students than before. The Jesuit colleges, and those founded by Gregory XIII., have been already mentioned. They were endowed at a large expense in that palmy state of the Roman see.

Universities in Italy.

59. Universities were founded at Altdorf and Leyden in 1575, at Helmstadt in 1576. Others of less importance began to exist in the same age. The University of Edinburgh derives its origin from the charter of James in 1582. Those of Oxford and Cambridge, reviving, as we have seen, after a severe shock at the accession of Elizabeth, continued, through her reign, to be the seats of a progressive and solid erudition. A few colleges were founded in this age. I should have wished to give some sketch of the mode of instruction pursued in these two universities; but sufficient materials have not fallen in my way: what I have been able to glean has already been given to the reader in some pages of the first volume. It was the common practice at Oxford, observed in form down to this century, that every candidate for the degree of bachelor of arts, independently of other exercises, should undergo an examination (become absolutely nominal) in the five sciences of grammar, logic, rhetoric, ethics, and geometry; every one for that of master of arts, in the additional sciences of physics, metaphysics, Hebrew, and some more. These were probably the ancient trivium and quadrivium; enlarged, perhaps after the sixteenth century, according to the increase of learning and the apparent necessity of higher qualifications.[1] But it would be, I conceive, a great mistake to imagine that the requisitions for academical degrees were ever much insisted upon. The universities sent forth abundance of illiterate graduates in every age; and as they had little influence, at least of a favorable sort, either on philosophy or polite literature, we are not to overrate their importance in the history of the intellectual progress of mankind.[2]

In other countries.

60. Public libraries were considerably enlarged during this period. Those of Rome, Ferrara, and Florence, in Italy, of Vienna and Heidelberg in Germany, stood much above any others. Sixtus V. erected the splendid Repository of the Vatican. Philip II. founded that of the Escurial, perhaps after 1580, and collected books with great labor and expense; all who courted the favor of Spain con-

Libraries.

1 [" The quadrivials — I mean arithmetic, music, geometry, and astronomy — are now little regarded in either of the universities." — Harrison's Description of England, p. 252. Hence we may infer, that the more modern division in use at Oxford was made after his time.—1842.]

2 Lord Bacon animadverts (De Cogitatis et Visis) on the fetters which the universities imposed on the investigation of truth; and Morhof ascribes the establishment of the academies in Italy to the narrow and pedantic spirit of the universities. — l. i. c. 14.

tributing also by presents of rarities.[1] Ximenes had established the library of Alcala; and that of Salamanca is likewise more ancient than this of the Escurial. Every king of France took a pride in adding to the Royal Library of Paris. By an ordinance of 1556, a copy of every book printed with privilege was to be deposited in this library. It was kept at Fontainebleau, but transferred to Paris in 1595. During the civil wars, its progress was slow.[2] The first Prince of Orange founded the public library of Leyden, which shortly became one of the best in Europe. The catalogue was published in 1597. That bequeathed by Humphrey, Duke of Gloucester, to the University of Oxford, was dispersed in the general havoc made under Edward VI. At the close of the century, the university had no public library. But Sir Thomas Bodley had already, in 1597, made the generous offer of presenting his own, which was carried into effect in the first years of the ensuing age.[3] In the colleges, there were generally libraries. If we could believe Scaliger, these were good: but he had never been in England; and there is no reason, I believe, to estimate them highly.[4] Archbishop Parker had founded, or at least greatly enlarged, the public library of Cambridge. Many private persons of learning and opulence had formed libraries in England under Elizabeth, some of which still subsist in the mansions of ancient families. I incline to believe, that there was at least as competent a stock of what is generally called learning among our gentry as in any continental kingdom: their education was more literary, their habits more peaceable, their religion more argumentative.

[1] Mariana, in a long passage wherein he describes the Escurial palace, gives this account of the library: "Vestibulo bibliotheca imposita, majori longitudine omnino pedum centum octoginta quinque, lata pedes triginta duos, libros servat præsertim Græcos manuscriptos, præcipuæ plerosque vetustatis; qui ex omnibus Europæ partibus ad famam novi operis magno numero confluxerunt: auro pretiosiores thesauri, *digni quorum evolvendorum major eruditis hominibus facultas contingeret. Quod enim ex captivis et majestate revinctis literis emolumentum?*"—De Rege et Regis Institutione, l. iii. c. 10. The noble freedom of Mariana breaks out, we see, in the midst of his praise of royal magnificence. Few, if any libraries, except those of the universities, were accessible to men of studious habits,—a reproach that has been very slowly effaced. I have often been astonished, in considering this, that so much learning was really acquired.

[2] Jugler's Hist. Literaria, c. iii. s. 5. This very laborious work of the middle of the last century contains the most ample account of public libraries throughout Europe that I have been able to find. The German libraries, with the two exceptions of Vienna and Heidelberg, do not seem to have become of much importance in the sixteenth century.

[3] Wood's Hist. and Ant., p. 922.

[4] Scalig. Secunda, p. 236. "De mon temps," he says, in the same place, "il y avoit à Londres douze bibliothèques *complètes*, et à Paris quatre-vingt." I do not profess to understand this epithet.

Perhaps we should make an exception for Italy, in which the spirit of collecting libraries was more prevalent.[1]

61. The last forty years of the sixteenth century were a period of uninterrupted peace in Italy. Notwithstanding the pressure of governments always jealous, and sometimes tyrannical, it is manifest that at least the states of Venice and Tuscany had grown in wealth, and in the arts that attend it. Those who had been accustomed to endure the license of armies found a security in the rule of law which compensated for many abuses. Hence that sort of property, which is most exposed to pillage, became again a favorite acquisition; and, among the costly works of art which adorned the houses of the wealthy, every relic of antiquity found its place. Gems and medals, which the books of Vico and Erizzo had taught the owners to arrange and to appreciate, were sought so eagerly, that according to Hubert Goltzius, as quoted by Pinkerton, there were in Italy 380 of such collections. The marbles and bronzes, the inscriptions of antiquity, were not less in request; and the well-known word *virtuosi*, applied to these lovers of what was rare and beautiful in art or nature, bespoke the honor in which their pursuits were held. The luxury of literature displayed itself in scarce books, elegant impressions, and sumptuous bindings.

Collections of antiquities in Italy.

62. Among the refined gentlemen who devoted to these graceful occupations their leisure and their riches, none was more celebrated than Gian Vincenzio Pinelli. He was born of a good family at Naples in 1538. A strong thirst for knowledge, and the consciousness that his birth exposed him to difficulties and temptations at home which might obstruct his progress, induced him to seek, at the age of twenty-four, the University of Padua, at that time the renowned scene of learning and of philosophy.[2] In this city he spent forty-three years, — the remainder of his life. His father was desirous that he should practise the law; but, after a short study of this, Pinelli resumed his favorite pursuits. His fortune, indeed, was sufficiently large to render

Pinelli.

[1] [Morhof, i. 3, mentions several large private libraries in Italy and France: that of the younger Aldus Manutius contained 80,000 volumes. — 1842].

[2] "Animadverterat autem hic noster, domi, inter amplexus parentum et familiarium obsequia, in urbe deliciarum plena, militaribus et equestribus, quam musarum studiis aptiore, non preventurum sese ad eam gloriæ metam quam sibi destinaverat, ideo gymnasii Patavini fama permotus," &c.—Gualdi, Vita Pinelli. This Life by a contemporary, or nearly such, is republished in the Vitæ Illustrium Virorum by Bates.

any sacrifice of them unreasonable; and it may have been out of dislike of his compulsory reading, that, in forming this vast library, he excluded works of jurisprudence. This library was collected by the labor of many years. The catalogues of the Frankfort fairs, and those of the principal booksellers in Italy, were diligently perused by Pinelli; nor did any work of value appear from the press on either side of the Alps which he did not instantly add to his shelves. This great library was regularly arranged; and, though he did not willingly display its stores to the curious and ignorant, they were always accessible to scholars. He had also a considerable museum of globes, maps, mathematical instruments, and fossils; but he only collected the scarcer coins. In his manners, Pinelli was a finely polished gentleman, but of weak health, and for this cause devoted to books, and seldom mingling with gay society, nor even belonging to the literary academies of the city, but carrying on an extensive correspondence, and continually employed in writing extracts or annotations. Yet he has left nothing that has been published. His own house was, as it were, a perpetual academy, frequented by the learned of all nations. If Pinelli was not a man of great genius, nor born to be of much service to any science, we may still respect him for a love of learning and a nobleness of spirit which has preserved his memory.[1]

Italian academies.

63. The literary academies of Italy continued to flourish even more than before: many new societies of the same kind were founded. Several existed at Florence; but all others have been eclipsed by the Della Crusca, established in 1582. Those of another Tuscan city, which had taken the lead in such literary associations, did not long survive its political independence: the jealous spirit of Cosmo extinguished the Rozzi of Sienna in 1568. In governments as suspicious as those of Italy, the sort of secrecy belonging to these meetings, and the encouragement they gave to a sentiment of mutual union, might appear sufficient reasons for watchfulness. We have seen how the Academy of Modena was broken up on the score of religion. That of Venice, perhaps for the same reason, was dissolved by the senate in 1561, and did not revive till 1593. These, how-

[1] Gualdi; Tiraboschi, vi. 214. The library of Pinelli was dispersed and in great part destroyed by pirates not long afterwards. That long since formed by one of his family is well known to book collectors.

ever, were exceptions to the rule; and it was the general policy of governments to cherish in the nobility a love of harmless amusements. All Lombardy and Romagna were full of academies: they were frequent in the Kingdom of Naples and in the ecclesiastical states.[1] They are a remarkable feature in the social condition of Italy, and could not have existed perhaps in any other country. They were the encouragers of a numismatic and lapidary erudition, elegant in itself, and throwing for ever its little sparks of light on the still ocean of the past, but not very favorable to comprehensive observation, and tending to bestow on an unprofitable pedantry the honors of real learning. This, indeed, is the inherent vice of all literary societies, accessible too frequently to those who, for amusement or fashion's sake, love as much knowledge as can be reached with facility, and from the nature of their transactions seldom capable of affording scope for any extensive research.

64. No academy or similar institution can be traced at this time, as far as I know, in France or Germany. But it is deserving of remark, that one sprung up in England, not indeed of the classical and polite character that belonged to the Infiammati of Padua, or the Della Crusca of Florence, yet useful in its objects and honorable alike to its members and to the country. This was the Society of Antiquaries, founded by Archbishop Parker in 1572. Their object was the preservation of ancient documents, illustrative of history, which the recent dissolution of religious houses and the shameful devastation attending it had exposed to great peril. They intended also, by the reading of papers at their meetings, to keep alive the love and knowledge of English antiquity. In the second of these objects, this society was more successful than in the first: several short dissertations, chiefly by Arthur Agard, their most active member, have been afterwards published. The Society comprised very reputable names, especially of lawyers, and continued to meet till early in the reign of James, who, from some jealousy, thought fit to dissolve it.[2]

Society of Antiquaries in England.

[1] Tiraboschi, viii. 125-179, is so full on this subject, that I have not recourse to the other writers who have, sometimes with great prolixity, investigated a subject more interesting in its details to the Italians than to us. Ginguéné adds very little to what he found in his predecessor.

[2] See Life of Agard, in Biogr. Brit. and in Chalmers. But the best account is in the Introduction to the first volume of the Archæologia. The present Society

New books, and catalogues of them

65. The chief cities on this side of the Alps, whence new editions came forth, were Paris, Basle, Lyons, Leyden, Antwerp, Brussels, Strasburg, Cologne, Heidelberg, Frankfort, Ingoldstadt, and Geneva. In all these and in many other populous towns, booksellers, who were generally also printers, were a numerous body. In London, at least forty or fifty were contemporaneous publishers in the latter part of Elizabeth's reign; but the number elsewhere in England was very small. The new books on the Continent, and within the Alps and Pyrenees, found their principal mart at the annual Frankfort fairs. Catalogues of such books began to be published, according to Beckmann, in 1554.[1] In a collective catalogue of all books offered for sale at Frankfort, from 1564 to 1592, I find the number in Latin, Greek, and German, to be about 16,000. No Italian or French appear in this catalogue, being probably reserved for another. Of theology in Latin there are 3,200; and, in this department, the Catholic publications rather exceed the Protestant. But of the theology in the German language, the number is 3,700, not one-fourth of which is Catholic. Scarcely any mere German poetry appears, but a good deal in both languages with musical notes. Law furnishes about 1,600 works. I reckon twenty-seven Greek and thirty-two Latin grammars, not counting different editions of the same. There are at least seventy editions of parts of Aristotle. The German books are rather more than one-third of the whole. Among the Latin I did not observe one book by a writer of this island. In a compilation by Clessius, in 1602, purporting to be a conspectus of the publications of the sixteenth century, formed partly from catalogues of fairs, partly from those of public libraries, we find, at least in the copy I have examined, but which seems to want one volume, a much smaller number of productions than in the former, but probably with more selection. The books in modern languages are less than 1,000, half French, half Italian. In this catalogue, also, the Catholic theology rather outnumbers the

of Antiquaries is the representative, but after long intermission, of this Elizabethan progenitor.

[1] Hist. of Inventions, iii. 120. "George Willer, whom some improperly call Viller, and others Walter, a bookseller at Augsburg, who kept a large shop, and frequented the Frankfort fairs, first fell upon the plan of causing to be printed every fair a catalogue of all the new books, in which the size and printers' names were marked." There seems to be some doubt whether the first year of these catalogues was 1554 or 1564: the collection mentioned in the text leads us rather to suspect the latter.

Protestant, which is perhaps not what we should have expected to find.

66. These catalogues, in the total absence of literary journals, were necessarily the great means of communicating to all the lovers of learning in Cisalpine Europe (for Italy had resources of her own) some knowledge of its progress. Another source of information was the correspondence of scholars with each other. It was their constant usage, far more than in modern times, to preserve an epistolary intercourse. If their enmities were often bitter, their contentions almost always violent, many beautiful instances of friendship and sympathy might be adduced on the other side: they deemed themselves a distinct caste, a priesthood of the same altar, not ashamed of poverty nor disheartened by the world's neglect, but content with the praise of those whom themselves thought worthy of praise, and hoping something more from posterity than they obtained from their own age.

Literary correspondence.

67. We find several attempts at a literary, or rather bibliographical, history of a higher character than these catalogues. The Bibliotheca Universalis of Gesner was reprinted in 1574, with considerable enlargements by Simler. Conrad Lycosthenes afterwards made additions to it, and Verdier published a supplement. Verdier was also the author of a Bibliothèque Française, of which the first edition appeared in 1584. Another, with the same title, was published in the same year by La Croix du Maine. Both these follow the strange alphabetical arrangement by Christian instead of family names, so usual in the sixteenth century. La Croix du Maine confines himself to French authors; but Verdier includes all who had been translated. The former is valued for his accuracy and for curious particulars in biography; the second, for the extracts he has given. Doni pretended to give a history of books in his Libreria; but it has not obtained much reputation, and falls, according to the testimony of those who are acquainted with it, below the compilations above mentioned.[1]

Bibliographical works.

68. The despotism of the state, and far more of the church, bore heavily on the press in Italy. Spain, mistress

[1] Morhof; Goujet; Biogr. Univ.

of Milan and Naples, and Florence under Cosmo I., were jealous governments. Venice, though we are apt to impute a rigid tyranny to its senate, appears to have indulged rather more liberty of writing on political topics to its subjects, on the condition, no doubt, that they should eulogize the wisdom of the republic; and, comparatively to the neighboring regions of Italy, the praise both of equitable and prudent government may be ascribed to that aristocracy. It had at least the signal merit of keeping ecclesiastical oppression at a distance: a Venetian might write with some freedom of the Papal court. One of the accusations against Venice, in her dispute with Paul V., was for allowing the publication of books that had been censured at Rome.[1]

Restraints on the press.

69. But Rome struck a fatal blow, and perhaps more deadly than she intended, at literature in the Index Expurgatorius of prohibited books. It had long been the regulation, that no book should be printed without a previous license. This was, of course, a restraint on the freedom of writing; but it was less injurious to the trade of the printer and bookseller than the subsequent prohibition of what he had published or purchased at his own cost and risk. The first list of books prohibited by the church was set forth by Paul IV. in 1559. His Index includes all Bibles in modern languages, enumerating forty-eight editions, chiefly printed in countries still within the obedience of the church. Sixty-one printers are put under a general ban; all works of every description from their presses being forbidden. Stephens and Oporinus have the honor of being among these.[2] This system was pursued and rigorously acted upon by the successors of the imperious Caraffa. The Council of Trent had its own list of condemned publications. Philip II. has been said to have preceded the pope himself in a similar proscription. Wherever the sway of Rome and Spain was felt, books were unsparingly burned; and to this cause is imputed the scarcity of many editions.

Index Expurgatorius.

70. In its principle, which was apparently that of preserving obedience, the prohibitory system might seem to have untouched many great walks of learning and

Its effects.

[1] Ranke, ii. 330.

[2] Schelhorn, Amœnit. Liter., vii. 98; viii. 342 and 485. The two dissertations on prohibited books here quoted are full of curious information.

science. It is, of course, manifest that it fell with but an oblique blow upon common literature. Yet, as a few words or sentences were sufficient to elicit a sentence of condemnation, often issued with little reflection, it was difficult for any author to be fully secure; and this inspired so much apprehension into printers, that they became unwilling to incur the hazard of an obnoxious trade. These occupations, says Galluzzi, which had begun to prosper at Florence, never recovered the wound inflicted by the severe regulations of Paul IV. and Pius V.[1] The art retired to Switzerland and Germany. The booksellers were at the mercy of an Inquisition, which every day contrived new methods of harassing them. From an interdiction of the sale of certain prohibited books, the church proceeded to forbid that of all which were not expressly permitted. The Giunti, a firm not so eminent as it had been in the early part of the century, but still the honor of Florence, remonstrated in vain. It seems probable, however, that after the death of Pius V., one of the most rigorous and bigoted pontiffs that ever filled the chair, some degree of relaxation took place.

71. The restraints on the printing and sale of books in England, though not so overpowering as in Italy, must have stood in the way of useful knowledge under Elizabeth. The Stationers' Company, founded in 1555, obtained its monopoly at the price of severe restrictions. The Star Chamber looked vigilantly at the dangerous engine it was compelled to tolerate. By the regulations it issued in 1585, no press was allowed to be used out of London, except one at Oxford, and another at Cambridge. Nothing was to be printed without allowance of the council; extensive powers both of seizing books and of breaking the presses were given to the officers of the crown.[2] Thus every check was imposed on literature; and it seems unreasonable to dispute that they had some efficacy in restraining its progress, though less, perhaps, than we might in theory expect, because there was always a certain degree of connivance and indulgence. Even the current prohibition of importing Popish books, except for the use of such as the council should permit to use them, must have affected the trade in modern Latin authors beyond the bounds of theology.

Restrictions in England.

72. These restrictions do not seem to have had any mate-

[1] Ist. del Gran Ducato, iii. 442.

[2] Herbert, iii. 1668

rial operation in France, in Germany, or the Low Countries. And they certainly tended very considerably to keep up the usage of writing in Latin; or rather, perhaps, it may be said, they were less rigorously urged in those countries, because Latin continued to be the customary tongue of scholars. We have seen that great license was used in political writings in that language. The power of reading Latin was certainly so diffused, that no secrecy could be affected by writing it; yet it seemed to be a voluntary abstaining from an appeal to the passions of the multitude, and passed better without censure than the same sense in a modern dress.

Latin more employed on this account.

73. The influence of literature on the public mind was already very considerable. All kinds of reading had become deeper and more diffused. Pedantry is the usual, perhaps the inevitable, consequence of a genuine devotion to learning, not surely in each individual, but in classes and bodies of men. And this was an age of pedants. To quote profusely from ancient writers seemed to be a higher merit than to rival them; they furnished both authority and ornament; they did honor to the modern, who shone in these plumes of other birds with little expense of thought; and sometimes the actual substance of a book is hardly discernible under this exuberance of rich incrustations. Tacitus, Sallust, Cicero, and Seneca (for the Greeks were in comparison but little read), and many of the Latin poets, were the books that directly, or by the secondary means of quotation, had most influence over the public opinion. Nor was it surprising that the reverence for antiquity should be still undiminished; for, though the new literature was yielding abundant crops, no comparison between the ancients and moderns could as yet fairly arise. Montaigne, fearless and independent as he was, gave up altogether the pretensions of the latter; yet no one was more destined to lead the way to that renunciation of the authority of the former which the seventeenth century was to witness. He and Machiavel were the two writers who produced the greatest effect upon this age. Some others, such as Guevara and Castiglione, might be full as much read; but they did not possess enough of original thought to shape the opinions of mankind. And the former two, to whom we may add Rabelais, seem to be the only writers of the sixteenth century, setting aside poets and historians, who are now much read by the world.

Influence of literature.

PART III.

ON THE LITERATURE OF THE FIRST HALF OF THE SEVENTEENTH CENTURY.

CHAPTER I.

HISTORY OF ANCIENT LITERATURE IN EUROPE, FROM 1600 TO 1650

SECTION I.

Decline of merely Philological, especially Greek, Learning — Casaubon — Viger — Editions of Greek and Latin Classics — Critical Writings — Latin Style — Scioppius — Vossius — Successive Periods of Modern Latinists.

1. IN every period of literary history, if we should listen to the complaints of contemporary writers, all learning and science have been verging towards extinction. None remain of the mighty; the race of giants is no more; the lights that have been extinguished burn in no other hands; we have fallen on evil days, when letters are no longer in honor with the world, nor are they cultivated by those who deserve to be honored. Such are the lamentations of many throughout the whole sixteenth century; and with such do Scaliger and Casaubon greet that which opened upon them. Yet the first part of the seventeenth century may be reckoned eminently the learned age rather, however, in a more critical and exact erudition with respect to historical fact, than in what is strictly called philology, as to which we cannot, on the whole, rank this so high as the preceding period. Neither Italy nor Germany maintained its reputation, which, as it has been already mentioned, had begun to wane towards the close of the sixteenth century. The same causes were at work, the same preference of studies very foreign to polite letters, metaphysical philosophy, dogmatic theology, patristic or mediæval ecclesiastical history, or,

Learning of 17th century less philological.

in some countries, the physical sciences, which were rapidly gaining ground. And to these we must add a prevalence of bad taste, even among those who had some pretensions to be reckoned scholars. Lipsius had set an example of abandoning the purest models; and its followers had less sense and taste than himself. They sought obsolete terms from Pacuvius and Plautus; they affected pointed sentences, and a studied conciseness of period, which made their style altogether dry and jejune.[1] The universities, and even the gymnasia, or schools of Germany, grew negligent of all the beauties of language. Latin itself was acquired in a slovenly manner, by help of modern books, which spared the pains of acquiring any subsidiary knowledge of antiquity; and this neglect of the ancient writers in education caused even eminent scholars to write ill, as we perceive in the supplements of Freinshemius to Curtius and Livy.[2]

Popularity of Comenius.

2. A sufficient evidence of this is found in the vast popularity which the writings of Comenius acquired in Germany. This author, a man of much industry, some ingenuity, and little judgment, made himself a temporary reputation by his Orbis Sensualium Pictus, and still more by his Janua Linguarum Reserata; the latter published in 1631. This contains, in 100 chapters subdivided into 1,000 paragraphs, more than 9,300 Latin words, exclusive, of course, of such as recur. The originality of its method consists in weaving all useful words into a series of paragraphs, so that they may be learned in a short time, without the tediousness of a nomenclature. It was also intended to blend a knowledge of things with one of words.[3] The Orbis Sensualium Pictus has the same end. This is what has since been so continually attempted in books of education, that some may be surprised to hear of its originality. No one, however, before Comenius, seems to have thought of this method. It must, unquestionably, have appeared to facilitate the early acquirement of knowledge in a very great degree; and even with reference to language, if a compendious mode of getting at Latin words were the object, the works of Comenius would answer the purpose beyond those of any classical author. In a country where Latin was a living and spoken tongue, as was in some

1 Biogr. Univ., art. "Grævius;" Eichhorn, iii. 1. 320.

2 Eichhorn, 326.

3 Biogr. Univ.

measure the case with Germany, no great strictness in excluding barbarous phrases is either practicable or expedient. But, according to the received principles of philological literature, they are such books as every teacher would keep out of the hands of his pupils. They were, nevertheless, reprinted and translated in many countries; and obtained a general reception, especially in the German Empire and similarly circumstanced kingdoms.[1]

3. The Greek language, meantime, was thought unnecessary; and few, comparatively speaking, continued to prosecute its study. In Italy it can merely be said that there were still professors of it in the universities; but no one Hellenist distinguishes this century. Most of those who published editions of Greek authors in Germany, and they were far from numerous, had been formed in the last age. The decline was progressive: few scholars remained after 1620; and a long blank ensued, until Fabricius and Kuster restored the study of Greek near the end of the century. Even in France and Holland, where many were abundantly learned, and some, as we shall see, accomplished philologers, the Greek language seems to have been either less regarded, or at least less promoted, by eminent scholars, than in the preceding century.[2]

Decline of Greek learning.

4. Casaubon now stood on the pinnacle of critical renown. His Persius in 1605, and his Polybius in 1609, were testimonies to his continued industry in this province.[3] But, with this latter edition, the philological la-

Casaubon.

[1] Baillet, Critiques Grammairiens, part of the Jugemens des Sçavans (whom I cite by the number or paragraph, on account of the different editions), No. 634, quotes Lancelot's remark on the Janua Linguarum, that it requires a better memory than most boys possess to master it, and that commonly the first part is forgotten before the last is learned. It excites disgust in the scholar, because he is always in a new country, every chapter being filled with words he has not seen before; and the successive parts of the book have no connection with one another.

Morhof, though he would absolutely banish the Janua Linguarum from all schools where good Latinity is required, seems to think rather better of the Orbis Sensualium Pictus, as in itself a happy idea; though the delineations are indifferent, and the whole not so well arranged as it might be. Polyhistor., lib. ii. c 4

[2] Scaliger, even in 1602, says: "Quis hodie nescit Græcè? sed quis est doctus Græcè? Non dubito esse aliquot, sed paucos, et quos non novi ne de nomine quidem. Te unum novi et memoriæ avorum et nostri sæculi Græcè doctissimum, qui unus in Græcis præstiteris, quæ post renatas apud nos bonas literas omnes nunquam præstare potuissent." He goes on to speak of himself, as standing next to Casaubon, and the only competent judge of the extent of his learning: "qui de præstantia doctrinæ tuæ certo judicare possit, ego aut unicus sum, aut qui cæteros hac in re magno intervallo vinco." — Scal. Epist., 72.

[3] The translation that Casaubon has here given of Polybius has generally passed for excellent; though some have thought him a better scholar in Greek than in Latin, and consequently not always able to render the sense as well as he conceived it. Baillet, n. 902. Schweig-

bors of Casaubon came to an end. In 1610 he accepted the invitation of James I., who bestowed upon him, though a layman, a prebend in the Church of Canterbury; and as some, perhaps erroneously, have said, another in that of Westminster.[1] He died in England within four years after, having consumed the intermediate time in the defence of his royal patron against the Jesuits, and in writing Animadversions on the Annals of Baronius; works ill suited to his peculiar talent, and in the latter of which he is said to have had but little success. He laments, in his epistles, the want of leisure for completing his labors on Polybius: the king had no taste but for theology, and he found no library in which he could pursue his studies.[2] "I gave up," he says, "at last, with great sorrow, my commentary on Polybius, to which I had devoted so much time; but the good king must be obeyed."[3] Casaubon was the last of the great scholars of the sixteenth century. Joseph Scaliger, who, especially in his recorded conversation, was very sparing of praise, says expressly, "Casaubon is the most learned man now living." It is not impossible that he meant to except himself; which would by no means be unjust, if we take in the whole range of erudition: but, in the exactly critical knowledge of the Greek language, Casaubon had not even a rival in Scaliger.

Viger de Idiotismis.

5. A long period ensued, during which no very considerable progress was made in Greek literature. Few books occur before the year 1650 which have obtained a durable reputation. The best known, and, as I conceive, by far the best of a grammatical nature, is that

hauser praises the annotations, but not without the criticism for which a later editor generally finds room in an earlier. Reiske, he says, had pointed out many errors.

[1] The latter is contradicted by Beloe, Anecdotes of Literature, vol. v. p. 126, on the authority of Le Neve's Fasti Ecclesiæ Anglicanæ.

[2] "Jacent curæ Polybianæ, et fortasse æternum jacebunt, neque enim satis commodus ad illa studia est locus." — Epist. 705. "Plura adderem, nisi omni librorum præsidio meorum deficerer. Quare etiam de commentariis Polybianis noli meminisse, quando rationes priorum meorum studiorum hoc iter mirificè conturbavit, ut vix sine suspirio ejus incepti possim meminisse, quod tot vigiliis mihi constitit. Sed neque adest mea bibliotheca, neque ea studia multum sunt ad gustum illius, cujus solius, quamdiu hic sum futurus, habenda mihi ratio." — Ep. 704 (Feb. 1611). "Rex optimus atque ευσεβεστατος rebus theologicis ita delectatur, ut aliis curis literariis non multum operæ impendat." — Ep. 872. "Ego quid hic agam, si cupis scire, hoc unum respondebo, omnia priora studia mea funditus interiisse. Nam maximus rex et liberalissimus unico genere literarum sic capitur, ut suum et suorum ingenia in illo detineat." — Ep. 753.

[3] "Decessi gemens a Polybiano commentario, quem tot laboribus concinnaveram; sed regi optimo parendum erat." Ep. 854. Feb., 1613.

of Viger de Idiotismis, Præcipuis Græcæ Linguæ, which Hoogeveen and Zeunius successively enlarged in the last century. Viger was a Jesuit of Rouen; and the first edition was in 1632. It contains, even as it came from the author, many valuable criticisms; and its usefulness to a Greek scholar is acknowledged. But, in order to determine the place of Viger among grammarians, we should ascertain by comparison with preceding works, especially the Thesaurus of Stephens, for how much he is indebted to their labors. He would probably, after all deductions, appear to merit great praise. His arrangement is more clear, and his knowledge of syntax more comprehensive, than that of Caninius or any other earlier writer; but his notions are not unfrequently imperfect or erroneous, as the succeeding editors have pointed out. In common with many of the older grammarians, he fancied a difference of sense between the two aorists, wherein even Zeunius has followed him.[1]

Weller's Greek Grammar.

6. In a much lower rank, we may, perhaps, next place Weller, author of a Greek grammar, published in 1638, of which its later editor, Fischer, says that it has always stood in high repute as a school-book, and been frequently reprinted; meaning, doubtless, in Germany. There is nothing striking in Weller's grammar: it may deserve praise for clearness and brevity; but in Vergara, Caninius, and Sylburgius there is much more instruction for those who are not merely schoolboys. What is most remarkable is, that Weller claims as his own the reduction of the declensions to three, and of the conjugations to one; which, as has been seen in another place,[2] is found in the grammar of Sylburgius, and is probably due to Ramus. This is rather a piece of effrontery, as he could scarcely have lighted by coincidence on both these innovations. Weller has given no syntax: what is added in Fisher's edition is by Lambert Bos.

Labbe and others.

7. Philip Labbe, a French Jesuit, was a laborious compiler, among whose numerous works not a few relate to the grammar of the Greek language. He had, says Niceron, a wonderful talent in multiplying titlepages: we

[1] An earlier treatise on Greek particles by Devarius, a Greek of the Ionian Islands, might have been mentioned in the last period. It was republished by Reusmann, who calls Devarius, "homo olim haud ignobilis, at hodie pæne neglectus." He is thought too subtle in grammar, but seems to have been an excellent scholar. I do not perceive that Viger has borrowed from him.

[2] Vol. ii. p. 29.

have fifteen or sixteen grammatical treatises from him, which might have been comprised in two or three ordinary volumes. Labbe's Regulæ Accentuum, published in 1635, was once, I believe, of some repute; but he has little or nothing of his own.[1] The Greek grammars published in this age by Alexander Scot and others are ill digested, according to Lancelot, without order or principle, and full of useless and perplexing things;[2] and that of Vossius, in 1642, which is only an improved edition of Clenardus, appears to contain little which is not taken from others.[3] Erasmus Schmidt is said by Eichhorn to be author of a valuable work on Greek dialects:[4] George Pasor is better known by his writings on the Hellenistic dialect, or that of the Septuagint and New Testament.

Salmasius de Lingua Hellenistica.

Salmasius, in his Commentarius de Hellenistica (Leyden, 1643), has gone very largely into this subject. This, he says, is a question lately agitated, whether there be a peculiar dialect of the Greek Scriptures; for, in the last age, the very name of Hellenistic was unknown to scholars. It is not above half a century old. It was supposed to be a Hebrew idiom in Greek words; which, as he argues elaborately and with great learning, is not sufficient to constitute a distinct dialect, none of the ancients having ever mentioned one by this name. This is evidently much of a verbal dispute, since no one would apply the word to the scriptural Greek in the same sense that he does to the Doric and Attic. Salmasius lays down two essential characteristics of a dialect: one, that it should be spoken by people of a certain locality; another, that it should be distinguishable by single words, not merely by idiom. A profusion of learning is scattered all round, but not pedantically or impertinently; and this seems a very useful book in Greek or Latin philology. He may perhaps be thought to underrate the peculiarities of language in the Old and New Testament, as if they were merely such as passed current among the contemporary Greeks. The second part of this Commentary relates to the Greek dialects generally, without reference to the Hellenistic. He denies the name to what is usually called the common dialect, spoken, or at least written, by the Greeks in general after the time of Alexander. This also is, of course, a question of words: perhaps Salmasius

[1] Niceron, vol. xxv.
[2] Baillet, n. 706.
[3] Baillet, n. 711.
[4] Geschichte der Cultur, iii. 325.

used a more convenient phraseology than what is often met with in grammarians.

8. Editions of Greek classics are not so numerous as in the former period. The Pindar of Erasmus Schmidt in 1614, and the Aristotle of Duval in 1619, may be mentioned: the latter is still in request, as a convenient and complete edition. Meursius was reckoned a good critical scholar, but his works as an editor are not very important. The chief monument of his philological erudition is the Lexicon Græco-Barbarum, a glossary of the Greek of the Lower Empire. But no edition of a Greek author published in the first part of the seventeenth century is superior, at least in magnificence, to that of Chrysostom by Sir Henry Savile. This came forth, in 1612, from a press established at Eton by himself, provost of that college. He had procured types and pressmen in Holland, and three years had been employed in printing the eight volumes of this great work; one which, both in splendor of execution and in the erudition displayed in it by Savile, who had collected several manuscripts of Chrysostom, leaves immeasurably behind it every earlier production of the English press. The expense, which is said to have been eight thousand pounds, was wholly defrayed by himself; and the tardy sale of so voluminous a work could not have reimbursed the cost.[1] Another edition, in fact, by a Jesuit, Fronto Ducæus (Fronton le Duc), was published at Paris within two years afterwards; having the advantage of a Latin translation, which Savile had imprudently waived. It has even been imputed to Ducæus, that, having procured the sheets of Savile's edition from the pressmen while it was under their hands, he printed his own without alteration; but this seems an apocryphal story.[2] Savile had the assist-

Greek editions: Savile's Chrysostom.

[1] Beloe's Anecdotes of Literature, vol. v. p. 103. The copies sold for £9 each, a sum equal in command of commodities to nearly £30 at present, and, from the relative wealth of the country, to considerably more. What wonder that the sale was slow? Fuller, however, tells us, that when he wrote, almost half a century afterwards, the book was become scarce. "Chrysostomus," says Casaubon, "a Savilio editur privata impensa, animo regio." — Ep. 738 (*apud* Beloe). The principal assistants of Savile were Matthew Bust, Thomas Allen, and especially Richard Montagu, afterwards celebrated in our ecclesiastical history as Bishop of Chichester, who is said to have corrected the text before it went to the press. As this is the first work of learning, on a great scale, published in England, it deserves the particular commemoration of those to whom we owe it.

[2] It is told by Fuller, and I do not know that it has any independent confirmation. Savile himself says of Fronto Ducæus, "Vir doctissimus, et cui Chrysostomus noster plurimum debet." Fuller, it may be observed, says, that the Parisian edition followed Savile's "in a few months," whereas the time was two years; and, as Brunet (Manuel du Libraire) justly observes, there is no appa-

ance, in revising the text, of the most learned co-adjutors he could find in England.

Greek learning in England.

9. A very few more Greek books were printed at Eton soon afterwards; and, though that press soon ceased, some editions of Greek authors, generally for schools, appeared in England before 1650. One of these, the Poetæ Minores of Winterton, is best known, and has sometimes been reprinted: it appears to differ little, if at all, from the collection printed by Crispin in 1570, and of which there had been many subsequent editions, with the title Vetustissimorum Autorum Georgica, Bucolica et Gnomonica: but the text, though still very corrupt, has been amended; and a few notes, generally relating to prosody, have been subjoined. The Greek language, however, was now much studied;[1] the age of James and Charles was truly learned; our writers are prodigal of an abundant erudition, which embraces a far wider range of authors than are now read; the philosophers of every class, the poets, the historians, and orators of Greece, to whom few comparatively had paid regard in the days of Elizabeth, seem as familiar to the miscellaneous writers of her next successors as the fathers of the church are to the theologians. A few, like Jeremy Taylor, are equally copious in their libations from both streams. But, though thus deeply read in ancient learning, our old scholars were not very critical in philology.

Latin editions: Torrentius.

10. In Latin criticism, the pretensions of the seventeenth century are far more considerable than in Greek. The first remarkable edition, however, that of Horace by Torrentius, a Belgian ecclesiastic, though it

rent necessity to suppose an unfair communication of the sheets, even if the text should be proved to be copied.

[1] It might appear, at first sight, that Casaubon intended to send his son Meric to Holland, under the care of Heinsius, because he could not get a good classical education in England. "Cupio in Græcis, Latinis, et Hebraicis literis ipsum serio exerceri. Hoc in Anglia posse fieri sperare non possumus; nam hic locupletissima sunt collegia, sed quorum ratio toto genere diversa est ab institutis omnium aliorum collegiorum." — Ep. 962 (1614). But possibly he meant, that, on account of his son's foreign birth, he could not be admitted on the foundation of English colleges, though the words do not clearly express this. At the king's command, however, Meric was sent to Oxford. One of Casaubon's sons went to Eton school; "Literis dat operam in gymnasio Etoniensi." — Ep. 737 (quoted in Beloe's Anecdotes: I had overlooked the passage). Theological learning, in the reign of James, opposed polite letters and philology. "Est in Anglia," says Casaubon, "theologorum ingens copia; eo enim fere omnes studia sua referunt." — Ep. 762. "Venio ex Anglia (Grotius writes in 1613), literarum ibi tenuis est merces; theologi regnant, leguleii rem faciunt; unus ferme Casaubonus habet fortunam satis faventem, sed, ut ipse judicat, minus certam. Ne huic quidem locus fuisset in Anglia ut literatori, theologum induere debuit." — Epist. Grot., p. 751.

appeared in 1602, being posthumous, belongs strictly to the preceding age. It has been said that Dacier borrowed much for his own notes from this editor; but Horace was so profusely illustrated in the sixteenth century, that little has been left for later critics except to tamper, as they have largely done, with his text. This period is not generally conspicuous for editions of Latin authors; but some names of high repute in grammatical and critical lore belong to it.

11. Gruter, a native of Antwerp, who became a professor in several German universities, and finally in that of Heidelberg, might have been mentioned in our history of the sixteenth century, before the expiration of which some of his critical labors had been accomplished. Many more belong to the first twenty years of the present. No more diligent and indefatigable critic ever toiled in that quarry. His Suspiciones, an early work, in which he has explained and amended miscellaneous passages, his Annotations on the Senecas, on Martial, on Statius, on the Roman historians, as well as another more celebrated compilation which we shall have soon to mention, bear witness to his immense industry. In Greek he did comparatively but little; yet he is counted among good scholars in that language. All others of his time, it has been said, appear mere drones in comparison with him.[1] Scaliger, indeed, though on intimate terms with Gruter, in one of his usual fits of spleen, charges him with a tasteless indifference to the real merit of the writers whom he explained, one being as good as another for his purpose, which was only to produce a book.[2] In this art, Gruter was so perfect that he never failed to publish one every year, and sometimes every month.[3] His eulogists have given him credit for acuteness and judgment, and even for elegance and an agreeable variety; but he seems not to have preserved much repute except for his laborious erudition.

Gruter

12. Daniel Heinsius, conspicuous as secretary of the synod of Dort, and a Latin poet of distinguished name, was also among the first philologers of his age. Many editions of Greek and Latin writers, or annotations upon them, Theocritus, Hesiod, Maximus Tyrius, Aristotle, Horace, Terence, Silius, Ovid, attest his critical skill. He is praised for

Heinsius.

1 Baillet, n. 483; Bayle; Niceron, vol. ix.

2 "Non curat utrum charta sit cacata, modo libros multos excudat." — Scalig. Secunda.

3 Bayle, art. "Gruter," note I.

a judicious reserve in criticism, avoiding the trifles by which many scholars had wearied their readers, and attending only to what really demanded the aid of a critic, as being corrupt or obscure. His learning was very extensive and profound, so that, in the panegyrical tone of the times, he is set above all the living, and almost above all the dead.[1]

Grotius.

13. Grotius contributed much to ancient philology. His editions of Aratus, Stobæus, the fragments of the lost Greek dramas, Lucan and Tacitus, are but a part of those which he published. In the power of illustrating a writer by parallel or resembling passages from others, his taste and fondness for poetry, as much as his vast erudition, have made him remarkable. In mere critical skill, he was not quite so great a master of the Greek as of the Latin language, nor was he equal to restoring the text of the dramatic poets.

Rutgersius; Reinesius; Barthius.

14. The Variæ Lectiones of Rutgersius, in 1618, whose premature death cut off a brilliant promise of erudition, are in six books, almost entirely devoted to emendation of the text, in such a miscellaneous and desultory series of criticisms as the example of Turnebus and other scholars had rendered usual.[2] Reinesius, a Saxon physician, in 1640, put forth a book with the same title, a thick volume of about 700 pages of multifarious learning, chiefly, but not exclusively, classical. He is more interpretative, and less attentive to restore corrupted texts, than Rutgersius.[3] The Adversaria of Gaspar Barthius are better known. This work is in sixty books, and extends to about 1,500 pages in folio. It is exactly like those of Turnebus and Muretus, an immense repertory of unconnected criticisms and other miscellaneous erudition. The chapters exceed in number the pages, and each chapter contains several articles. There is, however, more connection, alphabetical or otherwise, than in Turnebus; and they are less exclusively classical, many relating to mediæval and modern writers. The sixtieth book is a comment-

1 Baillet, n. 517.

2 "This work," says Niceron (vol. xxxii.), "is in esteem: the style is neat and polite, the thoughts are just and refined; it has no more quotations than the subject requires."

3 Bayle observes of the writings of Reinesius in general, that "good judges of literature have no sooner read some pages, but they place him above those philologers who have only a good memory; and rank him with critics who go beyond their reading, and know more than books have taught them. The penetration of their understanding makes them draw consequences and form conjectures which lead them to discover hidden treasures. Reinesius was one of these, and made it his chief business to find out what others had not said."

ary on a part of Augustin de Civitate Dei. It is difficult to give a more precise notion of Barthius: he is more *æsthetic* than Turnebus, but less so than Muretus; he explains and corrects fewer intricate texts than the former, but deals more in parallel passages and excursive illustration.[1] Though Greek appears more than in Turnebus, by far the greater part of Barthius's Adversaria relates to Latin, in the proportion of at least fifteen to one. A few small poems are printed from manuscripts for the first time. Barthius, according to Morhof, though he sometimes explains authors very well, is apt to be rash in his alterations, hasty in his judgments, and has too much useless and frivolous matter. Bayle is not more favorable. Barthius published an edition of Statius, and another of Claudian.

Other critics—English.

15. Rigault or Rigaltius, Petit, Thysius, and several more, do honor to France and the Low Countries during this period. Spain, though not strong in classical philology, produced Ramiresius de Prado, whose Πεντηκονταρχος, sive Quinquaginta Militum Ductor, 1612, is but a book of criticism with a quaint title.[2] In Latin literature we can hardly say that England made herself more conspicuous than in Greek. The notes of John Bond on Horace, published in 1606, are properly a work of the age of Elizabeth: the author was long a schoolmaster in that reign. These notes are only little marginal scholia for the use of boys of no great attainments, and in almost every instance, I believe, taken from Lambinus. This edition of Horace, though Antony Wood calls the author a most noted critic and grammarian, has only the merit of giving the observations of another concisely and perspicuously. Thomas Farnaby is called by Baillet one of the best scholiasts, who says hardly any thing useless, and is

[1] The following are the heads of the fourth chapter of the first book, which may serve as a specimen of the Adversaria: — "Ad Victoris Uticensis librum primum notæ et emendationes. Limites. Collimitia. Quantitas. H. Stephanus notatur. Impendere. Totum. Omnimodè. Dextrales. Asta. Francisii Balduini audacia castigatur. Tormenta antiqua. Liguamem Arx Capitis. Memoriæ. Cruciari. Balduinus denuo aliquoties notatur." It is true that all this farrago arises out of one passage in Victor of Utica, and Barthius is far from being so desultory as Turnebus; but 3,000 columns of such notes make but a dictionary without the help of the alphabet. Barthius tells us himself that he had finished two other volumes of Adversaria, besides correcting the first. See the passage in Bayle, note K. But he does not stand on very high ground as a critic, on account of the rapidity with which he wrote; and, for the same reason, has sometimes contradicted himself. Bayle; Baillet, n. 528; Niceron, vol. vii.; Morhof, lib. v. l. 10.

[2] This has been ascribed by some to his master Sanctius, author of the Minerva; Ramirez himself having been thought unequal to such remarks as we find in it. Baillet, n. 527.

very concise.[1] He has left notes on several of the Latin poets. It is possible that the notes are compiled, like those of Bond, from the foreign critics. Farnaby also was a schoolmaster, and schoolmasters do not write for the learned. He has, however, been acknowledged on the Continent for a diligent and learned man. Wood says he was "the chief grammarian, rhetorician, poet, Latinist, and Grecian of his time; and his school was so much frequented, that more churchmen and statesmen issued thence than from any school taught by one man in England."[2]

16. But the greatest in this province of literature was Claude Saumaise, best known in the Latin form Salmasius, whom the general suffrage of his compeers placed at their head. An incredible erudition, so that it was said, what Salmasius did not know was beyond the bounds of knowledge; a memory such as none but those great scholars of former times seem to have possessed; a life passed, naturally enough, in solitary labor, — were sufficient to establish his fame among the learned. His intellectual strength has been more questioned: he wrote, it has been alleged, on many subjects that he did not well understand; and some have reduced his merit to that of a grammatical critic, without altogether rating this so highly as the world has done.[3] Salmasius was very proud, self-confident, disdainful, and has consequently fallen into many errors, and even contradictions, through precipitancy. In his controversy with Milton, for which he was little fitted, he is rather feeble, and glad to escape from the severity of his antagonist by a defence of his own Latinity.[4] The works of Salmasius are numerous, and on very miscellaneous subjects: among the philological, his Annotations on the Historiæ Augustæ Scriptores seem to deserve mention. But the most remarkable, besides the commentary on the Hellenistic Dialect, of which an account has been given, is the Plinianæ Exercitationes, published in 1629. These remarks, nominally on Pliny, are, in the first instance, on Solinus.

Salmasius.

[1] N. 521.

[2] Athenæ Oxonienses, vol. iii.

[3] Baillet, n. 511, is excessively severe on Salmasius; but the homage due to his learning by such an age as that in which he lived cannot be extenuated by the censure of a man like Baillet, of extensive but rather superficial attainments, and open to much prejudice.

[4] Milton began the attack by objecting to the use of *persona* for an individual man; but, in this mistaken criticism, uttered himself the solecism *vapulandum*. See Johnson's Lives of the Poets. This expression had previously been noticed by Vavasseur.

Salmasius tells us that he had spent much time on Pliny; but, finding it beyond the powers of one man to write a commentary on the whole Natural History of that author, he had chosen Solinus, who is a mere compiler from Pliny, and contains nothing from any other source. The Plinianæ Exercitationes is a mass of learning on the geography and natural history of Pliny in more than 900 pages, following the text of the Polyhistor of Solinus.[1]

17. It had been the desire of those who aspired to reputation for taste and eloquence to write well in Latin, the sole language, on this side of the Alps and Pyrenees, to which the capacity of choice and polished expression was conceded. But, when the French tongue was more cultivated and had a criticism of its own, this became the natural instrument of polite writers in France; and the Latin fell to the merely learned, who neglected its beauties. In England it had never been much studied for the purposes of style; and, though neither in Germany nor the Low Countries it was very customary to employ the native language, the current Latin of literature was always careless and often barbarous. Even in Italy, the number of good writers in that language was now very scanty. Two deserve to be commemorated with praise, both historians of the same period. The History and Annals of Grotius, in which he seems to have emulated, with more discretion than some others, the nervous brevity of Tacitus, though not always free from a certain hardness and want of flow, nor equal, consequently, in elegance to some productions of the sixteenth century, may be deemed a monument of vigorous and impressive language. The Decades of Famianus Strada, a Roman Jesuit, contain a history of the Flemish war, not written certainly in imitation of Tacitus, whom the author depreciated, but with more classical spirit than we usually find in that age. Scarcely any Latin, however, of this period is equal to that of Barclay in the Argenis and Euphormio.

Good writers of Latin.

1 "Nemo adeo ut propriam, suumque veluti regnum, sibi criticen vindicatum ivit, ac Claudius Salmasius, qui, quemadmodum nihil unquam scripsit, in quo non insignia multa artis criticæ vestigia deprehendas, ita imprimis, ut auctores cum notis et castigationibus absolutissimis editos taceamus, vasto illo Plinianarum Exercitationum opere, quantum in eo eruditionis genere valeret demonstratum dedit." — Morhof, liv. v. c. 1, § 12. The Jesuits Petavius and Harduin, who did not cordially praise any Protestant, charged this book with passing over real difficulties, while a mass of heterogeneous matter was foisted in. Le Clerc (or La Croze) vindicates Salmasius against some censures of Harduin in Bibl. Univ., vol. iv

His style, though rather diffuse, and more florid than that of the Augustan age, is perhaps better suited to his subjects, and reminds us of Petronius Arbiter, who was probably his model.

Scioppius.

18. Of the grammatical critics, whose attention was solely turned to the purity of Latin style, two are conspicuous, — Gaspar Scioppius and Gerard Vossius. The first, one of those restless and angry spirits whose hand is against all the world, lived a long life of controversy and satire. His productions, as enumerated by Niceron, mostly anonymous, are about one hundred; twenty-seven of which, according to another list, are grammatical.[1] The Protestants whom he had abandoned, and the Jesuits whom he would not join, are equally the objects of his anger. In literature he is celebrated for the bitterness of his attacks on Cicero, whom he spared as little as he did his own contemporaries. But Scioppius was an admirable master of the Latin language.

His Philosophical Grammar.

All that is remembered of his multifarious publications relates to this. We owe to him a much improved edition of the Minerva of Sanctius. His own Grammatica Philosophica (Milan, 1628), notwithstanding its title, has no pretensions to be called any thing more than an ordinary Latin grammar. In this I observed nothing remarkable but that he denies the gerund and supine to be parts of the verb, considering the first as passive participles, and the second as nouns substantive.

His Infamia Famiani.

19. The Infamia Famiani of Scioppius was written against Famianus Strada, whom he hated both as a Jesuit, and as one celebrated for the beauty of his style. This book serves to show how far those who wrote with some eloquence, as Strada certainly did, fell short of classical purity. The faults pointed out are often very obvious to those who have used good dictionaries. Scioppius is, however, so fastidious as to reject words employed by Seneca, Tacitus, and even Phædrus, as of the silver age; and sometimes, probably, is wrong in his dogmatic assertion of a negative, that no good authority can be found for them.

Judicium de Stylo Historico.

20. But his most considerable work is one called Judicium de Stylo Historico, subjoined to the last, and published after his death in 1650. This treatise con-

1 Niceron, vol. xxxv ; Biogr. Univ.

sists chiefly of attacks on the Latin style of Thuanus, Lipsius, Casaubon, and other recent authors; but, in the course of it, we find the remarks of a subtle and severe observer on the ancients themselves. The *silver* age he dates from the latter years of Augustus, placing even Ovid within it. The *brazen* he carries up to Vespasian. In the silver period, he finds many single words as well as phrases not agreeable to the usage of more ancient authors. As to the moderns, the Transalpine writers, he says (speaking as an Italian), are always deficient in purity; they mingle the phraseology of different ages as preposterously as if they were to write Greek in a confusion of dialects; they affect obscurity, a broken structure of periods, a studied use of equivocal terms. This is particularly perceived in the school of Lipsius, whose own faults, however, are redeemed by many beauties even of style.[1] The Italians, on the contrary, he proceeds to say, read nothing but what is worthy of imitation, and shun every

[1] "Transalpinis hominibus ex quotidiano Latini sermonis inter ipsos usu, multa sive barbaræ, sive plebeiæ ac deterioris notæ, sic adhærescere solent, ut postea cum stylum arripuere, de Latinitate eorum dubitare nequaquam iis in mentem veniat. Inde fit ut scripta eorum plerumque minus puritatis habeant, quamvis gratia et venustas in iis minimè desideretur. Nam hæc natura duce melius fiebant, quam arte aut studio. Accedit alia causa cur non æquè pura sit multorum Transalpinorum oratio, quod nullo ætatis discrimine ac delectu in autorum lectione versantur, et ex omnium commixtione varium quoddam ac multiforme pro suo quisque ingenio dicendi genus effingunt, contempto hoc Fabii monito: 'Diu non nisi optimus quisque et qui credentem sibi minime fallat, legendus est, sed diligenter ac pæne ad scribendi solicitudinem; nec per partes modo scrutanda omnia, sed perlectus liber utique ex integro resumendus.' Itaque genus illud corruptæ orationis, seu κακοζῆλιας, effugere nequeunt, quod κοινιστηον vocant, quæ est quædam mista ex variarum linguarum ratione oratio, ut si Atticis Dorica, Ionica, Æolica etiam dicta confundas; cui simile est si quis sublimia humilibus, vetera novis, poetica vulgaribus, Sallustiana Tullianis, æneæ et ferreæ ætatis vocabula aureis et argenteis misceat, qui Lipsio deductisque ab eo viris, solennis et jam olim familiaris est morbus. In quibus hoc amplius, verba maxime impropria, comprehensionem obscuram, compositionem fractam, aut in frustula concisam, vocum similium aut ambiguarum puerilem captationem passim animadvertas. Magnis tamen, non nego, virtutibus vitia sua Lipsius redimit, imprimis acumine, venere, salibus (ut excellens viri ingenium ferebat) tum plurimis lectissimis verbis loquendique modis, ex quibus non tam facultatem bene scribendi, ejusque, quod melius est, intellectum ei deesse, quam voluntatem, quo minus rectiora malit, ambitiuscule, plaususque popularis studio præpediri intelligas. Italorum longè dispar ratio. Primum enim non nisi optimum legere et ad imitandum sibi proponere solent; quod judicio quo cæteras nationes omnium consensu superant, imprimis est consentaneum. Deinde nihil non faciunt, ut evitent omnia unde aliquid injucundæ et contaminandæ orationis periculi ostenditur. Latinè igitur nunquam loquuntur, quod fieri vix posse persuasum habeant, quin quotidianus ejus linguæ usus ad instar torrentis lutulentus fluat, et cujusque modi verborum sordes secum rapiat, quæ postea quodam familiaritatis jure sic se scribentibus ingerant, ut etiam diligentissimos fallant, et haud dubie pro Latinis habeantur. Hoc eorum consilium cum non intelligant Transalpini, id eorum inscitiæ perperam assignant. Sic rectè Paulo Manutio usu venit, ut quoniam vix tria verba Latina in familiari sermone proferre poterat, eum Germani complures, qui loquentem audituri ad eum venerunt, vehementer præ se contemnerent. Huic tamen nemo qui sanus sit ad puritatis et elegantiæ Latinæ summam quicquid defuisse dixerit." — p. 65.

expression that can impair the clearness and purity of a sentence. Yet, even in Manutius and in the Jesuit Maffei, he finds instances of barbarism, much more in the French and German scholars of the sixteenth age; expressing contempt upon this account for his old enemy, Joseph Scaliger. Thuanus, he says, is full of modern idioms; a crime not quite unpardonable, when we remember the immensity of his labor, and the greater importance of other objects that he had in view.

Gerard Vossius: De Vitiis Sermonis.

21. Gerard Vossius, a far greater name in general literature than Scioppius, contributed more essentially to these grammatical rules; and to him, perhaps, rather than to any other one man, we may refer the establishment of as much correctness of writing as is attainable in a dead language. Besides several works on rhetoric and poetry, which, as those topics were usually treated in ages of more erudition than taste or philosophy, resolved themselves into philological disquisitions, looking only to the language of the ancient writers, we have several more strictly within that province. The long use of Latin in writings on modern subjects, before the classical authors had been studied, had brought in a host of barbarisms, that even yet were not expelled. His treatise, De Vitiis Sermonis et Glossematis Latino-barbaris, is in nine books: four published in 1645, during the author's life; five, in 1685. The former are by far the most copious. It is a very large collection of words in use among modern writers, for which there is no adequate authority. Of these, many are plainly barbarous, and taken from the writers of the middle ages, or, at best, from those of the fifth and sixth centuries. Few such would be used by any tolerable scholar. He includes some, which, though in themselves good, have a wrong sense given to them. Words, however, occur, concerning which one might be ignorant without discredit, especially before the publication of this treatise, which has been the means of correcting the ordinary dictionaries.

22. In the five posthumous books, which may be mentioned in this place, having probably been written before 1650, we find chiefly what the author had forgotten to notice in the former, or had since observed. But the most valuable part relates to the *falso suspecta*, which fastidious critics have unreasonably rejected, generally because they do not appear

in the Augustan writers. Those whom he calls *Nizoliani verius quam Ciceroniani*, disapproved of all words not found in Cicero.[1] It is curious to perceive, as Vossius shows us, how many apparently obvious words do not occur in Cicero; yet it would be mere affectation to avoid them. This is, perhaps, the best part of Vossius's treatise.

His Aristarchus.

23. We are indebted to Vossius for a still more important work on Grammar, the Aristarchus, sive de Arte Grammatica, which first appeared in 1635. This is in seven books: the first treats of grammar in general, and especially of the alphabet; the second, of syllables, under which head he dwells at great length on prosody;[2] the third (which, with all the following, is separately entitled De Vocum Analogia), of words generally, and of the genders, numbers, and cases of nouns. The same subject occupies the fourth book. In the fifth, he investigates verbs; and in the sixth, the remaining parts of speech. The last book relates to syntax. This work is full of miscellaneous observations, placed for the most part alphabetically under each chapter. It has been said that Vossius has borrowed almost every thing in this treatise from Sanctius and Scioppius. If this be true, we must accuse him of unfairness; for he never mentions the Minerva. But the edition of this grammar by Scioppius was not published till after the death of Vossius. Salmasius extolled that of the latter above all which had been published.[3]

Progress of Latin style.

24. In later times, the ambition of writing Latin with accuracy and elegance has so universally declined, that the diligence of Scioppius and Vossius has become hardly valuable except to schoolmasters. It is, however, an art not contemptible, either in respect to the taste and discernment for which it gives scope in composition, or for the

[1] Paulus Manutius scrupled to use words on the authority of Cicero's correspondents, such as Cælius or Pollio; a ridiculous affectation, especially when we observe what Vossius has pointed out, that many common words do not occur in Cicero. It is amazing to see the objections of these Ciceronian critics.

[2] In this we find Vossius aware of the rule in Terentianus Maurus, but brought to light by Dawes, and now familiar, that a final vowel is rarely short before a word beginning with *s* and a mute consonant.

[3] "Tuum de grammatica à te accepi exactissimum in hoc genere opus, ac cui nullum priorum aut prisci ævi aut nostri possit comparari." — Apud Blount in Vossio. Daunou says of the grammatical and rhetorical writings of Vossius, "Ces livres se recommandent par l'exactitude, par la méthode, par une littérature très-étendue. Gibert en convient, mais il trouve de la prolixité. D'autres pourraient n'y voir qu'une instruction sérieuse, souvent austère, et presque toujours profitable." — Biogr. Univ.

enhanced pleasure it reflects on the pages of ancient writers. We may distinguish several successive periods in its cultivation since the first revival of letters. If we begin with Petrarch, since before his time there was no continuous imitation of classical models, the first period will comprise those who desired much, but reached little, — the writers of the fourteenth and fifteenth centuries, destitute of sufficient aids, and generally incapable of clearly discriminating the pure from the barbarous in Latin. A better era may be dated from Politian; the ancients were now fully known, and studied with intense labor; the graces of style were frequently caught, yet something was still wanting to its purity and elegance. At the end of a series of improvements, a line marked by Bembus, Sadolet, and Longolius, we arrive at a third period, which we may call that of Paulus Manutius, the golden age of modern Latinity. The diligence in lexicography of Robert Stephens, of Nizolius, of Manutius himself, and the philological treatises of their times, gave a much greater nicety of expression; while the enthusiasm with which some of the best writers emulated the ancients inspired them with a sympathetic eloquence and grace. But towards the end of the century, when Manutius and Muretus and Maphæus, and others of that school, had been removed by death, an age of worse taste and perhaps of more negligence in grammar came on, yet one of great scholars and of men powerful even in language, — the age of Lipsius, of Scaliger, of Grotius. This may be called the fourth period; and in this apparently the purity of the language, as well as its beauty, rather declined. Finally, the publications of Scioppius and Vossius mark the beginning of another period, which we may consider as lasting to the present day. Grammatical criticism had nearly reached the point at which it now stands; the additions, at least, which later philologers — Perizonius, Burman, Bentley, and many others — have made, though by no means inconsiderable, seem hardly sufficient to constitute a distinct period, even if we could refer them properly to any single epoch. And the praise of eloquent composition has been so little sought, after the close of the years passed in education, or attained only in short and occasional writings which have left no durable reputation behind, that the Latin language may be said, for this purpose, to have silently expired in the regions of polite literature.

SECTION II.

Antiquities of Rome and Greece — Gruter — Meursius — Chronology.

25. THE antiquities of Greece and Rome, though they did not occupy so great a relative space in the literature of this period as of the sixteenth century, were, from the general increase of erudition, not less frequently the subject of books than before. This field, indeed, is so vast, that its harvest had in many parts been scarcely touched, and in others very imperfectly gathered by those we have already commemorated, — the Sigonii, the Manutii, the Lipsii, and their fellow-laborers in ancient learning. The present century opened with a great work, the Corpus Inscriptionum, by Gruter. A few endeavors had long before been made[1] to collect the ancient inscriptions, of which the countries once Roman, and especially Italy, were full. The best work hitherto was by Martin Smetius of Bruges, after whose death his collection of inscriptions was published at Leyden in 1588, under the superintendence of Dousa and Lipsius.

Gruter's collection of inscriptions.

26. Scaliger first excited his friend Gruter to undertake the task of giving an enlarged edition of Smetius.[2] He made the index for this himself, devoting the labor of the entire morning for ten months (*a summo mane ad tempus cœnæ*) to an occupation from which so little glory could accrue. "Who," says Burman, "would not admire the liberal erudition and unpretending modesty of the learned of that age, who, worn as they were by those long and weary labors, of which they freely complain in their correspondence with each other, though they knew that such occupations as these could gain for them no better name than that of common clerks or mere drudges, yet hesitated not to abandon for the advantage of the public those pursuits which a higher fame might be expected to reward? Who in these times would imitate the generosity of Scaliger, who, when he might have ascribed to himself this addition to the work of Smetius,

Assisted by Scaliger.

[1] See vol. i., p. 331.

[2] Burman in Præfatione ad Gruteri Corpus Inscript. Several of Scaliger's epistles prove this, especially the 405th, addressed to Gruter.

gave away his own right to Gruter, and declined to let his name be prefixed either to the index which he had wholly compiled, or to the many observations by which he corrects and explains the inscriptions, and desired, in recompense for the industry of Gruter, that he alone should pass with posterity as the author of the work?"[1] Gruter, it is observed by Le Clerc, has committed many faults; he often repeats the same inscriptions, and still more frequently has printed them from erroneous copies; his quotations from authors, in whom inscriptions are found, sometimes want exactness; finally, for which he could not well be answerable, a vast many have since been brought to light.[2] In consequence of the publication of Gruter's Inscriptions, the learned began with incredible zeal to examine old marbles for inscriptions, and to insert them in any work that had reference to antiquity. Reinesius collected as many as make a respectable supplement.[3] But a sort of era in lapidary learning was made, in 1629, by Selden's description of the marbles brought by the Earl of Arundel from Greece, and which now belong to the University of Oxford. These contain a chronology of the early times of Greece, on which great reliance has often been placed; though their antiquity is not accounted very high in comparison with those times.

Works on Roman antiquity.

27. The Jesuit Donati published, in 1633, Roma Vetus et Nova, which is not only much superior to any thing previously written on the antiquities of the city, but is preferred by some competent judges to the later and more known work of Nardini. Both these will be found, with others of an earlier date, in the third and fourth volumes of Grævius. The tenth volume of the same collection contains a translation from the History of the Great Roads of the Roman Empire, published in French by Nicolas Bergier in 1622; ill arranged, it has been said, and diffuse, according to the custom of his age, but inferior, Grævius declares, in variety of learning, to no one work that he has inserted in his numerous volumes. Guther, whose treatise on the pontifical law of Rome appears in the fifth volume,

[1] Burman, p. 6.

[2] Bibl. Choisie, vol. xiv. p. 51. Burman, *ubi supra*, gives a strange reason for reprinting Gruter's Inscriptions with all their blemishes, even the repetitions; namely, that it was convenient to preserve the number of pages which had been so continually referred to in all learned works; the simple contrivance of keeping the original numeration in the margin not having occurred to him.

[3] Burman, *ubi supra*.

was, says the editor, "a man of various and extended reading, who had made extracts from every class of writers, but had not always digested his learning or weighed what he wrote. Hence, much has been found open to criticism in his writings, and there remains a sufficient harvest of the same kind for any one who should care to undertake it." The best work on Roman dress is by Octavius Ferrarius, published partly in 1642, partly in 1654. This has been called superficial by Spanheim; but Grævius, and several other men of learning, bestow more praise.[1] The Isiac tablet, covered with emblems of Egyptian antiquity, was illustrated by Pignoria, in a work bearing different titles in the successive editions from 1605; and his explanations are still considered probable. Pignoria's other writings were also in high esteem with the antiquaries.[2] It would be tedious to enumerate the less important productions of this kind. A minute and scrupulous criticism, it has been said, distinguished the antiquaries of the seventeenth century. Without, perhaps, the comprehensive views of Sigonius and Panvinius, they were more severely exact. Hence forgery and falsehood stood a much worse chance of success than before. Annius of Viterbo had deceived half the scholars of the preceding age. But when Inghirami, in 1637, published his Etruscarum Antiquitatum Fragmenta, monuments of Etruscan antiquity, which he pretended to have discovered at Volterra, the imposture was speedily detected.[3]

Geography of Cluverius.

28. The Germania Antiqua of Cluverius was published in 1616; and his Italia Antiqua, in 1624. These form a sort of epoch in ancient geography. The latter, especially, has ever since been the great repertory of classical illustration on this subject. Cluverius, however, though a man of acknowledged ability and erudition, has been thought too bold an innovator in his Germany, and to have laid down much on his own conjecture.[4]

Meursius.

29. Meursius, a native of Holland, began when very young, soon after the commencement of the century, those indefatigable labors on Grecian antiquity, by which he became to Athens and all Hellas what Sigonius had been to Rome and Italy. Niceron has given a list of his publi-

[1] Niceron, v. 80; Tiraboschi, xi. 300.

[2] Niceron, vol. xxi.; Biogr. Univ.

[3] Salfi (Continuation de Ginguéné), xi.

[4] Blount; Niceron, vol. xxi.; Biogr. Univ.

cations, sixty-seven in number, including some editions of ancient writers, but, for the most part, confined to illustrations of Greek usages; some also treat of Roman. The Græcia feriata, on festivals and games; the Orchestra, on dancing; the Eleusinia, on that deeply interesting, and in his time almost untouched subject, the ancient mysteries, — are collected in the works of this very learned person, or scattered through the Thesaurus Antiquitatum Græcarum of Gronovius. "Meursius," says his editor, "was the true and legitimate mystagogue to the sanctuaries of Greece." But his peculiar attention was justly shown to "the eye of Greece," Athens. Nothing that bore on her history, her laws and government, her manners and literature, was left by him. The various titles of his works seem almost to exhaust Athenian antiquity: De Populis Atticæ — Athenæ Atticæ — Cecropia — Regnum Atticum — Archontes Athenienses — Pisistratus — Fortuna Attica — Atticarum Lectionum Libri IV. — Piræeus — Themis Attica — Solon — Areopagus — Panathenæa — Eleusinia — Theseus — Æschylus — Sophocles et Euripides. It is manifest that all later learning must have been built upon his foundations. No one was equal to Meursius in this province; but the second place is perhaps due to Ubbo Emmius, professor of Greek at Groningen, for his Vetus Græcia Illustrata, 1626. The facilities of elucidating the topography of that country were by no means such as Cluverius had found for Italy; and, in fact, little was done in respect to local investigation in order to establish a good ancient geography till recent times. Samuel Petit, a man placed by some in the very first list of the learned, published, in 1635, a commentary on the Athenian laws, which is still the chief authority on that subject.

Ubbo Emmius.

30. In an age so peculiarly learned as this part of the seventeenth century, it will be readily concluded that many books must have a relation to the extensive subject of this section; though the stream of erudition had taken rather a different course, and watered the provinces of ecclesiastical and mediæval still more than those of heathen antiquity. But we can only select one or two which treat of chronology, and that chiefly because we have already given a place to the work of Scaliger.

31. Lydiat was the first who, in a small treatise on the various calendars, 1605, presumed in several respects to

differ from that of the dictator of literature. He is, in consequence, reviled in Scaliger's Epistles as the most stupid and ignorant of the human race, a portentous birth of England, or at best an ass and a beetle, whom it is below the dignity of the author to answer.[1] Lydiat was, however, esteemed a man of deep learning, and did not flinch from the contest. His Emendatio Temporum, published in 1609, is a more general censure of the Scaligerian chronology; but it is rather a short work for the extent of the subject. A German, Seth Calvisius, on the other hand, is extolled to the skies by Scaliger for a chronology founded on his own principles. These are applied in it to the whole series of events, and thus Calvisius may be said to have made an epoch in historical literature. He made more use of eclipses than any preceding writer; and his dates are reckoned as accurate in modern as in ancient history.[2]

Chronology of Lydiat. Calvisius.

32. Scaliger, nearly twenty years after his death, was assailed by an adversary whom he could not have thought it unworthy of his name to repel. Petau, or Petavius, a Jesuit of uncommon learning, devoted the whole of the first of two large volumes, entitled Doctrina Temporum, 1627, to a censure of the famous work De Emendatione Temporum. This volume is divided into eight books: the first on the popular year of the Greeks; the second on the lunar; the third on the Egyptian, Persian, and Armenian; the fourth on the solar year; the fifth treats of the correction of the paschal cycle and the calendar; the sixth discusses the principles of the lunar and solar cycles; the seventh is entitled an introduction to computations of various kinds, among which he reckons the Julian period; the eighth is on the true motions of the sun and moon, and on their eclipses. In almost every chapter of the first five books, Scaliger is censured, refuted, reviled. It was a retribution upon his own arrogance; but published thus after his death, with no justice done to his great learning and ability, and scarcely the common terms of respect towards a mighty name, it is impossible

Petavius.

[1] "Ante aliquot dies tibi scripsi, ut scirem ex te quis sit Thomas Lydiat iste, quo monstro nullum portentosius in vestra Anglia natum puto; tanta est inscitia hominis et confidentia. Ne semel quidem illi verum dicere accidit." And again: "Non est similis morio in orbe terrrarum. Paucis asinitatem ejus perstringam ut lector rideat. Nam in tam prodigiosè imperitum scarabæum scribere, neque nostræ dignitatis est, neque otii." — Scalig. Epist. 291. Usher, nevertheless, if we may trust Wood, thought Scaliger worsted by Lydiat. Ath. Oxon., iii. 187.

[2] Blount; Biogr Univ.

not to discern in this work of Petavius both signs of an envious mind, and a partial desire to injure the fame of a distinguished Protestant. His virulence, indeed, against Scaliger becomes almost ridiculous. At the beginning of each of the first five books, he lays it down as a theorem to be demonstrated, that Scaliger is always wrong on the particular subjects to which it relates; and, at the close of each, he repeats the same in geometrical form as having been proved. He does not even give him credit for the invention of the Julian period, though he adopts it himself with much praise, positively asserting that it is borrowed from the Byzantine Greeks.[1] The second volume is in five books, and is dedicated to the historical part of chronology, and the application of the principles laid down before. A third volume, in 1630, relating to the same subjects, though bearing a different title, is generally considered as part of the work. Petavius, in 1633, published an abridgment of his chronological system, entitled Rationarium Temporum, to which he subjoined a table of events down to his own time, which in the larger work had only been carried to the fall of the empire. This abridgment is better known and more generally useful than the former.

Character of this work

33. The merits of Petavius as a chronologer have been differently appreciated. Many, of whom Huet is one, from religious prejudices rejoiced in what they hoped to be a discomfiture of Scaliger, whose arrogance had also made enemies of a large part of the literary world. Even Vossius, after praising Petavius, declares that he is unwilling to decide between men who have done for chronology more than any others.[2] But he has not always been so favorably dealt with. Le Clerc observes, that as

[1] Lib. vii. c. 7.

[2] Vossius *apud* Niceron, xxxvii. 111. "Dionysius Petavius permulta post Scaligerum optime observavit. Sed nolim judicium interponere inter eos, quorum uterque præclare adeo de chronologia meritus est, ut nullis plus hæc scientia debeat. . . . Qui sine affectu ac partium studio conferre volet quæ de temporibus scripsere, conspiciet esse ubi Scaligero major laus debeatur, comperiet quoque ubi longe Petavio malit assentiri; erit etiam ubi ampliandum videatur; imo ubi nec facile veritas à quoquam possit indagari." The chronology of Petavius was animadverted upon by Salmasius with much rudeness, and by several other contemporaries engaged in the same controversy. If we were to believe Baillet, Petavius was not only the most learned of the order of Jesuits, but surpassed Salmasius himself *de plusieurs coudées*. Jugemens des Sçavans, n. 513. But, to judge between giants, we should be a little taller ourselves than most are. Baillet, indeed, quotes Henry Valois for the preference of Petavius to any other of his age; which, in other words, is much the same as to call him the most learned man that ever lived; and Valois was a very competent judge. The words, however, are found in a funeral panegyric.

Scaliger is not very perspicuous, and Petavius has explained the former's opinions before he proceeds to refute them, those who compare the two will have this advantage, that they will understand Scaliger better than before.[1] This is not very complimentary to his opponent. A modern writer of respectable authority gives us no reason to consider him victorious. "Though the great work of Petavius on chronology," says M. St. Martin, "is certainly a very estimable production, it is not less certain that he has in no degree contributed to enlarge the boundaries of the science. The author shows too much anxiety to refute Scaliger, whether right or wrong: his sole aim is to destroy the edifice perhaps too boldly elevated by his adversary. It is not unjust to say, that Petavius has literally done nothing for positive chronology: he has not even determined with accuracy what is most incontestable in this science. Many of the dates which he considers as well established are still subject to great doubt, and might be settled in a very different manner. His work is clear and methodical; and, as it embraces the whole of chronology, it might have become of great authority: but these very qualities have rendered it injurious to the science. He came to arrest the flight, which, through the genius of Scaliger, it was ready to take; nor has it made the least progress ever since: it has produced nothing but conjectures, more or less showy, but with nothing solid and undeniable for their basis."[2]

[1] Bibl. Choisie, ii. 186. A short abstract of the Petavian scheme of chronology will be found in this volume of Le Clerc.

[2] Biogr. Univ., art. "Petavius."

CHAPTER II.

HISTORY OF THEOLOGICAL LITERATURE IN EUROPE, FROM 1600 TO 1650.

Claim of Popes to temporal Power — Father Paul Sarpi — Gradual Decline of Papal Power — Unpopularity of Jesuits — Controversy of Catholics and Protestants — Deference of some of the Latter to Antiquity — Wavering in Casaubon — Still more in Grotius — Calixtus — An opposite School of Theologians — Daillé — Chillingworth — Hales — Rise of the Arminian Controversy — Episcopius — Socinians — Question as to Rights of Magistrates in Religion — Writings of Grotius on this Subject — Question of Religious Toleration — Taylor's Liberty of Prophesying — Theological Critics and Commentators — Sermons of Donne and Taylor — Deistical Writers — English Translation of the Bible.

Temporal supremacy of Rome.

1. The claim of the Roman see to depose sovereigns was like the retractile claws of some animals, which would be liable to injury were they not usually sheathed. If the state of religion in England and France towards the latter part of the sixteenth century required the assertion of these pretended rights, it was not the policy of a court, guided as often by prudence as by zeal or pride, to keep them for ever before the eyes of the world. Clement VIII. wanted not these latter qualities, but they were restrained by the former; and the circumstances in which the new century opened did not demand any direct collision with the civil power. Henry IV. had been received back into the bosom of the church: he was now rather the ally, the favored child, of Rome, than the object of her proscription. Elizabeth, again, was out of the reach of any enemy but death; and much was hoped from the hereditary disposition of her successor. The temporal supremacy would therefore have been left for obscure and unauthorized writers to vindicate, if an unforeseen circumstance had not called out again its most celebrated champion. After the detection of the gunpowder conspiracy, an oath of allegiance was imposed in England, containing a renunciation, in strong terms, of the tenet, that princes excommunicated by the pope might be deposed or murdered by their subjects. None of the English Catholics refused allegiance to James; and most of them,

probably, would have felt little scruple at taking the entire oath, which their arch-priest, Blackwell, had approved. But the see of Rome interfered to censure those who took the oath; and a controversy singularly began with James himself, in his Apology for the Oath of Allegiance. Bellarmin answered, in 1610, under the name of Matthew Tortus; and the duty of defending the royal author was devolved on one of our most learned divines, Lancelot Andrews, who gave to his reply the quaint title, Tortura Torti.[1] But this favorite tenet of the Vatican was as ill fitted to please the Gallican as the English Church. Barclay, a lawyer of Scottish family, had long defended the rights of the crown of France against all opponents. His posthumous treatise on the temporal power of the pope with respect to sovereign princes was published at London in 1609. Bellarmin answered it next year in the ultramontane spirit which he had always breathed: the parliament of Paris forbade the circulation of his reply.[2]

2. Paul V. was a pope imbued with the arrogant spirit of his predecessors, Paul IV. and Pius V.: no one was more prompt to exercise the despotism which the Jesuits were ready to maintain. After some minor disputes with the Italian states, he came, in 1605, to his famous conflict with the republic of Venice, on the very important question of the immunity of ecclesiastics from the civil tribunals. Though he did not absolve the subjects of Venice from their allegiance, he put the state under an interdict, forbidding the celebration of divine offices throughout its territory. The Venetian clergy, except the Jesuits and some other regulars, obeyed the senate rather than the pope. The whole is matter of known history. In the termination of this

Contest with Venice.

[1] Biogr. Britann., art. "Andrews;" Collier's Ecclesiastical History; Butler's English Catholics, vol. i. Matthew Tortus was the almoner of Bellarmin, whose name he thought fit to assume as a very slight disguise.

[2] "Il pretesto," says Father Paul of Bellarmin's book, "è di scrivere contra Barclajo; ma il vero fine si vede esser per ridurre il papa al colmo dell' omnipotente. In questo libro non si tratta altro, che il suddetto argumento, e più di venti cinque volte è replicato, che quando il papa giudica un principe indegno per sua colpa d' aver governo, overo inetto, ò pur conosce, che per il bene della chiese sia cosa utile, lo può privare. Dice più volte, che quando il papa comanda, che non sia ubbidito ad un principe privato da lui, non si può dire, che comandi che principe non sia ubbidito, ma che privata persona, perchè il principe privato dal papa non è più principe. E passa tanto inanzi, che viene à dire, il papa può disponere secondo che giudica ispediente de' tutti i beni di qual si voglia Christiano, ma tutto sarebbe niente, se solo dicesse che tale è la sua opinione; dice, ch' è un articolo della fede catholica ch' è eretico, chi non sente così, e questo con tanta petulantia, che non vi si può aggiungere." — Lettere di Sarpi, 50.

dispute, it has been doubted which party obtained the victory; but, in the ultimate result and effect upon mankind, we cannot, it seems, well doubt that the see of Rome was the loser.[1] Nothing was more worthy of remark, especially in literary history, than the appearance of one great man, Fra Paolo Sarpi, the first who, in modern times and in a Catholic country, shook the fabric not only of Papal despotism, but of ecclesiastical independence and power. For it is to be observed, that, in the Venetian business, the pope was contending for what were called the rights of the church, not for his own supremacy over it. Sarpi was a man of extraordinary genius, learning, and judgment: his physical and anatomical knowledge was such as at least to have caused several great discoveries to be assigned to him;[2] his reasoning was concise and cogent, his style perspicuous and animated. A treatise, Delle Materie Beneficiarie, — in other words, on the rights, revenues, and privileges, in secular matters, of the ecclesiastical order, — is a model in its way. The history is so short and yet so sufficient, the sequence so natural and clear, the proofs so judiciously introduced, that it can never be read without delight, and admiration of the author's skill. And this is more striking to those who have toiled at the verbose books of the sixteenth and seventeenth centuries, where tedious quotations, accumulated, not selected, disguise the argument they are meant to confirm. Except the first book of Machiavel's History of Florence, I do not remember any earlier summary of facts so lucid, and pertinent to the object. That object was, with Father Paul, neither more nor less than to represent the wealth and power of the church as ill-gotten and excessive. The Treatise on Benefices led the way, or rather was the seed thrown into the ground, that ultimately produced the many efforts both of the press and of public authority to break down ecclesiastical privileges.[3]

Father Paul Sarpi.

3. The other works of Sarpi are numerous; but none

[1] Ranke is the best authority on this dispute, as he is on all other matters relating to the Papacy in this age. Vol. ii. p. 324.

[2] He was supposed to have discovered the valves of the veins, the circulation of the blood, the expansion and contraction of the pupil, the variation of the compass. "A quo," says Baptista Porta of Sarpi, "aliqua didicisse non solum fateri non erubescimus, sed gloriamur, cum eo doctiorem, subtiliorem, quotquot adhuc videre contigerit, neminem cognovimus ad encyclopædiam." — Magia Naturalis, lib. vii., *apud* Ranke.

[3] A long analysis of the Treatise on Benefices will be found in Dupin, who does not blame it very much. The treatise is worth reading through, and has been commended by many good judges of history.

require our present attention, except the most celebrated, his History of the Council of Trent. The manuscript of this, having been brought to London by Antonio de Dominis, was there published in 1619, under the name of Pietro Soave Polano, the anagram of Paolo Sarpi Veneto. It was quickly translated into several languages, and became the text-book of Protestantism on the subject. Many incorrectnesses have been pointed out by Pallavicini, who undertook the same task on the side of Rome; but the general credibility of Father Paul's history has rather gained by the ordeal of hostile criticism. Dupin observes, that the long list of errors imputed by Pallavicini, which are chiefly in dates and such trifling matters, make little or no difference as to the substance of Sarpi's history; but that its author is more blamable for a malicious disposition to impute political motives to the members of the council, and idle reasonings which they did not employ.[1] Ranke, who has given this a more minute scrutiny than Dupin could have done, comes nearly to the same result. Sarpi is not a fair, but he is, for those times, a tolerably exact historian. His work exhibits the general excellences of his manner,—freedom from redundancy; a clear, full, agreeable style; a choice of what is most pertinent and interesting in his materials. Much has been disputed about the religious tenets of Father Paul: it appears to me quite out of doubt, both by the tenor of his history, and still more unequivocally, if possible, by some of his letters, that he was entirely hostile to the church, in the usual sense, as well as to the court of Rome; sympathizing in affection, and concurring generally in opinion, with the reformed denomination.[2] But as he continued in the exercise of his functions

History of Council of Trent.

1 Hist. Eccles. Cent. 17.

2 The proofs of this it would be endless to adduce from the history: they strike the eye in every page, though it cannot be expected that he should declare his way of thinking in express terms. Even in his letters he does not this. They were printed, with the date at least of Verona, in 1673. Sully's fall he laments, "having become partial to him on account of his firmness in religion."—Lett. 53. Of the republic of the United Provinces he says, "La nascenza di quale si come Dio ha favorito con grazie inestimabili, così pare che la malizia del diavolo oppugni con tutte le arti."—Lett. 23. After giving an account of one Marsilio, who seems to have been a Protestant, he adds: "Credo se non fosse per ragion di stato, si trovarebbono diversi, che saltarebbono da questo fosso di Roma nella cima dell riforma; ma chi teme una cosa, chi un' altra. Dio però par che goda la più minima parte dei pensieri umani. So ch' ella mi intende senza passar più oltre."—Lett. 81. Feb., 1612. Sarpi speaks with great contempt of James I., who was occupied like a pedant about Vorstius and such matters. "Se il re d' Inghilterra non fosse dottore, si potrebbe sperare qualche bene, e sarebbe un gran principio, perchè Spagna non si può vincere, se non levato il pretesto della religione, ne questo si leverà se non introducendo i reformati nell' Italia. E si il rè sapesse fare, sarebbe facile e in Torino, e quì."—Lett. 88. He

as a Servite monk, and has always passed at Venice more for a saint than a heretic, some of the Gallican writers have not scrupled to make use of his authority, and to extenuate his heterodoxy. There can be no question but that he inflicted a severe wound on the spiritual power.

Gallican liberties. Richer.

4. That power, predominant as it seemed in the beginning of the seventeenth century, met with adversaries besides Sarpi. The French nation, and especially the parliament of Paris, had always vaunted what were called the liberties of the Gallican Church; liberties, however, for which neither the church itself nor the king, the two parties interested, were prone to display much regard. A certain canonist, Richer, published in 1611 a book on ecclesiastical and political power, in which he asserted the government of the church to be a monarchy tempered with aristocracy; that is, that the authority of the pope was limited in some respects by the rights of the bishops. Though this has since become a fundamental principle among the Cisalpine Catholics, it did not suit the high notions of that age; and the bishops were content to sacrifice their rights by joining in the clamor of the Papal party. A synod assembled by Cardinal du Perron, Archbishop of Sens, condemned the book of Richer, who was harassed for the rest of his life by the persecution of those he had sought to defend against a servitude which they seemed to covet. His fame has risen in later times. Dupin concludes a careful analysis of Richer's treatise with a noble panegyric on his character, and style of writing.[1]

wrote, however, a remarkable letter to Casaubon much about this time; hinting at his wish to find an asylum in England, and using rather different language about the king: "In eo, rarum, cumulatæ virtutes principis ac viri. Regum idea est, ad quam forte ante actis sæculis nemo formatus fuit. Si ego ejus protectione dignus essem, nihil mihi deesse putarem ad mortalis vitæ felicitatem. Tu, vir præstantissime, nihil te dignius efficere potes, quam tanto principi mea studia commendare." — Casaubon, Epist. 811. For *mea* in another edition is read *tua;* but the former seems preferable. Casaubon replied, that the king wished Paul to be a light to his own country; but, if any thing should happen, he had written to his ambassador, "ut nulla in re tibi desit."

[The above collection of letters, published at Geneva, with the date of Verona, is said by a late biographer of Sarpi, and one very far from Catholic orthodoxy, to have been most incorrectly printed, and even interpolated, for the purpose of giving a more Protestant cast to his opinions; so that, though in the main his own, they cannot be quoted in evidence. Vita di Sarpi, per Bianchi-Giovini, Bruxelles, 1836, vol. ii. p. 191. But the letter to Casaubon is certainly genuine; and we have no proof of interpolation in those of Geneva, though we may have of incorrectness. The History, however, is sufficient to demonstrate Sarpi's Protestantism. — 1847.]

[1] Hist. Eccles. Cent. 17, l. ii. c. 7; Niceron, vol. xxvii. The Biographie Universelle talks of the republican principles of Richer: it must be in an ecclesiastical sense; for nothing in the book

5. The strength of the ultramontane party in the Gallican Church was Perron, a man of great natural capacity, a prodigious memory, a vast knowledge of ecclesiastical and profane antiquity, a sharp wit, a pure and elegant style, and such readiness in dispute that few cared to engage him.[1] If he did not always reason justly, or upon consistent principles, these are rather failings in the eyes of lovers of truth, than of those, and they are the many, who sympathize with the dexterity and readiness of a partisan. He had been educated as a Protestant; but, like half the learned of that religion, went over from some motive or other to the victorious side. In the conference at Fontainebleau with Du Plessis Mornay, it has been mentioned already that he had a confessed advantage; but victory in debate follows the combatant rather than the cause. The supporters of Gallican liberties were discouraged during the life of this cardinal. He did not explicitly set himself against them, or deny, perhaps, the principles of the Council of Constance; but, by preventing any assertion of them, he prepared the way, as it was hoped at Rome, for a gradual recognition of the whole system of Bellarmin. Perron, however, was neither a Jesuit, nor very favorable to that order. Even so late as 1638, a collection of tracts by the learned brothers Du Puy, on the liberties of the church, was suppressed at the instance of the nuncio, on the pretext, that it had been published without permission. It was reprinted some years afterwards, when the power of Rome had begun to decline.[2]

Perron.

6. Notwithstanding the tone still held by the court of Rome and its numerous partisans, when provoked by any demonstration of resistance, they generally avoided aggressive proceedings, and kept in reserve the tenets which could not be pleasing to any civil government.

Decline of Papal power.

I think, relates to civil politics. Father Paul thought Richer's scheme might lead to something better, but did not highly esteem it. "Quella mistura del governo ecclesiastico di monarchia e aristocrazia mi pare una composizione di oglio e acqua, che non possono mai mischiarsi insieme." — Lettere di Sarpi, 109. Richer entirely denies the infallibility of the Pope in matters of faith, and says there is no authority adduced for it but that of the popes themselves. His work is written on the principles of the Jansenizing Gallicans of the eighteenth century, and probably goes farther than Bossuet, or any one who wished to keep on good terms with Rome, would have openly approved. It is prolix, extending to two volumes 4to. Some account of Richer will be found in Histoire de la Mère et du Fils, ascribed to Mezeray or Richelieu.

[1] Dupin.

[2] Dupin, l. iii. c. 1; Grot. Epist. 1105. "Liber de libertatibus ecclesiæ Gallicanæ ex actis desumptus publicis, quo regis regnique jura contra molitiones pontificias defenduntur, ipsius regis jussu vendi est prohibitus." — See also Epist. 519

We should, doubtless, find many assertions of the temporal authority of the pope by searching into obscure theology during this period: but, after Bellarmin and Perron were withdrawn from the stage, no prominent champions of that cause stood forth; and it was one of which great talents and high station alone could overcome the intrinsic unpopularity. Slowly and silently the power of Rome had much receded before the middle of the seventeenth century. Paul V. was the last of the imperious pontiffs who exacted obedience as sovereigns of Christendom. His successors have had recourse to gentler methods, to a paternal rather than regal authority: they have appealed to the moral sense, but have rarely or never alarmed the fears of their church. The long pontificate of Urban VIII. was a period of transition from strength to weakness. In his first years, this pope was not inactively occupied in the great cause of subduing the Protestant heresy. It has been lately brought to light, that, soon after the accession of Charles I., he had formed a scheme, in conjunction with France and Spain, for conquering and partitioning the British islands: Ireland was to be annexed to the ecclesiastical state, and governed by a viceroy of the holy see.[1] But he afterwards gave up these visionary projects, and limited his ambition to more practicable views of aggrandizement in Italy. It is certain that the temporal principality of the popes has often been an useful diversion for the rest of Europe: the Duchy of Urbino was less in our notions of importance than Germany or Britain; but it was quite as capable of engrossing the thoughts and passions of a pope.

Unpopularity of the Jesuits.

7. The subsidence of Catholic zeal before the middle of this age deserves especially to be noted at a time, when, in various directions, that church is beginning to exalt her voice, if not to rear her head, and we are ostentatiously reminded of the sudden revival of her influence in the sixteenth century. It did undoubtedly then revive; but it is equally manifest that it receded once more. Among the leading causes of this decline in the influence, not only of what are called ultramontane principles, but of the

[1] Ranke, ii. 518. It is not at all probable that France and Spain would have seriously coalesced for any object of this kind: the spoil could not have been safely divided. But the scheme serves to show the ambition, at that time, of the Roman see.

zeal and faith that had attended them, a change as visible, and almost as rapid, as the re-action in favor of them which we have pointed out in the latter part of the sixteenth century, we must reckon the increasing prejudices against the Jesuit order. Their zeal, union, indefatigable devotion to the cause, had made them the most useful of allies, the most formidable of enemies; but in these very qualities were involved the seeds of public hatred and ultimate ruin. Obnoxious to Protestant states for their intrigues; to the lawyers, especially in France, for their bold theories of political power and encroaching spirit; to the Dominicans for the favor they had won,—they had become, long before the close of this period, rather dangerous supporters of the see of Rome.[1] Their fate, in countries where the temper of their order had displayed itself with less restraint, might have led reflecting men to anticipate the consequences of urging too far the patience of mankind by the ambition of an insulated order of priests. In the first part of this century, the Jesuits possessed an extensive influence in Japan, and had re-united the kingdom of Abyssinia to the Roman Church. In the course of a few years more, they were driven out from both: their intriguing ambition had excited an implacable animosity against the church to which they belonged.

Richelieu's care of Gallican liberties.

8. Cardinal Richelieu, though himself a theological writer, took great care to maintain the liberties of the French crown and church. No extravagance of Hildebrandic principles would find countenance under his administration. Their partisans endeavored sometimes to murmur against his ecclesiastical measures: it was darkly rumored that he had a scheme of separating the Catholic Church of France, something in the manner of Henry VIII., from the supremacy of Rome, though not from her creed; and one Hersent published, under the name of Optatus Gallus, a book, so rapidly suppressed as to be of the greatest rarity, the aim of which was to excite the public apprehension of this schism.[2] It was in defence of the Gallican liberties, so far as it was yet prudent to assert them, that

[1] Clement VIII. was tired of the Jesuits, as we are told by Perron, who did not much love them. Perroniana, pp. 286, 288.

[2] Biogr. Univ.; Grot. Epist. 982, 1354. By some other letters of Grotius, it appears that Richelieu tampered with those schemes of reconciling the different religions which were then afloat, and all which went on setting the pope nearly aside. Ruarus intimates the same. Epist Ruar., p. 401.

De Marca was employed to write a treatise, De Concordantiâ Sacerdotii et Imperii. This book was censured at Rome; yet it does not by any means come up to the language afterwards used in the Gallican Church: it belongs to its own age, the transitional period in which Rome had just ceased to act, but not to speak, as a mistress. De Marca was obliged to make some concessions before he could obtain the bulls for a bishopric. He rose, however, afterwards to the see of Paris. The first part of his work appeared in 1641; the second, after the death of the author.

Controversy of Catholics and Protestants.

9. In this most learned period, according to the sense in which the word was then taken, that Europe has ever seen, it was of course to be expected that the studious ecclesiastics of both the Romish and Protestant denomination would pour forth a prodigal erudition in their great controversy. It had always been the aim of the former to give an historical character to theological inquiry: it was their business to ascertain the faith of the Catholic Church as a matter of fact, the single principle of its infallibility being assumed as the basis of all investigation. But their opponents, though less concerned in the issue of such questions, frequently thought themselves competent to dispute the field; and, conversant as they were with ecclesiastical antiquity, found in its interminable records sufficient weapons to protract the war, though not to subdue the foe. Hence, partly in the last years of the sixteenth century, but incomparably more in the present, we find an essential change in the character of theological controversy. It became less reasoning, less scriptural, less general and popular, but far more patristic (that is, appealing to the testimonies of the fathers), and altogether more historical, than before. Several consequences of material influence on religious opinion sprang naturally from this method of conducting the defence of Protestantism. One was, that it contracted very greatly the circle of those, who, upon any reasonable interpretation of the original principle of personal judgment, could exercise it for themselves: it became the privilege of the deeply learned alone. Another, that, from the real obscurity and incoherence of ecclesiastical authorities, those who had penetrated farthest into that province of learning were least able to reconcile them; and, however they might disguise it from the world while the pen was in their

Increased respect for the fathers.

hands, were themselves necessarily left, upon many points, in an embarrassing state of doubt and confusion. A third effect was, that, upon these controversies of Catholic tradition, the Church of Rome had very often the best of the argument; and this was occasionally displayed in those wrestling-matches between religious disputants, which were held, publicly or privately, either with the vain hope of coming to an agreement, or to settle the faith of the hearers. And from the two last of these causes it arose, that many Protestants went over to the Church of Rome, and that a new theological system was contrived to combine what had been deemed the incompatible tenets of those who had burst from each other with such violence in the preceding century.

Especially in England. Laud.

10. This retrocession, as it appeared, and as in spirit it was, towards the system abandoned in the first impetuosity of the Reformation, began in England about the conclusion of the sixteenth century. It was evidently connected with the high notions of ecclesiastical power, of an episcopacy by unbroken transmission from the apostles, of a pompous ritual, which the rulers of the Anglican Church took up at that time in opposition to the Puritans. It rapidly gained ground in the reign of James, and, still more, of his son. Andrews, a man far more learned in patristic theology than any of the Elizabethan bishops, or perhaps than any of his English contemporaries except Usher, was, if not the founder, the chief leader, of this school. Laud became afterwards, from his political importance, its more conspicuous head; and from him it is sometimes styled. In his conference with the Jesuit Fisher, first published in 1624, and afterwards with many additions in 1639, we find an attempt, not feeble, and, we may believe, not feigned, to vindicate the Anglican Protestantism, such as he meant it to be, against the Church of Rome, but with much deference to the name of Catholic and the authority of the ancient fathers.[1] It is

[1] "Ce qu'il y a de particulier dans cette conférence, c'est qu'on y cite beaucoup plus les pères de l'église, que n'ont accoutumé de faire les Protestans de deça la mer. Comme l'église Anglicane a une vénération toute particulière pour l'antiquité, c'est par là que les Catholiques Romains l'attaquent ordinairement. Bibl. Univ., i. 336. Laud, as well as Andrews, maintained "that the true and real body of Christ is in that blessed sacrament" Conference with Fisher, p. 299 (edit. 1639). And afterwards, "for the Church of England, nothing is more plain than that it believes and teaches the true and real presence of Christ in the eucharist." Nothing is more plain than the contrary, as Hall, who belonged to a different school of theology, though the friend of Laud, has in equivalent words observed. Hall's Works (Pratt's edition), vol. ix. p. 374.

unnecessary to observe, that this was the prevalent language of the English Church in that period of forty years which was terminated by the civil war; and that it was accompanied by a marked enhancement of religious ceremonies, as well as by a considerable approximation to several doctrines and usages of the Romanists.

Defections to the Catholic Church.

11. The progress of the latter church for the first thirty years of the present century was as striking and uninterrupted as it had been in the final period of the sixteenth. Victory crowned its banners on every side. The signal defeats of the elector-palatine and the King of Denmark, the reduction of Rochelle, displayed an evident superiority in the ultimate argument to which the Protestants had been driven, and which silences every other; while a rigid system of exclusion from court favor and of civil discouragement, or even of banishment, and suppression of public worship, as in the Austrian dominions, brought round the wavering and flexible to acquiesce with apparent willingness in a despotism which they could neither resist nor escape. The nobility, both in France and Germany, who at the outset had been the first to embrace a new faith, became afterwards the first to desert it. Many also of the learned and able Protestants gave evidence of the jeopardy of that cause by their conversion. It is not, however, just to infer that they were merely influenced by this apprehension. Two other causes mainly operated: one, to which we have above alluded, the authority ascribed to the traditions of the church as recorded by the writers called fathers, and with which it was found very difficult to reconcile all the Protestant creed; another, the intolerance of the reformed churches, both Lutheran and Calvinistic, which gave as little latitude as that which they had quitted.

Wavering of Casaubon,

12. The defections, from whatever cause, are numerous in the seventeenth century. But two, more eminent than any who actually renounced the Protestant religion, must be owned to have given evident signs of wavering, — Casaubon and Grotius. The proofs of this are not founded merely on anecdotes which might be disputed, but on their own language.[1] Casaubon was staggered by the

[1] In his correspondence with Scaliger, no indications of any vacillation as to religion appear. Of the unfortunate conference between Du Plessis Mornay and Du Perron, in the presence of Henry IV., where Casaubon himself had been one of

study of the fathers, in which he discovered many things, especially as to the eucharist, which he could not in any manner reconcile with the tenets of the French Huguenots.[1] Perron used to assail him with arguments he could not parry. If we may belive this cardinal, he was on the point of declaring publicly his conversion before he accepted the invitation of James I. to England; and, even while in England, he pro-

the umpires, he speaks with great regret, though with a full acknowledgment that his champion had been worsted. "Quod scribis de congressu Diomedis cum Glauco, sic est omnino, ut tu judicas rectè. Vir optimus, si eum sua prudentia orbi Gallico satis explorata non defecisset, nunquam ejus certaminis aleam subiisset." After much more, he concludes: "Equidem in lacrymas prope adducor, quoties subit animo tristissima illius diei species, cum de ingenua nobilitate, de excellenti ingenio, de ipsa denique veritate pompaticè adeo vidi triumphatum." — Epist. 214. (Oct., 1600.) See also a letter to Heinsius on the same subject. Casaub. Epist. 809. In a letter to Perron himself, in 1604, he professed to adhere to Scripture alone, against those who "vetustatis auctoritatem pro ratione obtendunt." — Epist. 417. A change, however, came gradually over his mind; and he grew fascinated by this very authority of antiquity. In 1609 he had, by the king's command, a conference on religion with Du Perron, but very reluctantly, and, as his biographer owns, "quibusdam visus est quodammodo cespitasse." Casaubon was, for several reasons, no match in such a disputation for Perron. In the first place, he was poor and weak, and the other powerful, which is a reason that might dispense with our giving any others; but, secondly, he had less learning in the fathers; and, thirdly, he was entangled by deference for these same fathers; finally, he was not a man of as much acuteness and eloquence as his antagonist. The issue of battle does not follow the better cause, but the sharper sword; especially when there is so much *ignoratio elenchi* as in this case.

1 Perron continued to persecute Casaubon with argument, whenever he met him in the king's library. "Je vous confesse (the latter told Wytenbogart) qu'il m'a donné beaucoup des scrupules qui me restent, et auxquels je ne sçais pas bien répondre . . . il me fâche de rougir. L'escapade que je prens est que je n'y puis répondre, mais que j'y penserai." — Casauboni Vita (ad edit. Epistolarum, 1709). And in writing to the same Wytenbogart, January, 1610, we find similar signs of wavering. "Me, ne quid dissimulem, hæc tanta diversitas a fide veteris ecclesiæ non parum turbat. Ne de aliis dicam, in re sacramentaria a majoribus discessit Lutherus, a Luthero Zuinglius, ab utroque Calvinus, a Calvino qui postea scripserunt. Nam constat mihi ac certissimum est, doctrinam Calvini de sacra eucharistia longe aliam esse ab ea quæ in libro observandi viri Molinæi nostri continetur, et quæ vulgo in ecclesiis nostris auditur. Itaque Molinæum qui oppugnant, Calvinum illi non minus objiciunt, quam aliquem è veteribus ecclesiæ doctoribus. Si sic pergimus, quis tandem erit exitus? Jam quod idem Molinæus, omnes veterum libros suæ doctrinæ contrarios respuit, ut ὑποβολιμαιους, cui mediocriter docto fidem faciet? Falsus illi Cyrillus, Hierosolymorum episcopus; falsus Gregorius Nyssenus, falsus Ambrosius, falsi omnes. Mihi liquet falli ipsum, et illa scripta esse verissima, quæ ille pronuntiat ψευδεπιγραφα." — Ep. 670. See also Ep. 1043, written from Paris in the same year. He came now to England, and, to his great satisfaction, found the church and its prelates exactly what he would wish. "Illud solatio mihi est, quod in hoc regno speciem agnosco veteris ecclesiæ, quam ex patrum scriptis didici. Adde quod episcopis ὁσημεραι συνδιαγω doctissimis, sapientissimis, ευσεβεστατοις, et quod novum mihi est, priscæ ecclesiæ amantissimis." — (Lond., 1611.) Ep. 703. His letters are full of similar language. See 743, 744, 772, &c. He combined this inordinate respect for authority with its natural concomitant, a desire to restrain free inquiry. Though his patristic lore should have made him not unfavorable to the Arminians, he writes to Bertius, one of their number, against the liberty of conscience they required. "Illa quam passim celebras, prophetandi libertas, bonis et piis hujus ecclesiæ viris mirum in modum suspecta res est et odiosa. Nemo enim dubitat de pietate Christiana actum esse inter vos, si quod videris agere, illustrissimis ordinibus fuerit semel persuasum, ut liberum unicuique esse velint, via regia relicta semitam ex animi libidine sibi aliisque aperire. Atqui ve-

moted the Catholic cause more thán the world was aware.[1] This is more than we can readily believe; and we know that he was engaged both in maintaining the temporal rights of the crown against the school of Bellarmin, and in writing animadversions on the ecclesiastical annals of Baronius. But this opposition to the extreme line of the ultramontanists might be well compatible with a tendency towards much that the reformers had denounced. It seemed, in truth, to disguise the corruptions of the Catholic Church by rendering the controversy almost what we might call personal; as if Rome alone, either by usurping the headship of the church, which might or might not have bad consequences, or by its encroachments on the civil power, which were only maintained by a party, were the sole object of that religious opposition which had divided one-half of Europe from the other. Yet if Casaubon, as he had much inclination to do, — being on ill terms with some in England, and disliking the country,[2] — had returned to

ritas, ut scis, in omnibus rebus scientiis et disciplinis unica est, et το φωνειν ταυτο inter ecclesiæ veræ notas, fateantur omnes, non est postrema. Ut nulli esse dubium possit, quin tot πολυσχιδεις semitæ totidem sint errorum diverticula. Quod olim de politicis rebus prudentissimi philosophorum dixerunt, id mihi videtur multo etiam magis in ecclesiasticis locum habere, την αγαν ελευθεριαν εις δουλειαν εξ αναγκης τελευτᾶν, et πασαν τυραννιδα αναρχιας esse κρειττην [sic!] et optabiliorem. . . . Ego qui inter pontificios diu sum in patri mea versatus, hoc tibi possum affirmare, nulla re magis stabiliri την τυραννιδα του χξζ, quam dissentionibus nostris et dissidiis."

Meric Casaubon's Pietas contra maledicos Patrii Nominis ac Religionis Hostes is an elaborate vindication of his father against all charges alleged by his adversaries. The only one that presses is that of wavering in religion. And here Meric candidly owns that his father had been shaken by Perron about 1610. (See this tract subjoined to Almeloveen's edition of the Epistles, p. 89.) But afterwards, by dint of theological study, he got rid of the scruples the cardinal had infused into him, and became a Protestant of the new Anglican school, admiring the first six centuries, and especially the period after Constantine: "Hoc sæculum cum duobus sequentibus ακμη της εκκλησιας, flos ipse ecclesiæ et ætas illius aurea queat nuncupari." — Prolegomena in Exercitationes in Baronium. His friend Scaliger had very different notions of the fathers. "The fathers," says he, in his blunt way, "are very ignorant, know nothing of Hebrew, and teach us little in theology. Their interpretations of Scripture are strangely perverse. Even Polycarp, who was a disciple of the apostles, is full of errors. It will not do to say, that, because they were near the apostolic age, they are never wrong." — Scaligerana Secunda. Le Clerc has some good remarks on the deference shown by Casaubon to the language held by the fathers about the eucharist, which shook his Protestantism. Bibl. Choisie, xix. 230.

[1] Perroniana; Grot. Epist., p. 939.

[2] Several of his letters attest his desire of returning. He wrote to Thuanus, imploring his recommendation to the queen-regent. But he had given much offence by writing against Baronius, and had very little chance of an indemnity for his prebend of Canterbury, if he had relinquished that on leaving England. This country, however, though he sometimes calls it μακαρων νησος, did not suit his disposition. He was never on good terms with Savile, the most presumptuous of the learned, according to him, and most scornful, whom he accused of setting on Montagu to anticipate his animadversions on Baronius, with some suspicion, on Casaubon's part, of stealing from him. Ep. 794, 848, 849. But he seems himself to have become generally unpopular, if we may trust his own account. "Ego mores Anglorum non capio. Quoscunque

France, it seems probable that he would not long have continued in what, according to the principles he had adopted, would appear a schismatical communion.

13. Grotius was, from the time of his turning his mind to theology, almost as much influenced as Casaubon by primitive authority, and began, even in 1614, to commend the Anglican Church for the respect it showed, very unlike the rest of the reformed, to that standard.[1] But the

And of Grotius.

habui notos priusquam huc venirem, jam ego illis sum ignotus, verè peregrinus, barbarus; nemo illorum me vel verbulo appellat; *appellatus silet.* Hoc quid sit, non scio. Hic —— [Henricus Wotton] vir doctissimus ante annos viginti mecum Genevæ vixit, et ex eo tempore literis amicitiam coluimus. Postquam ego e Galliis, ille Venetiis huc convenimus, desii esse illi notus; meæ quoque epistolæ responsum dedit nullum; an sit daturus nescio." — Ep. 841. It seems difficult to account for so marked a treatment of Casaubon, except on the supposition that he was thought to pursue a course unfavorable to the Protestant interest. He charges the English with despising every one but themselves, and ascribes this to the vast wealth of their universities, — a very discreditable source of pride in our ancestors, if so it were. But Casaubon's philological and critical skill passed for little in this country, where it was not known enough to be envied. In mere ecclesiastical learning, he was behind some English scholars.

[1] Casaubon himself hailed Grotius as in the right path. "In hodiernis contentionibus in negotio religionis et doctè et piè judicat, et in veneratione antiquitatis cum iis sentit, qui optimè sentiunt." — Epist 883. See also 772, which is addressed to him. This high respect for the fathers and for the authority of the primitive church grew strongly upon him, and the more because he found they were hostile to the Calvinistic scheme. He was quite delighted at finding Jerome and Chrysostom on his side. Grot. Epist. 29. (1614.) In the next year, writing to Vossius, he goes a great length. "Cæterum ego reformatarum ecclesiarum miseriam in hoc maximè deploro, quod cum symbola condere catholicæ sit ecclesiæ, ipsis inter se nunquam eam in rem convenire sit datum, atque interim libelli apologetici ex re nata scripti ad imperatorem, reges, principes, aut ut in concilio œcumenico exhiberentur, trahi cœperint in usum longè alienum. Quid enim magis est alienum ab unitate catholica quam quod diversis in regionibus pastores diversa populo tradere coguntur? Quam mirata fuisset hoc prodigium pia antiquitas! Sed hæc aliaque multa mussitanda sunt nobis ob iniquitatem temporum." — Epist. 66. He was at this time, as he continued till near the end of his life, when he moved on farther, highly partial to the Anglican Church. He was, however, too Erastian for the English bishops of the reign of James, as appears by a letter addressed to him by Overall, who objected to his giving, in his treatise, De Imperio circa Sacra, a definitive power in controversies of faith to the civil magistrate, and to his putting Episcopacy among non-essentials, which the bishops held to be of divine right. Grotius adhered to his opinion, that Episcopacy was not commanded as a perpetual institution; and thought, at that time, that there was no other distinction between bishops and priests than of precedency. "Nusquam meminit," he says in one place, "Clemens Romanus exsortis illius episcoporum auctoritatis quæ ecclesiæ consuetudine post Marci mortem Alexandriæ, atque eo exemplo alibi, introduci cœpit, sed planè ut Paulus Apostolus, ostendit ecclesias communi presbyterorum, qui iidem omnes et episcopi ipsi Pauloque dicuntur, consilio fuisse gubernatas." Even in his latter writings, he seems never to have embraced the notions of some Anglican divines on this subject, but contents himself, in his remarks on Cassander, — who had said, singularly as it may be thought, "Convenit *inter omnes* olim Apostolorum ætate inter episcopos et presbyteros discrimen nullum fuisse, sed postmodum ordinis servandi et schismatis evitandi causa episcopum presbyteris fuisse præpositum," — with observing, "Episcopi sunt presbyterorum principes; et ista προστασια (præsidentia) a Christo præmonstrata est in Petro, ab Apostolis vero, ubicunque fieri poterat, constituta, et a Spiritu Sancto comprobata in Apocalypsi." — Op. Theolog., iv. 579, 621.

But to return from this digression to our more immediate purpose. Grotius

ill usage he sustained at the hands of those who boasted their independence of Papal tyranny; the caresses of the Gallican

for several years continued in this insulated state, neither approving of the Reformation nor the Church of Rome. He wrote, in 1622, to Episcopius against those whom he called Cassandrians, "Qui etiam plerosque Romanæ ecclesiæ errores improbantibus auctores sunt, ne ab ejus communione discedant."—Ep. 181. He was destined to become Cassandrian himself, or something more. The infallibility of the church was still no doctrine of his. "At illa auctoritas ecclesiæ αναμαρτητον, quam ecclesiæ, et quidem suæ, Romanenses ascribunt, cum naturali ratione non sit evidens, nam ipsi fatentur Judaicam ecclesiam id privilegium non habuisse, sequitur ut adversus negantes probari debeat ex sacris literis." — Epist. secunda series, p. 761. (1620.) And again: "Quæ scribit pater de restituendis rebus in eum statum, qui ante concilium Tridentinum fuerat, esset quidem hoc per multum; sed transubstantiatio et ei respondens adoratio pridem Lateranensi concilio definita est, et invocatio peculiaris sanctorum pridem in omnes liturgias recepta." — p. 772. (1623.)

Grotius passed most of his latter years at Paris, in the honorable station of ambassador from the court of Sweden. He seems to have thought it a matter of boast that he did not live as a Protestant. See Ep. 196. The Huguenot ministers of Charenton requested him to communicate with them, which he declined, pp. 854, 856. (1635.) He now was brooding over a scheme of union among Protestants: the English and Swedish churches were to unite, and to be followed by Denmark. "Constituto semel aliquo tali ecclesiarum corpore, spes est subinde alios atque alios se aggregaturos. Est autem hæc res eo magis optanda protestantibus, quod quotidie multi eos deserunt et se cœtibus Romanensium addunt, non alia de causa, quam quod non unum est eorum corpus, sed partes distractæ, greges segreges, propria cuique sua sacrorum communio, ingens præterea maledicendi certamen." — Epist. 866. (1637.) See also p. 827. (1630.) He fancied that by such a weight of authority, grounded on the ancient church, the exercise of private judgment, on which he looked with horror, might be overruled. "Nisi interpretandi sacras literas," he writes to Calixtus, "libertatem cohibemus intra lineas eorum, quæ omnes illæ non sanctitate minus quam primæva vetustate venerabiles ecclesiæ ex ipsa prædicatione scripturis ubique consentiente hauserint, diuque sub crucis maximè magisterio retinuerint, nisi deinde in iis quæ liberam habuere disputationem fraterna lenitate ferre alii alios discimus, quis erit letium sæpe in factiones, deinde in bella erumpentium finis?" — Ep. 674. (Oct., 1635.) "Qui illam optimam antiquitatem sequuntur ducem, quod te semper fecisse memini, iis non eveniet, ut multum sibi ipsis sint discolores. In Angliâ vides quam bene processerit dogmatum noxiorum repurgatio, hac maximè de causa quod qui id sanctissimum negotium procurandum suscepere nihil admiscuerunt novi, nihil sui, sed ad meliora sæcula intentam habuere oculorum aciem." — Ep. 966. (1638.)

But he could not be long in perceiving that this union of Protestant churches was impossible from the very independence of their original constitution. He saw that there could be no practicable re-union except with Rome itself, nor that, except on an acknowledgment of her superiority. From the year 1640, his letters are full of sanguine hopes that this delusive vision would be realized. He still expected some concession on the other side; but, as usual, would have lowered his terms according to the pertinacity of his adversaries, if indeed they were still to be called his adversaries. He now published his famous annotations on Cassander, and the other tracts mentioned in the text, to which they gave rise. In these he defends almost every thing we deem Popery, such as transubstantiation (Opera Theologica, iv. 619), stooping to all the nonsensical evasions of a spiritual mutation of substance and the like; the authority of the pope (p. 642), the celibacy of the clergy (p. 645), the communion in one kind (ibid.), and, in fact, is less of a Protestant than Cassander. In his epistles he declares himself decidedly in favor of purgatory, as at least a probable doctrine, p. 930. In these writings he seems to have had the countenance of Richelieu. "Cardinalis quin ἑνωσεως negotium in Gallia successurum sit, dubitare se negat." — Epist. sec. series, p. 912. "Cardinalis Ricelianus rem successuram putat. Ita certè loquitur multis. Archiepiscopus Cantuariensis pœnas dat honestissimi consilii, quod et aliis bonis sæpe evenit." — p. 911. Grotius is now run away with by vanity, and fancies all will go according to his wish, showing much ignorance of the real state of things. He was left by some from whom he had entertained hopes, and thought the Dutch Arminians timid. "Vossius, ut video, præ metu, forte et ex Anglia sic jussus, auxilium suum mihi

clergy after he had fixed his residence at Paris; the growing dissensions and virulence of the Protestants; the choice that

subtrahit." — p. 908. "Salmasius adhuc in consiliis fluctuat. Est in religionis rebus suæ parti addictior quam putabatur." — p. 912. "De Episcopio doleo; est vir magni ingenii et probus, sed nimium cupidus alendæ partis." But it is probable that he had misinterpreted some language of these great men, who contemplated with regret the course he was taking, which could be no longer a secret. "De Grotii ad papam defectione," a French Protestant of some eminence for learning writes, "tanquam re certa, quod fama istuc distulit, verum non est. Sed non sine magno metu eum aliquid istiusmodi meditantem et conantem quotidie inviti videmus. Inter Protestantes cujuslibet ordinis nomen ejus ascribi vetat, quod eos atrocius sugillavit in Appendice de Antichristo, et Annotatis ad Cassandri consultationem." — Sarravii Epistolæ, p. 58. (1642.) And again he expresses his strong disapprobation of one of the later treatises. "Verissimè dixit ille qui primus dixit Grotium papissare." p. 196; see also pp. 31, 53.

In 1642, Grotius had become wholly averse to the Reformation. He thought it had done more harm than good, especially by the habit of interpreting every thing on the Papal side for the worse. "Malos mores qui mansere corrigi æquum est. Sed an non hoc melius successurum fuerit, si quisque semet repurgans pro repurgatione aliorum preces ad Deum tulisset, et principes et episcopi correctionem desiderantes, non rupta compage, per concilia universalia in id laborassent. Dignum est de quo cogitetur." — p. 938. Auratus, as he calls him, that is D'Or, a sort of chaplain to Grotius, became a Catholic about this time. The other only says, "Quod Auratus fecit, idem fecit antehac vir doctissimus Petrus Pithæus; idem constituerat facere Casaubonus si in Gallia mansisset, affirmavit enim id inter alios etiam Cordesio." — p. 939. Of Casaubon he says afterwards, "Casaubonus multo saniores putabat Catholicos Galliæ quam Carentonianos. Anglos autem episcopos putabat a schismatis culpa posse absolvi." — p. 940. Every successive year saw him now draw nearer to Rome. "Reperio autem quicquid communiter ab ecclesia occidentali quæ Romanæ cohæret recipitur, idem reperiri apud Patres veteres Græcos et Latinos, quorum communionem retinendam esse vix quisquam neget. Si quid præter hoc est, id ad liberas doctorum opinationes pertinet; in quibus suum quis judicium sequi potest, et communionis jus non amittere." — p. 958. Episcopius was for limiting articles of faith to the creed. But Grotius did not agree with this, and points out that it would not preserve uniformity. "Quam multa jam sunt de sacramentis, de ecclesiarum regimine, in quibus, vel concordiæ causa, certi aliquid observari debet. Alioqui compages ecclesiæ tantopere nobis commendata retineri non potest." — p. 941. It would be endless to quote every passage tending to the same result. Finally, in a letter to his brother in Holland, he expresses his hope, that Wytenbogart, the respectable patriarch of Arminianism, would turn his attention to the means of restoring unity to the church. "Velim D. Wytenbogardum, ubi permiserit valetudo, nisi id jam fecerit, scriptum aliquid facere de necessitate restituendæ in ecclesia unitatis, et quibus modis id fieri possit. Multi pro remedio monstrant, si necessaria a non necessariis separentur, in non necessariis sive creditu sive factu relinquatur libertas. At non minor est controversia, quæ sint necessaria quam quæ sint vera. Indicia, aiunt, sunt in scripturis. At certè etiam circa illa loca variat interpretatio. Quare nondum video an quid sit melius, quam ea quæ ad fidem et bona opera nos ducunt retinere, ut sunt in ecclesia catholica; puto enim in iis esse quæ sunt necessaria ad salutem. In cæteris ea quæ conciliorum auctoritate, aut veterum consensu recepta sunt, interpretari eo modo quo interpretati sunt illi qui commodissimè sunt locuti, quales semper aliqui in quaque materia facile reperientur. Si quis id a se impetrare non possit, ut taceat, nec propter res de quibus certus non est, sed opinationem tantum quandam habet, turbet unitatem ecclesiæ necessariam, quæ nisi retinetur ubi est, et restituitur ubi non est, omnia ibunt in pejus." — p. 960. (Nov., 1643.) Wytenbogart replied very well: "Si ita se res habet, ut indicia necessariorum et non necessariorum in scripturæ reperiri nequeant, sed quæri debeant in auctoritate conciliorum aut veterum consensu, eo modo quo interpretati sunt illi qui commodissimè locuti sunt, prout Excellentia tua videtur existimare, nescio an viginti quinque anni, etiamsi illi mihi adhuc restarent, omnesque exigui ingenii corporisque mei vires in mea essent potestate, sufficerent ut maturo cum judicio perlegam et expendam omnia quæ eo pertinent." This letter is in the Epistolæ Præstantium et Eruditorum Virorum, edited by Limborch in 1683, p. 826. And Grotius's answer is in the same collection. It is that of a man who throws off a mask he had reluctantly worn. There was, in

seemed alone to be left in their communion, between a fanatical anarchy, disintegrating every thing like a church on the one hand, and a domination of bigoted and vulgar ecclesiastics on the other, — made him gradually less and less averse to the comprehensive and majestic unity of the Catholic hierarchy, and more and more willing to concede some point of uncertain doctrine, or some form of ambiguous expression. This is

fact, no other means of repelling Wytenbogart's just observation on the moral impossibility of tracing for ourselves the doctrine of the Catholic Church as an historical inquiry. Grotius refers him to a visible standard. "Quare considerandum est, an non facilius et æquius sit, quoniam doctrina de gratia, de libero arbitrio, necessitate fidei bonorumque operum obtinuit in ecclesia quæ pro se habet universale regimen et ordinem successionis, privatos se in aliis accommodare, pacis causa, iis quæ universaliter sunt recepta, sive ea aptissimis explicationibus recipiendo, sive tacendo, quam corpus illud catholicum ecclesiæ se in articulo tolerantiæ accommodare debere uniuscujusque considerationibus et placitis. Exempli gratiâ: Catholica ecclesia nemini præscribit ut precetur pro mortuis, aut opem precum sanctorum vita hac defunctorum imploret; solummodo requirit, ne quis morem adeo antiquum et generalem condemnet." The church does, in fact, rather more than he insinuates.

I have trespassed on the patience of the general reader in this very long note, which may be thought a superfluous digression in a work of mere literature. But the epistles of Grotius are not much read; nor are they in many private libraries. The index is also very indifferent, so that, without the trouble I have taken of going over the volume, it might be difficult to find these curious passages. I ought to mention that Burigny has given references to most of them, but with few quotations. Le Clerc, in the first volume of the Bibliothèque Universelle, reviewing the epistles of Grotius, slides very gently over his bias towards Popery; and I have met with well-informed persons in England, who had no conception of the lengths to which this had led him. It is of far more importance, and the best apology I can offer for so prolix a note, to perceive by what gradual, but, as I think, necessary steps, he was drawn onward by his excessive respect for antiquity, and by his exaggerated notions of Catholic unity, preferring at last to err with the many than to be right with the few. If Grotius had learned to look the hydra schism in the face, he would have had less fear of its many heads, and at least would have dreaded to cut them off at the neck, lest the source of life should be in one of them.

That Grotius really thought as the fathers of Trent thought upon all points in dispute cannot be supposed. It was not in the power of a man of his learning and thoughtfulness to divest himself of his own judgment, unless he had absolutely subjugated his reason to religious awe, which was far from being the case. His aim was to search for subtle interpretations, by which he might profess to believe the words of the church, though conscious that his sense was not that of the imposers. It is needless to say, that this is not very ingenuous; and even, if it could be justifiable relatively to the person, would be an abandonment of the multitude to any superstition and delusion which might be put upon them. "Via ad pacem expeditissima mihi videtur, si doctrina, communi consensu recepta, commodè explicetur, mores sanæ doctrinæ adversantes, quantum fieri potest, tollantur, et in rebus mediis accommodet se pars ingenio totius." — Epist. 1524. Peace was his main object: if toleration had been as well understood as it was afterwards, he would perhaps have compromised less.

Baxter having published a Treatise of the Grotian Religion, wherein he imputed to Grotius this inclination towards the Church of Rome, Archbishop Bramhall replied, after the Restoration, with a vindication of Grotius, in which he does not say much to the purpose, and seems ignorant of the case. The epistles indeed were not then published.

Besides the passages in these epistles above quoted, the reader who wishes to follow this up may consult Epist. 1108, 1460, 1561, 1570, 1706, of the first series; and, in the second series, pp. 875, 896, 940, 943, 958, 960, 975. But there are also many to which I have made no reference. I do not quote authorities for the design of Grotius to have declared himself a convert if he had lived to return to France, though they are easily found; because the testimony of his writings is far stronger than any anecdote.

abundantly perceived, and has often been pointed out, in his Annotations on the Consultation of Cassander, written in 1641; in his Animadversions on Rivet, who had censured the former treatise as inclining to Popery; in the Votum pro Pace Ecclesiasticâ; and in the Rivetiani Apologetici Discussio: all which are collected in the fourth volume of the theological works of Grotius. These treatises display an uniform and progressive tendency to defend the Church of Rome in every thing that can be reckoned essential to her creed; and, in fact, he will be found to go farther in this direction than Cassander.

14. But if any one could put a different interpretation on these works, which would require a large measure of prejudice, the epistles of Grotius afford such evidence of his secession from the Protestant side, as no reasonable understanding can reject. These are contained in a large folio volume, published in 1687, and amount to 1,766 of one series, and 744 of another. I have quoted the former, for distinction's sake, by the number, and the latter by the page. Few, we may presume, have taken the pains to go through them, in order to extract all the passages that bear upon this subject. It will be found that he began, as I have just said, by extolling the authority of the Catholic or Universal Church, and its exclusive right to establish creeds of faith. He some time afterwards ceased to frequent the Protestant worship, but long kept his middle path, and thought it enough to inveigh against the Jesuits and the exorbitances of the see of Rome. But his reverence for the writers of the fourth and fifth centuries grew continually stronger; he learned to protest against the privilege claimed by the reformers, of interpreting Scripture otherwise than the consent of the ancients had warranted; visions, first of an union between the Lutheran and English Churches, and then of one with Rome itself, floated before his eyes; he sought religious peace with the latter, as men seek it in opposition to civil government, by the redress of grievances, and the subsequent restoration of obedience. But, in proportion as he perceived how little of concession was to be obtained, he grew himself more ready to concede; and though at one time he seems to deny the infallibility of the church, and at another would not have been content with placing all things in the state they were before the Council of Trent, he came ultimately to think such a favorable sense

might be put on all the Tridentine decrees, as to render them compatible with the Confession of Augsburg.

15. From the year 1640, his course seems to have been accelerated; he intimates no disapprobation of those who went over to Rome; he found, as he tells us, that whatever was generally received in the Church of Rome had the authority of those Greek and Latin fathers, whose communion no one would have refused; and at length, in a remarkable letter to Wytenbogart, bearing date in 1644, he puts it as worthy to be considered, whether it would not be more reasonable for private men, who find the most essential doctrines in a church of an universal hierarchy and a legitimate succession, to waive their differences with it for the sake of peace, by putting the best interpretations they can, only keeping silence on their own opinions, than that the Catholic Church should accommodate itself to the separate judgment of such men. Grotius had already ceased to speak of the Arminians as if he were one of themselves, though with much respect for some of their leaders.

16. Upon a dispassionate examination of all these testimonies, we can hardly deem it an uncertain question, whether Grotius, if his life had been prolonged, would have taken the easy leap that still remained; and there is some positive evidence of his design to do so. But, dying on a journey and in a Protestant country, this avowed declaration was never made, — fortunately, indeed, for his glory; since his new friends would speedily have put his conversion to the proof, and his latter years might have been spent, like those of Lipsius, in defending legendary miracles, or in waging war against the honored dead of the Reformation. He did not sufficiently remember that a silent neutrality is never indulged to a suspicious proselyte.

17. It appears to me, nevertheless, that Grotius was very far from having truly subjected his understanding to the Church of Rome. The whole bent of his mind was to effect an exterior union among Christians; and, for this end, he did not hesitate to recommend equivocal senses of words, convenient explanations, and respectful silence. He first took up his reverence for antiquity, because he found antiquity unfavorable to the doctrine of Calvin. His antipathy to this reformer and to his followers led him on to an admiration of the episcopal succession, the organized hierarchy, the ceremo-

nial and liturgical institutions, the high notions of sacramental rites, which he found in the ancient church, and which Luther and Zwingle had cast away. He became imbued with the notion of unity as essential to the Catholic Church; but he never seems to have gone the length of abandoning his own judgment, or of asserting any positive infallibility to the decrees of man. For it is manifest, that, if the Councils of Nice or of Trent were truly inspired, it would be our business to inquire what they meant themselves, not to put the most convenient interpretations, nor to search out for some author or another who may have strained their language to our own opinion. The precedent of Grotius, therefore, will not serve those who endeavor to bind the reason of the enlightened part of mankind, which he respected like his own. Two predominant ideas seem to have swayed the mind of this great man in the very gradual transition we have indicated: one, his extreme reverence for antiquity and for the consent of the Catholic Church; the other, his Erastian principles as to the authority of the civil magistrate in matters of religion. Both conspired to give him an abhorrence of the "liberty of prophesying," the right of private men to promulgate tenets inconsistent with the established faith. In friendly conversation or correspondence, even perhaps, with due reserve, in Latin writings, much might be indulged to the learned: room was to be found for an Erasmus and a Cassander; or, if they would themselves consent, for an Episcopius and a Wytenbogart, at least for a Montagu and a Laud; but no pretext was ever to justify a separation. The scheme of Grotius is, in a modified degree, much the same as that of Hobbes.

Calixtus.

18. In the Lutheran Church we find an eminent contemporary of Grotius, who may be reckoned his counterpart in the motives which influenced him to seek for an entire union of religious parties, though resembling him far more in his earlier opinions than in those to which he ultimately arrived. This was George Calixtus, of the University of Helmstadt, a theologian the most tolerant, mild, and catholic in his spirit, whom the Confession of Augsburg had known since Melanchthon. This university, indeed, which had never subscribed the Form of Concord, was already distinguished by freedom of inquiry, and its natural concomitant, a large and liberal spirit. But in his own church, generally, Calixtus found as rigid schemes of orthodoxy, and

perhaps a more invidious scrutiny into the recesses of private opinion, than in that of Rome, with a less extensive basis of authority. The dream of good men in this age, the re-union of Christian churches in a common faith, and, meanwhile, the tolerance of differences, were ever the aim of Calixtus. But he fell, like the Anglican divines, into high notions of primitive tradition; placing, according to Eichhorn and Mosheim, the unanimity of the first six centuries by the side of Scripture itself. He was assailed by the adherents of the Form of Concord with aggravated virulence and vulgarity: he was accused of being a Papist and a Calvinist, reproaches equally odious in their eyes, and therefore fit to be heaped on his head; the inconsistency of calumnies being no good reason with bigots against uttering them.[1]

His attempts at concord.

19. In a treatise, published long after his death, in 1697, De Tolerantia Reformatorum circa Quæstiones inter ipsos et Augustanam Confessionem professos controversas Consultatio, it is his object to prove that the Calvinists held no such tenets as should exclude them from Christian communion. He does not deny or extenuate the reality of their differences from the Confession of Augsburg. The Lutherans, though many of them, he says, had formerly maintained the absolute decrees of predestination, were now come round to the doctrine of the first four centuries.[2] And he admits that the Calvinists, whatever phrases they may use, do not believe a true and substantial presence in the eucharist.[3] But neither of these errors, if such they are, he takes

[1] Eichhorn, vol. vi. part ii. p. 20; Mosheim; Biogr. Univ.

[2] "Nostri e quibus olim multi ibidem absolutum decretum approbarunt, paulatim ad sententiam primorum quatuor sæculorum, nempe decretum juxta præscientiam factum, receperunt. Qua in re multum egregiè laboravit Ægidius Hunnius. Difficile autem est hanc sententiam ita proponere, ne quid Pelagianismo habere affine videatur."—p. 14.

[3] "Si tamen non tam quid loquantur quam quid sentiant attendimus, certum est eos veri corporis et sanguinis secundum substantiam acceptorum præsentiam non admittere. Rectius autem fuerit utramque partem simpliciter et ingenuè, quod sentit, profiteri, quam alteram alteri ambiguis loquendi formulis imponere. Qualem conciliandi rationem inierunt olim Philippus et Bucerus, nempe ut præscriberentur formulæ, quarum verba utraque pars amplecteretur, sed singulæ suo sensu acciperent ac interpretarentur. Quem conatum, quamvis ex pio eoque ingente concordiæ desiderio et studio profectum, nulla successûs felicitas excepit."—p. 70. This observation is very just in the abstract; but, in the early period of the Reformation, there were strong reasons for evading points of difference, in the hope that the truth would silently prevail in the course of time. We, however, who come later, are to follow the advice of Calixtus, and in judging, as well as we can, of the opinions of men, must not altogether regard their words. Upon no theological controversy, probably, has there been so much of studied ambiguity as on that of the eucharist. Calixtus passes a similar censure on the equivocations of some great men of the preceding century in his other treatise mentioned in the text.

to be fundamental. In a shorter and more valuable treatise, entitled Desiderium et Studium Concordiæ Ecclesiasticæ, Calixtus proposes some excellent rules for allaying religious heats. But he leans far too much towards the authority of tradition. Every church, he says, which affirms what others deny, is bound to prove its affirmation: first, by Scripture, in which whatever is contained must be out of controversy; and, secondly (as Scripture bears witness to the church that it is the pillar and foundation of truth, and especially the primitive church which is called that of the saints and martyrs), by the unanimous consent of the ancient church, above all, where the debate is among learned men. The agreement of the church is therefore a sufficient evidence of Christian doctrine, not that of individual writers, who are to be regarded rather so far as they testify the Catholic doctrine, than as they propound their own.[1] This deference to an imaginary perfection in the church of the fourth or fifth century must have given a great advantage to that of Rome, which is not always weak on such ground, and doubtless serves to account for those frequent desertions to her banner, especially in persons of very high rank, which afterwards occurred in Germany.

High-church party in England.

20. The tenets of some of those who have been called High-church Anglicans may in themselves be little different from those of Grotius and Calixtus. But the spirit in which they have been conceived is altogether opposite. The one is exclusive, intolerant, severe, dogmatical, insisting on uniformity of faith as well as of exterior observances; the other, Catholic in outward profession, charitable in sentiment, and in fact one mode, though a mode as imprudent as it was oblique, in which the latitudinarian principle was manifested. The language both of Grotius and Calixtus bears this out; and this ought closely to be observed,

[1] "Consensu itaque primæ ecclesiæ ex symbolis et scriptis manifesto doctrina Christiana rectè confirmatur. Intelligimus autem doctrinam fundamentalem et necessariam, non quasvis appendices et quæstiones, aut etiam quorundam scripturæ locorum interpretationes. De talibus enim unanimis et universalis consensus non poterit erui vel proferri. Et magis apud plerosque spectandum est, quid tanquam communem ecclesiæ sententiam proponunt, quam quomodo eam confirmant aut demonstrant." — p. 85. I have not observed, in the little I know of Calixtus, any proof of his inclination towards the Church of Rome.

Gerard Vossius, as Episcopius wrote to Vorstius in 1615, declared, in his inaugural lecture as professor of theology, his determination to follow the consent of antiquity, "in explicatione Scripturarum et controversiarum diremtionibus diligenter examinare et expendere catholicum et antiquissimum consensum, cum sine dubio illud quod a pluribus et antiquissimis dictum est, verissimum sit." — Epist. Virorum Præstantium, p. 6.

lest we confound the real laxity of one school with the rigid orthodoxy of the other. One had it in view to reconcile discordant communions by mutual concession, and either by such explication of contrarieties as might make them appear less incompatible with outward unity, or by an avowed tolerance of their profession within the church: the other would permit nothing but submission to its own authority; it loved to multiply rather than to extinguish the risks of dissent, in order to crush it more effectually: the one was a pacific negotiator, the other a conquering tyrant.

Daillé on the Right Use of the Fathers.

21. It was justly alarming to sincere Protestants, that so many brilliant ornaments of their party should either desert to the hostile side, or do their own so much injury by taking up untenable ground.[1] Nothing, it appeared to reflecting men, could be trusted to the argument from antiquity: whatever was gained in the controversy on a few points was lost upon those of the first importance. It was become the only secure course to overthrow the tribunal. Daillé, himself one of the most learned in this patristic erudition whom the French Reformed Church possessed, was the first who boldly attacked the new school of historical theology in their own stronghold, not occupying their fortress, but razing it to the ground. The design of his celebrated Treatise concerning the Right Use of the Fathers, published in 1628, is, in his own words, to show "that they cannot be the judges of the controversies in religion at this day between the Papist and the Protestant," nor, by parity of reasoning, of many others: "1. Because it is, if not an impossible, yet at least a very difficult thing to find out what their sense hath been touching the same. 2. Because that their sense and judgment of these things, supposing it to be certainly and clearly understood, not being infallible, and without all danger of error, cannot carry with it a sufficient authority for the satisfying the understanding."

[1] It was a poor consolation for so many losses, that the famous Antonio de Dominis, Archbishop of Spalato, came over to England, and by his book De Republica Ecclesiastica, as well as by his conversation, seemed an undisguised enemy to the Church of Rome. The object of his work is to prove that the pope has no superiority over other bishops. James gave De Dominis the deanery of Windsor and a living; but whether he, strictly speaking, belonged to the Church of England, I do not remember to have read. Preferments were bestowed irregularly in that age. He returned, however, to the ancient fold; but did not avoid suspicion, being thrown into prison at Rome; and, after his death, the imputations of heresy against him so much increased, that his body was dug up and burned. Neither party has been ambitious to claim this vain and insincere though clever prelate.

22. The arguments adduced by Daillé in support of the former of these two positions, and which occupy the first book of the treatise, are drawn from the paucity of early Christian writers, from the nature of the subjects treated by them having little relation to the present controversies, from the suspicions of forgery and interpolation affecting many of their works, the difficulty of understanding their idioms and figurative expressions, the habit of some of the fathers to say what they did not believe, their changes of mind, the peculiar and individual opinions of some among them, affording little evidence of the doctrine of the church; finally, the probability that many who differed from those called the fathers, and whose writings have not descended to us, may have been of as good authority as themselves.

23. In the second book, which in fact has been very much anticipated in the first, he shows that neither the testimony nor the doctrine of the fathers is infallible (by which word he must be understood to mean that it raises but a slight presumption of truth), proving this by their errors and contradictions. Thus he concludes, that, though their negative authority is considerable, since they cannot be presumed ignorant of any material doctrine of religion, we are to be very slow in drawing affirmative propositions from their writings, and much more so in relying upon them as undoubted verities.

24. It has been said of this Treatise on the Right Use of the Fathers, that its author had pretty well proved they were of no use at all. This, indeed, is by no means the case; but it has certainly diminished, not only the deference which many have been wont to pay to the opinion of the primitive writers, but, what is still more contended for, the value of their testimony, whether as to matters of fact, or as to the prevailing doctrines of the Christian Church. Nothing can be more certain, — though, in the warmth of controversy, men are apt to disregard it, — than that a witness, who deposes in any one case what can be disproved, is not entitled to belief in other assertions which we have no means of confuting, unless it be shown that the circumstances of his evidence render it more trustworthy in these points than we have found it before. Hence such writers as Justin and Irenæus, for example, ought not, except with great precaution, to be quoted in proof at all, or at least with confidence; their falsehood, not probably wilful, in assertions that have been brought to a test

rendering their testimony very precarious upon any other points. Daillé, it may be added, uses some circumspection, as the times, if not his own disposition, required, in handling this subject, keeping chiefly in view the controversies between the Romish and Protestant Churches; nor does he ever indulge in that tone of banter or acrimony which we find in Whitby, Barbeyrac, Jortin, and Middleton, and which must be condemned by every one who reflects that many of these writers exposed their lives, and some actually lost them, in the maintenance and propagation of Christianity.

Chillingworth's Religion of Protestants.

25. This well-timed and important book met with a good reception from some in England, though it must have been very uncongenial to the ruling party. It was extolled and partly translated by Lord Falkland; and his two distinguished friends, Chillingworth and Hales, found in it the materials of their own bold revolt against church authority. They were both Arminians, and, especially the former, averse in all respects to the Puritan school. But, like Episcopius, they scorned to rely, as on these points they might have done, on what they deemed so precarious and inconclusive as the sentiments of the fathers. Chillingworth, as is well known, had been induced to embrace the Romish religion, on the usual ground, that a succession of infallible pastors, that is, a collective hierarchy, by adhering to whom alone we could be secure from error, was to be found in that church. He returned again to the Protestant religion on being convinced that no such infallible society could be found. And a Jesuit, by name Knott, having written a book to prove that unrepenting Protestants could not be saved, Chillingworth published, in 1637, his famous answer, The Religion of Protestants a Safe Way to Salvation. In this he closely tracks the steps of his adversary, replying to every paragraph, and almost every sentence.

Character of this work.

26. Knott is by no means a despicable writer: he is concise, polished, and places in an advantageous light the great leading arguments of his church. Chillingworth, with a more diffuse and less elegant style, is greatly superior in impetuosity and warmth. In his long parenthetical periods, as in those of other old English writers, in his copiousness, which is never empty or tautological, there is an inartificial eloquence, springing from strength of intellect, and

sincerity of feeling, that cannot fail to impress the reader. But his chief excellence is the close reasoning which avoids every dangerous admission, and yields to no ambiguousness of language. He perceived, and maintained with great courage, considering the times in which he wrote and the temper of those whom he was not unwilling to keep as friends, his favorite tenet, — that all things necessary to be believed are clearly laid down in Scripture. Of tradition, which many of his contemporary Protestants were becoming as prone to magnify as their opponents, he spoke very slightingly; not denying, of course, a maxim often quoted from Vincentius Lirinensis, that a tradition strictly universal and original must be founded in truth, but being assured that no such could be shown; and that what came nearest, both in antiquity and in evidence of Catholic reception, to the name of apostolical, were doctrines and usages rejected alike by all denominations of the church in modern times.[1] It will be readily conceived, that his method of dealing with the controversy is very different from that of Laud in his treatise against Fisher, wherein we meet chiefly with disputes on passages in the fathers, as to which, especially when they are not quoted at length, it is impossible that any reader can determine for himself. The work of Chillingworth may at least be understood and appreciated without reference to any other, — the condition, perhaps, of real superiority in all productions of the mind.

27. Chillingworth was, however, a man versed in patristical learning; by no means less so, probably, than Laud. But he had found so much uncertainty about this course of theological doctrine, seducing as it generally is to the learned, — "fathers," as he expresses it, "being set against fathers, and councils against councils," — that he declares, in a well-known passage, the Bible exclusively to be the religion of Protestants, and each man's own reason to be, as from the general tenor of his volume it appears that he held it, the

[1] "If there were any thing unwritten which had come down to us with as full and universal a tradition as the unquestioned books of canonical Scripture, that thing should I believe as well as the Scripture: but I have long sought for some such thing, and yet I am to seek; nay, I am confident no one point in controversy between Papists and Protestants can go in upon half so fair cards, for to gain the esteem of an apostolic tradition, as those things which are now decried on all hands; I mean the opinion of the Chiliasts and the communicating infants." — Chap. iii. § 82. He dilates upon this insecurity of tradition in some detached papers subjoined to the best editions of his work.

interpreter of the Bible.[1] It was a natural consequence, that he was a strenuous advocate not so much for toleration of separate churches, as for such an "ordering of the public service of God, that all who believe the Scripture, and live according to it, might, without scruple or hypocrisy, or protestation against any part, join in it,"[2] — a scheme, when practicable, as it could not perhaps be often rendered, far more eligible than the separation of sects; and hence the favorite object of Grotius and Taylor, as well as of Erasmus and Cassander. And, in a remarkable and eloquent passage, Chillingworth declares that "Protestants are inexcusable if they did offer violence to other men's consciences;" which Knott had said to be notorious, as in fact it was, and as Chillingworth ought more explicitly to have admitted.[3] "Certainly," he observes in another place, "if Protestants are faulty in this matter [of claiming authority], it is for doing it too much, and not too little. This presumptuous imposing of the senses of men upon the words of God, the special senses of men upon the general words of God, and laying them upon men's consciences together, under the equal penalty of death and damnation; this vain conceit, that we can speak of the things of God better than in the words of God; this deifying our own interpretations, and tyrannous enforcing them upon others; this restraining of the word of God from that latitude and generality, and the understandings of men from that liberty wherein Christ and the apostles left them, — is and hath been the only fountain of all the schisms of the church, and that which makes them immortal;[4] the common incendiary of Christendom, and that which tears in pieces, not the coat, but the bowels and members, of Christ. Take away these walls of separation, and all will quickly be one. Take away this persecuting, burning, cursing, damning of men for not subscribing the words of men as the words of God; require

[1] This must always be understood with the condition, that the reason itself shall be competently enlightened: if Chillingworth meant more than this, he carried his principle too far, as others have done. The case is parallel in jurisprudence, medicine, mechanics, and every human science: any one man, *primâ facie*, may be a competent judge; but all men are not so. It is hard to prove that there is any different rule for theology; but parties will always contend for extremes, — for the rights of bigots to think for others, and the rights of the ignorant to think for themselves.

[2] Chap. iii. § 81.

[3] Chap. v. § 96.

[4] "This persuasion," he says in a note, "is no singularity of mine, but the doctrine which I have learned from divines of great learning and judgment. Let the reader be pleased to peruse the 7th book of Acontius de Stratagematibus Satanæ, and Zanchius his last oration delivered by him after the composing of the discord between him and Amerbachius, and he shall confess as much."

Christians only to believe Christ, and to call no man master but him only; let those leave claiming infallibility that have no title to it; and let them that in their words disclaim it, disclaim it also in their actions; in a word, take away tyranny;"[1] &c.

28. It is obvious that in this passage, and indeed throughout the volume, Chillingworth contravenes the prevailing theories of the Anglican Church full as distinctly as those of the Roman. He escaped, however, unscathed by the censure of that jealous hierarchy: his private friendship with Laud, the lustre of his name, the absence of factious and sectarian connections, and still more, perhaps, the rapid gathering of the storms that swept both parties away, may be assigned as his protection. In later times, his book obtained a high reputation; he was called the immortal Chillingworth; he was the favorite of all the moderate and the latitudinarian writers, of Tillotson, Locke, and Warburton. Those of opposite tenets, when they happen to have read his book, can do nothing else but condemn its tendency.

29. A still more intrepid champion in the same cause was John Hales; for his little tract on Schism, not being in any part directed against the Church of Rome, could have nothing to redeem the strong protestations against church authority, "which," as he bluntly expresses it, "is none,"—words that he afterwards slightly qualified. The aim of Hales, as well as of Grotius, Calixtus, and Chillingworth, was to bring about a more comprehensive communion; but he went still farther: his language is rough and audacious;[2] his theology, in some of his other writings, has a

Hales on Schism.

[1] Chap. iv. § 17.

[2] "I must for my own part confess that councils and synods not only may and have erred, but, considering the means how they are managed, it were a great marvel if they did not err; for what men are they of whom those great meetings do consist? Are they the best, the most learned, the most virtuous, the most likely to walk uprightly? No: the greatest, the most ambitious, and many times men of neither judgment nor learning; such are they of whom these bodies do consist. Are these men, in common equity, likely to determine for truth?"—Vol. i. p. 60, edit. 1765.

"Universality is such a proof of truth as truth itself is ashamed of; for universality is but a quainter and a trimmer name to signify the multitude. Now, human authority at the strongest is but weak; but the multitude is the weakest part of human authority: it is the great patron of error, most easily abused, and most hardly disabused. The beginning of error may be, and mostly is, from private persons; but the maintainer and continuer of error is the multitude. Private persons first beget errors in the multitude, and make them public; and publicness of them begets them again in private persons. It is a thing which our common experience and practice acquaints us with, that when some private persons have gained authority with the multitude, and infused some error into them and made it public, the publicness of the error gains authority to it, and interchangeably pre-

scent of Racow; and, though these crept slowly to light, the was enough in the earliest to make us wonder at the hi name, the epithet Ever-memorable, which he obtained in t English Church.

Controversies on grace and free-will. Augustinian scheme.

30. It is unnecessary to say that few disputes in theolog have been so eagerly conducted, or so extensive ramified, as those which relate to the free-will c man, and his capacity of turning himself towar God. In this place, nothing more will be expecte than a brief statement of the principal questio doing no injustice by a tone of partiality to either side. A shades of opinion, as it seems, may be reduced to two, whic have long divided and will long divide the Christian worl According to one of these, the corrupt nature of man i incapable of exerting any power towards a state of acceptanc with God, or even of willing it with an earnest desire, unti excited by preventing (*præveniens*) grace; which grace i vouchsafed to some only, and is called free, because God is not limited by any respect of those persons to whom he accords this gift. Whether those who are thus called by the influence of the Spirit are so irresistibly impelled to it, that their perseverance in the faith and good works which are the fruits of their election may surely be relied upon, or, on the other hand, may either at first obdurately resist the divine impulses, or finally swerve from their state of grace, is another question, upon which those who agree in the principal doctrine have been at variance. It is also controverted among those who belong to this class of theologians, whether the election thus freely made out of mankind depends upon an eternal decree of predestination, or upon a sentence of God following the fall of man. And a third difference relates to the condition of man after he has been aroused by the Spirit from a state of entire alienation from God: some holding that the completion as well as commencement of the work of conversion is wholly owing to the divine influence; while others maintain a co-operation of the will, so that the salvation of a sinner may in some degree be ascribed to himself. But the essential principle of all whom we reckon in this category of

vails with private persons to entertain it. The most singular and strongest part of human authority is properly in the wisest and most virtuous; and those, I trow, are not the most universal." —iii. 164.

The treatise on Schism, from which these last passages are *not* extracted, was printed at Oxford in 1642, with some animadversions by the editor. Wood's Athenæ, iii. 414.

vines is the necessity of preventing grace; or, in other words, that it is not in the power of man to do any act, in the first instance, towards his own salvation. This, in some or other of its modifications, used to be deemed the orthodox scheme of doctrine: it was established in the Latin Church by the influence of Augustin; it was generally held by the schoolmen, by most of the early reformers, and seems to be inculcated by the decrees of the Council of Trent, as much as by the Articles of the Church of England. In a loose and modern acceptation of the word, it often goes by the name of Calvinism; which may perhaps be less improper, if we do not use the term in an exclusive sense; but, if it is meant to imply a particular relation to Calvin, leads to controversial chicane, and a misstatement of the historical part of the question.

31. An opposite class of theological reasoners belong to what is sometimes called the Semi-Pelagian school. These concur with the former in the necessity of assistance from the Spirit to the endeavors of man, towards subduing his evil tendencies and renewing his heart in the fear and love of God, but conceive that every sinner is capable of seeking this assistance, which will not be refused him, and consequently of beginning the work of conversion by his own will. They, therefore, either deny the necessity of preventing grace, except such as is exterior; or, which comes effectively to the same thing, assert that it is accorded in a sufficient measure to every one within the Christian Church, whether at the time of baptism, or by some other means. They think the opposite opinion, whether founded on the hypothesis of an eternal decree or not, irreconcilable with the moral attributes of the Deity, and inconsistent with the general tenor of Scripture. The Semi-Pelagian doctrine is commonly admitted to have been held by the Greek fathers; but the authority of Augustin and the decisions of the Western Church caused it to assume the character of an heresy. Some of the Scotists among the schoolmen appear to have made an approach to it by their tenet of grace *ex congruo.* They thought that the human virtues and moral dispositions of unregenerate men were the predisposing circumstances, which, by a sort of fitness, made them the objects of the Divine Goodness in according the benefits of his grace. Thus their own free-will, from which it was admitted that such qualities and actions might proceed, would be the real,

Semi-Pelagian hypothesis.

though mediate, cause of their conversion. But this w rejected by the greater part, who asserted the absolute irı spective freedom of grace, and appealed to experience for i frequent efficacy over those who had no inherent virtues merit it.

32. The early reformers, and none more than Luthe maintained the absolute passiveness of the huma will; so that no good actions, even after conversio could be ascribed in any proper sense to man, bı altogether to the operation of the Spirit. Not only, howeve: Melanchthon espoused the synergistic doctrine; but the Lu theran Church, though not in any symbolic book, has bee thought to have gone a good way towards Semi-Pelagianism or what passed for such with the more rigid party.[1] In th reformed church, on the contrary, the Supralapsarian tenet of Calvin, or the immutable decrees of election and repro bation from all eternity, were obviously incompatible witl any hypothesis that made the salvation of a sinner depend upon himself. But, towards the close of the sixteenth century, these severer notions (which it may be observed, by the way, had always been entirely rejected by the Anabaptists, and by some of greater name, such as Sebastian Castalio) began to be impugned by a few learned men. This led in England to what are called the Lambeth Articles, drawn up by Whitgift, six of which assert the Calvinistic doctrine of predestination, and three deny that of the Semi-Pelagians. But these, being not quite approved by the queen or by Lord Burleigh, were never received by authority in our church. There can nevertheless be no reasonable or even sincere doubt that Calvinism, in the popular sense, was at this time prevalent: even Hooker adopted the Lambeth Articles with verbal modifications that do not affect their sense.

Tenets of the reformers.

33. The few who in England, or in the reformed churches upon the Continent, embraced the novel and heterodox opinions, as they were then accounted, within the sixteenth century, excited little attention in comparison with James Arminius, who became professor of theology at Leyden in 1604. The controversy ripened in a few years:

Rise of Arminianism.

[1] Le Clerc says, that the doctrine of Melanchthon, which Bossuet stigmatizes as Semi-Pelagian, is that of the Council of Trent. Bibl Choisie, v. 341. I should put a different construction upon the Tridentine canons; but, of course, my practice in these nice questions is not great.

was intimately connected, not, of course, in its own nature, by some of those collateral influences which have so often ermined the opinions of mankind, with the political relans between the Dutch clergy and the States of Holland, as was afterwards with the still less theological differences of t government with its stadtholder: it appealed, on one e, to reason; on the other, to authority and to force; an equal conflict, till posterity restore the balance. Arminius d in 1609: he has left works on the main topics of debate; t, in theological literature, the great chief of the Arminian or monstrant Church is Simon Episcopius. The principles of iscopius are more widely removed from those of the Austinian school than the five articles, so well known the leading tenets of Arminius, and condemned the Synod of Dort. Of this famous assembly it is difficlt to speak in a few words. The copious history of Brandt perhaps the best authority; though we must own that the posite party have a right to be heard. We are here, hower, on merely literary ground; and the proceedings of ecclestical synods are not strictly within any province of literary story. Episcopius.

34. The works of Episcopius were collectively published in 350, seven years after his death. They form two olumes in folio, and have been more than once reinted. The most remarkable are the Confessio Remonstranum, drawn up about 1624; the Apology for it against a cenre of the opposite party; and, what seems to have been a ter work and more celebrated, his Institutiones Theologicæ. hese contain a new scheme of religion, compared with that f the established churches of Europe; and may justly be eemed the representative of the liberal or latitudinarian theogy. For though the writings of Erasmus, Cassander, Castao, and Acontius, had tended to the same purpose, they were ither too much weakened by the restraints of prudence, or too bscure and transitory, to draw much attention, or to carry any veight against the rigid and exclusive tenets which were susained by power. His writings.

35. The earlier treatises of Episcopius seem to speak on everal subjects less unequivocally than the Theological Institutions; a reserve not perhaps to be censured, and which all parties have thought themselves waranted to employ, so long as either the hope of agreement with Their spirit and tendency.

a powerful adversary, or of mitigating his severity, sho remain. Hence the Confession of the Remonstrants explic states, that they decline the Semi-Pelagian controversy, c tenting themselves with asserting that sufficient grace is stowed on all who are called by the gospel to comply with t divine call and obey its precepts.[1] They used a form of wor which might seem equivalent to the tenet of original sin; they did not avoid or refuse that term. But Episcopius aft wards denies it, at least in the extended sense of most theo gians, almost as explicitly as Jeremy Taylor.[2] It was comm in the seventeenth century, to charge the Arminians, a especially Episcopius, with Socinianism. Bossuet, who see to have quarrelled with all parties, and is neither Molinist r Jansenist, Calvinist nor Arminian, never doubting but th there is a firm footing between them, having attacked Episc pius and Grotius particularly for Semi-Pelagianism and So nianism, Le Clerc entered on their defence. But probab he would have passed himself with Bossuet, and hardly car if he did pass, for a heretic, at least of the former denomin tion.[3]

Great latitude allowed by them.

36. But the most distinguishing peculiarity in the writin of Episcopius was his reduction of the fundament doctrines of Christianity far below the multitudino articles of the churches, confining them to prop sitions which no Christian can avoid acknowledging witho manifest blame; such, namely, wherein the subject, the pr dicate, and the connection of the two, are found in Scriptu by express or equivalent words.[4] He laid little stress on th authority of the church, notwithstanding the advantage h

[1] Episcop. Opera, vol. i. p. 64. "De eo nemini litem movent Remonstrantes." I am not sure that my translation is right; but I think it is what they meant. By prevenient grace they seemed to have meant only the exterior grace of the gospel's promulgation, which is equivalent to the Semi-Pelagian scheme, p. 189. Grotius latterly came into this opinion, though he had disclaimed every thing of the kind in his first dealings with theology. I have found the same doctrine in Calixtus; but I have preserved no reference as to either.

[2] Instit. Theolog., lib. iv. sect. v. c. 2. "Corruptionis istius universalis nulla sunt indicia nec signa; imo non pauca sunt signa ex quibus colligitur naturam totam humanam sic corruptam non esse." The whole chapter, "Ubi de peccato, quod v cant, originis agitur, et præcipua S. loca quibus inniti creditur, examinantur, appears to deny the doctrine entirely but there may be some shades of distin tion which have escaped me. Limbor (Theolog. Christiana, lib. iii. c. iv.) allow it in a qualified sense.

[3] Bibl. Choisie, vol. v.

[4] "Necessaria quæ scripturis continen tur talia esse omnia, ut sine manifest hominis culpa ignorari, negari, aut i dubium vocari nequeant; quia videlic tum subjectum, tum prædicatum, tu subjecti cum prædicato connexio neces saria in ipsis scripturis est, aut expressè aut æquipollenter."—Inst. Theol., l. iv c. 9.

ght have gained by the Anti-Calvinistic tenets of the fathers; mitting, indeed, the validity of the celebrated rule of Vintius Lirinensis, in respect of tradition, which the upholders primitive authority have always had in their mouths, but ding that it is utterly impossible to find any instance wherein can be usefully applied.[1]

37. The Arminian doctrine spread, as is well known, in spite of obloquy and persecution, over much of the otestant region of Europe. The Lutheran churches re already come into it; and in England there is a predisposing bias in the rulers of the church towards e authority of the primitive fathers, all of whom, before the e of Augustin, and especially the Greek, are generally acowledged to have been on that side which promoted the owth of this Batavian theology.[2] Even in France, it was t without considerable influence. Cameron, a divine of umur, one of the chief Protestant seminaries, desed a scheme of conciliation, which, notwithstanding uch opposition, gained ground in those churches. It was pported by some highly distinguished for learning, Amyraut, aillé, and Blondel. Of this scheme it is remarkable, that hile in its literal purport it can only seem a modification of e Augustinian hypothesis, with an awkward and feeble adixture of the other, yet its tendency was to efface the former degrees, and to slide into the Arminian hypothesis, which

Progress of Arminianism.

Cameron.

[1] Instit. Theolog., l. iv. sect. i. c. 15. upin says of Episcopius: "Il n'a emoyé dans ses ouvrages que des passages l'écriture sainte qu'il possédoit partement. Il avoit aussi lu les Rabbins; ais on ne voit pas qu'il eût étudié les res ni l'antiquité ecclésiastique. Il rit nettement et méthodiquement, pose s principes, ne dissimule rien des objecons qu'on peut faire contre, et y répond mieux qu'il peut. On voit en lui une lérance parfaite pour les Sociniens, quoiu'il se déclare contre eux; pour le parti Arminius, jamais il n'a eu de plus zélé de plus habile défenseur." — Bibliohèque des Auteurs séparés de l'Eglise omaine, ii. 495.

The life of Episcopius has been written y Limborch. Justice has been done to his eminent person, and to the Arminian arty which he led, in two recent English orks, Nicholls's Calvinism and Arminiansm displayed, and Calder's Life of Episcoius (1835). The latter is less verbose and nore temperate than the former, and may be recommended, as a fair and useful production, to the general reader. Two theological parties in this country, though opposite in most things, are inveterately prejudiced against the Leyden school.

[2] Gerard Vossius, in his Historia Pelagiana, the first edition of which, in 1618, was considerably enlarged afterwards, admitted that the first four centuries did not countenance the predestinarian scheme of Augustin. This gave offence in Holland; his book was publicly censured; he was excommunicated, and forbidden to teach in public or private. Vossius, like others, remembered that he had a large family, and made, after some years, a sort of retractation, which, of course, did not express his real opinion. Le Clerc seems to doubt whether he acted from this motive, or from what he calls simplicity, an expression for weakness. Vossius was, like his contemporary Usher, a man of much more learning, than strength of intellect Bibliothèque Universelle, xvii. 312, 329; Niceron, vol. xiii.

ultimately became, I believe, very common in the Reforr Church.

Rise of Jansenism.

38. These perplexities were not confined to Protestant th logy. The Church of Rome, strenuous to maint the tenets of Augustin, and yet to condemn th who did the same, has been charged with exerting plenitude of her infallibility to enforce the belief of an in herent syncretism. She had condemned Baius, as giving much efficacy to grace: she was on the point of condemni Molina for giving too little. Both Clement VIII. and P V. leaned to the Dominicans against the Jesuits in this co troversy; but the great services and influence of the lat order prevented a decision which would have humbled the before so many adversaries. It may, nevertheless, be sa that the Semi-Pelagian or Arminian doctrine, though cons nant to that of the Jesuits, was generally ill received in t Church of Rome, till the opposite hypothesis, that of August and Calvin, having been asserted by one man in more u limited propositions than had been usual, a re-action to place, that eventually both gave an apparent triumph to t Molinist party, and endangered the church itself by t schism to which the controversy gave rise. The Augustin of Jansenius, Bishop of Ypres, was published in 1640, and the very next year was censured at Rome. But, as the gre controversy that sprang out of the condemnation of this boc belongs more strictly to the next period, we shall defer it fc the present.

Socinus; Volkelius.

39. The Socinian academy at Racow, which drew to itsel several proselytes from other countries, acquired con siderable importance in theological literature afte the beginning of the century. It was not likely that a sec regarded with peculiar animosity would escape, in the genera disposition of the Catholic party in Poland to oppress the dis sidents whom they had long feared: the Racovian institutio was broken up and dispersed in 1638, though some of it members continued to linger in that country for twenty year longer. The Bibliotheca Fratrum Polonorum, published a Amsterdam (in the titlepage, Irenopolis) in 1658, contains chiefly the works of Socinian theologians who belong to this first part of the century. The Prælectiones Theologicæ of Faustus Socinus himself, being published in 1609, after his death, fall within this class. They contain a systematic theo-

gy according to his scheme, and are praised by Eichhorn r the acuteness and depth they often display.[1] In these, mong his other deviations from the general orthodoxy of hristendom, Socinus astonished mankind by denying the evi-ences of natural religion, resolving our knowledge, even of a eity, into revelation. This paradox is more worthy of those who have since adopted it, than of so acute a reasoner as So-inus.[2] It is, in fact, not very congenial to the spirit of his heology, which, rejecting all it thinks incompatible with rea-on as to the divine attributes, should at least have some es-ablished notions of them upon rational principles. The later Socinians, even those nearest to the time, did not follow their master in this part of his tenets.[3] The treatise of Volkelius, son-in-law of Socinus, De Vera Religione, is chiefly taken from he latter's writings. It was printed at Racow in 1633, and again in Holland in 1641: but, most of the Dutch impression having been burned by order of the magistrates, it is a very scarce book; and copies were formerly sold at great prices. But the hangman's bonfire has lost its charm; and forbidden books, when they happen to occur, are no longer in much request. The first book out of five in this volume of Volke-lius, on the attributes of God, is by Crellius.

40. Crellius was, perhaps, the most eminent of the Racovian school in this century.[4] Many of its members, like himself, were Germans; their sect having gained ground in some of the Lutheran States about this time, as it did also in the United Provinces. Grotius broke a lance with him in his treatise De Satisfactione Christi, to which he replied in another with the same title. Each retired from the field with the courtesies of chivalry towards his antagonist. The Dutch Arminians in general, though very erroneously supposed to concur in all the leading tenets of the Racovian

Crellius; Ruarus.

[1] Eichhorn, vi. part 1, p. 283. Simon, however, observes that Socinus knew little Greek or Hebrew, as he owns himself; though he pretends to decide questions which require a knowledge of these languages. I quote from Bibliothèque Universelle, vol. xxiii. p. 498.

[2] Tillotson, in one of his sermons (I cannot give the reference, writing from memory), dissents, as might be expected, from this denial of natural religion, but with such encomiums on Socinus as some archbishops would have avoided.

[3] "Socinum sectæ ejus principes nuper Volkelius, nunc Ruarus non probant, in eo quod circa Dei cognitionem petita e natura rerum argumenta abdicaverit." — Grot. Epist., 964. See, too, Ruari Epist., p. 210.

[4] Dupin praises Volkelius highly, but says of Crellius, "Il avoit beaucoup étudié, mais il n'étoit pas un esprit fort élevé." — Bibl. des Auteurs séparés, ii. 614, v. 628. Simon, on the contrary (*ubi suprà*), praises Crellius highly, and says no other commentator of his party is comparable to him.

theologians, treated them with much respect.[1] Groti was often reproached with the intimacies he kept up amor these obnoxious sectaries; and many of his letters, as we as those of Curcellæus and other leading Arminians, bear wi ness to the personal regard they felt for them.[2] Sever proofs of this will be also found in the Epistles of Ruarus, book which throws much light on the theological opinions o the age. Ruarus was a man of acuteness, learning, and piety not wholly concurring with the Racovians, but not far re moved from them.[3] The Commentaries of Grotius on th

[1] The Remonstrants refused to anathematize the Socinians. Episcopius says, on account of the apparent arguments in their favor, and the differences that have always existed on that head. Apologia Confessionis; Episc. Op., vol. i. His own tenets were probably what some would call Arian: thus he says, "Personis his tribus divinitatem tribui, non collateraliter aut co-ordinatè, sed subordinatè." — Inst. Theol., l. iv. c. 2, 32. Grotius says, he finds the Catholics more *tractable* about the Trinity than the Calvinists.

[2] Grotius never shrunk from defending his intimacy with Ruarus and Crellius; and, after praising the former, concludes, in one of his letters, with this liberal and honest sentiment: "Ego vero ejus sum animi, ejusque instituti, ut mihi cum hominibus cunctis præcipue cum Christianis quantumvis errantibus necessitudinis aliquid putem intercedere, idque me neque dictis neque factis pigeat demonstrare." — Epist. 860. "Hæretici nisi aliquid haberent veri ac nobiscum commune, jam hæretici non essent." — 2da Series, p. 873. "Nihil veri eo factum est deterius, quod in id Socinus incidit." — p. 880. This, he thought, was the case in some questions, where Socinus, without designing it, had agreed with antiquity. "Neque me pudeat consentire Socino, si quando is in veram veteremque sententiam incidit, ut sanè fecit in controversia de justitia per fidem, et aliis nonnullis." — Id., p. 797. "Socinus hoc non agens in antiquæ ecclesiæ sensus nonnunquam incidit, et eas partes, ut ingenio valebat, percoluit feliciter. Admiscuit alia quæ etiam vera dicenti auctoritatem detraxere." — Epist. 936. Even during his controversy with Crellius, he wrote to him in a very handsome manner. "Bene autem in epistola tua, quæ mihi longè gratissima advenit, de me judicas, non esse me eorum in numero, qui ob sententias salva pietate dissentientes, alieno a quoquam sim animo, aut boni alicujus amicitiam repudiare. Etiam in libro de vera religione [Volkelii], quem jam percurri, relecturus et posthac multa invenio summo cum judicio observata; illud vero sæculo gratulor, repertos homines, qui neutiquam in controversiis subtilibus tantum ponunt, quantum in vera vitæ emendatione, et quotidiano ad sanctitatem profectu." — Epist. 280. (1631.) He wrote with kindness and regret on the breaking-up of the establishment at Racow in 1638. Ep. 1006. Grotius has been as obnoxious on the score of Socinianism as of Popery. His Commentaries on the Scriptures are taxed with it; and in fact he is not in good odor with any but the Arminian divines; nor do they, we see, wholly agree with him.

[3] Ruarus nearly agreed with Grotius as to the atonement; at least, the latter thought so. "De satisfactione ita mihi respondit, ut nihil admodum controversiæ relinqueretur." — Grot. Epist., 2da Series, p. 881. See also Ruari Epistolæ, pp. 148, 282. He paid also more respect to the second century than some of his brethren, pp. 100, 439, and even struggles to agree with the Ante-Nicene fathers; though he cannot come up to them, pp. 275, 296. But, in answer to some of his correspondents who magnified primitive authority, he well replies: "Deinde quæro quis illos fixit veritati terminos? quis duo illa prima sæcula ab omni errore absolvit? Annon ecclesiastica historia satis testatur, nonnullas opiniones portentosas jam tum inter eos qui nomen Christi dederant, invaluisse? Quin ut verum fatear, res ipsa docet nonnullos posterioris ævi acutius in enodandis Scripturis versatos; et ut de nostra ætate dicam, valde me pœniteret Calvini vestri ac Bezæ si nihilo solidius sacras literas interpretarentur, quam video illos ipsos, quos tu mihi obducis, fecisse." — p. 183. He lamented the fatal swerving from Protestantism into which reverence for antiquity was leading his friend Grotius: "Fortassis et antiquitatis veneratio, quæ gravibus quibusdam Pontificiorum erroribus præluxit, ultra lineam eum perduxit," p. 277 (1642); and

criptures have been also charged with Socinianism; but he leaded that his interpretations were those of the fathers.

41. Two questions of great importance, which had been aised in the preceding century, became still more interesting in the present, on account of the more requent occasion that the force of circumstances gave for neir investigation, and the greater names that were engaged n it. Both of these arose out of the national establishment of hurches, and their consequent relation to the commonwealth. One regarded the power of the magistrate over the church he ecognized: the other involved the right of his subjects to issent from it by nonconformity, or by a different mode of vorship.

Erastianism

42. Erastus, by proposing to substitute for the ancient discipline of ecclesiastical censures, and especially for excommunication, a perpetual superintendence of the civil power over the faith and practice of the church, had given name to a scheme generally denominated Erastianism, though in some respects far broader than any thing he seems to have suggested. It was more elaborately maintained by Hooker in his Ecclesiastical Polity, and had been, in fact, that on which the English Reformation, under Henry, was originally founded. But as it was manifestly opposed to the ultramontane pretensions of the see of Rome, and even to the more moderate theories of the Catholic Church, being, of course, destructive of her independence, so did it stand in equal contradiction to the Presbyterian scheme of Scotland and of the United Provinces. In the latter country, the States

Maintained by Hooker

in answer to Mersenne, who seems to have had some hopes of his conversion, and recommended to him the controversy of Grotius with Rivet, he plainly replies, that the former had extenuated some things in the Church of Rome which ought to be altered. — p. 258. This he frequently laments in the course of his letters, but, in comparison with some of the sterner Socinians, treats him with gentleness. It is remarkable that even he and Crellius seem to have excluded the members of the Church of Rome, except the "vulgus ineruditum et Cassandri gregales," from salvation; and this while almost all churches were anathematizing themselves in the same way. Ruar. Epist., p. 9, and p. 167.

This book contains two centuries of epistles, the second of which is said to be very scarce; and I doubt whether many have read the first, which must excuse my quotations. The learning, sense, and integrity of Ruarus, as well as the high respect which Calixtus, Curcellæus. and other great men, felt for him, render the book of some interest. He tells us that while he was in England, about 1617, a professorship at Cambridge was offered to him, worth £100 per annum, besides as much more from private pupils. — p. 71. But he probably mistook the civil speeches of individuals for an offer: he was not eminent enough for such a proposal on the part of the university; and at least he must have been silent about his Socinianism. The morality of the early Socinians was very strict, and even ascetic; proofs of which appear in these letters. — p. 306, *et alibi.*

of Holland had been favorable to the Arminians, so far least as to repress any violence against them: tl clergy were exasperated and intolerant; and th raised the question of civil supremacy, in which Grotius, l one of his early works, entitled Pietas Ordinum Hollandi published in 1613, sustained the right of the magistrate inhibit dangerous controversies.

And Grotius.

43. He returned, after the lapse of some years, to the sam theme in a larger and more comprehensive work, D Imperio Summarum Potestatum circa Sacra. It i written upon the Anglican principles of regal su premacy, which had, however, become far less popular wit the rulers of our church than in the days of Cranmer, Whit gift, and Hooker. After stating the question, and proving th ecclesiastical power of the magistrate by natural law, Scrip ture, established usage, agreement of Heathen and Christian writers, and the reason of the thing, he distinguishes control over sacred offices from their exercise, and proceeds to inquire whether the magistrate may take the latter on himself; which, though practised in the early ages of the world, he finds inconvenient at present, the manners required for the regal and sacerdotal character being wholly different.[1]

His treatise on ecclesiastical power of the state.

44. Actions may be prescribed or forbidden by natural divine law, positive divine law, or human law; the latter extending to nothing but what is left indefinite by the other two. But, though we are bound not to act in obedience to human laws which contradict the divine, we are also bound not forcibly to resist them. We may defend ourselves by force against an equal, not against a superior, as he proves, first, from the Digest, and, secondly, from the New Testament.[2] Thus the rule of passive obedience is unequivocally laid down. He meets the recent examples of resistance to sovereigns, by saying that they cannot be approved where the kings have had an absolute power; but where they are bound by compact or the authority of a senate or of estates, since their power is not unlimited, they may be resisted on just grounds by that authority.[3] "Which I remark," he proceeds to say, "lest any one, as I sometimes have known, should disgrace a good cause by a mistaken defence."

[1] Cap. 4.

[2] Cap. 3.

[3] "Sin alicubi reges tales fuere, qui pactis sive positivis legibus et senatus alicujus aut ordinum decretis adstringerentur, in hos, ut summum imperium non obtinent, arma ex optimatum tanquam superiorum sententia sumi justis de causis potuerunt." — Ibid.

45. The magistrate can alter nothing which is definitely laid down by the positive law of God; but he may regulate the circumstantial observance even of such; and, as to things undefined in Scripture, he has plenary jurisdiction, such as the temporalities of the church, the convocation of synods, the election of pastors. The burden of proof lies on those who would limit the civil power by affirming any thing to be prescribed by the divine law.[1] The authority attributed in Scripture to churches does not interfere with the power of the magistrate, being persuasive, and not coercive. The whole church has no coercive power by divine right.[2] But, since the visible church is a society of divine institution, it follows, that whatever is naturally competent to a lawful society is competent also to the church, unless it can be proved to be withdrawn from it.[3] It has, therefore, a legislative government (*regimen constitutivum*), of which he gives the institution of the Lord's Day as an example. But this does not impair the sovereign's authority in ecclesiastical matters. In treating of that supremacy, he does not clearly show what jurisdiction he attributes to the magistrate; most of his instances relating to the temporalities of the church, as to which no question is likely to arise.[4] But, on the whole, he means undoubtedly to carry the supremacy as far as is done in England.

46. In a chapter on the due exercises of the civil supremacy over the church, he shows more of a Protestant feeling than would have been found in him when he approached the latter years of his life;[5] and declares fully against submission to any visible authority in matters of faith, so that sovereigns are not bound to follow the ministers of the church in what they may affirm as doctrine. Ecclesiastical synods he deems often useful, but thinks the magistrate is not bound to act with their consent, and that they are sometimes pernicious.[6] The magistrate may determine who shall compose such synods,[7] — a strong position, which he endeavors to prove at

[1] Cap. 3.

[2] Cap. 4.

[3] "Quandoquidem ecclesia cœtus est divina lege non permissus tantum sed et institutus, de aspectabili cœtu loquor, sequitur ea omnia quæ cœtibus legitimis naturaliter competunt, etiam ecclesiæ competere, quatenus adempta non probantur." — Ibid.

[4] Cap. 5.

[5] Cap. 6. He states the question to be this: "An post apostolorum ætatem aut persona aut cœtus sit aliquis aspectabilis, de quâ quove certi esse possimus ac debeamus, quæcunque ab ipsis proponantur, esse indubitatæ veritatis. Negant hoc Evangelici; aiunt Romanenses."

[6] Cap. 7.

[7] "Designare eos, qui ad synodum sunt venturi."

great length. Even if the members are elected by the church, the magistrate may reject those whom he reckons unfit: he may preside in the assembly; confirm, reject, annul its decisions. He may also legislate about the whole organization of the established church.[1] It is for him to determine what form of religion shall be publicly exercised; an essential right of sovereignty, as political writers have laid it down. And this is confirmed by experience; "for if any one shall ask why the Romish religion flourished in England under Mary, the Protestant under Elizabeth, no cause can be assigned but the pleasure of these queens, or, as some might say, of the queens and parliaments." To the objection from the danger of abuse in conceding so much power to the sovereign, he replies, that no other theory will secure us better. On every supposition, the power must be lodged in men, who are all liable to error. We must console ourselves by a trust in Divine Providence alone.[2]

47. The sovereign may abolish false religions, and punish their professors, which no one else can. Here again we find precedents instead of arguments; but he says that the primitive church disapproved of capital punishments for heresy, which seems to be his main reason for doing the same. The sovereign may also enjoin silence in controversies, and inspect the conduct of the clergy without limiting himself by the canons; though he will do well to regard them. Legislation and jurisdiction, that is, of a coercive nature, do not belong to the church, except as they may be conceded to it by the civil power.[3] He fully explains the various kinds of ecclesiastical law that have been gradually introduced. Even the power of the keys, which is by divine right, cannot be so exercised as to exclude the appellant jurisdiction of the sovereign; as he proves by the Roman law, and by the usage of the parliament of Paris.[4]

48. The sovereign has a control (*inspectionem cum imperio*) over the ordination of priests, and certainly possesses a right of confirmation; that is, the assignment of an ordained

[1] Cap. 8. "Nulla in re magis elucescit vis summi imperii, quam quod in ejus arbitrio est quænam religio publicè exerceatur, idque præcipuum inter majestatis jura ponunt omnes qui politicè scripserunt. Docet idem experientia; si enim quæras cur in Anglia Maria regnante Romana religio, Elizabetha vero imperante, Evangelica viguerit, causa proxima reddi non poterit, nisi ex arbitrio reginarum, aut, ut quibusdam videtur, reginarum ac parlamenti." — p. 242.

[2] Cap. 8.

[3] Ibid.

[4] Cap. 9.

minister to a given cure.[1] And, though the election of pastors belongs to the church, this may, for good reasons, be taken into the hands of the sovereign. Instances in point are easily found; and the chapter upon the subject contains an interesting historical summary of this part of ecclesiastical law. In every case, the sovereign has a right of annulling an election, and also of removing a pastor from the local exercise of his ministry.[2]

Remark upon this theory.

49. This is the full development of an Erastian theory, which Cranmer had early espoused, and which Hooker had maintained in a less extensive manner. Bossuet has animadverted upon it, nor can it appear tolerable to a zealous churchman.[3] It was well received in England by the lawyers, who had always been jealous of the spiritual tribunals, especially of late years, when, under the patronage of Laud, they had taken a higher tone than seemed compatible with the supremacy of the common law. The scheme, nevertheless, is open to some objections, when propounded in so unlimited a manner, none of which is more striking than that it tends to convert differences of religious opinion into crimes against the state, and furnishes bigotry with new arguments as well as new arms in its conflict with the free exercise of human reason. Grotius, however, feared rather that he had given too little power to the civil magistrate than too much.[4]

Toleration of religious tenets

50. Persecution for religious heterodoxy, in all its degrees, was, in the sixteenth century, the principle as well as the practice of every church. It was held inconsistent with the sovereignty of the magistrate to permit any religion but his own; inconsistent with his duty to suffer any but the true. The Edict of Nantes was a compromise between belligerent parties; the toleration of the dissidents in Poland was nearly of the same kind: but no state

[1] Cap. 10. "Confirmationem hanc summæ potestati acceptam ferendam nemo sanus negaverit."

[2] Ibid.

[3] See Le Clerc's remarks on what Bossuet has said. Bibliothèque Choisie, p. 349.

[4] "Ego multo magis vereor, ne minus quam par est magistratibus, aut plusquam par est pastoribus tribuerim, quam ne in alteram partem iterum (?) excesserim, nec sic quidem illis satisfiet qui se ecclesiam vocant."—Epist. 42. This was in 1614, after the publication of the Pietas Ordinum Hollandiæ. As he drew nearer to the Church of Rome, or that of Canterbury, he must probably have somewhat modified his Erastianism. And yet he seems never to have been friendly to the temporal power of bishops. He writes in August, 1641, "Episcopis Angliæ videtur mansurum nomen prope sine re, accisa et opulentia et auctoritate. Mihi non displicet ecclesiæ pastores et ab inani pompa

powerful enough to restrain its sectaries from the exercise of their separate worship had any scruples about the right and obligation to do so. Even the writers of that century, who seemed most strenuous for toleration, — Castalio, Celso, and Koornhert, — had confined themselves to denying the justice of penal, and especially of capital, inflictions for heresy: the liberty of public worship had but incidentally, if at all, been discussed. Acontius had developed larger principles, distinguishing the fundamental from the accessory doctrines of the gospel; which, by weakening the associations of bigotry, prepared the way for a Catholic tolerance. Episcopius speaks in the strongest terms of the treatise of Acontius, De Stratagematibus Satanæ, and says that the remonstrants trod closely in his steps, as would appear by comparing their writings; so that he shall quote no passages in proof, their entire books bearing witness to the conformity.[1]

51. The Arminian dispute led, by necessary consequence, to the question of public toleration. They sought at first a free admission to the pulpits; and in an excellent speech of Grotius, addressed to the magistrates of Amsterdam in 1616, he objects to a separate toleration as rending the bosom of the church. But it was soon evident that nothing more could be obtained; and their adversaries refused this. They were driven, therefore, to contend for religious liberty; and the writings of Episcopius are full of this plea. Against capital punishments for heresy he raises his voice with indignant severity, and asserts that the whole Christian world abhorred the fatal precedent of Calvin in the death of Servetus.[2] This indicates a remarkable change already wrought in the sentiments of mankind. No capital punishments for heresy seem to have been inflicted in Pro-

Claimed by the Arminians;

et a curis sæcularium rerum sublevari." — p. 1011. He had a regard for Laud, as the restorer of a reverence for primitive antiquity, and frequently laments his fate; but had said, in 1640, "Doleo quod episcopi nimium intendendo potentiæ suæ nervos odium sibi potius quam amorem populorum pariunt." — Ep. 1390.

[1] Episcop. Opera, i. 301 (edit. 1665).

[2] "Calvinus signum primus extulit supra alios omnes, et exemplum dedit in theatro Gebennensi funestissimum, quodque Christianus orbis merito execratur et abominatur; nec hoc contentus tam atroci facinore, cruento simul animo et calamo parentavit." — Apologia pro Confess. Remonstrantium, c. 24, p. 241. The whole passage is very remarkable, as an indignant reproof of a party who, while living under Popish governments, cry out for liberty of conscience, and deny the right of punishing opinions; yet in all their writings and actions, when they have the power, display the very opposite principles. [The Council of Geneva, in 1632, little ashamed of the death of Servetus, had condemned one Nicolas Antoine to be strangled and burned for denying the Trinity. Bibliothèque Raisonnée, ii. 156. I do not distinctly recollect any later case in Protestant countries of capital punishment for mere heresy — 1842.]

stant countries after this time; nor were they as frequently as boldly vindicated as before.[1]

52. The Independents claim to themselves the honor of having been the first to maintain the principles of general toleration, both as to freedom of worship and immunity from penalties for opinion. But that the Arminians were not as early promulgators of the same noble tenets, seems not to have been proved. Crellius, in his Vindiciæ pro Religionis Libertate, 1636, contended for the Polish dissidents, and especially for his own sect.[2] The principle is implied, if not expressed, in the writings of Chillingworth, and still more of Hales; but the first famous plea in this country for tolerance in religion, on a comprehensive basis and on deep-seated foundations, was the Liberty of Prophesying, by Jeremy Taylor. This celebrated work was written, according to Taylor's dedication, during his retirement in Wales, whither he was driven, as he expresses it, "by this great storm which hath dashed the vessel of the church all in pieces;" and published in 1647. He speaks of himself as without access to books: it is evident, however, from the abundance of his quotations, that he was not much in want of them; and from this, as well as other strong indications, we may reasonably believe that a considerable part of his treatise had been committed to paper long before.

By the Independents; And by Jeremy Taylor.

53. The argument of this important book rests on one leading maxim, derived from the Arminian divines, as it was in them from Erasmus and Acontius, that the fundamental truths of Christianity are comprised in narrow compass, not beyond the Apostles' Creed in its literal meaning; that all the rest is matter of disputation, and too uncertain, for the most part, to warrant our condemning those

His Liberty of Prophesying.

1 "De hæreticorum pœnis quæ scripsi, in iis mecum sentit Gallia et Germania, ut puto, omnis." — Grot. Epist., p. 941. (1642.) Some years sooner, there had been remains of the leaven in France. "Adversus hæreticidia," he says in 1626, "satis ut arbitror plane locutus sum, certè ita ut hic multos ob id offenderim." — p. 789. Our own Fuller, I am sorry to say, in his Church History, written about 1650, speaks with some disapprobation of the sympathy of the people with Legat and Wightman, burned by James I., in 1614; and this is the more remarkable, as he is a well-natured and not generally bigoted writer. I should think he was the latest Protestant who has tarnished his name by such sentiments.

2 This short tract, which will be found among the collected works of Crellius, in the Bibliotheca Fratrum Polonorum, contains a just and temperate pleading for religious liberty, but little which can appear very striking in modern times. It is said, nevertheless, to have been translated and republished by D'Holbach about 1760. This I have not seen; but there must, I presume, have been a good deal of *condiment* added to make it stimulating enough for his school.

who differ from us, as if their error must be criminal. Th one proposition, much expanded, according to Taylor's diffu style, and displayed in a variety of language, pervades th whole treatise; a small part of which, in comparison wi the rest, bears immediately on the point of political toleratio as a duty of civil governments and of churches invested wit power. In the greater portion, Taylor is rather arguin against that dogmatism of judgment which induces men, eithe singly or collectively, to pronounce with confidence wher only a varying probability can be attained. This spirit is th religious, though not entirely the political, motive of intole rance; and, by chasing this from the heart, he inferred, no that he should lay wide the door to universal freedom, bu dispose the magistrate to consider more equitably the claim of every sect. "Whatsoever is against the foundation of faith or contrary to good life and the laws of obedience, or destruc tive to human society and the public and just interests of bodies politic, is out of the limits of my question, and does no pretend to compliance or toleration: so that I allow no indifferency, nor any countenance to those religions whose principles destroy government, nor to those religions, if there be any such, that teach ill life."

Boldness of his doctrines.

54. No man, as Taylor here teaches, is under any obligation to believe that in revelation, which is not so revealed but that wise men and good men have differed in their opinions about it. And the great variety of opinions in churches, and even in the same church "there being none that is in prosperity," as he with rather a startling boldness puts it, "but changes her doctrines every age, either by bringing in new doctrines or by contradicting her old," shows that we can have no term of union but that wherein all agree, — the creed of the apostles.[1] And hence though we may undoubtedly carry on our own private inquiries as much farther as we see reason, none who hold this fundamental faith are to be esteemed heretics, nor liable to punishment. And here he proceeds to reprove all those oblique acts which are not direct persecutions of men's persons, — the

[1] "Since no churches believe themselves infallible, that only excepted which all other churches say is most of all deceived, it were strange if, in so many articles, which make up their several bodies of confessions, they had not mistaken, every one of them, in some thing or other." This is Taylor's fearless mode of grappling with his argument; and any other must give a church that claims infallibility the advantage.

estruction of books, the forbidding the publication of new ies, the setting out fraudulent editions and similar acts of ilsehood, by which men endeavor to stifle or prevent religious iquiry. "It is a strange industry and an importune diligence iat was used by our forefathers: of all those heresies which ave them battle and employment, we have absolutely no reord or monument, but what themselves, who are adversaries, ave transmitted to us; and we know that adversaries, especially such who observed all opportunities to discredit both the ersons and doctrines of the enemy, are not always the best ecords or witnesses of such transactions. We see it now in his very age, in the present distemperatures, that parties are o good registers of the actions of the adverse side; and if we cannot be confident of the truth of a story now, — now I say that it is possible for any man, and likely that the interested adversary will discover the imposture,— it is far more unlikely that after-ages should know any other truth, but such as serves the ends of the representers."[1]

55. None were accounted heretics by the primitive church, who held by the Apostles' Creed, till the Council of Nice defined some things, rightly, indeed, as Taylor professes to believe, but perhaps with too much alteration of the simplicity of ancient faith, so that "he had need be a subtle man who understands the very words of the new determinations." And this was carried much farther by later councils, and in the Athanasian Creed, of which, though protesting his own persuasion in its truth, he intimates not a little disapprobation. The necessary articles of faith are laid down clearly in Scripture; but no man can be secure, as to mysterious points, that he shall certainly understand and believe them in their true sense. This he shows, first, from the great discrepancy of readings in manuscripts (an argument which he overstates in a very uncritical and incautious manner); next, from the different senses the words will bear, which there is no certain mark to distinguish, the infinite variety of human understandings, swayed, it may be, by interest, or determined by accidental and extrinsical circumstances, and the fallibility of those means by which men hope to attain a clear knowledge of scriptural truth. And after exposing, certainly with no extenuation, the difficulties of

His notions of uncertainty in theological tenets.

1 Vol. vii. p. 424, Heber's edition of Taylor.

interpretation, he concludes, that, since these ordinary mear of expounding Scripture are very dubious, "he that is th wisest, and by consequence the likeliest to expound truest, i all probability of reason, will be very far from confidence and therefore a wise man would not willingly be prescribed t by others; and, if he be also a just man, he will not impos upon others; for it is best every man should be left in tha liberty, from which no man can justly take him, unless h could secure him from error; so here there is a necessity to conserve the liberty of prophesying and interpreting Scripture, — a necessity derived from the consideration of the difficulty of Scripture in questions controverted, and the uncertainty of any internal medium of interpretation."

His low opinion of the fathers.

56. Taylor would in much of this have found an echo in the advocates of the Church of Rome, and in some Protestants of his own communion. But he passes onward to assail their bulwarks. Tradition, or the testimony of the church, he holds insufficient and uncertain, for the reasons urged more fully by Daillé; the authority of councils is almost equally precarious, from their inconsistency, their liability to factious passions, and the doubtful authenticity of some of their acts; the pope's claim to infallibility is combated on the usual grounds; the judgment of the fathers is shown to be inconclusive, by their differences among themselves, and their frequent errors; and, professing a desire that "their great reputation should be preserved as sacred as it ought," he refers the reader to Daillé for other things; and "shall only consider that the writings of the fathers have been so corrupted by the intermixture of heretics, so many false books put forth in their names, so many of their writings lost which would more clearly have explicated their sense, and at last an open profession made, and a trade of making the fathers speak not what themselves thought, but what other men pleased, that it is a great instance of God's providence, and care of his church, that we have so much good preserved in the writings which we receive from the fathers, and that all truth is not as clear gone as is the certainty of their great authority and reputation."[1]

[1] It seems not quite easy to reconcile this with what Taylor has just before said of his desire to preserve the reputation of the fathers sacred. In no writer is it more necessary to observe the *animus* with which he writes; for, giving way to his impetuosity, when he has said any thing that would give offence, or which he thought incautious, it was not his custom, so far as we can judge, to ex-

57. The authority of the church cannot be any longer lleged when neither that of popes and councils, nor f ancient fathers, is maintainable; since the diffuve church has no other means of speaking, nor can e distinguish by any extrinsic test the greater or better ortion of it from the worse. And thus, after dismissing repectfully the pretences of some to expound Scripture by the Spirit, as impertinent to the question of dictating the faith of thers, he comes to the reason of each man, as the best judge, or himself, of religious controversies, — reason, that may be xercised either in choosing a guide, if it feel its own incompetency, or in examining the grounds of belief. The later has great advantages; and no man is bound to know any hing of that concerning which he is not able to judge for himself. But reason may err, as he goes on to prove, without being culpable; that which is plain to one understanding being obscure to another; and among various sources of error which he enumerates as incidental to mankind, that of education being "so great and invincible a prejudice, that he who masters the inconvenience of it is more to be commended than he can justly be blamed that complies with it." And thus, not only single men, but whole bodies, take, unhesitatingly and unanimously, opposite sides from those who have imbibed another kind of instruction: and "it is strange that all the Dominicans should be of one opinion in the matter of predestination and immaculate conception, and all the Franciscans of the quite contrary; as if their understandings were formed in a different mould, and furnished with various principles by their very rule." These and the like prejudices are not absolute excuses to every one, and are often accompanied with culpable dispositions of mind; but the impossibility of judging others renders it incumbent on us to be lenient towards all, and neither to be peremptory in denying that those who differ from us have used the best means in their power to discover the truth, nor to charge their persons, whatever we may their opinions, with odious consequences which they do not avow.

Difficulty of finding out truth.

58. This diffuse and not very well-arranged vindication of

punge or soften it, but to insert something else of an opposite color, without taking any pains to harmonize his context. This makes it easy to quote passages, especially short ones, from Taylor, which do not exhibit his real way of thinking; if indeed his way of thinking itself did not vary with the wind that blew from different regions of controversy

diversity of judgment in religion, comprised in the fir twelve sections of the Liberty of Prophesying, is th proper basis of the second part, which maintains th justice of toleration as a consequence from the former prin ciple. The general arguments, or prejudices, on which pun ishment for religious tenets had been sustained, turned o their criminality in the eyes of God, and the duty of th magistrate to sustain God's honor, and to guard his own sub jects from sin. Taylor, not denying that certain and know idolatry, or any sort of practical impiety, may be punishe corporally, because it is matter of fact, asserts that no mat ter of mere opinion, no errors that of themselves are not sins are to be persecuted or punished by death or corporal inflic tion. He returns to his favorite position, "that we are no sure not to be deceived;" mingling this, in that inconsequent allocation of his proofs which frequently occurs in his writings, with other arguments of a different nature. The governors of the church, indeed, may condemn and restrain, as far as their power extends, any false doctrine which encourages evil life, or destroys the foundations of religion: but if the church meddles farther with any matters of question, which have not this tendency, so as to dictate what men are to believe, she becomes tyrannical and uncharitable; the Apostles' Creed being sufficient to conserve the peace of the church and the unity of her doctrine. And, with respect to the civil magistrate, he concludes that he is bound to suffer the profession of different opinions, which are neither directly impious and immoral, nor disturb the public peace.

Grounds of toleration.

59. The seventeenth chapter, in which Taylor professes to consider which among the sects of Christendom are to be tolerated, and in what degree, is written in a tone not easily reconciled with that of the rest. Though he begins by saying that diversity of opinions does more concern public peace than religion, it certainly appears, in some passages, that on this pretext of peace, which with the magistrate has generally been of more influence than that of orthodoxy, he withdraws a great deal of that liberty of prophesying which he has been so broadly asserting. Punishment for religious tenets is doubtless not at all the same as restraint of separate worship; yet we are not prepared for the shackles he seems inclined to throw over the latter. Laws of ecclesiastical discipline, which, in Taylor's age, were under-

Inconsistency of one chapter.

ood to be binding on the whole community, cannot, he holds, e infringed by those who take occasion to disagree, without ndering authority contemptible; and if there are any as ealous for obedience to the church, as others may be for their pinions against it, the toleration of the latter's disobedience ay give offence to the former: an argument strange enough n this treatise! But Taylor is always more prone to accu- ulate reasons than to sift their efficiency. It is indeed, he hinks, worthy to be considered, in framing a law of church iscipline, whether it will be disliked by any who are to obey t; but, after it is once enacted, there seems no further indul- gence practicable than what the governors of the church may grant to particular persons by dispensation. The laws of liscipline are for the public good, and must not so far tolerate a violation of themselves as to destroy the good that the pub- ic ought to derive from them.[1]

His general defence of toleration.

60. I have been inclined to suspect that Taylor, for some cause, interpolated this chapter after the rest of the treatise was complete. It has as little bearing upon, and is as inconsistent in spirit with, the following sections as with those that precede. To use a familiar illustration, the effect it produces on the reader's mind is like that of coming on deck at sea, and finding, that, the ship having put about, the whole line of coast is reversed to the eye. Taylor, however, makes but a short tack. In the next section, he resumes the bold tone of an advocate for freedom; and, after discussing at great length the leading tenet of the Anabaptists, concludes, that, resting as it does on such plausible though insufficient grounds, we cannot exclude it by any means from

1 This single chapter is of itself conclusive against the truth of Taylor's own allegation, that he wrote his Liberty of Prophesying in order to procure toleration for the Episcopal Church of England at the hands of those who had overthrown it. No one ever dreamed of refusing freedom of opinion to that church: it was only about public worship that any difficulty could arise. But, in truth, there is not one word in the whole treatise which could have been written with the view that Taylor pretends.

[It has been suggested by an anonymous correspondent, that I have put a wrong construction on this seventeenth chapter, and that Taylor's design was to withstand that Puritan party within the church who refused to submit to the established laws of ecclesiastical discipline. It is certain that much which he has said will bear that construction; but, if he meant only this, he has not expressed himself with uniform clearness and consistency, as indeed is too common with him. He is so far from being distinct in the whole treatise as to what he aims at, that his editor, Heber, imagines him to have contended, under the name Liberty of Prophesying, not for toleration of sectaries, but of an exemption from fixed articles of faith for the clergy themselves. I conceive this to be a mistake; but Heber was not deficient in acuteness, and could hardly have misunderstood a plain meaning. The hypothesis of my correspondent, it may be observed, strengthens the presumption that the Liberty of Prophesying was chiefly written while the Church of England was still in the ascendant. — 1842.]

toleration, though they may be restrained from preachir their other notions of the unlawfulness of war, or of oath or of capital punishment; it being certain that no goc religion teaches doctrines whose consequences would destro all government. A more remarkable chapter is that in whic Taylor concludes in favor of tolerating the Romanists, excep when they assert the pope's power of deposing princes or o dispensing with oaths. The result of all, he says, is this "Let the prince and the secular power have a care th commonwealth be safe. For whether such or such a sect o Christians be to be permitted, is a question rather politica than religious."

61. In the concluding sections, he maintains the right of particular churches to admit all who profess the Apostles Creed to their communion, and of private men to communicate with different churches, if they require no unlawful condition. But "few churches, that have framed bodies of confession and articles, will endure any person that is not of the same confession; which is a plain demonstration that such bodies of confession and articles do much hurt." "The guilt of schism may lie on him who least thinks it; he being rather the schismatic who makes unnecessary and inconvenient impositions, than he who disobeys them, because he cannot do otherwise without violating his conscience."[1] The whole treatise on the Liberty of Prophesying ends with the celebrated parable of Abraham, found, as Taylor says, "in the Jews' books," but really in an Arabian writer. This story, Franklin, as every one now knows, rather unhandsomely appropriated to himself; and it is a strange proof of the ignorance as to our earlier literature which then prevailed, that for many years it continued to be quoted with his name. It was not contained in the first editions of the Liberty of Prophesying; and indeed the book from which Taylor is supposed to have borrowed it was not published till 1651.

62. Such is this great pleading for religious moderation; a production not more remarkable in itself than for the quarter from which it came. In the polemical writings of Jeremy Taylor, we generally find a stanch and uncompromising adherence to one party; and, from the abundant use he makes of

[1] This is said also by Hales, in his tract on Schism, which was published some years before the Liberty of Prophesying It is, however, what Taylor would have thought without a prompter.

uthority, we should infer that he felt a great veneration for t. In the Liberty of Prophesying, as has appeared by the general sketch rather than analysis we have just given, there s a prevailing tinge of the contrary turn of mind, more striking than the comparison of insulated passages can be. From what motives, and under what circumstances, this treatise was written, is not easily discerned. In the dedication to Lord Hatton of the collective edition of his controversial writings after the Restoration, he declares, that, "when a persecution did arise against the Church of England, he intended to make a reservative for his brethren and himself, by pleading for a liberty to our consciences to persevere in that profession which was warranted by all the laws of God and our superiors." It is with regret we are compelled to confess some want of ingenuousness in this part of Taylor's proceedings. No one reading the Liberty of Prophesying can perceive that it had the slightest bearing on any toleration that the Episcopal Church, in the time of the civil war, might ask of her victorious enemies. The differences between them were not on speculative points of faith, nor turning on an appeal to fathers and councils. That Taylor had another class of controversies in his mind is sufficiently obvious to the attentive reader of his work; and I can give no proof in this place to any other.

63. This was the third blow that the new school of Leyden had aimed in England at the positive dogmatists, who, in all the reformed churches as in that of Rome, labored to impose extensive confessions of faith, abounding in inferences of scholastic theology, as conditions of exterior communion, and as peremptory articles of faith. Chillingworth and Hales were not less decisive; but the former had but in an incidental manner glanced at the subject, and the short tract on Schism had been rather deficient in proof of its hardy paradoxes. Taylor, therefore, may be said to have been the first who sapped and shook the foundations of dogmatism and pretended orthodoxy; the first who taught men to seek peace in unity of spirit rather than of belief; and, instead of extinguishing dissent, to take away its sting by charity, and by a sense of human fallibility. The mind thus freed from bigotry is best prepared for the public toleration of differences in religion; but certainly the despotic and jealous temper of governments is

Effect of this treatise.

not so well combated by Taylor as by later advocates of religious freedom.

64. In conducting his argument, he falls not unfrequently into his usual fault. Endowed with a mind of prodigious fertility, which a vast erudition rendered more luxuriant, he accumulates without selection whatever presents itself to his mind: his innumerable quotations, his multiplied reasonings, his prodigality of epithets and appositions, are poured along the interminable periods of his writings, with a frequency of repetition, sometimes of the same phrases, which leaves us to suspect that he revised but little what he had very rapidly composed. Certain it is, that, in his different works, he does not quite adhere to himself; and it would be more desirable to lay this on the partial views that haste and impetuosity produce, than on a deliberate employment of what he knew to be insufficient reasoning. But I must acknowledge, that Taylor's fairness does not seem his characteristic quality.

Its defects

65. In some passages of the Liberty of Prophesying, he seems to exaggerate the causes of uncertainty, and to take away from ecclesiastical antiquity even that moderate probability of truth which a dispassionate inquirer may sometimes assign to it. His suspicions of spuriousness and interpolation are too vaguely sceptical, and come ill from one who has no sort of hesitation, in some of his controversies, to allege as authority what he here sets aside with little ceremony. Thus, in the Defence of Episcopacy, published in 1642, he maintains the authenticity of the first fifty of the apostolic canons, all of which, in the Liberty of Prophesying, a very few years afterwards, he indiscriminately rejects. But this line of criticism was not then in so advanced a state as at present; and, from a credulous admission of every thing, the learned had come sometimes to more sweeping charges of interpolation and forgery than would be sustained on a more searching investigation. Taylor's language is so unguarded, that he seems to leave the authenticity of all the fathers precarious. Doubtless there is a greater want of security as to books written before the invention of printing than we are apt to conceive, especially where independent manuscripts have not been found; but it is the business of a sagacious criticism, by the aid of internal or collateral evidence, to distinguish, not dogmatically as most are wont, but with a rational though

ited assent, the genuine remains of ancient writers from incrustations of blundering or of imposture.

Great erudition of this period

66. A prodigious reach of learning distinguishes the theologians of these fifty years, far greater than even in the sixteenth century; and also, if I am not mistaken, more critical and pointed, though in these latter qualities it was afterwards surpassed. And, in this erudition, the Protestant churches, we may perhaps say, were, upon the whole, more abundant than that of Rome. But it would be unprofitable to enumerate works which we are incompetent to appreciate. Blondel, Daillé, and Salmasius on the Continent, Usher in England, are the most conspicuous names. Blondel maintained the equality of the Apostolic Church both against the primacy of Rome, and the episcopacy for which the Anglicans contended: Salmasius and Daillé fought on the same side in that controversy. The writings of our Irish primate, Usher, who maintained the antiquity of his order, but not upon such high ground as many in England would have desired, are known for their extraordinary learning, in which he has perhaps never been surpassed by an English writer. But for judgment, and calm appreciation of evidence, the name of Usher has not been altogether so much respected by posterity as it was by his contemporaries. The Church of Rome had its champions of less eminent renown: Gretser, perhaps the first among them, is not very familiar to our ears; but it is to be remembered, that some of the writings of Bellarmin fall within this period. The Dogmata Theologica of the Jesuit Petavius, though but a compilation from the fathers and ancient councils, and not peculiarly directed against the tenets of the reformed, may deserve mention as a monument of useful labor.[1] Labbe, Sirmond, and several others, appear to range more naturally under the class of historical than theological writers. In mere ecclesiastical history, — the records of events rather than opinions, — this period was far more profound and critical than the preceding. The Annals of Baronius were abridged and continued by Spondanus.

Usher; Petavius.

67. A numerous list of writers in sacred criticism might easily be produced. Among the Romanists, Cornelius à Lapide

[1] The Dogmata Theologica is not a complete work: it extends only as far as the head of free-will. It belongs to the class of Loci Communes. Morhof, ii. 539.

has been extolled above the rest by his fellow-Jesuit, A
Sacred criticism. drès. His Commentaries, published from 1617
1642, are reckoned by others too diffuse; but
seems to have a fair reputation with Protestant critics.[1] T
Lutherans extol Gerhard, and especially Glass, author of t
Philologia Sacra, in hermeneutical theology. Rivet was t
highest name among the Calvinists. Arminius, Episcopi
the Fratres Poloni, and indeed almost every one who had
defend a cause, found no course so ready, at least among P
testants, as to explain the Scriptures consistently with
Grotius; Coccejus. own tenets. Two natives of Holland, opposite
character, in spirit, and principles of reasoning, a
consequently the founders of opposite schools of discipl
stand out from the rest, — Grotius and Coccejus. Luth
Calvin, and the generality of Protestant interpreters in t
sixteenth century, had, in most instances, rejected with so
contempt the allegorical and multifarious senses of Scriptu
which had been introduced by the fathers, and had prevail
through the dark ages of the church. This adherence to t
literal meaning was doubtless promoted by the tenet they a
professed, the facility of understanding Scripture. That whi
was designed for the simple and illiterate was not to requi
a key to any esoteric sense. Grotius, however, in his Ann
tations on the Old and New Testament, published in 1633, –
the most remarkable book of this kind that had appeare
and which has had a more durable reputation than any pe
haps of its precursors, — carried the system of literal inte
pretation still farther, bringing great stores of illustrativ
learning from profane antiquity, but merely to elucidate th
primary meaning, according to ordinary rules of criticism
Coccejus followed a wholly opposite course. Every passage
in his method, teemed with hidden senses; the narratives
least capable of any ulterior application, were converted int
typical allusion, so that the Old Testament became throughou
an enigmatical representation of the New. He was als
remarkable for having viewed, more than any precedin
writer, all the relations between God and man under the form
of covenants, and introduced the technical language of jurisprudence into theology. This became a very usual mode of

[1] Andrès; Blount. Simon, however, says he is full of an erudition not to the purpose; which, as his Commentaries on the Scriptures run to twelve volumes is not wonderful.

;ating the subject in Holland, and afterwards in England. ie Coccejans were numerous in the United Provinces, ough not perhaps deemed quite so orthodox as their adver-ries, who, from Gisbert Voet, a theologian of the most lexible and polemical spirit, were denominated Voetians. ieir disputes began a little before the middle of the century, d lasted till nearly its close.[1] The Summa Doctrinæ of occejus appeared in 1648; and the Dissertationes Theolo-cæ of Voet, in 1649.

68. England gradually took a prominent share in this ranch of sacred literature. Among the divines of is period, comprehending the reigns of James and harles, we may mention Usher, Gataker, Mede, ightfoot, Jackson, Field, and Leigh.[2] Gataker stood, per-aps, next to Usher, in general erudition. The fame of Iede has rested, for the most part, on his interpretations f the Apocalypse. This book had been little commented pon by the reformers; but, in the beginning of the seven-eenth century, several wild schemes of its application to resent or expected events had been broached in Germany. England had also taken an active part, if it be true what Grotius tells us, that eighty books on the prophecies had been ublished here before 1640.[3] Those of Mede have been eceived with favor by later interpreters. Lightfoot, with extensive knowledge of the rabbinical writers, poured his copious stores on Jewish antiquities, preceded in this by a more obscure laborer in that region,—Ainsworth. Jackson had a considerable name; but I do not think that he has been much quoted in modern times.[4] Field on the Church has been much praised by Coleridge: it is, as it seemed to me, a more temperate work in ecclesiastical theory than some have represented it to be, and written almost wholly against Rome. Leigh's Critica Sacra can hardly be reckoned, nor does it

English commentators.

1 Eichhorn, vi. part i. p. 264; Mosheim.

2 "All confess," says Selden, in the Table-talk, "there never was a more learned clergy: no man taxes them with ignorance." In another place, indeed, he is represented to say, "The Jesuits and the lawyers of France, and the Low Country-men, have engrossed all learning: the rest of the world make nothing but homilies." As far as these sentences are not owing to difference of humor in the time of speaking, he seems to have taken learning in a larger sense the second time than the first. Of learning not theological, the English clergy had no extraordinary portion.

3 "Si qua in re libera esse debet sententia, certè in vaticiniis, præsertim cum jam Protestantium libri prodierint fermè centum (in his octoginta in Anglia sola, ut mihi Anglici legati dixere) super illis rebus, inter se plurimum discordes."—Grot. Epist. 895.

4 [The entire works of Jackson have been reprinted at Oxford within a few years.—1853.]

claim to be, more than a compilation from earlier theologia it is an alphabetical series of words from the Hebrew a Greek Testaments, the author candidly admitting that he w not very conversant with the Latin language. Leigh, should be added, was a layman.

Style of preaching.

69. The style of preaching before the Reformation h been often little else than buffoonery, and seldc respectable. For the most part, indeed, the clerg wrote in Latin what they delivered to the multitude in tl native tongue. A better tone began with Luther. His la guage was sometimes rude and low, but persuasive, artles powerful. He gave many useful precepts, as well as exan ples, for pulpit eloquence. Melanchthon and several other both in the sixteenth and seventeenth centuries, as well in tl Lutheran as in the Reformed Church, endeavored by system tic treatises to guide the composition of sermons. The forme could not, however, withstand the formal, tasteless, and pol mical spirit that overspread their theology. In the latter, superior tone is perceived. Of these, according to Eichhor the Swiss preachers were most simple and popular, the Dutc most learned and copious; the French had most taste an eloquence, the English most philosophy.[1] It is more tha probable, that in these characteristics he has meant to com prise the whole of the seventeenth century. Few Continenta writers, as far as I know, that belong to this its first moiety have earned any remarkable reputation in this province of theology. In England several might be distinguished ou of a large number. Sermons have been much mor frequently published here than in any other country; and, from the beginning of the seventeenth century, form a large proportion of our theological literature. But it is, of course, not requisite to mention more than the very few which may be said to have a general reputation.

English sermons:

Of Donne;

70. The sermons of Donne have sometimes been praised in late times. They are undoubtedly the productions of a very ingenious and a very learned man; and two folio volumes by such a person may be expected to supply favorable specimens. In their general character, they will not appear, I think, much worthy of being rescued from oblivion. The subtilty of Donne, and his fondness for such

[1] Eichhorn, vi. part ii. p. 219, *et post*

onclusive reasoning as a subtle disputant is apt to fall into, as through all of these sermons at which I have looked. His rning he seems to have perverted in order to cull every pertinence of the fathers and schoolmen, their remote analoes, their strained allegories, their technical distinctions; and these he has added much of a similar kind from his own nciful understanding. In his theology, Donne appears often incline towards the Arminian hypotheses, which in the st years of James and the first of his son, the period in hich these sermons were chiefly preached, had begun to be counted orthodox at court: but I will not vouch for his nsistency in every discourse. Much, as usual in that age, levelled against Rome. Donne was conspicuously learned that controversy; and, though he talks with great respect antiquity, is not induced by it, like some of his Anglican ntemporaries, to make any concession to the adversary.[1]

71. The sermons of Jeremy Taylor are of much higher eputation; far, indeed, above any that had preceded hem in the English Church. An imagination essenially poetical, and sparing none of the decorations which, by ritical rules, are deemed almost peculiar to verse; a warm one of piety, sweetness, and charity; an accumulation of ircumstantial accessories whenever he reasons or persuades r describes; an erudition pouring itself forth in quotation ill his sermons become in some places almost a garland of lowers from all other writers, and especially from those f classical antiquity, never before so redundantly scattered rom the pulpit, — distinguish Taylor from his contemporaries y their degree, as they do from most of his successors by heir kind. His sermons on the Marriage Ring, on the House of Feasting, on the Apples of Sodom, may be named without lisparagement to others, which perhaps ought to stand in equal place. But they are not without considerable faults, some of which have just been hinted. The eloquence of Taylor is great, but it is not eloquence of the highest class: it is far too Asiatic, too much in the style of the declaimers

Of Jeremy Taylor.

[1] Donne incurred some scandal by a book entitled Biathanatos, and considered as a vindication of suicide. It was published long after his death in 1651. It is a very dull and pedantic performance, without the ingenuity and acuteness of paradox: distinctions, objections, and quotations from the rabble of bad authors whom he used to read, fill up the whole of it. It is impossible to find a less clear statement of argument on either side No one would be induced to kill himself by reading such a book, unless he were threatened with another volume

of the fourth century, by the study of whom he had proba
vitiated his taste; his learning is ill-placed, and his argume
often as much so; not to mention that he has the comm
defect of alleging nugatory proofs: his vehemence loses
effect by the circuity of his pleonastic language; his sentenc
are of endless length, and hence not only altogether unm
sical, but not always reducible to grammar. But he is st
the greatest ornament of the English pulpit up to the midd
of the seventeenth century; and we have no reason to believ
or rather much reason to disbelieve, that he had any comp
titor in other languages.

Devotional writings of Taylor

72. The devotional writings of Taylor, several of whi
belong to the first part of the century, are by n
means of less celebrity or less value than his se
mons. Such are the Life of Christ, the Holy Livin
and Dying, and the collection of meditations called the Go
den Grove. A writer as distinguished in works of practic

And Hall.

piety was Hall. His Art of Divine Meditation, h
Contemplations, and indeed many of his writing
remind us frequently of Taylor. Both had equally pious an
devotional tempers; both were full of learning, both ferti
of illustration; both may be said to have had strong imagina
tion and poetical genius, though Taylor let his predominate
little more. Taylor is also rather more subtle and argumen
tative; his copiousness has more real variety. Hall keep
more closely to his subject, dilates upon it sometimes mor
tediously, but more appositely. In his sermons there is som
excess of quotation and far-fetched illustration, but less tha
in those of Taylor. In some of their writings, these tw
great divines resemble each other, on the whole, so much, tha
we might for a short time not discover which we were reading. I do not know that any third writer comes close to
either. The Contemplations of Hall are among his most
celebrated works. They are prolix, and without much of that
vivacity or striking novelty we meet with in the devotional
writings of his contemporary, but are perhaps more practical
and generally edifying.[1]

73. The religious treatises of this class, even those which, by their former popularity or their merit, ought to be mentioned in a regular history of theological literature, are too

[1] Some of the moral writings of Hall were translated into French by Chevreau in the seventeenth century, and had much success. Niceron, xi. 348.

ıerous for these pages. A mystical and ascetic spirit ɪsed itself more over religion, struggling some- es, as in the Lutherans of Germany, against the nal orthodoxy of the church, but more often in subordination ts authority, and co-operating with its functions. The writ- s of St. Francis de Sales, titular Bishop of Geneva, ecially his treatise on the Love of God, published in 1616, ke a sort of epoch in the devotional theology of the Church Rome. Those of St. Teresa, in the Spanish language, owed some years afterwards: they are altogether full of a stical theopathy. But De Sales included charity in his eme of divine love; and it is to him, as well as others of age, that not only a striking revival of religion in France, ich had been absolutely perverted or disregarded in the teenth century, was due, but a reformation in the practices monastic life, which became more active and beneficent, th less of useless penance and asceticism, than before. New stitutions sprang up with the spirit of association, and all ıer animating principles of conventual orders, but free from e formality and torpor of the old.[1]

In the Roman

74. Even in the German churches, rigid as they generally ere in their adherence to the symbolical books, me voices from time to time were heard for a more iritual and effective religion. Arndt's Treatise of rue Christianity, in 1605, written on ascetic and devotional inciples, and with some deviation from the tenets of the ery orthodox Lutherans, has been reckoned one of the first otests against their barren forms of faith;[2] and the mystical ıeologians, if they had not run into such extravagances as id dishonor to their name, would have been accessions to the ıme side. The principal mystics or theosophists have gene- ılly been counted among philosophers, and will therefore nd their place in the next chapter. The German nation is onstitutionally disposed to receive those forms of religion which address themselves to the imagination and the heart. Much, therefore, of this character has always been written, nd become popular in that language. Few English writings f the practical class, except those already mentioned, can be aid to retain much notoriety. Those of George Herbert are best known: his Country Parson, which seems properly

And Lutheran Church

[1] Ranke, ii. 430.

[2] Eichhorn, vi. part i. p. 355; Biogr. Univ.; Chalmers.

to fall within this description, is, on the whole, a pleas little book; but the precepts are sometimes so overstrain according to our notions, as to give an air of affectation.

Infidelity of some writers.

Charron.

75. The disbelief in revelation, of which several sympto had appeared before the end of the sixteenth c tury, became more remarkable afterwards both France and England, involving several names obscure in literary history. The first of these, point of date, is Charron. The religious scepticism of t writer has not been generally acknowledged, and indeed seems repugnant to the fact of his having written an elabor defence of Christianity; yet we can deduce no other concl sion from one chapter in his most celebrated book, t Treatise on Wisdom. Charron is so often little else than transcriber, that we might suspect him in this instance also have drawn from other sources; which, however, would lea the same inference as to his own tenets; and I think th chapter has an air of originality.

Vanini.

76. The name of Charron, however, has not been general associated with the charge of irreligion. A mo audacious and consequently more unfortunate writ was Lucilio Vanini, a native of Italy, whose book De Adm randis Naturæ Reginæ Deæque Mortalium Arcanis, printe at Paris in 1616, caused him to be burned at the stake by decree of the parliament of Toulouse, in 1619. This treatis as well as one that preceded it, Amphitheatrum Æterna Providentiæ, Lyons, 1615, is of considerable rarity; so tha there has been a question concerning the atheism of Vanin which some have undertaken to deny.[1] In the Amphithea trum I do not perceive any thing which leads to such an im putation, though I will not pretend to have read the whole of a book full of the unintelligible metaphysics of the later Aris totelians. It professes, at least, to be a vindication of the being and providence of the Deity. But the later work, which is dedicated to Bassompierre, and published with a royal privilege of exclusive sale for six years, is of a very different complexion. It is in sixty dialogues, the interlocutors being styled Alexander and Julius Cæsar; the latter representing Vanini himself. The far greater part of these dialogues relate to physical, but a few to theological subjects.

[1] Brucker, v. 678.

the fiftieth, on the religion of the heathens, he avows his sbelief of all religion, except such as Nature, which is God, ing the principle of motion, has planted in the hearts of an; every other being the figment of kings to keep their bjects in obedience, and of priests for their own lucre and onor;[1] observing plainly of his own Amphitheatrum, which a vindication of Providence, that he had said many things it which he did not believe.[2] Vanini was infatuated with

1 "In quanam religione verè et piè eum coli vetusti philosophi existimâ-int? In unica Naturæ lege, quam ipsa atura, quæ Deus est (est enim princi-ium motûs), in omnium gentium animis iscripsit; cæteras vero leges non nisi gmenta et illusiones esse asserebant, non cacodæmone aliquo inductas, fabulosum amque illorum genus dicitur a philo-ophis, sed a principibus ad subditorum ædagogiam excogitatas, et a sacrificulis b honoris et auri aucupium confirmatas, on miraculis, sed scriptura, cujus nec riginale ullibi adinvenitur, quæ miracu-a facta recitet, et bonarum ac malarum ctionum repromissiones polliceatur, in utura tamen vita, ne fraus detegi possit." p. 366.

2 "Multa in eo libro scripta sunt, qui-bus a me nulla præstatur fides. Così va il mondo. — ALEX. Non miror, nam ego crebris vernaculis hoc usurpo sermoni-bus: Questo mondo è una gabbia de' matti. Reges excipio et pontifices. Nam de illis scriptum est: Cor regis in manu Domini," &c. — Dial. LVI. p. 428.

The concluding pages are enough to show with what justice Buhle and Tenne-mann have gravely recorded Vanini among philosophers. "Quæso, mi Juli, tuam de animæ immortalitate sententiam explices. — J. C. Excusatum me habeas rogo. — AL. Cur ita? — J. C. Vovi Deo meo quæs-tionem hanc me non pertractaturum, an-tequam senex dives et germanus evasero. — AL. Dii tibi Nestoreos pro literariæ rei-publicæ emolumento dies impertiant: vix trigesimum nunc attigisti annum et tot præclaræ eruditionis monumenta admira-bili cum laude edidisti. — J. C. Quid hæc mihi prosunt? — AL. Celebrem tibi lau-dem comparârunt. — J. C. Omnes famæ rumusculos cum uno amasiæ basiolo com-mutandos plerique philosophi suadent. — AL. At alter ea perfrui potest. — J. C. Quid inde adimit? . . . — AL. Uberrimos voluptatis fructus percepisti in Naturæ arcanis investigandis. — J. C. Corpus mihi est studiis enervatum exhaustumque; ne-que in hac humana caligine perfectam rerum cognitionem assequi possumus; cum ipsummet Aristotelem philosophorum Deum infinitis propemodum locis halluci-natum fuisse adverto, cumque medicam facultatem præ reliquis certissimam adhuc incertam et fallacem experior, subscribere cuperem Agrippæ libello quem de scientia-rum vanitate conscripsit. — AL. Laborum tuorum præmium jam consecutus es; æternitati nomen jam consecrâsti. Quid jucundius in extremo tuæ ætatis curri-culo accipere potes, quam hoc canticum? Et superest sine te nomen in orbe tuum. — J. C. Si animus meus una cum corpore, ut Athei fingunt, evanescat, quas ille ex fama post obitum delicias nancisci pote-rit? Forsitan gloriolæ voculis, et fidiculis ad cadaveris domicilium pertrahatur? Si animus, ut credimus libenter et spera-mus, interitui non est obnoxius, et ad superos evolabit, tot ibi perfruetur cupe-diis et voluptatibus, ut illustres ac splen-didas mundi pompas et laudationes nec pili faciat. Si ad purgatorias flammas descendet, gratior erit illi illius orationis, Dies iræ, dies illa, mulierculis gratissima recitatio, quam omnes Tulliani glossuli, dicendique lepores, quam subtilissimæ et pene divinæ Aristotelis ratiocinationes: si Tartareo, quod Deus avertat, perpetuo carceri emancipatur, nullum ibi solatium, nullam redemptionem inveniet. — AL. O utinam in adolescentiæ limine has rationes excepissem! — J. C. Præterita mala ne cogites futura ne cures, præsentia fugias. — AL. Ah! — J. C. Liberaliter inspiras. — AL. Illius versiculi recordor. Perduto è tutto il tempō, che in amor non si spende. — J. C. Eja quoniam inclinato jam die ad vesperam perducta est disputatio (cujus singula verba divino Romanæ ecclesiæ oraculo, infallibilis cujus interpres a Spiri-tu Sancto modo constitutus est Paulus V., serenissimæ Burghesiæ familiæ soboles, subjecta esse volumus, ita ut pro non dictis habeantur, si quæ forsitan sunt, quod vix crediderim, quæ illius placitis ad amussim non consentiant), laxemus paulisper animos, et a severitate ad hilari-tatem risumque traducamus. Heus pueri! lusorias tabulas huc adferte." The wretch-ed man, it seems, had not much reason to think himself a gainer by his specula tions; yet he knew not that the worst was still behind.

presumption, and, if he resembled Jordano Bruno in th respect, fell very short of his acuteness and apparent inte rity. His cruel death, and perhaps the scarcity of his work has given more celebrity to his name in literary history tha it would otherwise have obtained.

Lord Herbert of Cherbury.

77. Lord Herbert of Cherbury, in his treatise De Veritat and still more in that De Religione Gentilium, ha been justly deemed inimical to every positive re ligion. He admits, indeed, the possibility of imme diate revelation from heaven, but denies that any traditio from others can have sufficient certainty. Five fundamen tal truths of natural religion he holds to be such as al mankind are bound to acknowledge, and damns those hea thens who do not receive them as summarily as any theo logian.[1]

Grotius de Veritate.

78. The progress of infidelity in France did not fail t attract notice. It was popular in the court of Louis XIII., and, in a certain degree, in that of Charles I But this does not belong to the history of literature. Among the writers who may have given some proofs of it, we may reckon La Mothe le Vayer, Naudé, and Guy Patin.[2] The writings of Hobbes will be treated at length hereafter. It is probable that this sceptical spirit of the age gave rise to those

[1] These five articles are: "1. Esse Deum summum.—2. Coli debere.—3. Virtutem pietatemque esse præcipuas partes cultûs divini.—4. Dolendum esse ob peccata, ab iisque resipiscendum.—5. Dari ex bonitate justitiaque divina præmium vel pœnam tum in hac vita, tum post hanc vitam. . . . Hisce quippe ubi superstitiones figmentaque commiscuerint, vel animas suas criminibus quæ nulla satis eluat pœnitentia, commaculaverint, a seipsis perditio propria, Deo vero summo in æternum sit gloria."—De Religione Gentilium, cap. 1.

[2] La Mothe le Vayer has frequently been reckoned among those who carried their general scepticism into religion. And this seems a fair inference, unless the contrary can be shown; for those who doubt of what is most evident will naturally doubt of what is less so. In La Mothe's fourth dialogue, under the name of Oratius Tubero, he pretends to speak of faith as a gift of God, and not founded on evidence; which was probably but the usual subterfuge. The Naudæana are full of broad intimations that the author was, as he expresses it, *bien déniaisé*; and Guy Patin's letters, except those near the end of his life, lead to a similar conclusion One of them has certainly the appearance of implicating Gassendi, and has been quoted as such by Sir James Mackintosh, in his Dissertation on Ethical Philosophy. Patin tells us, that Naudé, Gassendi, and he were to sup together the following Sunday. "Ce sera une débauche, mais philosophique, et peut-être quelque chose d'avantage, pour être tous trois guéris du loup-garou, et être délivrés du mal des scrupules qui est le tyran des consciences, nous irons peut-être jusque fort près du sanctuaire. Je fis l'an passé ce voyage de Gentilly avec M. Naudé, moy seul avec luy, tête-à-tête; il n'y avoit point de témoins, aussi n'y en faloit-il point; nous y parlâmes fort librement de tout, sans que personne en ait été scandalisé."—p. 32. I should not, nevertheless, lay much stress on this letter, in opposition to the many assertions of belief in religion which the writings of Gassendi contain. One of them, indeed, quoted by Dugald Stewart, in note Q to his first Dissertation, is rather suspicious, as going too far into a mystical strain for his cold temperament

ications of revealed religion which were published in the ent period. Among these, the first place is due to the -known and extensively circulated treatise of Grotius. s was originally sketched in Dutch verse, and intended the lower classes of his countrymen. It was published in in in 1627.[1] Few if any books of the kind have been so uently reprinted; but some parts being not quite so close critical as the modern state of letters exacts, and the uments against Jews and Mahometans seeming to occupy much space, it is less read than formerly.

'9. This is not a period in which many editions or versions he Scriptures were published. The English translaon of the Bible had been several times revised, re-made, since the first edition by Tyndale. It ally assumed its present form under the authority James I. Forty-seven persons, in six companies, meeting Westminster, Oxford, and Cambridge, distributed the labor iong them; twenty-five being assigned to the Old Testament, een to the New, seven to the Apocrypha. The rules imsed for their guidance by the king were designed, as far as ssible, to secure the text against any novel interpretation; e translation, called the Bishops' Bible, being established as e basis, as those still older had been in that; and the work each person or company being subjected to the review of e rest. The translation, which was commenced in 1607, as published in 1611.[2]

English translation of the Bible.

80. The style of this translation is in general so enthusistically praised, that no one is permitted either to ualify or even explain the grounds of his approbaion. It is held to be the perfection of our English language. shall not dispute this proposition; but one remark as to a natter of fact cannot reasonably be censured, that, in consequence of the principle of adherence to the original versions which had been kept up ever since the time of Henry VIII., t is not the language of the reign of James I. It may, in the eyes of many, be a better English, but it is not the English of Daniel or Raleigh or Bacon, as any one may easily perceive. It abounds, in fact, especially in the Old Testament, with obsolete phraseology, and with single words long since abandoned, or retained only in provincial use. On the **more**

Its style.

1 Niceron, vol. xix.; Biogr. Univ.

2 Fuller's Church History

important question, whether this translation is entirely, with very trifling exceptions, conformable to the orig text, it seems unfit to enter. It is one which is seldom cussed with all the temper, and freedom from oblique vie which the subject demands, and upon which, for this reas it is not safe, for those who have not had leisure or me to examine it for themselves, to take upon trust the te mony of the learned. A translation of the Old Testam was published at Douay in 1609, for the use of the Engl Catholics.

END OF VOL. II.

Cambridge: Press of John Wilson & Son.